Johann Peter and Anna Katharina Krug Family

Front Row: Louise, Johann Peter, Anna Katharina, John George

Second Row: Anna, John August, Elizabeth, William, Katharina "Katie"

Back Row: Henry, Adam, John Daniel

GERMAN SETTLERS of IOWA

Their Descendants and European Ancestors

—THIRD EDITION—

Margaret Krug Palen

HERITAGE BOOKS
2009

HERITAGE BOOKS

AN IMPRINT OF HERITAGE BOOKS, INC.

Books, CDs, and more—Worldwide

For our listing of thousands of titles see our website
at
www.HeritageBooks.com

Published 2009 by
HERITAGE BOOKS, INC.
Publishing Division
100 Railroad Ave. #104
Westminster, Maryland 21157

Other books by the author:
Genealogical Guide to Tracing Ancestors in Germany
Genealogical Research Guide to Germany
German Settlers of Iowa: Their Descendants and European Ancestors
German Settlers of Iowa: Their Descendants and European Ancestors, Revised Edition

International Standard Book Numbers
Paperbound: 978-1-55613-981-9
Clothbound: 978-0-7884-8291-5

Dedicated to Susan and Richard
Andrea and Thomas

TABLE OF CONTENTS

PREFACE

There is great interest in genealogy today along with an increasing search for family health history. A family's genetic background can be enlightening. The search of family history may reveal the illnesses to which one might be predisposed, and that offers advantages not previously known. A knowledge of family cancer, glaucoma, diabetes and other diseases—along with technological advances for genetic testing—can lead to early detection and treatment. Then it is possible to take advantage of the new understandings scientists have about genetics. You will discover by reading the pages in this dictionary that it is a chronicle of the past centuries including wars, disease, and longevity of life.

This dictionary may help you finally settle the "cousins" question. The children of your first cousins are your first cousins once removed. The children of your first cousins are second cousins to each other. The lineage then proceeds through third and fourth cousins. It is an accurate and quick way of identifying common ancestors. The method used over the years to give each generation a number starting with one caused confusion in identifying grandparents, and great-grandparents. One of the relatives I was explaining this to observed, "All my cousins are removed! I don't ever see them."

Take time to study the abbreviation page in the forefront of the data before beginning a search for names. Abbreviations make it possible to collect a large amount of genealogy in a small volume that can be kept at hand where it can be quickly available. It documents information in primary sources such as German church register books, Iowa church and cemetery records, and secondary sources, i.e. gravestones. Once you become familiar with the form it is quicker to search the index and find information in this volume than in other genealogy programs.

To assist in tracing immigrant ancestors and their related ancestors in Germany an asterisk (*) at the beginning of a name designates that person in a family lineage. When two asterisks (**) appear before a name it indicates an ancestral descendant of Iowa German immigrants currently residing in Germany. This is a simple aid to assist travelers planning to visit European heritage villages.

If you fail to find a name of an older person, if it is a male, determine if the name begins with Johann or Johannes. In Germany, it was customary to give all male births the first name Johann or Johannes. After immigration to the USA, many German men dropped their first name and used their second name to prevent confusion in identification. In past centuries, European males in Germany were given the same name as their father as a method of clarifying family genealogy from generation to generation.

In the earliest primary source records of Germany there are no middle names; however, after The Reformation more than one middle name was given to gift the name of each baptismal sponsor to the child. This dictionary records accurate names, and the spelling of names, as they appear in research of the primary source records in Germany. In the 17th, 18th and 19th centuries babies were baptized the day they were born, therefore, baptismal record dates are also the only recorded date of birth. Immigrants did not bring birth certificates with them to America, and it is common that descendants are unfamiliar with the accurate recorded name, spelling, and date of birth of their ancestors causing mistakes in family history and on engravings for burial markers.

When a wife's name is listed first in the identification of parents, it recognizes, whenever possible, the parent that has the closest relationship to the German settlers of Iowa. Children of married female ancestors and descendants are always listed with surnames to assist in locating and recognizing family lines, whereas, children born to male descendants need only first and middle names to follow the lineage.

Designation of state location of birth, marriage and death is by the current two letter abbreviation. ND can mean either North Dakota or No Date; and MD can mean Maryland or Medical Doctor, NE is Nebraska. In each instance, the context of the abbreviation clarifies the meaning. Location given after birth is the place of birth unless specified as place of residence. Iowa data has three Iowa locations making it necessary to abbreviate: the State of Iowa: IA; Iowa County: Co; and Iowa Township: Twp.

In North America, immigrants translated the German spelling of their surname to the English language by inserting the "e" vowel. Henry Michel was naturalized Henry Michael in Volume I, page 166 Benton County, Iowa, Courthouse Recorders Office. It is common when translating the German language into English to add "e" when the German name contains vowels with an umlaut (two dots).

To continue my German heritage search, I returned to the European villages of my Krug, Happel, Moeller, Michel, Paar families in 2003. A reporter from the Frankenberg, Germany newspaper interviewed me in Löhlbach and wrote a story with my photograph about this search for ancestral "roots." A reception was held for me in the pub setting of the Löhlbach Alt Schule with a picture program of the village in the years before emigration of my great-grandparents to the USA.

Thank you to everyone that updated family information for this edition. Acknowledgement for contributing research: Al and Lola Maye Brehm Krug, Mary Jane Woodson Krug, Erna Rinderknecht, Dale Grabau, Gregory Michel, Art Taschner, Harriet Keiper Rinderknecht and Marlene Böhle (Germany).

In focusing on forbearers I become evermore grateful for their lives and am determined to make as much as possible of the present time as they did so honorably.

Margaret Krug Palen

PHOTO Fig. 1: Krug 4th cousins meeting in Huddingen, Germany
Left, author Margaret Krug Palen. Right, Lena Höhl Happe

In Search of Family Lineage

A massive migration of Germans to North America began in the 1830's and grew; by the 1880's 1.4 million Germans had come to the United States of America. From the 1830's through the 1850's most immigrants came from Prussia, a large German state that was authoritarian, militaristic, and economically backward. In Prussia peasants faced a hard life, and some were still tied to the land like medieval serfs. Germany was wracked repeatedly by revolutions and men faced conscription into the Prussian army. Thousands of Prussians left Bremen, Germany on American ships bound for New York with their sights on acquiring land and a home in the developing Middle West.

Throughout the 19th Century German immigrants generally were welcomed to America, however, anti-immigrant feelings began to grow at the turn of the 20th Century. World War I sparked strong anti-German sentiment which spilled over to affect attitudes toward German-Americans. Gradually, German families that continued speaking the German language and customs of their culture became a part of the "melting pot" that is America.

During the 20th century, there were parallels in family life in Germany and America. Genealogical data collected in Germany, back to 1678, documents the frequency of more than one sibling of a family marrying into the same family. In the village life in Germany, and in rural communities of Iowa, more than one marriage between two families occurred when life in German families was centered in a small geographical area. In the 17th, 18th and 19th centuries in Germany, families did not have cars or own a horse or bicycle. The only means of travel was by foot. Men were the wage earners of the family and walked to wherever they worked while wives managed the chores of farmyard animals, as well as the garden, household work and children. Diets during winter months were mainly milk and potatoes. Village families in Germany had little to eat when the potato rot disease spread throughout Europe in the 19th century. This provided the incentive for emigration to America where promoters were painting a glorious picture of opportunity in a developing country.

PHOTO Fig. 2: Rev. G.F. Dressler (left) and Richard Palen (right) searching records in Germany for data about ancestors that immigrated to Iowa.

PHOTO Fig. 3: House No. 70 Löhlbach, Germany, the Krug ancestral home. Note the U-shaped Bauerhof complex (village farm).

PHOTO Fig. 4:   House No. 43 Löhlbach, Germany, Möller (Moeller) ancestral home. Note slate (native to the area) siding.

PHOTO Fig. 5: House No.10 Löhlbach, Germany, Paar ancestral home.

PHOTO Fig. 6:   House No. 48 Löhlbach, Germany, Michel ancestral home.

We traveled along the forest road to (os Alt Hein) Altenhaina through many beech, oak, and maple trees on the way to the ancestral Happel homes. When the Happel ancestors lived there, they walked this road to Löhlbach to attend church and village events. There is a junction where funeral biers were carried by horse and wagon from Alt Heim, then lifted at the junction by men to walk the steep trail uphill over a mountain to the Löhlbach cemetery for burial. There was no cemetery in Alt Heim until the 20th century.

We stopped to see the two Happel houses in Altenhaina of two generations of Happels, House #5 and the house where Andreas Happel was born, and where his ten children were born, was built by Andreas' parents, Johann Peter Happel and his wife Anna Gertrude in 1813. The inscription (Balkeninschrift) on the beam across the front of the house —"Gott allein die Ehre Johann Peter Happel und Anna Gertraut seine Ehefrau die haben Gott vertraut und dieses Haus gebaut im Jahr 1813 denzten July gehoben Zimmermeister Bickhard von Löhlbach"; English translation: "To God alone the honor (ns: by the grace of God) Johann Peter Happel and Anna Gertraut his wife have placed confidence in God and built this house in the year 1813 7 July. Master carpenter Bickhard of Löhlbach." This Fachwerk Happel home was in beautiful restoration in 1984 when we first saw it. In 1990, the trees in front of the house had grown so tall it was difficult to take photos of the inscription. In October 1995, the leaves were off the trees and photos of the inscription were clear, but the trees had grown even taller covering the front of the house, and the paint was aging so the house appeared to need repainting.

PHOTO Fig. 7: Happel ancestral home located in (os Alt Heim) Altenhaina, Germany. Note the inscription on the house. Willie Hackel, left; Rev. G.F. Dressler, right.

PHOTO Fig. 8: Werning descendant Margaret Krug Palen standing in front of the Werning ancestral home built 1835 in Dankerode-on-der-Fulda.

PHOTO Fig. 9: Werning descendant Margaret Krug Palen, right, with communion ware and baptismal bowl used by her Werning ancestors in Dankerode-on-der-Fulda Church, Germany. The pewter ware has been in continuous use to the present day. Left, Willie Knierin, Werning-Brehm relative of the author.

PHOTO Fig. 10: Brehm descendant Willie Knierin standing in front of the Brehm ancestral home in Dankerode-on-der-Fulda, Germany.

Dankerode-on-der-Fulda is a small farming village located about forty-five kilometers southeast of Kassel, Germany and about eight kilometers north of Rotenberg. It is approximately fifteen kilometers from what was at one time the East Germany border in the State of Hessen, the area called Hessen-Kassel. Frau Maria Schmidt was postmistress of the village when we visited. Her grandfather Conrad Brehm was a brother of Johana Jeanette Brehm (b 28 Sept 1817, d 21 Sept 1882 Benton Co IA) married 12 Jan 1840 to Johann Adam Werning (b 23 Aug 1812, d 14 Dec 1879 Benton Co IA) the author's great-great grandparents.

When 19th Century migration to the USA occurred, thirty people from Dankerode-on-der-Fulda, including the Werning family, parents and nine children emigrated in two sailings via Bremen, Germany, arriving in New York in spring of 1869 and March 1870. The Knierin family bought the forty acre farm owned by Valentin Werning, and Willie and Hildegard Knierin resided in the original house built by Valentin Werning in 1835, and renovated in 1964. A foundation stone engraved with Valentin's name and 1835 date remains visible.

Twelve km from Haina is Moischeid, where history records the name Krug as landowners in 1301 A.D. Castlestreet exists today where the Krug family dwelled in a castle to defend the nobility, and the street still bears the name. The land along on the way to Haina is Old Vohl (land farmed by Krugs).

A common thread found in the author's heritage villages of Germany is the reference to the Holy City of Jerusalem:

> Last night as I lay sleeping,
> I dreamed I stood in Old Jerusalem beside the
>   Temple.
> I heard the children singing.
> I thought the voice of angels from Heaven was
>   answering.
> And then my dream changed.
> The streets no longer rang as the children sang.
> The sun grew dark, the morn was cold.
> A cross arose upon a lonely hill.
> Once again my dream changed.
> I saw the Holy City
> The light of God was on the streets.

The gates were open wide,
All could enter; nobody was denied.
It was the New Jerusalem
That would not pass away.
The blessings of that scene,
Remain with me to this day.

A passionate loyalty to a new home in the USA was evident in the first two generations of American-born Germans even though English was their second language. As long as German was spoken as the first language, the cultural values of Germany were maintained. When it was decided that the next generation born in America would have English as their first language, erosion of German cultural values occurred.

Equal parts of frugality, thriftiness (some prefer the expression, conservatism), and the ambition of German-American families contributed greatly to the development of communities in the USA. Education, once not important to German immigrant families and their immediate descendants due to unlimited economic opportunities to make money beginning at a young age, became a more important value in the last half of the 20th century. Education was necessary to qualify for employment opportunities other than those existing in agriculture.

The 21st century brought with it a nostalgic return to one's "roots" that has become increasingly popular. Little has been written about the ordinary lives of ordinary farm people in either Germany or the USA. The searching of German family lineage contributes greatly to the history and understanding of this important segment of the population of the United State of America.

There is something satisfying about searching for, and finding, information about relatives of generations past. It validates our own existence, it makes us feel good because we are honoring our ancestors, and we just feel better knowing where we came from.

ABBREVIATIONS

Abt	about
Aft	after
ae	age
aka	known as
b	born
Bef	before
bpt	baptized
bur	buried
CdrMem	Cedar Memorial Cemetery, Cedar Rapids
cf	cross reference
Ch	church
con	confirmation
d	died
d/o	daughter of
dec'd	deceased
DVD	divorced
GS	gravestone
Hosp	hospital
Hse	house
JP	Justice of the Peace
Luth	Lutheran
m	married
mbr(s)	member(s)
MD	medical doctor
nee	maiden family name
ND	no date
NFR	no further record
NN	no name
ns	new style
os	old style
prob	probably
Rev	Reverend
s/o	son of

St.And .... St. Andrew Luth Church, Van Horne, IA
St.John .... St. John Lutheran Church, Newhall, IA
St.John Cem...... St. John Luth Cemetery, Newhall, IA
St.Steph............. St. Stephen Luth Church, Atkins, IA
St.Steph Cem .... St. Stephen Luth Cemetery, Atkins, IA
TrinCR .... Trinity Luth Church, Cedar Rapids, IA
TrinVT .... Trinity Lutheran Church, Vinton, IA
wid/o .... widow of
wid/er .... widower
wit .... witness
* .... ancestor in/from Germany
** .... latest generation in Germany

GERMAN SETTLERS OF IOWA
THEIR DESCENDANTS AND EUROPEAN ANCESTORS

*August Heinrich ABRAHAM SR. s/o Peter Abraham & Anna Katherina nee Stein; b 1838 Lunden Schlewswig, Germany, d 1923 Benton Co IA bur Vinton, IA Evergreen Cem; freight vessel helmsman twelve years; 1867 emigrated to USA; Highland, WI farm laborer; m 1868 Rosena Louisa Kramer (b Germany 1842, d 1924 bur Vinton, IA Evergreen Cem; 1852 WI immigrant). Moved to farm purchased in Eden Twp. Benton Co IA; 1898 retired in Vinton, IA. Children:
  Dora – m August Broendel
  Emma – NFR
  Peter – m Emma Knuth; son Loren
  Mary – b 1877, d 1959 bur Evergreen Cem Vinton, IA;
      m 1899 Charles Frank Knuth
  George SR. – m Anna Averhof.
  August Heinrich JR. – m 1910 Louise Weichman
  Alma – NFR

George ABRAHAM SR. s/o August Heinrich Abraham SR. & Rosena Louisa nee Kramer; m Anna Averhof. Children:
  Margaret – m Overan Lund, Minneapolis, MN
  George JR. – NFR
  Willard – Newhall, IA
  Wayne – Lamont, IA

Kent Myron ADAMS s/o Barbara Juliann Haerther & Herbert "Howard" Adams; b 28 Jun 1956 Cavalier, ND; Occupation: Pressman; m 21 Jul 1990 Holy Cross Luth Ch Kansas City, MO to Laurie Ann Gish (b 08 Oct 1964 KS) d/o Roger Eli Gish & Elaine Louise nee Ohlde. Children:
  Christopher Martin John – b 02 Aug 1991 Kansas City
  Andrew Kent Avery – b 01 Nov 1993 Kansas City, MO

Marchelle Lynn ADAMS d/o Barbara Juliann Haerther & Herbert "Howard" Adams; b 10 Apr 1955 Cavalier, ND; m 24 Sept 1988 Monterey, CA to Curtis Hins Carleton III (his 2nd m; b 12 Jul 1941 San Mateo, CA; US Army Vietnam; Vice-President Medical Supply Co.) s/o Curtis Hins

1

Carleton II & Florence Katherine nee Herzog.
>STEPSON:
>Gregory Scott Carleton – b 27 Dec 1965 San Jose, CA

Alvin ALBERS s/o Hartwig A. Albers & Anna nee Witt; m Velma Frahm. Children:
>Larry – Children: Beth, Tina
>Allen – NFR

Donald ALBERS s/o Hartwig A. Albers & Anna nee Witt; m Betty Feuerbach. Children:
>Mark – m 1973 Cynthia Thompson
>Kevin – NFR
>Sheila Ann – b 31 Mar 1959; m 27 Aug 1977 Randall Ray Krug

*Hartwig ALBERS came to Benton Co IA in 1874 from Holstein, Germany; 1876 purchased 80 acres Section 15 Homer Twp Benton Co IA; m 23 Sept 1877 Katharina Groth from Holstein, Germany. Children:
>Hartwig A. – m Anna Witt
>John – m Katharina Scheel
>Herman – m Elsie Junge
>Jacob Henry – m Emma Witt
>Celia – m Gustov Witt
>Margaret – b 07 Dec 1888 Keystone, IA d 14 Jun 1984;
>>m 27 Dec 1911 Henry J. Sindt

Hartwig A. ALBERS s/o Hartwig Albers & Katharina nee Groth; m Anna Witt. NFR Children:
>Alvin – m Velma Frahm
>Arthur – m Kathryn Carter
>Donald – m Betty Feurbach

Margaret ALBERS d/o Hartwig Albers & Katharina nee Groth; b 07 Dec 1888 near Keystone Benton Co IA, d 14 Jun 1984 ae77y 20d; m 27 Dec 1911 Henry J. Sindt (b 26 Apr 1888, d 14 Jun 1984 ae96y 1m 19d) s/o Wilhelm Sindt & Katharina nee Wunder of rural Keystone. Farmers in Kane Twp Benton Co IA retiring in 1941. Members St. John Luth Ch, Keystone, IA. Children:
>Wilbert H. Sindt – b 24 Nov 1912
>Lester Sindt -b 04 Oct 1914; m Dorothy Sullivan, Belle Plaine, IA

Elmer Sindt – b 10 Feb 1917; m Lylas Witt, Keystone, IA

Mark ALBERS s/o Donald Albers & Betty nee Feuerbach; m 1973 Cynthia Thompson (b 1949) d/o Russell Thompson & LaVonne nee Koopman. Children:
   Amy – b 1977
   Brad – b 1980
   Juston – NFR

Shiela Ann ALBERS d/o Donald Albers & Betty nee Feuerbach: cf Randall Ray Krug.

David L. ALBERTSON s/o Donald G. Albertson & Kay Frances nee Pickering; b 30 Jul 1957; 1st m 22 Jul 1978 Patricia Vitek (b 13 Jun 1958). Children:
   Adam Roy – b 17 Jan 1979
   TWINS: Nichole – b 24 Mar 1981
              Valerie – b 24 Mar 1981
2nd m 05 Dec 1990 David L. Albertson to Coreen Petrasalka (b 18 Mar 1968).

Vince ALBRECHT: cf Doris Schmidt, d/o Frieda Gertrude nee Happel & Richard Schmidt.

Craig Daniel ANDERSON s/o Betty Jean nee Koopman & John Hasbrouck Anderson; b 07 Feb 1969; m 03 Aug 1996 Teresa Kay Buchanan. Children:
   Ethan John – b 10 Feb 1997
   Caleb Joseph – b 15 Nov 1999

James Peter ANDERSON s/o Lydia Mary nee Buchmann & Peter Anderson; b 05 Apr 1954; m 29 Sept 1972 Corinna Rollins. Children:
   Stacy Lynn – b 28 Nov 1972
   Jason – b 13 Dec 1973

Dennis Ray ANDREW s/o Arlene Lucille nee Wilhlemi & Virgil Meyer Andrew; b 1942; m Judy Mattson. Children:
   Kimberley – b 1964; m Robert Stewart
   Kristina Rae – b 1966; m Craig Stilson
   Karmen – b 1967; m Steve Miller
   Jason – 1971

3

Julie – b 1972; m Rick Lundvall

Kay Lynn ARMSTRONG d/o Alice Marie nee Deklotz & Lenard James Armstrong; b 27 Jul 1962 St.Lukes Hosp Cedar Rapids, IA bpt 18 Aug 1962 and con 11 Apr 1976 St.Steph; m 03 Sept 1988 Ed Bartholomew s/o Paul & Ann Bartholomew of Ft.Madison, IA. Montrose, IA. Residence. Children:
    Megan Bartholomew – b 09 Apr 1990
    Bryce Bartholomew – b 27 Mar 1993

Kimberly ARMSTRONG d/o Alice Marie nee Deklotz & Lenard James Armstrong; b 19 May 1958 St.Lukes Hosp Cedar Rapids, IA bpt 15 Jun 1958 and con 21 Mar 1972 St.Steph; m 04 Apr 1987 St.Steph to Gary Spiess s/o Robert & Ann Speiss of Ft. Lauderdale, Fl. Lisbon, IA residence. Children:
    Nicole Spiess – b 19 Feb 1989
    Alison Spiess – b 24 Jun 1991

Barbara Jean BACHMANN d/o Robert Louis Bachmann & Frances Lorraine nee Lingwood; b 23 Aug 1941; m 04 Jun 1961 James LaVern Hankins (b 02 Dec 1941). Children:
    Karla Kay Hankins – b 13 Nov 1965
    Kimony Jo Hankins – b 03 Nov 1968

Carol Ann BACHMANN d/o Donald William Bachmann & Ruth Elaine nee Reynick; b 08 Aug 1953; m 22 Apr 1978 Bruce Leland Marxsen (b 09 Jul 1951). Children:
    Jamie Leigh Marxsen – b 31 Jul 1981
    Cale Shawn Marxsen – b 31 May 1984

Donald William BACHMANN s/o Louise Dorothea Katherine nee Brehm & Julius H. Bachmann; b 20 Oct 1926; m 21 Aug 1949 Ruth Elaine Reynick (b 21 Nov 1930). Children:
    Lance Alan – b 02 May 1951;
        m 25 Sept 1974 Perla Tina Praxedes Delina
    Carol Ann – b 08 Aug 1953; m 22 Apr 1978 Bruce Leland Marxsen
    Kathleen Marie – b 28 Apr 1956;
        m 29 Nov 1975 Anthony Clarence Storbeck

Dorothy Katherine BACHMANN d/o Louise Dorothea Katherine nee

Brehm & Julius H. Bachmann; b 26 Oct 1924; m 03 Jun 1956 Herbert H. Bade (d 21 Sept 1987). Children:

Ralph Edward Bade – b 29 Aug 1959;
    m 27 Jun 1981 Kathleen Ann Brady
Paul Andrew Bade – b 05 Nov 1958
Priscilla Faith Bade – b 08 Feb 1961
Lawrence Mark Bade – b 20 Aug 1963;
    m 30 Mar 1996 Natasha Renee Sutliff

Helen Louise BACHMANN d/o Louise Dorothea Katherine nee Brehm & Julius H. Bachmann; b 01 Jan 1931; m 01 Oct 1950 James Rae Wilson JR. (b 14 Jun 1929, d 27 Jun 2002 ae71y 13d). Children:

Wendy Ann Wilson – b 26 Sept 1955;
    m 31 Jul 2002 Timothy Joe Martin
James Rae Wilson III – b 15 Dec 1958

James Robert BACHMANN s/o Robert Louis Bachmann & Frances Lorraine nee Lingwood; b 09 Nov 1957; m 23 Jun 1979 Sally Marie Marshall (b 25 Nov 1960). Children:

Isaac Theodore – b 05 Aug 1980

Julius Jacob Theodore BACHMANN s/o Louise Dorothea Katherine nee Brehm & Julius H. Bachmann; b 29 Oct 1918, d 08 Mar 2001 ae82y 4m 7d); m Dorothy Agnes Reed (b 19 Aug 1916, d 09 Feb 2002 ae85y 5m 21d). Children:

Robert Reed – b 30 Oct 1953;
    1st m 26 Jun 1983 Catherine Rose Underwood DVD
    2nd m 24 Jun 1998 Vickie Jo Frank

Kathleen Marie BACKMANN d/o Donald William Bachmann & Ruth Elaine nee Reynick; b 28 Apr 1956; m 29 Nov 1975 Anthony Clarence Storbeck (b 04 Jan 1956). Children:

Nathan Anthony Storbeck – 14 Jan 1980
Nicholas Arthur Storbeck – b 08 Mar 1981
Breanna Katherine Storbeck – b 24 Sept 1984

Lance Alan BACHMANN s/o Donald William Bachmann & Ruth Elaine nee Reynick; b 02 May 1951; m 25 Sept 1974 Perla Tina Praxedes Delina (b 21 Jul 1950). Children:

Christina Lee – b 06 Jan 1976

Donald Charles – b 05 Feb 1980

Marilyn Kay BACHMANN d/o Robert Louis Bachmann & Frances Lorraine nee Lingwood; b 22 Feb 1943; m 08 Jan 1966 Mickey Calvin Myrick (13 Feb 1942). Children:
    Melanie Kay Myrick (Adopted) – b 21 Mar 1971
    TWINS: Jill Renee Myrick – b 20 Aug 1975
            Julie Kay Myrick – b 20 Aug 1975

Robert Reed BACHMANN s/o Julius Jacob Theodore Bachmann & Dorothy Agnes nee Reed; b 30 Oct 1953; 1st m 26 Jun 1983 Catherine Ross Underwood (b 03 Jul 1958) DVD. Child:
    Ashley Brooke – b 10 Mar 1988
2nd m 24 Jun 1998 Robert Reed Bachmann to Vickie Jo Frank (b 29 Sept 1955).

Saundra Ann BACHMANN d/o Robert Louis Bachmann & Frances Lorraine nee Lingwood; b 04 Dec 1954; m 24 Nov 1978 Cliff Roy Roberts (b 28 Sept 1951). Children:
    Jason Michael Roberts – b 25 Nov 1975
    Philip Matthew Roberts – b 03 Jul 1980

Ralph Edward BADE s/o Dorothy Katherine nee Bachmann & Herbert H. Bade; b 29 Aug 1959; m 27 Jun 1981 Kathleen Ann Brady (b 05 Jan 1959). Children:
    Nicole Elizabeth – b 10 Oct 1982
    Tara Ann – b 06 Nov 1983

Joyce May BAKENHUS d/o Evelyn Hettie nee Rammelsberg & Ora Oscar Bakenhus; b 30 Sept 1954; m 25 Nov 1973 Wayne B. Stone. Children:
    Angela Denise Stone – b 24 Jul 1979
    Michelle Leigh Stone – b 14 Feb 1985

Amelia BALHORN d/o Joachin Balhorn JR. & Dora; b 1892; m 1913 Louis Koep (b 1885, d 1951). Residence Belle Plaine, Benton Co IA. Children:
    Stanley Koep – m Jean Minish, Belle Plaine, IA
    Mildred Koep – m Dick Schild
    Dorothy Koep – m Tom Miller

Anna BALHORN d/o August J.W. Balhorn & Anna nee Bender; b 1899; m

Arthur Hamann (b 1899, d 1970). Children:
  Harlan Hamann – b 1922; m Lois Crombaugh
  Donna Mae Hamann – b 1925; m William P. Malloy

August J. W. BALHORN s/o Carl Balhorn & Sophia nee Hennings; b 1872, d 1926; attended Tilford Academy; m Anna Bender (b 14 Jun 1872, d 30 May 1964 ae91y 11m 14d). Children:
  Charles W. – b 1892, d 1969; m Elnora Margaret Hamann
  William – b 1893, d 1969; m Antonette (Tony) Albertson
  Sophia – b 1895; m Alfred Bockholt
  John – b 1898; m Pearl Struve
  Anna – b 1899; m Arthur Hamann

*Carl BALHORN s/o Joackin Balhorn & Sophia nee Nieman; b 14 Apr 1843 Mecklenburg, Germany, d 15 Oct 1892 ae49y 6m; came to USA about 1858; m Sophia Hennings (b 1844 d 1923). Farmed in Big Grove Twp Benton Co IA. Children:
  August J.W. – b 1872, d 1926; m Anna Bender
  Annie – m NN Seeck

Charles BALHORN s/o Joachin Balhorn JR. & Dora; b 1883, d 1967; m 1906 Clara Knuth. Child:
  Merrill – m Helen Primus, Vinton, IA residence

Charles W. BALHORN s/o August J. W. Balhorn & Anna nee Bender; b 1892, d 1969; attended Tilford Academy; Mt. Vernon College; US Army World War I, Camp Dodge, Des Moines, IA; m Elnora Margaret Hamann (b 1893 d 1976) Farmed north of Keystone, Benton Co IA. Children:
  Dean William – b 1921; m Gayle Armstrong
  Richard Charles – b 1925; m Betty Wagmer
  Elaine Eleanor-b 1928; m Robert E.B. Beadle

Dean William BALHORN s/o Charles W. Balhorn & Elnora Margaret nee Hamann; b 1921; m Gayle Armstrong of Atkins, Benton Co IA. Children:
  Randall – NFR
  Linda – NFR

Elaine Eleanor BALHORN d/o Charles W. Balhorn & Elnora Margaret nee Hamann b 1928; m Robert E.B. Beadle of IN. Children:
  Natalee Beadle – m NN Marquardt. Children: Brooke, Luke

Matthew Beadle – m Ann; Children: Shannon, Tyler

*Joachin BALHORN JR.s/o Joachin Balhorn SR. & Sophia nee Nieman; b 1850 Germany; 1880 came to USA from Bremen, Germany, with parents and wife Dora (b 1860, d 1946). Moved to CA prob 1916 where both are buried. Children:
    Charles – b 1883, d 1967; m 1906 Clara Knuth
    John – b 1885, d 1904, bur Luth Cemetery
    August – b 1888, d 1978; bur CA
    Anna – b 1890; m Orville Bowman; residence CA
    Amelia – b 1892; m 1913 Louis Koep

*Joachin BALHORN SR. b 21 Feb 1813 Mecklenburg, d 29 Nov. 1902 ae89y 9m 8d bur St.John Cem; 1880 came to USA; m Sophia Nieman (b 16 Dec. 1816 Mecklenburg, Germany, d 29 Jun 1895 ae78y 6m 13d bur St.John Cem). Retired from farming 2 miles north and 1/2 mile east of Newhall, Eldorado Twp Benton Co IA. Children:
    Joachin JR. – b 1850; m Dora NN
    John – NFR
    Carl – b 1843; m Sophia Hennings
    Minnie – NFR

John BALHORN s/o August J.W. Balhorn & Anna nee Bender; b 1898. Invented and patented corn picker; m Pearl Struve. Children:
    Vincent – m Bernice Wilkins
    Milo – b 1923; m Dorliss Witt

Milo BALHORN s/o John Balhorn & Pearl nee Struve; b 1923; m Dorliss Witt. Invented a cement loader. Waterloo, IA residence. Children:
    Jean Ann – NFR
    Linda – NFR
    Barbara – NFR

Richard Charles BALHORN s/o Charles W. Balhorn & Elnora Margaret nee Hamann; b 1925; m Betty Wagmer of Keystone, Benton Co IA. Children:
    Camille – NFR
    Gary – NFR
    Glenda – NFR
    Jackoelyn – NFR

Sophia BALHORN d/o August J. W. Balhorn & Anna nee Bender; b 1895; m Alfred Bockholt. Children:
  LaVerne (Bucky)Bockholt – d 09 Nov 1942 Invasion of North Africa World War II; m Olive Boehmke
  Marlus Bockholt – b 1921; m Robert Buck. Children:
    Marcia, Holst, Ronald, Barbara

Vincent BALHORN s/o John Balhorn & Pearl nee Struve; Computer Manager Data Point Corp. San Antonio, TX; 1st m Bernice Wilkins. Children:
  Carl – NFR
  Dean – NFR
  Nancy – NFR
  Diane – NFR
2nd m Vincent Balhorn to Pat NN

James BARTHOLOMEW s/o NFR; b 20 Jun 1954; m 28 Jul 1972 Lisa Ann Boots (b 18 Apr 1956). Children:
  Brandy Jo – b 08 Mar 1973
  Brock James – b 23 Sept 1976

Michelle Lea BAUMAN d/o Carol Marie nee Rammelsberg & 2nd m Ralph Bauman; b 01 Sept 1970; m 10 Sept 1994 Mark Riley. Children:
  Macey Grae Riley – b 11 Oct 2000
  Maximim Anthony Riley – b 14 Sept 2002

Vicky Lynn BAUMILLER d/o Marvin Baumiller & Elda nee Werning; b 10 May 1963; Nurse; m 18 Feb 1989 Our Savior's Luth Ch Aberdeen, SD to Earl Willis Maier JR. s/o Earl Maier SR. & Marcella of Eureka, SD. Earl was State of SD Diesel Mechanic. Child:
  (Daughter) NN Maier – b 09 Aug 1989

Delmar Elwood BAYER s/o Martin Fredrick Bayer & Elda Gertrude Louise nee Rinderknecht; b 20 Apr 1947 Guernsey, IA; m 27 Mar 1971 Homestead, IA Rose Marie Thompson (b 07 Oct 1951 Jackson, MS) d/o Otto Thompson. Occupation: Farmer; Feed Store. Children:
  Denise Michelle – b 28 Dec 1972 Grinnell, IA
  Matthew Joseph – b 09 Jan 1975 Grinnell, IA
  Lukas Nathan – b 20 Aug 1979 Grinnell, IA

Paula Marie – b 03 Feb 1981 Grinnell, IA

Doris Elaine BAYER d/o Martin Fredrick Bayer & Elda Gertrude Louise nee Rinderknecht; b 18 Jan 1939 Guernsey, IA; m 28 Oct 1962 TrinCR to Marvin Jerome Stanek (b 21 Dec 1939 Cedar Rapids, IA; Machinist) s/o Leo Stanek & Nellie nee Primmer. MN Resort Owners. Children:
>Lori Sue Stanek – b 15 May 1963 Cedar Rapids, IA;
>>m 27 Nov 1993 Robert Newton
>Wesley David Stanek – b 30 Mar 1965 CR, IA;
>>m 19 Sept 1992 Cyndi Hollerman
>Dawn Marie Stanek – b 19 Feb 1970 Cedar Rapids, IA;
>>m 29 Jun 1966 Matt Koenig
>Joan Renee Stanek – b 10 Nov 1971 Cedar Rapids, IA;
>>m 30 Jul 1994 Paul Matchan

Julia Marie BAYER d/o Friedrich Henry Bayer & Dorothy Marie nee Krug; b 26 Oct 1959 Marengo, Iowa Co IA, bpt Marengo Luth Ch; m 20 Jun 1981 Terry L. Warnick (b 27 Apr 1956). Child:
>Renee Marie Warnick – b 04 Jun 1982; m 25 May 2006 Dietrich Maas

Linda Ann BAYER d/o Martin Fredrick Bayer & Elda Gertrude Louise nee Rinderknecht; b 10 Nov 1956 Victor, IA US Air Force in England; d 26 Apr 1995 ae38y 5m 16d; m 25 Aug 1979 Luth Ch Victor, IA to James William Mortell (b 17 Aug 1937 Clinton, IA) s/o Charles Henry Mortell & Roberta Patricia nee Amjach. Children:
>Patrick Martin Mortell – b 19 Aug 1981 Madison, IN
>Philip August Mortell -b 29 Nov 1982 Louisville, KY

Lucille Jean BAYER d/o Martin Fredrick Bayer & Elda Gertrude Louise nee Rinderknecht; b 07 Jul 1950 Guernsey, IA; m 11 Nov 1972 Victor, IA to James Allen Tuttle (b 29 Dec 1946 Manly, IA; Railroad Engineer) s/o Howard Allen Tuttle & Bernidane Ann nee Amonson. Children:
>Jason Edward Tuttle – b 22 Mar 1975 CR, IA
>Jamie Nicole Tuttle – b 19 Oct 1979 Des Moines, IA; d 26 Dec 1987
>>Victor, IA, bur Altoona, IA

Marine Mae BAYER d/o Martin Fredrick Bayer & Elda Gertrude Louise nee Rinderknecht; b 23 May 1943 Guernsey, IA; 1st m 04 Aug 1961 Chicago, IL to Dennis Edward Keys (b 04 Aug 1940 Chicago, IL) s/o Charles Keys (mother's maiden name Hawk). DVD. Child:

Edward Ronald Keys – b 04 Jun 1962 Chicago, IL

2nd m 11 Feb 1984 Trinity Luth Ch Tama, IA, Marine Mae nee nee Bayer Keys to Darold Dean Timm(b 20 Jul 1949) s/o Glenn Albert & Esther Florence Timm.

Martin Eldred BAYER s/o Martin Fredrick Bayer & Elda Gertrude Louise nee Rinderknecht; b 07 Feb 1937 Guernesey, IA; m 08 Mar 1964 Cedar Rapids, IA to Betty Jean Hershey (b 08 Apr 1943 Atkins Benton Co IA) d/o George William Hershey & Anna Gertrude nee Lockhart. Farmers. Children:

Jeffrey Martin – b 07 Jan 1966 Marengo, IA

Joel Roger – b 16 May 1968 Marengo, IA

David Lee – b 23 Jun 1972 Marengo, IA

Deborah Jean – b 06 Nov 1974 Marengo, IA

Pearl Evelyn BAYER d/o Martin Fredrick Bayer & Elda Gertrude Louise nee Rinderknecht; b 26 Jan 1935 Guernsey, Iowa Co IA; m 29 May 1960 St.John Luth Ch Victor, IA to Arlo Hans Fredrick Suhr (b 05 Apr 1936 Battle Creek, IA; Farmer; Carpenter) s/o Hans Suhr & Elsa nee Koster. Children:

Mark Allen Suhr – b 19 Apr 1961 Correctionville, IA

m 01 Oct 1994 Kim Robinson

Annette Marie Suhr – b 30 Sept 1963 Correctionville

m 19 Dec 1982 Greg Allen Nelson

Donna Rae Suhr – b 05 Sept 1965 Correctionville, IA

m 27 May 1988 Clark Trent Davis

Phyllis Lucille BAYER d/o Martin Fredrick Bayer & Elda Gertrude Louise nee Rinderknecht; b 20 Jun 1945 Guernsey, IA; m 20 Aug 1966 Des Moines, IA to Bernard John Dahlhauser JR. (b 19 Aug 1943 Algona, IA, d 02 Nov 1989 ae46y 2m 14d) s/o Bernard John Dahlhauser SR. & Ruthy nee Mucky. Children:

Joelle Ruth Dahlhauser – b/d 01 Oct 1967 Des Moines, IA

Sean David Dahlhauser – b 17 Jan 1969 Des Moines, IA;

m 13 Oct 1987 Carrie Hernandez

Rev. Robert Fredrich BAYER s/o Friedrich Henry Bayer & Dorothy Marie nee Krug; b 15 Feb 1950 Marengo, Iowa Co IA, bpt Marengo Luth Ch; 03 Jul 1977 ordained Missouri Synod Luth clergyman, parishes Marion and Hillsboro KS; Correctionville, IA; Libertory, NE; Livonia, MI; m 09 Jun

1979 Amy Dormer (b 23 Feb 1952). Children:
    Timothy Paul (Adopted) – b 14 Feb 1983
    Paul Thomas (Adopted) – b 15 Aug 1985
    Rebecca Lynn (Adopted) – b 27 Aug 1987

Violette Janette BAYER d/o Martin Fredrick Bayer & Elda Gertrude Louise nee Rinderknecht; b 17 Dec 1940 Guernsey, IA; m 01 Nov 1959 Victor, IA to Roger Eugene Hall (b 06 May 1937 Grinnell, IA d 22 Jul 2005 ae68y 2m 16d) s/o Gene Orlando Hall (b 18 Aug 1906) & Ahlea nee Wylie (b 17 Jul 1906). Children:
    Kathleen Lynn Hall – b 11 May 1960 Marengo, IA
    Kelly Jo Hall – b 24 Oct 1963 Marengo, IA;
        m 26 Sept 1987 Russell Lee Emanuel
    Sherrie Lee Hall – b 01 Feb 1967 Marengo, IA;
        m 21 Oct 1989 Paul Stolz

Austin BECK s/o Jacob Beck JR. & Addie Fellows; b 1868, d 1934; m 1890 Liberty, PA to Lilliam Sheffer. Moved to IA and farmed 640 acres with 12 horses. Children:
    TWINS: Milton – b 1890, d 1952; m Hazel Files
              Florence – premature b/d 1890
    Ethel – b 1892, d 1950; m Leland Marsh; 2 children
    Hazel – b 1897; m Eugene McLeod
    Mabelle – b 1899; m Chuck Upah; Adopted daughter
    Burdette – b 1901 d 1973; m Jennie Koch; 7 children
    Lucille – b 1903; m John Marsh; 2 children

Jacob BECK JR. s/o Jacob Beck SR. & Catharine nee Miller; b 1827, d 1906; m Addie Fellows; moved west to Iowa where land prices were lower than PA. Purchased 320 acres Sections 30 and 31, Kane Twp Benton Co IA extending into Tama Co IA. Children:
    Austin – b 1868, d 1934; m Lillian Sheffer
    Florence – b 1866, d 1954
    Emma – b 1871, d 1968

Jacob BECK SR. b 1794, d 1875; Blacksmith; JP; m Catharine Miller. Seven children including:
    Jacob Beck JR. – b 1827, d 1906; m Addie Fellows

Amy Elizabeth BECKER d/o Deanne Kay nee Krug & Andrew Joseph

Becker; b 08 Jan 1975; m 25 Sept 2004 Andrew Robert Volz (b 11 Dec 1970) s/o Jim & Annie Volz of Amana, IA.

Sarah Marie BECKER d/o Deanne Kay nee Krug & Andrew Joseph Becker; b 30 Jan 1983; m 02 Sept 2006 Geoffrey Michael Seifert (b 17 Jul 1981) s/o Michael & Patricia Seifert of Urbandale, IA.

Mary Lou BEHRENS d/o Louise Martha nee Haerther & Walter Behrens; b 17 Feb 1937; m 21 Feb 1959 Eugene Felix Doran (b 04 Sept 1931). Children:
  Lori Lou Doran – b 02 Oct 1959
  Gary Eugene Doran – b 15 Feb 1961
  Gina Marie Doran – b 25 Jan 1970

William Henry BEHRENS s/o Louise Martha nee Haerther & Walter Behrens; b 04 Jun 1940; m 31 Dec 1959 Margaret Judith Kapfer (b 08 Apr 1940). Children:
  Michael William – b 08 Jul 1960
  Mark David – b 26 Jun 1961
  Mathew Anthony – b 04 Feb 1975

Angeline Kay BENDER d/o Elnora nee Juhnke & LeRoy Theodore Bender; b 23 Jun 1957 Freeman, SD; 1st m 09 Jun 1979 Hillsdale United Ch of Christ to Donald R. Ewen (b 14 Nov 1955) s/o Jean & Jackie Ewen JR. of Portland, OR. DVD 1993. OR residence. Children:
  Autumn Leigh Ewen – b 19 Jun 1984
  Sara Melissa Ewen – b 17 May 1989
2nd m 06 Aug 1995 Mt. Tabor Park Amphitheater, Portland, OR Angeline Kay nee Bender Ewen to Steve Pringle (b 07 Nov 1958) s/o Ronald Pringle and Karen nee Obrist. Steve's children from 1st m:
  STEPCHILDREN:
  Richard Pringle – b 17 Nov 1984
  Christina Pringle – b 17 Apr 1987
  Amber Pringle – b 05 Aug 1990

Amanda BENDER d/o Wilhelmina nee Heyer & Edward Bender; b 1896, d 1988; m Henry Allers. Farmers. Children:
  Carol Allers – m NN Olson
  Donald Allers – NFR

Debra Ann BENDER d/o Elnora nee Juhnke & LeRoy Bender; b 31 Aug 1955 Freeman, SD; m 31 Aug 1974 Hillsdale United Ch of Christ to Larry Syme s/o Robert & Leona Syme. OR residence. Children:
  Nathanial Jay Syme – b 06 Apr 1976;
    m 27 May 1995 Alicia Lynn Kearns
  Karrah Ann Syme – b 12 Feb 1978; m 21 Feb 1998 James Savage
  Katie Marie Syme – b 01 Nov 1983; m 26 Jun 2004 Dustin Moon
  Kami Joy Syme – b 03 Aug 1985; m 19 May 2007 Jeff Tam Sing

Lizzie BENDER d/o Wilhelmina nee Heyer & Edward Bender; b 1893, d 1975; m John Steinford. Farmers. Children:
  Henrietta Steinford – m NN Kuehl
  Leonard Steinford – NFR
  Russell Steinford – NFR
  Ina Mae Steinford – m NN Radloff
  Dorothy Steinford – m NN Ohde
  Duane Steinford – NFR
  Margil Steinford – NFR

Robert BENDER s/o Wilhelmina nee Heyer & Edward Bender; b 1901, d 1980; m Esther Seeck; owned Bender Implement in Keystone, IA until 1942 move to Cedar Rapids, IA. Children:
  Joann – m NN Schweitzer
  Charlene – m NN Hansen
  Sarah – m NN Breidert
  Connie – m NN Frost
  Robert – NFR
  Jerry – NFR

Carol Ann BERGEN d/o Edna Frieda Marie nee Husted & Robert John Bergen; b 17 May 1943; m 14 Nov 1962 Darold Dean Junge. Children:
  Darren Dean Junge – b 15 Mar 1964; m 30 Jul 1994 Sherri Ganzar
  Steven Robert Junge – b 27 Dec 1967;
    1st m 06 Aug 1987 Michelle Kopecky DVD
    2nd m 08 Oct 2005 Sandra McChesney

Steven Robert JUNGE s/o Carol Ann nee Bergen & Darold Dean Junge; b 27 Dec 1967; 1st.m 06 Aug 1987 Michelle Kopecky DVD.
2nd m 08 Oct 2005 Steven Robert Junge to Sandra McChesney. Child:
  Zander – b 09 May 2007

Susan Jean BERGEN d/o Edna Frieda Marie nee Husted & Robert John Bergen; b 14 Feb 1947; m 24 Feb 1970 Norman Eugene Cross (b 22 Jul 1934 d 09 Sept 1995 ae61y 1m 18d). Children:
Raymond Eugene Cross – b 05 May 1974;
m 07 Oct 2000 Tonya Kay Duby
Marie Ann Cross – b 05 Jun 1978

Anna Martha BEYER d/o Simon Beyer & Anna Elisabeth nee Vaupel: cf Konrad Daume.

*Anna Karoline BEYER d/o Maria nee Gross & Johann Peter Beyer; b 15 Feb 1915 Löhlbach, Germany; bpt and con 1929 Löhlbach Ch; d 20 Dec 1997 Löhlbach, Germany ae82y 10m 5d; m 10 Mar 1939 Löhlbach Ch to Jakob Wickert (b 01 Nov 1914 Löhlbach, Germany, d 27 Aug 1949 ae35y 9m 16d Nordhorn, Germany, funeral in Löhlbach Ch; World War II Germany Army). First relative to recognize Author in 1984 on first visit in Löhlbach, Germany. Child:
**Marlene Wickert – b 17 Apr 1939 Löhlbach Hse #33;
m 14/15 Apr 1961 Heinz Bohle

*Johannes BEYER, Germany; m Anna Gertrude Rose. Child:
Simon – b 19 Oct 1819, d 16 Mar 1881; m Anna Elisabeth Vaupel

Simon BEYER s/o Johannes Beyer & Anna Gertrude nee Rose; b 19 Oct 1819, d 16 Mar 1881 ae61y 4m 25d; m Anna Elisabeth Vaupel (b 1815, d 20 May 1891). Child:
Anna Martha BEYER – b 09 Dec 1844, d 14 Apr 1931;
m 03 Mar 1867 Konrad Daume

Kent Daniel BIENLIEN s/o Lois Ruth nee Rammelsberg & William Walter Bienlien; b 13 May 1964; m 31 May 1986 Sarah Martley (b 21 Feb 1967). Children:
Jared Daniel – b 29 Nov 1986
Hannah Elizabeth – b 25 Jul 1988
Lydia Mae – b 02 Jun 1990
Prisca Charity – b 27 Jun 1994

*Carl Heinrich (Henry Carl) BIERSCHENK s/o Jacob Bierschenk & Anna Martha nee George: cf Eizabeth Kranz.

15

Christina Elizabeth BIERSCHENK d/o Carl Heinrich (Henry Carl) Bierschenk & Elizabeth nee Kranz; b 23 Oct 1896 near Newhall, IA d 1948; m 1922 St.John Benton Co IA to Carl J. Heppe (b 1889 d 1967) s/o Martin Heppe & Dorothea nee Bierschenk. Carl returned to IA with his parents in 1909 from PA; Carl and Christina rented land to farm before 1941 purchase of Carl Heinrich (Henry Karl) & Elizabeth nee Kranz Biershenck farm northwest of Newhall in Eden Twp Benton Co IA. Children:
    Robert Heppe – b 1924; m Virginia Harper
    Dwain C. Heppe – b 1927; m Reta Leimberer
    Arlene Heppe – b 1928, d 1951

Daryl Wayne BIERSCHENK s/o James Conrad Bierschenk & Christine nee Anderson; b 24 Jul 1966 (Adopted Luth Family Services, Ft.Dodge, IA); m 27 Sept 1997 Michelle Sherwood. Child:
    Braden Ward – b 23 Jun 1999

Dean Allen BIERSCHENK s/o James Conrad Bierschenk & Christina Julianna nee Andersen; b 10 Feb 1959 (Adopted Luth Family Services, Ft.Dodge, IA); Graduated ISU; 1st m 11 Aug 1984 Gloria Dei Luth Ch Des Moines, IA to Dawn Ellen Thornton (b 17 Feb 1962; Graduated ISU) d/o Richard Thornton & Marlys nee Anderson of Des Moines, IA.
2nd m Dean Allen Bierschenk to Laurie NN. Denver, IA residence.

*Dorthea "Dora" BIERSCHENK d/o John Heinrich Bierschenk & Anna Katherine nee Gier; b 1864 Datterode, Hessen, Germany, d 1935 Benton Co IA; m 1885 Martin Heppe (b Kuchen, Germany, d 1920 Newhall, IA). Martin and Dorthea with daughter Kathrina came to USA pro 1889, settled northwest of Newhall, Benton Co IA. The family later moved to Latrobe, PA where Martin Heppe worked in coal mines. 1909 return to Benton Co IA and farmed northwest of Newhall, IA. Children:
    Kathrina Heppe – b 1886, d 1947; m Carl Vaupel
    Carl J. "Charlie" Heppe – b 1889, d 1967;
        m 1922 Christina Elizabeth Bierschenk
    Elizabeth Heppe – b 1891; m Irvin Knuth
    Emma Heppe – b 1895; m August Schultz
    Henry J. Heppe – b 1902; m Marie Barney

Dorthea Katharina BIERSCHENK d/o John Heinrich Bierschenk & Anna Katherine nee Gier: cf Jacob Brehm.

16

Elaine Elizabeth BIERSCHENK d/o Fred William Bierschenk & Esther Katherine nee Rinderknecht Bierschenk Froehlich; b 10 Oct 1931 north of Newhall, Eden Twp Benton Co IA, bpt 1931 St.John, d 27 Mar 1981 University Hosp Iowa City, IA ae49y 5m 17d bur 30 Mar 1981 St.John Cem; m 17 Feb 1952 St.John to Delbert Henry Paulsen (b 05 Mar 1929 Eldorado Twp Benton Co IA) s/o George H. Paulsen & Ellen nee Broendel. Children:

    Shirley Ann Paulsen – b 01 May 1953 Vinton, IA;
        m 27 Apr 1974 Ricky Eugene Dawes
    Daniel Wayne Paulsen – b 06 Aug 1957 Vinton, IA
    Joyce Elaine Paulsen – b 09 Aug 1959 Vinton, IA;
        m 03 Mar 1984 Ronald Lee Wendt

2nd m 04 May 1985 Delbert Henry Paulsen to Isabel Irene nee Emerson Hammond (b 27 Mar 1924 Coggon, IA) d/o William James Emerson & Ellea Mae nee Todd.

Gary Wayne BIERSCHENK s/o Kenneth Conrad Bierschenk & Lorene Ann nee Weiss; b 25 Nov 1953 Virginia Gay Hosp Vinton, IA; m 10 Nov 1973 Grace Luth Ch Blairstown, IA to Phyllis Jane Heitshusen (b 04 Mar 1953 St.Lukes Hosp Cedar Rapids, IA) d/o Erwin George William Heitshusen & Madora Gesina nee Sandersfeld of Blairstown, IA. Farmers north of Blairstown, Benton Co IA. Children:

    Brian Conrad – b 13 May 1975 St.Lukes Hosp Cedar Rapids, IA
    Bridget Marie – b 10 Jan 1978 St.Lukes Hosp Cedar Rapids, IA
    Brandee Lynn – b 26 Apr 1981 St.Lukes Hosp Cedar Rapids, IA

George A. BIERSCHENK s/o Carl Heinrich (Henry Carl) Bierschenk & Elizabeth nee Kranz; b 03 Sept 1898, d 1976; m 1927 Gertrude Broendel (b 1904) d/o Henry & Lena nee Greve Broendel. Farmers, retired 1946 in Newhall, IA. No children.

Harry A. Martin BIERSCHENK s/o Carl Heinrich (Henry Carl) Bierschenk & Elizabeth nee Kranz; b 05 Feb 1906 Eden Twp Benton Co IA, bpt 15 Mar 1906 St.John, d 14 Mar 1957 ae51y 1m 9d Mercy Hosp Cedar Rapids, Linn Co IA, bur 18 Mar 1957 St.John Cem; m 11 Feb 1930 St.John to LaVerna Anna Gertrude Rinderknecht (b 23 Mar 1911 near Van Horne Eldorado Twp Benton Co IA, bpt 23 Apr 1911 St.John, d 19 Nov 1995 [Cancer] ae84y 7m 27d Virginia Gay Hosp Vinton, IA bur St.John Cem) d/o Conrad Martin Rinderknecht & Elizabeth Anna nee Krug. Farmers.

Children:
James Conrad – b 10 Sept 1931 Eden Twp Benton Co, IA
    d 25 Jun 2001; m 15 Feb 1953 Christine Julianna Andersen
Marlys Elizabeth – b 18 Jul 1935 Eden Twp Benton Co IA;
    m 27 Feb 1955 Leonard Edward Geater
Karen Margaret – b 23 Aug 1938 Eden Twp Benton Co IA;
    m 08 Jun 1958 Roger Earl Inman

James Conrad BIERSCHENK s/o Harry Martin Bierschenk & LaVerna Anna Gertrude nee Rinderknecht; b 10 Sept 1931 Eden Twp Benton Co IA, bpt 1931 St.John, d 25 Jun 2001 ae69y 9m 15d; m 15 Feb 1953 American Luth Ch Jesup, IA to Christine Julianna Andersen (b 27 Feb 1932 Eden Twp Benton Co IA) d/o Ernest Andersen & Marie Martha nee Froehlich. Farmers, retired 1996. Adopted three children:
Dean Allen (Adopted) – b 10 Feb 1959 Luth.Family Service
    Ft. Dodge, IA; 1st m 11 Aug 1985 Dawn Ellen Thorton DVD;
    2nd m Laurie NN
Renee Marie (Adopted) – b 17 May 1961 Luth.Family Service
    Ft. Dodge, IA
Daryl Wayne (Adopted) – b 24 Jul 1966 Luth.Family Service
    Ft. Dodge, IA; m 27 Sept 1997 Michelle Sherwood

Johann "Jake" BIERSCHENK s/o John Heinrich Bierschenk & Anna Katherine nee Gier; b 1862, d 1934; m 1890 Catherine Kestner. Children:
(Katie) Dorthea – NFR
William – NFR
Anna M.K. – dec'd in infancy
Anna – NFR
Martha – NFR
Reinhard – NFR
Marie – dec'd in infancy

*John Heinrich BIERSCHENK b 1837 Datterode, Hessen Kassel, Germany, d 1920 Benton Co IA; m Anna Katherine Gier (b 1839 Datterode, Germany, d 1904 Benton Co IA). John crossed Atlantic Ocean seven times visiting some of his children who came abroad ahead of him and bringing the rest of the family to America; later also going back to Germany to visit after he emigrated. Purchased 320 acres to farm 3/4 mile north of Newhall, IA. Land later farmed by great-grandson, Terry Hertle s/o Arnold Hertle. Children born in Germany before coming to USA in 1889:

*Johann "Jake" – b 1862, d 1934; m 1890 Anna Katherine Gier
*Dorthea "Dora" – b 1864, d 1935 Benton Co IA;
    m 1885 Martin Heppe
*Reinhardt – b 1868, d 1901
*Dorthea Katherina – b 1879, d 1949 Benton Co IA;
    m 1891 Jacob Brehm
*Carl – b 1872; m 1917 Elizabeth Wieditz
*Elizabeth – b 1875; m 1899 Conrad Vaupel
*Martha Elizabeth – b 12 Oct 1877 Hessen, Germany; d 04 Jul 1945
    IA; m 16 Dec 1903 August Sebastian Hertle
Henry – b 1888, d 4 days after arrival in USA

Karen Margaret BIERSCHENK d/o Harry A. Martin Bierschenk & LaVerna Anna Gertrude nee Rinderknecht; b 23 Aug 1938 Eden Twp Benton Co IA, bpt 1938 con St.John; m 08 Jun 1958 St.John to Roger Earl Inman (b 09 Jul 1937 Virginia Gay Hosp Vinton, IA; Spec. 5th Class US Army Reserves) s/o Myron Clarence Inman & Flossie Muriel nee Kucker of Vinton, IA. Farmers. Children:
    Lee Alan Inman – b 07 Jul 1960; Virginia Gay Hosp Vinton, IA;
        1st m 06 Nov 1982 Linda Marie Heitz DVD;
        2nd m 21 Nov 1987 Nancy Ann Madden
    Denise Ann Inman – b 02 Apr 1963; Virginia Gay Hosp Vinton, IA;
        m 25 Nov 1988 Glenn Robert Parker DVD
    David Robert Inman – b 02 Sept 1966; Virginia Gay Hosp Vinton, IA;
        m 05 Sept 1987 Brenda Lee Hagen

Kenneth Conrad BIERSCHENK s/o Fred William Bierschenk & Esther Katherine nee Rinderknecht; b 05 Nov 1928 north Newhall, Eden Twp. Benton Co IA, bpt 1928 Parent's Farm, Eden Twp Benton Co IA; US Army Cpl. Korean Conflict; m 09 Oct 1952 St.Paul's Luth Ch Williamsburg, IA to Lorene Ann Weiss (b 08 Oct 1929 Troy Twp Iowa Co) d/o Laurel Emil Weiss SR. & Amanda Gesina Rebecca nee Koester of Williamsburg. Farmers northwest of Newhall, IA; Farm Services Board of Directors, Benton Co IA Farm Bureau; Pork Producers; American Legion. Children:
    Gary Wayne – b 25 Nov 1953 Virginia Gay Hosp Vinton, IA
        m 10 Nov 1973 Phyllis Jane Heitshusan
    Sandra Kay – b 14 Feb 1957 Virginia Gay Hosp Vinton, IA
        m 12 Aug 1977 Ted Eldo Miller
    Mark Allen – b 25 Aug 1958 Virginia Gay Hosp Vinton, IA
        m 03 Dec 1983 Holly June Bischof

Paul Steven- b 30 Apr 1960 Virginia Gay Hosp Vinton, IA
 m 10 Feb 1990 Joellen Kay Anderson
David Thomas – b 18 Jan 1962; Virginia Gay Hosp Vinton, IA
Mary Sue – b 06 Dec 1963 Virginia Gay Hosp Vinton, IA

Mark Alan BIERSCHENK s/o Kenneth Conrad Bierschenk & Lorene Ann nee Weiss; b 25 Aug 1958 Virginia Gay Hosp Vinton, IA; Farmers; m 03 Dec 1983 St.Paul's Methodist Cedar Rapids, IA to Holly June Bischof (b 25 Dec 1959 St.Lukes Hosp Cedar Rapids, IA; Nurse) d/o Norman LaVerne Bischof SR. & Betty June nee Midkiff of Cedar Rapids, IA. Children:
    Courtney June – b 22 Dec 1989 Mercy Hosp Cedar Rapids, IA
    Blaine Alan – b 27 Dec 1991 Mercy Hosp Cedar Rapids, IA

Marlys Elizabeth BIERSCHENK d/o Harry A. Martin Bierschenk & LaVerna Anna Gertrude nee Rinderknecht; b 18 Jul 1935 Eden Twp Benton Co IA, bpt 1935 con St.John; m 27 Feb 1955 St.John to Leonard Edward Geater (b 20 Oct 1931 Vinton, IA; US Army Cpl Korean Conflict) s/o Robert Geater & Esther nee Johnson of Vinton, IA. Children:
    Diana Elaine Geater – b 26 Jun 1957 Vinton, IA;
        m 04 Nov 1978 Dennis Leroy Landrus
    Debra Lynn Geater – b 23 Jun 1959 Vinton, IA;
        m 25 Aug 1984 Lorus John Readle JR.

Niles BIERSCHENK s/o Melvin Bierschenk & Viola nee Buettner; Hawkeye Community College; Belle Plaine, IA Police Department; m Dixie NN. Van Horne, IA residence. Child:
    Trisha Sue – m 18 Dec 1999 St.John to Kristopher Jon Hudson
        s/o Kenneth & Joan Hudson, Belle Plaine, IA

Paul Steven BIERSCHNEK s/o Kenneth Conrad Bierschenk & Lorene Ann nee Weiss; b 30 Apr 1960 Virginia Gay Hosp Vinton, IA; 1980 Graduate Ellsworth Comm College, Iowa Falls, IA; Farmer; m 10 Feb 1990 St.John to Joellen Kay Anderson (b 23 Jun 1959 Marshalltown, IA; 1981 B.A. Central College, Pella, IA; Teacher; 1st m to Kirk Ahrends) d/o Roger Dean Anderson & June Leona nee Roephke of Marengo, IA. DVD. Children:
    Deborah Joellen – b 16 Nov 1990 St.Lukes Hosp Cedar Rapids, IA
    Jonathon Paul – b 03 Jun 1992 St.Lukes Hosp Cedar Rapids, IA
    Jacob Steven – b 07 Mar 1996 St.Lukes Hosp Cedar Rapids, IA

Sandra Kay BIERSCHENK d/o Kenneth Conrad Bierschenk & Lorene Ann nee Weiss; b 14 Feb 1957 Virginia Gay Hosp Vinton, IA Graduate ISU, Teacher; m 12 Aug 1977 St.John to Ted Eldo Miller (b 10 Jan 1957 Story Co, Nevada, IA). Farmers east of Williamsburg, IA. Children:

Lynelle Jane Miller- b 20 Aug 1978 Marshalltown, IA

Sara Jo Miller – b 01 Sept 1982 St.Lukes Hosp Cedar Rapids, IA

Lana Joy Miller- b 29 Jun 1991 Mercy Hosp Iowa City, IA

Brenda Jean BLOESER d/o Berdina Ann nee Happel & Floyd Bloeser; b 04 Dec 1956; m Michael Carrol. Children:

Andy Michael Carrol – b Nov 1987

Laura Elizabeth Carrol – b 13 Jul 1990

Laverne "Bucky" BOCKHOLT s/o Sophia nee Balhorn & Alfred Bockholt; [Killed] 09 Nov 1942 World War II Invasion of North Africa; m Olive Boehmke d/o William Boehmke & Anna nee Kramer. Child:

James Lee – b 1942 Palo Alto, CA; m Mako Iwaashashi

Marlus BOCKHOLT d/o Sophia nee Balhorn & Alfred Bockholt; b 1921; m Robert Buck. Children:

Marcia Buck– NFR

Holst Buck – NFR

Ronald Buck – NFR

Barbara Buck – NFR

*Albert A. BODDICKER, SR. s/o John Boddicker & Elizabeth nee Jacobi; b 1843 Brelon, Germany, d 1915 Benton Co IA, bur St.Patrick Cem near Watkins, IA; Oct 1865 came to USA with parents, three sisters and two brothers; m 1870 Antonette "Nettie" Pieper (b 1852 Germany, came to New York ae7y, d 1935 IA) d/o Casper Pieper. Farmers north of Newhall, IA; members St.Paul's Catholic Ch; Nettie moved into Newhall and lived with daughter Ida Matson. Eleven children:

Anna – b 1872; m James C. Stuart, 3 children

Elizabeth – b 1874; m 1895 Otto A. Koopman, 5 children

Joseph A. – b 1876; m Bertha Seltrecht, 1 child

Mary – b 1880; m Jesse Johnson, 9 children

Albert A. "Fish"-b 1883; m Julia Sevening, 7 children

John Henry "Jack"-b 1885; m Anna Trojousky, 6 children

Bertha – m Frank Schulte, 7 children

Emma – b 1895; m Fermin Weichman, 4 children

William – b 1892; m Oralie Jones

Henry John – b 1890; m Lena Sevening, 1 son
Ida Pauline – b 1901; m Edwin Matson, 6 children

Elwood BODDICKER s/o Henry John Boddicker & Lena nee Sevening; b 1919 Benton Co; d 26 Oct 2000 ae81y; m 1945 Marjorie Meyer of Van Horne, IA. Took over family farm for his father. Children:
   Randell – residence Cedar Rapids, IA
   Rhonda – b 1950; m Barry Franck
   Jolene – residence Scottsdale, AZ

Henry John BODDICKER s/o Albert A. Boddicker SR. & Antonette Nettie nee Pieper; b 1890 north of Newhall, IA; m 1916 Lena Sevening (b 1893, d 1950) d/o Jacob Sevening & Lena nee Smith of Norway, IA. 1923 purchased family farm. Child:
   Elwood – b 1919; m Marjorie Meyer

Janel Lynn BODDICKER d/o James Leroy Boddicker & Janet Lynn nee Webert; b 26 Jul 1963 Mercy Hosp Cedar Rapids, IA; m 24 Jul 1982 St.Paul Catholic Ch Newhall, IA to Douglas Jay Rathbun (b 09 Sept 1956 Independence, IA) s/o Herbert & Shirley Rathbun of Independence IA. Farmers. Children:
   Nichole Elizabeth Rathbun – b 22 Dec 1982; Independence, IA
   Corinne Elizabeth Rathbun – b 11 Jan 1987; Independence, IA

Marie BODDICKER d/o Albert J. Boddicker & Caroline nee Weichman; b 1914, d 26 Jan 2007 ae83y; m 08 Feb 1937 St.Paul's Catholic Ch Newhall, IA to Donald D. Campbell (b 27 Dec 1913 Vinton, IA d 23 Apr 1999 ae85y 3m 27d Cedar Rapids, IA bur Watkins, IA, St. Patrick & Paul Cem; World War II Engineers Corps Europe & Pacific Theaters) s/o William McKinley Campbell & Anna nee Luwe. Both born, raised, educated, residence Newhall, IA area. Children:
   Robert Lee Campbell – b 1937; m Jan McRoberts; Vinton, IA
   Donald Albert Campbell – b 1939; m Pat Owens; CA
   David Duaine Campbell – b 1940;
      m Linda Gregory; Salt Lake City, UT
   Donna Marie Campbell – b 1948; m Jan Mattson; Newhall, IA
   Sharon Kay Campbell – b 1950; m 1978 Mike Gilman

Rhonda BODDICKER d/o Elwood Boddicker & Marjorie nee Meyer; b 07 Apr 1950 Benton Co IA; m 20 Oct 1973 Barry Franck (b 01 Feb 1950) s/o

George Harlan Franck & Marian Frances nee Braksiek. Children:
Robbie Franck – b 15 Jul 1974
Jodie Franck – b 15 May 1977
Karrie Franck – b 05 Jul 1980

Nadine V. BODZEIN d/o Laurel Bodzein & Viola nee Schrader; b 1927; m Clifford Wax. Children:
Sharyln Wax – b 1947; m James Munn

*William BOEHMKE s/o Detlef & Sophia Boehmke; b 1885 Schleswig-Holstein, Germany, d 1934 IA; 1890's came to USA with parents; m 1911 Anna Kramer d/o Fritz & Catherine Kramer (b 1891 Varflet, Germany). Rented farm land in Big Grove Twp Benton Co IA. All eight children confirmed St.John Parochial School; all graduated from Keystone High School:
Lynold – 1st m Thelma Criswell, 3 sons; 2nd m Ann Reed
Walter – m Quinnever Hoffman, 2 daughters
Olive – 1st m LaVerne "Bucky" Bockholt, 1 son
    2nd m Kenneth Kramer, 3 children
Dorothy – 1st m Arthur Franzenburg, 4 children; 2nd m Leonard Brecht
Wilma – m Leslie Linn, 2 adopted children
Arlene – 1st m Karl Behrens, 9 children; 2nd m Marvin Titler
William – m Carolyn White, CA residence
Bob – m Ruby Whiting

**Ingolf BOHLE s/o Marlene nee Wickert & Heinz Böhle; b 22 Apr 1972 Bad Wildungen, Germany; bpt 18 Jun 1972 Löhbach Ch & con Löhlbach Ch; m 28 May 2005 Civil Registry Office to Michaela Waid (b 16 Sept 1974). Child:
**Philipp – b 03 Mar 2004

**Torsten BOHLE s/o Marlene nee Wickert & Heinz Böhle; b 22 Sept 1961 Bad Wildungen, Germany; bpt 05 Nov 1961 Löhlbach Ch & con 25 Löhlbach Ch; m 28 Sept 1989 Civil Ceremony/30 Sept 1989 Löhlbach Ch to Carola Schafer (b 05 Jun 1962 Frankenau, Germany (bpt & con 25 Apr 1976 Frankenau, Germany). Author visited in home of this cousin 1999, 2003. Children:
**Laura – b 21 Feb 1990 Bad Wildungen, Germany; bpt 13 May 1990 Löhlbach Ch
**Lukas – b 26 Jan 1993 Bad Wildungen, Germany; bpt 23 May 1993

Löhlbach Ch

Lynn BOLTE d/o Phyllis Ann nee Schnadt & Ralph Bolte; b 19 Jul 1964; m 02 May 1987 Thomas Anderson (b 03 Apr 1964). Child:
    Dain Anderson – b 21 Nov 1992

Jacqueline Marie BONE d/o Kay Ann nee Rinderknecht & Dennis D. Bone; b 18 Jan 1976 Mercy Hosp Cedar Rapids, IA; m Dan Fitzgerald. Child:
    Madeline Fitzgerald – b ND

Lisa Ann BOOTS d/o Donna nee Happel & Ray D. Boots; b 18 Apr 1956; m 28 Jul 1972 James Bartholomew (b 20 Jun 1954). Children:
    Brandy Jo Bartholomew – b 08 Mar 1973
    Brock James Bartholomew – b 23 Sept 1976

Susan Rae BOOTS d/o Donna nee Happel & Ray D. Boots; b 24 Aug 1954; m 25 Oct 1975 Kevin Gillett (b 10 Jan 1952).Children:
    Aaron Robert Gillett – b 08 Jun 1983
    Douglas James Gillett – b 20 Mar 1987

*Johanna Elisabeth BORNSCHEUER d/o NN Bornscheuer of Dainrode, Germany; m 15 May 1781 Johannes Daniel Möller (b 08 Mar 1757 Hse #43 Löhlbach, Germany, d 23 Mar 1830, Löhlbach, Germany, ae73y 15d). Child:
    *Johannes Georg Möller – b 21 Sept 1782 Löhlbach, Germany;
        m 21 Jan 1808 Maria Katharina Stremme

*Karoline BORNSCHEUER of Altenhaina Kreis Frankenberg, Germany, d/o Johann Daniel Bornscheuer & Anna Elisabeth nee Schmittmann; b 19 Oct 1822 os Alt Hein ns Altenhaina, Germany, d 16 May 1861 Löhlbach, Germany ae39y 6m 27d; m 20 Sept 1846 Löhlbach Ch to Johannes Georg Möller, farmer in Löhlbach, Germany(b 18 Jul 1820 Löhlbach, Germany, Hse #43, bpt & con Löhlbach Ch, d 25 Jul 1892 ae72y 7d IA) s/o Johannes Möller & Maria Katharina nee Stremme. 2nd m Johannes Georg Möller to Wilhelmina Krug. The living children of Johannes Georg Möller and Karoline nee Bornscheuer emigrated to USA 12 Nov 1861. Daniel Möller was confirmed in Löhlbach Ch just before the family left for America. Arrived 01 Feb 1862 in IA at home of brother John Möller who resided eight miles west of Cedar Rapids, IA. The countryside was as yet a wilderness and the Civil War was waging. Children of Karoline nee
24

Bornscheuer and Johannes Georg Möller born in Hse #43, Löhlbach, Germany, and baptized in Löhlbach Ch before emigrating to USA:

    *Johann Daniel Möller – b 01 Sept 1847
        Löhlbach, Germany; bpt 05 Sept 1847 & con Löhlbach Ch;
        m USA 19 Sept 1867 Anna Elisabeth Krug
    Hartmann Wilhelm Möller – b 04 Dec 1849 Löhlbach, Germany;
        d 21 Nov 1850 Löhlbach, Germany
    Maria Elisabeth Möller– b 03 Jan 1852 Löhlbach, Germany;
        d 20 Oct 1852 Löhlbach, Germany
    *Johannes Adam Möller – b 04 Aug 1853 Löhlbach, Germany;
        bpt 14 Aug 1853 Löhlbach Ch;
        m USA 05 Mar 1876 Anna Elisabeth Michel
    *Louise Kristine Möller – b 07 Dec 1855 Löhlbach, Germany;
        bpt 16 Dec 1855 Löhlbach Ch;
        m USA 26 Jan 1873 Henry Gerhold SR.
    *Andreas Heinrich Möller – b 21 Apr 1860 Löhlbach, Germany;
        bpt 05 May 1860 Löhlbach Ch;
        m USA 06 Sept 1883 Maria Gerber

Dennis Lee BRAKSIEK s/o Paul Henry Karl Braksiek & Naomi Grace nee Kuelper; b 29 Jul 1946 Belle Plaine, IA; m 26 Jun 1971 Susan Jane Dubes. Children:
    Robert Jay – b 11 Oct 1972
    Andrew Kent – b 21 Jan 1975

Evelyn Anna Marie BRAKSIEK d/o Frank Benjamin Braksiek & Maria (Marie) Elizabeth nee Happel; b 13 Dec 1914 Van Horne, IA; m 07 Dec 1932 Luth Parsonage, Keystone, IA to Roy Pickering (b 15 May 1911) s/o George Pickering & Margaret nee Ohde of Van Horne, IA. Children:
    Joan Margaret Pickering – Stillborn 10 Oct 1934
    Kay Frances Pickering – b 09 Sept 1935; m 1953 Donald G.Albertson
    Lynn Franklyn Pickering – b 11 Jun 1937; m 1956 Delores Schirm
    Larry Lee Pickering- b 1940; m 1962 Karen K. McIllrath

Julie Denise BRAKSIEK d/o Richard Dean Braksiek & Delores F. nee Hoydt; b 31 Jul 1955; 1st m 28 Jun 1975 her Werning cousin Thomas John Werning (b 21 Jan 1954) s/o Lawrence Werning & Maxine nee Boddicker. Julie Denise Braksiek's Great-Grandmother: Katherina Elisabeth Werning; Thomas John Werning's Great-Grandfather: Justus Werning (brother of Katherina Elisabeth Werning) DVD. Children:

Rachel Marie Werning – b 28 Nov 1978 Cedar Rapids, IA
Gregory John Werning – b 04 May 1982 Cedar Rapids, IA
2nd m 11 May 1991 St.John Luth Ch, Keystone, IA Julie Denise nee Braksiek Werning to Mark Wayne Andresen of Keystone s/o Marlyn Andresen (dec'd) & Marge Severin of Keystone. Keystone, IA residence.

Lurline Ann BRAKSIEK d/o Stanley Fred Adam Braksiek & Goldie Caroline nee Ahrens; b 11 Sept 1937 Davenport, Scott Co IA; bpt Nov 1937; 1st m 26 May 1955 Craig Ford (d 20 May 1957). Child:
    Michael Dean Ford Gardeman – b 08 Aug 1957;
        m 10 Sept 1988 Angela Schoetmer
2nd m 13 Sept 1959 Lurline Ann nee Braksierk Ford to Douglas Gardeman (b 07 Jun 1934) s/o Merle Gardeman & Evelyn nee Kunstorf. Farmers one mile east and ¾ mile south of Newhall. Douglas Gardeman adopted Michael Dean Ford. Child:
    Kim Ellen Gardeman – b 01 Aug 1960;
        m 04 May 1985 Timothy Ray Leidigh (Happel cousin)

Marian Francis BRAKSIEK d/o Frank Benjamin Braksiek & Maria (Marie) Elizabeth nee Happel; b 06 Sept 1926 Keystone, IA, bpt 1926 St.And; m 19 Nov 1944 St.John Luth Ch, Keystone to George Harlan Franck (b 05 Jul 1922 Winthrop, Buchanan Co IA, bpt Spring 1944 St.John Luth Ch, Keystone, d 07 Sept 2000 ae78y 2m 2d) s/o George & Julia Franck & Julia Marie nee Fest of Winthrop, Buchanan Co IA. Celebrated 55th Wedding Anniversary. Children:
    Sally Rae Franck – b 10 Mar 1946; m 1964 Douglas Wendel
    Douglas Kenn Franck – b 29 Nov 1947; m 1970 Becky Bare
    Barry Kim Franck – b 01 Feb 1950; m 1973 Rhonda Boddicker
    Scott Dean Franck – b 11 Jun 1953; m 1972 Nancy Peterson
    Roxanne Franck- b 21 May 1955; m 1955 Anthony Rieder

Maxine Lorraine BRAKSIEK d/o Stanley Fred Adam Braksiek & Goldie Caroline nee Ahrens; b 03 Feb 1934 Davenport, Scott Co IA, bpt 1934; m 13 Dec 1952 Melvin G. Happel (b 20 Sept 1929 Benton Co IA, bpt 1929 St.John Luth Ch, Keystone, IA) s/o Paul Happel & Emma nee Boettcher of Vinton, IA. Children:
    Carol Ann Happel – b 19 Dec 1953; m 25 Jun 1976 David Prather
    Cindy Sue Happel – b 01 Jun 1957;
        m 03 Sept 1975 Douglas Furler, DVD
    Gary Allen Happel – b 10 Dec 1961; m 15 Jun 1985 Jill Coghlin

Paul Henry Karl BRAKSIEK s/o Frank Benjamin Braksiek & Maria (Marie) Elizabeth nee Happel; b 10 Feb 1913 Braksiek Home, Van Horne, IA bpt 1913 St.And, d 14 Apr 1982 Cedar Rapids, IA ae69y 2m 4d bur 17 Apr 1982 Oak Hill Cem, Belle Plaine, IA; m 09 Sept 1941 Luth Parsonage, Keystone, IA to Naomi Grace Kuelper (b 08 Mar 1915 bpt 1915 Bethany Evangelical Ch) d/o Henry Kuelper & Mary nee Upah of Belle Plaine, IA. Child:

Dennis Lee – b 29 Jul 1946; m 26 Jun 1971 Susan Jane Dubes

Richard Dean BRAKSIEK s/o Frank Benjamin Braksiek & Maria (Marie) Elizabeth nee Happel; b 21 Jun 1932 Keystone, IA bpt 1932 St.And; m 26 Oct 1952 Delores F. Hoydt (d 14 Nov 1987). Residence rural Elberon, IA. Children:

Michelle – b 13 Jun 1954; m 29 Jul 1978 Donald Joseph Temeyer
(b 02 Jun 1952)
Julie Denise – b 31 Jul 1955; 1st m 28 Jun 1975 Thomas John Werning
(her Werning cousin) DVD; 2nd m 1991 Mark Wayne Andresen
Angela – Stillborn 05 May 1960
Gary Dean – b 10 Jan 1963; m 25 Jun 1993 Susan Jones

Stanley Fred Adam BRAKSIEK s/o Frank Benjamin Braksiek & Maria (Marie) Elizabeth nee Happel; b 15 Oct 1911 Van Horne, IA d 24 Dec 1997 ae86y 2m 9d; m 10 Mar 1937 Luth Parsonage, Rock Island, IL to Goldie Caroline Ahrens (b 22 Aug 1914, bpt 1914 St.John Luth Ch, Keystone, d 21 Oct 2001 ae87y 2m 1d) d/o Hans Ahrens & Elfrieda Viola nee Rohr of Hawkeye, IA. Children:

Maxine Lorraine – b 23 Feb 1934; m 13 Dec 1952 Melvin G. Happel
Lurline Ann – b 11 Sept 1937; 1st m 26 May 1955 Craig Ford, dec'd;
2nd m 13 Sept 1959 Douglas Gardeman

August BRAMOW s/o Ludwig Bramow & Minnie nee Warner: cf Matilda Werning.

*August Christoff BRAMOW s/o Louis Bramow & Fredericka nee Sissler; b 1869 Ceasendorf, Mecklenberg, Germany, d 1944 SD, bur St.John Luth Cem, Howard, SD; came to USA 1891 with widowed mother and 4 sisters via Bremerhaven and New York City; m 1895 St. Martin's Luth Ch S.W. of Watkins, IA Sophia Bross (b 1876, d 1941) d/o Johann Bross & Mary nee Raabe. Farmed near Winfred, SD 1920's-1940's. Ten daughters:

27

Emma – b 1895; m Lloyd Orwig, Twin Falls, ID
Martha – b 1889; m Ora Vandagrift, Medford, OR
Mary – dec's in infancy
Clara – b 1899; m Harrison Kruger, Mt.Auburn, IA
Alma – b 1901; m August Timm, Huron, SD
Elsie – b 1904; m Warren Waller, Alpena, SD
Wilma – b 1906; m Harvey Halvorsen, SD
Lillian – b 1907; m William Docken, SD
Hazel Bernice Marie – b 1912; m Myron Edwin Taschner, SD
Alvina – b 1914; m Lawrence Jacobsen, SD

*Frederika BRAMOW b in Germany; wid/o Louis BRAMOW (b and d Mecklenberg, Germany); Came to USA with children 1891 leaving Bremerhaven on ship "Rezicka"; traveled from New York City to IA; d & bur Luth Cem south of Canova, SD. Children:
   *August Christoff Bramow – b 1869 Germany, d 1944 IA;
      m 1895 Sophia Bross
   *Dorothea Bramow – m Fred Zulk, Canova, SD
   *Louise Bramow – m NN Jarmuth, MI residence
   *Sophia Bramow – m Fred Bruger, Riceville, IA
   *Anna Bramow – m John Miller, Van Horne, IA residence
   *Louis Bramow – m Minnie Summerville, Canova, SD

*Ludwig BRAMOW b 1872 Mecklenburg, Germany, d 1958 Benton Co IA; m Minnie Warner (b 1874, d 1933). Started farming 1910 on 120 acres in Eldorado Twp. Sections 3 and 4 Benton Co IA; Luth. Children:
   August – b 25 Dec 1893; m 14 Feb 1915 Matilda Werning,
   Herman – b 1896; m Elfrieda Wutzke, 3 children
   Ella – b 1902; m Rudolph Henkel, 3 children

Iver BRECHT s/o Edgar Brecht & Elma Ellen nee Weichman; b 1916; m 1945 Mary Bissel. Muscatine, IA residence. Children:
   Bonita – m James Delehoy
   Robert C. – NFR
   Susan – m David Scheets
   Mary Lynn – NFR
   Kathryn – NFR
   Richard – NFR
   Teresa – NFR

James Rolland BRECHT s/o Rolland Brecht & Marian nee Dill; b 1948; US Army 1972-74; m 1976 Rachelle Barquist. Both school teachers; Mt.Vernon, IA residence. Children:
   TWINS: Nathan – NFR
              Nicholas – NFR

Rolland BRECHT s/o William Brecht & Amelia Weichman; b 1920; US Army World War II; m 1948 Vinton, IA to Marian Dill d/o Arthur Dill & Bertha nee Sturtz. Moved to farm two miles east and one-fourth mile south of Newhall, IA. His grandmother Weichman born on farm owned partly by her and partly by an uncle, Irvin (Dick) Weichman; moved to Newhall 1968. Children:
   James Rolland – b 1948; m 1976 Rachelle Barquist
   William Arthur – b 1950; m 1973 Teresa Youngren
   Larry Edward – b 1952; Solon, IA residence; Deputy Sheriff
   Gerald Wayne – b 1957; Cedar Rapids, IA residence

William Arthur BRECHT s/o Rolland Brecht & Marian nee Dill; b 1950; m 1973 Teresa Youngren. Both teachers. St.Peters, MO residence. Child:
   Daniel – NFR

Adam Reinhard Louis aka Louis A. BREHM s/o Jacob Brehm & Katherina nee Bierschenk; b 23 Jun 1896 north of Newhall, IA d 03 Jan 1987 ae90y 6m 11d; hired farm laborer until drafted World War I; m 22 Dec 1926 Elsie Anna Strellner (b 27 Jan 1906 Keystone, IA, d 25 Sept 1994 ae88y 7m 29d) d/o Julius D. Strellner & Julia nee Waterstradt; 1946 purchased farm east of Shellsburg, Canton Twp Benton Co IA. Retired in Shellsburg, IA. Celebrated 60th Wedding Anniversary. Children:
   Lola Maye – b 03 Sept 1929 near Garrison, IA;
       m 13 Nov 1954 Albert Martin Krug
   Franklin Louis – b 18 Jul 1932 near Garrison, IA; d 13 Feb 1995;
       m 05 Jun 1960 Mary Louise Roll DVD
   Russell Dean – b 05 Nov 1935 near Garrison, IA;
       d 29 Jul 1987 Cheyenne, WY;
       m 26 Aug 1960 Roselyn Edith Brown
   Ronald Lee – b 19 Dec 1938 near Garrison, IA;
       1st m 20 Nov 1960 Ann Marie Deal DVD
       2nd m 27 Jan 1989 Sandra Sue Spenser Grimm

Andrew John BREHN s/o Edwin Carl Brehm & Leota Clara Anna nee

Guider; b 26 Sept 1959; m 05 Dec 1983 Yana Roxanna Yanria Ortiz Garcia. Children:
  Andrea Lynne Stanley – b 25 Feb 1991
  Jillian Eleanore – b 28 Feb 1997

*Anton BREHM b 23 Feb 1794 Breitenbach, Germany, d 09 Jun 1860 ae 66y 3m 16d; 1st m 21 April 1816 Dankerode-on-der-Fulda, Germany to Anna Katherina Pfaffenbach (b 22 Feb 1798, d 07 Mar 1837 ae39y). Children:
  Jeanette – b 1817 Dankerode-on-der-Fulda
  Martin – d ae23y
  *Justus – b 1828 Dankerode-on-der-Fulda
  George – d ae19y
2nd m 16 Aug 1840 Anton Brehm to Anna Margarethe (Borschel) Sandrock.

August Justus Henry BREHM s/o Jacob Brehm & Dorthea Katherina Bierschenk; b 01 Jul 1907, d 26 Dec 1971; m 08 Oct 1932 Geraldine E. Evans (b 02 Aug 1912, d 23 Oct 2006). Children:
  Lynwood Allen – b 19 Jun 1938; m 16 Apr 1961 Rose Alice Malloy
  Dennis Evans – b 30 Jan 1941; m 28 Dec 1965 Marijean Pudenz

Bonita Mae BREHM d/o Herman Conrad Brehm & Mildred Matilda nee Fry; b 27 Sept 1931; m 29 Aug 1952 William Keith Wilson (b 12 Jun 1926). Children:
  Julie Rae Wilson – b 11 Jan 1954; m 04 Aug 1979 Jay Dee Villont
  William John Wilson – b 19 Dec 1956; m 18 Jun 1994 Ronda Houck

Crystal Lynne BREHM d/o Thomas Lyn Brehm & Sharon Colleen Wooten; b 03 Feb 1985 Cedar Rapids, IA; m 09 Jun 2007 Mark Manos (b 18 Dec 1984).

David John BREHM s/o Donald John Brehm & Margaret Martha; b 07 Aug 1955; m 28 Oct 1978 Susan Marie Berg (b 20 Jul 1953). Children:
  Laura Ann – b 29 Mar 1983
  John Alan – b 04 Nov 1986

Dennis Evans BREHM s/o August Justus Henry Brehm & Geraldine E. nee Evans; b 30 Jan 1941; 1st m 28 Dec 1965 Marijean Pudenz (b 16 Nov 1942, d 25 Jul 1976 ae33y 8m 9d . Children:
  Elizabeth Marie "Beth" – b 19 Feb 1967

Christophey Dennis – b 13 Jan 1970
2nd m 05 Jan 2001 Dennis Evans Brehm to Pamela E. Johnson (b 29 Jan 1951, d 10 Apr 2004).

Donald James BREHM s/o Donald John Brehm & Margaret Martha; b 09 Nov 1956; m 15 Sept 1984 Corrine Steffen (b 18 Mar 1959). Children:
    Amanda Margaret – b 18 Dec 1987
    Evan James – b 22 May 1992

Donald John BREHM s/o Rev. John Jacob Conrad Brehm & Bertha Wilhelmina nee Heup; b 09 Jul 1928; m 20 Jun 1954 Margaret Martha (b 01 Aug 1930). Children:
    David John – b 07 Aug 1955; m 28 Oct 1978 Susan Marie Berg
    Donald James – b 09 Nov 1956; m 15 Sept 1984 Corrine Steffen
    Jeffrey Daniel – b 20 Jan 1958
    Steven Paul – b 11 Sept 1959

Edwin Carl BREHM s/o Jacob Brehm & Katherina nee Bierschenk; b 13 Jul 1912 north of Newhall, IA; rural mail carrier 26y; d 14 Apr 1982 ae69y 9m 1d; m 1934 Leota Clara Anna Guider (d 27 Aug 2000) d/o Andrew Guider & Martha nee Bruger of Van Horne, IA; Leota Vice-President Peoples Bank & Trust Co. Newhall, IA office of Cedar Rapids Peoples Bank. Child:
    Roger Kent – b 02 Sept 1935;
        1st m 05 Feb 1959 Elizabeth Ruth Anderson;
        2nd m 06 Sept 1969 Rose Marie Augspurger;
        Canadagua, NY residence

Eunice Maye BREHM d/o Rev. John Jacob Conrad Brehm & Bertha Wilhelmina nee Heup; b 04 Sept 1926; m 17 Jul 1949 Theodore Charles Knauff (b 14 Jun 1926). Children:
    David Alan Knauff – b 10 May 1951;
        m 28 Dec 1978 Evelyn Ruth Anderson
    Karen Maye Knauff – b 11 Jul 1953;
        1st m 29 Jul 1973 Jeffrey William Bittner DVD 1975
        2nd m 12 May 1979 Lloyd Luther Ward
    Barbara Joanne Knauff – b 28 Dec 1954;
        m 16 Jan 1982 Kevin William King
    Daniel James Knauff – b 02 Jul 1956
    Sharon Ruth Knauff – b 03 Mar 1958;

m 09 May 1981 Kenneth John Krall
Jonathan Mark Knauff – b 30 Oct 1962

Evelyn Matilda BREHM d/o Herman Conrad Brehm & Mildred Matilda nee Fry; b 17 Dec 1943; m 07 Aug 1965 Larry Lee Wiebke (b 18 Jan 1938). Children:
Melissa Lynn Wiebke (Adopted) b 24 Nov 1975;
m 04 Oct 1997 Jeremy Jay Jurgens

Franklin Louis BREHM s/o Adam Reinhardt Louis aka Louis A. Brehm & Elsie nee Strellner; b 18 Jul 1933, near Garrison, Benton Co IA, d 13 Feb 1995 ae61y 6m 26d; US Army May 1954-Apr 1956 served in Germany; m 05 Jun 1960 Mary Louise Roll (b 27 Sept 1940 Vinton, IA d 13 Feb 2007 ae66y 4m 17d) DVD. Farmed parents farm east of Shellsburg, IA. Children:
Thomas Lyn – b 01 May 1962 Vinton, IA;
m 18 Jun 1983 Sharon Colleen Wooten
Scott Lawrence – b 03 Oct 1963 Vinton, IA;
1st m 16 Feb 1985 Susan Margarette Haerther DVD
2nd m 09 Jan 1993 Rochelle D. Neal

Frieda Katherine Elizabeth BREHM d/o Jacob Brehm & Dorthea Katherine nee Bierschenk; b 20 Feb 1895, d 06 Dec 1998 ae103y 9m 16d; m 16 Dec 1917 Theodore Geiken (b 26 May 1890, d 19 Aug 1955 ae65y 2m 24d). Children:
Anna Margaret Geiken – b 09 Sept 1918, d 28 Jul 1987;
m 05 Feb 1946 Fredrick Waldo Obermueller
Myron Bernard Louis Geiken – b 06 May 1922, d 21 Aug 1977;
m 18 Aug 1953 Greta Lou Witmer
Harold Lloyd Geiken – b 12 Jan 1925
Eleanor Kathleen Geiken – b 10 Feb 1935;
m 13 Nov 1954 Norman George Geiger

Herman Conrad BREHM s/o Jacob Brehm & Dorthea Katherine nee Bierschenk; b 18 Dec 1909, d 26 Jan 1969 ae59y 1m 8d; m 24 Oct 1930 Mildred Matilda Fry (b 15 Feb 1910, d 24 Apr 1971 ae61y 2m 9d). Children:
Bonita Mae – b 27 Sept 1931; m 29 Aug 1952 William Keith Wilson
Judith Mildred – b 29 Nov 1938;
m 12 Aug 1962 Donald Andrew Ernest Kuch
Lynda Frances – b 29 Jan 1942; 1st m 29 May 1971 Craig Allen Smith

DVD; 2nd m 24 Aug 1992 Richard Hachmann
Evelyn Matilda – b 17 Dec 1943; m 07 Aug 1965 Larry Lee Wiebke
Joel Edward – b 24 Apr 1955; m 17 Nov 1984 Sheryl Sue Werning
DVD

*Jacob BREHM s/o Justus Brehm & Martha Juliann nee George; b 1861 Dankerode-on-der-Fulda, Germany, d 1941; came to USA ae14y with parents and family; m 1891 Dorthea Katherina Bierschenk (b 1879 d 1949) d/o John Heinrich Bierschenk & Anna Katherine nee Gier. Lifetime farmers in Benton Co IA. Children:
Louise Dorothea – b 11 Jan 1892, d 07 Jul 1983;
    m 06 Feb 1918 Julius H. Bachman, 5 children
Anna – b 09 Sept 1893, d 09 Nov 1965;
    m 1917 Roy Husted, 2 daughters
Freida Katherine Elizabeth – b 20 Feb 1895, d 06 Dec 1998;
    m 16 Dec 1917 Theodore Geiken, 4 children
Adam Reinhard Louis – b 23 Jun 1896, d 03 Jan 1987;
    m 22 Dec 1926 Elsie Anna Strellner,4 children
Carl – b 04 Mar 1898, d 12 Mar 1980; Never Married
Rev. John Jacob Conrad- b 07 Sept 1900, d 10 Dec 1979;
    m 15 Nov 1925 Bertha Wilhelmina Heup, 3 children
Fredrich – b 15 Jun 1903, d 29 Jun 1966;
    1st m 01 Jan 1931 Mary Scheib, DVD;
    2nd m 05 Apr 1945 Roberta Clark Dunek DVD (d 02 May 1956);
    3rd m 08 Mar 1957 Yola Gray Pidgeon (d 12 Aug 1966)
August Justus Henry – b 01 Jul 1907, d 26 Dec 1971;
    m 08 Oct 1932 Geraldine E. Evans, 2 sons
Herman – b 18 Dec 1909, d 26 Jan 1969;
    m 24 Oct 1930 Mildred Matilda Fry, 5 children
Edwin Carl – b 13 Jul 1912, d 14 Apr 1982;
    m 17 Mar 1934 Leota Clara Anna Guider, one son

Rev. John Jacob Conrad BREHM s/o Jacob Brehm & Dorthea Katherina nee Bierschenk; b 07 Sept 1900, d 10 Dec 1979; m 15 Nov 1925 Bertha Wilhelmina Heup (b 10 Jul 1901, d 26 Jan 1988). Children:
Eunice Maye – b 04 Sept 1926;
    m 17 Jul 1949 Theodore Charles Knauff
Donald John – b 09 Jul 1928; m 20 Jun 1954 Margaret Martha
Marvin Marlow – b 19 Feb 1933, d 11 Jan 1997;
    m 08 Jul 1956 Pauline Elinore Adams

Joel Edward BREHM s/o Herman Conrad Brehm & Mildred Mathilda nee Fry; b 24 Apr 1955; m 17 Nov 1984 Sheryl Sue Werning (b 23 Nov 1960)DVD d/o Donald Werning & Martha Joanna nee Baldwin. Children:
Evan Tyler – b 23 Oct 1989
Ethan Garrett – b 09 Nov 1992

Judith Mildred BREHM d/o Herman Conrad Brehm & Mildred Matilda nee Fry; b 29 Nov 1938; m 12 Aug 1962 Donald Andrew Ernest Kuch (b 11 Dec 1933). Children:
Marc Donald Kuch – b 13 Jan 1964;
1st m 27 Feb 1988 Lisa Maree Williams DVD
2nd m 31 Jan 1998 Sally Classen Campbell DVD
Terry Lynn Kuch – b 14 Feb 1965
Lori Jo Kuch – b 04 Mar 1970;
m 04 Jan 1992 Chandler Timothy Woodward
Pamela Joy Kuch – b 17 Dec 1971;
m 11 Jun 1994 Rand Charles Harman

*Justus BREHM s/o Anton Brehm & Anna Katharina Pfaffenback; b March 1828 Dankerode on-der-Fulda, Hessen, Germany, d 1918 Benton Co IA; m Martha Julianna George (b Nov 1834, d 1904 Benton Co IA). Children:
Martha – m Wm. Katz
Conrad – m Dorothy Katz
Christine – m Herman Diers
Eliza – m Fred Stelling
Adam – m Lena Schlueter
Jacob – b 1861; d 1941; m 1891 Dorthea Katherina Bierschenk
Louise – m Edward Schlueter
Elizabeth – m Ludwig Schlotfeld
Maria – Never Married

Katharine Elizabeth BREHM d/o Roger Kent Brehm & Elizabeth Ruth nee Anderson; b 25 Aug 1962 (TWIN: Martha Ruth Brehm); m 31 Jan 1985 Patrick McKean. Children:
Kirk Andrew McKean – b 04 Oct 1984
Charles Patrick McKean – b 30 May 1986
Benjamin Isaac McKean – b 12 Nov 1987
Desiree Hope McKean – b 20 Sept 1989

Kevin Douglas BREHM s/o Lynwood Allan Brehm & Rose Alice nee Malloy; b 02 Nov 1966; m 10 Apr 1993 Charity NN. Child:
Danielle – NFR

Louise Dorothea Katherine BREHM d/o Jacob Brehm & Dorothea Katherine nee Bierschenk; b 11 Jan 1892, d 07 Jul 1983 ae91y 5m 27d); m 06 Feb 1918 Julius H. Bachmann (b 09 Sept 1892, d 05 Feb 1953 ae60y 4m 27d). Children:
Julius Jacob Theodore Bachmann – b 29 Oct 1918,
    d 08 Mar 2001; m Dorothy Agnes Reed
Robert Louis Bachmann – b 19 Sept 1920, d 06 Sept 2002;
    m 05 Jan 1941 Frances Lorraine Lingwood DVD
Dorothy Katherine Bachmann – b 26 Oct 1924;
    m 03 Jun 1956 Herbert H. Bade
Donald William Bachmann – b 20 Oct 1926;
    m 21 Aug 1949 Ruth Elaine Reynick
Helen Louise Bachmann – b 01 Jan 1931;
    m 01 Oct 1950 James Rae Wilson JR.

Lynda Frances BREHM d/o Herman Conrad Brehm & Mildred Matilda nee Fry; b 29 Jan 1942; 1st m 29 May 1971 Craig Allen Smith DVD 17 Dec 1981. Child:
Erik Allen Smith – b 13 Jul 1975;
2nd m 24 Aug 1992 Lynda Frances nee Brehm Smith to Richard Hachman (b 25 Oct 1937).

Lynwood Allan BREHM s/o August Justus Henry Brehm & Geraldine E. nee Evans; b 19 Jun 1938; m 16 Apr 1961 Rose Alice Malloy (b 28 Jan 1941). Children:
Jody Lynn – b 22 Apr 1962
Todd Allan – b 29 Aug 1963; m 18 Apr 1987 Andrea Dee Little
Kevin Douglas – b 02 Nov 1966; m 10 Apr 1993 Charity NN

Martha Ruth BREHM d/o Roger Kent Brehm & Elizabeth Ruth nee Anderson; b 25 Aug 1962 (TWIN: Katharine Elisabeth Brehm); m Dec 1986 Ralph Stanley DVD 1992. Child:
Ian James Stanley – b 11 May 1985

Marvin Marlow BREHM s/o Rev. John Jacob Conrad Brehm & Bertha Wilhelmina nee Heup; b 19 Feb 1933, d 11 Jan 1997 ae63y 10m 23d; m 08

Jul 1956 Pauline Elinore Adams (b 10 Jan 1933). Children:
   Amala – b 04 Feb 1959
   Paul – b 09 Jan 1961
   Elizabeth – b 15 May 1963

Renee Lynn BREHM d/o Ronald Lee Brehm & Ann nee Deal; b 13 Mar 1970 ND; 1991 Combat Medic Operation Desert Storm; m 13 Dec 1991 Daniel Joe Williams (b 15 Jun 1965). Children:
   Brianna Marguerite Williams – b 18 Sept 1992
   Ariel Kay Williams – b 13 Dec 1993

Richard Louis BREHM s/o Ronald Brehm & Anna Marie nee Deal; b 11 May 1964 Cedar Rapids, IA; 1st m 07 Jun 1985 Grace Luth Ch Blairstown, Benton Co IA to Karmen Jane Reinhardt (b 01 Sept 1963 Marengo, IA con 1977; Kirkwood Comm College) d/o Robert Karl Reinhardt & Ardith Elizabeth nee Kreutner. DVD Sept 1991.
2nd m 02 Mar 1996 Richard Louis Brehm to Some Meuxayanakhoma, DVD 2000.
3rd m 03 Nov 2004 Richard Louis Brehm to Nicole Dawn Collins (b 02 Apr 1974). Child:
   Phoenix Louis – 08 Feb 2005
   STEPCHILDREN:
   Wayne Meuxayanakham – b 23 Dec 1981
   Bend Meuxayanakham – b 01 Mar 1983
   Kellie Meuxayakham – b 28 Feb 1987

Rodney Lee BREHM s/o Ronald Lee Brehm & Anna Marie nee Deal; b 22 Nov 1961; m 21 Aug 1982 Angela Kay Becker (b 05 Nov 1959). Children:
   Ashley Marie – b 27 Jul 1983 Cedar Rapids, IA
   Ryan Louis – b 03 May 1985 Cedar Rapids, IA

Roger Kent BREHM s/o Edwin Carl Brehm & Leota Clara Anna nee Guider; b 02 Sept 1935; 1st m 05 Feb 1959 Elizabeth Ruth Anderson (b 10 Jun 1936) DVD 29 Feb 1968. Children:
   Andrew John – b 26 Sept 1959;
       m 05 Dec 1983 Yana Roxanna Yanria Ortiz Garcia
   Timothy Edwin – b and d Mar 1961
   TWINS: Martha Ruth – b 25 Aug 1962;
       m Dec 1986 Ralph Stanley DVD 1992
           Katharine Elizabeth – b 25 Aug 1962;

m 31 Jan 1985 Patrick McKean
2nd m 06 Sept 1969 Roger Kent Brehm to Rose Marie Augspurger.

Ronald Lee BREHM s/o Adam Reinhard Louis aka Louis A. Brehm & Elsie nee Strellner; b 19 Dec 1938 near Garrison, Benton Co IA; Occupation: Carpenter; 1st m 20 Nov 1960 Ann Marie Deal (b 21 Jan 1943 Ft. Benning, GA) d/o M/Sgt US Army Retired C.L.& Mrs. Deal. DVD. Children:

Rodney Lee – b 22 Nov 1961 Cedar Rapids, IA;
    m 21 Aug 1982 Angela Kay Becker
Richard Louis – b 11 May 1964 Cedar Rapids, IA;
    1st m 1985 Karmen Reinhardt, DVD Sept 1991
    2nd m 02 Mar 1996 Some Meuxayanakham DVD 2000
    3rd m 03 Nov 2004 Nicole Dawn Collins
Renee Lynn – b 13 Mar 1970; m 13 Dec 1991 Daniel Joe Williams
2nd m 27 Jan 1989 Ronald Lee Brehm to Sandra Sue Spenser Grimm (b 24 Jun 1944).

STEPCHILDREN:

Melissa Marie Grimm – b 12 Dec 1963;
    m 07 Jul 1986 Andrew George Zinser.
    Parents of Levi Andrew Zinser b 22 Apr 1988
Ronald La Monte Grimm JR. – b 17 Nov 1965
Melinda Sue -b 13 Jan 1968; m 25 Nov 1985 Russell Dean Shelton.
    Children: Suela Marie Shelton b 31 May 1986; Jonathan Russell
    Shelton b 28 May 1989; Sara Elizabeth Shelton b 18 Apr 1991

Russell Dean BREHM s/o Adam Reinhard Louis aka Louis A. Brehm & Elsie nee Strellner; b 05 Nov 1935 Benton Co IA, d 29 Jul 1987 ae51y 8m 24d attending "Frontier Days" Cheyenne, WY; US Army in Germany Jun 1958-Mar 1960; m 26 Aug 1960 Roselyn Edith Brown. No children.

Scott Lawrence BREHM s/o Franklin Louis Brehm & Mary Louise nee Roll; b 03 Oct 1963 Vinton, IA; 1st m 16 Feb 1985 Shellsburg, IA to Susan Margarette Haerther (b 12 Mar 1959) DVD.
2nd m 09 Jan 1993 Scott Lawrence Brehm to Rochelle D. Neal.
    STEPSON: Jonathan – NFR

Thomas Lyn BREHM s/o Franklin Louis Brehm & Mary Louise nee Roll; b 01 May 1962; m 18 Jun 1983 Sharon Colleen Wooten (b 09 May 1962). Children:

Crystal Lynne – b 03 Feb 1985 Cedar Rapids, IA;
    m 09 Jun 2007 Mark Alan Manos (b 18 Dec 1984)
    s/o Harry Manos III & Pamela
Samantha Colleen – b 22 Aug 1989 Cedar Rapids, IA

Todd Allan BREHM s/o Lynwood Allan Brehm & Rose Alice nee Malloy; b 29 Aug 1963; m 18 Apr 1987 Andrea Dee Little. Children:
    Alexandria – b 08 Mar 1988
    Duston – b 16 Mar 1989

Juli Hope BREHMER d/o Mary Lou nee Haerther & Rev. Charles Alvin Brehmer; b 13 Nov 1961 St. Louis, MO; m 06 Jun 1992 St.John Luth Ch Bakersfield CA to Jonathan Andrew Blanke (b 21 Dec 1961). Children:
    Sarah Margaret Blanke – b 08 Jul 1993 Okinawa, Japan
    Joel Robert Blanke – b 15 Apr 1995 Okinawa, Japan

*Anna Mae BROCK b 1859 Germany, d 1931 Benton Co IA; came to USA with widowed father, three sisters, and two brothers in 1873; m 1879 Oxford, IA to Albert Husted (b 1855 Oxford, IA d 1930 Benton Co IA). 1899 moved to Benton Co making Newhall, IA home; In 1929 Celebrated 50th Golden Wedding Anniversary. Children:
    Martha Husted – dec'd at birth
    Frederick "Fred" Husted – b 1881, d 1959;
        m 1914 Elizabeth Seilhamer
    Bert Husted – b 1884, d 1925; m Amelia Freeman
    George Husted – b 1886, d 1906
    Jennie Alice Husted – b 1888; m 1909 Henry O. Johnson
    Anna Marie "Dolly" Husted – b 1891, d 1927; m 1915 Eugene Kohler
    Roy Husted – b 1892, d 1974; m 1917 Anna Brehm
    John Husted – b 1897; m 1917 Esther Happel
    Marjorie Husted – b 1899; m 1920 Clarence Kelly
    Frank Husted – b 1901, d 1972; m 1920 Elizabeth Rasmussen
    Lillian Husted – b 1903, d 1980; m 1921 Herman Becker
    Melvin Husted – b 1907, d 1981; m Stella Johnson

Elmer BROENDEL s/o Henry Broendel & Lena nee Greve; b 1896, d 1948; m 29 Nov 1927 Rose Wiese (b 1897, d 12 Jul 2000 ae103y). Farmers Eden Twp Benton Co IA until 1940 Newhall, IA retirement. Children:
    Lucille – b 1918; m George Good
    Phyllis – b 1929; m Don Ebert

Ernest BROENDEL s/o Hans Broendel & Anna nee Hassee; b ND on farm in Eden Twp Benton Co IA; m Mary Eggers (b Germany, d 1951 Newhall, IA) d/o Rolf Eggers & Anna nee Unrau. Farmers northwest of Newhall, retiring about 1919 in Newhall, IA. Luth. No children.

*Hans BROENDEL b 1824 Schleswig-Holstein, Germany, d 1907 Benton Co IA; m 1857 Anna Hassee (b 1836 Schleswig-Holstein, Germany, d 1886). Came to USA settling on farm near Newhall, IA. Six children, all except John, lived on farms near Newhall, IA:
    Alvena – NFR
    Elte – b 1861, d 1930; m Charles Grovert
    Ernest – m Mary Eggers
    August – NFR
    Henry – b 1873, d 1942; 1st m Lena Greve, 3 children;
        2nd m 1924 Emma nee Stien Richter
    John – m Tina Seeman, residence Rock Island, IL

Henry BROENDEL s/o Hans Broendel & Anna nee Hassee; b 1873 on farm in Eden Twp Benton Co IA d 1942; 1st m Lena Greve (b 1871 d 1915). Farmers in Eden Twp until 1917 retirement in Newhall, IA. Children:
    Elmer – b 1896, d 1948; m 29 Nov 1927 Rose Wiese
    Ellen – m George Paulsen (b 1898, d 1981)
    Gertrude – NFR
2nd m 1924 Henry Broendel to Emma nee Stien Richter. Mbrs Luth Ch.

*Johann BROSS b 1846 Mecklenberg, Germany, d 1929; emigrated to USA 1872; farmed near Marengo, IA; 1st m 1876 Mary Raabe (b 1856 Germany, d 1879 IA) d/o Johann Joachim Frederick Raabe & Louisa nee Brockman. Residence Big Amana, IA 1872-1876. Mary died giving birth to Caroline; daughter Sophia lived with maternal aunt, Henry and Dorothea Haacker of Marengo, IA. Children:
    Sophia – b 1876, d 1941; m 1895 August Christoff Bramow
    Caroline – b 1879
2nd m 1886 Johann Bross to Fredericka Bauman (b 1856 d 1946). Children:
    Anna – b 1888; m Herman Johnson, 3 children
    Kathryn – b 1890; m Roy Moore, 4 children
    Henry – b 1892; m Alvena Knock, 4 children
    Charles – b 1892; m Letta Roggentine, 3 children
    Ida – b 1898; m Bernard Meyer, no children

Jason Robert BRUCE s/o Sally Ann nee Hanson Bruce & Steve Dale Bruce; b 17 Nov 1976; m 06 Jun 2000 Erica Louise Tompkins. Child:
Sammie Bruce – b 01 Apr 2004

Frank Arthur BRYNER SR. s/o James Monroe Bryner & Sarah Caroline nee Gordon; b 13 Sept 1875 Mt. Auburn farm Benton Co IA, bpt 03 Feb 1934 Tabernacle Salt Lake City, UT, con 04 Feb 1934; d 28 Dec 1955 [Stroke]Salt Lake City, UT ae80y 3m 15d bur 30 Dec 1955 City Cem, Salt Lake City, UT; 1st m 01 Jan 1900 Newhall, Benton Co IA to Inez Vivian Tanner (b 30 Jan 1877 Eldorado Twp Benton Co IA, d 03 Jan 1966 Cedar Rapids IA [Pneumonia] 89y 11m 27d bur 06 Jan 1966 CdrMem Masoleum) d/o Benton Co IA Pioneers William Allen Tanner (1841-1880) & Mary Janette nee Muirhead (1852-1938). DVD Sept 1927. Children:
Hope Lovaire – b 10 Feb 1901 Urbana, Benton Co IA;
    d 26 Sept 1970 Long Beach CA ae69y 7m 16d;
    m 13 Aug 1923 Leroy James Warner
Enid Muriel – b 08 Jun 1903 Eldorado Twp Benton Co;
    d 17 Nov 1986 Luth Home, Vinton IA ae83y 5m 9d;
    m 09 Sept 1925 Walter William August Krug
Jay Muirhead – b 31 May 1907 Salina KS;
    d 08 Jul 2000 Niagara WI ae93y 1m 9d
    m 09 Aug 1929 Margaret Emma Chamberlain
Frank Arthur JR. – b 15 Nov 1909 Kipp KS; d 11 Aug 1987
    King Co. WA ae77y 8m 27d; m 15 Nov 1933 Mary Helene Hunt
Mary Caroline – b 22 Dec 1914 Afton, Union Co.IA; d 26 Sept 2005
    Cedar Rapids IA ae90y 9m 4d;
    m 31 May 1946 Clifford Leroy Parmater
2nd m 01 Jan 1934 Salt Lake City, UT, Frank Arthur Bryner SR. to Ellen Sophie Sundstrom (b 02 May 1893 Salt Lake City, UT d 1966 bur City Cem Salt Lake City UT) d/o John August Sundstrom & Hedvig Gustava nee Bredenberg.

James Monroe BRYNER s/o David Leonidas Bryner & Sarah nee Bodkin; b 22 May 1829 Wharton Twp Fayette Co PA, d 02 Dec 1911 ae72y 6m 10d Canon City, Fremont Co CO, bur 11 Dec 1911 Evergreen Cem Vinton, Benton Co IA; m 04 Oct 1861 Monmouth Warren Co IL to Sarah Caroline Gordon (b 04 Aug 1835 McDonough Co IL, d 07 Oct 1907 ae69y 2m 3d Benton Co IA, bur 09 Oct 1907 Evergreen Cem Vinton, Benton Co IA) d/o William Smith Gordon & Anne nee Wilson. 1873 moved to Benton Co IA and farmed Mt. Auburn, IA. Children:

Estella Grace – b 26 Jul 1862 Kewanee, Henry Co IL d 30 May 1933
Newton, Jasper Co IA; m 1883 John Warren Brewer

Ferman Gordon – b 14 Aug 1864 Kewanee, Henry Co IL
d 10 Mar 1933 Long Beach, CA bur 16 Mar 1933 Evergreen Cem
Vinton, IA; m 07 Sept 1892 Ida Mae Chenoweth

Zee – b 04 Apr 1870 Monmouth, Warren Co IL; d 06 Jun 1936
Antigo, Langlade Co WI; m Lucy Evers Davis (d 03 Nov 1930)

Nellie Ethyl –b 18 Apr 1873 Cambridge, Henry Co IL d 27 Dec 1948
Brandon, Buchanan Co IA; m 25 Nov 1891 Rufus Elvin Bower

Frank Arthur SR. – b 13 Sept 1875 Mt. Auburn, IA; d 28 Dec 1955
Salt Lake City, UT; 1st m 01 Jan 1900 Inez Vivian Tanner
DVD Sept 1927; 2nd m 01 Jan 1934 Ellen Sophie Sundstrom

Mary Caroline BRYNER d/o Frank Arthur Bryner SR. & Inez Vivian nee
Tanner; b 22 Dec 1914 Afton, Union Co IA; bpt 17 Apr 1927 Cedar Rapids,
IA d 26 Sept 2005 ae90y 9m 4d bur CdrMem; m 31 May 1946 St.James
Methodist Ch Cedar Rapids, IA to Clifford Leroy Parmater (b 26 Apr 1914
Vinton, IA, d 31 Mar 1986 Cedar Rapids, IA ae72y 11m 26d bur CdrMem;
World War II U.S. Army Pacific Theatre Medical Corps) s/o Clifford Earl
Parmater & Elizabeth Helen nee Ross of Vinton, IA. Mary: employed Cedar
Rapids Quaker Oats Company; Clifford Leroy: Parts Manager LaPlant
Choate Manufacturing Company/Allis-Chalmers. Child:

Nancy Sue Parmater – b 21 Apr 1947 St.Lukes Hosp Cedar Rapids, IA
d 13 Sept 1985 [Airplane Crash in AL] bur CdrMem;
1st m 29 Nov 1968 Robert Craig Alcorn DVD;
2nd m 17 Jan 1978 William Dean Champion; d 13 Sept 1985
[Airplane Crash in AL] bur CdrMem

Esther Martha BUCHMANN d/o Elfrieda nee Werning & Ruben
Buchmann; b 20 Mar 1937; m 30 Jun 1968 Marvin Mullennex (b 08 Jan
1925, d 16 Jan 1977 ae52y 8d) s/o Julius Mullennex & Anna nee Witt of
Lemars, IA.

Harold Robert BUCHMANN s/o Elfrieda nee Werning & Ruben
Buchmann; b 20 Aug 1944; 1st m 13 Feb 1965 Carol Moehlman (b 28 Mar
1945) d/o Albert Moehlman & Violet nee Mangelson. DVD 1976. Children:

Melisse Lee – b 25 Feb 1970
Brian Will – b 02 Jun 1971
Cary Lynn – b 15 Oct 1973

2nd m Jun 1980 Harold Robert Buchmann to NN.

Lydia Mary BUCHMANN d/o Elfrieda nee Werning & Ruben Buchmann; b 20 May 1931; m 24 Sept 1946 Peter Anderson (b 05 Sept 1925) s/o Ray Anderson & Mattie nee Kruson. Children:
    Joan Elaine Anderson – b 07 Feb 1953; m 22 Jun 1974 Lonnie NN
    James Peter Anderson – b 05 Apr 1954; m 1972 Corinna Rollins
    Kathy Ann Anderson – b 23 Dec 1958
    John Robert Anderson – b 11 May 1961

Ruth Mathilda BUCHMANN d/o Elfrieda nee Werning & Ruben Buchmann; b 01 Sept 1943; m 21 Oct 1963 Robert Wood (b 13 Nov 1933, d 24 Jul 1980 ae46y 8m 11d) s/o Thomas Wood & Elisabeth nee Franks.

Dale Warren BUCKLER s/o John Buckler & Margaret nee Harnisch; b 15 Jul 1957; m 01 Jan 1981 Sue Wiescke. Child:
    Jonathan Carl – b 25 May 1982

Mary Margaret BUCKLER d/o John Buckler & Margaret nee Harnisch; b 16 Oct 1954; m 21 Jun 1981 Steve Glenn (b 28 May 1954) s/o Patrick & Marilee Glenn. Children:
    Brenna Marie Glenn – b 16 Jul 1982
    Haley Nicole Glenn – b 20 Sept 1985

Delbert BUEHNER s/o Leonard Buehner & Alice nee Dannenbring; b 15 Sept 1951; m 23 Jun 1972 Vicki M. Kitchen d/o Shirley L. Kitchen. Children:
    Steffanie – NFR
    Nichola – NFR
    Jonathan – b Apr 1987

Donald BUEHNER s/o Leonard Buehner & Alice nee Dannenbring; b 25 Jun 1942; m 15 May 1966 Judy Waage (b 30 Dec 1945) d/o Thomas Waage & Mabel nee Kroger. Children:
    Duwayne – b 27 May 1968
    Kristi Lynn – b 13 Feb 1971

Evelyn BUEHNER d/o Leonard Buehner & Alice nee Dannenbring; b 16 Dec 1945; m 18 Apr 1965 Larry Ondrozeck (b 16 Dec 1944) s/o Waldo Ondrozeck & Anna nee Beisel. Child:

Juli Ann Ondrozeck – b 01 Oct 1971

Gloria BUEHNER d/o Leonard Buehner & Alice nee Dannenbring; b 04 Oct 1954; m 17 Aug 1974 at Zion Luth Ch Canistota, SD to Michael Waechter. Madison, SD residence. Children:
    Matthew Waechter – b 31 Dec 1978
    Michelle Waechter – b 17 Aug NFR

Linda BUEHNER d/o Leonard Buehner & Alice nee Dannenbring; b 26 Feb 1948; m 24 Nov 1967 Randall R. Parry (b 19 Jun 1948) s/o Art Parry & Ella nee Schaeffer. Children:
    Michelle Parry – b 03 Oct 1968
    (Son) NN Parry – b 06 Aug 1972

Lois BUEHNER d/o Leonard Buehner & Alice nee Dannenbring; b 08 May 1944; m 26 May 1963 Eugene Taylor (b 17 Nov 1942) s/o Arnold Taylor & Opal nee Deucher. Children:
    Kimberly Taylor – b 09 May 1969
    Lisa Ann Taylor – b 11 Sept 1972

Judy Joyce BUELOW d/o Leo William Buelow & Anna Elizabeth nee Happel; b 30 Aug 1955 Vinton, IA bpt Oct 1955 Grace Luth Ch, Blairstown, IA; 1st m 30 Mar 1974 Kenneth Joe Ginther s/o Arlo Ginther. DVD.
2nd m 26 Sept 1987 Judy Joyce nee Buelow Ginther to Ronald Conried. Child:
    Whitney Lynn Conried – b 21 Jan 1989

Terry Lee BUELOW s/o Leo William Buelow & Anna Elizabeth nee Happel; b 14 Feb 1947 Vinton, IA bpt 23 Mar 1947 TrinVT; m 24 Oct 1970 Mary Lynne Weaver (b 22 Feb 1949) d/o Sidney Weaver. Children:
    Greg Michael – b 19 Apr 1972
    Julie Lynn – b 10 Apr 1975; m 19 Jun 1999 Michael Justin Kasper

Beverly CAMPBELL d/o LeRoy Campbell & Mathilda nee Harnisch; b 19 Dec 1946; m 31 Dec 1965 Daniel Dortt (b 09 Feb 1944) s/o Burle Dortt & Velma nee Lynch. Children:
    Daryl Allan Dortt – b 18 Dec 1968; m 1987 Susan Eisenbraun
    Denise Renae Dortt – b 21 Mar 1973

Christopher James CAMPBELL s/o Ruth Marie nee Rinderknecht & Clement Ambrose Campbell; b 19 Oct 1954; m 11 Mar 1978 Janet Lynne Wiker (b 25 Oct 1956, d 16 May 1984 ae27y 6m 21d). Children:
    Bryan Justin – b 21 Jul 1978
    Todd William – b 27 Feb 1980

Clara CAMPBELL d/o LeRoy Campbell & Mathilda nee Harnisch; b 20 Aug 1940; m 16 Aug 1959 Robert White (b 29 Jun 1941) s/o Ward White & nee Mayer. Children:
    Kevin Dale White – b 23 May 1961
    Kyle E. White – b 25 Nov 1963
    Kelly White – b 16 Aug 1965

Daniel Joseph CAMPBELL s/o Ruth Marie nee Rinderknecht & Clement Ambrose Campbell; b 25 Dec 1950; m 19 Apr 1975 Mary Ann Plut (b 28 Sept 1952). Children:
    Katrina Lynne – b 16 Jul 1985
    Joseph Augustine – b 31 Dec 1988

David Duaine CAMPBELL s/o Donald Campbell & Marie nee Boddicker; b 1940; m Linda Gregory; Salt Lake City, UT residence. Children:
    Shelly – NFR
    David – NFR
    Brian – NFR

Donald Albert CAMPBELL s/o Donald Campbell & Marie nee Boddicker; b 1939; 1st m NN. Children:
    Donald Lynn – NFR
    Debra Leslie – NFR
2nd m Donald Albert Campbell to Pat Owens; CA residence. Children:
    Lisa – NFR
    Todd – NFR
    Chad – NFR

Donna Marie CAMPBELL d/o Donald D. Campbell & Marie nee Boddicker; b 1948; m 1972 Jan Mattson s/o Art Mattson & Lucille nee Wyant. Newhall, IA residence. Children:
    Brooke Renee Mattson – b 1975;
        m 10 Oct 1998 Benjamin Earl Osborn
    Matthew Jan Mattson – b 1978

John Albert CAMPBELL JR. s/o John Albert Campbell SR. & M. Christine nee Kline; b 30 Mar 1966; m 02 Jun 1990 Julie Strode (b 15 Jan 1966). Child:
    Megan Elizabeth – b 08 Jan 1994

John Albert CAMPBELL SR. s/o Ruth Marie nee Rinderknecht & Clement Ambrose Campbell; b 15 Apr 1948; m 05 Nov 1965 M. Christine Kline (b 09 Jan 1950). Children:
    John Albert JR. – b 30 Mar 1966; m 02 Jun 1990 Julie Strode
    Keith Allen – b 07 Feb 1970
    Brad David – b 06 Oct 1971
    Kyle Curtis – b 28 Jan 1976

Kevin Paul CAMPBELL s/o Ruth Marie nee Rinderknecht & Clement Ambrose Campbell; b 13 Apr 1961; m 23 May 1980 Lori Jo Watkins. Children:
    Chadwick Paul – b 02 Oct 1980
    Cory Jo – b 11 Oct 1981
    Marrisa Ann – b 17 Mar 1993
    Ryan Michael – b 09 Jun 1994

Lawrence Charles CAMPBELL s/o Ruth Marie nee Rinderknecht & Clement Ambrose Campbell; b 04 Nov 1949; m 28 Nov 1969 Patricia Lois Hice (b 26 Jul 1950). Children:
    Monica Jean – b 30 May 1970
    Jude Patrick – b 10 Aug 1973

Marjorie CAMPBELL d/o LeRoy Campbell & Mathilda nee Harnisch; b 10 Nov 1942; 1st m 17 Sept 1959 Richard Van Vleck DVD. Children:
    Tamara Kay Van Vleck – b 30 May 1960; m 1983 David Manson
    Troy Dean Van Vleck – b 30 Oct 1964; m 1988 Misty NN
    Timothy Lee Van Vleck – b 03 Jan 1969; m 1981 Alta Gayle Stanley

Mark Patrick CAMPBELL s/o Ruth Marie nee Rinderknecht & Clement Ambrose Campbell; b 06 Oct 1959; 1st m 09 Jun 1979 Sara Jane Watkins (b 12 Feb 1961). Children:
    Brandi Nicole – b 11 Nov 1981
    Nathaniel Patrick – b 31 Oct 1983
2nd m 14 Feb 1991 Mark Patrick Campbell to Morna Ed Barrie (b 23 Mar

1961). Child:
    Victoria Cecile Campbell – b 15 Mar 1992

Mary Margaret CAMPBELL d/o Ruth Marie nee Rinderknecht & Clement Ambrose Campbell; b 06 May 1957; m 19 Jun 1975 Ronald Bellinger (b 03 Aug 1956). Child:
    Thomas Albert Bellinger – b 22 Nov 1975

Richard Dean CAMPBELL s/o Ruth Marie nee Rinderknecht & Clement Ambrose Campbell; b 31 Jan 1966; m 27 Jun 1989 Lisa Ann Sierra (b 07 Apr 1966). Children:
    Sierra Kristina – b 06 Nov 1989
    Erick George – b 15 Aug 1995

Rita Ann CAMPBELL d/o Ruth Marie nee Rinderknecht & Clement Ambrose Campbell; b 16 Jan 1956; m 01 Jul 1974 Timothy Lawrence Sierra (b 30 Jun 1956). Children:
    Veronica Ruth Sierra – b 20 Jul 1974
    Katherine Ambrosia Sierra – b 31 Mar 1977;
        m 10 Dec 1993 Joseph Clarence Walters
    Philip Timothy Sierra – b 30 Dec 1980
    Daniel Julien Sierra – b 10 Mar 1983

Robert Lee CAMPBELL s/o Donald D. Campbell & Marie nee Boddicker; b 1937; m Jan McRoberts (b 1939). Vinton, IA area residence. Children:
    Cindy – m Kevin Thumma
    Gregory – US Air Force
    Tina – NFR

Sharon Kay CAMPBELL d/o Donald D. Campbell & Marie nee Boddicker; b 1950; 1st m 26 Apr 1969 George Leon Woodson DVD 1974. Children:
    Debbie Ann Woodson – b 08 Oct 1969
    Wendy Renee Woodson – b 11 Jul 1972
2nd m 1978 Sharon Kay nee Campbell Woodson to Mike Gilman.

Stephen Francis CAMPBELL s/o Ruth Marie nee Rinderknecht & Clement Ambrose Campbell; b 04 Nov 1962; m 01 Aug 1986 Carolyn Mae Wertz (b 02 Apr 1954). Children:
    Stephanie Marie – b 17 Nov 1984
    Sean Stephen – b 26 Dec 1986

Therese Marie CAMPBELL d/o Ruth Marie nee Rinderknecht & Clement Ambrose Campbell; b 04 Jun 1952; m 29 Jul 1977 Hayden Lee Wayne Powers (b 03 Aug 1938). Child:
Nova Lynn Powers – b 26 Aug 1988

Patricia Lee CHRISTY d/o Leta Mae nee Reiss & Richard Raymond Christy; b 29 Dec 1966; m 18 Feb 1989 Kelly Alan Freese (b 22 Apr 1964). Children:
Rebekah Anne Freese – b 20 Jun 1995
Abigail Lee Freese – b 30 Aug 1997

Susan Lynette CHRISTY d/o Leta Mae nee Reiss & Richard Raymond Christy; b 12 Apr 1960; m 24 Sept 1983 David Lee Fuls (b 03 Nov 1959). Children:
John Richard Fuls – b 01 Mar 1990
Rachel Ann Fuls – b 09 Jul 1993
Matthew James Fuls – b 22 Jul 1999

Michael CARROLL s/o NFR; m Brenda Jean Bloeser (b 04 Dec 1956). Children:
Andy Michael – b Nov 1987
Laura Elizabeth – 13 Jul 1990

Edith Frieda CORPORON d/o Frieda Emma Barbara nee Kerkman & Frank Theodore Corporon; b 1937; 1st m Edward Everett Biggart JR. (b 1935). Children:
Ted Calvin Biggart – b 1957; 1st m Cindy Lou McCarthney;
2nd m Cristine Marie Krogman Krisofate
Patricia Frieda Biggart – b 1961; m Dennis Lee Pohlman (b 1959)
Gail Lois Biggart – b 1964; m Bradley Jerome Goedken (b 1963)
2nd m Edith Frieda Corporon to Lewis Arthur Pearson (b 1928).

Leo Frank CORPORON s/o Frieda Emma Barbara nee Kerkman & Frank Theodore Corporon; b 1935; 1st m Meredith Ann Reed (b 1937, d 1985). Children:
Steven Russell – b 1960; m Sarah Towle Weston (b 1962)
Sheri Lynne – b 1962; m Douglas Bryan Brunner (b 1960)
Jon Michael – b 1967
2nd m Leo Frank Corporon to Corrine Dorothy nee Nichols Ballam (b 1933).

Max Arvin CORPORON s/o Frieda Emma Barbara nee Kerkman & Frank Theodore Corporon; b 1942; 1st m Nancy Irene Bartusch (b 1942). Children:
    Max Allen – b 1966; m Sherri Gilliland (b 1969)
    Amanda Ann – b 1967
    Laura Lynn – b 1969
2nd m Max Arvin Corporon to Magdelene Slone (b 1942).

Timothy Thomas CORPORON s/o Frieda Emma Barbara nee Kerkman & Frank Theodore Corporon; b 1941; m Ruth Ann Heiken (b 1941). Children:
    Scott James – b 1961; m Joan Hagg (b 1960)
    Thomas John – b 1963; m Kim Machholz (b 1965)
    Richard "Rick" Allen – b 1965; m Lori Hitchings (b 1966)
    Jerome Noel – b 1968

Raymond Eugene CROSS s/o Susan Jean nee Bergen & Norman Cross; b 05 May 1974; m 08 Oct 2000 Tonya Kay Duby. Child:
    Allison Frances – b 19 May 2005

Lisa Kay CULPEPPER d/o Kay Elaine nee Rammelsberg & Terry Culpepper; b 25 Aug 1974 Seward AK; m 21 Aug 1993 Reno, NV to Lance Caddell (b 12 Jan 1967). Child:
    Joshua Caddell – b 22 Nov 1994 Reno, NV

Sean David DAHLHAUSER s/o Phyllis Lucille nee Bayer & Bernard John Dahlhauser; b 17 Jan 1969 Des Moines, IA; US Navy; m 13 Oct 1987 Colton, CA to Carrie Hernandez (b 03 Sept Colton, CA) d/o Jesse & Joyce Hernandez. Child:
    Kelli Jo – b 17 Jan 1988 Colton, CA

*George DAMM s/o Johannes Damm & Elisabeth nee Borkhard; b 1814 Germany; d 06 Feb 1890 Germany; m Katharina Roder (d 06 Apr 1896 Germany) d/o Johann Heinrich Roder & Anna Maria nee Ochse. Child:
    Karoline – d 01 Apr 1897

Alice DANNENBRING d/o Otto Dannenbring & Martha nee Werning; b 02 Apr 1916; m 19 May 1940 Leonard Buehner (b 06 Jun 1917) s/o George Buehner & Frieda nee Rose. Children:
    Donald Buehner – b 25 Jun 1942; m 15 May 1966 Judy Waage
    Lois Buehner – b 08 May 1944; m 26 May 1963 Eugene Taylor

Evelyn Buehner – b 16 Dec 1945; m 18 Apr 1965 Larry Ondrozeck
Linda Buehner – b 26 Feb 1948; m 24 Nov 1967 Randall R. Parry
Delbert Buehner – b 15 Sept 1951; m 23 Jun 1972 Vicki Kitchen
Gloria Buehner – b 04 Oct 1954; m 17 Aug 1974 Michael Waechter

Arthur DANNENBRING s/o Otto Dannenbring & Martha nee Werning; b 31 Mar 1923; m 22 Oct ND Leola Huber (b 02 Jul 1923) d/o Albert Huber & Lilly nee Schulz. Children:
Joanna – b 23 Oct 1945; m 1970 Leslie Sterling
James – b 18 Dec 1948; m 1970 Kathy Wuetzer
Joyce – b 02 Oct 1953

Diana DANNENBRING d/o Leonhard Dannenbring & Leona nee Huber; b 17 Sept 1947; m 09 Aug 1970 Thomas Agnitsch (b 16 Mar 1943) s/o Frances Agnitsch & Eileen nee Murphy. Aberdeen, SD residence. Children:
Nicole Lee Agnitsch – b 13 May 1973
Marni Jo Agnitsch – b 14 Nov 1979
Lindsay Dianne Agnitsch – b 11 Apr 1984

Dorothy DANNENBRING d/o Leonhard Dannenbring & Leona nee Huber; b 01 May 1944; 1st m 08 May 1964 Wayne Conrad (b 22 Jan 1943) s/o Earl Conrad & Irene nee Guerke. DVD. Children:
Tamara Kay Conrad – b 26 Oct 1964
Charity Eve Conrad – b 11 Sept 1972
2nd m Dorothy nee Dannenbring Conrad to Chris Acklam. Denver, CO residence.

Harvey DANNENBRING s/o Leonhard Dannenbring & Leona nee Huber; b 16 Dec 1949; m 17 Oct 1987 Debra Ann Eitenmiller of IL. Clayton, SD residence.

James DANNENBRING s/o Arthur Dannenbring & Leola nee Huber; b 18 Dec 1948; m 02 Aug 1970 Kathy Wuetzer (b 07 Jan 1951) d/o Louis Wuetzer & Lillian nee Fischer. Child:
Jason James – b 23 Dec 1972

Janet Josephine DANNENBRING d/o Leonhard Dannenbring & Leona nee Huber; b 05 Feb 1956; m 03 Aug 1985 Daniel Brown. Seattle, WA residence.

Joanna DANNENBRING d/o Arthur Dannenbring & Leola nee Huber; b 23 Oct 1945; m 26 May 1970 Leslie Sterling (b 21 Apr 1944) s/o Jack Vincent Sterling & Dorothy Louise nee Stickling of Oaklawn, IL. Children:
    Laura Sterling – b 28 Oct 1971
    (Son) Sterling – NFR

Leonhard DANNENBRING s/o Otto Dannenbring & Martha nee Werning; b 13 Dec 1913, d 1989; m 15 Dec 1940 Leona Huber (b 01 May 1919 Clayton Twp, SD, bpt 08 Jun 1919 St.Peter's Luth Ch, Clayton, SD, d 24 Aug 1989 ae70y 3m 8d bur St.Peter's Luth Cem Clayton, SD) d/o Reinhold Huber & Josephine nee Langle. Children:
    Marvin – b 20 Nov 1942; 1st m 29 Dec 1967 Claudia VanderHamm;
        2nd m Feb 1987 NFR
    Dorothy – b 01 May 1944; 1st m 08 May 1964 Wayne Conrad DVD;
        2nd m Chris Acklam
    Diana – b 17 Sept 1947; m 09 Aug 1970 Thomas Agnitsch
    Harvey – b 16 Dec 1949; m 17 Oct 1987 Debra Ann Eitenmiller
    Twyla Lee – b 26 Jan 1953; m 24 Aug 1974 Ralph Richter
    Daniel Otto – b 14 Feb 1958; Platte, SD residence
    June Leona – b 04 Mar 1960; Seattle, WA residence

Marvin DANNENBRING s/o Leonhard Dannenbring & Leona nee Huber; b 20 Nov 1942; 1st m 29 Dec 1967 Claudia VanderHamm (b 13 Apr 1947, d 12 Nov 1984) d/o Cellen VanderHamm & Wilma nee Calsbeek. Clayton, SD residence. Children:
    Patricia Ann – b 11 Oct 1968
    Matthew Marvin – b 29 Aug 1970
    Lucas Len – b 09 Mar 1976
2nd m Feb 1987 Marvin Dannenbring to NFR.

Olga DANNENBRING d/o Otto Dannenbring & Martha nee Werning; b 15 Apr 1928; m 19 Jan 1947 Ivan Ibis (b 22 Dec 1922, d Jun 1997) s/o Arthur Ibis & Sara nee Kunkel. Children:
    Sandria Ibis – b 22 Oct 1947; m 1972 Gorden Krause
    Charles Ibis – b 10 Nov 1950; m 1976 Cynthia Burdine

Twyla Lee DANNENBRING d/o Leonhard Dannenbring & Leona nee Huber; b 26 Jan 1953; m 24 Aug 1974 Ralph Richter. Henderson, NV residence. Child:
    Jacky Ryan Richter – b 05 Jun 1980

*Anna Katharina Elisabeth DAUME d/o Konrad Daume & Anna Martha nee Beyer; b 04 Aug 1867 Löhlbach Hse #120 Germany, d 06 Mar 1946 ae78y 7m 2d Löhlbach Hse #38½ Germany; m 22 Mar 1894 Johann Heinrich Thielmann (b 02 Jan 1867 Löhlbach Hse #4 Germany, d 27 Oct 1951 ae84y 9m 25d Löhlbach, Germany). Children:

Conrad Daume Thielmann – b 20 May 1887 Löhlbach, Germany

Conrad Heinrich Thielmann- b 30 Oct 1894 Löhlbach,
    d 1915 in World War I

Anna Martha Thielmann – b 07 Nov 1896 Löhlbach, Germany;
    m 16/18 Sept 1921 Wilhelm Keute (b 24 Feb 1893)

TWINS: Marie Sophie Thielmann – b 18 Sept 1901
    Löhlbach, Germany
       *Elisabeth Thielmann – b 18 Sept 1901 Löhlbach, Germnany;
    d 14 May 1986 Löhlbach, Germany;
    m 9/11 Jan 1935 Heinrich Paar (b 08 Oct 1901)

Anna Thielmann – b 17 Nov 1903 Löhlbach, Germany

*Johann Adam DAUME, Germany, m Anna Katharina Schneider. Child:
    *Konrad – b 01 Sept 1841 Germany, d 26 Jun 1918 Germany;
    m Anna Martha Beyer d/o Simon Beyer & Anna nee Vaupel

*Konrad DAUME s/o Johann Adam Daume & Anna Katharina nee Schneider; b 01 Sept 1841 Löhlbach, Germany, d 26 Jun 1918 ae76y 8m 26d Löhlbach, Germany; m 03 Mar 1867 Anna Martha Beyer (b 09 Dec 1844 Löhlbach Hse #39, d 14 Apr 1931 ae92y 4m 5d Löhlbach #39) d/o Simon Beyer & Anna Elisabeth nee Vaupel. Child:
    *Anna Katharina Elisabeth – b 24 Aug 1867, d 06 Mar 1946;
    m 22 Mar 1894 Heinrich Thielemann

*Henry J. DAVIS SR. b 1837 Baden, Germany, d 1892 Benton Co IA; 1853 emigrated to USA with parents; settled at Marion, Linn Co IA; m 1861 Louisa Baker who was born in Prussia and came to America with sister in 1858. Louisa met Henry in Linn Co IA; 1863 moved to Benton Co IA after marriage; purchased farmland two miles east of Newhall, IA. Henry lived rest of his life on the farm. Children:

Henry J. JR. – m Lena Ockenfels

Mary – b 1864 Benton Co IA, d 1950; m 1883 John Weichman

Lena L. – b Benton Co IA, d 1939; m 1888 Lewis Deklotz

Bertha – m William Means

Louisa – m John T. Smith
Elizabeth – m Ferman Lucas

James Edward DAY s/o Nina Mae nee Rinderknecht & Lloyd Wilmer Day; b 29 Feb 1952; Owner Commercial Upholstery business, San Jose, CA; 1st m 13 Dec 1974 Anita Weitz DVD. Children:
　James Edward II – b 09 Jul 1975
　Sarah Autumn – b 31 Dec 1976; m 1997 Frank McMillan. Children:
　　Frankie Mae McMillan (b 17 Jun 1998);
　　Jaime Sierra McMillan(b 16 Sept 1999)
2nd m 25 Apr 1988 James Edward Day to Patty Avery

Janet Ellen DAY d/o Nina Mae nee Rinderknecht & Lloyd Wilmer Day; b 24 Sept 1948; City Tem Ministries missionary, San Jose, Ca; 1st m 12 Aug 1973 John Douglas Hanson DVD. Children:
　Karen Lynn Hanson – b 07 Feb 1974;
　　m 14 Feb 2002 Lawrence Jay Perlman
　Mary Elizabeth Hanson – b 27 Dec 1977;
　　m 11 May 1998 Peter John Hintze

Thomas Allen DAY s/o Nina Mae nee Rinderknecht & Lloyd Wilmer Day; b 13 Nov 1950, d 24 Sept 1995; m 25 Jul 1969 Sandra Lundy DVD. Children:
　Tina Marie – b 22 Feb 1970; m Trent Kenney (b 12 Mar 1967). Child:
　　Cali – b 20 Jul 2000
　Lisa Lynette – b 30 Aug 1972

**Karl Heinrich DEBUS s/o Anni Elisabeth nee Hecker & Walter Debus; b 17 Mar 1958 Germany; Civil Engineer; m Jutta Erika Hesse (b 25 May 1960 Germany; Bank employee). Children:
　**Simon Fabian – b 25 Oct 1987
　**Michael – b 13 Nov 1989

**Richard Konrad DEBUS s/o Anni Elisabeth nee Hecker & Walter Debus; b 09 Jul 1959 Germany; Customs employee; m Christel Friederike (b 03 Jan 1958 Lieberum, Germany). Children:
　**Pierre – b 09 Jan 1982
　**Johanna – b 20 Jul 1987
　**Theresa – b 21 Jun 1991

Alice Marie DEKLOTZ d/o Ralph Louis Deklotz & Amelia Louise nee Fix; b 07 Jul 1931; bpt 26 Jul 1931 St.Step Sponsors: Mrs. John Fix, Mildred Seeman; con 25 Mar 1945 St.Steph; 1949 Class Atkins High School; d 27 Apr 1997 [Cancer] ae65y 9m 10d; cremate bur St.Steph Cem; m 07 May 1957 St.Steph to Lenard James Armstrong s/o Elton Armstrong & Mildred nee Yileck. Farmers on land of Armstrong father and grandfather, north of Atkins, Benton Co IA. Children:

Kristy Ann Armstrong – b 30 Oct 1956 St.Lukes Hosp CR, IA; bpt 18 Nov 1956 & con 22 Mar 1970 St.Steph; Atkins, IA residence

Kimberly Sue Armstrong – b 19 May 1958 St.Lukes Hosp CR, IA; m 04 Apr 1987 Gary Spiess of Lisbon, IA

Kay Lynn Armstrong – b 27 Jul 1962 St.Lukes Hosp CR, IA; m 03 Sept 1988 Edward Bartholmew of Montrose, IA

2nd m 01 Jan 1999 St.Steph Lenard James Armstrong to Dorothy Olive Gillis Rathje (b 05 Jul 1936; 1st m Alan Henry Rathje, DVD) Children: cf Alan Henry Rathje.

Douglas Dennis DEKLOTZ s/o Wayne John Deklotz & Marie Elizabeth nee Gerhold; b 28 Jun 1951 Cedar Rapids, IA bpt 29 Jul 1951 St.Steph Sponsors: Wilbert Rinderknecht & George Gerhold, con 11 Apr 1965 St.Steph; m 15 Feb 1985 Sharon Frederick (b 24 Apr 1953). Child:

Daniel Douglas – b 02 Mar 1987, bpt 19 Apr 1987 St.Steph; Sponsors: Michael Deklotz & Debbie Lefebure

Edward John DEKLOTZ s/o Lewis Deklotz & Lena L. nee Davis; b 1894, d 1976; m Minnie Hessenius (b 1893 Germany) d/o Herman Hessenius & Gesina Klover. Child:

Louis John SR. – b 16 Jul 1920, d 19 Nov 1997; m 24 Apr 1943 Margaret (Peg) Millburn

Gary DEKLOTZ s/o Louis John Deklotz SR. & Margaret (Peg) nee Millburn; b 18 Feb 1950; 1st m Mary Rhinehard. DVD. Child:

Olivia – b 14 Nov 1975

2nd m 11 Oct 1980 Gary Deklotz to Rae Wonderlich. Child:

Cole – b 09 Jan 1985

*John DEKLOTZ s/o B. Deklotz & Anna M; b 1828 Germany, d 1906 Benton Co IA, [Killed by Chicago & Northwestern Railroad train on eve of 50th Wedding Anniversary]; 1854 emigrated to USA; 1859 moved from

Galion, OH to Tipton, IA; 1861 moved to Norway, IA where he was one of founders of Catholic Ch; m 1856 Elizabeth Petter (b 1828 d 1923) d/o John & Elizabeth Petter of Sixhelden, Germany. Children:

> Frank – b 1859 d 1945; banker IA; Farmer ID
> Fannie – b 1860 d 1920; organist at Catholic Ch
> Lewis – b 1862 d 1941; m 1888 Lena Davis

Lewis DEKLOTZ s/o John Deklotz & Elizabeth nee Petter; b 1862 Cedar Co IA., d 1941 Benton Co IA bur Mound Cem, Watkins, IA; attended Tilford Academy; teacher St. Clair and Florence Twp Benton Co IA; m 1888 Lena Davis (b Benton Co IA, d 1939 bur Mound Cem, Watkins, IA) d/o Henry & Louisa Davis. Same year bought 160 acres of farmland in Eldorado Twp Benton Co; 1904 cashier of Newhall, IA Savings Bank; 1905 purchased additional 80 acres of farmland; charter mbr Newhall St. Paul's Catholic Ch. Children:

> Mabel Elizabeth – b 1890, d 1972; m John Seeman, Newhall, IA
> Edward John – b 1894, d 1976; m Minnie Hessenius,
> Ralph Lewis – b 21 Feb 1896, d 1973;
> > m Amelia Louise Fix, Atkins, IA
> Gilbert Henry – b 1898, d 1977; m Velma Reisser
> Roy – b 1902, d 1943; m Grace Sovern, Burlington, IA
> Merril – b 1904; lived in Newhall, IA all his life

Linda DEKLOTZ d/o Louis John Deklotz SR. & Margaret (Peg) nee Millburn. b 08 Nov 1955; m 03 Jul 1980 Jim Herzberger. Children:

> Stephanie Herzberger – b 10 Aug 1981, d 15 Feb 1982
> Adam Herzberger – b 04 May 1983
> Tara Herzberger (Adopted) – b 20 Mar 1985

Louis John DEKLOTZ JR. s/o Louis John Deklotz SR. & Margaret (Peg) nee Millburn; b 02 Jul 1943; 1st m 1965 Karen Radeke DVD. Children:

> Regina – b 20 Sept 1967
> Rikki – b 16 Jul 1969
> Brenda 28 Jul 1972

2nd m 06 Aug 1987 Louis John Deklotz JR. to Judy Hartz and adopted her daughter Stephanie b 16 Nov 1974.

Louis John DEKLOTZ SR. s/o Edward John Deklotz & Minnie nee Hessenius; b 16 Jul 1930; 1937 High School Graduation; Entered World War II U.S. Army Jan 1943. Overseas Apr 1943 – Nov 1945; d 19 Nov

1997 ae77y 4m 3d bur Oakwood Cemetery, Shellsburg, IA; m 24 Apr 1943 in San Francisco, CA to Margaret (Peg) Millburn. Farmed in Shellsburg, IA area; had Louis Deklotz & His Toe Teasing Tempos orchestra from 1945 – 1971. Mbrs St.Steph, Atkins, IA. Children:

Louis John JR. b 02 Jul 1943; 1st m 1965 Karen Radeke DVD;
2nd m 06 Aug 1987 Judy Hartz

Sharon – b 04 Jul 1947; m Dennis Young

Gary – b 18 Feb 1950; 1st m Mary Rhinehart DVD;
2nd m 11 Oct 1980 Rae Wonderlich

Margaret (Margie) – b 15 Mar 1952; m 17 Mar 1973 Dennis Lohrer

Linda – b 08 Nov 1955; m 03 Jul 1980 Jim Herzberger

Margaret (Margie) DEKLOTZ d/o Louis John Deklotz SR. & Margaret (Peg) nee Millburn; b 15 Mar 1952; m 17 Mar 1973 Dennis Lohrer. Children:

Chad Lohrer – b 07 Aug 1973

Brian Lohrer – b 26 Aug 1975

Eric Lohrer – b 04 Jan 1978

Carrie Lohrer – b 05 Jan 1980

Michael Wayne DEKLOTZ s/o Wayne John Deklotz & Marie Elizabeth nee Gerhold; b 25 Mar 1949 bpt 17 Apr 1949 and con 07 Apr 1963 St.Steph; Farmed Deklotz farm owned by grandfather Lewis and farmed by father Wayne; m 24 Jun 1973 United Methodist Ch Chillicothe, MO to Patricia Hawkins (b 30 Dec 1949 bpt 18 May 1951, con 02 Apr 1978 Mt. Calvary Ch, Eagle Grove,IA) d/o Robert S. Hawkins & Darlene C. nee Crane, Chillicothe, MO. Child:

Jennifer Lee – b 27 Feb 1978, bpt 02 Apr 1978 and con St.Steph;
m 31 Jul 1999 Joseph Michael Eason, Red Oak, IA
Pennington, NJ residence.

Ralph Louis DEKLOTZ s/o Lewis Deklotz & Lena L. nee Davis; b 21 Feb 1896 Eldorado Twp Benton Co IA, d 1973 Benton Co IA; m Amelia Louise Fix (b 13 Jul 1896, d 1946 [Cancer] Benton Co IA) d/o John Phillip Fix & Meta nee Axelsen. Farmers west of Atkins, IA beginning 1916 when purchased first parcel of land from father-in-law. Children:

Margaret Ella – b 31 Dec 1916, d 15 Nov 1951 bur St.Steph Cem;
m 01 Jun 1938 Wilbert Heinrich Julius Rinderknecht

Wayne John – b 25 Jul 1922 Fremont Twp farm near Atkins, IA
d 05 Dec 1999 bur St.Steph Cem;

m 09 Mar 1947 Marie Elizabeth Gerhold
Alice Marie – b 07 Jul 1931, d 27 Apr 1997 bur St.Steph Cem;
m 07 May 1957 Lenard James Armstrong

Ronald Alan DEKLOTZ s/o Wayne John Deklotz & Marie Elizabeth nee Gerhold; b 27 Nov 1954 Cedar Rapids, IA bpt 19 Dec 1954 St.Steph Sponsors: Wilbert Gerhold & Mrs. Bernard Graham, con 30 Mar 1969 St.Steph; d 10 May 2007 [Infection] ae 52y 5m 14d bur St.Steph Cem; 1973 Class Benton Community High School; 1977 B.S. Iowa State University; Master's Degree Industrial Engineering; Community College Instructor; Realtor; m 31 Dec 1996 in WI to Jeannie Utitus (b 29 Jun 1961).

Sharon DEKLOTZ d/o Louis John Deklotz SR. & Margaret (Peg) nee Millburn; b 04 Jul 1947; m 06 May 1967 Dennis Young. Children:
    Jennifer Young – b 23 Dec 1967
    Richard Young – b 02 Feb 1974

Wayne John DEKLOTZ s/o Ralph Louis Deklotz & Amelia Louise nee Fix; b 25 Jul 1922, bpt 15 Aug 1922 and con 05 Apr 1936 St.Steph, d 04 Dec 1999 ae77y 4m 9d Marengo Memorial Hosp, Marengo, IA [Cancer; Parkinsons Disease; Congestive Heart Failure] bur St.Steph Cem; m 09 Mar 1946 Marie Elizabeth Gerhold (b 24 Mar 1924 Atkins, IA bpt and con St.Steph; Graduate Atkins High School;d 25 Feb 2007 ae82y 11m 1d bur 01 Mar 2007 St.Steph Cem) d/o Adam Gerhold & Elizabeth nee Rinderknecht. Farmed land of his father 30 years until 1977 when built a new home in Atkins, IA. Wayne: Mayor of Atkins; active in Atkins Little League. Children:
    Michael – b 25 Mar 1949 Cedar Rapids, IA;
        m 24 Jun 1973 Patricia Hawkins of Chillicothe, MO
    Douglas Dennis – b 28 Jun 1951 Cedar Rapids, IA;
        m 15 Feb 1985 Sharon Frederick
    Ronald Alan – b 27 Nov 1954 Cedar Rapids, IA; d 10 May 2007
    m 31 Dec 1996 Jeannine Utitus

Ada Marie DETLEFSEN d/o Amanda nee Senne & Carl Lehrer Detlefsen; b 1919; m Robert Henry Traver (b 1918). Child:
    Michael Robert Traver – b 1957; 1st m Jean Lubben (b 1961);
        2nd m Mary Kaye Porter (b 1961). Children: Julie Marie (b 1981),
        Christopher Michael (b 1984), Daniel Robert (b 1985)

Lois DETLEFSEN d/o Amanda nee Senne & Carl Lehrer Detlefsen; b
1925; m Richard Marks (b 1923). Children:
  Bruce Thomas Marks – b 1945; m Pamela Walker (b 1946). Children:
    1. Kevin (b 1967); m Cindy Garrett (b 1966). Child:
    Jordan Ashley (b 1993); 2. Steven (b 1971, d 1989)
  Leslie Anne Marks – b 1947; m Jeffery Heefner (b 1945). Children:
    Timothy Allen Heefner (b 1971); Kara Marie Heefner (b 1973)
  TWINS: Dennis Paul Marks – b 1948; 1st m Kathleen Solem (b 1949)
    Children: 1. Andrea Danielle (b1973); m Sean Meyer;
    2. Sarah Marie (b 1978);
    2nd m Karen Matthews (b 1945)
      Terry Niel Marks – b 1948; m Susan Kay McIntosh (b 1949).
    Children: 1. Richard Jason (b 1971); m Kimberly Krumholz
    (b 1971). Child: Richard Jacob b1992);
    2. Matthew Travis (b1973); 3. Angela Marie (b 1976)
    4. Nathan Andrew (b 1981)

Paul DETLEFSEN s/o Amanda nee Senne & Carl Lehrer Detlefsen; b 1912,
d 1971; m Leona Schumann (b 1913). Children:
  Margaret Jean – b 1936, d 1996; m Donald Bendewald (b 1935);
    Children: Thomas Paul Bendewald (b 1963);
    Dawn Marie Bendewald (b 1964); Jill Annette Bendewald
    (b 1968)
  Janet Ann – b 1943; m Paul Berkowitz (b 1943); Child:
    Zachary Michael Paul Berkowitz (b 1981)
  Ellen Leona – b 1944; m Robert Worthington JR. (b 1945).
    Children: Darrin John Worthington (b 1970)
    Brian Paul Worthington (b 1975)

Ruth DETLEFSEN d/o Amanda nee Senne & Carl Lehrer Detlefsen: b
1915; m Harold Kammerer (b 1913, d 1991). Children:
  Carol Ann Kammerer – b 1940; m Robert Price SR. (b 1937)
    Children: 1. Robert Price JR. (b 1961); m Donna Jean Anderson
    (b 1954). Child: Matthew Robert Price(1992); 2. Debra Jo Price
    (b 1962); m Dean Allen Shipe SR.(b 1965). Children:
    Dean Allen Shipe JR. (b1988); Laurie Anne Shipe (b 1990)
    3. Sheryln Ann Price (b 1963); m Anthony Stump (b 1954).
    Child: Tyler Paul Stump (b 1990)
  Phyllis Jean Kammerer – b 1943; 1st m Edwin Isbell (b 1947)
    Child: Steven Isbell (b 1969); m Kristi Wright

2nd m Gerald Lockwood

Ronald Harold Kammerer – b 1946; 1st m Diane Masters (b 1950)
Child: Lori Kammerer (b/d 1969)
2nd m LuAnne McCarty. Children: Kelly (b 1978); Melinda
(b 1981); Brian Michael(b 1985)

Walter Philip DETLEFSEN SR. s/o Amanda nee Senne & Carl Lehrer
Detlefsen; b 1914, d 1974; m Ida Wolter (b 1912). Children:
Walter Philip JR. – b 1948; m Cheryle Marie Solbert. Children:
Jennifer Marie (b 1974); Karen Sueanne (b 1977)
Joan Ruth – b 1950; m Joseph Roger Kleinmaier (b 1948). Children:
Sarah Jo Kleinmaier (b 1977); Susan Kleinmaier (b 1980)
Eunice – b 1952

Dennis DICKENSON s/o NFR; b 15 Feb 1952; m 07 Aug 1976 Suzanne
Happel (b 29 Oct 1954). Children:
Amanda – b 23 Oct 1979
Ryan – b 01 Dec 1981
Andria – b 25 Jul 1984

Donovan Martin DIETRICH s/o Walter William Dietrich & Anna Christina
nee Happel; b 18 Oct 1916 Van Horne, IA; m 28 Jun 1942 TrinCR to
Lenora Mae Meineke (b 01 Apr 1921 bpt 29 Mar 1942 TrinCR, d 26 Jun
2004 ae83y 2m 25d bur St.John Cem) d/o Paul George Meineke & Lillie
Mae nee Lyons of Olin, Jones Co IA. Celebrated 50th and 60th Wedding
Anniversary. Children:
Verlee Ann – b 01 Aug 1944; m 07 Nov 1964 Dennis Schiel
Pamela Jean – b 11 Dec 1946; m 24 Sept 1946 Darrel L. Honnold
Larry Robert – b 17 Jul 1950; 1st m 11 Jan 1976 Shirlee Weed DVD;
2nd m 24 Dec 1995 Kaye Schadle

Glenn Howard DIETRICH s/o Walter William Dietrich & Anna Christina
nee Happel; b 06 Jan 1919 Van Horne, IA, bpt 1919 St.And; m 21 Mar
1942 Fort Snelling Army Chapel, MN to Lois Catherine Husted (b 10 Jun
1919 near Van Horne, IA bpt Aug 1919 St.And) d/o Roy Husted & Anna
Margaret Elizabeth nee Brehm of Shellsburg, IA. Celebrated 50th and 60th
Wedding Anniversary. Children:
Max Allen – b 16 May 1943; 1st m 07 Dec 1966 Judith Pope;
2nd m 02 Jan 2004 Jacqueline Humfield
Randy Lee – b 03 Nov 1949 in Vinton, IA bpt 19 Nov 1949

Larry Robert DIETRICH s/o Donovan Martin Dietrich & Lenora Mae nee Meineke; b 17 Jul 1950 Cedar Rapids, IA bpt 1950; 1st m 11 Jan 1976 Shirlee Weed (b 17 Dec 1947)DVD. Van Horne, IA residence. Children:
  Dake Mathew – b 10 Sept 1976; m 14 Jun 1997 Kathy Brown
    (b 08 Mar 1977)
  Cole Christopher – b 25 Aug 1977
  Amy Jo – b 07 Sept 1979
2nd m 24 Dec 1995 Larry Robert Dietrich to Kaye Schadle:
  STEPDAUGHTERS:
    Kelly – b 19 Sept 1971; m 23 Sept 1995 Bret Burkart;
    Daughter: Hannah Nichole – b 10 Nov 1999
    Valerie – b 10 Nov 1975; Daughter: Miranda – b 26 Nov 1997

Marilyn Ruth DIETRICH d/o Walter William Dietrich & Anna Christina nee Happel; b 25 Mar 1931 Parent's Home, Van Horne, IA bpt 1931 St.And; m 30 Jan 1955 TrinCR to Alan F. Young. Marilyn employed by Martin-Roasa Tractor & Equipment Co. Cedar Rapids, IA; Alan employed by Lynch Transfer & Storage Co. Children:
  Jeffrey Alan Young – b 22 Feb 1961 (Adopted 10 May 1961);
    m 23 Sept 1995 Jody Ryker(b 24 Aug 1962)
  Colleen Young – b 13 Sept 1963 (Adopted Nov 1963)
    m 04 Aug 1984 Russ Alan Williams DVD

Max Allen DIETRICH s/o Glenn Howard Dietrich & Lois Catherine nee Husted; b 16 May 1943 Nevada, Vernon Co MO, bpt 11 Aug 1943; 1st m 17 Dec 1966 Judith Pope (b 27 Jan 1945) DVD. Children:
  Timothy Allen – b 06 Nov 1975; m 21 Mar 2003
  Craig Alex – b 15 Jan 1980
2nd m 02 Jan 2004 Max Allen Dietrich to Jacqueline Humfield.

Pamela Jean DIETRICH d/o Donovan Martin Dietrich & Lenora Mae nee Meineke; b 22 Dec 1946 Cedar Rapids, IA bpt Feb 1947; m 24 Sept 1966 Darrel L. Honnold (b 20 Jul 1946). Westfield, WI residence. Children:
  Darren L. Honnold – b 04 Mar 1968; m 04 Nov 1996 Kelly Murphy
  Tamitha J. Honnold – b 16 Nov 1970; m 18 Jun 1994 Brian Janke

Verlee Ann DIETRICH d/o Donovan Martin Dietrich & Lenora Mae nee Meineke; b 01 Aug 1944 Cedar Rapids, IA bpt Sept 1944; m 07 Nov 1964 Dennis Schiel. Rogers, AR residence. Children:

Brett Schiel – b 08 May 1967
Dawn Renee Schiel – b 29 Apr 1969

*Christian DOEBEL b 1821 Holstein, Germany, d 1881 Benton Co IA; 1852 came to USA landing at New Orleans, worked on Illinois Central Railroad. Returned to Louisiana and floated timber in the swamps netting $400 in gold with which to establish his life. In 1854 purchased 320 acres of land, Section 8, Fremont Twp Benton Co IA; 1857 built a house of split rails covered with a straw roof on the land; m 1862 Maria Busoker (b 1837 Mecklenburg, Germany, d 1901 Benton Co IA). He was Postmaster in the summertime. Children:
    Minnie – b/d 1863
    Mary – b 1864, d 1935; m 1883 Louis C. Gardemann, 10 children
    Annie – b 1866, d 1917; m C.H. Schlotterbeck, 5 children
    Christian – b & d 1868
    Fred – b & d 1869
    Lizzie – b 1870, d 1938; m A.J. Lloyd, 2 children
    Charles – b 1873, d 1935; m Sadie McGranahan, 2 children
    George – b 1876, d 1953; Never Married
    Frank – b 1879, d 1955; m Bertha Tedrick, son:Frank

*Amelia DOOSE (DOHSE) b 1851 East Germany; m 08 Nov 1877 in Germany to Johann Jochim Christian Doose (b 1852 East Germany, d 1901 Germany). Wid/Amelia came to USA in 1902 with seven children:
    *Emma Doose – m NN Kiesel
    *Ida Dorthea (Dora) Doose – b 1880's, d 1936;
        m 05 Jul 1902 Henry Grau SR.
    *August Doose – Never Married
    *Augusta Doose – m NN Kiesel
    *Gustave Doose – m NN Chaloupek
    *John Doose – m NN Roland
    *Marie Doose – 1st m NN Rogers; 2nd m NN Callahan

*Ida Dorthea (Dora) DOOSE (DOHSE) d/o Amelia & Johann Jochim Christian Doose, b 1880's Hollenbeck, Germany; changed name to Dora Amelia after immigrating to USA with mother in 1902; d 1936; m 05 Jul 1902 Henry Grau (b 1864, d 1924). Eight children: two dying in infancy-bur Keystone IA Cem:
    Alvina Grau – m NN Sturtz-Myers
    George Grau – m NN Mathiason

Henry Grau – d 1974, m NN Turner-Vogt
William Grau – d 1971, m NN Johnson
Walter Grau – m NN Wilson
Clara Grau – m NN Wutzke

Daryl Allan DORTT s/o Daniel Dortt & Beverly nee Campbell; b 18 Dec 1968; m 04 Jan 1987 Susan Eisenbraun. Child:
Rawley John – b 12 Apr 1987

Denise Michele DRAHN d/o Sharon Louise nee Harris & Don Lloyd Drahn; b 06 Sept 1969 Cedar Rapids, IA; m 28 Jul 1990 St.Paul Luth Ch Postville, IA to Craig Marvin Adams (b 28 Jan 1967 Postville, IA) s/o Marvin Adams & Janice nee Guese. Children:
Adrian Craig Adams – b 17 Aug 1991 Waukon, IA

John Allen DRISCOLL s/o Loreen Marie nee Happel & Oakley H. Driscoll; b 30 Jul 1945 Vinton, IA; m 16 Jun 1973 Judith Kay Brooks d/o John Brooks & Helen nee Turner. Children:
Carrie Loreen – b 15 Jun 1979
Krista Marie – b 17 May 1982

Catherine Lea EDMONDS d/o Leslie August Edmonds & Wilma Henrietta nee Hudson; b 29 Aug 1931 Cedar Rapids, IA bpt 11 Sept 1931 Parent's Home, Cedar Rapids, IA; m 31 Aug 1950 Leon Leslie Durham. Children:
TWINS(Adopted): Douglas Leslie Durham – b 07 Aug 1958
David Leon Durham – b 07 Aug 1958
Debbie Durham – b 08 Apr 1960

Jacqueline Marie EDMONDS d/o Leslie August Edmonds & Wilma Henrietta nee Hudson; b 26 Apr 1930 Cedar Rapids, IA bpt 23 Jun 1930 at home, Cedar Rapids, IA; 1st m 18 Nov 1949 First Methodist Ch, Ottumwa, IA to Dr. Charles Ray Phelps SR.(b 16 Aug 1915 Ft.Scott, KS, d 11 Jan 1969 ae53y 4m 26d Ottumwa, IA) s/o Harry John Phelps & Dora nee Pear of Fort Scott, KS. Residence Siesta Key, FL. Children:
Charles Ray Phelps JR. – b 28 Aug 1950; m 30 Dec 1971 Jeannine Hatt
Victor Leslie Phelps – b 26 Jan 1952; m 12 Jun 1972 Rachel NN
Gregory Lynn Phelps – b 23 Jan 1954;
m 02 Jun 1978 Jacquelyn Threadgill
Terry Kay Phelps – b 27 Aug 1957; m 19 Aug 1979 James Meara
2nd m Jacqueline Marie nee Edmonds Phelps to Billy Stonefield DVD.

3rd m Jacqueline Marie nee Edmonds Phelps Stonefield to Don Jones DVD.

Leslie August EDMONDS s/o Prescott Samuel Edmonds & Katharina Wilhemina nee Happel Gilbert; b 01 Jul 1907 Van Horne, Union Twp Benton Co IA; d 03 Sept 1990 TX ae83y 2m 2d; m 29 Dec 1927 Parsonage TrinCR to Wilma Henrietta Hudson (b 30 Mar 1909 Cedar Rapids, IA bpt 22 Dec 1927 Parsonage TrinCR, d 03 Sept 1990 Denison, TX ae81y 6m 4d bur Fairview Cem, Denison, TX) d/o Everett Raymond Hudson & Marie nee Sommers of Cedar Rapids, IA. Cedar Rapids Appliance dealer; Collins Radio Company (Rockwell-Collins International). Moved to TX, retiring in Denison. Children:
>   Jacqueline Marie – b 26 Apr 1930 Cedar Rapids, IA;
>>   1st m 18 Nov 1949 Dr.Charles Phelps(d 11 Jan 1969)
>>   2nd m Billy Stonefield DVD; 3rd m Don Jones DVD
>   Catherine Lea – b 29 Aug 1931 Cedar Rapids, IA;
>>   m 31 Aug 1950 Leon Leslie Durham
>   Leslie Everett (Corky) – b 13 Aug 1935 Cedar Rapids, IA;
>>   m 07 Sept 1957 Patricia Mae Brown

Leslie Everett EDMONDS s/o Leslie August Edmonds & Wilma Henrietta nee Hudson; b 13 Aug 1935 Cedar Rapids, IA bpt 04 Nov 1935 Parent's Home, Cedar Rapids, IA; m 07 Sept 1957 St.Paul Methodist Ch, Cedar Rapids, IA to Patricia Mae Brown (b 19 Jun 1937) d/o Harold H. Brown of Cedar Rapids. Braniff Airline pilot; Liquor store business; Dennison, TX residence. Children:
>   Leslie Alan – b 28 Jul 1955
>   Brian – b 11 Aug 1960
>   Craig – b 28 May 1962
>   Daniel – b 01 May 1970

Prescott Williard EDMONDS s/o Prescott Samuel Edmonds & Katharina Wilhelmina nee Happel Gilbert; b 18 Dec 1909 Carlisle, ND, bpt 04 Sept 1910 St.And, d 01 Aug 1940 at his home, Van Horne, IA ae30y 7m 13d bur 03 Aug 1940 St.John Cem; Occupation: Painter & Paperhanger; m 07 Dec 1932 Helen Margaret Mess (b 09 Jun 1912 Keystone, IA) d/o Ernest Mess & Emma nee Brand of Keystone, IA. Children:
>   Darrell Dean – Stillborn 12 Feb 1934 bur St.John Cem
>   Roger Wayne – b 21 Mar 1936;
>>   m 27 Jun 1959 Frances Norma Glidden

Roger Wayne EDMONDS s/o Prescott Williard Edmonds & Helen Margaret nee Mess; b 21 Mar 1936; m 27 Jun 1959 Frances Norma Glidden (b 07 Apr 1941). Children:
Darrell James – b 01 Aug 1960
Cheryl Lynn – b 05 Dec 1961

*Rolf EGGERS b 1838 Drage, Schleswig-Holstein, Germany, d 1919 Benton Co IA; m Anna M. Unrau (b 1836, d 1895). 1870 Rolf & Anna sailed to USA on steamship "Holsatia" with two young daughters; traveled to Keystone, IA by train; 1880 moved to farm north of Newhall, IA purchased for $50 an acre where three boys were born. Bought land in SD for $27 an acre. Children:
Mary – b 1866, d 1951; m Ernest Broendel of Newhall, IA
Dora – b 1868; m John Zornig of Elberon, IA
Henry – b 1872; m Dorothea Haack, SD, CA
William – b 1875; m Emma Junge, Keystone, IA
John – b 1878; m Clara Boysen, Cedar Rapids, IA

Frederick Julius EHLERS s/o Anna Elisabeth nee Happel & Rev. Fred Ehlers; b 15 Feb 1886 Estherville, IA, d 13 August 1966 ae80y 5m 29d; m 30 October 1917 West Bend, IA to Mary Matilda Mueller.

(Henry) Johannes Heinrich Andreas Nicholas EHLERS s/o Anna Elisabeth nee Happel & Rev. Fred Ehlers; b 23 Dec 1882 Adair, IA d 27 Jan 1964 ae81y 1m 4d; m 13 Feb 1908 Storm Lake, Grant Twp IA to Bertha Anna Margaret Ripke.

Marie Gertrude EHLERS d/o Anna Elisabeth nee Happel & Rev. Fred Ehlers; b 14 Feb 1893 Knierim, Calhoun Co IA bpt 1893, d 10 Jun 1962 ae68y 10m 27d; m 25 Dec 1924 Centerville, SD to Leo Henry Boettcher (b 22 Aug 1891 Storm Lake, IA). Children:
Loretta Boettcher – b 28 May 1928 Belvidera, SD
Gertrude Boettcher – b 02 Feb 1930 Belvidera, SD
Clara Boettcher – b 20 Jan 1932 Belvidera, SD

*George John ENGEL s/o John George Engel & Eva Rosina nee Keller; b 12 Jan 1869 Germany; m in Germany to Johanna Kale d/o Martin & Katherina Kale. 1850 emigrated to USA when daughter Mary was 3y; settled on farm two miles west of Covington, Linn Co IA. Children:
Mary – b 1847 Germany; m John Saha

Joe – Atkins resident; owned team of Shetland ponies

*John George ENGEL s/o George Engel & Anna Marie nee Koehl; b 03 Oct 1845 Bahlingen, Baden, Germany, d 03 Dec 1926 Vinton, IA ae81y 2m; 1856 emigrated to USA with grandfather, J. Martin Koehl, and lived in Fremont Twp Benton Co IA; a year later his parents, brothers and sisters followed to America; John joined them on a farm in Clinton Twp Linn Co IA; m 02 Apr 1868 Eva Rosina Keller(b 25 Sept 1846 Rosenberg, Baden, Germany, d 25 Aug 1921 ae74y 11m Vinton, IA) d/o Johann Andreas Keller & Katharina Margaretha nee Schweizer. The Kellers in Rosenberg, Germany, for many generations were weavers, tailors, blacksmiths, bakers, innkeepers, and farmers. Eva's great-grandfather served as judge and many years as town mayor. In 1866 Eva left Germamy to join her sister, Mrs. Kate Walthers in the Amana Colonies, IA. Eva worked in the kitchen at Homestead, IA. In 1897, John and Eva retired in Atkins, IA. Children:
George John – b 12 Jan 1869; m Johanna Kale
Charles – b 01 Aug 1872
Ida – b 08 Aug 1875
Rosa Marie Elizabeth – b 18 Dec 1879; m Jacob Schirm

*Mary ENGEL d/o George John Engel & Johanna nee Kale; b 1847 in Germany; 1850 came to USA from Germany with parents at ae3y; m John Saha and Mar 1883 purchased farm midway between towns of Atkins, IA and Palo, IA. Mary's parents made their home with them. The land for Raetz Cemetery was donated by Martin Kale's son-in-law Peter Fritz. The Saha family had a butter and egg route in Cedar Rapids, IA. Fresh vegetables were also delivered in season. A special team of driving horses and surry was used for the route. Butter was packed in ice, sawdust and straw to keep it chilled throughout the summer. Children:
George Saha – NFR
Etta Saha – NFR
John D. Saha – b 1879; m Blanche Ellen Beatty
Katie Saha – NFR
Edward Saha – NFR
Anna Saha – NFR

Kim Marie ENGLUND d/o Marion nee Juhnke & Dallis Englund; b 16 Apr 1963; m 07 Nov 1987 John Leonard Schulz (b 06 Aug 1962). Children:
Scott Englund Schulz – b 30 Jan 1991
Lucas Englund Schulz – b 10 Jun 1992

Todd Michel ENGLUND s/o Marion nee Juhnke & Dallis Englund; b 17 Mar 1962; 1st m 18 Jan 1985 Lynn Sorenson of Sioux Falls, SD. DVD. Children:
    Jamie Lynn – b 11 Feb 1987
    Sahara – b 06 Nov 1990
2nd m Todd Michel Englund to Kris Krinis

*Joseph John ERGER b 1880 Padberg, Germany, d 1952 Benton Co IA; m Gertrude Flammaug (b 1877 Dahnen, Germany, d 1951 Benton Co IA). 1918 purchase of farm north of Newhall, IA. Ten children:
    Lucy Katherine – b 1906, d 1974; m Lee Swanson
    Oscar Joseph – b 1907, Cedar Rapids, IA; Never Married
    Cecelia Margaret – b 1908; m Francis Baker, MN
    Viola Gertrude – b 1910; m Wencil Kulish
    Alvin Nicholas – b 1912; m Lucille Dietrich
    Henry Alphonse – b 1913; m Marie Voss
    Juliette Marie – b 1916; m Earl Harvigsen
    Elenora Julie – b 1916; m Vernon Samuelson
    Frances Elizabeth – b 1918; m Millard Buchanan
    Donald William – b 1922, d 1926 [Farm Accident]

*Anna Katharina ERNST d/o Johannes Ernst & Anna Elisabeth nee Maurer; b 10 Aug 1819 Löhlbach, Germany Hse #68; one child born out of wedlock in Löhlbach, Germany:
    *Tobias Friedrich Ernst – b 13 Jan 1842 Löhlbach Hse #68;
        bpt 16 Jan 1842 Godfather: Tobias Ernst, mother's brother;
        1857 emigrated to USA with his mother.
Anna Katharina Ernst m Edward F. Franke in USA and had five children; lived in Coudersport PA until her death. Recorded name of only one child:
    Frederick Franke – NFR

**Emilie ERNST d/o Justus Ernst & Helene nee Hesse; b 21 Dec 1933 Löhlbach, Germany; m 06 Dec 1952 Löhlbach, Germany to Karl Stocker (d 04 Feb 1985). Children:
    **Wolfgang Stocker – b 19 Feb 1958;
        m 02 Sept 1980 Karin Schneider
    **Ralf Stocker – b 08 Aug 1963; m 30 May 1987 Martina Möller

**Erna ERNST d/o Justus Ernst & Helene nee Hesse; b 03 Aug 1939

Löhlbach, Germany; m 03 Nov 1961 Löhlbach, Germany to Ludwig Noll (b 28 Mar 1932). Children:

Heike – b 01 Oct 1962; m 25 Jul 1985 Peter Weber (b 28 Nov 1957).
Two children: Sarah – b 17 Jan 1987; Theresa – b 24 Apr 1993
Volker – b 30 Jul 1967

*Johannes ERNST s/o Johann Just Ernst & Anna Guida nee Möller; b 03 Jul 1783 Löhlbach, Germany Hse #33, bpt 06 Jul 1783 Löhlbach Ch Godfather: Johannes Möller, d 20 Sept 1844 ae61y 2m 17d Löhlbach Hse #68; herdsman; m 24 Jun 1808 Löhlbach Ch to Anna Elisabeth Maurer (b 11 Jun 1788 Löhlbach Hse #68, bpt 15 Jun 1788 Godmother: Anna Elisabeth, her father's sister, d 02 Jan 1860 ae71y 7m Löhlbach Hse #68). Children:

Johann Daniel – b 07 Mar 1802; m 1838 Schille Michel
*Johann Conrad – b 04 Jul 1809 Löhlbach, d 23 Mar 1883;
    m 13 Nov 1836 Anna Elisabeth Beyer
*Tobias – b 24 Aug 1814; m 1842 Anna Elisabeth Schmidt
*Johann Heinrich – b 22 Sept 1816, d 13 Dec 1889 Löhlbach;
    m 1839 Katharina Elisabeth Losekamm
Anna Katharina – b 10 Aug 1819; m Edward F. Franke
*Johann Heinrich – b 09 May 1822, d 15 Jun 1875 Battenhausen;
    m 19 Dec 1849 Marie Landau
Katharina Elisabeth – b 24 Nov 1824, d 26 Dec 1824
*Johann Christopher – b 06 Dec 1828, d 12 Jan 1894 Löhlbach;
    m 03 Oct 1852 Elisabeth Beyer

*Johann Christopher ERNST s/o Johannes Ernst & Anna Elisabeth nee Maurer; b 06 Dec 1828 Löhlbach Germany Hse #68, d 12 Jan 1894 ae65y 1m 6d Löhlbach Hse #39; m 03 Oct 1852 Elisabeth Beyer (b 07 Feb 1827 Löhlbach Hse #39, d 18 April 1902 ae65y 2m 10d Löhlbach Hse #39).

*Johann Conrad ERNST s/o Johannes Ernst & Anna Elisabeth nee Maurer; b 04 Jul 1809 Löhlbach, Germany Hse #68, d 23 Mar 1883 ae73y 8m 9d Löhlbach Hse #68; m 13 Nov 1836 Anna Elisabeth Beyer (b 25 Dec 1809 Löhlbach, d 21 Sept 1870 ae60y 3m 3d Löhlbach, Germany).

*Johann Heinrich ERNST s/o Johannes Ernst & Anna Elisabeth nee Maurer; b 22 Sept 1816 Löhlbach, Germany Hse #68, d 13 Dec 1889 ae73y 2m 21d Löhlbach Hse #104; m 16 Sept 1839 Katharina Elisabeth Losekamm (b 06 Apr 1812, d 16 Feb 1873 ae60y 10m 10d).

*Johann Heinrich ERNST s/o Johannes Ernst & Anna Elisabeth nee Maurer; b 09 May 1822 Löhlbach, Germany Hse #68, d 15 Jun 1875 ae53y 1m 6d Battenhausen, Germany; m 19 Dec 1849 Marie Landau (b 14 Feb 1831 Löhlbach, Germany).

*Tobias ERNST s/o Johannes Ernst & Anna Elisabeth nee Maurer; b 24 Aug 1814 Löhlbach, Germany Hse #68, bpt 28 Aug 1814 Löhlbach Ch Godfather: Tobias Vaupel the herdsman's son; herdsman; m 21 Aug 1842 Löhlbach Ch to Anna Elisabeth Schmidt (b 10 Jun 1820 Löhlbach Hse #56, bpt 18 Jun 1820 Löhlbach Ch, Godmother: Anna Elisabeth Schmidt, father's sister, her aunt) d/o Balthasar Schmidt and Anna Guida nee Scholl of Löhlbach, Germany. 1853 Tobias Ernst family emigrated to USA residing at Coudersport, PA 16 years before moving a short distance to Sartwell Creek. Some descendants live on the farm where they settled. Children:
    *Wilhelm Heinrich – b 04 Aug 1845 Löhlbach Hse #68;
        bpt 10 Aug 1845 Löhlbach Ch; Godfather: Johann Conrad Ernst
        brother of his father
    *Christoph Friedrich – b 05 Apr 1848 Löhlbach Hse #68;
        bpt 04 Apr 1848 Löhlbach Ch;
        Godfather: Johann Christoph Ernst, brother of his father

*Anna Gertrud FACKINER d/o Johann Justus Fackiner & Anna Christina nee Grack; b 31 Jul 1790, Altenhaina, Germany, d 02 Apr 1849 ae58y 8m 2d Altenhaina, Germany; m 12 Jul 1812 Johann Peter Happel (b 23 Oct 1784 os Alt Heim ns Altenhaina, Germany d 27 Apr 1828 ae43y 6m 4d os Alt Heim ns Altenhaina, Germany) s/o Johann Jost & Regina nee Menkel. Children:
    Johann Justus Happel – b 12 Oct 1812, d 1812 os Alt Heim ns
        Altenhaina, Germany
    *Johann Baltsar Happel – b 29 Dec 1814 os Alt Heim ns Altenhaina,
        Germany remained resident of Altenhaina Happel home
    Anna Elisabeth Happel – b 25 Sept 1816, d Mar 1817 ae6m 1d
    *Andreas Happel – b 27 Mar 1821 os Alt Heim ns Altenhaina,
        Germany; d 03 Dec 1895 Atkins, IA;
        m 29 May 1843 Maria (Marie) Elisabeth Möller
    Anna Katharina Happel – b 31 Dec 1823, d 15 Dec 1826 Germany

*Johann Justus FACKINER s/o Johannes Fackiner of Dornholzhausen,

Germany; (b 17 Jun 1762, Dornholzhausen, Germany, d 29 Mar 1825 ae62y 9m 12d os Alt Heim ns Altenhaina, Germany; m 08 Apr 1785 Löhlbach Ch to Anna Christina Grack (b 24 Feb 1767 os Alt Heim ns Altenhaina, Germany d 11 Jul 1836 ae69y 4m 17d os Alt Heim ns Altenhaina, Germany).Children:

    *Anna Gertrud – b 31 Jul 1790, d 02 Apr 1849 Germany;
        m 12 Jul 1812 Löhlbach, Germany to Johann Peter Happel
    Katharina Elisabeth – b 12 Nov 1799 os Alt Heim ns Altenhaina,
        Germany

Ann Lucille FARMER d/o Lucille nee Grote & Wayne J. Farmer; b 1937; Iowa State Teachers College; m 1959 James E. Sage (b 1932 Waterloo, IA) s/o Ernest E. Sage & Frances nee Rainbow. Farmers of Rainbow Farms, Inc. Waterloo, IA. Children:

    Timothy Sage – b 1960; Van Horne, IA residence
    Amy Sage – b 1962; Kansas City, KS residence
    Craig Sage – b 1964; Waterloo, IA residence
    Patrick Sage – b 1974; Waterloo, IA residence

*Anna Gertrud FELS d/o Konrad Fels & Marie Katherine nee Ernst; b 30 May 1860 Löhlbach, Germany, bpt 1860 Löhlbach Ch, d 10 Mar 1936 ae75y 9m 11d Bremer Co IA; 1st m 01 Nov 1881 St.Steph Luth Ch to Henry Happel(b 24 Oct 1855 os Alt Heim ns Altenhaina, Germany, bpt 1855 Löhlbach Ch Germany, d 20 Apr 1888 ae32y 5m 27d Benton Co IA) s/o Andreas (Andrew) Happel and Maria (Marie) Elisabeth nee Möller. Children:

    Andrew John Happel – b 02 Aug 1882, d 27 Jun 1948;
        m 19 Dec 1907 Louise Sophia Wente
    Conrad August William Happel – b 15 Apr 1884, d 25 Oct 1951;
        m 16 Jan 1908 Anna Kreutner
    William Hartman Peter Happel – b 27 Sept 1885, d 1953;
        m 14 Sept 1910 Dorothea Poock
    Henry George August Happel – b 04 Jan 1889, d 22 Jul 1969;
        m 14 Jun 1914 Hulda Caroline Nolting

2nd m 27 Sept 1890 Anna Gertrude nee Fels Happel to Fredrick Johan Heinrich Sass s/o John Sass SR. & Frieda nee Huebner. Children:

    Frieda Sass – b 06 Jun 1898, d 18 Mar 1991;
        m 1921 Arthur Henry Huebner
    John Sass – b 20 May 1892, d 31 Jul 1976;
        m 09 Dec 1914 Emma Kreutner

Bertha Sass – b 1901, d 1906

**Frederich FELS s/o Konrad Fels & Karoline nee Nobis; b 29 May 1904 Löhlbach, Germany; m 22 Feb 1952 Lina Siegfried (b 09 Oct 1934); Löhlbach, Germany residents. Children:
  **Klaus – b 15 Jun 1952 Löhlbach, Germany
  **Bernard – b 21 May 1960, d 01 Apr 1968 Löhlbach, Germany
  **Markus – b 19 May 1969 in Germany

*Hans Jacob FELS s/o NFR; b 1614 Germany, d 1678 Germany, ae64y; m Anna Kath. Children:
  *Paul – b 23 Aug 1657, d 07 May 1702;
    m 1683 Ann Elisabeth (b 1663, d 27 Jul 1729 ae66y)

*Johann Justus FELS s/o Konrad Fels & Marie Katherine nee Ernst; b 28 Nov 1864 Löhlbach, Germany, d 22 Jun 1937 ae73y 6m 25d Löhlbach, Germany; m 30 Mar 1891 Ann Elisabeth Landau (b 26 Aug 1866 Löhlbach, Germany, d 10 May 1941 ae74y 9m 14d Löhlbach, Germany). Children:
  Anna Martha – b 02 Jan 1892;
    m Frederick Krebs in Bad Wildungen, Germany
  Marie Gertrud – b 18 Aug 1894, d Dec 1987 Löhlbach, Germany
  Henriette – b 01 Aug 1897, d 11 Jan 1915
  Anna Elisabeth – b 31 Aug 1907 Löhlbach, Germany
  Konrad – b 20 May 1904; Löhlbach, Germany residence

*Johannes FELS JR. s/o Johannes Fels SR. & Annie Elisabeth nee Deisel; b 25 Jan 1752 Löhlbach, Germany, d 23 Apr 1815 ae63y 2m 24d Löhlbach, Germany; m 02 Oct 1772 Barbara Kath Möller (b 18 Oct 1748 Löhlbach Germany, d 10 May 1813 ae64y 6m 22d). Child:
  *Johannes Adam – b 17 Aug 1774 Löhlbach, d 27 Jan 1812 Löhlbach;
    m 09 Apr 1795 Anna Christina Ritter

*Johannes FELS SR. s/o Paul Fels & Ann Elisabeth; b 26 May 1696 Dornholzhausen, Germany, d 18 Nov 1775 ae49y 5m 23d Löhlbach, Germany; m 25 Apr 1748 Annie Elisabeth Deisel (b 07 Apr 1715 Löhlbach,Germany d 22 Nov 1775 Löhlbach, Germany) d/o Johana Diesel. Child:
  *Johannes JR. – 25 Jan 1752 Löhlbach, d 23 Apr 1815 Löhlbach;
    m 02 Oct 1772 Löhlbach Ch Barbara Kath Möller

*Johannes Adam FELS s/o Johannes Fels & Barbara Kath nee Möller; b 17 Aug 1774 Löhlbach, Germany, d 27 Jan 1812 ae37y 5m 10d Löhlbach, Germany; m 09 Apr 1795 Anna Christina Ritter (b 11 Jun 1772 Löhlbach,Germany, d 06 Dec 1834 ae62y 5m 25d Löhlbach, Germany). Child:
>   *Karl Jacob – b 26 Apr 1812 Löhlbach, d 16 Feb 1881 Löhlbach;
>   m 12 Jul 1835 Anna Kathrina Faust

*Karl Jacob FELS s/o Johannes Adam Fels & Anna Christina nee Ritter; b 26 Apr 1812 Löhlbach, Germany, d 16 Feb 1881 ae68y 8m 21d Löhlbach, Germany; m 12 Jul 1835 Anna Kathrina Faust (b 08 Dec 1812 Löhlbach, Germany d 10 Nov 1878 ae65y 11m 2d Löhlbach, Germany). Child:
>   *Konrad – b 14 Dec 1835 Löhlbach, Germany d 02 Mar 1907
>   Löhlbach, Germany; m 11 Mar 1860 Marie Katherine Ernst.

*Konrad FELS s/o Karl Jacob Fels & Anna Kathrina nee Faust; b 14 Dec 1835 Löhlbach, Germany, d 02 Mar 1907 ae71y 2m 16d Löhlbach, Germany; m 11 Mar 1860 Löhlbach to Marie Katherine Ernst (b 09 Sept 1835 Löhlbach, Germany d 28 Jan 1915 ae29y 4m 19d Löhlbach, Germany). Children:
>   *Anna Gertrud – b 30 May 1860 Löhlbach, Germany;
>   d 10 Mar 1936 IA; 1st m 01 Nov 1881 Henry Happel, dec'd;
>   2nd m 27 Sept 1890 Fredrick Johann Heinrich Sass
>   Anna Elisabeth – b 21 Dec 1862, d 12 Sept 1867 Löhlbach, Germany
>   Johann Justus – b 28 Nov 1864, d 22 Jun 1937 Löhlbach, Germany;
>   m 1891 Ann Elisabeth Landau, Löhlbach, Germany
>   Catherine Elisabeth – b 29 Jul 1867, d 07 Jan 1870 Löhlbach
>   *Marie Gertrud Elisabeth – b 11 Mar 1870; emigrated to America;
>   believed to be Chicago, IL
>   Fredericka Elisabeth Charlotte – b 04 Aug 1872 Löhlbach, Germany
>   m 14 Feb 1896 Heinrich Ernst, Frankenberg, Germany
>   Adam – b Jul 1875 Löhlbach, Germany;
>   m 31 Mar 1902 Anna D.C. Vampel

**Konrad FELS s/o Johann Justus Fels & Ann Elisabeth nee Landau; b 29 May 1904 Löhlbach, Germany; m 29 Mar 1931 Löhlbach Ch to Karoline Nobis (b 02 Dec 1906, dec'd) Löhlbach, Germany residence. Children:
>   Heinrich – b 15 Sept 1931 Löhlbach, Germany
>   Friedrich-b 13 Oct 1932; m 22 Feb 1952 Lina Siegfried
>   Konrad – b 05 May 1935 Löhlbach, Germany

Elisabeth – b 18 Aug 19ND Löhlbach, Germany

*Paul FELS s/o Hans Jacob Fels & Anna Kath; b 23 Aug 1657 Germany, d 07 May 1702 Germany; m 1683 Ann Elisabeth (b 1663, d 27 Jul 1729, ae 66y). Child:
    *Johannes – b 26 May 1696 Dornholzhausen, Germany;
        d 18 Nov 1775 Löhlbach, Germany;
        m 25 Apr 1748 Annie Elisabeth Deisel

Debra Sue FENNELL d/o Marcia Diane nee Bennett & Joseph Fennell; b 15 May 1966; 1st m NN Mata. Children:
    Joseph Gabriel Mata – b 11 Sept 1986
    Jonathan Manual Mata – b 20 Oct 1988
2nd m 1990 Debra Sue nee Fennel Mata to Manuel Tortoledo. Children:
    Alex William Tortoledo – b 14 Apr 1991
    Christine Juanita Tortoledo – b 13 Jan 1995

Wendy Kay FENNELL d/o Marcia Diane nee Bennett & Joseph Fennell; b 29 Dec 1964; m Oreste Locatelli (b 28 Dec 1964). Child:
    Makayla Diane Locatelli – b 13 Jul 1993

August Henry FENNERN s/o August Reimer Fennern & Sophia Marie nee Carstens; b 1900, d 1972; m 01 Jan 1925 Avova, IA to Josephine Anna Pauley (b 1904) d/o Joseph Pauley & Gusta nee Sohl; farmers in Shelby Co & Pottawattamie Co before moving south of Vinton, IA to Mud Creek; 1966 retired in Vinton, IA. Children:
    Audrey LaVerne – b 1927; m 1946 Frank Arthur Mayhew
    Lorrene Mae – b 1929; m 1949 Warren Carl Anderson
    Marlene Ann – b 1937; m 1957 Lee Richard Overton

*August Reimer FENNERN s/o Heinrich C. Fennern & Margaretha nee Ahrens; b 1884 Germany, d 1966 bur Shelby, IA; 1880 came to USA; m 23 Feb 1897 Sophia Marie Carstens (b 1877 Germany, 1881 came to USA, d 1966 bur Shelby) d/o Heinrich Carstens & Sophia Marie nee Hoppe. August and Sophia were small children with their parents when they came to America. August settled with family at Davenport, IA. Sophia settled with family on a farm at Minden, IA. They married at Harlan, IA and farmed near Shelby and Avoca, IA until moving to Garrison in Benton Co. A.R. Fennern and sons bred Shorthorn cattle and showed them for many years. A.R. and Sophia retired in 1949 and moved to the Luth Home in Vinton.

Eight children:
Anna Matilda – b 1898, d 1931; Never Married
August Henry – b 1900, d 1972; m Josephine Pauley
Harry William – b 1902; m 1928 Evelyn Bauer
Walter Frederick – b 1903; m 1930 Hertha Peters
Edward Harvey – b 1907, d 1985; m Margaret Dannen
Leone Marie – b 1910; m 1943 Carl Christensen
Edna Margaret – b 1913, d 1977; m Howard Hoffman
Erwin Carl – b 1917; m 1952 Rachel Cashman Bramow

Edna Margaret FENNERN d/o August Reimer Fennern & Sophia nee Carstens; b 1913, d 1977; m 1940 Howard Hoffman. Child:
Carol Jean Hoffman – b 1943; San Diego, CA residence

Edward Harvey FENNERN s/o August Reimer Fennern & Sophia nee Carstens; b 1907, d 1985; m 1943 Margaret Muller Dannen (b 1916, d 1961). Children:
Marlys – b 1940
TWINS: Barbara – b 1945
        Eugene – b 1945, d 1950
Sandra – b 1948

Harry William FENNERN s/o August Reimer Fennern & Sophia Marie nee Carstens; b 1902; m 1928 Evelyn Bauer (b 1906). Farmers until retiring to Garrison, IA. Ten children:
Robert – b 1928; m Maryann NN, Ventura CA
Lila Jean – b 1929, d 1930
Jack – b 1930; Norway, IA residence
Donald – b 1932; m Dianne NN Cedar Rapids, IA residence
Marvin – b 08 Sept 1933 Shelby Co IA, d 10 Jan 2000;
        m 06 Oct 1956 Shirley Dunker
Joan – b 1934; m Keith Abernathy, Vinton IA residence
Jeanette – b 1936; m Bill Wilson, Walker IA residence
Richard – b 1939, d 19??
Jon – b 1941, Garrison IA residence
Mary Lou – b 1948; m Gerald Schoettmer, Shellsburg IA residence

Leone Marie FENNERN d/o August Reimer Fennern & Sophia Marie nee Carstens; b 1910; m 1943 Carl Christensen (b 1902, d 1988); residents of Avoca, IA. Child:

Charles Christensen – b 1945

Lorrene Mae FENNERN d/o August Henry Fennern & Josephine nee Pauley; b 1929; m Warren Carl Anderson (b 1927) s/o William Carl Anderson & Cora Vlasta nee Barta. Lorrene's residence in Vinton, IA; Warren's residence CA. Child:
Collene Elaine Anderson – b 1951; m 1971 Wayne David Forristall

Marvin C. FENNERN s/o Harry William Fennern & Evelyn nee Bauer; b 08 Sept 1933 Shelby Co IA, d 10 Jan 2000 in his home ae76y 4m 2d bur 13 Jan 200 Keystone IA Cem; m 06 Oct 1956 St.John Luth Ch Keystone to Shirley Dunker, d/o Elfrieda Hunker of Keystone IA. Marvin employed 35 years IDOT. Children:
Brian – NFR
Lynne m to NN Cumming; Children: Brandon and Shaina

Walter Frederick FENNERN s/o August Reimer Fennern & Sophia Marie nee Carstens; b 1903, d 1984; m 1930 Hertha Peters (b 1909). Mt. Auburn, Benton Co IA farm residence. Children:
Lorna – b 1931
Deane – b 1937

*Christian FIEBELKORN b 1837, Germany, d 1918 IA; came to USA in his youth and settled on a farm northwest of Newhall, Benton Co IA; m Ernestine Hageman (b 1851 IL, d 1934). Retired 1901 in Newhall, IA. Children:
William – b 21 Aug 1875, d Jul 1965;
    m 09 Mar 1899 Christine Werning
Herman – b 1877, d 1957; m 14 Feb 1901 Maria (Mary) Werning
Robert – dec'd as young man

Doris FIEBELKORN d/o Waldmar Conrad Fiebelkorn & Linda L. W. nee Bierschenk; b 1944; m 1980 LaVerne Kriz. Cedar Rapids, IA residence.
STEPCHILDREN:
Jeffry Kriz – b 1963
Douglas Kriz – b 1964

Elfrieda FIEBELKORN d/o Herman Fiebelkorn & Maria (Mary) nee Werning; b 1913 Eden Twp Benton Co IA; d 13 Dec 1999; m Clarence Conrad J. Hertle (b 1910, d 1977) Pioneer Seed Corn Saleman) s/o August

Hertle & Martha nee Bierschenk. Luth. Children:
  Francine Hertle- b 1936; m Daryl Daker, Cedar Rapids, IA
  Richard Hertle – b 29 Oct 1938, Eden Twp Benton Co IA
      d 21 Mar 2000; m 02 Dec 1967 Judy Webert, Newhall, IA
  Dennis Hertle – b 1942; m Sandra Blough, Atkins, IA

Elvira FIEBELKORN d/o Herman Fiebelkorn & Maria (Mary) nee
Werning; b ND; m William Alpers (d 18 Aug 1955, bur St.John Cem).
Children:
  Pearl Alpers – m Lester J. Schuldt
  Robert Alpers – m Dorothy Rowe
  Gerold Alpers – NFR

Herman FIEBELKORN s/o Christian Fiebelkorn & Ernestine nee
Hageman; b 1877 farm northwest of Newhall, IA d 1957; m 14 Feb 1901
Maria (Mary) Werning (b 07 Jun 1880, d 03 Aug 1950 ae70y 1m 27d) d/o
Conrad Werning & Wilhelmina nee Keiper. Children:
  Elvira – m William Alpers
  Waldemar Conrad – b 1905; m 12 Feb 1931 Linda L. W. Bierschenk
  Elfreida – b 1913, d 13 Dec 1999; m Clarence Conrad J. Hertle

Stanley FIEBELKORN s/o Waldemar Conrad Fiebelkorn & Linda L. W.
nee Bierschenk; b 1932, d 1953 on board ship going to Korea; m Shirley
Boyles. Child:
  Steven – b 1954; m Debbie Robinson

Steven FIEBELKORN s/o Stanley Fiebelkorn & Shirley nee Boyles; b
1954; m Debbie Robinson. Shellsburg, IA residence. Children:
  Denise – b 1974
  Stephanie – b 1976

Waldemar Conrad FIEBELKORN s/o Herman Fiebelkorn & Maria (Mary)
nee Werning; b 1905 Eden Twp farm northwest of Newhall, IA; m 12 Feb
1931 Linda L. W. Bierschenk (b 24 Jan 1908, d 1967) d/o Carl Heinrich
(Henry Carl) Henry Bierschenk & Elizabeth nee Kranz. Farmed home-place
in Eden Twp, Benton Co until 1964 retirement in Newhall, IA. Children:
  Stanley – b 1932, d 1953; m Shirley Boyles
  Roger – b 1937; m 1966 Marjorie Harkemeyer
  Leroy – b 1940; m 1964 Marie Chris Kranz
  Doris – b 1944; m 1980 LaVerne Kriz

Wilma FIEBELKORN b 14 Jun 1918; m 1945 Clair Johnson (b 1920, d 1973) s/o Henry O. Johnson & Jennie A. nee Husted. Children:
Kathy Johnson – NFR
Becky Johnson – NFR
Richard Johnson – NFR

Sharon Arlene FISH d/o Patricia Lou nee Krug & Rad Fish; b 20 Mar 1947; m 15 Aug 1987 Mark Aaron Basten (b 04 Jun 1966). Children:
Emily Basten – b 02 Aug 1994
Collin Basten – b 04 Oct 1997

Edward Lee FIX s/o Paul William Fix & Ruth Ann nee Foley; b 15 May 1952 Vinton IA; US Air Force Major; m 23 Nov 1974 Janice Marie Ritchie (b 12 Apr 1952) d/o Joseph Ritchie & Wilma nee Maass. OH residence. Children:
Andrew William – b 29 May 1981 Minot ND
Emily Ruth – b 21 Jul 1988

*Georg Jakob FIX s/o Johann (GS John P.) Fix and wife Margaretha nee Nees; b 18 Oct 1830 Edelbach, Germany, d 04 Nov 1901 ae71y 17d Norway, Benton Co IA; came to USA in 1850's; a cooper, worked in a distillery in Iowa City, IA and many other cities before settling in Benton Co IA; purchased eighty acres of farmland across the road from his father. Shortly before Fredrick Gardemann died in 1864 he asked his neighbor Jacob Fix to take care of his young widow and three sons. Georg Jakob m 24 Dec 1864 wid/o Fredrick F. Gardemann, Christina Magdelene nee Schneckloth Gardemann (b 1839. d 1926) d/o Claus Schneckloth & Magdelene nee Meyer. Eight children:
John Phillip – b 23 Dec 1865 Newhall IA d 28 Dec 1942 Newhall IA;
    m 10 Oct 1988 Meta Axelsen
Henry Joseph – b 15 Dec 1867 Newhall IA d 11 Jan 1882 Newhall IA
Philip Karl – b 30 Dec 1869; 1st m 13 Jun 1894 Emma Schneckloth;
    2nd m 1913 Flo Harger Shellsburg, IA
    3rd m 1914 Bertha Battles Cedar Rapids, IA
Oliver Bruno – b 23 Feb 1873; m Etta Axelsen
Louise Margaretha – b 03 Sept 1874, d 29 Mar 1882
Bertha Katherine – b 24 Oct 1879, d 22 Jan 1964; m Jacob Krumm JR.
Maria Christina – b 12 Aug 1882, d 24 Feb 1883
Elizabeth Veronica – b 20 Sept 1884, d 04 Dec 1969; 1st m Al Strawn;

2nd m 1964 Jacob Krumm JR.

James Dean FIX s/o Paul William Fix & Ruth Ann nee Foley; b 10 Sept 1953 Vinton, IA; m 14 Dec 1974 Rita Carol Harrison. Dairy Farmer Fix home farm, Vinton, IA; Children:
Sarah Anne – b 10 Dec 1978 Vinton IA
Paul James – b 21 Aug 1980 Vinton IA

*Johann FIX, b 28 Feb 1800 Edelbach, Germany, d 14 Mar 1875 ae75y 1m 14d Norway, IA IA bur Norway Catholic Cem; m 24 Jul 1828 Schollkrippen, Germany to Margaretha Nees, d/o Andreas Nees & Anna nee Ostheimer. After his wife died 1950's in Germany he came to USA with their son Georg Jakob:
Catharina – b 06 Feb 1826
*Georg Jakob – b 18 Oct 1830 Edelbach, Germany,
d 05 Nov 1901 Norway, Benton Co IA;
m 24 Dec 1864 Christina nee Schneckloth Gardemann,
wid/o Fredrich F. Gardemann

John Edward FIX s/o Emma Anna Marie nee Moeller & Louis Frederick Fix; b 09 Dec 1925 Newhall, IA bpt and con St.Steph; m 08 Dec 1946 Vinton IA to Mildred Donley Daughhetee (b 14 Apr 1925) d/o Guy Daughhetee & Ada nee Donley. Retired Colorado Springs, CO. Children:
John Neil – b 24 Sept 1947; m 19 Jul 1970 Linda Wright
Peggy Mae – b 17 Jul 1949; m 20 Jul 1972 Kenneth Clark
Forrest Edward – b 27 Oct 1956; m 24 May 1985 Papatya (Pat) Cetin
Fredrick Louis – b 13 Jun 1958
Philip Guy – b 15 Oct 1960; m 31 Sept 1994 Joann NN

John Neil FIX s/o John Edward Fix & Mildred Donley nee Daughhetee; b 24 Sept 1947 Vinton, IA; m 19 Jul 1970 Linda Kay Wright (b 27 May 1947) d/o William Wright & Hazel nee Spencer. LaPorte, IN residence. Children:
Daniel Wayne – b 05 Jul 1977 LaPorte, IN
Mark Allen – b 13 Jul 1979 LaPorte, IN
David Eugene – b 25 Jan 1984 LaPorte, IN

John Phillip FIX s/o Georg Jakob Fix & Christina Magdelene nee Schneckloth; b 23 Dec 1865 Newhall, IA; d 28 Dec 1942 Newhall, IA ae77y 4d [Killed by a train south of Newhall, IA]; m 10 Oct 1888 Atkins,

IA to Meta Axelsen d/o Heinrich Axelsen & Mary nee Schaefer. Children:
Mary M. – b 13 Jan 1890, d 27 Sept 1976; m Louis Paulsen
Louis Frederich – b 11 Sept 1892, d 26 Jun 1980 Vinton, IA;
    m 11 Feb 1923 Emma Anna Maria Moeller
Amelia Louise – b 13 Jul 1896, d 04 Mar 1946;
    m 01 Nov 1916 Ralph Louis Deklotz
Ella Mae – b 03 May 1900, d 05 Feb 1996, Belle Plaine, IA;
    m 08 Jan 1925 Henry Eberhard Valentin Rinderknecht

Lois Ann FIX d/o Emma Anna Marie nee Moeller & Louis Frederick Fix; b 05 Jul 1931 Vinton, IA bpt and con 02 Apr 1944 St. Steph; m 14 Aug 1955 Newhall, IA to Russell Stanley Wunschel (b 26 Mar 1927 Early, IA) s/o Rudolph August Wunschel (b 19 Feb 1886 Early, IA, d 15 Oct 1956 Early) & Ruth Elizabeth nee Adams (b 05 Mar 1897 Elgin, NE, d 31 Aug 1981 Early). Celebrated 50th Wedding Anniversary. Children:
DeeAnn Kay Wunschel – b 08 Dec 1959 Carroll, IA;
    1st m 10 Aug 1985 Brian Taylor DVD Dec 1987;
    2nd m 31 Dec 1992 Jeffery Crouse
Steven Rudy Wunschel – b 03 Feb 1962 Carroll, IA;
    m 04 Nov 2000 Beka Cox
Lori Lynn Wunschel – b 18 Nov 1964 Carroll, IA;
    m 05 Nov 1989 Steven Blair Elliott
David Scott Wunschel – b 14 Jul 1969 Carroll, IA
    m 09 Jun 2001 Sand Point, ID to Sharon
Kristine Elizabeth Wunschel – b 11 May 1972 Carroll, IA
    m 01 Sept 2004 Dublin, Ireland to Joe Elliott

Paul William FIX s/o Emma Anna Marie nee Moeller & Louis Frederick Fix; b 09 Sept 1924 Vinton, IA bpt and con St.Steph; U.S. Army World War II; 1st m 08 Feb 1950 Spencer, IN to Ruth Ann Foley (d 08 Jan 1977) d/o Clarence Foley & Eunice nee Sanders. Children:
Edward Lee – b 15 May 1952; m 23 Nov 1974 Janice Ritchie
James Dean – b 10 Sept 1953; m 14 Dec 1974 Rita Carol Harrison
Susan Marie – b 19 Aug 1959; m 05 Sept 1981 Brent Russell Larson
    DVD
2nd m 25 Mar 1978 Paul William Fix to Lorraine Stock-Bettin of Odebolt, IA. Retired farmer, wood worker; Mission, TX residence.

Peggy Mae FIX d/o John Edward Fix & Mildred Donley nee Daughhetee; b 17 Jul 1949 Vinton, IA; m 20 Jul 1972 Colorado Springs, CO to Kenneth

Clark. Mobile Park owners, Ruidoso, NM; Children:
    Wendy Jo Clark – b 22 Feb 1973 Colorado Springs, CO
    Randy Wayne Clark – b 22 Mar 1977 Alamogordo, NM

Philip Guy FIX s/o Forrest Edward Fix & Papatya (Pat) nee Cetin; b 15 Oct 1960 Denver, CO; m 30 Sept 1994 Colorado Springs, Co to Joann Lorraine Apostolides. Children:
    Connor Philip – b 12 Sept 1995 Colorado Springs, CO
    Sierra Rhiannon – b 08 Mar 1998 Colorado Springs, CO

Susan Marie FIX d/o Paul William Fix & Ruth Ann nee Foley; b 19 Aug 1959; m 05 Sept 1981 Vinton, IA to Brent Russell Larsen (b 21 Aug 1959) DVD 1993. Houston, TX residence.

Paula Rae FLECK d/o Dianne Caye nee Mohr & William Jon Fleck; b 02 Jul 1966; m 21 Jul 1990 Joseph Gourley (b 13 Jan 1955). Children:
    Nathan Alan Gourley – b 25 May 1986
    Jeremy Lou Gourley – b 09 Aug 1992

Dean A. FOLKMANN s/o Gladys Marie nee Rammelsberg & Richard Folkmann; b 02 Jul 1956; m 20 Jun 1998 Julian Lynn Gaddis (b 24 Aug 1962).Child:
    Katelyn Elizabeth – b 02 Feb 2000

Steven Warren FORRISTALL s/o Wayne David Forristall & Colleen Elaine nee Anderson; b 1961, d 1988; m 1983 Tina Marie Lute. Child:
    Tonaleen Joy – b 1985

Wayne David FORRISTALL s/o Dona nee Eastman & NN Forristall; b 1947; m Colleen Elaine Anderson (b 1951) d/o Lorrene Mae nee Fennern & Warren Carl Anderson. Children:
    David Wayne – b 1974, Sarasota, FL residence
    Steven Warren – b 1961, d 1988; m 1983 Tina Marie Lute

Barry Kim FRANCK s/o George Harlan Franck & Marian Frances nee Braksiek; b 01 Feb 1950 St.Lukes Hosp Cedar Rapids, IA; m 20 Oct 1973 Rhonda Boddicker (b 17 Apr 1950) d/o Elwood Boddicker & Marjorie nee Meyer. Children:
    Robbie Jan – b 15 Jul 1974
    Jodi Jean – b 15 May 1977;

m 11 Nov 2000 St.John Ch Wesley Mitchell Obermueller
s/o Don & Nita Obermueller, Vinton IA
Kari Kim – b 05 Jul 1980 at Cedar Rapids, IA

Clayton FRANCK s/o Gilbert Franck & Dorthy nee Peyton; b 1939; m 1959 Barbara Deklotz (b 1939) d/o Gilbert Deklotz & Velma nee Reisser Dairy farmers in Eldorado Twp Benton Co IA. Children:
Randall Gilbert – b 1963; m 1984 Elaine Barbera, De Witt, IA
    Farmers and have son: Ryan Randall (b 1986)
Ronald Edward – b 1965; m 1988 Joan Anderson, Newhall, IA
Richard Arthur – b 1967; m 29 May 1993 Anne-Marie Streeter
Rachel Marie – b 1969
Rhonda Kay – b 1971

Douglas Kenn FRANCK s/o George Harlan Franck & Marian Frances nee Braksiek; b 29 Nov 1947 St.Lukes Hosp Cedar Rapids, IA; m 02 May 1970 Becky Bare (b 10 Mar 1950). Children:
Shonda – b 16 Nov 1970
Shane Aaron – b 08 Nov 1974;
    m 10 Sept 1999 Charla Francine Herman d/o Mr.& Mrs.
    Jay Herman, Van Horne IA
Seth Adam – b 04 Feb 1977

Gilbert FRANCK s/o George W. Franck (b 1882 d 1937) & Julia Marie nee Fest(b 1893, d 1972); b 1912, d 1988; m Dorthy Peyton (b 1912 Troy Mills, IA) d/o Jacob E. Peyton & Ica D. Sauer. Gilbert came to Benton Co IA, pro 1912, to husk corn with a team and wagon for Joe G. Boddicker. Farmed Joe Boddicker farm twenty-two years. Children:
Gordon – b 1938; m Kathleen Gerhold (b 1941)
Clayton – b 1939; m 1959 Barbara Deklotz (b 1939)

Roxanne FRANCK d/o George Harlan Franck & Marian Frances nee Braksiek; b 21 May 1955; m 09 Sept 1973 Anthony Rieder. Children:
Ryan Anthony Rieder – b 19 Feb 1974
Tami Melissa Rieder – b 25 Nov 1975

Sally Rae FRANCK d/o George Harlan Franck & Marian Frances nee Braksiek; b 10 Mar 1946 Peoples Hosp Independence, Buchanan Co IA bpt 07 Apr 1946 St.John Luth Ch, Keystone, IA; m 27 Jun 1964 Douglas Wendel (b 04 Sept 1943; Carpenter; 01 Jan 1978 owned business

corporation) s/o Loren Wendel & Glenda nee Melhus. Children:
  Kelly Rae Wendel – b 1966; m 1988 Steven James Heistoffer
  Amy Rae Wendel – b 30 Apr 1969

Scott Dean FRANCK s/o George Harlan Franck & Marian Frances nee Braksiek; b 11 Jun 1953 St.Lukes Hosp Cedar Rapids, IA, bpt Jul 1953; m 01 Apr 1972 Nancy Peterson (b 03 Jun 1953). Children:
  James Dean – b 09 Sept 1972
  Darci Sue – b 03 Oct 1975
  Larry John – b 13 Aug 1979 Cedar Rapids, IA

Cecil FRANK s/o Clarence Frank & Clarine nee Williams; b 1937; LaPorte City High School; m 1960 in Waterloo, IA to Judith Buehner. Farmers in Cedar Twp Benton Co IA. Children:
  Diane – NFR
  Debra – NFR

Clarence FRANK s/o Philip & Henreitta Frank; b ND, d 1967; m 1936 Clarine Williams (d 1975)of Fountain Run, KY. Children:
  Cecil – b 1937; m 1960 Judith Buehner
  Ella – b 1938; m 1962 Alvin Wubbena of Ackley, IA
  Russell – b 1940

Ella FRANK d/o Clarence Frank & Clarine nee Williams; b 1938; LaPorte City High School; Iowa State Teachers College; taught school Garrison, IA; m 1962 Alvin Wubbena of Ackley, IA. Farmers in Monroe Twp Benton Co IA. Children:
  Kevin Wubbena – m Tracy NN
  Kim Wubbena – NFR
  Korey Wubbena – NFR
  Kristy Wubbena – NFR

Kimberly Nichole FRANK d/o Carolyn Sue nee Rammelsberg & Stacey S. Frank; b 02 Jul 1979. Child:
  Orion Frank-Little – b 15 Apr 1999 (Father: Dennis Little)

*Claus FRANZENBURG of Schleswig-Holstein, Germany; m Hiemke Albers of Schleswig-Holstein. Emigrated to USA. Eleven children all born on farm in Kane Twp Benton Co IA. NFR of nine of the children:
  John – b 05 Jun 1888; m 22 Mar 1911 Louise Garbers

Herman – m Lena Wiese

Faye FRANZENBURG d/o Howard Franzenburg & Norma nee Pickering; m to William Nolan of Van Horne, IA. Farmers. Children:
Michelle Nolan – m Keith Hartkemeyer
Kevin Nolan – m Andrea Stueck
Greg Nolan – m Linda Jacobi

Gary FRANZENBURG s/o Howard Franzenburg & Norma nee Pickering; m and had two daughters, Fort Lauderdale, FL residence:
Carol – NFR
Jennifer – NFR

Gene FRANZENBURG s/o Howard Franzenburg & Norma nee Pickering; b ND, d 1986; m Dorothy Bates of Keystone. Farmed Franzenburg Homestead. Children:
Darold – NFR
Darren – NFR
Gina – NFR

Herman FRANZENBURG s/o Clause Franzenburg & Heimke nee Albers; m Lena Wiese d/o Fred Wiese & Margaretha nee Meinert Zornig. Child:
Robert – m Nola Feuerbach

Howard FRANZENBURG s/o John Franzenburg & Louise nee Garbers; b 17 May 1913, d 1961; m 1936 Norma Pickering; Farmed Franzenburg homestead until building a new home in Keystone, IA. Children:
Faye – m William Nolan of Van Horne, IA
Gary – m and two daughters, FL residence
Gene – d 1986; m Dorothy Bates of Keystone, IA
James – m Dorothy Walters of Watkins, IA

James FRANZENBURG s/o Howard Franzenburg & Norma nee Pickering; m Dorothy Walters of Watkins, IA. Van Horne, IA residence where Dorothy operated a beauty shop. Children:
Carrie – NFR
Jeffrey – NFR
TWINS: Jessica – NFR
Jason – NFR

John FRANZENBURG s/o Claus Franzenburg & Hiemke nee Albers; b 05 Jun 1888, Keystone, IA, d 20 May 1970 ae81y 11m 15d; m 22 Mar 1911 Louise Garbers (b 22 Dec 1888, d 11 Apr 1974 ae85y 3m 20d) d/o William Garbers & Anna nee Hartman. Louise, a twin, had five sisters and four brothers born on farm north of Van Horne, IA. Children:

Howard – b 17 May 1913, d 1961; m 1936 Norma Pickering
TWINS: Ruby – b 22 Jan 1922; m Henry Rice
        Ruth – b 22 Jan 1922; m Donald Paulsen

Robert FRANZENBURG s/o Herman Franzenburg & Lena nee Wiese; b Farm near Keystone, IA; m 11 Nov 1942 St. John's Luth Parsonage to Nola Feuerbach d/o William (Mike) Feuerbach (parents came from Echzell near Hessendarmstadt, Germany in 1853)& Mary nee Junge. Farmers until moving 1978 to Keystone, Benton Co IA. Both Keystone High School graduates. Children:

Donald – NFR
Joan – NFR
Dean – NFR
Janet – NFR

Ruby FRANZENBURG d/o John Franzenburg & Louise nee Garbers; b 1922 (TWIN: Ruth Franzenburg) m Henry Rice of Waterloo, IA. Children:

Michael Rice – m Barbara Larsen, MN residence
Marla Rice – m Russell Betts, Waterloo, IA residence
Marcia Rice – m Michael Daly, Iowa City, IA residence

Ruth FRANZENBURG d/o John Franzenburg & Louise nee Garbers; b 1922 (TWIN: Ruby Franzenburg) m Donald Paulsen of Keystone, IA U.of I. Medical School, Cedar Rapids, IA anesthesiologist. Children:

Gretchen Paulsen – m William Enke, 2 children
Gregory Paulsen – m Mary Coan, 3 children
Glenda Paulsen – d 1976 [Killed in Car Accident]
Gordon Paulsen – Kirkwood's Radio Station employee

Amelia FREEMAN d/o August Freeman & Mary nee Kine; b 1882, d 1976; m Bert Husted s/o Albert Husted & Anna Mae nee Brock. Children:

William Husted – NFR
Charles Husted – NFR
Esther Husted – NFR

*August FREEMAN s/o Henry Freeman & Sophia nee Smith; b 1855 in Germany; 1857 came to USA with parents; lived in Cedar Rapids, IA; moved to Newhall, IA area; d 1916; m 1880 Mary Kine (b 1862 near Robins, Linn Co IA, d 1949) d/o Henry Kine and Mary nee Beck. Children:
   Henry – b 1881, d 1899
   William – b 1882, d 1980; m Mary Jane Johnson
   Amelia – b 1883, d 1976; m Bert Husted
   Gussie J. – b 1885, d 1974; m 1913 Pharo Meyer
   Charles – b 1887, d 1960; m Elsie L. Miller
   George "Gerry" – b 1895, d 1955; m Matilda Ann "Tillie" Koopman

Charles FREEMAN s/o August Freeman & Mary nee Kine; b 1887, d 1960; m Elsie L. Miller of Louisa. Moved to farm west of Atkins, IA; later moved to Atkins and ran the elevator for several years; 1934 opened and operated tavern for twenty years on east side of Main Street Atkins in building that once was the Farmers Savings Bank. Children:
   Howard S. – b 01 Jun 1918, d 08 Jul 2002;
      m 29 Sept 1946 Lila B. Snyder
   Marion V. – b 1911, d ND; m 1938 Edna Barnoske

Corleen FREEMAN d/o George Freeman & Matilda nee Koopman; m 1950 Alden Morrison (b 1929) s/o Leonard Morrison & Olga nee Strimnoen of Decorah, IA. Lived five years in Marshalltown and Fort Dodge before moving to Newhall, IA; operated Alcor Trailer Sales of Newhall selling and servicing recreational vehicles; Alden Newhall Mayor pro-tem four years and on Newhall Fire Department twenty years serving as Chief; chairperson of the Newhall Centennial Committee and president of Newhall Commercial Club. Luth. Children:
   Sue Morrison – b 1950; m Jim Wubben of Buffalo Center, IA
   Amy Morrison – b 1958; Registered Nurse,
      Cedar Rapids, IA residence

Dorothy FREEMAN d/o George Freeman & Matilda nee Koopman; m Charles Hanneman of Van Horne, IA. Children:
   Mary Jo Hanneman – m Dick Vilhauer, Iowa City
   Thomas Hanneman – m Kathy Furler, Iowa City

George "Gerry" FREEMAN s/o August Freeman & Mary nee Kine; b north of Newhall, IA 1885, d 1955; m 1915 Matilda Ann "Tillie" Koopman d/o Otto Koopman & Elizabeth nee Boddicker. Farmed until 1934 when moved to Newhall, IA and worked for Wheeler Construction Co; 1939 formed own construction company and self-employed remainder of life; built many Newhall homes and farm buildings. Chief of Newhall Fire Department eight years and served fire department nineteen years. Children:

Dorothy – m Charles Hanneman of Van Horne, IA

Corleen – m 1950 Alden Morrison

Gussie J. FREEMAN s/o August Freeman & Mary nee Kine; b 1885 Farm Fremont Twp Benton Co IA, began carpenter work ae17y, d 1974; m 1913 Pharo Meyer and lived in new home he built; learned blacksmithing trade. Children:

James – b 1916; m Ione Knain

Virgil – b 1919; m Ann Nagy, one son

*Henry FREEMAN b 1831 in Germany, d 1892 IA; m Sophia Smith. Moved to Cedar Rapids IA pro 1855; later moved northeast of Newhall, IA. Children:

August – b 1855, d 1916; m 1880 Mary Kine

Charles – b 1864, d 1944

Herman – NFR

Julias – NFR

Howard S. FREEMAN s/o Charles Freeman & Elsie L. nee Miller; b 01 Jun 1918 Newhall, IA d 08 Jul 2002 ae84y bur CdrMem ; graduate Atkins High School; 1941 drafted US Army; m 29 Sept 1946 Cedar Rapids, IA to Lila B. Snyder; owner Freeman electrical business sixteen years in same building where wife operated beauty salon. 1962 sold building; Howard electrician at Cedar Rapids IA Quaker Oats Company 21 years. Retired 1981. No children.

James FREEMAN s/o Gussie J. Freeman & Pharo nee Meyer; b 1916 Newhall IA; US Army Lieutenant; m Ione Knain. Taught school forty years; Cedar Rapids, IA resident. Children:

Douglas – NFR

Gordon – NFR

Richard – NFR

Ronald – NFR

Marion V. FREEMAN s/o Charles Freeman & Elsie L. nee Miller; b 1911; m 1938 Edna Barnoske. Moved to Cedar Rapids, IA. Employed at LaPlant

Choate Manufacturing Company; Allis-Chalmers and Harnischfeger in 1952. Child:
Roger (adopted) NFR.

William FREEMAN s/o August Freeman & Mary nee Kine; b 1882, d 1980; m Mary Jane Johnson d/o Cassina & Mary Johnson. Farmed in Newhall, IA area. Child:
Carolyn – NFR

Lori FRENCH d/o Donna Mae nee Steege & Larry French; b 10 May 1968; m Thomas Jeffrey Price III. Children:
Megan Price – b 14 Feb 1991
Larry Price – b 19 Sept 1992

*Heinrich FREITAG, Germany; m Aug 1774. Child:
*Jacob Freitag – b 03 Feb 1782 Geismar, Germany; d 11 Nov 1843
Geismar, Germany;
m 27 Feb 1807 Katharina Elisabeth Leinweber

*Jacob FREITAG s/o Heinrich Freitag; b 03 Feb 1782 Geismar, Germany, d 11 Nov 1843 ae 61y 9m 13d Geismar, Germany; m 27 Feb 1807 Katharina Elisabeth Leinweber(b 02 Nov 1787 Geismar, Germany) d/o Emanuel Leinweber & Anna Elisabeth nee Garde (m 03 Aug 1882). Child:
*Anna Elisabeth Freitag – b 06 Dec 1808 Geismar, Germany;
m 19 Mar 1829 Johann Peter Michel

August "GUS" FRITZ s/o Peter Fritz & Anna nee Kahl; b 20 Apr 1864 Fremont Twp Benton Co IA, d 1946 Atkins, IA; m 27 Sept 1884 Anna Fox (d Jan 1935) d/o John Fox. 1912 retired in Atkins; served many years as street commissioner. Mbr Atkins Pleasant Hill Presbyterian Ch. Children:
Mary – m LeRoy Stanke
Matilda "Tilly" – d 04 Jan 1968; m 20 Mar 1913 Louis Lensch
John – m Augusta Hegewald
Magdalena – m Robert Hegewald
Emma – m Edward Hegewald
Augusta – d 1917 ae16y

*Peter FRITZ of Hessen, Germany; m Anna Kahl and emigrated to Fremont Twp Benton Co IA. Early settlers. Child:
August – b 20 Apr 1864 Fremont Twp Benton Co IA, d 1946

Atkins, IA; m 27 Sept 1884 Anna Fox

Dale Carl FROEHLICH s/o Hugo Herman Froehlich & Esther Katherine nee Rinderknecht Biershenk; b 03 Nov 1946 Eden Twp Benton Co IA; Banker; m 03 Sept 1966 St.Thomas Moore Chapel, Iowa City, IA. to Ruth Ann Duncalf(b 30 Nov 1946 Vinton, IA; Nurse) d/o Delbert George Duncalf & Agnes Marie nee Nolan of Van Horne, IA. Children:
   Lori Ann – b 23 Dec 1970 Davenport, IA
   Susan Marie – b 06 Feb 1973 Davenport, IA.
   Kari Lynn – b 19 Jan 1978 St.Lukes Hosp Cedar Rapids, IA

Hugo Herman FROEHLICH s/o John Froehlich & Sophia nee Wendlandt: cf Esther Katherine Rinderknecht (Bierschenk).

*John FROEHLICH b 1865 in Germany, d 1949 Iowa; m in Germany to Sophia Wendlandt (b 1858 Germany, d 1931 IA) and came to USA in 1880. Worked as hired man on farms until purchasing a farm six miles northwest of Newhall, IA where Hugo was born. Two sons died in infancy in addition to the following children:
   Mary – m Ernest Anderson
   Anna – m Howard Staab
   Hedwig – m Willie Holm
   Ernest – Killed in France in World War I
   Hugo Herman – b 06 Oct 1898 Eden Twp Benton Co IA;
      d 24 Dec 1987 bur St.John Cem;
      m 21 Sept 1941 Esther Katherine nee Rinderknecht Bierschenk

Loren Hugo FROEHLICH s/o Hugo Herman Froehlich & Esther Katherine nee Rinderknecht Bierschenk; b 26 Jan 1943 Eden Twp Benton Co IA, bpt 1943 & con St.John; US Army Psych. Social Worker; PhD Education; m 28 Aug 1965 Memorial Luth Ch Ames, IA to Helen Marie Hovde (b 04 Mar 1942 Roland, IA Story Co). Children:
   John Hugh – b 15 Oct 1970 St.Lukes Hosp Cedar Rapids, IA
   Laura Marie – b 11 Aug 1972 St.Lukes Hosp Cedar Rapids, IA

Sharon FROEHLICH d/o Hugo Herman Froehlich & Esther Katherine nee Rinderknecht Bierschenk; b 15 Aug 1944 Eden Twp Benton Co IA, bpt 1944 con St.John; m 29 Jan 1966 St.John to David Alan Hintze (b 01 Sept 1943 Cedar Rapids, Linn Co IA). Children:
   Liza Ann Hintze – b 01 Oct 1968 Irwin Army Hosp Junction City, KS

Michelle Lynn Hintze – b 29 Dec 1970 Mercy Hosp Cedar Rapids, IA

Cynthia Marie GALLO d/o Dorothy Gertrude nee Schanbacher & Virgil LaClare Gallo; b 11 Jul 1950; m 31 Jul 1971 Mark David Virtue (b 09 May 1951). Children:
    Heather Christine Virtue – b 18 Aug 1977
    Christopher David Virtue – b 29 Sept 1980
    Peter David Virtue – b 10 Feb 1982

Janee' Ann GALLO d/o Dorothy Gertrude nee Schanbacher & Virgil LaClare Gallo; b 20 Feb 1954; m 22 Sept 1990 Dennis Linn. Child:
    Andrew Moon – b 21 Jun 1983

Sue Ellen GALLO d/o Dorothy Gertrude nee Schanbacher & Virgil LaClare Gallo; b 22 Aug 1955; m 14 Oct 1976 Michael Edward Davis. Children:
    Bethany Ann Davis – b 08 Apr 1981
    Jeremy Michael Davis – b 11 Jul 1984
    Cristy Lynn Davis – b 21 Oct 1985

Edward L. GARBERS s/o Henry Garbers & Eleonora nee Karg; b 1891, d 1969; m Stella Andrews d/o John & Cora Andrews. Farmed Garbers homestead west of Van Horne, IA. Children:
    TWINS: Henry L. – b 1916; m 1921 Geraldine Young
            John L. – b 1916
    Irene – b 1918; m Robert Cranston

*Henry GARBERS s/o John & Marie Garbers; b Holstein, Germany; with younger brother, Wilhelm, emigrated to USA as stowaways to join older brothers Christopher and Frederick in Keystone, Benton Co IA; m Eleonora Karg. Children:
    Edward L. – b 1891, d 1969; m Stella Andrews
    George – NFR

Kim Ellen GARDEMAN d/o Douglas Gardeman & Lurline Ann nee Braksiek: cf Timothy Ray Leidigh.

Beth GARDEMANN d/o Donald H.C. Gardemann & Kathryn M. nee Jack; b 1959; m 12 Sept 1981 Stephen Rathje. Children:
    Scott Rathje – NFR
    Holly Rathje – NFR

Charles A. GARDEMANN s/o Louis A.C. Gardemann & Mary nee Doebel; b 1891, d 1972; m 1915 Hattie A. Schlotterbeck (b 1894, d 1986) d/o William Schlotterbeck & Josephine nee Weichman. Farmed near Newhall, Atkins, and Shellsburg, IA forty-three years; 1958 retirement in Atkins, IA. Children:

> Donald H.C. – b 31 Oct 1915, d 19 Dec 1992;
> > m 20 Feb 1941 Kathryn M. Jack
> Dorothy Louise – b 09 Nov 1917 Newhall, Benton Co IA;
> > 1st m 21 Feb 1940 Paul Henry Rinderknecht;
> > 2nd m 27 Jul 1973 Raymond Jensen

Danny GARDEMANN s/o Donald H.C. Gardemann & Kathryn M. nee Jack; b 1951; m 11 Jul 1970 Jacqueline Gibney. Palo, IA residence. Children:

> Rhonda – NFR
> Chad – NFR

Donald H. C. GARDEMANN s/o Charles A. Gardemann & Hattie A. nee Schlotterbeck; b 31 Oct 1915, d 19 Dec 1992; 1934 Class Newhall High School; m 20 Feb 1941 Kathryn M. Jack (b 24 Mar 1920) d/o Niles Verne Jack & Mary nee Bowman. Farmers near Newhall and Shellsburg, IA. Children:

> Niles – b 1942; m 15 Oct 1961 Diane Anderson
> Donald Craig – b 1945; m 02 Aug 1965 Sandra Zeller
> Garth – b 1950; m 14 Oct 1977 Vickie L. Wilhelmi
> Danny – b 1951; m 11 Jul 1970 Jacqueline Gibney
> Beth – b 1959; m 12 Sept 1981 Stephen Rathje

Donald Craig GARDEMANN s/o Donald H. C. Gardemann & Kathryn M. nee Jack; b 1945; m 02 Aug 1965 Sandra Zeller. Cedar Rapids, IA residence. Children:

> Brian – NFR
> Stephanie – NFR
> Rodney – NFR

Dorothy Louise GARDEMANN d/o Charles A. Gardemann & Hattie A. Schlotterbeck: cf Paul Henry Rinderknecht.

*Fredrick F. GARDEMANN, b 1819 Schleswig, Germany where he lived until ae15y; 1834 came to USA; lived in Davenport, IA and other cities before moving to Fremont Twp Benton Co IA where he purchased eighty acres of prairie land; d 1864 [Pneumonia] after 4y of marriage; m 1860 Christina Schnecloth (b 1839, d 1926). Children:

Louis C. – b 1861, d 1937; m 1883 Mary Doebel
William – b 1862, d 1959; m Ella Jungclaus
August – b 1864, d 1939; m Anna C. Schminke (b 1867, d 1926)

Garth GARDEMANN s/o Donald H. C. Gardemann & Kathryn M. nee Jack; b 1950; m 14 Oct 1977 Vickie LaVonne Wilhelmi (b 16 Jan 1954 St.Lukes Hosp Cedar Rapids, IA bpt 14 Feb 1954 St.Steph and con Steph) d/o Edward Leroy Wilhelmi & LaVonne Wiebold. Children:

Lori Joyce – b 16 Nov 1979
Larry Dean – b 06 Feb 1982
Dennis Donald Karl – b 07 Aug 1985

John GARDEMANN s/o Louis C. Gardemann & Mary nee Doebel; b 1887, d 1960; m Clara Schlotterback (b 1887, d 1979) d/o William Schlotterback & Josephine nee Weichman. Children:

Merle – NFR
Melba – NFR

Louis C. GARDEMANN, s/o Fredrick F. Gardemann & Christina nee Schnecloth; b 1861, d 1937; Tilford Academy Vinton, IA; began carpenter work ae18y. With brother William established Newhall, IA general merchandise store eight years. Louis returned to farming; school director, director of Atkins Savings Bank; m 1883 Mary Doebel (b 1864, d 1935) d/o Christian Doebel & Maria nee Busoker. Mbrs of St.Steph. Retired 1927 and moved to Newhall, IA. Ten children:

Fred – b 1885, d 1942; m Tillie Schlotterback
John – b 1887, d 1960; m Clara Schlotterback
Frances – b 1889, d 1946; m 1910 John Schlotterback
Charles A. – b 1891, d 1972; m 1915 Hattie A. Schlotterback
Harry – b 1894, d 1957; m Laura Ray
George – b 1898; m Mabel Ray
Irving – b 1900; m Opal Van Deusen
Louise – b 1903, d 1980; m Victor Niebuhr
Marie – b 1906, d 1980; m Wm. P. Spitz
Luella – b 1911; m Cyril Boddicker

Niles GARDEMANN s/o Donald H. C.Gardemann & Kathryn M. nee Jack; b 1942; m 15 Oct 1961 Dianne Anderson (d Jun 1999) Cedar Rapids, IA residence. Children:
    Jefferey – NFR
    Sherry – NFR

*Johann Daniel GARTHE, Germany; m Maria Kramer. Child:
    *Caroline Garthe – b 07 Nov 1874 Ellenhausen, Germany,
        d 30 Jan 1904 ae29y 2m 23d; m 10 Mar 1899 Heinrich Paar
        (b 08 Oct 1901, d 17 Jul 1967 ae65y 9m 9d Löhlbach, Germany).

*John Jacob "Jake" GASSER SR. b 04 May 1860 Germany, d 29 Sept 1934 ae74y 4m 25d [Automobile Accident in MN] bur St.Steph Cem; came to Cedar Rapids, IA in middle 1800's from Germany; 1st m Magdelena Romisch (b 30 Mar 1860, d 15 Jan 1914 ae53y 1m 16d Atkins, IA bur St.Steph Cem) from Alsace-Lorraine, France. Settled in Atkins; operated hotel and saloon followed by a butcher shop taken over by Jacob (Jake) Gasser JR. Butchered, harvested and stored ice. Children:
    Maggie – m Joe Beatty
    Fredricka – m Bill Risch
    Lillian – m Lawrence Johnsen
    Bill – m Reba NN
    Jake B. JR. – b 1886, d 1971 bur St.Steph Cem; m Elsie NN
In 1914 Jake Gasser SR. and daughter Lillian went to Germany to visit. While there Jake met Maria Boos in Baden, Germany.
2nd m 1916 John Jacob "Jake" Gasser SR. to Maria Boos (d Oct 1950 ae74y) when she came to Atkins, IA. Child:
    Walter Martin – b 05 Jan 1929; m Frances NN

Debra Lynn GEATER d/o Leonard Edward Geater & Marlys Elizabeth nee Bierschenk; b 23 Jun 1959 Virginia Gay Hosp Vinton, IA; m 25 Aug 1984 St.John to Loras John Beadle JR.(b 09 May 1955 Dubuque, IA) s/o Loras John Beadle SR. & Leta Beadle. Children:
    Elizabeth Ann Beadle – b 18 Sept 1986 Iowa City, IA
    Andrew Loras Beadle – b 06 Dec 1989 Iowa City, IA

Diana Elaine GEATER d/o Leonard Edward Geater & Marlys Elizabeth nee Bierschenk; b 26 Jun 1957 Virginia Gay Hosp Vinton, IA; m 04 Nov 1978 Bride's home, Vinton, IA to Dennis Leroy Landrus (b 16 Nov 1956 his 2nd m) s/o Ronald Landrus. Children:

STEP-CHILD: Virginia Landrus – b 16 Nov 1976
Amy Lee Landrus – b 14 Apr 1982 Mercy Hosp Cedar Rapids, IA
Holly Renee Landrus – b 04 Mar 1985
Lindsey Kay Landrus – b 17 Mar 1988

Eugene Earl GEIGER s/o Norman George Geiger & Eleanor Kathleen nee Geiken; b 08 Jul 1955; 1st m 25 May 1980 Gina Swayse DVD. Child:
   Christina Renee – b 18 May 1980;
      m 03 Jun 2002 Darren Eugene Wolfanger
2nd m 24 Feb 1989 Eugene Earl Geiger to Wendy Jo LaSeur (10 Aug ND). Children:
   Lea Marie – b 30 May 1989
   Brian William – b 16 Apr 1990
   Alan Eugene – b 06 Jul 1994

Suzanne Kay GEIGER d/o Norman George Geiger & Eleanor Kathleen nee Geiken; b 10 Jun 1956; 1st m 11 Aug 1974 Ronald Hugh Bonar (b 03 Jul 1953) DVD. Children:
   Kimberly Ann Bonar – b 25 May 1973
   Keith Allen Bonar – b 23 Mar 1974; m 05 Aug 2006 Rachel Kramer
   Nicole Renee Bonar – b 18 Jan 1984;
      m 04 Feb 2006 Dustin Arlo Hinton (b20 Jun 1984)
   Shaina Marie Bonar – b 15 Jul 1986
2nd m 02 Sept 1995 Suzanne Kay nee Geiger Bonar to David Herr (b 23 Mar 1974). Children:
   Adin Nathaniel Herr – b 24 Nov 1997
   Levi Zachery Herr – b 21 Jul 2000
   Kaylee Ann Herr – 24 Nov 2003

Anna Margaret GEIKEN d/o Frieda Katherine Elizabeth nee Brehm & Theodore Geiken; b 09 Sept 1918, d 28 Jul 1987 ae68y 10m 22d; m 05 Feb 1946 Frerick Waldo Obermueller (b 06 Mar 1922, d 18 Apr 1974 ae52y 1m 12d). Children:
   Nancy Jean Obermueller – b 28 Aug 1947;
      1st m 16 Dec 1966 Ronald Hamilton DVD;
      2nd m 01 Nov 1987 Darris Pickering DVD 2005
   Donald Lee Obermueller – b 06 Jun 1952;
      m 24 Jun 1972 Juanita Thompson
   Anerea Leigh Obermueller – b 18 Jun 1979;
      m 14 Feb 2001 Jaxon James Klostermann

Alana Rae Obermueller – b 22 Dec 1982

Deanna Marie GEIKEN d/o Myron Bernard Louis Geiken & Greta Lou nee Witmer; b 07 Sept 1960; m 28 Dec 1978 Tom Yocum. Children:
Jeremy Delbert Yocum – b 06 Jan 1977
Tommy Merle Yocum – b 04 Mar 1979
Christine Marie Yocum – b 23 Nov 1981; m Casey Wightman

Debbie Kay GEIKEN d/o Myron Bernard Louis Geiken & Greta Lou nee Witmer; b 25 Jan 1955; m 05 Apr 1975 Robert Steven Fenton (b 22 Nov 1954). Children:
Brian Robert Fenton – b 26 Jun 1981;
    m 16 Sept 2006 Sheila Rae Jessen
Natalie Lynn Fenton – b 12 Mar 1957

Denise Ellen GEIKEN d/o Myron Bernard Louis Geiken & Greta Lou nee Witmer; b 03 Mar 1957; m 10 May 1975 Randie Ray Brodigan (b 15 Jul 1956) DVD. Child:
Kellie Raye Brodigan (Adopted) b 09 Mar 1988

Dixie Lee GEIKEN d/o Myron Bernard Louis Geiken & Greta Lou nee Witmer; b 20 May 1958; m 28 May 1977 Kent Sturtz DVD. Children:
Jill Marie Sturtz – b 16 May 1979
Ryan Steven Sturtz – b 12 Feb 1983

Eleanor Kathleen GEIKEN d/o Frieda Katherine Elizabeth nee Brehm & Theodore Geiken; b 10 Feb 1935; m 13 Nov 1954 Norman George Geiger (b 01 Nov 1934). Children:
Eugene Earl Geiger – b 08 Jul 1955;
    1st m 25 May 1980 Gina Swayze DVD;
    2nd m 24 Feb 1989 Wendy Jo LaSeur
Suzanne Kay Geiger – b 10 Jun 1956;
    1st m 11 Aug 1974 Ronald Hugh Bonar DVD;
    2nd m 02 Sept 1995 David Herr
Ricky Norman Geiger – b 05 Dec 1958;
Elizabeth Ann Geiger – b/d 09 Sept 1959
Linda Luanne Geiger – b 06 Sept 1960;
    m 05 Oct 1985 Michael David Fish

Myron Bernard Louis GEIKEN s/o Frieda Katherine Elizabeth nee Brehm

& Theodore Geiken; b 06 May 1922, d 21 Aug 1977 ae55y 3m 15d; m 18 Aug 1953 Greta Lou Witmer (b 11 Jul 1930). Children:

Debbie Kay – b 25 Jan 1955; m 05 Apr 1975 Robert Steven Fenton
Denise Ellen – b 03 Mar 1957; m 10 May 1975 Randie Ray Brodigan
Dixie Lee – b 20 May 1958; m 28 May 1977 Kent Sturtz DVD
Deanna Marie – b 07 Sept 1960; m 28 Dec 1976 Tom Yocum
Steven Allen – b 12 Dec 1967;
    m 18 Aug 1990 Kimberly Alice Poldberg

Steven Allen GEIKEN s/o Myron Bernard Louis Geiken & Greta Lou Witmer; b 12 Dec 1967; m 18 Aug 1990 Kimberly Alice Poldberg (b 20 Sept 1968). Children:

Lucas Aaron – b 02 Oct 1994
Cassandra Leigh – b 04 May 1998

*Johann Philip (GS St.Steph Cem George Philip) GEITZ, b 01 Feb 1801 Germany, d 14 Jul 1883 IA ae 82y 5m 13d bur St.Steph Cem Fremont Twp Benton Co IA; m 25 Apr 1824 Katharina Elisabeth Fackiner(b 12 Nov 1799 os Alt Heim ns Altenhaina, Germany, d 17 Sept 1847 ae47y 10m 7d). Child:

Anna Elisabeth – b 29 Aug 1835 Löhlbach, Germany

*Jacob GERBER JR. s/o Jacob Gerber SR. & Christina; b 1857 Baden, Germany; learned farming from his parents in Germany before coming to USA at ae13y. Worked for William Rinderknecht in Benton Co IA before buying 160 acres of land; m Emma Fritz d/o Peter Fritz & Anna nee Kale of Benton Co IA; organizer and director of Newhall Savings Bank, Atkins Savings Bank and original Peoples Savings Bank in Cedar Rapids, IA. Children:

Clara Ida – d 27 Mar 1909;
    m 14 Feb 1901 John Harry Lensch of Benton Co IA
Jacob III – NFR
Charles – NFR
Christina – NFR

Adam F. GERHOLD s/o Henry Gerhold SR. & Louise Kristine nee Moeller; b 01 Mar 1884, d 11 Apr 1960 ae76y 1m 10d bur St.Steph Cem; m 26 Jan 1910 to Elizabeth Anna Rinderknecht (b 07 Jan 1886 Benton Co., d 03 Nov 1967 ae81y 9m 27d Cedar Rapids, IA. bur St.Steph Cem) d/o William Rinderknecht & Mary nee Happel. Children:

Wilbert – b ND Atkins, IA d ND;
   m 12 Oct 1951 Alice Hughes Warren
Elva M. – b 13 Mar 1912 Farm near Atkins, IA; d 01 Apr 1999
   Luth Home Vinton; Never Married
George Martin – d 23 Sept 1978; m 16 Feb 1938 Wilma C. Licht
Louis C. – b 1918 Parent's Farm, d 23 Sept 1979;
   m 16 Nov 1948 Helen A. Slaby
Marie – b 24 Mar 1924 Atkins, IA d 25 Feb 2007 Atkins, IA;
   m 09 Mar 1947 Wayne John Deklotz
Loretta – m 16 Nov 1949 Bernard Graham

Anna Sophia Maria Elizabeth GERHOLD d/o Henry Gerhold SR. & Louise Kristine nee Möller; b 06 Apr 1880 at Adair, IA con 1894; d 03 Jun 1967 Atkins, IA ae87y 1m 28d, bur St. Steph Cem; m 06 Sept 1900 St.Steph to George William Frederick Rinderknecht (b 10 Feb 1876 Fremont Twp Benton Co IA, d 10 Aug 1960 Atkins ae84y 6m bur St.Steph Cem) s/o Karl Rinderknecht & Anna Katherine nee Happel. Farmed the Rinderknecht homestead one and one-half miles east of Atkins until retiring in Atkins, IA. Ten children all born on farm east of Atkins, Fremont Twp Benton Co IA.:
   Arnold Karl Heinrich Rinderknecht – b 22 Jun 1902; d 27 Feb 1992,
      bur St.Steph Cem; m 10 Jul 1930 Catherine Louise Lenz
   John Henry William Conrad Rinderknecht – b 21 Mar 1904;
      d 28 Sept 1989; 1st m 10 Jun 1928 Lora Lena Lea Boettcher;
      2nd m 13 Oct 1970 Ella Marie O'Brien
   Alfred August Heinrich Rinderknecht – b 02 Oct 1905;
      d 20 Dec 1986; m 12 Dec 1934 Irene Katherine Elizabeth Krug
   Erna Louise Catherine Rinderknecht – b 05 Nov 1908;
      d 15 Apr 2007 bur St.Steph Cem; Never Married
   Herbert Adam August Rinderknecht – b 08 Feb 1911, d 28 Feb 1994;
      m 18 Oct 1947 Odetta Marie (Eutsler) Glick
   Helen Caroline Gertrude Rinderknecht – b 09 Feb 1913;
      d 22 May 1982 Des Moines, IA;
      m 12 Jul 1941 Ernest Philip Schwartz
   Rose Marie Elizabeth Rinderknecht – b 23 Jul 1915, d 28 Feb 1993
      [Cancer]; bur St.Steph Cem; Never Married
   Eda Barbara Elizabeth Rinderknecht – b 17 Dec 1917;
      m 14 Sept 1940 Wilbert Martin Schanbacher
   Otto Henry Carl Rinderknecht – b 17 Dec 1919, d 12 May 1999;
      m 06 Sept 1941 Edna Alice Railsback
   Elsie Katherine Louise Rinderknecht – b 21 Aug 1922;

m 22 Aug 1943 Alvin Ernest Polk (formerly Poock)

Arlen GERHOLD s/o Carl Henry Gerhold SR. & Emma Elisabeth nee Happel; b 04 Jun 1935 Atkins, IA bpt 1935 St.Steph; m 11 Feb 1961 Barbara Joan Sandler (b 03 Mar 1936 Cedar Rapids, IA) d/o Edward Max Sandler SR. & Phyliss nee Hoehn. Cedar Rapids Real Estate salesman. Children:
  Curtis Allen – b 12 May 1962 Cedar Rapids, IA;
      m 03 Aug 1985 Lori Sue Behounek (b 11 Dec 1962)
  Kathryn Ann – b 30 May 1964 Cedar Rapids, IA;
      m 25 Nov 1995 James Thomas Maddox (b 12 Dec 1959)
  Susan Kay – b 07 Dec 1965 Cedar Rapids, IA;
      bpt 19 Dec 1965, con 30 Mar 1980 St.Steph;
      m 29 Sept 2001 Christopher Gerald Dolan
  Sally Jo – b 10 Mar 1968 Cedar Rapids, IA;
      bpt 31 Mar 1968, con 04 Apr 1982 St.Steph;
      m 23 Oct 1993 St.Steph Matthew David Polansky
  Dianna Lynn – b 15 Apr 1971 Cedar Rapids, IA;
      bpt 09 May 1971, con 31 Mar 1985 St.Steph;
      m 17 Oct 1998 Bradley Scott Svoboda Murrells Inlet, SC

Carl Henry GERHOLD JR. s/o Carl Henry Gerhold SR. & Emma Elisabeth nee Happel; b 11 Jul 1925 Atkins, IA d 1973 [Cancer] bur St.Steph Cem; m 14 Nov 1953 Mary Rosdail(b 23 Sept 1929 Cedar Rapids, IA); Farmed Gerhold farm southwest of Atkins. Children:
  Randall – b 29 Oct 1954
  Lynette – b 04 Jul 1957
  Carl III – b 31 May 1959
  Thomas Donovan – b 21 Jun 1961; m 1991 Patricia Elaine Palmer
  TWINS: Judy – b 31 Mar 1963
          Jony – b 31 Mar 1963

Carl Henry GERHOLD SR. s/o Henry Gerhold SR. & Louise Kristine nee Möller; b 05 Oct 1892 Atkins, IA d 04 Aug 1974 ae81y 9m 30d, bur St. Steph Cem; m 09 Feb 1921 Emma Elisabeth Happel (b 13 Apr 1891 Linn Co IA d 04 May 1974 ae83y 21d bur St.Steph Cem) d/o August A. Happel & Martha nee Young. Farmed southwest of Atkins, IA. Children:
  Martha – b 22 Nov 1922 Atkins, IA;
      2nd m 26 Dec 1957 Howard Burns of CA
  Carl Henry JR. – b 11 Jul 1925 Atkins; d 1973 bur St.Steph Cem;

m 14 Nov 1953 Mary Rosdail
Lolita Marie – b 12 Oct 1927 Atkins, IA;
   m 07 Sept 1947 Gilmore Julius Schanbacher
Arlen – b 04 Jun 1935 Atkins, IA;
   m 11 Feb 1961 Barbara Joann Sandler

Curtis Allen GERHOLD s/o Arlen Gerhold & Barbara Joan nee Sandler; b 12 May 1962 Cedar Rapids, IA bpt 10 Jun 1962 TrinCR & con 11 Apr 1976 St.Steph; m 03 Aug 1985 Chelsea, IA Lori Sue Behounek (b 11 Dec 1962 Marshalltown, IA). Children:
Lindsey Marie – b 16 Oct 1987
Ashley Nicole – b 04 Oct 1989
Kelsey Jo – b 25 Jan 1994
Matthew Curtis – b 17 May 1996

Dianna Lynn GERHOLD d/o Arlen Gerhold & Barbara Joan nee Sandler; b 15 Apr 1971 Shellsburg, IA; m 17 Oct 1998 Bradley Scott Svoboda (b 31 Sept 1970) s/o Lynn Bading, Cedar Rapids, IA. Children:
Zachary James Svoboda – b 07 May 2002
Allison Nicole Svoboda – b 02 Jul 2006

Elsie GERHOLD d/o Henry Gerhold JR. & Sophie nee Rinderknecht;b 07 Feb 1909 Linn Co IA; m 28 Feb 1932 Karl Kray. Residence Newhall, IA. Children:
Virgil Kray – b 08 Oct 1935 Shellsburg, IA
Delbert Kray – b 04 Dec 1939 Shellsburg, IA

Emma K. GERHOLD d/o Henry Gerhold SR. & Louise Kristine nee Möller; b 13 Mar 1898 Benton Co IA, bpt St.Steph, d 23 Jun 1979 Atkins, IA ae81y 3m 10d, bur St.Steph Cem; m 12 Feb 1920 Karl Jacob Happel (b 29 Sept 1895 Linn Co IA, bpt St.Steph, d 10 Dec 1928 ae33y 2m 12d [Brain Abscess] bur St.Steph Cem) s/o August A. Happel & Martha nee Young; farmers east of Atkins, IA. Children:
Karl Henry August Happel JR. – b 13 Jul 1921 Linn Co IA;
   d 30 May 1999; m 05 Jul 1967 Phyllis nee Pecka McLinden
Herbert Louis Happel – b 04 Jan 1926 Linn Co IA; d 09 Jan 2005;
   m 25 Oct 1956 Geraldine Edsburn
Eleanor May Happel – b 25 May 1928 Linn Co IA;
   m 06 Jun 1948 Raymond Wichman

George GERHOLD s/o Adam F. Gerhold & Elizabeth Anna nee Rinderknecht; b 14 Jun 1913, d 23 Sept 1978; m 16 Feb 1938 Wilma C. Licht (b 23 Jan 1910). Farmers near Van Horne, IA until moving to Cedar Rapids, IA. Child:
   Kathleen Ann – NFR

Henry GERHOLD III, s/o Henry Gerhold JR. & Sophie nee Rinderknecht; b 08 Dec 1913 Palo, IA d 03 May 1970; m 11 Dec 1936 Esther Reding(b 21 Jun 1916). Farmers near Center Point IA. Children:
   Barbara – NFR
   Lora Lee – b 03 Jun 1940 Cedar Rapids, IA
   Henry John – NFR
   Cheryl Linn – NFR

Henry GERHOLD JR. s/o Henry Gerhold SR. & Louise Kristine nee Möller; b 1881 Adair, IA d 1975 Atkins, IA bur St.Steph; m 28 Feb 1907 his Möller (Moeller) cousin Sophie Rinderknecht (b 14 Oct 1882 Benton Co IA, d 16 Apr 1966 ae83y 6m 2d) d/o William (Wilhelm) Rinderknecht & Maria Happel. Henry Gerhold JR.'s Grandfather: Johannes Georg Möller (George Moeller); Sophie Rinderknecht's Grandmother: Maria Möller (Marie Moeller). Johannes George Möller and Maria Möller bro/sis; Farmers in Palo, IA area. Children:
   Erma – Never Married [Born Hearing Impaired] b 22 Dec 1907
   Elsie – b 07 Feb 1909; m Karl Kray of Newhall, IA
   Henry III – b 08 Dec 1913, d 03 May 1970;
        m 11 Dec 1936 Esther Reding
   Eldred – b 15 Mar 1918; Never Married [Born Blind]

*Henry GERHOLD SR. s/o Conrad George Gerhold & Anna Katherine nee Holz; b 14 Aug 1847 Hessen Kassel, Germany; 1868 came to USA landing on his twenty-first birthday; visited cousin in Philadelphia, PA, stopped in Chicago, IL before settling near Cedar Rapids, IA where he farmed in 1873; d 21 Nov 1943 Atkins, IA ae96y 3m 7d bur 23 Nov 1943 St.Steph Cem; m 26 Jan 1873 Louise Kristine Möller (b 07 Dec 1855, Löhlbach, Germany, bpt 16 Dec 1855 Löhlbach Ch,con St.Paul's Ev Luth Ch Luzerne, IA d 31 Dec 1928 Atkins, IA ae73y 24d bur St.Steph Cem) d/o Johannes Georg Möller aka George Moeller & Karoline nee Bornscheuer. 1861 Louise Kristine ae6y came to America. In 1875 they moved to Gutherie Co near Adair, IA where other relatives and friends settled. They farmed there eight years and lost three children in infancy from diptheria; they moved back to

Benton Co southwest of Atkins, IA where seven more children were born:
    Anna Sophia Marie Elizabeth – b 06 Apr 1880 Adair, IA;
        d 03 Jun 1967 Atkins, IA;
        m 06 Sept 1900 George William Frederick Rinderknecht
    Henry JR. – b 1881 Adair, IA d 1975 Atkins, IA;
        m 28 Feb 1907 Sophie Rinderknecht
    Adam F. – b 01 Mar 1884 Atkins, IA d 11 Apr 1960;
        m 26 Jan 1910 Elizabeth Anna Rinderknecht
    Caroline (Carrie) – b 1886, d 1967 Atkins, IA bur St.Steph Cem;
        Never Married
    Mary – b 30 Mar 1888 Atkins, IA d 01 Sept 1976; m William Ehlers
    Elizabeth – b 1890, d 1981 Atkins, IA bur St.Steph Cem;
        Never Married
    Carl H. SR. – b 05 Oct 1892 Atkins, IA; d 04 Aug 1974;
        m Emma Elisabeth Happel
    Louise Christina – b 11 Jan 1895 Atkins, IA
        d 18 Oct 1979;m Albert Henry Rathje
    Emma K. – b 13 Mar 1898 Benton Co IA, d 23 Jun 1979 Atkins IA;
        m 12 Feb 1920 Karl Jacob Happel

Kathryn Ann GERHOLD d/o Arlen Gerhold & Barbara Joan nee Sandler; b 30 May 1964 Cedar Rapids IA, bpt 21 Jun 1964 & con 19 Mar 1978 St.Steph; m 25 Nov 1995 Concordia Luth Ch Cedar Rapids, IA to James Thomas Maddox (b 12 Dec 1959 South Fulton, TN; d 22 Mar 2000 ae40y 3m 10d St.Lukes Hosp Cedar Rapids, IA bur 25 Mar 2000 Mount Calvary Cem; Washington High School Assistant Football Coach) s/o James & Leatha Maddox, Cedar Rapids, IA. Child:
    MacKenzie Nicole Maddox – b 10 Apr 1997

Loretta GERHOLD d/o Adam F. Gerhold & Elizabeth Anna nee Rinderknecht; m 16 Nov 1949 Bernard Graham. Cedar Rapids, IA residence. Children:
    Steven Graham – NFR
    Kenneth Graham – NFR
    Beth Graham – NFR

Louis C. GERHOLD s/o Adam F. Gerhold & Elizabeth Anna nee Rinderknecht; b 1918 on parent's farm, 160 acres on south edge of Atkins, IA purchased from Elizabeth's father, William Rinderknecht; d 23 Sept 1979, bur St.Steph Cem; m 16 Nov 1948 Helen A. Slaby; farmed east of

Atkins. 1970 moved to parents' farm on south edge of Atkins. Children:
Linda – NFR
Mary Ellen – NFR

Louise Christina GERHOLD d/o Henry Gerhold SR. & Louise Kristine nee Möller; b 11 Jan 1895 Atkins, IA d 18 Oct 1979 ae84y 9m 7d, bur St.Steph Cem; Teacher until marriage; m Albert Henry Rathje (b 03 Oct 1894, d 06 Dec 1970 bur St.Steph Cem). Farmers near Atkins, IA. Children:
Arlene Rathje – m Paul McMann, Blairstown, IA residence
Maurine Rathje – Salt Lake City, UT residence
(Daughter) Rathje – b 11 Jun 1929, dec'd
Alan Henry Rathje – b 29 Mar 1931,
1st m 04 Jun 1960 Dorothy Olive Gillis DVD; 2nd m Judy Snider

Martha GERHOLD d/o Carl Henry Gerhold SR. & Emma Elizabeth nee Happel; b 22 Nov 1922 Atkins, IA bpt St.Steph; 1st m NN. Child:
Marilyn – b 29 Jul 1950 in CA
2nd m 26 Dec 1957 Martha nee Gerhold to Howard Burns (b 05 Dec 1924 TX).

Mary GERHOLD d/o Henry Gerhold SR. & Louise Kristine nee Möller; b 30 Mar 1888 Atkins, IA d 01 Sept 1976 ae88y 5m 1d; m 07 Dec 1911 William John August Ehlers (b 24 Feb 1884, d 09 Jun 1947; Luth School Teacher) d/o Rev. Fred Ehlers SR. & Elizabeth nee Happel. MN residence. Children:
Wilma Ehlers – b 17 Sept 1914; m 31 Oct 1953 Edwin Friend
Herbert Ehlers – b 14 Jul 1920
Loretta Ehlers – b 20 Sept 1922

Sally Jo GERHOLD d/o Arlen Gerhold & Barbara Joan nee Sandler; b 10 Mar 1968; m 23 Oct 1993 St. Steph to Matthew David Polansky (b 14 Dec 1968). Children:
William Matthew Polansky – b 12 Dec 2000
Nathan David Polansky – b 29 Dec 2003

Susan Kay GERHOLD d/o Arlen Gerhold & Barbara Joan nee Sandler; b 07 Dec 1965; m 29 Sept 2001 Concordia Luth Ch, Cedar Rapids, IA to Christopher Gerard Dolan (b 08 Dec 1959). Child:
Andrew James Dolan – b 21 Jun 2003
Christopher Gerard Dolan's children from 1st m:

Nicholas Henry – b 02 Jan 1986
Lukas Charles – b 19 Aug 1987
Samuel David – b 18 Jul 1991

Thomas Donovan GERHOLD s/o Carl Henry Gerhold JR. & Mary nee Rosdail; b 21 Jun 1961; m 06 Oct 1990 United Methodist Ch, Britt, IA to Patricia Elaine Palmer d/o Stephen & Linda Palmer of rural Britt, IA. Patricia Registered Nurse, U. of IA College of Nursing, employed by Veterans Administration Medical Center; Thomas: Central Sterilizing Technician employed by U. of IA Hospitals and Clinics. Iowa City, IA residence.

Wilbert GERHOLD s/o Adam F. Gerhold & Elizabeth Anna nee Rinderknecht; m 12 Oct 1951 Alice Hughes Warren. Farmers on south edge of Atkins, IA until moving to Cedar Rapids, IA. Child:
    Richard Warren – NFR

Terry Lee GEWECKE s/o Shirley Ann nee Rammelsberg & Dennis Gewecke; b 26 Aug 1964 bpt 1964 St.John; m 15 Aug 1986 Lori Ann Newton (b 20 Sept 1968). Atkins, IA residence. Children:
    Rachel Kay – b 02 Jun 1988
    Brooke Nicole – b 12 Sept 1990

Alan William GIELAU s/o Anna Marie nee Happel & Albert Henry Gielau; b 10 Mar 1948; 1st m 31 Jul 1970 Renae Barnes (b 17 Dec 1949)DVD 1975. Children:
    Jeffrey Alan – b 16 Dec 1970
    Amy Renae – b 25 Jul 1972
2nd m 22 Sept 1990 Alan William Gielau to Sharon Kallenbeck (b 05 May 1956). Children:
    TWINS: Tyler Jeffrey Gielau – b 31 Jan 1993
           Bryan Alan Gielau – b 31 Jan 1993
    STEPCHILDREN:
    Amy Kallenbeck – b 12 Nov 1976
    Elizabeth Kallenbeck – b 20 Aug 1979

Irma Jean GIELAU d/o Anna Marie nee Happel & Albert Henry Gielau; b 11 Apr 1953; 1st m Rich Hubbard DVD 02 Sept 1972.
2nd m 30 Jul 1977 to Keith Allen Lee (b 17 Oct 1950). Children:
    Jason Alan Lee – b 04 Jan 1980

Lisa Jean Lee – b 23 Oct 1981
Heather Marie Lee – b 11 Nov 1983

Robert Alan GIELAU s/o Anna Marie nee Happel & Albert Henry Gielau; b 16 May 1964; m 29 Aug 1987 Cheryl Christopher (b 04 Apr 1964). No children.

Vicky Marie GIELAU d/o Anna Marie nee Happel & Albert Henry Gielau; b 12 Nov 1950; m 17 Oct 1970 Franklin Tribon (b 30 Dec 1948). Children:
    Laura Ann Tribon – b 24 Jan 1977
    Zachary Arthur Tribon- b 13 Feb 1979, d 13 Apr 1983
    Seth Theodore Tribon – b 26 May 1982
    Thomas Mark Tribon (Adopted) b 25 Jan 1984

Wesley Ray GIELAU s/o Anna Marie nee Happel & Albert Henry Gielau; b 14 Oct 1957; m 11 Sept 1982 Barbara Wylam (b 06 Jul 1959). Children:
    Adam Wesley – b 12 Nov 1984
    Jacquelyn Kristine – b 20 Aug 1986
    Rachel Mae – b 13 Apr 1988
    Emily Ann – b 26 Aug 1990

Joel David GLASGOW s/o Audrey Ann nee Krug & David L. Glasgow; b 04 Jan 1971; m 29 Apr 2000 Kari Ann Dumblauskas (b 11 Aug 1970) d/o Paul Dumblauskas & Gail nee Rundle. Children:
    Ella Mikalena – b 28 Jul 2004
    Henrick Elsworth – b 13 Feb 2007

Michael John GLICK s/o Galen Eugene Glick & Delores Ann nee Krug Tibben; b 08 May 1964 St.Lukes Hosp Cedar Rapids, IA bpt 31 May 1964 St.Steph; m 21 June 1985 TrinCR to Alice M. Beltz (b 19 Feb 1966 University Hosp, Iowa City, IA her 2nd m) d/o Ronald & Linda Hartson. Children:
    STEPSON: Jarod Ryan Beltz – b 06 Nov 1983, Cedar Rapids, IA
    Jennifer Marie Glick – b 19 Jan 1986, Phoenix, AZ
    Joseph Tyler Glick – b 26 Jun 1990

Shari Lynn GLICK d/o Galen Eugene Glick & Delores Ann nee Krug Tibben; b 09 Jan 1963 St.Lukes Hosp Cedar Rapids, IA bpt 10 Feb 1963 St.Steph; American West Airline Flight Attendant; m 17 Jan 1987 King of Glory Luth Ch, Tempe, AZ to Stuart Nechanicky (b 30 Oct 1961 Cedar

Rapids, IA bpt Dec 1961 St.Jude Catholic Ch, Cedar Rapids, IA; d 14 Jan 2008 Phoenix, AZ ae46y 2m 15d) DVD s/o Robert Nechanicky & Kathryn nee Hough. AZ residence. Children:
    Ashley Ann Nechanicky – b 13 Jun 1987 Tempe, AZ
    Amber Marie Nechanicky – b 28 Jan 1990 Tempe, AZ

Helen GLUESING d/o John Gluesing & Hannah nee Senne; b 1923, d 1996; m John Schreckengast (b 1925). Children:
    Dennis F. Schreckengast – b 1949; m Terese Joy Alt (b 1950).
        Children: 1. Dennis Franklin (b 1969); m Julia Catherine Bernhard
        (b 1971); 2. Tamara Lynn (b 1974); m Chad McLaud. Child:
        Bret Louis McLaud (1996); 3. Robert John (b 1982)
    Rex Randall Schreckengast – b 1951; m Debbie Hohensee (b 1956)
        Children: 1. Kevin (b 1977); 2. Tara (b 1974); 3. Elizabeth Kay
        (b 1982); 4. Ashley Liana (b 1988)
    Michael John Schreckengast – b 1952; m Julie Kay Heldt (b 1954)
        Children: 1. Cal Duffy (b 1982); 2. Jess Heldt (b 1984)
    Stacy Schreckengast – b 1954; m Sharon Swalley (b 1956). Children:
        1. Benjamin Lee (b 1982); 2. Katherine Kay (b 1984);
        3. Leanna Una (b 1985)

Jacquelyn Rae GLUESING d/o Paul Gluesing & Norma nee Voeltz; b 1946; m Alan Norris (b 1940). Children:
    Scott Alan Norris – b 1967; m Melinda Mueller (b 1968). Children:
        Kyle Scott Norris (b 1988); Kaylie Suzanne Norris (b 1991)
    Kristen Jay Norris – b 1970
    Nicole Norma Norris – b 1975

JoAnn GLUESING d/o Gilbert Gluesing & Madeline nee Weichman; b 1937; m Jack Phelps (b 1937) Mesa, AZ residence. Children:
    Daniel Jack Phelps – b 1964
    Donald Scott Phelps – b 1966; m Deborah Darlene Bowers. Child:
        Hannah Darlene Phelps (1996)

Karmen Noreen GLUESING d/o Paul Gluesing & Norma nee Voeltz; b 1942; m Richard Kimm (b 1942). Children:
    James Allen Kimm – b 1962; m Lori Schlarbaum (1965). Child:
        Kelsey Lee Kimm (b 1993)
    Sonja Kay Kimm – b 1973; m Jeremy Lerch (b 1974). Child:
        Annthaneeya Lerch (b 1993)

Paul GLUESING s/o John Gluesing & Hannah nee Senne; b 1915; m Norma Voeltz (b 1919, d 1991). Children:
Karmen Noreen – b 1942; m Richard Kimm
Jacquelyn Rae – b 1946; m Alan Norris
Paulette Sue – b 1951; m Dennis Lee Brown. Children:
Kevin Neal Brown (b 1974); Denise Vania Brown (b 1979)

Shirley GLUESING d/o Gilbert Gluesing & Madeline nee Weichman; b 1935; m Eldo Meyer (b 1932). Garrison, IA residence. Children:
Steven Lynn Meyer – b 1956; m Teresa Block. Children:
Amy Beth Block (b 1989)
Connie Jean Meyer – b 1959; m Randy Mortvedt. Children:
Criston Kay Meyer (b 1987); Rachel Marie Meyer (b 1996)

Deborah Joyce GOETZ d/o Caroline Mary nee Haerther & Donald Charles Goetz; b 30 Aug 1956 Minneapolis, MN; m 11 Jul 1981 Grace Luth Ch, Gas City, IN to Mark Hadden Lugar (b 31 Oct 1958 Indianapolis, IN) s/o Richard Green Lugar & Charlene nee Smeltzer. Occupation: Sales. Children
Tye Ashley Green Lugar – b 28 Nov 1982, Indianapolis, IN
Taylor Charles Goetz Lugar – b 07 Dec 1985, Indianapolis, IN
Trent Hadden Haerther Lugar – b 14 Nov 1987 Nashua, NH
Tory Marie Lugar – b 25 Jan 1993

Douglas John GOETZ S/O Caroline Mary nee Haerther & Donald Charles Goetz; b 15 Feb 1963 Minneapolis, MN; m 12 Jun 1993 Birmingham MI to Elaine Constance Rawley (b 16 Jan 1967 Birmingham, MI) d/o Joe & Ethel Rawley of Birmingham, MI. Children:
Ryan Charles – b 04 Apr 1995
Dustin Thomas – b 19 Oct 1997

Jacqueline Marie GOETZ d/o Caroline Mary nee Haerther & Donald Charles Goetz; b 12 Jul 1966 Hartford City, IN; m 24 Jun 1990 Indianapolis, IN to Thomas Charles Bell (b 01 Aug 1967 South Bend, IN) s/o Robert Bell & Margaret nee Chrastil. Occupation: Teacher/Coach. Children:
Madison Margaret Bell – b 20 Apr 1994
Baylee Theresa Bell – b 01 Feb 1996
Brent Bell Bell – b Aug 1998

Therese Carol GOETZ d/o Caroline Mary nee Haerther & Donald Charles Goetz; b 01 Feb 1960 Minneapolis, MN; m 24 Jun 1989 Upland, IN to Douglas Eugene Miller. Children:
    Rhianna Carolyn Miller – b 08 Feb 1993
    Ian Douglas Miller – b 07 Nov 1994

James GOOD s/o John Good & Audrey nee Paulsen; b 1946; m Bonnie Baker of Cedar Rapids, IA. Newhall, IA residence; Occupation: Realtor. Children:
    Kimberly – b 1967
    Wade – b 1973

Joanne GOOD d/o John Good & Audrey nee Paulsen; b 1954; m James Smith. North English, IA residence. Children:
    Justin Smith – b 1978
    Jesse Smith – b 1980

Judy GOOD d/o John Good & Audrey nee Paulsen; b 1950; m Laverne Upah. Elberon, IA residence. Children:
    Chad Upah – b 1972
    Heidi Upah – b 1976
    Travis Upah – b 1979

Dorothy Griswold GOUGH d/o Louise Marie nee Mohr & William Griswold Gough; b 01 Sept 1922; m 21 Mar 1948 Brian Earl Bigley (b 19 Aug 1930). Children:
    William Brian Bigley – b 26 Sept 1948
    Carol Michelle Bigley – b 17 Aug 1954
    Deborah Ann Bigley – b 05 Oct 1956
    Rebecca Joy Bigley – b 06 Feb 1958
    Brette Lee Bigley – b 25 Jul 1959

Elsie Louise GOUGH d/o Louise Marie nee Mohr & William Griswold Gough; b 18 Oct 1920; m 26 Jan 1952 Derk Newell Gysbers (b 31 Mar 1924). Children:
    TWINS: Tor Merrill Gysbers – b 28 Jun 1953
                Linda Diane Gysbers – b 28 Jun 1953
    Bonnie Sue Gysbers – b 02 Apr 1956

*Anna GRABAU d/o Claus Heinrich (Henry) Grabau SR. & Katherine nee

Schroeder; b 08 Nov 1882 Kolheim, Germany, d 10 Oct 1947 Cedar Rapids, Linn Co IA; m 23 Mar 1905 Otto E. Strauss (b Berlin, Germany) s/o Henry Strauss & Wilhelmina nee Hartwick. Children:
Richard – NFR
Christina M. – b 1904
Edward A. – b 1906, d 1929
Almore L. – b 1907, d 1993
Florence M. – b 1910, d 1982
Robert – b 1916

Arthur Charles GRABAU s/o Herman Grabau JR. & Marie nee Michel; b 30 Nov 1902 Boone, IA d 20 Aug 1975 ae72y 8m 21d bur 23 Aug 1975 CdrMem; Occupation: Salesman; 1st m 20 Nov 1926 Cedar Rapids, IA to Hilda Gertrude Schirm (b 01 Sept 1905 Newhall, Benton Co IA d 27 Feb 1983 ae77y 5m 26d Moline, IL bur CdrMem) d/o Henry Schirm & Katherine nee Rinderknecht. Children:
Dale Allan – b 07 Oct 1928 Cedar Rapids, Linn Co IA;
　　1st m 09 Mar 1951 Lois N. Austin;
　　2nd m 07 Feb 1970 Irene Louise Hannenfent
Dalene Marie – b 20 Jul 1930 Cedar Rapids, Linn Co IA
2nd m 223 Mar 1955 Angola, IN Arthur Charles Grabau to Mary E. nee Salerno Starbuck (b 20 Mar 1919, d 30 Nov 1961 ae43y 8m 10d).

Byron Zane GRABAU s/o Leonard Henry Adam Grabau & Ora Lee nee Noland; b 21 Nov 1937 Boone, IA; m 13 Feb 1966 Marion IA Frances Ellen Sauer (b 10 May 1940 Quasqueton, IA) d/o Earnest George Sauer & Vesta Alice nee Smith. Children:
Walter Boyce – b 14 Mar 1967 Linn City, IA
Dietrich Earl Zane – b 03 May 1968 Linn City, IA
Mimz Anna – b 27 Jun 1969 Linn City, IA
Gordon Douglas Kite – b 21 Apr 1971 Linn City, IA

Carol Renea GRABAU d/o Harold Walter Adam Grabau & Arlene nee Silvey; b 02 Mar 1952 Boone, IA; m 02 Aug 1975 Boone, IA to Dennis Leroy Hamman (b 15 Dec 1952 Red Oak, IA) s/o Rodney Hamman & Pearl nee White. Children:
Justin Tanar Hamman – b 25 Aug 1980 Story City, IA
Kesey Vaun Hamman – b 05 Oct 1983 Story City, IA

Christopher GRABAU JR. s/o Louise Caroline Marie nee Moeller &

Christopher Dietrich Grabau SR.; b 28 Nov 1924 Boone, IA; m 09 Jun 1944 Des Moines, IA to Gretchen Marie Price (b 21 Jan 1926 Boone, IA) d/o Dan Price & Anthia nee Lewis. Children:
> Maureen Kay – b 09 Oct 1944 Boone, IA;
>> m 05 Sept 1964 Thomas Lightfoot
> Kathleen Marie – b 24 Sept 1949 Boone, IA

*Claus GRABAU s/o Hinrich Grabau & Margaret nee Blomen; b 1694 Otterstedt, Germany, bpt 05 Mar 1697 Otterstedt, Germany d 25 Sept 1761 Dipshorn, Germany; m 28 Nov 1726 Anneke Westermann (b 01 Oct 1695 Dipshorn, Germany). Children:
> Johann – b 16 Feb 1728 Dipshorn, Germany; d 06 Dec 1769
>> Ostersode, Germany; m 17 Nov 1757 Gesche Huckfeldt
> Dierck – b 18 May 1730 Dipshorn, Germany
> Claus – b 14 Sept 1732 Dipshorn, Germany
> Gretje – b 21 Dec 1735, d 08 May 1750 Dipshorn, Germany
> Annete – b 13 Apr 1737, d 21 Oct 1765 Dipshorn, Germany
> Becke – b 28 May 1739 Dipshorn, Germany
> Tibke – b 14 Apr 1742, d 18 Mar 1743 Dipshorn, Germany

*Claus GRABAU s/o Johann Grabau & Catherine (Trine) Otten; b 15 Oct 1793 Ostersode, Germany, d 16 Jan 1864 ae70y 3m 1d Ostersode, Germany; m 06 Feb 1816 Gnarrenburg, Germany to Margarete Schnakenberg (b 11 Nov 1796 Ostersode, Germany, d 15 Feb Ostersode, Germany) d/o Jorgen Schnakenberg & Gretje (Margarete) nee Blanken. Children:
> *Dietrich – b 25 Sept 1822 Ostersode, Germany;
>> d 19 Sept 1908 Boone, IA;
>> m 1847 Kolheim, Germany to Adelheid (Ollie) Hasstedt
> Claus – b 26 Dec 1824 Ostersode, Germany
> Catherine – b 08 Mar 1827 Ostersode, Germany
> Herman – b 09 Feb 1830 Ostersode, Germany
> Meta – b 17 Aug 1832 Ostersode, Germany
> Gerd – b 13 mar 1836 Ostersode, Germany

*Claus Heinrich (Henry) GRABAU SR. s/o Dietrich Grabau & Adelheid (Ollie)Kathryn nee Hasstedt; b 31 Aug 1848 Kolheim, Germany, d 24 Jul 1922 ae73y 10m 23d Boone, IA bur 28 Jul 1922 Linwood Park Cem Boone, IA Occupation: Chicago & NW Railroad; 1st m 11 Nov 1902 in Germany to Margaretha nee Mair Moris. Children:

*Meta Grabau – b 09 Nov 1876 Kolheim, Germany; d 21 Jan 1936
 Fremont Twp Benton Co. IA; m 11 Feb 1902 Adam John Michel
*Herman JR. – b 28 Oct 1877 Kolheim, Germany; d 04 May 1939
 Cedar Rapids, Linn Co IA; m 18 Sept 1901 Marie Michel
2nd m 09 Apr 1881 Hanover, Germany, Claus Henry Grabau to Katherine Schroeder (b 22 Jan 1856 Hanstedt, Germany, d 13 Feb 1935 ae79y 22d Boone, IA bur 16 Feb 1935 Linwood Park Cem Boone, IA Occupation: Maid) s/o George & Adelheid Schroeder. Children:
*Adelheid (Ollie) Grabau – b 24 Feb 1881 Kolheim, Germany;
 d 04 Feb 1965 Madrid, IA
*Anna Grabau – b 08 Nov 1882 Kolheim, Germany; d 10 Oct 1947
 Cedar Rapids, Linn Co IA; m 23 Mar 1905 Otto E. Strauss
Katherine Grabau – b 14 Jun 1886 Boone, IA; d Dec 1960
 Schleswig, IA
Minnie Grabau – b 26 Jan 1890 Boone,IA; d 07 Sept 1977 Perry, IA
Maria Grabau – b 11 Jun 1892 Boone, IA; d 01 Nov 1955
 Des Moines, IA
Claus Henry Grabau JR. – b 30 Dec 1895 Boone, IA; d 26 Oct 1957
 Boone, IA

Dale Allan GRABAU s/o Arthur Charles Grabau & Hilda Gertrude nee Schirm; b 07 Oct 1928 Cedar Rapids, IA; Occupation: Tool Engineer; 1st m 09 Mar 1951 Rock Island, IL to Lois Neil Austin (b 10 Jun 1930). Children:
Scott Allan – b 18 Feb 1953 Rock Island, IL;
 m 17 Nov 1984 Lynetta Burkead
Douglas Lee – b 16 Oct 1955 Rock Island, IL;
 m 27 Sept 1986 Deborah Versluis Stombaugh (b 23 Jun 1956)
Jeffrey Neal – b 12 Jun 1959 Rock Island, IL;
 1st m 10 Jul 1982 Rajean A. German;
 2nd m 26 May 1990 Catherine Ann Goodall
Brian Dean – b 05 Oct 1961 Rock Island, IL; m Pamela Ryser
2nd m 07 Feb 1970 Moline, IL Dale Allan Grabau to Irene Louise Hannenfent (b 12 Mar 1932).

*Dietrich GRABAU s/o Claus Grabau & Margarete Schnakenberg; b 25 Sept 1822 Ostersode, Germany, d 19 Sept 1908 ae85y 11m 25d Boone, IA bur 22 Sept 1908 Linwood Park Cem Boone, IA; m 1847 Kolheim, Germany to Adelheid (Ollie) Kathryn Hasstedt (b 1824 Kolheim, Germany, d 20 Nov 1882 ae58y Boone, IA bur Linwood Park Cem Boone, IA). Children:

*Claus Heinrich (Henry) SR. – b 32 Aug 1848 Kolheim, Germany;
    d 24 Jul 1922 Boone, IA;
    1st m 11 Nov 1902 Margaretha nee Mair Moris;
    2nd m 09 Apr 1881 Hanover, Germany Katherine Schroeder
*John – b 22 Feb 1850 Kolheim, Germany, d 04 Oct 1936 Boone, IA
*Henry Claus – b 23 Oct 1852 Kolheim, Germany;
    d 09 Jul 1936 Boone, IA
*Dietrich – b 14 Nov 1855 Kolheim, Germany;
    d 14 Aug 1941 Boone, IA
*Adelheid – b 05 Feb 1858 Kolheim, Germany;
    d 16 May 1910 Boone, IA
*Herman – b 23 Feb 1862 Kolheim, Germany,
    d 03 Jan 1917 Boone, IA
*Katherine – b 13 Oct 1864 Kolheim, Germany;
    d 15 Oct 1953 Boone, IA

Elizabeth Louise GRABAU d/o Louise Caroline Marie nee Moeller & Christopher Dietrich Grabau; b 25 Jan 1918 Boone, IA; m 15 Jul 1942 Des Moines, IA to Vernon Wickstrom (b 09 Jan 1907 Boone, IA, d 19 Jan 1974 ae67y 10d Boone,IA bur Linwood Park Cem Boone, IA) s/o Nels Wickstrom & Anna nee Erickson.

Harold Walter Adam GRABAU s/o Louise Caroline Marie nee Moeller & Christopher Dietrich Grabau; b 10 Sept 1916 Boone, IA; Farmer; m 10 Jun 1942 St.Joseph, MO to Arlene Silvey (b 26 Jul 1921 Boone, IA) d/o Fred Silvey & Florence nee Brandt. Child:
    Carol Renea – b 02 Mar 1952 Boone, IA;
        m 02 Aug 1975 Dennis Leroy Hamman

*Heinrich GRABAU s/o Hinrich & Tibke Grabau; b ND, d 12 Apr 1753; m 13 Oct 1694 Otterstedt, Germany to Margaret Blomen (b 10 Nov 1675, d 17 Feb 1717 Otterstedt, Germany). Children:
    Tibke – NFR
    *Claus – b 1694 Otterstedt, Germany; d 25 Sept 1761
        Dipshorn, Germany; m 28 Nov 1726 Anneke Westermann
    Heinrich – NFR
    Otrav – NFR
    Didrich Wilhelm – NFR
    Tibcke – NFR
    Heinrich – NFR

*Heinrich Claus GRABAU s/o Dietrich Grabau & Adelheid (Ollie) Kathryn nee Hasstedt; b 23 Oct 1852 Kolheim, Germany, d 09 Jul 1936 Linwood Cem Boone, IA; m 30 Apr 1877 Boone IA to Minna Dehn (b 13 Jan 1862 Luneberg, Germany, d 03 Aug 1935 Boone Co.IA). Children:
    Anna – NFR
    Frederich Henry – b 1877, d 1945
    Chistopher Dietrich – b 1881, d 1948
    Wilhelmina Marie Meta – b 1884, d 1957
    Heinrich (Henry) Claus Martin JR. – b 1886, d 1946
    Herman George – b 1892, d 1961;
        m 16 Sept 1914 Hilda Christina Claussen
    Walter Martin – b 1893, d 1944

*Herman GRABAU JR. s/o Claus Heinrich (Henry) Grabau & Margaretha nee Mair Moris; b 28 Oct 1877 Kolheim, Germany, d 04 May 1939 ae61y 6m 6d Cedar Rapids, IA bur 06 May 1939 CdrMem; Occupation: Blacksmith; m 18 Sept 1901 Atkins, IA to Marie Michel (b 21 Aug 1877 Fremont Twp Benton Co IA d 12 Mar 1963 ae85y 6m 19d Cedar Rapids, IA bur 15 Mar 1963 CdrMem) d/o Johann Heinrich (Henry) Adam Michel & Anna Elisabeth Geitz. Children:
    Arthur Charles – b 30 Nov 1902 Boone, IA d 20 Mar 1975
        Cedar Rapids, IA; 1st m 20 Nov 1926 Hilda Gertrude Schirm;
        2nd m 23 Mar 1955 Mary E. nee Salerno Starbuck
    Ruth Katherine – b 19 Apr 1912, d 2001

Jeffrey Neal GRABAU s/o Dale Allan Grabau & Lois Nell nee Austin; b 23 Jun 1959 Rock Island, IL; 1st m 10 Jul 1982 Rajean A. German (b 09 Nov 1960). Child:
    Jeffrey Allan – b 1984
2nd m 26 May 1990 Rock Island, IL Jeffrey Neal Grabau to Catherine Ann Columbia Goodall (b 03 Oct 1963).

Jill Crisann GRABAU d/o Leonard Morris Grabau & Norma Jean Robertson; b 26 Aug 1969 Linn Co IA; 1st m 23 May 1992 Central City, IA to Gregory Young s/o Don & Dione Young.

*Johann GRABAU s/o Claus Grabau & Anneke nee Westermann; b 16 Feb 1728 Dipshorn, Germany, d 06 Dec 1769 Ostersode, Germany; m 17 Nov 1757 Gesche Huckfeldt (b 28 Jul 1732 Tarmstedt, Germany). Children:

Claus – b 19 Apr 1760 Tarmstedt, Germany
*Johann – b 29 Sept 1761 Ostersode, Germany; d 13 Mar 1832
   Ostersode, Germany;
   m 12 Nov 1786 Hambergen, Germany Catherine (Trine)Otten

*Johann GRABAU s/o Johann Grabau & Gesche nee Huckfeldt; b 29 Sept 1761 Ostersode, Germany, d 13 Mar 1832 ae70y 5m 14d Ostersode, Germany; m 12 Nov 1786 Hambergen, Germany to Catherine (Trine) Otten (b 31 Dec 1766 Ostersode, Germany, d 08 Oct 1815 ae48y 9m 8d Ostersode, Germany) d/o Claus & Tibke Otten. Children:
   Gesche – b 14 Nov 1788 Hambergen, Germany
   Claus – b 15 Oct 1793 Ostersode, Germany; d 16 Jan 1864
      Ostersode, Germany; m 06 Feb 1816 Margarete Schnakenberg
   Johann – b 22 Oct 1795 Ostersode, Germany
   Hinrich – b 15 Jan 1798 Ostersode, Germany
   Titje – b 18 Jul 1801 Ostersode, Germany
   Dirk – b 31 Oct 1803 Ostersode, Germany
   Gerd – b 28 Oct 1807 Ostersode, Germany

Leonard Henry Adam GRABAU s/o Christopher Dietrich Grabau & Louise Caroline Marie nee Moeller; b 07 Feb 1919 Boone, IA d 18 Feb 1987 ae68y 11d Cedar Rapids, IA bur 21 Nov 1987 CdrMem. Occupation: Collins Radio; m 06 Jun 1934 Woodward IA to Ora Lee Noland (b 05 Sept 1910) d/o Morris & Anna Noland. Children:
   Leonard Morris Grabau – b 21 Apr 1935 Boone, IA;
      m 09 Jun 1957 Norma Jean Robertson
   Byron Zane Grabau – b 21 Nov 1937 Boone, IA;
      m 13 Feb 1966 Frances Ellen Sauer

Leonard Morris GRABAU s/o Leonard Henry Adam Grabau & Ora Lee nee Noland; b 21 Apr 1935 Boone, IA Occupation: Quaker Oats Co.; m 09 Jun 1957 Marion, IA to Norma Jean Robertson (b 26 May 1937 Iowa City, IA) d/o James Robertson & Violet nee Wilson. Children:
   Elizabeth Lee Grabau – b 22 Oct 1961 Linn Co IA
   Morris Allen Kite Grabau – b 17 Nov 1962 Linn Co IA;
      m 12 Apr 1962 Linda Jean Kilberger
   Joel Scott Grabau – b 29 Nov 1967 Linn Co IA
   Jill Crisann Grabau – b 26 Aug 1969 Linn Co IA;
      m 23 May 1992 Gregory Young

Maureen Kay GRABAU d/o Christopher Grabau JR. & Gretchen Marie nee Price; b 09 Oct 1944 Boone, IA; m 05 Sept 1964 Boone, IA to Thomas Lightfoot s/o Harold Lightfoot. Children:
    Jeffrey Scott Lightfoot – b 22 Feb 1969 Boone, IA
    Shawn Dietrich Lightfoot – b 26 Aug 1971 Iowa City, IA

*Meta GRABAU d/o Claus Heinrich (Henry) Grabau & Margaretha nee Mair Moris: cf Adam John Michel SR.

Mildred Anne Minnie GRABAU d/o Louise Caroline Marie nee Moeller and Christopher Dietrich Grabau; b 16 Oct 1913 Boone, IA; m 14 Jul 1938 Des Moines, IA to Eugene Koppenhaver (b 27 Nov 1911 Boone, IA) s/o Leon Koppenhaver & Pauline nee Doeder

Morris Allen Kite GRABAU s/o Leonard Morris Grabau & Norma Jean nee Robertson; b 17 Nov 1962 Linn Co IA; m 12 Apr 1986 Cedar Rapids, IA to Linda Jean Kilberger d/o Marvin & Marlene Kilberger.

Scott Allan GRABAU s/o Dale Allan Grabau & Lois Nell nee Austin; b 18 Feb 1953 Rock Island, IL; m 17 Nov 1984 Lynetta Burkhead (b 23 Oct 1953). Children:
    Kimberly Donne – b 1985
    Anthony Scott – b 1987

*Johannes Jacob GRACK s/o Johannes Grack & Anna Katharina nee Möller; b 27 Jan 1744 Altenhaina, Germany, d 14 May 1812 ae68y 3m 17d os Alt Heim ns Altenhaina, Germany; m 17 Jun 1763 Löhlbach Ch to Anna Elisabeth Webelhuth of Grusen, Germany (b 04 Nov 1745, d 13 Apr 1811 ae65y 5m 9d os Alt Heim ns Altenahaina, Germany House #6) d/o Johannes Webelhuth & Anna Elisabeth. Child:
    *Anna Christina – b 24 Feb 1767 os Alt Heim ns
        Altenhaina, Germany; d 11 Jul 1836 ae 69y 4m 17d os Alt Heim
        ns Altenhaina, Germany; m 08 Apr 1785 Löhlbach Ch to
        Johann Justus Fackiner s/o Johannes Fackiner of Dornholzhausen,
        Germany

Alfred GREASER s/o Levi Henry Greaser & Emma nee Mackie; b 1892, d 1955; m 17 Jun 1917 Anna Grace Martin (b 1897, d 1981) d/o Robert E. Martin & Bessie nee O'Wreatha (Scott). Benton Co IA farmers. Children:
    Charlotte – b 1918, d 1985; m to NN Caslavka, Waterloo, IA

Harold – m Edna Johnson, Cedar Rapids IA
Helen – m Myron Walthart, Vinton IA
Ray – m June Biram, Vinton IA
Carl – m Margaret Lindeman

Carl GREASER s/o Alfred Greaser & Anna Grace nee Martin; m Margaret Lindeman. Third generation farming Greaser farm. Children:
Marilyn – m NN Yedlik, children: Sara, Carrie
Janice – m NN Mino, children: Rebecca, Michelle
James – two sons: Daniel, Christy (b 25 Jan 1988)

Charlotte GREASER d/o Alfred Greaser & Anna Grace nee Martin; b 1918, d 1985; m NN Caslavka. Waterloo, IA residence. Children:
Craig Caslavka – NFR
Curtis Caslavka – NFR
Sharon Caslavka- m NN Sicra, children: Steve, Ron
Graydon Caslavka – b 1947, d 1978

Harold GREASER s/o Alfred Greaser & Anna Grace nee Martin; m Edna Johnson. Cedar Rapids, IA residence. Children:
Gary – NFR
Douglas – NFR
Gregg – NFR

Helen GREASER d/o Alfred Greaser & Anna Grace nee Martin; m Myron Walthart of Vinton, IA. Children:
Linda Walthart – m NN Nannen
Duane Walthart – NFR
Larry Walthart – NFR
David Walthart – NFR
Kimberly Walthart – m NN Frank
Lori Walthart – NFR

*Johann Georg GREASER, b 1791 Hesse-Darmstadt, Germany, d 1881; m Agnesia Kotzenmayer (b 1804, d 1877) and sailed from Bremen, Germany to Baltimore, MD and farmed in Blair Co PA. Eleven children:
*Philip – b 1822, d 1914, m 1847 Elizabeth Dilling
George – NFR
Katherine – NFR
Agnes – NFR

Barbara – NFR
Susan – NFR
Anna – NFR
Elizabeth – NFR
Margaret – NFR
Maria – NFR
John – NFR

Levi Henry GREASER s/o Philip Greaser & Elizabeth nee Dilling; m 20 Mar 1889 Emma Mackie d/o Robert & Mary Mackie. Farmed west of Vinton, IA. Children:
    Idella – b 1890, d 1952
    Alfred – b 1892, d 1855, m Anna Grace Martin
    Lewis – b 1894, d 1967, m Elizabeth Sage

*Philip GREASER s/o Johann Georg Greaser & Agnesia nee Kotzenmayer; b 1822 Ellenbach, Hesse-Darmstadt, Germany, d 1914 IA; 1831 emigrated to USA; settled with family in Blair County, PA; 1st m 1847 Elizabeth Dilling (d 1866) d/o John Dilling & Elizabeth nee Acker. 1851 moved to Iowa, bought farmland near Shellsburg, IA. Children:
    Katherine -NFR
    Maria – NFR
    Agnes – NFR
    George – NFR
    Emma – NFR
    Levi Henry – m Emma Mackie
2nd m Philip Greaser to Susan Miller

Ray GREASER s/o Alfred Greaser & Anna Grace nee Martin; m June Biram. Vinton, IA residence. Children:
    Lisa – NFR
    Lana – NFR

Arno GREENLEAF s/o Vernon Greenleaf & Dorothy nee Happel; b 12 Jun 1947 in CA; m 28 May 1972 Karen A. Rando (b 04 Jul 1951). Children:
    Kenneth Allen – b 19 Feb 1986
    Ashley Lauren – b 21 Mar 1989

Delmar Lewis GREENLEAF s/o Vernon Greenleaf & Dorothy nee Happel; b 27 May 1951 in CA; m 22 Dec 1979 Michelle Whitehead (b 13 Jun

1951). Children:
    Nichole Clara Michelle – b 23 Jun 1981
    Jolle (Adopted) – NFR
    Brian Kettering – b 07 Apr 1983
    Melanie – b 23 Sept 1987

Bruner Lovaire GROFF s/o Calvin Groff & Margaret Lovaire nee Wilson, b 14 Feb 1858 Lancaster, PA; moved to Iowa pro 1880's; d 08 Jun 1933 ae75y 3m 25d, 1610 C Ave NW, Cedar Rapids, IA, bur 11 Jun 1933 Mound Cem Watkins, IA; Newhall Cattle Buyer & Meat Market, 1912-14 Newhall Councilman; 1916-1920 Mayor of Newhall, IA; m 07 Oct 1891 Mary Janette nee Muirhead Tanner (b 20 Sept, 1852 Udina, Kane Co IL, d 01 Mar 1938 ae85y 5m 9d Cedar Rapids, IA bur 03 Mar 1938 Mound Cem, Watkins, IA) d/o George Muirhead & Mary nee Morrison, Plato Center, IL. Raised Granddaughter Enid Muriel Bryner from premature birth 08 Jun 1903 to m 09 Sept 1925 to Walter William August Krug.

*Anna Dorothea GROSS d/o Anna Elisabeth nee Paar & Johann Wilhelm Gross; b 07 Dec 1887, d 27 Jul 1956 ae68y 7m 20d; m Henrich Ritter (b 20 Sept 1888, d 07 Jan 1954 ae65y 3m 18d, Bricklayer. Children:
    Nikolaus Ritter – b 08 Nov 1887, d 1918 [Diptheria]
    Wilhelm Ritter – b 01 May 1916, d Aug 1945 in France;
        m Franziska Eckmuller
    **Helene – b 26 Nov 1919, d 14 May 1999; m Karl Friedrich Hecker,
        Butcher & Landlord

*Maria GROSS d/o Anna Elisabeth nee Paar & Johann Wilhelm Gross; b 24 Jan 1890 Löhlbach, Germany Hse # 106, bpt & con Löhlbach Ch; d 31 Aug 1961 ae71y 7m 7d Löhlbach Hse #33; m 13 Nov 1914 Löhlbach Ch to Johann Peter Beyer (b 21 Apr 1888 Löhlbach, Germany Hse #33 bpt & con Löhlbach Ch; Maurer, d 14 Jan 1975 ae86y 8m 24d Löhlbach Hse #33). Children:
    *Anna Karoline Beyer – b 15 Feb 1915 Löhlbach, Germany; bpt and
        con 1929 Löhlbach Ch; d 20 Dec 1997 Löhlbach, Germany;
        m 10 Mar 1939 Löhlbach Ch to Jakob Wickert
    *Helene Beyer – b 23 Mar 1920 Löhlbach, Germany
    *Heinrik Beyer – m Liesel Homberger

*August Henry GROTE s/o J. Heinrich Grote & Fredricka nee Hille; b 1830 Hanover, Germany, d 1898 Benton Co IA; 1858 emigrated to Davenport,

IA; enlisted in Union Army, served three years during Civil War; m 1864 Rebecca Fry (b 1845 Lehigh Co PA, d 1934) d/o Edward Fry & Paulina nee Reinhardt of Jackson Co IA. 1868 August and Rebecca Grote moved to Benton Co near Van Horne, IA and farmed. Ten children; only six survived:

Sarah – NFR
Henry L. – b 1872, d 1964; m 1896 Emma Dora Werner
Clara – NFR
Harriet – NFR
John – NFR
Emma – NFR

Henry L. GROTE s/o August Henry Grote & Rebecca nee Fry; b 1872, south of Van Horne, IA d 1964; m 1896 Emma Dora Werner (b 1876 Will Co. IL, d 1958) d/o Henry Werner & Christine nee Mausehund. Members Evangelical United Brethren Ch. Farmers. Children:

Carrie – school teacher Davenport, IA
Ralph – b 1898, d 1937; m 1930 Esther McCandless
Ethel – Hospital Dietitian, Oak Park, IL
Lucille – b 1908, d 1978; m 1935 Wayne J. Farmer

Lucille GROTE d/o Henry L. Grote & Emma Dora nee Werner; b 1908, d 1978; m 1935 Wayne J. Farmer (b 1906 Edgewood, IA, d 1978) s/o Willard Farmer & Lettie nee Hockaday. Farmers east of Van Horne, IA. Members United Methodist Ch. Child:

Ann Lucille Farmer – b 1937; m 1959 James E. Sage

Charles GROVERT s/o Henry J. Grovert & Antje nee Luehr; b 1861 Eden Twp Benton Co IA, d 1945; m Elta Broendel (b 1861, d 1930) d/o Hans Broendel & Anna nee Hassee. 1904 retired from farming in Eldorado Twp Benton Co IA, moved to Newhall, IA started a garage and sold Fords and Studebakers. Members Luth Ch. Spent many winters in CA following sport of horseshoes year round. Children:

William Henry – b 09 Dec 1888, d 02 Jul 1970;
    m 03 May 1916 Elfriede C. Werning
Rose A. – b 10 Dec 1890 Eldora Twp Benton Co IA d 16 Jan 1994;
    m 16 Mar 1919 Chris Werning

Dale GROVERT s/o William H. Grovert & Elfriede C. nee Werning; b 1925; Air Force Lieutenant World War II; Data Processing Manager General Motors at Detroit, MI; m to Dortha Stuart d/o Albert Stuart & Anna

nee Garbers Tuttle. Child:
    Stuart Dale – b 1956

Donald C. GROVERT s/o William H. Grovert & Elfriede C. nee Werning; b 30 May 1923 Newhall, IA; Coe College; World War II Infantry in Europe receiving Bronze Star and Croix de Guerre (French Medal of Honor); m 1947 Joan Morr (b 1947 Akron, Ohio) d/o Clarence Morr & Anna nee Zornig. Joan World War II Army Nurse in Phillipines. Donald took over Chevrolet Garage from his father in 1947; active fireman, councilman, American Legion, Commercial Club in Newhall IA. Luth. Celebrated 60th Wedding Anniversary. Children:
    Susan – b 1948; m 1971 Clyde William Much
    William M. – b 1950; m 1971 Linda Padilla
    Patricia – b 1954; m 1986 Michael Creech

George GROVERT s/o Henry J.Grovert & Antje nee Luehr; b 1857 Eden Twp Benton Co IA, d 1934, bur St.John Cem; 1st m 1881 Alvine Broendel (d 1882) 2nd m 1888 Constance Rammelsberg (b 1867, d 1945) d/o Hugo Rammelsberg & Bertha nee Hauschild. Farmers north of Newhall, IA until retiring 1927; Director of Newhall Farmers Telephone Company. Luth. Children:
    Hugo – b 1890, d 1918; m 1916 Eleanor Weed
    Herald Robert – b 1900; m 1927 Florence Young

George Lewis GROVERT s/o Gertrude Mary Christina nee Happel & Maurice Henry Grovert; b 21 Oct 1941 Mercy Hospital Cedar Rapids, IA bpt 07 Dec 1941; m 14 Sept 1969 Pauline Marquardt (b 31 Oct 1946) d/o Herman Marquardt. Children:
    Paul Eugene – b 07 Aug 1971
    Lori Christine – b 06 Apr 1975

*Henry J. GROVERT s/o John Grovert & Wiebke nee Dethlefs; b 1832 Schleswig-Holstein, Germany, d 1920; m 1853 in Germany to Antje Luehr(d 1900 Van Horne, IA). 1854 came to USA to Davenport, IA; 1855 purchased land in Eden Twp Benton Co IA and took possession 1857; retired in 1893 Van Horne, IA; Luth. Children:
    George – b 1857; d 1934; m 1881 Alvina Broendel
    Charles – b 1861; d 1945; m Elta Broendel
    Amelia "Emilie" – b 1863, d 1952;
        m Conrad H. "Cooney" Kerkman JR.

Mary – b 1866, d 1960; m Wilbur Nevin, CA
Mathilda – b 1870, d 1950; m John August Taschner, CA
Henry – b 1873, d 1952; m Louise Rammelsberg

Herald Robert GROVERT s/o George Grovert & Constance nee Rammelsberg; b 1900 Eden Twp Benton Co IA; m 1927 Florence Young (b 1903, d 1997; Public School Teacher) d/o Frank Young & Mathilda nee Kerkman. Herald farmed with his father. The 1936 Iowa State Corn Husking Contest sponsored by Wallace's Farmer was held on Herald's farm in a field of Vinton Hybrid Corn. 1957 retired in Newhall, IA; 1977 celebrated 50th Golden Wedding Anniversary. Children:
Mary Lou – b 1928, d 09 Feb 2007; Never Married
Richard – b 1933; m Marjorie Kaestner

Lola GROVERT d/o William Henry Grovert & Elfriede C. nee Werning; b 1917; m Milton Krumm (b 1912, d 1978 US Army in Europe World War II) s/o Jacob Krumm & Bertha nee Fix. Both graduates Coe College, Cedar Rapids, IA; both teachers Newhall High School 1947-1951. Milton was principal New Hampton High School at time of his death. Child:
Michael Krumm – b 1949; m Melinda Miller, Cedar Rapids, IA

Richard GROVERT s/o Herald Robert Grovert & Florence nee Young; b 1933; m Marjorie Kaestner. Children:
Cathy – m Kevin Kilawee
Jane – m Scott Hagen
Robert – NFR

Rose A. GROVERT d/o Charles Grovert & Elta nee Broendel: cf Chris Werning.

Susan GROVERT d/o Donald C. Grovert & Joan nee Morr; b 1948; Teacher; m 1971 Clyde William Much (b Burlington) s/o Alvin Much & Irene nee Thomas. Newhall, IA residence owning Newhall Lumber and Hardware. Luth. Children:
Nicole Much – b 1972 Rockford, IL
Melissa Much – b 1979 Cedar Rapids, IA

William Henry GROVERT s/o Charles Grovert & Elta nee Broendel: cf Elfriede C. Werning.

William M. GROVERT s/o Donald C. Grovert & Joan nee Morr; b 1950; Arizona State U. graduate; m 1971 Linda Padilla at Phoenix, AZ. Scottsdale, AZ residence. Children:

    Jason – b 1978

    Ashley – b 1982

Donald Dean GRUMMER s/o Wilma Elizabeth Ruth nee Rinderknecht & James William Grummer; b 03 Sept 1943 St.Lukes Hosp Cedar Rapids, IA; US Navy 1968-71; m 17 Feb 1972 Whittier, CA to Pamela Eileen Roberts (b 12 Mar 1949 Whittier, CA) d/o James Andrew Roberts & Eloise Virigina nee Allen. Children:

    Deanna Wreve – b 01 Dec 1975 Fountain Valley, CA

    Bryan James – b 20 May 1977 Fountain Valley, CA

    Colleen Elizabeth – b 15 Nov 1979 Orange, CA

Duane William GRUMMER s/o Wilma Elizabeth Ruth nee Rinderknecht & James William Grummer; b 18 Oct 1946 St.Lukes Hosp Cedar Rapids, IA; m 14 Sept 1968 Ames, IA to Sue Faber (b 15 Jun 1945) d/o Les & Maxine Faber. DVD 1977. Alameda, CA residence.

Gary James GRUMMER s/o Wilma Elizabeth Ruth nee Rinderknecht & James William Grummer; b 22 Feb 1950 St.Lukes Hosp Cedar Rapids, IA; m 10 Jun 1973 Cedarville, IL to Mary Ann Southwick (b 05 Nov 1950 Cedarville, IL) d/o Edwin Southwick & Polly Bethel nee Yeagle. WI residence. Child:

    Ericka Beth – b 01 Jul 1976 Madison, WI; m Chris Page, Dubuque, IA

Alice GUERICKE d/o Alice nee Werning & Arthur Guericke SR.; b 11 Feb 1936; m 29 Jun 1955 John Holzworth (b 12 Dec 1932) s/o Theador Holzworth & Pauline nee Frey. Children:

    Marcia Ann Holzworth – b 30 Jun 1956;

        m 23 Sept 1978 Steven Wayne Schuldt

    Irene Alice Holzworth – b 21 Aug 1958;

        m 16 Apr 1983 Jeffrey Dean Nelson

    Paulette Pauline Holzworth – b 12 Mar 1963;

        m 01 Jun 1985 Roger Oleson

    Todd Theador Holzworth – b 10 Jan 1970

Alma GUERICKE d/o Alice nee Werning & Arthur Guericke SR.; b 17 Nov 1932; m 16 Dec 1956 Roland Presyler (b 12 Oct 1932) s/o Hubert

Presyler (d 28 Sept 1976) & Helen nee Koerner. Children:
    Charlene Alice Presyler – b 05 Oct 1957
    Cynthia Helen Presyler – b 23 Nov 1959

Alvert GUERICKE s/o Walter Guericke; m 13 Oct 1963 Lula Logan. Children:
    Alvert Conrad – b 02 Nov 1962
    Walter Wallace – b 04 Dec 1965

Arthur GUERICKE JR. s/o Alice nee Werning & Arthur Guericke SR.; b 04 Aug 1930; m 17 Feb 1957 Arlene Stoebner (b 20 Oct 1938) d/o Emanuel Stoebner (d 12 May 1973) & Alma nee Renner. Alexandria, SD residence. Children:
    Daniel Mark – b 22 Oct 1957; m 1979 Jane Oberembt
    Douglas Arthur – b 26 Jul 1959
    David Jon – b 30 Sept 1960

Daniel Mark GUERICKE s/o Arthur Guericke & Arlene nee Stoebner; b 22 Oct 1957; Hanson High School; U. of SD; m 27 Oct 1979 Jane Oberembt d/o James Oberembt of Mitchell, SD. Jane graduate Mitchell High School and Stewarts School of Hairstyling. Children:
    Mark Daniel – b 24 Aug 1983
    Laurie Marie – b 19 Nov 1986

Donald GUERICKE s/o Mary nee Werning & Ernest Guericke; b 16 Mar 1940; m 11 Mar 1962 Charlotte Wuetzer (b 08 Dec 1943) d/o Louis Wuetzer & Lillian nee Fischer. Children:
    Steven Don – b 23 Jun 1963; m 14 Mar 1987 Kelli Marie Reisbick,
        Salt Lake City, UT d/o Fredric Reisbick
    Susan Dawn – b 24 Jul 1965; m 12 Apr 1986 Jack Korten, Tabor, SD

Emma GUERICKE d/o Mary nee Werning & Ernest Guericke; b 01 Feb 1926; m 25 Jun 1947 Edmund Rose (b 15 May 1920, d 17 Nov 1983 ae63y 6m 2d) s/o Otto Rose & Bertha nee Drewitz. Children:
    Milton Rose – b 04 Apr 1949; m 07 Jul 1973 Christine Martitz
    Ronald Rose -b 15 Dec 1950; m 03 Apr 1971 Jolene LaDue
    Karen Rose – b 11 Nov 1955; m 1977 Lonnie Bair

Evelyn GUERICKE d/o Mary nee Werning & Ernest Guericke; b 05 Jan 1942; m 26 Dec 1960 Gary Walter (b 12 May 1939) s/o Ferd Walter &

Clara nee Guenther. Children:
    Timothy J. Walter – b 26 Sept 1961
    Tommy Walter – b 15 Apr 1965
    Kristi Walter – b 18 May 1971

Gilbert GUERICKE s/o Alice nee Werning & Arthur Guericke SR.; b 04 Sept 1941; m 18 Jun 1961 Carol Wenzel (b 28 Mar 1942) d/o Herbert Wenzel & Johannes Edna nee Fryer of Parkston, SD. Residence Fort Dodge, IA, and Norcross, GA. Children:
    Micheal Jay – b 14 Jul 1962; m 1985 Beth Ann Harris
    Joalyce Jean – b 13 Nov 1964
    Judson Gilbert – b 01 Apr 1967; m 1988 Michelle Rene Childs
    Heidi Joy – b 03 Dec 1971

Harold GUERICKE s/o Mary nee Werning & Ernest Guericke; b 16 Mar 1940, m 03 Nov 1963 Sharon Gerlach (b 08 Feb 1941) d/o Emil Gerlach & Helen nee Dahlke. Children:
    Brian Lee – b 11 Apr 1965
    Jeffrey Jon – b 23 Nov 1967
    Jamie Allen – b 07 Feb 1973

Judson Gilbert GUERICKE s/o Gilbert Guericke & Carol nee Wenzel; b 01 Apr 1967; m 06 Aug 1988 at Memorial Luth Ch, Ames, IA to Michelle Rene Childs d/o Michael & Diane Childs of Ames, IA.

Lena GUERICKE d/o Alice nee Werning & Arthur Guericke SR.; b 07 Aug 1938; m 07 Dec 1958 Maynard Winter (b 14 Jul 1934) s/o Solomon D. Winter (d 1985) & Theresa nee Uttecht. Children:
    Nancy Jo Winter – b 03 Mar 1960; m 1984 Joseph F. Long
    Connie Sue Winter – b 22 Feb 1961; m 1985 Michael Miller
    TWINS: Jody Lee Winter – b 02 Feb 1965; m 1989 John Voyta
                Julie Lynn Winter – b 02 Feb 1965

Luverne GUERICKE s/o Mary nee Werning & Ernest Guericke; b 01 Nov 1943; m 01 Aug 1986 at Huron, SD to Gloria Pontzer (b 24 May 1958) d/o John & Jean Pontzer of St.Mary, PA. Pierre, SD residence.

Margaret GUERICKE d/o Mary nee Werning & Ernest Guericke; b 06 Oct 1945; m 18 Mar 1977 at West Wood Luth Church, West Wood, KS to John Bartell s/o L.C. Bartell of Niagara Falls, Ontario, Canada. Margaret

graduated Parkston, SD High School. Scotland Honeymoon. Both Trans World Airlines employees. Eugene, OR residence. Children:
Mary Elizabeth Bartell (Adopted) – b 21 Sept 1990
Sarah Jane Bartell (Adopted) – b 06 Sept 1991

Martin GUERICKE s/o Mary nee Werning & Ernest Guericke; b 07 Sept 1928; m 26 Feb 1950 Ladeen Jansen (b 28 May 1930) d/o Henry Jansen & Lena nee Jelsen. Children:
Nancy Ann – b 08 Jun 1956; 1st m 1976 Michael Knudson;
    2nd m 02 Jul 1995 S. Larry Fodor
Martin Dean – b 28 Jan 1958

Michael Jay GUERICKE s/o Gilbert Guericke & Carol nee Wenzel; b 14 Jul 1962, m 15 Jun 1985 at Fort Dodge, IA to Beth Ann Harris d/o Ken Harris of Dayton, IA. Children born at Ramstein Air Force Base, Germany when Michael was US Air Force Lieutenant:
Michael Austin – b 27 Jan 1987 in Germany
Dustin Grey – b 29 May, 1989 in Germany

Nancy Ann GUERICKE d/o Martin Guericke & Ladeen nee Jansen; b 08 Jun 1956; m 15 May 1976 Pomona, CA to Michael Knudson. Children:
Suzanne Elaine Knudson – b 29 Oct 1976
Michael Knudson JR. – b 31 May 1978

**Gerhardt HACKEL s/o Karoline nee Thielemann & Wilhelm Hackel; b 16 Nov 1958 Löhlbach, Germany; m 15 May 1985 Karin Kraushaar (b 07 Feb 1969 Huddingen, Germany). Huddingen, Germany farmers. Children:
**Markus – b 15 Oct 1985
**Stefan – b 10 Feb 1988

**Walter HACKEL s/o Karoline nee Thielemann & Wilhelm Hackel; b 12 Nov 1953 Löhlbach, Germany; Electrical Engineer; m 07 Jun 1980 Doris Berg (b 03 Apr 1953 Medebach, Germany). Children:
**Melanie – b 06 Jun 1977
**Alexander – b 09 Jun 1981

Albert Eberhardt HAERTHER s/o Christian Eberhardt Haerther & Sophia Barbara Rinderknecht; b 07 Feb 1899 Northwest of Atkins, IA, d 08 Jun 1969 ae70y 4m 1d Longmont, CO; m 15 Feb 1922 Caroline Johanna Michel (b 11 Jul 1900, d 03 Jun 1971 ae70y 10m 23dLongmont, CO) d/o

Johannes Heinrich Michel & Anna Elisabeth nee Geitz. Children:
  Marilyn Marie – b 06 Feb 1923; m 14 Jun 1942 William R.Bennett
  Daryl Willard – b 17 Jan 1926; m 23 Jun 1946 Bette Mae Fagin

Barbara Juliann HAERTHER d/o Rev. Martin Johannes Haerther & Adina
Juliann nee Biberdorf; b 03 Apr 1937 Rugby, ND; m 12 Mar 1955 Cavalier,
ND to Herbert "Howard" Adams (b 24 May 1936 Cavalier,ND)
s/o Herbert Carter Adams & Althea Marie nee Robbie. Occupation: Quality
Control, Lipton Tea. Children:
  Marchelle Lynn Adams – b 10 Apr 1955 Cavalier, ND;
    m 24 Sept 1988 Curtis Hins Carleton
  Kent Myron Adams – b 28 Jun 1956 in Cavalier, ND;
    m 21 Jul 1990 Laurie Ann Gish

Barbara June HAERTHER d/o Donald Henry Haerther & Violet June nee
Ronnenberg; b 26 Jan 1960 St.Lukes Hosp Cedar Rapids, IA; Degree 1988
U. of Iowa; Masters of Social Work; m 19 Jun 1982 home place Fremont
Twp sec 22 Benton Co IA to Charles Edward DuMond (b 12 Jul 1959
England: Ryslit Air Force Base; 1981 Central College, Pella IA; PhD
Statistics) s/o Edward Leighton DuMond & Genelle Mae nee Zack of San
Luis Obispo, CA. Child:
  Jennifer Johanna DuMond – b 13 Aug 1986 Mercy Hosp
    Iowa City, IA
  Emily Gabriel DuMond – b 15 May 1993 San Mateo, CA

Bertram William HAERTHER s/o Rev. Martin Johannes Haerther & Adina
Juliann nee Biberdorf; b 10 Feb 1933 Rugby, ND; m 15 Sept 1968 Odgen,
IA to Patricia Ann Lackney (b 16 Mar 1943 Erie, PA) d/o William Edward
Lackney & Gertrude Ilene nee Symeski. Occupation: Insurance; Children:
  Lisa Denise – b 14 Jun 1970 Mt.View, CA
  Stacey Ann – b 23 Mar 1972 Redwood City, CA;
    m 27 May 1995 Valparaiso, IN Scott Mitchell Petcu

Bonnie Lou HAERTHER d/o Roger William Haerther & La Dean Meta nee
Glandorf; (TWIN: Connie Sue Haerther) b 08 Jan 1961 St.Lukes Hosp
Cedar Rapids, IA bpt 05 Feb 1961 & con 23 Mar 1975 St.Steph; 1st m 24
Oct 1981 St.Steph to Steven Lester Rhodes (b 24 Sept 1953) DVD 1996.
Children:
  Joshua John William Rhodes (Adopted 1994) – b 22 Mar 1985
  Lacey Lynn Anna Rhodes (Adopted 1994) – b 30 Mar 1989

2nd m 15 Mar 1997 Jerusalem Luth Ch Wadsworth, OH Bonnie Lou nee Haerther Rhodes to Patrick Michael Thompson (b 17 Feb 1955). Children:

Scott Michael Thompson – b 27 Sept 1983 in Wadsworth, OH
Bryan Lee Thompson – b 03 Sept 1989 St.Lukes Hosp CR, IA
Ross Edward Thompson – b 12 Sept 1997 in Wadsworth, OH

Brian Keith HAERTHER s/o Roger William Haerther & LaDean Meta nee Glandorf; b 19 Apr 1967 (Adopted) Ft.Dodge, IA; bpt 30 Apr 1967 St.Paul Garner, IA & 02 Jul 1967 St.Steph; con 12 Apr 1981 St.Steph; National Guard Service; m 29 Nov 1986 St.Steph to Kelly Jo Schoettmer (b 26 Nov 1968 Vinton, IA bpt 26 Jan 1969 con 14 Dec 1986 St.Steph) d/o Louis John Schoettmer & Vickie Lee nee Craft of Shellsburg, IA. Children:

Nicholas James – b 17 Mar 1987 St.Lukes Hosp Cedar Rapids, IA;
    bpt 26 Apr 1987 St.Steph
Andrew William – b 24 Jul 1992 St.Lukes Hosp Cedar Rapids, IA;
    bpt 23 Aug 1992 St.Steph

Carl George HAERTHER s/o Wilhelm Gottlob Haerther & Gertrude Katharina Maria nee Rinderknecht; b 27 Mar 1902 Lenox Twp Iowa Co So. Norway IA, con 16 Apr 1916 St.Steph; d 15 Mar 1960 Atkins, IA ae57y 11m 16d [Leukemia] bur St.Steph Cem; m 03 Sept 1930 Blairstown, IA to Anna Martha Wendel (b 08 Jan 1906 Canton Twp Benton Co, d 17 Oct 1988 ae82y 9m 9d St.Lukes Hosp Cedar Rapids, IA bur St.Steph Cem) d/o Gus Wendel & Louise nee Krahling. Farmed until 1959 retirement in Atkins, IA. Children:

Mary Louise – b 29 Feb 1936 (Adopted Ft. Dodge, IA);
    m 13 Aug 1960 Rev. Charles Alvin Brehmer
Roger William – b 02 Feb 1938;
    m 12 Jun 1959 LaDean Meta Glandorf

Caroline Mary HAERTHER d/o Elmer August Henry Haerther & Johanna Sylvia nee Beiberdorf; b 25 Nov 1936 Fremont Twp Benton Co; m 30 Nov 1957 St.Steph to Donald Charles Goetz (b 09 Sept 1933 Riverside, IA; Military Reserves; Chemical Engineer) s/o George Joseph Goetz & Clara Mary nee Shradel. Children:

Deborah Joyce Goetz – b 30 Aug 1958 Minneapolis, MN;
    m 21 Jul 1981 Mark Hadden Lugar
Theresa Carol Goetz – b 01 Feb 1960 Minneapolis, MN;
    m Douglas Eugene Miller
Douglas John Goetz – b 15 Jan 1963 Minneapolis MN

Jacqueline Marie Goetz – b 12 Jul 1966 Hartford City, IN;
    m 01 Aug 1990 Thomas Charles Bell, IN

Christ HAERTHER s/o Christian Haerther & Sophie nee Rinderknecht: cf Walter Christian George Haerther.

*Christian Eberhardt HAERTHER s/o Johann Georg Haerther & Wilhelmine Margarethe nee Bernhardt; b 20 Sept 1862 Ehningen, Germany, d 01 Nov 1900 Atkins, IA [Shortly after kicked by a horse] ae38y 1m 12d, bur St.Steph Cem; 1879 came to USA ae17y; Butcher by trade in Germany; farmer in Parkers Grove, IA area; m 24 Mar 1892 Sophia Barbara Rinderknecht (b 14 Mar 1867, d 15 Dec 1936 ae69y 9m 1d, bur St.Steph Cem) d/o Johann Rinderknecht & Barbara Mead. 1896 moved to farm four miles northwest of Atkins, IA. Children:
    Marie Wilhelmina Katherine – b 13 Aug 1893, d 29 Apr 1984;
        m 10 Mar 1918 Albert Frederick Hartman Rinderknecht
    Sophia Christine – b 28 Jan 1895, d 04 Oct 1967;
        1stm 10 Jun 1914 George Fredrick Williams
        2nd m 19 Mar 1940 Arnold George Gafeller
    Henry Fredrick – b 11 Sept 1896, d 17 Mar 1975 Newhall, IA;
        m 02 Jun 1920 Elizabeth Salome Kokemiller
    Albert Eberhardt – b 07 Feb 1899, d 08 Jun 1969 Longmont, CO;
        m 15 Feb 1922 Caroline Johanna Michel
    Walter Christian George – b 22 Jun 1900; d 18 Aug 1990;
        m 22 Feb 1922 Marie Matilda Barbara Fox
2nd m Sophia Barbara nee Rinderknecht Haerther to NN Schnarr.

Christine Wilhelmine HAERTHER d/o Johann Georg Haerther & Margaretha Wilhelmina nee Bernhardt: cf William Wilhelm H. Rinderknecht.

Connie Sue HAERTHER d/o Roger William Haerther & LaDean Meta nee Glandorf; (TWIN: Bonnie Lou Haerther) b 08 Jan 1961 St.Lukes Hosp Cedar Rapids, IA; bpt 05 Feb 1961 & con 23 Mar 1975 St.Steph; 1st m 24 Mar 1990 St.Steph to Allen Lee Wimer (b 30 Dec 1952 Mahaska Co Hosp Oskaloosa, IA; Metal Fabricator 1st m 09 Feb 1972 Barbara Burkes. Children: Becky Lynn Wimer – b 15 Apr 1978 Mercy Hosp Cedar Rapids, IA; m 19 Sept 1998 Steven Lee Harford. Kimberly Ann Wimer – b 09 Jul 1981 St.Lukes Hosp CR, IA) s/o Jerry Alvin Wimer & Eleanor Janet nee Kading, Cedar Rapids, IA. DVD.

2nd m 17 Jun 2006 Cedar Rapids, IA Connie Sue nee Haerther Wimer to Jeffrey Robert McQuistin (b 23 Jul 1956) s/o William & LaVelle McQuistin.

Dale William HAERTHER s/o Herman Wilhelm Haerther & Edna Katherine Elizabeth nee Krug; b 28 Apr 1930 Parent's farm north of Atkins, IA bpt 18 May 1930 St.Steph Sponsors: Grandfathers Wm.G.Haerther & August Krug, con 23 Apr 1943 St.Steph; 1947 Class Atkins High School; US Air Force Greenland, Alaska, TX, FL, Korean Conflict Veteran; m 15 Feb 1959 Salem E.U.B. Ch Cedar Rapids to Jane Ann Gardner(b 30 Jun 1932 Mercy Hosp Cedar Rapids, bpt 06 Nov 1932 Salem EUB Ch Cedar Rapids, IA con 22 Mar 1964 St.Steph; d 02 Apr 2007 ae74y 9m 4d Mc Allen, TX bur St.Steph Cem) d/o Paul Leroy Gardner & Faye Irene nee Holley. Moved to McAllen,TX. Children:

Paul William (Adopted) – b 03 Jan 1968 Iowa City, IA;
m 18 Apr 1988 Cheryl Jane Lloyd
Holley Catherine (Adopted) – b 17 Jan 1971 Webster Co IA;
bpt 22 Jan 1971 Ft.Dodge, IA

Darlene Elizabeth HAERTHER d/o Henry Fredrick Haerther & Elizabeth Salome nee Kokemiller; b 13 Apr 1921; m 11 Sept 1946 Arthur Carl Koering (b 28 Apr 1919). Children:

James Arthur Koering – b 27 Jul 1947; m 03 Oct 1970 Sally Hass
Lester H. Koering – b 09 Jun 1949;
m 12 Aug 1978 Kathy Marie Anderson
Jeffrey Allen Koering – b 11 Jan 1951;
m 14 Mar 1980 Kathleen Marie Oehler

Daryl Willard HAERTHER s/o Albert Eberhardt Haerther & Caroline Johanna nee Michel; b 17 Jan 1926; m 23 Jun 1946 Bette Mae Fagin (b 11 May 1925). Children:

Susan Lynn – b 30 Jan 1948;
m 24 Mar 1968 Loren (Lonnie) Leslie Losh (b 27 May 1946)
Children: Christopher Losh (b 28 Sept 1968);
Jeffrey Losh (b 08 Dec 1970)
Linda Jean – b 12 Apr 1949; 1st m 26 Jul 1969 David Bloomquist
DVD; Children: Travis Bloomquist (b 11 Jul 1970);
Jessica Bloomquist (b 17 Feb 1972); Jonathan Bloomquist
(b 30 Apr 1978)
2nd m 10 Jan 1993 George Lowell Huffman

Carol Ann – b 07 Dec 1950;
    m 16 Sept 1979 Russell Atha III (b 22 Aug 1949)

Dean William HAERTHER s/o Glenn August Haerther & Mary Caroline nee Long; b 19 May 1966 St.Lukes Hosp Cedar Rapids, IA; bpt 10 Jul 1966 & con St.Steph; m 08 Mar 1992 St.Steph to Kelli Kathleen Kline (b 07 Apr 1964 Burlington Medical Center, Burlington, IA) d/o Hubert Husted Kline & Ada Jean nee McClure. Occupation: Computer Repair; Trucking; Farming. Children:
    Zachary Dean – b 12 Feb 1996 Mercy Hosp Cedar Rapids, IA;
        bpt 07 Jul 1996 St.Steph
    Benjamin Kline – b 26 Aug 1997 Mercy Hosp Cedar Rapids, IA;
        bpt 19 Sept 1997 TrinCR

Debra Sue HAERTHER d/o LeRoy Herman Haerther & Susan Betty nee Schaer; b 01 Oct 1962 South Shore, Chicago, IL; m 09 Sept 1989 St.Paul Luth Ch, Boca Raton, FL to Richard Leslie Lee (b 19 Nov 1960 Lincoln Park, MI) s/o Jack Swaney Lee & Ruby Ann nee Brund. Occupation: IBM. Children:
    Alex Jordan Lee – b 07 Mar 1992, FL
    Suzanne Nicole Lee – b 16 Jan 1996, FL

Dennis Glenn HAERTHER s/o Glenn August Haerther & Mary Caroline nee Long; b 21 Aug 1964 St.Lukes Hosp. Cedar Rapids, IA bpt 27 Sept 1964 St.Steph con 19 Mar 1978 St.Steph; Central Luth School Class 1978; Benton Community School Class 1982; m 19 Jul 1986 St.Steph to Kerrie Sue Kruse (b 01 Dec 1962 St.Lukes Hosp Cedar Rapids, IA) d/o Richard Wayne Kruse & Bonnie Jean nee Hamman. Farmer/Trucking. Children:
    Jessica Kay – b 25 Oct 1987 St.Lukes Hosp Cedar Rapids, IA;
        bpt 15 Nov 1987 St.Steph
    Brittanie Jean – b 15 Oct 1990 Mercy Hosp Cedar Rapids, IA;
        bpt 04 Nov 1990 St.Steph
    Joshua Dennis – b 22 Jun 1998 Mercy Hosp Cedar Rapids, IA;
        bpt 08 Jul 1998 St.Steph

Diane Lynn HAERTHER d/o Lester William Haerther & Irene Mae nee Pingel; b 26 Sept 1950; m 12 Aug 1972 Charles Richard Haynor (b 02 May 1972). Children:
    Benjamin Charles Haynor – b 28 May 1978
    John William Haynor – b 21 Mar 1981

Nathan David Haynor – b 29 Dec 1983

Donald Henry HAERTHER s/o George Jacob Haerther & Edna Katharina Magdalena nee Schminke; b 11 Apr 1932 Fremont Twp Sec 22 Benton Co IA, bpt and con 1945 St.Steph; 1949 Class Atkins High School; US Army Korean Conflict; d 06 Feb 1974 [Farm Accident] ae41y 9m 17d, bur St.Steph Cem; m 01 Sept 1956 TrinCR to Violet June Ronnenberg (b 20 Mar 1934 Cedar Rapids, IA d 08 Sept 1986 ae52y 5m 19d Cedar Rapids, IA bur St.Steph Cem) d/o William Charles Ronnenberg & Adelia Ruth nee Ward. Farmed (milked cows) his father's farm southwest of Atkins, IA. Children:

    Kristina Lynn – b 10 Oct 1957 St.Lukes Hosp Cedar Rapids, IA;
        m 09 Oct 1976 David James Carte
    William Donald – b 03 Sept 1958 St.Lukes Hosp Cedar Rapids, IA;
        1st m 07 Jul 1979 Susan Margarite Wooten DVD
        2nd m 02 Mar 1991 Pamela Kay Randall
    Barbara June – b 26 Jan 1960 St.Lukes Hosp Cedar Rapids, IA;
        m 19 Jun 1982 Charles Edward DuMond
    Linda Jean – b 12 Jul 1961 St.Lukes Hosp Cedar Rapids, IA;
        m 06 Aug 1983 Kevin John Leaven

Dorothy Mae HAERTHER d/o Paul Julius Haerther & Erma Magdalene nee Schminke; b 25 Mar 1936; m 26 Jun 1965 Rudolf Ludwig (b 27 Feb 1937). Residence Roselle, IL. Children:
    Thomas Richard Ludwig – b 03 Oct 1966;
        m 26 Nov 1994 Michelle Bauer (b 13 Nov 1973)
    Susan Marie Ludwig – b 01 Sept 1969 Rock Island, IL residence

Dorothy Kay HAERTHER d/o Marilyn Marie nee Haerther & William R. Bennett; b 27 Apr 1945 Excelsior Springs, MO; m 14 Jun 1967 Kansas City, MO to Robert Ritter (b 02 Dec 1943). Children:
    Lisa Marie Ritter – b 20 Nov 1969; 1st m 09 Nov 1996 Steven Werner
        (d 26 Jan 1998); 2nd m 02 Jan 1999 Jeffery Alan Delaney
    Shelby Lynn Ritter – b 05 Aug 1972; m 14 Feb 1997 Joseph Neil Peck

Duane John HAERTHER s/o Walter Christian George Haerther & Marie Matilda Barbara nee Fox; b 28 Apr 1929; m 03 Aug 1957 Marquerite Ann Christensen (b 03 May 1933). Children:
    Christopher John – b 08 May 1962, d 28 Mar 1967
    Patricia Jane – b 13 Jul 1966; m 16 Sept 1989 Mark Allen Crogham

Kathryn Ruth – b 13 Apr 1969;
    m 31 Jul 1993 Charles Robert Kreikemeir

Elmer August Heinrich HAERTHER s/o Wilhelm Gottlob Haerther & Gertrude Katharina Maria nee Rinderknecht; b 23 Oct 1910 NW Atkins, Fremont Twp Benton Co IA, d 11 Mar 1975 Cedar Rapids, IA ae64y 4m 15d bur St.Steph Cem; m 01 Sept 1935 Emmanuel Ch Willow City, ND to Johanna Sylvia Biberdorf(b 16 Aug 1912 Willow City, ND, d 15 Dec 1992 ae89y 3m 15d Cary, NC bur 19 Dec 1992 St.Steph Cem) d/o John G. Biberdorf & Mary nee Hehn. Farmed near Atkins, IA and actioneered; retired 1960 in Atkins. Children:
    Caroline Mary – b 25 Nov 1936 Fremont Twp Benton Co IA;
        m 30 Nov 1957 Donald Charles Goetz, IN
    Joyce Gertrude – b 13 May 1941 St.Lukes Hosp Cedar Rapids, IA;
        m 28 Dec 1968 Shrikant Kulkarni, TN

Emma Gertrud HAERTHER d/o Henry August Gottlieb Haerther & Marie (Mary) Dorothea nee Schanbacher: cf Henry Carl Rathje.

Esther Wilhelmine HAERTHER d/o Heinrich(Henry) August Gottlieb Haerther & Mary Dorothea nee Schanbacher; b 28 Dec 1914 Fremont Twp Benton Co IA, d 10 Oct 2003 ae88y 9m 12d; m 15 Jan 1938 St.Steph to Marvin Adam Moeller (b 21 Nov 1910, d 26 Aug 1996 Boone, IA bur Linwood Park Cem Boone, IA). Children:
    Janet Carol Moeller – b 07 Apr 1939 Boone, IA;
        m 21 Dec 1958 Myron Wilson Hasstedt
    David Lee Moeller – b 12 Aug 1943 Boone, IA;
        m 20 Jun 1970 Boone, IA to Kim Tran Thi Xe

George Jacob HAERTHER s/o Henry August Gottlieb Haerther & Marie (Mary) Dorothea nee Schanbacher; b 23 May 1900 Lennox Twp Iowa Co IA d 04 May 1983 ae82y 11m 11d Luth Home Vinton, IA bur St.Steph Cem; m 26 May 1927 St.Steph to Edna Katharina Magdalena Schminke(b 03 Apr 1905 Fremont Twp Benton Co IA bpt 40 Apr 1905 con 24 Mar 1919, d 02 Oct 1988 ae83y 6m Atkins, IA bur St.Steph Cem) d/o August Heinrich (Henry) George Schminke & Elisabeth "Lizzie" Katharina Anna nee Rinderknecht. Farmed two miles southwest Atkins, IA; insurance sales until retiring 1957 in Atkins, IA. Children:
    Kathryn Marie – b 14 Dec 1929 Fremont Twp Benton Co IA;
        m 28 Nov 1953 Warren Walter Waterman

Donald Henry – b 11 Apr 1932 Fremont Twp Benton Co IA;
d 06 Feb 1974 bur St.Steph Cem;
m 01 Sept 1956 Violet June Ronnenberg

Geraldine Edna HAERTHER d/o Herman Wilhelm Haerther & Edna Katherine Elizabeth nee Krug; b 24 Jul 1941 Fremont Twp Benton Co IA, bpt 24 Aug 1941 at home, con St.Steph; m 14 Aug 1965 St. Steph to Kay Louis Lenaburg(b 14 Jun 1941 Van Horne, IA US Army 3 years TX & Germany) s/o Edward Theodore Lenaburg & Alma nee Schliemann. Cedar Rapids residence. Children:

Craig Louis Lenaburg- b 16 Sept 1966 St.Lukes Hosp CR, IA;
m 08 Aug 1992 Marie R. King
Keith Louis Lenaburg – b 31 Oct 1968 St.Lukes Hosp CR, IA;
m 18 Aug 2001 Zay Christine Rugland

Glenn August HAERTHER s/o Herman Wilhelm Haerther & Edna Katherine Elizabeth nee Krug; b 04 Apr 1933 Fremont Twp Benton Co IA, bpt 29 Apr 1933 at home, con 14 Apr 1946 St.Steph; 1950 Class Atkins High School; US Army Veteran, d 07 Jan 2007 ae74y 9m 3d bur St.Steph Cem; m 05 Aug 1962 TrinCR to Mary Caroline Long (b 14 Oct 1938 Mercy Hosp Cedar Rapids, IA; con 17 May 1964 St.Steph; d 04 Jul 2006 ae67y 8m 20d bur St.Steph Cem; Teacher) d/o Emerson Clayton Long & Georgia Pauline nee Louvar of Cedar Rapids. Glenn farmed his father's farm, sold hybrid seed corn and did custom corn shelling, tiling, backhoeing, combining. Luth. Children:

Dennis Glenn – b 21 Aug 1964 St.Lukes Hosp Cedar Rapids, IA;
m 19 Jul 1986 Kerrie Sue Kruse
Dean William – b 19 May 1966 St.Lukes Hosp Cedar Rapids, IA;
m 08 Mar 1992 Kelli Kathleen Kline

Gloria Susan HAERTHER d/o Rev. Martin Johannes Haerther & Adina Juliann nee Biberdorf; b 11 Dec 1942 Jamestown, North Dakota; m 02 Sept 1976 Mill Valley, CA to Richard Jule Cavanaugh (his 2nd m; b 10 Oct 1944 Center Fall, RI; US Air Force 1963-67) s/o Richard Jule Cavanaugh & Doris nee Murphy. Child:
STEPDAUGHTER:
Lori Jeanne Cavanaugh- b 18 Jun 1972, Wellsley, MA

*Heinrich (Henry) August Gottlieb HAERTHER s/o Johann Georg Haerther & Wilhelmine Margarethe nee Bernhardt; b 05 May 1874

Ehningen, Germany, d 20 May 1945 ae71y 15d Atkins, IA bur St.Steph Cem; came to America ae9y with his family to live on farm four miles south of Norway, IA; m 15 Oct 1896 Norway, IA to Marie (Mary) Dorothea Schanbacher (b 01 Mar 1876 Boebblingen, Wittenberg, Germany, d 13 Nov 1965 ae89y 8m 12d Atkins, IA bur St.Steph Cem) d/o Jacob Schanbacher & Maria M. nee Keller. 1911 moved to farm southwest of Atkins, IA; 1929 retired to Atkins where Henry was Mayor two terms. Children:

Marie Heinrike – b 05 Aug 1897 Lenox Twp Iowa Co Norway, IA;
    d 14 Sept 1916 Atkins, IA bur St.Steph Cem;
George Jacob – b 23 May 1900 Lenox Twp Iowa Co Norway, IA;
    d 04 May 1983 Atkins, IA bur St.Steph Cem;
    m 26 May 1927 Edna Katherine Magdalene Schminke
Christ William – b 05 Jan 1902 Lenox Twp Iowa Co Norway IA;
    d 10 Mar 1952 Atkins, IA bur St.Steph Cem; Never Married
Paul Julius – b 08 Sept 1904 Lenox Twp Iowa Co Norway, IA;
    d 01 Feb 1972 Atkins, IA bur St.Steph Cem;
    m 30 Jan 1929 Erma Magdalena Schminke
Emma Gertrude – b 06 Dec 1906 Lenox Twp Iowa Co Norway, IA;
    d 27 Oct 1977 Cedar Rapids, IA bur CdrMem;
    m 10 Feb 1929 Henry Carl Rathje
Louise Martha – b 10 Dec 1910 Lenox Twp Iowa Co Norway, IA;
    d 27 Feb 1944 Atkins, IA bur St.Steph Cem;
    m 19 Jan 1936 Walter Behrens
Esther Wilhelmine – b 28 Dec 1914 Fremont Twp Benton Co IA;
    d 10 Oct 2004; m 15 Jan 1938 Marvin Adam Moeller

Heinrika Louise HAERTHER d/o Johann Georg Haerther & Wilhelmine Margarethe nee Bernhardt: cf Louise Heinrika "Ricke" Haerther.

Henry Fredrick HAERTHER s/o Christian Eberhardt Haerther & Sophia Barbara nee Rinderknecht; b 11 Sept 1896 Farm northwest of Atkins, IA, d 17 Mar 1975 Newhall, IA ae79y 2m 6d bur St.John Cem; m 02 Jun 1920 Elizabeth Salome Kokemiller (b 27 Sept 1896, d 30 Nov 1976 ae 80y 2m 3d Newhall, IA bur St.John Cem). Children:

Darlene Elizabeth – b 13 Apr 1921;
    m 11 Sept 1946 Arthur Carl Koering
Mildred Arlene – b 14 Jul 1922;
    m 07 Apr 1947 Richard Fredrick Homan
Kathryn Adele – b 12 Feb 1927, d 25 Feb 1933
Waldo Henry – b 22 May 1930; m 01 Sept 1951 Shirley Ann Lutz

Herman Wilhelm HAERTHER s/o Wilhelm Gottlob Haerther & Gertrude Katharina Maria nee Rinderknecht; b 10 Jun 1904 Lenox Twp Iowa Co IA south of Norway, IA (Tauf Reg p.132) bpt 10 Jul 1904 and con 24 Mar 1918 St.Steph; d 12 May 1995 Cedar Rapids IA ae90y 11m 29d bur St.Steph Cem; 1st m 20 Jun 1928 St.Steph to his Happel cousin Edna Katharina Elizabeth Krug (b 10 May 1904 Parent's Farm Fremont Twp Benton Co, bpt 12 Jun 1904 and con 24 Mar 1918 St.Steph d 14 Dec 1969 ae65y 7m 4d Cedar Rapids, IA [Heart Failure] bur St.Steph Cem) d/o John August Henry Krug & Elizabeth Jeanette nee Happel. Herman Wilhelm Haerther's Great-Grandparents Andreas (Andrew) Happel & Maria (Marie) Elisabeth nee Mo (e)ller; Edna Katherina Elizabeth Krug's Great-Grandparents: Andreas (Andrew) Happel & Maria (Marie) Elisabeth nee Mo(e)ller. Farmers one-half miles northwest of Atkins 1928-1962 until retiring in Atkins, IA. Children all born on the farm NW of Atkins, Fremont Twp Benton Co IA.:

Dale William – b 28 Apr 1930 Fremont Twp Benton Co IA;
    m 15 Feb 1959 Jane Ann Gardner
Glenn August – b 04 Apr 1933 Fremont Twp Benton Co IA
    d 07 Jan 2007 his farm home;
    m 05 Aug 1962 Mary Caroline Long
Leroy Herman – b 28 Jul 1935 Fremont Twp Benton Co IA;
    m 25 Nov 1961 Susan Betty Schear
Geraldine Edna – b 24 Jul 1941 Fremont Twp Benton Co IA;
    m 14 Aug 1965 Kay Louis Lenaburg
Norma Jean – b 13 Mar 1943 Fremont Twp Benton Co IA;
    m 10 July 1965 Grant Louis Voth

2nd m 01 Sept 1974 St.Steph Herman Wilhelm Haerther to Gaythel Edna nee Howard Loberg (b 23 Dec 1913 Thornburg, Arkansas, d 30 Sept 2006 ae92y 9m 7d Mason City, IA bur Silver Lake Cem, Norwood, IA). Atkins, IA residence.

*Johan Conrad HAERTHER s/o Joseph Fredrick & Christine Catherine nee Bek; b 09 Dec 1799 Germany, d 03 Nov 1854 ae54y 10m 25d Germany; m 03 Nov 1829 Germany to Eva Catherine Klein (b 18 Oct 1796 Germany, d 09 Mar 1862 ae65y 4m 20d Germany). Children:

TWINS: Johamer – b 29 Oct 1830 Germany, d 16 Nov 1830 Germany
        Christine Catherine – b 29 Oct 1830, d 02 Nov 1830
Eva Marie – b 25 Dec 1831 Germany, d 06 Jan 1832 Germany
John Frederick – b 22 Apr 1833 Germany, d 03 May 1833 Germany

Gottfried Wilhelm – b 26 Sept 1834 Germany, d 13 Oct 1834
*Johann Georg – b 30 Apr 1837 Germany, d 17 Jan 1919 Atkins, IA;
   m 22 May 1859 Germany Wilhemine Margarethe Bernhardt

*Johann Georg HAERTHER s/o Johan Conrad Haerther & Eva Catherine nee Klein; b 30 Apr 1837 Ehningen, Wuerttenberg, Germany, d 17 Jan 1919 ae81y 8m 18d Atkins,IA bur Norway, IA Lenox (4 miles south Norway); 1883 came to USA settling on farm south of Norway, IA; m 22 May 1859 in Ehningen, Wuerttenberg, Germany to Wilhelmine Margarethe nee Bernhardt (b 06 Nov 1834 Germany, d 12 Dec 1893 ae59y 1m 6d Norway, IA bur Norway, IA Lenox Cem) d/o Georg Bernhardt & Marie Agnes nee Koenig. Four children died in infancy. Johann Georg moved to Atkins, IA in 1907. Five living children:
   Wilhelmine – b & d 20 Apr 1860 Ehningen, Germany
   Wilhelm Heinrike – b 06 May 1861, d 03 Jun 1861
      Ehningen, Germany
   *Christian Eberhardt – b 20 Sept 1862 Ehningen, Germany;
      d 01 Nov 1900 Atkins, IA, bur St.Steph Cem;
      m 24 Mar 1892 Sophia Barbara Rinderknecht
   *Louise Heinrike "Ricke" – b 02 Jul 1864 Ehningen, Germany;
      d 10 Aug 1896, bur near Iowa City, IA;
      m 02 Feb 1887 Jacob Mohr
   Marie Wilhelmine – b 31 May 1866, d 17 Sept 1866 Ehningen
   Mary Luise – b 09 Aug 1867, d 21 Aug 1877 Ehningen, Germany
   *Christine Wilhelmine – b 09 Dec 1869 Ehningen, Germany;
      d 18 Dec 1955 Atkins, IA, bur St.Steph Cem;
      m 15 Oct 1896 (William) Wilhelm H. Rinderknecht
   *Heinrich August Gottlieb – b 05 May 1874 Ehningen, Germany;
      d 20 May 1945 Atkins, IA, bur St.Steph Cem;
      m 15 Oct 1896 Mary Dorothea Schanbacher
   *Wilhelm Gottlob – b 14 Aug 1876 Ehningen, Germany;
      d 09 Nov 1956 Atkins, IA, bur St.Steph Cem;
      m 22 Dec 1898 Gertrude Katharina Maria Rinderknecht

*Joseph Fredrick HAERTHER b 17 Feb 1761 Hassbach, Germany, d 30 Oct 1834 ae73y 8m 13d Germany; 1st m 11 May 1784 Ehningen, Germany to Marie Hounker (d 07 May 1796); 2nd m 21 Nov 1796 Christine Catherine Bek (b 30 Mar 1758 Ehningen, Wuerttenberg, Germany, d 07 Apr 1824 ae66y 8d Germany). Children:
   Johan Fredrick – b 19 Jan 1785 Germany

Marie Katherine – b 20 Jul 1786 Germany
Anna Magdalene – b 08 Jan 1788 Germany
Christine Barbara – b 16 Aug 1790 Germany
*Johan Conrad – b 09 Dec 1799 Germany, d 03 Nov 1854 Germany;
    m 03 Nov 1829 Eva Catherine Klein, Germany
    (Ancestors of Haerthers in Benton Co IA)

Joyce Gertrude HAERTHER d/o Elmer August Henry Haerther & Johanna Sylvia nee Beiberdorf; b 13 May 1941 St.Lukes Hosp.Cedar Rapids, IA; m 28 Dec 1968 St.Steph to Shrikant Vishnu Kulkarni (b 25 Mar 1937 Nagpur, India; Occupation: Chemist) s/o Vishnu Kulkarni & Sushila nee Chorghade. Children:
    Kimberly Kumud Kulkarni – b 04 Sept 1970 Ottawa, Canada;
        m 05 Aug 1995 John Bernard Morch III
        (b 01 Apr 1970 Milwaukie,WI) Cary, NC
        s/o John Bernard Morch II & Mary nee Casey
    Sonya Carol Kulkarni – b 06 Sept 1974 Chicago, IL;
        m 24 Apr 1999 David Owen Miller (b 02 Feb 1973 PA) in
        Cary, NC s/o Ralph & Shelia Miller

Kathryn Marie HAERTHER d/o George Jacob Haerther & Edna Katharina Magdalena nee Schminke; b 14 Dec 1930 Fremont Twp Benton Co IA; bpt and con 1943 St.Steph; 1947 Class Atkins High School; m 28 Nov 1953 St.Steph to Warren Walter Waterman (b 23 Dec 1922 Palo, IA; 1943-1946 Combat Engineers-Okinawa, d 23 Oct 2000 ae78y 10m bur St.Steph Cem) s/o Walter George Waterman & Alice Martha Sophia nee Kramer. Waterman Oil Company; Atkins, IA residence. Children:
    James Warren Waterman – b 02 Jun 1956 St.Lukes Hosp CR, IA.;
        m 03 Aug 1985 Loretta Jo Benson
    Kathy Ann Waterman – b 05 Dec 1957 St.Lukes Hosp CR, IA;
        m 21 Jul 1979 Gorden Lewis Jacobsen
    Karen Sue Waterman – b 31 Dec 1959 St.Lukes Hosp CR, IA;
        m 18 Nov 1989 Thomas Joseph Timmerman

Kristina Lynn HAERTHER d/o Donald Henry Haerther & Violet June nee Ronnenberg; b 10 Oct 1957 St.Lukes Hosp Cedar Rapids, IA; m 09 Oct 1976 St.Steph to David James Carte (b 26 Nov 1956 St.Lukes Hosp Cedar Rapids, IA) s/o Clifford Eugene Carte & Lela Jean nee Knight. Children:
    Sara Lynn Carte – b 16 Apr 1976 St.Lukes Hosp Cedar Rapids, IA
        Child: Marcial James Carte (b 22 Jun 1998)

Douglas Donald Carte – b 17 Aug 1982 St.Lukes Hosp CR, IA
m 19 Nov 2000 Tara Jean Shaw DVD. Children:
Payton Alexander West (b 14 Jun 1996);
Adrianna Katherine Carte (b 18 Feb 2001)

Leroy Herman HAERTHER s/o Herman Wilhelm Haerther & Edna Katherine Elizabeth nee Krug; b 28 Jul 1935 Fremont Twp Benton Co IA, bpt 18 Aug 1935 St.Steph, con St.Steph, Class 1953 Atkins High School; m 25 Nov 1961 Roseland Ev. Mission Ch Chicago, IL to Susan Betty Schaer (b 27 Jun 1941 Illinois Central: Chicago, IL) d/o Gerald Richard Schaer & Lillian Elizabeth nee Hendrickson. Boca Raton, FL residence. Children:
Debra Sue – b 01 Oct 1962 South Shore, Chicago, IL;
m 09 Sept 1989 Richard Leslie Lee
Daniel Lee – b 14 May 1966 Evergreen Park, IL;
m 10 Oct 1998 Carolynne Colosimo

Lester William HAERTHER s/o Walter Christian George Haerther & Marie Matilda Barbara nee Fox; b 26 Mar 1923; m 26 Sept 1945 St.Johns Ch, Keystone, IA to Irene Mae Pingel (b 17 Jan 1924) d/o John H.Pingel & Caroline nee Koelle. Children:
Sandra Lee – b 28 Nov 1947; m 10 Jul 1981 Stephen Bruce Siepman
Diane Lynn – b 26 Sept 1950;
m 12 Aug 1972 Charles Richard Haynor
Steve William – b 15 Oct 1953; m 02 May 1982 Susan Glanz Bennett
David Chris – b 25 Dec 1956

Linda Jean HAERTHER d/o Daryl Willard Haerther & Bette Mae nee Fagin; b 12 Apr 1949; 1st m 26 Jul 1969 David Bloomquist (b 22 Apr 1949). Children:
Travis Neal Bloomquist – b 11 Jul 1970
Jessica Jean Bloomquist – b 17 Feb 1972;
m 23 Jul 1994 Leslie Arnold Heywood (b 24 Aug 1969)
Jonathan David Bloomquist – b 30 Apr 1978
2nd m 10 Jan 1993 Linda Jean nee Haerther Bloomquist to George Lowell Huffman (b 02 Feb 1944)

Linda Jean HAERTHER d/o Donald Henry Haerther & Violet June nee Ronnenberg; b 12 Jul 1961 St.Lukes Hosp Cedar Rapids, IA; Graduate Kirkwood Community College, Cedar Rapids, IA; m 06 Aug 1983 St.Steph to Kevin John Leaven (b 20 Dec 1959 People Hosp Independence, IA) s/o

Kenneth John Leaven & Lorene "Flora" nee Andrews. Children:
Joshua John Leaven – b 03 Jan 1984 St.Lukes Hosp CR, IA
TWINS: Kyle Lawrence Leaven – b 02 Mar 1987
    Lucas Donald Leaven- b 02 Mar 1987

*Louise Heinrika "Ricke" HAERTHER d/o Johann George Haerther & Wilhelmine Margaretha nee Bernhardt; b 02 Jul 1864 Ehningen, Germany; d 10 Aug 1896 IA ae32y 1m 8d, bur Iowa City, IA Oakland Cem; m 02 Feb 1887 Jacob Mohr (b 13 May 1860 Germany, d 13 Feb 1899 ae38y 9m bur Iowa City, IA Oakland Cem). Children:
Wilhelmine Heinrike Mohr – b 25 Nov 1887, d 01 Nov 1955;
    bur CdrMem;
    m 30 Apr 1908 August George Johann "Gus" Rinderknecht
William Mohr – b 06 May 1889 Iowa City, IA; d 04 Oct 1889
    Iowa City bur Oakland Cem
Louise Marie Mohr – b 19 Aug 1890, d 28 Jul 1981;
    bur Fullerton, CA; m 24 Nov 1919 William Griswold Gough
Henry Gustave Mohr – b 14 Aug 1892, d 31 Jul 1952;
    bur Evergreen Cem, Vinton, IA;
    m 12 Feb 1918 Anna Katherine Kokemiller
Katherine Ruth Mohr – b 27 Sept 1894, d 20 Apr 1981
    bur St.Steph Cem; m 03 Feb 1920 Roy Carl Jacob Rammelsberg

Louise Martha HAERTHER d/o Henry August Gottlieb Haerther & Mary Dorothea nee Schanbacher; b 10 Dec 1910 Lenox Twp Iowa Co Norway, IA, d 27 Feb 1944 ae33y 2m 17d Atkins, IA bur St.Steph Cem; m 19 Jan 1936 Walter Behrens (b 05 Apr 1905, d 24 Apr 1970 ae65y 9d Williamsburg, IA bur Williamsburg, IA South Section Oak Hill Cem) s/o Claus Behrens & Anna nee Matter. Children:
Mary Lou Behrens – b 17 Feb 1937 Fremont Twp Benton Co IA;
    m 21 Feb 1959 Eugene Felix Doran
William Henry Behrens – b 04 Jun 1940 Fremont Twp Benton Co IA;
    m 31 Dec 1959 Margaret Judith Kapfer
Henry Walter Behrens – b 11 Oct 1943 Fremont Twp Benton Co IA;
    d 15 Jul 1953 Victor, IA bur Victor,IA St.Johns Luth Cem

Mabel Marie HAERTHER d/o Paul Julius Haerther & Erma Magdalena nee Schminke; b 23 Mar 1932 Fremont Twp Benton Co IA, bpt and con 1945 St.Steph, 1949 Class Atkins High School; Bethany Luth College, Mankato, MN; m 02 Aug 1959 St.Steph to Rev. Lawrence Arthur Schmidt, Missouri

Synod Luth Clergyman (b 25 Nov 1932) s/o Theodore H. Schmidt & Marie Karoline nee Steinbronn. Children:
    Lisa Marie Schmidt – b 06 Apr 1963
    Gretchen Ann Schmidt – b 11 Apr 1968
    Julie Kay Schmidt – b 03 Nov 1969;
        m 12 Oct 1996 Davenport IA Craig Alan Dueker

Marie (Minnie) Wilhelmina Katherine HAERTHER d/o Christian Eberhardt Haerther & Sophia Barbara nee Rinderknecht: cf Albert Frederick Hartman Rinderknecht.

Marilyn Haerther d/o Paul Julius Haerther & Erma Magdalena nee Schminke; b 03 Feb 1941; m 18 Feb 1984 John Thiel (b 06 Jun 1943). Chicago, IL residence.

Marilyn Marie HAERTHER d/o Albert Eberhardt Haerther & Caroline Johanna nee Michel; b 06 Feb 1923; m 14 Jun 1942 William R. Bennett (b 21 Nov 1922). Children:
    Dorothy Kay Bennett – b 06 Feb 1945; m 14 Jun 1967 Robert Ritter
    Marcia Diane Bennett – b 28 Oct 1946;
        1st m 18 May 1962 Joseph Fennell;
        2nd m 29 Jun 1980 Ronald Allen Datnauskus;
        3rd m 22 Apr 1995 William J. Carlock
    Gloria Ann Bennett – b 13 Aug 1948;
        m 28 Dec 1968 John Edward Maddox
    Bonnie Jo Bennett – b 08 Apr 1951;
        1st m 16 Nov 1968 Richard Brook Knuckey DVD;
        2nd m 15 Jul 1978 Douglas Leroy Rogers DVD;
        3rd m 09 Jul 1979 Jerry Sickler DVD;
        4th m 23 Jun 1990 Ernest Shippen
    John Mark Bennett – b 16 Aug 1959;
        1st m 27 Sept 1980 Kimberley J. Falkins
        2nd m 23 Jun 1991 Amy Katherine Velasquez, DVD

Rev.Martin Johannes HAERTHER s/o Wilhelm Gottlob Haerther & Gertrude Katharina Maria nee Rinderknecht; b 24 Jun 1906 NW of Atkins, Fremont Twp Benton Co IA (Tauf p.135), d 03 Apr 1977 Kansas City, MO [Lung Cancer] ae70y 9m 10d bur St.Steph Cem; m 03 Jun 1932 Emmanuel Ch Willow City, North Dakota to Adina "Deena" Juliann Beiberdorf (b 16 Mar 1912, d 1971 bur St.Steph Cem) d/o Herman Biberdorf & Hulda nee

Hehn. Children:

    Bertram William – b 10 Feb 1933 Rugby, North Dakota;
        m 15 Sept 1968 Ogden, IA Patricia Ann Lackney
    Barbara Juliann – b 03 Apr 1937 Rugby, North Dakota;
        m 12 Mar 1955 Cavalier, North Dakota to Herbert Howard Adams
    Gloria Susan – b 11 Dec 1942, Jamestown, North Dakota;
        m 02 Sept 1976 CA, to Richard Jule Cavanaugh

Mary Louise HAERTHER d/o Carl George Haerther & Anna Martha nee Wendel; b 29 Feb 1936 (Adopted) Ft. Dodge, IA; bpt & con St.Steph; Graduate Atkins High School; m 13 Aug 1960 St.Step to Rev Charles Alvin Brehmer (b 10 Jun 1937 Minneapolis, MN) s/o Alvin Franz Karl Brehmer & Dorothea nee Meir. Missionary: Luth Bible Translators. Children:

    Juli Hope Brehmer – b 13 Nov 1961 St.Louis, MO;
        m 06 Jun 1992 Rev Jonathon Andrew Blanke
    Charles Robert (Chip) Brehmer – b 07 Oct 1966 Cedar Rapids, IA;
        m 16 May 1992 Graciela Maria Gambetta
    Theodore Alvin Brehmer – b 18 Jun 1972 Jos, Nigeria, Africa;
        d 20 Jun 1972 Jos, Nigeria, Africa
    Jeremy Carl Brehmer – b 05 Sept 1974 Jos, Nigeria, Africa

Mildred Arlene HAERTHER d/o Henry Fredrick Haerther & Elizabeth Salome nee Kokemiller; b 14 Jul 1922; m 07 Apr 1947 Richard Fredrick Homan (b 21 Dec 1924). Children:

    Kathleen Jo Homan – b 13 Jan 1951;
        m 01 Sept 1973 Walter Anton Powers
    Susan Elisabeth Homan – b 05 Sept 1952;
        m 02 Apr 1987 Alberto Cruz
    Cynthia Marie Homan – b 31 Jan 1957;
        m 25 Jun 1977 John Benjamin Jacobs
    Celeste Joyce Homan – b 06 Oct 1958;
        m 04 Oct 1986 Timothy Paul Magnani
    Lynn Adele Homan – b 06 Mar 1961;
        m 02 Sept 1995 John Anthony Mila

Nicole Suzanne HAERTHER d/o William Donald Haerther & Susan Margarite nee Wooten; b 12 Apr 1980 St.Lukes Hosp Cedar Rapids, IA; m 24 Jun 2000 Salem United Methodist Ch Van Horne, IA to David Hofmann of Tama IA s/o Lawrence & Kathleen Hofmann of Tama, IA

Norma Jean HAERTHER d/o Herman Wilhelm Haerther & Edna Katherine Elizabeth nee Krug; b 13 Mar 1943 Fremont Twp Benton Co IA, bpt 09 Apr 1943 St.Steph; m 10 Jul 1965 St.Steph to Grant Louis Voth (b 18 Jan 1943 Red Wing, MN) s/o Marvin Frank Voth & Waldena Helen nee Lemke. Pacific Grove, CA residence. Child:

Sharon Elizabeth Voth – b 20 Mar 1968 Ft.Wayne, IN;
B.A. 1990 Santa Clara University, CA

Patricia Jane HAERTHER d/o Duane John Haerther & Marquerite Ann nee Christensen; b 13 Jul 1966; m 16 Sept 1989 Mark Allen Crogham (b 27 Feb 1961). Child:

Court Christopher Crogham – b 26 Mar 1993

Paul Julius HAERTHER s/o Heinrich (Henry) August Gottlieb Haerther & Marie (Mary) Dorothea nee Schanbacher; b 08 Sept 1904 Iowa Co IA, d 01 Feb 1972 Benton Co IA ae67y 4m 23d, bur St.Steph Cem; moved with parents to Benton Co IA in 1911 and lived on Haerther homestead 61y; m 30 Jan 1929 St.Steph to Erma Magdalene Schminke (b 03 Mar 1909 in ND, d 21 Nov 1992 Atkins, IA ae83y 8m 8d bur St.Steph Cem) d/o Frederick Schminke & Lillie May nee Wieneke. Children:

Mabel Marie – b 23 Mar 1932;
m 02 Aug 1959 Rev. Lawrence Schmidt
Dorothy Mae- b 25 Mar 1936;
m 26 Jun 1965 Rudolf Ludwig, Roselle, IL
Marilyn Erma – b 03 Feb 1941;
m 18 Feb 1984 John Thiel, Chicago, IL

Paul William HAERTHER s/o Dale William Haerther & Jane Ann nee Gardner; b 03 Jan 1968 (Adopted 15 Aug 1968 Luth Home, Ft.Dodge, IA bpt 18 Aug 1968 St.Steph); m 18 Apr 1988 San Benito, TX to Cheryl Jane Lloyd (b 05 Oct 1967 Owensboro, KY) d/o William Edward Lloyd & Nell Jean nee Bassett. Children:

STEPCHILD: James Edward Lloyd – b 25 Jan 1984 Brownsville, TX
Erica Nicole – b 13 Jan 1991 Harlingen, TX
Andrea Faye – b 12 Nov 1996

Rodney Carl HAERTHER s/o Roger William Haerther & LaDean Meta nee Glandorf; b 11 Apr 1968 St.Lukes Hosp Cedar Rapids, IA bpt 12 May 1968 and con 04 Apr 1982 St.Steph; m 04 Apr 1992 Julie Christine Mahoney (b 27 Dec 1968 Cedar Rapids, IA) d/o LeRoy Mahoney & Mary nee

Bellendier. Children:
  Kelsey Ann – b 22 Jul 1993 Mercy Hosp Cedar Rapids, IA
  Timothy Roger – b 26 Jul 1996 Mercy Hosp Cedar Rapids, IA

Roger William HAERTHER s/o Carl George Haerther & Anna Martha nee Wendel; b 02 Feb 1938 Canton Twp Benton Co IA; m 12 Jun 1959 Immanuel Luth Ch, York Twp Williamsburg, IA to LaDean Meta Glandorf (b 28 Nov 1938 York Twp Williamsburg, IA) d/o Arthur Fredrick Glandorf & Johanna Dorthea nee Wardenburg. Farmed Haerther land where Carl lived from 1930 to 1959, six miles northwest of Atkins, IA. Milk Route. Children:
  TWINS: Bonnie Lou – b 08 Jan 1961 St.Lukes Hosp CR, IA;
      1st m 24 Oct 1981 Steven Lester Rhodes, DVD 1996
      2nd m 15 Mar 1997 Patrick Michael Thompson
          Connie Sue – b 08 Jan 1961 St.Lukes Hosp CR, IA;
      1st m 24 Mar 1990 Allen Lee Wimer DVD
      2nd m 17 Jun 2006 Jeffrey Robert McQuistin
  Brian Keith – b 19 Apr 1967 (Adopted) Ft.Dodge, IA;
      m 29 Nov 1986 Kelly Jo Schoettmer
  Rodney Carl – b 11 Apr 1968 St.Lukes Hosp, Cedar Rapids, IA;
      m 04 Apr 1992 Julie Christine Mahoney

Roxanne Elizabeth HAERTHER d/o Waldo Henry Haerther & Shirley Ann nee Lutz; b 28 Apr 1957; m 19 Jun 1976 Gilbert Leathman (b 04 Feb 1954). Children:
  Melissa Beth Leathman – b 10 Nov 1976
  Allison June Leathman – b 12 Aug 1980
  Kristin Ashley Leathman – b 30 Apr 1982

Sandra Lee HAERTHER d/o Lester William Haerther & Irene Mae nee Pingel; b 28 Nov 1947; m 10 Jul 1981 Stephan Bruce Siepman (b 19 Nov 1954). Children:
  Kathleen Marie Siepman – b 07 Aug 1983
  Thomas Stephan Siepman – b 02 Mar 1986

Sophia Christine HAERTHER d/o Christian Eberhardt Haerther & Sophia Barbara nee Rinderknecht; b 28 Jan 1895 Lenox Twp Iowa Co Norway, IA; d 04 Oct 1967 ae72y 8m 6d bur St.Steph Cem; 1st m 10 Jun 1914 St.Steph to George Fredrick Williams (b 08 Sept 1879 Farm 3 miles SW of Atkins, IA; had the tile factory at Atkins; d 03 Apr 1928 ae48y 6m 26d bur St.Steph

Cem) Children:

Eleanor Sophia Wilhelmine Williams – b 13 Jun 1915;
    m 21 Sept 1941 J. Neill Delaat
Vernon Frederick Williams – b 19 Feb 1919, d 30 Jan 1951 Atkins;
    m 25 Jul 1941 Viola Mae Fry
2nd m 19 Mar 1940 Hyde Park Ch, Chicago, IL Sophia Christine nee Haerther Williams to Arnold George Gafeller (b 26 Aug 1891, d 14 Aug 1961 ae69y 11m 19d bur St.Steph Cem)

Steve William HAERTHER s/o Lester William Haerther & Irene Mae nee Pingel. b 15 Oct 1953; m 02 May 1982 Susan Glanz Bennett (b 24 Nov 1954). Children:
    STEPCHILD: Courtney Bennett – b 25 Sept 1975
    Cody Lee – b 14 Jul 1983
    Casey Logan – b 05 Oct 1987

Susan Lynn HAERTHER d/o Daryl Willard Haerther & Bette Mae nee Fagin; b 30 Jan 1948; m 24 Mar 1968 Loren Leslie Losh (b 27 May 1946). Children:
    Christopher Leslie Losh – b 28 Oct 1968
    Jeffrey Alan Losh – b 08 Dec 1969; m 22 Jul 1995 Jennifer Love Bibb

Waldo Henry HAERTHER s/o Henry Fredrick Haerther & Elizabeth Salome nee Kokemiller; b 22 May 1930; m 01 Sept 1951 Shirley Ann Lutz (b 24 Aug 1931). Children:
    Marshall Lee – b 22 Oct 1953
    Richard David – b 23 Dec 1954
    Roxanne Elizabeth – b 28 Apr 1957; m 19 Jun 1976 Gilbert Leathman
    Dale Fredrick – b 12 Apr 1961
    Christopher Henry – b 10 Jul 1966

Walter Christian "Christ" George HAERTHER s/o Christian Haerther & Sophie nee Rinderknecht; b 22 Jun 1900 Benton Co IA, d 18 Aug 1990 ae90y 1m 27d McAllen, TX, bur St.Steph Cem); m 22 Feb 1922 Cedar Rapids, IA to Marie Matilda Barbara Fox (b 10 Aug 1902, d 07 Dec 1989 ae87y 3m 27d bur St.Steph Cem) d/o John & Barbara Fox of Cedar Rapids, IA. Atkins, IA residence; Carpenter with own construction crew. "Snowbirds" in retirement spending part of each year in McAllen, TX. Six children:

Lester William – b 26 Mar 1923;

m 26 Sept 1945 Irene Mae Pingel, Cedar Rapids, IA
Doris Barbara – b 02 Sept 1924, d 04 Nov 1924, bur St.Steph Cem
Dorothy Ann – b & d 02 Jan 1927
Duane John – b 28 Apr 1929 in NE;
 m 03 Aug 1957 Marguerite Ann Christensen
Verda Marie – b 12 Oct 1932; Never Married; Atkins, IA residence
Lois Mae – b 21 Feb 1935, d 25 Jul 1937 bur St.Steph Cem

*Wilhelm Gottlob HAERTHER s/o Johann Georg Haerther & Wilhelmine Margarethe nee Bernhardt; b 14 Aug 1876 Ehningen, Germany, d 09 Nov 1956 Atkins, IA ae80y 2m 25d [Heart Attack] bur St.Steph Cem; 1883 came to Norway, IA; m 22 Dec 1898 St.Steph to Gertrude Katharina Maria Rinderknecht (b 25 Feb 1878 Fremont Twp Benton Co IA, d 16 May 1965 Atkins ae 87y 2m 21d [Heart Attack] bur St.Steph Cem) d/o Karl Rinderknecht & Katharina Elisabeth nee Happel. Moved to Fremont Twp Benton Co IA farm in 1905 three miles northwest of Atkins. Retired in Atkins, IA. Children:
 Margaret Katharina Wilhelmine – b 20 Apr 1900 Lenox Twp Iowa Co
  d 04 Dec 1983 Cedar Rapids, IAS bur St.Steph Cem;
  Never Married; retired in Atkins, IA
 Carl George – b 27 Mar 1902 Lenox Twp Iowa Co Norway IA;
  d 15 Mar 1960 Atkins, IA bur St.Steph Cem;
  m 03 Sept 1930 Anna Martha Wendel
 Herman Wilhelm – b 10 Jun 1904 Lenox Twp Iowa Co Norway, IA;
  d 12 May 1995 Cedar Rapids, bur St.Steph Cem;
  1st m 20 Jun 1928 Edna Katharine Elizabeth Krug;
  2nd m 01 Sept 1974 Gathel Edna nee Howard Loberg
 Rev.Martin Johannes – b 24 Jun 1906 Farm northwest Atkins, IA;
  d 03 Apr 1977 Kansas City, bur St.Steph Cem;
  m 03 Jun 1932 Adina Juliann Biberdorf
 Elmer August Heinrich – b 23 Oct 1910 Farm northwest Atkins, IA;
  d 11 Mar 1975 Cedar Rapids, bur St.Steph Cem;
  m 01 Sept 1935 Johanna Sylvia Biberdorf

William Donald HAERTHER s/o Donald Henry Haerther & Violet June nee Ronnenberg; b 03 Sept 1958 St.Lukes Hosp Cedar Rapids, IA; 1st m 07 Jul 1979 Susan Margarite Wooten (b 12 Mar 1959 Omaha, NE) d/o Carroll Maynard Wooten & Irma nee Walpus. DVD 1984. Child:
 Nicole Suzanne – b 12 Apr 1980 St.Lukes Hosp Cedar Rapids, IA;
  m Jun 2000 David Hofmann

2nd m 02 Mar 1991 St.Steph William Donald Haerther to Pamela Kay Randall (b 13 Aug 1963 Ottumwa, IA; Cosmetology Graduate) d/o Charles Ernest Randall II & Verna Dean nee Lewis, of Marion, IA.

STEPCHILD: Sondra Kay Randall – b 06 Dec 1981 Iowa City, IA
Jordan William – b 30 Apr 1993, St.Lukes Hosp Cedar Rapids, IA
Amber Marie – Stillborn 09 Oct 1995; St.Lukes Hosp
  Cedar Rapids, IA bur St.Steph Cem
Cameron Mitchell – b 16 Sept 1996; St.Lukes Hosp Cedar Rapids, IA

Kathleen Lynn HALL d/o Violette Janette nee Bayer & Roger Eugene Hall; b 11 May 1960 Marengo, IA. Children:
Allison Hall – b 19 Oct 1984 Iowa City, IA
Abbie Nicolyn Hall – b 09 Nov 1988 Iowa City, IA

Kelly Jo HALL d/o Violette Janette nee Bayer & Roger Eugene Hall; b 24 Oct 1988 Cedar Rapids, IA; m 26 Sept 1987 Luth Ch Blairstown, IA to Russell Lee Emanuel (b 24 Oct 1963 Marengo, IA) s/o Larry Emanuel & Bonnie nee Kirby. Child:
Eric Lee Emanuel – b 24 Oct 1963 Marengo, IA

Sherri Lee HALL d/o Violette Janette nee Bayer & Roger Eugene Hall; b 01 Feb 1967 Marengo, IA; m 21 Oct 1989 Paul Stolz. Children:
Hilary Stolz – b 28 Sept 1992
Dakota Stolz – b 08 Jul 1995

Sharon Ann HALWEG d/o Alvera Gertrude nee Happel & Elmer Halweg; b 04 Feb 1942; m 15 Aug 1964 Ronald Jack Abram (b 16 Jun 1939). Children:
Eric Ryan Abram – b 23 Oct 1973
Andrew Timothy Abram – b 07 Dec 1983

Allen HAMANN s/o Harlan Hamann & Lois nee Crombaugh; b 1947; US Navy 1965-1968; m Julie Kramer. Cedar Rapids, IA residence. Children:
Heather – NFR
Bradley – NFR
Eric – NFR

Arthur HAMANN s/o Ferdinand (Fred) Hamann & Alvena nee Schluntz; b 1899, d 1970; m Anna Balhorn (b 1898). Farmed 1921-1946. Children:
Harlan – b 1922; m Lois Crombaugh

Donna Mae – b 1925; m William Malloy

Beverly HAMANN d/o Harlan Hamann & Lois nee Crombaugh; b 1948; m George Gibson, DVD. Beverly's residence Denver, CO. Child:
    Stacee Gibson – NFR

Donna Mae HAMANN d/o Arthur Hamann & Anna nee Balhorn; b 1925; m William Malloy (b 1921). Cedar Rapids, IA residence. Children:
    Dennis Malloy – b 1953; m Julia Martinusen, Des Moines, IA
    Julie Malloy – b 1953; m David Wilkinson, Chicago, IL
    Steve Malloy – b 1956; WA state residence

Edna HAMANN d/o Ferdinand (Fred) Hamann & Alvena nee Schluntz; b 1895, d 1978; m Glen Lang (b 1900, d 1969). CA residence. Children:
    Thomas Lang – NFR
    Patricia Lang – NFR

Ferdinand (Fred) HAMANN s/o William Hamann & Maria nee Nieman; b 1866, d 1929; m Alvena Schluntz. Children:
    William – b 1891, d 1918; m Mabel Shireman
    Elnora Margaret – b 1893, d 1976; m Charles Balhorn
    Edna – b 1895, d 1978; m Glen Lang
    Arthur – b 1899, d 1970; m Anna Balhorn

Harlan HAMANN s/o Arthur Hamann & Anna nee Balhorn; b 1922; m Lois Crombaugh (b 1925). Children:
    Allen – b 1947; m Julie Kramer, Cedar Rapids, IA
    Beverly – b 1948; m George Gibson, Denver, CO
    Janis – b 1952; m William Osterlund, Sioux City, IA
    Lori – b 1954; Nurse, Golden, CO

*William HAMANN b 1883 Mecklenberg, Germany, d 1901 IA; dentist, blacksmith, agriculturist; m in Germany to Maria Nieman (b 1835, d 1913). 1868 emigrated to Scott Co IA; 1869 moved to Benton Co IA. Child:
    Ferdinand (Fred) – b 1866, d 1929; m Alvena Schluntz

Edward R. HANSON s/o Norma L. nee Rammelsberg & Oscar R. Hanson; b 20 Nov 1958; 1st m 25 Sept 1984 Dea Hettinger DVD.
2nd m 21 Apr 1990 Edward R. Hanson to Rhonda Tuttle. Child:
    Jarret Robert – b 28 Jan 1991

Sally Ann HANSON d/o Norma L. nee Rammelsberg & Oscar R. Hanson; b 26 Jan 1956; m 05 Oct 1974 Steve Dale Bruce. Child:
  Jason Robert Bruce – b 17 Nov 1976;
    m 06 Jun 2000 Eric Louise Tompkins
  Stacy Ann Bruce – b 06 Sept 1985

**Uwe HAPPE s/o Willi Happe & Lina nee Hohl(Author's 4th cousin); b 07 Mar 1969 Bad Wildungen, Germany; m 06 Jan 1994 Jolante Kotyezka (b 17 Jun 1966 Gleinitz, Germany). Author met this generation of Krug cousins in Germany in 1999. Children:
  **Vanessa – b 04 Jul 1994 Bad Wildungen, Germany
  **Patrick – b 23 Jan 1996 Bad Wildungen, Germany

Adam Martin Andrew HAPPEL s/o Johann Peter Happel & Katharine Elizabeth nee Werning; b 25 Sept 1875, Farm Fremont Twp Benton Co IA, bpt 16 Oct 1875, d 23 Feb 1933 ae57y 4m 29d [Stroke] at his Vinton, IA home, bur 26 Feb 1933 St.John Cem; m 25 Feb 1902 Katharina Barbara Rinderknecht (b 24 Feb 1882 Eden Twp Benton Co IA, bpt 1882 St.John, d 26 Apr 1983 ae101y 2m 2d Luth Home, Vinton, IA bur 28 Apr 1983 St.John Cem) d/o Chris Rinderknecht & Ann nee Nell. Children:
  Jeanette Anna Elizabeth – b 24 Mar 1903, d 08 Oct 1938;
    m 07 Aug 1929 Rev. Elmer Widmann
  Alfred August Christ – b 17 Dec 1904; d 24 Apr 1994
    m 30 Jun 1936 Margaret Louise Edwards
  Gertrude Mary Christina – b 16 Dec 1906;
    m 22 Feb 1936 Maurice Henry Grovert
  Loreen Marie – b 06 Jun 1910; m 11 Sept 1939 Oakley H. Driscoll
  Ervin Henry John – b 09 Feb 1913;
    m 17 Nov 1946 Dorothy Claire Boeyink
  George Andrew – b 08 Feb 1916, d 21 Jun 1986;
    m 29 Sept 1955 Esther Kaiser (d 18 Aug 1978)
  Fred Martin – b 19 Feb 1924, bpt 25 Feb 1924; d 25 Feb 1924
    bur St.John Cem

Albert C. HAPPEL s/o August A. Happel & Martha nee Young; b 31 May 1908 Linn Co IA, bpt & con St.Steph; d 21 Oct 1959 ae51y 4m 21d bur St.Steph Cem; m St.Steph 15 Jan 1930 Ruth Rickels (b 22 Jul 1907 Rockwell City, IA, d 02 Apr 1990 ae96y 8m 11d Denver, CO Presbyterian Hosp, bur St.Steph Cem) Adopted d/o Rev Gerjansef Rickels and Lena nee

Holstenberg of St.Steph Luth Ch. Farmers and Raleigh Products salesman. After Albert's death Ruth's home in Aurora, CO. Children:

Kenneth – b 22 Dec 1931; m 22 Jul 1951 Donna Zimmerman

James – b 25 Dec 1937; m 07 Nov 1961 Arlene Bader DVD

Alfred August Christ HAPPEL s/o Adam Martin Andrew Happel & Katharina Barbara nee Rinderknecht; b 17 Dec 1904 Eden Twp Benton Co IA, bpt Jan 1905 St.John; Benton County IA Auditor, d 24 Apr 1994 ae89y 4m 7d; m 30 Jun 1936 Margaret Louise Edwards (b 07 Sept 1910 near Brooklyn, Poweshiek Co IA, bpt 1910 Presbyterian Ch, d 05 Jan 2004 ae93y 3m 29d bur Evergreen Cem Vinton IA) d/o David Albert Edwards & Carrie Mae nee Tranter. Vinton, IA residence. Child:

David Edward – b 18 Apr 1939 Mercy Hosp Cedar Rapids, IA;
    bpt 14 May 1939. School Athletic Coach.

Alfred W. HAPPEL s/o Conrad Happel & Anna nee Kreutner; b 11 Oct 1908 Benton Co IA; m 26 Apr 1934 LaVera Hagenow (b 08 Sept 1914 Bremer Co IA). Children:

Rita Jane – b 11 May 1935; m Aug 1957 Virgil Kray

Yvonne Marie – b 01 Jun 1937; m 05 Aug 1956 Glenn Wehrkamp

Charles Conrad – b 29 Sept 1938; m 14 Oct 1961 Jane Miller

Mary Ann – b 17 Jul 1940; m 10 Jun 1962 Hilbert Mixdorf

Donald Alfred – b 08 Mar 1942; m 20 Jun 1965 Donna McDougal

Robert – b 28 Sept 1943; m 10 Jun 1972 Margaret Wood

Richard – b 16 Feb 1950; m 02 Feb 1975 Nancy Hesse

Glenda – b 10 Jan 1952; m 06 Jul 1974 Glen Slack

Cheryl – b 18 Mar 1959; m 06 Oct 1979 Rodney Bergman

Alvera Gertrude HAPPEL d/o Henry George Happel & Hulda Caroline nee Nolting; b 15 Sept 1917; 1st m 14 Aug 1938 Elmer Halweg (b 05 Jan 1913, d 02 May 1948). Child:

Sharon Ann Halweg – b 04 Feb 1942;
    m 15 Aug 1964 Ronald Jack Abram
2nd m 01 Mar 1969 Alvera Gertrude nee Happel Halweg to Cecil William Harvey (b 24 Sept 1909).

*Andreas (Andrew) HAPPEL s/o Johann Peter Happel & Anna Gertrud nee Fackiner; b 27 Mar 1821 os Alt Heim Prussia, ns Altenhaina Germany, bpt 1821 Löhlbach Ch (Godfather: Andreas Möller, Hse #69 Löhlbach) con Löhlbach Ch, d 03 Dec 1895 Atkins, IA ae 74y 8m 6d(Todten reg. p 282) bur St.Steph Cem; Farmer; m Poenitentes 29 May 1843 Löhlbach Ch, Germany to Maria (Marie) Elisabeth Möller (b 08 May 1822 Hse #43 Löhlbach, Germany, bpt 1822 Löhlbach Ch, d 30 Aug 1892 Linn Co IA ae 70y 3m 27d, bur St. Steph Cem) d/o Johannes Möller & Maria Katharina nee Stremme. 1864 emigrated with ten children to America settling on farm in Linn Co IA where they lived until the death of Maria; Andrew made his home in later years with youngest daughter Anna. Children:

*Johann Georg – b 11 Dec 1842 Löhlbach, Germany; d 09 May 1923
Benton Co IA, bur St.Steph Cem;
1st m Jan 1864 Sophia Katharina Elisabeth Rinderknecht;
2nd m 06 Dec 1891 Marie Richter
*Anna Gertrud – b 19 Oct 1844 os Alt Heim ns Altenhaina, Germany;
d 10 Sept 1919 Benton Co IA, bur St.Steph Cem;
m 25 Sept 1866 Friedrich Rinderknecht
*Johann Hartman – b 27 Sept 1846 os Alt Heim, Germany;
d 03 Jun 1925 Benton Co IA, bur St.Steph Cem;
m 24 Jul 1879 Katharina Elisabeth Michel
*Maria Katherina – b 14 Oct 1848 os Alt Heim, Germany;
d 26 Nov 1924 Atkins, IA, bur St.Steph Cem;
m 06 Mar 1869 Friedrich Wilhelm Rinderknecht
*Johann Peter – b 04 Mar 1851 os Alt Heim ns Altenhaina, Germany;
d 13 May 1902 Benton Co IA, bur St.Steph Cem;
m 03 Jul 1874 Katharina Elisabeth Werning
*Anna Katherina – b 04 May 1853 os Alt Heim, Germany;
d 14 Apr 1933 Benton Co IA, bur St.Steph Cem;
m 21 Feb 1872 Karl Rinderknecht
*Johann Heinrich – b 24 Oct 1855 os Alt Heim, Germany;
d 20 Apr 1888 Benton Co IA, bur St.Steph Cem;
m 11 Nov 1881 Anna Gertrud Fels
*August A. – b 21 Feb 1859 os Alt Heim ns Altenhaina, Germany;
d 28 Jun 1921 Benton Co IA, bur St.Steph Cem;
m 12 Feb 1888 Martha Young
*Anna Elisabeth – b 01 Nov 1861 os Alt Heim, Germany;
d 15 May 1939; m 01 Nov 1881 Rev Fred Ehlers
*Anna Katherina – b 21 Jan 1864 os Alt Heim, Germany;
d 28 Jul 1947 Benton Co IA, bur St.Steph Cem;
m 12 Feb 1888 George Rinderknecht JR.
Unnamed Boy – b & d Linn Co IA

Andrew John (Johann George Andrew) HAPPEL s/o Johann Heinrich

Happel & Anna Gertrud nee Fels; b 02 Aug 1882 Fremont Twp Benton Co IA, bpt 1882 St.Steph; d 27 Jun 1948 ae65y 10m 25d Bremer Co IA, bur 30 Jun 1948 Harlington Cem, Waverly, Bremer Co IA; m 19 Dec 1907 Evangelical Ch, Diggens, MO to Louise Sophia Wente (b 22 Sept 1886, d 10 Mar 1972 ae85y 5m 16d bur Harlington Cem, Waverly, Bremer Co IA). Farmers. Children:

Frieda Gertrude – b 26 Oct 1908 Marshfield, MO; m Richard Schmidt

Elsie Minnie – b 21 Sept 1910 Tower City, SD, d 08 Dec 1972;
    m 08 Sept 1935 Reinhardt Fred Steege

Elmer Ernest – b 26 Jan 1913 Tower City, SD; d 16 Jan 1981
    Blackhawk Co IA; m 25 Oct 1936 Elaine Thurm

Walter Herman – b 06 Aug 1917 Park City, MN;
    m 06 Feb 1947 Eleanora Matilda Musch

Anna Christina HAPPEL d/o Johann Peter Happel & Katharine Elisabeth nee Werning; b 22 Oct 1895 Parent's Farm Eldorado Twp Benton Co IA, bpt 1895 & con St.John, Eldorado Twp, d 19 Dec 1981 ae86y 1m 27d Benton Co IA, bur St.John Cem; m 29 Mar 1915 Walter William Dietrich (b 14 May 1891 Van Horne, IA d 27 Apr 1963 ae71y 11m 17d Cedar Rapids, IA bur 30 Apr 1963 CdrMem) s/o Andrew Dietrich & Minnie nee Hameister. Children:

Donovan Martin Dietrich – b 18 Oct 1916 Van Horne, IA;
    m 28 Jun 1942 Lenora Mae Meineke

Glenn Howard Dietrich – b 06 Jan 1919 Van Horne, IA;
    m 21 Mar 1942 Lois Catharine Husted

Leona Mae Dietrich – b 25 Apr 1921, d 02 May 1975 Never Married

Marilyn Ruth Dietrich – b 25 Mar 1931; Van Horne, IA;
    m 30 Jan 1955 Alan F.Young

*Anna Elisabeth HAPPEL d/o Andreas (Andrew) Happel & Maria (Marie) Elisabeth nee Möller (Moeller); b 01 Nov 1861 os Alt Heim ns Altenhaina, Germany, bpt 1861 Löhlbach Ch, Germany, 1864 emigrated to Iowa with parents and siblings, d 15 May 1939 ae77y 6m 14d; m 01 Nov 1881 Benton Co IA to Rev. Fred Ehlers, Luth Clergyman (b 08 Feb 1857 Morgan Co MO). Children:

(Henry) Johannes Heinrich Andreas Nicholas Ehlers – b 23 Dec 1882
    Adair, IA, d 27 Jan 1964;
    m 13 Feb 1908 Bertha Anna Margaret Ripke

William John August Ehlers – b 24 Feb 1884 Adair, d 08 Jun 1947;
    m 07 Dec 1911 Mary Gerhold

Frederick Julius Ehlers – b 15 Feb 1886 Estherville, IA;
    d 13 Aug 1966; m 30 Oct 1917 Mary Matilda Mueller
George Christian Ehlers – b 28 Jan 1888 Adair, IA;
    m 26 Sept 1918 Esther Wilma Henrietta Mueller
John Peter Hartman Ehlers – b 09 Aug 1890 Adair, IA;
    m Bertha Hausreth
Marie Gertrude Ehlers – b 14 Feb 1893 Knierim, Calhoun Co IA;
    d 10 Jun 1962; m 25 Dec 1924 Leo Henry Boettcher
Karl George William Ehlers – b 02 Jul 1897 Knierim Calhoun Co IA
    d 08 Dec 1970; m 12 Oct 1924 Nell Augusta Peetzee
    (b 01 Apr 1902)

Anna Elizabeth HAPPEL d/o Heinrich August Happel & Elizabeth Christina nee Krug; b 24 Sept 1917 Parent's Farm South of Vinton, IA bpt 04 Nov 1917 Parent's Farm Home, South of Vinton, IA; m 23 Aug 1942 Parent's Farm Home to Leo William Buelow (b 12 Feb 1917, Iowa Co bpt 09 Mar 1917 Parent's Farm Home, Iowa Co d 15 Aug 2007 ae90y 7m 3d) s/o Louis & Augusta nee Willinbrock Iowa Co. Celebrated 50th Wedding Anniversary. Children:
    Terry Lee Buelow – b 14 Feb 1947;
        m 24 Oct 1970 Mary Lynne Weaver DVD
    Betty Ann Buelow – b 25 Mar 1951; m 27 Dec 1970 Ted L. King
        DVD
    Judy Joyce Buelow – b 30 Aug 1955;
        1st m 30 Mar 1974 Kenneth Joe Ginther DVD;
        2nd m 26 Sept 1987 Ronald Conried

*Anna Gertrud HAPPEL d/o Andreas (Andrew) Happel & Maria (Marie) Elisabeth nee Möller (Moeller); b 19 Oct 1844 os Alt Heim ns Altenhaina, Germany, bpt 1844 Löhlbach Ch, Germany, 1864 emigrated to Iowa with parents and siblings; d 10 Sept 1919 ae74y 10m 27d Benton Co IA, bur St.Steph Cem; m 25 Sept 1866 Luzerne Luth Ch Benton Co to Friedrich Rinderknecht (b 26 Sept 1841 Wachbach, Germany, d 14 Jun 1927 ae85y 8m 20d IA bur St.Steph Cem) s/o George Martin Rinderknecht & Maria Barbara nee Spoerer. Farmers Benton Co, IA. Children:
    Maria Elizabeth Gertrude Rinderknecht – b 09 Jun 1867; d 1945
        ae 78y Cedar Rapids, IA;
        m 11 Mar 1886 St.Steph Valentine Keiper
    (William) Wilhelm H. Rinderknecht – b 13 Jan 1873, d 29 Aug 1949;
        m 15 Oct 1896 Christine Wihelmine Haerther

Barbara Maria Rinderknecht – b 11 Jan 1875, d 11 Jun 1960;
   m 25 Apr 1895 Tobias Wilhelmi
Karl George Martin Rinderknecht – b 11 Aug 1878; d 05 May 1896
   ae19y (Diptheria) (Todten Bk p.282)

*Anna Katherina HAPPEL d/o Andreas (Andrew) Happel SR. & Maria
(Marie) Elisabeth nee Möller (Moeller): cf George Rinderknecht JR.

Anna Katherina HAPPEL d/o Andreas (Andrew) Happel & Maria (Marie)
Elisabeth nee Möller (Moeller): cf Karl Rinderknecht

Anna Maria HAPPEL d/o Johann Hartmann Happel & Katharina Elisabeth
Michel; b 29 Nov 1879, d 12 Nov 1962 ae82y 11m 14d, bur St.Steph Cem;
m 25 Feb 1904 Adolph Theis (b 28 Jan 1882 Spring, TX, lived in Norman,
OK; 1900 came to Atkins, IA d 02 Jan 1970 Atkins ae91y 11m 5d). Farmers
near Norway, IA and on Happel Homestead, Linn Co IA; 1913 purchased
Hartmann Happel farm; 1937 retired in Atkins. Children:
   Olga Theis – b 31 Jan 1905, d 15 Mar 1918 ae13y; bur St.Steph Cem
   Lydia Theis – m Apr 1950 Lamont Larrabee
   Wilmer Theis – b 1914, d 1996 bur St.Steph Cem;
      m 20 Dec 1936 Clara Sessler

Anna Marie HAPPEL d/o William (Hartmann Peter William) Happel and
Dorothea nee Poock; b 16 Apr 1926 Waterloo, IA; m 27 Oct 1946 in CT to
Albert Henry Gielau (b 04 May 1921). Children:
   Alan William Gielau – b 10 Mar 1948;
      1st m 31 Jul 1970 Renae Barnes DVD;
      2nd m 22 Sept 1990 Sharon Kallenbeck
   Sharon Ann Gielau – b 16 May 1949, d 13 Oct 1951
   Vicky Marie Gielau – b 12 Nov 1950; m 17 Oct 1970 Frank Tribon
   Irma Jean Gielau – b 11 Apr 1953; 1st m Rich Hubbard
      DVD 02 Sept 1972; 2nd m 30 Jul 1977 Keith Allen Lee
   Randy Albert Gielau – b 28 Jun 1955
   Wesley Ray Gielau – b 14 Oct 1957; m 11 Sept 1982 Barbara Wylam
   Robert Alan Gielau – b 18 May 1964;
      m 29 Aug 1987 Cheryl Christopher

Arlen HAPPEL s/o Elmer Ernest Happel & Elaine nee Thurm; b 03 Mar
1952; m 16 Jun 1973 St.John Catholic Ch Black Hawk Co IA to Mary
Condon (b 10 Jul 1953). Child:

149

Brenden Lucas – b 05 Dec 1989

Arnold Christian HAPPEL s/o Henry George Happel & Hulda Caroline nee Nolting; b 27 Aug 1915; m 30 Aug 1941 Sophie Renzelman (b 12 Oct 1914). Children:
    Steven Kent – b 26 Sept 1949
    Jerry Douglas – b 28 Feb 1953; m and DVD
    Geraldine – b 28 Feb 1953; m 05 Dec 1976 Russell Knox
    Philip – NFR

Audrey HAPPEL d/o William Happel & Esther nee Matthias; b 02 Aug 1937; m Norbert Schmidt. Children:
    Jeff Schmidt – 28 Oct 1961; m 02 Nov 1985 Penny Hagenow
    Pam Schmidt – b 15 Feb 1965
    Scott Schmidt – 30 Nov 1966; m 09 Jun 1990 Keith Meier
        (b 14 Oct 1966)
    Berry Schmidt – b 10 Nov 1974

Audrey Louise HAPPEL d/o Walter Herman Happel & Eleanora Mathilda nee Musch; b 05 Apr 1951 Waterloo, IA bpt 1951 Waterloo; m 26 May 1973 Robert E. Hill (b 11 Jul 1951) s/o Eddie Hill & Waneita nee Wallin. Celebrated 25th Silver Wedding Anniversary. Children:
    Elizabeth Ann Hill – b 17 Jan 1978 Waterloo, IA;
        m 11 Aug 2000 Chris Wickman
    Erin Michelle Hill – b 14 Dec 1980 Independence, IA
    Laura Kristine Hill – b 25 Aug 1985 Waterloo, IA

*August A. HAPPEL s/o Andreas (Andrew) & Maria (Marie) Elisabeth nee Möller (Moeller); b 21 Feb 1859 os Alt Heim ns Altenhaina, Germany, bpt 1859 Löhlbach Ch, d 28 Jun 1921, Benton Co IA ae62y 4m 7d bur St.Steph Cem; 1864 emigrated to Iowa with parents and siblings; m 12 Feb 1888 St.Steph Benton Co IA to Martha Young (b 24 Feb 1868 New York City, NY, d 06 Jun 1952 ae84y 3m 13d on farm Fremont Twp Benton Co IA bur 08 Jun 1952 St.Steph Cem) d/o Jakob Young & Sophia nee Rinderknecht. Farmers in Linn Co IA two and one-half miles southeast of Atkins, IA where all children were born:
    Sophia Marie Elisabeth – b 04 Sept 1889; d 19 Apr 1976,
        bur St.Steph Cem; m 30 Jan 1910 Henry Kreutner SR.
    Emma Elisabeth – b 13 Jul 1891; d 04 Apr 1974, bur St.Steph Cem;
        m 09 Feb 1921 Carl H. Gerhold SR.

Herman Andreas Johann George – b 19 Jul 1893; d 19 May 1899
   bur St.Steph Cem
Karl Jacob – b 29 Sept 1895, d 10 Dec 1928 ae33y 2m 11d
   [Brain Abscess]) bur St.Steph Cem;
   m 12 Feb 1920 Emma K. Gerhold
Louis Peter Georg – b 03 Oct 1900 Linn Co IA; d 27 Jul 1928 ae27y
   [fell off barn roof]; bur St.Steph Cem; Never Married
Martin George Valentine – b 12 Jun 1903; d Oct 1987,
   bur St.Steph Cem; m 20 Feb 1929 Dorothy Gertrude Poock
Albert C. – b 31 May 1908, d 21 Oct 1959, bur St.Steph Cem;
   m 15 Jan 1930 Ruth Rickels

August Anton HAPPEL s/o Johann Peter Happel & Katharine Elisabeth nee Werning; b 01 Apr 1885, bpt 1885 St.Steph, d 30 May 1965 ae80y 1m Cedar Rapids, IA bur 03 Jun 1965 CdrMem; 1st m 15 Feb 1906 St.And to Marie Louise Kraft (b 22 Jan 1888 Van Horne, IA bpt 1889 St.And, d 20 Jan 1947 at her home Cedar Rapids, IA ae58y 11m 29d, bur 23 Jan 1947 CdrMem) d/o Benjamin Kraft & Katharine Louise nee Siek. Founder of Happel & Sons Farm Implement Inc. Cedar Rapids, IA. Children:
   Marvin Benjamin – b 10 Aug 1909, d 16 Apr 1964;
      1st m 14 Jun 1928 Kathleen Pettycourt DVD;
      2nd m 26 Nov 1938 Nina Smith
   Raymond John Henry – b 06 Dec 1912, d 28 Jan 1972;
      m 05 Nov 1932 Neoma Margaret Biskup
2nd m 31 Mar 1951 Holy Family Ch, Davenport August Anton Happel to Esther Catherine Mullin (b 14 Mar 1902, d 07 Nov 1990 ae92y 7m 24d) d/o Frank Mullin & Catharine nee Daly.

Becky Jo HAPPEL d/o Loren Ernest Happel & Joan nee Day; b 25 Mar 1960 Cedar Rapids; m 24 Sept 1976 in Winston-Salem, NC to Robert Jake Hamby (b 14 Jun 1959 Winston-Salem, NC). Children:
   Michael Gray Hamby – b 28 Jan 1977 Winston-Salem, NC
   Timothy Lee Hamby – 04 Oct 1978 Winston-Salem, NC
   Matthew Brian Hamby – b 14 Sept 1981 Winston-Salem, NC

Berdina Ann HAPPEL d/o Henry George Happel & Hulda Caroline nee Nolting; b 01 Oct 1919, d 24 Nov 1970; m 08 Sept 1955 Floyd Bloeser (b 01 Oct 1921). Children:
   Brenda Jean Bloeser- b 04 Dec 1956; m Michael Carrol
   Sheryl Rae Bloeser – b 15 Jul 1959

Betty Lou HAPPEL d/o Elmer Ernest Happel & Elaine nee Thurm; b 26 Sept 1941 Black Hawk Co.; m 08 Jul 1961 at St.Paul Luth Ch, Black Hawk Co. to Jerry Walter (b 06 Jan 1942). Children:
 Doreen Walter – b 02 May 1962; m 02 Jun 1984 Mark Boss
 Brian Walter – b 13 Feb 1965
 Daniel Walter – b 17 Nov 1970

Beverly HAPPEL d/o William John Happel & Lenora nee Bock; b 26 Jan 1948; m 15 Mar 1969 Gene Wehr (b 26 Nov 1944). Child:
 Charlotte Wehr – b 13 Nov 1969

Carol Ann HAPPEL d/o Melvin G. Happel & Maxine Lorraine nee Braksiek; b 19 Dec 1953 Benton Co IA; m 25 Jun 1976 David Prather (b 02 Apr 19??). Children:
 Greg Alan Prather – b 09 Dec 1979
 Shawn David Prather – b 26 Mar 1984

Charles Conrad HAPPEL s/o Alfred W. Happel & LaVera nee Hagenow; b 29 Sept 1938, m 14 Oct 1961 Jane Miller. Children:
 Gregory – b 12 Mar 1962; m 05 May 1984 Deb Wonderlick
 Teresa Jane – b 14 Jul 1963; m Sept 1983 Joe Stafford

Cheryl HAPPEL d/o Alfred W. Happel & LaVera nee Hagenow; b 18 Mar 1959; m 06 Oct 1979 Rodney Bergman. Children:
 Travis Bergman – b 29 Nov 1986
 Lisa Bergman – b 10 Dec 1990

Cindy Sue HAPPEL d/o Melvin G. Happel & Maxine Lorraine nee Braksiek; b 01 Jun 1957; 1st m 13 Sept 1975 Douglas Raye Furler (b 22 Nov 1955) DVD. Child:
 Chris Alan Furler – b 12 Aug 1979
2nd m 09 Apr 1983 Cindy Sue nee Happel Furler to Steve Mumn.

(Conrad) August Konrad William HAPPEL s/o Johann Heinrich Happel & Anna Gertrud nee Fels; b 15 Apr 1884 Atkins, IA, d 25 Oct 1951 ae76y 6m 10d Bremer Co IA; m 16 Jan 1908 at Atkins, IA to Anna Kreutner (b 30 May 1888, d 05 Dec 1986 ae98y 6m 5d) d/o William Kreutner & Maria nee Moeller. Children:
 Alfred W. – b 11 Oct 1908; m 26 Apr 1934 LaVera Hagenow

William – b 05 Apr 1910; m 07 Sept 1933 Esther Matthias
Victor – b 25 Aug 1912; m 10 Jun 1934 Lucinda Wittenberg
Marie – b 09 Sept 1915, d 29 Nov 1993;
    m 29 Nov 1993 Elmer Schnadt

David Lee HAPPEL s/o Leroy Happel & Margaret Ann nee Buss; b 18 Jul 1952; m 19 Aug 1972 Dianne Williams (b 07 Jun 1953). Children:
    Alison Leigh – b 20 Dec 1975
    Lesley Kay – b 11 Apr 1980

Dean Alan HAPPEL s/o Kendall Gene Happel & Linda nee Wright; b 09 Nov 1965; m 19 Jan 1991 Dawn Durr. Child:
    (Daughter) – b 04 May 1993

Delores Marie HAPPEL d/o Henry George Happel & Hulda Caroline nee Nolting; b 05 Apr 1926; m 10 Oct 1947 DeWayne Steege (b 07 Jan 1926). Children:
    Craig Wayne Steege – b 13 Jan 1949; m 04 Oct 1980 Ann Hageman
    David Lee Steege – b 15 Aug 1950; m 18 Oct 1975 Debbie Knipfel
    Daniel Allen Steege – b 17 Aug 1953
    Kimberly Kay Steege – b 12 Mar 1959; m 25 Aug 1981 Rick Shannon
    Michael Jon Steege – b 21 Sept 1961

Denise HAPPEL d/o Eldon Happel & Bonnie nee Larsen; b 20 Feb 1966; m 01 Oct 1988 Perry Gerloff (b 14 May 1965). Child:
    Blake Gerloff – b 06 May 1990

Dennis Harold HAPPEL s/o Harold Conrad Happel & Carolyn Louise nee Harms; b 07 May 1958; m 22 May 1977 Ronda Jean Swales (b 02 Jun 1958). Children:
    Brian Dennis – b 05 Oct 1977
    Neil Alan – b 12 Nov 1980
    Kristin Ann – b 04 Oct 1983
    Derch John – b 05 Apr 1986

Diane Carolyn HAPPEL d/o Harold Conrad Happel & Carolyn Louise nee Harms; b 24 Jan 1956; m 29 Dec 1972 Bernard William Farrel (b 07 Apr 1954). Children:
    Brandy Alexandra Farrel – b 31 May 1973
    Carrie Jo Farrel – b 17 Dec 1977

Donald Alfred HAPPEL s/o Alfred W. Happel & LaVera nee Hagenow; b 08 Mar 1942; m 20 Jun 1965 Donna McDougal. Children:
Jason – b 22 Aug 1971
Alison – b 29 Sept 1980

Donna Mae HAPPEL d/o (William) Hartmann Peter William Happel & Dorothea nee Poock; b 18 Apr 1930 Waterloo, IA; d 18 Jul 1992; 1st m 26 Oct 1952 Ray Dale Boots (d 21 Mar 1982). Children:
Susan Rae Boots – b 24 Aug 1954; m 25 Oct 1975 Kevin Gillett
Lisa Ann Boots- b 18 Apr 1956; m 28 Jul 1972 Jim Bartholomew
2nd m 14 Apr 1984 Donna nee Happel Boots to Robert L. Paulsen (d 20 Jul 1992).

Dorothy HAPPEL d/o William Martin Happel & Marie nee Dornseif; b 11 Feb 1913 Eldorado Twp Benton Co IA, bpt 1913 St.John, d 07 Mar 1990 in CA ae77y 29d; m 09 Nov 1940 in CA to L. Vernon Greenleaf (b 10 Jan 1914, d 01 Aug 1987 in CA ae73y 6m 22d). Dorothy moved to CA with mother and sister after death of father in farm accident while oats harvesting on Happel homestead. Children:
Arno Greenleaf – b 12 Jun 1947; m 28 May 1972 Karen A. Rando
Wayne Vernon Greenleaf – b 09 Nov 1948, d 26 Dec 1971
Delmar Lewis Greenleaf – b 27 May 1951;
    m 22 Dec 1979 Michelle Whitehead

Dorothy Marie HAPPEL d/o William Happel & Dorothea nee Poock; b 07 Oct 1932 Waterloo, IA; d 17 Nov 1981; m 14 Sept 1950 James Holdiman (b 02 Jul 1932). Children:
Linda Holdiman – b 22 Feb 1952; m 24 Jun 1972 Robert Dart
Nancy Holdiman – b 01 Nov 1953; m 26 Aug 1972 Jerry Koester
Thomas Holdiman – b 20 Oct 1959; m 1979 Paula Church

Edwin John HAPPEL s/o Walter Happel & Martha nee Lippert; b 30 May 1921 Cedar Rapids, IA d 27 Aug 1978 his home in Cedar Rapids, IA ae57y 2m 28d, bur Linwood Cem Cedar Rapids; employed 30 years FMC where he was safety director before retirement in 1977. Mbr TrinCR; graduate Washington High School; US Navy World War II; m 25 Jun 1949 Edna Hudson DVD. Child:
Jerry Wayne – b 17 Nov 1951 Cedar Rapids, IA resident

Elda HAPPEL d/o William (Hartmann Peter William) Happel & Dorothea nee Poock; b 10 Aug 1911 Dunkerton, IA; d 13 Sept 1984; m 01 Feb 1931 Walter Warneke (b 08 Jul 1906). No children.

Eldon HAPPEL s/o Elmer Ernest Happel & Elaine nee Thurm; b 28 Mar 1937 Bremer Co IA; m 02 Aug 1964 St.Paul Luth Ch, Evansdale, IA to Bonnie Larson (b 08 Oct 1944). Children:
    Denise – b 20 Feb 1966; m 01 Oct 1988 Perry Gerloff
    Kent – b 21 Jan 1967;
        m 19 Jun 1993 Heidi S. Kuesperf (b 08 Jul 1968)
    Joel – b 17 Dec 1972

Eleanor May HAPPEL d/o Karl Jacob Happel & Emma K. nee Gerhold; b 25 May 1928 Linn Co IA, bpt 1928 & con 1942 St.Steph; 1946 Class Atkins High School; m 06 Jun 1948 Raymond Wichman (b 29 May 1927 Iowa Co IA). Children:
    Richard Ray Wichman – b 07 Jul 1949 Cedar Rapids, IA
    Diane May Wichman – b 26 Dec 1950 Iowa Co IA
    Kenneth Karl Wichman – b 21 Jun 1953 Iowa Co IA

Elmer aka Derald Elmer HAPPEL s/o Elmer Henry Adam Happel & Mildred Esther nee Stevenson; b 15 May 1936 Virginia Gay Hosp, Vinton, IA bpt 1936 TrinVT; m 31 May 1958 Wesley United Methodist Ch Vinton to Brenda Joyce Hagerty (b 31 May 1940) d/o Wayne Edward Hagerty & Aletha Dale nee Yost of Waverly, Bremer Co IA. Children:
    Ricky Allen – b 10 Dec 1958; 1st m 13 Feb 1976 Laura Jo Oliver,
        DVD; 2nd m 06 Mar 1981 Diane L. Hanson
    Douglas – b 19 Jul 1967

Elmer Ernest HAPPEL s/o Andrew John Happel & Louise Sophia nee Wente; b 26 Jan 1912 Tower City, SD, d 16 Jan 1981 ae68y 11m 21d Blackhawk Co IA; m 25 Oct 1936 at St.Peter Luth Ch, Denver, IA to Elaine Thurm (b 16 Feb 1914 Altenburg, MO) d/o Paul & Rose Thurm. Children:
    Eldon – b 28 Mar 1937; m 02 Aug 1964 Bonnie Larson
    Harvey – b 08 Feb 1939; 1st m Connie Bettis, DVD 29 Jan 1961;
        2nd m Kathleen Coburn
    Betty Lou – b 26 Sept 1941; m 08 Jul 1961 Jerry Walter
    Jane Ann – b 25 Jan 1944; m 29 Nov 1969 Lester William Hambly III
    Karen Jean – b 29 Jul 1949; m 08 Jan 1972 Gerald Gardner
    Arlin – b 03 Mar 1952; m 17 Jun 1973 Mary Condon
155

Elmer Henry Adam HAPPEL s/o Heinrich August Happel & Elizabeth Christina nee Krug; b 25 Nov 1907 Parent's Farm Eden Twp Benton Co IA bpt 25 Jan 1908 St.And; d 12 Feb 1989 ae81y 2m 18d; 1st m 07 Mar 1935 NW of Vinton, IA to Mildred Esther Stevenson (b 22 Jan 1916 rural Vinton, IA bpt 1916 Pratt Creek, d 17 Nov 1982) d/o Wilbert Roy Stevenson & Maude Estelle nee Taylor. Children:

> Elmer Derald – b 15 May 1936;
>> m 31 May 1958 Brenda Joyce Hagerty
> Vernon Ray – b 10 Aug 1941; m 27 Jul 1963 Betty L. Wendel

2nd m 18 Jun 1984 Elmer Henry Adam Happel to Margaret Hoffman (b 17 Jun 1915).

Elsie Minnie HAPPEL d/o Andrew John Happel & Louise Sophia nee Wente; b 21 Sept 1910 Tower City, SD, d 08 Dec 1972 ae62y 2m 17d Parkersburg bur 11 Dec 1972 Waverly, IA; m 08 Sept 1935 Ev.Luth Ch Klinger, Bremer Co IA to Reinhardt Fred Steege (b 04 Jun 1911 Readlyn, Bremer Co, d 23 May 1990 Des Moines, IA ae80y 11m 19d bur 26 May 1990 Waverly, Bremer Co IA). Children:

> Verla Mae Steege – b 11 Aug 1936; m 15 Oct 1955 Clarence Redin
>> (b 25 Jun 1930)
> Darlene Gladys Steege – b 08 Dec 1938;
>> 1st m 18 Sept 1960 Leonard Leisinger;
>> 2nd m 11 May 1985 Ray Smith
> Donna Mae Steege – b 14 Feb 1946, m 1967 Larry R. French

Ervin Henry John HAPPEL s/o Adam Martin Andrew Happel & Katharina Barbara nee Rinderknecht; b 09 Feb 1913 Eden Twp near Vinton, IA bpt 1913 St.And; m 17 Nov 1946 Parsonage, Vinton Luth Ch to Dorothy Claire Boeyink (b 01 Dec 1917 Sioux Center, IA, bpt Jan 1918, d 03 Apr 1983) d/o John Boeyink & Clara nee Muilenberg. Children:

> John David – b 25 May 1947; m 13 Jan 1968 Becky Sue Lewis
> James Ervin – b 17 Oct 1949; m 17 Feb 1976 Paula Fuehrer

Erwin Henry HAPPEL s/o Henry George Happel & Hulda Caroline nee Nolting; b 12 May 1923; m 19 Jan 1943 Dorothy Fern Renner (b 07 Oct 1923). Children:

> Verilyn Ferne – b 01 Sept 1943; 1st m 26 Mar 1960 Donald Garner
>> DVD; 2nd m 02 Jun 1990 Terry Savage
> Kendall Gene – b 03 Feb 1947; 1st m 1965 Linda Wright DVD;

2nd m 1970 Donna Weitzkamp DVD; 3rd m 1981 Darles Vance
   Raydean Lee – b 18 Jun 1949; m 07 Sept 1968 Susan Eskridge
   Janelle Anne – b 06 Jun 1957; m 25 Oct 1980 Lonnie Bibler

Esther HAPPEL d/o William (Hartmann Peter William) Happel & Dorothea nee Poock; b 05 Apr 1916 Waterloo, IA; 1st m 30 Nov 1933 to Melvin Matthias (b 07 Nov 1915, d 07 Nov 1989 ae74y) DVD Jul 1959. Children:
   Janet Jean Matthias – b 14 Nov 1935; m Mark Steven Taylor
   Carol Joyce Matthias – b 26 Jan 1937; m Harry Risvold
   Maxine Dorothy Matthias – b 29 Dec 1938; m William Edward Layne
   Kenneth Melvin Matthias – b 09 Aug 1940, d 10 Apr 1959
   Leroy William Matthias – b 22 Nov 1943
2nd m 01 Nov 1975 Esther nee Happel Matthias to Harold Spooner (d 16 Apr 1984).

Fred HAPPEL s/o Johann George Happel SR. & Katharina Elisabeth nee Rinderknecht; b 16 Jul 1879 Linn Co IA, d 19 Dec 1932; m 09 May 1908 Hattie Toepher (b 02 Feb 1888 Bozeman, MT). Children:
   Arthur – b 1908
   Lawrence – b 1909
   Lora – b 1912
   Arnold – b 1913
   Harold – b 1917
   Fred JR. – b 1923

Frieda Gertrude HAPPEL d/o Andrew John Happel & Louise Sophia nee Wente; b 26 Oct 1908 Marshfield, MO; m Richard Schmidt (b 11 May 1905 Klinger, Bremer Co IA; d 11 Jan 1992) s/o Oswald & Botha Schmidt. Children:
   Leona Schmidt – 08 Jan 1927; m 29 Aug 1927 Henry Standridge
   Doris Schmidt – 14 Dec 1930; m 29 Aug 1953 Vincent Albrecht
   Norman Schmidt – 29 Dec 1932; m 30 Dec 1958 Linda Shoemaker

Friedrich Hartmann Happel s/o Hartmann Johann Balthaser Happel & Anna Katharina nee Seibel; b 04 Mar 1852, d 12 Jan 1935 ae82y 10m 2d; m Auguste Katharina Christ (b 18 Dec 1856, d 02 Aug 1913 ae56y 7m 15d). Child:
   Johann Balthaser – b 15 Sept 1889, d 05 Oct 1978

Gary Allen HAPPEL s/o Melvin G. Happel & Maxine Lorraine nee

Braksiek; b 10 Dec 1961; m 15 Jun 1985 Jill Coghlin. Child:
    Tyler Alan – b 06 Aug 1986

*George HAPPEL s/o Heinrich Happel & Anna Katharina Hayner; b 07 Nov 1690 Grusen, Germany; m 07 Nov 1720 Eva Katherina Weiss. Child:
    **Wilhelm – b NFR

Gerald Marvin HAPPEL s/o Marvin Benjamin Happel & Kathleen nee Pettycourt; b 06 Sept 1931 Cedar Rapids, IA; m 04 Feb 1950 Betty Louise LeHue (b 04 Feb 1932). Children:
    Debra Lynn – b 21 Jun 1951
    Starr Layne – b 11 May 1953
    Janna Myrtice – b 16 Aug 1954
    Sandra Kay – b 07 Nov 1959
    Brian Christopher – b 11 Mar 1966

Geraldine HAPPEL d/o Arnold Christian Happel & Sophie nee Renzelman; b 28 Feb 1953; m 05 Dec 1976 Russell Knox (b 26 Aug 1948). Child:
    Philip Knox – b NFR

Gertrude Mary Christina HAPPEL d/o Adam Martin Andrew Happel & Katharina Barbara nee Rinderknecht; b 16 Dec 1906 Eden Twp near Vinton, IA bpt Jan 1907 St.John, Newhall, IA; m 22 Feb 1936 Parsonage of Luth Ch, Morrison, IL to Maurice Henry Grovert (b 02 Nov 1902) s/o Henry Grovert & Louise nee Rammelsberg. Vinton, IA farmers. Children:
    Thomas Milton Grovert – b 10 Mar 1940; d 19 May 1941
        bur St.John Cem
    George Lewis Grovert – b 21 Oct 1941;
        m 14 Sept 1969 Pauline Marquardt
    Gretchen Louise Grovert – b 23 Sept 1947 St.Lukes Hosp
        Cedar Rapids, IA bpt 09 Nov 1947;
        1st m 09 Jun 1973 Robert Weitermann, (b 17 May 1947) DVD;
        2nd m 21 May 1983 Thomas Randall (b 02 Jul 1941)

Gertrude Katherina HAPPEL d/o Johann Heinrich Happel & Anna Gertrud nee Fels; b 26 Feb 1887 Atkins, Benton Co, IA d 13 Dec 1969 Atkins, IA ae82y 9m 17d bur St.Steph Cem; m 24 Jan 1906 Immanuel Luth Ch Klimger, Bremer Co IA to Ernest Poock (b 19 Jan 1884, d 02 Feb 1951 ae64y 14d Klinger, Bremer Co IA, bur St.Steph Cem) s/o Henry Poock. Owned grocery store in Atkins, IA during 1940's. Children:

158

Dorothy Gertrude Poock – b 06 Feb 1908, d 26 Apr 1986;
    bur St.Steph Cem;
    m 20 Feb 1929 Martin George Valentine Happel
Harold Ernest Poock – b 01 Jan 1912, d 11 Nov 1953;
    m Helen A. Block
Elda Anna Dorothea Poock – b 12 Aug 1915;
    1st m 22 Jun 1938 Paul Charles Henry Michel;
    2nd m Merle Green DVD 06 Sept 1988
Leona Frieda Poock – b 16 Sept 1920; m 23 Aug 1940 Eldo Schirm
Alvin Ernest Poock (name legal changed to Polk) – b 03 Jun 1922;
    m 22 Aug 1943 Elsie Katherine Louise Rinderknecht

Glenda HAPPEL d/o Alfred W. Happel & LaVera nee Hagenow; b 10 Jan 1952; m 06 Jul 1974 Glen Slack. Child:
    Erica Slack – b 01 Oct 1982

Gordon HAPPEL s/o William Happel & Esther nee Matthias; m 05 Jul 1939 Ruth Detterding. Children:
    Todd – NFR
    Susan – NFR

Grace Gertrude HAPPEL d/o Martin George Valentine Happel & Dorothy Gertrude nee Poock; b 23 Mar 1934 Happel homestead in Linn Co IA, bpt 1934 and con 1948 St.Steph; m 25 Jun 1955 St.Steph to Thomas William Copley (b 26 Oct 1936 Grundy Center, IA). Des Moines, IA residence. Children:
    Thomas David Copley – b 03 Oct 1959 Des Moines, IA
    Ann Grace Copley – b 13 Oct 1961 Cedar Falls, IA
    Beth Marie Copley – b 14 May 1963 Cedar Falls, IA

Gregory HAPPEL s/o Charles Conrad Happel & Jane nee Miller; b 12 Mar 1962; m 05 May 1984 Deb Wonderlick. Child:
    Rachael – b 28 Feb 1988

Harlan James HAPPEL s/o William Happel & Esther nee Matthias; b 16 Feb 1935; m 07 Aug 1960 Luann Ruth Diercks (b 19 May 1938). Children:
    Mark Orville – b 07 Dec 1960
    TWINS: Lisa Jean – b 23 Jul 1964;
        m 25 Oct 1986 Barry James Wittenburg
            Laura Jean – b 23 Jul 1964;

m 04 Apr 1987 Brian James Bockholt
Kevin Jo – b 12 Jun 1967; 1st m Tracie Ann Kammeyer
    (b 09 Oct 1967) DVD 03 Jul 2002;
    2nd m Apr 2004 Kami Leigh Fuller
Allen James – b 10 Dec 1968

Harold Conrad HAPPEL s/o Henry George Happel & Hulda Caroline nee Nolting; b 29 Jun 1931, d 12 Mar 2004 ae72y 8m 14d bur Harlington Cem Waverly IA; m 24 Jul 1955 Carolyn Louise Harms (b 10 Jun 1935). Children:
    Diane Carolyn – b 24 Jan 1956;
        m 29 Dec 1972 Bernard William Farrel
    Dennis Harold – b 07 May 1958; m 22 May 1977 Ronda Jean Swales

Harold John August HAPPEL s/o Heinrich August Happel & Elizabeth Christina nee Krug; b 16 Mar 1916 Parent's Farm south of Vinton, IA bpt 1916 St.And; d 21 Oct 1966 ae50y 7m 5d; m 17 Sept 1939 Methodist Parsonage, Vinton, IA to Shirley A. Markland (b 18 Feb 1922 Marshalltown, IA d 17 Apr 1986 ae64y) d/o Samuel F. Markland & Madeline Frances nee Scott of Vinton, IA. Children:
    Kathy Joan – b 31 Dec 1946; m 18 Sept 1971 William H. Duermyer
        (b 08 Sept 1947)
    Sharen Kay – b 25 Apr 1956; m NN
    Mark – b 04 Nov 1957; m 25 Feb 1978 Rhonda Flickinger

*Hartmann Johann Balthaser HAPPEL s/o Johann Hartmann Happel & Anna Elisabeth nee Lingelbach; b 30 Sept 1821 Sehlen, Germany, d 01 Nov 1869 Sehlen, Germany; m Anna Katharina Seibel (b 12 Nov 1825 Germany, d 20 Mar 1894 ae68y 4m 8d Germany). Child:
    Friedrich Hartmann – b 04 Mar 1852 Germany; d 12 Jan 1935
        Germany; m Augusta Katharina Christ

Harvey HAPPEL s/o Elmer Ernest Happel & Elaine nee Thurm; b 08 Feb 1939 Bremer Co IA; 1st m 29 Jan 1961 Connie Bettis (b 26 Sept 1944) DVD. Children:
    Scott – b 20 Jun 1963
    Steven – b 21 Nov 1965
2nd m 20 Jun 1986 Little Brown Ch, Nashua, Chickasaw Co IA, Harvey Happel to Kathleen Coburn (b 26 Apr 1937).

*Heinrich HAPPEL s/o Catharina Hayner (bur 17 Sept 1678 Grusen, Germany); b Sebbeterode, Germany; Meister Blacksmith; bur 01 Feb 1706 at Grusen, Germany; m 16 Jun 1670 Grusen, Germany to Anna Catharina Hayner(b 14 Jun 1620 Grusen, Germany bur 19 Apr 1710 Grusen, Germany) d/o Hans Hayner. Heinrich was master blacksmith and metal worker at Grusen, Germany. 8 children (6 boys, 2 girls):

Johann Heinrich – bpt 03 Apr 1671; m Bef 1705
Elisabeth – bpt 1673; bur 27 Oct 1735, ae62y;
    m 05 Dec 1702 Joh. George Roder
*Johann Balthaser – bpt 04 Dec 1677 Grusen, Germany;
    bur Easter Day 1732 Sehlen, Germany, ae54y;
    Poenitentes 25 May 1799
Henrich – bpt 07 Nov 1680 Grusen, Germany
A. Elisabeth – bpt 03 Mar 1685, Godfather #1 brother
Johann Heinrich – m 08 Nov 1707 George Mengel
Johann George – bpt 10 Apr 1689 Grusen, Germany, bur 01 Oct 1689
*Johann George – bpt 07 Nov 1690 Grusen, Germany;
    m 07 Nov 1720 Eva Catharina Weise, Mohnhausen, Germany
Johann Henrich – bpt 13 Jul 1694, bur 16 Sept 1701

Heinrich August aka Henry HAPPEL s/o Johann Peter Happel & Katharine Elizabeth nee Werning; b 04 Feb 1881 north Atkins, Fremont Twp Benton Co IA, bpt 20 Mar 1881 St.Steph, d 06 Apr 1963 ae82y 2m 2d Benton Co IA, bur 09 Apr 1963 St.John Cem; m 06 Dec 1906 St.Steph to Elizabeth Christina Krug (b 07 Jun 1882 south Atkins, Fremont Twp Benton Co IA, bpt 26 Jun 1882 Atkins, IA d 19 Feb 1986 ae103y 8m 12d Luth Home, Vinton, IA bur 21 Feb 1986) d/o Johann Heinrich Krug & Louise nee Krahling. Children:

Elmer Henry Adam – b 25 Nov 1907, d 12 Feb 1989;
    m 07 Mar 1935 Mildred Esther Stevenson
Mildred Louise – b 17 Feb 1910, d 25 Nov 2000;
    m 25 Nov 1939 Henry Balthasar Jessen
Elvira Marie Christina – b 23 May 1913, d 27 Oct 1923
    bur St.John Cem
Harold John August – b 16 Mar 1916, d 21 Oct 1966;
    m 17 Sept 1939 Shirley Markland
Anna Elizabeth – b 24 Sept 1917, d 21 Oct 1966;
    m 23 Aug 1942 Leo William Buelow

Henry (George August Henry) HAPPEL s/o Johann Heinrich Happel &

Anna Gertrud nee Fels; b 04 Jan 1889 Atkins Fremont Twp Benton Co. IA, d 22 Jul 1969 ae80y 6m 18d Waterloo, IA; m 14 Jun 1914 St.John Luth Ch Benington Twp to Hulda Caroline Nolting (b 24 Jun 1893, d 10 Sept 1938 ae45y 7m 17d Ft. Morgan, CO, bur Denver, IA). Children:

    Arnold Christian – b 27 Aug 1915; m 30 Aug 1941 Sophie Renzelman

    Alvera Gertrude – b 15 Sept 1917; 1st m 14 Aug 1938 Elmer Halweg;
        2nd m 01 Mar 1969 Cecil William Harvey

    Berdina Ann – b 01 Oct 1919, d 24 Nov 1970;
        m 08 Sept 1955 Floyd Bloeser

    Erwin Henry – b 12 May 1923; m 19 Jan 1943 Dorothy Fern Renner

    Delores Marie – b 05 Apr 1926, m 10 Oct 1947 DeWayne Steege

    Wilma Malinda – b 29 Feb 1928; m 29 Sept 1946 Leroy Steege

    Harold Conrad – b 29 Jun 1931; m 24 Jul 1955 Carolyn Louise Harms

    Marvin John – b 16 May 1936; m 26 Oct 1958 Arnetta Westendorf

    Lester Carl – b 29 Aug 1938; m 05 Jul 1959 Suzanne Seward

Herbert Louis HAPPEL s/o Karl Jacob Happel & Emma K. nee Gerhold; b 04 Jan 1926 Linn Co IA, bpt St.Steph, d 09 Jan 2005 ae79y 5d bur St.Steph Cem; m 25 Oct 1956 Geraldine Edaburn (b 14 Feb 1928 Linn Co IA, dec'd). Child:

    Jay Lynn – b 24 Sept 1964 Cedar Rapids, IA; m Julie

Hilda HAPPEL d/o William (Hartmann Peter William) Happel & Dorothea nee Poock; b 16 Mar 1914 Waterloo, IA; d 19 Jul 1942 ae28y 3m 3d; m 26 Nov 1937 Harold Meyer (b 01 Jun 1914). Children:

    Dale Herold Meyer – b 09 Jul 1938; m Julien Tegmeier

    Jean Dorothy Meyer – b 22 Dec 1940, d Jan 1941

    Merle William Meyer – b 20 Feb 1942, d 12 Jun 1962

James Albert HAPPEL s/o Albert C. Happel & Ruth nee Rickels; b 25 Dec 1937 Linn Co IA, bpt and con St.Steph; Realtor; President Happel's Gormet Foods; m 07 Nov 1959 St.Steph to Arlene Bader (b 07 Nov 1941 Springville) DVD. Cedar Rapids, IA residence. Children:

    Tamara Sue – b 26 Mar 1960 Williamsburg, IA;
        m 30 May 1993 David Lawrence Garman, Cedar Rapids, IA

    Julie Ann – b 28 Jun 1964 in Atkins, IA;
        m 13 Jul 1991 Theodore Joseph Collins, Cedar Rapids, IA

James Ervin HAPPEL s/o Ervin Henry John Happel & Dorothy Claire nee Boeyink; b 17 Oct 1949 Virginia Gay Hosp Vinton, IA bpt Dec 1949

TrinVT; m 17 Feb 1976 Paula Fuehrer (b 31 Oct 1953). Children:
Adam – b 25 May 1979
Brian James – b 02 Feb 1981 Cedar Rapids, IA

James Richard HAPPEL s/o Richard Henry Happel & Florene nee Koelling; b 22 Nov 1940; m 27 Apr 1963 Carolyn Sue Schmidt (b 03 Mar 1942). Children:
Todd James – b 13 Jan 1966
Kristin Sue – b 22 Oct 1967
Shannon Lee – b 15 Mar 1969; m 16 Dec 1989 Wade Klamer

Jane Ann HAPPEL d/o Elmer Ernest Happel & Elaine nee Thurm; b 25 Jan 1944 Black Hawk Co IA; m 29 Nov 1969 St.Paul Luth Ch, Black Hawk Co IA to Lester William Hambly III (b 15 Feb 1944). Children:
Dean L. Hambly – b 26 Apr 1970
Ann M. Hambly – b 04 Apr 1971

Janelle Anne HAPPEL d/o Erwin Henry Happel & Dorothy Fern nee Renner; b 06 Jun 1957; m 25 Oct 1980 Lonnie Bibler. Child:
Wade Nicholas Bibler – b 14 Feb 1982

Jeanette Anna Elizabeth HAPPEL d/o Adam Martin Andrew Happel & Katharina Barbara nee Rinderknecht; b 24 Mar 1903 Eden Twp, near Vinton, IA bpt Apr 1903 Farm Home Eden Twp Benton Co IA, d 08 Oct 1938 ae35y 6m 15d Hills Retreat, Des Moines, IA bur 12 Oct 1938 St.John Cem; m 07 Aug 1929 at TrinVT to Rev. Elmer H. Widmann of Iona, MN (b 12 Dec 1902 Luth clergyman; Ute, IA and Ogden, IA). Jeanette taught Luth school at Webster City, IA where she met Rev. Widmann. Children:
Richard Warren Widmann – b 22 Oct 1931 Iona, MN;
m 22 Jun 1958 Eileen Kane
Dorothy Vergene Widmann – b 03 Apr 1933 Ute, IA, bpt 09 Apr 1933
m 29 Aug 1999 Cedar Rapids, IA to Ed Statton

Jeanne K. HAPPEL d/o Leroy Happel & Margaret Ann nee Buss; b 21 Dec 1948; m 28 Sept 1969 Eugene Heineman (b 22 Nov 1945). Children:
Amy Ann Heineman – b 27 Sept 1972
Ann Lee Heineman – b 13 Apr 1976

*Johann Balthaser HAPPEL s/o Johann Henrich Happel, master blacksmith from Sebbeterode & wife Anna Catharina nee Hayner; b/bpt Grusen,

163

Germany, d 04 Dec 1677, bur 1732 Sehlen, Germany Easter Monday 1732 ae54y; Poenitentes 27 May 1699 Eulalia Elisabeth Rose (bpt 04 May 1673 Sehlen, Germany, bur 1st Epiphany 1737 ae64y) d/o Johannes Rose & NN nee Struube. Eight children:

Johann Henrich – b/bpt 02 Jul 1699, bur 31 Oct 1699
    Sehlen, Germany
*Johann Heinrich –b/bpt 14 Nov 1700 Sehlen,
    d/bur 22/24 Feb 1766 65y;
    1st m 11 Feb 1721 Anna Elisabeth Volmer
    2nd m 04 Aug 1730 A. Elisabeth;
A. Kunigunde – b/bpt 24 Jun 1703
A. Elisabeth – b/bpt 20 Nov 1705, bur 22 Jun 1708
Joh. Hartmann – b/bpt 07 Oct 1708;
    m 09 Jun 1733 Grusen, Germany to Gerdruth Groll
A. Elisabeth – b/bpt 26 May 1711;
    m 29 Oct 1734 Daniel Wirthzusch Ernst
NN – b/d 23 Mar 1714 Sehlen, Germany
Joh.Jost – bpt 30 Jun 1715 Sehlen, Germany; m NN Guida
A.Catharina – b/bpt 22 Jan 1719,
    d/bur 07/08 Oct 1741 ae22y 8 mo 18 d

*Johann Balthaser HAPPEL s/o Friedrich Hartmann Happel & Auguste Katharina nee Christ; b 15 Sept 1889, d 05 Oct 1978; m Karoline Klinge (b 15 Jan 1890, d 02 May 1961 ae71y 3m 17d). Child:
    **Johann Peter – b 22 Jan 1920; m Gertrud Heide

*Johann Georg HAPPEL SR. s/o Andreas (Andrew) Happel & Maria (Marie) Elisabeth nee Möller (Moeller); b 11 Dec 1842 Löhlbach, Germany, bpt 1842 Löhlbach Ch, d 09 May 1923, ae80y 4m 29d Benton Co IA, bur St.Steph Cem; 1st m Jan 1864 Sophia Katharina Elisabeth Rinderknecht (TWIN: William Rinderknecht; b 06 Jul 1844 Wachback, Germany, d 09 May 1886 ae41y 10m 3d Benton Co IA bur St.Steph Cem) d/o George Martin Rinderknecht SR. & Maria Barbara nee Spoerer. Farmers. Ten children:

Annie – b 29 Jun 1864 Rock Island, IL; d 08 Apr 1893;
    m 21 Dec 1884 Georg Friedrick Michel
George Carl – b 02 Jul 1868 Rock Island, IL; d 20 Dec 1922 ae54y
    [Automobile Accident]; m 26 Oct 1893 Rosa Fritz
Katherina Elisabeth- b 17 Apr 1870 Linn Co IA; d 03 Nov 1922;
    m 17 Sept 1891 Fred Kokemiller

Mary – b 31 Dec 1871 Linn Co IA; d 30 Mar 1948;
m 29 Jun 1893 St.Steph Wilhelm Christopher (Will) Kanmin
John – b 13 Jan 1874 Linn Co IA; d 22 Oct 1948;
m 27 Apr 1899 Elizabeth Moeller
Barbara – b 20 Oct 1875 Linn Co IA; d 20 Sept 1878
Elizabeth – b 24 Sept 1877 Linn Co IA; d 31 May 1954;
m Georg Friedrick Michel
Fred – b 16 Jul 1879 Linn Co IA; d 19 Dec 1932;
m 09 May 1908 Hattie Toepher
Carl – b 24 Sept 1881 Linn Co IA; d 10 Sept 1895
Christina – b 15 Dec 1883 Linn Co IA; d 11 Sept 1957;
m 26 May 1909 Carl Fred Stoll
2nd m 06 Dec 1891 Johann Georg Happel SR. to Marie Richter (b 27 May 1860, d 26 Mar 1932 ae71y bur St.Steph Cem). Five children all born in Linn Co IA:
Clara Sophie Anna Elisabeth – b 17 Jul 1892; d 05 Jun 1983;
m 19 Sept 1920 Fred Schroeder,
Latimer, Franklin Co IA residence
Ernest – b 22 Dec 1894, d 14 Sept 1895 bur St.Steph Cem
Theodore George – b 02 Oct 1896, d 14 Nov 1952 Latimer, IA;
m 27 Mar 1921 Clara Clausen, Latimer,Franklin Co IA residence
Paul Friedrich Heinrich – b 12 Apr 1898, d 23 Feb 1970
bur St.Steph Cem; m 09 Aug 1925 Emma Henrietta Boettcher
Walther Johann Heinrich Phillip – b 27 May 1900; d 03 Aug 1952
bur Linwood Cem Cedar Rapids, IA;
m 19 Dec 1919 Martha Lippert

*Johann Hartmann HAPPEL s/o Johann Heinrich Happel & Anna Elisabeth nee Lower; b 13 Jan 1737 Sehlen, Germany, d 06 Dec 1811 ae73y 10m 23d bur 09 Dec 1811 Sehlen, Germany; in 1776 Duke of Saxony (Germany was indebted to England by Treaty)contracted with King George III to send 12,000 Hessian soldiers to fight for Great Britain in American Revolution. Johann Hartman Happel was one of three soldiers from Sehlen that went to America. He returned to Germany and continued his Tailor trade; m 1763 Engel Magdalena Hupen (b 15 Oct 1736, d 10 Feb 1787 ae50y 3m 26d bur 12 Feb 1787 Sehlen, Germany). Children:
*Johann Jost – b 20 Sept 1763 Sehlen, Germany, d 23 May 1824;
m 01 Aug 1790 Grusen, Germany to Anna Martha Rose
of Sehlen, Germany
Johannes – b 13 Jun 1766, d 16 Jun 1766 Sehlen, Germany ae4d

*Katharina – b 18 Dec 1767 Sehlen, Germany;
  1st m 31 Jul 1791 Grusen, Germany Johann Rose;
  2nd m at Grusen 27 Dec 1802 J. Baltsar Rose.
Johann Jost – b 07 Dec 1769 Sehlen, Germany

*Johann Hartmann HAPPEL of Sehlen, Germany, s/o Johann Jost Happel (Ackermann: farmhand) & Anna Martha nee Rose; b 17 Apr 1796 Sehlen Germany, d 23 May 1871 ae74y 6d Sehlen, Germany; m Anna Elisabeth Lingelbach (b 08 Feb 1801, d ND) d/o Johann Lingelbach (ackermann: farmhand) & Anna Elisabeth nee Henkel. Children:
  Hartmann Johann Balthaser-b 30 Sept 1821 Sehlen, d 01 Nov 1869
  Elisabeth – b 03 Nov 1823 Sehlen, Germany; d 23 Oct 1892
    Grusen, Germany; m Johann Schunk.
  Johann Balthasar – b 20 Dec 1827 Sehlen, d Sehlen 05 Aug 1829.
  Anna Martha – b 13 Dec 1830 Sehlen, Germany d 18 Mar 1877
  Anna Magdalena Caroline – b 12 Jan 1840 Sehlen, d 11 Feb 1916;
    m 01 Feb 1863 Heinrich Wilhelm Scholl.

*Johann Hartmann HAPPEL s/o Andreas (Andrew) Happel & Maria (Marie) Elisabeth nee Möller (Moeller); b 27 Sept 1846 os Alt Heim ns Altenhaina, Germany, bpt 1846 Löhlbach ch, 1864 emigrated to Iowa with parents and siblings; d 03 Jun 1925, Benton Co IA ae78y 8m 7d [Heat Stroke] (Todtn Bk.p.343) bur St.Steph Cem; m 24 Jul 1870 St.Steph to Katharina Elisabeth Michel (b 18 Nov 1846 Geismar, Germany, d 27 Aug 1922 ae75y 9m 9d bur St.Steph Cem) d/o Johann Peter (Henry) Michel & Anna Elisabeth nee Freitag. Farmed 160 acres 1½ miles southwest of Atkins (across from St.Stephen Luth Church & Cem) retired and built new home on their farm in 1911. Son William farmed the land for two years. Nine children born Benton Co IA:
  Andrew – b 16 Dec 1871; m 29 Mar 1894 Emma Ahrens
  Katherina Maria- b 21 Feb 1873, con 1887 St.Steph; d 15 Apr 1950
    bur St.Steph Cem; m 16 Apr 1896 Henry Nell
  George Fritz – b 06 Aug 1874, d 23 Aug 1963; bur St.Steph Cem;
    m 28 Sept 1899 St.Steph to Emma Kunstorf
  Henry – b 18 Mar 1876, con 1889 St.Steph; d 26 Feb 1946
    bur St.Steph Cem; m 11 Jan 1906 Katherine Keiper (Twin)
  Maria (Mary) – b 04 Jan 1878, con 1891 St.Steph, d 04 Apr 1935;
    m 13 Mar 1902 St.Steph to Henry Theis
  Anna (Annie) Maria – b 29 Nov 1879, d 12 Nov 1962
    bur St.Steph Cem; m 25 Feb 1904 Adolph Theis

Karl Wilhelm (William C.) – b 27 Apr 1881, d 1973;
    con 1895 St.Steph; m 03 Feb 1910 Bertha Keiper
Gertrud Anna Elizabeth – b 21 May 1885; con 1898 St.Steph;
    d 12 Oct 1941; m 03 Feb 1910 George Moeller
Rev. Peter Heinrich Wilhelm – b 31 Mar 1887, con 1899 St.Steph;
    m 03 Jun 1910 Adelle Franz

*Johann Heinrich HAPPEL, master blacksmith from Sebbeterode, Germany, d 01 Feb 1706 Grusen, Germany; m 14 Jun 1670 Grusen, Germany to Katharine Hayner from Grusen, Germany (d 19 Apr 1710 Grusen, Germany). Child:
    *Johann Baltsar – b 04 Dec 1677 Grusen, d 1732 bur Easter Monday
        Sehlen, Germany; Poenitentes 27 May 1699 with
        Eulalia Elisabeth Rose and had eight children
    *George – b 07 Nov 1690 Grusen, Germany;
        m 07 Nov 1720 Eva Catherine Weise

*Johann Heinrich HAPPEL s/o Johann Balthasar Happel & Eulalia Elisabeth nee Rose; bpt 14 Nov 1700 Sehlen, Germany; d/bur Lehnhausen, Germany 22/24 Feb 1766 ae65y 3m; 1st m 11 Feb 1721 Anna Elisabeth Volmar (bpt 16 Aug 1696 at Sehlen, Germany d/bur 28 Feb 1727 Sehlen, Germany ae30y) d/o Heinrich Volmar & Catharina nee Ocus. Children:
    A Konigunda – b/bpt 08 Mar 1722 Sehlen, Germany;
        m 08 Dec 1747 Johann Hartmann Schneider
    Eva Catharina – b/bpt 12 Mar 1724 Sehlen, Germany;
        bur 3rd Epiphany Sunday 1725 Sehlen
    A. Martha – b/bpt 14 Apr 1726 Sehlen, Germany
        bur 23 Sept 1728 Sehlen, Germany
2nd m 04 Aug 1730 Herbelhausen, Germany, Johann Heinrich Happel to Anna Elisabeth Lower (b 05 May 1709 Herbelhausen, Germany, d 22 Feb 1774, bur 24 Feb 1774 ae64y 9m 21d) d/o Johannes Lower & Margaretha nee Schneider. Children:
    *Magdalena – b/bpt 22 Apr 1731 Sehlen, Germany;
        m 18 Jan 1754 Mohnhausen, Germany to Johann Peter Eckhard
    Anna Elisabeth – b/bpt 21 Dec 1732 Sehlen, d on St.Thomas 1733
    Anna Catharina – b/bpt 21 Dec 1734 Sehlen, Germany;
        m 14 Oct 1770 Grusen to Hartmann Mebus of Sehlen
    *Johann Hartmann – b/bpt 13 Jan 1737 Sehlen, Germany; in 1776 he
was one of 12,000 Hessian soldiers the Duke of Saxony contracted to Great Britain to fight in America against the colonist in Revolutionary War. He

returned to Germany; m 1763 Engel Magdalena Hupen; d 06 Dec 1811 Sehlen, Germany. Maybe his talk about American freedom and American Dream to his nephew Johann Peter Happel influenced Johann's son Andreas to emigrate to USA.

    *Johann Jost – b/bpt 14 Jan 1739 Sehlen, Germany, d 22 Jul 1793;
        1st m 19 Nov 1763 Anna Gertrud (d 05 Oct 1774);
        2nd m 18 Apr 1775 Altenhaina to Regina Menkel.
        Godfather 1766 for nephew Johann Jost Eckhard
        (oldest sister Magdalena's son)
    Johann Balthasar – b/bpt 16 Jul 1741 Sehlen, Germany;
        d 12 Jul/bur 13 Jul 1744 Sehlen, Germany
    Johann Daniel – b/bpt 13 Apr 1743 Sehlen, Germany;
        d 24 Feb/bur 26 Feb 1752 Sehlen, Germany

*Johann Heinrich HAPPEL s/o Andreas (Andrew) and Maria (Marie) Elisabeth nee Mo(e)ller; b 24 Oct 1855 os Alt Heim ns Altenhaina, Germany, bpt 1855 Löhlbach Ch Germany, d 20 Apr 1888 ae32y 5m 27d Benton Co IA, bur St.Steph Cem; 1864 emigrated to Iowa with parents and siblings; m 11 Nov 1881 St.Steph to Anna Gertrud Fels (b 30 May 1860 Löhlbach, Germany, bpt 1860 Löhlbach Ch, d 10 Mar 1936 ae75y 9m Bremer Co IA, bur Denver, IA Bremer Co) d/o Conrad Fels & Marie Catherina nee Ernst. Children:

    (Andrew John) Johann George Andrew – b 02 Aug 1882 Fremont
        Twp; 27 Jun 1948; m 19 Oct 1907 Louise Sophia Wente
    (Conrad) August Konrad William – b 15 Apr 1884 Fremont Twp;
        d 25 Oct 1951; m 1908 Anna Kreutner
    (William) Hartmann Peter William – b 27 Sept 1885; Fremont Twp
        Benton Co IA, d 26 Oct 1953; m 14 Sept 1910 Dorothea Poock
    Gertrude Katherina – b 26 Feb 1887 Fremont Twp Benton Co IA;
        d 13 Dec 1969; m 24 Jan 1906 Ernest Carl Poock
    (Henry) George August Henry – b 04 Jan 1889 Fremont Twp;
        d 22 Jul 1969; m 14 Jun 1914 Hulda Caroline Nolting

*Johann Jost HAPPEL s/o Johann Heinrich Happel & 2nd m Anna Elizabeth nee Lower; bpt 14 Jan 1739 Sehlen, Germany; d 22 Jul 1793 Hse #5 ae 54y 6m 8d os Alt Heim ns Altenhaina, Germany, bur Altenhaina, Germany; 1st m 19 Nov 1763 Anna Gertrud (b 05 Jan 1744, d 10 May 1774 ae30y 4m 5d); 2nd m 18 Apr 1775 os Alt Heim ns Altenhaina, Germany to Regina Menkel (b 24 Jun 1755 os Alt Heim ns Altenhaina, Germany, d 23 Sept 1806 Hse #5 ae51y 3m Altenhaina, Germany, bur Altenhaina) d/o

Johann Peter Menkel of Upper Mill, Germany. Child:

*Johann Peter – b 23 Oct 1784 os Alt Heim ns Altenhaina, Germany;
    d 27 Apr 1828 oa Alt Heim ns Altenhaina, Germany;
    m 27 Dec 1812 Anna Gertrud Fackiner

*Johann Jost HAPPEL of Sehlen, Germany, s/o Johann Hartmann Happel & Engel Magdalena nee Hupen; b 20 Sept 1763 Sehlen, Germany, d 23 May 1824 ae60y 8m 3d Sehlen, Germany; m Grusen, Germany 01 Aug 1790 to Anna Martha Rose of Sehlen, Germany (b 03 May 1772, d 05 Sept 1815 ae43y 4m 2d bur 07 Sept 1815) d/o Johann Adam Rose & Anna Martha nee Happel(Sehlen). Eight children:

Anna Martha – b 03 Aug 1792 Sehlen, Germany;
    m 30 Jan 1820 Johann Peter Vaupel.
*Johann Hartmann – b 17 Apr 1796 Sehlen, d 23 May 1871 Sehlen;
    m 18 Jun 1820 Anna Elisabeth Lingelbach
Anna Catharina – b 18 Nov 1799, d 22 Jun 1800
Anna Margaretha – b 16 Nov 1801, d 10 Dec 1805
Johann Balthasar – b 29 Dec 1804
Fredrich – b 01 Dec 1807
Anna Katharina – b 10 Sept 1811, d 11 Aug 1818
Johann Wilhelm – b 22 Jun 1814

*Johann Peter HAPPEL s/o Johann Jost Happel & Regina nee Menkel; b 23 Oct 1784, os Alt Heim ns Altenhaina, Germany d 27 Apr 1828 ae43y 6m 4d os Alt Heim ns Altenhaina, Germany; m 12 Jul 1812 Löhlbach, Germany to Anna Gertrud Fackiner of os Alt Heim ns Altenhaina, Germany (b 31 Jul 1790 os Alt Heim ns Altenhaina, Germany, d 02 Apr 1849 ae58y 8m 2d os Alt Heim ns Altenhaina, Germany) d/o Johann Justus Fackiner & Anna Christina nee Grack. Six children:

Johann Justus – b 12 Oct 1812 os Alt Heim ns Altenhaina,
    d 1812 Altenhaina, Germany
Johann Baltsar – b 29 Dec 1814 remained in Altenhaina house,
    had one daughter (her name vanished)
Anna Elisabeth- b 25 Sept 1816, d 26 Mar 1817 ae6m 1d
Anna Katharina – b 14 Aug 1818 os Alt Heim ns Altenhaina
*Andreas Happel – b 27 Mar 1821 Altenhaina (Prussia) Germany
    d 03 Dec 1895 Atkins, IA;
    m 29 May 1843 Maria (Marie)Elisabeth Möller;
    1864 emigrated with 10 children to Iowa.
Anna Kathrina – b 31 Dec 1823 os Alt Heim ns Altenhaina

d 15 Dec 1826 os Alt Heim ns Altenhaina

*Johann Peter HAPPEL s/o Andreas (Andrew) Happel SR. & Maria (Marie) Elisabeth nee Möller (Moeller); b 04 Mar 1851 os Alt Heim ns Altenhaina, Germany (Althaina Kreiz Frankenberg), bpt 1851 Löhlbach Ch, Germany; 1864 came to USA with parents and siblings; d 13 May 1902 ae51y 2m 9d on his farm, Eldorado Twp Benton Co IA, bur 16 May 1902 St.Steph Cem; m 03 Jul 1874 St.Steph, Atkins to Katharina Elisabeth Werning (b 24 Jan 1854 Dankerode-on-der-Fulda, Hessen Nassau Germany, bpt 1854 Dankerode Ch, came to America March 1870; d 13 Jul 1937 ae83y 5m 19d at her home in Van Horne, IA, bur St.Steph Cem) d/o Johann Adam Werning & Johana Jeanette nee Brehm. Farmers in Fremont Twp and farm north of Newhall. Ten children:

Adam Martin Andrew – b 25 Sept 1875 Atkins IA; d 23 Feb 1933
    ae 58y near Newhall, bur St.John Cem;
    m 25 Feb 1902 Katharina Barbara Rinderknecht

Christina Marie – b 13 Feb 1877 Atkins, IA; d 17 Mar 1934
    ae57y Farm Clinton Twp Linn Co IA bur St.Steph Cem
    (Todten Bk p.347); m 09 Mar 1989 Henry John Krug

Elizabeth Jeanette – b 27 Dec 1878 Atkins, IA; d 30 Jun 1967
    ae89y Atkins, IA bur St.Steph Cem;
    m 18 Feb 1903 John August Henry Krug

Heinrich August – b 04 Feb 1881 Atkins, IA; d 06 Apr 1963
    ae82y Newhall, IA bur St.John Cem;
    m 06 Dec 1906 Elizabeth Christina Krug

Katharina Wilhelmina – b 11 Jan 1883 Newhall, IA;
    d 11 Oct 1970 ae87y bur St.John Cem;
    1st m 08 Mar 1906 Prescott Samuel Edmonds, DVD;
    2nd m 26 May 1921 Claude C. Gilbert

August Anton – b 01 Apr 1885 Newhall, IA; d 30 May 1965
    ae80y bur CdrMem; 1st m 15 Feb 1906 Marie Louise Kraft;
    2nd m 31 Mar 1951 Esther Catherine Mullin

William Martin – b 29 Jan 1888 Newhall, IA; d 17 Jul 1914
    ae26y farm near Newhall, bur St.John Cem;
    m 08 Apr 1912 Marie Dornseif

Maria Elizabeth – b 25 Dec 1890 Newhall IA; d 05 Jan 1965
    ae75y Newhall, bur St.John Cem;
    m 25 Dec 1910 Frank Benjamin Braksiek

Andrew Adam JR.- b 03 Jun 1893 Newhall, IA; d 31 Aug 1963
    ae70y bur St.John Cem; Never Married

Anna Christina Elizabeth – b 22 Oct 1895 Newhall, IA;
   d 19 Dec 1981 ae86y bur St.John Cem;
   m 29 Mar 1915 Walter William Dietrich

**Johann Peter HAPPEL s/o Johann Balthaser Happel & Karoline nee Klinge; b 22 Jan 1920 Sehlen, Germany; m Gertrud Heide (b 26 Dec 1924) Sehlen, Germany. Author visited in their home 1990, 1995. Children:
   **Margita – b 02 Feb 1950 Sehlen, Germany;
      m 25 Oct 1969 Friedhelm Grotecke
   **Peter – b 28 Oct 1954 Sehlen, Germany; m Inge Werum

John David HAPPEL s/o Ervin Henry John Happel & Dorothy Claire nee Boeyink; b 25 May 1947 Virginia Gay Hosp Vinton, IA bpt 30 Aug 1947 TrinVT; m 13 Jan 1968 Becky Sue Lewis (b 16 Sept 1948) d/o Leonard Lewis. Child:
   Michael John – b 02 Jun 1971

Judith Kay HAPPEL d/o Raymond John Henry Happel & Neoma Margaret nee Biskup; b 08 Apr 1942 Cedar Rapids, IA bpt 1942 TrinCR; m 22 Feb 1960 Russell Clare Leidigh (b 05 Oct 1942). Children:
   Timothy Ray Leidigh – b 04 Jul 1960;
      m 04 May 1985 Kim Ellen Gardeman
   Laurie Ann Leidigh – b 09 Oct 1962; m 09 May 1987 Mark Schuyller
   Thomas Russell Leidigh – b 24 Dec 1963; m 07 Jul 1989 Lisa L.Hess
   John William Leidigh – b 23 Nov 1969

Julie Ann HAPPEL d/o James Albert Happel of Cedar Rapids, IA & Arlene nee Bader of San Francisco, CA; b 28 Jun 1964 bpt 13 Jul 1964 St.Steph, con May 1978 Bethany Luth Ch Cedar Rapids, IA; m 13 Jul 1991 at home of bridegroom's parents Mr. & Mrs. Thomas Collins SR. of Cedar Rapids, IA to Theodore Joseph Collins (b 03 Nov 1964; Drake University Law School, employed by Shuttleworth & Ingersoll). Cedar Rapids, IA residence. Children:
   Lauren Elizabeth Collins – b 16 Apr 1992 Cedar Rapids, IA
   Grace Danielle Kripa Collins – b 15 Apr 1994 in Delhi, India
      (Adopted 03 Aug 1995)

Karen Jean HAPPEL d/o Elmer Ernest Happel & Elaine nee Thurm; b 29 Jul 1949 Black Hawk Co IA; m 08 Jan 1972 St.Paul Luth Ch Black Hawk Co IA to Gerald Gardner (19 Jan 1948). Children:

Tracie Lynne Gardner – b 04 Dec 1973
Adam Gerald Gardner – b 18 Sept 1975

Karl Jacob HAPPEL s/o August A. Happel & Martha nee Young: cf Emma K. Gerhold.

Karl Henry August HAPPEL s/o Karl Jacob Happel & Emma K. nee Gerhold; b 13 Jul 1921 Linn Co IA, bpt 05 Aug 1921 & con 14 Apr 1935 St.Steph, d 30 May 1999 ae77y 10m 17d; m 05 Jul 1967 Phyllis nee McLinden Peeka (1st m Peeka). No children.

Katharina Wilhelmina HAPPEL d/o Johann Peter Happel & Katharine Elizabeth nee Werning; b 11 Jan 1883 Parent's Farm Eldorado Twp Benton Co IA, bpt 1883, d 11 Oct 1970 ae87y 9m Vinton, bur 14 Oct 1970 St.John Cem; 1st m 08 Mar 1906 Prescott Samuel Edmonds (02 Feb 1887, d 1940)DVD; s/o John Edmonds of Vancouver, WA. Children:
    Leslie August Edmonds – b 01 Jul 1907, d 03 Sept 1990;
        m 29 Dec 1927 Wilma Henrietta Hudson
    Prescott Williard Edmonds – b 18 Dec 1909, d 01 Aug 1940;
        m 07 Dec 1932 Helen Margaret Mess
2nd m 26 May 1921 Katharina Wilhelmina nee Happel Edmonds to Claude C. Gilbert (b 11 Oct 1888)Cedar Rapids, IA.

Kathryn Elizabeth HAPPEL d/o Marvin Benjamin Happel & Kathleen nee Pettycourt; b 24 Nov 1929 Cedar Rapids, IA; m 21 Apr 1951 Garland E. Wagner. Temple City, CA residence. Children:
    Linda Kay Wagner – b 11 Mar 1952 Temple City, CA
    Garland Wagner – b 04 Jun 1954 Temple City, CA

Kendall Gene HAPPEL s/o Erwin Henry Happel & Dorothy Fern nee Renner; b 03 Feb 1947; 1st m 05 Jun 1965 Linda Wright, DVD. Children:
    TWINS: Dean Alan – b 09 Nov 1965, m 19 Jan 1991 Dawn Durr
        Dale Adam – b 09 Nov 1965, m 1991 Beth NN
2nd m May 1970 Kendall Gene Happel to Donna Weitzkamp DVD; Children:
    Jason – b 19 Oct 1970
    Jodi Lynn – b 04 Dec 1973, d 01 May 1992
3rd m 28 May 1981 Kendall Gene Happel to Darles Wurtz Vance and adopted her child:
    Jesse James Vance Happel – b 16 Oct 1973

Kenneth HAPPEL s/o Albert C. Happel & Ruth nee Rickels; b 22 Dec 1931 Linn Co IA, bpt 1931 and con 1945 St.Step; m 22 Jul 1951 Donna Zimmerman (b 21 Feb 1932 Iowa City, IA). Cedar Rapids, IA residence; Kenneth employed at Rockwell Collins. Children:
    Gary – b 14 Nov 1951 Linn Co IA
    Rickey – b 17 Jan 1953 Linn Co IA
    Rodney – b 14 Nov 1955 Linn Co IA
    Stacy – b 01 Mar 1957 Linn Co IA
    Kendall – b 15 May 1959 Cedar Rapids, IA
    Thomas – b 04 Jan 1961 Cedar Rapids, IA
    Brenda – b 20 May 1963 Cedar Rapids, IA

Kevin Jon HAPPEL s/o Harlan James Happel & Luann Ruth nee Diercks; b 12 Jun 1967; 1st m 27 Oct 1990 Tracie Ann Kammeyer (b 09 Oct 1967)DVD 03 Jul 2002. Child:
    Alan James – b NFR
2nd m Kevin Jon Happel 20 Apr 2004 St.Steph to Kami Leigh Fuller d/o Woody & Judy Steinbeck, Waterloo, IA

Kimberly Sue HAPPEL d/o Loren Ernest Happel & Joan Patricia nee Day; b 01 Feb 1962; m 20 Apr 1985 David Lawrence Titzlaff. Children:
    Brian Lawrence Titzlaff – b 26 Sept 1987
    Adam Michael Titzlaff – b 05 Jun 1990

Laura Jean HAPPEL d/o Harlan James Happel & Luann Ruth nee Diercks; (TWIN: Lisa Jean Happel) b 23 Jul 1964; m 04 Apr 1987 Brian James Bockholt (b 26 Oct 1956). Child:
    Brady James Bockholt – b 27 Mar 1990

Leroy HAPPEL s/o William (Hartmann Peter William) Happel & Dorothea nee Poock; b 27 Dec 1920 Waterloo, IA; d 23 Aug 1971; m 02 Dec 1945 Margaret Ann Buss (b 07 Aug 1922). Children:
    Jeanne Kay – b 21 Dec 1948; m 28 Sept 1969 Eugene Heineman
    David Lee – b 18 Jul 1952; m 19 Aug 1972 Diane Williams

Lester Carl HAPPEL s/o Henry George Happel & Hulda nee Caroline Nolting; b 29 Aug 1938, m 05 Jul 1959 Suzanne Seward (b 26 Mar 1938) DVD 10 Oct 1971. Children:
    Cynthia Kay – b 18 Jan 1960

Michael Harvey – b 29 Apr 1961

Lisa Jean HAPPEL d/o Harlan James Happel & Luann Ruth nee Diercks; (TWIN: Laura Jean Happel) b 23 Jul 1964; m 25 Oct 1986 Barry James Wittenburg (b 11 Jun 1956). Child:
Alana Jo Wittenburg – b 04 Jan 1989

Loreen Marie HAPPEL d/o Adam Martin Andrew Happel & Katharina Barbara nee Rinderknecht; b 06 Jun 1910 Eden Twp near Vinton, IA bpt 1910 St.And; m 11 Sept 1939 LaPorte City, IA to Oakley H. Driscoll (b 27 Sept 1909, d 21 Aug 1985) s/o John Driscoll & Julia nee Harrington. Farmers near LaPorte City, IA. Children:
Norma Jane Driscoll – b 25 Nov 1942;
m 30 Jul 1965 James Lee Ballheim (b 10 Jun 1941)
John Allen Driscoll – b 30 Jul 1945;
m 16 Jun 1973 Judith Kay Brooks

Loren Ernest HAPPEL s/o Martin George Valentine Happel & Dorothy Gertrude nee Poock; b 21 Jul 1931 Happel Homestead Linn Co IA, bpt 1931 and con 1945 St.Steph, 1949 Class Atkins High School, d 10 Oct 1987 ae56y 2m 20d Winston-Salem, NC; Corporate Credit Manager, R.J.Reynolds Industrial, Winston-Salem, NC; m 01 Feb 1957 Joan Patricia Day (b 18 Aug 1931 Ollie, IA). Children:
Jeffrey Lynn – b 25 Nov 1957 Cedar Rapids, IA
Becky Jo – b 25 Mar 1960 Cedar Rapids, IA;
m 24 Sept 1976 Robert Jake Hamby
Kimberly Sue – b 01 Feb 1962 Cedar Rapids, IA;
m 20 Apr 1985 David Lawrence Titzlaff
Bradley Martin – b 26 May 1963 Cedar Rapids, IA

Loren W. HAPPEL s/o Walter Happel & Martha nee Lippert; b 16 Aug 1928 Monticello, IA; Wilson High School, Cedar Rapids, IA d 07 May 1978 ae49y 8m 21d Chariton, IA; retired employee Iowa Department of Transportation; 1st m 24 Jun 1957 Mildred Collins DVD. Children:
Roxanne – b 18 Sept 1958 Irving, TX resident
Daughter – m James Scott, Des Moines, IA resident
Edward – Des Moines, IA resident
2nd m 1968 Loren W. Happel to Arlene Tuttle.

Lydia HAPPEL d/o William Martin Happel & Marie nee Dornseif; b 13

Dec 1914 Van Horne, IA bpt St.And; m 26 Jun 1941 John E. Lecraw. Children:

Donald Lecraw – b 30 Sept 1944; m 31 Oct 1980 to NN
Adrienne Lecraw – b 14 Jun 1946;
    m 08 Oct 1977 John Philip Polychron

Lyle William HAPPEL s/o James Richard Happel & Carolyn Sue nee Schmidt; b 03 Jun 1943; m 01 Oct 1967 Sally Rae Brettman (b 26 Sept 1946). Children:

Dana Rae – b 24 May 1972
Amber Lynn – b 09 Aug 1975

*Magdalena HAPPEL d/o Johann Heinrich Happel & Anna Elisabeth nee Lower; b 22 Apr 1731 Sehlen, Germany; m 18 Jan 1754 Mohnhausen, Germany to Johann Peter Eckhard. Children:

NN Eckhard – b 1754, Godmothers: Anna Catharina Happel,
    Grandmother Margaretha Happel (Schneider)
NN Eckhard – b 1770, Godmothers: Anna Elisabeth Happel,
    Grandmother Margaretha Happel (Schneider)
Johann Jost Eckhard – b 1766, Godfather Johann Jost Happel

**Margita HAPPEL d/o Johann Peter Happel & Gertrud nee Heide; b 20 Feb 1950 Sehlen, Germany; m 25 Oct 1969 Sehlen Luth Ch Germany to Friedhelm Grotecke (b 30 Oct 1944 Muhlhausen, Germany) s/o Hildegard Grotecke. Children:

**Christina Grotecke – b 11 Jan 1970, Korbach Hosp, Germany
**Gabriel Grotecke – b 20 Apr 1971, Korbach Hosp, Germany
**Michaela Grotecke – b 15 Dec 1972, Korbach Hosp, Germany
**Oliver Grotecke – b 16 Nov 1975, Korbach Hosp, Germany
1995 Author visited in home of this family at Mulhausen, Germany.

Maria (Marie) Elizabeth HAPPEL d/o Johann Peter Happel & Katharina Elisabeth nee Werning; b 25 Dec 1890 Happel Farm, Eldorado Twp Benton Co IA, bpt 1891 & con St.John Luth Ch, Eldorado Twp d 05 Jan 1965 ae74y 11d St.Lukes Hosp Cedar Rapids, IA bur 08 Jan 1965 St.John Cem; m 10 Dec 1910 Parent's Farm Home, Eldorado Twp Benton Co IA to Frank Benjamin Braksiek (b 22 Feb 1890 Van Horne, IA bpt 22 Feb 1890 Van Horne, IA d 27 May 1956 ae66y 3m 5d Keystone, IA bur 30 May 1956 St.John Cem) s/o Adam Braksiek & Elisabeth nee Siek of Van Horne, IA. Child:

Stanley Fred Adam Braksiek – b 15 Oct 1911;
     m 10 Mar 1937 Goldie Caroline Ahrens
Paul Henry Karl Braksiek – b 10 Feb 1913;
     m 09 Sept 1941 Naomi Grace Kuelper
Evelyn Anna Marie Braksiek – b 13 Dec 1914;
     m 07 Dec 1932 Roy Pickering
Lolita Elizabeth Braksiek – b 29 Aug 1918; d 03 Jul 1922
     bur St.John Cem
Marian Frances Braksiek – b 06 Sept 1926;
     m 19 Nov 1944 George Harlan Franck
Richard Dean Braksiek – b 21 Jun 1932;
     m 26 Oct 1952 Delores F. Hoydt

Maria (Mary) Katherina HAPPEL d/o Andreas (Andrew) Happel & Maria (Marie) Elisabeth nee Möller (Moeller): cf Friedrich William (Wilhelm) Rinderknecht.

Marie HAPPEL d/o Conrad Happel & Anna nee Kreutner; b 09 Sept 1915, d 29 Nov 1993 ae78y 2m 20d; m 16 Jan 1935 Elmer Schnadt (b 05 May 1912). Children:
     Arlin Conrad Schnadt – b 06 Jan 1936, d 12 Jan 1936
     Ronald Lee Schnadt – b 03 Jan 1937
     Phyllis Ann Schnadt – b 22 Feb 1939; m 02 Sept 1962 Ralph Bolte
     Dale James Schnadt – b 26 Jul 1947; m 27 Jun 1987 Sue Hoeger

Mark HAPPEL s/o Harold John August Happel & Shirley A. nee Markland; b 04 Nov 1957; m 25 Feb 1978 Rhonda Flickinger. Children:
     Kelly Marie – b 21 Jun 1978
     John Keith – b 12 Jun 1984

Martin HAPPEL grandson of Johann George Happel & Katharina Rinderknecht; m Dorothy Poock. Children:
     Edwin John – b 30 May 1921, d 27 Aug 1978; Cedar Rapids, IA
          residence
     Loren W. – b 16 Aug 1928, d 1978; m Arlene NN; Chariton, IA
          residence
     Marvin – NFR Vinton, IA residence
     Dorothy – NFR Cedar Rapids, IA residence
     Elda – m to NN Vileta, Cedar Rapids, IA residence

Martin George Valentine HAPPEL s/o August Happel & Martha nee Young; b 12 Jun 1903 Happel Homestead Linn Co IA, bpt 1903 and con St.Steph, d 13 Oct 1987 ae84y 4m 1d, bur St.Steph Cem; m 20 Feb 1929 to his Happel cousin Dorothy Gertrude Poock (b 06 Feb 1908 Orisha, ND; d 26 Apr 1986 ae78y 2m 20d bur St.Steph Cem) d/o Ernest Poock & Gertrude K. nee Happel. Martin and Dorothy's common Grandparents: Andreas (Andrew) Happel & Maria (Marie) Elisabeth nee Mo(e)ller; Farmed Happel Linn Co IA homestead. Children:

Loren Ernest – b 21 Jul 1931, d 10 Oct 1987;
m 01 Feb 1957 Joan Patricia Day
Grace Gertrude – b 23 Mar 1934;
m 25 Jun 1955 Thomas William Copley
Merle Martin – b 21 Sept 1936; m 11 Aug 1960 Beverly Ann Hagan

Marvin Benjamin HAPPEL s/o August Anton Happel & Marie Louise nee Kraft; b 10 Aug 1909 Eldorado Twp. Benton Co IA, bpt Sept 1909 St.And, d 16 Apr 1964 ae54y 8m 6d Cedar Rapids, IA bur 20 Apr 1964 CdrMem; 1st m 14 Jun 1928 First Christian Ch, Cedar Rapids, IA to Kathleen Pettycourt (b 15 Jun 1912) d/o Claude L. Pettycourt & Ella M. nee Miller of Cedar Rapids, IA. DVD. Partner in farm implement business with his father. At time of death he was secretary-treasurer of Happel & Sons Inc. offices, Cedar Rapids and Central City, IA. Children:

Kathryn Elizabeth – b 24 Nov 1929;
m 21 Apr 1951 Garland E. Wagner
Gerald Marvin – b 06 Sept 1931; m 04 Feb 1950 Betty Louise LeHue
2nd m 26 Nov 1938 Marvin Benjamin Happel to Nina Laura Smith (b 30 Mar 1916 Coconut Grove FL) of Cedar Rapids.

Marvin John HAPPEL s/o Henry George Happel & Hulda Caroline nee Nolting; b 16 May 1936; 1st m 26 Oct 1958 Arnetta Westendorf (b 22 Nov 1936) DVD 24 Apr 1979. Children:

Renee Ann – b 12 Feb 1959
Ronda – b 23 May 1960; m James Konrad
Jon – b 28 Mar 1962
2nd m 08 Aug 1984 Marvin John Happel to Elizabeth Ordonez (b 08 Aug 1959). Children:
Enrique Edward – b 09 Nov 1984
Christina – b 22 Sept 1986

Mary Ann HAPPEL d/o Alfred W. Happel & LaVera nee Hagenow; b 17

Jul 1940; m 10 June 1962 Hilbert Mixdorf. Children:
Denise Mixdorf – b 03 May 1967; m 1989 Mark Ryan
Chad Mixdorf – b 23 Mar 1973

Melvin G. HAPPEL s/o Paul Happel & Emma nee Boettcher: cf Maxine Lorraine Braksiek.

Merle Martin HAPPEL s/o Martin George Valentine & Dorothy Gertrude nee Poock; b 21 Sept 1936 Happel Homestead Linn Co IA, bpt 1936 and con St.Steph, Graduate Atkins High School; Branch Manager Iowa National Mutual Insurance Company, Cedar Rapids; m 11 Aug 1960 Beverly Ann Hagan (b 07 Aug 1938 Shellsburg, IA Graduate Atkins High School) d/o Gordon Hagan & Doris nee Pickerill. Children:
Timothy Gordon – b 20 Apr 1962 Cedar Rapids, IA;
m 27 May 1989 Eydie Faye Campbell
Karina Ann – b 07 Aug 1970 Omaha, NE

Mildred Louise HAPPEL d/o Heinrich August Happel & Elizabeth Christina nee Krug; b 17 Feb 1910 Parent's Farm south Vinton, IA bpt 27 Mar 1910 St.And; d 25 Nov 2000 ae90y 9m 8d; m 25 Nov 1939 Parsonage Vinton, IA Luth Ch to Henry Balthasar Jessen (b 08 Dec 1911 Cedar Bluffs, NE; d 30 Mar 1978 ae66y 3m 22d University Hosp, Iowa City, IA bur 03 Apr 1978 CdrMem) s/o Sonke Jessen, Cedar Bluffs, NE. Child:
Lois Ann Jessen – Stillborn 03 Apr 1951

Milton Eugene HAPPEL s/o Victor Happel & Lucinda nee Wittenberg; b 24 May 1936; m Kim McElhose (b 26 Sept 1936). Children:
David – b 09 Sept 1959; m 17 Jun 1978 to NN (b 18 Feb 1960)
Martin – b 03 May 1963
Andrea – b 26 Feb 1969

Nancy Lue HAPPEL d/o Raymond John Henry Happel & Neoma Margaret nee Biskup; b 18 Feb 1935 St.Lukes Hosp Cedar Rapids, IA bpt Easter Sunday 1935 First Baptist Ch, Cedar Rapids, IA; 1st m 13 Jun 1954 First Baptist Ch, Cedar Rapids, IA to Glenn Eldon Lutz (b 03 Jul 1932 State Center, Marshal Co IA, bpt First Baptist Ch Cedar Rapids) s/o Louis Carl Lutz & Pearl nee Moore of State Center, Marshall Co IA. DVD 1975. Children:
Tamara Rae Lutz – b 13 Feb 1955; m 1980 Craig Lien
Joette Kay Lutz – b 20 Mar 1958

178

2nd m 23 Jun 1984 Nancy Lue nee Happel Lutz to John L. Kaufman (b 31 Jan 1935)

Paul Friedrich Heinrich HAPPEL s/o Johann Georg Happel & Marie nee Richter; b12 Apr 1989 d 23 Feb 1970 bur St. Steph Cem; m 09 Aug 1925 Emma Henrietta Boettcher at Zion Luth Ch, Storm Lake, IA to Emma Henrietta Boettcher (b 02 Aug 1894 in Buena Vista Co, IA, d 02 Jul 1991 ae 96y at her Van Horne, IA residence bur St.Steph Cem) d/o William Boettcher & Ella nee Buchholtz. Members St.Andrew's Luth Ch, Van Horne, IA. Children:
    Marie – Van Horne, IA residence
    Robert – m to Luanna NN, Atkins, IA residence
    Melvin G. – b 20 Sept 1929 Benton Co IA;
        m Maxine Lorraine Braksiek, Victor, IA residence

**Peter HAPPEL s/o Johann Peter Happel & Gertrud nee Heide; b 28 Oct 1954 Sehlen, Germany; m Sehlen, Germany to Inge Werum (b 31 Dec 1955). Children:
    **Jens – b 10 Oct 1976 Sehlen, Germany
    **Bianca Stefanie – b 05 Feb 1978 Sehlen, Germany

Raydean Lee HAPPEL s/o Erwin Henry Happel & Dorothy Fern nee Renner; b 18 Jun 1949; m 07 Sept 1968 Susan Eskridge DVD 1990. Children:
    Jeffery Alan – b 27 Feb 1969
    Jeremy – b 10 May 1971
    TWINS: Marcus – b 29 Jan 1976
           Matthew – b 29 Jan 1976

Raymond John Henry HAPPEL s/o August Anton Happel & Marie Louise nee Kraft; b 06 Dec 1912 Eldorado Twp Benton Co IA, bpt 28 Jan 1913 St.And, d 28 Jan 1973 60y 1m 22d Cedar Rapids, IA bur 30 Jan 1972 CdrMem; Partner with father and brother in Happel & Sons Inc. farm implement business; President at time of death; All-Iowa Fair Board; Board of Directors Cedar Rapids Baseball Assn; Chamber of Commerce; Elks Lodge; m 05 Nov 1933 TrinCR to Neoma Margaret Biskup (b 17 Sept 1911, d 25 Jun 2001 ae89y bur CdrMem) d/o Louis Biskup & Nellie nee Lofferty of Cedar Rapids. Members First Baptist Ch; Children:
    Nancy Lue – b 18 Feb 1935; 1st m 13 Jun 1954 Glenn Eldon Lutz
        DVD 1975; 2nd m 23 Jun 1984 John L. Kaufman

William Raymond – b 15 Jul 1936; m 17 Aug 1957 Catherine Culver
DVD
Judith Kay – b 08 Apr 1942; m 22 Feb 1960 Russell Clare Leidigh

Richard HAPPEL s/o Alfred W.Happel & LaVera nee Hagenow; b 16 Feb
1950; m 02 Feb 1975 Nancy Hesse. Children:
Matthew – b 11 Jul 1975
Lucas – b 11 Mar 1977
Kelli – b 02 Dec 1980
Abbi – b 02 Jun 1983

Richard Henry HAPPEL s/o William (Hartmann Peter William) Happel &
Dorothea Poock; b 17 Aug 1918 Waterloo, IA; m 30 Nov 1939 Florene
Koelling (b 12 Oct 1919). Children:
James Richard – b 22 Nov 1940; m Carolyn Schmidt
Lyle William – b 03 Jun 1943; m Sally Rae Brettman
Bruce William – b 22 Jul 1945, d 25 Nov 1956

Ricky Allen HAPPEL s/o Elmer Derald Happel & Brenda Joyce nee
Hagerty; b 10 Dec 1958 Vinton, IA bpt 11 Jan 1959 TrinVT; 1st m 13 Feb
1976 Laura Jo Oliver (b 12 Apr 1958) DVD 22 Nov 1995. Children:
Renee Jo Lynn – b 21 Jun 1976
Rebecca Lea – b 30 Dec 1978; 1st m NN;
Michael Lynn – b 19 Mar 1983
2nd m 03 Sept 1996 Ricky Allen Happel to Chari Kisling (b 11 Apr 1966).
STEPCHILDREN:
Heather Kisling Happel – b 14 Jan 1984
Sara Kisling Happel – b 07 Aug 1989

Rita J. HAPPEL d/o Alfred W. Happel & LaVera nee Hagenow; b 11 May
1935; 1st m Aug 1957 Virgil Kray DVD. Children:
Michael J. Kray – b 20 Jan 1959; m 30 May 1987 Laurie NN
Jeffrey Kray – b 06 Apr 1960
Kathy Kray – b Oct 1961; m 21 Mar 1987 Duc Tran, DVD
2nd m 19 Apr 1988 Rita J. nee Happel Kray to Dean Frey

Robert HAPPEL s/o Alfred W. Happel & LaVera nee Hagenow; b 28 Sept
1943; m 10 Jun 1972 Margaret Wood. Children:
Jessie – b 23 Jun 1974
Lynn – b 28 Oct 1977

Ronda HAPPEL d/o Marvin John Happel & Arnetta nee Westendorf; b 23 May 1960; m James Konrad. Child:
Kyle Leon Konrad – b 17 Aug 1991

Shannon Lee HAPPEL d/o James Richard Happel & Carolyn Sue nee Schmidt; b 15 Mar 1969; m 16 Dec 1989 Wade Klammer (b 25 Jul 1969). Children:
Kory Dean Klammer – b 18 Mar 1990
Justin Klammer – b 02 Jul 1993

Suzanne HAPPEL d/o William John Happel & Lenora nee Bock; b 29 Oct 1954; m 07 Aug 1976 Dennis Dickenson (b 15 Feb 1952). Children:
Amanda Dickenson – b 23 Oct 1979
Ryan Dickenson – b 01 Dec 1981
Andrea Dickenson – b 25 Jul 1984

Tamara Sue HAPPEL d/o James Albert Happel & Arlene nee Bader; b 26 Mar 1960 Williamburg, IA, bpt 10 Apr 1960 Williamburg, IA, con May 1974 Bethany Luth Ch Cedar Rapids, IA; 1983 U. of IA; m 30 May 1993 David Lawrence Garman (b 04 May 1958 Hawkeye Tech College, Self-employed Artist). Children:
Jakob Albert Stewart Garman – b 18 Dec 1993 Cedar Rapids, IA
David Andrew Garman – b 25 Dec 1998
Emma Elizabeth Garman – b21 Jan 2001

Teresa Jane HAPPEL d/o Charles Conrad Happel & Jane nee Miller; b 14 Jul 1963; m Sept 1983 Joe Stafford. Children:
Justin Stafford – b 12 Jul 1986
Darin Joe Stafford – b 27 May 1989

Verilyn Ferne HAPPEL d/o Erwin Henry Happel & Dorothy Fern nee Renner; b 01 Sept 1943; 1st m 26 Mar 1960 Donald Duane Garner; DVD. Children:
Scott Allan Garner – b 11 Sept 1960; m 03 Nov 1990 Lynn Herliscka
Laurie Jo Garner – b 01 Feb 1963
Timothy David Garner – b 20 Mar 1967
2nd m 02 Jun 1990 Verilyn Ferne nee Happel Garner to Terry Savage.

Vernon HAPPEL s/o William Happel & Dorothea nee Poock; b 22 Mar

1928, m 16 Aug 1963 Betty Eilers (b 04 Apr 1932). Children:
  Sherry – b 04 Apr 1965
  Lori – b 28 Aug 1967

Vernon Ray HAPPEL s/o Elmer Henry Adam Happel & Mildred Esther nee Stevenson; b 10 Aug 1941 Virginia Gay Hosp Vinton, IA bpt 09 Nov 1941 TrinVT; m 27 Jul 1963 Betty L. Wendel (b 23 Oct 1941) d/o Loren Wendel & Glenda nee Melhus. Children:
  Scott – b 06 Aug 1965; m NFR
  Dennis – b 17 Oct 1967

Victor HAPPEL s/o Conrad Happel & Anna nee Kreutner; b 25 Aug 1912; m 10 Jun 1934 Lucinda Wittenburg (b 10 Jun 1916). Child:
  Milton Eugene – b 24 May 1936; m Kim McElhose (b 26 Sept 1936)

Walter HAPPEL s/o Johann George C. Happel & 2nd m Marie nee Richter; b 27 May 1900 Linn City, IA, d 03 Aug 1952 ae52y 2m 7d; m 19 Dec 1919 Martha Lippert (b 12 Oct 1901 Linn City, IA, d 08 Oct 1963 ae61y 11m 26d). Children:
  Marvin – b 16 Jan 1920 Cedar Rapids, IA;
      m 30 Mar 1941 Aretha Shimek
  Edwin – b 30 May 1921 Cedar Rapids, IA d 27 Aug 1978;
      m 25 Jun 1949 Edna Hudson
  Elda Ann – b 27 Apr 1923 Cedar Rapids, IA;
      m 29 Jun 1941 Leo C. Vileta (b 19 Apr 1917)
  Dorothy – b 26 Jan 1926 Cedar Rapids, IA
  Loren W. – b 16 Aug 1928 Monticello, IA;
      d 07 May 1978 Chariton, IA; 1st m 24 Jun 1957 Arlene Tuttle;
      2nd m Mildred Collins

Walter Herman HAPPEL s/o Andrew John Happel & Louise Sophia nee Wente; b 06 Aug 1917 Park Rapids, MN; bpt 1917 d 02 Feb 2000 82y 5m 27d; John Deere Co. employee; m 06 Feb 1947 St.Peter Luth Ch Denver, Bremer Co IA to Eleanora Mathilda Musch (b 26 Sept 1914). Celebrated 50th Golden Wedding Anniversary; Waterloo, IA residence. Aft Walter's death Eleanora moved to :2603 Orchard Drive, Cedar Falls, IA. Child:
  Audrey Louise – b 05 Apr 1951; m 26 May 1973 Robert E. Hill

Wilhelm HAPPEL s/o George Happel & Anna Katherina nee Hayner. Children:

Thomas – b 1970
Diana – b 1971
Armin – b 1974

William HAPPEL s/o Conrad Happel & Anna nee Kreutner; b 05 Apr 1910; m 07 Sept 1933 Esther Matthias. Children:
Harlan James – b 16 Feb 1935; m 07 Aug 1960 Luann R. Diercks
Audrey – b 02 Aug 1937; m 09 Aug 1959 Norbert Schmidt
Gordon – b 05 Jul 1939; m Ruth Detterding

William John HAPPEL s/o (William) Hartmann Peter William Happel & Dorothea nee Poock; b 26 Nov 1924, d 05 Feb 1972; m 06 Apr 1947 Lenora Bock (b 06 Aug 1922). Children:
Beverly Kay – b 26 Jan 1948; m 15 Mar 1969 Gene Wehr
Darwin Eugene – b 24 Jul 1949
Eileen Joyce – b 22 Sept 1950, d 29 Jul 1985
Suzanne – b 29 Oct 1954; m 07 Aug 1976 Dennis Dickenson

(William) Hartmann Peter William HAPPEL s/o Johann Heinrich Happel & Gertrud nee Fels; b 27 Sept 1885 Fremont Twp Benton Co IA, d 1953 ae68y; m 14 Sept 1910 Dorothea Poock (b 29 Nov 1890 Klinger, IA). Ten children:
Elda – b 10 Aug 1911 Dunkerton, IA; d 13 Sept 1984;
    m 01 Feb 1931 Walter Warneke (b 08 Aug 1906)
Hilda – b 16 Mar 1914 Waterloo, IA; d 19 Jul 1942;
    m 26 Nov 1937 Harold Meyer
Esther – b 05 Apr 1916 Waterloo, IA;
    1st m 30 Nov 1933 Melvin Matthias, DVD;
    2nd m 01 Nov 1975 Harold Spooner
Richard Henry – b 17 Aug 1918 Waterloo, IA;
    m 30 Nov 1939 Florene Koelling
Leroy – b 27 Dec 1920 Waterloo, IA; d 23 Aug 1971;
    m 02 Dec 1945 Margaret Ann Buss
William John – b 26 Nov 1924 Waterloo, IA; d 05 Feb 1972;
    m 06 Apr 1947 Lenora Bock
Anna Marie – b 16 Apr 1926 Waterloo, IA;
    m 27 Oct 1946 in CT Albert Henry Gielau
Vernon – b 22 Mar 1928 Waterloo, IA; m 16 Aug 1963 Betty Eilers
Donna Mae – b 18 Apr 1930 Waterloo, IA; d 18 Jul 1992;
    1st m 26 Oct 1952 Robert Dale Boots;

2nd m 14 Apr 1984 Robert L. Paulsen
Dorothy Marie – b 07 Oct 1932 Waterloo, IA; d 17 Nov 1981;
    m 14 Sept 1950 James Holdiman

William Martin HAPPEL s/o Johann Peter Happel & Katharine Elisabeth
nee Werning; b 29 Jan 1888 Family Farm, Eldorado Twp Benton Co IA, bpt
1888 & con St.John, Newhall, IA d 17 Jul 1914 ae26y 5m 18d Family
Farm, Eldorado Twp Benton Co IA, [Bled to death in oat field of his farm
following runaway horses that knocked him into the cutting blades of the
oat binder] bur Jul 1914 St.John Cem; m 08 Apr 1912 St.John Luth Ch,
Newhall to Marie Dornseif (b 02 Jul 1886 Fort Dodge, IA, bpt 1886, d 22
May 1967 in CA) d/o Rev Philip Dornseif & Marie nee Guenther of Fort
Dodge, IA. Wid/o and young daughters made home with Henry & Christina
nee Happel Krug in Clinton Twp Linn Co IA until moving to CA residence.
Children:
    Dorothy – b 11 Feb 1913 Benton Co IA, d 07 Mar 1990 in CA
        m 09 Nov 1940 L. Vernon Greenleaf, CA
    Lydia – b 13 Dec 1914 Benton Co IA;
        m 26 Jun 1941 John E. Lecraw, CA
2nd m in CA Marie nee Dornseif Happel to Arthur Adrian

William Raymond HAPPEL SR. s/o Raymond John Henry Happel &
Neoma Margaret nee Biskup; b 15 Jul 1936 Cedar Rapids, IA bpt 1936
TrinCR; m 17 Aug 1957 First Presbyterian Ch, Cedar Rapids IA to
Catherine Culver (b 03 Oct 1936) d/o William Clarke Culver of Cedar
Rapids. DVD Children:
    Jana Lynn – b 10 May 1960
    William Raymond JR. – b 13 Dec 1963; m 22 Mar 1986 Tamie Jo Hese
    Robert Quinton – b 29 Oct 1965

Wilma Malinda HAPPEL d/o Henry George Happel & Hulda Caroline nee
Nolting; b 29 Feb 1928; m 29 Sept 1946 Leroy Steege (b 20 Nov 1921).
Children:
    Gregory Lynn Steege – b 08 Aug 1947;
        m 27 Aug 1969 Susan Mae Wente
    Debra Ann Steege – b 23 Sept 1950;
        m 19 Oct 1968 Duane Paul St.John
    Jolyne Kay Steege – b 31 Jan 1954; m 06 Apr 1973 Daniel Matthias
        DVD 1975
    Mark Leroy Steege – b 30 Apr 1960; m 21 Aug 1982 Teresa Kosted

Yvonne Marie HAPPEL d/o Alfred W. Happel & LaVera nee Hagenow; b 01 Jun 1937; m 05 Aug 1956 Glenn Wehrkamp. Children:
   Donald D. Wehrkamp – b 30 Jul 1957; m 23 Aug 1980 Karen NN
   Pamela Wehrkamp – b 12 Jul 1959; m 10 Aug 1985 Steve Egli
   Beth Marie Wehrkamp – b 18 Dec 1962;
      m Aug 1990 Robert McWilliams
   Kristin Wehrkamp – b 11 March 1970

Alice HARNISCH d/o William Harnisch & Emma nee Werning; b 12 Jul 1935; m 09 Jun 1956 Maurice Richard Schumacher (b 01 May 1935) s/o Maurice Schumacher & Mrs. Virgil (Bertha Day) Bunce.

Esther HARNISCH d/o William Harnisch & Emma nee Werning; b 04 Jun 1930; m 24 Jun 1950 Elry Hoefs (b 30 Jul 1928) s/o Edward Hoefs & Clara nee Sether. Child:
   Debra Hoefs – b 13 May 1952

Helen HARNISCH d/o William Harnisch & Emma nee Werning; b 06 Aug 1927; m 26 Sept 1953 Earl Slovak (b 28 Feb 1923) s/o John Slovak & Emma nee Buckolz. Child:
   William Slovak – b 06 Jul 1955; m 1982 Pennie Lou Hamm

Leonard HARNISCH s/o William Harnisch & Emma nee Werning; b 06 Jan 1933; m 28 Oct 1967 to Yvonne Erickson (b 10 Oct 1941) d/o Theodore Erickson & Hilda nee Benson. Children:
   William – b 11 Apr 1969
   Eric Lenard – b 08 Nov 1971

Margaret HARNISCH d/o William Harnisch & Emma nee Werning; b 20 Aug 1925; m 26 Sept 1953 John Buckler JR. (b 19 Mar 1925) s/o John Buckler SR. & Nellie nee Koorman. Children:
   Mary Margaret Buckler – b 16 Oct 1954
   Alan Dean Buckler – b 07 Feb 1956
   Dale Warren Buckler – b 15 Jul 1957
   Lora Marie Buckler – b 13 May 1966

Mathilda HARNISCH d/o William Harnisch & Emma nee Werning; b 19 Mar 1918, d Jun 1997; m 12 Sept 1939 LeRoy Campbell (b 04 Nov 1911, d 08 Jan 1969) s/o Rufus Campbell & Della nee Bedford. Children:

185

Clara May Campbell – b 20 Aug 1940; m 1959 Robert White

Marjorie Campbell – b 10 Nov 1942; 1st m 1959 Richard VanVleck
   DVD; 2nd m 1986 Marion Paulsen

Beverly Campbell- b 19 Dec 1946; m 1965 Daniel Dortt

Gregory Alan HARRIS s/o Velma Louise nee Rinderknecht & Thurman Cloyd Harris; b 24 Jan 1955 St.Lukes Hosp Cedar Rapids, IA; m 07 Sept 1980 All Saint's Ch Cedar Rapids to Carolyn Ann Wilson (b 19 Jun 1959 Cedar Rapids, IA) d/o Harold Joseph Wilson & Jane Ganoe nee Jensen. Children:

Nichole Louise – b 16 Nov 1983 Cedar Rapids, IA

Nathan Wilson – b 11 Jun 1989 Cedar Rapids, IA

Nadine Jane – b 01 Oct 1991 Cedar Rapids, IA

Robert Dwain HARRIS s/o Velma Louise nee Rinderknecht & Thurman Cloyd Harris; b 23 Feb 1950 St.Lukes Hosp Cedar Rapids, IA; 1st m 26 Jun 1971 TrinCR to Kristine Kay Beatty (b 01 Jul 1954) DVD. Child:

Brad Alan – b 15 Nov 1972 St.Lukes Hosp Cedar Rapids, IA

2nd m 29 Sept 1978 Robert Dwain Harris to Patricia Elaine Tudeen (b 17 Jun 1952 Cedar Rapids, IA) d/o Clarence Bernard Tudeen & Joann nee Miller. Children:

Amy Suzanne – b 13 Sept 1979 Mercy Hosp Cedar Rapids, IA

Erica Renee – b 11 Jan 1982 Mercy Hosp Cedar Rapids, IA

Lisa Marie – b 28 Jan 1985 Cedar Rapids, IA

Sharon Louise HARRIS d/o Velma Louise nee Rinderknecht & Thurman Cloyd Harris; b 30 Mar 1946 St.Lukes Hosp Cedar Rapids, IA; m 29 Jul 1967 TrinCR to Don Lloyd Drahn (b 15 Mar 1944 Monroe, IA) s/o Glender Arthur Drahn & Irene Ann nee Williamson. Children:

Jeffery David Drahn – b 24 May 1968 Olin, IA

Denise Michele Drahn – b 06 Sept 1969 Cedar Rapids, IA;
   m 28 Jul 1990 Craig Marvin Adams

Chad Harris Drahn – b 07 Feb 1973 Postville, IA

Alfred L. HARTKEMEYER s/o William C. Hartkemeyer & Jennie nee Stammer; b 1919, d Jul 1979 bur St.Steph Cem; m Helen L. Bascom (b 1919, d Jan 1980 bur St.Steph Cem) d/o Albert Bascom SR. of Newhall, IA. 1946 moved to Atkins, IA from Blairstown, IA. Alfred worked for Benton Co IA as maintainer operator; 1960-62 purchased a gas station in Atkins. They also bought into the Atkins drugstore and ran it until closing in 1967.

Alfred also worked for the Milwaukee Railroad and Midland Forge in Cedar Rapids, IA until his death. Helen worked in Cedar Rapids for Killian department store and Collins Radio Company. Children:

Elaine – b 1942; Memphis, TN residence, 4 children

David – b 1945; Charlestown, SC residence, one daughter

Dick – b 1947; m NN Miles & had two sons

Eileen – b 15 Jan 1950 Vinton, IA; 1st m Jan 1970 Bernard Heyer JR. DVD; 2nd m 17 Mar 2000 Las Vegas, NV to John Schanbacher

Eileen HARTKEMEYER d/o Alfred L. Hartkemeyer & Helen L. nee Bascom; b 15 Jan 1950 Vinton, IA; bpt 19 Feb 1950, con 22 Mar 1964; 1st m Jan 1970 Bernard Heyer JR. DVD. Children:

Brenda – m 29 Apr 1999 David Huber

Julie – m 09 Oct 1999 Wayne Farmer

2nd m 17 Mar 2000 Las Vegas, NV Eileen nee Hartkemeyer Heyer to John Schanbacher s/o Wilbert Schanbacher & Eda nee Rinderknecht.

*William C. HARTKEMEYER b 21 Mar 1876 Westphalia, Laverne, Germany, d 04 Apr 1948 IA ae72y 14d; came to USA with his mother, three brothers, and three sisters. His father came earlier and found living quarters for the family in Cincinnati, OH. The family moved to Luzerne, IA and Belle Plaine, Benton Co. IA; m Jennie Stammer (d 09 Jun 1973) of Belle Plaine, IA. Her parents also came from Germany. They moved to Atkins, IA 08 Dec 1941 from the Keystone, IA and Van Horne, IA area. Children:

Eldo – dec'd NFR

Elmer – Cedar Rapids, IA resident

Laura C. – d 28 Mar 2002;
    m 1954 Arthur George Wilhelm (Bud) Rinderknecht

Leona – Never Married; Atkins, IA resident, housework employment

Edna – Never Married; Atkins, IA resident, local employment

Alfred L. – b 1919, d Jul 1979, bur St.Steph Cem;
    m Helen L. Bascom, moved to Atkins, IA

Leonard J. HARTL s/o Fred Hartl & Laverna nee Rinderknecht; b 18 Sept 1936 Cedar Rapids, IA; d 12 Jun 2004 St.Mary's Hosp Rochester MN [Car Accident near West Union IA]; 1954 Class Roosevelt High School Cedar Rapids; farmer and grain trucker; teacher of physics Davenport & Eastern Iowa Community College; m NN. Children:

Julie – Nevada IA residence

Dan – m Melissa, Calamar, IA residence

Herbert HARTZ s/o Virgil Hartz & Ruth E. nee Schmidt; b 1943; m Sally Curtis; Cedar Rapids, IA residence. Children:
Julie Anne – b 1966
Jennifer Kay – b 1969

Mary HARTZ d/o Virgil Hartz & Ruth E. nee Schmidt; b 1936; m Dr. William R. Cotton MD. Chevy Chase, MD residence. Child:
Caroline Ruth Cotton – b 1976

Joel Craig HASSTEDT s/o Janet Carol nee Moeller & Myron Wilson Hasstedt; b 09 Dec 1960; m 21 May 1988 First Methodist Ch Plainwell, MI to Denise Elaine Headley (b 05 Oct 1957). Children:
Ryan Craig – b 02 May 1990
Ashley Elaine – b 13 Feb 1992

Todd Alan HASSTEDT s/o Janet Carol nee Moeller & Myron Wilson Hasstedt; b 20 Mar 1963; m 12 Aug 1989 Timothy Episcopal Ch, West Des Moines, IA to Andrea Ramah Camenzend (b 15 Mar ND). Children:
Nathan Alan – b 19 Apr 1994
TWINS: Nicole Ann – b 14 Jul 1996
             Joshua Tyler – b 14 Jul 1996

Jane Elaine HAUSKINS d/o Edna Elizabeth nee Moeller & Carl Julius Hauskins; b 09 Mar 1937; 1st m 23 May 1963 Donald Lincoln Wallin, DVD 1967. 2nd m 17 Jul 1970 Jon Allen Jernigan (b 14 Nov 1939) Petaluma, CA residence.

Joan Edna HAUSKINS d/o Edna Elizabeth nee Moeller & Carl Julius Hauskins; b 16 Sept 1930 Cedar Rapids, IA; m 08 Dec 1950 George Luppert Pyle (b 29 Dec 1926; Retired Insurance Audit Manager). Naples, FL residence. Children:
James George Pyle – b 18 Jul 1951;
      m 29 Nov 1987 Janet Maria Richard
Susan Jane Pyle – b 22 Aug 1952;
      1st m 25 Sept 1976 John Henry Fusan JR. DVD Oct 1979;
      2nd m 09 Jun 1990 Stephen Pierson
Robert Carl Pyle – b 17 Jun 1960; Indianapolis, IN residence
David William Pyle – b 24 Oct 1966; Morgans Point, TX residence

**Anni Elisabeth HECKER d/o Helene nee Ritter & Karl Friedrich Hecker; b 04 Nov 1939 Löhlbach, Germany; m Walter Debus, Bricklayer, Male Nurse (b 16 Oct 1934). 1999 Author met Anni in Löhlbach the first time.. Children:

    **Karl Heinrich Debus – b 12 Mar 1958, Civil Engineer;
        m Jutta Erika Hesse, bank employee
    **Richard Konrad Debus – b 09 Jul 1959, customs employee;
        m Christel Friederike
    **Ute Charlotte Helene Debus – b 29 Oct 1962;
        Choral Director, Organist

Clement HECKT s/o Ernst Heckt & Emma nee Ohde; b 1907, d 1979; m Fleta Shirley. Children:
    James Ernst – NFR
    Shirley – NFR

Ernst HECKT s/o Joachim Heckt & Anna nee Dierks; b 1880 Tama Co IA, d 1926 Keystone, Benton Co IA; moved to Keystone, IA ae12y; m 04 Feb 1903 at home of her parents Keystone, IA to Emma Ohde (b 1882, d 1940) d/o William Ohde & Caroline nee Wiese; 1903-1924 business: Heckt Hardware and Furniture Store, Keystone, IA Funeral Director; founded Heckt Oil Company. Children:
    Raymond – b 1904, d 1967; m Ruth Rucker
    Clement – b 1907, d 1979; m Fleta Shirley
    Herbert – b 1912; m Beryl McGoff
    Phyllis – b 1917; m Ronald England

Herbert HECKT s/o Ernst Heckt & Emma nee Ohde; b 1912; m Beryl McGoff. Children:
    Sherwyn – NFR
    William – NFR
    Carole – NFR

*Joachim HECKT s/o Margarita Heckt of Hafen Laboe, Germany; b 1843 Hafen Laboe, Germany, d 1929 Benton Co IA; m Anna Dierks (d 1890 IA) residence Hafen Laboe, seaport village close to Denmark, where Joachim was carpenter working on ships; 1880 emigrated to Tama Co IA. Child:
    Ernst- b 1880 IA, d 1926 Benton Co IA; m 1903 Emma Ohde

Phyllis HECKT d/o Ernst Heckt & Emma nee Ohde; b 1917; m Ronald England. Children:

Jacqueline England – m NN Schoettmer
Duane England – NFR
Michael England – NFR
Rodney England – NFR
Robin England – Ernst Heckt Homestead, IA residence

Raymond HECKT s/o Ernst Heckt & Emma nee Ohde; b 1904, d 1967; m Ruth Rucker. Child:

Rosemary – NFR

*August HEINRICH b 1849 Tusheim, Madgeburg province, Germany; ae21y, 1870 emigrated to Milwaukee, WI with two brothers, Gustav and Frederich; parents and another brother William came later, stayed one year and returned to Germany; 1871 August moved to Blairstown area, Benton Co IA; m Susan Wolf. Purchased 160 acre farm in 1876. Children:

Emma – NFR
Mae – NFR
Amanda – NFR
George – NFR

*Frederich HEINRICH b 1852 when parents lived in South Australia; 1870 emigrated to Milwaukee, WI with two brothers, August and Gustav; parents and brother William came later, stayed one year and returned to Germany; pro 1870's moved to Blairstown area, Benton Co IA; farm laborer; m 1880 Mary LoBean. 1890 purchased 160 acre farm; sold farm and moved to Cedar Rapids, IA. Children:

Hattie – NFR
Clara – NFR
Alfred – NFR

*Gustav HEINRICH – b 1855 Tusheim, Madgeburg province, Germany; 1870 emigrated to Milwaukee, WI with two brothers, August and Frederich; parents and brother William came later, stayed one year and returned to Germany; 1873 moved to Benton Co IA; farm laborer; m Matilda Becker. Purchased Benton Co IA farms 1878 and 1882. Children:

NN infant – dec'd
Arthur – m Daisy Baker
Laurance – m Meta Coombs

Frank – m Mabel McGranahan, sons: Howard, Wallace
Jennie – m Arthur Brown
Elsie – Never Married
Charlie – m Tilla Stien
Laura – m Dr. Wold
Mrytle – m Gerald Woodill
Raymond – m Ethel Bell
Edith – m Carlyle Richards

Elmer HEITMANN s/o Louis Heitmann & Mary nee Boehmke; b 1902, d 1980; 1942-1945 World War II US Army; m 1945 Edna Olmsted of McGregor, IA. Teacher in Keystone, IA beginning in 1942. Children:
Jean – b 1948; m Glenn Neely
Mary – b 1951; m Gene Welch
Neill – b 1953; Ames, IA residence
Gale – b 1954; m 1980 Sue Walton
Alice – b 1957; Des Moines, IA residence

Gale HEITMANN s/o Elmer Heitmann & Edna nee Olmsted; b 1954; m 1980 Sue Walton. Fourth generation farmers on Hitmann land, Century Farm since 1984. Children:
Luke – b 1980
Will – b 1984

*John HEITMANN SR. b 1840 Ackland, Germany, d 1925 Keystone, Benton Co IA; April 1865 emigrated to Benton Co IA; purchased 80 acres Benton Co land, returned to Germany 18 months later to m Lena Rosburg (b 1838 Germany, d 1917 Keystone, Benton Co IA). Kane Twp Benton Co IA farmers until 1904 retirement in Keystone, IA. Ten children:
Heinrich – b 1867, d 1894
Lena – b 1869, d 1900; m Fred Lahn
Herman – b 1870, d 1943; m Margretha Franzenburg
Cecilia – b 1872, d 1946; m Hans Willer, Akron, IA
Maria – b 1873, d 1955; m John Albertsen
Alvena – b 1875, 1927; m Peter Junge
Martin – b 1877, d 1877
Johann – b 1878, d 1931; m Caroline Mussman
Louis – b 1881, d 1964; m Mary Boehmke
Wilhelm – b 1883, d 1933; Katie Holm, Remsen, IA

Louis HEITMANN s/o John Heitmann & Lena nee Rosburg; b 1881; m 1964 Mary Boehmke. Farmed Heitmann land until 1941 retirement in Keystone. Children:
    Elmer – b 1902, d 1980
    Francis – d 1936

Mary HEITMANN d/o Elmer Heitmann & Edna nee Olmstead; b 1951; B.S. ISU; Teacher Coordinator Omaha Public Schools; m Gene Welch. Children:
    David Welch – b 1978
    John Welch – b 1981

Karen Marie HEITSHUSEN d/o Milda Katherine nee Keiper & Willard Anton Heitshusen; (TWIN: Kaye Ann Heitshusen) b 21 Jun 1952 Belle Plaine, IA; m 30 Jul 1971 St.John to Joseph Andrew Wheeler s/o Don & Joyce Wheeler. Separated 1984. Children:
    Chad Joseph Wheeler – b 01 Feb 1972 St.Lukes Hosp CR, IA
    Timothy Melvin Wheeler- b 04 Dec 1974 St.Lukes Hosp CR, IA
    Scott Alan Wheeler – b 30 Jan 1978 St.Lukes Hosp CR, IA

Kaye Ann HEITSHUSEN d/o Milda Katherine nee Keiper & Willard Anton Heitshusen (TWIN: Karen Ann Heitshusen) b 21 Jun 1952 Belle Plaine, IA; m 03 Mar 1973 St.John to Richard Allen Less (b 31 Aug 1951 Cedar Rapids, IA) s/o Vernon Charles Less & Josephine nee Hauser. Children:
    Rachel Ann Less – b 14 May 1975 Lincoln, NE
    Ryan Allen Less – b 18 Jun 1977 Lincoln, NE

*Joseph HENSING b 04 Dec 1924 Derden, Keets Hochester, Loenigreich, os Prussia, ns Germany; 1852 emigrated to USA; m Freeport, IL to Elizabeth Jaeger. 1875 moved to Benton Co IA and purchased 160 acre Taylor Twp farm remaining in Hensing name 91 years; sons took over farm when Joseph returned to Freeport, IL to retire. Children:
    Joseph A. – b 1861, d 1927; m 1894 Emma Miller
    TWINS: George – NFR
               Charles -NFR
    William – NFR
    Kate – NFR
    Frances – NFR

*Joseph A. HENSING s/o Joseph Hensing & Elizabeth nee Jaeger; b 1861 [Hospitalized 28 years after kicked by horse] d 1927; m 1894 Emma Miller of Newhall, IA. Emma rented the Hensing farm and moved to SD where her sons were educated; returned to Iowa farm when they were old enough to start farming. Children:

Fred Joseph – b 1896; continued farming Hensing land
Arthur – b 1898; moved to CA

Carl J. "Charlie" HEPPE s/o Martin Heppe & Dorthea nee Bierschenk; b 1889 near Newhall, IA d 1967; m 1922 St.John Luth Ch in Eldorado Twp to Christina Elizabeth Bierschenk (b 23 Oct 1896, d 1948) d/o Carl Heinrich (Henry Carl) Bierschenk & Elizabeth nee Kranz. Rented farm land near Vinton, Garrison, and Atkins Benton Co IA areas before 1941 purchasing from her parents farm located in Eden Twp northwest of Newhall, IA. Carl farmed until his death. Children:

Robert – b 1924; m Virginia Harper; Cedar Rapids, IA residence
Dwain C. – b 1927; m Reta Leimberer; Newhall, IA farmers
Arlene – b 1928, d 1951

Dewain C. HEPPE s/o Carl Heppe & Christina Elizabeth nee Bierschenk; b 1927 Vinton, IA d 17 Oct 1986; two years US Army in Wiesbaden, Germany; occupational forces during Korean Conflict; returned to farm and bought his father's farm in 1954; m 27 Jul 1958 Reta Leimberer (b 04 Apr 1934, d 07 Apr 1999 ae65y 3d; taught school in Poweshiek and Benton Co IA twenty-five years, later a social worker). Child:

Brian (Adopted) – b 1966; m/DVD; daughter: Stephanie

*Kathrina HEPPE d/o Martin Heppe & Dorthea nee Bierschenk; b 1886 in Germany, d 1947 IA; m Carl Vaupel. Children:

Henry Vaupel – NFR
Louise Vaupel – NFR
Alfred Vaupel – NFR
Anna Vaupel – NFR
Emma Vaupel – NFR
Martha Vaupel – NFR
Arnold Vaupel – NFR

Robert HEPPE s/o Martin Heppe & Dorthea nee Bierschenk; b 1924; m Virginia Harper (b 1925). Cedar Rapids, IA residence. Children:

Kristine – b 1949

193

Kendall – b 1950
Karl – b 1952
Karol E. – dec'd 1954
Kyle – b 1955
Karol V. – b 1958

Lois HERETH d/o Martha nee Seene & Conrad Hereth; b 1916, d 1988
(TWIN: Lydia Hereth); m Eugene Wisman (b 1917, d 1989). Child:
Jay Wisman – b 1939; m Mary Ann Denniss. Child:
    Mary Jaylene Wisman (b 1970); m Eric Wecks. Child:
    Lillian Grace Wecks (b 1999)

Martha HERETH d/o Martha nee Senne & Conrad Hereth; b 1909; m
Henry Brandes (b 1901, d 1977). Children:
John Brandes – b 1933; m Helen Bressler (b 1934). Child:
    Leona Kathleen; 1st m Kenneth Wing; 2nd m Gary Smith
Martha Jane Brandes – b 1945; m Lester Franks. Child:
    Donna Jean Franks (b 1966, d 1985)

Ruth HERETH d/o Martha nee Senne & Conrad Hereth; b 1911; m Carl
Koss (b 1908, d 1997). Children:
Noel Koss – b 1942; m Linda R. I. Lee (b 1943). Children:
    1. Konrad Nikolaus (b 1969); m Juliane Soreano. Children:
    Ethan (b 1997); Katelyn Rose (b 1998)
    2. Kristin Leanne (b 1971); m Kevin Flandreau
    3. Eric Steiner (b 1972); 4. Jenniver Lynn (b 1973)
Mary Koss – b 1946; m William Branom (b 1945). Children:
    1. Mark William Branom (b 1971); m Susanne North
    2. Jonathan David Branom (b 1977); 3. Christina Marie Branom
    (b 1984); 4. Robert Timothy Branom (b 1986)
Timothy Koss – b 1950; m Kathleen Prine (b 1951). Child:
    Amanda Marie Koss (b 1976)

*Anna HERTLE d/o John Hertle & Rosina nee Frank; b 1875 Germany, d
1966 Benton Co IA; 1st m Gottlieb Raetz. Children:
Clarence Raetz – NFR
John Raetz – NFR
Emma Raetz – NFR
Wilma – dec'd ae3y

2nd m Anna nee Hertle Raetz to William Meissner.

Arnold William Martin HERTLE s/o August Hertle & Martha nee Bierschenk; b 03 Sept 1919 on grandparent Bierschenk's farm north of Newhall, Eden Twp Benton Co IA; bpt and con St.John; Class 1936 Newhall High School; d 31 Mar 2007 ae87y 6m 28d Shellsburg, IA Rock Ridge Care Center, bur St.John; m 10 May 1944 Keystone, IA to Lois G. Schoelerman (b 19 Jul 1924, d 21 May 2001 ae76y 10 m 2d) d/o George Schoelerman & Rosa nee Kuhl of Keystone, IA. Farmed Hertle Homestead north of Newhall. 1964 moved into home built in Newhall and continued farming. 1972 purchased Schoelerman homestead north of Keystone, IA. Children:
  Terry – b 09 Jan 1945; m 27 Sept 1964 Judith Sindt
  Eloise – b 1946; m 1965 John Timmerman

*August Sebastian HERTLE s/o John Hertle & Rosina nee Franck; b 19 Mar 1881 Sackenfleur-Baden, Germany, d 19 Jan 1964 ae82y 10m, bur St.John Cem. In 1892, ae11y came to USA with parents and two sisters to live with other sisters and brothers settled near the Amana Colonies; m 16 Dec 1903 Martha Elizabeth Bierschenk (b 12 Oct 1877 Datterode Hessen, Germany, d 04 Jul 1945 ae67y 8m 24d IA) d/o John Heinrich Bierschenk & Anna Katherine nee Gier. Built farmstead four and one-fourth miles north of Newhall, IA where they farmed until 1944 retirement in Newhall. August served as Township Trustee and two terms on Benton County IA Board of Supervisors. Seven children:
  Carl – b 1905, d 1915 ae10y
  Ilma – b 1907; d NFR; m 1924 John George Koopman
  Clarence Conrad J. – b 1910, d 1977; m Elfrieda Fiebelkorn
  Luella – b 1911, d 1912
  Leola Anna Elizabeth – b 25 Jun 1913, d 18 Sept 2002;
      m 27 Jun 1934 Irvin August Krug
  Elfreida – b 1917; d NFR; 1st m 1936 Jay McKinstry;
      2nd m 1959 Hartley McHattie
  Arnold – b 03 Sept 1919; d 31 Mar 2007;
      m 10 May 1944 Lois Schoelerman

Dennis HERTLE s/o Clarence C.J. Hertle & Elfrieda nee Fiebelkorn; b 1942; m Sandra Blough. Atkins, IA residence. Children:
  Michael – b 1966
  Michelle – b 1968

Melissa – b 1970

Elfrieda HERTLE d/o August Hertle & Martha nee Bierschenk; b 1917; d ND; 1st m 1936 Jay McKinstry (dec'd).
Children:
  Sharon McKinstry – NFR
  Sheila McKinstry – NFR
2nd m 1959 Elfrieda nee Hertle McKinstry to Hartley McHaffie. Des Moines, IA residence.

Eloise HERTLE d/o Arnold William Martin Hertle & Lois nee Schoelerman; b 1946; m 1965 John Timmerman (b 1944, d 1970) s/o Walter & Elna Timmerman of Newhall, IA. Newhall, IA residence.
Children:
  David Timmerman – m Rachelle, Fairfax, IA residence
  Mark Timmerman – m Stephanie, Van Horne, IA residence

*George HERTLE s/o John Hertle & Rosina nee Frank; b 1865 Germany, d 1952 IA; m 1888 Sophie Preis. Children:
  Mary – NFR
  Emma – NFR
  Bertha – NFR
  Anna – NFR

Ilma HERTLE d/o August Hertle & Martha nee Bierschenk: cf John George Koopman.

*John HERTLE b 10 Jul 1836 Sacksenfleur, Baden, Germany, d 28 Oct 1908 ae72y 3m 18d Newhall, IA bur St.John Cem; baker by trade in Germany; m 11 Nov 1859 Rosina Frank (b 12 Mar 1841 Germany, d 18 May 1925 ae84y 2m 6d Benton Co IA bur St.John Cem). 01 May 1892 emigrated with three children to Iowa settling near the Amana Colonies; 1897 moved to farm near Atkins, Benton Co and later to farm near Newhall, Eldorado Twp Benton Co IA. Mbrs St.John. Children:
  *Katharine – b 1860 Germany, d 1945 Atkins, IA;
      m 1886 John W. Matter in Germany
  *George – b 1865, d 1952; m 1888 Sohpie Preiss
  *William – b 1867, d 1931; m 1892 Friederike Schumann
  *Rosina – b 1870, d 1945; m 1891 William Wiese
  John – b 1871, d 1889

Lena – dec'd Germany

Sopfie – dec'd Germany ae18y

Albert – dec'd Germany

*Anna – b 1875, d 1966; 1st m Gottlieb Raetz;
   2nd m William Meissner

*August Sebastian – b 19 Mar 1881, d 19 Jan 1964;
   m 16 Dec 1903 Martha Elizabeth Bierschenk

*Louise – b 1884, d 1914; m 1902 Claus Behrens

*Louise HERTLE d/o John Hertle & Rosina nee Frank; b 1884 Germany, d 1914 Atkins, IA; 1st m 1902 Claus Behrens (d Atkins bur St.John Cem). Farmers south of Atkins, Benton Co IA. Children:

John Behrens – NFR

Harry Behrens – NFR

Mae Behrens – NFR

Louis Behrens – NFR

2nd m 1915 Claus Behrens to Anna Matter (d Atkins, IA bur St.John Cem). Children:

Pauline Behrens – b 26 Jan 1919, d 25 Dec 2000 in Floyd, IN
   m 12 Jan 1940 Albert Kreutner

Walter Behrens – b 05 Apr 1905, d 24 Apr 1970 Williamsburg, IA
   m 19 Jan 1936 Louise Martha Haerther

Carl Behrens – NFR

Elmer Behrens – d 1999

Richard HERTLE s/o Clarence C.J. Hertle & Elfreida nee Fiebelkorn; b 29 Oct 1938 Eden Twp Benton Co IA; m 02 Dec 1967 Judy Webert d/o Melvin Webert & Eleanor nee Rinderknecht. Farmers north of Newhall. Children:

Brad – b 1968

Shonda – b 1972

Rosina HERTLE d/o John Hertle & Rosina nee Frank: cf William Wiese.

Terry HERTLE s/o Arnold William Martin Hertle & Lois nee Schoelerman; b 09 Jan 1945 Belle Plaine, IA; Newhall High School; m 27 Sept 1964 at Keystone Judith Sindt (b 04 Mar 1944 Belle Plaine; Keystone High School; American Institute of Business) d/o Lester & Dorothy Sindt of Keystone, IA. Fourth generation farmers on Hertle homestead. Members St.John. Children:

Kevin – b 29 Aug 1965; Hotel Manager, St.Louis, MO
Denise – b 11 Apr 1967

*William HERTLE s/o John Hertle & Rosina nee Frank; b 1867 Germany, d 1931 IA; m 1892 Friederike Schumann. Children:
    Bill – NFR
    Henry – NFR
    Ewald – NFR
    Otto – NFR
    Frieda – NFR
    Carl – NFR
    Ted – NFR
    Elmer – NFR

*Simon HESSE b 09 July 1841 Löhlbach, Germany, d 14 Jan 1917 ae75y 6m 5d Germany; m 20 Feb 1870 Marie Debus (b 07 Oct 1845 Löhlbach, Germany, d 12 Jan 1934 Germany). Child:
    *Wilhelm – b 16 Sept 1873 Löhlbach, Germany; d 17 Nov 1961
        Löhlbach, Germany; m Helene Grunewald

*Wilhelm HESSE s/o Simon Hesse & Marie nee Debus, Löhlbach, Germany; b 16 Sept 1873 Löhlbach, Germany, d 17 Nov 1961 ae88y 2m 1d Germany; m Helene Grunewald (b 05 Mar 1894, d 10 Nov 1970 ae84y 8m 5d) d/o Georg Grunewald & Henriette nee Schmidt). Child:
    *Emilie – b 08 Nov 1923; m 18 Nov 1950 Philipp Wickert II
        (Parents of Roland Wickert; m Marlene Paar)

*Herman HESSENIUS b 1863 Westrhauderfehn, Germany, d 1930 Newhall, IA; 1910 came to USA and settled in Newhall, IA area with wife Gesina Klover (b 1864, d 1935 Newhall). Farmers north of Newhall until 1928 retirement in Newhall. Children:
    TWINS: *Marie J. – b 1891 Germany, d 1970 Benton Co IA;
        m 1912 Gerhardt R. Miessner
            *Margaret – b 1891 Germany
    *Minnie – b 1893; m Edward John Deklotz
    *Heinrika – b 1896
    *Henry – b 1899
    *John – b 1902

*Marie J. HESSENIUS d/o Herman Hessenius & Gesina nee Klover; b

1891 Westrhauderfehn, Germany, d 1970 Benton Co IA; 1910 came to America with parents; m 1912 Gerhardt R. Meissner (b 1880 New Minden, IL, d 1955 Newhall, IA). Farmers northwest of Newhall until 1937 move to Newhall to operate restaurant and dance hall. Gerhardt sold Rawleigh products until 1950; Marie cooked at Newhall school until 1958; mbrs St.John. Children:

Dale Meissner – b 1920; m Delores Kacer; Cedar Rapids, IA residence
Hillis Meissner – b 1926; m Verla Moore; Little Rock, AK residence

*Elisabeth HEYER d/o Ludwig Heyer SR. & Margaretha; b 1847 Krofdorf, Hesse, Germany, d 1913 Benton Co IA; m John Krohnke (b 1839, d 1894) 1881 owned first grist mill in Keystone, IA. Children:

Alvin Krohnke – b 1872, d 1947; m Indiana "Anna" Keenan
Meta Krohnke – b 1874, d 1951; m Henry Harder

*Katrina HEYER d/o Ludwig Heyer SR. & Margaretha; b 1859 Krofdorf, Hesse, Germany, d 1941; m Pete Paulsen. Farmers Big Grove Twp Benton Co IA. Children:

Elizabeth Paulsen – b 1880, d 1976; m to Fredrich Herman Schneider
Anna Paulsen – b 1885, d 1952; m Will Sindt
Dora Paulsen – b 1886, d 1986; m William Meinert
Herman Paulsen – b 1888, d 1974; m 10 Feb 1915 Ella Tecklenburg

*Ludwig HEYER SR. b 1818 Krofdorf, Hesse, Germany, d 1904 Benton Co IA; m in Germany to Margaretha NN; 1881 emigrated to Benton Co IA with three children: Carl, Katrina, Wilhelmina and Katrina's daughter Elisabeth to join four children who preceded them to Iowa:

Louise – b 1845 Germany, d 1921 Germany;
    m Johann Adam Krombach, Krofdorf residence; did not emigrate;
    six children--three later immigrated to USA.
*Elisabeth – b 1847 Germany, d 1913 IA; m John Krohnke
*Ludwig JR. – b 1849, d 1923; m Margaretha Dammon
*Phillip – b 1852, d 1940 Benton Co IA; m Augusta Thiessen
*Wilhelm – b 1857, d 1925; Never Married
*Carl – b 1854 Germany, d 1907; Never Married
*Katrina – b 1859 Germany, d 1941 IA; m Pete Paulsen
*Wilhelmina – b 1862 Germany, d 1944; m Edward Bender

*Ludwig HEYER JR. s/o Ludwig Heyer SR. & Margaretha; b 1849 Krofdorf, Hesse, Germany; 1867 emigrated to Benton Co IA (cf

Naturalization May 1874 Benton Co Courthouse Recorder's Office); 1874 purchased Kane Twp farm; d 1923; m 1874 Margaretha Dammon. 1893 moved to Elgin, IL; employed by Elgin Watch Company.

Paul – b 1875

*Phillip HEYER s/o Ludwig Heyer SR. & Margaretha; b 1852 Krofdorf, Hesse, Germany, d 1940 Benton Co IA; 1868 emigrated to Benton Co IA; purchased and farmed land in Big Grove Twp until moving to Lyon Co IA, pro 1890; m Augusta Thiessen. Seven children born in Benton Co IA; (two bur Bender Cem):

Ferdinand – b 1877, d 1948
Louis – b 1879, d 1957
Bertha – b 1880, d 1947
Amanda – b 1883, d 1969
Herman – b 1886, d 1961

*Wilhelmina HEYER d/o Ludwig Heyer SR. & Margaretha; b 1862 Krofdorf, Hesse, Germany, d 1944 IA; m Oct 1892 Edward Bender. Children:

Lizzie Bender – b 1893, d 1975; m John Steinford
Amanda Bender – b 1896, d 1988; m Henry Allers
Robert Bender – b 1901, d 1980; m Esther Seeck

Elizabeth Ann HILL d/o Audrey Louise nee Happel & Robert E. Hill; b 17 Jan 1978 Waterloo IA; m 11 Aug 2000 Chris Wichman. Child:

Taylor Nicole Wichman – b 05 Mar 2004

Debra HOEFS d/o Elry Hoefs & Esther nee Harnisch; b 13 May 1952; m 06 Jun 1970 Steven Robert Deal (b 06 Jul 1952) s/o Robert Deal & Marlene nee Brick. Children:

Crystal Kay Deal – b 25 Dec 1970
Craig Kenneth Deal – b 06 Jun 1978

Erwin Carl HOFFMAN s/o Howard Hoffman & Edna Margaret nee Fennern; b 1917; m 1952 Rachel Cashman Bramow (b 1924). Children:

Larry – b 1949
Nancy – b 1953
Anita – b 1956
Daniel – b 1960, d 1981

*Charlotte Luise HOHL d/o Heinrich Hohl & Catharina nee Beyer of Löhlbach, Germany; b 22 Jul 1881 Löhlbach, Germany, d 01 Jan 1970 ae88y 5m 10d Löhlbach, Germany; m 04 Mar 1906 Löhlbach Ch to Balthasar Schengel (b 08 Mar 1879 Löhlbach, Germany, d 1917 World War I at Flanders, France). Children:

    Catharina Marie Schengel – b 20 Jun 1907 Löhlbach, Germany;
        m 17 Oct 1935 Conrad Dingel

    Johann Peter Schengel – b 02 Aug 1910 Löhlbach, Germany;
        m Minna Schnellbiaher

    *Heinrich Peter Schengel – b 30 Sept 1912 Löhlbach, Germany;
        d 04 Sept 1996 ae83y 11m 5d Löhlbach, Germany;
        m 16 Mar 1946 Maria Katharina Gerke

1995 Author's first reunion of Krug fourth cousins since 1865 emigration of Johann Justus Krug III. Heinrich Schengel: descendant of Johann Justus Krug's sister Anna Elisabeth, lifelong resident of Löhlbach, Germany

*Heinrich HOHL s/o Andreas Hohl & Wilhelmina nee Schuler of Löhlbach, Germany; b 04 Aug 1857 Löhlbach, Germany d 04 Dec 1938 Löhlbach, Germany; m 08 Feb 1881 Catharina Beyer. Children:

    *Charlotte Luise Hohl – b 22 Jun 1881, d 01 Jan 1970;
        m Lohbach Ch 04 Mar 1906 Bathasar Schengel

    Johann Peter Hohl – b 07 Jan 1888, NFR

*Johann Justus Paulus HOHL s/o Paulus Hohl & Wid/ Karolina Dippel; b 10 Apr 1913 Löhlbach,Germany d 1943 in Russia World War II [Missing in Action]; m 02 May 1940 Löhlbach Ch to Luise Elisabeth Rohleder (b 20 Feb 1919 Dilforshof, Germany) d/o Wilhelm Rohleder & Marie nee Stormer. Child:

    **Lina Hohl – b 06 Aug 1940 Germany; m 26 Mar 1967 Wille Happe;

2nd m 11 Apr 1953 Luise Elisabeth nee Rohleder to Heinrich Reitze (d 05 Jul 1991). Children:

    Ingrid Reitze – m 26 Mar 1977 Gutar Bettinghausen
    Helen Reitze – b 15 Sept 1956

**Lina HOHL d/o Johann Justus Paulus Hohl & Luise Elisabeth nee Rohleder; b 06 Aug 1940 Dilforshof, Germany; m 26 Mar 1967 Wille Happe (b 20 Nov 1937 Huddingen, Germany, d 19 Apr 1987 ae49y 5m bur Huddingen Ch, Germany). Residence: Laubachweg 2, 34537 Bad Wildungen, Huddingen, Germany. Author visited in home of this Krug fourth cousin, Lina Hohl, 1995 and 1999 in Huddingen (6 km from

Löhlbach). Children:
 **Uwe Happe – b 07 Mar 1969; m 06 Jan 1996 Jolante Kotyezka
 **Elke Happe – b 26 May 1970

*Paulus HOHL s/o Andreas Hohl & Wilhelmina nee Schuler of Löhlbach, Germany; b 13 Nov 1848 Löhlbach, Germany, d 17 Jun 1931 ae82y 7m 4d Löhlbach, Germany; 1st m 16 Feb 1873 Löhlbach Ch; No children; 2nd m 20 Apr 1912 to Wid/ Karoline Dippel nee Möller (13 Mar 1872, d 20 Apr 1934). Children:
 *Johann Justus Paulus Hohl – b 10 Apr 1913 Löhlbach, Germany;
  d [Missing in action in Russia World War II];
  m 02 May 1940 Luise Elisabeth Rohleder

Linda HOLDIMAN d/o Dorothy Marie nee Happel & James Holdiman; b 22 Feb 1952; m 24 Jun 1972 Robert Dart (b 05 Mar 1951). Children:
 Jason Dart – b 06 Aug 1974
 Jeff Dart – b 07 Oct 1976

Nancy HOLDIMAN d/o Dorothy Marie nee Happel & James Holdiman; b 01 Nov 1953; m 26 Aug 1972 Jerry Koester (b 21 Mar 1953). Children:
 Shelley Lynn Koester – b 06 Nov 1977
 Heidi Marie Koester – b Nov 1982

Thomas HOLDIMAN s/o Dorothy Marie nee Happel & James Holdiman; b 20 Oct 1959; 1st m 1979 Paula Church (b 27 Mar 1958) DVD 1991. No children.
2nd m 14 Feb 1993 Thomas Holdiman to Peggy Lynn Martin (b 19 Dec 1958). Child:
 Benjamin Thomas Holdiman – b 03 Nov 1993

Connie HOLMES d/o Martha nee Rammelsberg & John Richard Holmes; b 02 Dec 1964; m 21 Jun 1986 Jeffrey Alan Palmer (b 06 Dec 1963). Children:
 Cody Alan Palmer – b 09 Jan 1992
 Sara Lynn Palmer – b 01 Nov 1994

Alfred HOLST s/o Claus Julius Holst & Hedwig nee Nieman; m Stella Holst. Children:
 Olga – NFR
 Ruth – NFR

Bryon – farmed original Holst homestead
Harvey – NFR
Lester – NFR
Carol – NFR

*Andrew Julius HOLST s/o Johann Andrew Julius Holst & Christena nee Carsten; b Germany, d 30 Dec 1935; m 02 Jun 1876 Victoria Nieman from Denmark (d 21 Aug 1944). Children:
Fred – NFR
Victor – NFR
Selma – m NN Albers
Alma – m NN Hartkemeyer
Christena – m NN Brieholtz
Hattie – m NN Brieholtz

*Claus Julius HOLST s/o Johann Andrew Julius Holst & Christena nee Carsten; b 1849, d 1930; m 1881 Hedwig Nieman, immigrant from Denmark. Children:
Dora – m George Nissen
John – m Effie Lorenz
Alfred – m Stella Holst
Lillie – Never Married
Anna – Never Married
Mary – Never Married

Dora HOLST d/o Claus Julius Host & Hedwig nee Nieman; m George Nissen. Children:
Lydia Nissen – NFR
Elmer Nissen – NFR
Hulda Nissen – NFR
Marie Nissen – NFR
Frank Nissen – NFR
Paul Nissen – NFR

*Johann Andrew Julius HOLST b 04 Oct 1805 Schwabstedt, Schleswig Holstein, os Prussia/ns Germany, d 07 Jan 1866 ae61y Benton Co IA; m Sept 1830 Christena Carstens (b 1805 Germany, d 1883 Benton Co. IA). May 1865 emigrated to Scott Co Davenport, IA to a German settlement before moving to farm near Keystone, Benton Co IA. Children:
Marie – Never Married

*Johann – m Katherina Nissen
*Elsabe Margaretha – m John Brieholtz
*Hans Jurgen – m Mary Dittlemuth
*Christina Margaretha – m Wilhelm Knoke
*TWINS: Andreas Julius – m Victoria Nieman
            Claus Julius – m Hedwig Nieman (Victoria's sister)

John HOLST s/o Claus Julius Holst & Hedwig nee Nieman; m Effie Lorenz. Children:
    Waldo – NFR
    Earl – NFR

Marcia Ann HOLZWORTH d/o Alice nee Guericke & John Holzworth; b 30 Jun 1956; m 23 Sept 1978 Steven Wayne Schuldt s/o Ivan Schuldt. Children:
    Jason Adam Schuldt – b 08 Aug 1979
    Rachel Renee Schuldt – b 22 Sept 1982

Paulette Pauline HOLZWORTH d/o Alice nee Guericke & John Holzworth; b 12 Mar 1963; m 01 Jun 1985 in Menno, SD to Roger Oleson. Child:
    Allison Oleson – b 01 Apr 1989

Celeste Joyce HOMAN d/o Mildred Arlene nee Haerther & Richard Fredrick Homan; b 06 Oct 1958; m 04 Oct 1986 Timothy Paul Magnani (b 02 Sept 1958). Child:
    Nicole Lynn Magnani – b 12 Aug 1989

Cynthia Marie HOMAN d/o Mildred Arlene nee Haerther & Richard Fredrick Homan; b 31 Jan 1957; m 25 Jun 1977 John Benjamin Jacobs (b 12 Jan 1956). Children:
    Sara Jo Jacobs – b 10 Sept 1981
    Evan Lee Jacobs – b 23 Aug 1988

Kathleen Jo HOMAN d/o Mildred Arlene nee Haerther & Richard Fredrick Homan; b 13 Jan 1951, d 22 Mar 1991; m 01 Sept 1973 Walter Anton Powers (b 26 Oct 1951). Children:
    Brian Frederick Powers – b 23 Jan 1980
    Eric Powers – b 11 Nov 1982
    Rebecca Erin Powers – b 24 Apr 1985

Susan Elizabeth HOMAN d/o Mildred Arlene nee Haerther & Richard Fredrick Homan; b 05 Sept 1952; m 02 Apr 1987 Alberto Cruz (b 16 Dec 1947). Children:
Ariana Lea Cruz – b 12 Jul 1987
Martin Ricardo Cruz – b 31 Oct 1989
Gabriel Dylan Cruz – b 07 Jun 1991

Darren L. HONNOLD s/o Pamela Jean nee Dietrich & Darrel L. Honnold; b 04 Mar 1968; m 04 Nov 1995 Kelly Murphy (b 10 Jun 1969). Children:
Michaela Jene – b 23 Dec 1997
Rylie Jean – b 29 Jul 1999

Tamitha J. HONNOLD d/o Pamela Jean nee Dietrich & Darrel L. Honnold; b 16 Nov 1970; m 18 Jun 1994 Brian Janke. Children:
Tyler Brian Janke – b 02 Jul 1996
Wyatt Brian Janke – b 08 Mar 1998

Diane HUBER d/o Harold Huber & Elma nee Werning; b 21 Dec 1951; m 16 Aug 1975 Steven Hurd (b 21 Sept NFR). Children:
Christopher Hurd – b 24 Apr 1977
Collin Reed Hurd – b 02 Feb 1980
Brent Steven Hurd – b 08 Mar 1982

Galynn Gary HUBER s/o Harold Huber & Elma nee Werning; b 18 Jul 1955; m 27 Jun 1981 Monica Schneider (b 07 Jul 1959) d/o Roy Schnieder of Farmer, SD & Carol A. Stieff of Salem, SD. Children:
Christine Marie – b 05 Mar 1982
Ashley Elisabeth – b 16 Jan 1984

James HUBER s/o Harold Huber & Elma nee Werning; b 05 May 1947; m 18 Nov 1972 Mary Johnson (b 06 Jul 1953) d/o John H. Johnson & Elizabeth nee Henderickson. Children:
Troy Donavon – b 10 Apr 1973
Jeremy James – b 24 Apr 1977

Royce Reinhold HUBER s/o Harold Huber & Elma nee Werning; b 02 Jul 1950; m 01 Jul 1979 Aberdeen, SD to Lana Rae Schuring of Aberdeen, SD d/o Robert Schuring of Andover, SD. FL residence. Children:
Laura Elma – b 28 Apr 1983
Justin Royce – b 20 Feb 1985

Bruce A. HUEBENER s/o LaVonne nee Krug & Albert T. Huebener; b 05 Mar 1960; m 12 May 1984 Teresa Robinson. Ottumwa, IA residence. Children:
>   Zachariah S. – b 18 Jan 1991 Iowa City IA
>   Jacob A. – b 19 Nov 1994

Gere Keith HUEBNER s/o Milton Henry Huebner & Margaret nee Tremaine; b 17 Oct 1942; m 27 Dec 1965 Virginia Balfour DVD. Children:
>   Tiffan Huebner – b 19 Jun 1970
>   Jade Huebner – b 07 Jul 1971
>   Douglas Arthur Huebner – b 07 Apr 1973

James Arthur HUEBNER s/o Arthur Henry Huebner & Frieda nee Sass; b 02 Apr 1929; m 08 Feb 1964 Nancy Holt (b 22 Jan 1932). No children.

Mary Lee HUEBNER d/o Arthur Henry Huebner & Frieda nee Sass; b 26 Dec 1932; m 22 Jun 1952 Ernie A. Meyer (b 04 Aug 1930). Children:
>   Randall Milton Meyer – b 30 May 1953; m 1976 Teresa L. Berry
>   Diane Lee Meyer – b 23 Nov 1954; m 1975 Bradley Semelroth DVD
>   Timothy Harold Meyer – b 31 Jan 1959; m 1979 Darcy Ann Gloede

Milton Henry HUEBNER s/o Arthur Henry Huebner & Frieda nee Sass; b 11 Jul 1922, d 25 Dec 1944 ae22y 5m 14d; m Margaret Tremaine (b 02 Jan 1942). Child:
>   Gere Keith – b 17 Oct 1942; m 27 Dec 1965 Virginia Balfour DVD

Anna Marie "Dolly" HUSTED d/o Albert Husted & Anna Mae nee Brock; b 1891, d 1927; m 1915 Eugene Kohler. Children:
>   Lillian Kohler – NFR
>   Madeline Kohler – NFR
>   Lucille Kohler – NFR

Bert HUSTED s/o Albert Husted & Anna Mae nee Brock; b 1884, d 1924; m Amelia Freeman (b 1883, d 1976) d/o August Freeman & Mary nee Kine. Children:
>   TWINS: Charles – NFR
>   Esther – NFR
>   William – NFR

Edna Frieda Marie HUSTED d/o Roy Husted & Anna nee Brehm; b 14 Jan 1922, d 17 Jan 1992 ae70y 3d; m 03 May 1942 Robert John Bergen (b 10 Sept 1918, d 30 Mar 1997 ae78y 6m 20d). Children:

    Carol Ann Bergen – b 17 May 1943;

        m 14 Nov 1962 Darold Dean Junge

    Susan Jean Bergen – b 14 Feb 1947;

        m 24 Feb 1970 Norman Eugene Cross

Frank HUSTED s/o Albert Husted & Anna Mae nee Brock; b 1901, d 1972; m 1920 Elizabeth Rasmussen. Children:

    LaVern – NFR

    Bernice – NFR

    Joyce – NFR

    George – NFR

Frederick "Fred" HUSTED s/o Albert Husted & Anna Mae nee Brock; b 1881, d 1959; m 1914 Elizabeth Seilhamer. Children:

    Robert F. – b 1916, d 1946

    Lucille (Adopted) – m NN Thompson, State of WA residence

Jennie Alice HUSTED d/o Albert Husted & Anna Mae nee Brock; b 1888; m 1909 Henry O. Johnson (b 1875, d 1969) s/o Lewis Johnson & Anna nee Austin. Worked for Wagner & Rosburg Store in Newhall, IA where the children all grew up and graduated from Newhall High School. In later years, Henry & Jennie moved to CA. Children:

    Everett Johnson – b 1909; m 1930 Maurine Olson; CA residence

    Evelyn Johnson – b 1912; m 1940 Thomas McNallen; CA residence

    Clair Johnson – b 1920, 1973; m 1945 Wilma Fiebelkorn

John HUSTED s/o Albert Husted & Anna Mae nee Brock; b 31 Mar 1897; m 31 Jan 1917 Esther R. Happel(b 03 Jul 1899). Cedar Rapids, IA residence, Child:

    Lloyd – b 29 Aug 1917 CA residence

Lillian HUSTED d/o Albert Husted & Anna Mae nee Brock; b 1903, d 1980; m 1921 Herman Becker. Children:

    Myron Becker – NFR

    Alberta Becker – NFR

    Donald Becker – NFR

    Wayne Becker – NFR

Bonnie Becker – NFR

Marjorie HUSTED d/o Albert Husted & Anna Mae nee Brock; b 1899; m 1920 Clarence Kelly (d ND). CA residence. Child:
LaVonne Kelly – CA residence

Melvin HUSTED s/o Albert Husted & Anna Mae nee Brock; b 1907, d 1981; m Stella Johnson. Children:
Merle – NFR
Audrey – NFR
Richard – NFR
Doris – NFR
Wayne – NFR

Roy HUSTED s/o Albert Husted & Anna Mae nee Brock; b 1892, d 1974; m 1917 Anna Brehm; Shellsburg, IA residence. Children:
Lois Catherine – b 10 Jun 1919 near Van Horne, IA;
m 21 Mar 1942 Glenn Howard Dietrich
Edna Frieda Marie – b 14 Jan 1922, d 17 Jan 1992
m 03 May 1942 Robert John Bergen

Charles IBIS s/o Ivan Ibis & Olga nee Dannenbring; b 10 Nov 1950; Court Service Worker, Fourth Judicial Circuit Court; m 23 Oct 1976 Augustana Luth Ch Sioux Falls, SD to Cynthia Burdine (Fourth Judicial Circuit Court Reporter) d/o Wallace Burdine of Sioux Falls, SD. Mitchell SD residence. Children:
Luke – b 05 Jan 1978
Sara Ann – b 24 Sept 1984

Sandria IBIS d/o Ivan Ibis & Olga nee Dannenbring; b 22 Oct 1947; m 02 Jul 1972 Gorden Krause. Child:
Elizabeth Joy Krause – b 08 Mar 1977

David Robert INMAN s/o Karen Margaret nee Bierschenk & Roger Earl Inman; b 02 Sept 1966 Virginia Gay Hosp Vinton; Ellsworth Comm College; m 05 Sept 1987 Trinity Luth Ch Conroy, IA to Brenda Lee Hagen (b 28 Jan 1966 Mercy Hosp Iowa City; St.Lukes School of Nursing C.R.) d/o Willard Waldo Hagen & Sharon Grace nee Wilhite of Marengo, IA. Children:
Joshua David – b 28 Jul 1991 St.Lukes Hosp Cedar Rapids, IA

Seth Allen – b 27 Dec 1993

Denise Ann INMAN d/o Karen Margaret nee Bierschenk & Roger Earl Inman; b 02 Apr 1963 Virginia Gay Hosp Vinton; m 26 Nov 1988 Newhall, IA to Glenn Robert Parker (b 08 Jan 1966) s/o Otis Robert Parker & Charlene nee Jones. DVD 1990

Lee Alan INMAN s/o Karen Margaret nee Bierschenk & Roger Earl Inman; b 07 Jul 1960 Virginia Gay Hosp Vinton; Central Luth School; Newhall High School; Ellsworth College; 1st m 06 Nov 1962 St.Patrick Catholic Ch Cedar Rapids, IA to Linda Marie Heitz (b 28 Mar 1959 Cedar Rapids) d/o John A. & Mary Lou Heitz of Cedar Rapids, IA. DVD Residence: Garden City, KS. 2nd m 21 Nov 1987 Paradise Park, Oahu Hawaiian Islands to Nancy Ann Madden (b 28 Jan 1959 St.Anthony's Hosp Carroll, IA) d/o John William Madden & Marlene nee Hutchison. Children:
    Alex Michael – b 28 May 1992 Humboldt, IA
    Marcus Alan – b 23 Mar 1996 Ft. Dodge, IA

Christian F. JANSSEN b. 1834, d 1904; m Amerila Burow (b 1852, d 1934). Farmers north of Newhall, IA. Children:
    Karl C. – b 1890, d 1942; m Alma Scholtfeldt; Newhall, IA farmers
    August George – b 25 Nov 1895, d 1978;
        m 22 Feb 1920 Wilhelmine Elizabeth Kranz

Gordon Otto JAROCH s/o Eleanor nee Taschner & Otto Jaroch; b 1919; m Lila Renner (b 1920, d 1996). Children:
    Roger MacArthur – b 1942, d 2004; m Deanna Dobos (b 1943).
        Children: Matthew John Jaroch (b 1967);
        Adam Michael Jaroch (b 1970); Sarah Jaroch (b 1984)
    Judy Olive – b 1946; m Thomas Byrne (b 1943). Children:
        Sean Bryne (b 1967); Shamus Byrne (b 1976)
    Scott John – b 1948, d 2001; 1st m Molly Sue; 2nd m Nancy Nelson
        (b 1954); 3rd m Barbara May (b 1948). Children:
        Scott John Jaroch JR. (b.1970); Neil Leon Jaroch (b.1975)

*Jurgen Friedrich JEBE b 1877 Jagel, Schleswig-Holstein, Germany, d 1968 Benton Co IA, bur Westview Cem, LaPorte City, IA. Following German military service emigrated to Tama Co IA; m Oct 1908 at Dysart, IA to Theresa Arp (d 1969 bur Westview Cem, LaPorte City) of Clutier, IA. Farmers in Monroe Twp and Bruce Twp Benton Co IA until retiring 1943 in Dysart, IA. Children:

NN – dec'd

Emil H. – m Norma Lureen Rupprich, Ann Arbor, MI residence

Wesley SR. – m 1932 Mabel Jurgens

Alice K. – m 1948 Henry Fleisher, Jebe farm residence

Mary Alyce JENNINGS d/o Esto Magdalene nee Keiper & Arthur William Jennings; b 23 Apr 1950 St.Lukes Hosp Cedar Rapids, IA; m 01 Jun 1974 St.Steph to Larry Edward Youngberg (b 11 Oct 1949 Oak Park, IL) s/o Edward Youngberg & Eleanor Hedwig nee Johnson. Park Forest, IL residence. Children:

Edward Arthur Youngberg – b 01 Apr 1978 Chicago Heights, IL

Amy Marie Youngberg – b 21 Mar 1980 Chicago Heights, IL

Jason Melvin Youngberg – b 21 Oct 1981 St.James Hosp,
Chicago Heights, IL

Michael Arthur JENNINGS s/o Esto Magdalene nee Keiper & Arthur William Jennings; b 30 Sept 1952 St.Lukes Hosp Cedar Rapids, IA; Vietnam War Military Service; m 24 Sept 1977 St.John's United Ch of Christ, Hebron, ND to Pamela Kay Wallin (b 29 Sept Bismark, ND) d/o Keith Harley Wallin & Harriet Marian nee Freise of Hebron ND. Children:

Aaron Michael – b 24 Dec 1980 St.Lukes Hosp Cedar Rapids, IA;
m 05 Nov 2005 May Elizabeth Hemesath

Kyle David – b 10 Jan 1986 St.Lukes Hosp Cedar Rapids, IA

Lindsay Joy – b 09 Nov 1987 St.Lukes Hosp Cedar Rapids, IA

David Lee JESSEN s/o Phyllis Marie nee Werning & Leroy Henry Jessen; b 27 Dec 1957 Minneapolis MN; m 01 Sept 1984 Holly Jean Hartloff (b 23 Jun 1960). Ankey, IA residence. Children:

Erik Dean – b 26 May 1989

Benjamin Lee – b 18 May 1991

Ryan Cole – b 31 Jan 1996

Jo Ellen JESSEN d/o Phyllis Marie nee Werning & Leroy Henry Jessen; b 05 Aug 1955 Minneapolis MN; m 31 Jul 1982 Mound NN to William David Ambrose (b 19 Jun 1954). Coon Rapids, MN residence; both teachers. Children:

Daniel Jessen Ambrose – b 18 May 1985

Laura Marie Ambrose – b 30 Aug 1988

Lee Ann JESSEN d/o Phyllis Marie nee Werning & Leroy Henry Jessen; b 04 Oct 1965 Minneapolis MN; m 27 Jun 1992 John Melin (b 28 Nov 1962). Minneapolis, MN residence. Child:
Jackson Thomas Melin – b 22 Aug 1996

Mark Henry JESSEN s/o Phyllis Marie nee Werning & Leroy Henry Jessen; b 28 Oct 1962 Minneapolis MN; m 20 Nov 1993 Margaret (Peggy) Ann Lynch (b 11 Sept 1963). Minneapolis, MN residence. Children:
Henry Charles – b 09 Jun 1996
Kelly Ann – b 05 May 1998

Charles Larry JOHNSON s/o Viola nee Kreutner & Cecil Edward Johnson; b 1940; m Mary Elizabeth Eppert. Children:
Andrea Jean – b 1963; 1st m Duane Bunning; 2nd m Jeffrey Powers
Pamela Kay – b 1967

Everett JOHNSON s/o Henry Johnson & Jennie Alice nee Husted; b 1909; m 1930 Maurine Olson (b 1909). Moved to CA. Children:
Patricia – NFR
James – NFR
Evelyn – NFR

Evelyn JOHNSON d/o Henry Johnson & Jennie Alice nee Husted; b 1912; 1st m 1940 Thomas McNallen (b 1902, d 1959). Children:
Robert H. McNallen – NFR
Thomas McNallen JR. – NFR
2nd m 1962 Evelyn nee Johnson McNallen to Bertram Becker.

Richard Edward JOHNSON s/o Viola nee Kreutner & Cecil Edward Johnson; b 1935; 1st m Helen Lee Bristow. Children:
Randy – b 1958; m Lori Hartzler (b 1962)
Larry Edward – b 1961; m Ann Brekke
Kenneth Dean – b 1964, d 1989
2nd m Richard Edward Johnson to Sharon Mendell

Thomas JOHNSON s/o Viola nee Kreutner & Cecil Edward Johnson; b 1947; m Donna Smith (b 1950). Children:
Jilayne Christine – b 1976
TWINS: Julien Susan – b 1979
Michelle Elaine – b 1979

Dorothy JUHNKE d/o Mathilda nee Werning & Albert Juhnke; b 18 Jun 1936 Clayton, SD; m 04 Dec 1955 Leland Schempp (b 31 Oct 1931) s/o Albert Schempp & Olga nee Martell. Rapid City, SD residence. Children:
>   Jane Marie Schempp – b 27 Dec 1956; m 1976 Jay Franklin Reniker
>   DVD 1985
>   Julie Ann Schempp – b 16 Apr 1960; m 1984 James Frankman
>   DVD 1989
>   Jerod Albert Lee Schempp – b 02 Jul 1969

Elnora JUHNKE d/o Mathilda nee Werning & Albert Juhnke; b 02 Jun 1933 Parkston, SD; m 29 Aug 1954 St.Peter Luth Ch, Clayton SD to LeRoy Theodore Bender (b 21 Mar 1931, d 04 Jan 2005 ae73y 9m 14d) s/o Theodore Bender & Lydia nee Keller. Celebrated 50th Wedding Anniversary. Beaverton, OR residence. Children:
>   Debra Ann Bender – b 31 Aug 1955 Freman, SD;
>   m 31 Aug 1974 Larry Syme, OR
>   Angeline Kay Bender-b 23 Jun 1957 Freman, SD;
>   1st m 09 Jun 1979 Donald R. Ewen DVD 1993
>   2nd m 06 Aug 1995 Ronald Pringle

Kevin Marvin JUHNKE s/o Marvin Juhnke & Sandra Kay nee Hodson; b 23 Jul 1967; m Candice NN. Children:
>   Travis Jacob – b 29 Jun 1991
>   Kyley Christopher – b 16 Feb 1993

Marion JUHNKE d/o Mathilda nee Werning & Albert Juhnke; b 10 Apr 1940 Clayton, SD; m 20 Aug 1961 Dallis Englund (b 31 Oct 1941) s/o Ernest Englund & Lavonne nee Johnson. Sioux Falls, SD residence. Children:
>   Todd Michel Englund- b 17 Mar 1962; 1st m 1985 Lynn Sorenson
>   DVD; 2nd m 03 May 1997 Chris Krinis
>   Kim Marie Englund – b 16 Apr 1963;
>   m 07 Nov 1987 John Leonard Schulz (b 06 Aug 1962)

Marvin JUHNKE s/o Mathilda nee Werning & Albert Juhnke; b 15 Mar 1945, d 01 Jan 1979 ae337 9m 17d Clayton, SD; m 29 May 1966 Sandra Kay Hodson (b 17 Aug 1946, d 01 Jan 1974 ae27y 4m 15d Clayton, SD) d/o Robert Clyde Hodson & Genevieve nee Grimm Ulmer. Child:
>   Kevin Marvin – b 23 Jul 1967; m Candice NN

2nd m 06 Nov 1976 Sioux Falls, SD Sandra Kay (Hodson) Juhnke to Michael W. Nyreen s/o C.W. Nyreen of Sioux City, IA

Mildred JUHNKE d/o Mathilda nee Werning & Albert Juhnke; b 22 Mar 1938 Clayton, SD; m 06 Apr 1958 Curt Smith (b 21 Jul 1936) s/o Dewey Smith & Ardith nee Blackwell. Marion, IA residence. Children:
    Douglas Curt Smith- b 08 Apr 1959; m 04 Jun 1982 Vickie Slater DVD
    Chris Jay Smith – b 24 Mar 1961; m 1983 Lisa Christine Sharks
    Allen Jane Smith – b 09 Aug 1962; m 1986 Carla Williams
    Jeanette Ann Smith – b 07 Jan 1964; m 1982 Kevin Wheeler

Curtis JUNGE s/o Louie Junge & Emma Esther nee Seeck; b 03 Jul 1920; m 08 Mar 1944 Ruth Lois Peterson of Newhall, IA (b 25 Apr 1924). Farmers near Keystone, IA. Children:
    Keith – NFR
    Coleen – NFR
    Carol – NFR
    Connie – NFR
    Kevin – NFR

Darren Dean JUNGE s/o Carol Ann nee Bergen & Darold Dean Junge; b 15 Mar 1964; m 30 Jul 1994 Sherri Ganzar. Children:
    Jenna Lee – b 10 Jun 1995
    Andrea Lynn – b 08 May 1997
    Evan Matthew – b 06 Oct 2000

Dorothy Anne JUNGE d/o Louie Junge & Emma Esther nee Seeck; b 29 Mar 1921, d 22 Mar 1974 [Cancer & Arthritis] ae52y 11m 22d; m 21 Mar 1941 Lloyd Petersen (b 11 Jan 1920). Farmers near Dysart, IA. Children:
    Lynn Petersen – NFR
    Neil Petersen – NFR
    Wayne Petersen – NFR
    Thomas Petersen – NFR
    Michael Petersen – NFR

*Hans JUNGE b Holstein, Germany; m Holstein, Germany to Gesche Dolling. 1893 emigrated to Keystone, IA area and farmed. Hans had four children before arrival and three more children were born in Iowa. Hans was naturalized 20 Sept 1899 after applying for citizenship 04 Jan 1892 (cf

Naturalization records Benton Co Courthouse Recorder's Office). They retired in Keystone, IA. NFR

Irvin John JUNGE s/o Louie Junge & Emma Esther nee Seeck; b 10 Nov 1925 Union Twp Benton Co IA; World War II military service; m 10 Mar 1947 Washington D.C. to Mary Elizabeth (Betty) Sizer (b 24 Aug 1927 Washington D.C.) d/o Charles Mills Sizer & Mary Agnes nee Kelly. Benton Co farmers and insurance agents. Children:
    Jerome (Jerry) – b 17 Jun 1948; m 21 Sept 1968 Karen Stark
    Teresa (Terry) – m 27 Jan 1979 Lonnie Carney
    Martin (Marty) – b 11 May 1954; m 29 Mar 1980 Kristie Jurgens

Jerome (Jerry) JUNGE s/o Irvin John Junge & Mary Elizabeth (Betty) nee Sizer; b 17 Jun 1948; 1966 Class Benton Community School; m 21 Sept 1968 Karen Stark (b 08 Sept 1950 Newhall) d/o Ted & Carolyn Stark. Children:
    Kristie Ann – b 02 Oct 1969 in SC
    Jeffrey Michael – b 05 Jan 1971 in SC

Lois Helena JUNGE d/o Louie Junge & Emma Esther nee Seeck; b 09 Dec 1923; m 25 Jun 1943 Delmar Charles Schlotterbeck (b 09 Nov 1914). Farmers and retired in Keystone, IA. Children:
    Darwin Lee Schlotterbeck – b 1945; m Marilyn Monroe Pugh (b 1947)
    Cheryl Ann Schlotterbeck – b 1947; m Steven Raub
    Beverly Kay Schlotterbeck – b 1952; m David Michael Stafford
    Anita Mae Schlotterbeck – b 1953; m Mark Adyniec
    Denise Dawn Schlotterbeck – b 1961; m Randy Nolan

Louie JUNGE s/o Hans & Helen Junge; b 26 Mar 1897; World War I Army service; m 12 Mar 1918 Emma Esther Seeck (b 20 Dec 1898) d/o John Seeck & Margaret nee Balhorn. Farmers northeast of Keystone, IA until retiring 1945 in Keystone, IA. Children:
    Curtis – b 03 Jul 1920; m 08 Mar 1944 Ruth Lois Peterson
    Dorothy Anne – b 29 Mar 1921, d 22 Mar 1974;
        m 21 Mar 1941 Lloyd Petersen
    Lois Helena – b 09 Dec 1923; m 25 Jun 1943 Delmar Schlotterbeck
    Irvin John – b 10 Nov 1925;
        m 10 Mar 1947 Mary Elizabeth (Betty) Sizer
    Marilyn – b 08 Jul 1931; m 03 Oct 1950 Russell Rieder

Marilyn JUNGE d/o Louie Junge & Emma Esther nee Seeck; b 08 Jul 1931; m 03 Oct 1950 Russell Rieder (b 30 Mar 1930; US Army Korean Conflict). Newhall, IA residence and Auto Repair Shop. Children:
    Pat Rieder – NFR
    Janet Rieder – NFR
    Douglas Rieder – NFR

Martin (Marty) JUNGE s/o Irvin John Junge & Mary Elizabeth (Betty) nee Sizer; b 11 May 1954; Benton Community School; Muscatine Community College; owner of O'Grady Chemical Company in Van Horne; m 29 Mar 1980 Kristie Jurgens (b 12 Dec 1955) d/o Dean Jurgens & Shirley nee Lund. Children:
    Nathan – b 24 Aug 1981
    Noah – b 21 Sept 1983
    Megan – b 17 Sept 1986

Teresa (Terry) JUNGE d/o Irvin John Junge & Mary Elizabeth (Betty) nee Sizer; Benton Community School; Paris Beauty Academy; m 27 Jan 1979 Lonnie Carney (b Cedar Rapids). Residence on Junge family farm. Teresa's child adopted by Lonnie Carney:
    Tracey Carney – b 27 Jul 1970

Betty Jean KAESTNER d/o Richard Kaestner & Mae Elaine nee Rinderknecht; b 15 Jul 1951; Teacher Belle Plaine, IA; m 09 Aug 1975 Louis Moeller (b 09 May 1952) s/o George Moeller & Elvira nee Schultz. Children:
    Matthew Louis Moeller – b 20 Apr 1979 Cedar Rapids, IA;
        m 31 Dec 2005 Thea Hoyer (b 26 Aug 1983)
    TWINS: Peter George Moeller – b 31 Jan 1983 Cedar Rapids, IA
            Kathleen Mae Moeller – b 31 Jan 1983 Cedar Rapids, IA

Daniel Lee KAESTNER s/o Richard Kaestner & Mae Elaine nee Rinderknecht; b 24 Aug 1952 St.Lukes Hosp Cedar Rapids, IA bpt Sept 1952 and con 03 Apr 1966 St.John; m 01 Sept 1973 St.John, Newhall, IA to Katherine Albers (b 03 Jan 1954 bpt 14 Feb 1954 Keystone, IA). Farmers three miles east and one mile north of Newhall. Children:
    David Daniel – b 23 Feb 1974 Cedar Rapids, IA;
        m 25 May 1996 Julie Miller
    Dawn Marie – b 02 Jun 1976 Cedar Rapids, IA
    Dustin William – b 29 Apr 1979 Cedar Rapids, IA;

m 08 Sept 2001 Kim Fintell
Daris Lee – b 03 Dec 1983 Cedar Rapids, IA

David Daniel KAESTNER s/o Daniel Lee Kaestner & Kathleen nee Albers;
b 23 Feb 1974 bpt Mar 1976 and con 27 Mar 1988 St.John; Teacher/Coach;
m 25 May 1996 Indianoloa,IA to Julie Miller (b 17 Dec 1975; Teacher).
Atkins, IA residence. Children:
Shelby Ann – b 07 May 2000
Sienna Marie – b 06 Jun 2002
Lane Daniel – b 18 Oct 2004

Dustin William KAESTNER s/o Daniel Lee Kaestner & Kathy nee Albers;
b 29 Apr 1979 Cedar Rapids, IA; m 08 Sept 2001 Kim Fintell. Child:
Cael Edward – b 10 Oct 2004

Judy Marie KAESTNER d/o Richard Kaestner & Mae Elaine nee
Rinderknecht; b 08 Sept 1962. Children's father: Reo Varnado (b 25 May
1955 Mississippi):
Justin Mercedes Varnado – b 26 Jan 1992
Joshua Daniel Varnado – b 25 Feb 1994

Patricia Kay KAESTNER d/o Richard Kaestner & Mae Elaine nee
Rinderknecht; b 02 Apr 1959; m 31 May 1980 St.John Luth Ch, Victor, IA
to Paul Kevin Pirkl (b 21 Sept 1958). Children:
Jared Paul Pirkl – b 28 May 1981 Grinnell, IA;
m 26 Aug 2006 Kelly Ann Watkins (b 13 Mar 1982)
Adam Lynn Pirkl – b 08 Mar 1983 Grinnell, IA
Laura Jo Pirkl – b 21 Apr 1985 Grinnell, IA
Rachel Lea Pirkl – b 15 Dec 1986 Grinnell, IA

Richard KAESTNER s/o Otto Kaestner & Pauline nee Weise: cf Mae
Elaine Rinderknecht.

Robert Richard KAESTNER s/o Richard Kaestner & Mae Elaine nee
Rinderknecht; b 06 Oct 1954; m 07 Jul 1979 Cindy Strellner (b 06 Dec
1955). Farmers 1/2 mile south of Newhall, IA. Children:
Eric Michael – b 12 May 1980 Cedar Rapids, IA;
m 28 Aug 2004 Keevan Schadle
Grant Andrew – b 18 Sept 1985 Cedar Rapids, IA

William Alan KAESTNER s/o Richard Kaestner & Mae Elaine nee Rinderknecht; b 03 Jun 1964; m 06 Jan 1990 Denise Kinzenbaw. Children:
Kaily Brooke – b 05 Dec 1992
Megan Nicole – b 17 Aug 1995

*Friederich KANKE s/o John & Dora Kanke from Mecklenburg, Germany; d Apr 1926 Van Horne, IA; emigrated with parents ae18y; m 1872 Dorothy Grimm (d ae38y). Eight children (two dec'd infancy):
Frederick August – b 1887, d 1947; m 1912 Wilhelmina Schilling

Frederick August KANKE s/o Friederich Kanke & Dorothy nee Grimm; b 1887, d 1947; m 1912 Wilhelmina Schilling (b 1893, d 1966). Benton Co farmers. Children:
Myron – b 1913, d 1987; m Veda Furler, one son: Wayne
Glenn – b 1915; m Irene Vogeler
Kenneth – b 1916; m Lavonne Kelly
Donald – b 1920; m Mabel Anderson, Vinton, No children
Warren – b 1922, d 1983; m Martha Taylor
Vernon – dec'd 1927 at birth

Glenn KANKE s/o Fredrick August Kanke & Wilhelmina nee Schilling; b 1915; m Irene Vogeler. Moved to Van Horne, IA after living in AR and Newhall, IA. Children:
Gordon – Everly, IA residence; children: Kevin, William, Brenda
Karen – m John James, Winfield, IL. Children: John, Julie, Jeffrey
Jean – Cedar Rapids, IA Children: Thomas, Kendra, Brett
Dennis – Cedar Rapids, IA. Children: Chad, Jennifer, Melissa, Jessica
Dick – Grand Prairie, TX. Child: Shana

Kenneth KANKE s/o Frederick August Kanke & Wilhelmina nee Schilling; b 1916; m Lavonne Kelly. Arleta, CA residence. Children and grandchildren live in Los Angeles, CA suburbs:
Darrel – m Marcella Johnson, Children: Deborah, Michael
Janice – dec'd infancy
Dean – Children: Sheryl, Steven, Jolene, Scott
Danny – Children: Gidget, Tiffany

Warren KANKE s/o Frederick August Kanke & Wilhelmina nee Schilling; b 1913, d 1983); m Martha Taylor (b 1927, d 1987). Children:
Joe – m Penny Carter, Chatsworth, CA; children: Janet, Jeri

217

Kathy – AK residence; children: Carly, Kody
Agatha – dec'd infancy
Sue Ann – dec'd infancy

Wayne KANKE s/o Myron Kanke & Veda nee Furler; m Linda Slaymaker. Marengo, IA residence. Children:
Stacy – NFR
Jock – NFR

Deborah Lynn KARR d/o Dennis Leroy Karr & Jo Ann nee Webert; b 30 Sept 1964 St.Lukes Hosp Cedar Rapids, IA; m 06 Aug 1983 St.John to Douglas Alan Stien (b 21 Apr 1962 St.Lukes Hosp Cedar Rapids, IA) s/o Howard William Stien & Edna nee Risdal. Farmers. Mbrs St.John. Children:
Jacob Douglas Stien – b 02 Feb 1984 St.Lukes Hosp Cedar Rapids, IA
Ryan Dennis Stien – b 31 Jul 1986 St.Lukes Hosp Cedar Rapids, IA
Lucas William Stien -b 15 Mar 1990 St.Lukes Hosp Cedar Rapids, IA

Bernice Marie KATZ d/o Arthur Katz & Cora Ann nee Pohlman; b 1911; m Leroy Hergenhahn (b 1910). Children:
Warren Lee Hergenhahan – b 1935; m Lynn Mae. Child:
Lisa Lynn Hergenhahn; m William Gigler
Allen Hergenhahn – b 1944; m Margaret. Children:
Lori, Aaron, Adam

Leona Mae KATZ d/o Arthur Katz & Cora Ann nee Pohlman; b 1921; m Luverne C. Feuerbach (b 1924, d 1992). Children:
Bruce C. Feuerbach – b 1948; m Velda Hepker
Susan Gail Feuerbach – b 1951; m Gary Valenta
Sara Anne Feuerbach – b 11 Nov 1954;
m 12 Jul 1975 Thomas Grant Wessling
Daniel Lee Feuerbach – b 1956

Marilyn Ann KATZ d/o Arthur Katz & Cora Ann nee Pohlman; b 1929; m Wilfred C. Junge (b 1929). Children:
Jennifer Junge – b 1952; m Andrew Fritzpatrick. Children: Brouice, Megan, Jill Fritzpatrick
Charles Dean Junge – b 1955; m Susan Hagen. Children: Angela, Wesley Junge
Roger Neal Junge – b 1957; m Diana: Child: Kelly Junge

(Adopted), Rachel Junge & Brian Junge
Janine Cora Junge – b 1959; m David Crowe. Children: Joshua, Luke, Gregory Junge
Bart Phillip Junge – b 1961; m Susan. Children: Kurt, Emily Junge

Ruth Lillian KATZ d/o Arthur Katz & Cora Ann nee Pohlman; b 1913, d 1987; m Ervin E. Numrich (b 1915, d 1977). Children:
John Arthur Numrich – b 1947
Monica ruth Numrich – b Jul ND

Sophia Dorathea KATZ d/o Anna M. nee Kerkman & Heinrich Christoph Katz; b 1867, d 1946; m Fred Saller. Children:
Herbert Saller – m Dorothy NN: Children: Herb "Bud" Saller, Charlene Saller
Lenore Saller – NFR
Alice Saller – m Fred Willenina: Children: Barbara, Frederich
Adeline Saller – m George Hudson: Children: Judy, Nancy, Mary

Alma M. KEIPER d/o Frederick Keiper JR. & Magdalena nee Schminke; b 17 Jan 1893 Keiper Homestead, Fremont Twp Benton Co, bpt and con St.Steph; Celebrated 100th birthday; m William G. "Bill" Koehn (b 1888, d 1961)of Victor, IA. Business in Atkins; blacksmith shop; implement store; garage. Children:
Merrell Koehn – b 1914, d 1916 ae2y
Leota Koehn – b 27 Jan 1918 Atkins, IA;
d 13 Apr 2002 Scottsdale, AZ; m Cpt. Glenn Paulson
Scottsdale, AZ residence
William George Koehn JR. – b 23 Apr 1932 Atkins, IA;
d 01 Mar 2005 Bradenton, FL;
m 06 Sept 1959 Allene Deanna Vondracek;
Bradenton, FL residence

Corrine Elsie KEIPER d/o Frances Magdalene Elizabeth Anna nee Schueler & Elmer Henry John Keiper; b 07 Nov 1930 Farm Fremont Twp Benton Co IA; bpt 07 Dec 1930 and con 02 Apr 1944 St.Steph; 1948 Class Atkins High School; m 14 Dec 1952 Joseph Walter Sutcliffe (b 14 May 1931 Cedar Rapids, IA bpt 09 Apr 1950 Covington, IA) s/o Walter William Sutcliffe & Margaret Amanda nee Harper. Celebrated 50th Wedding Anniversary. Children:
Thomas Joel Sutcliffe – b 05 Aug 1958 Newton, IA;

m 05 Oct 1984 Catherine Mary McCubbins
Jean Susan Sutcliffe – b 25 Aug 1964 Wichita, KS;
    m 12 May 1990 Gregory Stephen Weiss

Donald Ray KEIPER s/o Raymond Conrad Keiper & Betty Jane nee Lensch; b 12 Jan 1955 St.Lukes Hosp Cedar Rapids, IA; B.S. Bowling Green State University; m 24 Aug 1974 Grace Episcopal Ch Cedar Rapids, IA to Barbra Jane Croy (b 11 Dec 1953 Mercy Hosp Cedar Rapids, B.S. Bowling Green State University) d/o Wayne Croy & Betty nee Shrame. DVD 1999. Child:
    Sara Jane – b 24 Jun 1982 St.Lukes Hosp Cedar Rapids, IA

Douglas Elton KEIPER s/o Irvin George Keiper & Delores Irene nee Melberg; b 13 Oct 1946 St.Lukes Hosp Cedar Rapids, IA bpt St.Steph, d 17 Jan 2006 [Cancer] ae59y 3m 4d bur Parker's Grove Cem, Shellsburg; m 25 Aug 1967 First Presbyterian Ch Cedar Rapids to Bonnie Lynn Hagan (b 13 Jun 1946 St.Lukes Hosp Cedar Rapids) d/o Charles Owens Hagan & LaVerne nee Risdale of Shellsburg, Benton Co; Farmers 5th generation on Keiper Homestead, Fremont Twp Benton Co IA. Observed 35th Wedding Anniversary 2002. Children:
    Matthew Clark – b 24 Jul 1970 St.Lukes Hosp Cedar Rapids, IA;
        m Paula Jo Welch d/o Paul & Barbara Welch, New Haven IN
    Melanie Suzanne – b 07 Mar 1973 St.Lukes Hosp Cedar Rapids, IA
    Mark Andrew – b 06 Feb 1979 St.Lukes Hosp Cedar Rapids, IA;
        m Kate NN

Elmer Henry John KEIPER s/o Frederick Keiper JR. & Magdalena nee Schminke; b 25 Aug 1906 Keiper Homestead, Fremont Twp Benton Co, bpt and con St. Steph, d 04 Jan 1974 [Cancer] ae67y 4m 10d bur St.Steph Cem; m 16 Nov 1926 St.Steph to Frances Magdalene Elizabeth Anna Schueler (b 26 Jan 1905, bpt and con St.Steph, d 31 Dec 1968 [Cancer] ae63y 11m 5d bur St.Steph Cem; farmed southwest of Atkins until 1942 until Elmer worked at Quaker Oats Company, later opened upholstery and repair shop until his death. Frances worked at Poock's Grocery Store in 1940's; St.Stephen Luth Parochial School Cook. Children:
    Harriet Charlene – b 04 Oct 1928 Fremont Twp Benton Co IA;
        m 05 Oct 1947 Arthur John Rinderknecht
    Corrine Elsie – b 07 Nov 1930 Fremont Twp Benton Co IA;
        m 14 Dec 1952 Joseph Walter Sutcliffe
    Josephine Magdalene – b 15 Dec 1932 Fremont Twp Benton Co IA;

d 22 Apr 1942 [Cancer] bur St.Steph Cem
Timothy Lynn – b 26 Sept 1948 St.Lukes Hosp Cedar Rapids, IA;
    m 22 Jun 1985 Susan Trachta Sojka

Esto Magdalene KEIPER d/o Henry Conrad Keiper & "Katie" Katherina Christina Magdalena nee Rinderknecht; b 23 Feb 1917 Keiper Homestead, Fremont Twp Benton Co IA, bpt 18 Mar 1917 and con 14 Apr 1930 St. Steph; m 15 May 1949 St.Steph to Arthur William Jennings (b 03 Mar 1911 Port Byron, IL; bpt Port Byron, IL, con 29 Mar 1949 St.Steph; World War II US Army Quartermaster & Medic European Theatre, d 1955 ae44y bur St.Steph Cem). Children:
Mary Alyce Jennings – b 23 Apr 1950 St.Lukes Hosp Cedar Rapids;
    m 01 Jun 1974 Larry Edward Youngberg
Michael Arthur Jennings – b 30 Sept 1952 St.Lukes Cedar Rapids;
    m 24 Sept 1977 Pamela Kay Wallin
Melvin Lee Jennings – b 26 Apr 1955 St.Lukes Hosp Cedar Rapids;
    d Jun 1972 ae17y [Tractor Accident] bur St.Steph Cem

Frederick Carl "Friz" KEIPER s/o Henry Conrad Keiper & "Katie" Katherina Christina Magdalene nee Rinderknecht; b 12 Nov 1911 Keiper Homestead, Fremont Twp Benton Co IA, bpt 10 Dec 1911 at home, con 05 Apr 1925 St.Steph; m 03 Aug 1933 St.John Luth Ch Victor, IA to Ella Charlotte Behrens (b 20 Dec 1910 Deep River, IA bpt 11 Jan 1911 Victor, IA con 05 Apr 1925 Victor, IA, d 08 May 2005 [Cancer] ae94y 4m 18d bur St.Steph Cem) d/o William Deitrick Behrens & Mary Katharine nee Rank. Occupation: Farming. Children:
Patricia Lou – b 29 Jan 1936 Atkins; d 21 Jun 1956 [Lupus]
    bur St.Steph Cem; m 22 Oct 1955 Jerry Orvelle Hansen
Sharon Kay – b 24 Dec 1938 Atkins;
    m 24 Jun 1961 William John Peters JR.

Frederick KEIPER JR. s/o Frederick Keiper SR. & Katharina nee Mauer; b 1855, bpt and con St.Steph, d 1933, bur St.Steph Cem; m 25 Nov 1884 to Magdalena Schminke (b 1855, bpt and con St.Steph, d 1961 bur St.Steph Cem) d/o Jacob Schminke & Anna Katherina nee Ibel. Purchased Keiper homestead. Nine children:
Frieda – m George Bayer; farmed near Marengo, IA
Henry Conrad – b 17 May 1887 Atkins, IA d 31 Mar 1982
    Cedar Rapids, IA; m 08 Dec 1910 Katherina "Katie" Christina
    Magdalena Rinderknecht

Alma M. – b 17 Jan 1893; m William G. Koehn from Victor;
moved to Atkins, IA
Hulda J. – 1895, d 1988 bur St.Steph Cem; m John H. Koehn, Victor;
moved to Atkins, IA
Hattie A. – b 1898, d 1988 bur St.Steph Cem;
1st m 10 Apr 1918 Frederick J. Schlotterback;
2nd m James Henry Dye
Magdalene Lillian – b 12 Apr 1904,d 03 Feb 1982;bur St.Steph Cem
m 03 Apr 1929 Peter J.McGivern, Marengo, IA
Elmer Henry John – b 25 Aug 1906, d 04 Jan 1974 bur St.Steph Cem
m 16 Nov 1926 Frances Magdalene Elizabeth Anna Schueler
Frederick – b 1901, d 1903 bur St.Steph Cem
Lila M. – b 1890, d 1896 bur St.Steph Cem

*Frederick KEIPER SR. b 30 Oct 1824 Reinfaltz, Germany, d 1881 Benton
Co IA; early 1860's emigrated to Iowa; 15 May 1867 purchased farm in
Fremont Twp Benton Co; m 1853 Katherina Mauer (b 1830, d 1925)
Children:
    *Wilhelmina – b 11 Oct 1850, d 1920;
        m 05 Apr 1875 Conrad Werning
    *Frederick JR. – b 1855, d 1933 bur St.Steph Cem;
        m 25 Nov 1884 Magdalena Schminke
    Valentine – b 11 Nov 1862, d 1953 bur St.Steph Cem;
        m 11 Mar 1886 Maria (Mary) Elizabeth Gertrude Rinderknecht
    John – m Anna Ehlers, Hutchinson Co. SD
    Elizabeth -NFR
    Anna – m William Schlueter; moved to Chicago, IL
    Caroline – Never Married

Frieda KEIPER d/o Frederick Keiper JR. & Magdalena nee Schminke; b
Keiper Homestead, Fremont Twp Benton Co, bpt St.Steph; m George Bayer
of Marengo, IA. Farmers near Victor, IA until retirement. Children:
    Martin Bayer – NFR
    Lilia Bayer – NFR
    Frederick Henry Bayer – b 04 Dec 1916;
        m 30 Sept 1948 Dorothy Marie Krug

Harriet Charlene KEIPER d/o Elmer Henry John Keiper & Frances
Magdalene nee Schueler: cf Arthur John Rinderknecht.

Hattie A. KEIPER d/o Frederick Keiper JR. & Magdalena nee Schminke: cf Frederick J. Schlotterback.

Henry Conrad KEIPER s/o Frederick Keiper JR. & Magdalena nee Schminke: cf "Katie" Katherina Christina Magdalena Rinderknecht.

Hulda J. KEIPER d/o Frederick Keiper JR. & Magdalena nee Schminke; b 1895 Keiper Homestead, Fremont Twp Benton Co IA, bpt and con St.Steph, d 1988 bur St.Steph Cem; m John H. Koehn (b 1892, d 1974 bur St.Steph Cem)of Victor, IA. Farmed in Poweshiek Co IA, and moved to Atkins, IA owner and operator Koehn Hardware store until retirement. Children:
>   Arlene Claire Koehn(Adopted) – b 04 Oct 1922 Davenport, IA;
>> d 28 Jan 2007 Cedar Rapids, IA; 1st m 20 Dec 1945 Jacob Lieb;
>> 2nd m 19 Apr 1950 William Keys Murray
>   Merlon F. Koehn – b 08 Jan 1917 Poweshiek Co. IA;
>> m 01 Jul 1943 Zoe Kathleen Beatty, Fairfax, IA

Irvin George KEIPER s/o Henry Conrad Keiper & "Katie" Katherina Christina Magdalena nee Rinderknecht; b 06 Oct 1913 Keiper Homestead, Fremont Twp Benton Co IA, bpt 15 Oct 1913 and con 10 Apr 1927 St.Steph; World War II Air Force Pacific Theatre; m 30 Jun 1938 Norway, IA to Delores Irene Melberg (b 22 May 1917 home S. of Norway; con 26 Aug 1938 St.Steph; Teacher). Farmed Keiper homestead. Celebrated 60th & 70th Wedding Anniversary. Children:
>   Douglas Elton – b 13 Oct 1946 St.Lukes Hosp Cedar Rapids, IA;
>> d 17 Jan 2006 [Non-Hodgkins Lymphoma];
>> m 25 Aug 1967 Bonnie Lynn Hagan
>   Janice Irene – b 10 Apr 1949 Cedar Rapids, IA;
>> m 14 Feb 1970 Karl Allen Nelson

James Charles KEIPER s/o Raymond Conrad Keiper & Betty Jane nee Lensch; b 03 Oct 1947 St.Lukes Hosp Cedar Rapids, bpt 26 Oct 1947 and con 1961 St.Steph; National Guard; m 14 Oct 1967 TrinCR to Wendy Kay Werning (b 15 Feb 1948 St.Lukes Hosp Cedar Rapids, bpt 14 Mar 1948 & con 15 Apr 1962 TrinCR) d/o Wilmer Paul Werning & Fern Katherine nee Bryant. Celebrated 25th Silver Wedding Anniversary. Children:
>   Scott Allan – b 18 Jun 1970 St.Lukes Hosp Cedar Rapids, IA;
>> bpt 12 Jul 1970 and con 18 Apr 1984 St.Steph;
>> m 27 Nov 1999 Heidi Wessling at St.John
>   Julie Ann – b 08 Sept 1973 St.Lukes Hosp Cedar Rapids, IA;

bpt 07 Oct 1973 and con 12 Apr 1987 St.Steph;
m 28 Aug 1999 Corey Lynn Ruehle at St.Steph
Lori Sue – b 22 Jun 1977 St.Lukes Hosp Cedar Rapids, IA;
bpt 03 Jul 1977 and con 05 May 1991 St.Steph
m Oct 2000 Jerry Farmer (b 26 Oct 1974)

Janice Irene KEIPER d/o Irvin George Keiper & Delores Irene nee Melberg; b 10 Apr 1949 Cedar Rapids, IA bpt and con St.Steph; m 14 Feb 1970 St.Steph to Karl Allen Nelson (b 26 Jul 1949 Rochester, MN; Attorney) s/o Jens Christian Nelson & Helen Irene nee Peterson of LeRoy, MN. Shell Rock, IA residence. Children:
Joel Andrew Nelson – b 28 Sept 1970 Decorah, IA
Stephanie Lynn Nelson – b 30 Apr 1975 Waterloo, IA

John KEIPER s/o John George Keiper & Hilda nee Schueler; b 1940 Newhall; m Jeanne Reiner of SD. Children:
John – b 1963
Kimberly – b 1965
Wendy – b 1972
Jayson – b 1974

John George KEIPER s/o John Keiper & Anna nee Arndt; b 1897 near Yankton, Hutchinson Co, SD; d 1961 Newhall, IA bur St.John Cem; m 1926 Hilda Schueler d/o Adam Schueler & Anna nee Krumm. John came to Iowa in 1922, known as "Jack" in Newhall area where he worked for Grovert Motor Co.; 1942 started own business selling Studebakers with garage until his death. Children:
Richard – b 1927
John – b 1940

Julie Ann KEIPER d/o James Charles Keiper & Wendy Kay nee Werning; b 08 Sept 1973 St.Lukes Hosp Cedar Rapids, IA bpt 07 Oct 1973 and con 12 Apr 1987 St.Steph; m 28 Aug 1999 St.Steph Corey Lynn Ruehle (b 06 Jul 1973) s/o Gary & Denise Ruehle, Ruthven, IA. Child:
Annalie Grace Ruehle (Adopted) – b 14 Jan 2005 in China
Landry Irvin Ruehle (Adopted) – b 19 Mar 2007 in Korea

June Ann KEIPER d/o Raymond Conrad Keiper & Betty Jane nee Lensch; b 27 Oct 1943 St.Lukes Hosp Cedar Rapids, bpt and con St.Steph; m 15 Jun 1963 St.Steph to Roger Henry Reed (b 31 Aug 1940 Radcliffe, Hamilton

Co IA) s/o Ralph Henry Reed & Arlene nee Thompson. Children:
  Carla Sue Reed – b 17 Sept 1965 Luth Hosp Des Moines, IA;
      m 15 Sept 1990 Todd Michael Chambers
  Krista Kay Reed – b 17 Oct 1971 Luth Hosp Des Moines, IA

Lawrence J. KEIPER s/o Fred J. Keiper & Anna Elizabeth nee Krug; b 15 Nov 1929 Atkins, IA, d 10 Feb 2005 ae75y 2m 26d Mercy Medical Center, Cedar Rapids, IA bur CdrMem; U.S. Air Force Korean War; m 20 Jan 1955 Munich, Germany to Maria Louisa Hofer. Child:
  Stan – m Cheryl; Cedar Rapids, IA residence Dau: Crystal Keiper

Lori Sue KEIPER d/o James Charles Keiper & Wendy Kay nee Werning; b 22 Jun 1977 St.Lukes Hosp Cedar Rapids, IA bpt 03 Jul 1977 con 05 May 1991 St.Steph; m 23 Sept 2000 Jerald Francis Farmer (b 26 Oct 1974) s/o John Farmer, Strawberry Point, IA & Kate Johnson, Rolfe, IA. Children:
  Shannon Evelyn Farmer – b 04 Mar 2004
  Kirsten Kay Farmer – b 11 Jan 2007

Louis KEIPER s/o Fred J. Keiper & Anna Elizabeth nee Krug; b 18 Jan 1927, bpt and con 17 Mar 1940 St.Steph; 1944 Class Atkins High School; m 03 Feb 1951 Fairfax, IA to Germaine Stallman. Children:
  Steven – m Sherry NN
  Greg – Cedar Rapids, IA residence
  Ann – m Rick Schulte, Amana, IA residence
  Becky – m Andrew Schulte, Watkins, IA residence
  Jayme Keiper – Palo, IA residence
  Terry Keiper – Palo, IA residence

Magdalene Lillian KEIPER d/o Frederick Keiper JR. & Magdalena nee Schminke; b 12 Apr 1904 Keiper Homestead, Fremont Twp Benton Co IA, bpt and con St.Steph; d 03 Feb 1982 [Bladder Cancer] ae77y 9m 22d bur St.Steph Cem; m 03 Apr 1929 pro St.Steph to Peter J. McGivern (b 20 Aug 1904 Marengo, IA, d 18 Sept 1980 ae76y 29d bur St.Steph Cem)of Marengo, IA. Members St.Steph Ch; both in Atkins Peoples Savings Bank. No children.

Marie KEIPER d/o Valentine Keiper & Mary Elizabeth nee Rinderknecht; b 31 May 1904 Linn Co IA; m 24 Oct 1924 Edwin Bruns (b 12 Dec 1898 Chicago, IL). Children:
  Donald Bruns – b 12 Jul 1927 Cedar Rapids, IA

David Bruns – b 26 Dec 1928 Cedar Rapids, IA
John Edwin Bruns – b 14 Jan 1937 Cedar Rapids, IA

Maj Matthew Clark KEIPER s/o Douglas Elton Keiper & Bonnie Lynn nee Hagan; b 24 Jul 1970 St.Lukes Hosp Cedar Rapids, IA; m Paula Jo Welchd/o Paul & Barbara Welch, New Haven, IN. Children:
    Kaitlin – NFR
    Lydia – NFR

Milda Katherine KEIPER d/o Henry Conrad Keiper & "Katie" Katherina Christina Magdalene nee Rinderknecht; b 05 Sept 1922 Keiper Homestead, Fremont Twp Benton Co, bpt and con St.Steph, d 24 May 2003 ae80y 8m 19d bur St.Steph Cem; m 17 Feb 1946 St.Steph to Willard Anton Heitshusen (b 01 Aug 1920 South Amana, IA, d 08 Feb 1976 ae55y 6m 7d Cedar Rapids bur St.John Cem) s/o Herman F. Heitshusen & Anna nee Bach of Williamsburg, IA. Farmers. Children:
    TWINS: Karen Marie Heitshusen – b 21 Jun 1952 Belle Plaine, IA;
        m 31 Jul 1971 Joseph Andrew Wheeler DVD 1984
            Kaye Ann Heitshusen – b 21 Jun 1952 Belle Plaine, IA;
        m 03 Mar 1973 Richard Allen Less

Nancy Lynne KEIPER d/o Raymond Conrad Keiper & Betty Jane nee Lensch; b 14 Jan 1951 St.Lukes Hosp Cedar Rapids, IA bpt 1950 St.Steph; m 25 Mar 1972 St.Steph to Edward Karl Wilhelmi (b 06 Sept 1951 St.Lukes Hosp Cedar Rapids, IA bpt 23 Sept 1951 St.Steph; Army Reserves) s/o Edward Leroy Wilhelmi & LaVonne nee Wiebold. Farmers. Celebrated 35th Wedding Anniversary. Children:
    Debra Rae Wilhelmi – b 23 Oct 1974 St.Lukes Hosp Cedar Rapids;
        m Aug 1998 Martin W. Gorkow of Norway, IA
    Kathy Dawn Wilhelmi – b 11 May 1977 St.Lukes Hosp Cedar Rapids;
        m 24 Jul 1999 Daniel G. Schneiderman
    Tami Renee Wilhelmi – b 14 Feb 1981 St.Lukes Hosp Cedar Rapids

Patricia Lou KEIPER d/o Frederick Carl Keiper & Ella Charlotte nee Behrens; b 29 Jan 1936 Atkins, IA bpt St.Steph, d 21 Jun 1956 ae20y 4m 23d St.Lukes Hosp Cedar Rapids, IA [Lupus] bur St.Steph Cem; m 22 Oct 1955 St.Steph to Jerry Orvelle Hansen of Palo (b 01 May 1936 Mitchell, SD, d 25 Feb 1990 ae53y 9m 24d) s/o Orvelle & Shirley Hanson. No Children.

Raymond Conrad William KEIPER s/o Henry Conrad Keiper & "Katie" Katherina Christina Magdalena nee Rinderknecht; b 13 Feb 1919 Keiper Homestead, Fremont Twp Benton Co, bpt 1919 and con 1932 St.Steph; m 24 May 1941 Betty Jane Lensch (b 10 Apr 1919 Fremont Twp Benton Co IA, bpt 1921 Cedar Rapids, con 1938 St.Steph) d/o John Harry Lensch & Bettie Philomena nee Weis. Linn Co IA farmers. Children:

    June Ann – b 27 Oct 1943 St.Lukes Hosp Cedar Rapids, IA;
        m 15 Jun 1963 Roger Henry Reed

    James Charles – b 03 Oct 1947 St.Lukes Hosp Cedar Rapids, IA;
        m 14 Oct 1968 Wendy Kay Werning

    Nancy Lynne – b 14 Jan 1951 St.Lukes Hosp Cedar Rapids, IA;
        m 25 Mar 1972 Edward Karl Wilhelmi

    Donald Ray – b 12 Jan 1955 St.Lukes Hosp Cedar Rapids, IA;
        m 24 Aug 1974 Barbara Jane Croy

Scott Allan KEIPER s/o James Charles Keiper & Wendy Kay nee Werning; b 18 Jun 1970 St.Lukes Hosp Cedar Rapids, IA; bpt 12 Jul 1970 St. Steph and con 18 Apr 1984 St.Steph; m 27 Nov 1999 St.John to Heidi Mae Wessling (b 17 Jan 1976 University Hosp, Iowa City, IA) d/o Thomas Grant Wessling & Sara Ann nee Feuerbach. Children:

    Caitlin Ann – b 25 Oct 2002
    Cameron James – b 04 Oct 2004
    Callan Mae – b 12 Oct 2007

Sharon Kay KEIPER d/o Frederick Carl Keiper & Ella Charlotte nee Behrens; b 24 Dec 1938 Atkins, IA bpt St.Steph; m 24 Jun 1961 St.Steph to William John Peters JR. (b 22 Nov 1935 Chicago, IL; National Guard 1962-68) s/o William John Peters SR. & Ann nee Kuschnereit. Occupation: Teacher. Children:

    Jennifer Suzanne Peters – b 05 Feb 1965 Cedar Rapids, IA
    William Frederick Peters – b 11 Jul 1969 Cedar Rapids, IA

Stan KEIPER s/o Lawrence J. Keiper & Maria; m Cheryl. Cedar Rapids, IA residence. Child:

    Crystal -NFR

Timothy Lynn KEIPER s/o Elmer Henry John Keiper & Frances Magdalene Elizabeth Anna nee Schueler; b 26 Sept 1948 St.Lukes Hosp Cedar Rapids, IA bpt 17 Oct 1948 and con 15 Apr 1962 St.Steph; m 22 Jun 1985 Susan nee Sojka Trachta (b 27 Sept 1953, bpt Oct 1953, con 09 Mar

1986; 1ˢᵗ m 24 Aug 1979). Atkins residence. Children:
>STEPSON: Blake Trachta – b 29 Sept 1978
>Kristin Frances – b 17 Aug 1986, bpt 14 Sept 1986

Valentine KEIPER s/o Frederick Keiper SR. & Katharina nee Mauer; b 11 Nov 1862, d 1953; m 11 Mar 1886 St.Steph to Maria (Mary) Elizabeth Gertrude Rinderknecht (b 09 Jun 1867 Benton Co, d 1945 ae78y Cedar Rapids, IA) d/o Friedrich Rinderknecht & Anna Gertrud nee Happel. South Dakota homesteaders, Hutchinson Co, before moving back to Iowa, and purchasing a farm two miles east of the Keiper homestead. Resided one mile from William & Gertrude (Rinderknecht) Schirm also homesteaders in SD, Hutchinson Co that returned to Iowa buying a farm just a mile inside Linn Co IA. Children:
>TWINS: Gertrude Marie – b 17 Dec 1886 in SD; (Double Wedding)
>>m 11 Jan 1906 Julius Schanbacher
>>>Katherine – b 17 Dec 1886 in SD; (Double Wedding)
>>m 11 Jan 1906 Henry Happel
>Carolena – b 28 Jul 1888 in SD; m 20 Dec 1911 Martin W. Schirm
>Frederick John – b 02 Jan 1890, d 27 Apr 1975;
>>m 04 Oct 1917 Anna Elizabeth Krug
>Bertha – b 13 Oct 1891; m 03 Feb 1909 William Happel
>Bernard – b 02 Feb 1894, d 18 Mar 1894
>Rev. Valentine II – b 11 Mar 1895, d 21 May 1957;
>>m 15 Jun 1919 Anna Schirm
>August – b 21 Apr 1897; m Jan 1920 Helen Ilten;
>>Winona, MN residence
>Meta – b 07 Sept 1899; m 15 Jun 1921 Lee Ilten,
>>Cedar Rapids, IA residence
>Otto – b 23 Dec 1901; 1ˢᵗ m Bernice Link;
>>2ⁿᵈ m Margaret Baker;Carlsbad, CA
>Maria – b 31 May 1904 Linn Co IA; m 24 Oct 1924 Edwin Bruns,
>>Pinellas Park FL residence
>TWINS: Olga – b 23 Sept 1907; m Rev. Fred Ilten,
>>Davenport, IA residence
>>>Amanda – b 23 Sept 1907, d 13 Nov 1907
>Amanda – b 19 Jun 1908
>Oswald John Tobias "O.J." – b 25 Feb 1909;
>>m 15 Sept 1934 Florence Hasenjaeger

*Richard KEMME b 1861 Germany; came to USA when a young boy, d

1929 Atkins, IA; m Christine Seeborg (b Germany). Cedar Rapids, IA residence until moving to rural Atkins, IA in 1895 to farm. Children:
- Charles – m Lizzie Schlotterback, 3 children
- Edward – m Margaret Seltrecht, 2 children
- William – 1st m Elizabeth Bartosh of Chain Lakes, IA;
    - 2nd m Anna Schnedler

Virginia Marie KEMME d/o William Kemme & Elizabeth nee Bartosh; b 1922 Atkins, IA Kemme farm; m 18 Sept 1945 Vernon William Kerkman (b 1920) s/o Fred Kerkman & Clara nee Kreutner. Farmed near Van Horne, IA until 1947. Moved to Kemme farm near Atkins, IA; 1977 moved to Newhall, IA when their son William took over the Kemme farm. Children:
- Rita Marie Kerkman – b 1951; m Bill Hammitt of Logan, IA
- William Fred Kerkman – b 15 Mar 1949 St.Lukes Hosp Cedar Rapids;
    - m 28 Sept 1974 Kathy Storty

William KEMME s/o Richard Kemme & Christine nee Seeborg; 1st m Elizabeth Bartosh of Chain Lakes, IA. Resided on Kemme farm, later buying additional eighty acres. Child:
- Virginia Marie – b 1922; m 18 Sept 1945 Vernon William Kerkman

2nd m Aft Elizabeth's death William Kemme to Anna Schnedler (b Germany, d Apr 1976 Cedar Rapids, IA). Moved to Cedar Rapids. William sold his home after Anna's death in 1976, and moved to Newhall, IA to live with his daughter and son-in-law.

Alma Ruth KERKMAN d/o Paul John Fred Kerkman & Gladys Elizabeth nee Brant; b 1949; m Richard Lee Golladay (b 1949). Children:
- William Golladay – b 1970; m Elvira Luna Gaviola (b 1968)
- Cheryl Ann Golladay – b 1972; m David Christopher Vander Meer
    - (b 1970)

Anita KERKMAN d/o Roy Kerkman & Orpha nee Zeman; b 1937; m Ralph L. Stimson. Children:
- Karie Stimson – b 1959; m Tyrone Meyer
- Kent Stimson – b 1960

Anna Emelie KERKMAN d/o Edward John Kerkman & Barbara nee Rinderknecht; b 1883, d 1959; m Willard Henry Alden (b 1877, d 1948). Children:
- Myrtle Irene Alden – b 1905, d 1990; m George Adam Fritz Moeller

Howard Budette Alden – b 1908, d 1987

Anna M. KERKMAN d/o Johan Conrad Kerkman & Anna Martha nee Werning Schumacher; b 1848, d 1895; m Heinrich Christoph Katz (b 1839, d 1913). Children:
    Sophia Dorathea Katz – b 1867, d 1946; m Fred Saller
    Johann Heine Katz – b 1868, d 1921;
    Louis Otto Katz – b 1870, d 1871;
    Marie Sophie Katz – b/d 1872
    Ida Dorothea Katz – b 1873; m Jack Fister
    Emma Katz – b 1875, d 1919
    Ernestine "Tina" Mary Katz – b 1877, d 1967; m NN Carstenson.
        Children: Helen; Owen
    Martha Mary Katz – b 1879, d 1964; Children: Anita, Myles, Leona
    William Katz – b 1882, d 1940
    Fred Katz – b 1884, d 1887
    Arthur Katz – b 1886, d 1960; m Cora Ann Pohlman
    Henry Katz – b 1889, d 1944
    Mathilda "Tillie" E. Katz – b 1890, d 1979; m Ralph Cassidy
    Lawrence Katz – b 1893, 1939; m Amanda; Children: Mildred, Ralph

Arthur Martin KERKMAN s/o Barbara nee Rinderknecht & Edward John Kerkman; b 1890, d 1963; m 1921 his Werning cousin Wilhelmina "Minnie" Ellen Werning (b 01 May 1894, d 1983) d/o Anton Werning & Alice nee Nell. Arthur Martin Kerkman & Wilhelmina "Minnie" Wernings's common Great-Grandparents: Johann Valentin Werning & Anna Martha nee Orth. Farmed southeast of Newhall until moving 1949 to Newhall, IA. Children:
    Lola Mae – b 1921, d 1991
    Doris Jean – b 1924, m 30 Jun 1946 Robert Dean Schlotterback

Bonnie KERKMAN d/o Harold George Kerkman & Maxine nee King; b 1950; m Tom Desotel. Children:
    Thomas Desotel – b 1966
    Lisa A. Desotel – b 1967; m Duane T. N. Johnson
    Tara L. Desotel – 1972; m Gregory K. Landsdown

Carl Edward KERKMAN s/o George John Edward Kerkman & Martha Bertha Marie nee Conrad: cf Lydia Martha Marie Kranz d/o Adam Kranz & Emma nee Emmick.

Clara KERKMAN d/o Edward John Kerkman & Barbara nee Rinderknecht: cf Peter Wilhelmi.

Conrad H. "Cooney" KERKMAN s/o Johan Conrad Kerkman & Anna Martha nee Werning Schumacher; b 1861, d 1938; m Amelia "Emilie" Grovert (b 1863, d 1952). Children:
    Gertrude M. – b 1886, d 1926; m George Charles Schrader
    Emily – NFR
    Julius "Jay" – b 1884, d 1921
    John – b 1888, d 1969
    Frank – b 1891, d 1948; m Dora Bobzien; Child: Luverne b 1926
    Hubert Karl – b 1900, d 1943

Dean KERKMAN s/o Hubert Karl Kerkman & Helen Rosalie nee Jenkins; b 1924; m Thelma Olga Wendel. Children:
    Dennis Dean – b 1952; 1st m Mary Pinon; Child: Amelia Rose; 2nd m Leslie Linscott; Child: Adam
    Renay Ellen – b 1954; m Kenneth Pohlmeier (b 1951)
    Amy Annette – b 1964; m Kenneth Manaugh

Diane Lee KERKMAN d/o Eldon George Kerkman & Mary Ann nee Kunch; b 1954; m Sidney Hass (b 1950). Children:
    Jennifer Lee Hass Kreigel – b 1974
    Brian Scott Hass Kreigel – b 1975; m Shannon Mara Langenbau (b 1972)

Doris Jean KERKMAN d/o Arthur Martin Kerkman & Wilhelmina "Minnie" nee Werning; b 1924; m 30 Jun 1946 Robert Dean Schlotterback (b 1925 d 03 Jun 2005) s/o William Frank Schlotterback & Anna E. nee Wallem. Farmers living on original Schlotterback farm. Children:
    Richard Robert Schlotterback – b 1948; m 1971 Mary L. Montague
    Linda Jean Schlotterback – b 1949; m 1971 Donald John Brecht

Edward John KERKMAN s/o Johan Conrad Kerkman & Anna Martha nee Werning Schumacher: cf Barbara Rindernecht.

Eldon George KERKMAN s/o George John Edward Kerkman & Martha Bertha Marie nee Conrad; b 1922, 1995; m Mary Ann Kunch (b 1924). Children:

231

Ronald Eldon – b 1949; m Rose Marie Underwood
Linda Marie – b 1951; m Charles Allen Morrison
Eldon Eugene – b 1952; m Ann Marie Jabens. Child:
    Kurtis Eldon Kerkman (b 1977)
Diane Lee – b 1954; m Sidney Hass
Martha Emma – b 1958; m Mike Steven Mumm

Emma KERKMAN d/o Edward John Kerkman & Barbara nee
Rinderknecht; b 1881, d 1959; m John Wilhelm Williams (b 1875, d 1939)
s/o Frederich Wilhelm Williams & Sophia nee Koch. Children:
    Clarence Williams – NFR
    Harold Williams – NFR
    Elmer G. Williams – b 1907; m Sylvia B. Voeltz
    Raymond Williams – b 1915; m Jean Marie Kell
    Elsie Barbra Williams – b 1917; m Myron Walter Knaack

Erna Martha Matilda KERKMAN d/o George John Edward Kerkman &
Martha Bertha Marie nee Conrad; b 1917; 1st m Hans John Clausen (b 1902,
d 1968). Children:
    Jeannette Clausen – b 1939; m Norman Duane McClintock (b 1937)
        Children: 1. Jo Dee McClintock (b 1960); m Scott A. Boots
        (b 1961); 2. Wayne David McClintock (b 1963);
        m Regina Renna Palas (b 1962); 3. Misti Lynn McClintock
        (b 1968); 1st m Brad Allen Ternus (b 1967); 2nd m Phil Hudephol
    George L. Clausen – b 1940; m Donna Harris. Child: Larry Clausen
        (b 1970)
2nd m Erna Martha Matilda nee Kerkman Clausen to Arnold Kranz (b 1916)

Ervin KERKMAN s/o Heinrich (Henry) Kerkman & Minna "Minnie" nee
Hausmann; b 1883, d 1968; m Bertha Meyer. Children:
    Marvin – m Leona; Children: Deloris, Dorothy, Darrell, Robert,
        Delbert
    Frances – m Harold Brecht, Children: Raymond, Betty
    Gladys – m Elzo Lint, Children: David, Dennis
    Roy – m Orpha Zeman, Children: Anita, Janet, Marlys, Galen

Evelyn KERKMAN d/o Hubert Karl Kerkman & Helen Rosalie nee
Jenkins; b 1921, d 1989; m Wayne Ohde (b 1916, d 1988). Children:
    Diane Ohde – b 1942
    Dale Ohde – b 1943; 1st m Andrea Ellen Himmah; Child:

Jade Lexus b 1992
2nd m Nancy Mcvey; Child: Shannon Kathleen b 1972
Jayne Helen Ohde – b 1945; m Robert Heise

Floyd KERKMAN s/o Henry C. Kerkman & Anna K. Hanneman; b 1913, d 1968; m Lolita Weichman (b 1915). Children:
Keith Gene – b 1935, d 1979; m Mae F. Dufresne (b 1935)
Children: Craig Edward (b 1956); Bryan Keith (b 1960)

Frieda Emma Barbara KERKMAN d/o George John Edward Kerkman & Martha Bertha Marie nee Conrad; b 1912; m Frank Theodore Corporon (b 1904, d 1984). Children:
Leo Frank Corporon – b 1935; 1st m Meredith Ann Reed;
2nd m Corrine Dorothy Nichols Ballam
Edith Frieda Corporon – b 1937; 1st m Edward Everett Biggart JR.;
2nd m Lewis Arthur Pearson
Timothy Thomas Corporon – b 1941; m Ruth Ann Heiken
Max Arvin Corporon – b 1942; 1st m Nancy Irene Bartusch;
2nd m Magdelene Slone

George John Edward KERKMAN s/o Edward John Kerkman & Barbara nee Rinderknecht; b 1878 Eden Twp Benton Co IA, d 1940; m 1905 Martha Bertha Marie Conrad (b 1885, d 1945). Farmers. Children:
Carl Edward – b 1905; d 1995; 1st m 1933 Lydia Martha Marie Kranz;
2nd m Ethel Todd Smith; 3rd m Margaret Haskins Wilder
Frieda Emma Barbara – b 1912; m Frank Theodore Corporon,
Marion, IA residence
Hilda Marie Emma – m Lester Henry Dolge, Blairstown, IA residence
Paul John Fred – 1st m Gladys Elizabeth Brant; 2nd m Lucille Grim;
3rd m Agnes Geissler Hollandsworth
Erna Martha Matilda – b 1917; 1st m Hans John Classen,
Shellsburg, IA residence; 2nd m Arnold Kranz
Viola Martha – b 1919, d 1996; m Earl Edward Grogan,
Cabool, MO residence
Eldon George – b 1922, d 1995; m Mary Ann Kunch,
Toledo, IA residence
Harold George – b 1923, d 1996; 1st m Maxine King,
Walker, IA residence; 2nd m Elsie A. Adair Wilsey

Gertrude M. KERKMAN d/o Conrad H. "Cooney" Kerkman & Amelia

"Emilie" nee Grovert: cf George Charles Schrader.

Glenn H. KERKMAN s/o Henry C. Kerkman & Anna K. nee Hanneman; b 1905, 1978; m Mildred F. Fisher. Children:
   Harold – b 1927; m Rita Quinn

Harold KERKMAN s/o Glenn H. Kerkman & Mildred F. nee Fisher; b 1927; m Rita Quinn (b 1930). Children:
   Lori – b 1945
   Diane – b 1948; m Robert Crawford
   Michael – b 1950; m Lorraine Coble

Harold George KERKMAN s/o George John Edward Kerkman & Martha Bertha Marie nee Conrad; b 1923, d 1996; m Maxine King (b 1925, d 1989). Children:
   Sharon Jean – b 1947; m William Mallison
   Roger – b 1948; 1st m Toni Baugh;
      2nd Kathryn "Kathy" Jean Elizabeth Rush Weber
   Bonnie – b 1950; m Tom Desotel
   Patricia Martha – b 1955; m Darrell Dean Engelking

Heinrich (Henry) KERKMAN s/o Johan Conrad Kerkman & Anna Martha nee Werning Schumacher; b 1857, d 1928; m Minna "Minnie" Hausmann. Children:
   Wilbert – m NN Child: Donald "Dutch" Kerkman (b 1914);
      m Helen Nelson. Children: Gordon (b 1936); m Marilyn Schirm.
      Connie (b 1945)
   Jessie – m Mable NN. Children: Lucille m NN Nelson;
      Vera m NN Hietman
   Mathilda – m Frank Young
   Henry C – b 1883, 1960; m Anna K. Hanneman
   Ervin – b 1883, d 1968; m Bertha Meyer

Henry C. KERKMAN s/o Heinrich (Henry) Kerkman & Minna "Minnie" nee Hausmann; b 1883, d 1960; m Anna K. Hanneman (b 1883, d 1950). Children:
   Glenn H. – b 1905, d 1978; m Mildred F. Fisher
   Blanche – b 1906, d 1987; m W. D. Ted Durant
   Floyd – b 1913, d 1968; m Lolita Weichman

Hilda Marie Emma KERKMAN d/o George John Edward Kerkman & Martha Bertha Marie nee Conrad; b 1914, d 1997; m Lester Henry Dolge (b 1908, d 1978). Child:
Donna Mae Dolge – b 1938; m Jerome Francis Wilhelm (b 1931).
Children: Debra Ann Wilhelm (b 1959); m Dennis Oris Coop
Julia Kay Wilhelm (b 1960); m Timothy James Rathje
Scott Francis Wilhelm (b 1963); m Christine Lynn Ure
Robert Lee Wilhelm (b 1966); m Tami Jo Meldrem

Hulbert Karl KERKMAN s/o Conrad "Cooney" Kerkman & Amelia "Emilie" nee Grovert; b 1900, d 1943; m Helen Rosalie Jenkins (b 1902). Children:
Ralph – b 1919; 1st m Charlotte Jackson; 2nd m Mariann Tecklenburg
Evelyn – b 1921, d 1989; m Wayne Ohde
Dean – b 1924; m Thelma Olga Wendel

*Johan Conrad KERKMAN s/o Johann Carl Kerkman (1788) & Engel Marie Charlotte nee Richers (1785); b 1817 Germany, d 1878; 1840 came to USA and settled in Wills Co IL, blacksmith by trade; m 1847 Anna Martha nee Werning Schumacher (b 1819 Widow with two sons; moved to Benton Co Eldorado Twp IA in 1871, d 1876). Charter Mbr St.John. Children:
Anna M. – b 1848, d 1895; m Heinrich Christoph Katz
Katherine – b 1850, d 1941; m John Senne
Edward John. – b 1855, d 1892; m Barbara Rinderknecht
Heinrich (Henry) – b 1857, d 1928; m Minna "Minnie" Hausman
Maria (Mary) – b 1859, d 1942; m Heinrich (Henry) Stien
Conrad H. "Coony" – b 1861, d 1938; m Amelia "Emilie" Grovert

John Paul KERKMAN s/o Paul John Fred Kerkman & Gladys Elizabeth nee Brant; b 1952; m Choe Lynda Jung (b 1960). Children:
Paul Robert – b 1980
Diva Elizabeth – b 1991

Katherine KERKMAN d/o Johan Conrad Kerkman & Anna Martha nee Werning Schumacher: cf John Senne.

Maria Mary KERKMAN d/o Johan Conrad Kerkman & Anna Martha nee Werning Schumacher: cf Heinrich Stien.

Marlin George KERKMAN SR. s/o Carl Edward Kerkman & Lydia Martha Marie nee Kranz; b 1938, d 1981; 1st m Mary Faye Pope Lormand (b 1941). Children:
    Marlin George JR. – b 1965; m Penny Jo Burton (b 1967)
    Karla Mary – b 1971
2nd m Marlin George Kerman SR. to Jeanice Schillig Seabrook (b 1940). Child:
    Heidi Lynn Weirich Kerkman – b 1979

Martha Emma KERKMAN d/o Eldon George Kerkman & Mary Ann nee Kunch; b 1958; m Mike Steven Mumm (b 1959). Children:
    Patricia Mary Mumm – b 1985
    Mathew Michael Mumm – b 1989

Mathilda KERKMAN d/o Heinrich (Henry) Kerkman & Minna "Minnie" nee Hausmann; m Frank Young. Children:
    Geraldine Young – m Henry Garbers
    Wesley Young – NFR
    Della Young – m John McConnaughey

Patricia Martha KERKMAN d/o Harold George Kerkman & Maxine nee King; b 1955; m Darrell Dean Engelking (b 1955). Children:
    Vincent Everly Engelking – b 1979
    Kyle Dean Engelking – b 1983
    Scott Evean Engelking – b 1985

Paul John Fred KERKMAN s/o George John Edward Kerkman & Martha Bertha Marie nee Conrad; m Gladys Elizabeth Brant (b 1919, d 1958). Children:
    Carol Ann – b 1943; m Robert E. Achey
    TWINS: Robert Dean – b/d 1947
                Robert Paul – b/d 1947
    Alma Ruth – b 1949; m Richard Lee Golladay
    TWINS: John Paul – b 1952; m Choe Lynda Jung
                James – b 1952
    Earl Dean – b/d 1954

Ralph KERKMAN s/o Hubert Karl Kerkman & Helen Rosalie nee Jenkins; b 1919; 1st m Charlotte Jackson. Children:
    Kay Riki – b 1951; m Max Jones; Child: Tim b 1980

Kyle Lynette – b 1955; m Steve Miller
Keely Denise – b 1959; m Gary Mcafee. Children: Brian b 1986;
    Jeremy b 1991
2nd m Ralph Kerkman to Mariann Tecklenburg.

Rita Marie KERKMAN d/o Vernon William Kerkman & Virginia Marie
nee Kemme; b 1951; m Bill Hammitt (b 1951). Children:
    Rebecca Marie Hammitt – b 1976
    Wesley William Hammitt – b 1979

Roger KERKMAN s/o Harold George Kerkman & Maxine nee King; b
1948; m Toni Baugh (b 1951). Children:
    Karla Kay – b 1970; m Bruce Lamar Miles (b 1964)
    Robert Wayne – b 1972

Ronald Eldon KERKMAN s/o Eldon George Kerkman & Mary Ann nee
Kunch; b 1949; m Rose Marie Underwood (b 1956). Children:
    Rebecca Marie – b 1982
    Dustin Robert – b 1986

Sharon Jean KERKMAN d/o Harold George Kerkman & Maxine nee King;
b 1947; m William Mallison (b 1950). Children:
    Dawn Michelle Kerkman – b 1969
    William Zachary Mallison (Adopted) – b 1990

Vernon William Kerkman s/o Fred Kerkman & Clara nee Kreutner: cf
Virginia Marie Kemme.

Viola Martha KERKMAN d/o George John Edward Kerkman & Martha
Bertha Marie nee Conrad; b 1919, d 1996; m Earl Edward Grogan (b 1914).
Children:
    Calvin Earl Grogan – b 1934; m Anna Miller (b 1936). Children:
        1. Calvin Edward Grogan (b 1955). 2. Elizabeth Ann Grogan
        (b 1957); m Melvin J. Latta (b 1951). 3. Susan Elaine Grogan
        (b 1971)
    Kenneth Grogan – b 1942; m Connie Crabtree (b 1938). Children:
        1. Pamela Sue Grogan (b 1958). 2. Terry Edward Grogan (b 1961)
        3. Scott Edward Grogan (b 1966) (d 1973).
        4. Sean Michael Grogan (b 1974); m Jennifer Delane Aeschliman
    Frieda Martha Grogan – b 1953; m Danny Dean. Child:

Kenny Lynn Dean (b 1977) m Chrystal Elaine Mckinley

William Fred KERKMAN s/o Vernon William Kerkman & Virginia Marie nee Kemme; b 15 Mar 1949 St.Lukes Hosp Cedar Rapids, IA bpt 10 Apr 1949 and con 07 Apr 1963 St.John; m 28 Sept 1974 Hope Luth Ch Germanville, IA to Kathy Stortz of Brighton, IA (b 1951). Lived near Van Horne, IA and farmed in partnership with his father until moving to the Kemme farm Oct 1977. Child:
    Erick William – b 26 Feb 1977 St.Lukes Hosp Cedar Rapids, IA;
        bpt 27 Mar 1977 & con 28 Apr 1991 St.John

Angie KERSTEN d/o Floy J. nee Rammelsberg & Donald Kersten; b 24 Dec 1962; m 07 Nov 1981 Mikal Seegmiller. Children:
    Jacob Mikal Seegmiller – b 20 Jul 1983
    Jason Donald Seegmiller – b 13 Oct 1987

Kelly Diane Kersten Hurst KING d/o Floy J. Rammelsberg & Donald Kersten; b 15 Jan 1961; 1st m 27 May 1989 Randall Hurst DVD; 2nd m 12 Jun 1993 Kelly Diane nee Kersten Hurst to Kent King. Children:
    Kersten King – b 17 Mar 1994
    Katie King – b 26 Apr 1995

*Ludwig KIRCHNER of Schwabendorf, Germany; m Marie Madeleine Badenin. Child:
    *Wilhemina Kirchner – b 1767, d 22 Nov 1855 Löhlbach Hse #70;
        m 18 May 1804 in Löhlbach Ch Johann Justus Krug II

*Jacob KLAR b 02 Jul 1878 Hesse, Germany, d 24 Jun 1951 at his home ae72y 11m 8d bur Westview Cem, LaPorte City, IA; 1895 emigrated to Dysart, IA where he met uncles, John and Paul Klar; farm laborer; m 17 Jan 1906 Eva Amelia Mengel (b 28 Feb 1883, d 14 Aug 1957 ae74y 5m 16d bur Westview Cem, LaPorte City) d/o Henry Mengel & Margaret nee Schreiber, immigrants from Germany. Farmers in Monroe Twp Benton Co IA. Children:
    George Wilbur – b 10 Oct 1906, d 24 Aug 1968
    Elmer Jerry – b 15 May 1908
    Paul Leroy – b 27 Feb 1910, d 06 Mar 1975
    Hazel Marie – b 03 Apr 1914; m Ralph W. Flemming
    Ella Mae – b 11 Jan 1927

Barbara Joanne KNAUFF d/o Eunice Maye nee Brehm & Theodore Charles Knauff; b 28 Dec 1954; m 16 Jan 1982 Kevin William King (b 26 Oct 1956). Child:
    Jennifer Irene King – b 24 Dec 1982

David Alan KNAUFF s/o Eunice Maye nee Brehm & Theodore Charles Knauff; b 10 May 1951; m 28 Dec 1978 Evelyn Ruth Anderson (b 28 Jul 1958). Children:
    Gregory Charles – b 12 Aug 1984

Karen Maye KNAUFF d/o Eunice Maye nee Brehm & Theodore Charles Knauff; b 11 Jul 1953; 1st m 29 Jul 1973 Jeffrey William Bittner (b 29 Feb 1952) DVD Dec 1975.
2nd m 12 May 1979 Karen Maye nee Knauff Bittner to Lloyd Luther Ward (b 13 Feb 1953). Children:
    Andrea Lynn Ward – b 15 Aug 1980
    Sarah Katherine Ward – b 10 Apr 1983

Sharon Ruth KNAUFF d/o Eunice Maye nee Brehm & Theodore Charles Knauff; b 03 Mar 1958; m 09 May 1981 Kenneth John Krall (b 03 Oct 1954). Child:
    Elizabeth Ann Krall – b 16 Jan 1985

Charles Frank KNUTH s/o William Knuth & Wilhelmina nee Niederbroecker; b 1872 Lee Co IL, d 1952, bur Evergreen Cem, Vinton; moved to Eden Twp Benton Co with his parents ae2y; m 1899 Mary Abraham (b 1877, d 1959, bur Evergreen Cem, Vinton) d/o August Heinrich Abraham SR. & Rosena Louisa nee Kramer. Farmed his parent's farm; moved on Abraham family farm; fed livestock, shipped carloads of cattle to Chicago market by rail from Newhall; hogs hauled by wagon on Saturday afternoon and cattle driven on foot with four or five men on horseback and a team/wagon with feed and bedding; animals were loaded in railcars by lanterns, arriving in Chicago for Monday market accompanied by Charles (returned later to Newhall, IA by passenger train). 1938 retired to Vinton, IA. Child:
    Viola – b 1912; m 1935 Lloyd Werning

*William KNUTH b Germany; 1856 emigrated to USA; served in Civil War Company D of IL infantry in battles of Fort Donnellson, Shiloh, Philips Creek and Corinth in which he was wounded and given Honorable

Discharge; m Wilhelmina Niederbroecker (b Germany). 1874 moved to Benton Co IA by wagon with two year old son; settled in Eden Twp five miles north and two miles west of Newhall, IA. Child:

Charles Frank – b 1872 in IL; m 1899 Mary Abraham

Arlene Claire KOEHN d/o Hulda J. nee Keiper & John H. Koehn; b 04 Oct 1922 (Adopted) Davenport, IA; Atkins High School; d 28 Jan 2007 ae84y 3m 24d Cedar Rapids, IA 1st m 20 Dec 1945 Jacob Lieb (b 02 Feb 1919, d 27 Jan 1947 [Airplane Accident] ae27y 11m 25d). Child:

Jay Edward Lieb – b 1946; m Cheryl NN Child: Joshua Edward Lieb

2nd m 19 Apr 1950 Arlene Claire nee Koehn Lieb to William "Billy" Keys Murray (b 18 Nov 1908 Storm Lake, IA, d 19 Dec 1998 ae90y 1m 1d Belle Plaine IA Care Center bur St.Steph Cem; Marion High School; Coe College) s/o Roy W. Murray & Louie Ethel nee Keys. Child:

Jean Ann Murray – m Rev. Dr. Gregory Hollis, Hilton Head, SC.
    Children: 1. Erick G. Hollis. 2. Heather Jean Hollis;
      m Bryan Edwards. Children: Kyle B.W. Edwards,
      Jacob Murray Edwards,
    3. Melinda Arlene Hollis

Karen Lee KOEHN d/o William "Bill" George Koehn JR. & Allene Deanna nee Vondracek; b 10 Nov 1966; m 12 Nov 1994 Mark Sullivan Ballard, DVD 2007.Children:

Shannon Lee Ballard – b 29 May 1998
Lauren Alyse Ballard – b 29 Mar 2000

Kristen Deann KOEHN d/o William "Bill" George Koehn JR. & Allene Deanna nee Vondracek; b 06 Oct 1962; m Robert Maxwell McLean (b 16 Oct 1967 Labrador, Canada).

STEPCHILDREN:
Cole Maxwell McLean – NFR
Emma McLean – NFR

Leota KOEHN – d/o William G. "Bill" Koehn & Alma M. nee Keiper; b 27 Jan 1918 Atkins, IA, d 13 Apr 2002 ae84y 2m 27d bur St.Steph Cem; m Cpt. Glenn Paulson, fighter pilot in US Air Force killed in Korea 1954 s/o Omar & Stella Paulson of Irregon, OR. After husband's death Leota moved to Miami, FL, then Scottsdale, AZ. Children:

Steve Paulson – [drug addiction death] bur St.Steph Cem
Sharyl Lee Paulson – b 07 Oct 1943 Cedar Rapids, IA;

m George Speaker, corporate lawyer, dec'd;
Scottsdale, AZ residence

William "Bill" George KOEHN JR. s/o William G. "Bill" Koehn & Alma M. nee Keiper; b 23 Apr 1932 Atkins, IA; bpt and con 1945 St.Steph; 1949 Class Atkins High School Class; banking (trust department), d 01 Mar 2005 ae72y 10m 6d Bradenton, FL; 04 Mar 2005 Memorial Service Hope Luth Ch, Bradenton, FL Cremate bur FL; m 06 Sept 1959 Allene Deanna Vondracek (b 24 Jan 1937 Cedar Rapids, IA) d/o Joseph Vondracek & Myrtle Frost of Cedar Rapids, IA. Children:
    TWINS: Kristin Deann – b 06 Oct 1962; m Robert Maxwell McLean
                Kraig William – b 06 Oct 1962
    Karen Lee – b 10 Nov 1966; m 12 Nov 1994 Mark S. Ballard,
        DVD 2007

Mildred KOEP d/o Amelia nee Balhorn & Louis Koep; m Dick Schild. Children:
    Ann Schild – NFR
    Donald Schild – NFR

Dorothy KOEP d/o Amelia nee Balhorn & Louis Koep; m Tom Miller. Children:
    (son) Miller – NFR
    (son) Miller – NFR
    (son) Miller – NFR

James Arthur KOERING s/o Darlene Elizabeth nee Haerther & Arthur Carl Koering; b 27 Jul 1947; m 03 Oct 1970 Sally Hass (b 27 Dec 1945). Children:
    TWINS: Susan Marie Koering – b 31 Mar 1975
                Amy Lynn Koering – b 31 Mar 1975

Jeffrey Allen KOERING s/o Darlene Elizabeth nee Haerther & Arthur Carl Koering; b 11 Jan 1951; m 14 Mar 1980 Kathleen Marie Oehler (b 21 Jan 1959). Children:
    Kelly Ann – b 26 Sept 1989
    Andrew Lee – b 04 Apr 1990

Lester H. KOERING s/o Darlene Elizabeth nee Haerther & Arthur Carl Koering; b 09 Jun 1949; m 12 Aug 1978 Kathy Marie Anderson (b 08 Aug

1953). Children:
    Jerald Arthur – b 08 Oct 1979
    Jason Andrew – b 13 Dec 1981

Alfred Otto KOOPMAN s/o Otto Koopman & Elizabeth nee Boddicker; b 1909, d 1976; lifelong resident of Eldorado Twp Benton Co IA; m 1931 Viola Werning (b 09 Jul 1909) d/o John C.A. Werning & Mathilda nee Schultz. Retired to Newhall in 1969 from their farm west of town. Children:
    Delbert – m Yvonne Fletcher; farmed home place
    Charles LeRoy – b 1936; m Mary Ann Beatty
    Janice – m Russell Knipp; residence near Keystone, IA
    Marilyn – m Jerry Johnson; CA residence
    TWINS: Karolyn – m Thomas McGinnis; residence near Fairfax, IA
              Marlyn – dec'd at birth

Betty Jean KOOPMAN d/o Harry Joe Koopman & Wilhelmina "Minnie" Gertrude nee Strellner; b 08 Mar 1940 near Shellsburg, IA; m 05 Nov 1966 Vinton, IA to John Hasbrouck Anderson (b 30 Jun 1926, d 08 Jun 1990 ae63y 11m 9d [Heart Attack]. Children:
    Craig Daniel Anderson – b 07 Feb 1969;
        m 03 Aug 1996 Teresa Kay Buchanan
    Kent Douglas Anderson – b 29 Jul 1973

Charles LeRoy KOOPMAN s/o Alfred Otto Koopman & Viola nee Werning; b 1936 near Newhall; m 1958 First Presbyterian Ch, Shellsburg, IA to Mary Ann Beatty (b 1939) d/o Joseph Charles Beatty & Minnie Ella nee Weis of Shellsburg, IA. Moved southwest of Newhall, IA to farm and raise hogs, cattle and sheep. Mary beautician in shop at her home. 1980 established Koopman & Sons Trucking business. Children:
    Dennis Lee – b 1959
    Daniel Ray – b 1960
    Brenda Ann – b 1962
    Dean Edward – b 1965
    Duane Alan – b 1968

Dale Wayne KOOPMAN s/o Stanley Harry Koopman & Phyllis Jean nee Lines; b 10 Jul 1957 Vinton, IA; m 19 Dec 1987 Marlene Suzanne Wiese. Children:
    Matt Wiese – NFR
    Missy Wiese – NFR

242

Delbert KOOPMAN s/o Alfred Otto Koopman & Viola nee Werning; m Yvonne Fletcher. Farmed the home place. Children:
 Terry – NFR
 Rochelle – NFR
 Tracy – NFR
 Holly – NFR

Delores KOOPMAN d/o John George Koopman & Ilma nee Hertle; b 1930; m 1948 Newhall, IA to Neils Schmidt. Dysart, IA residence. Children:
 Kristi Schmidt – b 1950; m 1973 Mike Hesse
 Randy Schmidt – b 1952; Dysart, IA residence
 Julie Schmidt – b 1955; Des Moines, IA residence

Donald John KOOPMAN s/o John George Koopman & Ilma nee Hertle; b 15 Dec 1927 rural Newhall, IA d 13 Sept 1999 ae71y 8m 29d Vinton Luth Home [Cancer] bur St.John Cem; 1935 Class Newhall High School; US Army Korean Conflict; m 18 Feb 1955 Mildred M. Dripps (b 1932, d 26 Jul 1997). Farmers on John G. Koopman home farm west of Newhall. Children:
 Ruth Ann – b 1956; m 1980 Bruce Cross; Atkins, IA residence
 Thomas – b 1957; US Army, Newhall, IA residence
 Jean – b 1959; m 1978 Robert Wild, Newhall, IA residence
 Robert – b 1963; Cedar Rapids, IA residence

Douglas Allen KOOPMAN s/o Merlyn Richard Koopman & Donna Lucille nee Roehr; b 31 Jul 1960 Cedar Rapids, IA; 1st m 20 Oct 1979 Wisconsin Rapids, WI to Kathleen Marie Kaminski (b 10 Oct 1959 Wisconsin Rapids, WI) DVD 15 Oct 1984 OK.
2nd m 22 Aug 1987 Guthrie, OK Douglas Allen Koopman to Susan Rae Cravens Gaither (b 13 Jun 1961 OK) DVD Jan 1999 in OK. Children:
 STEPDAUGHTER: Lexie Kay Gaither – b 01 Nov 1979 in OK
 Rachel Nicole – b 19 Sept 1990 Edmund, OK

Harry Joe KOOPMAN s/o Otto A. Koopman & Elizabeth nee Boddiker; b 07 May 1896, d 23 Sept 1955 59y 4m 16d; m 27 Sept 1922 at Van Horne, IA to Wilhelmina "Minnie: Gertrude Strellner (b 25 Mar 1904, d 23 Jan 1995 ae90y 9m 29d) d/o Julius Strellner & Julie Fredericka Amelia nee Waterstradt. Farmers in Union Twp and Canton Twp Benton Co IA. Children:
 Mardene Lorraine – b 07 Jul 1923 near Newhall, IA d 09 Jan 1986;

1st m 12 May 1942 Albert Gustave Buettner;
2nd m 14 Jun 1972 Robert Schade Council Bluffs
Stanley Harry – b 12 Sept 1928 near Newhall, IA; d 05 Feb 2000;
m 07 Oct 1951 Phyllis Jean Lines
Merlyn Richard – b 11 Oct 1934 near Keystone, IA;
m 18 Jul 1953 Donna Lucille Roehr
Betty Jean – b 08 Mar 1940 near Shellsburg, IA;
m 05 Nov 1966 John Hasbrouck Anderson

Jean KOOPMAN d/o Donald John Koopman & Mildred M. nee Dripps; b 1959; m 1978 Robert Wild. Newhall, IA residence. Children:
Brian Wild – b 1980
Marcy Wild – NFR
Sarah Wild – NFR

JoAnne Elaine KOOPMAN d/o Meril Albert Koopman & Agnes Emma nee Senne: cf Merlyn Melvin Schanbacher.

John George KOOPMAN s/o Otto Koopman & Elizabeth nee Boddicker; b 1903 d NFR; m 1924 at Newhall, IA to Ilma Hertle (b 1907 d NFR) d/o August Hertle & Martha nee Bierschenk. Residence west of Newhall, bought Koopman home farm in 1937; retired Newhall, IA in 1955; members St.John. Children:
LaVonne – b 1926; m 1947 Russell Thompson
Donald John – b 15 Dec 1927; d 13 Sept 1999 Vinton, IA;
m 18 Feb 1955 Mildred M. Dripps
Delores – b 1930; m 1948 Neils Schmidt

Judith Ann KOOPMAN d/o Meril Albert Koopman & Agnes Emma nee Senne; b 1942; 1st m Carl B. Morgan (b 1939). Children:
Andrea Sue Morgan – b 1962, d 1975
Diana Lynn Morgan – b 1965; m Daniel Preston Slaughter (b 1964)
2nd m Judith Ann Koopman to Stephen Paul Cope.

*Juergen KOOPMAN b 1833 Germany, d 1904 Benton Co. ae71y; 1866 emigrated with wife Annie C. Albers (b 1836, d 1904 Benton Co) locating in Davenport, IA before moving to Benton Co IA; purchased eighty acres northwest of Newhall, IA in Eldorado Twp spring of 1867 when it was raw prairie land; wolves prowled around and stole chickens. Juergen carpenter and cabinetmaker in Germany, built a home and farmed until his death.

Children:
- Otto A. – b 1871, d 1951; m Elizabeth Boddicker; rural Newhall, IA residence.
- Emyl – Never Married; Pipestone, MN residence
- Anne – m Peter Kahler; Eldorado Twp Benton Co IA residence
- Minnie – m Okke Boomgarden; Union Twp Benton Co IA residence

Karen Lee KOOPMAN d/o Stanley Harry Koopman & Phyllis Jean nee Lines; b 18 Nov 1955; m 16 Aug 1975 Robert Louis Schulte (b 07 Dec 1955). Child:
- Bret Allen Schulte – b 03 Mar 1980

Kay Ann KOOPMAN d/o Merlyn Richard Koopman & Donna Lucille nee Roehr; b 27 Feb 1954 Vinton, IA; 1st m 22 Sept 1973 Plaver, WI to Roderich Stuart Schmelter (b 30 Aug 1951 Marshfield WI, d 26 Mar 1975 [Spleen Cancer] ae23y 6m 24d). Child:
- Matthew Scott Schmelter – b 11 Dec 1974; m 06 Jun 1998 Michelle Sue Amelse

2nd m 17 May 1980 Kay Ann nee Koopman Schmelter to Robert Glen Hargett DVD 18 Nov 1993. Child:
- Marcus Robert Hargett – b 25 Jul 1980 Wisconsin Rapids, WI

3rd m 03 Sept 1994 Wisconsin Rapids, WI Kay Ann nee Koopman to Jeffery Romaine Wunrow (b 07 Apr 1966).

Larry Dean KOOPMAN s/o Merlyn Richard Koopman & Donna Lucille nee Roehr; b 20 Sept 1955 Vinton; 1st m 01 Jan 1979 Jane Louise Ferguson, DVD Jun 1985 Chicago, IL.

2nd m 05 Dec 1987 Wisconsin Rapids, WI Larry Dean Koopman to Cynthia Marie nee Knoll Cesare.
- STEPDAUGHER:
- Marna Marie Cesare – 03 Jun 1969 Wisconsin Rapids, WI

LaVonne KOOPMAN d/o John George Koopman & Ilma nee Hertle; b 1926; m Newhall, IA 1947 to Russell Thompson. Newhall residence. Children:
- Cynthia Thompson – b 1949; m 1973 Mark Albers; Decorah, IA residence
- Douglas Thompson – b 1952; Koopman home farm residence

Mardene Lorraine KOOPMAN d/o Harry Joe Koopman & Wilhelmina

"Minnie" Gertrude nee Strellner; b 07 Jul 1923 near Newhall, d 09 Jan 1986 ae62y 6m 2d; 1st m 12 May 1942 Shellsburg, IA to Albert Gustave Buettner (b 25 Mar 1916, d 07 Dec 1964 [Broke neck in fall from haymow] ae48y 8m 12d). Children:

    Garry Richard Buettner – b 11 Oct 1945 near Vinton, IA;
        m 31 May 1969 Claudia Barber

    DeWayne Albert Buettner – b 04 Jan 1948 Vinton, IA; d 17 Dec 1974
        [Accident]

2nd m 14 Jun 1972 Council Bluffs, IA. Mardene Lorraine nee Koopman Buettner to Robert Schade (b 24 Jun 1930, d 23 Jul 1989 ae58y 11m 1d)

Meril Albert KOOPMAN s/o Otto Koopman & Elizabeth nee Boddicker; b 23 Sept 1911 northwest of Newhall, d 21 Apr 1992 ae80y 6m 29d Virginia Gay Hosp Vinton, bur 24 Apr 1992 St.John Cem; m 02 Oct 1935 at St.John to Agnes Emma Senne (b 1912, d 1980) d/o Fred Senne & Elsie M. nee Bierschenk. Farmed home place ten years; 1945 purchased farm from his father. Meril served nine years on Newhall Public School Board; forty consecutive years as officer of St.John Luth Ch. 1972 retired; 1974 moved to Newhall, IA. Children:

    James Lowell – b 1939; m Carolyn Peterson; Deery, NH residence

    Judith Ann – b 1942; 1st m Carl B. Morgan; 2nd m Stephen Cope;
        Robins, IA residence

    Joanne Elaine – b 02 Apr 1949;
        m 16 Aug 1969 Merlyn Melvin Schanbacher;
        rural Newhall, IA residence

Merlyn Richard KOOPMAN s/o Harry Joe Koopman & Wilhelmina "Minnie" Gertrude nee Strellner; b 11 Oct 1934 near Keystone, IA; m 18 Jul 1953 in Shellsburg, IA to Donna Lucille Roehr (b 05 Jan 1937 Cripple Creek, CO). Celebrated 50th Wedding Anniversary. Children:

    Kay Ann – b 27 Feb 1954 Vinton, IA;
        1st m 22 Sept 1973 Roderich Stuart Schmelter (d 1975);
        2nd m Jeffery Wanrow; 3rd m 17 May 1980 Robert Hargett DVD

    Larry Dean – b 20 Sept 1955 Vinton, IA;
        1st m 01 Jan 1979 Jane Ferguson DVD;
        2nd m 05 Dec 1987 Cynthia Marie Asare

    Vickie Lee – b 24 Jul 1957 Cedar Rapids, IA;
        1st m 27 Nov 1976 Dale Ray Pierce DVD;
        2nd m 03 May 1984 Joe Lanzi JR.

    Douglas Allen – b 31 Jul 1960;

246

1st m 20 Oct 1979 Kathleen Marie Kaminski DVD 1984;
2nd m 22 Aug 1987 Susan Rae Cravens Gaither DVD 1999

Otto A. KOOPMAN s/o Juergen Koopman & Annie C. nee Albers; b 1871 near Newhall, d 1951; educated Tilford Academy, Vinton; m 1895 Elizabeth Boddicker (b 1874) d/o Albert A. Boddicker & Antonette Nettie nee Pieper. Otto had small business in Newhall and served about three years as road supervisor while still farming; sold Auburn automobiles. After retiring he had Oliver and Allis Chalmers implement dealership. Children:
Harry Joe – b 07 May 1896, d 23 Sept 1955;
    m 27 Sept 1922 Wilhelmina "Minnie" Gertrude Strellner
Matilda Ann "Tillie" – b 1899, d 1983; m George "Gerry" Freeman
John George – b 1903; m 1924 Ilma Hertle
Alfred Otto – b 1909, d 1976; m 1931 Viola Werning
Meril Albert – b 23 Sept 1911, d 21 Apr 1992;
    m 02 Oct 1935 Agnes Senne

Ruth Ann KOOPMAN d/o Donald John Koopman & Mildred M. nee Dripps; b 1956; m 1980 Bruce Cross. Children:
Jessi Cross – NFR
Luke Cross – NFR
Daniel Cross – NFR

Sandra Jean KOOPMAN d/o Stanley Harry Koopman & Phyllis Jean nee Lines; b 01 Mar 1954 Vinton, IA; m 28 Oct 1977 in Germany to Stephen Salviati (b 04 Dec 1956 Boston, MA) DVD 1988. Children:
Stephen Paul Salviati – b 15 Apr 1978 in Germany
Jennifer Jean Salviati – b 15 Apr 1982 Cedar Rapids, IA
Jessica Elise Salviati – b 29 Apr 1986 Cedar Rapids, IA

Stanley Harry KOOPMAN s/o Harry Joe Koopman & Wilhelmina "Minnie" Gertrude nee Strellner; b 12 Sept 1928 near Newhall, d 05 Feb 2000 ae71y 4m 24d; m 07 Oct 1951 Phyllis Jean Lines (b 01 Apr 1931). Children:
Sandra Jean – b 01 Mar 1954 Vinton, IA;
    m 28 Oct 1977 in Germany to Stephen Salviati
Karen Lee – b 18 Nov 1955 Vinton, IA;
    m 16 Aug 1975 Robert Louis Schulte
Dale Wayne – b 10 Jul 1957;
    m 19 Dec 1987 Marlene Suzanne Wiese

Vickie Lee KOOPMAN d/o Merlyn Richard Koopman & Donna Lucille nee Roehr; b 24 Jul 1957 Cedar Rapids, IA; 1st m 27 Nov 1976 Wisconsin Rapids, WI to Dale Ray Pierce DVD 25 Mar 1981 Wisconsin Rapids, WI; 2nd m 03 May 1984 Wisconsin Rapids, WI to Joseph James Lanzi JR. (b 11 Feb 1952). Children:
    Kristi Lynn Lanzi – b 23 Apr 1985 Wisconsin Rapids, WI
    Stepson Jeff Lanzi – b 23 May 1972 Wisconsin Rapids, WI

*Johann Peter KRAFT b Germany; m 11 Jun 1784 Germany to Katharina Elisabeth Battefeld. Child:
    *Anna Margaretha Kraft – b 12 Dec 1779 Geismar, Germany;
        d 27 Jun 1836 Geismar, Germany;
        m 21 Apr 1804 Johann Heinrich Michel

*Conrad KRAHLING s/o Johann Daniel Krahling & Anna Gerdraut nee Krahling; b 04 Apr 1846 Allendorf, Germany, con Easter Sunday 1860 Allendorf Luth Ch, 24 Jun 1865 ae19y departed parental home to emigrate, sailing 08 Jul 1865 Bremen, Germany to Baltimore, MD arrival 13 Sept 1865; Washington D.C. baker and tailor two years to repay emigration expense debt borrowed from his uncle; Sept 1867 to Benton Co IA where older brother Johann Peter lived; d 04 Feb 1934 ae87y 10m bur Luth Cem George, IA; m 28 Dec 1873 St.Steph Luth Ch to Christina Engel (b 03 Jun 1850 Bahlingen, Groszogthun, Baden, Germany; emigrated 1857 with parents to Benton Co. IA; d 04 Feb 1915 ae64y 8m 1d bur Luth Cem George, IA) d/o George & Anna M. Engel (both dec'd ae54) 1870 bur Raetz Cem, Atkins, IA. Moved to farm southwest of Atkins, IA in 1867. Moved to cheaper farm land in Lyon Co IA 02 Mar 1885 settling six miles west of Ashton and east of George, IA. Eleven children:
    John William – b 08 Nov 1874 Fremont Twp Benton Co IA
        d 20 Jan 1929 bur Zion Luth Cem George, IA;
        m 09 Aug 1899 Gertrude "Gertie" Addengast
    Anna Elizabeth – b 06 Oct 1876
    Louisa Maria – b 27 Aug 1878
    Adam Daniel – b 26 Jun 1880
    Conrad George – b 28 Mar 1882
    August Henry – b 12 Nov 1884, d 06 Mar 1900
    Christina Maria – b 02 Oct 1886
    Henry William – b 04 Feb 1889
    Wilhelmina Lydia "Minnie L." – b 23 Dec 1890

William August – b 18 Jun 1892
George Henry – b 08 May 1895

*Johann Daniel KRAHLING s/o Konrad Krahling & Anna Gerdraut nee Seibel; b 06 Aug 1810 Dainrode (less than 5 miles south of Allendorf) Frankenberg,Hessen-Nassau, Germany, bpt 07 Aug 1810; Wirt und Ackermann (innkeeper & farmer); 1st m 17 Jan 1836 Maria Elisabeth Krahling (b 21 Nov 1819, d 20 Sept 1839 ae19y 10m week after birth of son). Child:
    *Johann Peter – b 13 Sept 1839
2nd m 21 Jun 1840 Johann Daniel Krahling to Anna Gerdraut Krahling, sister of 1st wife, (b 07 Sept 1821). Children:
    *Conrad – b 04 Apr 1846 Allendorf, Germany, d 1934 Atkins, IA;
        m Christina Engel
    *Gertrude – b 27 May 1850 Allendorf, Germany
    *Peter – b Apr 15 1854 Allendorf, Germany
    Anna Katharina – b 21 Aug 1857, d 21 Feb 1877, Allendorf, Germany

John William KRAHLING s/o Conrad Krahling & Christina nee Engel; b 08 Nov 1874 farm Fremont Twp Benton Co IA later owned by Adam Krug, Dale Vogt. John moved to Lyon Co IA to obtain cheaper farmland; d 20 Jan 1929 bur Zion Luth Cem George, IA; m 09 Aug 1899 Gertrude "Gertie" Addengast (19 May 1877 Ridott, Stephenson Co IL, d 18 Aug 1959 bur Zion Luth Cem Ashton, IA). Twelve children.
    Allie Christine – b 16 Oct 1899, d 11 Feb 1970;
        m 27 Dec 1951 Robert B. McCandless
        (b 01 Nov 1885, d 11 Mar 1958)
    Anna Alice – b 28 Dec 1900 George, IA; d 23 Aug 1949;
        m 15 Dec 1921 Arthur George Wilhelm (Bud)Rinderknecht
    Augusta Elizabeth – b 05 Jun 1902
    Daniel Conrad – b 18 Oct 1903
    Christine A. – b 09 Mar 1905
    Gertie Marie – b 20 Sept 1906
    John Dirk – b 13 May 1908
    Henry Peter – b 02 Mar 1910
    William John – b 26 Jul 1911
    Carl Edward – b 12 Feb 1913
    Glenn George – b 09 Aug 1915
    Zaida Johann Gertrude – b 14 Apr 1917

*Adam KRANZ s/o George Kranz & Anna Christina nee Werning; b 27 Dec 1862 Germany, d 08 Mar 1941 ae78y 2m 8d Benton Co; m 24 Feb 1891 his cousin Emma Emmick (b 12 Mar 1873, d 25 Sept 1955 ae82y 6m 13d) d/o Justus Emmick & Elisabeth nee Werning. Emma's Grandparents: Johann Adam Werning & Johana Jeanette nee Brehm; Adam Kranz's Grandparents: Johann Adam Werning & Johana Jeanette nee Brehm. Children:

Christina – b 02 Feb 1892, d 20 May 1958; Never Married
Heinrich George – b 07 Aug 1894, d 08 Oct 1894
Wilhelmine Elizabeth – b 02 Jul 1895, d 1967;
    m 22 Feb 1920 August George Janssen
Maria A. – b 10 Jun 1897, d 18 Jan 1955; Never Married
George C.M. – b 02 Oct 1899, d 21 Jan 1980; m Hilda Moeller
Anna – b 12 Aug 1902; d 29 Apr 1902
Edna A. – b 15 Aug 1903, d 1976; Never Married
Lydia M. – b 17 Oct 1905; d 1981; m 1933 Carl Edward Kerkman
Elfriede Martha – b 12 Sept 1907, d 20 Apr 1967; m Herman Senne
Hulda C.- b 10 Jan 1912; m Francis Oehlert
Arnold J.William – b 19 Dec 1915; Never Married

Elfrieda Martha KRANZ d/o Adam Kranz & Emma nee Emmick; b 12 Sept 1907, d 20 Apr 1989 ae81y 7m 8d; m Herman Senne (b 1899, d 1967) s/o Fred Senne & Elsie M. nee Bierschenk. Owned and farmed Fred Senne land in Benton Co until retirement. Son Donald purchased farm making it a fourth generation farm. Children:

Lenore Senne – 1928
Donald Senne – b 1931; m Anita Franzenburg (b 1932). Children:
    1. Cynthia Sue Senne (b 1954); m Gary Edwin Muench (b 1949).
    Children: Nicholas Andrew Muench (b 1979),
    Katherine Christine Muench (b 1981),
    Matthew Douglas Muench (b 1983),
    Emily Elizabeth Muench (b 1994)
    2. Douglas Herman Senne (b 1957)
Gladene Senne – b 1934

Elisabeth KRANZ d/o George Kranz & Anna Christina nee Werning; b 21 Nov 1873, d 13 Nov 1960 ae86y 11m 23d; m 23 Mar 1893 Carl Heinrich (Henry Carl) Bierschenk (b 1865 Heyrode, Germany, d 1930 Benton Co, IA bur St.John Cem) s/o Jacob Bierschenk & Anna Martha nee George. Children:

Jacob George Bierschenk – b 05 Apr 1894, d 1930; War Veteran
Christina Elizabeth Bierschenk – b 23 Oct 1896, d 1948;
    m 1922 Carl J."Charlie" J.Heppe
George A.Bierschenk – b 03 Sept 1898, d 1976;
    m 1927 Gerturde Broendel
Fred William Bierschenk – b 12 Oct 1900, d 30 Jul 1939;
    m 1926 Esther Katherine Rinderknecht
A.M.Alma Bierschenk – b 21 Feb 1903, d 05 May 1978;
    Never Married
Harry A.Martin Bierschenk – b 05 Feb 1906, d 14 Mar 1957;
    m 11 Feb 1930 LaVerna Anna Gertrude Rinderknecht
Linda L.W. Bierschenk – b 24 Jan 1908, d 1967;
    m 12 Feb 1931 Waldemar Conrad Fiebelkorn
Martha M.E.Bierschenk – b 03 Jan 1910, d 27 Jun 1970;
    m 29 Jan 1930 Roy Schminke
TWINS: Marvin Bierschenk – b 09 Oct 1912, d 30 Apr 1917
    Melvin Bierschenk – b 09 Oct 1912; m 1935 Villa Buethner

George KRANZ JR. s/o George Kranz SR. & Anne Christina nee Werning;
b 1899. d 1980; m 1929 Hilda Moeller (b near Wilton Junction, IA) d/o
Charles Moeller & Lizzie nee Miller. Children:
    Merlon G. – b 1934; m 1952 Joyce Ford
    Wilbert E. – b 1942, d 1958

*George KRANZ SR. s/o John Kranz & Elizabeth nee Wagner; b 1834
Dankerode-on-der-Fulda, Hessen Nassau, Germany, bpt and con Dankerode
Luth Ch, d 1912 Benton Co; m 1861 in Dankerode Ch to Anna Christiana
Werning (b 1840 Dankerode-on-der-Fulda, bpt and con Dankerode Luth
Ch, d 1922 Benton Co IA) d/o Johann Adam Werning & Jeanette nee
Brehm. 1869 emigrated to USA and lived near Gibsonburg, OH almost
three years. 1871 came west by train when the Great Chicago Fire was in
progress, settling on a farm one and one-half miles northwest of Newhall,
IA. Later built a home further west and north on the same farm. Children:
    *Adam – b 27 Dec 1862 in Germany, d 08 Mar 1941 Benton Co IA;
        m 24 Feb 1891 Emma Emmick
    Elizabeth – b 1873 in Benton Co IA;
        m Carl Heinrich (Henry Carl) Bierschenk

Lydia Martha Marie KRANZ d/o Adam Kranz & Emma nee Emmick; b 17
Oct 1905, d 1981; m 1933 Carl Edward Kerkman (b 1905 Terrill, Dickinson

Co IA) s/o George John Edward Kerkman & Martha Bertha Marie nee Conrad. Carl: farmer, auto mechanic, carpenter, stone and brick mason; Newhall Fire Dept. for thirty years; Benton Co Disaster Service for ten years; operated stationary steam engine each year at Old Thresher's Reunion. Children:

    Nadine Marie Kerkman – b 1934

    Walter Carl Kerkman – b 27 Aug 1935, d 18 Jun 2007

    (Stillborn) Kerkman – b/d 1937

    Marlin George Kerkman SR. – b 1938, d 1981;

        1st m Mary Faye Pope Lormand; 2nd m Jeanice Schillig Seabrook

Mariam Jean KRANZ d/o Merlon G. Kranz & Joyce nee Ford; b 1957; Occupational Therapist Assistant; m 1978 George Simpson. Child:

    Marie Simpson – b 1980

Merlon G. KRANZ s/o George Kranz JR. & Hilda nee Moeller; b 1934; m 1952 Joyce Ford (b 1934) d/o Charles Ford & Alma nee Kellerhale. Children:

    Kathy Jo – b 1954; Registered Nurse in Corpus Christi, TX

    Mariam Jean – b 1957; m 1978 George Simpson; Mason City, IA

    Mark Wilbert – b 1960; Iowa City, IA residence

    Martin Lee – b 1964

    Steven Marion – b 1968

Wilhelmine Elizabeth KRANZ d/o Adam Kranz & Emma nee Emmick; b 02 Jul 1895, d 1967; m 22 Feb 1920 August George Janssen (b 25 Nov 1895, d 1978 US Army cook in France World War I (1917-19) s/o Christian F. Janssen & Amelia nee Burow. Farmers 33 years retiring 1953 to Newhall. Mbrs St.John. Children:

    Bernice Janssen – m Charles L. Cottrell, Benton Co IA farmers

    Ruth Janssen – m Elmer Scheetz; Benton Co IA farmers

    Hilbert Janssen – m Mary Leclere of Cedar Rapids, IA

    Lawrence Janssen – 1st m Donella Shields

Dallas KRAY s/o William Kray & Laura nee Anderson; b 28 Sept 1938; m Pat Marshall. Story City, IA residence. Child:

    Tammy Sue – m Jon Ollendick, Grimes, IA residence

*Fred KRAY b 10 Jan 1873 Baden, Germany; 1891 came to USA where brother Jake and sister Mary Vail resided, d 04 Apr 1965 ae92y 2m 25d

Atkins, IA bur St.Steph; m 28 Oct 1903 Elizabeth Kreutner (b 18 May 1884, d 05 Dec 1955 ae71y 6m 17d bur St.Steph) d/o William Kreutner & Maria (Mary) nee Moeller of Atkins, IA. Settled in Atkins area after living briefly near Newhall, IA. Children:

    William – b 24 Jul 1904 Fremont Twp Benton Co IA, d 12 Oct 1972;
        m 26 Feb 1930 Laura Anderson, Newhall, IA residence

    Karl – b 20 May 1909 Fremont Twp Benton Co IA, d 04 Oct 1982;
        m 28 Feb 1932 Elsie Gerhold, Newhall, IA residence, 2 sons

    Rosa Marie – b 26 Jul 1916 farm Canton Twp Benton Co IA;
        m 15 Jan 1936 Roy Joseph August Popenhagen

Harry Carl KRAY s/o William Carl Frederick Kray & Meda nee Shenenberger; b 22 Sept 1899 Cedar Rapids, IA; m 14 Aug 1929 Lincoln, NE to Vera Ruth Everett (b 10 Dec 1901 Ocheyden, IA, d 01 Jul 1971 ae69y 6m 21d) d/o Alfred Vernon Everett & Lucille nee McIsaac. Child:

    Patricia Jean – b 26 Apr 1931; m Beryl W. Layton, Cedar Rapids, IA

Kathy KRAY d/o Virgil Kray & Rita J. nee Happel; b Oct 1961; m 21 Mar 1987 Duc Tran. Child:

    Michon Katrina Tran – b 22 Sept 1987

Karl KRAY s/o Fred Kray & Elizabeth nee Kreutner; b 20 May 1909 Fremont Twp Benton Co IA, d 04 Oct 1982 ae73y 4m 14d; m 28 Feb 1932 Elsie Gerhold and eventually settled in Newhall, IA. Elsie's residence Chariton, IA in 1999. Children:

    Virgil – b 08 Oct 1935; m Bernie Landrey,
        Baton Rouge, LA residence.

    Delbert – b 14 Dec 1939; m Karen Schuldt, Chariton, IA residence

Michael J. KRAY s/o Virgil Kray & Rita J. nee Happel; b 20 Jan 1959; m 30 May 1987 Laurie NN. Child:

    Katey Jane – b Nov 1991

Patricia Jean KRAY d/o Harry Carl Kray & Vera Ruth nee Everett; b 26 Apr 1931; m Beryl W. Layton; Engineer. Cedar Rapids, IA residence. Children:

    John Bradley Layton – b 04 Jun 1958
    Susan Marie Layton – b 15 Jul 1960;
        m Daniel V. Qualls, Saginaw, MI

Rosa Marie aka Rose KRAY d/o Fred Kray & Elizabeth nee Kreutner: cf Roy Joseph Popenhagen.

Russell Earl KRAY s/o William Carl Frederick Kray & Meta nee Shenenberger; b 14 Dec 1909 Benton Co IA; 1ˢᵗ m 1932 Edith Kucker of Troy, SD DVD 1945. Children:
     William Russell – b 18 Aug 1937
     James Earl – b 12 Jan 1943
2ⁿᵈ m 02 May 1947 Russell Earl Kray to Ruth Roberts of Reinbeck, IA. Farmer and truck driver. Children:
     Janet Elaine – b 09 Oct 1948
     David Roberts – b 23 Aug 1954

Virgil KRAY s/o Karl Kray & Elsie nee Gerhold; b 08 Oct 1935; m Bernie Landrey. Residence Baton Rouge, LA. Children:
     Michael – NFR
     Jeffrey – NFR
     Kathy – NFR

William KRAY s/o Fred Kray & Elizabeth nee Kreutner; b 24 Jul 1904 Fremont Twp Benton Co IA, d 12 Oct 1972 ae68y 2m 18d; m 26 Feb 1930 Laura Anderson and settled in Newhall, IA. Laura resident Vinton, IA Luth Home 1999. Child:
     Dallas – b 28 Sept 1938; m Pat Marshall, Story City, IA residence
     Tammy Sue – m Jon Ollendick, Grimes, IA residence

*William Carl Frederick KRAY s/o Frederick Kray a ferryman from Lenzen, Germany; b 26 Oct 1873 Germany, d 04 Nov 1945 ae72y 9d bur Pleasant Hill Cem, Blairstown, IA; 1881 emigrated to Iowa with mother and infant brother. Naturalized 24 Sept 1896; m 14 Dec 1989 at Cedar Rapids to Meda Shenenberger (b 06 Sept 1877, d 07 Feb 1959 ae81y 5m 1d bur Pleasant Hill Cem, Blairstown, IA) d/o Sylvanus A. Shenenberger & Naomi nee Mosier. Sold seed corn; director of Federal Land Bank, organizer and director of Farmers Elevator, Vinton, IA. Children:
     Harry Carl – b 22 Sept 1899; m 14 Aug 1929 Vera Ruth Everett
     Elsie Elizabeth – b 22 Apr 1901, d 04 Aug 1982
     Merl Andrew – b 05 Aug 1903, d 27 Sept 1908
     Esther Mae – b 25 Jan 1908, d 27 Dec 1958
     Russell Earl – b 14 Dec 1909; 1ˢᵗ m 1932 Edith Kucker;
          2ⁿᵈ m 02 May 1947 Ruth Roberts

George Arthur – b 04 Mar 1912, d 26 Apr 1916
Ruth Marie – b 14 Jun 1914
Helen Lucille – b 28 Feb 1918

Albert KREUTNER s/o Henry Kreutner SR. & Sophie Maria Elisabeth nee Happel; b 15 Mar 1915 Shellsburg, IA; bpt 1915 St.Steph; d 19 Dec 1980 ae65y 9m 4d bur St.Steph Cem; m 12 Jan 1940 Pauline Behrens (b 26 Jan 1919 Newhall, IA, d 25 Dec 2000 in Floyd, IN). Children:
Carol Ann – b 03 Aug 1942; m 06 Apr 1968 Jack Mason
Donald – b 25 Jan 1945; m 15 Sept 1968 Janet Bard
Susan – b 19 Mar 1955; m Derk Mullinger

Ardith Elizabeth KREUTNER d/o William August Kreutner & Margaret Elisabeth nee Rinderknecht; b 21 Mar 1937 Virginia Gay Hosp Vinton, IA bpt 1937; m 05 Jun 1960 St.John to Robert Karl Reinhardt (b 02 Apr 1939 Blairstown Benton Co IA) DVD 1986. Children:
Pamela Ann Reinhardt – b 07 Aug 1961 Cedar Rapids, IA;
      m Duane England, Keystone, IA
Karmen Jane Reinhardt – b 01 Sept 1963 Marengo, IA;
      1st m 07 Jun 1985 Richard Louis Brehm DVD 1991;
      2nd m Jeff Stramer, Maple Grove, IA residense

Bernard KREUTNER s/o Henry Kreutner SR. & Sophia Marie Elisabeth nee Happel; b 03 Oct 1912 on farm northwest of Atkins, IA in Parkers' Grove area, bpt and con St.Steph, d 02 Sept 1995 ae82y 11m bur St.Steph Cem; m 06 Jun 1940 Immanuel Luth Ch Klinger, Bremer Co IA to Marie Bruch (b 18 Jul 1913)of Dunkerton, IA. Farmers in Dunkerton area for five years; Mar 1945 moved to farm north of Atkins and farmed until 23 Jan 1962 when moved to Atkins, IA; Salesman for Terra Eastern Fertilizer Company. Retired 01 Jan 1978. Mayor of Atkins 1970 to 1980. Children:
David Lee – b 01 Mar 1941 Waterloo, IA;
      m 02 Sept 1967 Bernice Christene Kelly
Loren – b 27 May 1942; Seattle, Retired Northwest Airlines
James – b 02 May 1944 Waterloo, IA;
      1st m 14 Sept 1965 Betty Jo Primrose DVD 1983;
      2nd m 17 Oct 1987 Christine Hintze
Leroy – b 06 Jan 1946; Atkins, IA residence
Wayne – b 08 Sept 1948; m Cynthia McCurry
Jeanne – b 28 Apr 1952 in Vinton, IA;
      m 22 Oct 1977 Murray Pommier, Redwood City, CA

Michael Paul – b 08 Jul 1953, d 09 Jul 1953

Carol Ann KREUTNER d/o Albert Kreutner & Pauline nee Behrens; b 03 Aug 1942 Cedar Rapids, IA; m 06 Apr 1968 Jack Mason. Cedar Rapids, IA residence. Children:
    Kevin Andrew Mason – b 25 Feb 1971 Michigan City, IN
    Andrea Catherine Mason – b 29 Aug 1978 Muscatine, IA

Clara KREUTNER d/o William Kreutner & Marie nee Moeller; b. 1891, d 1969; m Fred Kerkman (b 1888, d 1968) s/o Edward John Kerkman & Barbara Rinderknecht. Children:
    Vernon William Kerkman – b 1920

Clarence KREUTNER s/o William Kreutner & Sophia nee Kerkman; b 1908, d 1974; m Helen Pottee (b 1912). Child:
    Ronald – b 1946; m Joyce Christoffer

David Lee KREUTNER s/o Bernard Kreutner & Marie nee Bruch; b 01 Mar 1941 Waterloo, IA, bpt 1941; Retired United Airlines Employee; m 02 Sept 1967 in Honolulu, Hawaii to Bernice Christene Kelly (b 22 Feb 1943 Needham, MA) d/o Elmer Evelyn Kelly & Willa Catherine nee MacLeod. Visited ancestral villages in Germany in 2000. Children:
    Heather Jeanne – b 27 Aug 1974 Palo Alto, CA;
        m 09 Aug 1997 Joseph Raymond Keller
    Melissa Anne – b 30 May 1976 Palo Alto, CA

Diane KREUTNER d/o Henry Kreutner JR. & Lillian nee Tranberg; b 19 May 1947 Cedar Rapids, IA; m 12 Aug 1972 James L. Brock. Children:
    Jason Thomas Brock – b 04 May 1977, d 18 May 1979 in OK
    Jillian Lee Brock – b 16 Feb 1979 in OK
    Justin James Brock – b 15 Apr 1982 in OK

Donald KREUTNER s/o Albert Kreutner & Pauline nee Behrens; b 25 Jun 1945 Cedar Rapids, IA; m 15 Sept 1968 Great Lakes Navy Base, IL to Janet Bard (b 08 Aug 1945) of LaPorte, IN. Children:
    Derek Sean – b 06 Jun 1969 in Puerto Rico
    Jay Robert – b 03 Jan 1971 in Puerto Rico

Emma Anna KREUTNER d/o William Kreutner & Marie nee Moeller: cf John A. Sass.

Floyd KREUTNER s/o William Kreutner & Sophia nee Kerkman; b 1907, d 1969; m Ruth Happel (b 1911). Children:

Doris Mae – b 1934; m Richard Staples. Children: Gina, Kendra, Allen Danny, Herchel

Sherry – 1942; 1st m Garry Blumberg; 2nd m NN Terrones Child: Tracy Terrones; 3rd m NN Children: Henry NFR; Louis NFR

Gerald William KREUTNER s/o William August Kreutner & Margaret Elisabeth nee Rinderknecht; b 15 Sept 1938 Taylor Twp Benton Co. IA bpt 1938; US Army Reserve Sgt.E 5; m 28 Nov 1964 Grace Luth Ch Blairstown, IA to Eileen Frieda Meyer (b 29 Feb 1945 St.Clair Twp Benton Co) d/o Theophil Meyer & Florence Lisetta nee Miller. Farmers. Children:

Tammy Sue – b 18 Sept 1965 St.Lukes Hosp Cedar Rapids, IA; m 26 Nov 1994 George Moffett Surface

Becky Ann – b 25 Feb 1968 St.Lukes Hosp Cedar Rapids, IA;

Brian Lee – b 14 Jul 1970 Virginia Gay Hosp Vinton, IA; m 22 Jun 1996 Jennifer Christine Peterson

Heather Jeanne KREUTNER d/o David Lee Kreutner & Bernice Christene nee Kelly; b 27 Aug 1974 Palo Alto, CA; m 09 Aug 1997 Portola Valley, CA to Joseph Raymond Keller (b 17 Oct 1974 Camden, NJ) s/o Louis John Keller & Mary Elizabeth nee McCann.

Henry KREUTNER JR. s/o Henry Kreutner SR. & Sophia Marie Elisabeth nee Happel; b 28 Jun 1919 Shellsburg, IA; m 18 Sept 1943 Lillian Tranberg (b 07 Mar 1921 Ettrick, WI). Children:

Diane – b 19 May 1947; m 12 Aug 1972 James L. Brock

Thomas – b 18 May 1952; m 28 Aug 1976 Linda Deklotz DVD

Henry KREUTNER SR. s/o William Kreutner & Marie Moeller b 04 Mar 1886 near Atkins, bpt 1886 St. Steph, con St.Steph, d 09 Jun 1952 ae66y 3m 5d; m 30 Jan 1910 Sophie Marie Elisabeth Happel (b 04 Sept 1889 Linn Co IA, d 19 Apr 1976 ae86y 7m 15d) d/o August A. Happel & Martha Young. Started farming on his parent's farm six miles northwest of Atkins, IA in Parker's Grove area. Children:

William August – b 07 Feb 1911, d 01 Feb 2005 bur St.John Cem m 07 Feb 1936 Margaret Elisabeth Rinderknecht

Bernard – b 03 Oct 1912, d 02 Sept 1995 bur St.Steph Cem; m 06 Jun 1940 Marie Bruch

Albert – b 15 Mar 1915 Shellsburg, IA, d 19 Dec 1980
    bur St.Steph Cem; m 12 Jan 1940 Pauline Behrens
Marvin Peter – b 16 Mar 1917, d 27 Feb 1987
    m 16 Mar 1944 Mary Ann Barbara Wilhelmi
Henry JR. – b 28 Jun 1919 Shellsburg, IA;
    m 18 Sept 1943 Lillian Tranberg

James KREUTNER s/o Bernard Kreutner & Marie nee Bruch; b 02 May 1944 Waterloo; 1st m 14 Sept 1965 Betty Jo Primrose (b 02 Apr 1946) DVD 1983. Children:
    Dawn Marie – b 21 Dec 1966
    Debra Jo – b 02 Nov 1967
    Donna Jean – b 19 Apr 1969
    Dana Therese – b 08 May 1970
    James David – b 18 Oct 1971
2nd m 17 Oct 1987 James Kreutner to Christine Hintze.

Jeanne KREUTNER d/o Bernard Kreutner & Marie nee Bruch; b 28 Apr 1952 Vinton, IA; m 22 Oct 1977 Murray Pommier (b 15 Feb 1953) of Currie, MN. Children:
    Benjamin John Pommier – b 19 Oct 1979 Redwood City, CA
    Angela Marie Pommier – b 08 Jul 19 Modesto, CA

John Edward KREUTNER s/o Marvin Peter Kreutner & Mary Ann Barbara nee Wilhelmi; b 11 Mar 1946 St.Lukes Hosp Cedar Rapids, IA bpt 07 Apr 1946 St.Steph; 1st m 21 Oct 1967 Sheryll Dauenbaugh (b 23 Jun 1947) DVD 1987. Children:
    Gary Lee – b 04 Jan 1970 Cedar Rapids, IA
    Scott Allyn – b 25 Jun 1974 Cedar Rapids, IA
2nd m 12 Feb 1993 John Edward Kreutner to Stephanie Bush (b 10 May 1950).

Leo Marvin KREUTNER s/o Marvin Peter Kreutner & Mary Ann Barbara nee Wilhelmi; b 23 Apr 1945 St.Lukes Hosp Cedar Rapids, IA bpt 13 May 1945 St.Steph; m 17 Jun 1972 Valerie Head (b 17 Jun 1948 Marengo, Iowa Co IA). Children:
    Karl Lee – b 26 Aug 1974 Cedar Rapids, IA
    Kristopher Allen – b 08 Aug 1975 Cedar Rapids, IA

Mildred KREUTNER d/o William Kreutner & Sophia nee Kerkman; b

1915, d 1986; m Leonard Vogler (b 1914, d 1987). Children:
  Loren Vogler – b 1940; m Eleanor Kreger. Children:
      1. Laura Vogler (b 1964); m Tim Schiller (b 1964)
      2. Kim Vogler (b 1967); m Joel Bohnenstingl
      3. Kathy Vogler (b 1969); m Keith Brace (b 1971)
  Janice Vogler – b 1942; 1st m Tracy Stoner; Son: Brent (b 1963);
      m Christy Barkley.
      2nd m Merle Ricks
  Donald Vogler – b 1946, d 1996; m Clare Gustafson (b 1949)
      Children: Abigal (b 1978), Sarah (b 1980)

Randy Lee KREUTNER s/o Marvin Peter Kreutner & Mary Ann Barbara nee Wilhelmi; b 21 Nov 1956; m 14 Sept 1983 Jeanette Hofer (b 27 Jun 1959).

Richard Karl KREUTNER s/o Marvin Peter Kreutner & Mary Ann Barbara nee Wilhelmi; b 09 May 1951 St.Lukes Hosp Cedar Rapids, IA bpt 03 Jun 1951 St.Steph; m 15 Mar 1974 St.Steph to his Kreutner and Krug cousin Delaine Sass (b 24 Jun 1953 Shellsburg, Benton Co IA) d/o Elmer W. Sass & Rose nee Vesley. Richard Karl Kreutner's Great-Grandfather: William Kreutner; Great-Great-Grandmother: Wilhelmina Krug. Delaine Sass' Great-Grandfather: William Kreutner; Great-Great Grandmother: Wilhelmina Krug. Children:
  Matthew Richard – b 05 Jan 1978 St.Lukes Hosp Cedar Rapids, IA;
      bpt 05 Feb 1978 & con 04 Apr 1993 St.Steph
  Michelle Ann – b 01 May 1980 St.Lukes Hosp Cedar Rapids, IA;
      bpt 29 May 1980 & con Mar 1995 St.Steph

Ronald KREUTNER s/o Clarence Kreutner & Helen nee Pottee; b 1946; m Joyce Christoffer. Children:
  Marcella Marie – b 1969; m Jeff Simington
  Matthew Ronald – b 1973
  Brandon William – b 1974
  Adam John – b 1986

Rosella KREUTNER d/o William Kreutner & Sophia nee Kerkman; b 1924, d 1997; m Frank Mills (b 1915, d 1964). Children:
  Rita Mills – b 1953; 1st m Steve Brannan; Child: Amanda Brannan;
      2nd m Richard Madison; Child: Brian Madison
  Rena Mills – b 1964; m Robert Eide; Children: Joshua (b 1983),

Jesse (b 1992)
Darwin Mills b 1951; 1ˢᵗ m Joyce Rinker; Child: Ryan (b 1975);
2ⁿᵈ m Kathy Holmes; Children: Chad (b 1980), Laura (b 1986)

Russell Harry KREUTNER s/o William August Kreutner & Margaret
Elisabeth nee Rinderknecht; b 28 Aug 1943 Taylor Twp Benton Co IA; m
08 Mar 1975 St.Matthew Catholic Ch Cedar Rapids, IA to Marie Ann
Craney (b 07 Nov 1949 Independence, IA) d/o Cecil Craney & Rita nee
Moroney. Children:
    Jeremy Michael – b 14 Oct 1976 Virginia Gay Hosp Vinton, IA
        m Kristi NN; New Hampton, IA residence
    Julie Marie – b 15 Mar 1979 St.Lukes Hosp Cedar Rapids, IA
        Longmont, CO residence

Susan KREUTNER d/o Albert Kreutner & Pauline nee Behrens; b 19 Mar
1955 Mt.Pleasant, IA; m Madison, WI to Derk Mullinger. Child:
    Nicole Mullinger – NFR

Thomas KREUTNER s/o Henry Kreutner JR. & Lillian nee Tranberg; b 18
May 1952 Cedar Rapids, IA; m 28 Aug 1976 Cedar Rapids, IA to Linda
Deklotz DVD.

Verna KREUTNER d/o William Kreutner & Sophia nee Kerkman; b 1910,
d 1996; m Jesse Nutt (b 1910, d 1965). Children:
    Melvin Nutt – b 1940; m Beverly Freeborn. Children: Teresa (b 1971),
        Tracy (b 1973)
    Mary Ann Nutt – b 1947; m Gaylord Swanson. Children: Christine
        (b 1969); m 1970 Bob Holms. Aaron (b 1973);
        m 1971 Nephani Schroeder
    Ilene Nutt –b 1948; m Jack Mustapha. Children: Curtis; Kelly

Viola KREUTNER d/o William Kreutner & Sophia nee Kerkman; b 1913;
m Cecil Edward Johnson. Children:
    Richard Edward Johnson – 1935; 1ˢᵗ m Helen Lee Bristow;
        2ⁿᵈ m Sharon Mendell
    Charles Larry Johnson – b 1940; m Mary Elizabeth Eppert
    Thomas Johnson – b 1947; m Donna Smith

*William KREUTNER b 18 Apr 1861 Baden-Baden, Germany; came to
USA in 1879; d 1937 Atkins, IA bur St.Steph Cem; m 1883 Marie Moeller

(b 17 Nov 1864, d [Stroke] 1919 Atkins bur St.Steph Cem) d/o Johannes Georg Möller & Wilhelmina nee Krug. Started farming 1/2 mile east of Atkins, IA and moved Mar 1886 to a farm purchased northwest of Atkins in Parkers' Grove area. They raised Bertha Bokorny (m Gus Brender)she lost her parents at ae2y. William & Marie retired 1917 in Atkins. Children:

    Elizabeth – b 18 May 1884, d 05 Dec 1955 bur St.Steph Cem;
        m 28 Oct 1903 Fred Kray
    Henry SR.-b 04 Mar 1886, d 09 Jun 1952 bur St.Steph Cem;
        m 30 Jan 1910 Sophie Marie Elisabeth Happel
    Anna – b 30 May 1888, d 05 Dec 1986;
        m 16 Jan 1908 (Conrad) August Konrad William Happel
    Clara – b 1891, d 1969; m Fred Kerkman
    Emma Anna – b 16 Dec 1895, d 10 May 1965 bur St.Steph Cem;
        m 09 Dec 1914 John A. Sass

William KREUTNER b 1882, d 1947; m Sophia Kerkman (b 1885, d 1962) d/o Edward John Kerkman & Barbara nee Rinderknecht. Children:

    Floyd – b 1907, d 1969; m Ruth Happel
    Clarence – b 1908, d 1974; m Helen Pottee
    Verna – b 1910, d 1996; m Jesse Nutt
    Viola – b 1913; m Cecil Edward Johnson
    Mildred – b 1915, d 1986; m Leonard Vogler
    Norman – b 1923, d 1976; 1st m Sophia Enich; 2nd m 1995 Jean NN
    Rosella – b 1924, d 1997; m Frank Mills

William Albert KREUTNER s/o William August Kreutner & Margaret Elisabeth nee Rinderknecht; b 22 Feb 1941 Taylor Twp Benton Co, bpt 1941, d 11 Sept 2001 ae50y 6m 19d; National Guard Sgt.E 5; m 14 Jun 1964 Luth Ch Maynard, IA to Linda Mae Bark (b 14 Jun 1944 Maynard, IA) d/o Floyd Bark & Bertha nee Bachley of Maynard, Fayette Co IA. Children:

    Sherri Lynn – b 25 Apr 1970 Virginia Gay Hosp Vinton, IA;
        m 13 May 1995 Jake Isbell
    Shawn William – b 22 Jul 1978 St.Lukes Hosp Cedar Rapids, IA;
        m 01 Sept 2007 Sara Michelle Schulte

William "Bill" August KREUTNER s/o Henry Adam Kreutner SR. & Sophia Marie Elisabeth nee Happel; b 07 Feb 1911 near Shellsburg Canton Twp Benton Co IA, bpt 1911 St.Steph and con St.Steph, d 01 Feb 2005 ae93y 11m 25d bur St.John Cem; m 07 Feb 1936 on farm near Van Horne his Happel first cousin-once-removed Margaret Elisabeth Rinderknecht (b 01 Jul 1913 north of Van Horne, Eldorado Twp Benton Co, bpt 1913 con St.John, Eldorado Twp Benton Co) d/o Conrad Martin Rinderknecht & Elizabeth Anna nee Krug. Their common Great-Grandparents: Andreas Happel & Maria (Marie)Elisabeth nee Möller; Farmers in Benton Co IA. 1975 retired in Newhall, IA. Mbrs St.John. Children:

Ardith Elizabeth-b 21 Mar 1937 Virginia Gay Hosp Vinton, IA;
m 05 Jun 1960 Robert Karl Reinhardt, DVD
Gerald William – b 15 Sept 1938 Taylor Twp Benton Co IA;
m 28 Nov 1964 Eileen Frieda Meyer
William Albert – b 22 Feb 1941 Taylor Twp Benton Co IA;
d 11 Sept 2001; m 14 Jun 1964 Linda Mae Bark
Russell Harry – b 28 Aug 1942 Taylor Twp Benton Co IA;
m 08 Mar 1975 Marie Ann Craney

Jody Sue KROENING d/o Nadine Marcel nee Krug & Donald LaVerne Kroening; b 04 Oct 1987 Kurt Anderson (b 12 Jun 1965). Racine, WI residence. Child:
Isabella Nicole Anderson – b 09 Jun 1999

Lori Kristine KROENING d/o Nadine Marcel nee Krug & Donald LaVerne Kroening; b 19 Mar 1959; m 30 Sept 1987 Norbert Julius (b 09 Feb 1962). Sussex, WI residence. Children:
Amanda Kristine Kroening – b 17 Jun 1991
Hannah Kristine Kroening – b 12 Sept 1993

Shelly Renee KROENING d/o Nadine Marcel nee Krug & Donald LaVerne Kroening; b 23 May 1962; m 01 May 1983 Allen James Milota. Cedar Rapids, IA residence. Children:
Jade Rui Milota – b 08 Jun 1966 Maoming, China
Jami Oiu Milota – b 09 Oct 1998 Hetei, China

Kurt Duane KROMMINGA s/o Elaine Leone nee Schminke & Duane Ferdinand Kromminga; b 25 Sept 1963 Cedar Rapids; m 08 May 1993 Jane Renae Tucker d/o Charles & Elaine Tucker. Children:
Hailey – b NFR
Ross –b- NFR

Lori Lynn KROMMINGA d/o Elaine Leone nee Schminke & Duane Ferdinand Kromminga; b 27 Nov 1958 Virginia Gay Hosp Vinton, IA;

262

Crowned 1980 Miss Iowa; Iowa State University; m 18 Jul 1981 St.John Luth Ch Keystone to Brian Winton McCulloh (b 03 Apr 1959 DeWitt, IA; Employment with Angus Association) s/o Winton Scott McCulloh & Cleone Rachel nee Olson, DeWitt, IA
Children:
    Ryan Jay McCulloh – b 15 Apr 1982 Roanoke, VA
    Matthew Calvin McCulloh – b 14 Jun 1984 LaCrosse, WI
    Allison Lynn McCulloh – b 08 Nov 1985 Viroqua, WI

Adam KRUG m Christina Schafer. Children:
    John – d 1884
    Martha – m NN Heibenthal, d 1891
    Charles – d May 1916
    Conrad – b 04 Feb 1827 or 37; m 18 Mar 1859 Anna Martha Reiss

Adam Andrew KRUG s/o Johann Peter Krug aka John Krug & Anna Katharina nee Michel; b 08 Jun 1889 Krug Homestead Fremont Twp Benton Co IA, bpt 23 Jun 1889 and con St.Steph, d 12 Jul 1960 ae71y 1m 4d St. Lukes Hosp Cedar Rapids, IA bur 14 Jul 1960 St.Steph Cem; m 27 Oct 1921 Cedar Rapids to Lucy Isabelle Snell (b 01 Aug 1894 near Fairfax, Clinton Twp Linn Co IA, bpt 1901 Fairview Methodist Ch, Linn Co IA, con St.Steph, d 15 Jan 1978 ae83y 5m 14d bur St.Steph Cem) d/o Julian Franklin Snell & Etta nee Elson. Farmers Fremont Twp Benton Co IA. Lucy retired in Atkins after Adam's death. Children:
    Noreen Etta – b 06 Aug 1923 Fremont Twp Benton Co IA;
        d 08 Dec 1996 Cedar Rapids, IA;
        m 17 Feb 1962 Claris Dean Utecht, DVD
    Phyllis Catherine – b 25 Nov 1929 Fremont Twp Benton Co IA;
        d 25 Mar 1966 [Cancer] bur St.Steph Cem;
        m 02 Sept 1950 Delbert Dale Vogt

Albert Martin KRUG s/o Fredrich William Krug & Juliet Elizabeth nee Swanson; b 22 Mar 1931 Krug farm, Fremont Twp Benton Co IA; bpt 03 May 1931 Sponsors: Martin Krug, Albert Werning; con St.Steph; 1948 Class Atkins High School; US Army 16 May 1952-20 Jun 1954; Newhall, IA City Clerk beginning Jan 1979; m 13 Nov 1954 Zion Luth Ch Shellsburg, IA to Lola Maye Brehm (b 03 Sept 1928 home near Garrison, IA, bpt 14 Oct 1928 Sponsors: Mrs. Jacob Brehm, Mrs Geo. St.Clair; con 29 Mar 1942 St.And; 1946 Class Shellsburg High School; Employed Rockwell-Collins 39 years, Cedar Rapids, IA) d/o Adam Reinhard Louis

Brehm, aka Louis Brehm & Elsie Anna nee Strellner. Newhall, IA residence. Celebrated 50th Wedding Anniversary. Children:

> Kathleen Ellen – b 29 Mar 1966 St.Lukes Hosp Cedar Rapids, IA;
> > m 24 Nov 2001 Eric Keith Goslinga
>
> Stephen Martin – b 03 Aug 1967 St.Lukes Hosp Cedar Rapids, IA;
> > m 30 Aug 2003 Margrate Rebecca Jones

Amy Sue KRUG d/o Roger Gerhardt Krug & Mary Jane nee Woodson; b 29 Oct 1973 St.Lukes Hosp Cedar Rapids, IA bpt 18 Nov 1973 and con 27 Mar 1988 St.Steph; 1992 Class St.Paul's Luth High School, Concordia, MO; 1996 Class Concordia Luth College, Seward, NE; Paralegal; m 13 Feb 1999 St.Steph to Craig Marc Hubbard (b 12 Dec 1968 Princeton, IL; Assistant Football Coach Mid-America University) s/o Rev. Roger & Mary Ann Hubbard of Wapello, IA. Children:

> Hannah Sue Hubbard – b 09 Feb 2000 Olathe Medical Center Kansas
> Caleb Marc Hubbard – b 16 Jan 2004 Olathe Medical Center Kansas

*Anna Elisabeth Krug d/o Johann Justus Krug II & Wilhelmina Kirchner, Löhlbach, Germany, b 27 Jan 1799 Schabendorf, Germany d 10 Apr 1879 ae80y 2m 14d Löhlbach Hse #70; m 16 Apr 1824 Andreas Schuler (b 25 May 1798 Löhlbach, Germany, d 20 Jan 1875 ae76y 7m 26d Löhlbach, Germany) s/o Luise Katharina nee Almus Schuler, Löhlbach, Germany. Children:

> *Wilhelmina Schuler – b 10 Oct 1824, d 18 Nov 1882;
> > m 16 Jan 1848 Löhlbach Ch Andreas Hohl
>
> Conrad Schuler – b 26 Mar 1830, d 1830 Löhlbach, Germany
> Johann Justus Schuler – b 08 Jul 1837, d 02 Jan 1868; m 17 Feb 1867;
> > No children

Anna Elisabeth KRUG d/o Johann Justus Krug III & Anna Elisabeth nee Paar: cf Johann Daniel Moeller, stepson of his wife's sister Wilhelmina Krug Moeller.

Anna Elizabeth KRUG d/o Johann Heinrich Krug & Louisa nee Krahling; b 14 Nov 1894 Krug Farm, two miles south of Atkins, Fremont Twp Benton Co IA bpt 02 Dec 1894 and con St.Steph; d 19 Aug 1961 ae66y 9m 5d Linn Co IA farm, bur 23 Aug 1961 St.Steph Cem; m 04 Oct 1917 Frederick John Keiper (b 02 Jan 1890, d 27 Apr 1975 ae85y 3m 25d bur St.Steph Cem). Farmers east of Atkins in Linn Co IA. Children:

> Wilma Keiper – b 18 Mar 1919; m Martin Sanders Child: Kenneth

Marie Keiper – b 02 Jan 1922; m James Bell
Louis Keiper – b 18 Jan 1927; m 03 Feb 1951 Germaine Stallman
Lawrence J. Keiper – b 15 Nov 1929, d 10 Feb 2005;
    m Maria Louisa Hofer in Munich, Germany

Anna Katherine KRUG d/o Johann Peter Krug aka John Krug & Anna
Katharina nee Michel; b 04 Jul 1870 Krug Homestead, Fremont Twp
Benton Co IA, bpt 14 Aug 1870 and con St.Steph, d 04 Aug 1927 ae57y 1m
on farm Fremont Twp Benton Co, bur 07 Aug 1927 St.Steph Cem; m 12
Mar 1896 St.Steph to William (Wilhelm) R. Rammelsberg (b 17 Jun 1864
near Atkins, IA d 14 Jan 1947 ae82y 6m 28d Cedar Rapids, IA bur 17 Jan
1947 St.StephCem) s/o Carl(Charles)Rammelsberg & Maria Katharina
Barbara nee Rinderknecht. Children:
    Elmer Henry David Rammelsberg – b 16 Sept 1896 Atkins, IA;
        d 29 May 1985 Cedar Rapids bur St.Steph Cem;
        1st m 15 Dec 1921 Goldie Etta Snell;
        2nd m 1961 Constance Jensen, Shellsburg, IA
    Ralph Leonard SR. Rammelsberg – b 25 Nov 1897 Atkins, IA;
        d 13 Oct 1940 [Farm Suicide]bur St.Steph Cem;
        m 24 Jan 1923 Louise May Schlotterback
    Laura Katherine Rammelsberg – b 26 Nov 1898 Fremont Twp
        Benton Co; d 08 Feb 2000 ae101y 2m 13d bur St.Steph Cem;
        m 16 Mar 1921 Karl Fredrich Wilhelmi
    John August Rammelsberg – b 14 Apr 1903, d 17 Feb 1994;
        m 21 Apr 1928 Bernice M. Hamilton
    Rose Elizabeth Rammelsberg- b 14 Aug 1905 Fremont Twp.;
        d 25 Jul 2006 ae100y 11m 11d Cedar Rapids, IA;
        m 15 Dec 1927 Walter Peter Valentine Wilhelmi
    Charles Fred Rammelsberg – b 20 Jan 1907 Atkins, d 07 Jul 1996;
        m 19 Mar 1930 Wilhemine (Wilma) I. Pheffer
    William (Bill) Henry Rammelsberg – b 14 Oct 1911 near Palo. IA,
        d 17 Jun 1992 Cedar Rapids, IA; m 01 May 1940 Ardis Sisley

Anna Maria (Mary) KRUG d/o Johann Heinrich Krug & Louisa nee
Krahling; b 13 Oct 1879 Krug Farm two miles south Atkins, Fremont Twp
Benton Co IA, bpt and con St.Steph, d 12 Mar 1945 Cedar Rapids, IA
ae65y 4m 27d; m 07 Mar 1907 John G. Rinderknecht. Farmers. Children:
    Erma Rinderknecht – m Leroy Riggs
    Gertrude Rinderknecht – m Hans Hansen
    Clarence Rinderknecht – m Esther Vavenka

Laverna Rinderknecht – m Fred Harti; Son: Leonard J. Harti
Edna Rinderknecht – m Homer Fryrear
Howard Rinderknecht – m three times, CA residence

Arthur John Peter KRUG s/o Henry John Krug & Christina Marie nee Happel; (TWIN: Emma Katherine Elizabeth nee Krug Rammelsberg) b 27 Sept 1899 Parent's farm near Atkins, Fremont Twp Benton Co IA) bpt 22 Oct 1899 and con 1913 St.Steph, d 26 Mar 1977 ae66y 5m 27d Cedar Rapids, IA bur 28 Mar 1977 Sisley Grove Cem Linn Co IA; 1st m 28 Aug 1926 St.Steph to Loretta Mae Housman (b 22 May 1904 Housman Farm near Walford, Benton Co IA, d 15 Nov 1991 ae87y 5m 24d bur Linwood-Murdock Cem, Cedar Rapids, IA) d/o Charles William Housman & Alta Maria nee Usher. DVD. Children:
  Arlene Mae – b 29 Apr 1928 Cedar Rapids, IA; Never Married
  Evelyn Leta – b 30 Nov 1930 Krug farm Fremont Twp Benton Co, IA;
      m 10 Jul 1948 William Raymond Neal SR.
  Raymond Henry – b 05 May 1932 Krug farm Fremont Twp
      Benton Co; 1st m 1954 Donna Lee Mitchell, DVD;
      2nd m 08 Jul 1978 Rena Milani, DVD
  Vera Eloise – b 01 Oct 1937 parents farm Fremont Twp Benton Co;
      Glendale CA residence; Never Married
2nd m 26 Oct 1951 Davenport, IA, Arthur John Peter Krug to Helen Teegen Hoover, DVD.
3rd m Arthur John Peter Krug to Kathleen Hogan, DVD.
4th m 25 Feb 1960 Arthur John Peter Krug to Frances D. Cuttright
2nd m 14 Feb 1945 Cedar Rapids, IA Loretta Mae nee Housman Krug to Kenneth Lemuel Tharp.

Audrey Ann KRUG d/o Harvey Adam Krug & Ella Wilhelmina nee Rinderknecht; b 28 Jul 1939 Parent's Farm Fremont Twp Benton Co IA, bpt 20 Aug 1939 Parent's home Fremont Twp Benton Co, con St.Steph; Atkins High School; m 15 Aug 1964 St.Steph to David L. Glasgow (b 26 Jun 1935). Children:
  Jodi Ann Glasgow – b 09 Dec 1967
  Joel David Glasgow – b 04 Jan 1971;
      m 29 Apr 2000 Kari Ann Dumblaukas

*Bernhart KRUG b Hesse-Kassel, Germany, (cf naturalization 29 Sept 1899, ae24y, Volume IV, Page 194 Benton Co IA Courthouse Recorders Office) brother of John M. Krug. West Bend, IA residence.

Beverlyn Kay KRUG d/o Elmer Henry Krug & Virginia nee Jolley; b 13 Jan 1946 Cedar Rapids, IA bpt and con St.Steph, Atkins High School; Psychiatric Nurse; m 20 Feb 1971 Madison, WI to James M. O'Connor (b 04 Feb 1944, Chicago School Superintendent). LaGrange, IL residence. Children:

> Christine Ann O'Connor – b 22 Aug 1973;
>> m 20 Feb 1971 James M. O'Conner
> Rebecca Lynn O'Connor – b 24 Jun 1976; B.A. Valparaiso U.
> Timothy James O'Connor – b 11 Jan 1979; IL Wesleyan U.

Charlotte Louise KRUG d/o Clarence John Adam August Krug & Gail Alein nee Harnisch; b 23 May 1933 Krug Farm Fremont Twp Benton Co IA bpt 18 Jun 1933 St.Steph, 1950 Class Atkins High School; 1st m 22 May 1956 St.James Methodist Ch, Cedar Rapids, IA to Dale L. Tuttle s/o Estel M. Tuttle of Danbury, DVD. No children.
2nd m 22 Jan 1960 Charlotte Louise nee Krug to William V. Petty (b 09 Nov 1931 dec'd) DVD. Residence Sioux City, IA.; in GA.

> STEPCHILDREN:
> Stephen V. Petty – b 05 Sept 1951; m 06 Sept 1970 Marsha Marta
>> (Sept 1951)
> James E. Petty – b 12 Aug 1955; m 01 Jun 1974 Deanna Durham
>> (b 28 Nov 1955)

Clarence John Adam August KRUG s/o Henry John Krug & Christina Marie nee Happel; b 06 Sept 1901 Krug farm near Atkins, Fremont Twp Benton Co IA, bpt 13 Oct 1901 and con 1915 St.Steph, d 03 Jul 1959 ae57y 9m 22d University Hosp Iowa City, IA [Injuries: fall off farm hayrack wagon] bur 06 Jul 1959 Sisley Grove Cem, Linn Co IA; m 14 Mar 1930 St.Stephen Luth School Hall to Gail Alein Harnisch (b 04 Jan 1906 Waterloo, IA, d 20 May 1987 ae81y 4m 16d Story City, IA bur 22 May 1987 Sisley Grove Cem, Linn Co IA) d/o Emil Frederick William Harnisch & Martha nee Degler. Gail continued farming after Clarence's death residing fifty-two consecutive years on same farm 1 ¼ miles east of Atkins, IA. Children:

> Ruth Marie – b 14 Apr 1931 Krug Farm Fremont Twp Benton Co IA;
>> m 05 Jun 1954 Frank Hudson
> Charlotte Louise – b May 1933 Krug Farm Fremont Twp Benton Co
>> 1st m 22 May 1956 Dale Tuttle, DVD;
>> 2nd m 22 Jan 1960 William V. Petty, DVD

Maynard Clarence – b 30 Jul 1935 Fremont Twp Benton Co IA;
m 1981 Vickie Hanson, DVD.
David Karl – b 20 Jun 1939 Krug Farm Fremont Twp Benton Co IA;
m 06 May 1967 Joyce Elaine Woodward
Thelma Karlein – b 22 Feb 1946 Mercy Hosp Cedar Rapids, IA;
m 15 Jun 1968 Robert Lloyd Huffer

David Karl KRUG s/o Clarence John Adam August Krug & Gail Alein nee Harnisch; b 20 Jun 1939 Krug Farm Fremont Twp Benton Co IA, bpt 23 Jul 1939 St.Steph Sponsor: Uncle Walter W.A. Krug; m 06 May 1967 Joyce Elaine Woodward (b 11 Jun 1943, d 10 Mar 1983 ae39y 8m 27d Omaha, NE). NE residence Children:
Karl Robert – b 05 Jan 1968; m NN
Kurtis John – b 19 Jun 1970; Career U.S. Navy, Pearl Harbor, HA

Deanne Kay KRUG d/o Melvin August Krug & Mary Ann nee Ludvicek; b 17 Feb 1951 St.Lukes Hosp Cedar Rapids, IA bpt 11 Mar 1951 and con St.Steph, Atkins High School; m 02 Sept 1972 St.Steph to Andrew Joseph Becker (b 28 Jul 1951; Teacher Benton Community High School) s/o Wilferd & Dorothy Becker of Atkins. Newhall, IA residence. Children:
Amy Elizabeth Becker – b 08 Jan 1975;
m 25 Sept 2004 Andrew Robert Volz
Kelly Anne Becker – b 26 May 1977;
m 29 Dec 2007 Daron Neil Buch
Nathan Andrew Becker – b 12 Jun 1980
Sarah Marie Becker – b 30 Jan 1983;
m 02 Sept 2006 Geoffrey Michael Seifert
s/o Michael & Patricia Seifert

Delbert John KRUG s/o John August Henry Krug & Elizabeth Jeanette nee Happel; b 14 Sept 1914 Parent's Farm Fremont Twp Benton Co IA, bpt 18 Oct 1914 and con St.Steph; d 07 Feb 1995 ae80y 4m 24d; m 23 Jun 1943 TrinCR (Double Ceremony with first cousin George Popenhagen) to Libbie Ann Cerveny (b 13 Oct 1922 rural Fairfax, IA bpt Easter Sunday 1943 TrinCR) d/o Wesley Cerveny & Ann nee Hynek, Cedar Rapids, IA. Farmed south of Atkins; raised and exhibited Polled Herefords. Celebrated 50th Wedding Anniversary. Five children bpt and confirmed at TrinCR:
Janice Kay – b 26 Apr 1944, d 10 Jun 2002 [Cancer]
m 12 Sept 1964 Kenneth C. Schatz
Patricia Lou – b 27 Jun 1947; m 12 Aug 1965 Rad Fish

Ronda Lee – b 11 May 1949; m 30 Jun 1973 Randall George Hess
Liberta Sue – b 18 Sept 1954;
    1st m 07 Aug 1976 Dr. Joel H. Hendrickson, DVD;
    2nd m 11 Jun 1983 Charles Ledder
Della Rae – b 18 Apr 1958; m 11 Jul 1981 Duane Petersen, DVD

Della Rae KRUG d/o Delbert John Krug & Libbie Ann nee Cerveny; b 18 Apr 1958 Cedar Rapids, IA bpt May 1958 TrinCR; m 11 Jul 1981 TrinCR to Duane Petersen (b 14 Nov 1948) DVD; s/o Sonke & Corrine Petersen of Stewartville, MN. Rochester, MN residence. Child:
Karl John Peterson – b 11 Oct 1986

Delores Ann KRUG d/o Gerhardt Henry Conrad Krug & Frances Marie nee Strellner; b 03 Jul 1941 Parent's Farm, Clinton Twp Linn Co IA, bpt 27 Jul 1941 and con 1954 St.Steph, 1958 Class Atkins High School; 1st m 17 Jun 1961 St.Steph to Galen Eugene Glick (b 26 May 1941 Aurora, IL, bpt 27 May 1949 Aurora, IL; Bricklayer) Stepson of Herbert Rinderknecht (Father: Fred H.Glick) & his mother Odetta Marie nee Eutsler Glick. DVD July 1968. Children:
Shari Lynn Glick – b 09 Jan 1963 Cedar Rapids, IA;
    m 07 Jan 1987 Stuart Nechanicky, DVD
Michael John Glick – b 08 May 1964 Cedar Rapids, IA;
    m 21 Jun 1985 Alice M. Beltz
2nd m 14 Aug 1975 Good Shepherd Luth Ch, Cedar Rapids, Delores Ann nee Krug Glick to John Tibben (b 18 Nov 1937 Marengo, IA bpt 12 Dec 1937 St.John Luth Ch, Marengo, IA; Iowa Co Commissioner) s/o Arthur H. Tibben & Bertha Marie nee Kummer. Charter flight service. Farmers. Child:
Anne Marna Marie Tibben – b 11 Dec 1977 Cedar Rapids, IA;
    m 19 Aug 2000 Bradley Dwayne Nelson

Dennis Elmer KRUG s/o Elmer Henry Krug & Virginia Beverlyn nee Jolley; b 24 Jun 1948 Cedar Rapids, IA bpt and con St.Steph, Atkins High School; 1974 Master's Degree Education, Western Oregon State College; m 24 Aug 1985 Carolyn Sue Eldred (b 24 Jul 1946). Austin, TX Contractor. Children:
Amanda Elizabeth – b 11 Mar 1986
Kelsey Suzanne – b 31 Jan 1990

Donald George August KRUG s/o John George Krug & Emma Bertha nee Daleske; b 22 Dec 1931 Krug Homestead Fremont Twp Benton Co IA. bpt

31 Jan 1932 and con St.Steph, 1949 Class Atkins High School; m 30 Jun 1954 St.Steph to Ila Jean Taschner, Howard, SD(b 28 Jul 1934 Howard, SD, d 30 Nov 2006 ae72y 4m 2d Cedar Rapids, IA bur St.Steph Cem) d/o Myron Taschner & Hazel nee Bramow of Cedar Rapids, IA. Farmed Krug Homestead of his father and immigrant grandfather Johann Peter Krug. Celebrated 50th Wedding Anniversary. Children:

 IDENTICAL TWINS: Richard Allan – b 03 Feb 1955
   Cedar Rapids, IA; m 24 Apr 1993 Janene Rae Symonds
    Randall Ray – b 03 Feb 1955 Cedar Rapids, IA;
  m 27 Aug 1977 Sheila Ann Albers
 John Jay – b 03 Jun 1957 Cedar Rapids, IA;
  m 08 Nov 1986 Cynthia Louise McGohan
 Jeffrey Donald – b 16 Apr 1960 Cedar Rapids, IA;
  m 20 Jul 1985 Linda Marie Selk
 James Curtis- b 10 Jul 1961 Cedar Rapids, IA;
  m 24 Jul 1985 "Gina" Deeanne Selk (Linda Marie Selk's cousin)

Donna Mae KRUG d/o Irvin August Krug & Leola Anna Elizabeth nee Hertle; b 24 Apr 1936 Parent's Farm Fremont Twp Benton Co IA, bpt 17 May 1936 and con 1949 St.Steph, 1953 Class Atkins High School; d 22 Jun 2007 ae71y 2m 29d bur St.Steph Cem; m 08 June 1957 St. Steph to Donald Gene Selken (b 29 Jan 1936) s/o Rudolph Selken of Keystone, IA. Farmers near Keystone. Children:

 Debra Sue Selken – b 28 Mar 1959; 1st m 11 Mar 1978 Rich Selk,
  DVD; 2nd m 13 Aug 1984 Douglas Yates of Palo
 David Jon Selken – b 19 Jan 1961; m 13 Apr 1985 Denise Grieder
  (b 01 Aug 1964)
 Dianne Marie Selken – b 20 Jul 1962;
  m 17 Dec 1982 Thomas Edward Barfels

Dorothy Marie KRUG d/o Fredrich William Krug & Juliet Elizabeth nee Swanson; b 01 Oct 1922 Krug farm, Fremont Twp Benton Co IA, bpt 03 Dec 1922 con St.Steph, Atkins High School; d 14 Aug 1990 ae71y 10m 13d; m 30 Sept 1948 St.Steph to Friedrich Henry Bayer of Marengo, IA(b 04 Dec 1916) s/o Frieda nee Keiper & George Bayer. Farmers near Marengo, Iowa Co IA. Children:

 Rev. Robert Fredrich Bayer – b 15 Feb 1950 Marengo, IA;
  m 09 Jun 1979 Amy Dormer
 Kenneth Martin Bayer – b 04 Jul 1953 Marengo, IA; Victor, IA farmer
 Julia Marie Bayer – b 26 Oct 1959 Marengo, IA;

m 20 Jun 1981 Terry L. Warnick

Edna Elizabeth Katherine KRUG d/o John August Henry Krug & Elizabeth Jeanette nee Happel: cf Herman William Haerther.

Elaine Enid KRUG d/o Walter William August Krug & Enid Muriel nee Bryner; b 30 Jul 1935 Krug Farm Fremont Twp Benton Co IA, bpt 08 Sept 1935 St.Steph Cousin Sponsor: Leslie & Wilma Edmonds, con 1949 St.Steph, 1953 Class Atkins High School; Beautician; Kirkwood Community College; m 02 Dec 1956 St.Steph to Allan Eugene Postel (b 12 Jul 1935 St.Lukes Hosp Cedar Rapids, IA; Retired 22y service Cedar Rapids Fire Department) s/o Gayle Osborn Postel & Thelma Evangeline nee Miller. Mbrs Concordia Luth Ch, Cedar Rapids, IA. Celebrated 50th Wedding Anniversary. Children:
  Thomas Allan Postel – b 26 Aug 1959, d 28 Aug 1959, bur CdrMem.
  Cynthia Ann Postel – b 16 May 1963 St. Lukes Hosp
    Cedar Rapids, IA. U of Iowa Registered Nurse
  Mark Allan Postel – b 24 Sept 1964 St.Lukes Hosp Cedar Rapids, IA;
    bpt 29 Nov 1964 and con Concordia Luth Ch

Elizabeth Anna KRUG d/o Johann Peter Krug aka John Krug & Anna Katherina nee Michel; b 15 Mar 1884 Krug Homestead, Fremont Twp Benton Co IA, bpt 11 Apr 1884 and con St.Steph; d 12 Jun 1972 ae88y 2m 28d Virginia Gay Hosp Vinton, IA bur 15 Jun 1972 St.John Cem; m 07 Feb 1907 St.Steph to Conrad Martin Rinderknecht (b 01 Aug 1882 Rinderknecht farm, Fremont Twp Benton Co IA, bpt 20 Feb 1882 St.Steph, d 10 Jan 1957 ae74y 5m 9d his home, Eldorado Twp Benton Co IA, bur 13 Jan 1957 St.John Cem) s/o Karl Rinderknecht & Anna Katherina nee Happel. Farmers in Benton Co. Children:
  Esther Katherine Rinderknecht-b 11 Apr 1908 Clinton Twp Linn Co
    d 24 Sept 1973; m 01 Feb 1928 Fred William Bierschenk
  LaVerna Anna Gertrude Rinderknecht – b 23 Mar 1911
    Eldorado Twp; d 19 Nov 1995;
    m 11 Feb 1930 Harry Martin Bierschenk
  Margaret Elizabeth Rinderknecht- b 01 Jul 1913 Eldorado Twp;
    m 07 Feb 1936 William August Kreutner
  Merl Carl Johannes Rinderknecht – b 01 Nov 1916 Eldorado Twp;
    d 21 Dec 2000; m 19 Sept 1942 Lois Mae Franzenburg
  Karl George Rinderknecht – b 14 Jun 1919 Eldorado Twp;
    d 16 Jan 2004; m 01 Jun 1948 Betty Jo Van Heiden

Eleanor Louise Barbara Rinderknecht – b 04 Dec 1922 Eldorado;
   d 15 Mar 1999; m 11 Jan 1942 Melvin Gottfried Webert
Robert Henry Rinderknecht – b 14 Sept 1926 Eldorado Twp;
   m 28 May 1950 Marcella Jean Hurst

Elma Ann Christina KRUG d/o John August Henry Krug & Elizabeth Jeanette nee Happel; b 15 Jun 1908 Parent's Farm Fremont Twp Benton Co IA, bpt 19 Jul 1908 and con St.Steph, d 31 Dec 2004 ae96y 6m 16d Vinton IA Lutheran Home bur St.Steph Cem; m 11 Jan 1933 St.Steph to Bernard Jacob Schanbacher (b 16 Mar 1907 Schanbacher Farm, Clinton Twp Linn Co IA, bpt 23 Jun 1907 and con St.Steph, d 20 Jun 1976 ae69y 3m 4d Atkins, IA bur 23 Jun 1976 St.Steph Cem) s/o Julius Schanbacher & Gertrude nee Keiper. Dairy farmers Fremont Twp Benton Co, IA until retiring in new home they built in Atkins. Children:
   Ronald August Schanbacher – b 15 Mar 1935 St.Lukes Hosp
      Cedar Rapids, IA; m 04 Jun 1955 Janet Sue Rosdail
   Allan Edward Schanbacher – b 12 Feb 1939 Fremont Twp Benton Co;
      m 30 May 1959 Joyce Elaine Piehl
   Merlyn Melvin Schanbacher – b 21 Sept 1946 St.Lukes Hosp
      Cedar Rapids, IA; m 16 Aug 1969 Joanne Elaine Koopman

Elmer Henry KRUG s/o Fredrich William Krug & Juliet Elizabeth nee Swanson; b 16 Dec 1914, Krug farm Fremont Twp Benton Co IA, bpt 17 Jan 1915 St.Steph, d 11 Aug 1981 ae66y 7m 26d bur St.Steph Cem; US Army World War II, Ascension Island; Retired Milwaukie Railroad Telegrapher, Atkins; m 20 Jun 1943 Parsonage St.Steph (both on US Army miliary leave World War II) to Lt.Virginia Beverlyn Jolley (b 25 Nov 1921, d 13 Jan 1985 ae63y 1m 19d bur St.Steph Cem). Atkins, IA residence. Children:
   Beverlyn Kay – b 13 Jan 1946 Cedar Rapids, IA;
      m 20 Feb 1971 James M. O'Connor at Madison, WI
   Dennis Elmer – b 24 Jun 1948 Cedar Rapids, IA;
      m 24 Aug 1985 Carolyn Sue Eldred

Elward William KRUG s/o John Daniel Krug & Carrie May nee Hein; b 07 Feb 1916 Parent's farm near Atkins, IA d 10 May 1987 [Suicide on his farm near Fairfax, IA] ae71y 3m 3d, bur 13 May 1987 Raetz Cem, Atkins, IA; m 12 Jun 1951 TrinCR to Emily Irene Ludvicek (b 06 Jun 1924 Linn Co IA, d 10 May 1987 ae62y 11m 4d Cedar Rapids [Gunshot wounds to head; shot by husband at farm where he was born, resided all of his life] bur 13 May

272

1987 Raetz Cem, Atkins, IA) d/o Joseph L. Ludvicek & Mary nee Herman of Center Point, Linn Co IA. Child:

> Troy Lee – b 14 Jun 1952 St. Lukes Hosp Cedar Rapids, IA;
> m 20 Jun 1981 Margaret Jean Henry

Emma Katherine Elizabeth KRUG d/o Henry John Krug & Christina Marie nee Happel; (TWIN: Arthur John Peter Krug) b 27 Sept 1899 Parent's Farm Fremont Twp near Atkins, Benton Co IA; bpt 22 Oct 1899 and con 1913 St.Steph, d 23 Sept 1988 ae88y 11m 27d Virginia Gay Hosp Vinton, IA bur 26 Sept 1988 St.John Cem; m 15 Feb 1928 St.Steph to Earl Edward Rammelsberg (b 28 Sept 1896 north of Atkins, Fremont Twp Benton Co IA, bpt 1896 Pleasant Hill Presbyterian Ch, Atkins, d 16 Jul 1988 ae91y 9m 18d Virginia Gay Hosp Vinton, IA bur 19 Jul 1988 St.John Cem) s/o Alphonsa Friedrich Emil (A.F.) Rammelsberg & Mary Jane nee Armstrong. Farmers one mile east of Newhall, IA. Children:

> Merle Rammelsberg – b & d 05 Feb 1930, bur St.Steph Cem
> Gladys Marie Rammelsberg – b 29 Jan 1933 Parent's farm;
> m 08 Dec 1954 Richard Folkmann
> Verla Emma Rammelsberg – b 02 Mar 1937, Never Married
> Shirley Ann Rammelsberg – b 10 Jan 1942 Parent's farm;
> d 18 May 1984 [Suicide]; m 14 Feb 1960 Dennis Gewecke,
> DVD 1984

Evelyn Leta KRUG d/o Arthur John Peter Krug & Loretta Mae nee Housman; b 30 Nov 1930 Krug Farm Fremont Twp Benton Co IA, bpt 04 Jan 1931 St.Steph, con 1944 TrinCR, 1948 Class Roosevelt High School Cedar Rapids, IA; Retired from Rockwell Collins International, Cedar Rapids, IA; m 10 Jul 1948 TrinCR to William (Bill) Raymond Neal SR. (b 30 Sept 1930 Deep River, IA; Retired 1992) s/o Christ Raymond Neal & Inez nee Van Dee of Bertram, IA. Lifelong residents of Cedar Rapids, IA. Children:

> William Raymond Neal JR. – b 14 Mar 1950 Cedar Rapids, IA;
> m 03 Jun 1972 Sheryl Dianne Elliot
> Brenda Kris Neal – b 23 Sept 1955 Cedar Rapids, IA;
> 1st m 01 Oct 1977 James Stepanek (b 13 Sept 1955) DVD;
> 2nd m 13 Jun 1992 Brian Garbe
> Connie Lou Neal – b 22 Feb 1959 Cedar Rapids, IA;
> m 21 May 1983 John Ray Caviness

Everett Harvey KRUG s/o Harvey Adam Krug & Ella Wilhelmina nee

Rinderknecht; b 09 Dec 1946 Cedar Rapids, IA bpt 05 Jan 1947 and con St.Steph, Atkins High School; m 22 Dec 1967 St.Steph to Krista Lynn Blattler (b 14 Dec 1946) d/o Charles Richard Blattler. Child:

Melissa Lynn – b 23 May 1968; m 24 Jun 1995 Steven Beckler

Fredrich William KRUG s/o Johann Heinrich Krug & Louisa nee Krahling; b 03 Oct 1889 Farm near Atkins Fremont Twp Benton Co IA, bpt 13 Oct 1889 and con St.Steph, d 02 Sept 1970 ae80y 10m 29d St.Lukes Hosp Cedar Rapids, IA bur 05 Sept 1970 St.Steph Cem; Farmed land where he was born; Carpenter; m 12 Feb 1914 Cedar Rapids to Juliet Elizabeth Swanson (b 05 Apr 1895 Belle Plaine, IA, bpt Easter Apr 1898 Belle Plaine, IA d 12 Feb 1962 ae66y 10m 2d St.Lukes Hosp Cedar Rapids, IA bur 14 Feb 1962 St.Steph Cem) d/o John Emmanuel Swanson & Augusta Christine nee Kolstrom. Moved to Atkins, IA residing on Main Street. Children:

Elmer Henry – b 16 Dec 1914, d 11 Aug 1981;
    m 20 Jun 1943 Virginia Beverlyn Jolley
Dorothy Marie – b 01 Oct 1922, d 14 Aug 1990;
    m 30 Sept 1948 Friedrich Henry Bayer
Albert Martin – b 22 Mar 1931, m 13 Nov 1954 Lola Maye Brehm

Gary Allan KRUG s/o Roger Gerhardt Krug & Mary Jane nee Woodson; b 02 Aug 1967 St.Lukes Hosp Cedar Rapids, IA; bpt 22 Aug 1967 St.Steph Sponsors: Uncle Roland & Aunt Bessie Burke, Victor, IA, con 12 Apr 1981 St.Steph, 1985 Class College Community High School; Occupation: Trucking; 1st m 13 Aug 1993 Carrie Schulte d/o Clarence & Hazel Schulte of rural Walford, IA. DVD 1996; 2nd m 28 Nov 1998 St.Steph to Tamara Suzanne Leisner Hess (b 02 Dec 1965 Sterling IL) d/o Frank & Sharon Leisner. IL residence.

STEPCHILDREN:
Dustin Gene Hess – b 13 Apr 1987 Sterling, IL
Elizabeth Marie Hess – b 31 Oct 1991 Sterling, IL
Kyle Richard Hess – b 06 Apr 1993 Dixon, IL

George Andrew KRUG s/o George Andrew August Krug & Betty Ann nee Knipp; b 08 Jun 1954 Linn Co IA; m 18 Aug 1979 All Saints Catholic Ch Cedar Rapids, IA to Denise Marie Erceg d/o Joseph N. Erceg of Cedar Rapids. Child:

Jessica Kay – b 14 Jan 1986

George Andrew August KRUG s/o John Daniel Krug & Carrie May nee

Hein; b 12 Jul 1918 Parent's farm near Atkins, Fremont Twp Benton Co IA, bpt 18 May 1925 St.Steph; m 01 Jun 1947 Betty Ann Knipp (b 09 Dec 1918). Children:

Pamela May – b 21 Apr 1948; m 28 Sept 1968 Richard Keith Ruhberg
Sheryl Kay – b 21 Mar 1952; m 22 Aug 1970 Dennis Lynn Dunston
George Andrew – b 08 Jun 1954; m 25 Aug 1979 Denise Marie Erceg
    (b 28 Aug 1959)
Kevin Kenneth – b 27 Jul 1955; m 1978 Jill L. NN, DVD

Gerhardt Henry Conrad KRUG s/o Henry John Krug & Christina Marie nee Happel; b 25 Apr 1909 Henry Krug Farm, Clinton Twp Linn Co IA, bpt 30 May 1909 and con 1923 St.Steph, d 22 May 1975 ae65y 27d Deer River, MN [Diabetic Coma on fishing trip]bur St.Steph Cem; m 29 Jan 1936 at Julius Strellner farm home, Big Grove Twp near Van Horne, IA to Frances Marie Strellner (b 31 Oct 1914 Big Grove Twp Benton Co IA, bpt 1914 and con St.And, d 20 Oct 1999 ae84y 11m 20d Vinton, IA Hosp bur 23 Oct 1999 St.Steph Cem) d/o Julius D. Strellner & Julia Fredericka Amelia nee Waterstradt. Owner of farm where he was born for sixty-two years until 1971 retirement in Atkins, IA. Children:

Roger Gerhardt – b 03 Mar 1939 St.Lukes Hosp Cedar Rapids, IA;
    m 08 Aug 1964 Mary Jane Woodson
Delores Ann – b 03 Jul 1941 Parents Farm Clinton Twp Linn Co IA;
    1st m 17 Jun 1961 Galen Eugene Glick, DVD Jul 1968;
    2nd m 14 Aug 1975 John Tibben

Harvey Adam KRUG s/o John August Henry Krug & Elizabeth Jeanette nee Happel; b 23 Jul 1906 Parent's Farm Fremont Twp Benton Co IA, bpt 19 Aug 1906 and con St.Steph, d 27 Nov 1957 ae57y 4m 4d [Tractor Accident] Fremont Twp Benton Co, bur 30 Nov 1957 St.Steph Cem; m 10 Jun 1936 St.Steph to Ella Wilhelmina Rinderknecht (b 09 Apr 1910 near Bancroft, Kossouth Co, IA, bpt 1910 Bancroft, IA d 05 Oct 1987 ae87y 5m 26d Atkins home [Cancer] bur 08 Oct 1987 St.Steph Cem; Retired Teacher Central Luth School) d/o Martin Fred Lenard Rinderknecht & Bertha Augusta nee Ehlers. Farmers near Atkins, IA. Children:

Karen Marie – 30 Sept 1937; m 08 Feb 1958 Paul R. Nielson
Audrey Ann – 28 Jul 1939; m 15 Aug 1964 David L. Glasgow
Inez Mae – b 11 Apr 1942; m 24 Aug 1963 David Charles Lensch
Everett Harvey – b 09 Dec 1946; m 22 Dec 1967 Krista Blattler

Heinrich Peter Martin KRUG s/o Johann Heinrich Krug & Emma Louise nee Raetz; b 04 Jun 1901 Farm near Atkins, IA bpt 23 Jun 1901 and con St.Steph, d 03 May 2001 ae99y 11m bur Linwood Cem Cedar Rapids IA; m 19 Feb 1928 Emma Louise Raetz (b 16 May 1903, d 24 Feb 1983 ae79y 9m 5d). Cedar Rapids, IA residence. Children:

LaVonne – b 14 Apr 1930; m 20 Nov 1955 Albert T. Huebener

Nadine Marcel – b 11 Jul 1937, d 03 May 2001;
   m 22 Jun 1958 Donald LaVerne Kroening

Henry John KRUG s/o Johann Peter Krug & Anna Katharina nee Michel; b 09 Feb 1872 Krug Homestead, Fremont Twp Benton Co IA, bpt 18 Feb 1872 St.Steph and con St.Steph, d 26 Dec 1955 ae82y 10m 17d Lutheran Home Vinton, IA bur 28 Dec 1955 St.Steph Cem; m 09 Mar 1898 St.Steph to Christina Marie Happel (b 13 Feb 1877, bpt 08 Apr 1877 St.Steph and con St.Steph, d 17 Mar 1934 ae57y 1m 4d [Stroke] Henry Krug farm, Clinton Twp Linn Co IA, bur 19 Mar 1934 St.Steph Cem) d/o Peter Johann Happel & Katharine Elisabeth nee Werning. Farmers in Fremont Twp Benton Co and Clinton Twp Linn Co IA; extended family farming operation 600 acres with four sons. Celebrated 25th Silver Wedding Anniversary. Children:

TWINS: Arthur John Peter – b 27 Sept 1899 Fremont Twp
   Benton Co; d 26 Mar 1977 Cedar Rapids, IA;
   1st m 28 Aug 1926 Loretta Mae Housman, DVD;
   2nd m 26 Oct 1951 Helen Teegen Hoover, DVD;
   3rd m Kathleen Hogan, DVD;
   4th m 25 Feb 1960 Frances D. Cuttright
      Emma Katherine Elizabeth – b 27 Sept 1899
   Fremont Twp IA; d 23 Sept 1988 Vinton, IA;
   m 15 Feb 1928 Earl Edward Rammelsberg
Clarence John Adam August- b 06 Sept 1901 Fremont Twp
   Benton Co; d 03 Jul 1959 Iowa City, IA;
   m 14 Mar 1930 Gail Alein Harnisch
Walter William August – b 02 Aug 1904 Clinton Twp Linn Co IA;
   d 08 Oct 1985 Iowa City, IA; m 09 Sept 1925 Enid Muriel Bryner
Gerhardt Henry Conrad – b 25 Apr 1909 Clinton Twp Linn Co IA;
   d 22 May 1975 Deer River MN;
   m 29 Jan 1936 Frances Marie Strellner

Inez Mae KRUG d/o Harvey Adam Krug & Ella Wilhelmina nee Rinderknecht; b 11 Apr 1942 Parent's Farm Fremont Twp Benton Co, bpt 10 May 1941, con St.Steph, Atkins High School; Bachelor's Degree U of

IA; m 24 Aug 1963 St.Steph to David Charles Lensch (b 10 Oct 1943 Cedar Rapids, IA bpt 1943 St.Steph; B.S. Degree ISU) s/o Charles Edward Lensch & Doris Mae nee Schlotterback. WI residence. Children:
Lori Ann Lensch – b 08 Jan 1967; m 06 Jul 1991 Michael Marcotti
Kristin Marie Lensch – b 16 Dec 1970;
    m 29 May 1999 Timothy S.Huebner

Irene Katherine Elizabeth KRUG d/o John August Henry Krug & Elizabeth Jeanette nee Happel: cf Alfred August Heinrich Rinderknecht.

Irvin August KRUG s/o John August Henry Krug & Elizabeth nee Happel; b 03 Apr 1912 Farm west of Atkins, IA bpt 12 May 1912 and con St.Steph; 1928 Class Atkins High School; d 31 Mar 1997 ae84y 11m 27d bur St.Steph Cem; m 27 Jun 1934 St. John Luth Ch, Eldorado Twp Benton Co IA to Leola Anna Elizabeth Hertle (b 25 June 1913 Farm north of Newhall, IA bpt 1913 St.John Luth Ch, Newhall; Teacher Eden Twp School #7, d 18 Sept 2002 ae89y 2m 24d bur St.Steph Cem) d/o August Sebastian Hertle & Martha nee Bierschenk. Farmers 1/2 mile west of Atkins, IA until 1969 retirement in Atkins home they built. Irvin: Feed salesman many years achieving 1966 top salesman honor in nation for Vigortone Company. Celebrated 50th Wedding Anniversary. Children:
Donna Mae – b 24 Apr 1936 Fremont Twp Benton Co IA;
    d 22 Jun 2007 Vinton, IA Lutheran Home;
    m 08 Jun 1957 Donald Gene Selken of Keystone, IA
Virgil Irvin – b 19 Sept 1941 Fremont Twp Benton Co IA;
    m 07 Dec 1968 Mary Jane Meroshek, Marion, IA

James Curtis KRUG s/o Donald George August Krug & Ila Jean nee Taschner; b 10 Jul 1961 St.Lukes Hosp Cedar Rapids, IA bpt 13 Aug 1961 St.Steph; Farmer; m 24 Aug 1985 St.John Luth Ch, Keystone, IA to "Gina" Deeanne Selk (b 05 Dec 1961; Rockwell Employee, Cedar Rapids, IA) d/o Kenneth & Elaine Selk of Keystone, IA (cousin of Linda Selk m Jeffrey Donald Krug). Children:
Tyler James – b 11 Sept 1990 Cedar Rapids, IA
Anna Elise – b 26 Jul 1993 Cedar Rapids, IA

Janice Kay KRUG d/o Delbert John Krug & Libbie Ann nee Cerveny; b 26 Apr 1944 Mercy Hosp Cedar Rapids, IA bpt 20 May 1944 TrinCR, d 10 Jun 2002 [Cancer] ae58y 1m 15d bur St.Steph Cem; m 12 Sept 1964 Kenneth C. Schatz. Sioux City, IA residence. Children:

Bradley Carl Schatz – b 27 Feb 1973, Chicago IL residence
Cynthia Kay Schatz – b 22 Oct 1977, Denver, Co residence

Jeffrey Donald KRUG s/o Donald George August Krug & Ila Jean nee Taschner; b 16 Apr 1960 St.Lukes Hosp Cedar Rapids, IA bpt 29 May 1960 St.Steph; Sales Representative; m 20 Jul 1985 St.John Luth Ch, Keystone, IA to Linda Marie Selk (b 14 Oct 1963; Teacher) d/o Delbert & Jeanette Selk, Keystone, IA. Child:
Rachel Marie – b 08 Jun 1993 Oskaloosa, IA

*Johann Hartmann KRUG s/o Johann Jost Krug & Marie Elisabeth Kraushaar Bornscheuer; b 23 Apr 1696 Altenhaina, Germany, bpt Löhlbach Ch Godfather: brother-in-law from Herbelhausen, Germany, d 11 Nov 1759 ae63y 6m 19d Löhlbach, Germany; 1st m 14 Apr 1723 Anna Guida Schween (b 19 Jun 1701 Löhlbach, Germany, d 25 Oct 1780 ae81y 4m 6d Löhlbach, Germany) d/o Tobias Johannes Schween (A miller b 08 Sept 1748) & Anna Gertrud nee Groll (b 04 Jun 1745). Seven children born in os Alt Heim ns Altenhaina, Germany:
*Johann Justus I – b 16 Sept 1725 os Alt Heim, d 04 Apr 1786
1st m 1753 Anna Gertrud nee Schween;
2nd m 10 May 1763 Anna Gertrude Möller;
3rd m 26 Aug 1779 Anna Kunigunde Möller
Anna Elisabeth – b 30 Oct 1729; Godmother: Aunt Anna Elisabeth
Schween d/o Tobias Johannes Schween & Anna Gertrud nee Groll
(cf Page 2 Löhlbach Ch 1729 Birth Records)
Tobias – b 10 Sept 1735, bpt 13 Sept 1735 Löhlbach Ch.
Johann Stephen – b 20 Jul 1742

*Johann Heinrich aka Henry KRUG s/o Johann Justus Krug III & Anna Elisabeth nee Paar; b 25 Jul 1850 Löhlbach, Germany, bpt 1850 Löhlbach Ch, Germany, con Löhlbach Ch, 1865 emigrated to Iowa with parents and siblings; naturalized 04 Mar 1873 Benton Co, d 28 Dec 1924 ae74y 5m 3d Atkins, IA home, bur 03 Jan 1925 St.Steph Cem; m 25 Jun 1876 St.Steph to Louise Krahling(b 28 May 1858 Allenborg, Germany, bpt 1858 Germany, d 06 Mar 1941 ae82y 9m 6d John G. Rinderknecht Home, Cedar Rapids, IA, bur 09 Mar 1941 St.Steph Cem) d/o Johann Peter Krahling & Elizabeth nee Binger (Father: Johann Binger). Seven children:
John Peter – b 07 May 1877, d 06 Oct 1967 bur St.Steph Cem;
m 19 Feb 1907 Clara Amelia Beitz
Anna Maria (Mary) – b 13 Oct 1879, d 12 Mar 1945;

m 07 Mar 1907 John G. Rinderknecht
Elizabeth Christina – b 07 Jun 1882, d 19 Feb 1986;
   m 06 Dec 1906 Heinrich August Happel
Conrad John Daniel – b 18 Feb 1887, d 20 Mar 1887;
   farm near Atkins, IA bur St.Steph Cem;
Fredrich William – b 03 Oct 1889, d 05 Sept 1970; bur St.Steph Cem;
   m 12 Feb 1914 Juliet Elizabeth Swanson
Anna Elizabeth – b 14 Nov 1894, d 19 Aug 1961 bur St.Steph Cem;
   m 04 Oct 1917 Frederick John Keiper
Heinrich Peter Martin – b 04 Jun 1901, d 03 May 2001;
   m 1928 Emma Louise Raetz

*Johann Jost KRUG s/o Jost Krug & Anna nee Bornscheuer, Haina, Germany, farmers; b/bpt 16 August 1668 Haina, Germany, d 16 Mar 1745 ae76y 7m os Alt Heim ns Altenhaina, Germany; m 18 May 1693 os Alt Heim ns Altenhaina Hse to Wid/o Conrad Bornscheuer (b 1655 os Alt Heim ns Altenhaina, d 24 May 1692 Haddenberg, [Slain by a shepherd]; m 22 Jan 1684 two sons, 2 daughters) to Marie Elisabeth Bornscheuer nee Kraushaar (b 1664 Bringshausen, d 28 Feb 1736 os Alt Heim ns Altenhaina, Germany) d/o Johannes Kraushaar, A miller at Bringshausen and had two sons, and three daughters of which two daughters died:
Martha Elisabeth – b os Alt Heim ns Altenhaina, Germany,
   prob 01 Mar 1694, bpt 01 Mar 1694
   Godmother: Mother of the father
   (cf Page 15 Löhlbach Ch 1694 Birth Records)
*Johann Hartmann – b 23 Apr 1696, d 11 Nov 1759;
   m 14 Apr 1723 Anna Guida Schween d/o Tobias Schween
   (b 08 Sept 1748) & Anna Gertrud nee Groll(b 04 Jun 1745).
Johann Adam – b 16 Mar 1699
Anna Katharina – b 31 Mar 1702
Maria Elisabeth – b 14 Jul 1707

*Johann Justus KRUG I s/o Johann Hartmann Krug & Anna Guida nee Schween, Löhlbach, Germany; b 16 Sept 1725, d 04 Apr 1786 ae60y 6m 19d Löhlbach, Germany; 1st m 1753 to Anna Gertrude Schween d/o Tobias Schween. Three children:
Johann Justus – b 31 Aug 1757, bpt 04 Sept 1757
   Godfather: Johann Just Schween from os Alt Heim ns Altenhaina,
   Germany, brother of mother.
   (cf Page 44 Löhlbach Ch 1757 Baptism Records) NFR

2nd m 10 May 1763 Johann Justus Krug I to Anna Gertrud Möller (b 05 Apr 1735 Halgehausen, Germany: 10 km from Löhlbach, con 1748 at Mohnhausen, Germany, d 18 Sept 1778 [Giving premature birth to daughter] bur 18 Sept 1778 Löhlbach, Germany) d/o Johannes Möller (b 19 Feb 1741 Battenhausen, Germany; oil mill worker (schlagmuller) m 18 Feb 1776 to Anna Gertrud nee Wilhelmi (d 27 Apr 1747). (cf Page 13 Löhlbach Ch 1763 Marriage Records) Six children:

Johann Philip – b 26 Oct 1764 Löhlbach, d ND Elberfeld

Johann Peter – 18 Nov 1766 Löhlbach;
    Godfather: Johannes Peter Möller of Halgehausen, Germany,
    son of Johann Peter The Elder

Anna Elisabeth – b 01 Sept 1769 Löhlbach, Germany

Johann Peter – b 12 Jan 1772 Löhlbach, Germany

*Johann Justus II – b 11 May 1775 Löhlbach Hse #70,
    Godfather: Johann Justus Rudolph from Herbelhausen, Germany,
    tilemaker for roofs, d 09 Apr 1847; m 18 May 1804 Löhlbach Ch
    to Wilhelmina Kirchner of Schwabendorf, Germany

Anna Gertrud – b 18 Sept 1778 Löhlbach, died same day immediately
    after baptism. (cf Page 72 Löhlbach Ch 1778 Death Records)

3rd m 26 Oct 1779 Johann Justus Krug I to Anna Kunigunde Möller d/o Conrad Möller, Cowherd Shepherd for Haina, Germany. One child. NFR

*Johann Justus KRUG II s/o Johann Justus Krug I & Anna Gertrud nee Möller of Löhlbach, Germany; b 11 May 1775 Löhlbach Hse #70, d 09 Apr 1847 ae71y 10m 29d Löhlbach, Germany; m 18 May 1804 Löhlbach Ch to Wilhelmina Kirchner (b 1769 Schwabendorf, Germany, d 22 Nov 1855 Löhlbach, Germany, Hse #70) d/o Ludwig Kirchner & Marie Madeleine nee Badonin of Schwabendorf, Germany. Children:

*Anna Elisabeth – b 27 Jan 1799 Schwabendorf, Germany,
    d 10 Apr 1879 Löhlbach Hse #70;
    m 16 Apr 1824 Andreas Schuler of Löhlbach

*Johann Justus III – b 18 Nov 1805 Löhlbach Hse #70;
    d 1879 Krug Homestead Benton Co IA;
    m 25 Dec 1835 Löhlbach Ch Anna Elisabeth Paar
    (b 16 Mar 1811 Löhlbach, Germany Hse #10, d 06 Oct 1882 IA)

Johann Conrad – b 14 Mar 1810, d 1815 Löhlbach, Germany, Hse #70

*Johann Justus KRUG III s/o Johann Justus Krug II (Soldier and Alderman cf Page 25 Löhlbach Ch 1805 Birth Records) & Wilhelmina nee Kirchner; b 18 Nov 1805 Hse #70 Löhlbach, Germany, during the night between 2-3

a.m. bpt 24 Nov 1805 Löhlbach Ch (Godfather: Johann Justus Möller, son of Johann Adam Möller, unmarried),cf Page 25 Löhlbach Ch 1805 Birth Records; con Löhlbach Ch; Occupation: bricklayer; d prob Bef Jun 1879 Krug Homestead, Fremont Twp Benton Co IA, bur 1879 St.Steph Cem; m 25 Dec 1833 Löhlbach Ch to Anna Elisabeth Paar (b 16 Mar 1811 Hse #10 Löhlbach, Germany, bpt 1811 Löhlbach Ch, con Löhlbach Ch, d 06 Oct 1882 ae71y 6m 20d Krug Homestead Fremont Twp Benton Co IA, bur Oct 1882 St.Steph Cem) d/o Johannes Paar & Anna Elisabeth nee Prachter. 1861 daughter Wilhelmina emigrated to Iowa followed by her parents and remaining living children in 1865. They sailed from Bremerhaven, Germany and it was six weeks to cross the Atlantic Ocean. Children of Johann Justus and Anna Elisabeth Paar:

*Wilhelmina – b 1835 Löhlbach, Germany bpt 04 Nov 1835
  Löhlbach Ch; d 25 Jun 1882 [Suicide] Fremont Twp
  Benton Co IA; m 1862 Johannes Georg Moeller
  (cf Löhlbach Reg Nr. 158)

Katharina Elisabeth – b 28 Sept 1837 Löhlbach, Germany
  bpt 01 Oct 1837 Löhlbach Ch,
  d 14 Jul 1854 at 7 o'clock in morning Löhlbach Hse #33
  ae16y, 9m, 16d, bur at 14 o'clock when bells rang.
  (cf Löhlbach Ch 1854 Death Records)

*Anna Elisabeth – b 22 Apr 1841 Löhlbach Hse # 70, Germany,
  bpt 25 Apr 1841 Löhlbach Ch; d Feb 1920 Guthrie Center, IA
  m 19 Sept 1867 Johann Daniel Mo(e)ller
  (cf Löhlbach Reg Nr. 348)

*Johann Peter – b 22 Jan 1844 Löhlbach Hse #70, Germany
  bpt 28 Jan 1844 Löhlbach Ch; d 21 Jun 1926 Farm Fremont Twp
  Benton Co IA; m 22 Aug 1869 Anna Katharina Michel
  (cf Löhlbach Reg Nr. 433)

Georg – b 06 Dec 1847 Löhlbach, Germany,
  d 06 Jan 1848 in night at 1 o'clock Löhlbach Hse #70 ae1m,
  bur 09 Jan 1848 in evening at 18 hours when bells rang.
  (cf Löhlbach Ch Reg Nr. 570; 1848 Death Records)

*Johann Heinrich – b 25 Jul 1850 Löhlbach Hse #33, Germany;
  bpt 1850 Löhlbach Ch (cf Löhlbach Reg Nr. 664)
  d 28 Dec 1924 Atkins, IA;
  m 25 Jun 1876 Atkins, IA to Louise Krahling

*Johann Peter KRUG aka John Krug (cf Naturalization 04 Mar 1873 Volume I, Page 215 Benton Co IA Courthouse Recorders Office) s/o

Johann Justus Krug III & Anna Elisabeth nee Paar; b 22 Jan 1844 (cf Löhlbach Ch Records)Löhlbach, Germany, bpt 28 Jan 1844 Löhlbach Ch, Germany, con Löhlbach Ch; Maurer (bricklayer); d 21 Jun 1926 ae82y 5m Krug Homestead, Fremont Twp Benton Co IA, bur Jun 24 1926 St.Steph Cem; m 22 Aug 1869 (cf Marriage Records Book C, Page 127 Benton Co IA Courthouse Recorders Office) St.Steph by Pastor Studt to Anna Katharina Michel (b 30 Sept 1847 at noon in Hse #19 Geismar, Germany, bpt 04 Oct 1847 Pferdgrund, con 1862 ae14y, 6m, 27d Geismar Ch, (cf No. 474, 1847 Geismar Ch record)d 27 May 1918 ae71y 8m Krug Homestead Fremont Twp Benton Co IA, bur 30 May 1918 St.Steph Cem) d/o Johann Peter Michel [Henry Michael] & Anna Elisabeth Freitag (cf Naturalization 06 Mar 1872, Volume I, Page 166, Benton Co IA Courthouse Recorders Office).Johann Peter emigrated to Iowa sailing on "Columbus" from Bremen, Germany with parents, sister Anna Elisabeth, brother Johann Heinrich arrived in New York 19 Jul 1865. 1862 Anna Katharina Michel emigrated to Iowa with her parents; naturalization automatic with husband's in 1873. Farmers owning 600+ acres of land in Fremont Twp Benton Co IA and Linn Co IA. Eleven children:

Anna Katherine – b 04 Jul 1870 Krug Homestead Fremont Twp;
 d 04 Aug 1927 Fremont Twp Benton Co IA Farm;
 m 12 Mar 1896 William (Wilhelm) R. Rammelsberg
Henry John – b 09 Feb 1872 Krug Homestead Fremont Twp
 Benton Co; d 26 Dec 1955 Luth Home Vinton, IA;
 m 09 Mar 1898 Christina Marie Happel
John August Henry – b 16 Feb 1874 Krug Homestead Fremont Twp;
 d 21 Nov 1944 on Farm Fremont Twp Benton Co;
 m 18 Feb 1903 Elizabeth Jeanette Happel
John Daniel – b 15 Sept 1876 Krug Homestead Fremont Twp;
 d 31 May 1926 on Farm Linn Co IA;
 m 17 Mar 1915 Carrie May Hein
TWINS: William Henry – b 23 Jun 1879 Krug Homestead
 Fremont Twp; d 31 Dec 1963 bur St.Steph Cem; Never Married
  Katharina Elizabeth -b 23 Jun 1879 Krug Homestead
 Fremont Twp; d 29 Jun 1979 Krug Homestead Fremont Twp
Elizabeth Anna – b 15 Mar 1884 Krug Homestead Fremont Twp;
 d 12 Jun 1972 Virginia Gay Hosp Vinton, IA;
 m 07 Feb 1907 Conrad Martin Rinderknecht
Katherina Elizabeth – b 04 Jan 1882 Krug Homestead Fremont Twp;
 d 14 Sept 1976 Luth Home Vinton, IA;
 m 18 Jan 1912 Wilhelm Fredrich Popenhagen

Louise Elizabeth-b 03 May 1886 Krug Homestead Fremont Twp;
    d 09 May 1979 St.Lukes Hosp Cedar Rapids, IA;
    m 22 Oct 1916 Henry Karl Rinderknecht
Adam Andrew – b 08 Jun 1889 Krug Homestead Fremont Twp
    Benton Co d 12 Jul 1960 St.Lukes Hosp Cedar Rapids, IA;
    m 27 Oct 1921 Lucy Isabelle Snell
John George – b 10 Nov 1892 Krug Homestead Fremont Twp
    Benton Co d 24 May 1983 St.Lukes Hosp Cedar Rapids, IA;
    m 23 Apr 1930 Emma Bertha Daleske

Johannes KRUG, landsiedler (land settler), bur 27 Oct 1692 [Cause of death: drowning]. On 27 Oct five persons drowned...they had been to a wedding at Haina, Germany, above Frankenberg, Germany, and on the way back they wanted to drive through the Eder and there drowned, their husbands and other people were saved by people taking risks, buried here in this place; the settlers daughter. (cf S./Nr.: 142v Haina Kloster Records)

*John KRUG, Germany; (cf naturalization 05 Mar 1877, ae minor, Volume II, Page 223 Benton Co IA Courthouse Recorders Office).

John August Henry KRUG s/o Johann Peter Krug aka John Krug & Anna Katharina nee Michel; b 16 Feb 1874 Krug Homestead Fremont Twp Benton Co IA, bpt 15 Mar 1874 and con St.Steph, d 21 Nov 1944 ae70y 9m 5d [Stroke] on his farm west of Atkins, Fremont Twp Benton Co IA, bur 25 Nov 1944 St.Steph Cem; m 18 Feb 1903 Farm north of Newhall, IA to Elizabeth Jeanette Happel (b 27 Dec 1878 Farm north of Atkins, Fremont Twp Benton Co IA, bpt 19 Jan 1879 St.Steph, d 30 Jun 1967 ae88y 1m 3d Atkins, IA bur 03 Jul 1967 St.Steph Cem) d/o Peter Johann Happel & Katharine Elizabeth nee Werning. Farmers 1/2 mile west of Atkins. 1948 Elizabeth retired in Atkins and lived on Main Street. Eight children:
Edna Elizabeth Katherine – b 10 May 1904 Parents Farm;
    d 14 Dec 1969 Fremont Twp Benton Co;
    m 20 Jun 1928 Herman William Haerther
Harvey Adam – b 23 Jul 1906 Parents Farm Fremont Twp Benton Co.
    d 27 Nov 1957 [Tractor Accident] bur St.Steph Cem;
    m 10 Jun 1935 Ella Wilhelmina Rinderknecht
Elma Ann Christina – b 15 Jun 1908 Parents Farm Fremont Twp;
    d 31 Dec 2004 Luth Home Vinton, IA;
    m 11 Jan 1933 Bernard Jacob Schanbacher
Irene Katherine Elizabeth- b 03 Sept 1910 Parents Farm;

m 12 Dec 1934 Alfred Rinderknecht

Irvin August – b 03 Apr 1912 Parents Farm Fremont Twp Benton Co;
    d 31 Mar 1997 bur St.Steph Cem;
    m 27 Jun 1934 Leola Anna Elizabeth Hertle

Delbert John – b 14 Sept 1914 Parents Farm Fremont Twp Benton Co
    d 07 Feb 1995 bur St.Steph Cem;
    m 23 Jun 1914 Libbie Ann Cerveny

Louise Marie Katherine – b 03 Feb 1918 Parents Farm Fremont Twp;
    d 04 Mar 2001;
    m 01 Jun 1941 Raymond Henry Martin Rinderknecht

Melvin August – b 02 Oct 1925 Parents Farm Fremont Twp
    Benton Co; m 02 Sept 1948 Mary Ann Ludvicek

John Daniel KRUG s/o Johann Peter Krug aka John Krug & Anna Katharina nee Michel; b 15 Sept 1876 Krug Homestead, Fremont Twp Benton Co IA, bpt 15 Oct 1876 and con St.Steph, d 31 May 1925 ae48y 8m 16d on his farm near Fairfax, Linn Co IA, bur 02 Jun 1925 St.Steph Cem; m 17 Mar 1915 at Cedar Rapids, IA to Carrie May Hein (b 17 Aug 1887 Marion, Linn Co IA, bpt and con 12 Feb 1926 St.Steph, d 25 Nov 1979 ae97y 3m 8d Cedar Rapids, IA bur 28 Nov 1979 Shiloh Cem, Linn Co IA) d/o Andrew Hein. Farmers. Children:

Elward William – b 07 Feb 1916 Parents Farm; d 10 May 1987
    [Suicide on his farm]; m 12 Jun 1951 Emily Ludvicek

George Andrew August – b 12 Jul 1918 Parents Farm;
    m 01 Jun 1947 Betty Knipp

John George KRUG s/o Johann Peter Krug aka John Krug & Anna Katharina nee Michel; b 10 Nov 1892 Krug Homestead, Fremont Twp Benton Co, bpt 27 Nov 1892 and con St.Steph, d 24 Jul 1983 ae90y 8m 14d St.Lukes Hosp Cedar Rapids, IA bur 27 May 1983 St.Steph Cem; m 23 Apr 1930 Eldora, IA to Emma Bertha Daleske (b 04 May 1899 bpt 1899 d 27 Dec 1997 ae98y 7m 23d bur St.Steph Cem) d/o Herman F. Daleske & Johanna nee Krause. Farmed Johann Peter Krug Homestead in Fremont Twp Benton Co IA, purchasing it in 1923. 1964 retired in Atkins, IA. Celebrated 50th Wedding Anniversary. Children:

Donald George August – b 22 Dec 1931 Krug Homestead
    Fremont Twp; m 30 Jun 1954 Ila Jean Taschner

Kenneth John – b 22 Oct 1934 Krug Homestead Fremont Twp;
    m 16 Sept 1956 Ann Delores McClintock

John Jay KRUG s/o Donald George August Krug & Ila Jean nee Taschner; b 03 Jun 1957 St.Lukes Hosp Cedar Rapids, IA bpt 14 Jul 1957 St.Steph; m 08 Nov 1986 at Mt.Pleasant, IA Luth Ch to Cynthia Louise McGohan (b 20 Aug 1961) d/o Donald & Helen McGohan, Mount Pleasant, IA). Children:

>   Lindsey Christine – b 24 Apr 1991 St.Lukes Hosp Cedar Rapids, IA
>   Lauren Elizabeth – Stillborn 12 Mar 1993 Omaha, NE;
>   bur Mar 1993 St.Steph Cem
>   Logan John – b 24 Mar 1995 Omaha, NE

*John M. KRUG s/o Bernard Krug & Lizzie nee Kilner; b 07 Mar 1864 Hesse-Kassel, Germany, 1881 emigrated ae17y with his mother to USA (his father never emigrated); (cf Naturalization 28 Oct 1889, Volume III, Page 431 Benton Co IA Courthouse Recorders Office) d 24 Nov 1947 ae83y 7m 17d Dysart, IA, bur Houghton Cem; painter and paper hanger; 1st m 1889 Katie Koch (b 1870, d 1900 in childbirth). Farmers. Children:

>   Harry – dec'd in infancy
>   George – dec'd in infancy
>   Mary – m Joe Barta
>   Edward – m Bertha Urmy
>   Christ – NFR
>   Katie – m Charles Schmidt

2nd m 1901 John M. Krug to Rose Tritten (b 1882 Lenke, Switzerland, d 1960) 1919 retired from farming to Dysart, IA; John was Dysart Town Marshal 20 years. Mbrs Evangelical United Brethren Ch. Children:

>   John – NFR
>   Otto – NFR
>   Walter – NFR
>   Roy – NFR
>   Lucille – m Edward Urhammer

John Peter KRUG s/o Johann Heinrich Krug & Louise nee Krahling; b 07 May 1877 Krug Farm near Atkins, Fremont Twp Benton Co IA, bpt 21 May 1877 and conf St. Steph; Lifelong resident of Fremont Twp Benton Co IA, d 06 Oct 1967 ae90y 5m Atkins, IA bur St.Steph Cem; m 04 Apr 1907 Clara Amelia Beitz (b 19 Feb 1890 Otter Creek Twp near Alburnett, IA; d 04 Aug 1992 ae102y Vinton IA Luth Home bur 02 Aug 1992 St.Steph Cem) d/o Julius Beitz & Nettie nee Pflueger. John Peter & Clara farmed one mile east of Atkins (Author born on this farm) until 1931 retirement in Atkins, IA. Celebrated 50th & 60th Wedding Anniversary. Children:

>   Nettie L. – b 30 Jan 1909, d 27 Nov 2005 Luth Home Vinton, IA;

285

m 05 Feb 1930 Melvin A. Rammelsberg
Leona A. – b 02 Mar 1912, d 21 May 1999;
m 14 Feb 1933 Ivan L. Rammelsberg
Grant Henry John – b 16 May 1917, d 21 Apr 1920 bur St.Steph Cem
Martha E. – b 23 Feb 1922; 1st m 31 Mar 1951 Will Pelton dec'd;
2nd m 10 Jan 1966 Raymond L. Edwards, FL residence

*Jost KRUG of Haina, Germany, S./Nr.: 88r (Haina Kloster Germany Records) b Kirchhaun, Germany; m 19 Nov 1657 Anna Bornscheuer of Haina, Germany, d/o Johannes Bornscheuer. Tennant farmer of land owned by Haina, Germany, Monastery (now a hospital) where records show Krugs from 1653 to 1690 (Page 39 Book 1690) paid 30 sheaves of corn and rye plus 23 x 60 straw to the monastery for farming their land. Children:
Johannes – b 13 Mar 1659, d ae8 weeks, bur 01 May 1659
(cf S./Nr.: 137v Haina Kloster Records)
Katharina – b 19 Aug 1660, d and bur 07 Jun 1661
(cf S./Nr.: 138v Haina Kloster Records)
Anna Martha – b 06 Jul 1662
Anna Katharina – b 30 Oct 1664
Anna Magdalena – b 12 Jun 1667, bur 16 Jun 1667,
Acts 14, verse 13 from Bible spoken at funeral.
(cf S./Nr.: 139v Haina Kloster Records)
*Johann Jost – b Haina bpt 16 Aug 1668
(cf S.Nr.: 7v Haina Kloster Records) d 16 Mar 1745;
m 18 May 1693 Wid/o Conrad Bornscheuer,
Marie Elisabeth nee Kraushaar (b 1664 Bringhausen,
d 28 Feb 1736 os Alt Heim ns Altenhaina, Germany).
Anna Kunigunda – b 08 Apr 1670, 13 Oct 1687 Johann Vohl
Anna Kunigunda – b 09 Apr 1671
Martha Elisabeth – b 22 Nov 1674, bur 26 Nov 1674,
(cf S./Nr.: 140v Haina Kloster Records)
Martha Elisabeth – b 12 May 1680
NN – b 16 Jun 1681

Karen Marie KRUG d/o Harvey Adam Krug & Ella Wilhelmina nee Rinderknecht; b 30 Sept 1937 Cedar Rapids, IA bpt 24 Oct 1937 and con St.Steph, Atkins High School; m 08 Feb 1958 St.Steph to Paul R. Nielson (b 17 Jan 1928) s/o P.M. Nielson of Springville, IA. Celebrated 50th Wedding Anniversary. Children:
Steven Nielson – b 05 Dec 1958 St.Lukes Hosp Cedar Rapids, IA

Sue Ellen Nielson – b 29 Mar 1961, 1st m 1981 Frederick Kraft, DVD 2nd m to Terry James Soukup

Karri Lynn KRUG d/o Virgil Irvin Krug & Mary Jane nee Meroshek; b 01 Apr 1975; m 112 Jun 1998 David W. Griffin. Children:
  Grant Galen Griffin – b 19 May 2000
  Olivia Marie Griffin – b 16 Apr 2003

Katherina "Katie" Elizabeth KRUG d/o Johann Peter Krug aka John Krug & Anna Katharina nee Michel; b 04 Jan 1882 Krug Homestead Fremont Twp Benton Co IA bpt 29 Jan 1882 St.Steph, d 14 Sept 1976 ae94y 8m 10d Luth Home Vinton, IA bur 17 Sept 1976 St.Steph Cem; m 18 Jan 1912 Wilhelm Fredrich Popenhagen (b 21 Mar 1881 Niles Center, IL d 24 Apr 1961 ae80y 1m 3d Newhall, IA bur 27 Apr 1961 St.Steph Cem) s/o Joseph Popenhagen & Fredricka. Farmers until retirement. Children:
  Roy Joseph August Popenhagen – b 24 Mar 1913, d 13 Apr 2002
    m 15 Jan 1936 Rose Marie Kray
  Bernice Ella Louise Popenhagen – b 25 Jul 1914
    m 23 Mar 1947 Harlan Thurston
  George Conrad Popenhagen – b 08 Mar 1916;
    m 23 Jun 1943 Leone Andrlik
  Henry Elmer Conrad Popenhagen – b 25 Mar 1917, d 26 May 2006
    m 15 Feb 1946 Emma Meyer

Kathleen Ellen KRUG d/o Albert Martin Krug & Lola Maye nee Brehm; b 29 Mar 1966 St.Lukes Hosp Cedar Rapids, IA bpt 17 Apr 1966 Sponsors: Beverlyn Krug, Elmer Krug, Franklin Brehm; con 30 Mar 1980 St.John; 1984 Class Benton Community High School; 1987 A.A. Degree Kirkwood Community College; B.A. 1991 University of Northern Iowa; Masters Degree; Teacher; m 24 Nov 1001 Eric Keith Goslinga (b 16 Sept 1965).

Kenneth John KRUG s/o John George Krug & Emma Bertha nee Daleske; b 22 Oct 1934 Krug Homestead, Fremont Twp Benton Co IA, bpt 25 Nov 1935 and con St.Steph, Atkins High School; m 16 Sept 1956 First Presbyterian Ch, Cedar Rapids, IA to Ann Delores McClintock (28 Feb 1934 Fairfax) d/o Lyle T. McClintock. Farmed land next to Krug Homestead in Fremont Twp Benton Co purchased by his father from his Uncle Henry John Krug. Celebrated 50th Wedding Anniversary. Children:
  Steven John (adopted) – b 27 Oct 1967;
    m 15 Jul 2000 Rhonda Kaye Haack; d/o Russell & Phyllis Haack,

Marengo, IA
Julie Ann (adopted) – b 30 Dec 1969

Kenneth Paul KRUG s/o Edward Krug & Bertha nee Urmy; b 1925 Dysart, IA; 1943 Class Dysart High School; employed Wilson Packing House, Cedar Rapids, IA; farm laborer; m 07 Mar 1946 Marjorie Ann Chizum (b 1927) d/o E. Clifford Chizum & Clarinda Isabelle nee Brewer of Garrison, IA. Farmers Big Grove Twp Benton Co IA. Children:
David – b 1948 Garrison, IA residence
Lloyd – b 1949 Remsen, IA farmer; m 1970 Renee Groepper
Connie – b 1951 Shellsburg, IA residence; m 1972 Milo Kearns
TWINS: Larry – b 1953 Long Grove, IA; m 1975 Allyn Richter
           Lyle – b 1953 Cedar Rapids, IA
Kathy – b 1956 Hiawatha, IA
Thomas – b 1959 US Navy

Kerri Lynn KRUG d/o Virgil Irvin Krug & Mary Jane nee Meroshek; (Adopted) b 01 Apr 1975; m 12 Jun 1998 David W. Griffin (07 Sept 1968) s/o Galen & Velda Griffin, Elkader, IA

Lavonne KRUG d/o Heinrich Peter Martin Krug & Emma Louise nee Raetz; b 14 Apr 1930 Cedar Rapids IA; m 20 Nov 1955 Albert T. Huebener. Marion IA residence. Children:
Bruce A. Huebener – b 05 Mar 1960;
    m 12 May 1984 Teresa Robinson
Scott W. Huebener – b 12 Jul 1961
Wayne S. Huebener – b 30 Jul 1962;
    m 21 Nov 1998 Christianne Twaddle
Mark A. Huebener – b 24 Sept 1966

Leona A. Krug d/o John Peter Krug & Clara Amelia Beitz; b 02 Mar 1912, d 21 May 1999 ae87y 2m 19d; m 14 Feb 1933 Ivan L. Rammelsberg (b 14 Jan 1909, d 21 Apr 1977 ae68y 3m 7d) s/o Alphonsa Fredrich Emil Rammelsberg & Mary Jane nee Armstrong. Farmers in Benton Co. IA. Children:
Carmen C. Rammelsberg – b 28 Dec 1933;
    m 29 May 1955 Paul Wirth
Floy J. Rammelsberg – b 07 Nov 1936;
    m 16 Jun 1957 Donald Kersten
Joan Lee Rammelsberg – b 05 Feb 1940;

m 05 Feb 1960 Denton Schultz

Liberta Sue KRUG d/o Delbert John Krug & Libbie Ann nee Cerveny; b 18 Sept 1954 Cedar Rapids, IA bpt Oct 1954 TrinCR; 1st m 07 Aug 1976 Dr. Joel H. Hendrickson (b 23 Jun 1954)DVD; s/o Alvin Hendrickson, Minneapolis, MN; 2nd m 11 Jun 1983 Charles Ledder. Children:
    Matthew Ledder – b 25 Nov 1984
    John Robert Ledder – b 24 Aug 1987

Louise Elizabeth KRUG d/o Johann Peter Krug aka John Krug & Anna Katharina nee Michel; b 03 May 1886 Krug Homestead, Fremont Twp Benton Co IA, bpt 23 May 1886 and con St.Steph, d 09 May 1979 ae93y 6d St.Lukes Hosp Cedar Rapids, IA bur 11 May 1979 St.Steph Cem; m 22 Oct 1916 St.Steph to Henry Karl Rinderknecht (b 01 Sept 1890 Parent's farm, Fremont Twp Benton Co IA bpt 1890 and con St.Steph, d 28 Jul 1982 ae91y 10m 27d home of his daughter Dorothy Lange, bur 30 Jul 1982 St.Steph Cem) s/o Karl Rinderknecht & Anna Katherina nee Happel. Farmers retiring in Atkins, IA; Henry: Owner Atkins Lumber Company. Celebrated 50th & 60th Wedding Anniversary. Children:
    Dorothy Catherine Rinderknecht – b 12 Aug 1917 Farm
        Fremont Twp; d 30 Aug 2000 [Cancer] Cedar Rapids;
        m 28 Jun 1941 Henry Donald Lange
    Edward John George Rinderknecht – b 27 Oct 1919 Fremont Twp;
        d 12 Jun 1987 Cedar Rapids;
        m 27 Oct 1941 Margaret Lorene Tow
    Velma Louise Rinderknecht – b 23 Apr 1923 Farm Fremont Twp;
        d 21 Jul 1971 Cedar Rapids;
        m 18 Feb 1946 Thurman Cloyd Harris
    Alberta Elizabeth Rinderknecht – b 19 Oct 1927 Farm Fremont Twp;
        m 19 Jul 1952 Gerald Nathan Welty

Louise Marie Katherine KRUG d/o John August Henry Krug & Elizabeth Jeanette nee Happel; b 03 Feb 1918 Parent's Farm Fremont Twp Benton Co IA, bpt 10 Mar 1918 and con St.Steph Luth Ch; d 04 Mar 2001 ae83y 1m 1d; m 01 Jun 1941 TrinCR to Raymond Henry Martin Rinderknecht (b 25 Dec 1912 Farm near Lone Rock, Kossuth Co IA, bpt 01 Jun 1913, d 12 Sept 1993 ae80y 8m 18d his home Vinton, IA bur 15 Sept 1993 TrinVT) s/o Martin Fred Lenard Rinderknecht & Bertha Augusta nee Ehlers of Dysart, IA. Farmers S.E. of Vinton, IA until 1977 retirement. Celebrated 50th Wedding Anniversary. Children (14 grandchildren):

Roger Raymond Rinderknecht – b 02 Jun 1942;
    m 27 Jun 1964 Rose Ann Kramer, Ames, IA residence
Verna Jane Rinderknecht – b 24 Sept 1944;
    m 24 Jun 1966 Reginald M.Muhl, Mt. Pleasant IA residence
Gene August Rinderknecht – b 29 Jul 1947;
    m 07 Jun 1969 Gail Ann Berndt, Newton IA residence
Jolene Louise Rinderknecht – b 12 Aug 1952;
    m 27 Jul 1974 Daniel Raymond Blanchard, Belle Plaine, IA
Luanne Rae Rinderknecht – b 22 Feb 1954;
    m 26 Jul 1975 Marc Meyer,Perry, IA residence

Margaret Lovaire KRUG d/o Walter William August Krug & Enid Muriel nee Bryner; b 14 May 1931 Krug Farm Fremont Twp Benton Co IA, bpt 28 Jun 1931 St.Steph Aunt Sponsors: Gail Alein nee Harnisch Krug, Emma Katherine Elizabeth nee Krug Rammelsberg, con 02 Apr 1944 St.Steph; 1948 Class Atkins High School; Bethany Luth College, Mankato, MN; B.S. Iowa State, Ames; M.S. Oregon State U.; PhD Education Research U. of British Columbia, Canada; Iowa State U. Staff; Oregon State U. Assistant Professor; m 01 Nov 1957 Redeemer Luth Ch, Portland, OR to Kenneth Raymond Palen (b 02 Oct 1926 Medford, OR, bpt/con 28 Apr 1956 Calvary Luth Ch, Hillsboro,OR; U.S. Army Infantry World War II; B.S. Oregon State U; 43 years professional forester State of Oregon; 33 degree Scottish Rite; York Rite Cross of Honor; Royal Order of Scotland; Al Kader Shrine; Order of Quetzalcoatl) s/o Lloyd Ira Palen & Mildred Cecil nee Persons. Salem, OR residence beginning 1970. Celebrated 25th Silver Wedding Anniversary; 30th in New Zealand; 35th vow renewal in Wedding Miracle Ch Cana, Israel; 40th in Nairobi, Kenya. Celebrated 50th Wedding Anniversary. Mbrs St.Mark Luth Ch Salem, OR. Children:
Nancy Ann Palen – Premature b/d 11 Jun 1958 Tuality Hosp;
    bpt 11 Jun 1958 by Rev. John L. Baglien bur 13 Jun 1958
    Fir Lawn Cem, Hillsboro, OR
Susan Laurel Palen – b 25 Jun 1959 Tuality Hosp Hillsboro, OR
    m 12 Jul 1986 Edward Peter McHugh
Richard Kenneth Palen – b 10 Apr 1961 Tuality Hosp Hillsboro, OR
    m 30 Oct 1993 Helen Polly Shaw

Martin aka Heinrich Peter Martin KRUG: cf Heinrich Peter Martin Krug s/o Johann Heinrich Krug & Louise nee Krahling.

Marvin KRUG s/o Edward Krug & Bertha nee Urmy; b 1918; World War II

Armed Forces in Cook Islands, South Pacific; m 08 Jun 1942 Nadine Boldt. Nadine taught in Benton Co IA rural schools. Farmers in Bruce Twp and Cedar Twp Benton Co IA. 1982 retired in Mt.Auburn, IA. Children:
  Jerry – b 1947; m 1969 Jo Ellen Bass (b 1947)
  Janet – b 1951; m 1971 Jerry Appleton (b 1950)

Mary Janette KRUG d/o Walter William August Krug & Enid Muriel nee Bryner; b 13 Jun 1927 Krug Farm Fremont Twp Benton Co IA, bpt 13 Jun 1927 Krug farm home Fremont Twp Benton Co, Sponsors: Grandmother Christina Krug, Meta Michel con 17 Mar 1940 St.Steph, 1944 Class Atkins High School; Bethany Luth College, Mankato, MN; Cadet Nurse World War II; m 29 Aug 1948 St.Steph to Ralph Emerson Wilson (b 13 Jun 1923 Hazel Green Twp Delaware Co IA, bpt/con 01 Mar 1951 St.Steph, d 25 Apr 2002 ae78y 10m 12d [Farm Accident]bur St.Steph Cem) s/o Charles Octavus Wilson & Mary Pauline nee Zid. Farmers Fremont Twp Benton Co IA. Mbrs St.Steph. Observed 50th Wedding Anniversary. Children:
  Donald William Wilson – b 11 Mar 1951 St.Lukes Hosp
      Cedar Rapids IA; bpt 15 Apr 1951 St.Steph
      Sponsors: Grandparents Walter William August Krug &
      Enid Muriel nee Bryner; Kirkwood Community College;
      Cedar Rapids Barber School.
  Carol Elaine Wilson – b 04 Apr 1954 St.Lukes Hosp
      Cedar Rapids, IA; bpt 02 May 1954 St.Steph
      Sponsors: Aunt Margaret Krug Palen & Aunt Elaine Krug Postel;
      Kirkwood Community College; Bachelor & Masters Degrees
      Hosp & Business Admin. University of Iowa, Iowa City, IA.
  Brian John Wilson – b 04 Apr 1960 St.Lukes Hosp Cedar Rapids, IA;
      bpt 19 Jun 1960 St.Steph Sponsors: Uncle Kenneth Palen &
      Uncle Allan Postel; Kirkwood Community College;
      m 18 Apr 1981 Nancy Ann Duvall, West Chester, IA.

Maynard Clarence KRUG s/o Clarence John Adam August Krug & Gail Alein nee Harnisch; b 29 Aug 1935 Krug Farm Fremont Twp Benton Co IA; bpt 29 Sept 1935 St.Steph; 1953 Class Atkins High School; B.S. Iowa State U.; m 05 Sept 1981 Vickie Hanson (b 25 May 1941, dec'd) DVD. No children.

Melvin August KRUG s/o John August Krug & Elizabeth Jeanette nee Happel; b 02 Oct 1925 Farm Fremont Twp Benton Co IA, bpt 25 Oct 1925 Parent's Farm Home Fremont Twp Benton Co IA, con 1939 St.Steph, 1943

Class Atkins High School; m 02 Sept 1948 St.Steph to Mary Ann Ludvicek(b 14 Apr 1930 near Fairfax, Johnson Co IA. bpt 07 Sept 1930 TrinCR, d 13 Jan 1990 ae59y 8m Cedar Rapids, IA bur 16 Jan 1990 St.Steph Cem) d/o Joseph L. Ludvicek & Mary nee Herman, Swisher IA. Child:

Deanne Kay – b 17 Feb 1951; m 02 Sept 1972 Andrew Joseph Becker

Nadine Marcel KRUG d/o Heinrich Peter Martin Krug & Emma nee Raetz; b 11 Jul 1937 Cedar Rapids, IA d 11 Oct 2003 ae66y 3m bur CdrMem; m 22 Jun 1958 Donald LaVerne Kroening (b 25 Sept 1938).Children:

Lori Kristine Kroening – b 19 Mar 1959;
m 30 Sept 1987 Norbert Julius
Shelly Renee Kroening – b 23 May 1962;
m 01 May 1983 Allen James Milota
Jody Sue Kroening – b 27 Nov 1965; m 04 Oct 1987 Kurt Anderson
Julie Ann Kroening – b 24 May 1967; m 11 Sept 1998 Jerry C. Brooks
(b 20 Apr 1967

Nettie L. KRUG d/o John Peter Krug & Clara Amelia Beitz; b 30 Jan 1909 Farm Fremont Twp Benton Co IA d 27 Nov 2005 ae96y 9m 28d Luth Home Vinton, IA bur Evergreen Cem Vinton IA; m 05 Feb 1930 Melvin A. Rammelsberg (b 03 Nov 1906, d 22 Jul 1961 ae54y 8m 19d) s/o Alphonsa Friedrich Emil Rammelsberg & Mary Jane nee Armstrong. Farmers Benton Co. Children:

Norma L. Rammelsberg – b 14 Dec 1930, d 26 Sept 1972;
m 14 Nov 1954 Oscar R. Hanson JR.
Hugo H. Rammelsberg – b 28 May 1934; m 20 May 1960 Joan Daily
Carol Marie Rammelsberg – b 06 Mar 1938;
1st m 09 Aug 1959 William Souto DVD;
2nd m 24 Jan 1970 Ralph Bauman
Alice Faye Rammelsberg – b 03 Nov 1941;
m 26 Apr 1964 Robert Whitlatch
Eunice Jean Rammelsberg – b 26 Aug 1946;
m 21 Sept 1974 Thomas Pingenot

Noreen Etta KRUG d/o Adam Andrew Krug & Lucy Isabelle nee Snell; b 06 Aug 1923 Parent's Farm bpt 07 Oct 1923 and con St.Steph, Atkins High School; d 08 Dec 1996 ae73y 4m 2d Cedar Rapids, IA; m 17 Feb 1962 Claris Dean Utecht (b 14 Aug 1928, d 21 Sept 1995 ae67y 1m 7d) DVD. Denver CO & Cedar Rapids, IA residence. Child:

Gary Dean Utecht – b 28 Jan 1964 Denver, CO

Pamela May KRUG d/o George Andrew August Krug & Betty Ann nee Knipp; b 21 Apr 1948; m 28 Sept 1968 Richard Keith Ruhberg (b 07 Jan 1947). Children:
Chad Michael Ruhberg – b 07 Apr 1972
Danielle Ann Ruhberg – b 30 Sept 1978

Patricia Lou KRUG d/o Delbert John Krug & Libbie Ann nee Cerveny; b 27 Jun 1947 St.Lukes Hosp Cedar Rapids, IA bpt 20 Jul 1947 TrinCR; m 12 Aug 1965 Rad Fish (b 16 Apr 1947). Coralville, IA area residence. Children:
Sharon Arlene Fish -b 20 Mar 1966;
    m 15 Aug 1987 Mark Aaron Basten
Theresa Fish – b 28 Jun 1967; m 12 Sept 1998 Hank Novak

Phyllis Catherine KRUG d/o Adam Andrew Krug & Lucy Isabelle nee Snell; b 25 Nov 1929 Parent's Farm Fremont Twp Benton Co IA, bpt 22 Jun 1930 and con St.Steph, 1946 Class Atkins High School; d 25 Mar 1966 ae36y 4m Cedar Rapids, IA bur 29 Mar 1966 Shellsburg, IA Cem; m 02 Sept 1951 Little Brown Church, Nashua, IA to Delbert Dale Vogt (b 18 Jun 1919 near Palo, IA; d 27 Sept 2007 ae88y 3m 9d bur Oakwood Cem, Shellsburg, IA) s/o Herman Vogt. Children:
Katherine Jean Vogt – b 19 Oct 1951 Vinton IA Hosp d 23 Oct 1951;
    bur 25 Oct 1951 Shellsburg, IA Cem
Ronald Dale Vogt – b 18 Sept 1952; 1st m 07 Jul 1972 Barbra Uridil,
    DVD 1975; 2nd m Jul 1980 Ellen Marie Day, DVD;
    3rd m 14 Apr 1984 Bonnie Zhanek, DVD
Donald Adam Vogt – b 18 Nov 1953;
    1st m 12 Feb 1977 Maureen Murray; [Suicide];
    2nd m Feb 1995 Andie Albert
Thomas Dean Vogt – b 12 Nov 1956; Nida; residence Frisco, TX
John Duane Vogt – b 25 May 1959; m Julie; residence Atkins,IA
Lonnie Edward Vogt – b 07 Jul 1963; residence Hiawatha, IA
2nd m Nov 1966 Delbert Dale Vogt to Jeanne Krsek. Dale Vogt Trucking and Salvaging business; farmed Adam Krug Farm.

Randall Ray KRUG s/o Donald George August Krug & Ila Jean nee Taschner; (IDENTICAL TWIN: Richard Allan Krug) b 03 Feb 1955 St.Lukes Hosp Cedar Rapids, IA bpt 06 Mar 1955 St.Steph; m 27 Aug 1977

St.John Luth Ch, Keystone, IA to Sheila Ann Albers (b 31 Mar 1957 Keystone, IA) d/o Donald & Betty Albers. Hiawatha, IA residence. Children:

  Ryan Randall – b 19 Aug 1981 Cedar Rapids, IA; m Angie
  Brandon Andrew – b 17 Jul 1985 Cedar Rapids, IA

Raymond Henry KRUG s/o Arthur John Peter Krug & Loretta Mae nee Housman; b 05 May 1932 Farm Fremont Twp Benton Co IA, bpt 28 Aug 1932 St.Steph, con TrinCR; 1st m 1954 First Congregational Ch, Blencoe, IA to Donna Lee Mitchell (b 29 Jun 1935) DVD. Child:

  Reva Marjorie – b 25 Nov 1961 Cedar Rapids, IA;
    m 25 Apr 1981 James P. Svoboda
2nd m 08 Jul 1978 Holy Trinity Catholic Ch, Des Moines Raymond Henry Krug to Rena Milani (b 28 Jun 1948) d/o Guiseppe Milani, Madrid, IA, DVD. Children:

  Rita Rae – b 18 Aug 1979 Cedar Rapids, IA
  Rebecca – b 02 Aug 1985 Cedar Rapids, IA

Reva Marjorie KRUG d/o Raymond Henry Krug & Donna Lee nee Mitchell; b 25 Nov 1961 Cedar Rapids, IA bpt 1961; m 25 Apr 1981 TrinCR to James P. Svoboda (b 29 May 1959, d 30 Jul 1983 ae24y 2m 1d) s/o Arthur Svoboda. Child:

  James Robert Michael Svoboda – b 08 Mar 1983

Richard Allan KRUG s/o Donald George August Krug & Ila Jean Taschner; (IDENTICAL TWIN: Randall Ray Krug) b 03 Feb 1955 St.Lukes Hosp Cedar Rapids, IA; m 24 Apr 1993 Luth Ch, Dysart, IA to Janene Rae Symonds (b 13 Dec 1967) d/o James & Karen Symonds. Children:

  Lexa Rae – b 22 Aug 1995 Waterloo, IA
  IDENTICAL TWINS: Trevor James – b 12 Jan 1998 Waterloo, IA
    Weston Richard – b 12 Jan 1998 Waterloo, IA

Roger Gerhardt KRUG s/o Gerhardt Henry Conrad Krug & Frances Marie nee Strellner; b 03 Mar 1939 IA St.Lukes Hosp Cedar Rapids, IA bpt 26 Mar 1939 St.Steph Uncle Sponsors: Uncle Arthur John Peter Krug and Uncle Harry Koopman, con 06 Apr 1952 St.Steph, 1956 Class Atkins High School; US Army 05 Oct 1958-04 Apr 1959 Ft.Leonard Wood, MO; 15 Oct 1961-10 Aug 1962 at 301st Field Hosp Ft.Ord, CA (Berlin Crisis Reserve Active Duty); m 08 Aug 1964 St.Steph to Mary Jane Woodson (b 30 Sept 1942, bpt St.Mary Catholic Ch, Vinton, IA con 22 Mar 1964 St.Steph) d/o

George Leon Woodson & Eleanor nee Farr. Farmers near Fairfax, IA. Celebrated 40th Wedding Anniversary. Children:
Gary Allan – b 02 Aug 1967 St.Lukes Hosp Cedar Rapids, IA;
    1st m 13 Aug 1993 Carrie Schulte, DVD 1996;
    2nd m 28 Nov 1998 Tamara Suzanne Leisner Hess
Amy Sue – b 29 Oct 1973 St.Lukes Hosp Cedar Rapids, IA;
    m 13 Feb 1999 Craig Marc Hubbard

Ronda Lee KRUG d/o Delbert John Krug & Libbie Ann nee Cerveny; b 11 May 1949, Cedar Rapids, IA bpt 31 May 1949 TrinCR; m 30 Jun 1973 Randall George Hess (b 16 Apr 1947). Residence near Amana, IA. Children:
Bret Randall Hess – b 11 Dec 1975
Gregory Hess – b 18 Aug 1978

Ruth Marie KRUG d/o Clarence John Adam August Krug & Gail Alein nee Harnisch; b 14 Apr 1931 Krug Farm Fremont Twp Benton Co IA, bpt 17 May 1931 St.Steph, 1949 Class Atkins High School; Bachelor Degree Wartburg College, Waverly, IA; m 05 Jun 1954 St.Mark Luth Ch, Cedar Rapids, IA to Frank Junior Hudson (b 05 May 1929, bpt 28 Feb 1954 St.Mark Luth, Cedar Rapids, IA; d 05 Nov 2007 ae78y 6m Phoenix, AZ) s/o Zail Howard Hudson & Minerva Ellen nee Korn. Meza, AZ residence. Children:
Marc Joel Hudson – b 31 Jan 1964 Meza, AZ
Faith A. Hudson – b 02 Jul 1966 Meza, AZ; m 1990 to NN Ballard

Sarah Marie KRUG d/o Virgil Irvin Krug & Mary Jane nee Merosheck; b 16 Sept 1976; m 04 Dec 1999 St.John to Justin Franklyn Gorsh (b 27 Mar 1976) s/o Carroll Gorsch, Williamsburg, IA & Donna Gorsch, Van Horne, IA. Child:
Jonah V. Gorsh – b 21 Dec 2006

Stephen Martin KRUG s/o Albert Martin Krug & Lola Maye nee Brehm; b 03 Aug 1967 St.Lukes Hosp Cedar Rapids, IA bpt 27 Aug 1967 Sponsors: Beverlyn Krug, Dennis Krug, Ronald Brehm con 12 Apr 1981 St.John; Class 1985 Benton Community High School; 1988 A.A. Degree Kirkwood Community College; U. of Northern Iowa; employed Victor Mfg. Co.; m 30 Aug 2003 Margrate Rebecca Jones (b 05 Feb 1962). Hartwick, IA residence Children:
Matthew Martin – b 27 Feb 2004

STEP-CHILDREN:
Miranda Kristina Jones – b 15 Jan 1986
Elijah Timothy Jones – b 08 Mar 1989

Steven John KRUG (Adopted) s/o Kenneth John Krug & Ann Delores nee McClintock; b 27 Oct 1967; m 15 Jul 2000 Rhonda Kaye Haack d/o Russell & Phyllis Haack, Marengo, IA. Child:
Owen Russell – b 04 Jan 2006

Thelma Karlein KRUG d/o Clarence John Adam August Krug & Gail Alein nee Harnisch; b 22 Feb 1946 Mercy Hosp Cedar Rapids, IA bpt 14 Apr 1946 St.Mark Methodist Ch, Cedar Rapids, IA; Atkins High School; m 15 Jun 1968 Trinity Methodist Ch, Cedar Rapids, to Robert Lloyd Huffer (b 18 May 1945; Attorney) s/o Ray Huffer of Shenandoah, IA. Story City, IA residence. Children:
James R. Huffer – b 13 May 1969
Duane Maynard Huffer – b 15 Aug 1974

Travis James A. KRUG s/o Virgil Irvin Krug & Mary Jane nee Meroshek; m 14 Jun 1996 Stephanie Nave (b 13 Jun 1972) d/o Dennis & Carolyn Nave, Joplin, MO. Children:
Jacob Aaron – b 25 May 1998 San Antonio, TX
Zachary Caleb – b 10 Jan 2001

Troy Lee KRUG s/o Elward William Krug & Emily Irene nee Ludvicek; b 14 Jun 1952 Cedar Rapids, IA; m 20 Jun 1981 Urbana, IA Christian Ch to Margaret Jean Henry (b 11 Nov 1951) d/o Delbert Henry of Vinton, IA. Child:
Weston – b 04 Mar 1985 Cedar Rapids, IA

Virgil Irvin KRUG s/o Irvin August Krug & Leola Anna Elizabeth nee Hertle; b 19 Sept 1941 Farm Fremont Twp Benton Co IA, bpt 19 Oct 1941 and con St.Steph, Atkins High School; m 07 Dec 1968 St.Steph to Mary Jane Meroshek (b 15 Jan 1945) d/o Charles Meroshek of Marion, IA. Farmed Irvin Krug land 1/2 mile west of Atkins. Children:
Travis James A.(Adopted) – b 13 May 1972;
    m 14 Jun 1996 Stephanie Nave
Kerri Lynn (Adopted) – b 01 Apr 1975;
    m 12 Jun 1998 David W. Griffin
Sarah Marie – b 16 Sept 1976; m 04 Dec 1999 Justin Franklyn Gorsh

Walter William August KRUG s/o Henry John Krug & Christina Marie nee Happel; b 02 Aug 1904 Henry Krug Farm Clinton Twp Linn Co, IA, bpt 04 Sept 1904 St.Steph Sponsors: Uncle August Anton Happel, Uncle William Krug, con 1918 St.Steph, Graduate Cedar Rapids Business College; d 08 Oct 1985 ae81y 2m 6d [Injury from a fall]University Hosp Iowa City, IA bur 12 Oct 1985 St.Steph Cem; m 09 Sept 1925 Bruner Groff Home, Cedar Rapids, IA to Enid Muriel Bryner (b 08 Jun 1903, bpt 13 Apr 1924 Trinity Methodist Ch, Cedar Rapids, IA con 1926 St.Steph, d 17 Nov 1986 ae83y 5m 9d Vinton IA Luth Home bur 20 Nov 1986 St.Steph Cem; Coe College; School Teacher). Farmed one mile east of Atkins, Fremont Twp Benton Co IA. Purchased cattle in Kansas City Stockyards, shipped them by railroad to farm, fed them grain and trucked them to Chicago Stockyards. When cattle sold, returned to farm by limousine. 1966 built new home and retired in Atkins. Walter: Secretary Atkins Telephone Company fifty years; St.Steph Christian Day School Board; Fremont Twp Farm Bureau Chairman; World War II Fremont Twp War Bond Chairman. Director/President Atkins Fremont Twp Consolidated School Board; President Atkins Community Club; Atkins Centennial Committee; Carlson Seed Corn Dealer; Raleigh salesman twenty years. Celebrated 25th, 40th, 50th and 60th Wedding Anniversary. Children:

    Mary Janette – b 13 Jun 1927 Fremont Twp Farm Benton Co IA;
        m 29 Aug 1948 Ralph Emerson Wilson
    Margaret Lovaire – b 14 May 1931 Fremont Twp Farm Benton Co IA;
        m 01 Nov 1957 Kenneth Raymond Palen
    Elaine Enid – b 30 Jul 1935 Fremont Twp Farm Benton Co IA;
        m 02 Dec 1956 Allan Eugene Postel

*Wilhelmina KRUG d/o Johann Justus Krug III & Anna Elisabeth nee Paar; b 29 Oct 1835 Löhlbach, Germamy, bpt 04 Nov 1835 Löhlbach Ch, con Löhlbach Ch, Germany, d 25 Jun 1882 ae46y 7m 27d Benton Co IA (page 277 St. Steph Ch book – Burial Scripture: 1 Samuel 15, 32 – Death occured by hanging) bur Jun 1882 St.Steph; m 1861 Löhlbach Ch, Germany to Johannes Georg Moeller (b 18 Jun 1820 Löhlbach, bpt 1820 Löhlbach Ch, d 25 Jun 1892 ae72y 7d Atkins, bur Jun 1892 St.Steph Cem) s/o Johannes Georg Möller & Maria Katharina nee Stremme. 12 Nov 1861 Wilhelmina and Johannes Georg Möller emigrated to Iowa with the Möller children born to Johannes Georg's 1st m to Karoline Bornscheuer. 01 Feb 1862 arrival in USA; added 'e' to name in English spelling, known thereafter as George Moeller. (cf naturalization Benton Co IA Courthouse). Children born in Iowa:

    Anna Moeller – b 02 Jul 1862, d Mar 1946; 1st m Conrad Schneider;
        2nd m 12 Dec 1904 Justus Werning

    Maria Moeller – b 17 Nov 1864, d 1919 [Stroke] bur St.Steph Cem;
        m 1883 William Kreutner

    August Moeller – dec'd infancy, family farm, Benton Co IA

    Elizabeth Moeller – 1st m Adam Hesse; 2nd m Rev Julius Deckman

    John H. Moeller – b 14 Jul 1869 Fremont Twp Benton Co IA;
        d 1959 bur St.Steph Cem; m 26 Feb 1901 Caroline E. Schueler

    Peter George Moeller – b 06 Dec 1870 Fremont Twp Benton Co IA;
        d 15 Oct 1949 Benton Co bur St.Steph Cem;
        m 17 Jan 1895 Anna Marie Rinderknecht

Anna KRUMM d/o Jacob Krumm SR. & NN nee Wirstlin; b 1872, d 1926; m Adam Schueler. Children:

    Arthur Schueler – NFR

    Esther Schueler – NFR

    Hilda Schueler – m John Keiper

    Louis Schueler – NFR

    Carl Schueler – Never Married; Newhall,IA residence

    Fred Schueler – NFR

    Walter Schueler – NFR

    Elsie Schueler – NFR

Jacob KRUMM JR. s/o Jacob Krumm SR. & Barbara nee Wirstlin; b 1887, d 1967; 1st m Bef 1909 Bertha Katherine Fix (b 24 Oct 1879, d 22 Jan 1964 ae84y 2m 29d) d/o Georg Jakob Fix & Christina Magdelene nee Schneckloth Gardemann wid/o Fredrick F. Gardemann. In 1905 Jake started harness shop in Newhall, IA; designed stock and water tanks, 1941 manufactured heating tanks. Children:

    Dero J. – b 23 May 1909, d 11 Apr 1967;
        m 1934 Opal Olson, Oklahoma City residence

    Milton – b 1912, d 1978; m Lola Grovert

    Cleora – b 15 Feb 1914, d 15 Sept 1972; m 1938 Earl Kline

2nd m Aft 1964 Jacob Krumm JR. to wid/o Al Strawn, Elizabeth Veronica nee Fix (b 20 Sept 1884, d 04 Dec 1969 ae85y 2m 14d) d/o Georg Jakob Fix & Christina Magdelene nee Schneckloth Gardemann wid/o Fredrick F. Gardemann.

*Jacob KRUMM SR. b 1845 Baden, Germany, d 1933 Benton Co IA; 1st m

in Germany to NN Wirstlin (dec'd sister of 2nd wife Barbara Wirstlin). Child:

Anna – b 1872, d 1926; m Adam Schueler

2nd m in Germany Jacob Krumm SR. to Barbara Wirstlin (b 1852 Germany, d 1932 IA). 1881 Jacob and Barbara came to USA. Barbara's mother, Anna Wirstlin and four children came to USA with them. Children of Jacob & Barbara:

Lena – b 1876, d 1959
Katherine – b 1887, d 1958
George – b 1880, d 1971
Rosa – b 1882, d 1971
Christina – b 1884
Louise – b 1886, d 1978
Jacob JR. – b 1887, d 1967; 1st m Bertha Katherine Fix;
    2nd m Elizabeth Veronica Fix
William – b 1889, d 1974
Fred – b 1891, d 1967
Barbara – b 1892, d 1979
Caroline – b 1895
Martin – b 1896

Michael KRUMM s/o Lola nee Grovert & Milton Krumm; b 1949 Superintendent of Jesup, IA Schools; m 1969 Melinda Miller of Cedar Rapids, IA. Children:

Marcy – b 1979
Andrew – b 1982
Amy – b 1984

Milton KRUMM s/o Jacob Krumm JR. & Bertha nee Fix; b 1912; US Army Captain World War II European Theatre, received Silver Star; d 1978 President Iowa Principals' Association and Principal of New Hampton High School at time of his death; m Lola Grovert (b 1917, Music Teacher at Charles City, IA) d/o William H. Grovert & Elfriede C. nee Werning of Newhall, IA. Child:

Michael – b 1949; m 1969 Melinda Miller

Lori Jo KUCH d/o Judith Mildred nee Brehm & Donald Andrew Ernest Kuch; b 04 Nar 1970; m 04 Jan 1992 Chandler Timothy Woodward (b 21 Jun 1970). Children:

Syrena Emma Lena Woodward – b 30 May 1998

Ryder William Woodward – b 11 Apr 2002

Marc Donald KUCH s/o Judith Mildred nee Brehm & Donald Andrew
Ernest Kuch; b 13 Jan 1964; 1st m 27 Feb 1988 Lisa Maree Williams (b 22
Mar 1965) DVD.
STEPCHILDREN:
Bradley – b 18 Jul 1985
Mallory – b 23 Jul 1987
Alison – b 14 Sept 1989
2nd m 31 Jan 1998 Marc Donald Kuch to Sally Classen Campbell DVD.

Pamela Jo KUCH d/o Judith Mildred nee Brehm & Donald Andrew Ernest
Kuch; b 17 Dec 1971; m 11 Jun 1994 Rand Charles Hartman (b 23 Dec
1971). Children:
Meghan Genevieve Hartman – b 03 May 1999
Nathan Earl Hartman – b 22 Jul 2002
Olivia Judith Hartman – b 17 Oct 2003

*Jochim KUHL b 08 Aug 1848 near Krempe, Holstein, Germany, d 26 Jan
1917 ae68y 5m 20d Benton Co IA; 1867 emigrated to Scott Co, Davenport,
IA; 1870 moved to Benton Co IA; m 15 Mar 1878 Big Grove Twp IA to
Anna Breiholz (b 08 May 1858 Nordhasdt, Holstein, Germany, d 08 Jan
1940 ae81y 8m emigrated with mother to USA ae6y) d/o Jacob & Maria
Breiholz. Farmers Big Grove Twp. Benton Co IA. Children:
Henry – b 1880, d 1959; m 1941 Margaret Sindt Schoelerman
Herman – b 1883, d 1943; m 1909 Martha Koch
Rosa – b 1886, d 1987; m 1909 George Schoelerman
Albert – b 1889, d 1964; m 1929 Henrietta Steinford
Frank – b 1892, d 1970; m 1917 Anna Breiholz
Lulu – b 1897; m 1933 Henry Converse

Charles KUNSTORF s/o Henry Kunstorf & Elizabeth nee Palas; b 1848, d
1943; purchased eighty acres of land from his father in 1888, one mile east
and 1/2 mile south of Newhall, IA; 1st m Jane Schlotterbeck (b 1855, d
1881). Child:
Emma – 1st m 28 Sept 1899 George Fritz Happel s/o Johann Hartmann
Happel. 2nd m Charles Kunstorf to Anna Weichman. Children:
William – b 1886, d 1979; m 22 Feb 19 ND Ida Vitt
d/o Joseph Vitt
Henry – b 1883, d 1936; m Dora Emcke

Charles KUNSTORF s/o Everett Kunstorf & Mabel nee Anderson; m Carol Werning d/o Lester Werning & Annis nee Schlotterback. From 1963-1967 owned-operated Chuck's 66 Gas Station on highway 30 near Atkins, IA; worked for L.P. Gas in Newhall, IA; 1968 worked for Morton Bldg; 1969-1972 partnership with Houser Bros. Newhall, IA; worked for Gibney & Risdal carpenters three years. 1974 worked for Virgil Alberts; 1975 purchased Alberts Oil Co.; 1977 built a service station on Railroad St. and built a home one mile east of Newhall, IA. Members of St. John. Children:
Todd – NFR
Timothy – NFR

Evelyn KUNSTORF d/o Henry Kunstorf & Dora nee Emcke; b 1911; m Merle Gardeman (b 1911). Children:
Douglas Gardeman – b 07 Jun 1934;
m 13 Sept 1959 Lurline Ann Braksiek
Joan Gardeman – m Vernon Pickerill; residence near Amana, IA

Everett KUNSTORF s/o Henry Kunstorf & Dora nee Emcke; b 1913, d 1974; m 1936 Mabel Anderson (b 07 Aug 1911 in Norway (Europe) d/o Henry Anderson & Gertrude nee Lundl. Farmers on family farm. Children (seven grandchildren):
Charlotte – m Richard Stanford; Hiawatha, IA residence
Charles – m Carol Werning
Curtis – m Nancy Allen; Everett, WA residence

*Henry KUNSTORF b 1821 Germany, d 1906 Benton Co IA; m in Germany to Elizabeth Palas (b 1816 Germany, d 1895 Benton Co IA) came to USA and settled 1873 in Benton Co IA. Children:
Charles – b 1848, d 1943; 1st m Jane Schlotterback;
2nd m Anna Weichman
Minnie – NFR
Mary – NFR

Henry KUNSTORF s/o Charles Kunstorf & Anna nee Weichman; b 1883, d 1936; m Dora Emcke (b 1882, d 1963). Settled on his father's farm; his father moved across the road. Children:
Evelyn – b 1911; m Merle Gardeman
Everett – b 1913; m Mabel Anderson

Alfred Hans LAHN s/o Fredrich Lahn & Lena nee Heitmann; d 09 Jan 1983 at his home; m 25 Aug 1928 Little Brown Church, Nashua, IA to Evelyn Johnson of Blairstown, IA. Farmers. Children:

Roger Johnson – m Jean MacLean, Boston, MA

Victor Fredrick – m Donna Newton, Luzerne, IA

John David – m Beverly Welch, Belle Plaine, IA

*Fredrick LAHN s/o Frerick Lahn & Weibke nee Albers; b 18 Mar 1870 Tensbuttal, Schleswig Holstein, Germany, d 08 Aug 1929 ae59y 4m 20d; emigrated to Belle Plaine, IA to live with Uncle & Aunt Hans & Doris Lahn; 1st m Feb 1892 Lena Heitmann (d 07 Aug 1900 Luzerne, IA) d/o John & Lena Heitmann. Children:

Alvena – m William Janss

John F – one son: Jack of Arrowhead, CA

2nd m Fredrick Lahn to Ordinancy Schluntz, d/o Hans Schluntz & Anna nee Miller. Children:

Alfred Hans – m 25 Aug 1928 Evelyn Johnson

Irene – m 24 Dec 1930 Blairstown, IA to Lewis Johnson

John David LAHN s/o Alfred Hans Lahn & Evelyn nee Johnson; m Beverly Welch of Belle Plaine, IA. Lived in Fairbanks AK; moved to IL. Officer with American Savings & Loan. Children:

Peter – m Sharon NN, Fredrick, MD residence

TWINS: Sarah – Anchorage, AK residence

Sam – Fairbanks, AK residence

Roger Johnson LAHN s/o Alfred Hans Lahn & Evelyn nee Johnson; m Jean MacLean of Boston, MA. Park City, UT residence; Roger: Captain Trans World Airlines 35 years. Children:

Susan – NFR

Leslie – m Stephan Beaks

Pamela – NFR

Victor Fredrick LAHN s/o Alfred Hans Lahn & Evelyn nee Johnson; m Donna Newton of Luzerne, IA. Pilot for Iowa Public Service 21 years. Children:

James – m Diane Woodward, two sons: Elliot and Zachary

David – m Christine Pottebaum, one daughter: Lauren

Angela Christine LANGE d/o Richard Wayne Lange & Cynthia Diane nee

Schoemaker; b 17 Dec 1970 St.Lukes Hosp Cedar Rapids, IA bpt 24 Jan 1971 and con 31 Mar 1985 St.Steph; m Billy Gammill. Children:
Parker Chase Gammill – b 30 Jun 2005
Brady Dixon Gammill – b 15 Jan 2007

David Henry LANGE s/o Thomas Henry Lange & Nancy Jean nee Schanbacher; b 15 Jun 1974 St.Lukes Hosp Cedar Rapids, IA bpt 30 Jun 1974 St.Steph Sponsor: Jim & Wendy Keiper; m 01 Apr 2000 St.Michael's Catholic Ch, Norway, IA to April Ann Stepanek (b 26 Mar 1977) d/o Patrick Eldon & Sharon Ann Stepanek. Children:
Drew David – b 12 Oct 2001
Ryan Patrick – b 28 Mar 2004
Luke Thomas – b 30 Oct 2006

Gary Thomas LANGE s/o Thomas Henry Lange & Nancy Jean nee Schanbacher; b 27 Feb 1970 St.Lukes Hosp Cedar Rapids, bpt 15 Mar 1970 St.Steph Sponsors: Jane nee Schanbacher, Upton & Richard Lange, con Mar 1984 St.Steph; m 06 Mar 1992 St.Steph to Suzanne Marie nee Havlik Corrigan (b 23 Sept 1961) d/o Raymond Gerald & Cathleen Mary Havlik. Children:
STEPCHILD: Benjamin Joseph Corrigan – b 21 May 1984;
     m 12 Aug 2006 Angela Kay Brockschink (b 13 Dec 1983)
Emily Suzanne – b 08 Apr 1994

Jay Michael LANGE s/o John Edward Lange & Janeen Kaye Weichman; b 21 Jan 1973, bpt 21 Jan 1973; m 28 Jan 1993 Jennifer Jack DVD 1996. Child:
Aaron Michael – b 07 Aug 1994

John Edward LANGE s/o Dorothy Katherine nee Rinderknecht & Henry Donald Lange; b 21 Dec 1946 St.Lukes Hosp Cedar Rapids, IA bpt 19 Jan 1947 St.Steph Sponsors: Raymond & Ruth Lange, con 16 Mar 1961 St.Steph; m 12 Sept 1969 St.John to Janeen Kaye Weichman (b 18 Jun 1951 St.Lukes Hosp Cedar Rapids, IA bpt 11 Mar 1965, con 11 Apr 1965) d/o Herbert Franklin Weichman & Gladys Myrtle nee Schukert. Palmetto, FL residence. Children:
Eric John – b 02 Apr 1971 Orange, CA; bpt 02 May 1971
Jay Michael – b 21 Jan 1973 St.Lukes Hosp Cedar Rapids, IA;
     m 28 Jan 1993 Jennifer Jack DVD 1996

Mark Edward LANGE s/o Thomas Henry Lange & Nancy Jean nee Schanbacher, b 07 Jul 1971 St Lukes Hosp Cedar Rapids, IA; bpt 25 Jul 1971 St.Steph Sponsors: Glenn Schanbacher & Cindy Lange (Mrs. Richard); con 31 Mar 1985 St.Steph; m 25 Apr 1998 Bethany Luth Ch Cedar Rapids, IA to Kathy Sue Piehl (b 05 Oct 1971) d/o Wayne Robert Piehl & Ileene Dora nee Brinkert. Child:

Darci Nicole – b 17 Aug 1999

Grant – b 03 Apr 2004

Richard Wayne LANGE s/o Dorothy Katherine nee Rinderknecht & Henry Donald Lange; b 12 Jun 1949 St.Lukes Hosp Cedar Rapids, bpt 03 Jul 1949 St.Steph Sponsors: Bill & Eda Schanbacher, con 07 Apr 1963 St.Steph; m 11 Jul 1969 St.Steph to Cynthia Diane Shoemaker (b 05 Mar 1951 Belle Plaine, Benton Co IA bpt 20 Dec 1969 and con 21 Dec 1969 TrinCR) d/o Robert & Darlene Schoemaker. Children:

Angela Christine – b 17 Dec 1970 St.Lukes Hosp Cedar Rapids, IA; m Billy Gammill

Robert Wayne – b 31 Oct 1972 St.Lukes Hosp Cedar Rapids, IA; bpt 19 Nov 1972 & con 12 Apr 1987 St.Steph; m 01 Aug 1998 Gwen Christensen

Robert Wayne LANGE s/o Richard Wayne Lange & Cynthia Diane nee Shoemaker; b 31 Oct 1972 St.Lukes Hosp Cedar Rapids, IA; bpt 19 Nov 1972 and con 12 Apr 1987 St.Steph; m 01 Aug 1998 Gwen Christensen (b 15 May ND). Children:

Leighton – b 13 Mar 2002

Quincy (Adopted) – b 30 Jun 2005

Thomas Henry LANGE s/o Dorothy Katherine nee Rinderknecht & Henry Donald Lange; b 16 Mar 1944 St.Lukes Hosp Cedar Rapids, bpt 22 Apr 1944 Parent's Atkins home & con St.Steph; m 01 Apr 1967 St.Steph to Nancy Jean Schanbacher (b 14 Mar 1945 St.Lukes Hosp Cedar Rapids, IA bpt 1945 and con St.Steph) d/o Edward Fredrick Schanbacher & Wilma Augusta Lensch. Occupation: Atkins Lumber Co. Celebrated 40th Wedding Anniversary. Children:

Gary Thomas – b 27 Feb 1970 St.Lukes Hosp Cedar Rapids, IA; m 06 Mar 1993 Suzanne Marie Havlik

Mark Edward – b 07 Jul 1971 St.Lukes Hosp Cedar Rapids, IA; m 25 Apr 1998 Kathy Sue Piehl

David Henry – b 15 Jun 1974 St.Lukes Hosp Cedar Rapids, IA;

m 01 Apr 2000 April Ann Stepanek

Loren LARRABEE s/o Lydia nee Theis & Lamont Larrabee; m Debra NN. St.Charles, IL residence. Children:
Benjamin – NFR
Joshua – NFR

Ervin J. LAUTERWASSER b 05 Jan 1901 northwest of Van Horne, IA d 24 Nov 1965 ae64y 10m 19d; m 27 Jan 1924 Irene K. Senne (b 21 Oct 1902 1/2 mile north of where Ervin was born, d 13 Apr 1953 ae50y 5m 23d). Children:
Dorothy – b/d 1924
Lewis F. – b 30 Mar 1927, d 09 Sept 1981; m 1950 Rozella Weichman
Kathleen – b 1929; m Harold Thompson
Kenneth – b 1933, d 1978; m Colleen Howe

John Emery LAUTERWASSER s/o Lewis F. Lauterwasser & Rozella nee Weichman; b 09 Jul 1962; m 23 Aug 1986 Shelley Beatty. Child:
Brandon – b 1991

Kenneth LAUTERWASSER s/o Ervin J. Lauterwasser & Irene K. nee Senne; b 1933, d 1978; m Colleen Howe (b 1934, d 1997). Children:
Debra Ann – b 1953; m William Michael Drahos. Children:
1. Lisa Ann Drahos (b 1971); m Travis Rush. Child:
Austin James Rush (b 1999)
2. Amy Marie Drahos (b 1976); m Jason Rupp
3. Heather Lynne Drahos (b 1977)
4. Brian Michael Drahos (b 1980)
Kent Ervin – b 1955; m Leslie Jean Delaney McDaniels
Diana Lynn – b 1960; m Mark Edward Stauffer
Douglas Gene – b 1967

Kathleen LAUTERWASSER d/o Ervin J. Lauterwasser & Irene K. nee Senne; b 1929; m Harold Thompson (b 1926). Children:
Susan Kay Thompson – b 1950; m David Drugg (b 1951)
Children: 1. Jeffrey David Drugg (b 1980),
2. Matthew Scott Drugg (b 1983)
Steven Thompson – b 1952; m Patricia Lynn Jones (b 1955)
Children: 1.Jason Roy (b 1976); m Robin Lorraine Bunton.
Children: Johanthan Roy (b 2001), Abigail Rose (b 2004)

2. Kimberly Denise (b 1977)

3.Christopher Davis (b 1980); m Barbara May Bowen

4. Josie Lynn (b 1981); m Allen Selck

Sandra Irene Thompson – b 1953; m David Henry Glienke (b 1953)
Children: 1. Lynn Marie Glienke (b 1980); m Matthew Palmer
(b 1969), 2. Kevin David Glienke (b 1982)

Sharon Mae Thompson – b 1954; m Marc Charles Moeller (b 1954)
Children: 1. Jill Marie Moeller (b 1984), 2. Tyler Charles Moeller
(b 1987), 3. Lisa Moeller (b 1991)

Scott Oren Thompson – b 1957; m Rebecca Lynn Heren (b 1969)
Children: 1. Andrew Scott (b 1996), 2. Hannah Margaret (b 1997),
3. Nicholas Arthur (b 1999), 4. Jacob Ray (b 2001),
5. Timothy Edward (b 2004)

Stella Marie Thompson – b 1958; m Calvin F. Wolter (b 1959)
Children: 1. Erik Thomas Wolter (b 1989),
2. Kelly Marie Wolter (b 1991)

Shirley Beth Thompson – b 1962; m Richard Joseph Paul (b 1956)
Children: 1. Emily Suzanne Paul (b 1990),
2. Natalie Elizabeth Paul (b 1994)

Sally Jane Thompson – b 1964; m John David York (b 1963)
Children: 1. Erin Ashley York (b 1987),
2. Michelle Kathleen York (b 1992)

Sara Sue Thompson – b 1966; m Gary Eugene Osborne (b 1966)

Lewis F. LAUTERWASSER s/o Ervin J. Lauterwasser & Irene K. nee
Senne; b 30 Mar 1927 northwest of Van Horne, IA d 09 Sept 1981 ae64y
5m 10d; drafted US Army Korean Conflict; m 02 Aug 1950 Rozella
Weichman (b 24 Sept 1930) d/o Emery J. Weichman & Ethel F. nee Farrell.
Farmers south of Van Horne, IA and north of Newhall, IA. Children:
Bruce Allen – b 22 Dec 1953, Newhall, IA residence
Mark Erwin – b 17 Nov 1955; m 09 Sept 1978 Sharon Balhorn
Mary Lou – b 19 Apr 1960; m 28 Aug 1982 Steven Young
John Emery – b 09 Jul 1962; m 23 Aug 1986 Shelley Beatty
Jane Ethel – b 02 Oct 1972

Mark LAUTERWASSER s/o Lewis F. Lauterwasser & Rozella nee
Weichman; b 17 Nov 1955; m 09 Sept 1978 Sharon Balhorn. Cedar Rapids,
IA residence. Children:
Steven Wayne – b 27 May 1979; Christina Poole
Ryan Cole – b 14 Jun 1983

Sara Lynette- b 16 Mar 1988

Mary Lou LAUTERWASSER d/o Lewis F. Lauterwasser & Rozella nee Weichman; b 19 Apr 1960; m 28 Aug 1982 Steven Young. Blairstown, IA residence. Children:
Amy Christine Young – b 19 Oct 1985
Daniel Joseph Young – b 18 Jun 1987

Roy Michael LAYNE s/o Maxine Dorothy nee Matthias & William Edward Layne; b 30 Sept 1958; 1st m Stacy Keith (b 09 Dec 1959)DVD. Child:
Benjamin Michael – b 23 Jan 1980
2nd m Roy Michael Layne to Ruth Trost (b 26 Jun 1962). Children:
Stephane Emma – b 10 Jan 1985
Casey William – b 05 Nov 1989

Jeffrey David LEASURE s/o Carol Ann nee Rinderknecht & John Edward Leasure; b 08 Sept 1967; m 26 Jun 1993 Paula Wehling (b 15 Jul 1964). Children:
Joshua David – b 11 Jan 1997
Rachel Nicole – b 25 Oct 1998

Adrienne LECRAW d/o John E. Lecraw & Lydia nee Happel; b 14 Jun 1946 in CA; m 08 Oct 1977 John Philip Polychron. Children:
Jason John Polychron – b 17 Jul 1979
Alexandra Adrienne Polychron – b 20 Nov 1981

Timothy Ray LEIDIGH s/o Russell Clare Leidigh & Judy Kay nee Happel; b 04 Jul 1960; m 04 May 1985 his cousin Kim Ellen Gardeman (b 01 Aug 1960) d/o Douglas Gardeman & Lurline Ann nee Braksiek Gardeman. Great-Grandparents in common: Andreas Happel & Maria (Marie) Elisabeth nee Moeller. Children:
Ashley Nicole – b 23 Dec 1986
Nathan Ray – b 28 Jun 1988

Craig Louis LENABURG s/o Geraldine Edna nee Haerther & Kay Louis Lenaburg; b 16 Sept 1966 St.Lukes Hosp Cedar Rapids, IA; bpt 16 Oct 1966 con 1981 TrinCR; US Marine Corps; 1st m 08 Aug 1992 Little White Chapel, Las Vegas, NV to Marie R. King (b 02 Feb 1965 in Phillipines)DVD. Children:
STEPCHILDREN:

Diana King – b 23 Mar 1987
Dawn King – b 30 Aug 1988
Carisza Marie Lenaburg – b 23 Aug 1993 in CA
2nd m 03 Mar 2007 Vista, CA Craig Louis Lenaburg to Lelia Antor nee Tocayon Wilmany (b 17 Nov 1960) d/o Felipe & Leonida Tocayon.

Keith Louis LENABURG s/o Geraldine Edna nee Haerther & Kay Louis Lenaburg; b 31 Oct 1968 St.Lukes Hosp Cedar Rapids, IA bpt 01 Dec 1968; m 18 Aug 2001 Zay Christine Rugland (b 06 Apr 1970) d/o Walter & Amelia Rugland. Children:
    Henry Kai – b 20 Oct 2004
    TWINS: Marta Christine – b 14 Jul 2006
            Amelia Louise – b 14 Jul 2006

Anna Jo LENSCH d/o Dennis Paul Lensch & Jolene Ann nee Rinderknecht; b 27 Feb 1975 Sioux Valley Hosp Sioux Falls, SD; bpt 08 Mar 1975 & con May 1989 Zion Luth Ch, Sioux Falls, SD; B.S. May 1997 Dental Hygiene; m 06 Feb 2000 Century Memorial Chapel, Naperville, IL to Matthew Benjamin Haber (b 12 Jan 1975 Elmhurst, IL Architectural Landscaper) s/o Fred Haber & Joyce nee Hanson.

Chad Michael LENSCH s/o Dennis Paul Lensch & Jolene Ann nee Rinderknecht; b 15 Jun 1972 Sioux Falls, SD bpt 25 Jun 1972 Zion Luth Ch Sioux Falls, SD; con May 1986 Glorio Dei Luth Ch Urbandale IA; 1999 Doctor of Dental Surgery, Ankeny, IA; m 28 Dec 2002 Hope Luth Ch Des Moines, IA to Cynthia Jo Hesse (b 07 Mar 1971 Hartley, IA bpt & con St.Paul Luth Ch Hartley, IA; Dental Hygienist). Children:
    Alex Jo – b 15 Feb 2004 bpt Hope Luth Ch Des Moines, IA
    Ava Charlene – b 06 Aug 2005 bpt Hope Luth Ch Des Moines IA

Charles Edward LENSCH s/o John Lensch & Bettie nee Weis; b 06 Dec 1917 family farm near Atkins, d 21 Apr 1999 ae81y 4m 15d St.Lukes Hosp Cedar Rapids, IA bur 24 Apr 1999 CdrMem; 1935 Class Atkins High School; m 22 Jan 1941 Doris Mae Schlotterback (b 31 Jul 1920; d 06 Jan 2008 ae87y 5m 6d bur CdrMem) d/o William Frank Schlotterback & Anna E. nee Wallem. Took over his parent's farm following the milking tradition of father and raised hogs, grain and hay crops, retiring in 1984; served on Board of Directors of Atkins Telephone Company from 1954. Children:
    David Charles – b 10 Oct 1943; m 24 Aug 1963 Inez Mae Krug
    Dennis Paul- b 26 Oct 1945; m 29 Aug 1970 Jolene Rinderknecht

308

Wayne Allen – b 01 Nov 1952; m 22 Sept 1973 Christine Orcutt

David Charles LENSCH s/o Charles Edward Lensch & Doris Mae nee Schlotterback; b 10 Oct 1943 Cedar Rapids, IA bpt St.Steph Sponsors: Betty Keiper & Robert Schlotterback; con St.Steph; B.S. U of Iowa; m 24 Aug 1963 St.Steph to Inez Mae Krug (b 11 Apr 1942 bpt and con St.Steph; B.S. IA State University) d/o Harvey Adam Henry Krug & Ella Wilhelmina nee Rinderknecht. Residence Cedar Rapids, IA; employed United Fire Group Ins. Co. Children:
Lori Ann – b 08 Jan 1967 Fort Wayne, IN;
 m 06 Jul 1991 Joseph Denis Michel Marcotte
Kristin Marie – b 16 Dec 1970 Indianapolis, IN;
 m 24 May 1999 Dr.Timothy Sloan Huebner

Dennis Paul LENSCH s/o Charles Edward Lensch & Doris Mae nee Schlotterback; b 26 Oct 1946 St.Lukes Hosp Cedar Rapids, IA bpt and con St.Steph; U.S. Air Force; m 29 Aug 1970 St.Steph to Jolene Ann Rinderknecht (b 21 Oct 1949 St.Lukes Hosp Cedar Rapids; bpt and con St.Steph; nurse; church secretary; dental assistant) d/o Arthur John Rinderknecht & Harriet Charlene nee Keiper. Dennis: Air Traffic Controller Bismark, ND; 1971 Sioux Falls, SD tower; Honolulu, Hawaii tower; 1978 Des Moines,IA tower; retired 2006. Members of Glori Dei Lutheran Ch, Urbandale, IA. Children:
Chad Michael – b 15 Jun 1972 Sioux Falls, SD;
 m 28 Dec 2002 Cynthia Jo Hesse
Anna Jo – b 27 Feb 1975 Sioux Falls, SD;
 m 06 Feb 2000 Matthew Benjamin Haber

John Harry LENSCH s/o William Matthew Lensch & Catherine nee Schmackels; b 1879, d 1960; 1st m 14 Feb 1901 Clara Ida Gerber (d 27 Mar 1909). Moved to farm two and 1/2 miles east of Atkins in Linn Co IA and had five children. 1909 fire destroyed their home, Dorothy, Catherine and Clara perished. John and remaining children moved 10 Dec 1910 to 240 acre farm on the Old Lincoln Highway known as the Simon Gongwer farm. Children:
Harold – ND
Esther – ND
Leslie – b 19 Feb 1905 Atkins, IA d 08 Sept 1991
 ae86y 6m 20d,Keystone, IA; Never Married
Dorothy – d 27 Mar 1909 in farmhouse fire

Catherine – d 27 Mar 1909 in farmhouse fire
2nd m 27 Sept 1916 John Harry Lensch to Bettie Weis d/o Edward & Theresa Weis. Lived on farm two and 1/2 miles northeast of Atkins, IA. John milked a herd of Holsteins; 1953 retired to Cedar Rapids. Children:

> Charles Edward – b 06 Dec 1917, d 21 Apr 1999 Cedar Rapids, IA;
>> m 22 Jan 1941 Doris Mae Schlotterback
> Betty Jane – b 10 Apr 1919;
>> m 24 May 1941 Raymond Conrad William Keiper

Kristin Marie LENSCH d/o David Charles Lensch & Inez Mae nee Krug; b 16 Dec 1970 Indianapolis, IN bpt Messiah Luth Ch Indianapolis, IN, con May 1985 Zion Luth Ch & School Wausau, WI; m 24 May 1999 St.George's Episcopal Ch, Germantown, TN to Timothy Sloan Huebner (b 13 Oct 1967). Child:

> Sloan Elizabeth Huebner – b 05 Sept 2001

Lori Ann LENSCH d/o David Charles Lensch & Inez Mae nee Krug; b 08 Jan 1967 Ft. Wayne, IN; bpt Holy Cross Luth Ch Ft. Wayne, IN; con May 1981 Zion Luth Ch & School Wausau, WI; m 06 Jul 1991 Zion Luth Ch Wausau, WI to Joseph Denis Michel Marcotte (b 05 Oct 1963). Children:

> Tristan David Marcotte – b 25 Jun 1992
> Sebastien Nicholas Marcotte – b 23 Nov 1993
> Renaud Alexander Marcotte – b 12 Sept 1995

Louis LENSCH s/o William Matthew Lensch & Catherine nee Schmackels; b 10 May 1884 Linn Co IA; m 20 Mar 1913 Cedar Rapids, IA to Matilda "Tilly" Fritz (d 04 Jan 1968) d/o August & Anna Fritz of Atkins, IA. Louis had Holstein dairy herd and farmed on the edge of Atkins for many years. He was the only Atkins milkman. With help of his family milked cows, bottled milk, and delivered it to customers in town and to many workers at the Milwaukee Railroad Yard east of Atkins. Active member of community affairs: served on Atkins Public School Board for years until they left Atkins in 1943 to farm a larger farm near Ely, IA. 1953 Louis and "Tilly" retired to a small place near Center Point, IA. After death of Louis, "Tilly" and their invalid daughter, Mary, returned to Atkins, IA to live. After "Tilly's" death Mary lived in a Care Center in Cedar Rapids, IA. Eight children:

> Mary – Invalid; Never Married
> Catherine – b 23 Jun 1915; m 12 Jun 1940 Albert Schirm
> Wilma Augusta – b 02 Mar 1917, bpt 09 Dec 1917, con 06 Jan 1938;

m 30 Nov 1940 Edward Frederick Schanbacher
Dorothy – m Martin Halbasch of Montrose
August Louis – b 1922, d 06 Jan 1999; m Joan Houser of Vinton, IA
Bertha – m George Furey of Mequon, WI
William – m Margaret Novak of Cedar Rapids, IA
Kenneth – m Mary Lou Kneeland of Marion, IA

Wayne Allen LENSCH s/o Charles Edward Lensch & Doris Mae nee Schlotterback; b 01 Nov 1952 Cedar Rapids, IA, bpt & con St.Steph, d 30 Sept 1982 ae29y 10m 29d [Farm Accident]; m 22 Sept 1973 Christine Orcutt. Residence on her parent's farm near Newhall, IA. Wayne and his father Charles farmed 600 acres as a Corporation. Children:
Tonya Leigh – b 11 Nov 1974; New York City, NY residence
Brian Charles – b 15 Oct 1977; Luther College, Decorah, IA

*William Matthew LENSCH b 1824 Schleswig-Holstein, Germany, d 1900 Iowa; m 12 Nov 1867 Catherine Schmackels (b 1847 Schleswig-Holstein, Germany, d 1927 IA). Immigrants from Prussia, Germany to Cedar Rapids, IA. Operated hotel and restaurant on First Street East and Third Avenue, Cedar Rapids, IA (present site of Municipal Parking Ramp). Residence on farm on Wilson Avenue S.W. Children:
John – b 1879, d 1960; 1st m 14 Feb 1901 Clara Ida Gerber;
    2nd m 27 Sept 1916 Bettie Weis
Louis – b 10 May 1884; m 20 Mar 1913 Matilda "Tilly" Fritz

*Andreas LOWER d 22 Oct 1680 ae66y Herbelhausen, Germany; m Anna NN (d 27 Jul 1690 Herbelhausen). Children:
Catharina – b 29 Jan 1654 Herbelhausen, Germany;
    m 09 Nov 1676 Johan Monch of Battenhausen, Germany
*Johannes Jost – b 10 Mar 1657, d 12 Apr 1714 Herbelhausen;
    m 29 Nov 1681 Gertraut Mebes
Heinrich – b Mar 1659 Herbelhausen, Germany;
    m 29 Nov 1681 Barbara Möller
Anna Elisabeth – b 23 Feb 1662 Herbelhausen, Germany;
    bur 03 Mar 1665
Magdalena – b 08 Jul 1664 Herbelhausen, Germany
Johan Daniel – b 31 Dec 1665 Herbelhausen, Germany
TWINS: Johan Adam – b 12 Aug 1670, bur 08 Sept 1670
    Johan Jacob – b 12 Aug 1670, bur 08 Sept 1670
Joh. Hartman – b 12 Apr 1669; Godfather Munch

bur 29 Jun 1694 Germany

Anna Elisabeth – b 2nd Trinity Sunday 1673; Godfather her brother
  Joh. Jost (2nd child above); bur 14 Jan 1783 ae65y Germany

Anna Martha – b prob 1673; 1st m 01 Dec 1692 Joh. Volmer;
  2nd m 29 Apr 1694 Joh. Croll;
  3rd m 17 Apr 1703 Joh. Jost Eyerdantz

*Johannes LOWER s/o J. Jost Lower & Gertraut nee Mebes; bpt 06 Jan 1686 Herbelhausen, Germany, Godfather 1737 Eyerdantz his grandfather, d 07 Jan 1771 bur 09 Jan 1771 ae85y 1d; 1st m 03 May 1709 Margaretha Schneider(bur 20 May 1718) from village Wohra, Germany. Children:

  *Anna Elisabeth – b/bpt 05 May 1709 Herbelhausen, Germany;
    m 04 Aug 1730 Herbelhausen, Joh. Henrich Happel,
    Sehlen,Germany

  Johann Jost – b/bpt 04 Mar 1711;
    m 11 Feb 1740 Margaret Elisabeth Kudding

  A. Magdalena – b/bpt 26 Feb 1713 Herbelhausen; d 21 Nov 1760;
    bur 23 Nov 1760 Herbelhausen, 45y 9m

  A. Gertraut – b/bpt 15 Sept 1715 Herbelhausen, Germany;
    m Grusen 09 Jun 1737 Johannes Eyerdantz,Lehnhausen, Germany

2nd m 28 Feb 1721 Johannes Lower to Anna Maria Muller (bpt 25 Jan 1693 Mohnhausen, Germany; bur 27 Feb 1722 ae29y after birth of twin boys); m one year. Children:

  TWIN boys – d at birth 03 Jan 1733 (mother also died at birth)

3rd m 02 Apr 1723 Johannes Lower to Anna Gertraut Becker (b prob 1698, d 26 Jan 1748 Herbelhausen, Germany, 20y, 1m) d/o Johannes & Elisabeth (Godmother 1724) of Halsdorf, Germany. Children:

  Maria Elisabeth – b/bpt 12 Feb 1724 at Herbelhausen, Germany

  Christian – b/bpt 30 Dec 1725 at Herbelhausen, Germany;
    m A. Gertrud Schmermund of Hattenberg, Germany

  A. Martha – b/bpt 07 Apr 1726 Herbelhausen, Germany

  Elisabeth – b/bpt 04 Jan 1731 Herbelhausen, Germany;
    m 25 Nov 1757 J. Jost Rudolph of Herbelhausen

  Johannes – b/bpt 17 Jul 1735 at Herbelhausen; Godfather: 1753
    Christian his Grusen, Germany, brother;
    m 21 May 1762 A. Magdalena Weller

*Johannes Jost LOWER s/o Andreas & Anna Lower of Sehlen, Germany; bpt Herbelhausen, Germany 10 Mar 1657, d 12 Apr 1714 ae57y 1m 2d Herbelhausen, Germany; m 29 Nov 1681 Gertraut Mebes (b prob 1661, d

312

Herbelhausen, Germany 1st Epiphany Sunday 1733 ae72y) d/o Hans Mebes of Haddenberg, Germany. Children:

    Johannes – b 06 Jan 1686 Herbelhausen, Germany;
        1st m 03 May 1708 Margaretha Schneider;
        2nd m 28 Feb 1721 A. Maria Muller
        3rd m 02 Apr 1723 A. Gertraut Becker
    Johan Jost – b 30 Dec 1688 Herbelhausen, Germany;
        m 24 Jan 1747 A. Catharina Schildwachter
    Johannes – b 13 Dec 1691; d 16 Dec 1691 Herbelhausen, Germany
    A. Elisabeth – bpt 01 Jan 1693 Herbelhausen, Germany;
        d 14 May 1693 Herbelhausen, Germany
    Joh. Henrich – b 09 Apr 1694 Herbelhausen, Germany
    Christianus – b 19 Dec 1697; m 21 Nov 1732 A.Catharina Rose
    Catharina – b 28 Oct 1706 Herbelhausen, Germany; d 14 Nov 1706

Thomas Richard LUDWIG s/o Dorothy Mae nee Haerther & Rudolf Ludwig; b 03 Oct 1966; m 26 Nov 1994 Michelle Bauer (b 13 Nov 1973). Child:

    Hannah Michelle – b 23 Oct 1997

Anna M. LUECKE d/o Heinrich F. Luecke & Margarethe nee Werning; b 21 Aug 1878, d May 1952 ae73y; m 24 Jun 1899 Gottleib Eberspecher (b 24 Jul 1871, d 03 Jul 1963 ae92y 21d) s/o Christ Eberspecher & Kath nee Kloepfer. Children:

    Floyd R. Eberspecher – b 21 Jun 1900
    Elmer Edwin Eberspecher – b 23 Mar 1903
    Myrtle S. Eberspecher – b 02 Jun 1904; m NN Wurst
    Florence May Eberspecher – b 04 May 1906; Registered Nurse
    John G.K. Eberspecher – b 12 Aug 1908
    Homer Hy Eberspecher – b 01 Mar 1911
    Harold G. Eberspecher – b 09 Aug 1912
    Luella A. Eberspecher – b 24 May 1915
    Phoebe K. Eberspecher – b 14 Jul 1918
    Verna L. Eberspecher – b 22 Aug 1919, d 31 Mar 1920

Emma S. LUECKE d/o Heinrich F.Luecke & Margarethe nee Werning; b 24 Oct 1889; m 06 Jul 1911 Henry Packard (b 28 Aug 1881) s/o George Packard & Mary Jane nee Gee. Children:

    Gerald Packard – NFR
    Doris Packard – NFR

Grace Packard – NFR

Fred M. LUECKE s/o Heinrich F. Luecke & Margarethe nee Werning; b 20 Jan 1875, d 1963 ae88y; m 03 Aug 1902 Nellie Bohlmann (b 02 Feb 1882) d/o Christ Bohlmann & Anna nee Klaussen. Child:
    Anita – b 02 Nov 1903

George C. LUECKE s/o Heinrich F. Luecke & Margarethe nee Werning; b 10 Jul 1880, d 30 Oct 1961 ae81y 3m 20d; m 24 Jun 1903 Aurelia Brust (b 18 May 1886, d 28 Oct 1918 ae32y 6m 10d) d/o William Brust & Margaret nee Lyon, Haxton, CO. Children:
    Lucille – NFR
    Glen – NFR
    Bruce – NFR
    George – NFR

Henry L. LUECKE s/o Heinrich F. Luecke & Margarethe nee Werning; b 17 Sept 1871; m 12 Feb 1896 Sophie Fuess, Chicago, IL (b 21 Nov 1875, d 04 Jun 1918 ae42y 6m 14d) d/o Phil Fuess & Anna nee Spirkel. Children:
    Earl – NFR
    Ruby – NFR
    Hazel – NFR
    Royal – NFR

Jeanette LUECKE d/o Heinrich F. Luecke & Margarethe nee Werning; b 09 Jul 1882; m 08 Feb 1905 George Raym (b 28 May 1893) s/o George Price & Laura nee Henderson. Children:
    Miriam Raym – NFR
    Roland Raym – NFR
    George Raym JR. – NFR
    Virgil Raym – NFR

Johann LUECKE s/o Heinrich F. Luecke & Margarethe nee Werning; b 26 Feb 1873, d 09 Aug 1962; m 05 Nov 1902 Mattie Buehler (b 10 Nov 1875) d/o John Buehler & Margaret nee Honnen. Children:
    Erwin Alvin – b 02 Feb 1896
    Neva Veda – b 28 Sept 1897
    Glen Gerald – b 21 Aug 1900
    Viva Margaret – b 20 Apr 1906

Mary C. LUECKE d/o Heinrich F.Luecke & Margarethe nee Werning; b 15 Sept 1884, d 04 Jun 1965 ae80y 8m 20d; m 29 Jan 1908 Paul Hahn (b 22 Jul 1882 Germany, d 13 Jun 1953 ae70y 10m 22d) s/o Jacob Hahn & Rosine nee Boehert. Children:
>   Wilbur Hahn – b 1918
>   Margaret Hahn – b 1912
>   Edith Hahn – b 1919

William LUECKE s/o Heinrich F. Luecke & Margarethe nee Werning; b 06 May 1870, d 1946; m 22 Feb 1899 Margaretha Oltmann (b 10 Feb 1874) d/o Anton Oltman & Kath nee Rademacher. Children:
>   Esther – b 1900
>   Gladys – b 1902

Tamara Rae LUTZ d/o Glenn Eldon Lutz & Nancy Lue nee Happel; b 13 Feb 1955; m 02 Aug 1980 Craig Lien (b 21 Sept 1956). Residence Phoenix, AZ. Child:
>   Justin Wayne Lien – b 23 Jun 1984 Phoeniz, AZ

*Albert LUWE s/o Wilhelm Luwe & Charlotte nee Smock; b 1858 Germany, d 1929 Benton Co IA; m in Germany to Anna Foote (b 1860 Germany, d 1941 Benton Co IA). Jul 1882 came to USA with his parents and their son Paul. They landed in New York and traveled to Newhall, IA. Albert, a stonemason, set up business immediately contracting work and doing all of the mason work for Wheeler Construction Co. Children:
>   Paul – b 1881 in Germany, d 1898 IA
>   Harry "Barney" – b 1886, d 1951
>   Emma – b 1889, d 1968; 1st m Clarence Weichman;
>   2nd m Morris Whitson
>   Albert "Mose" – b 1891, d 1951
>   Henry – b 1893; m Mabel Ashing of Wellsburg, IA
>   William – b 1895; 1st m Rose Fox, DVD;
>   2nd m Charlotte Farrish of Mankato, MN
>   Anna – b 1898; m William McKinley Campbell
>   Carl – b 1900, dec'd infancy
>   Arnold – b 1902, d 1968; m Lucille Schlotterback

Anna LUWE d/o Albert Luwe & Anna nee Foote; b 1898; m William McKinley Campbell. Children:
>   Donald Campbell – m Marie Boddicker; Newhall, IA residence

Cleota Campbell – m Virgil Alberts; Newhall, IA residence

Arnold LUWE s/o Albert Luwe & Anna nee Foote; b 1902, d 1968; m Lucille Schlotterback. Child:
    Delores – NFR

Emma LUWE d/o Albert Luwe & Anna nee Foote; b 1889, d 1968; 1st m Clarence Weichman (d 1918). Children:
    Leona Weichman – NFR
    Elsie Weichman – NFR
    Audrey Weichman – NFR
    Henry Weichman – NFR
    Clarence Weichman JR. – NFR
2nd m Emma nee Luwe Weichman to Morris Whitson.

Henry LUWE s/o Albert Luwe & Anna nee Foote; b 1893; m Mabel Ashing of Wellsburg, IA. Wellsburg, IA residence. Children:
    Vinson – NFR
    Kathryn – NFR
    Leland – NFR

William LUWE s/o Albert Luwe & Anna nee Foote; b 1895; 1st m Rose Fox. Child:
    Dale – NFR
2nd m William Luwe to Charlotte Farrish of Mankato, MN

Jane Anne LYONS d/o Eileen Isabel Schlotterbeck & Harry Lyons; b 1950; 1st m Glen Michael Jacobsen. Children:
    Erick Michael Jacobsen – b 1970
    Dain Glenn Jacobsen – b 1972
2nd m Jane Anne Lyons to C. T. Harbourne (b 1944). Child:
    Jaime Farrah Harbourne – b 1977

Karen Eileen LYONS d/o Eileen Isabel Schlotterbeck & Harry Lyons; b 1946; m Gaylan Roy Brunssen (b 1944). Children:
    Angela Karen Brunssen – b 1967
    Kirk Alan Brunssen – b 1970
    Ryan Brunssen – b 1975

Loren Harry LYONS s/o Eileen Isabel Schlotterbeck & Harry Lyons; b

1944; 1st m Judith Juanita Gwinn (b 1943). Children:
    Andrew – b 1963; m Anna
    Matthew David – b 1965; m Karen
2nd m Loren Harry Lyons to Carol J. Swenby. Child:
    Daniel Loren Lyons – b 1983
3rd m Loren Harry Lyons to Peni Lavigne. Children:
    A'Mae Karissa Nicole Lyons – b 1988
    Kari Ann Lyons – b 1991

Roger Gene LYONS s/o Eileen Isabel Schlotterbeck & Harry Lyons; b 1949; 1st m Patricia Eileen Strampe (b 1949). 2nd m Linda Warner (b 1952). Child:
    Steve – b 1979

Sharon Kae LYONS d/o Eileen Isabel Schlotterbeck & Harry Lyons; b 1942; m Philip Dean Ridenour (b 1941). Children:
    Philip Shawn Ridenour – b 1963
    Kristin Michelle Ridenour – b 1964; m Sean Patrick Doran (b 1968)
    Heather Danielle Ridenour – b 1970; 1st m Refik Ismali;
        2nd m Amber Ali Shah
    Shane Michael Ridenour – b 1974

Daryl Dean MAGEE s/o Velma nee Moeller & Loraine James aka Joe Magee; b 21 Sept 1941; m 16 Dec 1962 Judy Kirkpatrick (b 01 Mar 1944). Children:
    Michelle Kay – b 10 Nov 1963; m 17 Aug 1985 Curtis David Behrens

David Joe MAGEE s/o Velma nee Moeller & Loraine James aka Joe Magee; b 29 Oct 1939, d 23 May 1992; m 17 Jun 1972 Lesa Lochard (b 05 May 1946, d 22 Jun 1982). Children:
    Colleen Mauree – b 30 Aug 1973;
        m 11 Aug 1992 Michael Dochscherr
    Darren Joe – b 19 Apr 1975
    Kevin James – b 15 Mar 1978

James Henry MAGEE s/o Velma nee Moeller & Loraine James aka Joe Magee; b 02 May 1938; m 08 Mar 1959 Kathy Muller (b 14 Jul 1937). Children:
    Tamara Jo – b 09 Sept 1959; m Stacy Wilson
    Randall James – b 05 Jun 1961; m 1982 Debra Meyer

Jeanette MAGEE d/o Velma nee Moeller & Loraine James aka Joe Magee; b 28 Feb 1937; m Rev. Donald Moll (b 27 Jun 1936). Children:
Debra Jane Moll – b 12 May 1959; m 25 Apr 1983 Don Zeiter
Sharon Kay Moll – b 22 Apr 1961; m Kurt Happel
Amy Jo Moll – b 15 Mar 1955

Keith Charles MAGEE s/o Velma nee Moeller & Loraine James aka Joe Magee; b 05 Feb 1946; m 01 Mar 1969 Jean Linder (b 28 Jan 1946). Children:
John James – b 25 May 1970
Joseph Karl – b 09 Feb 1974

Mary Jane MAGEE d/o Velma nee Moeller & Loraine James aka Joe Magee; b 21 Jun 1948; m 01 Jul 1967 Sam Weidman (b 16 Feb 1949). Children:
Stasha Lynn Weidman – b 26 Feb 1974
Melinda Jo Weidman – b 28 Aug 1980

Randall James MAGEE s/o James Henry Magee & Kathy nee Muller; b 05 Jun 1961; m 24 Apr 1982 Debra Meyer (b 14 Aug 1962). Children:
Breann – b 24 Mar 1986
Kisley Lorrine – b 02 Mar 1988
Elaine James – b 1990

Carol MATTHIAS d/o Esther nee Happel & Melvin Matthias; b 26 Jan 1937; m Harry Risvold (b 10 Jan 1932). Children:
Larry Risvold – b 20 Mar 1956; m Sheri NN (b 01 Mar 1963)
Laura Lyn Risvold – b 10 Jan 1959; m Tony H. Abbott

Janet MATTHIAS d/o Esther nee Happel & Melvin Matthias; b 14 Nov 1935; 1st m 07 Dec 1953 Mark Steven Taylor (b 18 Sept 1925) DVD Jun 1980. Children:
William Stanley Taylor – b 14 Nov 1954
Robert Steven Taylor – b 18 Sept 1956;
m 14 Aug 1976 Darlene May Dietz
Joel Gene Taylor – b 06 Jan 1959
2nd m 04 Sept 1991 Janet nee Matthias Taylor to Paul Gene Anderson.

Maxine Dorothy MATTHIAS d/o Esther nee Happel & Melvin Matthias; b

29 Dec 1938; m William Edward Layne (b 15 Sept 1934). Child:
  Roy Michael Layne – b 30 Sept 1958; 1st m Stacy Keith; DVD;
    2nd m Ruth Trost

*John W. MATTER b 1861 in Germany, d 1941 Atkins, Benton Co IA; m
in Germany to Katharina Hertle (b 1860, d 1945 Atkins, IA) d/o John Hertle
& Rosina Frank. Emigrated to Iowa Co IA, then Hartley, IA and moved to
farm north of Atkins, Benton Co IA. Children:
  Bill – NFR
  John – m Alice Kocker; farmed with brother Charles
  Anna – d Atkins, IA bur St.John Cem; m 1915 Claus Behrens;
    farmers south of Atkins, IA
  Charles – Never Married; farmed north of Atkins, IA

*Johannes MAURER b 19 Oct 1750 Löhlbach, Germany, d 19 Dec 1811
ae61y 2m Löhlbach, Germany Hse #68; m 02 Nov 1787 Anna Guida
Menke (b 1752 Allendorf, Germany, d 03 Dec 1809 Löhlbach Hse #68).
Children:
  *Anna Elisabeth – b 11 June 1788; m 1808 Johannes Ernst

Nadine Ann MAURER d/o Walter William Maurer & Hilda Gertrude Anna
nee Schminke; b 24 Jun 1938 Cedar Rapids, IA; m 20 Sept 1957 TrinCR to
Larry Dean Schultz (b 04 Nov 1936 Military Service 2yr CA) s/o Alfred
Schultz & Clara nee Dakota. Children:
  Randal Lee Schultz – b 10 Nov 1959 Sacramento, CA;
    m 29 Dec 1985 Ruth Ann Hove
  Robert Dean Schultz – b 27 Jan 1962 St.Lukes Hosp Cedar Rapids;
    m 27 Oct 1984 Sheryl LaValley

Frank Arthur MAYHEW s/o Merrill Emerson Mayhew & Sarah Louise nee
Haines; b 1922; m 1946 Audrey LaVerne Fennern (b 1927) d/o August
Henry Fennern & Josephine nee Pauley. Children:
  Marcia Jo – b 1948; m 1970 Steven Gilliland
  Denette Helen – b 1951; m 1971 Steven Keenon
  Benjamin Merrill – b 1961; residence Hillsboro, OR
  Andrew Frank – b 1964; residence Hillsboro, OR

Carol Leona MELHUS d/o Leona Barbara Lillian nee Schminke &
Clarence Arnold Melhus; b 18 Dec 1946 St.Lukes Hosp Cedar Rapids, IA;
1st m 02 Jul 1966 Luth Ch Morris, IL to Charles Irvin Schirm, DVD (b 12

Oct 1941; 1st m 26 Feb 1961 Beverly Cowan; 3rd m 24 Oct 1981 Susan Lytten) s/o Irvin Schirm & Zolina nee Myers, Newhall, IA. Children:
  Brian Charles Schirm – b 28 Nov 1966 St.Lukes Hosp Cedar Rapids
  Jeffery Allen Schirm – b 02 Jun 1973 St.Lukes Hosp Cedar Rapids
2nd m Carol Leona nee Melhus Schirm to Less Abodeely s/o Leslie Abodeely, Cedar Rapids, IA.

Kathleen Ann MELHUS d/o Leona Barbara Lillian nee Schminke & Clarence Arnold Melhus; b 22 Jun 1939 Mercy Hosp Cedar Rapids, IA; m 09 Mar 1958 Trinity Luth Ch Norway, IA to William Charles Stickney (b 26 Nov 1938 Cedar Rapids, IA; Air Force: Kansas/Maine) s/o Charles Stickney & Myrtle nee Sharon. Children:
  Steven William Stickney – b 18 Jun 1959 Salinas, KS
  Stacy Elizabeth Stickney – b 11 Jul 1960 St.Lukes, Cedar Rapids;
      m 04 Feb 1983 Steven James Myers
  Jon Charles Stickney – b 29 Oct 1964 St.Lukes Hosp Cedar Rapids

Kenneth Clarence MELHUS s/o Leona Barbara Lillian nee Schminke & Clarence Arnold Melhus; b 04 Nov 1942 St.Lukes Hosp Cedar Rapids, IA; US Army Vietnam; m 06 Sept 1975 First Luth Ch Cedar Rapids, IA to Sheila Gay Rodies (b 25 Apr 1947 Manchester, IA) d/o Wayne Ernest Rodies & Alma Alberta nee Wolfe. Occupation: Northwestern Bell Telephone Co. Children:
  Kendra Denise – b 01 May 1977 Des Moines, IA
  Michael Jason – b 04 Mar 1979 Des Moines, IA

*Johann Winter MENKEL s/o Eckardt Menkel & Anna Katharina NN prob of Dainrode, Germany; b 1676 Dainrode, Germany, d Löhlbach, Germany; m 1707 Löhlbach Ch to Anna Martha Möller d/o Herman Möller of Löhlbach; had two sons and three daughters:
  *Anna Marie – b 17 May 1721 prob Löhlbach, Germany,
      d 11 Apr 1753 Löhlbach, Germany;
      m 11 Jan 1743 Löhlbach Ch to Johannes Roder b 02 Jun 1720
      s/o Hartman Roder, Sehlen, Germany

Judith Ann MERRITT d/o Ardith Mae nee Rathje & Jack Dillard Merritt; b 26 Jan 1960 Cedar Rapids, IA; m 27 Jun 1981 Hiawatha, IA Zion Luth Ch to Paul Bryan Patrick (b 08 Apr 1959). Children:
  Amanda Jo Patrick – b 24 Feb 1983
  Paul Bryan Patrick – b 04 Nov 1986

Meghan Mae Patrick – b 25 Feb 1995

Dale MEYER s/o Harold Meyer & Hilda nee Happel; b 09 Jul 1938; m 19 Jun 1960 Julien Tegmeier. Children:
Janet – b 19 Jun 1961
Michael – b 14 Nov 1962
Gregg – b 08 Feb 1966

Diane Lee MEYER d/o Mary Lee nee Huebner & Ernie A. Meyer; b 23 Nov 1954; 1st m 20 Jun 1975 Bradley Semelroth (b 03 Aug 1955)DVD. Children:
Adam (A.J.) John Semelroth – b 30 Jun 1976
Abby Jo Semelroth – b 23 Feb 1980
2nd m 03 Aug 1985 Diane Lee nee Meyer Semelroth to Timothy Brase (b 17 Oct 1959).

*Ernst H.F. MEYER b 1843 Germany, d 1929 Benton Co IA, bur St.John Cem; m 1865 in Germany to Elisa Strankman (b 1849 Germany, d 1923 Benton Co, bur St.John Cem). Upon arrival in Iowa purchased farmland in Eldorado Twp Benton Co dated 23 Nov 1867. Purchased additional land in Eldorado Twp IA and in MN. Director Eldorado Twp School Board 1898-1899, Director Newhall Savings Bank 1909-1913. Children:
Henry – b 1866, d 1944
Anna – b 1868, d 1949; m Henry Hemme
Ida – b 1869, d 1957; m Henry Backhaus
Ernest – b 1871, d 1956
Herman – b 1877, d 1947
Clara – b 1879, d 1950; m Louis Warkenthine
Mathilda – b 1881, d 1929; m Frank Natzel
John – b 1883, d 1948
Bertha – b 1885, d 1956; m Ervin Kerkman
Emma L. – b 1887, d 1968; m Irvin A. Andrew
Otto – b 1889, dec'd
Elizabeth Maria – b 1891, d 1964; m 1914 Harry Edward Weichman

Randall Milton MEYER s/o Mary Lee nee Huebner & Ernie A. Meyer; b 30 May 1953; m 31 Jul 1976 Teresa L. Berry (b 25 May 1959). Children:
Travis Earl – b 11 Mar 1980
Jillian Louise – b 03 Aug 1982

Timothy Harold MEYER s/o Mary Lee nee Huebner & Ernie A. Meyer; b 31 Jan 1959; m 02 Sept 1979 Darcy Ann Gloede (b 14 Aug 1958). Children:
Samuel James – b 13 Sept 1985
Annie Jean – b 03 Jun 1988

Adam John MICHEL SR. aka Henry Michel s/o Johann Heinrich (Henry) Adam Michel aka Henry Michael & Anna Elisabeth Geitz; b 20 May 1868 Fremont Twp Farm Benton Co IA farm, bpt 14 Jun 1868, d 11 Feb 1920 ae51y 7m 22d Fremont Twp Farm Benton Co IA bur St.Steph Cem; m 11 Feb 1902 Boone, IA to Meta Grabau (b 09 Nov 1876 Kolheim, Germany, d 21 Jan 1936 ae59y 2m 12d Fremont Twp Benton Co IA bur St.Steph Cem; her 2nd m) d/o Claus Henry Grabau & Margaretha nee Mair Moris. Children:
George Andreas – b 26 Oct 1903 Fremont Twp Benton Co IA;
d 02 Dec 1947 CA; Never Married
Adam John JR. – b 14 Nov 1905, d 15 Jul 1950 bur St.Steph Cem;
m 06 May 1929 Arlyne Strickell
Peter Herman Wilhelm – b 13 Sept 1907 Fremont Twp Benton Co IA
d 1964; m 02 Mar 1927 Ione Larson, DVD; 2nd m Luella Jacobsen
Paul Charles Henry – b 29 Mar 1909 Fremont Twp Benton Co IA;
d 28 May 1973 Anamosa, Jones Co IA;
m 22 Jun 1938 Elda Anna Dorothea Poock
Margaret Jane – b 1913 Fremont Twp Benton Co IA, d 1960 CA;
m 1943 John Whitehead, CA residence

Adam John MICHEL JR. s/o Adam John SR. aka Henry Michel & Meta nee Grabau; b 14 Nov 1905 Michel farm SE Atkins, Fremont Twp Benton Co IA, bpt & con St.Steph, d 15 Jul 1950 ae45y 8m 1d St.Lukes Hosp Cedar Rapids, Linn Co IA, bur 17 Jul 1950 St.Steph Cem; m 06 May 1929 St.Steph Parsonage, Fremont Twp Benton Co to Arlyne Strickell (b 08 Jul 1910 at Marion, Linn Co, d 06 Nov 2004 San Diego, CA ae94y 3m 29d bur St.Steph Cem) d/o Charles & Hattie Strickell. Farmers in Fremont Twp Benton Co IA; operated restaurant on Atkins, IA Main Street until Adam's death. Arlene and children moved to San Diego, CA. Children:
Patsy Lee – b 19 Aug 1931; 1st m Dorance Scheer DVD;
2nd m Jun 1954 Henry Howell DVD
Ronald Devall – b 30 Jul 1935, d 30 May 1953 CA (Auto Accident)

Andreas MICHEL Geismar, Germany m Anna Gertud Schmitmann. Child:

Johann Heinrich – b 07 Nov 1781 Geismar, Germany d 22 Nov 1848
  Germany; m 21 Apr 1804 Anna Margreta Kraft

Anna Elisabeth "Lizzie" MICHEL d/o Johann Heinrich (Henry) Adam Michel & Anna Elisbeth nee Geitz: cf Johannes Adam Möller aka John Adam Moeller aka Adam Moeller SR.

Anna Katharina MICHEL d/o Johann Peter (Henry) Michel & Anna Elisabeth nee Freitag: cf Johann Peter Krug

Benjamin Aaron MICHEL s/o Gregory Alan Michel & Marianne nee Holland; b 19 May 1970 St.Mary's Clayton, MO; 1992 BFA School of Art Institute Chicago, IL; Interactive Media Developer; m 19 Oct 1993 St.Petri Ch Story City, IA to Bonnie Sue Broekemeier (b 15 Jan 1972 Art Graduate) d/o Richard Gerald Broekemeier & Fortuna Tina Juan. Child:
  Duncan Boyd – b 04 Oct 2003 Evanston NW Medical Center, IL

Caroline Johanna MICHEL d/o Johannes John Heinrich Michel & Susanna nee Klippel: cf Albert Eberhardt Haerther.

Daryl MICHEL s/o Paul Charles Henry Michel & Elda Anna Dorothea nee Poock; b 17 Dec 1942 Michel Homestead, Benton Co IA, bpt 1943 St.Steph, d 30 Apr 1989 ae46y 4m 13d Valentine, NE [Heart Failure] bur Greewood Cem, Cedar Falls, Black Hawk Co; m 01 Oct 1966 Redeemer Luth Ch, Cedar Falls, IA to Joan Andrews. Children:
  Tanya Jo – b 19 Jan 1969 Cedar Falls, IA
  Tyler Andrew – b 20 May 1973 Cedar Falls, IA
  Tara Marie – b 22 Sept 1979 Postville, IA

Dennis Paul MICHEL s/o Paul Charles Henry Michel & Elda Anna Dorothea nee Poock; b 01 Jul 1944 St.Lukes Hosp Cedar Rapids, Linn Co IA; bpt 1944 St.Steph, d 15 Nov 2004 ae60y 4m 14d Methodist Hosp Rochester, MN bur Greenwood Cem Cedar Falls, IA; 1962 State Teachers College High School; m 04 Jun 1972 Hudson, Black Hawk Co IA to Kathleen Marie nee England Bibb. Dennis retired in 2000 Capt. of Cedar Falls Fire Dept. Children:
  John Lyn – b 16 Apr 198? Waterloo, Black Hawk Co IA
  STEP-DAUGHTERS:
  Dawn Rae Bibb – m Brian Heath. No Children
  Wendy Marie Bibb – m Jeff Mulanax, Waterloo, IA. 3 children:

Steven, Jessica, Christopher
Penny – m Scott Lindholm, Mineral Point, WI residence

Dorothy Caroline MICHEL d/o George Conrad Michel & Clara Caroline nee Peter; b 06 Feb 1919 Harrison Twp Boone, IA; Teacher; m Herschel Robert Tietjen (b 29 Jul 1920 Harrison Twp Boone, IA). Children:
Duane Robert Tietjen – b 21 Jun 1944; Airline Dispatcher;
m 19 Jun 1971 Janet Lucille Chausse (b 07 Jul 1947). Children:
1. Darin Robert Tietjen (b 02 Nov 1973 Des Moines, IA);
1st m Kay Carlson; Child: Elisabeth (b 30 Oct 1998);
2nd m 25 Jun 2001 Lisa Marie Guay (b 30 Sept 1972). Children:
Lauren Michelle Tietjen (b16 Apr 2003),
Katelyn Marie Tietjeen (b 28 Jul 2006)
2. Paul Edward Tietjen (b 10 Jun 1977);
m 08 Jun 2002 in MI Danielle Waller (b 12 Jul 1979). Children:
Noah Robert Tietjen (b 02 Sept 2005), Caleb Michael Tietjen
(b 23 Apr 2007)
3.Stephen Ray Tietjen (b 16 Jul 1980);
m 12 Jul 2003 Andrea Hedding (b 07 1978 MN)
Connie Lynn Tietjen – b 30 Apr 1947;
1st m 09 Sept 1973 Dennis Hutchins DVD. Child:
Sara Lynn Hutchins (b 22 Jan 1976); m Damon Farrington.
Children: Hailey Anne Farrington (b 24 May 2002),
Cade William Farrington (b 05 Dec 2003)
2nd m Gene Pollman

Erick John MICHEL s/o Gregory Alan Michel & Marianne nee Holland; b 26 May 1966 St.Joseph's Milwaukee WI; 1992 B.S. Iowa State University, 1997 PhD Northwestern in Electrical engineering; m 25 Feb 1989 Memorial Luth Ch Ames, IA to Christine Mae Burden (b 12 Aug 1967 Mt. Pleasant IA; Occupational Therapist) d/o Kenneth Chris Burden & Marjorie Ann nee DeBont. Child:
Sadie Elizabeth – b 22 Sept 2000 Reading, PA
Jack Martin – b 25 Sept 2002 Reading, PA

George Andreas MICHEL s/o Adam John SR. aka Henry Michel & Meta nee Grabau; b 26 Oct 1903 Fremont Twp Benton Co IA, bpt and con St.Steph, d 02 Dec 1947 ae44y 1m 6d San Diego, CA hospital after a long illness. Graduate Cedar Rapids Business College; secretary to aircraft company in San Diego, CA. Lifelong member St.Steph; services and bur

St.Steph Cem. Never Married.

George Conrad MICHEL s/o Johannes John Heinrich Michel & Susanna nee Klippel; b 20 Mar 1889 Vermillion, SD; d 24 Mar 1953 ae64y 4d Wheatridge, Co bur St.Paul Luth Cem Boone, IA; Farmer; m 08 Feb 1911 St.Paul Luth Ch, Boone, IA to Clara Caroline Christine Peter (b 29 Jun 1888 Boone Co. IA, d 02 Apr 1984 Arvada, Co) d/o Frederick Carl (Fritz) Peter (b 15 Sept 1847 Gross-Werther, Germany) & Sophia nee Duever(b 13 Nov 1853 Boedenstedt, Hanover, Germany). Children:
    Verda Erma Anna – b 15 Apr 1912;
        1st m 17 Dec 1933 Albert Mindeman (b 1912);
        2nd m 30 Jun 1951 Reinhold Karl Brinkman
    Wilbert John Henry – b 09 Apr 1915, d 1987;
        m 08 Apr 1942 Bette Caroline Fick
    Martin Arnold – b 02 Apr 1917 rural Boone Co IA, d 04 Dec 1996
        bur St.Paul Luth Cem, Boone, IA;
        m 09 Feb 1941 St.Paul Luth Ch to Bernice Louise Grabau
    Dorothy Caroline – b 06 Feb 1919; m Herschel Tietjen (b 29 Jul 1920)
    Leonard – b 13 Jan 1928; m 20 Aug 1950 JoAnn Olson

George Friedrich MICHEL s/o Johann Heinrich Adam Michel & Anna Elisabeth nee Geitz; b 05 Jul 1859 bpt 13 Jun 1859 Löhlbach Ch Godfather: Georg Philipp Geitz; 1st m 21 Dec 1884 Annie Happel (b 29 Jun 1864 Rock Island, IL, d 08 Apr 1893 ae38y 9m 10d) d/o Johann Georg Happel SR. 2nd m George Friedrich Michel to Elizabeth Happel (b 24 Sept 1877, d 31 May 1954 ae76y 8m 6d). Child:
    John – m Ella Stoll; Children: 1. Kenneth; m Marian NN. Children:
        1. Rodney, 2 Paula; m Paul Volga, 2. Karl, 3. Loren

Gregory Alan MICHEL s/o Martin Arnold Michel & Bernice Louise nee Grabau; b 22 Sept 1941 Boone Co Hosp, Boone, IA; 1963 B.S. Iowa State University; m 02 Sept 1962 Our Savior's Luth Ch Leland, IA to Marianne Holland (b 30 Sept 1941 Forest City Hosp Forest City, IA) d/o Herbert Boyd Holland (1910-2006) & Mary Jane nee Sankot(1913-2003). Gregory visited Michel ancestral home in Löhlbach, Germany in 1999. Children:
    Jennifer Lynn – b 27 Mar 1963 Ames, IA;
        m 15 Oct 1989 Kurt William Lauer
    Erick John – b 26 May 1966 Milwaukee, WI;
        m 25 Feb 1989 Mt.Pleasant, IA to Christine Mae Burden
    Benjamin Aaron – b 19 May 1970 St.Louis, MO;

m 19 Oct 1993 Story City, IA to Bonnie Sue Broekmeier

Henry MICHEL s/o Johann Heinrich (Henry) Adam Michel & Anna Elisabeth nee Geitz; b 18 Aug 1873 Fremont Twp Benton Co IA; m 11 Feb 1902 Adelheid (Ollie) Grabau (b 24 Feb 1881, d 04 Feb 1965) d/o Claus Heinrich (Henry) Grabau SR. & Margaretha nee Mair Moris. Children:
    Charles J. – b 1903, d 1968
    Elenore – b 1905, d 1973
    Kathryn E. – b 1909
    Henry G JR. – b 1914, d 1982

Janice Kay MICHEL d/o Paul Charles Henry Michel & Elda Anna Dorothea nee Poock; b 05 Aug 1948 St.Lukes Hosp Cedar Rapids,IA bpt 1948 St.Steph; m 29 Jul 1972 St.Edwards, Waterloo, Black Hawk Co IA to Michael Joseph Girsch. Children:
    Theresa Maureen Girsch – b 22 Nov 1974 Cedar Rapids, IA
    Michael Paul Girsch – b 23 Nov 1977 Cedar Rapids, IA
    Matthew Joseph Girsch – b 01 Dec 1983 Cedar Falls, IA

Jennifer Lynn MICHEL d/o Gregory Alan Michel & Marianne nee Holland; b 27 Mar 1963 Mary Greeley Hosp, Ames, IA; 1985 B.S, Iowa State University; m 14 Oct 1989 Memorial Luth Ch, Ames, IA to Kurt William Lauer (b 21 Apr 1963 Ingalls Memorial Hosp Harvey, IL; Dentist) s/o Rolland William Lauer & Paula Louise nee Schiffer. Children:
    Elsa Anne Lauer – b 01 Aug 1995 Evanston Hosp Evanston, IL
    Greta Hope Lauer – b 04 Sept 1998 Evanston Hosp, Evanston, IL

*Johann Daniel MICHEL s/o Johannes Michel & Maria nee Schmittmann, Geismar, Germany; b 05 May 1808; m 17 May 1840 Maria Magdalena Scholl (b 20 Jun 1813, d 29 Dec 1884 ae71y 6m 9d) d/o Johannes Scholl & Maria Spor nee Hanbern. Child:
    *Anna Maria Michel – b Aug 1848 Geismar, Germany

* Johann Heinrich MICHEL s/o Johannes Adam Michel & Anna Gertrude nee Schmittmann; b 07 Nov 1781 Geismar, Germany, d 22 Nov 1848 ae67y 15d Geismar,Germany; m 21 Apr 1804 Geismar,Germany, Anna Margreta Kraft (b 12 Dec 1779 Geismar, Germany d 27 Jun 1836 57y 6m 15d Geismar,Germany) d/o Johann Peter Kraft & Katharina Elisabeth nee Battefeld. Children:
    Johann Adam – b Geismar, Germany

Johannes Nicolaus b Geismar, Germany:
*Johann Peter (Henry) – b 25 Jun 1805 Geismar, Germany
    d 19 Jun 1879 Michel Homestead Fremont Twp Benton Co IA;
    m 19 Mar 1829 Anna Elisabeth Freitag

*Johann Heinrich (Henry) Adam MICHEL s/o Johann Peter (Henry) Michel & Anna Elisabeth nee Freitag; b 19 Aug 1829 Geismar, Germany (10 km/6 miles from Löhlbach, Germany, bpt Löhlbach Ch d 29 Sept 1892 ae63y 1m 10d Fremont Twp Benton Co, IA, bur St.Steph Cem; Cartwright in Germany; m 04 Nov 1855 Löhlbach Ch Germany to Anna Elisabeth Geitz (b 29 Aug 1835 Löhlbach, Germany Hse #48, d 14 Sept 1922 ae87y 16d Fremont Twp Benton Co IA, bur St.Steph Cem) d/o Johann Georg Philip Geitz (Georg Philipp Geitz GS St.Steph Cem)& Katharina Elisabeth nee Fackiner. Emigrated 1865 with three oldest living children and father-in-law (farmer) from Löhlbach, Germany, sailing from Bremen, Germany on ship "Columbia." Also on board the Johann Justus Krug III family. Arrived in New York 19 Jul 1865 and traveled by train to Iowa.
    *Anna Elizabeth "Lizzie" – b 18 Aug 1856 Löhlbach, Germany;
        d 28 Sept 1940 Boone, IA; m 05 Mar 1876 Johannes Adam Möller
        aka John Adam Moeller aka Adam Moeller SR.
    *Georg Friedrick – b 05 Jun 1859 Löhlbach, Germany;
        1st m 21 Dec 1884 Annie Happel (1864-1893);
        2nd m Aft 1893 Elizabeth Happel (1877-1954)
        d/o Johann Georg Happel SR. & Katharina Elisabeth
        nee Rinderknecht
    Johann Adam – b 15 Jan 1862 bpt 21 Jan 1862 Löhlbach Ch;
        Godfather: Johann Adam Michel
        d 12 Feb 1862 Löhlbach, Germany
    *Johannes John Heinrich – b 05 Feb 1863 Löhlbach, Germany;
        d 31 Dec 1946 Boone, IA; m 26 Jan 1888 Susanna Klippel
    Adam John SR. – b 20 May 1868 Fremont Twp Farm Benton Co IA;
        d 11 Feb 1920 Fremont Twp Farm Benton Co IA;
        m 11 Feb 1902 Boone, IA Meta Grabau
    Andrew – b 1865 Fremont Twp Farm Benton Co IA;
        m Matilda Maine (b 05 Jun 1868, d 14 Jan 1961)
    Katherine "Katie" – b 1870 Fremont Twp Farm Benton Co;
        m Charles Carl Michael Ahrens; son: Andrew Ahrens
    Henry – b 18 Aug 1873 Fremont Twp Farm Benton Co IA;
        m Adelheid (Ollie) Grabau
    Marie – b 21 Aug 1877 Fremont Twp Farm Benton Co IA;

d 12 Mar 1963 Cedar Rapids, bur 15 Mar 1963 CdrMem;
m 18 Sept 1901 Herman Grabau JR.

*Johann Peter (Henry) Michel (GS St.Steph) of Geismar, Germany, Ackermann: farmhand; naturalized Henry Michael 06 Mar 1872, (Volume I, page 166, Benton Co Recorder, Courthouse, Vinton, IA);s/o Johann Heinrich Michel & Anna Margreta nee Kraft; b 25 Jun 1805 Geismar, Germany, d 19 Jun 1879 ae73y 11m 25d Michel Homestead, Fremont Twp Benton Co IA bur St.Steph Cem; m 19 Mar 1829 in Germany to Anna Elisabeth Freitag(b 06 Dec 1808 Geismar, Germany) d/o Jacob Freitag(1782-1843) & Katherina Elisabeth nee Leinweber. 1862 emigrated to Iowa(Page 98 Jacob, Otto Löhlbach records). Listed in first census in Fremont Twp Benton Co IA. Children:
*Johann Heinrich (Henry) Adam – b 19 Aug 1829 Geismar, Germany,
d 09 Sept 1890 Fremont Twp Benton Co IA;
m 04 Nov 1855, Löhlbach Germany Anna Elisabeth Geitz
*Johann Jost – b 31 Jan 1831 Geismar, Germany
*Katharina Elisabeth – b 18 Nov 1846 Geismar, Germany,
d 27 Aug 1922 Benton Co IA;
m 24 Jul 1870 St.Steph toJohann Hartman Happel
*Anna Katharina – b 30 Sept 1847 Geismar, Germany, d 30 May 1918
Fremont Twp Benton Co IA;
m 22 Aug 1869 St.Steph to Johann Peter Krug

*Johannes John Heinrich MICHEL s/o Johann Heinrich (Henry) Adam Michel & Anna Elisabeth nee Geitz; b 05 Feb 1863 Hse #48 Löhlbach, Germany, bpt 15 Feb 1863 Löhlbach Ch Godfather: Johannes Nicolaus Michel from Geismar, Germany d 31 Dec 1946 Boone, IA ae83y 10m 26d ; m 26 Jan 1888 Atkins, IA to Susanna Klippel (b 18 Nov 1867 Herkimer Co NY, d 21 Feb 1953 ae86y 3m 3d) d/o Conrad Klippel (1837-1911) & Anna Elizabeth nee Wilhelm (1838-1914). Following immigration lived on farm near Atkins, IA until 1884. Purchased/pioneered farm with his father near Vermillion, SD. Children:
George Conrad – b 20 Mar 1889 Vermillion, SD, d 24 Mar 1953;
m 08 Feb 1911 Clara Caroline Peter
Mary – b 10 Dec 1891; m Henry Peter
Arnold – m Rose Mindeman
Caroline Johanna – b 11 Jul 1900, d 03 Jun 1971 Longmont, CO;
m 15 Feb 1922 Albert Eberhardt Haerther
Henry – m 11 Feb 1902 Adelheid (Ollie) Grabau; (b 24 Feb 1881,

d 04 Feb 1965)
Adam – NFR

Katharina Elisabeth MICHEL d/o Johanna Peter (Henry) Michel & Anna Elisabeth Freitag: cf Johann Hartmann Happel.

Katherine Elizabeth MICHEL d/o Johann Heinrich (Henry) Adam Michel & Anna Elisabeth nee Geitz; m 07 Sept 1890 Charles Carl Michael Ahrens (b 15 Feb 1870, d 28 Apr 1950). Children:
  Emma Katherine Johanna Ahrens – NFR
  Andrew Ludwig Benjamin Ahrens – NFR
  Edwin Ahrens – NFR
  Mary Rose Ahrens – NFR
  Albert Herman Martin Ahrens – NFR
  Arthur Henry Conrad Ahrens – NFR
  Mildred Vesta Otilla Ahrens – NFR

Kay Karleen MICHEL d/o Martin Arnold Michel & Bernice Louise nee Grabau; b 26 Jun 1957 Story City Hosp Story City, IA; B.S. Concordia College, Seward, NE; Bank Teller; m 16 Jun 1979 St.Paul Luth Ch rural Boone, IA to Dale Kermit Anderson (b 17 Jun 1951) s/o Walter Anderson & Mae nee Nelson (1912-1995). Children:
  Tyler David Anderson – b 12 Aug 1983, d 09 Oct 2001
    [Auto Accident] bur Mackey Cem
  Laura Ann Anderson – b 09 Apr 1985 Story City IA Hosp
  Axel Anderson – b 11 Mar 1987 Story City, IA Hosp; Farmer

Leonard MICHEL s/o George Conrad Michel & Clara Caroline nee Peter; b 13 Jan 1928 Harrison Twp Boone Co IA; m 20 Aug 1950 JoAnn Olson (b 17 Jan 1928 Randall, IA) d/o Lester E. Olson & Lela W. nee Christianson. Children:
  Kevin – b 18 Jun 1955; m 18 Mar 1976 Anne Nelson. Child:
    Matthew Nelson (b 31 Mar 1990)
  Kristie Lee – b 23 Apr 1960; m 04 Apr 1987 Ferlan Whaley

Marie MICHEL d/o Johann Heinrich (Henry) Adam Michel & Anna Elisabeth nee Geitz: cf Herman Grabau JR.

Martin Arnold MICHEL s/o George Conrad Michel & Clara Caroline nee Peter; b 02 Apr 1917 Rural Home Boone Co IA, d 04 Dec 1996 ae79y 8m

329

2d bur St.Paul Luth Cem Boone, IA; Farmer; m 09 Feb 1941 St.Paul Luth Ch rural Boone IA to Bernice Louise Grabau (b 28 Apr 1920 rural Boone IA) d/o Herman George Grabau & Hilda Christine nee Claussen. Children:
>Gregory Alan – b 22 Sept 1941 Boone Co Hosp, Boone, IA;
>>m 02 Sept 1962 Marianne Holland
>Kay Karleen – b 26 Jun 1957 Story City Hosp, Story City, IA;
>>m 16 Jun 1979 Dale Kermit Anderson

Mary MICHEL d/o Johannes John Heinrich Michel & Susanna nee Klippel; b 10 Dec 1891; m Henry Peter (b 29 May 1883, d 29 Apr 1975) s/o Frederick Carl (Fritz) Peter (1847-1935) & Maria Sophia Duever (1853-1945). Child:
>Cleo Peter (Adopted) – m Vesta Blaes. Children:
>>1. JoAnn Peter m Robert Shuey. Children: Kathy Shuey, Carol Shuey.
>>2. Beverly Peter – m Larry Coghlin. Children: Kim Coghlin, David Coghlin, John Coghlin
>>3. Dale Peter

Patsy Lee MICHEL d/o Adam John Michel JR. & Arlyne nee Strickell; b 19 Aug 1931 St.Lukes Hosp. Cedar Rapids, Linn Co IA; bpt 1931 St.Steph, con 1945 St.Steph; 1949 Class Atkins High School; 1st m 1949 St.Steph to Dorance Scheer DVD.
2nd m Jun 1954 St.Steph Parsonage, Atkins, IA Patsy Lee nee Michel Scheer to Henry Howell DVD. San Diego, CA residence with her mother. Child:
>Debra Lynn Howell – b 06 Mar 1955 US Naval Hosp, San Diego, CA

Paul Charles Henry MICHEL s/o Adam John Michel SR. aka Henry Michel & Meta nee Grabau; b 29 Mar 1909 Michel Homestead, Fremont Twp Benton Co IA, bpt 1909 and con St.Steph, d 28 May 1973 ae64y 2m 1d Anamosa, Jones Co IA; bur 30 May 1973 St.Steph Cem; m 22 Jun 1938 St.Steph to Elda Anna Dorothea Poock (b 12 Aug 1915 Denver, IA, bpt 19 Sept 1915 Denver, IA) d/o Ernest Poock & Gertrude K. nee Happel. Farmed Michel homestead; 1955 sold farm; moved to Waterloo, IA; Paul employed by John Deere Tractor Co. Children:
>Vernon Paul – b 11 Mar 1940 Michel Homestead;
>>m 02 Jun 1961 Edwina M.Shelton, Cedar Falls, IA
>Daryl – b 17 Dec 1942 Michel Homestead; d 30 Apr 1989 NE;
>>m 01 Oct 1966 Joan Andrews, Cedar Falls, IA
>Dennis Paul – b 01 Jul 1944 St.Lukes Hosp Cedar Rapids, IA;

d 15 Nov 2004 Methodist Hosp Rochester, MN;
    m 04 Jun 1972 Kathie Engel Bibb at Hudson, IA
Janice Kay – b 05 Aug 1948 St.Lukes Hosp Cedar Rapids, IA;
    m 29 Jul 1972 Michael Girsch at Waterloo, IA
Steven Allen – b 16 Jun 1954 Cedar Falls, IA;
    m 31 Jan 1988 Jimi Jo Parker at Nashua, IA
2nd m Elda Anna Dorothea nee Poock Michel to Merle Green DVD 06 Sept 1988.

Peter Herman Wilhelm MICHEL s/o Adam John SR. aka Henry Michel & Meta nee Grabau; b 13 Sept 1907 Michel homestead Fremont Twp Benton Co IA, bpt 1907 and con St.Steph; d 28 Nov 1964, Cedar Rapids, IA; bur CdrMem; 1st m 02 Mar 1927 Ione Larson DVD. Child:
    Betty Jane – b 1930 Cedar Rapids, IA
2nd m Peter Herman Wilhelm Michel to Luella Jacobsen. Child:
    Herman JR. – b 1948 Cedar Rapids, IA

Terri Lynn MICHEL d/o Vernon Michel & Edwina M. nee Shelton; b 25 Feb 1964 Cedar Falls, IA; m 27 Mar 1987 Gregory Mason. Child:
    Taylor Michel Mason – b 14 Feb 1988 Cedar Falls, IA
    Stephanie Mason – b 25 Aug 1991

Verda Erma Anna MICHEL d/o George Conrad Michel & Clara Caroline nee Peter; b 15 Apr 1912; 1st m 17 Dec 1933 Albert Mindeman (b 1912)DVD Jul 1949. Child:
    Eileen Rose Mindeman – b 18 Feb 1938;
        1st m 19 Aug 1961 Lester Strasbaugh (b 07 Nov 1937). Child:
        Cindy Lou Strasbaugh (b 29 Jul 1963);
        m 20 Dec 1985 Gary Wayne Shuster. Child:
        Christopher Wayne Shuster (b 12 Jun 1988)
        2nd m 10 Apr 1981 Ted Spencer(b 25 Feb 1941)
2nd m 30 Jun 1951 Emmaus Luth Denver, Co Verda Erma Anna nee Michel Strasbaugh to Reinhold Karl Brinkman (b 04 Nov 1908).

Vernon Paul MICHEL s/o Paul Charles Henry Michel & Elda Anna Dorothea nee Poock; b 11 Mar 1940 Michel homestead, Fremont Twp Benton Co IA; bpt 1940 and con St.Steph, Atkins IA; m 02 Jun 1961 College Hill Luth Ch, Cedar Falls, Black Hawk Co IA to Edwina M. Shelton. Children:
    Trent Tyler – b 06 May 1962 Cedar Falls, IA

Terri Lynn – b 25 Feb 1964 Cedar Falls, IA;
    m 27 Mar 1987 Gregory Mason
Todd Vernon – b 20 Sept 1967 Cedar Falls, IA

Wilbert John Henry MICHEL s/o George Conrad Michel & Clara Caroline nee Peter; b 09 Apr 1915 Boone Co IA, d 15 Mar 1987 bur Crown Hill Cem, Wheatridge, Co; Financial Officer; m 08 Apr 1942 Bette Caroline Fick (b 07 Jan 1919 Boone, IA) d/o Rudolph Christian Fick(1891-1961) & Pauline Louisa Augusta nee Mueller(1895-1978). Children:

Sandra Lee – b 26 Apr 1946 Wheatridge, CO; News Reporter;
    1st m 17 Jun 1973 James Oscar (Sam) Branson DVD 1978;
    2nd m 20 Feb 1983 Lookout Mt. Golden CO to John Boyd Nance
    (b 21 Jan 1943 Wichita, KS) s/o Paul & Erma Nance
    Child: Tracy Michel Nance (b 18 Aug 1988)
Jacqueline Gail – b 18 Mar 1949; Educator;
    m 25 Jun 1977 Richard Marvin Will (b 09 Apr 1947). Children:
    Timothy Richard Will (b 18 Jul 1981),
    Jeffrey Douglas Will(b 23 Sept 1984)
Debra Lynn – b 26 Jan 1954; Artist;
    m 25 Apr 1981 Robert King Wall (b 09 Apr 1947). Children:
    Allison Caroline Wall (b 15 Jul 1983),
    Travis Cartwright Wall (b 12 Sept 1987)

Gerhardt R. MIESSNER b 1880 New Minden, IL; moved to Newhall, IA when young; m 1912 Marie J. Hessenius (b 1891 Westrhauderfehn, Germany, 1910 came with parents to Newhall, d 1970 Newhall, IA) d/o Herman Hessenius & Gesina nee Klover. Farmers northwest of Newhall, IA until moving to Newhall in 1937 to operate restaurant and dance hall. Rawleigh products salesman until 1950 retirement; Marie was school cook until 1958. Members Luth Ch. Children:

Dale – b 1920; m Delores Kacer, Cedar Rapids, IA residence
Hillis – b 1926; m Verla Moore, Little Rock, AR residence

Henry MILLER s/o John A. Miller & Louisa nee Vornholt; b 1890, d 1977; US Army Sergeant World War I; farmer 1/2 mile east of Newhall, IA; m 1922 Carolyn "Tina" Freeman d/o William Freeman & Mary nee Johnson. Children:

William "Bill" – b 1922; m Hazel Kemerer, NJ residence
Wayne – b 1924; m 1952 Alice McNulty

*John MILLER b 1817 Germany, emigrated to Sandusky, OH; moved to Linn Co IA, then to Newhall, Benton Co IA; m Elizabeth Maurer. Eight children:
    John A. – b 1863, d 1946; m 1890 Louisa Vornholt
    NFR

John A. MILLER s/o John Miller & Elizabeth nee Maurer; b 1863; m 1890 Louisa Vornholt d/o William Vornholt & Catherine nee Heiber. 1890 started farming on father's farm; John organized Newhall, IA Savings Bank, served as JP, school director, township trustee. Children:
    Henry – b 1890, d 1977; m 1922 Carolyn "Tina" Freeman
    Clara E. – b 1893, d 1958
    Clarence – dec'd ae2y

Wayne MILLER s/o Henry Miller & Carolyn "Tina" nee Freeman; b 1924; Korean Conflict Veteran; m 1952 Alice McNulty d/o Gerald McNulty & Lillian nee Boddicker. Children:
    Terry – b 1953; m Diane Rinderknecht; Van Horne, IA residence
    Craig – b 1954; one child, Atkins, IA residence
    Diane – b 1956; m David Berger, one child, Atkins, IA residence
    Catherine – b 1958; m Ted Davis, two children, Newhall, IA
    Gerald "Jerry" – b 1961
    Steven – b 1966

os Möller in Germany; ns Moeller in Iowa with insertion of letter 'e' English translation.

*Adam MOLLER b 11 Nov 1651 Löhlbach, Germany, d 24 Feb 1698 ae47y 3m 13d Löhlbach, Germany; m 11 Nov 1686 Löhlbach Ch to Anna Maria Schween (b 1661 Germany, d 09 Mar 1696 Löhlbach, Germany). Parents of:
    *Johannes Nicolaus – b 01 Apr 1694 Löhlbach, Germany;
        d 05 Oct 1761 Löhlbach, Germany;
        m 02 Dec 1793 Anna Catherine Molus

Adam MOELLER s/o Johannes Adam Moeller SR. & Anna Elisabeth nee Michel; b 10 Sept 1891 Fremont Twp Farm Benton Co, IA, d 17 Feb 1971 ae79y 5m 7d bur Linwood Park Cem Boone, IA; m 11 Apr 1917 Maria Magdalena (Lena) Graubau (b 23 Aug 1892 Boone, IA, d 18 Jun 1969 ae76y 9m 26d Boone, IA bur 21 Jun 1969 Linwood Park Cem Boone, IA)

d/o Herman Grabau & Wilhelmina nee Uhrbroch. 2 Children, 3 Grandchildren:
  Ruth Darlene – b 19 Oct 1919 Boone, IA
  Clarence – b 05 Sept 1948 Boone, IA;
    m 05 Sept 1948 Lois M. Aspengren

*Andreas MOLLER m 29 Apr 1797 Anna Elisabeth Happel. Parents of:
  *Balthasar Möller – b 24 Jan 1808 Löhlbach, Germany;
    d 04 Nov 1875 Löhlbach, Germany;
    m 23 Apr 1832 Anna Elisabeth Jager

*Andreas Heinrich MOLLER aka Henry Moeller s/o Johannes Georg & Karoline nee Bornscheuer; b 21 Apr 1860 Löhlbach, Germany, bpt 05 May 1860 Löhlbach Ch, Germany; 1861-1862 emigrated USA, d 17 Jul 1918 ae58y 2m 26d [Killed in car-train accident Dewar, IA] died at St.Francis Hosp Waterloo, IA [Internal Injuries]; 17 Jul 1918 services held at family home 901 Linden Ave Waterloo, bur Immanuel Luth Cem, Klinger, Bremer Co; m 06 Sept 1883 Atkins, IA to Maria (Marie) Gerber (b 08 Mar 1858 Kirchensruhe, Baden, Germany, d 16 Jul 1944 ae86y 4m 8d[Complications of old age following 8 month illness in home of daughter Hilda Moeller Knief]Waterloo, Black Hawk Co; 20 Jul 1944 services held at Henry Schutte home and Immanuel Luth. Ch, Klinger, bur Immanuel Luth Cem, Klinger, Bremer Co) d/o Martin Gerber & Salome aka Selma nee Reis. Moved from Atkins, Benton Co IA to Black Hawk Co IA. Children:
  Louise Elizabeth Salome – b 17 Jun 1884, d 08 Jul 1966;
    m 02 Jun 1904 Heinrich J. Schuette
  Anna Marie Barbara – b 03 Dec 1885, bpt 26 Dec 1885 St.Steph;
    d 19 Oct 1895
  Daniel Heinrich Martin – b 15 Aug 1887, d 09 Dec 1960;
    m 26 Feb 1912 Martha Poock
  Anna Elizabeth Caroline – b 23 Mar 1889; d 18 Nov 1970;
    m 01 Dec 1910 John Poock
  Martin Adam – b 15 Jan 1891, d 20 Nov 1981;
    m 02 Mar 1915 Marie Cecelia Clabby
  John Fredrich Wilhelm – b 22 Nov 1892, bpt 11 Dec 1892 St.Steph
  Peter Fredrich Heinrich – b 28 Aug 1893, d 29 Aug 1893
  Walter Wilhelm – b 08 Nov 1895, d 26 May 1985;
    m 20 Feb 1917 Martha Johanna Sundermeyer
  Hilda Anna Marie Sophia – b 18 Nov 1897, d 30 Apr 1969;
    m 06 May 1917 Edwin George Friedrich Knief

Bernard Fred – b 01 Jul 1900, d 25 Jun 1989;
    m 26 Jun 1922 Hulda Sophia Boderman
2nd m Maria (Marie) nee Gerber Möller to her brother-in-law William
Kreutner and moved back to Atkins, IA. When William Kreutner died she
moved back to Black Hawk Co IA and lived with her children.

Anna MOELLER d/o Johannes Adam Moeller SR. & Anna Elisabeth nee
Michel; b 17 Sept 1894, d 13 Oct 1931 ae37y 26d; m 12 Sept 1918 Harold
Smith (b 27 Apr 1897); 3 Children, 7 Grandchildren:
    Robert Smith – NFR
    Elaine Smith – NFR
    Elizabeth Smith – NFR

Anna Elizabeth Caroline MOELLER d/o Andreas Heinrich Möller (Henry
Moeller) & Marie nee Gerber; b 23 Mar 1889 Benton Co IA bpt 07 Apr
1889 St.Steph Sponsors: Anna Schneider, Elizabeth Happel con 1902
Immanuel Luth Ch Klinger, Bremer Co, d 18 Nov 1970 ae81y 7m 26d; m
01 Dec 1910 Immanuel Luth Ch Klinger, Bremer Co to John Poock.

Anna Marie Barbara MOELLER d/o Andreas Heinrich Möller (Henry
Moeller) & Maria (Marie) nee Gerber; b 03 Dec 1885 Benton Co, bpt 26
Dec 1885 St.Steph Luth Ch Sponsors: Maria Kreutner, Anna NN, Barbara
Lindbar, Fredericka NN, d 19 Oct 1895 ae9y 10m 16d Klinger, Bremer Co.

*Balthasar MOLLER s/o Andreas Möller & Anna Elisabeth nee Happel of
Löhlbach, Germany; b 24 Jan 1808 Löhlbach, d 04 Nov 1875 ae67y 9m 11d
Löhlbach; m 23 Apr 1832 Anna Elisabeth Jager (b 09 Mar 1809, d 13 Jan
1844 ae34y 10m 4d Löhlbach) d/o Daniel Jager & Anna Guida nee Weller.
Child:
    *Konrad – b 16 Jul 1836 Löhlbach, Germany d 03 Mar 1916 Löhlbach
        m 01 Apr 1860 Anna Elisabeth Schmidt

Berdina MOELLER d/o Daniel Heinrich Martin (Henry) Moeller & Martha
nee Poock; b 01 Mar 1923, d 10 Nov 1975 ae52y 8m 9d; m Alden Mathias
(b 10 Mar 1917). Children:
    Dennis Mathias – b 12 Sept 1942; Children: Theresa & Mark
    Tim Mathias – b 09 Dec 1945
    Angela Mathias – b 12 Aug 1955; m Rick Ervin: 2 children

Bernard Fred MOELLER s/o Andreas Heinrich Möller (Henry Moeller) &

Maria (Marie) nee Gerber; b 01 Jul 1900 Black Hawk Co, bpt 28 Jul 1900 Immanuel Luth Ch Klinger, Bremer Co, con 1914 Immanuel Luth Ch Klinger, Bremer Co, d Jun 1989 ae88y 11m; m 26 Jun 1922 Spring Fount Ch Sumner, IA to Hulda Sophia Boderman (b 11 Sept 1898, d 10 Apr 1991 ae92y 7m). Children:
    Virgil Dale – b 27 Apr 1923; m 1943 Evelyn Zander
    Robert Wayne – b 10 Apr 1925; m 1957 Mary Ellen Berlin
    Jean Marie – b 27 Jul 1927; m 1947 Leslie Elston Hoppenworth
    Loren Lee – b 23 Nov 1928; m 1954 Lois Elaine Blasberg

Bonnie Kaye MOELLER d/o Virgil Dale Moeller & Evelyn nee Zander; b 31 Aug 1945; m 18 Sept 1966 Charles Herman Steege (b 22 Sept 1942). Children:
    Scott Charles Steege – b 19 Jun 1967; m 23 May 1992 Sonja Wold
    Kristie Kaye Steege – b 08 May 1969
    Darin Dean Steege – b 27 May 1971

Carl William MOELLER s/o Peter George Moeller & Anna Marie nee Rinderknecht; b 07 Feb 1917 Benton Co IA, d 04 Feb 1988 ae70y 11m 28d Greenwood, SC; m 16 Mar 1947 Lorraine Trueblood Marsh (b 14 Feb 1921). Children:
    STEPCHILD: James Richard Marsh – b 28 Dec 1941 (Adopted) Benton Co IA; m 27 May 1963 Alva Jean Padgett
    Anne Marie – b 04 Jul 1948; m 11 Jul 1970 David Miller McClintock
    Steven Carl – b 05 Jul 1950; m 28 May 1972 Patsy Joyce Yochem, DVD 1988
    Judith Lee – b 11 Jul 1952; 1st m 14 Jul 1973 Donald Alfred Long, DVD 1983; 2nd m 27 Dec 1987 Dalmer Porter Sercy

Caroline MOELLER d/o Johannes Adam Moeller SR. & Anna Elisabeth nee Michel; b 02 Jul 1883, d 26 Apr 1962 ae78y 8m 24d; m 02 Feb 1905 Louis Peter (b 04 Nov 1881, d 08 Feb 1957 ae75y 3m 4d). 5 Children, 10 Grandchildren:
    Arthur Peter – NFR
    Ann Peter – NFR
    Bernard Peter – NFR
    Verna Peter – NFR
    Infant – Dec'd

Clarence MOELLER s/o Adam Moeller & Maria Magdalena (Lena) nee

Grabau; b 05 Jan 1922 Boone, IA; m 05 Sept 1948 Lois M. Aspengren (b 05 Mar 1928 Boone, IA, d 19 Nov 1975 ae47y 8m 14d Des Moines, IA bur St.Paul's Luth Cem Boone, IA) d/o Albin H. Aspengren & Violet M. Phipps. Children:

    Stephen Adam – b 06 Mar 1951; m 27 Jun 1981 Sandra Foster

    Susan Carol – b 25 Sept 1954; m 21 Sept 1974 Rodney Ullestad

    Laurie Mae – b 14 Apr 1961; m 03 Jun 1984 Brian R. Peterson

Daniel Heinrich Martin (Henry) MOELLER s/o Andreas Heinrich Möller (Henry Moeller) & Maria (Marie) nee Gerber; b 15 Aug 1887 Benton Co IA, bpt 22 Aug 1887 St.Steph Sponsors: Heinrich Gerhold, Martin Gerber, d 09 Dec 1960 ae73y 3m 25d Black Hawk Co; m 26 Feb 1912 Immanuel Luth Ch Waterloo to Martha Poock. Children:

    Velma – b 14 May 1914; m 21 Jun 1936 Loraine James

        aka Joe Magee

    Lucille – b 08 Aug 1918; m Edgar Muller

    Berdina – b 01 Mar 1923, d 10 Nov 1975; m Alden Matthias

    Gorden – b 08 Oct 1929; m Annetta Nye

Daniel Martin MOELLER s/o Lawrence Martin Moeller & Joanne Ruth nee Wiebold; b 15 Aug 1967 Vinton, IA; employed Brovert Motor, Newhall, IA; m 08 Jun 1991 St.John to Denise Lachenmier. Child:

    Evan Martin – b 06 Mar 1997

David Lee MOELLER s/o Esther Wilhelmine nee Haerther & Marvin Adam Moeller; b 12 Aug 1943 Boone, IA; m 20 Jun 1970 Kim Tran Thi Xe (b 17 Apr 1951). Children:

    Sherri Kim – b 24 Apr 1971;

        m 09 Jul 1994 Ames, IA to Monte Francis Taylor

        (b 23 Sept 1970)

    Lani Lee – b 05 Apr 1977

Edna Elizabeth MOELLER d/o Peter George Moeller & Anna Marie nee Rinderknecht; b 10 Apr 1903 Benton Co IA, d 11 Aug 1976 Cedar Rapids, IA; m 11 Sept 1926 Carl Julius Hauskins (b 19 Jun 1902, d 20 Jun 1990). Children:

    Jean Carol Hauskins – b 06 Nov 1927, d Jun 1933

    Joan Edna Hauskins – b 16 Sept 1930;

        m 08 Dec 1950 George Luppert Pyle

    Jane Elaine Hauskins – b 09 Mar 1937;

1st m 23 May 1963 Donald Lincoln Wallin DVD;
2nd m 17 Jul 1970 Jon Allen Jernigain, Petaluma,CA

Elizabeth MOELLER d/o John Adam Moeller SR. & Anna Elisabeth "Lizzie" nee Michel; b 23 Nov 1879, d 30 Jan 1959 ae79y 2m 7d; m 27 Apr 1899 John Happel (b 13 Jan 1874, d 22 Oct 1948 ae74y 9m 9d) s/o Hohann Georg Happel SR. & Katharina Elisabeth Rinderknecht. No Children.

Elmer Martin MOELLER s/o Peter George Moeller & Anna Marie nee Rinderknecht; b 22 May 1911 Benton Co IA, d 28 Aug 2004 ae93y 3m 6d Valley Baptist Hosp Harlingen, TX bur St.Steph Cem; 1st m 25 Mar 1940 Cedar Rapids, IA to Alice Margaret Mumma (b 17 Apr 1912 Bennett, IA, d 10 Aug 1995 Cedar Rapids, IA) d/o Oscar Delavan Mumma & Mary Rose nee O'Shea. Farmed northeast of Newhall until retirement to Newhall, IA and Harlingen, TX. Mbrs of St.John Ch Newhall. Children:
    Mary Jon – b 15 Feb 1941 Cedar Rapids, IA;
        m 21 Jun 1980 William Clifton Gernaat, Great Falls, MT
    Lawrence Martin "Larry" – b 06 May 1942 Atkins, Benton Co IA;
        m 09 Jun 1963 Joanne Ruth Wiebold
    Peter George II – b 17 Jul 1944 Newhall, Benton Co IA;
        m 27 Dec 1966 Janice Elaine Bracher
    Thomas Elmer – b 28 Mar 1950 Cedar Rapids, IA;
        1st m 14 Aug 1971 Joyce Shirley Werning, d 1983;
        2nd m 05 Jun 1993 Connie Kay Peters DVD;
        3rd m 24 Jul 2001 Ksenia Nosikova
2nd m 16 Mar 1996 Meza, AZ Elmer Martin Moeller & Leone Marie Blake.

Elsie Minnie MOELLER d/o John George Adam Moeller & Magdalena nee Peter; b 10 Dec 1904, d 31 Mar 1970; m John Stolte (b 29 May 1942). Children:
    Myron Dean Stolte – b 28 Jan 1935; m Donna Loy Ryan
        (b 11 Apr 1939). Children: Stephanie Ann Stolte(b 07 Oct 1965),
        Faith Stolte (b 20 Jul 1967), Jennifer Lynn Stolte (b 23 Jan 1968),
        Jason Christopher Stolte
    Ronald Leigh Stolte – b 16 Aug 1939; 1st m Virginia Blunck.
        Children: Michael John Stolte (b 21 Apr 1965),
        Robert Lee Stolte (b/d 04 Jan 1969)
        2nd m Patricia Lynch. Child: Maureen
    Sharon Kay Stolte – b 30 Jul 1942; 1st m Bill Gilliam. Children:
        Gregory James Gilliam (b 20 Feb 1963), Matthew Dean Gilliam

(b 23 Jan 1965)

2nd m Jim Clarahan. Child: Grant Dean Clarahan (b 06 Aug 1987)

Lavonne Alma Stolte – b 03 Jun 1936, d 25 Dec 1936

Emma Marie MOELLER d/o Peter George Moeller & Anna Marie nee Rinderknecht; b 18 Oct 1895 Newhall, d 06 Jun 1982 ae86y 7m 19d Vinton; m 11 Feb 1923 Newhall, IA to Louis Frederick Fix (b 11 Sept 1892 Newhall, IA d 23 Jun 1980 ae87y 9m 12d [Old Age] Vinton, IA) s/o John Phillip Fix & Meta nee Axelsen. Celebrated 50th Wedding Anniversary. Children:

Paul William Fix – b 09 Sept 1924 Newhall, IA;
   1st m 08 Feb 1950 Ruth Ann Foley, dec'd;
   2nd m 25 Mar 1978 Lorraine Stock-Bettin
John Edward Fix – b 09 Dec 1925 Newhall, IA;
   m 08 Dec 1946 Mildred Donley Daughhetee
Lois Ann Fix – b 05 Jul 1931 Vinton, IA;
   m 14 Aug 1955 Russell Stanley Wunschel

Gary Dean MOELLER s/o Robert Wayne Moeller & Mary Ellen nee Berlin; b 20 Mar 1962; m 07 Feb 1980 Kathy Jane Liddle. Children:

Jessica Ann – b 05 Aug 1980
Mathew Dean – b 22 Mar 1985
Adam Dean – b 22 May 1989

George MOELLER s/o Johannes Adam Moeller SR. & Anna Elisabeth "Lizzie" nee Michel; b 23 Jul 1881, d 22 Oct 1924 ae43y 2m 30d; m 03 Feb 1910 Gertrud Anna Elizabeth Happel (b 21 May 1885, d 12 Oct 1941) d/o Johann Hartmann Happel & Katharina Elisabeth nee Michel. 2 Children, 4 Grandchildren:

Marvin – NFR
Helen – NFR

Gladys E. MOELLER d/o Walter Wilhelm Moeller & Martha Johanna nee Sundermeyer; b 29 Dec 1917 Black Hawk Co IA con 1931 Immanuel Ch Klinger; 1ST m 30 Jun 1936 Immanuel Luth Ch Klinger, Bremer Co to Gerald (Jerry) Wingert, DVD Child:

Roger Wingert – b 09 Mar 1946;
   Con 10 Apr 1960 Grace Luth Waterloo

2nd m 27 Jun 1954 Grace Luth Ch Waterloo, IA Gladys E. nee Moeller Wingert to Harry Frank Miller DVD

3rd m 26 Aug 1971 Grace Luth Ch Waterloo, IA Gladys E. nee Moeller Wingert Miller to Elmer L. Schuldt

Gorden MOELLER s/o Daniel Heinrich Martin aka Henry Moeller & Martha nee Poock; b 08 Oct 1929; m Annetta Nye. Children:
    Andy – b 30 Nov 1951
    Thomas – b 30 Nov 1957
    Philip – b 09 Mar 1958

Henry MOELLER s/o Johannes Adam Moeller SR. & Anna Elisabeth nee Michel; b 25 Nov 1887, d 20 Sept 1975 ae87y 9m 25d; m 08 Jun 1913 Tene Tietjen (b 30 Nov 1890, 26 Apr 1976 ae85y 5m 6d). 2 Children, 6 Grandchildren:
    Harold – NFR
    Virgil – NFR

Hilda Anna Marie Sophia MOELLER d/o Andreas Heinrich Möller (Henry Moeller) & Maria (Marie) nee Gerber; b 18 Nov 1897 Dunkerton, Black Hawk Co, bpt 12 Dec 1897 Immanuel Luth Ch Klinger, Bremer Co IA, con 1911 Immanuel Luth Ch Klinger, Bremer Co IA, d 30 Apr 1969 ae71y 5m 12d [Cerebral Arteriosclerosis/bathtub accident] at 440 Cherry St. Waterloo, IA; m 06 May 1917 Immanuel Luth Ch Waterloo, IA to Edward George Friederich Knief.

Hilda Catherine MOELLER d/o Peter George Moeller & Anna Marie nee Rinderknecht; b 15 Dec 1908 Benton Co IA; m 23 Oct 1942 Los Angeles CA to William Fred Ploetz (b 02 Sept 1913, d 25 Dec 1993 ae80y 3m 23d). Sacramento, CA residence. Children:
    Carol Jean Ploetz – b 24 Feb 1944;
        m 13 Nov 1971 John Wesley Phillips
    Sandra Rose Ploetz – b 07 Nov 1951;
        m 21 Sept 1980 Kenneth L. Niemczyk

Jane Ann MOELLER d/o Wilfred Walter (Billy) Moeller & Alice Verna nee Traetow; (TWIN: Joel Dean Moeller) b 28 Nov 1955 Bremer Co; m 03 Sept 1983 Grace Luth ch DeWitt, IA to Michael Robert Buege (b 15 Jun 1952 Milwaukee Co, WI). Child:
    Stephen Michael Buege – b 20 Jul 1987 DuPage Co, IL

James Richard Marsh MOELLER s/o Carl William Moeller & Lorraine

Trueblood nee Marsh; b 28 Dec 1941; 1st m 27 May 1963 Benton Co IA
Alva Jean Padgett(b 15 Jan 1942, d 01 Mar 198?). Children:
    Meredith Liegh – b 10 Dec 1964
    Elisa Jennifer – b 23 Aug 1976. Child: Christian James Bass
        (b 22 Mar 1996)
2nd m 14 May 1988 James Richard Marsh Moeller to Cindy Laughey (b 09
Feb 1948) Waxhaw, NC residence.

Janet Carol MOELLER d/o Esther Wilhelmine nee Haerther & Marvin
Adam Moeller; b 07 Apr 1939 Boone, IA; m 21 Dec 1958 Myron Wilson
Hasstedt (b 28 Jan 1932). Children:
    Mark Wayne Hasstedt – b 05 Jun 1959
    Joel Craig Hasstedt – b 09 Dec 1960;
        m 21 May 1988 Denise Elaine Headley
    Todd Alan Hasstedt – b 20 Mar 1963;
        m 12 Aug 1989 Andrea Ramah Camenzend

Jean Marie MOELLER d/o Bernard Fred Moeller & Hulda Sophia nee
Boderman; b 27 Jul 1927; m 11 May 1947 Leslie Elston Hoppenworth (b
05 Jun 1924). Children:
    Bruce Allen Hoppenworth – b 06 May 1952, d 27 Jul 1952
    Gloria Jean Hoppenworth – b 24 Apr 1954;
        m 1974 Nile Dielschneider
    Carol Ann Hoppenworth – b 04 Dec 1956; m 1980 David Hilsabeck

Joel Dean MOELLER s/o Wilfred Walter (Billy) Moeller & Alice Verna
nee Traetow; (TWIN Jane Ann Moeller) b 28 Nov 1955 Bremer Co; m 14
Nov 1975 St.Anns Cath Ch Welton, IA to Maureen Ann Burke (b 18 Jan
1957 Clinton Co, IA) Children:
    Devin Joel – b 27 Apr 1976 Johnson Co, IA
    Byron David – b 26 Jun 1978 Johnson Co, IA
    Andrew Jason – b 23 Oct 1981 Clinton Co, IA

*Johann Daniel MOLLER s/o Johannes Möller (b 09 Dec 1671, d 30 Mar
1739 ae65y 3m 21d) & Magdalena nee Ernst; b 02 Feb 1672, d 23 Dec
1750 ae78y 10m 21d Löhlbach, Germany; m 19 Nov 1717 in Frankenau Ch
Germany to Anna Christina Scharschmidt (b 1692 Frankenau, Germany, d
01 Mar 1762 Löhlbach, Germany) d/o Johannes & Anna Elisabeth
Scharschmidt. Parents of:
    *Anna Christina Möller – b 23 Sept 1735 Löhlbach,Germany,

d 22 Jun 1772 ae36y 8m 9m Löhlbach, Germany;
m 06 Feb 1756 Löhlbach Ch Johannes Möller (b 03 Sept 1724
Löhlbach, Germany, d 13 Nov 1803 ae79y 2m 10d Löhlbach,
Germany).

*Johann Daniel MOLLER b 14 Mar 1717 Battenhausen, Germany, d 17
Nov 1773 ae56y 7m 23d Battenhausen, Germany; m 05 Dec 1762 Anna
Elisabeth Weber (b 19 Oct 1727 Battenhausen, Germany, d 18 May 1818
ae90y 7m Battenhausen, Germany) d/o Johannes Weber & Susanne Hauck
of Battenhausen, Germany. Parents of:
    *Anna Katharina Möller – b 15 Jul 1754, d 12 May 1811
    ae56y 9m 27d; m 10 Apr 1787 Johannes Stremme
    (b 1724 Battenhausen, Germany, d 04 Apr 1804)
    Parents of Maria Katharina Stremme b 10 Nov 1787;
    m Johannes Möller b 21 Sept 1782.

*Johann Daniel MOELLER aka John Moeller s/o Johannes Georg Möller &
Karoline nee Bornscheuer; b 01 Sept 1847 Löhlbach Hse #43 Germany, bpt
05 Sept 1847 Löhlbach Ch; con Löhlbach Ch last Sunday in Sept 1861
before the family emigrated 12 Nov 1861 to USA, arriving in Iowa 01 Feb
1862. The Civil War was raging and much of Iowa was still a wilderness; d
Adair Co IA; m 19 Sept 1867 Benton Co IA to Anna Elisabeth Krug (b 22
Apr 1841 Löhlbach Hse #70, Germany, bpt 25 Apr 1841 Löhlbach Ch;
emigrated to Iowa from Bremen, Germany aboard ship "Columbus"
arriving with her parents and siblings in New York 19 Jul 1865, d Adair Co
IA; d Feb 1920 ae78y Guthrie Center, IA) d/o Johann Justus Krug III &
Anna Katharina Elisabeth nee Paar. Johann Daniel Mo(e)ller was stepson of
his wife's sister Wilhelmina Krug. To prevent intermarriage among close
relatives in future years they moved 1976 permanently to farm home in
Adair Co IA. They lost three children to [Diptheria]. Johann Daniel aka
John Moeller suffered severe stroke in 1888. They bought and moved 1889
to a home in Adair, IA where they helped organize Immanuel Luth Ch in
Adair, IA with Pastor Ellers. Seven children:
    John Henry – d 1880 [Diptheria]
    Wilhelmina – 1880 [Diptheria]
    Anna Katharina – b 12 Sept 1869, bpt 26 Sept 1869, d 25 Sept 1951
    John Adam – d ae6 months [Diptheria]
    Infant – dec'd
    Louise Maria – b 18 Sept 1872; m NN Guttenfelder
    Carolina Maria Magdalena – b 20 Mar 1874, bpt 31 Mar 1874;

m NN Fage and had 10 children

*Johannes MOLLER s/o Johannes Nicolaus Möller & Anna Catherine Molus; b 03 Sept 1724 Hse #43 Löhlbach, Germany, d 13 Nov 1803 ae74y 2m 10d Löhlbach, Germany. m Anna Christina nee Möller (b 23 Sept 1735 Löhlbach, d 22 Jun 1772 ae36y 9m Löhlbach) d/o Johann Möller & Anna nee Scharrchmidt. Parents of:
>*Johannes Daniel – b 08 Mar 1757; d 23 Mar 1830
>>Löhlbach, Germany;
>>m 15 May 1781 Johanna Elisabeth Bornscheuer

*Johannes MOLLER s/o Johannes Daniel Möller, Ackermann: agriculture worker/farmhand in Löhlbach & Johanna Elisabeth nee Bornscheuer; b 21 Sept 1782 Löhlbach, Germany, Hse #43, d 09 Feb 1835 ae52y 4m 19d Löhlbach, Germany, bur Löhlbach Cem; m 21 Jan 1808 Maria Katharina nee Stremme Wid/o Gross from Battenhausen, Germany (b 10 Nov 1787 Battenhausen, Germany, d 13 Dec 1851 ae64y 1m 3d Löhlbach, Germany, Hse #43, bur Löhlbach Cem) d/o Johannes Stremme & Anna Katharina nee Möller. Children:
>NN – b 1809, d 1810 Löhlbach, Germany, Hse #43
>NN – Stillborn 13 Aug 1813 Löhlbach, Germany, Hse #43
>Anna Gertrud – b 29 Mar 1815 Löhlbach, Germany Hse #43
>Anna Katharina – b 24 Oct 1816, d 06 Nov 1816 Löhlbach Hse #43
>Johann (John) – b 13 Dec 1817 Löhlbach, Germany Hse #43,
>>emigrated to Cedar Rapids, IA USA
>TWINS: Johannes Heinrich – b 18 Jul 1820, d 19 Jul 1820 Hse #43
>>*Johannes Georg – b 18 Jul 1820 Löhlbach, Germany Hse
>>#43; d 25 Jul 1892 Benton Co IA bur St.Steph Cem;
>>1st m 20 Sept 1846 Karoline Bornscheuer; 2nd m Wilhelmina Krug
>*Maria Elisabeth – b 08 May 1822 Löhlbach, Germany Hse #43;
>>d 30 Aug 1892 Linn Co IA bur St.Steph Cem;
>>m 29 May 1843 Andreas Happel
>Katharina Elisabeth – b 28 Nov 1828 Löhlbach, Germany Hse #43

*Johannes Adam MOLLER aka John Adam Moeller aka Adam Moeller SR. s/o Johannes Georg Möller (George Moeller) & Karoline nee Bornscheuer; b 02 Aug 1853 Löhlbach, Germany, House #43, bpt 14 Aug 1853 Löhlbach Ch; ae8y emigrated 1861 on three month journey with family, father and stepmother, Wilhelmina Krug, to Iowa; con 04 Apr 1869 St.Paul Evangelical Luth Ch Luzerne, IA; d 07 Nov 1930 ae77y 3m 3d,

Boone, IA [Embolism following strangulated hernia surgery] bur St.Paul Evangelical Luth Ch Cem, Mackey; m 05 Mar 1876 St.Steph Ch to Anna Elisabeth "Lizzie" Michel (b 18 Aug 1856 Löhlbach, Germany, bpt 31 Aug 1856 Löhlbach Ch Godmother: Anna Elisabeth nee Freitag Michel, ae9y emigrated with parents and brothers George and John at end of Civil War to settle on farm near Atkins, IA; con 02 Apr 1871 St.Steph Luth Ch; d 28 Sept 1940 ae84y 1m 10d Boone, IA; [Pneumonia following fractured hip] bur 01 Oct 1940 St.Paul Evangelical Luth Cem, Mackey, IA) d/o Johann Heinrich (Henry) Adam Michel & Anna Elisabeth nee Geitz. They moved from Benton Co to Adair Co IA, to make their home, but being dissatisfied, returned within the year to a farm one mile from Atkins, later managing a hotel where they furnished board and room for men constructing the first railroad west of the Mississippi River. The family lived in Benton Co sixteen years where first eight children were born and baptized. Spring of 1892 Adam, ae39y, and Elizabeth, ae36y, with family of eight children left Benton Co and located on a 320 acre farm at Mackey, near Boone, IA, their permanent family location. Four more children were born at Mackey. Fall 1915 Adam, ae62y, and Elizabeth, ae59y, retired with three youngest daughters to live directly across the street from Trinity Luth Ch, Boone, IA. Celebrated 50th Wedding Anniversary joined by their family in a special church service followed by reception at their newly built home. Twelve Children:

John George Adam – b 30 Apr 1878, d 19 Feb 1948;
    m 10 Apr 1901 Magdalena Peter
Elizabeth – b 23 Nov 1879, d 30 Jan 1959;
    m 27 Apr 1899 John Happel
George – b 23 Jul 1881, d 22 Oct 1924;
    m 03 Feb 1910 Gertrud Anna Elizabeth Happel
Caroline "Carrie" – b 02 Jul 1883, d 26 Apr 1962;
    m 02 Feb 1905 Louis Peter
Louise Caroline Marie – b 02 Feb 1885, d 12 Nov 1973
    Cedar Rapids, IA; bur Linwood Park Cem, Boone, IA;
    m 28 Apr 1909 Christopher Dietrich Grabau
Henry – b 25 Nov 1887, d 20 Sept 1975; m 08 Jun 1913 Tena Tietjen
Katherine – b 01 Apr 1889, d 1976; m 13 Sept 1911 Chris Lutjen
Adam – b 10 Sept 1891 Fremont Twp Benton Co IA,
    d 17 Feb 1971 bur Linwood Park Cem, Boone, IA;
    m 11 Apr 1917 Maria Magdalena (Lena) Grabau
Infant – b 24 Aug 1892, dec'd 28 Aug 1892 [Diptheria]
Anna – b 17 Sept 1894, d 13 Oct 1931; m 12 Sept 1918 Harold Smith

Mathilda (Adel)- b 15 Mar 1898; m 20 Dec 1922 Julius C. Ehmann
   Children: Richard and Curtis
Marie – b 06 Aug 1903, d 20 Mar 1961 ae57y 7m 14d

*Johannes Daniel MOLLER s/o Johannes Möller & Anna Christina nee Möller; b 08 Mar 1757 Löhlbach, Germany, Hse #43, d 23 Mar 1830 ae73y 15d Löhlbach Hse #43 bur Löhlbach; Ackermann: farmhand in Löhlbach, Germany; m 15 May 1781 in Löhlbach Ch to Johanna Elisabeth Bornscheuer of Dainrode, Germany (b 30 Apr 1757, d 11 Apr 1832 ae74y 11m 12d Löhlbach Hse #43 bur Löhlbach, Germany) d/o Johann Daniel Bornscheuer of Dainrode, Germany. Parents of:
   *Johannes – b 21 Sept 1782 House #43 Löhlbach, Germany,
      d 09 Feb 1835 ae52y 4m 19d, Löhlbach, Germany;
      m 21 Jan 1808 Maria Katharina Stremme, Battenhausen, Germany

*Johannes Georg MOLLER aka George Moeller s/o Johannes Möller & Maria Katharina nee Stremme; b 18 Jul 1820 House #43 Löhlbach Germany, bpt Löhlbach Ch Germany, d 25 Jul 1892 Atkins, IA ae71y 7d; 1st m 20 Sept 1846 Löhlbach Ch to Karoline Bornscheuer (b 19 Oct 1822 Altenhaina Germany, d 16 Mar 1861 ae38y 4m 28d Löhlbach House #43) d/o Johann Daniel Bornscheuer & Anna Elisabeth nee Schmittmann. Six children:
   *Johann Daniel – b 01 Sept 1847 Löhlbach, Germany Hse #43;
      d Adair Co IA; m USA 19 Sept 1867 Anna Elisabeth Krug
   Hartmann Wilhelm – b 04 Dec 1849, d 21 Nov 1850
      Löhlbach,Germany
   Marie Elisabeth – b 03 Jan 1852, d 20 Oct 1852 Löhlbach, Germany
   *Johnnes Adam – b 02 Aug 1853 Löhlbach, Germany Hse #43;
      d 07 Nov 1930 Boone, IA;
      m 05 Mar 1876 Anna Elisabeth "Lizzie" Michel
   *Louise Kristine – b 07 Dec 1855 Löhlbach, Germany,
      d 31 Dec 1928 IA bur St.Steph Cem;
      m USA 26 Jan 1873 Henry Gerhold SR.
   *Andreas Heinrich – b 21 Apr 1860 Löhlbach, Germany;
      m USA 06 Sept 1883 Maria (Marie) Gerber
2nd m 1861 Johannes Georg Möller at Löhlbach Ch to Wilhelmina Krug d/o Johann Justus Krug III & Anna Elisabeth nee Paar; sold three buildings plus 12 hectares of land and emigrated USA 12 Nov 1861 arriving 01 Feb 1862 at his brother John's home in Cedar Rapids IA; bought land in Section 25 Fremont Twp Benton Co and farmed (Author born and raised to ae21y on

this farm purchased 1930 by Henry John Krug). Johannes Georg known as George Moeller in America. Six children of George & Wilhelmina born in Iowa:

Anna – b 02 Jul 1862 Fremont Twp Benton Co IA; d Mar 1946;
1st m Conrad Schneider; 2nd m 12 Dec 1904 Justus Werning
Maria – b 17 Nov 1864, d 1919 bur St.Steph Cem;
m 1883 William Kreutner
August – dec'd in infancy, family farm, Benton Co IA
Elizabeth – 1st m Adam Hesse; 2nd m Rev. Julius Deckman
John H. – b 14 Jul 1869, d 1959 bur St.Steph Cem;
m 26 Feb 1901 Caroline E. Schueler, MN residence
Peter George – b 06 Dec 1870, d 14 Oct 1949 bur St.Steph Cem;
m 17 Jan 1895 Anna Marie Rinderknecht

*Johannes Nicolaus MOLLER s/o Adam Möller & Anna Maria nee Schween; b 01 Apr 1694 Löhlbach, Germany, d 05 Oct 1761 ae67y 6m 4d Löhlbach, Germany; m 02 Dec 1723 Löhlbach Ch to Anna Catherine Molus (b 03 Apr 1698 Löhlbach, Germany, d 26 Apr 1734 ae46y 23d Löhlbach, Germany) d/o Peter Molus & Marie Elisabeth nee Schafer. Child:

*Johannes – b 03 Sept 1724, Löhlbach Hse #43 Germany,
d 13 Nov 1803 Lölbach, Germany;
m Anna Christina Möller of Lölbach, Germany

John Frederich Wilhelm MOELLER s/o Andreas Heinrich Möller (Henry Moeller) & Maria (Marie) nee Gerber; b 22 Nov 1892 Benton Co IA, bpt 11 Dec 1892 St.Steph, bur St.Steph Cem. NFR

John George Adam MOELLER s/o Johannes Adam Moeller aka John Adam aka Adam Moeller SR. & Elisabeth "Lizzie" nee Michel; b 30 Apr 1878 Benton Co IA, con 05 Apr 1891 St.Steph, d 19 Feb 1948 ae69y 9m 19d; m 10 Apr 1901 Magdalena Peter (b 02 Jul 1879). Six Children (11 Grandchildren):

George Adam Fritz – b 02 Apr 1902, d 11 Jun 1987;
m Myrtle Irene Alden;
Elsie Minnie – b 10 Dec 1904, d 31 mar 19701970; m John Stolte;
Caroline Clara – b 16 Mar 1906; m Arthur Krug (b 10 Jan 1905,
d 10 Feb 1944)). Child: Roger Krug (b 04 Mar 1943);
m Sue Schmidt (b 25 May 1942). Children: Laura Suzanne Krug
(b 19 Aug 1967), Steve Roger Krug (b 13 Mar 1972)
Henry – b 1911

Albert Adam – b 21 Mar 1913; m Dorothy Alden (b 18 Dec 1916);
 Children: 1. Gary Albert (b 02 Jul 1945); m Nancy Lou Huntley
 (b 23 Sept 1954). Children: Heather Jane (b 03 Feb 1978),
 Stacy Ann (b 23 Jan 1982)
 2. Joyce Jean (b 28 Jun 1948); m David O. Durlam
 (b 14 Mar 1947). Children: Adam Clark Durlam (b 10 Jun 1973),
 Jonathan David Durlam (b 18 Mar 1976)
Dorothea Mathilda – b 10 Nov 1918; m Lee Poynter (b 25 Jul 1908,
 d 1990). Child: Bryce Lee Poynter (b 25 Mar 1952);
 m Laura Jean Callaway (b 13 Jul 1957). Children:
 Brian Michael Callaway (b 08 Nov 1981),
 Jason Christopher Callaway (b 26 Mar 1984)

John H. MOELLER s/o Johann Georg Möller aka George Moeller &
Wilhelmina nee Krug; b 14 Jul 1869 1 mile east of Atkins, IA d 1959; m 26
Feb 1901 Caroline E. Schueler (b 13 Apr 1873 Löhlbach, Germany, d 1964
IA) d/o Johannes Schuler & Anna nee Landau of Löhlbach, Germany; MN
residence. Children:
 (Daughter) – m C.F. McKinney
 Albert – NFR
 Walter – NFR
 Fredrich Carl – NFR

Judith Lee MOELLER d/o Carl William Moeller & Lorraine Trueblood nee
Marsh; b 07 Nov 1952; 1st m 14 Jul 1973 Donald Alfred Long (b 24 Jun
1952) DVD Dec 1983; 2nd m 27 Dec 1987 Dalmer Porter Sercy. Columbia
SC residence.

Julie Kay MOELLER d/o Wilfred Walter (Billy) Moeller & Alice Verna
nee Traetow; b 14 Aug 1950 Bremer Co IA; m 17 Jun 1972 Grace Luth Ch
DeWitt, IA to Mitchell Krukow (b 06 Feb 1943). Children:
 Cory Jon Krukow – b 14 Jan 1976 Clinton Co IA
 Ryan Mitchell Krukow – b 26 Oct 1977 Clinton Co IA
 Kellie Jane Krukow – b 24 May 1982 Clinton Co IA

Katherine MOELLER d/o Johannes Adam Moeller SR. & Anna Elisabeth
nee Michel; b 01 Apr 1889; m 13 Sept 1911 Chris Lutjen (b 14 Apr 1888, d
28 May 1965). 4 Children, 8 Grandchildren:
 Elsie Lutjen – NFR
 Irene Lutjen – NFR

LaVerne Lutjen – NFR

Infant – dec'd

*Konrad MOLLER s/o Balthasar Möller & Anna Elisabeth nee Jager; b 16 Jul 1836 Löhlbach, Germany, d 03 Mar 1916 ae79y 7m 15d Löhlbach, Germany; m 01 Apr 1860 Anna Elisabeth Schmidt (b 10 May 1835 Löhlbach, Germany, d 21 Apr 1891 ae56y 11m 11d Löhlbach, Germany) d/o Johannes Schmidt & Anna Magdalina Leininger. Child:

    *Karoline – b 13 Mar 1872; 1st m NN Dippel;

        2nd m 20 Apr 1912 wid/er Paulus Hohl

Larry Lee MOELLER s/o Virgil Dale Moeller & Evelyn nee Zander; b 05 Aug 1944; m 31 May 1964 Elinor Eileen Stumme (b 01 Feb 1944). Children:

    Rhonda Sue – b 23 Mar 1965; 22 Aug 1987 Richard Gilbert

    Brian Lee – b 22 May 1966; m 07 Mar 1992 Marcie Williams

    Roxanne Kay – b 19 Feb 1969

    Becki Lyn – b 06 Mar 1970

    Deann Lea – b 26 Jun 1973

Lawrence MOELLER m Joanne Wiebold (b 1945) d/o Erwin Wiebold & Louise nee Warner. Children:

    Michael – b 1964; m Michelle Rowan

    Daniel Martin – b 1967; m Denise M. Lachenmaier. Child:

        Evan Martin Moeller (b 1997)

Lawrence "Larry" Martin MOELLER s/o Elmer Martin Moeller & Alice Margaret nee Mumma; b 06 May 1942 Atkins, IA; m 09 Jun 1963 St.John to Joanne Ruth Wiebold(b 18 Feb 1945) d/o Erwin Wiebold & Louise nee Warner. Farmed Elmer Moeller land. Children:

    Michael James – b 03 Mar 1964 Vinton, IA;

        m 17 Jun 1991 Cedar Rapids Michelle Marie Rowan

    Daniel Martin – b 15 Aug 1967 Vinton, IA;

        m 08 Jun 1991 St.John Denise Lachenmier

Loren George MOELLER s/o George Adam Fritz Moeller & Myrtle Irene nee Alden; b 02 Jun 1930; m Mabel Frances Strutz (b 21 May 1930). Children:

    Wendell Loren – b 08 Sept 1954; m Diane Sansgaard (b 02 Jun 1955).

        Children: Chad Wendell (b 13 Nov 1975),

Kristin Michelle (b 25 Mar 1981)
Kendall Jay – b 09 Jan 1957; m Robin Ross (b 31 Dec 1956).
  Children: Kira Jo (b 25 Jul 1981), Landon Jay (b 14 Dec 1985)
Pattilee Renae – b 18 Aug 1959; 1st m Doug Hocking;
  2nd m Mitch Frei (b 23 Feb 1959)
Danelle Frances – b 14 May 1964; m Jeffery Allen McBirnie

Loren Lee MOELLER s/o Bernard Fred Moeller & Hulda Sophia nee Boderman; b 23 Nov 1928; m 24 Oct 1954 Lois Elaine Blasberg (b 11 Sept 1935). Children:
  Mark Lynn – b 07 Nov 1955; m 26 Jul 1980 Terri Nuss
  Timothy Loren – b 20 Jul 1957; m 25 Oct 1980 Karla Kueker
  Gail Sue – b 30 Dec 1960
  Nathan Lee – b 13 Oct 1965

Louis MOELLER s/o George Moeller & Elvira nee Schultz: cf Betty Jean Kaestner

Louise Caroline Marie MOELLER d/o Johannes Adam Moeller SR. & Elisabeth nee Michel; b 02 Feb 1885 Fremont Twp Farm Benton Co IA d 12 Nov 1973 ae88y 9m 10d, bur 15 Nov 1973 Linwood Park Cem Boone, IA; m 28 Apr 1909 to Christopher Dietrich Graubau (b 09 Jan 1881 Boone, IA, d 23 Nov 1948 ae67y 10m 19d Boone, IA bur 26 Nov 1948 Linwood Park Cem Boone, IA) s/o Henry Claus Grabau & Minna nee Dehn. 5 Children & 5 Grandchildren:
  Leonard Henry Adam Graubau – b 07 Feb 1910 Boone, IA;
    d 18 Feb 1987 Cedar Rapids, IA; m 06 Jun 1934 Ora Lee Noland
  Mildred Anne Minnie Graubau – b 16 Oct 1913 Boone, IA;
    m 14 Jul 1938 Eugene Koppenhaver
  Harold Walter Adam Graubau – b 10 Sept 1916 Boone, IA;
    m 10 Jun 1942 Arlene Silvey
  Elizabeth Louise Graubau – b 25 Jan 1918 Boone, IA;
    m 15 Jul 1942 Vernon Wickstrom
  Christopher Graubau JR. – b 28 Nov 1924 Boone, IA;
    m 09 Jun 1944 Gretchen Marie Price

Louise Elizabeth Salome MOELLER d/o Andreas Heinrich Möller (Henry Moeller) & Maria (Marie) nee Gerber; b 17 Jun 1884 Atkins, Benton Co IA; bpt 29 1884 St.Steph Sponsors: Louise Gerhold, Elizabeth Moeller, Salome Kreutner, d 08 Jul 1966 ae82y 22d Waterloo, Black Hawk Co; m 02 Jun

1904 Schuette Home, Crane Creek, Black Hawk Co IA to Heinrich (Henry) J. Schuette (b 25 Apr 1891, d 23 May 1964 ae73y 28d).

Louise Kristine MOLLER d/o Johannes Georg Möller (George Moeller) & Karoline nee Bornscheuer: cf Henry Gerhold SR.

Louise Maria MOELLER d/o Johann Daniel Moeller aka John Moeller & Anna Elizabeth nee Krug; b 18 Sept 1872; m NN Guttenfelder. Children:
    Bertha Guttenfelder – NFR
    Martha – Guttenfelder – NFR

Lucille MOELLER d/o Daniel Heinrich Martin aka Henry Moeller & Martha nee Poock; b 08 Aug 1918; m Edgar Muller (b 24 Apr 1916). Children:
    Donald Muller – b Sept 1942; m Sept 1967 Sue Meyer
    Carole Muller – b 31 Dec 19; m Erlisrv Ehling

Maria (Marie) Elisabeth MOELLER d/o Johannes Möller & Maria Katharina nee Stremme: cf Andreas (Andrew) Happel.

Marie Elizabeth MOELLER d/o Peter George Moeller & Anna Marie nee Rinderknecht; b 10 Jul 1914 Benton Co IA; m 05 Aug 1935 Spencer, IA to Kenneth Gerald Skersick (b 11 Apr 1914 Retired Violinist). Paradise CA residence; Children:
    David Peter Skersick – b 02 Oct 1938; m 08 Oct 1976 Sara Post
    Richard Kenneth Skersick – b 25 Jul 1943;
        1st m 24 Dec 1970 Christe Cameron Smith, DVD;
        2nd m 10 Aug 1981 Pamela Wurzbacher

Marilyn Jean MOELLER d/o Walter Wilhelm Moeller & Martha Johanna nee Sundermeyer; b 09 Jan 1932 con 02 Apr 1944 Immanuel Luth Ch Waterloo; m 19 Feb 1950 Forrest William Droster (b 07 Feb 1929). Children:
    Sandy Droster – b 03 May 1951; m 24 Feb 1979 Gary Lee Patrick
    Mark Allen Droster – b 03 May 1954; m 30 Sept 1977 Jill Epping
    Dianne Marie Droster – b 13 Jun 1960

Mark Lynn MOELLER s/o Loren Lee Moeller & Lois Elaine nee Blasberg; b 07 Nov 1955; m 26 Jul 1980 Terri Nuss (b 13 Aug 1955). Child:
    Lisa Lyn – b 29 Oct 1981

Martin Adam MOELLER aka Andrew Martin Moeller (cf St.Steph Ch records) s/o Andreas Heinrich Möller (Henry Moeller) & Maria (Marie) nee Gerber; b 15 Jan 1891 Benton Co IA, bpt 15 Feb 1891 St.Steph Sponsors: Andrew Moeller, Martin Gerber, Martin Kreutner, con 1905 Immanuel Luth Ch Klinger, Bremer Co IA, d 20 Nov 1981 ae90y 10m 5d; 1st m 02 Mar 1915 Marie Cecelia Clabby.
2nd m Martin Adam Moeller aka Andrew Martin Moeller to Juanita Shimp.

Mary Ann MOELLER d/o George Adam Fritz Moeller & Myrtle Irene Alden; b 15 Feb 1938; 1st m Richard Smith. Children:
  Lorri Sue Smith – b 21 Dec 1958; 1st m John Gill;
      2nd m Douglas Chance
  Kimberly Suzanne Smith – b 10 Mar 1960; m Jeff Goethals
      (b 01 Apr 1956)
  Natalie Ann Smith – b 25 Dec 1961;
      m Forrest Stevens (b 08 Aug 1959). Child: Tanner Adam Stevens
      (b 27 Jul 1987)
2nd m Mary Ann Moeller to Gary Robert Granzberg (b 26 Feb 1940). Children:
  Milinda Bess Granzberg – b 27 Apr 1970
  Angela Sophia Granzberg – b 04 May 1972

Mary Jon MOELLER d/o Elmer Martin Moeller & Alice Margaret nee Mumma; b 15 Feb 1941 Cedar Rapids; retired Home Economics Teacher; m 21 Jun 1980 Great Falls, MT to William Clifton Gernaat (b 12 Jan 1943; Rancher, retired Industrial Arts Teacher). Great Falls, MT residence.
  STEPCHILDREN:
  Michele Ann Gernaat – b 13 Oct 1968;
      m 17 Jun 1989 Rev. Larry Goyette, MT
  Laurice Diane Gernaat – b 24 Mar 1971;
      m 12 Jun 1992 George Clayton, DVD

Mathilda MOELLER d/o John Adam Moeller & Anna Elisabeth nee Michel; b 15 Mar 1898; m 20 Dec 1922 to Julius Ehman (b 17 May 1902). Children:
  Richard Ehman – NFR
  Curtis Ehman – NFR

Merle Richard MOELLER s/o George Adam Fritz Moeller & Myrtle Irene

nee Alden; b 15 Feb 1932; m Carol Sue Bricker (b 17 Jan 1936). Children:
Kevin Lee – b 01 Oct 1958; m Melinda Ann Rosdal (b 02 Oct 1959).
Children: Samantha Jo (b 03 Apr 1983),
Sabrina Nicole (b 30 Aug 1986)
Kurtis Merle – b 02 Jun 1961;
m Roxann Rae nee Johnson Abraham (b 1967)
Jon Todd – 04 May 1966
Tamara Jo – b 12 Mar 1975

Peter George MOELLER s/o Johannes Georg Moeller & Wilhelmina nee Krug; b 06 Dec 1870 Farm Fremont Twp Benton Co IA, d 14 Oct 1949 ae78y 10m 8d Benton Co IA bur St.Steph Cem; m 17 Jan 1895 St.Steph to Anna Maria Katharina (Annie) Rinderknecht (b 29 Nov 1874 Benton Co IA, con 1888, d 11 Oct 1947 ae72y 10m 12d bur St.Steph Cem) d/o William Rinderknecht & Mary nee Happel. Farmers northwest of Atkins until 1940 retirement in Atkins, IA. Seven children:
Emma Anna Marie – b 18 Oct 1895 Newhall, IA d 06 Jun 1982
Vinton, IA; m 11 Feb 1923 Louis Frederick Fix
Rose Marie – b 03 May 1898 Newhall, IA d 31 May 1999
ae101y 28d Minneapolis, MN;
m 15 Dec 1921 Elmer Henry Werning
Edna Elizabeth – b 10 Apr 1903 Benton Co IA; d 11 Aug 1976;
Cedar Rapids, IA; m 11 Sept 1926 Carl Julius Hauskins
Hilda Catherine – b 15 Dec 1908 Benton Co IA;
m 23 Oct 1942 William Fred Ploetz
Elmer Martin – b 22 May 1911 Atkins, IA; d 28 Aug 2004
Harlingen, TX; 1st m 25 Mar 1940 Alice Margaret Mumma,
d 10 Aug 1995; 2nd m 16 Mar 1996 Leone Marie Blake
Marie Elizabeth- b 10 Jul 1914 Benton Co IA;
m 05 Aug 1935 Kenneth Gerald Skersick
Carl William – b 07 Feb 1917 Benton Co IA d 04 Feb 1988
Greenwood SC; m 16 Mar 1947 Lorraine Trueblood Marsh

Peter George MOELLER II s/o Elmer Martin Moeller & Alice Margaret nee Mumma; b 17 Jul 1944 Newhall, IA; USAF Captain; m 27 Dec 1966 St.John to Janice Elaine Bracher(b 06 Jul 1943 Coffeyville, KS; Teacher) d/o Martin & Dorothy Bracher of Coffeyville, KS. Children:
Eric Lee – b 22 Nov 1968; US Air Force
Jeffrey Scott – b 04 Aug 1973; 1995 Grad. Calif. Luth College

Ricky Allen MOELLER s/o Wilfred Walter (Billy) Moeller & Alice Verna nee Traetow; b 18 Feb 1952 Bremer Co IA; m 12 Aug 1978 Gl. Christie Luth Ch Greeley, CO to Dianne Marie Schram (b 12 Jun 1949 Toledo, OH). Child:
Eiron Marie – b 11 Sept 1980
Dianne Marie Schram's child from former marriage:
Dustin Bengtson – b 26 Dec 1970

Robert Wayne MOELLER s/o Bernard Fred Moeller & Hulda Sophia nee Boderman; b 10 Apr 1925; m 10 Jan 1957 Mary Ellen Berlin (b 24 Dec 1940). Children:
Steven Wayne – b 24 Apr 1957; m 1992 Tami Benham
Max Marvin – b 15 Jan 1960
Gary Dean – b 30 Mar 1962; m 07 Feb 1980 Kathy Jane Liddle

Rose Marie MOELLER d/o Peter George Moeller & Anna Marie nee Rinderknecht: cf Elmer Henry Werning.

Steven Carl MOELLER s/o Carl William Moeller & Lorraine Trueblood nee Marsh; b 05 Jul 1950; Millwright; m 28 May 1972 Patsy Joyce Yochem (b Sept 1952) DVD 04 Feb 1988. Greenwood, SC residence. Children:
Marcus Carl – b 02 Feb 1977
Kristen Joyce – b 30 Dec 1981

Steven Wayne MOELLER s/o Robert Wayne Moeller & Kathy Jane nee Liddle; b 24 Apr 1957; m 1992 Tami Benhem. Child:
Collin – b 18 May 1992
STEPCHILDREN:
Ashlea Benham NFR
Seph Benham NFR

Thomas Elmer MOELLER s/o Elmer Martin Moeller & Alice Margaret nee Mumma; b 28 Mar 1950 Cedar Rapids, IA; 1st m 14 Aug 1971 St.John to Joyce Shirley Werning (b 13 May 1952 Cedar Rapids, d 28 Mar 1983 ae30y 10m 15d [Auto Accident west of Shellsburg, Benton Co IA], bur St.John Cem; Master's Degree U.of IA; part-time Pyschology Instructor Kirkwood Community College, Cedar Rapids, & U.of IA) d/o Delbert Anton Werning & Lusann Florence Garnet nee Zobel; Peter George Moeller farm residence. Children:
TWINS: Christopher Martin – b 02 Apr 1975 Cedar Rapids, IA

Aaron Thomas – b 02 Apr 1975 Cedar Rapids, IA
Samantha Werning – b & d 28 Mar 1983
[Auto Accident killing her mother & grandmother]
2nd m 05 Jun 1993 in Newhall Thomas Elmer Moeller to Connie Kay nee Peters Mango (b 28 Nov 1951) d/o Victor & LaDonna Peters of Readlyn, IA DVD.
3rd m 24 Jul 2001 in Hawaii Thomas Elmer Moeller to Dr.Ksenia Nosikova, University of Iowa Professor. Child:
Katya Tatyana Alice Moeller – b 02 May 2004 U of IA Hosp

Velma MOELLER d/o Daniel Heinrich Martin aka Henry Moeller & Martha nee Poock; b 24 May 1914, m 21 Jun 1936 Loraine James aka Joe Magee (b 28 Aug 1915, d 29 Jun 1982). Children:
Jeanette – b 28 Feb 1937; m Rev. Donald Moll
James Henry – b 02 May 1938; m 1959 Kathy Muller
David Joe – b 29 Oct 1939; m 1972 Lesa Lochard
Daryl Dean – b 21 Sept 1941; m 1962 Jody Kirckpatrick
Keith Charles – b 05 Feb 1946; m 1969 Jean Linder
Mary Jane – b 21 Jun 1948; m 1967 Sam Weidman

Virgil Dale MOELLER s/o Bernard Fred Moeller & Hulda Sophia nee Boderman; b 27 Apr 1923; m 28 Nov 1943 Evelyn Zander (b 02 Mar 1925). Children:
Larry Lee – b 05 August 1944; m 31 May 1964 Elinor Eileen Stumme
Bonnie Kaye – b 31 August 1945; m 18 Sept 1966 Charles Steege

Walter Wilhelm MOELLER s/o Andreas Heinrich Möller aka Henry Moeller & Maria nee Gerber; b 08 Nov 1895 Black Hawk Co IA; con 1909 Immanuel Luth Ch Klinger, d 26 May 1985 ae89y 6m 18d Cedar Falls, Black Hawk Co IA bur 29 May 1985 Garden of Mem, Waterloo, IA; m 20 Feb 1917 Immanuel Luth Ch Klinger, Bremer Co IA to Martha Johanna Sundermeyer (b 05 Apr 1894 Peosta, IA, d 16 Sept 1985 ae91y 5m 11d Waterloo, Black Hawk Co IA, bur 20 Sept 1985 Garden of Mem. Waterloo, IA). Children:
Gladys E. – b 29 Dec 1917; 1st m 30 Jun 1936 Gerald Wingert DVD;
2nd m 27 Jun 1954 Harry Frank Miller DVD;
3rd m 26 Aug 1971 Elmer L. Shuldt
Wilfred Walter (Billy) – b 27 May 1924; m Alice Verna Traetow
Marilyn Jean – b 09 Jan 1932; m 1950 Forest William Droster

Wilfred Walter (Billy) MOELLER s/o Walter Wilhelm Moeller & Martha Johann nee Sundermeyer; b 27 May 1924 Black Hawk Co IA; m 30 May 1946 St.John Luth Ch, Waverly, IA to Alice Verna Traetow (b 22 Oct 1925). Children:

    Julie Kay – b 14 Aug 1950; m 1972 Mitchell Krukow

    Ricky Allen – b 18 Feb 1952; m 1978 Dianne Marie Schram

    TWINS: Joel Dean – b 28 Nov 1955; m 1975 Maureen Ann Burke

            Jane Ann – b 28 Nov 1955; m 1983 Michael Robert Buege

Dianne Caye MOHR d/o Werner Frederick Mohr & Pauline A. C. nee Hermann; b 27 Sept 1947; 1st m 22 Jan 1966 William Jon Fleck (b 25 Jan 1946). Children:

    Paula Rae Fleck – b 02 Jul 1966; m 21 Jul 1990 Joseph Gourley

    Trent Jon Fleck – b 22 Jun 1971

2nd m 16 Jun 1978 Dianne Caye nee Mohr fleck to Charles Arthur Rager (b 07 May 1939).

Henry Gustav MOHR s/o Heinrika Louise nee Haerther & Jacob Mohr; b 14 Aug 1892, d 31 Jul 1952 ae59y 11m 14d bur Evergreen Cem Vinton, IA; m 12 Feb 1918 Anna Katherine Kokemiller (b 20 Jun 1892, d 26 Aug 1976 ae84y 2m 6d, bur Evergreen Cem, Vinton, IA). Children:

    Werner Fredrick – b 07 Jan 1919, d 03 Nov 1973;

        m 26 Jun 1941 Pauline A.C.Hermann

    Verla Anna – b 11 Nov 1922; m 20 Jun 1947 Andrew C.Schnack II

Louise Marie MOHR d/o Heinrika Louise nee Haerther & Jacob Mohr; b 19 Aug 1890, d 28 Jul 1981 ae90y 11m 9d bur Fullerton, CA; m 24 Nov 1919 William Griswold Gough (b 04 May 1896, d 04 Aug 1981 ea85y 3m bur Fullerton, CA). Children:

    Elsie Louise Gough – b 18 Oct 1920;

        m 26 Jan 1953 Derk Newell Gysbers

    Dorothy Griswold Gough – b 01 Sept 1922;

        m 21 Mar 1948 Brian Earl Bigley

    William Griswold Gough – b 02 Jul 1924, d 20 Jan 1945

        Belgium World War II

Sherry Lyn MOHR d/o Werner Frederick Mohr & Pauline A. C. nee Hermann; b 08 Oct 1944; m 14 Nov 1964 Paul Michael Elliott (b 17 May 1945). Children:

    Kent Anthony Elliott – b 25 May 1965

Timothy Mark Elliott – b 20 Aug 1968
Amy Michelle Elliott – b 01 Jul 1971

Verla Anna MOHR d/o Henry Gustav Mohr & Anna Katherine nee
Kokemiller; b 11 Nov 1922; m 20 Jun 1947 Andrew C. Schnack II
(b 13 Jun 1923). Children:
  Andrew C. Schnack III – b 22 Feb 1949; 1ˢᵗ m 31 Jul 1971 Jane Oerly;
     2ⁿᵈ m 30 Oct 1982 Bonnie Huffman
  Cathryn Ann Schnack – b 30 Aug 1951; m 06 Jun 1981 Fred Guerrero

Werner Frederick MOHR s/o Henry Gustav Mohr & Anna Katherine nee
Kokemiller; b 07 Jan 1919, d 03 Nov 1973; m 26 Jun 1941 Pauline A.C.
Hermann (b 30 Mar 1920). Children:
  Sherry Lyn – b 08 Oct 1944; m 14 Nov 1964 Paul Michael Elliott
  Dianne Caye – b 27 Sept 1947; 1ˢᵗ m 22 Jan 1966 William Jon Fleck;
     2ⁿᵈ m 16 Jun 1978 Charles Arthur Rager

Peter MOLUS b 1657 Germany, d 28 Jul 1727; m 01 Sept 1691 Löhlbach
Ch to Maria Elisabeth Schafer (b 19 May 1701 Germany). Child:
  Anna Catherina – b 03 Apr 1698 Löhlbach, Germany d 26 Apr 1734
     Löhlbach, Germany;
     m 02 Dec 1723 Löhlbach Ch to Johannes Nicolaus Möller

Carole MULLER d/o Lucille nee Moeller & Edgar Muller; b 31 Dec 1944;
m Erlisrv Ehling. Children:
  Judy Ehling – NFR
  Stephanie Ehling – NFR

Donald MULLER s/o Lucille nee Moeller & Edgar Muller; b 11 Sept 1942;
m Sept 1967 Sue Meyer (b Sept 1944). Children:
  Sandy – NFR
  Debra – NFR
  Gregg – NFR

*Marx NAEVE b 1852 Germany; m Johanna Kay (b 1864, d 1893).
Maintained store two miles north and two miles west of Newhall, IA;
moved to Newhall, operated Newhall's first general store when railroad
went through town. After Newhall fire wiped out main street, Marx moved
to New Glarus, WI. Children:
  Anna – b 1886; m Henry Martin, moved to Bryant, SD

Ella – b 1890; m Art Schuett, moved to New Glarus, WI

Connie Lou NEAL d/o William Raymond Neal SR. & Evelyn Leta nee Krug; b 22 Feb 1959 Cedar Rapids, IA bpt 25 Mar 1959 Holy Redeemer Luth Ch, Cedar Rapids, IA; m 21 May 1983 Holy Redeemer Luth Ch, Cedar Rapids to John Ray Caviness (b 12 Apr 1958). Children:
 Jordan Neal Caviness – b 01 May 1987 Cedar Rapids, IA
 Brent James Caviness – b 03 Mar 1989 Cedar Rapids, IA

William "Bill" Raymond NEAL JR. s/o William Raymond Neal SR. & Evelyn Leta nee Krug; b 14 Mar 1950 Mercy Hosp Cedar Rapids, IA bpt 1950; m 03 Jun 1972 Sheryl Dianne Elliot (b 07 Jan 1951). Bill teacher and coach at Williamsburg, also their residence. Children:
 Amy Marie – b 01 Nov 1978
 Beth Ann – b 22 Feb 1983

Betty NESS d/o Leona Barbara Anna nee Schlotterbeck & Wallace Richard Ness; b 1939; m Richard Novotney. Children:
 Becky Novotney – NFR
 Mark Novotney – NFR
 Michael Novotney – NFR
 Scott Novotney – NFR

Ronald W. NESS s/o Leona Barbara Anna nee Schlotterbeck & Wallace Richard Ness; b 09 Dec 1939 Atkins, IA d 10 Sept 2002 St.Lukes Hosp Cedar Rapids, IA; employed Rockwell Collins 37 years, retired 1995. mbr St.Paul's Luth Ch, Marion, IA 1st m Joyce Lange. DVD. Children:
 Steven – Marion, IA residence
 Douglas – m Shelly; children: Ashley and Lauren
 Renee – m James Stribling; children: James and Justin
2nd m 10 Jun 1989 Little Brown Church Nashua, IA Ronald W. Ness to Carol Brown.

Kevin NOLAN s/o Faye nee Franzenburg & William Nolan; m Andrea Stueck. Child:
 Danniell – NFR

Michelle NOLAN d/o Faye nee Franzenburg & William Nolan; m Keith Hartkemeyer. Blairstown, Benton Co IA residence. Children:
 Brandon Hartkemeyer – NFR

Tiffany Hartkemeyer – NFR
Emily Hartkemeyer – NFR

Christine Ann O'CONNOR d/o Beverlyn Kay nee Krug & James M. O'Connor; b 22 Aug 1973; 1995 Valparaiso University; Dr. of Medicine 1999 Northwestern University; m 01 Sept 2002 Chad Eric Bonhomme (b 27 Jan 1973) s/o William L. & Judy Bonhomme. Child:
Reece O'Connor Bonhomme – b 18 Sept 2006

Rebecca Lynn O'CONNOR d/o Beverlyn Kay nee Krug & James M. O'Connor; b 24 Jun 1976; B.A. 1998 Magna Cum Laude Valparaiso University; m 29 Jun 2002 Gregory John Sandman (b 02 Jan 1973) s/o Jack & Judy Sandman. Children:
Connor Gregory Sandman – b 29 Jul 2004
Greta Louise Sandman – b 20 Jun 2006

Anerea Leigh OBERMUELLER d/o Donald Lee Obermueller & Juanita nee Thompson; b 18 Jun 1979; m 14 Feb 2001 Bryon Klostermann. Children:
Jaxon James Klostermann – b 17 Jul 1999
Brylee Ann Klostermann – b 07 Dec 2001
Kale David Klostermann – b 21 Aug 2003

Donald Lee OBERMUELLER s/o Anna Margaret nee Gieken & Fredrick Waldo Obermueller; b 06 Jun 1952; m 24 Jun 1972 Juanita Thompson (b 28 May 1954). Children:
Wesley Mitchell – b 22 Dec 1976;
m 11 Nov 2000 Jodie Jeanne Franck
Anerea Leigh – b 18 Jun 1979; m 14 Feb 2001 Bryon Klostermann
Alana Rae – b 22 Dec 1982

Wesley Mitchell OBERMUELLER s/o Donald Lee Obermueller & Juanita nee Thompson; b 22 Dec 1976; m 11 Nov 2000 Jodie Jeanne Franck (b 15 May 1977). Children:
Cade Mitchell – b 28 Jul 2003
Drake Wesley – b 01 May 2007

Harry W. OEHLERICH s/o Claus Oehlerich & Anna nee Popp, Schleswig-Holstein, Germany; b Homer Twp northwest of Keystone; farm laborer; Civilian Conservation Corps; US Army World War II 1942-1945; m 1951

Lucille Rieck d/o Henry Rieck & Emma nee Kluss from Luzerne, Iowa Twp Benton Co IA. Members St.John, Keystone, IA. Children:

Judith – Cedar Rapids, IA residence

Jay – m 1975 Joyce Ripperton, Walford, IA residence

Kim Denise OEHLERICH d/o Ruth Ilma nee Schminke & Darwin Ray Oehlerich; b 22 Jul 1960 Virginia Gay Hosp Vinton, IA; Graduate Benton Community; U.N.I. Teacher; m 26 Nov 1983 St.John Luth Ch Keystone, Benton Co to Michael Ray Mollenhauer (b 02 Apr 1961 Vinton; Graduate Benton Community; Central College, Pella IA) s/o Marvin Ray Mollenhauer & Lila Marie nee Ferguson. Children:

Abby Marie Mollenhauer – b 18 Oct 1986 Forest City, IA

Jenna Rae Mollenhauer – b 16 Oct 1989 Mason City, IA

*Henry OHLEN b 1849 Germany, d 1944 Benton Co. IA; m 1881 to Christine Abraham (b 1860 Germany, d 1941 Newhall, IA). Farmers in Eldorado Twp Benton Co IA until 1914 retirement in Newhall, IA. Children:

August – b 1882, d 1958; m Mae Hauser; Benton Co IA farmers

Henry F. – b 1883, d 1961; m Anna Thode; Benton Co IA farmers

Dora – b 1885, d 1953; m George Warnke; Scranton, ND & IA
    farmers

Herman OHRT s/o John Ohrt & Rosa nee Ballheim; b 13 Nov 1893 LaPorte City, IA, d 1960 [Hodgkin's Disease] bur Westview Cem, LaPorte City; m 26 Dec 1916 LaPorte City, IA to Leta Mae Wright (b 1897 Nora Springs, IA, d 26 Dec 1974 bur Westview Cem, LaPorte City) d/o Lewis N. Wright & Emma R. nee Watts. Farmers LaPorte City, IA, Mt. Auburn, IA, Vinton, IA. Children:

Harold L. – b 1918

Margaret – b 1919, d 1987

Donald L. – b 1921

Robert Herman – b 27 May 1922; m 1949 Kathryn Jean Welton

Zelda M. – b 1925

Ruth M. – b 1938

*Johann OHRT b Germany; farmer and harness maker, d Germany; m Margaretha Delfs (b 1834 Germany, d 1902 Benton Co IA bur Greenwalt Cem, Mt.Auburn, IA). After Johann's death Margaretha and children emigrated to Iowa. Children:

*John – b 1862, d 1951; m 22 Sept 1887 Rosa Ballheim

Anna – NFR

Henry – NFR

2nd m 1872 Vinton, IA Margaretha nee Delfs Ohrt to Frederick Wandschneider (b 1832 MacKlenburg, Germany, d 1892 Mt.Auburn, IA [Stomach Cancer] bur Greenwalt Cem, Mt.Auburn, IA). Frederick emigrated 1852 to Rock Island, IL; fought in major Civil War battles; 1866 moved to Iowa; Benton Co IA farmers. Children:

Otto Wandschneider – b 1873, d 1936

Charles Wandschneider – b 1875, d 1933

Mary Wandschneider – b 1876, d 1958

*John OHRT s/o Johann Ohrt & Margaretha nee Delfs; b 1862 Schleswig-Holstein, Germany, d 1951 Benton Co IA bur Westview Cem, LaPorte City, IA; emigrated ae10y with widowed mother and siblings to Mt.Auburn, Benton Co IA; naturalized 06 Oct 1884 (cf Benton Co Courthouse Recorder's Office Naturalization Records); m 22 Sept 1887 Rosa Ballheim (b 1862 Menomonee Falls, WI, d 1958 bur Westview Cem, LaPorte City, IA) d/o Michael & Anna Ballheim (1885 IA immigrants). Farmers near LaPorte City in Black Hawk Co IA & Benton Co IA retiring in 1919. Children:

Albert J. – b 1888, d 1974

Kuno – b 1890, d 1968

Herman – b 13 Nov 1893, d 1960; m 26 Dec 1916 Leta Mae Wright

Louis H. – b 1896

Theodore R. – b 1902

Rickie Duane OHRT s/o Robert Herman Ohrt & Kathryn Jean nee Welton; b 1953; m Penny M. Cumberlin. Child:

Jama Marie – b 1983

Robert Herman OHRT s/o Herman Ohrt & Leta Mae nee Wright; b 27 May 1922 Mt. Auburn, IA; m 1949 Dallas, TX, to Kathryn Jean Welton (b 1929 Mt. Auburn, IA) d/o Ernest C Welton & Stells M. Schnoor. Farmed retiring 1982. DVD 1972. Children:

Betty Jo – Stillborn 1950

Cheryl Rae – b 1951; m Randy L. Smith

Rickie Duane – b 1953; m Penney M.Cumberlin

Donita Sue – b 1954

Roger Lynn – b 1956; m Lori J.Stellmach

Roger Lynn OHRT s/o Robert Herman Ohrt & Kathryn Jean nee Welton; b 1956; m Lori J. Stellmach. Child:
Tana Joyce – b 1979

Lee Richard OVERTON s/o Milford Overton & Marjorie Ruth nee Worthington; b 1938; m 1957 Marlene Ann Fennern (b 1937) d/o August Henry Fennern & Josephine nee Pauley. Children:
Mark Lee – b 1958; m 1984 Kathryn Ann Steiner
Diane Marlene – b 1960; m 1984 Jeffrey John Hanft
Ann Marlene – b 1961
Mary Marlene – b 1964

Mark Lee OVERTON s/o Lee Richard Overton & Marlene Ann nee Fennern; b 1958, m 1984 Kathryn Ann Steiner d/o David Steiner & Marilyn nee Obermeyer. Cedar Rapids, IA residence. Children:
Jamie Kathryn – b 1985
Robert Mark – b 1986

Diane Marlene OVERTON d/o Lee Richard Overton & Marlene Ann nee Fennern; b 1960, m 1984 Jeffrey John Hanft (b 1956) s/o John R. Hanft & Dorothy Mae nee Beckman. Cedar Rapids, IA residence. Children:
Matthew John Hanft – b 1979
Elizabeth Marie Hanft – b 1985

*Adolf Heinrich PAAR s/o Georg Heinrich Paar & Karoline Gertrud nee Damm; b 15 Apr 1876, Germany d 01 Jan 1955 ae79y 8m 17d; 1st m 03 Oct 1899 Karoline Garthe (b 07 Nov 1871 Ellenhausen, Germany, d 30 Jan 1904 ae92y 2m 23d. Parents of:
*Heinrich Paar I – b 08 Oct 1901, d 17 Jul 1967;
m 09 Jan 1925 Elisabeth Thielemann

*Anna Elisabeth PAAR d/o Johannes Paar II and 2nd m Anna Kunigunde nee Fackiner; b 26 Mar 1857 Löhlbach, Germany, Hse #10, bpt & con Löhlbach Ch; d 23 Mar 1941 ae84y 11m 25d Löhlbach, Germany Hse #106; m 20 Feb 1887 Johann Wilhelm Gross (b 27 Nov 1855 Löhlbach, Germany, Hse #07, d 30 Nov 1931 ae76y 3d Löhlbach, Germany, Hse #106. Children:
*Anna Dorothea Gross – b 12 Jul 1887, d 27 Jul 1956;
m Heinrich Ritter, bricklayer

*Maria Gross – b 24 Jan 1890 Löhlbach, Germany Hse #106,
    d 31 Aug 1961 Löhlbach, Germany, Hse #33;
    m 13 Nov 1914 Löhlbach Ch Johann Peter Beyer
    (Marlene Wickert Bohle's grandparents)
Helene Gross – NFR
Georg Gross – NFR

*Anna Gertrud PAAR d/o Johannes Paar & Anna Elisabeth Schellberg, Löhlbach, Germany; b 07 Apr 1815, d 16 Aug 1886 ae71y 4m 9d; m 26 Dec 1836 Justus Vaupel (b 04 Sept 1809, d 05 Apr 1886 ae76y 7m 1d). Children:
    *Katharina Vaupel – b 18 Oct 1837, d 27 Apr 1907;
    m 28 May 1860 Justus Thielemann

*Georg Heinrich PAAR s/o Johannes Paar II & Anna Kunigunde Fackiner; b 20 May 1849 Löhlbach, Germany, Hse #10, d 09 Dec 1926 ae77y 6m 19d Löhlbach, Germany, Hse #10; m 26 Dec 1872 Karoline Gertrud Damm (b 20 Jan 1850 Löhlbach, Germany, Hse #57, d 01 Apr 1897 ae37y 2m 12d Löhlbach, Germany, Hse #10). Nine Children:
    Johann Heinrich – b 22 Apr 1873, d 21 Oct 1873
    Anna Elisabeth Karoline – b 14 Mar 1874, d 08 Sept 1889
    Adolf Heinrich – b 15 Apr 1876; 1st m 12 Mar 1899 Karoline Garthe;
        2nd m 10 Mar 1905 Elisabeth Faust
    Johann Heinrich – b 21 Mar 1878, d 26 Apr 1887
    Johann Daniel – b 01 May 1880, con 1826
    Anna Dorothea – b 10 Oct 1881, d 07 Aug 1898
    Anna Gertrud – b 17 May 1887, d 03 May 1952
    *Jacob – b 26 Sept 1889, d 01 Jul 1980 Löhlbach, Germany, Hse
        #144; m 04 Apr 1919 Elisabeth Marie Wickert (b 30 Oct 1892,
        d 07 Oct 1963)
    Sophie Friedericke – b 20 Apr 1891, d 18 Nov 1893

Heinrich Paar I (b 08 Oct 1901 at Heinstrasse #10, Löhlbach, Germany, d 17 Jul 1967 ae65y 9m 9d; m 08 Jan 1925 Elisabeth Thielmann (b 18 Sept 1901, d 13 May 1986 ae84y 7m 25d). Child:
    Heinrich II – b 10 Mar 1925, d 15 Aug 1987;
    m 22/24 May 1953 Helene Wilhelmi

Heinrich PAAR II s/o Heinrich Paar I & Elisabeth nee Thielemann, Löhlbach, Germany; b 10 Mar 1925, d 15 Aug 1987; m 22/24 May 1953

Helene Wilhelmi (b 03 Feb 1926 Löhlbach, Germany) Children:
  **Marlene Martha – b 22 Oct 1953; m 8/9 Oct 1971 Roland Wickert
  **Herta Elfriede – b 24 Nov 1957;
    m 13/17 May 1980 Burkhard Tropper (b 04 May 1956)

*Johann Daniel PAAR of Löhlbach, Germany, Hse #10; s/o Johann Georg
Paar & Anna Katharina nee Schellberg b 18 Dec 1749 Allendorf, Germany,
d 12 Jun 1819 ae69y 5m 25d Löhlbach, Germany, Hse #10; 1st m 02 Aug
1774 Löhlbach Ch to Katharina Elisabeth Roder of Löhlbach (b 01 Mar
1750 Löhlbach, Germany, d 11 Nov 1808 ae58y 8m 10d Löhlbach,
Germany) d/o Johannes Roder & Anna Marie nee Menkel. Seven Children:
  *Johannes I – b 20 Oct 1789 Löhlbach, Germany Hse #10;
    d 04 Jan 1856 Löhlbach, Germany, Hse #10;
    1st m 31 Mar 1807 Löhlbach Ch Katharina Elisabeth Prachter
    (Author's Paar lineage)
2nd m 09 Sept 1814 Johann Daniel Paar to Anna Elisabeth Schellberg
(**Marlene Martha Paar Wickert & **Marlene Wickert Bohle's lineage)

*Johann Georg PAAR b 1790 Grusen, Germany; m 19 Oct 1811 Anna
Katharina nee Schellberg (b 14 Sept 1791 Löhlbach, Germany, d 02 Apr
1854 ae62y 6m 18d Grusen). Parents of:
  Johann Daniel Paar – b 18 Dec 1749 Allendorf, Germany
    d 12 Jun 1819 Löhlbach, Germany;
    m 02 Aug 1774 Katharina Elisabeth Roder

*Johannes PAAR I, Ackerman (farm hand) s/o Johann Daniel Paar &
Katharina Elisabeth nee Roder of Löhlbach, Germany, Hse #10; b 20 Oct
1789 Löhlbach Hse #10, d 04 Jan 1856 ae66y 2m 15d Löhlbach, Germany,
bur Löhlbach; 1st m 31 Mar 1807 Löhlbach Ch to Katharina Elisabeth
Prachter (b 08 Jan 1786 os Alt Heim ns Altenhaina, Germany, d 17 Feb
1814 ae28y 1m 9d Löhlbach, Germany) d/o Johann Peter Prachter of os Alt
Heim ns Altenhaina, Germany & Anna Katharina nee Ochse (b 06 Jan 1763
Halzenhausen, Germany). Children:
  Katharina Elisabeth – b 08 Jan 1808 Löhlbach, Germany;
    d 23 Aug 1869 Löhlbach, Germany
  Johann Peter – b 13 Aug 1809 Löhlbach, d 03 May 1832
  *Anna Elisabeth – b 16 Mar 1811 Löhlbach Hse #10,bpt 21 Mar 1811
  Löhlbach Ch Godmother: Elisabeth, sister of her mother
    (cf Page 61 Löhlbach Ch 1811 Baptism Record)
    d 06 Oct 1882 Krug Homestead Benton Co IA;
363

m 25 Dec 1833 Löhlbach Ch Johann Justus Krug III
(b 18 Nov 1805 Löhlbach, Germany, Hse #70,
d 1879 Krug Homestead Benton Co IA)
Andreas – b 09 Feb 1813 Löhlbach, Germany
2nd m 09 Sept 1814 Löhlbach Ch Johannes Paar I to Anna Elisabeth Schellberg (b 04 Jun 1787 Löhlbach, Germany, Hse #22, d 16 Oct 1841 ae54y 4m 12d Löhlbach, Germany, Hse #10). Children:
 Anna Gertrud – b 07 Apr 1815, d 16 Aug 1886; m 1836 Justus Vaupel
 Anna Katharina – b 12 Sept 1817 Löhlbach, Germany; d 06 Sept 1818
 Johannes II – b 11 Jul 1819, d 05 Jul 1872;
  m 13 Sept 1844 Anna Kunigunde Fackiner
  (Marlene Bohle's lineage)
 Tobias – b 28 Sept 1821 Löhlbach, Germany, con 1835
 Georg – b 29 Sept 1823 Löhlbach, Germany, con 1837
 Johann Heinrich – b 10 Jun 1826 Löhlbach, Germany, con 1840
 Johann Adolf – b 18 Apr 1829, con 1843

*Johannes PAAR II Ackermann (farm hand) s/o Johannes Paar I & Anna Elisabeth nee Schellberg; b 11 Jul 1819 Löhlbach, Germany Hse #10, d 05 Jul 1872 ae53y 11m 25d Löhlbach Hse #10; 1st m 13 Feb 1842 Katharina Elisabeth Paar (b 16 Mar 1815 Allendorf, Germany, d 20 Oct 1843 ae28y 7m 4d Löhlbach Hse #10). No Children.
2nd m 13 Sept 1844 Johannes Paar II to Anna Kunigrunde Fackiner
(b 09 Feb 1817 Sehlen, Germany, d 04 Nov 1869 ae52y 8m 26d Löhlbach Hse #10). Eight Children:
 Katharina Elisabeth – b 21 Aug 1845, d 31 Dec 1854
 Johann Justus – b 03 Feb 1847, d 31 Jan 1869
 Georg Heinrich – b 20 May 1849, d 09 Dec 1926;
  m 26 Dec 1872 Karoline Damm
 Anna Katharina – b 17 Apr 1852, d 11 Jun 1852
 NN – b 01 Apr 1853
 Adolf Heinrich – b 24 Jun 1854
 *Anna Elisabeth – b 26 Mar 1857, d 23 Mar 1941;
  m 20 Feb 1887 Wilhelm Gross;
  (Marlene Wickert Bohle's lineage)
 Anna Dorothea – b 13 Nov 1859, d 03 Jan 1927; m 22 Oct 1882 to
  Ludwig Kente (b 05 Oct 1860, d 17 Nov 1925)

**Marlene Martha PAAR d/o Heinrich Paar I & Helene nee Wilhelmi, Löhlbach, Germany; b 22 Oct 1953 Löhlbach, Germany, bpt 06 Dec 1953 con Löhlbach Ch; m 08/09 Oct 1971 Löhlbach Ch to Roland Wickert(b 01 Jun 1951 Löhlbach, Germany; bpt 14 Jul 1951 Löhlbach Ch; nurse at Haina Kloster) s/o Philipp Wickert II & Emilie nee Hesse of Mittelgasse 34, Löhlbach, Germany. Residence: Bachgasse 1, 3559 Löhlbach, Germany. The Author visited this family ancestral home 1984, 1999 where Johann Justus Krug III and Johann Peter Krug were born. Children:

   **Karsten Wickert – b 23 Nov 1972, bpt 09 Jan 1972;
     m Claudia Schmermund (b 24 Jun 1968). son:
     Marius Wickert – b 16 Nov 2002
   **Dirk Wickert – b 02 Mar 1976, bpt 04 Apr 1976; Male Nurse

Richard Kenneth PALEN s/o Margaret Lovaire nee Krug Palen & Kenneth Raymond Palen; b 10 Apr 1961 Tuality Hosp Hillsboro, OR, bpt 16 Jul 1961 Calvary Luth Ch, Hillsboro, OR Sponsors: Milford & Jean Reed; con 06 Jun 1976 St.Mark Luth Ch, Salem, OR; 1979 Class South Salem High School Honor Society; Boy Scouts of America Eagle Rank; Gannett Foundation Scholarships; 1984 B.S. Magna cum laude Oregon State University; Master's Degree Western Oregon State University; Science Teacher Alsea, OR; St.Helens, OR; Mbr St.Mark Luth Ch Salem, OR; m 30 Oct 1993 Portland, OR to Helen Polly Shaw (b 11 Oct 1953 NY, B.S. Cornell University, Ithaca, NY; Teacher; Licensed Massuese) d/o Milton Roberts Shaw & Ruth Marie nee McCurdy, Ithaca, NY.

Susan Laurel PALEN d/o Margaret Lovaire nee Krug Palen & Kenneth Raymond Palen; b 25 Jun 1959 Tuality Hosp Hillsboro, OR, bpt 09 Aug 1959 Calvary Luth Ch, Hillsboro, OR Sponsors: Grandparents Walter William August Krug & Enid Muriel nee Bryner; con 26 May 1974 St.Mark Luth Ch Salem, OR; 1975 Bethel #43 Queen; Willamette Demolay Sweetheart; 1977 Class South Salem High School Honor Society; 1981 B.S. University of Oregon, Delta Delta Delta Sorority; Master's Degree Western Oregon State University; Special Education Teacher; m 12 Jul 1986 St.Matthew Luth Ch, Beaverton, OR to Edward Peter McHugh (b 08 Sept 1959 Nashua, NH, bpt and con Nashua, NH; President/CEO Active Marketing, West Linn, OR) s/o Raymond McHugh (d 1991) & Elizabeth nee Hicks (d 1996) St.Petersburg, FL. Children:

   Andrea Michelle McHugh – b 29 Nov 1986 Tuality Hosp
     Hillsboro,OR bpt 12 Jul 1987 Prince of Life Luth Ch,
     Oregon City, OR Sponsor: Uncle Richard Kenneth Palen;
     Girls Scouts of America Aquarius Project;
     2005 Class West Linn High School;

Oregon State University Honors Program;
Delta Delta Delta Sorority.
Thomas Edward McHugh – b 27 Dec 1988 Tuality Hosp Hillsboro,
OR; bpt 28 May 1989 St.Matthew Luth Ch, Beaverton, OR
Sponsor: Uncle Richard Kenneth Palen;
2007 Class West Linn High School; Oregon State University.

Arlo PAULSEN s/o John Fred Paulsen & Clara Marie nee Warner; b 1932;
m Dona Price. Child:
Beth – NFR

Audrey PAULSEN d/o George Paulsen & Ellen nee Broendel; b 1925; m
John Good s/o Elmer Good & Winnie nee Lunger. John & Audrey had
grocery store in Newhall, IA. Children:
James Good – b 1946; m Bonnie Baker; Newhall, IA residence
Judy Good – b 1950; m Lavern Upah; Elberon, IA residence
Jo Anne Good – b 1954; m James Smith, North English, IA residence

Delbert PAULSEN s/o George Paulsen & Ellen nee Broendel; b 1929; m
Elaine Bierschenk (b 1931, d 1981) d/o Fred Bierschenk & Esther nee
Rinderknecht. Farmers north of Newhall, IA. Children:
Shirley – b 1953
Daniel – b 1957
Joyce – b 1959

Eldo PAULSEN s/o William Paulsen & Maria (Mary) nee Senne; b 1903, d
1980; m Sophia Schnarr (b 1907, d 1979). Children:
Eugene – b 1926, d 1989; m Rose Fry (b 1928)
Deloris – b 1930
Ardis Rose – b 1932, d 1991; m Carlton Winstone Trice (b 1932).
Child: Lenora Trice (b 1953); m Randy Laswell (b 1933)
Darwin – b 1934; m Doris M. Darby (b 1934). Children:
James Darwin Paulsen (b 1953); m Sue Jong Sek. Children:
Kay Dee Paulsen (b 1973), Richard James Paulsen (b 1974),
David Paulsen (b 1976)
Lawrence Neil – b 1955, d 1963

Emily PAULSEN d/o William Paulsen & Maria (Mary) nee Senne; b 1915,
d 1977; m Fred Lange (b 1909, d 1962). Children:
Lola Katherine Lange – b 1937; m Herbert Dean Nosker (b 1936);

Children: 1.Kimberly Beth Nosker (b 1958);
m Stephen Joseph Nester SR. (b 1958). Children: Stephen JR.
(b 1989), Michael Dean (b 1991), Rachel Elizabeth(b 1993)
2. Robin Carol Nosker (b 1960); m Michael Harry Skordos
(b 1967)
Alice Lange – b 1945; m Ronald A. Westergaard (b 1940);
Children: 1.Eric Andrew Westergaard (b 1966);
m Terry Lynn St.Aubin (b 1966). Child: Brandon Andrew
(b 1992)
2. Debra Westergaard (b 1970)
Fred Lawrence Lange – b 1949; m Lynn Marie Mabie (b 1950).
Children: 1. Jared Steven Lange (b 1976),
2. Jennifer Lynn Lange (b 1981),
3. Andrew James Lange (b 1982)
Nanette Lange – b 1952; 1st m Anthony James Piwowarski (b 1952).
Children: Allen Jason Piwowarski (b 1971)
Kristofer Steven Piwowarski (b1978); 2nd m Danny D. Taylor
(b 1952)

Frieda PAULSEN d/o William Paulsen & Maria (Mary) nee Senne; b 1901,
d 1988; m William Warner SR. (b 1899, d 1973). Children:
Louise Warner – b 1921, d 1999; m Erwin Wiebold
Thelma Warner – b 1923; m Richard Wise
William Warner JR. – b 1929; m Elizabeth (Bunny) Morning

George PAULSEN s/o Heinrich Paulsen & Alvina nee Grovert; b 1898, d
1981; m Ellen Broendel (b 1900) d/o Henry Broendel & Lena nee Greve;
farmers near Newhall, IA until 1947 retirement in Newhall. Children:
Audrey – b 1925; m John Good
Delbert – b 1929; m Elaine Bierschenk

Gregory PAULSEN s/o Ruth nee Franzenburg & Donald Paulsen; graduate
U. of I. Medical School; Internal Medicine practice in Lansing, MI; m Mary
Coan of Princeton, NJ. Children:
Elizabeth – NFR
Lucas – NFR
Ben – NFR

Gretchen PAULSEN d/o Ruth nee Franzenburg & Donald Paulsen; m
William Enke, Attorney. Fort Dodge, IA residence. Children:

Erika – NFR
Kristen – NFR

*Heinrich PAULSEN s/o Marx Paulsen & Mary nee Bone; b 1864
Schleswig-Holstein, Germany, d 1912 Eldorado Twp ae52; came to USA as
young man and settled in Benton Co IA; m Alvina Grovert (b 1862
Schleswig-Holstein, Germany, d 1921 Newhall, IA). Farmers in Eldorado
Twp Benton Co IA until Alvina retired in Newhall, IA in 1917 with her
daughters:
>   Mathilda – b 10 Mar 1889, d 1965 bur St.John Cem;
>   m 06 Mar 1912 Conrad H. J. Werning
>   John Fred – b 1891, d 1975; m Clara Marie Warner
>   Emma – b 13 Feb 1893, d 06 Apr 1960;
>   m 12 Dec 1915 Leonard Werning
>   George – b 1898, d 1981; m Ellen Broendel
>   Elte – b 1896; m John Alpers

Herman PAULSEN s/o Peter Paulsen & Katherine nee Heyer; b 1888
Benton Co IA, d 1974; m 10 Feb 1915 Ella Tecklenburg (b 1894, d 1971
[Auto Accident Injuries]). Farmers Big Grove Twp Benton Co IA; moved to
Keystone, IA. Children:
>   Ruby – m Joe Tefer, Cedar Rapids, IA residence
>   Dorothy – m Wilfred Drahos, Belle Plaine, IA residence
>   Dr. Donald – Shueyville, IA residence
>   Herman JR. – farmed Paulsen Big Grove Twp Benton Co IA
>   homeplace

Irma PAULSEN d/o William Paulsen & Maria (Mary) nee Senne; b 1902, d
1999; m Espa Jones (b 1905, d 1979). Children:
>   Shirley Ann Jones – b 1929; m Louis C. Harrod (b 1929). Children:
>   1. Sharon Louise Harrod (b 1953), 2. David W. Harrod (b 1959),
>   3. Dana L.Harrod (b 1960)
>   Dorothy May Jones – b 1931; 1st m Leon Jones (b 1931);
>   2nd m John Fields (b 1922). Children: Timothy Estill Fields
>   (b 1958), Brian Scott Fields (b 1953)
>   William E. Jones – b 1933, d 1952
>   James Lee Jones – b 1935; m Elizabeth A. Bogie (b 1938). Children:
>   Pamela Sue Jones (b 1956), Charlotte Lee Jones (b 1973)
>   Edward B. Jones – b 1937; m Nancy Bowles. Children:
>   Dorothy Ann Jones (b 1959), Karen Sue Jones (b 1962),

Ralph Edward Jones (b 1965)
Raymond Warner Jones – b 1942; m Beulah Johnson (b 1941). Child: Angela Jones (b 1969)

John Fred PAULSEN s/o Heinrich Paulsen & Alvina nee Grovert; b 1891 Eldorado Twp Benton Co IA; m 1917 Clara Marie Warner (b 1896 on farm northwest of Newhall, IA d 1974) d/o Charles Warner & Fredaricka nee Wendt. Children:
Lloyd – b 1920, d 1978; m Marjory Willet of England
Ruth – b 1922; m Charles McSweeney
Melba – b 1925; m Donald Davison
Robert J. – b 1927; m Dorothy Rammelsberg
Marlys – b 1929; m Earl Taylor
Arlo – b 1932; m Dona Price

Lloyd PAULSEN s/o John Fred Paulsen & Clara Marie nee Warner; b 1920, d 1978; m Marjory Willet of England. Children:
Gail – NFR
Lesley – NFR
Allen – NFR
Ian – NFR

Marlys PAULSEN d/o John Fred Paulsen & Clara Marie nee Warner; b 1929; m Earl Taylor. Child:
Barbara Taylor – m Michael Fortune

Melba PAULSEN d/o John Fred Paulsen & Clara Marie nee Warner; b 1925; m Donald Davison. Children:
James Davison – NFR
Jean Davison – NFR
Bobby Davison – NFR

Mildred PAULSEN d/o William Paulsen & Maria (Mary) nee Senne; b 1910, d 1999; m Ray Meyer (b 1904, d 1974). Children:
Charles Meyer – b 1932; m Donna Schrader (b 1938). Child:
Jamie Meyer (b 1958); m Donna Jean Treadwell (b 1963).
Child: Abegail Meyer (b 1997)
Evelyn Meyer – b 1934; m Harry Schminkey (b 1929). Children:
1. Gregory Schminkey (b 1957), 2. Dwayne Schminkey (b 1958);
m Janet Coberly (b 1965). Children: Seth Michael (b1992),

Austin (b 1994), 3. Debra Sue Schminkey (b 1959);
m Dale Trumblee (b 1958). Children: Quentun Trumblee (b1982),
Britney Trumblee (b1986), 4. Lawanna Jean Schminkey (b1970);
1st m Johnie Scewc JR. (b1966); 2nd m Chad Hawker. Child:
NN Hawker (b 1998)
Ruth Meyer – b 1938; 1st m Harlan Hocken (b 1934, d 1986). Child:
Mark William Hocken (b 1968); 2nd m John Hartwig (b 1934)

*Peter PAULSEN b 1856 Ostechavetaft, Germany, d 1943; 1876 emigrated to Big Grove Twp Benton Co IA; m Katherine Heyer (b 1859, d 1941). Children:
Elizabeth – b 1880, d 1976; m Herman Schneider
Anna – b 1885, d 1952; m William Sindt
Dora – b 1886, d 198?; m William Meinert
Herman – b 1888 Benton Co IA, d 1974; m 10 Feb Ella Tecklenburg

Robert J. PAULSEN s/o John Fred Paulsen & Clara Marie nee Warner; b 1927; m Dorothy Rammelsberg d/o Arthur J. Rammelsberg & Elizabeth nee Van Voy; Paulsen homestead residence northwest of Newhall, IA. Children:
Terry Lee – b 1954
Gary Lee – b 1955
Kathy Lee – b 1957; m Robert Clemens JR.

Ruth PAULSEN d/o John Fred Paulsen & Clara Marie nee Warner; b 1922; m Charles McSweeney. Children:
Richard McSweeney – m Sandy Button
Michael McSweeney – NFR
Timothy McSweeney – NFR

James Patrick PEACOCK s/o Harold John Peacock & Iris May nee Rammelsberg; b 14 Mar 1946; m 09 Nov 1964 Betty Lou Leoffler (b 24 Sept 1944). Children:
Patricia Lee – b 30 Apr 1965; 1st m 1982 Stan Clang DVD 1985;
2nd 08 Jul 1989 Jon B. Smith
Steven Patrick – b 22 Jul 1966; m 11 Jul 1987 Cindi Roseberry
Rebecca Lynne – b 28 Sept 1969; m 04 Jan 1992 Timothy Stovie

Joan Kay PEACOCK d/o Harold John Peacock & Iris May nee Rammelsberg; b 08 Dec 1947; 1st m 20 Jul 1968 Patrick Henry White (b 08 Nov 1948) DVD. Children:

Tammy Kay White – b 19 May 1969; m 10 Sept 1988 Rick McSparen
Joseph William White – b 30 Nov 1971
2nd m 23 May 1992 Joan Kay nee Peacock White to Harold Schrader (b 02 Jun 1938).

Michael John PEACOCK s/o Harold John Peacock & Iris May nee Rammelsberg; b 13 Jun 1942 Mercy Hosp Cedar Rapids, IA; m 17 Oct 1970 Linda Jean Andrews McClurg (b 08 Sept 1941)DVD. Children:
Christopher Michael – b 14 Dec 1972
STEPCHILDREN:
Susan L. Andrews – b 01 Jul 1964
James A. Andrews – b 11 Feb 1966

Alfred M. PETERSEN s/o John F. Petersen & Augusta W. nee Kallsen; b 1884 Keystone, Benton Co IA, d 1963; 1902 moved to Newhall, IA with parents; helped father build house sometimes working by kerosene lantern; m 1914 Harriette Primrose (b 1887, d 1934) d/o James Primrose & Dora M. nee Miller; purchased family home from his mother. Children:
Everett – b 1915; m Leone Rudd
John Martin – b 1917; USAF World War II

Everett PETERSEN s/o Alfred M. Petersen & Harriette nee Primrose; b 1915; residence with parents until 1939 when went to CA; Douglas Aircraft employee thirty-six and a half years; m 1943 Leone Rudd (b 1924) d/o Leo H. & Isabelle Rudd. Children:
Lynda – NFR
Patricia – NFR

*John F. PETERSEN b 1863 Germany, d 1911 Benton Co IA; apprentice painter four years before leaving Germany to emigrate to USA; settled in Keystone, Benton Co IA where met wife; m Augusta W. Kallsen (b 1859, d 1920; sewing teacher) moved to Van Horne, IA; 1902 moved to Newhall, IA. John made many beautiful paintings on walls of churches and homes. Children:
Alfred M. – b 1884, d 1963; m 1914 Harriet Primrose
Chris George – b 1886, d 1976; m 1912 Delia Zornig
Anna – b 1888; m 1909 George Wheeler
Lillian – b 1896; m 1915 Emlyn Bergerson, Newhall, IA School Supt.

Charles Ray PHELPS JR. s/o Jacqueline Marie nee Edmonds & Dr. Charles

Ray Phelps SR.; b 29 Aug 1950 Ottumwa, IA; m 30 Dec 1971 Jeannine Hatt (b 25 Aug 1950). Children:
Benjamin Ryan – b 15 Jun 1975
Sarah Jane – b 28 Aug 1979

Gregory Lynn PHELPS s/o Jacqueline Marie nee Edmonds & Dr. Charles Ray Phelps SR. b 23 Jan 1954, bpt Nov 1954; m 02 Jun 1978 Jacquelyn Threadgill (b 19 Oct 1954).

Victor Leslie PHELPS s/o Jacqueline Marie nee Edmonds & Dr. Charles Ray Phelps SR.; b 16 Jan 1952 Ottumwa, IA; m 12 Jun 1972 Rachel NN(b 17 Jan 1954). Children:
Jennifer Renee – b 17 Jun 1976
Jessica Lynn – b 24 May 1978

Kay Frances PICKERING d/o Roy Pickering & Evelyn Anna Marie nee Braksiek; b 09 Sept 1935 St.Lukes Hosp Cedar Rapids, IA; m 22 Nov 1953 Donald G. Albertson (b 30 Jul 1934) s/o Ewald Albertson. Children:
Peggy Ann Albertson – b 18 Sept 1954;
    m 20 Jun 1975 Farlen Oelmann (b 14 May 1954)
David L. Albertson – b 30 Jul 1957; m 1978 Patricia Vitek DVD
Craig A. Albertson – b 25 Nov 1958; m 1988 Joanne Finchen

Larry Lee PICKERING s/o Roy Pickering & Evelyn Anna Marie nee Braksiek; b 09 Sept 1940 Cedar Rapids, IA; m 14 Jul 1962 Karen K. McIllrath (b 17 Jul 1944) d/o Floyd McIllrath. Children:
Trace Douglas – b 17 Dec 1965; m 17 Jul 1989 Kim Nelson
    (b 12 Mar 1967)
Tara Lyn – b 05 Oct 1969; m 25 Jul 1990 Mark Noe (b 24 Dec 1968)
Tiffany Ann – b 05 Oct 1980

Lynn Franklyn PICKERING s/o Roy Pickering & Evelyn Anna Marie nee Braksiek; b 11 Jun 1937 Cedar Rapids, IA; m 31 Aug 1956 St.John to Delores Schirm (b 18 Nov 1938) d/o Irvin Schirm & Zenolia nee Meier. Children:
Mark A. – b 06 Aug 1960, d 19 Nov 1977
Tami J. – b 02 Mar 1970
Jodi – b 10 Jun 1971

*Franz PIEPER s/o Kasper & Anna Marie; b 1847 Germany, Stonemason, d 1925 Benton Co IA, bur Evergreen Cem Vinton, IA; came with parents to USA and settled in Watkins, IA and Norway, IA area as farmers; m 1875 Clementine Boon (b 1858 Belgium, d 1928 bur Evergreen Cem Vinton, IA) d/o Henry & Mary Boon; farmed two and one-half miles west of Newhall, IA. Celebrated 50th Golden Wedding Anniversary in Vinton, IA. Children:

Frank – m Elizabeth Becker; MN residence

Mary Anne – m Anton Rieder; Watkins Boon Homestead, IA residence

Elizabeth – m Edward Kueny; residence northeast of Van Horne, IA

Sophia – m John Boisen; residence SD & Van Horne, IA

Bernard – m Effie Nenabor; residence SD & MN

Joseph SR. – m Mary Becker; residence northeast of Van Horne, IA

Mary – m W.Peter Miller; residence near Walker, Cedar Rapids, IA

George – Never Married; disabled World War I veteran; IN residence

Clara – m Milo Kearns; residence SD & Vinton, IA

John – m Lena Spratte; MN residence

Louis – m Marie Spratte; residence Pieper farm west of Newhall, IA

Joseph Albert PIEPER JR. s/o Joseph Pieper SR. & Mary nee Becker (descendant House of Brandenburg(Brandenburg Gate in Berlin, Germany); b 15 Jul 1916 near Van Horne, IA; Van Horne High School; World War II US Army; m 29 Aug 1942 Ft. Meade, SD to Arlene Wright (b 18 May 1920) d/o Alfred Wright & Emma nee Dietrich. Farmers. Children:

Gary James – b 14 May 1947; Air Force, Frankfurt, Germany

Marcia Jane – b 02 Feb 1953; m/DVD, son: Matthew Boies

Jolene Ellen – b 22 Dec 1956; teacher

Joe – NFR

Arlene – three children, one grandson NN

*Claus H. PINGEL b 1843 Schleswig-Holstein, Germany, d 1929 CA; m 1867 in Germany to Anna Detlefs (d pro 1883); 1873 emigrated to Scott Co IA, then to farm southwest of Keystone, Kane Twp Benton Co IA. Anna's mother came from Germany to keep house for the family. Following 1911 farm sale Claus, sons Peter J. and Henry moved to CA. Children (three children unknown):

John H. – b 1878; m Caroline Koelle

Henry – moved to CA

Dora – m to NN Bokholt, Belle Plaine, IA residence

Peter J. – moved to CA

Margaret – NFR

*John H. PINGEL s/o Claus H. Pingel & Anna nee Detlefs; b 1870 Schleswig-Holstein, Germany; 1873 emigrated to Scott Co IA; moved near Keystone, Kane Twp Benton Co IA; m 1913 Santa Ana, CA to Caroline Koelle (b 1888 Bonnigheim, Germany, 1910 immigrant Denison, IA, d 1968) 1915 moved to Iowa farm. Children:
Frieda – d 1961; m Waldo Holst
Rudolph – Pingel family farm resident
Helen – m Douglas Preston (d 1977)
Esther – d 1952; m Howard Hinrichs (d 1986
Irene Mae – b 17 Jan 1924; m 26 Sept 1945 Lester William Haerther
Lillian – Keystone, IA resident

Carol Jeaan PLOETZ d/o Hilda Catherine nee Moeller & William Fred Ploetz; b 24 Feb 1944; m 13 Nov 1971 John Wesley Phillips (b 28 May 1936). Cupertina, CA residence. Children:
Matthew James Phillips – b 29 May 1976
TWINS: Andrew Scott Phillips – b 08 May 1979
Heather Anne Phillips – b 08 May 1979

Sandra Rose PLOETZ d/o Hilda Catherine nee Moeller & William Fred Ploetz; b 07 Nov 1951; m 21 Sept 1980 Kenneth L. Niemczyk (b 02 Aug 1943). Woodstock VT residence. Children:
Megan Rose Niemczyk – b 01 Aug 1984
Katherine Marie (Kate) Niemczyk – b 21 Oct 1986

Nancy Ann POELZER d/o Audrey Ann nee Werning & George John Poelzer; b 25 Nov 1959 Milwaukee, WI; m 13 Jun 1987 Douglas John Olson (b 10 Oct 1956) Woodstock, IL residence. Children:
Leslie Rose Olson – b 02 Feb 1991
Natalie Susan Olson – b 19 Mar 1993

Susan Jane POELZER d/o Audrey Anne nee Werning & George John Poelzer; b 20 Sept 1952 Milwaukee, WI; m 14 Feb 1981 Eric Bruce Weeder (b 07 Aug 1949). McHenry, IL residence. Child:
Calvin Magpie Christian Weeder – b 21 Jul 1992

Thomas George POELZER s/o Audrey Anne nee Werning & George John Poelzer; b 19 Sept 1953; m 29 Aug 1976 Milwaukee, WI to Sally Ann

Kludt(b 17 Dec 1952). Children:
    Michael Thomas – b 09 May 1980
    Steven Andrew – b 17 Nov 1982
    Joseph John – b 20 Feb 1985

Dennis Delmar POHLMAN s/o Lenore Katherine nee Wilhelmi & Delmar Pohlman; b 16 Apr 1959; m 29 Nov 1986 Patricia Frieda Biggart (b 22 Feb 1961) d/o Edward Everett Biggart & Edith Frieda nee Corporon. Children:
    Mary Freida – b 11 Jan 1988
    Megan Angie – b 25 Dec 1989
    Matthew James – b 06 May 1993

Gloria POHLMAN d/o Lenore Katherine nee Wilhelmi & Delmar Pohlman; b 20 Nov 1960; m 21 Jun 1986 Mark Imhoff (b 30 Jan 1961). Child:
    Kathryn Ann Imhoff – b 18 Jul 1992

Larry Edward POHLMAN s/o Lenore Katherine nee Wilhelmi & Delmar Pohlman; b 23 Mar 1950 Belle Plaine, IA; bpt 16 Apr 1950 St.Steph; m 12 Sept 1970 Marilyn Hagan (b 12 May 1951). Children:
    Brian Edward – b 21 Mar 1974
    Bradley James – b 15 Sept 1977
    Aaron Andrew – b 02 Nov 1981

Steven Delmar POHLMAN s/o Lenore Katherine nee Wilhelmi & Delmar Pohlman; b 08 Jun 1953 Belle Plaine, IA; bpt 28 Jun 1953 St.Steph; m 15 Jul 1972 Marie Weisert (b 27 Jan 1954). Children:
    Bridgett Marie – b 30 May 1974
    Renee Ann – b 01 Jul 1976
    Tanya Rachelle – b 24 Apr 1981
    Lacey Justine – b 17 Oct 1982

James Herold POLK s/o Alvin Ernst Polk (changed Poock name) & Elsie Katherine Louise nee Rinderknecht; b 02 Apr 1955 Milwaukee, WI; m 31 Aug 1986 Monona, WI to Joanne Louise Kinney (b 21 May 1951 Pullman, WA) d/o Frank Lawrence Kinney & June Maxine nee Harding. Children:
    Jeffrey Michael – b 22 Jun 1987 Madison, WI
    Jordan James – b 09 Apr 1990 Madison, WI

Jane Ellen POLK d/o Alvin Ernst Polk (changed Poock name) & Elsie

Katherine Louise nee Rinderknecht; b 18 May 1958 Milwaukee, WI; m 04 Oct 1986 Salt Lake City, UT to Gary Robert Bucher (b 25 Nov 1948 Casper, WY; Petroleum Engineer) s/o Frederick M. Miller/Robert M. Bucker & Carol Melissa nee Schrater.

Alvin Ernest POOCK (changed name to POLK) s/o Ernest Poock & Gertrude K. nee Happel; b 03 Jun 1922 Eland, WI; m 22 Aug 1943 St. Steph to Elsie Katherine Louise Rinderknecht (b 21 Aug 1922 Fremont Twp. Benton Co IA) d/o George William Frederick Rinderknecht & Anna Sophia Marie Elizabeth nee Gerhold. Occupation: Self-employed. Children:
>   Jerry Wayne – b 08 Oct 1953 Milwaukee, WI
>   James Herold – b 02 Apr 1955 Milwaukee, WI; m Joanne Kinney
>   Jane Ellen – b 18 May 1958 Milwaukee, WI; m Gary Bucher

Carol Rae POOCK d/o Harold Ernest Poock & Helen A. nee Block; b 13 Sept 1936; m 09 Nov 1957 Clintonville, WI to Dale William Schoepke (b 24 Apr 1935). Children:
>   Chris Ann Schoepke – b 09 Dec 1959; m 21 Jun 1986 Brian Lapham
>   Daniel Dale Schoepke – b 02 Dec 1960
>   Mark Harold Schoepke – b 02 Dec 1964

Harold Edward POOCK s/o Harold Ernest Poock & Helen A. nee Block; b 15 Sept 1936 Sumner, IA; m 05 Sept 1959 Wittenberg, WI to Sandra A. Bloecher. Children:
>   Kyle Edward – b 28 Dec 1960 Wittenberg, WI
>   Dr.Scott Ervin – b 29 Dec 1961 Wittenberg, WI;
>   m 29 Sept 1990 Angie Smith in Elk City, OK
>   Infant – b 14 Oct 1965
>   Timothy Steven – b 19 Dec 1966 Almond, WI
>   Amylin Elizabeth – b 12 Oct 1971 Almond, WI

Harold Ernest POOCK s/o Ernest Poock & Gertrude K. nee Happel; b 01 Jan 1912 Orisha, ND, d 11 Nov 1953 ae41y 10m 10d Wittenberg, WI; m 22 Sept 1932 Wittenberg, WI to Helen A. Block (b 14 Feb 1912). Children:
>   Carol Rae – b 13 Sept 1936 Sumner, IA; m 1957 Dale Schoepke
>   Harold Edward – b 15 Sept 1936 Sumner, IA;
>   m 1959 Sandra A. Bloecher
>   Norma Lee – b 11 Feb 1943 Readlyn, IA;
>   m 08 Aug 1964 Jack Kitzmann

Leona Frieda POOCK d/o Ernest Poock & Gertrude K. nee Happel; b 16 Sept 1920 Eland, WI; d 07 Aug 1994 ae73y 10m 22d bur CdrMem; m 23 Aug 1940 St.Steph to Eldo August Schirm (b 23 Dec 1918 Atkins, IA, d 04 Jun 2007 ae88y 5m 12d bur CdrMem; 1936 Class Atkins High School; with his brothers and cousins started their own baseball team; retired Jan 1994 Anamosa Reformatory Supervisor) s/o Martin William Schirm & Carolina "Lena" B. nee Keiper. Children:

David Schirm – m 01 Dec 1951 Janice Hupfield, Richardson, TX
Mark Schirm – m Sue NN, MT residence
Marcia Schirm – m Ervin Oltmann, Marion, IA residence
Danny Schirm – m Kay NN, Mt. Vernon, IA residence
Debbie Schirm – m Bryon Ahrendsen, Anamosa, IA residence

Norma Lee POOCK d/o Harold Ernest Poock & Helen A. nee Block; b 11 Feb 1943 Readlyn, IA; m 08 Aug 1964 Jack Kitzmann. Children:

Ricky Kitzmann – b 25 Aug 1965; m 25 Aug 1965 NN
Marcie Kitzmann – b 12 Nov 1966
Andrew Kitzmann – b 02 Feb 1972

Bernice Ella Louise POPENHAGEN d/o Wilhelm Fredrich Popenhagen & Katherina Elizabeth nee Krug; b 25 Jul 1914 Parent's farm Fremont Twp Benton Co IA, bpt 16 Aug 1914 Parent's farm home, Fremont Twp Benton Co IA; m 23 Jun 1947 TrinCR Parsonage to Harlan Thurston(b 09 Dec 1915) s/o A.H. Thurston of Cedar Rapids, IA. Both Bernice and Harlan employed by National Oats Company, Cedar Rapids, IA. Children:

Marcella Thurston – b 19 Jun 1949 Cedar Rapids, IA;
1st 28 Feb 1969 Ronald Warren DVD 1979;
2nd m 31 Aug 1993 Jerry Emerson
David Thurston – b 03 Sept 1953 Cedar Rapids, IA;
m 14 May 1988 Shirley Biloszly
Steven Thurston – b 13 Jul 1956 Cedar Rapids, IA;
m 19 Dec 1976 Sherri Wonick

*Frederick John Martin POPENHAGEN s/o John Peter Popenhagen & Katherine Marie nee Koenning; b 15 Feb 1856 in Reinsdorf, Germany, d 03 Mar 1932 ae76y 17d Fayette Co IA, bur West Union, IA cem; member Luth Ch at 14y; 1873 emigrated to USA ae17y settling near Chicago, IL; 1884 move to Iowa; m 15 Apr 1885 Ella Sophie Lembke (b 20 Mar 1868 Du Page Co IL, d 17 Sept 1905 ae39y 5m 28d, funeral United Brethern Ch, Wadena, IA, bur Wadena, IA Cem) d/o John Lembke & Sophia nee Scherf (b Germany, d Jan 1899 Sumner, IA, funeral at German Luth Ch). Farmers in Windsor Twp. Ten Children:

>Louis Carle – b 30 May 1886 Fayette Co IA, d 03 Mar 1949;
>>m 25 Dec 1907 Elsie Sarah Hannah Cline

>Emma – b 26 Aug 1887 Fayette Co IA; m Harry Earle

>Amanda – b 08 Mar 1889 Fayette Co IA, d 15 Nov 1921;
>>m Ralph Walter Emerson Everett

>Ella Sophie Hannah – b 16 Nov 1890 Fayette Co IA, d 11 Feb 1970
>>Elgin, IA; m 16 Nov 1910 Myron M. Moore

>Otto George – b 07 Jul 1892, d Jan 1969;
>>m 21 Dec 1915 Grace Vochell

>George William – b

10 Mar 1894 Fayette Co IA; d 27 Nov 1967
>>bur Fayette, IA; m 11 Dec 1919 Ethel Josephine Beckwith

>Lida Johanna – b 13 Jun 1896 Fayette Co IA; d 11 Jan 1970,
>>bur Elgin, IA; m 15 Feb 1921 Herman C. Larson SR.

>John – b 04 Apr 1898 Fayette Co IA, d 1924 bur Lima, IA;
>>m Nellie Landas Reed

>Fred Herman – b 16 Jul 1900 Fayette Co IA, d Apr 1982 Fayette Co
>>m 21 Mar 1923 Loretta Corbin

>Joy Harold – b 01 Jan 1904; m 25 Oct 1923 Fern Melissa Ward

George Conrad POPENHAGEN s/o Wilhelm Fredrich Popenhagen & Katherina Elizabeth nee Krug; b 08 Mar 1916 Parent's farm Fremont Twp Benton Co IA, bpt 16 Apr 1916 Parent's farm home, Fremont Twp Benton Co IA; m 23 Jun 1943 TrinCR to Leone Andrlik (b 27 Feb 1924) d/o Joseph Andrilk of North Liberty, IA, double ceremony with first cousin Delbert Krug & Libbie Cerveny. Farmers. Child:

>Cynthia Jolene – b 23 Nov 1957; m 24 Sept 1983 Jeffrey Scott White

Henry Elmer POPENHAGEN s/o Wilhelm Fredrich Popenhagen & Katherina Elizabeth nee Krug; b 25 Mar 1917 parent's farm Fremont Twp Benton Co IA, d 26 May 2006 ae89y 2m 1d; m 15 Feb 1946 Chatfield, MN to Emma C. Meyer (b 31 Jan 1915) d/o Theodore & Alvina Meyer.

Jeffrey Karl POPENHAGEN s/o Norman Karl Popenhagen & Margie J. nee Hildebrand; b 12 Mar 1975; m 02 Aug 1997 Elisabeth Ann Seeton Ch, Hiawatha, IA to Carrie Campbell (b 15 Oct 1973) d/o Gary Campbell. Child:

>Dane – b 17 Feb 1999

Ella – NFR
Kade – NFR

Jennifer Marie POPENHAGEN d/o Norman Karl Popenhagen & Margie J. nee Hildebrand; b 27 Sept 1971; m 06 Sept 1997 Concordia Luth Ch Cedar Rapids, IA to Thomas Simmons (b 18 Jul 1970) s/o Craig Simmons. Child:
    Drew Simmons – Marion, IA

*Joseph POPENHAGEN born in Germany; 1st m in USA to Frederika Jacob (b 1846 Germany, d 1922 bur St.Steph Cem)2nd m Fredricka NN (b 1857, d 1930 bur St.Steph Cem)and settled in Niles Center(Skokie), IL. 1887 came to Iowa and settled in Benton Co Atkins area. Five children:
    Fred – b IL, d IA bur Linwood Cem, Cedar Rapids, IA;
        m and moved to Cedar Rapids, IA
    Wilhelm Fredrich – b 21 Mar 1881 Niles Center IL;
        d 24 Apr 1961 Newhall, IA bur St.Steph Cem;
        m 18 Jan 1912 Katherina Elizabeth Krug
    Joseph C. – b 1885 IL, d 1957 IA, bur St.Steph Cem;
        m Marie R. and moved to Shellsburg, IA
    Lena – b IL; m and moved to Center Point, IA
    Ella – b Atkins; m and moved to rural Marion, IA

Kenneth William POPENHAGEN s/o Roy Joseph August Popenhagen & Rosa Marie nee Kray; b 09 Aug 1939 north of Van Horne, Eden Twp Benton Co IA, bpt 27 Aug 1939 St.Steph; m 11 Jan 1969 Carol Jean Moore(b 22 Aug 1949). Kenneth: Benton Co IA Sheriff-retired after thirty-two years in office. Children:
    Richard Roy – b 10 Jan 1970 Cedar Rapids, IA; m Ellen NN
    Robert James – b 21 Jan 1975 Cedar Rapids, IA

Louis Carle POPENHAGEN s/o Frederick John Martin Popenhagen & Ella Sophie nee Lembke; b 30 May 1886 Fayette Co IA; buttermaker 22 ½ years for Iowa creameries; Guard at Anamosa, IA Reformatory five years; worked five years LaPlante Choates, Cedar Rapids, IA; worked at Schneider Turkey Farm & Capper's Hatchery; 1919 joined United Brethern Ch, Wadena, IA; 1924 joined Presbyterian Ch, Wadena, IA; five years gospel team mbr for Methodist Ch, Coggan, IA; member St.Paul's Methodist Ch, Elgin, IA at time of death; m 25 Dec 1907 Elsie Sarah Hannah Cline. Six children (one girl, two boys dec'd in infancy):
    LaVerle – m Arthur Groth, Decorah, IA

Leona – m Walter Medberry

Norman Karl POPENHAGEN s/o Roy Joseph August Popenhagen & Rosa Marie nee Kray; b 03 May 1944 S.E. of Atkins, Fremont Twp Benton Co IA, bpt 21 May 1944 St.Steph; Linn Co IA Risk Manager; d 14 Nov 2006 ae62y 6m 11d [Multiple Sclerosis] bur St.Steph Cem; m 29 Mar 1970 St. Matthew Luth Ch, Concordia, MO to Margie J. Hildebrand (b 15 Jul 1945, Preschool Teacher) d/o Clarence Hildebrand. Children:
    Jennifer Marie – b 27 Sept 1971; m 06 Sept 1997 Thomas Simmons
    Jeffrey Karl – b 12 Mar 1974; m 02 Aug 1997 Carrie Campbell

Roy Joseph August POPENHAGEN s/o Wilhelm Fredrich Popenhagen & Katherina Elizabeth nee Krug; b 24 Mar 1913 Parent's farm, Fremont Twp Benton Co IA, bpt 27 Aug 1913 Parent's Farm Home, Fremont Twp Benton Co IA; d 13 Apr 2002 ae89y 20d bur St.Steph Cem; m 15 Jan 1936 St.Steph to his Krug cousin Rosa Marie Kray (b 26 Jul 1916 Parent's Farm, Fremont Twp Benton Co IA, bpt 1916 St.John Luth Ch, Eldorado Twp. Benton Co IA, d 02 Oct 2006 ae90y 2m 6d bur St.Steph Cem) d/o Fred Kray & Elizabeth nee Kreutner. Roy Joseph August Popenhagen's Great-Grandparents: Johann Justus Krug & Anna Elisabeth nee Paar; Rosa Marie Kray's Great-Great-Grandparents: Johann Justus Krug & Anna Elisabeth nee Paar. Farmers until retirement. Children:
    Richard Roy – b 20 Jan 1937, d 27 Jan 1937 bur St.Steph Cem
    Kenneth William – b 09 Aug 1939; m 11 Jan 1969 Carol Jean Moore
    Norman Karl – b 03 May 1944, d 14 Nov 2006 bur St.Steph Cem;
        m 29 Mar 1970 Margie J. Hildebrant

*Frederick POSSEHL s/o Jacob Possehl of Medow bei Goldberg, Germany; m in Germany to Katrina Bobzein. Children:
    *Christian – b 1805 Germany, d 1876 IA; Clayton Co IA immigrant
    *Johann – b 1810 Germany, d 1875 IA; Amana Colonies, IA
        immigrant
    *Wilhelm – b 1818 Germany, d 1881 IA; Iowa Co IA resident
    *Carl – b 1822 Germany, d 1911 IA; Iowa Co IA resident

*Johann POSSEHL s/o Frederick Possehl & Katrina nee Bobzein; b 1810 Germany, d 1875 IA; m in Germany to Maria Rohdoz; 1868 emigrated with family to Amana Colonies, IA. Children:
    *Heinrich – b 1849 Germany
    *Karl – b 1847 Germany; 1st m Sophia Mueller (d 1891);

2nd m 1892 Louise Doerzman Bessinger
*Joachim – b Germany
*Sophia – b Germany; m John Dahnke, children: Henry and Minnie
*Dorothea – b Germany

*Karl POSSEHL s/o Johann Possehl & Maria nee Rohdoz; b 1847 Germany; 1st m Sophia Mueller (d 1891). Farmers Marengo, IA area before moving to Benton Co IA. Children:
Gustav – b 03 Jul 1881
Emma Katherine – b 22 Oct 1883
Louis Heinrich – b 25 Jan 1884
George John Henry – b 13 Jun 1887;
      m Mahala NN; Benton Co farmers
2nd m 1892 Karl Possehl to Louise Doerzman Bessinger. Children:
Vera – b 10 Apr 1893, d 1909 ae16y
Lydia – b 03 Aug 1894
Arthur – b 06 Apr 1896
Pearl Ethel – b 1912

*Johann Peter PRACHTER JR. of os Alt Heim ns Altenhaina, Germany, s/o Johann Peter Prachter SR. (Layman Judge in os Alt Heim ns Altenhaina, Germany) & Katharina Elisabeth Möller; b 11 Jan 1763 os Alt Heim ns Altenhaina, Germany, d 11 Feb 1836 ae73y 1m os Alt Heim ns Altenhaina, Germany; m 13 Jan 1785 os Alt Heim ns Altenhaina House to Anna Katharina Ochse (b 06 Jan 1763 Halgehausen, Germany, d 25 Sept 1825 ae62y 8m 9d) d/o Konrad Ochse, Layman Judge in Halgenhausen, Germany. Child:
*Anna Elisabeth – b 03 Jan 1786 os Alt Heim ns
      Altenhaina, Germany; d 19 Feb 1814 Löhlbach, Germany;
      m 31 Mar 1807 Löhlbach Ch Johannes Paar of Hse #10

*Johann Peter PRACHTER SR. Layman Judge in os Alt Heim ns Altenhaina, Germany; b 1723 d 26 Jul 1792; m 27 Dec 1758 Katharina Elisabeth Möller (b 1726 d 09 Sept 1797) d/o Nicholas Möller of Löhlbach, Germany. Child:
Johann Peter Prachter JR. – b 11 Jan 1763 os Alt Heim ns Altenhaina,
      Germany; d 11 Feb 1836 os Alt Heim ns Altenhaina, Germany;
      m 13 Jan 1785 Anna Katharina Ochse

James George PYLE s/o Joan Edna nee Hauskins & George Luppert Pyle; b

18 Jul 1951 Orthopedic Surgeon; m 29 Nov 1987 Janet Maria Richard (b 10 Jun 1955; Physical Therapist). Morgans Point, TX residence. Children:
Christopher James – b 26 Feb 1989
Scott Richard – b 15 Feb 1991

Susan Jane PYLE d/o Joan Edna nee Hauskins & George Luppert Pyle; b 22 Aug 1952; 1st m 25 Sept 1976 John Henry Fusan JR. DVD Oct 1979. 2nd m 09 Jun 1990 Susan Jane nee Pyle Fusan to Stephen Pierson (b 26 Jul 1954). North Andover, MA residence. Children:
Matthew Richard Pierson – b 01 Nov 1992
Chrisanne Joan Pierson – b 13 Jun 1994

Alfred QUASS JR. s/o George Quass SR. & Laura nee McMahan; b 02 Nov 1920; m 05 Jan 1942 Dorothy Hagan. World War II Military Police 1942-1946; Farmed Linn and Benton Co IA land of Quass grandfather. Children:
Stanley – b 11 Nov 1942; m Donna Weseloh, Ft.Myers, FL residence
James – b 21 Mar 1947; m Teresa Pippert, Cedar Rapids, IA residence

Alfred QUASS SR. s/o John G. Quass & Wilhelmina nee Kraejen; b 20 Jan 1860 Fremont Twp Benton Co IA, d 1931; m Mary Sutcliffe (b 1859, d 1934) d/o Ephraim & Hannah Sutcliffe of Linn Co IA. Farmed land in Clinton Twp Linn Co and Benton Co IA. Children:
George – b 1891, d 1986
Joe Edward – b 1884, d 1904 ae21y

Beulah Marie QUASS d/o George Quass & Laura nee McMahan; b 09 Nov 1912 Fremont Twp Benton Co IA; m 13 Aug 1933 George Clark. Farmers Clinton and Fayette Twp Linn Co near Springville, IA. Children:
Patricia Clark – b 15 Jul 1934; m Glenn Ament, Cedar Rapids, IA
Shirley Clark – b 16 Mar 1937; m Don Lewis, Riverside, IA
Bryon Clark- b 14 Mar 1940; m Norma Gefaller, Hawkeye, IA farmers

Doris Pauline QUASS d/o George Quass & Laura nee McMahan; b 22 Feb 1926 Fremont Twp Benton Co IA; Atkins High School; m 21 Sept 1947 Arthur Allen. Children:
Sheila Kay Allen – b 01 Nov 1951;
    m James Dvorak, Cedar Rapids, IA
Robert Louis Allen – b 29 Oct 1957

George QUASS JR. s/o Alfred Quass SR. & Mary nee Sutcliffe; b 1891, d 1986; m 24 Jan 1912 Shellsburg, IA to Laura McMahan (b 1893 Shellsburg, IA, d 1974) d/o James McMahan & Mary nee Jay. Farmed Alfred Quass homesite until 1946 retirement in Cedar Rapids, IA. Children:

Beulah Marie – b 09 Nov 1912; m 13 Aug 1933 George Clark
Dorothy May – b Jan 1915, d 1924 [Measles]
(George) Alfred JR. – b 02 Nov 1920; m 05 Jan 1942 Dorothy Hagan
Doris Pauline – b 22 Feb 1926; m 21 Sept 1947 Arthur Allen

*John G. QUASS b 1833 Saxon Aldenburg, Germany, d 1914 Linn Co IA; 1853 emigrated to Linn Co IA; 1855 moved to Rapids Twp Linn Co; 1st m 17 Apr 1859 Wilhelmina Kraejen (b 1843 Baden, Germany, d 1868 IA). Children:

Alfred SR.- b 20 Jan 1860
Edward – b 09 Nov 1861
Elizabeth – b 19 Jul 1865

2nd m 1875 John G. Quass to NN. Clinton Twp Linn Co IA residence

*Joachin Frederich RAABE b 1830 Zidderick, Mecklenberg, Germany, d 1907 Marengo, IA; m 1855 in Germany to Louisa Brockman (1830-1907). Emmigrated to USA 1872. Children:

*Mary – b 1856, d 1879
*Dorothea – b 1859, d 1942
*John – b 1862, d 1946, m Sophia Workenstien
*Fred – b 1866, d 1942, m Christina NN

Alice Faye RAMMELSBERG d/o Nettie L. nee Krug & Melvin A. Rammelsberg; b 11 Mar 1941; m 26 Apr 1964 Robert Whitlatch. Children:

Sarah Whitlatch – b 13 Sept 1941; m 20 Jan 1990 John Gaeta
Brenda Whitlatch –b 13 Jun 1967; m 03 Jun 1999 Mark Prohosky
Melanie Whitlatch – b 26 Aug 1974
Brian Whitlatch – b 24 Jul 1981

*Alphonsa Friedrich Emil RAMMELSBERG s/o Hugo Herman Friedrich Rammelsberg & Emiline nee Toedter; b 1861, d 1953; 1st m Mary Jane Armstrong (b 1873, d 1946) d/o Thomas Graham Armstrong b Ballinamallard, Fermanagh Co. Ireland) & Sarah nee Fawcett (b Belmont Co. OH). Residence on Thomas Armstrong farm three miles north and two miles east of Newhall, IA known as "Elm Hill Stock Farm". Children:

Arthur – b 1895, d 1979; Iowa City, IA residence

Earl Edward – b 28 Sept 1896 north of Atkins, Benton Co IA,
    d 16 Jul 1988 Virginia Gay Hosp Vinton, IA;
    m 15 Feb 1928 Emma Katherine Elizabeth Krug
Matilda – b Dec 1898
Julia – b 1900; m Lynn Nicodemus, Vinton, IA residence
Cecil – b 1901 Canton Twp Benton Co IA; m Dec 1925 Esther Thomas
Infant – dec'd Dec 1904
Melvin A. – b 11 Mar 1906, d 22 Jul 1961; m Nettie L. Krug
Ivan L. – b 14 Jan 1909, d 21 Apr 1977; m Leona A. Krug
Ruby – b 1912; Moline, Illinois residence
Marinda – b 1914; Everett, Washington
Loren – b 1916, d 1975; Independence residence
2nd m Aft 1946 Alphonsa Friedrich Emil Rammelsberg to Bertha Hauschild
(b 1845, d 1922).

Bernadine RAMMELSBERG d/o John August & Bernice M. nee Hamilton;
b 11 May 1931; 1st m Robert Ward. Child:
    Steven Ward (Hoyt) – b 12 Nov 1951
2nd m 16 Jun 1956 Bernadine Rammelsberg to William Hoyt (b 27 May
1930). Children:
    William Hoyt – b 21 Apr 1957
    Jennifer Hoyt – b 25 Apr 1959
    Terence Hoyt – b 27 Jun 1962

Brian RAMMELSBERG s/o Harold Roy Rammelsberg & Kathleen Rose
nee Kahler; b 15 Jul 1952 Atkins; m 10 Jun 1978 to Jeanne Parker (b 10
Dec 1951). Atkins, IA residence. Children:
    Daniel John – b 28 May 1981
    Michael Allen – b 18 Jun 1984
    Matthew Carl – b 06 Jul 1988

Bruce Thomas RAMMELSBERG s/o Ralph Leonard Rammelsberg &
Louise May Schlotterback b 25 Apr 1931, m 24 Jul 1970 Ellen Pauline
Bowers (d 24 Aug 1979).

Carl (Charles) RAMMELSBERG: cf Maria Katharina Barbara
Rinderknecht d/o George Martin Rinderknecht & Maria Barbara nee
Spoerer.

Carol Marie RAMMELSBERG d/o Nettie L. nee Krug & Melvin A.

Rammelsberg; b 06 Mar 1938, d 24 Dec 1971 ae33y 9m 18d; 1st m 09 Aug 1959 William Souto DVD. Children:

Jeffrey Nelson Souto – b 28 Feb 1960; m 22 Nov 1986 Suzanne Ryan

Gary Melvin Souto – b 04 Sept 1961; m 04 Jul 1986 Robin Lane

2nd m 24 Jan 1970 Carol Marie nee Rammelsberg Souto to Ralph Bauman. Child:

Michelle Lea Bauman – b 01 Sept 1970; m 10 Sept 1994 Mark Riley

Carolyn Sue RAMMELSBERG d/o Vernon David Rammelsberg & Barbara Jean nee Miller; b 23 Jul 1956 Cedar Rapids, IA bpt 02 Sept 1956; 1st m 29 Nov 1975 Stacey Allen Frank (b 24 May 1956) DVD. Children:

Kimberly Nichole Frank – b 02 Jul 1979;

1st m 31 Dec 2002 Dennis Little. Children: Orion Frank Little (b 15 Apr 1999), Alex Little (b 01 May 2005)

Kyle Allen Frank – b 05 Feb 1982; m Jessika NN. Child:

Lydia Frank (b 20 May 2006)

2nd m 11 Jan 1997 Carolyn Sue Rammelsberg to Jay Quimby. Children:

Brad Quimby – b NFR

Matt Quimby – b NFR

Cecil RAMMELSBERG s/o Alphonsa Friedrich Emil Rammelsberg & Mary Jane nee Armstrong; b 1901 Canton Twp Benton Co IA; m Dec 1925 Esther Thomas (b 1905 Benton Twp Benton Co IA, d 1987) d/o Herman Graham Thomas & Mary Ellen nee Nabholz of Shellsburg, IA. Farmed four miles north and one mile east of Newhall, IA. Children:

Beulah – m James Moloney; Marion residence

Mildred – dec'd

Fern – m James Bauman; Fargo, ND residence

Kathryn – m Keith Knaack; Vinton, IA residence, daughter:Karolyn

Cecil Faye – m Clydene Finch; Branson, MO residence

Roxy – m Wayne Roster; Vinton, IA residence

Darlene – m Donald Lawler; Chicago, IL residence

Esther Mae – m Charles Johnson; Goodhue, MN residence

Dale – m Caryl Fredrick; Cedar Rapids, IA residence

Glen – m Billie Alcott; Blairstown, IA residence

Cecil Faye RAMMELSBERG s/o Cecil Rammelsberg & Esther nee Thomas; m Clydene Finch. Branson, MO residence. Children:

Jason – NFR

Ava – NFR

Charles Fred RAMMELSBERG s/o William R. Rammelsberg & Anna Katherine nee Krug; b 20 Jan 1907 Atkins, IA bpt 06 Oct 1907 St.Steph, d 07 Jul 1996 ae89y 5m 17d; m 19 Mar 1930 TrinCR to Wilhelmine (Wilma) I. Pheffer (b 03 May 1909 East Amana, IA d 14 Jun 1972 ae63y 1m 11d Cedar Rapids, IA bur 16 Jun 1973 Linwood Cem, Cedar Rapids, IA). Child:
>   Marlene Ann – b 24 Aug 1934, bpt 21 Oct 1934; m Robert John
>   Horton

Christopher Lee RAMMELSBERG s/o Vernon David Rammelsberg & Barbara Jean nee Miller; b 16 Feb 1973; 1st m 24 Mar 1994 Rhonda Jean Aaron (b 28 May 1974)DVD. Children:
>   STEPCHILD: Chelsea – b 13 Aug 1992
>   Austin – b 20 Jul 1995

2nd m 12 Apr 2002 Christopher Lee Rammelsberg to Lynae DePascalis (b 14 Jun ND). Children:
>   STEPCHILD: Ryan DePascalis – b 31 Jan 2000
>   Cody – b 10 Feb 2005
>   Owen Chris – b 18 Mar 2006

Darlene RAMMELSBERG d/o Cecil Rammelsberg & Esther nee Thomas; m Donald Lawler. Chicago, IL residence. Children:
>   Philip Lawler – NFR
>   Brian Lawler – m Angela Ferraro
>   Tracy Lawler – NFR

David RAMMELSBERG s/o Carl (Charles) Rammelsberg & Barbara nee Rinderknecht; b 26 Apr 1863 Benton Co IA, d Aug 1900; m 26 Mar 1894 Magdalena (Lena) Nell. Farmed south of Atkins, IA. In 1892, purchased an eighty-acre farm 1/2 mile southeast of Atkins. Children:
>   Leonard – moved to Story City, IA
>   Roy Carl Jacob- m 1920 Katherine Ruth Mohr, Atkins, IA farmers
>   Elizabeth – m Herbert Van Voy, Newhall, IA resident

David Henry RAMMELSBERG s/o Vernon David Rammelsberg & Barbara Jean nee Miller; b 24 Sept 1951 Cedar Rapids, IA bpt 14 Oct 1951 St.Steph; m 17 Mar 1973 Cathy Rae Clark (b 20 May 1952). Children:
>   Brooke Lee – b 01 Nov 1974; m 13 Jul 2005 Fred Agan
>   Josie Ann – b 20 Nov 1977; m 20 May 2000 Mark Norton. Child:
>   Jackson Ray Norton (b 31 Jul 2004)

Kyla Kay – b 24 May 1981; m 08 Oct 2005 Todd Sergeant

Doris Ann RAMMELSBERG d/o Elmer Henry David Rammelsberg & Goldie Etta nee Snell; b 25 Mar 1929 St.Lukes Hosp Cedar Rapids, IA bpt 19 May 1929 St.Steph, con St.Steph, 1946 Class Atkins High School; m 24 Jun 1948 St.Steph to Wendell Creston Williams (b 09 Nov 1923; Truck Driver) s/o Ward Williams & Georgina nee Beard. Residence Fremont Twp Benton Co IA. Celebrated 50th Golden Wedding Anniversary. Children:

Linda Anna Williams – b 08 Feb 1949;
    m 15 Jul 1972 Ralph Leroy Root
William Craig Williams – b 15 Sept 1951;
    m 07 Jul 1979 Victoria Elaine Reed
Robert Gene Williams – b 07 Oct 1952; d 11 Dec 1974;
    m 27 Oct 1973 Cheryl Ann Pfiffner
James Creston Williams – b 04 Apr 1955;
    1st m 25 Sept 1976 Stacy Kay Zanka DVD;
    2nd m 01 Jun 1983 Sandra L. Kirby
Sherri Lynn Williams – b 08 May 1956;
    m 23 Sept 1978 Scott Michael Peters DVD
Charles Dean Williams – b 25 Nov 1962;
    m 24 Aug 1985 Valerie Renee Serbousek
Dennis Scott Williams – b 10 Oct 1964;
    m 28 Aug 1993 Teresa Ann Brown DVD

Dorothy Jean RAMMELSBERG d/o James William Rammelsberg & Lurel Jean nee Blackwell; b 30 Jul 1949; 1st m 1967 Kenneth Kettleson. Children:

Billy Kettleson – b 20 Nov 1968
Brian Scott Kettleson – b 1969
2nd m 1970 Dorothy Jean nee Rammeslberg Kettleson to Carl Witt SR. Child:
Carl Witt JR. – b 1972

Elmer Henry David RAMMELSBERG s/o William R. Rammelsberg & Anna Katherine nee Krug; b 16 Sept 1896 Atkins, IA bpt 21 Feb 1897 St.Steph, con St.Steph, d 29 May 1985 ae88y 8m 13d Cedar Rapids, IA bur 31 May 1985 St.Steph Cem; 1st m 15 Dec 1921 Cedar Rapids to Goldie Etta Snell (b 13 Sept 1896, d 28 Apr 1961 ae65y 7m 15d St.Lukes Hosp, Cedar Rapids, IA bur 02 May 1961 St.Steph Cem) d/o Julian Franklin Snell & Etta nee Elson. Farmers in Linn Co. Children:

Vernon David – b 21 Sept 1927 Farm Clinton Twp Linn Co IA

d 22 Feb 2005 at TX home; m 15 Oct 1950 Barbara Jean Miller
Doris Ann – b 25 Mar 1929 St.Lukes Hosp Cedar Rapids, IA;
m 24 Jun 1948 Wendell Creston Williams
2nd m 1961 Elmer Henry David Rammelsberg to Constance Jensen (d 28 Feb 1998)of Shellsburg, IA met arranging 1st wife's gravestone. Cedar Rapids, IA residence.

Esther Mae RAMMELSBERG d/o Cecil Rammelsberg & Esther nee Thomas; m Charles Johnson. Goodhue, MN residence. Children:
Brenda Johnson – m Russell Ehlers, daughters: Laura and Katie
Karen Johnson – m Larry Sorensen
Nancy Johnson – NFR
David Johnson – dec'd

Eunice Jean RAMMELSBERG d/o Nettie L. nee Krug & Melvin A. Rammelsberg; b 26 Aug 1946; m 21 Sept 1974 Thomas Pingenot (b 03 Feb 1944). Children:
Mark Joseph Pingenot – b 02 Dec 1975; m 07 Jun 2003 Carrie Yedlik
Aaron Thomas Pingenot – b 03 Dec 1978

Evelyn Hettie RAMMELSBERG d/o Ralph Leonard Rammelsberg SR. & Louise May nee Schlotterback; b 04 Sept 1929 Fremont Twp Benton Co IA; m 18 Jul 1947 Ora Oscar Bakenhus (b 21 Oct 1919) s/o Oscar Adolph Bakenhus & Martha nee Otte of R#1 Leigh, NE. DVD. Children:
Lorna Louise Bakenhus – b 14 Dec 1948
Oscar Adolph Bakenhus – b 30 Aug 1950, d 27 Mar 1991
bur Nettleton Cem, Jonesboro, AR
Orville Allen Bakenhus – b 07 Jun 1952
Joyce May Bakenhus – b 30 Sept 1954;
m 25 Nov 1973 Wayne B. Stone

Fern RAMMELSBERG d/o Cecil Rammelsberg & Esther nee Thomas; m James Bauman. West Fargo, ND residence. Children:
Craig Bauman – m Marie Erstad, daughter: Sarah
Scott Bauman – m Sanra Norman, daughter: Rachel
Jeffrey Bauman – m Evalina Sotelo
Faythe Bauman – m David Irvin, sons: Timothy, TWINS: Michael, Bryan
Kerry Bauman – NFR

Gerald Lee RAMMELSBERG s/o Vernon David Rammelsberg & Barbara Jean nee Miller; b 02 Apr 1953 Cedar Rapids, IA, bpt 10 May 1953 Parent's Home, Clinton Twp. Linn Co IA; m 03 Sept 1972 Carol Ann Rutan (b 01 Mar 1954). Children:

> Christopher Lee – b 16 Feb 1973;
>> 1st m 24 Mar 1994 Rhonda Jean Aaron DVD;
>> 2nd m 12 Apr 2002 Lynae DePascalis
> Eric Gerald – b 08 Feb 1975; m 13 May 1995 Stacey L. Wittman (b 12 May 1974)
> Marcy Ann – b 23 Feb 1980; m 22 Jun 2000 Gustavo A. Munoz

Gladys Marie RAMMELSBERG d/o Earl Edward Rammelsberg & Emma Katherine Elizabeth nee Krug; b 29 Jan 1933 Parent's farm east of Newhall, bpt 05 Mar 1933 con St.John, Graduate Newhall High School; m 08 Dec 1954 St.John Luth Ch, to Richard Folkmann (b 1928) s/o Christian H. Folkmann & Sophia nee Baack. Farmers on Great-Grandfather Hugo Rammelsberg's land. Observed 50th Wedding Anniversary. Children:

> Dean A. Folkmann – b 02 Jul 1956; m 20 Jun 1998 Julie Lynn Gaddis
> Diana Kay Folkmann – b 26 Aug 1959 Cedar Rapids, IA residence

Glen RAMMELSBERG s/o Cecil Rammelsberg & Esther nee Thomas; m Billie Alcott. Blairstown, IA residence. Children:

> Dori – NFR
> Robert – NFR

Harold Roy RAMMELSBERG s/o Roy Carl Jacob Rammelsberg & Katherine Ruth nee Mohr; b 25 Sept 1923; U.S. Navy World War II in Iwo Jima, Okinawa, Japan on aircraft carrier USS WASP. Atkins Postmaster 02 Feb 1948 retiring Nov 1978; 1st m 03 Sept 1950 Cedar Rapids, IA to Kathleen Rose Kahler (b 17 Sept 1926 Palo, IA, d 30 Apr 1989 [cancer] St.Lukes Hosp Cedar Rapids, IA ae62y 7m 13d bur St.Steph Cem; Atkins School Vocal/Band teacher) d/o Fred Kahler & Rose Mae nee Hollenbeck. Children:

> Brian Karl – b 15 Jul 1952, m 10 Jun 1978 Jeanne Parker, Atkins, IA residence
> Sarah Louise – b 25 Jul 1955, medical technologist; residence Coppell, Texas

2nd m 15 May 1993 Harold Roy Rammelsberg to Hazel Wahl (b 20 Apr 1921).

Hugo H. RAMMELSBERG s/o Nettie L. nee Krug & Melvin A. Rammelsberg; b 28 May 1934; m 20 May 1960 Joan Daily. Children:
John – b 25 Feb 1961;m 02 Mar 1987 Leona Scott DVD
Anne Marie – b 21 Nov 1966
Ruth Ellen – b 25 Feb 1969; m 05 Aug 1995 Bill Paarmann

*Hugo Herman Friedrich RAMMELSBERG s/o Frederich Rammelsberg & Charlotte nee Schreiber; b 1827 Magdeburg, os Prussia ns German, d 1879 Shellsburg, Benton Co IA; sailed to USA landing in New Orleans 1847; stayed with his Uncle Henry Kuhnholz who emigrated a few years earlier. Hugo learned the barber trade in New Orleans. In 1849, he established a mercantile business in Yazoo City, MS. 1854 he came to Iowa and entered 1280 acres in Section 18 and 19, Fremont Twp Benton Co IA, then returned to the South. 1855 his brother Alphonsa and his cousin Charles (Carl) arrived from Germany. He brought them to Iowa and located them on the land he had entered and again returned to the South. 1857 he closed out his business in Yazoo City, MS; moved to Iowa and engaged in farming. Hugo married twice. 1st m Scott Co IA to Emiline Toedter (b 1836 Holstein, Germany, d 1863). Children:
Ottillie – b 1859; m John Armstrong
Alphonsa Friedrich Emil – b 1861; d 1953 IA; m Mary Armstrong
2nd m Aft 1863 Hugo Herman Friedrich Rammelsberg to Bertha Hauschild (b 1845, d 1922). Children:
Constance – b 1867, d 1945; m 1888 George Grovert
Louise – b 1873, d 1916; m Henry Grovert
Julia – b 1875, d 1949; m Otto B. Schmidt
Elfriede – b 1880, d 1963; m Rex Shannon

Iris May RAMMELSBERG d/o Ralph Leonard Rammelsberg SR. & Louise May nee Schlotterback; b 11 May 1924 Farm north Atkins, Fremont Twp Benton Co IA, bpt at home 1924; m 06 Nov 1941 Harold John Peacock (b 18 Oct 1920, d 26 Nov 1987 ae67y 1m 8d) s/o James Peacock. Children:
Michael John Peacock-b 23 Jun 1942;
    m 17 Oct 1970 Linda Jean Andrews McClurg; DVD
Son NN – b Jul 1944, d Jul 1944
James Patrick Peacock – b 14 Mar 1946;
    m 09 Nov 1964 Betty Lou Leoffler
Joan Kay Peacock – b 08 Dec 1947;
    1st m 20 Jul 1968 Patrick Henry White DVD;
390

2nd m 23 May 1988 Harold Schrader

James William RAMMELSBERG s/o Ralph Leonard Rammelsberg SR. & Louise May nee Schlotterback; b 02 Feb 1927 Fremont Twp Benton Co IA; 1st m 1946 Lurel Jean Blackwell (b 1927) DVD. Children:
    Mary Ann – b 14 Jun 1947; m NN Blackwell; Cedar Rapids, IA
    Albert Edwin – b 08 May 1948
    Dorothy Jean – b 03 Jul 1949; 1st m 1967 Kenneth E. Kettleson; DVD;
        2nd m 1970 Carl Witt; 3rd m NN Henry; Ellsworth, KS
    Ralph Leonard II- b 07 Nov 1950, m 1970 Donna Fay; DVD
2nd m 28 Mar 1959 Iowa City, IA James William Rammelsberg to Mildred Winifred Glover (b 15 Aug 1934, d 01 Oct 2006 ae72y 1m 16d bur St.Steph Cem).

John RAMMELSBERG s/o Hugo H. Rammelsberg & Joan nee Daily; b 25 Feb 1961; m 02 Mar 1987 Leona Scott DVD. Children:
    Rachelle Danielle – b 23 Jul 1988
    TWINS: Jordan Paul – b 20 Mar 1991
           Jacob Steven – b 20 Mar 1991

John August RAMMELSBERG s/o William R. Rammelsberg & Anna Katherine nee Krug; b 14 Apr 1903 Atkins, IA bpt 05 Jul 1903, d 17 Feb 1994 ae90y 10m 3d; m 21 Apr 1928 Bernice M. Hamilton (b 13 Dec 1903, d 12 Apr 1995 ae91y 4m). Children:
    John B.- b 19 Feb 1930, m 08 Oct 1955 Ruth Brouse
    Bernadine – b 11 May 1931, 1st m Robert Ward DVD;
        2nd m 16 Jun 1956 William Hoyt
    Martha R. – b 06 Sept 1937, m 28 Jul 1956 John Richard Holmes

John B. RAMMELSBERG s/o John August Rammelsberg & Bernice M. nee Hamilton; b 19 Feb 1930; m 08 Oct 1955 to Ruth Brouse (b 09 Oct 1932). Children:
    Paul G. – b 1956, m 1976 Monica Ann Lynch
    John Charles – b 28 Sept 1957, m 02 Jun 1977 Brenda Sue Nessit
    Celeste – b 11 Nov 1958
    Andrew – b 19 Aug 1960, m 28 May 1988 Lisa K. Lamb

Karla Marie RAMMELSBERG d/o Marvin Fred Rammelsberg & Elaine Laura nee Nuechterlein; b 15 May 1957 Indianapolis, IN; m 26 Jun 1976 Anaheim, CA to Ronald Roberts (b 11 May 1954). Children:

Andrew Michael Roberts – b 05 Jun 1981 Santa Ana, CA
Aaron Matthew Roberts – b 11 Sept 1984 Fallbrook, CA
Alexis Marie Roberts – b 28 Sept 1986 Fallbrook, CA

Kathryn RAMMELSBERG d/o Cecil Rammelsberg & Esther nee Thomas; m Keith Knaack. Vinton, IA residence. Child:
  Karolyn Knaack – NFR

Kay Elaine RAMMELSBERG d/o Marvin Fred Rammelsberg & Elaine Laura nee Nuechterlein; b 18 Aug 1952 Valparaiso, IN; 1st m 16 Jun 1973 Terry Culpepper. Child:
  Lisa Kay Culpepper – b 25 Aug 1974 Seward, AK;
    m 21 Aug 1993 Reno, NV to Lance Caddel
2nd m 29 Mar 1980 Kay Elaine nee Rammelsberg Culpepper to Kevin Brown (b 28 Dec 1951).Children:
  James Mirari Brown – b 04 May 1987 Paradise CA
  TWINS: Lael Anne Brown – b 24 May 1989 Sacramento, CA
    Kathrin Terra Brown – b 24 May 1989 Sacramento, CA

Kenneth Carl RAMMELSBERG s/o Roy Carl Jacob Rammelsberg & Katherine Ruth nee Mohr; b 06 Aug 1936, d 26 Sept 1988 ae52y 1m 20d[Car/Truck Accident] bur St.Steph Cem; m 10 Jun 1962 Florence Ellen Zeadow (b 04 Mar 1942). Atkins, IA residence; Kenneth: section worker and foreman for Chicago Milwaukee St.Paul & Pacific Railroad; Florence: radio operator-dispatcher Chicago & Northwestern Railroad. Children:
  Tammy Jo – b 03 Dec 1962; m 04 Sept 1988 Joseph M. Carmody
  Todd Kenneth- b 22 Nov 1964
  Troy Kenneth – b 13 Aug 1968, d 19 Apr 1987 [Car Accident]
    bur St.Steph Cem

Kenneth Ralph RAMMELSBERG s/o Ralph Leonard Rammelsberg SR. & Louise May nee Schlotterback; b 12 May 1928 Fremont Twp Benton Co IA d 27 Nov 1996; m Nov 1948 in Austria/Jan 1955 USA to Anna Marie Schoenauer (b 22 Nov 1916 Austria, d 03 Jul 1982 ae65y 7m 10d). Child:
  Marie Louise – b 10 June 1950 in Austria

Kurt Marvin RAMMELSBERG s/o Marvin Fred Rammelsberg & Elaine Laura nee Nuechterlein; b 08 Apr 1960 Anaheim, CA; m 15 Jun 1985 Carol Ann Bulthius (b 09 Dec 1961). Children:
  James Everett – b 13 Nov 1989 Anaheim, CA

Stephen Chet – b/d 17 Nov 1993 Orange CA
Benjamin Kurt – b 26 Jun 1996 Orange, CA

Laura Katherine RAMMELSBERG d/o William R. Rammelsberg & Anna Katherine nee Krug; b 26 Nov 1898 Fremont Twp Benton Co IA, bpt 30 Jul 1899 St.Steph, con St.Steph; d 08 Feb 2000 ae101y 2m 13d bur 12 Feb 2000 St.Steph Cem; m 16 Mar 1921 St.Steph to Karl Fredrich Wilhelmi (b 13 Dec 1896 Fremont Twp Benton Co, bpt and con St.Steph, d 26 Jul 1985 ae88y 7m 13d, bur 29 Jul 1985 St.Steph Cem) s/o Tobias Wilhelmi & Barbara Maria nee Rinderknecht. Farmers west of Atkins, IA. Children:
    Mary Ann Barbara Wilhelmi – b 13 Oct 1924;
        m 16 Mar 1944 Marvin Peter Kreutner
    Lenore Katherine Wilhelmi – b 28 Oct 1926;
        m 27 Feb 1949 Delmar Pohlman
    Edward Leroy Wilhelmi – b 23 Dec 1929;
        m 29 Oct 1950 LaVonne Wiebold

Lois Ruth RAMMELSBERG d/o Roy Carl Jacob Rammelsberg & Katherine Ruth nee Mohr; b 19 Oct 1927; m 02 Jun 1959 William Walter Bienlien (b 05 Jun 1932). Children:
    Jacqueline Ruth Bienlien – b 29 Mar 1961
    Mark William Bienlien – b 21 Apr 1963;
        m 15 Aug 1987 Clare McDonald (b 04 Jun 1964)
    Kent Daniel Bienlien – b 13 May 1964;
        m 31 May 1986 Sarah Martley
    Janeen Lois Bienlien – b 19 Apr 1968;
        m 30 Dec 1995 Corey Mark Wakeland (b 23 Sept 1971)

Marlene Ann RAMMELSBERG d/o Charles Fred Rammelsberg & Wilhelmine (Wilma) I. nee Pheffer; b 24 Aug 1934 Linn Co IA, bpt 21 Oct 1934; m Robert John Horton (b 25 Apr 1929). Children:
    Jay Robert Horton (Adopted) – b 10 Jun 1968
    Dee Ann Horton – b 01 Aug 1969;
        m 22 Aug 1992 John Michael Warren

Martha R. RAMMELSBERG d/o John August Rammelsberg & Bernice M. nee Hamilton; b 06 Sept 1937; m 28 Jul 1956 John Richard Holmes (b 22 Apr 1933). Children:
    Brian Holmes – b 17 Aug 1961; m 06 Sept 1986;
        m C. Marie Anderson DVD 1995

Connie Holmes – b 02 Dec 1964, m 21 Jun 1986 Jeffrey Alan Palmer

Marvin Fred RAMMELSBERG s/o Roy Carl Jacob Rammelsberg & Katherine Ruth nee Mohr; b 10 Dec 1920; m 25 Aug 1951 Elaine Laura Nuechterlein (b 25 Apr 1930). Children:

Kay Elaine – b 18 Aug 1952 Valparaiso, IN;
1st m 16 Jun 1973 Terry Culpepper;
2nd m 29 Mar 1980 Kevin Brown
Karen Ruth – b 05 Jul 1954 Valparaiso, IN;
m 09 Aug 1975 Anaheim, CA Douglas Gerth(b 11 May 1954)
Karla Marie – b 15 May 1957 Indianapolis, IN;
m 26 Jun 1976 Anaheim, CA Ronald Roberts
Kurt Marvin – b 08 Apr 1960 Anaheim, CA;
m 15 Jun 1985 Carol Ann Bulthius

Norma L. RAMMELSBERG d/o Nettie L. nee Krug & Melvin A. Rammelsberg; b 14 Dec 1930, d 26 Sept 1972 ae41y 9m 12d; m 14 Nov 1954 Oscar R Hanson JR. (b 11 Jul 1932, d 12 Jan 2003 ae70y 6m 1d). Children:

Edward R Hanson – b 20 Nov 1958; 1st m 25 Sept Dea Hettinger DVD
2nd m 21 Apr 1990 Rhonda Tuttle
Sally Ann Hanson – b 26 Jan 1956; m 05 Oct 1974 Steve Dale Bruce
Richard John Hanson – b 19 Jul 1960, d 09 Jun 1980

Paul G. RAMMELSBERG s/o John B. Rammelsberg & Ruth nee Brouse; b 08 May 1956; 1st m 22 Sept 1976 Monica Ann Lynch (b 28 Apr 1957) DVD. Child:

Kyle L.- b 01 Apr 1977
2nd m Paul G. Rammelsberg to Kelly J. NN

Ralph Leonard RAMMELSBERG SR. s/o William R. Rammelsberg & Anna Katharine nee Krug; b 25 Nov 1897 Atkins, IA bpt 24 Apr 1898 Atkins, d 13 Oct 1940 ae42y 10m 18d[Farm Suicide near Atkins] bur 16 Oct 1940 St.Steph Cem; m 24 Jan 1923 Atkins, IA to Louise May (b Helen Louise) Schlotterback (b 09 Nov 1901, bpt Jul 1911 Atkins Presbyterian Ch, d 22 Oct 1974) d/o Fred Bert Armstrong & Elizabeth nee Pransky/Adoption Parents:Albert Schlotterback & Hettie May nee Armstrong. Farmers owning six farms. Children:

Iris May – b 11 May 1924; m 24 Jan 1941 Harold John Peacock
Albert Edwin – b 14 Nov 1925; d 09 Oct 1944 Kansas City

James William – b 02 Feb 1927; 1st m 1946 Lurel Jean Blackwell
 DVD; 2nd m 28 Mar 1958 Mildred Winifred Glover
Kenneth Ralph – b 12 May 1928;
 m Nov 1948 Anna Maria Schoenauer
Evelyn Hattie – b 04 Sept 1929; m 18 Jul 1947 Ora Bakenhus DVD
Bruce Thomas – b 25 Apr 1931; m 24 Jul 1970 Ellen Pauline Bowers
2nd m Louise May nee Schlotterback Rammelsberg to John Clifford Wilkins.
3rd m Louise May nee Schlotterback Rammelsberg Wilkins to Hobart Clark.

Ralph Leonard RAMMELSBERG II s/o James William Rammelsberg & Lurel Jean nee Blackwell; b 07 Nov 1950 Fremont Twp Benton Co IA; m 1970 Donna Fay NN (b 1950) DVD 22 Mar 1979. Children:
 Issac William – b 21 Mar 1973
 Ona Lea – b 01 Jun 1974
 Randy – b 15 Jul 1975
 Kevin Ray – b 28 Feb 1977

Rose Elizabeth RAMMELSBERG d/o William R. Rammelsberg & Anna Katherine nee Krug; b 14 Aug 1905 Fremont Twp Benton Co IA, d 25 Jul 2006 ae100y 11m 19d bur St.Steph Cem; m 15 Dec 1917 Walter Wilhelmi (b 06 Dec 1901 Fremont Twp Benton Co IA, d 22 Feb 1995 ae93y 2m 16d bur St.Steph Cem) s/o Tobias Wilhelmi & Barbara Maria nee Rinderknecht. Children:
 Donald Wilhelmi – b 03 Feb 1929; m 22 Jul 1951 Mae Alpers
 Richard Walter Wilhelmi – b 08 Sept 1934, d 06 Jul 1995
  bur St.Steph Cem; m 14 Feb 1959 Betty Sue McShane
 Carol Wilhelmi – b 15 Apr 1939;
  m 28 Mar 1959 John Lenard Edwards

Roxy RAMMELSBERG d/o Cecil Rammelsberg & Esther nee Thomas; m Wayne Roster. Vinton, IA residence. Children:
 Renea Roster – m William Daringer; Waterloo, IA residence
 Curtis Roster – m Barbara Tharp: TWIN dau: Julie and Jennifer
 Kristy Roster – m Russell Haefner; Vinton, IA residence
 David Roster – m Tracy Steinberg: children: Adam and Megan Lou

Roy Carl Jacob RAMMELSBERG s/o David Rammelsberg & Lena nee Nell; b 28 Jul 1897, d 07 Jan 1980 ae82y 5m 10d, bur St.Steph; m 03 Feb 1920 Katherine Ruth Mohr (b 27 Sept 1894, d 07 Apr 1981 ae86y 6m 11d bur St.Steph Cem). Farmed two miles south of Atkins, also farmed eighty-acre Rammelsberg homestead near Atkins, IA. Children:

Marvin Fred – b 10 Dec 1920;
    m 25 Aug 1951 Elaine Nuechterlein, CA
Harold Roy – b 25 Sept 1923;
    1st m 03 Sept 1950 Kathleen Rose Kahler, Palo, IA;
    2nd m 15 May 1993 Hazel Wahl
Victor David – b 25 Apr 1926;
    m 20 Jun 1959 Laverne Rose Zimmerman, IN residence
Lois Ruth – b 19 Oct 1927; m 02 Jun 1959 William Walter Bienlien,
    Davenport, IA
Leanna Rose – b 14 Oct 1930; m 11 Nov 1953 Leland Floyd
    (b 23 Aug 1971)
Kenneth Carl – b 06 Aug 1936, d 26 Sept 1988, bur St.Steph Cem;
    m 10 Jun 1962 Florence Ellen Zeadow

Selma Ann RAMMELSBERG d/o William (Bill) Henry Rammelsberg & Ardis nee Sisley; b 02 Aug 1948; m 02 Aug 1975 Donald Walser (b 27 Sept 1948). Cedar Rapids, IA residence. Children:

Mathew Donald Walser – Stillborn Oct 1978
Curtis Mathew Walser – b 02 Nov 1979
Mitchell Walser – b 03 Mar 1984;
    m 09 Jun 2007 Jennifer Diane Velky

Shirley Ann RAMMELSBERG d/o Earl Edward Rammelsberg & Emma Katherine Elizabeth nee Krug; b 10 Jan 1941 Parent's farm east of Newhall, bpt 22 Mar 1942 St.John, con St.John, Newhall High School, d 18 May 1984 ae43y 4m 8d [Suicide] Eldorado Twp Benton Co IA, bur 21 May 1984 St.John Cem; m 14 Feb 1960 St.John to Dennis Gewecke (b 13 Jul 1940) s/o Sterling Gewecke (b 10 Sept 1912, d 23 Jul 2006 ae93y 10m 13d) & Kathryn nee Hagen. 1984 DVD. Children:

Cindy Kay Gewecke – b 20 Sept 1961
Terry Lee Gewecke -b 26 Aug 1964, m 1986 Lori Ann Newton

Tammy Jo RAMMELSBERG d/o Kenneth Carl Rammelsberg & Florence Ellen nee Zeadow; b 03 Dec 1962; m 04 Sept 1988 Joseph Carmody (b 01 May 1963). Children:

Erin Kathleen Carmody – b 01 Aug 1990
Thomas Joseph Carmody – b 22 Nov 1992
Allison Elizabeth Carmody – b 22 Jun 1995

Todd Kenneth RAMMELSBERG s/o Kenneth Carl Rammelsberg & Florence Ellen nee Zeadow; b 15 Jan 1964; m NN. Child:
    Kandace Taylor Hampton – b 13 Feb 1990

Verla Emma RAMMELSBERG d/o Earl Edward Rammelsberg & Emma Katherine Elizabeth nee Krug; b 02 Mar 1937 Parent's farm east of Newhall, IA bpt 28 Mar 1937 St.John, con St.John, Newhall High School; residence Hollywood, CA. Never Married.

Vernon David RAMMELSBERG s/o Elmer Henry David Rammelsberg & Goldie Etta nee Snell; b 21 Sept 1927 Parent's Farm, Clinton Twp Linn Co IA, bpt 08 Jan 1928 St.Steph, con 1941 St.Steph. 1945 Class Atkins High School; d 22 Feb 2005 ae77y 5m 1d at TX winter home, bur St.Steph Cem; m 15 Oct 1950 Barbara Jean Miller (b 19 May 1930) d/o Henry N. Miller of Marion. Farmered Elmer Rammelsberg farm in Linn Co IA forty years. Children:
    David Henry – b 24 Sept 1951 St.Lukes Hosp Cedar Rapids, IA;
        m 17 Mar 1973 Cathy Rae Clark
    Gerald Lee – b 02 Apr 1953 St.Lukes Hosp Cedar Rapids, IA;
        m 03 Sept 1972 Carol Ann Rutan
    Carolyn Sue – b 23 Jul 1956 St.Lukes Hosp Cedar Rapids, IA;
        1st m 29 Nov 1975 Stacey Allen Frank DVD;
        2nd m 10 Jan 1997 Jay Morgan Quimby

Victor David RAMMELSBERG s/o Roy Carl Jacob Rammelsberg & Katherine Ruth nee Mohr; b 25 Apr 1926; m 20 Jun 1959 Laverne Rose Zimmerman (b 11 Mar 1928). Children:
    Paul David – b 31 Aug 1960; m 07 Nov 1987 Joanne Mentor
        (b 18 Aug 1958)
    Dianne Rose – b 04 Jan 1962
    Stephen Carl – b 30 Jun 1964
    Susan Kay – b 17 Jan 1967; m 05 Oct 1991 Leo Frey

William Edward RAMMELSBERG s/o William (Bill) Henry Rammelsberg & Ardis nee Sisley; b 03 May 1945 St.Lukes Hosp Cedar Rapids, IA; m Dec 1978 Susan Orhman (b 11 Oct ND). Children:
    Kristi Kaye – b 06 Jun 1981 Pullman, WA
    Eric – b 26 Oct 1984

William (Bill) Henry RAMMELSBERG JR s/o William R. Rammelsberg & Anna Katherine nee Krug; b 14 Oct 1911 near Palo, Linn Co IA, bpt 17 Dec 1911, d 17 Jun 1992; m 01 May 1940 Nashua, IA to Ardis Sisley (b 29 Dec 1913, d 20 Apr 1996) d/o Edgar Sisley. Farmers in Fremont Twp Benton Co IA. Celebrated 50th Wedding Anniversary. Children:
>   William Edward-b 03 May 1945; m Dec 1978 Susan Ohrman;
>>   Pullman WA
>   Selma Ann – b 02 Aug 1948; m 02 Aug 1975 Donald Walser,
>>   Cedar Rapids, IA

Alan Henry RATHJE s/o Louise nee Gerhold & Albert H. Rathje; b 29 Mar 1931 bpt 26 Apr 1931 St.Steph con 02 Apr 1944 St.Steph; farmed parents farm west of Atkins, IA; 1st m 04 Jun 1960 TrinCR to Dorothy Olive Gillis DVD. Children:
>   Marvin – b NFR, m Sandy NN
>   Melvin Leland – b 02 Dec 1958 Cedar Rapids, IA;
>>   m 26 Sept 1985 Elaine Marie nee Tharp Hrdlicka
>   Jeffrey Alan – b 17 Jan 1961 Vinton, IA;
>>   m 31 Jul 1982 Tammy Kay Schminke
>   Jolene Louise – b 25 Jun 1964 Cedar Rapids, IA

2nd m Alan Henry Rathje to Judy Snider, Cedar Rapids, IA residence.
>   STEPCHILDREN:
>   Dale Snider – NFR
>   Charles Snider – NFR
>   Kim Snider – NFR
>   Christa Snider-Holtz – NFR

2nd m 01 Jan 1999 Dorothy Olive nee Gillis Rathje to Lenard James Armstrong.

Craig Allen RATHJE s/o Glen Edward Rathje & Dixie Lee nee Pierce; b 22 Sept 1961 Newhall, IA; 1st m Caroline Rask. Children:
>   Chad Alan – b 01 May 1983, d 29 May 1983,
>>   bur Linwood Cem, Cedar Rapids, IA
>   Candice – b 1984 or 1985

2nd m 17 Sept 1994 Cedar Rapids, IA Craig Allen Rathje to Karolyn Kay Robinson.

Glen Edward RATHJE s/o Henry Carl Rathje & Emma Gertrude nee Haerther; b 20 Jul 1935 Van Horne Benton Co IA d 24 Jun 2005 [Cancer] ae69y 11m 4d bur St.Joseph Cem; 1st m 27 Feb 1955 Atkins, IA to Dixie

Lee Pierce (b 13 Jul 1936) DVD. Children:
    Kristie Kay – b 04 Dec 1955 Newhall, IA;
        1st m 07 Oct 1972 Fred Christensen DVD;
        2nd m 03 Jul 1976 Clark Leslie Wagner DVD;
        3rd m Jerry Sauer
    Daniel Edward – b 17 Aug 1960 Newhall, IA; 1st m Dawn NN;
        2nd m Tammy Stoddard
    Craig Allen – b 22 Sept 1961 Newhall, IA; 1st m Caroline Rask DVD;
        2nd m 17 Sept 1994 Karolyn Kay Robinson
2nd m 06 Nov 1976 Glen Edward Rathje to Eldora Glick (b 31 Dec 1928) DVD.
3rd m 23 Oct 1989 Naples, FL Glen Edward Rathje to Arlys Van Langen Feaker (b 1932).

*Henry RATHJE b 1860 Uttendorf, Germany, d 1910 Benton Co IA; m Anna Suberger (b Germany, d Benton Co IA). Family came to Cedar Rapids, IA; later settled on a farm near Newhall, Benton Co IA. Children:
    Katharine – m Arthur Ford
    John C. – b 03 Jul 1887, d 1976; m 24 Sept 1913 Elizabeth Werning
        d/o Justus Werning & Maria nee Krahling
    Emma – m Arthur Richie
    Martha A. – b 26 Feb 1892, d 30 Jan 1944;
        m 23 Feb 1916 Albert W. Werning s/o Justus Werning &
        Maria nee Krahling
    Albert Henry – b 03 Oct 1894, d 06 Dec 1970 bur St.Steph Cem;
        m Louise Christina Gerhold
    Arthur – m Albia Pokay
    Marvin – m Maxine Barlow
    Henry Carl – b 28 Sept 1905, d 10 Apr 1975;
        m 10 Feb 1929 Emma Gertrude Haerther

Henry Carl RATHJE s/o Henry Rathje & Anna nee Suberger; b 28 Sept 1905 Cedar Rapids, IA, d 10 Apr 1975 Cedar Rapids, bur CdrMem; m 10 Feb 1929 St.Steph to Emma Gertrude Haerther (b 06 Dec 1906, d 27 Oct 1977 Cedar Rapids, bur CdrMem) d/o Henry August Gottlieb Haerther & Marie (Mary) Dorothea nee Schanbacher; Benton Co IA Farmers. Children:
    Ardith Mae – b 09 Feb 1930; m 28 Jun 1953 Jack Dillard Merritt
    Henry Charles – b 20 Mar 1933;
        m 24 May 1953 Jeanne Marilyn Simmer
    Glenn Edward – b 20 Jul 1935; d 24 Jan 2005 [Cancer];

1st m 27 Feb 1955 Dixie Lee Pierce;
2nd m 06 Nov 1976 Eldora Glick;
3rd m 23 Oct 1989 Arlys Van Langen Feaker
Lee Arthur – b 02 Mar 1940; m 09 Aug 1959 Joann Catherine Bascom

Henry Charles RATHJE s/o Henry Carl Rathje & Emma Gertrude Haerther; b 20 Mar 1933 Van Horne, Benton Co IA; m 24 May 1953 Atkins, IA to Jeanne Marilyn Simmer (b 12 Jan 1935 Fremont Twp) d/o Charles Simmer. Celebrated 40th and 50th Wedding Anniversary. Children:
Jonie Lee – b 09 Feb 1957 Robins, IA;
1st m 06 Dec 1975 Thomas Lou Witter; 2nd m Matthew Flynn
Julie Lynn – b 02 Apr 1960 Robins, IA;
1st m 23 May 1981 Gary Lee Parker;
2nd m Everett Anthony (Sam) Nemer;
3rd m 11 May 1996 Gary Puckett
Jerry Alan – b 26 Aug 1965 Robins, IA; m 04 Sept 1992 Kay Lynch
(b 04 Sept 1964)

Jeffrey Alan RATHJE s/o Alan Henry Rathje & Dorothy Olive nee Gillis; b 17 Jan 1961 Vinton, IA bpt 04 Mar 1961 Zion Luth Ch Shellsburg, IA con 23 Mar 1975 St.Steph; m 31 Jul 1982 St.John Ch to Tammy Kay Schminke (b 12 Sept 1963 Vinton, IA bpt 29 Sept 1963 StJohn con 03 Apr 1977 St.John). Children:
Matthew Alan – b 26 Aug 1984 Cedar Rapids, IA bpt 23 Sept 1984
& con 25 Apr 1999 St.John
Joshua Virgil – b 06 Oct 1986 Cedar Rapids, IA
bpt 16 Nov 1986 St.John
Adam Jeffrey – b 16 Sept 1989 Cedar Rapids, IA bpt 24 Sept 1989
Robert Merle – b 11 Oct 1993. bpt 07 Nov 1993

Jerry Alan RATHJE s/o Henry Charles Rathje & Jeanne Marilyn nee Simmer; b 26 Aug 1965 Robins, IA; m 04 Sept 1992 Cedar Rapids St.Pius Catholic Ch to Kay Marie Lynch (b 04 Sept 1964) d/o Paul & Carol Lynch. Child:
Andrea Marie – b 10 Jul 1998 Hiawatha, IA

*Johann Heinrich RATHJE b 1860 Uttendorf, Germany, d 1910 Benton Co IA; m Anna Rebecca Katherina Seeborger (b Germany, d Benton Co IA). Family came to Cedar Rapids, IA and later settled on farm near Newhall Benton Co IA. Children:

Katharine – m Arthur Ford

John C. – b 03 Jul 1887; m 24 Sept 1913 Elisabeth Werning
    d/o Justus & Maria nee Krahling

Emma – m Arthur Richie

Martha A. – b 26 Feb 1892, d 30 Jan 1944;
    m Albert W. Werning s/o Justus & Maria nee Krahling

Albert Henry – b 03 Oct 1894, d 06 Dec 1970 bur St.Steph Cem;
    m Louise Christina Gerhold

Arthur – m Albia Pokay

Marvin – m Maxine Barlow

Henry Carl – b 28 Sept 1905 Cedar Rapids, IA
    d 10 Apr 1975 Cedar Rapids, IA bur CdrMem;
    m 10 Feb 1929 Emma Gertrude Haerther

John C. RATHJE s/o Johann Heinrich Rathje & Anna Rebecca nee Seeborger: cf Elizabeth Werning.

Jolene Louise RATHJE d/o Alan Henry Rathje & Dorothy Olive nee Gillis; b 25 Jun 1964 Cedar Rapids, IA bpt 19 Jul 1964 St.Steph con 19 Mar 1978 St.Steph. Occupation: Cedar Rapids X-Ray technician.

Jonie Lee RATHJE d/o Henry Charles Rathje & Jeanne Marilyn nee Simmer; b 09 Feb 1957 Newhall, IA; 1st m 06 Dec 1975 Zion Luth Ch Hiawatha, IA to Thomas Lou Witter (b 07 May 1956 Cedar Rapids, IA) DVD. Child:
    Jenifer Lynn Witter – b 30 Sept 1983 Sarasota, FL
2nd m Jonie Lee nee Rathje Witter to Matthew Flynn. Child:
    Heather Renee Flynn – b 21 Mar 1990 Sarasota, FL

Julie Lynn RATHJE d/o Henry Charles Rathje & Jeanne Marilyn nee Simmer; b 02 Apr 1960 Atkins, IA; 1st m 23 May 1981 Hiawatha, IA Zion Luth Ch to Gary Lee Parker (b 27 Aug 1956 Cedar Rapids, IA) DVD.
2nd m Julie Lynn nee Rathje Parker to Everett Anthony Nemer DVD. Child:
    Mary Kristine Nemer – b 09 Jan 1990 Cedar Rapids, IA
3rd m 11 May 1996 Little Brown Church, Nashua, IA Julie Lynn nee Rathje Parker Nemer to Gary Lee Puckett (b 26 Jan 1960 Hillsboro, IL).

Kristie Kay RATHJE d/o Glen Edward Rathje & Dixie Lee nee Pierce; b 04 Dec 1976 Newhall, IA; 1st m 07 Oct 1972 Fred Christensen. Child:
    Kelly Lee Christensen – b 10 Feb 973

2nd m 03 Jul 1976 Kristie Kay nee Rathje to Clark Leslie Wagner (b 06 Apr 1955). Child:
    Cameron Wagner – NFR
3rd m Kristie Kay nee Rathje Wagner to Jerry Sauer.

Lee Arthur RATHJE s/o Henry Carl Rathje & Emma Gertrude nee Haerther; b 02 Mar 1940 Newhall, IA; m 09 Aug 1959 Atkins, IA to Joann Catherine Bascom (b 03 Apr 1939). Children:
    Ricky Lee – b 03 Mar 1961; m 21 Jul 1984 Rebel Ann Bideaux
    Randy Lee – b 26 May 1963 Cedar Rapids, IA
    Renee Jo – b 22 Feb 1965l m 10 Sept 1989 Daniel Ellsworth

Martha A. Rathje d/o Johann Heinrich Rathje & Anna Rebecca Katherina nee Seeborger: cf Albert W. Werning

Martin RATHJE s/o Paul Justus Rathje & Lillian nee Carter; m Roxanne Brandt of Waverly, IA. Ankeny, IA residence. Children:
    Elizabeth – NFR
    Jonathan – NFR

Marvin RATHJE s/o Alan Henry Rathje & Dorothy Olive nee Gillis; m Sandy NN. Child:
    Melissa – b.01 28 1980, bpt 17 Feb 1980, con 26 Apr 1994
    Marsha – b 12 Apr 1981, bpt 03 May 1981, con 25 Apr 1995
    Amanda – b 01 Mar 1985, bpt 24 Mar 1985, con 24 Apr 1999

Melvin Leland RATHJE s/o Alan Henry Rathje & Dorothy Olive nee Gillis; b 02 Dec 1958 Cedar Rapids, bpt 04 Mar 1961 Zion Luth Ch Shellsburg, IA, con 15 Apr 1973 St.Steph; m 26 Sept 1985 Elaine Marie nee Tharp Hrdlicka (b 25 Mar 1942 bpt 08 Mar 1986 con 09 Mar 1986 St.Steph) d/o Clarence V. Tharp & Pauline L. nee Rayner.
    STEPCHILDREN:
    David Dochterman – b 31 Aug 1961
    Mark Dochterman – b 24 Oct 1963

Paul Justus RATHJE s/o John C. Rathje & Elizabeth nee Werning; m 29 Aug 1947 Little Brown Church, Nashua, IA to Lillian C. Carter (b 16 Aug 1919 Vinton, IA; graduate Lincoln High School, Vinton, IA; d 26 Aug 2002 ae83y 10d bur St.John Cem) d/o Martin Carter & Myrtle nee Fary. Residence on the family farm. 1981 Retired in Newhall, IA. Children:

Martin – m Roxanne Brandt; Ankeny, IA residence

Mary Elizabeth – 1st m NN Soukup; 2nd m Gordon Kennedy,
    Cedar Rapids, IA residence

Steven – m Beth NN; Atkins, IA residence

Timothy – 1st m Julia Wilhelm DVD; residence near Newhall, IA;
    2nd m Tammy NN; Atkins, IA residence

Renee Jo RATHJE d/o Lee Arthur Rathje & Joann Catherine nee Bascom; b 22 Feb 1965 Cedar Rapids, IA; m 10 Sept 1989 Cedar Rapids to Daniel Ellsworth. Child:
    Ross James Ellsworth – b 26 Jul 1992

Ricky Lee RATHJE s/o Lee Arthur Rathje & Joann Catherine nee Bascom; b 03 Mar 1961 Newhall, IA; m 21 Jul 1984 Cedar Rapids to Rebel Ann Bideaux (b 21 Apr 1964). Children:
    Angelica Renee – b 21 Jun 1987 Cedar Rapids, IA
    Chelsea Rose – b 05 Apr 1990 Cedar Rapids, IA
    Tanner Lee – b 20 Feb 1996 Cedar Rapids, IA

*Heinrich RAUDENBUSCH arrived in PA; sailed from Germany aboard the ship "Dragon" in 1732. Farmer in York Co. PA. Ten children. NFR of children except:
    Jacob – farmer in Rockingham Co. VA and Carroll Co. OH

Jacob RAUDENBUSCH s/o Heinrich Raudenbusch; name of mother unknown; b York Co. PA; became a miller, staying in VA where name was changed to "Roudabush". Gereon Roudabush, a farmer, moved from VA to Iowa settling at Belle Plaine, Benton Co IA.

Carla Sue REED d/o June Ann nee Keiper & Roger Henry Reed; b 17 Sept 1965 Luth Hosp Des Moines, IA; B.S. Iowa State University; m 15 Sept 1990 Gloria Dei Luth Ch Urbandale, IA to Todd Michael Chambers (b 10 Sept 1965 Mercy Hosp Des Moines, IA) s/o Gary Lee Chambers (b 19 Apr 1941 Guthrie Center, IA) & Carolyn Jean nee Hirschberg (b 27 Aug Yale, IA). Children:
    Ashlie Reed Chambers – b 21 Jun 1995 Des Moines, IA

*Anna Julianne REISS d/o Jacob Reiss SR. & Anna Juliane nee Schafer; b Reichensachsen, Germany, d in daughter's child birth; came to USA Apr 1847 with two sisters and one brother; m John C. Geyer. Children:

John Geyer – b 28 Oct 1855
James Geyer – b 06 Dec 1856
George Franklin – b 21 Dec 1858
Alice Geyer – b 06 Sept 1860

*Anna Martha REISS d/o Jacob Reiss SR. & Anna Juliane nee Schafer; b Reichensachsen, Germany; 1847 came to USA with parents, two sisters and one brother; d 13 Dec 1911 [Cancer]; m 18 Mar 1859 Conrad Krug SR. Farmed in Bradford Twp IL. Children:
Sophia Krug – b 17 Aug 1860, d 06 Jan 1900
Martha Krug – b 01 Feb 1863, d 25 Apr 1954
Julia Krug – b 10 Dec 1864, d 20 Jun 1949
Christina Krug – b 29 Feb 1868, d 19 Apr 1923
Elizabeth Krug – b 25 Feb 1870, d 20 Jan 1945
Anna Krug – b 06 Sept 1872, d 11 Aug 1936
Minnie Krug – b 18 Mar 1875, d 26 Mar 1954
Mary Krug – b lived a few weeks

*Anna Sophia REISS – d/o Jacob Reiss SR. & Anna Juliane nee Schafer; b 11 May 1845 Hesse-Darmstadt, Germany; 1847 came to USA with parents and two older sisters and one brother; d 26 Dec 1883 ae 38y 7m 15d bur Ashton Cem; m Jan 1863 Jacob Wagner SR. (b 20 Oct 1840 Reichensachsen, Kurhessen, Germany, 13 Apr 1916 Dixon, IL ae 75y bur Ashton Cem). Children:
Martha Wagner – b Nov 1863, d 17 Feb 1930
Charles Wagner – b 13 May 1864, d 13 Jul 1939
John J. Wagner – b 15 Feb 1864, d 16 Mar 195?
George Wagner – b 01 Oct 1868, d 13 Apr 1945
Anna Wagner – b 09 Oct 1870, d 26 Feb 1947
Jacob Wagner Jr – b 11 Nov 1872, d 14 Mar 1955
Mary Martha Wagner – b 10 Nov 1875, d 1947
Emma Sophia Wagner – b 18 Jan 1878, d 15 Oct 1964
Sarah Elizabeth Wagner – b 13 Sept 1879, d 15 Jul 1979
Minnet Henrietta Wagner – b 15 Apr 1881, d 07 Nov 1964
2nd m 16 Feb 1887 Jacob Wagner SR. to Anna Fernau (b Aug 1849). Child:
Frederick C. Wagner – b Oct 1888, d 01 Jul 1959.

Charles REISS s/o Jacob Reiss SR. & Anna Juliane nee Schafer; b 1847, d 17 Jul 1908 ae60y 11m.bur Ashton Cem; 1st m 1873 Christina Thiel. Child:
Lena –b 1872 Deaf/Dumb, d 1879 ae6y

2nd m 11 Mar 1879 Charles Reiss to Eva Elizabeth nee Muelhaus Langlo. Child:

    Martha Magdalena – b Nov 1880, d 15 Dec 1940;
        m Edward Fred Klenke (b 1880, d 1950)

Ernest John REISS s/o John Fredrick Reiss & Anna Dora nee Brandt; b 03 Aug 1901; m 06 Jun 1926 Ethel Lundin (b 01 Mar 1902). No Children.

Jeffrey John REISS s/o John Ivan Reiss & Ardis Kay nee Cowlishaw; b 19 Nov 1962; 1st m 03 Jun 1985 Brenda Malone (b 14 Aug 1940)DVD 1986; 2nd m 14 Feb 1992 Ann Marie Langelier Ewoldt (b 06 May 1964) Children:

    STEPCHILD: Amanda Marie Ewoldt – b 26 Dec 1988
    Katelyn Renee Reiss – b 11 Nov 1992

George REISS s/o Jacob Reiss & Anna Juliane nee Schafer; b 08 Oct 1840 Lee Co. IL, d 13 Jul 1934 Benton Co. IA ae84y, 9 m, 5d; m Wilhelmina Anthes (b 15 Oct 1850) d/o Kaspar John Anthes & Louisa Emma nee Just. Louisa Emma Just was sister of Wilhelmina Just Maas, mother of Jacob Reiss (George's father). Farmers near Ashton, IL until moving to Benton Co. Garrison, IA in 1883. Children:

    TWINS: Anna – b 23 Dec 1873, d 04 Apr 1948
           Emma – b 23 Dec 1873, d 13 Jul 1936
    John Fredrick– b 21 Sept 1875, d 12 Jun 1952;
        m 05 Apr 1899 Anna Dora Brandt. (Parents of Ivan Brandt Reiss)
    Martha Anna– b 19 Mar 1877, d 21 Mar 1938
    Mary Henrietta– b 04 Jul 1879, d 05 May 1969
    Ezra Charles – b 14 May 1882, d 25 Jan 1969
    Josephine Elizabeth – b 10 Jul 1886, d 30 Dec 1963

George Dean REISS s/o Ivan Brandt Reiss & Esther Florence nee Strellner; b 16 Dec 1946; m 13 Nov 1976 Carma Sue Mortland (b 27 Jan 1949). Children:

    Elizabeth Ann – Stillborn 18 Nov 1979
    TWINS: Brandt Ivan – Stillborn 09 Jan 1981
           Brian William – Stillborn 09 Jan 1981
    Sarah Elizabeth – b 08 Nov 1982
    Heather Marie – b 07 May 1984

Harry Ezra REISS s/o John Fredrick Reiss & Anna Dora nee Brandt; b 05 Dec 1899, d 18 Sept 1978; m 09 Jun 1938 Erma Wilhelmina Hall (b 01 Jun

1903, d 1998). Children:
    Edith Ann – b 30 Nov 1941
    George Edward – b 27 Apr 1943
    Mary Arlene – b 21 May 1944

Ivan Brandt REISS s/o John Fredrick Reiss & Anna Dora Brandt; b 23 Jun 1907 Benton Co IA, d 15 Jul 1980 ae73y 22d Vinton, IA; m 09 Jun 1934 Esther Florence Strellner (b 31 Dec 1912 Big Grove Twp Benton Co IA d 25 Apr 2002 ae89y 3m 25d) d/o Julius Strellner & Julia nee Waterstradt. Benton Co IA farmers. Children:
    Leta Mae – b 14 Feb 1935; m 12 Feb 1956 Richard Raymond Christy
    John Ivan – b 16 Dec 1939; m 30 Sept 1961 Ardis Kay Cowlishaw
    George Dean – b 16 Dec 1946; m 13 Nov 1976 Carma Sue Mortland

Jacob REISS JR. s/o Jacob Reiss SR. & Anna Juliane nee Schafer; b 11 Mar 1851 Lee Center, Lee Co IL, d 30 May 1926 ae75y 2m 19d [Injuries from runaway horse team] bur Canby, MN; m 1878 Louisa Maas (b 1853, d 19 May 1938 [Broken Hip]ae85y bur Canby, MN). Children:
    Jennie Leah – b 09 May 1890, d 01 Dec 1958
    William Henry – b 25 Mar 1892, d 07 Sept 1979
    Charles Jacob – b 23 Jul 1894, d 17 Aug 1964

*Jacob REISS SR. b 19 Feb 1806 Reichensachsen, Germany, d Sept 1852 or 1853 bur farm south of Franklin Grove, IL; m 16 Apr 1837 Anna Juliane "Julie" Schafer (d 14 Oct 1871 bur Beck Cem). 1847 economic/political conditions in Europe were in a state of havoc; great crop failure, famine, unrest caused great numbers of people to flee to the promises of the New World. To leave Germany permission from local police and government officials plus the parish pastors had to be obtained. Then travel to the nearest port to wait for a ship willing to carry them to the new land. Jacob and family left Germany April 1847, crossed the Atlantic Ocean in six weeks. There is no record of Carl dying, but he may have died enroute to USA. A number of neighbors from Reichensachsen were with them including Reinhardt Gross whom they fostered. His true relationship to the family is unknown, if he was blood kin. They went to Chicago, IL by wagon—drawn by ox teams and settled south of Franklin Grove, IL. Their 80 acre homestead was long grass prairie located south half of the south half of the northwest quarter of section 24, Twp 21, north of range 10 east. About 1848, Julia's half-brother George Schafer came to USA and lived with her and Jacob until he became established.   The German name Reis or Reiss means "rice." Shafer translated into the word "shepherd" in English. Children:

Anna Juliane b- Reichensachsen, Germany,
  d IL in child birth (daughter); m John C. Geyer.
Anna Martha – b Reichensachsen, Germany, d 13 Dec 1911ae70y
  [Cancer]; m 18 Mar 1859 Conrad Krug SR.
*George – b 08 Oct 1840 Lee Co IL, d 13 Jul 1934 Benton Co IA;
  m Wilhelmina Anthes.
Sophia – b 11 May 1845 Hesse-Darmstadt, Germany;
  d 26 Dec 1883 IL; m Jan 1863 Jacob Wagner SR.
Charles – b 1847, d 17 Jul 1908; 1st m 1873 Christina Thiel;
  2nd m 11 Mar 1879 Eva Elisabeth nee Muehlhaus Langlo
Jacob JR. – b 11 Mar 1852 Lee Center near Lee Co IL d 30 May 1926
  [Injuries from runaway horse team]; m 1878 Louisa Maas

Jeffrey John REISS s/o John Ivan Reiss & Brenda nee Malone; b 19 Nov 1962; 1st m 03 Jun 1985 DVD 1986; 2nd m 14 Feb 1992 Ann Marie nee Langelier Ewoldt (b 06 May 1964).
  STEPCHILD: Amanda Marie Ewoldt – b 26 Dec 1988
  Katelyn Renee – b 11 Nov 1992

John Fredrick REISS s/o George Reiss & Wilhelmina nee Anthes; b 21 Sept 1875, d 12 Jun 1952; m 05 Apr 1899 Anna Dora Brandt (b 24 Oct 1875, d 05 Jun 1930). Benton Co IA farmers. Children:
  Harry Ezra – b 05 Dec 1899, d 18 Sept 1978;
    m 09 Jun 1938 Erma Wilhelmina Hall
  Ernest John – b 03 Aug 1901, m 06 Jun 1926 Ethel Lundin.
    No Children
  Leola Wilhelmina – b 18 Jun 1903; m 08 Jun 1927 Cecil R. Fry
  Ivan Brandt – b 23 Dec 1907, d 15 Jul 1980;
    m 09 Jun 1934 Esther Florence Strellner

John Ivan REISS s/o Ivan Brandt Reiss & Esther Florence nee Strellner; b 16 Dec 1939; m 30 Sept 1961 Ardis Kay Cowlishaw (b 13 August 1940). Children:
  Jeffrey John – b 19 Nov 1962; 1st m 03 Jun 1985 Brenda Malone
    DVD 1986; 2nd m 14 Feb 1992 Ann Marie Langelier Ewoldt
  Kathryn Kay – b 01 Sept 1964; m 1984 Scott Lockwood
    DVD 26 Mar 1997

Kathryn Kay REISS d/o John Ivan Reiss & Ardis Kay nee Cowlishaw; b 01 Sept 1964; m 1984 Scott Lockwood (b 27 Feb 1962)DVD 26 Mar 1997. Children:
    Aaron Marcus Lockwood – b 02 Sept 1987
    Haley Kathryn Lockwood – b 02 Jun 1993
    Connor Scott Lockwood – b 02 Nov 1994

Leola Wilhelmina REISS d/o John Fredrick Reiss & Anna Dora nee Brandt; b 18 Jun 1903; m 08 Jun 1927 Cecil R. Fry (b 18 May 1903). Children:
    Jack Reiss Fry – b 30 Mar 1932

Leta Mae REISS d/o Ivan Brandt Reiss & Esther Florence nee Strellner; b 14 Feb 1935; m 12 Feb 1956 to Richard Raymond Christy (b 12 Sept 1931). Benton Co IA farmers. Children:
    Susan Lynette Christy – b 12 Apr 1960, m 24 Sept 1983 David Fuls
    Diane Kay Christy – b 05 May 1962
    Patricia Lee Christy – b 29 Dec 1966; m 18 Feb 1989 Kelly Freese

Arthur John REISSER s/o Henry Reisser & 2nd wife Margaret nee Rupp; b 1877 near Blairstown, IA d 1978; 1902 moved to O'Brien Co, IA; 1st m 1903 Elsie Schulze (b 1884, d 1918 Sioux City, IA) d/o Herman Schulze & Minnie nee Waldersdorf. 1909 moved to SD; 1912 moved to Sioux City, IA. 1921-1947 Arthur John lived in TX and Sioux City, IA; after 1947 he lived winters in McAllen, TX. Children:
    Velma – b 1908; m Gilbert Deklotz, Newhall, IA
    Lillian – b 1910; m Laurence Dick, Sibley, IA residence
    Ervin – b 1915; m Arleta Murphy, Weslaco, TX residence
    Erma – b 1917, d 1918
2nd m 1927 Arthur John Reisser to Elizabeth Albers (d 1943). Children:
    Mabel – m Glenn Moore, AR residence
    Irene – m Richard Cook, AR residence

*Henry REISSER s/o Carl & Elisabeth Reisser; b 1831 near Frankfurt, Germany, d 1914; 1851 emigrated to Baltimore, MD, later NJ; 1864 moved to Clayton Co IA, then Leroy Twp Benton Co IA; 1st m 1857 Mary Miller from Saxony, Germany (d 1864 ae26y Clayton Co. IA). Children:
    William – NFR
    Herman – NFR
2nd m Henry Reisser to Margaret Rupp (b 1844 Frankfort-on-the-Rhine, Germany; 1850 emigrated USA, d 1932). Children:

Harry – b 1869, d 1917
Mary – b 1871, d 1968; m John Blahauvietz, two children
Margaret – b 1873, 1933; m John Britton
Elinor – b 1875; m Alfred Vogelgesang, four children
Arthur – b 1877, d 1987; 1st m Elsie Schulze, four children;
    2nd m Elizabeth Albers, two children
Christian – b 1879, d 1950; m Flossie Schulze, four children
Martha – b 1882, 1953; m Dave Shaw
Otto – b 1885, d 1950; m Mabel Neibhor, one child
Edward – b 1887, d 1887

James Edward REYNOLDS s/o Barbara Jean nee Rinderknecht & Philip Anthony Reynolds I; b 30 Jul 1963 Naval Hosp Norfolk VA; m 24 Sept 1988 Clinton OH to Kimberly Rae Good (b 19 Aug 1964) d/o Wilber & Janet Good.

Philip Anthony REYNOLDS II s/o Barbara Jean nee Rinderknecht & Philip Anthony Reynolds I; b 07 Feb 1965 OH; m 05 Sept 1987 Fairlawn Luth Ch Akron, OH to Stacy Deneen Britton (b 30 Jul 1964) d/o Dean & Dorothy Britton. Children:
    Zachary Philip – b 10 Jul 1988

Marcia RICE d/o Henry Rice & Ruby nee Franzenburg; m Michael Daly of Des Moines, IA. Marcia graduated from U.N.I. Michael graduated from I.S.U. became landscape consultant. Iowa City, IA residence. Child:
    Noelle Daly – NFR

Marla RICE d/o Henry Rice & Ruby nee Franzenburg; m Russell Betts of Oelwein, IA. Waterloo, IA residence; John Deere employment. Marla & Russell both graduated fron U.N.I. Child:
    Katie Betts – NFR

Michael RICE s/o Henry Rice & Ruby nee Franzenburg; m Barbara Larsen. Egan, MN residence. Michael in electronics. Children:
    Jennifer – NFR
    Jeffrey – NFR

Albert Frederick Hartman RINDERKNECHT s/o George Rinderknecht JR. & Anna Katharina nee Happel; b 11 Nov 1888 Atkins, IA d 10 Aug 1937 ae48y 9m[Scarlet Fever] bur St.Steph Cem; 1st m Minnie Mitchell. Child:

Minnie Lois – b 17 Sept 1912; m 02 Sept 1939 Joe Yock
2nd m 10 Mar 1918 Albert Frederick Hartman Rinderknecht to (Minnie) Marie Wilhelmina Katherine Haerther (b 13 Aug 1893 Lenox Twp Iowa Co IA north of Norway, IA d 29 Apr 1984 ae90y 8m 16d Heritage Acres Care Center, Cedar Rapids, IA bur St.Steph Cem). Children:

> Dean Albert Arthur – b 01 Jan 1919; d 28 Aug 1993; residence
>> Port Charlotte, FL; 1st m 28 Oct 1951 Eleanor Elizabeth Fischer
>> (b 22 Nov 1924, d 14 Nov 1968);
>> 2nd m 14 Feb 1983 Marian Grodson (b12 Oct 1919)
> Eugene Henry Carl – b 10 Sept 1920; d 27 Mar 1992; residence
>> Bath, IL; 1st m 14 Feb 1948 Patricia Ann Bostick;
>> 2nd m Marie Rich
> George Christian Otto – b 16 Sept 1922, d 14 May 1923
> Ruth Marie – b 25 Feb 1925; Pekin, IL residence;
>> m 24 Jan 1948 Clement Ambrose Campbell
> Albert Paul – b 23 Jul 1927; residence Marion, IA;
>> m 07 Aug 1960 Bethel Jean Burmeister
> David Merle – b 05 Aug 1930; residence Arvada, CO;
>> m 24 Jun 1961 Nancy Alleyne Hendryx
> Paul George – b 16 Apr 1935 (retarded), Never Married
>> d 15 Nov 1972 1972 bur St.Steph Cem

Albert Paul RINDERKNECHT s/o Albert Frederick Hartman Rinderknecht & (Minnie) Marie Wilhelmina Katherine nee Haerther; b 23 Jul 1927; m 07 Aug 1960 Bethel Jean Burmeister (b 30 Dec 1931). Children:

> Douglas Albert – b 26 Aug 1963;
>> m 12 Aug 1995 Marion IA Lisa Charlene Crull
> Tracy Lynn – b 18 Jun 1965;
>> m 19 Mar 1988 Michael Raymond Robinson
> Brad Louis – b 07 May 1967; m 29 Aug 1992 Lee Ann Cady

Alberta Elizabeth RINDERKNECHT d/o Henry Karl Rinderknecht & Louise Elizabeth nee Krug; b 19 Oct 1927 Fremont Twp Benton Co. bpt 07 Nov 1927 St.Steph, con St.Steph; m 19 Jul 1952 St.Steph to Gerald Nathan Welty (b 28 Dec 1929 Oxford Junction IA) s/o Cale Welty & Anna Lavina nee Fritcher. Occupation: Accountant. Children:

> Scott Alan Welty – b 26 May 1959 (Adopted) Guttenberg, IA;
>> m 10 Jul 1988 Amy Kathleen Mitchell
> Sherri Lynn Welty – b 28 Jul 1962 (Adopted) Davenport, IA;
>> m 28 Aug 1982 Timothy David Patton

Alice Ann RINDERKNECHT d/o Donald Alvin William Rinderknecht & Betty Jean nee Birky; b 06 Sept 1963; m 05 May 1990 Jeffrey Albert Dillon (b 10 Oct 1962 Anoka Hennepin School District #11 Custodian). Milaca, MN residence. Children:

Hannah Marie Dillon – b 06 Aug 1992

Katherine Lois – b 03 Sept 1994

Alfred August Heinrich RINDERKNECHT s/o George William Frederick Rinderknecht & Anna Sophia Marie Elizabeth nee Gerhold; b 02 Oct 1905 Rinderknecht Homestead Fremont Twp Benton Co., bpt 27 Oct 1905 St.Steph, con St.Steph, d 20 Dec 1986 ae81y 2m 18d (Tauf Reg p. 134-48) bur CdrMem Cedar Rapids, IA; m 12 Dec 1934 St.Steph his Happel cousin Irene Katherine Elizabeth Krug (b 03 Sept 1910 Parent's Farm Fremont Twp Benton Co IA, bpt 02 Oct 1910 St.Steph, con St.Steph) d/o John August Henry Krug & Elizabeth Jeanette nee Happel. Alfred August Rinderknecht's Great-Grandfather: Andreas Happel; Irene Katherine Elizabeth Krug's Great-Grandfather: Andreas Happel; farmers near Marion until retiring to Cedar Rapids, IA. Children:

Betty Anne – b 21 Dec 1936; m 1963 James R. Madan

Richard Wayne – b 19 Jun 1938; m 1958 Sandra Gay Fillenworth

Carol Rae – b 06 Mar 1942; m 05 Jun 1965 Scott Bruntjen

David Lee – b 19 May 1943; m 24 Nov 1976 to Kathy Jo Schrader

Donald Gene – b 20 Nov 1944; m 23 Dec 1972 Priscill Bushaw

Anna Gertrude Katherina RINDERKNECHT (TWIN: Maria (Mary) Rinderknecht Young) d/o William Rinderknecht & Maria (Mary) Katharina nee Happel; b 09 Dec 1870 Fremont Twp Benton Co IA bpt 26 Dec 1870 St.Steph (tauf p. 660), d 11 Nov 1937 ae66y 11m 28d Cedar Rapids, IA bur St.Steph Cem; m 16 Mar 1890 St.Steph to Heinrich (Henry) Schirm (b 27 Jun 1863 Baden, Germany, d 23 Jun 1939 ae75y 11m 17d Cedar Rapids, IA bur St.Steph Cem) s/o George Martin Schirm & Anna Maria Gerber. Had eight children:

Otto William Schirm – b 13 Jul 1895 Newhall, Benton Co IA
   d 11 Oct 1953 Cedar Rapids, IA;
   m 08 Apr 1917 Maria Dorthea Ernst

Hilda Gertrude Schirm – b 01 Sept 1905 Newhall, Benton Co IA
   d 27 Feb 1983 Moline, IL;
   m 20 Nov 1926 Cedar Rapids Arthur Charles Grabau

411

Anne Elizabeth RINDERKNECHT d/o Robert Henry Rinderknecht & Marcella Jean nee Hurst; b 02 Sept 1957 St.Lukes Hosp Cedar Rapids, IA; 1st m 19 Aug 1978 St.John to David Dale Arnold (b 16 Nov 1956 Cedar Rapids, IA) s/o Walter S. Arnold & Ione nee Butz. DVD; 2nd m 02 Aug 1986 TrinCR to Glenn Orville Manderscheid (b 24 Sept 1952 Maquoketa, IA Jackson Co.) s/o Orville John Manderscheid & Marie Catherine nee Ryan of Zingle, IA

Arnold Karl Heinrich RINDERKNECHT s/o George William Frederick Rinderknecht & Anna Maria nee Gerhold; b 22 Jun 1902 Farm Fremont Twp. Benton Co IA, bpt 13 Jul 1902, con 16 Apr 1916 St.Steph, d 27 Feb 1992 ae89y 8m 5d Woodbury Care Center, West Des Moines, IA bur St.Steph Cem; m 10 Jul 1930 Burlington, IA to Catherine Louise Lenz (b 11 Mar 1905 d 06 Aug 2003 ae98y 4m 26d bur St.Steph Cem; School Teacher) d/o William Frederich Lenz & Louise nee Klepp. Atkins residence; owned electrical business. Child:
    Norman Keith – b 05 Mar 1934 Atkins, IA;
        m 03 Sept 1955 Eloise Colleen Hagan of Atkins, IA

Arthur George Wilhelm "Bud" RINDERKNECHT (Twin) s/o George Rinderknecht JR. & Anna Katharina nee Happel; b 02 Jul 1896 Atkins, bpt St.Steph, con St.Steph, d 25 Jan 1969 Atkins home ae72y 6m 23d bur St.Steph Cem; 1st m 15 Dec 1921 George, IA to Anna Alice Krahling (b 28 Dec 1900, d 23 Aug 1949 ae48y 7m 16d) d/o John William Krahling & Gertrude "Gertie" nee Addengast. Lived in St.Paul, MN for three years when he was professional heavyweight fighter (6 ft.10 inches tall); lived in Storm Lake, IA eleven years before returning to Atkins, IA for remainder of his life; associated with Atkins Lumber Company, he designed and built portable buildings called "correct buildings"; retired from Wilson Company, Cedar Rapids, IA. Children:
    Lois Ann – b 28 Jul 1922 St.Paul MN;
        1st m 14 Jun 1946 Hilbert Christian Schaefer;
        2nd m 24 Nov 1984 Bill Randolph,
    Nina Mae – b 26 Dec 1924 Atkins, IA;
        m 11 Jul 1947 Lloyd Wilmer Day
    Arthur John – b 15 Aug 1926 Atkins, IA;
        m 05 Oct 1947 Harriet Charlene Keiper
    Donald Alvin William – b 10 Apr 1929 Storm Lake, IA
        d 13 Aug 2004 Milaca, MN; m 07 May 1950 Betty Jean Birky
2nd m 1954 Arthur George Wilhelm "Bud" Rinderknecht to Laura

C.Harkemeyer (d 28 Mar 2002).

Arthur John RINDERKNECHT s/o Arthur George Wilhelm (Bud) Rinderknecht & Anna Alice nee Krahling; b 15 Aug 1926 Atkins, IA; bpt 12 Sept 1926 & con 17 Mar 1940 St.Steph; 1944 Class Atkins High School; U.S. Army 1944-1946 Saipan & Iwo Jima World War II; Knutson Construction Co. Superintendent Cedar Rapids, IA; m 05 Oct 1947 St.Steph to Harriet Charlene Keiper (b 04 Oct 1928 Farm Fremont Twp Benton Co IA bpt 28 Oct 1928 & con 30 Mar 1942 St.Steph; 1946 Class Atkins High School; Atkins Peoples Saving Bank beginning 1949) d/o Elmer Henry John Keiper & Frances Magdalene Elizabeth Anna nee Schueler. Celebrated 50th and 60th wedding anniversary. Atkins, IA residence. Children:
Jolene Ann – b 21 Oct 1949 St.Lukes Hosp Cedar Rapids, IA;
 m 29 Aug 1970 Dennis Paul Lensch
Jon Arthur – b 21 Oct 1953 Mercy Hosp Cedar Rapids, IA;
 m 21 Oct 1989 Nancy Kay Waterman

August Georg Johann "Gus" RINDERKNECHT s/o Karl Rinderknecht & Katherina nee Happel; b 07 Jul 1884, Fremont Twp. Benton Co IA d 01 Nov 1955 ae71y 3m 24d Cedar Rapids, IA bur CdrMem Cedar Rapids, IA; m 30 Apr 1908 Wilhelmine Heinrike "Minnie" Mohr (b 25 Nov 1887 Iowa City, IA bur CdrMem) d/o Jacob Mohr (b 13 May 1860 d 13 Feb 1899 ae38y 9m) & Louise Heinrike nee Haerther (b 02 Jul 1864 d 10 Aug 1896 ae32y 1 m 8d). Farmed thirty-two years. Moved to Rosehill Farm in 1916 until 1940; retired in Cedar Rapids, IA. Children:
Lorane Kathrine Wilhelmine – b 20 May 1909 Fremont Twp
 d 12 Apr 1994; 1st m 14 Mar 1945 Lloyd Spencer Parker;
 2nd m 17 Feb 1972 Ernest William Demmel
Elda Gertrude Louise – b 17 Jan 1913 home place;
 m 25 Jan 1934 Martin Fredrick Bayer
Paul Heinrich – b 01 Oct 1916 Farm, Linn Co. d 15 Oct 1968
 Bronx, New York; m 21 Feb 1940 Dorothy Louise Gardemann
Wilma Elizabeth Ruth- b 12 Jun 1920 Farm, Linn Co.;
 m 24 Sept 1941 to James William Grummer

Barbara RINDERKNECHT d/o John Rinderknecht & Barbara nee Mead; b 1859, d 1948; 1st m Edward John Kerkman (b 1855, d 1892). Eight children:
George John Edward Kerkman – b 1879 Eden Twp Benton Co IA
 d 1940; m 1905 Martha Berth Marie Conrad
Marie K. M. Kerkman – b 1880, d 1881

Emma Kerkman – b 1881, d 1959, m John Wilhelm Williams

Anna Emilie Kerkman – b 1883, d 1959, m Willard Henry Alden

Sophia Kerkman – b 1885, d 1962, m William Kreutner

Clara Kerkman – b 1886, d 1975, m Peter Wilhelmi

Fred Kerkman – b 1888, d 1968; m Clara Kreutner

Arthur Martin Kerkman – b 1890, d 1963;
> m 1921 Werning cousin Wilhelmina "Minnie" Ellen Werning

Amelia Christian Kerkman – b 22 Dec 1892, d 14 Mar 1976;
> m 18 Sept 1912 George Johann Carl Schlotterbeck

2nd m 1895 Barbara nee Rinderknecht Kerkman to Ludwig (Lewis) L. Lauterwasser (b 1869, d 1946). Retired 1924 in Atkins, IA. Celebrated Golden 50th Wedding Anniversary in 1945. Two children:

Tillie Lauterwasser – b 1898, m NN Hessenius

Ervin J. Lauterwasser – b 05 Jan 1901 northwest of Van Horne, IA
> d 24 Nov 1965; m 27 Jan 1924 Irene Senne

Barbara Jean RINDERKNECHT d/o Edward John George Rinderknecht & Margaret Lorene nee Tow; b 06 Jul 1942 St.Lukes Hosp Cedar Rapids, IA bpt 02 Aug 1942 St. Steph, Atkins High School; m 19 Apr 1963 South Mills, NC to Phillip Anthony Reynolds I (b 29 Apr 1943; U.S.Navy) s/o Robert Thomas & Gloria nee Jenkins Reynolds Thomas of Elyria, OH. Barbara employed by Pan American Airlines. Medina, OH residence. Children:

James Edward Reynolds – b 30 Jul 1963 Naval Hosp Norfolk, VA;
> m 24 Sept 1988 Kimberly Rae Good

Philip Anthony Reynolds II- b 07 Feb 1965 OH;
> m 05 Sept 1987 Stacy Deneen Britton

Michael William Reynolds – b 30 Jul 1969 OH

Ryan Andrew Reynolds – b 18 Dec 1975 Medina, OH

Becky Lee RINDERKNECHT d/o Edward John George Rinderknecht & Margaret Lorene nee Tow; b 15 Apr 1953 St.Lukes Hosp Cedar Rapids, IA bpt 03 May 1953 St.Steph, Atkins High School; 1st m 14 Jul 1973 St.Steph to Robert Herman "Casey" Snavely(b 02 Nov 1952; U.S.Air Force, Germany) s/o Herman Snavely & Doris nee Smith; Occupation: Carpenter. Child:

Nicholas Robert Snavely b 04 Oct 1979 St.Lukes Hosp Cedar Rapids

2nd m 06 Aug 1988 King of Kings Luth Ch Cedar Rapids, IA Becky Lee nee Rinderknecht Snavely to Craig Barr. Occupation:Computer Electrician.

Betty Anne RINDERKNECHT d/o Alfred August Rinderknecht & Irene Katherine Elizabeth nee Krug; b 21 Dec 1936 St.Lukes Hosp Cedar Rapids, IA bpt Jan 1937; m 21 Dec 1963 St.Paul's Luth Ch Marion, IA to James R. Madan (b 31 Dec 1936 in India). Residence: New York State. Children:
Jennifer Ann Madan – b 04 May 1969, NY
James Clark Madan – b 13 Mar 1972, NY

Brad Louis RINDERKNECHT s/o Albert Paul Rinderknecht & Bethel Jean nee Burmeister; b 07 May 1967; m 29 Aug 1992 in Coraoplis to Lee Ann Cady (b 24 Oct 1965). Child:
Jack Mason – b 20 Oct 1995

Carol Ann RINDERKNECHT d/o Wilbert Heinrich Julius Rinderknecht & Margaret Ella nee Deklotz; b 07 Apr 1943, Cedar Rapids, IA bpt and con St. Steph; m 18 Jun 1966 St. Steph to John Leasure (b 16 Jun 1942). Residence Champaign, IL Children:
Jeffrey David Leasure – b 08 Sept 1967;
    m 26 Jun 1993 Paula Wehling
Daniel Steven Leasure- b 21 Dec 1969

Carol Rae RINDERKNECHT d/o Alfred August Henry Rinderknecht & Irene Katherine Elizabeth nee Krug; b 06 Mar 1942 St.Lukes Hosp Cedar Rapids, bpt 12 Apr 1942; m 05 Jun 1965 St.Paul's Luth Marion, IA to Scott Bruntjen (b 10 Sept 1943; U.S.Army Vietnam) s/o Stanley & Ginnis Bruntjen. Programmer/College Library Pittsburg, PA.

Charles Albert RINDERKNECHT s/o Eugene Henry Carl Rinderknecht & Patricia Ann nee Bostick; b 01 Nov 1948; m Nancy Halverson (b 09 Oct 1950). Children:
Christine Ann – b 01 Apr 1975; m 17 Mar 1994 Christopher Wagner
Connie Joan – b 22 Oct 1976

Charles Richard RINDERKNECHT s/o Paul Henry Rinderknecht & Dorothy Louise nee Gardemann; b 24 Mar 1943 Cedar Rapids, IA; m 10 Sept 1966 Darlene Mary Stien (b 17 Mar 1943 Newhall, Benton Co IA) d/o Richard Henry Stien & Mary nee Dvorak. DVD. Occupation: farming Rosehill Farm Fremont Twp Benton Co south of Atkins, IA. Child:
Tricia Sue – b 19 Mar 1970 Cedar Rapids, bpt 19 Mar 1970 St.Steph
    Sponsors: Renne Rinderknecht & Donald Stien;
    m 31 Dec 1995 Christopher David Johnson

2nd m 30 Aug 1996 Charles Richard Rinderknecht to Maria G. Coleman.
2nd m Darlene Mary nee Stien Rinderknecht to Ron Ribble

Christian RINDERKNECHT s/o Johann Rinderknecht & Barbara nee Mead; b 1853, d 1904; m Anna Nell. Children:
    Martin – NFR
    Chris – NFR
    George – NFR
    Mary – NFR
    Emma – NFR
    Henry C. – NFR
    Katharine – b 1882, d 1983
    John E. – b 1885, d 1950

Christine Ann RINDERKNECHT d/o Charles Albert Rinderknecht & Christopher Wagner; b 01 Apr 1975; m 17 Mar 1994 Christopher Wagner (b 24 Nov 1969). Children:
    Christian James Wagner – b 06 Aug 1994
    Kirsten Renee Wagner – b 01 Sept 1995

Christine Katherina Barbara RINDERKNECHT d/o George Rinderknecht JR. & Anna nee Happel; b 25 Dec 1899; m 25 Sept 1925 John England. Moved to Muscatine, IA. Children:
    Beatrice Ella England – b 15 May 1926; m NN O'Reilly
    John Franklyn England – b 16 Sept 1927 Niles Center, IL
    Roberta Frances England – b 30 Jul 1929 Niles Center;m NN Dierks
    Frederick Louis England – b 23 Mar 1931 Atkins, IA
    William Thomas England – b 16 Sept 1936 Atkins, IA

Clara Elisabeth Barbara RINDERKNECHT d/o George Rinderknecht JR. & Anna nee Happel; b 20 Mar 1892 Atkins, IA; bpt St.Steph; d 10 Jun 1960 ae68y 2m 21d; m 08 Oct 1913 Charles Esch JR.(b 15 Feb 1886 Niles Center, IL). Lived in Chicago, IL; moved to Wenatchee, WA; retired in Atkins, IA. Children:
    Alvin Esch – b 10 Apr 1909 Atkins
    Karl Esch – b 07 Jul 1914 Atkins; dec'd
    Viola Esch – b 14 Jul 1916 Atkins; m 11 Nov 1939 Henry Kreegier

Connie Sue RINDERKNECHT d/o Otto Henry Carl Rinderknecht & Edna Alice nee Railsback; b 13 Nov 1952 St.Lukes Hosp. Cedar Rapids, IA;

1st m 02 Oct 1971 Concordia Lutheran Ch Cedar Rapids to Terry Edward Sindelar (b 10 Feb Cedar Rapids, IA) s/o (Carl) Charles Martin Sindelar & Bernadine Elsie nee Brunce. Occupation: Farming & Construction.
2nd m 25 Jun 1988 Sioux City, IA Connie Sue nee Rinderknecht Sindelar to 2nd m for Dennis Raymond Weathers (b 09 May 1952 Kingsley, IA) s/o Richard Joseph Weathers & Phyllis Margaret nee Christensen. Occupation: Account Consultant. Residence: Council Bluffs, IA.
STEPCHILDREN:
Nathanial Charles Weathers – b 09 Jan 1976 Cedar Falls, IA
Tieg Raymond Weathers – b 17 Mar 1979, Sioux City, IA

Conrad Martin RINDERKNECHT s/o Karl Rinderknecht & Anna Katherina nee Happel: cf Elizabeth Anna Krug

David Eugene RINDERKNECHT s/o Charles Albert Rinderknecht & Nancy nee Halverson; b 02 Apr 1954; m 09 Nov 1974 Wendy Gail Lewis (b 15 May 1956). Children:
David Eugene II – b 16 Nov 1975
Jason Michael – b 10 Aug 1977
Valerie Ann – b 13 May 1979; Child: Victoria Nicole Rinderknecht
(b 30 Dec 1995)
John Charles – b 05 Sept 1981

David John RINDERKNECHT s/o Robert Henry Rinderknecht & Marcella Jean nee Hurst; b 08 Sept 1951 St.Lukes Hosp Cedar Rapids, IA; m 23 Jan 1971 St.John to Patricia Jean Elsner (b 28 Nov 1950 Mercy Hosp Cedar Rapids, IA). Occupation: Draftsman. Children:
Mathew Jay (Adopted) – b 05 Jul 1974 Dubuque, IA
Bethany Jo – b 14 May 1976 Mercy Hosp Cedar Rapids, IA
Zachary James – b 12 Sept 1979 Mercy Hosp Cedar Rapids,IA

David Lee RINDERKNECHT s/o Wilbert Heinrich Julius Rinderknecht & Margaret Ella nee Deklotz; b 04 Apr 1940 Cedar Rapids, IA; School Teacher; m 22 Jul 1967 TrinCR to Jane Myrl Weiss (b 28 Feb 1940) d/o Clarence Henry Weiss & Viola Minnie nee Floerchinger of rural Deep River, IA. NJ residence. Children:
Michael David – b 07 May 1968; m 29 Jun 1991 Michelle McVey
Kimberly Jo – b 14 Jan 1970; m 15 May 1993 Stephen Miklandric

David Lee RINDERKNECHT s/o Alfred August Henry Rinderknecht &
417

Irene Katherine Elizabeth nee Krug; b 19 May 1943 St.Lukes Hosp. Cedar Rapids, IA; m 24 Nov 1976 Rockford, IL to Kathy Jo Schrader (b 23 Feb 1947 Oregon, IL) d/o Joseph & Kitty Schrader. Occupation: Auditor. Residence Chana, IL. Children:

    Kae Dee – b 18 Jan 1978 Rockford, IL
    Jad Lee – b 16 Aug 1979 Rockford, IL

David Merle RINDERKNECHT s/o Albert Frederick Hartman Rinderknecht & (Minnie) Marie Wilhelmina Katherine nee Haerther; b 05 Aug 1930; bpt and con 02 Apr 1944 St.Steph; 1948 Class Atkins High School; High School Teacher & Coach; Coors employe; m 24 Jun 1961 to Nanch Alleyne Hendryx. Arvada, CO residence. Children:

    Dana Lyn – b 29 Dec 1963
    Danice Marie – b 05 Nov 1965

Rev.Daniel Wayne RINDERKNECHT s/o Donald Alvin William Rinderknecht & Betty Jean nee Birky; b 15 Oct 1954; Luth Pastor since 1983 Alberta, Canada; Billings MT; m 29 Jan 1977 Cathryn Schiefelbein (b 16 Apr 1955; Registered Nurse). Children:

    Kesssie – b 29 Sept 1978
    Holly – b 29 Dec 1979
    Ditza – b 25 Oct 1981
    Luke – b 14 Dec 1984

Donald Alvin William RINDERKNECHT s/o Arthur George Wilhelm (Bud) Rinderknecht & Anna Alice nee Krahlimg; b 10 Apr 1929, d 13 Aug 2004 Foley MN bur 17 Aug 2004 Glory Luth Ch Blaine, MN; Construction worker; m 07 May 1950 Betty Jean Birky (b 02 Mar 1930). Children:

    Philip John – b 01 Jan 1953; m 1978 Julie Lawson DVD
    Daniel Wayne – b 15 Oct 1954; m 29 Jan 1977 Cathryn Schiefelbein
    Michael William – b 20 Jan 1959; m 22 Apr 1978 Pamela Meyer
    Donald Matthew – b 19 Dec 1960; m 28 Dec 1984 Penney Chapin
    Alice Ann – b 06 Sept 1963; m 05 May 1990 Jeffrey Albert Dillon

Donald Gene RINDERKNECHT s/o Alfred August Henry Rinderknecht & Irene Katherine nee Krug; b 20 Nov 1944 St.Lukes Hosp Cedar Rapids, IA; U.S.Army Vietnam; m 23 Dec 1972 St.Paul's Luth Ch Marion, IA to Priscilla Anne Bushaw (b 30 Mar 1945 Edgewood, IA) d/o William Jason Bushaw & Helen B. nee Smith. Occupation: Realtor.

Donald Matthew RINDERKNECHT s/o Donald Alvin William Rinderknecht & Betty Jean nee Birky; b 19 Dec 1960; National Weather Service Meterorologist, Norman OK; m 28 Dec 1984 Penney Chapin (b 12 Sept 1962; Registered Nurse).

Donna Marie RINDERKNECHT d/o Otto Henry Carl Rinderknecht & Edna Alice nee Railsback; b 21 Nov 1945 St.Lukes Hosp. Cedar Rapids, IA; m 06 Sept 1969 Trinity Luth Ch Cedar Rapids to Steven Garnett. Child:
Theodore "Teddy" Lynn – b 22 Jun 1970 Kansas City, MO

Dorothy Katherine RINDERKNECHT d/o Henry Karl Rinderknecht & Louise Elizabeth nee Krug; b 12 Aug 1917 Parent's farm, Fremont Twp Benton Co IA, bpt 1917 St.Steph, con St.Steph, d 30 Aug 2000 ae83y 22d [Cancer] Westridge Care Center, Cedar Rapids, IA bur 03 Sept 2000 St.Steph Cem; m 28 Jun 1941 TrinCR to Henry Donald Lange (b 22 Mar 1913 Muscatine, IA; World War II Air Corps, d 10 Nov 1998 ae85y 7m 19d Vinton, IA bur ST.Steph Cem)double ceremony with her brother Edward & Margaret Tow. Occupation: Owner/Operator Atkins Lumber Co. Children:
Thomas Henry Lange – b 16 Mar 1944 St.Lukes Hosp
Cedar Rapids, IA; m 01 Apr 1967 Nancy Jean Schanbacher
John Edward Lange – b 21 Dec 1946 St.Lukes Hosp Cedar Rapids;
m 12 Sept 1969 Janeen Kaye Weichman
Richard Wayne Lange – b 12 Jun 1949 St.Lukes Hosp Cedar Rapids;
m 11 Jul 1969 Cynthia Diane Shoemaker

Douglas Charles RINDERKNECHT s/o Robert Henry Rinderknecht & Marcella Jean nee Hurst; b 01 Sept 1953 St.Lukes Hosp Cedar Rapids, IA; m 22 Jul 1973 St.John Ch Keystone, IA to Dixie Rae Junge (b 29 Oct 1953 St.Lukes Hosp Cedar Rapids, IA) d/o Corley John Junge & Hazel Arlene nee Peterson. Farmers. Children:
Melisa Diane – b 15 Apr 1975 St.Lukes Hosp Cedar Rapids, IA
Nicholas Conrad – b 24 Sept 1978 St.Lukes Hosp Cedar Rapids, IA

Duane Alan RINDERKNECHT s/o Robert Henry Rinderknecht & Marcella Jean nee Hurst; b 09 Oct 1959 St.Lukes Hosp Cedar Rapids, IA; m 08 Dec 1984 St.John to Danielle Marie Van Hamme (b 05 Jun 1961 Victor, IA, Victor High School; Kirkwood Comm College) d/o Eugene Peter Van Hamme & Iowa Ann nee Van Dee. Children:
Daren Michael – b 28 Nov 1986 Cedar Rapids, IA
Devin Steven – 24 May 1990 Cedar Rapids, IA

Eda Barbara Elizabeth RINDERKNECHT d/o George William Frederick Rinderknecht & Anna Sophia Marie Elizabeth nee Gerhold; b 17 Dec 1917 bpt and con St. Steph; m 14 Sept 1940 St.Steph to "Bill" Wilbert Martin Schanbacher (b 06 Feb 1916 Farm home Linn Co IA, d 03 Nov 2002 ae86y 8m 28d bur St/Steph Cem) s/o Julius Daniel Schanbacher & Gertrude Marie nee Keiper. Farmed with Wilbert's twin brother on Schanbacher homestead in Linn County, east of Atkins, IA until retiring in Solon, IA. Children:

Barbara Ann Schanbacher – b 03 Mar 1943 Nurse at Iowa City, IA

Patricia Sue Schanbacher – b 24 Apr 1944;
   m 29 Jun 1968 Ivan Lee Lauck, West Bend residence

John Wilbert Schanbacher – b 17 Sept 1951, Atkins residence;
   m 17 Mar 2000 Eileen Ann nee Hartkemeyer Heyer

Edward John George RINDERKNECHT s/o Henry Karl Rinderknecht & Louise Elizabeth nee Krug; b 27 Oct 1919 Parent's farm, Fremont Twp Benton Co IA, bpt 1919 St.Steph, con St.Steph, Atkins High School, d 12 Jun 1987 ae67y 7m 16d Cedar Rapids, IA bur 15 Jun 1987 St.Steph Cem; m 28 Jun 1941 TrinCR to Margaret Lorene Tow (b 20 Jan 1918 Cedar Rapids, bpt Norway, IA) d/o Elmer Tow & Elizabeth McGregor nee Russell of Norway, IA. Double ceremony with his sister Dorothy & Henry Lange. Farmed their Rinderknecht homestead. Children:

Barbara Jean – b 06 Jul 1942 St.Lukes Hosp Cedar Rapids, IA;
   m 19 Apr 1963 Philip Anthony I Reynolds, OH

Elizabeth Louise – b 29 Oct 1943 St.Lukes Hosp Cedar Rapids, IA;
   m 30 Jul 1965 Douglas Lee Winders

William Edward- b 04 Feb 1947 St.Lukes Hosp Cedar Rapids, IA;
   1st m 22 Jul1967 Connie Rae Offedahl DVD;
   2nd m 21 Dec 1974 Barbara Sue Robinson

Nancy Ellen – b 19 Apr 1951 St.Lukes Hosp Cedar Rapids, IA;
   m 21 Oct 1972 Dennis Robert Deklotz, Shellsburg, IA

Rebecca Lee – b 15 Apr 1953 St.Lukes Hosp Cedar Rapids, IA;
   1st m 14 Jul 1973 Robert Herman Snavely;
   2nd m 06 Aug 1988 Craig Barr

Elda Gertrude Louise RINDERKNECHT d/o August Georg Johann "Gus" Rinderknecht & Wilhelmine Heinrike "Minnie" nee Mohr; b 17 Jan 1913 Fremont Twp. Benton Co IA (Tauf 146); m 25 Jan 1934 St.Steph to Martin Fredrick Bayer (b 25 Jun 1909 Victor, IA). Occupation: Farmer. Children:

Pearl Evelyn Bayer – b 26 Jan 1935 Guernsey, Iowa Co IA;

m 29 May 1960 Arlo Hans Fredrich Suhr

Martin Eldred Bayer – b 07 Feb 1937 Guernsey, Iowa Co IA;
    m 08 Mar 1964 Betty Jean Hershey

Doris Elaine Bayer – b 18 Jan 1939 Guernsey, Iowa Co IA;
    m 27 Oct 1962 Marvin Jerome Stanek

Violette Janette Bayer – b 17 Dec 1940 Guernsey, Iowa Co IA
    m 01 Nov 1959 Roger Eugene Hall

Marine Mae Bayer – b 23 May 1943 Guernsey, Iowa Co IA;
    1st m 04 Aug 1961 Dennis Edward Keys;
    2nd m 11 Feb 1984 Darold Dean Timm

Phyllis Lucille Bayer – b 20 Jun 1945 Guernsey, Iowa Co IA;
    m 20 Aug 1966 Bernard John Dahlhauser

Delmar Elwood Bayer – b 20 Apr 1947 Guernsey Iowa Co IA;
    m 27 Mar 1971 Rose Marie Thompson

Lucille Jean Bayer – b 07 Jul 1950 Guernsey, Iowa Co IA;
    m 11 Nov 1973 James Allen Tuttle

Linda Ann Bayer – b 10 Nov 1956 Victor, IA;
    m 25 Aug 1979 James William Mortell

Eleanor Louise Barbara RINDERKNECHT d/o Conrad Martin Rinderknecht & Elizabeth Anna nee Krug; b 04 Dec 1922 Farm north of Van Horne Eldorado Twp Benton Co IA, bpt 26 Dec 1922 St.John, Newhall, [Polio 1946] d 15 Mar 1999 ae76y 3m 11d Newhall, IA bur 17 Mar 1999 St.John Cem; 1940 Class Newhall High School; m 11 Jan 1942 St.John to Melvin Gottfried Webert (b 23 Jan 1919 Williamsburg, IA d 14 May 1988 ae68y 3m 21d bur 17 May 1988 St.John Cem) s/o Fred Peter Webert & Mathilda Meta nee Schwating. Farmed until 1947; Newhall Lumberyard; Insurance. Children:

Janet Lynn Webert – b 18 Nov 1942 St.Lukes Hosp Cedar Rapids, IA;
    m 20 Oct 1962 James Leroy Boddicker

Jo Ann Webert – b 12 Jul 1945 Virginia Gay Hosp Vinton, IA;
    m 07 Mar 1964 Dennis Leroy Karr

Judy Louise Webert – b 22 Oct 1948 St.Lukes Hosp Cedar Rapids, IA;
    m 02 Dec 1967 Richard Clarence Hertle

Elizabeth "Lizzie" Katharina Anna RINDERKNECHT d/o Karl Rinderknecht & Anna Katharina nee Happel; b 09 Apr 1880 Fremont Twp. Benton Co. bpt 25 Apr 1880 St.Steph (Tauf p.86) con, d 04 Aug 1969 ae89y 3m 26d bur St.Steph Cem; m 27 Feb 1902 August Heinrich (Henry) George Schminke (b 02 Apr 1876 Atkins; d 26 Nov 1964 Vinton Hosp.

ae88y 7m 24d bur St.Steph Cem) s/o Jacob Schminke & Anna Katerina nee Ibel. Farmed Jacob Schminke land and lived there 45 years until retirement in Atkins, IA. Celebrated 60 years of marriage (Text: Joshua:24:15). Eight children born on the farm in Fremont Twp. Benton Co IA.:

Walter Karl Jacob Schminke – b 15 Jun 1903, d 21 Oct 2003;
 m 08 Sept 1927 Ilma Mildred Werning
Edna Katharina Magdalena Schminke – b 03 Apr 1905, d 02 Oct 1988
 m 26 May 1927 George Jacob Haerther
Edwin Frederick George Schminke – b 07 Feb 1908, d 02 Sept 1990;
 m 21 Sept 1933 Amanda Katherina Marie Schanbacher
Hilda Gertrude Anna Schminke – b 12 Feb 1910;
 m 20 Sept 1934 Walter William Maurer
Leona Barbara Lillian Schminke – b 24 Mar 1912;
 m 31 Aug 1938 Clarence Arnold Melhus
Henry Conrad Schminke – b 14 Oct 1914, d 29 Mar 2005;
 1st m 25 Sept 1940 Audrey Laura Hartz;
 2nd m 15 Nov 1975 Pauline Anna Catherine Mohr
Wilmer Frederick August Schminke – b 15 Jun 1917, d 11 Oct 2001;
 1st m 01 Dec 1947 Helen Cecelia Blaha;
 2nd m 28 Aug 1982 Joan Marie (Kiernan)Shipley
Carl August Henry Schminke – b 20 Mar 1920, d 27 Apr 2002;
[Legal change to Carl Henry August]- m 14 Sept 1947 Lillian Koss

Elizabeth Louise RINDERKNECHT d/o Edward John George Rinderknecht & Margaret Lorene nee Tow; b 29 Oct 1943 St.Lukes Hospital, Cedar Rapids, IA bpt 20 Nov 1943 St.Steph, Atkins High School; m 30 Jul 1965 St.Steph to Douglas Lee Winders (b 11 Sept 1943 Cedar Rapids, IA bpt Jun 1966 St.Steph). Children:

Deborah Lynn Winders – b 17 May 1967 Knoxville, IA
 bpt 18 Jun 1967; m 13 Aug 1988 William Lee Settlage
Rodney Alan Winders – b 21 May 1968 St.Lukes Hosp
 Cedar Rapids, IA

Esther Katherine RINDERKNECHT d/o Conrad Martin Rinderknecht & Elizabeth Anna nee Krug; b 11 Apr 1908 Farm Clinton Twp Linn Co IA, bpt 17 May 1908 St.John, d 25 Sept 1973 ae65y 5m 14d Newhall, IA bur 28 Sept 1973 St.John Cem; 1st m 01 Feb 1928 St.John, Eldorado Twp Benton Co IA to Fred William Bierschenk (b 12 Oct 1900 Bierschenk Farm, Eden Twp Benton Co IA, bpt 1900 St.John, d 30 Jul 1939 ae38y 9m 18d Mercy Hosp Cedar Rapids, IA bur 01 Aug 1939 St.John Cem) s/o Carl Heinrich

(Henry Carl) Rinderknecht & Elizabeth nee Kranz. Farmers Eldorado Twp Benton Co IA. Children:

    Kenneth Conrad Bierschenk – b 05 Nov 1928 Eden Twp
        Benton Co IA; m 09 Oct 1952 Lorene Ann Weiss
    Elaine Elizabeth Bierschenk- b 10 Oct 1931 Eden Twp Benton Co IA
        d 27 Mar 1981 Iowa City, IA bur St.John;
        m 17 Feb 1952 Delbert Henry Paulsen

2nd m 21 Sept 1941 St.John Esther Katherine nee Rinderknecht Bierschenk to Hugo Herman Froehlich (b 06 Oct 1898 Eden Twp Benton Co IA, bpt St.John d 24 Dec 1987 ae89y 2m 18d, bur St.John Cem) s/o John D. Froehlich & Sophia nee Wendlandt. Benton Co IA Farmers. Children:

    Dr. Loren Hugo Froelich – b 26 Jan 1943 Eden Twp Benton Co IA;
        m 28 Aug 1965 Helen Marie Hovde
    Sharon Laverna Froelich – b 15 Aug 1944 Eden Twp Benton Co IA;
        m 29 Jan 1966 David Alan Hintze
    Dale Carl Froelich – b 03 Nov 1946 Eden Twp Benton Co IA;
        m 03 Sept 1966 Ruth Ann Duncalf

Eugene Henry Carl RINDERKNECHT s/o Albert Frederick Hartman Rinderknecht & (Minnie) Marie Wilhelmina Katherine nee Haerther; b 10 Sept 1920, d 27 Mar 1992 ae71y 6m 17d; 1st m 14 Feb 1948 Patricia Ann Bostick (b 22 Nov 1926, d 06 Apr 1982 ae55y 4m 15d). Child:

    Charles Albert – b 01 Nov 1948; m 02 Jul 1972 Nancy Halverson
    Katherine Josine – b 08 Oct 1950; m 14 Feb 1971 Berry Evan Wright
    LeAnne Marie – b 08 may 1953; m 08 Jan 1972 Terry Sadler
    David Eugene – b 02 Apr 1954; m 09 Nov 1974 Wendy Gail Lewis
    Valarie Susan – b & d 31 May 1962

2nd m Eugene Henry Carl Rinderknecht to Marie Rich (d 1995).

Friedrich RINDERKNECHT s/o Georg Martin Rinderknecht & Maria Barbara nee Spoerer: cf Anna Gertrud Happel d/o Andreas Happel & Maria Elisabeth nee Möller.

*Friedrich (William) Wilhelm RINDERKNECHT s/o Georg Martin Rinderknecht & Maria Barbara nee Spoerer; (Twin: Katherina Elisabeth) b 06 Jul 1844 Wachbach, Baden, Germany bpt Godparents: Friedrich Spoerer and Georg Wilhelm, came to USA in 1861 with his parents and eight siblings settling near Waubeek, Linn Co IA, later moving to a farm two miles southeast of Atkins, IA; d 01 Dec 1927 ae83y 4m 25d Cedar Rapids, IA, bur St.Steph Cem; m 06 Mar 1869 St.Steph to (Mary) Maria Katherina

Happel (b 14 Oct 1848 os Alt Heim ns Altenhaina, Germany, d 26 Nov 1924 ae76y 1m 12d Benton Co IA bur St.Steph Cem) d/o Andreas Happel & Maria (Marie) Elisabeth Möller. In 1868, William purchased 200 acres of land in Fremont Twp Benton Co IA for $7.25 per acre and turned the furrows with five oxen and a big prairie plow of twenty-eight inches. He was able to break about four acres of prairie soil a day. Later an additional 200 acres was purchased. The town of Atkins,IA was built on a part of his land when he sold forty acres to the Chicago & Milwaukee Railroad to establish the town. They were members of St.Stephen Luth Church which was built on part of their farm near Atkins. In 1901, William & Maria moved to Atkins and built a new home about 1/2 block from their farm where he made his home until 06 Jan 1911 when they moved to Cedar Rapids, IA; William was President Cedar Rapids State Bank that he opened 16 Nov 1912. Ten children:

Anna Gertrude Katherina – b 01 Jun 1869 Benton Co IA,
    d 19 Feb 1951 bur St.Steph Cem; m 11 Mar 1887 William Schirm
TWINS: Maria (Mary) Katharina – b 09 Dec 1870 Benton Co IA,
    d 15 Aug 1902 bur St.Steph Cem; m John Philip Young
        Anna Gertrude Katherina – b 09 Dec 1870 Benton Co IA,
    d 11 Nov 1937 bur St.Steph Cem;
    m 16 Mar 1890 Heinrich (Henry) Schirm
George A. – b 09 Sept 1872 Benton Co IA, d 17 Apr 1901
    bur St.Steph Cem
Anna Maria Katharina – b 29 Nov 1874 Benton Co IA, d 11 Oct 1947
    bur St.Steph Cem; m 17 Jan 1895 Peter George Moeller
Martin Fred Lenard – b 30 Dec 1877 Benton Co IA, d 30 Aug 1953;
    m 05 Mar 1903 Bertha Augusta Ehlers
Christina Elizabeth – b 18 May 1880 Benton Co IA, d 17 Apr 1973
    bur St.Steph Cem; m 20 Feb 1902 Fred Christian Gunzenhouser
Sophia – b 14 Oct 1882 Benton Co IA, d 16 Apr 1966
    bur St.Steph Cem; m 28 Feb 1907 Henry Gerhold
Elizabeth Anna – b 07 Jan 1886 Benton Co IA d 03 Nov 1967
    bur St.Steph Cem; m 26 Jan 1910 Adam F. Gerhold
William (Wilhelm Hartmann George) JR. – b 15 Feb 1891 Benton Co
    d 30 Oct 1974; m 20 Mar 1916 Gertrude W. Bachman
    (b 01 Mar 1889)

Gene August RINDERKNECHT s/o Raymond Henry Martin Rinderknecht & Louise Marie Katherine nee Krug; b 29 Jul 1947 Vinton, IA Hosp, bpt 24 Aug 1947 TrinVT; m 07 Jun 1969 Gail Ann Berndt d/o Herbert Berndt.

DVD. Children:
Wade Martin – b 09 Jun 1973
TWINS: Eric Gene – b 10 Sept 1974
Joel Jay – b 10 Sept 1974
Luke – b 28 May 1978

*Georg RINDERKNECHT JR. youngest s/o George Martin Rinderknecht & Maria Barbara nee Spoerer; b 06 Oct 1857 Wachbach, Germany, bpt Germany, 1863 emigrated to USA, d 03 Nov 1920 ae63y 28d Fremont Twp Benton Co IA bur St.Steph Cem; came to Benton Co. in 1863 with his parents and siblings. One of five in his family to marry into the neighboring Happel family; m 12 Feb 1888 St.Steph to Anna Katherina Happel (b 21 Jan 1864 Altenhaina, Germany, bpt Löhlbach Ch, Germany, d 28 Jul 1947 ae83y 6m 7d Benton Co IA bur St.Steph Cem) d/o Andreas (Andrew) Happel SR. & Maria (Marie) Elisabeth nee Möller. George: businessman in lumber, hardware, coal. All children born at Atkins, IA:
Albert Frederick Hartmann – b 11 Nov 1888, con 1901
(Taufe Reg.p.174); d 10 Aug 1937 ae48y (Scarlet Fever);
1st m Minnie Michel;
2nd m 10 Mar 1918(Minnie) Marie Wilhelmina Katherine Haerther
Clara Elisabeth Barbara – b 20 Mar 1892, con 1905, d 1960;
m 08 Oct 1913 Charles Esch JR.
TWINS: Arthur George Wilhelm – b 02 Jul 1896, d 25 Jan 1969;
1st m 15 Dec 1921Anna Alice Krahling;
2nd m 1954 Laura C. Hartkemeyer
NN son – Stillborn 02 Jul 1896
Christine Katherina Barbara – b 25 Dec 1899; m John England

*Georg Martin RINDERKNECHT SR. s/o Johann Georg Rinderknecht & Anna Marie nee Kober; b 27 Mar 1805 Wachbach, Baden, Germany (village near Stuttgart:Province of Saxony), bpt 28 Mar 1805 Sponsors: Martin Wilhelm and Georg Florian Hagelstein, con 1819; d 04 Jun 1887 ae82y 2m 8d Benton Co IA bur St.Steph Cem; weaver & farmer in Germany; farmer in Benton Co IA; m 02 May 1837 Maria Barbara Spoerer (b 22 Jun 1816 Wachbach, Germany, bpt 24 Jun 1816 Godparents: Eva Barbara Gacker, Maria Katharina Neils, Baria Katharina Gegel, con 1830, d 23 Mar 1886 ae69y 9m 1d Benton Co. IA bur St.Steph Cem) d/o Johann Martin Spoerer & Maria Margaretha nee Hammel. Emigrated 09 Feb 1861 from Bremen, Germany to Waubeek, IA; came to Benton Co IA in 1863. Forty-two days crossing Atlantic Ocean. Four children were left in New

York for brief period until money could be accumulated for them to come to Dubuque, IA. Children:

    *Maria Sophia Barbara – b 12 Sept 1837 Wachbach, Germany
        d 01 Mar 1924 Benton Co IA; m Jacob Young in New York
    *Johann W – b 02 Sept 1839 Wachbach, Germany; d (disappeared);
        m Elisabeth Heilman
    *Friedrich – b 26 Sept 1841 Wachbach, Germany
        d 13 Jun 1927 Atkins, Benton Co IA bur St.Steph Cem;
        m 25 Sept 1866 Anna Gertrude Happel
    TWINS: *(William)Friedrich Wilhelm – b 06 Jul 1844
        Wachbach, Germany; d 01 Dec 1927, Atkins, IA
        bur St.Steph Cem; m Mary (Maria) Happel
            *Sophia Katharina Elisabeth – b 06 Jul 1844
        Wachbach, Germany; d 09 May 1886 Atkins, IA
        bur St.Steph Cem; m Johann George C. Happel
    *Maria Katharina Barbara – b 25 Jan 1847 Wachbach, Germany;
        d 10 Nov 1906 [Typhus)Atkins, IA bur St.Steph Cem;
        m 1862 Carl (Charles) Rammelsberg
    *Karl – b 10 Mar 1849 Wachbach, Germany;
        d 23 Dec 1918 Atkins, IA bur St.Steph Cem;
        m 22 Feb 1872 Anna Katherina Happel
    *Martin – b 30 Dec 1854 Wachbach; d 03 Nov 1920 bur St.Steph Cem
        1st m 13 Jun 1879 Christina Gerber;
        2nd m 17 Jun 1917 Mary Garthoff
    *Georg JR. – b 06 Oct 1857 Wachbach, Germany
        d 03 Nov 1920 Fremont Twp Benton Co IA bur St.Steph Cem;
        m 12 Feb 1888 Anna Katharina Happel
    Infant – d 17 Apr 1901, bur St.Steph Cem

*Georg Peter RINDERKNECHT s/o Heinrich Rinderknecht; m 29 Jan 1760 Anna Maria Heindrich d/o Heinrich Heindrich. Children:
    Georg Peter – b 02 Feb 1766 Wurttemberg, Germany
    *Johann Georg – b 21 Apr 1770 Wurttemberg. Germany
        d 03 Oct 1846 Baden, Germany;
        m 19 Jun 1804 Anna Maria Kober

George William Frederick RINDERKNECHT s/o Karl Rinderknecht & Anna Katherine nee Happel: cf Anna Sophia Maria Elizabeth Gerhold.

Gertrude Katharina Maria RINDERKNECHT d/o Karl Rinderknecht &

Katharina Elisabeth nee Happel: cf Wilhelm Gottlob Haerther s/o Johann Haerther & Wilhelmine Haerther.

Helen Caroline Gertrude RINDERKNECHT d/o George William Frederick Rinderknecht & Anna Sophia Marie Elizabeth nee Gerhold; b 09 Feb 1913, d 22 May 1982 Des Moines, IA home ae69y 3m 13d, bur Glendale Cem Des Moines, IA; m 12 Jul 1941 Omaha, Nebraska to Ernest Philip Schwartz (b 13 Aug 1892, d 15 Feb 1981 ae88y 6m 2d Wesley Acres Care Center bur Glendale Cem Des Moines, IA; Occupation: Circulation Manager Des Moines Register Newspaper) s/o Henry S. Schwartz & Clara Johanna nee Sentz. Schwartzträuben name changed to Schwartz except for legal papers. No children.

Henry Eberhard Valentine RINDERKNECHT s/o William H. Rinderknecht & Christine nee Haerther; b 31 Dec 1901 Fremont Twp, bpt St.Steph, con St.Steph; d 17 Dec 1979 ae77y 11m 16d Cedar Rapids, IA bur 20 Dec 1979 St.Steph Cem; m 08 Jan 1925 Ella Mae Fix (b 03 May 1900 Atkins, bpt St.Steph, con St.Steph d 05 Feb 1996 ae95y 9m 2d bur St.Steph Cem) d/o John Philip Fix & Meta nee Axelsen. Farmers west of Atkins, IA; retired and built new home across the street from St.Steph Ch in Atkins. Child:
    Mae Elaine – b 15 Jul 1930 Atkins, IA;
        m 30 Aug 1950 Richard Kaestner

Henry Karl RINDERKNECHT s/o Karl Rinderknecht & Anna Katherina nee Happel: cf Louise Elizabeth Krug d/o Johann Peter Krug aka John Krug & Anna Katharina nee Michel.

Herbert Adam August RINDERKNECHT s/o George William Frederick Rinderknecht & Anna Sophia Marie Elizabeth nee Gerhold; b 08 Feb 1911 Farm Fremont Twp Benton Co IA, d 28 Feb 1994 ae83y 20d bur St.Steph Cem; m 18 Oct 1947 Iowa City, IA to Odetta Marie nee Eutsler Glick (b 02 Mar 1905 Muscatine, IA d 06 Sept 1985 ae80y 6m 4d St.Lukes Hosp Cedar Rapids, IA bur St.Steph Cem) d/o Fred Marrison Eutsler & Sarah Gertrude nee Piggott. Farmers Benton Co IA.
    STEPSON: Galen Eugene Glick – b 26 May 1941;
        1st m 17 Jun 1961 Delores Ann Krug DVD; 2nd m NFR

James Carl RINDERKNECHT s/o Karl George Rinderknecht & Betty Jo nee Van Heiden; b 15 Nov 1955 St.Lukes Hosp Cedar Rapids, IA; m 01 Dec 1984 St.John Luth Ch Marengo, IA to Tammara Jo Patterson d/o Larry

"Butch" & Dianne Patterson of Marengo, IA. Children:
  Joshua James – b 17 Jul 1987 St.Lukes Hosp Cedar Rapids, IA
  Molly Jo – b 21 Nov 1990 St.Lukes Hosp Cedar Rapids, IA

*Johann RINDERKNECHT b 17 Mar 1817 Wachbach, Baden, Germany, con 1828, d 08 Sept 1904 ae87 y 5m 22d Benton Co IA bur St.Steph Cem; m Barbara Mead (b 02 Feb 1827 Germany, d 25 Feb 1911 ae84y 23d Benton Co IA bur St.Steph Cem). 1864 emigrated to Atkins, IA area. Six children:
  Fred – NFR
  Christian – b 1853, d 1904; m Anna Nell
  Barbara – 1859, d 1948; 1st m Edward K. Kerman;
        2nd m 1895 Ludwig (Lewis) L. Lauterwasser
  Katharina – b 25 Dec 1864, d 1933; m 22 Mar 1882 Martin Werning
  Sophia Barbara – b 14 Mar 1867, d 15 Dec 1936 bur St.Steph Cem;
        1st m 24 Mar 1892 Christian Eberhardt Haerther;
        2nd m NN Schnarr
  George – NFR

*Johann Georg RINDERKNECHT s/o Georg Peter Rinderknecht & Anna Maria nee Heindrich; b 21 Apr 1770 Wurttenberg, Baden, Germany, bpt Godparent: Johann Peter Freiderich and Heinrich Friedrich, d 03 Oct 1846 Baden Germany; m 19 Jun 1804 Anna Maria Kober (b/bpt 06 Apr 1781 Godparents: Anna Maria Sebor and Anna Catharina Kober, d 07 Nov 1850 Wachbach, Germany) d/o Peter Kober & Maria Margaretha nee Hanemann. Children:
  *Georg Martin – b 27 Mar 1805 Wachbach, Baden, Germany
        d 04 Jun 1887 Atkins, Benton Co IA;
        m 02 May 1837 Maria Barbara Spoerer
  Catharina Barbara – b 09 1808 Wachbach, Baden, Germany
  Johann Martin – b 12 Aug 1811 Wachbach, Baden, Germany
        d 30 Jan 1814 Wachbach, Baden, Germany
  Johann Martin –b 29 May 1814 Wachbach, Baden, Germany
  *Johann – b 18 May 1817 Wachbach, Baden, Germany
        d 08 Sept 1904 Benton Co IA; m Barbara Mead
  Georg Peter – b 16 Jul 1820 Wachbach, Baden, Germany
  Catharina Fredericka – b 28 Aug 1824 Wachbach, Baden, Germany
  Anna Catharina – b 29 Jun 1827 Wachbach, Baden, Germany

John Henry William Conrad "Jack" RINDERKNECHT s/o Georg William

Frederick Rinderknecht & Anna Maria nee Gerhold; b 21 Mar 1904 Farm Fremont Twp. Benton Co IA bpt 17 Apr 1904 St.Steph Sponsors: Wilhelm Haerther, Konrad Rinderknecht, Heinrich Gerhold, con 01 Apr 1917 St.Steph; d. 28 Sept 1989 ae85y 6m 7d Mercy Medical Center, Cedar Rapids, IA bur St.Steph Cem; Owned Atkins Grocery Store. 1st m 10 Jun 1926 Lora Lena Lea Boettcher(b 03 Oct 1906 Albert City, IA, d 08 Apr 1969 [Heart Attack]ae62y 6m 5d Atkins, IA bur St.Steph Cem) d/o William Boettcher & Ella nee Bucholz No Children.

2nd m 03 Oct 1970 "Jack" John Henry William Conrad Rinderknecht to Ella Marie O'Brian (b 04 Jul ND) d/o Frederick O'Brian & Louise nee Pagel. Residences: Atkins, Newhall, Van Horne, IA

Jolene Ann RINDERKNECHT d/o Arthur John Rinderknecht & Harriet Charlene nee Keiper: cf Dennis Paul Lensch.

Jolene Louise RINDERKNECHT d/o Raymond Henry Martin Rinderknecht & Louise Marie Katherine nee Krug; b 12 Aug 1952 Vinton, IA Hosp, bpt 14 Sept 1952 TrinVT; m 27 Jul 1974 Daniel Raymond Blanchard (b 10 Dec 1952) s/o Lyman A. Blanchard. Children:
    TWINS: Perry Raymond Blanchard – b 24 Apr 1979
           Burke Daniel Blanchard – b 24 Apr 1979
    Ross Joseph Blanchard – b 27 Jan 1983

Jon Arthur RINDERKNECHT s/o Arthur John Rinderknecht & Harriet Charlene nee Keiper; b 21 Oct 1953 Mercy Hosp Cedar Rapids, IA bpt & con St.Steph; Construction Superintendent Taylor-Larson Co. Cedar Rapids, IA; m 21 Oct 1989 Nancy Kay Waterman (b 04 Jan 1955 St.Lukes Hosp Cedar Rapids, IA bpt & con St.Steph; Junior High School Teacher, Cedar Rapids, IA) d/o Norman Keith Waterman & Evelyn nee Hatter. Atkins, IA residence. Child:
    Catherine Ann – b 18 Apr 1991 St.Lukes Hosp Cedar Rapids, IA
    bpt 05 May 1991 St.Steph con 20 Mar 2005 St.Steph

Judy Kay RINDERKNECHT d/o Paul Henry Rinderknecht & Dorothy Louise nee Gardemann; b 05 Oct 1948 St.Lukes Hosp Cedar Rapids, IA bpt 1948 St.Steph Sponsors: Margaret & Edna Rinderknecht, con 1961 St.Steph; m 02 Feb 1970 St.Steph to John Gatlin Boatwright (b 06 Sept 1947 Marion, SC; d 15 Oct 1968 Bronx, NY; Welder/Trucker) s/o John D. Boatwright & Sarah nee Mattox. Florence, SC residence. Children:
    Tonya Sue Boatwright – b 09 Feb 1970 Marion, SC;

m 05 Jun 1994 Todd Stewart
Therese Ann Boatwright – b 17 Feb 1973 Cedar Rapids, IA

*Karl RINDERKNECHT s/o Georg Martin Rinderknecht SR. & Maria Barbara nee Spoerer; b 10 Mar 1849 Wachbach(near Stuttgart), Germany, d 23 Dec 1918 ae69y 9m 13d Atkins, IA [Operation & Rheum] (Influenza-Todten p.292) bur St.Steph Cem; came to USA with his parents and siblings leaving Bremen, Germany 09 Feb 1861 where he was farmer and weaver near Stuttgart. They were forty-two days crossing the Atlantic Ocean. Destination: Waubeek, IA where a brother of his father, Martin, resided. Family finances were limited and there was not enough money for all to travel to Waubeek so four children were left in New York for a brief period until money could be sent for their travel to Iowa. A farm of 190 acres was rented near Waubeek, Linn County IA for three years before purchasing eighty acres in Fremont Twp Benton Co IA. They built a house on the farm where Karl lived until his death in 1887. m (21) 22 Feb 1872 St/Steph (Trau Reg.p.245) to Anna Katherina Happel (b 04 May 1853 os Alt Heim ns Altenhaina, Germany, bpt Löhlbach, Germany, con Rock Island, IL, d 14 Apr 1933 ae79y 11m 10d bur St.Steph Cem) d/o Andreas (Andrew) Happel & Maria (Marie) nee Möller). Settled on the Rinderknecht home place and farmed until retirement in Atkins, IA. Ten Children born on farm in Fremont Twp. Benton Co.:

Frederick Georg Johann – b 09 Jan 1872 Fremont Twp Benton Co IA
    d 11 Mar 1873 ae1y 2m 2dbur St.Steph Cem
(John) Johannes Andreas Wilhelm- b 13 May 1874; Never Married;
    d 25 Nov 1896 [Diptheria] bur St.Steph Cem (Todten Bl.p.282)
George William Frederick – b 10 Feb 1876, d 10 Aug 1960
    bur St.Steph Cem; m 06 Sept 1900 Anna Sophia Maria Gerhold
Gertrude Katharina Maria – b 25 Feb 1878, d 16 May 1965;
    m 22 Dec 1898 Wilhelm Gottlob Haerther
Elizabeth Katherina Anna – b 09 Apr 1880, d 04 Aug 1969;
    m 27 Feb 1902 Heinrich (Henry) Schminke
Konrad Martin – b 01 Aug 1882, d 10 Jan 1957 bur St.John Cem;
    m 07 Feb 1907 Elizabeth (Lizzie) Anna Krug
August Johann Georg – b 07 Jul 1884, d 01 Nov 1955 bur CdrMem;
    m 30 Apr 1908 Wilhemine (Minnie) Heinrike Mohr
Barbara Anna Sophia – b 07 Sept 1886 Fremont Twp Benton Co IA
    d 01 Dec 1967 bur St.Steph Cem; Never Married.
Katherina "Katie" Christina Magdalene – b 19 Sept 1888,
    d 23 Apr 1977 bur St.Steph Cem;

m 08 Dec 1910 Henry Conrad Keiper

Henry Karl – b 01 Sept 1890; d 28 Jul 1982 Cedar Rapids,
   bur St.Steph Cem; m 22 Oct 1916 Louise Elizabeth Krug

Margaretha Marie Gertrudt-b 09 Jan 1893 Fremont Twp Benton Co IA
   d 17 May 1893 [Diptheria]ae3y 4m 8d bur St.Steph Cem

Karl George RINDERKNECHT s/o Conrad Martin Rinderknecht &
Elizabeth Anna nee Krug; b 14 Jun 1919 Farm north of Van Horne,
Eldorado Twp Benton Co IA bpt 13 Jun 1919 St.John; 1937 Class Newhall
High School; Military Service World War II; d 16 Jan 2004 ae85y 2d
Mercy Medical Center, Cedar Rapids, IA bur St.John Cem; Farmer;
Owner/Operater Rinderknecht Plumbing & Heating, Van Horne, IA; m 01
Jun 1948 Grand Center Luth Ch Iowa Falls, IA to Betty Jo Van Heiden (b
10 May 1925 Ackley, IA home). Mbrs St.And; Tara Hills Country Club.
Children:

Stephen Craig – b 30 Mar 1949 St.Lukes Hosp Cedar Rapids, IA;
   1st m 1983 Allyson Leigh DVD; 2nd m 21 Aug 1992 Jody Pence

Kay Ann – b 22 Oct 1950 St.Lukes Hosp Cedar Rapids, IA;
   m 07 Dec 1974 Dennis D. Bone

Keith Jay – b 20 Oct 1954 St.Lukes Hosp Cedar Rapids;
   m 29 Mar 1978 Lois Mary Burlage

James Carl – b 15 Nov 1955 St.Lukes Hosp Cedar Rapids;
   m 01 Dec 1984 Tammara Jo Patterson

Katherina "Katie" Christina Magdalene RINDERKNECHT d/o Karl
Rinderknecht & Anna Katherina nee Happel; b 19 Sept 1888 Fremont Twp
Benton Co IA d 23 Apr 1977 St.Lukes Hosp Cedar Rapids ae88y 7m 4d bur
St.Steph Cem; m 08 Dec 1910 St.Steph to Henry Conrad Keiper (b 17 May
1887 Atkins, IA, d 31 Mar 1982 Cedar Rapids ae94y 10m 14d bur St.Steph
Cem) s/o Frederick Keiper JR. & Magdalena nee Schminke. Farmers;
retired in Atkins 10 years. Celebrated 66th Wedding Anniversary Children:

Frederick Carl "Fritz" Keiper – b 12 Nov 1911 Farm Atkins, IA;
   m 03 Aug 1933 Ella Charlotte Behrens

Irvin George Keiper – b 06 Oct 1913 Farm Atkins, IA;
   m 30 Jun 1938 Dolores Irene Melberg

Esto Magdalene Keiper – b 23 Feb 1917 Farm Atkins, IA;
   m 15 May 1949 Arthur William Jennings

Raymond Conrad William Keiper – b 13 Feb 1919 Farm Atkins, IA;
   m 24 May 1941 Betty Jane Lensch

Milda Katherine Keiper – b 05 Sept 1922 Farm Atkins, IA

d 24 May 2003; St.John Cem;
m 17 Feb 1946 Willard Anton Heitshusen

Katherine Josine RINDERKNECHT d/o Charles Albert Rinderknecht & Nancy nee Halverson; b 08 Oct 1950; m 14 Feb 1971 Barry Evan Wright (b 05 Jan 1945). Children:
Brian Lewis Wright – b 22 Jul 1971
Carrie Ann Wright – b 04 Apr 1978

Kay Ann RINDERKNECHT d/o Karl George Rinderknecht & Betty Jo nee Van Heiden; b 22 Oct 1950 St.Lukes Hosp Cedar Rapids, IA; m 07 Dec 1974 St.And to Dennis D.Bone (b 24 Oct 1946 Harlan, IA) s/o Boyd & Marie Bone. Children:
Jacquline Marie Bone – b 18 Jan 1976 Mercy Hosp Cedar Rapids, IA; m Dan Fitzgerald
Kathelyn Elizabeth Bone- b 16 Aug 1981 Mercy Hosp Cedar Rapids, IA; m Chad Rainwater
Allyson Leigh Bone – b 01 Sept 1983 Mercy Hosp Cedar Rapids, IA

Keith Jay RINDERKNECHT s/o Karl George Rinderknecht & Betty Jo nee Van Heiden; b 20 Oct 1954 St.Lukes Hosp Cedar Rapids, IA; m 29 Mar 1978 Cedar Rapids to Lois Mary Burlage (b 12 Jan 1952 Dyersville, IA) d/o Elmer & Dorothy Burlage. Children:
Andrew Stephen – b 08 Oct 1982 Royal Oak, MI
Bradley James – b 02 Nov 1984 Royal Oak, MI

Keith Wayne RINDERKNECHT s/o Otto Henry Carl Rinderknecht & Edna Alice nee Railsback; b 06 Jan 1950 St.Lukes Hosp Cedar Rapids, IA; bpt St.Steph; 1st m 13 Oct 1973 in FL to Cheri Fester DVD 1979.
2nd m 22 Jul 1983 Keith Wayne Rinderknecht to Cindy Johnson.

Kimberly Kay RINDERKNECHT d/o Norman Keith Rinderknecht & Eloise Colleen nee Hagan; b 31 Oct 1961 Iowa City, IA; m 29 Nov 1986 Gloria Dei Lutheran Ch, Des Moines, IA to Leif Daniel Erickson (b 01 Oct 1961 Sioux City, IA) s/o Dr. Ernest Daniel Erickson & Helen Martha nee Bachrodt. Occupation: Law. Child:
Audrey Christine Erickson – b 20 Feb 1991

Luverna RINDERKNECHT m Fred Hartl. Child:
Leonard J. Hartl – b 18 Sept 1936 Cedar Rapids, IA d 12 Jun 2004
432

St.Mary's Hosp, Rochester MN [Car Accident Injuries]
bur 16 Jun 2004 Dupont Cem, Swisher, IA

Lawrence Ray RINDERKNECHT s/o Otto Henry Carl Rinderknecht & Edna Alice nee Railsback; b 18 Dec 1942 St.Lukes Hosp. Cedar Rapids, IA; Lt.Col. U.S.Air Force; m 02 Oct 1969 Wichita, KS to Paulette Marie Lebescat (b 22 Sept 1945 France) d/o Jean(pro John) & Marie Lebescat, France. Children:
    Lisa Marie – b 17 May 1971 Riverside, CA
    Christopher Lewis – b 02 Oct 1978 Montgomery, AL

LeAnne Marie RINDERKNECHT d/o Charles Albert Rinderknecht & Nancy nee Halverson; b 08 May 1953; m 08 Jan 1972 Terry Sadler (b 10 Mar 1951). Child:
    Megan Elizabeth Sadler – b 05 Jan 1978

Lois Ann RINDERKNECHT d/o Arthur George Wilhelm (Bud) Rinderknecht & Anna Alice nee Krahling; b 28 Feb 1922; Bethany Luth College, Mankato, MN; Homestead, IA Teacher; 1st m 14 Jun 1946 Hilbert Christian Schaefer (b 03 Aug 1922, d 17 Nov 1983 ae61y 3m 14d). Children:
    Bethann Alice Schaefer – b 11 Apr 1947;
        m 17 Aug 1968 Stanley Teggatz
    Mary Margaret Schaefer – b 20 Dec 1951;
        m 24 Feb 1974 Douglas Fast
    William Arthur Schaefer – b 28 Jul 1953; m 21 Jul 1979 Robyn Maas
2nd m 24 Nov 1984 Lois Ann nee Rinderknecht Schaefer to Bill Randolph (b 14 Dec 1921, d 14 Jul 2004 ae82y 7m; U.S. Navy World War II 1940-1946; retired building contractor).

Lorane Kathrine Wilhemine RINDERKNECHT d/o August Georg Johann "Gus" Rinderknecht & Wilhelmine Heinrike "Minnie" nee Mohr; b 20 May 1909 Fremont Twp. Benton Co IA, d 12 Apr 1994 ae84y 10m 23d; 1st m Lloyd Spencer Parker (b 14 Sept 1910 Benton Co IA, d 01 Jun 1968 ae57y 8m 18d Iowa City, IA bur Vinton, IA).
2nd m 17 Feb 1972 Lorane Katherine Wilhemine to Ernest William Demmel (b 31 Mar 1916 Vinton, IA d 08 Aug 1994 ae78y 4m 8d).

Luanne Rae RINDERKNECHT d/o Raymond Henry Martin Rinderknecht & Louise Marie nee Krug; b 21 Feb 1954 Vinton, IA Hosp bpt 07 Mar 1954

TrinVT; m 26 Jul 1975 Marc Meyer (b 09 May 1953). Children:
    Matthew Marc Meyer – b 17 Jun 1979
    Andrea Beth Meyer – b 01 Nov 1981

Lynn Merle RINDERKNECHT s/o Merl Carl Johannes Rinderknecht & Lois Mae nee Franzenburg; b 10 Feb 1948 St.Lukes Hosp Cedar Rapids, IA; B.S. Wartburg College, Waverly IA; Farmer; Teacher; m 22 Jun 1974 Peace United Ch of Christ Gladbrook, IA to Peggy Jean Hoing (b 13 Aug 1948 Marshalltown, IA) d/o Wilford Hoing & Amy nee Delfs. Children:
    Danae Rachel – b 28 Nov 1976 St.Lukes Hosp Cedar Rapids, IA
    Scott Merl – b 22 Dec 1979 St.Lukes Hosp Cedar Rapids, IA
    Trent Jacob – b 19 Sept 1989 St.Lukes Hosp Cedar Rapids, IA

Mae Elaine RINDERKNECHT d/o Henry Eberhardt Valentine Rinderknecht & Ella Mae Anna nee Fix; b 15 Jul 1930, bpt & con 02 Apr 1944 St.Steph; 1948 Class Newhall High School; m 20 Aug 1950 Richard Kaestner (b 01 Jun 1931, d 22 Aug 2003 ae72y 2m 21d) s/o Otto Kaestner & Pauline nee Weise. Farmers in Newhall and Belle Plaine, Benton Co IA. Celebrated 50th Wedding Anniversary. Mae retired 2006 in Newhall, IA. Children:
    Betty Jean Kaestner – b 15 Jul 1951; m 09 May 1952 Louis Moeller
    Daniel Lee Kaestner – b 24 Aug 1952; m 01 Sept 1973 Kathy Albers
    Robert Richard Kaestner – b 06 Oct 1954;
        m 06 Dec 1955 Cindy Strellner
    Patricia Kay Kaestner – b 02 Apr 1959; m 31 May 1980 Paul Pirkl
    Judy Marie Kaestner – b 08 Sept 1962
    William Alan Kaestner – b 03 Jun 1964;
        m 06 Jan 1990 Denise Kinzenbom

*Maria Katharina Barbara RINDERKNECHT d/o George Martin Rinderknecht & Maria Barbara Spoerer; b 25 Jan 1847 Wachbach, Germany; emigrated to USA 1861, d 19 Nov 1906 ae59y 9m 25d Atkins, IA (Typhus, Todten Bk p.287) bur St.Steph Cem; m 1862 Carl (Charles) Rammelsberg (b 17 Mar 1830 Brannschweg, Germany; emigrated to USA 1855 ae25y; d 05 Dec 1909 ae79y 8m 18d Benton Co IA bur St.Steph Cem).Carl's (Charles) cousin Hugo Rammelsberg, native of Magdeburg, os Prussia ns Germany, 1847 immigrant located Charles on land Hugo had entered in Fremont Twp Benton Co IA in 1854. Charles operated a drugstore in Cedar Rapids, IA, and later moved to farm southeast of Cedar Rapids. 1874 moved to another farm, retired in Atkins to house their son

William built and stands today as the Mobil Station on Main Street. Eight children born in Benton Co IA.:

David Rammelsberg – b 26 Apr 1863, d Aug 1900;
 m 26 Mar 1894 Magdalena (Lena) Nell
William R. (Wilhelm) Rammelsberg – b 17 Jun 1864, d 14 Jan 1947;
 m 12 Mar 1896 St.Steph Anna Katherine Krug
TWINS: Sophie Rammelsberg – b 11 May 1866;
 1st m 1884 Lenard Nell; 2nd m 1928 William Mealhauser
  Anna Rammelsberg – b 11 May 1866;
 m 02 Mar 1886 Matthew Schirm
Emma Rammelsberg – b 14 Feb 1870;m 02 Apr 1891 Carl Schuldt,
 Atkins Blacksmith
Mathilda Katherine Karolina Rammelsberg- b 27 Jun 1875, con 1888
 d 18 Dec 1908 Cedar Rapids (Typhus Todten p.288)
 bur St.Steph Cem; Never Married
Carolina Catharine Marie Rammelsberg – b 13 Apr 1878,
 d 14 Jan 1955 ae76y 9m 1d [Heart]bur St.Steph;
 m 18 Dec 1902 Fred C. Truckenmiller
Rosina Sophia Katharina Christine Rammelsberg – b 06 Jul 1883,
 con 1894 St.Steph; m 25 Aug 1924 Thomas Berryman

*Maria Sophia Barbara RINDERKNECHT d/o Georg Martin Rinderknecht SR. & Maria Barbara nee Spoerer; b 12 Sept 1837 Wachbach, Baden Germany, con 1851 Wachbach, Germany; d 01 Mar 1924 ae86y 5m bur St.Steph Cem(Totem Bk II p.342); m 20 Sept 1863 Jakob Young (b 02 Sept 1832 Germany, d 29 Sept 1880 ae58y 27d). Children:

John Philip Young – b 03 Nov 1865 New York City;
 1928 declared legally dead by Chicago, IL Court;
 m 1890 Marie (Mary) Rinderknecht
Martha Young – b 24 Feb 1868 New York City;
 d 06 Jun 1952 Benton Co IAbur St.Steph Cem;
 m 12 Feb 1888 St.Steph August A. Happel
Jacob George Young – b 29 Aug 1872 New York City;
 Never Married; d 01 Mar 1927 ae55y 6m

*Martin RINDERKNECHT s/o George Martin Rinderknecht & Barbara Spoerer; b 30 Dec 1854 Wachbach, Germany, d 03 Nov 1920 ae65y 10m 3d bur St.Steph Cem; 1st m 13 Jun 1879 St.Steph to Christina Gerber (b 13 Jan 1857). Children:

Maria Sophia Barbara – b 20 Mar 1880, con 1894 (p.167)

435

d 12 Apr 1919; m 20 Jun 1898 Henry Oltrogge
  Anna Martha Elisabeth – b 14 Aug 1881, con 1895 (p.168)
    d 1915; m Henry Nolting
  Fred – b 18 Jul 1884; m 07 Sept 1905 Barbara Fink
  Otto – b 23 Oct 1886, d 19 Mar 1940; 1st m 29 Oct 19ll Anna Trost;
    2nd m Margaret Murbach
  Matilda – b 31 Mar 1889; m 20 Mar 1912 Bert Mize
  Louie – b 29 Apr 1891; m 02 Sept 1915 Maude Thompson
  Martin – b 30 Jan 1899; m 17 Dec 1919 Sophe Voehl
2nd m 17 Jun 1917 Martin Rinderknecht to Mary Garthoff.

Mary Lee RINDERKNECHT d/o Merl Carl Johannes Rinderknecht & Lois
Mae nee Franzenburg; b 17 Aug 1945 St.Lukes Hosp Cedar Rapids, IA; m
22 Feb 1974 Our Lady of Lourdes Ch, Waterbury, CT to Dr.Anthony
Luciano M.D. (b 22 Jun 1945 Italy). Children:
  Danielle Elizabeth Luciano – b 27 Mar 1975 New Britain, CT
  Michael Gennaro Luciano – b 25 Apr 1978 Southington, CT
  Joseph Salvatore Luciano – b 15 Nov 1979 Iowa City, IA

Merl Carl Johannes RINDERKNECHT s/o Conrad Martin Rinderknecht &
Elizabeth Anna nee Krug; b 01 Nov 1916 Eldorado Twp Benton Co IA, bpt
03 Dec 1916 St.John, Eldorado Twp Benton Co, d 02 Jan 1987 ae70y 2m
1d bur St.John Cem; 1st m 19 Sept 1942 Parsonage of Keystone Luth Ch to
Lois Mae Franzenburg (b 23 May 1924 Keystone, IA, d 02 Jan 1986 ae61y
7m 10d [Car Accident enroute to Vinton, IA] bur St.John Cem) d/o Herman
Franzenburg & Lena Margaret nee Wiese. Farmers. Children:
  Rita Jane – b 20 Jan 1944 Mercy Hosp Cedar Rapids, IA;
    m 20 Jan 1976 Peter Thomas Hussey SR. DVD
  Mary Lee – b 17 Aug 1945 St.Lukes Hosp Cedar Rapids, IA;
    m 22 Feb 1974 Anthony Adolfo Luciano
  Lynn Merle – b 10 Feb 1948 St.Lukes Hosp Cedar Rapids, IA;
    m 22 Jun 1974 Peggy Jean Hoing, Van Horne, IA
  Connie Ann – b 26 Jun 1949 St.Lukes Hosp Cedar Rapids, IA
    d 21 Oct 1950 [Drownd] Eldorado Twp Benton Co IA
    bur St.John, Newhall, IA
  Michael Adam – b 26 Dec 1950 St.Lukes Hosp Cedar Rapids, IA;
    m 02 May 1970 Angela Gertrude Boddicker
2nd m 11 Dec 1987 Newhall,IA Merl Carl Johannes Rinderknecht to Irene
nee Buelow Veenstra (b 14 Jun 1919 Vinton, IA d 13 Jul 1991 ae72y 1m
Luth Home Vinton, IA) d/o Louis Buelow & Augusta nee Willenbrook.

Michael Alan RINDERKNECHT s/o Merl Carl Johannes Rinderknecht & Lois Mae nee Franzenburg; b 26 Dec 1950 St.Lukes Hosp Cedar Rapids, IA; m 02 May 1970 St.Paul Catholic Ch Newhall, IA to Angela Gertrude Boddicker (b 06 Oct 1951 Mercy Hosp Cedar Rapids, IA; d 30 Oct 2007 ae56y 24d) d/o Wallace Boddicker & Helen nee Anderson. Newhall, IA residence. Children:

  Todd Michael – b 23 Oct 1970 Mercy Hosp Cedar Rapids, IA
  Nita Nikkole – b 13 Aug 1972 Mercy Hosp Cedar Rapids, IA
  Jayd Wallace – b 07 Nov 1978 Mercy Hosp Cedar Rapids, IA
  Kortney Anne – b 03 Nov 1980 Cedar Rapids, IA

Michael David RINDERKNECHT s/o David Lee Rinderknecht & Jane nee Weiss; b 07 May 1968; m 29 Jun 1991 Michelle McVey (b 04 Jun 1968); Children:

  Lindsey Michelle – b 26 Apr 1995
  Katelin Marie – b 15 Oct 1997

Michael William RINDERKNECHT s/o Donald Alvin William Rinderknecht & Betty Jean nee Birky; b 20 Jan 1959; Business Owner; m 22 Apr 1978 Pamela Meyer (b 18 Oct 1958). Coon Rapids, MN residence. Children:

  Andrew William – b 27 Aug 1981
  Peter Lee – b 17 Sept 1983

Nancy Ellen RINDERKNECHT d/o Edward John George Rinderknecht & Margaret Lorene nee Tow; b 19 Apr 1951 St.Lukes Hosp Cedar Rapids, bpt 06 May 1951 St.Steph, Atkins High School; m 21 Oct 1972 St.Steph to Dennis Robert Deklotz (b 30 Jul 1946 Mercy Hosp Cedar Rapids 1st m Carol Voss) s/o Robert Herman Deklotz & Faye Evelyn nee Erland. Farmers near Shellsburg. Children:
STEPCHILDREN:

  Ann Marie Deklotz – b 10 Jan 1966 Mercy Hosp Cedar Rapids, IA;
      m 17 Sept 1988 Mitch Leon Goodell
  Scott Allan Deklotz – b 01 May 1967 Mercy Hosp Cedar Rapids, IA
  Nathan Robert Deklotz – b 05 May 1973; St.Lukes Hosp
      Cedar Rapids, IA

Nina Mae RINDERKNECHT d/o Arthur George Wilhelm (Bud) Rinderknecht & Anna Alice nee Krahling; b 26 Dec 1924; m 11 Jul 1947

Lloyd Wilmer Day (b 08 Jul 1924 U.S. Navy Jun 22 1944-June 04 1946 World War II; d 17 Jun 1999). Nina's residence: Morgan Hill, CA. Children:

 Janet Ellen Day – b 24 Sept 1948;
  1st m 12 Aug 1973 John Douglas Hanson DVD;
  2nd m 30 Dec 1998 Leonard Turner
 Thomas Allen Day – b 13 Nov 1950; d 24 Sept 1995;
  m 25 Jul 1969 Sandra Lundy DVD
 James Edward Day – b 29 Feb 1952; 1st m 13 Dec 1974 Anita Weitz
  DVD; 2nd m 25 Apr 1988 Patty Avery
 Robert Bruce Day – b 06 Aug 1955;
  m 11 Feb 1989 Bernadette Seyboldt;
  Adopted Child: Spencer Thomas Day (b 30 Oct 1997)

Norman Keith RINDERKNECHT s/o Arnold Karl Heinrich Rinderknecht & Catherine Louise nee Lenz; b 05 Mar 1934 Atkins, bpt & con St.Steph; 1950 class Atkins High School; 1958 U.S. Air Force; University of Iowa Medical School; Gynocologist practicing Des Moines, IA; m 03 Sept 1955 Cedar Rapids, IA to Eloise Colleen Hagan (b 08 Apr 1934 Shellsburg, IA) d/o Gordon Hagan & Doris nee Pickerill of Shellsburg, IA. Children:

 Randall Keith – b 21 Mar 1958 Iowa City, IA;
  m 09 Jun 1983 Ames, IA to Jennifer Kaye Bluhm
 Stephen Bradley – b 16 Oct 1959 Manhattan, KS;
  m 06 Jun 1981 Des Moines, IA to Danette Lee Baldwin
 Kimberly Kay – b 31 Oct 1962 Iowa City, IA;
  m 29 Nov 1986 Des Moines IA to Leif Daniel Erickson

Otto Henry Carl RINDERKNECHT s/o George William Frederick Rinderknecht & Anna Sophia Marie Elizabeth nee Gerhold; b 17 Dec 1919 Farm Fremont Twp Benton Co IA, d 12 May 1999 ae79y 4m 25d Lourdes Hosp Paducah, KY [Lung Cancer] bur CdrMem; Atkins High School graduate; m 06 Sept 1941 TrinCR to Edna Alice Railsback (b 10 Sept 1922 St.Lukes Hosp. Cedar Rapids, IA d 04 Feb 2001 ae78y 4m 25d) d/o Gary Railsback & Mae nee Lewis of Palo, IA. Farmed Rinderknecht homestead until moving to Cedar Rapids, IA; relocated to Tucson, AZ for retirement; moved to Murray, KY in 1996. 50th Wedding Anniversary. Children:

 Laurence Ray – b 18 Dec 1942 St.Lukes Hosp Cedar Rapids, IA;
  m 02 Oct 1969 Paulette Marie Lebescat
 Donna Marie – b 21 Nov 1945; m 06 Sept 1969 Stephen L. Garnett
 Keith Wayne – b 06 Jan 1950 St.Lukes Hosp Cedar Rapids, IA;

1st m 13 Oct 1973 Cheri Fester DVD 1979;

2nd m 22 Jul 1983 Cindy Johnson

Connie Sue – b 13 Nov 1952 St.Lukes Hosp Cedar Rapids, IA;

1st m 02 Oct 1971 Terry Edward Sindelar;

2nd m 25 Jun 1988 Dennis Weathers

Paul Henry RINDERKNECHT s/o August Georg Johann "Gus" Rinderknecht & Wilhelmine Heinrike "Minnie" nee Mohr; b 01 Oct 1916 Fremont Twp. Benton Co IA, d 15 Oct 1968 Bronx, New York ae52y 14d [Parkinson's Disease] bur St.Steph Cem; m 21 Feb 1940 Dorothy Louise Gardemann (b 09 Nov 1917 Newhall IA Benton Co IA) d/o Charles Albert Gardemann & Hatie Annie nee Schlotterback. Farmers. Children:

Charles Richard – b 24 Mar 1943 Cedar Rapids, IA;

m 10 Sept 1966 Darlene Mary Stien

Ronald Paul – b 18 Nov 1945 Cedar Rapids, IA;

m 23 Sept 1983 Miriam Kareen Heggen

Judy Kay – b 05 Oct 1948 Cedar Rapids, IA;

m 02 Feb 1970 John Gatlin Boatwright

Renee Ann – b 23 Sept 1953 Cedar Rapids, IA;

1st m 29 Sept 1984 Mark Wand Johnson DVD;

2nd m 15 Apr 1995 Samuel McHaffy

2nd m 27 Jul 1973 Dorothy Louise nee Gardemann Rinderknecht to Raymond Jensen. Celebrated 25th Silver Wedding Anniversary.

Randall Keith RINDERKNECHT s/o Norman Keith Rinderknecht & Eloise Colleen nee Hagan; b 21 Mar 1958 Iowa City, IA; Commercial Real Estate; Bankers Life Co.; m 09 Jun 1983 Ames, IA to Jennifer Kaye Bluhm (b 20 Aug 1960 Ames, IA) d/o Delwyn Donald Bluhm & Gloria Lee nee Summers. Child:

Alyssa Marie – b 28 Aug 1989

Rebecca Lee RINDERKNECHT d/o Edward John George Rinderknecht & Margaret nee Tow; b 15 Apr 1953 Cedar Rapids, IA bpt 03 May 1953 St.Steph; 1st m 14 Jul 1973 Robert Snavely (b 02 Nov 1952). Cedar Rapids, IA residence. Child:

Nicholas Robert Snavely – b 04 Oct 1979

2nd m 06 Aug 1988 Rebecca Lee nee Rinderknecht Snavely to Craig Louis Barr (b 18 Oct 1950).

Renee Ann RINDERKNECHT d/o Paul Henry Rinderknecht & Dorothy

Louise nee Gardemann; b 23 Sept 1953 St.Lukes Hosp Cedar Rapids, IA; bpt 1953 Sponsor: Lorane Parker, con 1965 St.Steph; Graduate Benton Comm High School; Iowa State University; 1st m 29 Sept 1984 Bridegroom's Father's Home, Ames, IA to Mark Wand Johnson(b 12 Oct 1948 Minneapolis, MN Occupation: Stockbroker) s/o Robert Walton Johnson & Irene Agatha nee Wand. DVD.

2nd m 15 Apr 1995 Renee Ann nee Rinderknecht Johnson to Samuel McHaffy (b 21 Aug 1953). Spokane, WA residence. Children:

> TWINS: Hanna McHaffy – b 18 May 1996
> Camiel McHaffy – b 18 May 1996

Richard Wayne RINDERKNECHT s/o Alfred August Rinderknecht & Irene Katherine Elizabeth nee Krug; b 19 Jun 1938 St.Lukes Hosp Cedar Rapids, IA bpt 10 Jul 1938; m 27 Jul 1958 St.Paul's Luth Ch, Marion, IA to Sandra Gay Fillenworth (b 06 Dec 1938) d/o Ralph Earl Fillenworth & Lucille nee Worden. Children:

> Debra Sue – b 04 Feb 1959, St.Lukes Hosp Cedar Rapids, IA
> Danna Ann – b 25 Sept 1960, Ames, IA;
> m 17 Nov 1990 Des Moines, IA to Christopher J. Randolph
> (b 06 Apr 1958)

Rita Jane RINDERKNECHT d/o Merl Carl Johannes Rinderknecht & Lois Mae nee Franzenburg; b 20 Jan 1944 Mercy Hosp Cedar Rapids, IA bpt 1944; m 14 Mar 1976 Chicago, IL to Peter Thomas Hussey SR. (b 10 May 1942 Chicago, IL Occupation: Greyhound Bus Driver) DVD. Children:

> Peter Thomas Hussey JR. – b 25 Apr 1975 Chicago, IL
> Paul Theodore Hussey – b 11 Jul 1976 Chicago, IL
> Phillip Timothy Hussey – b 23 Jun 1982 Chicago, IL

Robert Henry RINDERKNECHT s/o Conrad Martin Rinderknecht & Elizabeth Anna nee Krug; b 14 Sept 1926 Farm north of Van Horne Eldorado Twp Benton Co IA, bpt 10 Oct 1926 St.John; m 28 May 1950 St.John to Marcella Jean Hurst (b 07 Dec 1927 Harrison Twp Benton Co IA) d/o Charles Raymond Hurst & Mary Esto nee King. Newhall, IA residence. Children:

> David John – b 08 Sept 1951 St.Lukes Hosp Cedar Rapids, IA;
> m 23 Jan 1971 Patricia Jean Elsner
> Douglas Charles – b 01 Sept 1953 St.Lukes Hosp Cedar Rapids, IA;
> m 22 Jul 1973 Dixie Rae Junge
> Ann Elizabeth – b 02 Sept 1957 St.Lukes Hosp Cedar Rapids, IA;

m 19 Aug 1978 David Dale Arnold DVD
Duane Alan – b 09 Oct 1959 St.Lukes Hosp Cedar Rapids, IA;
    m 08 Dec 1984 Danelle Marie Van Hamme

Roger Raymond RINDERKNECHT s/o Raymond Henry Martin Rinderknecht & Louise Marie Katherine nee Krug; b 02 Jun 1941 Vinton, IA Hosp, bpt 21 Jun 1942 TrinVT; m 27 Jun 1964 Rose Ann Kramer (b 28 Feb 1943) d/o Kenneth Kramer. Children:
    Leslie Ranee – b 20 Nov 1967
    Reed Roger – b 02 Jan 1970
    Randal Kent – b 14 May 1971

Ronald Paul RINDERKNECHT s/o Paul Henry Rinderknecht & Dorothy Louise nee Gardemann; b 18 Nov 1945 Cedar Rapids, IA; bpt 1945 and con 1958 St.Steph; Airline Pilot; m 16 Sept 1983 Park City Golf Course, Salt Lake City, UT to Miriam Kareen Heggen (b 20 May 1943 Waterloo, IA) d/o William Rennard Svanoe & Myrtle nee Stadem. UT residence. Children:
    Chad Joshua Paul – b 27 Sept 1984 Salt Lake City, UT
    Tiffany Nicole (Adopted) – b 10 Sept 1990

Ruth Marie RINDERKNECHT d/o Albert Frederick Hartman Rinderknecht & (Minnie) Marie Wilhelmina Katherine nee Haerther; b 25 Feb 1925; m 24 Jan 1948 Clement Ambrose Campbell (b 30 Mar 1921). Children:
    John Albert Campbell SR.– b 15 Apr 1948;
        m 05 Nov 1965 M. Christine Kline
    Lawrence Charles Campbell – b 04 Nov 1949;
        m 28 Nov 1969 Patricia Lois Hice
    Daniel Joseph Campbell – b 25 Dec 1950;
        m 19 Apr 1975 Mary Ann Plut
    Therese Marie Campbell – b 04 Jun 1952;
        m 29 Jul 1977 Hayden Lee Wayne Powers
    Michael David Campbell – b 08 Jul 1953
    Christopher James Campbell – b 10 Oct 1954;
        m 11 Mar 1978 Janet Lynne Wiker
    Rita Ann Campbell – b 16 Jan 1956;
        m 01 Jul 1974 Timothy Lawrence Sierra
    Mary Margaret Campbell – b 06 May 1957;
        m 19 Jun 1975 Ronald Bellinger
    Mark Patrick Campbell – b 06 Oct 1959;

m 09 Jun 1979 Sara Jane Watkins

Kevin Paul Campbell – b 13 Apr 1961;

    m 23 May 1980 Lori Jo Watkins

Stephen Francis Campbell – b 04 Nov 1962;

    m 01 Aug 1986 Carolyn Mae Wertz

Richard Dean Campbell – b 31 Jan 1966;

    m 27 Jun 1989 Lisa Ann Sierra

Stephen Bradley RINDERKNECHT s/o Norman Keith Rinderknecht & Eloise Colleen nee Hagan; b 16 Oct 1959 Manhattan Kansas; Medical Student; m 06 Jun 1981 Des Moines, IA to Danette Lee Baldwin (b 04 Feb 1960 Burlington, IA) d/o Roger Allen Baldwin & Carolyn nee Richardson. Children:

    Erin Jo – b 16 Jun 1983 Iowa City, IA

    Robert Gordon – 26 Aug 1989

Tracy Lynn RINDERKNECHT d/o Albert Paul Rinderknecht & Bethel Jean nee Burmeister; b 18 Jun 1965; m 19 Mar 1988 Michael Raymond Robinson (b 19 Aug 1961). Children:

    Seon Michael Robinson – b 25 Mar 1989

    Taylor Albert Robinson – b 25 Jun 1990

    Bethany Lynn Robinson – b 15 Sept 1993

Velma Louise RINDERKNECHT d/o Henry Karl Rinderknecht & Louise Elizabeth nee Krug; b 23 Apr 1923 Fremont Twp Benton Co IA, bpt 13 May 1923 St.Steph and con St.Steph, d 21 Jul 1971 ae48y 2m 28d Cedar Rapids, IA bur 24 Jul 1971 CdrMem; m 18 Feb 1946 Davenport IA to Thurman Cloyd Harris (b 30 Mar 1925 Blythedale, MO; U.S. Army; Head of Wilson & Co. Cafeteria) s/o Charles D. Harris & Grace Marie nee Mohr. Children:

    Sharon Louise Harris – b 30 Mar 1946 St.Lukes Hosp

        Cedar Rapids, IA; m 29 Jul 1967 Don Lloyd Drahn

    Robert Dwain Harris – b 23 Feb 1950 St.Lukes Hosp

        Cedar Rapids, IA; 1st m 26 Jun 1971 Kristine Beatty DVD;

        2nd m 29 Sept 1978 Patricia Elaine Tudeen

    Gregory Alan Harris – b 24 Jan 1955 St.Lukes Hosp Cedar Rapids, IA

        m 07 Sept 1980 Carolyn Ann Wilson

2nd m 11 Feb 1973 Thurman Cloyd Harris to Grace Smith

Verna Jane RINDERKNECHT d/o Raymond Henry Martin Rinderknecht

& Louise Marie Katherine nee Krug; b 24 Sept 1944 Vinton, IA Hosp, bpt 22 Oct 1944 TrinVT; m 24 Jun 1966 Reginald M. Muhl (b 24 Apr 1944). Children:

Regina Jane Muhl – b 24 Aug 1973
Christopher Muhl – b 05 Jul 1974

Wilbert Heinrich Julius RINDERKNECHT s/o William H. Rinderknecht & Christine Wilhelmine nee Haerther; b 24 Apr 1907 Rinderknecht Farm near Atkins, Benton Co IA, bpt and con St.Steph; d 05 Oct 1993 ae86y 5m 12d bur St.Steph Cem; 1st m 01 Jun 1938 St.Steph to Margaret Ella Deklotz (b 31 Dec 1916, d 15 Nov 1951 ae34y 10m 15d Atkins, IA bur St.Steph Cem) d/o Ralph Deklotz & Amelia nee Fix. Farmed family farm until 1973 retirement. Children:

David Lee – b 04 Apr 1940; m 22 Jul 1967 Jane Weiss
Carol Ann – b 07 Apr 1943; m 18 Jun 1966 John Edward Leasure
Virgil Henry – b/d 17 Jan 1946 Cedar Rapids, IA bur St.Steph Cem
2nd m 21 Apr 1967 Wilbert Heinrich Julius Rinderknecht to Lucille Meyer(b 05 Jun 1916).

William Edward RINDERKNECHT s/o Edward John George Rinderknecht & Margaret Lorene nee Tow; b 04 Feb 1947 St.Lukes Hosp Cedar Rapids, IA bpt 09 Mar 1947 St.Steph, Atkins High School; U.S. Army Reserves; 1st m 22 Jul 1967 Norway, IA to Connie Rae Offedahl (b 20 Jan 1948 St.Lukes Hosp Cedar Rapids, IA) d/o Ervin Oftedahl & Joanne nee McKechnie. DVD. Children:

Heath William – b 01 May 1970 St.Lukes Hosp Cedar Rapids, IA;
    1988 Class Prairie High School;
    1991 Airman Lackland Air Force Base, TX;
    m 17 Oct 1998 Sandra Ann Heatherwick
2nd m 21 Dec 1974 William Edward to Barbara Sue Robinson (b 01 Oct 1953) d/o Frank Robinson & Margaret nee State. Children:
Jeremy Edward – b 18 Jun 1977 St.Lukes Hosp Cedar Rapids, IA
Todd Christopher – b 23 Mar 1979 St.Lukes Hosp Cedar Rapids, IA
Joshua John – b 05 Nov 1984 Cedar Rapids, IA

William Wilhelm H. RINDERKNECHT s/o Friedrich Rinderknecht & Anna Gertrud nee Happel; b 13 Jan 1873 Benton Co IA, d 29 Aug 1949 ae76t 7m 16d bur St.Steph Cem; m 15 Oct 1896 Christine Wilhelmine Haerther(b 09 Dec 1869 Ehningen, Germany, d 18 Dec 1955 ae86y 9d Atkins, IA bur St.Steph Cem) d/o Johann Georg & Wilhelmine Margarethe

nee Haerther. Farmers near Atkins, IA. Mbrs St. Steph Children:
- Carl George Fredrick – b 07 Sept 1897, d 15 Oct 1977;
    Never Married; bur St.Steph Cem
- Heinrike Marie Sophie – b 03 Feb 1900; Never Married
- Henry Eberhardt Valentine – b 31 Dec 1901, d 17 Dec 1979;
    m 08 Jan 1925 Ella May Fix
- Fred Tobias Wilhelm – b 01 May 1905, d 22 Aug 1935;
    Never Married; bur St.Steph Cem
- Wilbert Heinrich Julius – b 24 Apr 1907, d 05 Oct 1993;
    1st m 01 Jun 1938 Margaret Ella Deklotz;
    2nd m 21 Apr 1967 Lucille Meyer
- Ernest August Fredrick b 20 Mar 1909, d 25 Sept 1925
    Never Married; bur St.Steph Cem
- Pauline Wilhelmine Louise – b 30 Jan 1911;
    m/Annulment Harvey Knock

Wilma Elizabeth Ruth RINDERKNECHT d/o August Georg Johann "Gus" Rinderknecht & Wilhelmine Heinrike "Minnie" nee Mohr;b 12 Jun 1920 Fremont Twp Benton Co IA; bpt 11 Jul 1920 St.Steph and con 09 Apr 1933 St.Steph; d 20 Oct 1999 [Cancer] ae79y 4m 8d bur 02 Nov 1999 CdrMem; 1937 Class Atkins High School; Cedar Rapids Business College; m 24 Sept 1941 TrinCR to James William Grummer (b 17 Jan 1920 Luzerne Benton Co IA). Farmers. Moved to Cedar Rapids 1970. Children:
- Donald Dean Grummer – b 03 Sept 1943 St.Lukes Hosp
    Cedar Rapids, IA; m 17 Feb 1972 Pamela Eileen Roberts
- Duane William Grummer– b 18 Oct 1946 St.Lukes Hosp
    Cedar Rapids, IA; m 14 Sept 1968 Sue Faber DVD
- Gary James Grummer – b 22 Feb 1950 St.Lukes Hosp
    Cedar Rapids, IA; m 10 Jun 1973 Mary Ann Southwick

August RIPPEL s/o John Rippel & Christina nee Bachman; b 1876 Benton Co IA d 1949; m Bena Goettsch (b 1885, d 1973). Farmed Sac Co IA before moving to Cedar Twp Benton Co IA. Children:
- Karl – b 1905 Sac Co IA, d 1965
- Pearl – b 1906 Sac Co IA; m Chester Dufresne
- Flossie – b 1908 Sac Co IA; m Louie Selk
- Fern – b 1910 Sac Co IA; m Jennings Kaiser
- Ross – b 1913 Sac Co IA; m Phyllis Shonka
- Vera – b 1915 Cedar Twp Benton Co IA; m Chris Selk
- Roy – b 1917 Cedar Twp Benton Co IA; m Florence Campbell

Lois – b 1923 Cedar Twp Benton Co IA; m Walter Polege
Donald – b 1926 Cedar Twp Benton Co IA; m Jeri Henry
Waldo – b 1928 Cedar Twp Benton Co IA; m Regina Hanneman

*John RIPPEL b 1834 Kur Hessen, Germany, d 1908 Benton Co IA; m Christina Bachman (b 1836 Germany, d 1921 Benton Co IA; 1864 parents and three oldest children emigrated to Lee Co. IL; 1868 moved to Shellsburg and Dysart, Benton Co. IA; 1878 moved to farm purchased in Sac Co. IA. Children:
    *Mary – b Kur Hessen, Germany
    *Henry – b Kur Hessen, Germany
    *Chris – b Kur Hessen, Germany
    Charles – b Benton Co. IA
    John – b Benton Co. IA
    Emma – b Benton Co. IA
    Katherine – b Benton Co. IA
    Elizabeth – b Benton Co. IA
    August – b Benton Co. Ia
    William – b Sac Co. IA
    Lena – b Sac Co. IA

Waldo RIPPEL s/o August Rippel & Bena nee Goettsch; b 1928 Cedar Twp Benton Co IA; m Regina Hanneman. Owned/operator Rippel farm. Children:
    Alan – Story City, IA residence
    Cynthia – Bettendorf, IA schoolteacher
    Douglas – NFR
    Steven – Mt.Auburn., IA

Jess John RISCH s/o William F. Risch & Fredrika nee Gasser; b 28 Oct 1903 Atkins, IA; worked twenty-four years as carpenter and security guard for Quaker Oats Company, Cedar Rapids, IA; m 06 Aug 1931 Gertrude Kathryn Beatty (b 1910 d ND). Child:
    Judy Ann – b 25 Aug 1940

*John RISCH b 1851 Germany, d 1938 Atkins, IA; m Fredrika Lorenz (b 1853 Germany, d 1949 Atkins, IA); Came to USA with son William Fredrick in 1880. Settled in Atkins and John worked for the Milwaukee Railroad. Children:
    *William Fredrick – b 1877 in Germany

Bertha – b Atkins, IA; m NN Marshall

Judy Ann RISCH d/o Jess John Risch & Gertrude Kathryn nee Beatty; b 25 Aug 1940; m 11 Nov 1961 Gary Humphrey. Lived in London, England. Children:
    Scott Andrew Humphrey – b 09 Nov 1962 London, England
    Timothy Jon Humphrey – b 23 Jul 1964 London, England

*William Fredrich RISCH s/o John Risch & Fredrika nee Lorenz; b 1877 in Germany; 1880 came to USA with his parents, settled in Atkins, IA; carpenter; m 21 Nov 1902 Fredrika Gasser (b 1883, d 1957). Child:
    Jesse John – b 28 Oct 1903, m Gertrude Kathryn Beatty

Donald Eugene RISDAL s/o Orville Risdal & Rose Milda nee Schueler; b 05 Mar 1932 Atkins, IA; bpt 22 Mar 1932 St.Steph Sponsors: Elmer Schueller & Casper Risdal; con 16 May 1947 St.Steph; m Joan Lee Shaw (b 16 Jun 1933 Lytton, IA bpt 1943 con 01 Apr 1957 St.John d 25 Oct 1978 [Cancer] ae45y 4m 9d) d/o Harold C. Shaw & Edith B. nee Griffith of Eldora. Joan: school teacher at Newhall; Donald: carpenter for Chris Haerther and later took over the business with partner Bill Gibney. Children:
    Sue Ellen – b 05 Nov 1959 Cedar Rapids, IA;
        m 07 Jun 1980 Richart Blattler
    Stacy Jean – b 12 Sept 1964 Cedar Rapids, IA;
        m Kevin Williams DVD

Elaine RISDAL d/o Orville Risdal & Rose Milda nee Schueler; b 13 Apr 1930 Atkins, IA bpt and con St.Steph; m 16 Apr 1955 Francis Daniel Voss (b 30 Oct 1928, d 25 Mar 1997 [Cancer] ae68y 4m 23d; two year Farm Operations at Iowa State University and farmed with his father in Linn Co IA) s/o Francis J. Voss & M. Valeria nee Womochil. Observed 25th Silver Wedding Anniversary in 1980. Children:
    Daniel Joseph Voss – m 23 Jul 1988 Susan L Waterman;
        Farmer & substitute mail carrier
    Jeanne Marie Voss – m 16 Apr 1999 Michael Wampler;
        United States Bank, Cedar Rapids, IA
    Ellen K. Voss – m 08 Nov 1986 James M. McDonald;
        Accountant in Chicago
    Thomas John Voss – m 06 Feb 1993 Jill Marie nee Grow Runde;
        Carpenter

James C. Voss – m 25 Jul 1998 Tamara Fuller

Stacey Jean RISDAL d/o Donald Eugene Risdal & Joan Lee nee Shaw; b 12 Sept 1964 Cedar Rapids, IA bpt 11 Oct 1964 St.Steph Sponsors: Mr. & Mrs. Douglas Gardemann con 19 Mar 1978 St.Steph; m Kevin Williams DVD. Child:
　Cody Williams – b Mar 1990, bpt 24 Sept 1990 St.Steph

Sue Ellen RISDAL – d/o Donald Eugene Risdal & Joan Lee nee Shaw; b 05 Nov 1959 Cedar Rapids, IA; bpt 29 Nov 1959 St.Steph Sponsors: Mr. & Mrs. Duane Haerther con 07 Apr 1974 St.Steph; m 07 Jun 1980 Tichart Blattler. Children:
　Christopher Ryan Blattler – b 07 Oct 1983, bpt 22 Dec 1983 St.Steph
　Kelsey Rose Blattler – b 22 Apr 1987, bpt 31 May 1987 St.Steph

Larry RISVOLD s/o Carol nee Matthias & Harry Risvold; b 20 Mar 1956; m Sheri NN (b 01 Mar 1963). Children:
　Matthew – b 21 Jun 1986
　Malinda – b 01 Aug 1989

Laura RISVOLD d/o Carol nee Matthias & Harry Risvold; b 10 Jan 195?; m Tony H. Abbott (b 05 Jan 1954). Children:
　Brian Abbott – b 15 Jul 1987
　Logan Abbott – b 13 Mar 1989
　Carolyn Abbott – 04 Jul 1993

*Helene RITTER d/o Anna Dorothea nee Gross & Heinrich Ritter; b 26 Nov 1919 Löhlbach, Germany, d 14 May 1999 Löhlbach, Germany ae79y 5m 18d; m Karl Friedrich Hecker, Butcher and Landlord,(b 17 Jul 1913, d 18 Feb 1935 Ostpreussen, Germany). Helene was Löhlbach Forester Hermann Simon & wife Edda's housekeeper opening their home and cooking meals for her Paar relative: Author Margaret Krug Palen in 1990, 1995. Child:
　**Anni Elisabeth Hecker – b 04 Nov 1939;
　　m Walter Debus, bricklayer, male nurse

Wilhelm RITTER s/o Anna Dorothea nee Gross & Heinrich Ritter; b 01 May 1916; Technician, d Aug 1945 in France World War II; m Franziska Eckmuller(b 13 Apr 1921). Child:
　**Heinrich Jurgen – b 21 Aug 1944

447

*Johannes RODER s/o Hartman Roder of Sehlen, Germany; b 02 Jun 1720 Sehlen, Germany, d 07 Nov 1790 ae70y 5m 5d Löhlbach, Germany; m 11 Jan 1743 Löhlbach Ch to Anna Marie Menkel (b 17 May 1721 pro Löhlbach, bur 11 Apr 1753 ae31y 10m Löhlbach, Germany) d/o Johann Winter Menkel & Anna Martha nee Möller of Löhlbach. Child:

> *Katharina Elisabeth -b 11 Mar 150 Löhlbach, d 14 Nov 1808
> ae58y 8m 3d Löhlbach; m 02 Aug 1774 Löhlbach Ch to
> Johann Daniel Paar s/o Johann Georg Paar
> (b 1790 Grusen, Germany) & Anna Katharina nee Schellberg
> (b 14 Sept 1791 Löhlbach, d 02 Apr 1854 ae62y 6m 18d Grusen,
> Germany).

*Georg J. ROEPSCH b Abt 1811 Bavaria, Germany, d Abt 01 Mar 1882 Dubuque, IA bur St.Peter & St.Paul Cem, Sherrill, IA; m Abt 1839 Catherine (d Abt Apr 1850). Children:

> *Joseph George – b 20 Mar 1840 Bavaria, Germany;
> d 15 Aug 1918 Sageville, IA home; m 1869 Catherine Kirschner
> Eva – b Abt 1845 Bavaria, Germany
> George Nicholas – b 25 Dec 1847 Sageville, IA home
> d 17 Apr 1929 Dubuque, IA; m 12 Feb 1872 Clara Roth

George Edward ROEPSCH s/o George Nicholas Roepsch & Frances Kay nee Lewis; b 24 Feb 1941 Xavier Hosp Dubuque, IA; m 13 Jul 1963 St.Theresa Cath Ch LaMotte, IA to Dorothy Susan Muenster (b 10 Jan 1937 Mercy Hosp Dubuque, IA) d/o Frank Joseph Muenster & Ida Catherine nee Klein. Children:

> Robert George – b 17 Apr 1964 Xavier Hosp Dubuque, IA;
> m 13 Jun 1992 Emily Jo McAlexander
> Linda Sue – b 25 Sept 1965 Xavier Hosp Dubuque, IA;
> m 31 Oct 1993 Gary Michael Wessels
> Karen Sue – b 15 May 1968 Xavier Hosp Dubuque, IA

George Joseph ROEPSCH s/o George Nicholas Roepsch & Clara nee Roth; b 29 Dec 1873 Dubuque, IA, d 28 Apr 1970 Dubuque, IA bur Mt.Calvary Cem Dubuque, IA; m 08 May 1901 Dubuque, IA Sacred Heart Cath Ch to Annie Maria Sartor (b 17 Oct 1881 Dubuque, IA, d 02 Mar 1956 Dubuque, IA bur Mt.Calvary Cem Dubuque, IA) d/o Nicholas Sartor & Magdalene nee Klein. Children:

> George Nicholas – b 02 Jan 1904, d 09 1977;

1st m 02 Jan 1922 Augusta M. Rusch;

2nd m 08 May 1937 Frances Kay Lewis

Leo Stephen – b 23 Nov 1905 Dubuque, IA d 16 Oct 1986
    Mercy Hosp Dubuque, IA; bur Mt.Calvary Cem Dubuque, IA;
    m 05 Jun 1928 Hazel C. Ginter

Joseph Clarence – b 26 Mar 1907 Dubuque, IA; d 28 Nov 1991
    Dubuque, IA bur Mt.Calvary Mausoleum, Dubuque, IA;
    m 05 Jun 1935 Jeanne Gertrude Gatton

Margaret Catherine – b 25 May 1911 Dubuque, IA d 08 Jul 1988
    Oceanside, CA; m 26 Jun 1929 Joseph W. Deggendorf

Mary Frances – b 27 Nov 1916 Rhomberg, Dubuque, IA;
    m 03 Jul 1935 Harold Louis Leitner

George Nicholas ROEPSCH s/o George J. Roepsch & Catherine; b 25 Dec 1847 Sageville, IA home, d 17 Apr 1929 Dubuque, IA bur Mt.Calvary Cem Dubuque, IA; m 12 Feb 1872 Dubuque Co IA to Clara Roth (b 02 Nov 1851 Leipzig, os Prussia, Germany d 14 Oct 1892 bur Mt.Calvary Cem Dubuque, IA) d/o Herman Joseph Roth SR. & Catherine nee Benz. Children:

Catherine – b 18 Nov 1872 IA, d 13 Oct 1873 Dubuque, IA

George Joseph – b 29 Dec 1873 Dubuque Co IA d 28 Apr 1970
    Dubuque, IA; m 08 May 1901 Annie Maria Sartor

Ckara M. – b 14 Feb 1875 IA; m 25 Apr 1894 Frank P. Schumacher

Magdelena K. – b 02 Jun 1878 IA, d 18 Apr 1951 IA;
    m 16 Feb 1909 Nicholas J. Schroeder

Jospeh J. – b 24 Jan 1880 Dubuque, IA d Abt 28 Jan 1951
    Dubuque, IA; 1st m 06 Feb 1912 Mary Steil;
    2nd m 1935 Gertrude Grace Yatton

George Nicholas ROEPSCH s/o George Joseph Roepsch & Annie Maria nee Sartor; b 02 Jan 1904 Dubuque, IA d 09 Jun 1977 Xavier Hosp Dubuque, IA bur Mt.Calvary Cem Dubuque, IA; 1st m 02 Jan 1922 Galena, IL to Augusta M. Rusch. No children.

2nd m 08 May 1937 George Nicholas Roepsch to Frances Kay Lewis (b 18 Nov 1912 Asbury, IA, d 02 Mar 2001 Luther Manor bur 05 Mar 2001 Asbury Methodist Cem, Asbury, IA) d/o Edward G. Lewis SR. & Laura E. nee Hutton. Children:

Mary Frances – b 01 Nov 1937 Dubuque, IA;
    m 20 Aug 1955 William Richard Henry JR.

Carol June – b 29 Nov 1938 Dubuque, IA; m Melvin Louis Leick

George Edward – b 24 Feb 1941;
    m 13 Jul 1963 Dorothy Susan Muenster
Donald David – b 29 Jun 1943 Dubuque, IA;
    m 04 Jul 1964 Theresa Mae Maiers
Louis Stephen – b 24 Aug 1944 Finley Hosp Dubuque, IA;
    m 16 Apr 1966 Anna Mae Philomena Muenster
Edward Joseph – b 26 Oct 1945 Dubuque, IA;
    m 08 Jul 1967 Kristine Mary Link

Johannes ROSE cabinetmaster and village official at Sehlen, Germany; Godfather 1673 Miller of Sehlen, bur 21 Aug 1693 at Sehlen; 1st m 22 Jun 1652 at Sehlen to Gertraut NN (bur 12 Jan 1670). Children:
    Johannes – b/bpt 19 Jun 1653 Sehlen, Germany; bur 23 Jun 1666
    Eula – b/bpt 24 Jun 1655 Sehlen, Germany
    Anna-b/bpt 17 Oct 1661 Sehlen, Germany;
        m 07 Feb 1689 Joh. Curt Bossenberger
    A. Elisabeth – b/bpt 09 Mar 1664 Sehlen; bur 12 Apr 1665 Sehlen
    Walpurg – bpt 20 Jan 1667; m 08 Feb 1694 Joh. Adam Achenbuch
    Johan Adam – b/bpt 14 Jan 1670
    Magdalena – b prob 1660; m 27 Dec 1680 Wigand Koch
    Catharina – m 27 Oct 1677 Adam Schmitt
2nd m End of 1670 Johannes Rose to NN Straube. Children:
    Johannes – b/bpt 08 Oct 1671, Godfather 1691 Koch his brother-
        in-law; m 02 Nov 1695 Grusen, Germany to A. Kuniganda Vohl
        of Ell, Germany.
    *Eulalia Elisabeth – bpt 04 May 1673 at Sehlen, Godparents 1687
        Jes Rosen Koch sister-in-law; Poenit. 27 May 1699 to
        Johann Balthasar Happel
    Johann Jacob – b/bpt 16 Jan 1676
    Margretha – b/bpt 28 Jul 1678, bur 06 Apr 1679
    Anna Elisabeth – b/bpt 20 Feb 1681,
        m 25 Jul 1706 Johannes Fischer
    Anna Elisabeth – b/bpt 17 Feb 1684 Sehlen, Germany
    Anna Martha – b/bpt 25 Jan 1687;
        m 06 Nov 1716 to Joh. Henrich Kitting of Sehlen
    Joh. Baltzar – b/bpt 26 Sept 1689 Sehlen,
        Godfather 1729 Joh. Rose of Bo, cousin and Miller of Sehlen;
        m 21 Feb 1726 A. Martha Kaufmann
    Anna Marie – b/bpt 10 Apr 1692 Sehlen;
        bur 15 Jan 1715 at Sehlen, Germany ae22y

Karen Kay ROSE d/o Emma nee Guericke & Edmund Rose; b 11 Nov 1955; m 26 Feb 1977 Lonnie Bair s/o Duane Bair of Sioux City, IA. Children:
  Shaun Bair – b 23 Jul 1977
  TWINS: Sheila – b 01 Oct 1981 in Germany
          Shannon – b 01 Oct 1981 in Germany

Milton ROSE s/o Emma nee Guericke & Edmund Rose; b 04 Apr 1949; m 07 Jul 1973 Christine Martitz d/o Francis J. Martitz of San Bernadino, CA. Children:
  Jennifer – b 07 Mar 1976
  Scott – b 13 Apr 1982

Ronald ROSE s/o Emma nee Guericke & Edmund Rose; b 15 Dec 1950; m 03 Apr 1971 Jolene LaDue d/o Wayne LaDue. Children:
  Michael Jon – b 09 Jan 1975
  Ronda – b 09 Nov 1978

Renea ROSTER d/o Roxy nee Rammelsberg & Wayne Roster; m William Daringer. Children:
  Neal Daringer – NFR
  Alison Daringer – NFR

Kristy ROSTER d/o Roxy nee Rammelsberg & Wayne Roster; m Russell Haefner of Vinton, IA. Children:
  Natalie Haefner – NFR
  Joel Haefner – NFR

Charles ROTHS s/o Martin Roths JR. & Mary nee Schlotterback; b 1897, d 1961; m Alta Meek (b 14 May 1899, d 29 Apr 1978 ae78y 11m 15d) d/o John Meek & Ida nee Beatty. Alta graduated Shellsburg High School; Iowa State Teachers' College and taught school four years. Charles graduated Atkins High School, studied at Tilford Academy, Vinton, IA. He was World War I veteran and charter member of Atkins, IA American Legion. Two children:
  Charles Keith – b 1923, m Gladys Wilson
  Paul Wayne – b 07 Jun 1925, d 03 May 2000 ae74y 11m

Charles Keith ROTHS s/o Charles Roths & Alta nee Meek; b 1923, d 1970;

Atkins, High School; farmed and served in Pacific U.S.Navy during World War II; m 1967 Gladys Wilson, Iowa County Recorder from Marengo, IA. Members of Gethsemane White Shrine, El Kadir Shrine and American Legion.

Martin ROTHS JR. b IA, d 1946 Atkins, IA; m Mary Schlotterback of Atkins; moved to farm two and 1/2 miles northeast of Atkins. In 1923, Martin & Mary purchased a house and moved to Atkins. Child:
    Charles – b 1897, d 1961; m Alta Meek

*Martin ROTHS SR. b Baden-Baden, Germany, d 1946, Atkins, IA; m 16 Dec 1872 in Germany to Barbara Mirklin (b 04 Jun 1840 Balingen Bagden, Germany, d 1910 Atkins, IA). Emigrated to USA in 1876 settling in Clinton Twp Linn County, IA. Eight children:
    Martin JR. – b IA d 1946; m Mary Schlotterback of Atkins
    Fred – NFR
    Rev George – NFR
    Kate – m A.S. Weyer
    Christy – m Newton Armstrong
    Lena – m Ed Kibbe
    Jenny – m William Kneeskern
    Barbara – m NN Heilman

Paul Wayne ROTHS s/o Charles Roths & Alta nee Meek; b 07 June 1925; farmed with his brother Charles Keith after graduating from Atkins High School; served in U.S. Army, Korean Conflict; member of American Legion; White Shrine; El Kadir Shrine. Owner and operator of Roths' farm three miles northeast of Atkins, rented land to raise cattle, a few hogs, and grain farm. Never Married.

Dean ROUDABUSH s/o Samuel Roudabush & Florence nee Fitzgerald; b Belle Plaine, IA; m 1957 Teresa VanThournout. Moved from Cedar Rapids to Atkins winter of 1969. Dean employed at Rockwell International (electronics) and Teresa beautician in Atkins, IA.
Five children that are tenth generation of Raudenbush family in America:
    Steve – University of Iowa
    Connie – m James Jacobsen, Atkins, IA residence
    Dannie – NFR
    Philip – NFR
    Tami – NFR

Samuel ROUDABUSH s/o Gereon Roudabush; m Florence Fitzgerald of Belle Plaine, IA where they owned and operated a hatchery. Child:
   Dean – m 1957 Teresa VanThournout

*John RUPP b 1806 Germany, d 1883 IA; vineyard man in Germany; 1849 emigrated to Canton, OH; 1850 his family joined him in USA; 1872 moved to Eldorado Twp Benton Co IA; m Madgalene Weber (b 1806 Germany, d 1880 IA); retired in Blairstown, IA. Children:
   John – OH resident
   Margaret – m Henry Reisser
   Mary – m W.J. Grunewald, Blairstown

Charles Daniel RUPPRICH s/o William Rupprich & Henrietta nee Luze; b 1883 near Franklin Grove, Lee Co. IL, d 1976 ae93y bur Westview Cemetery, LaPorte City, IA; m 1909 home of parents of bride to Florence Agusta Frank (b 1887, d 1984 ae97y bur Westview Cemetery, LaPorte City, IA) d/o Philip Frank (b 1853, d 1905) & Henrietta nee Rahr (b 1853, d 1933). Bruce and Cedar Twp Benton Co IA farmers. 1938 retired in LaPorte City, IA. Children:
   Noma Lurreen – m Emil H. Jebe
   Glade – dec'd infancy

*William RUPPRICH b 1848 Schlessinger, Germany, d 1927 Iowa; m 1874 in Germany to Henrietta Luze (b 1851 Bischhausen, Hessen-Nassau, Germany, d 1913 IA). 1881 emigrated with two daughters to Lee Co. IL near Franklin Grove; 1884 moved to farm near Dysart, IA; moved to farm Bruce Twp Benton Co IA; 1907 retired to Dysart, IA. Children:
   Wilhelmine – b Germany; emigrated 1881
   Mathilde – b Germany; emigrated 1881
   Charles Daniel – b 1883 Franklin Grove, Lee Co. IL, d 1976
   Rose – b Bruce Twp Benton Co. IA

*Frederick SAEGEBRECHT b 1835 Germany; emigrated 1881 to USA going directly to Newhall, IA; m Sophia "Tonka" Rossoa (b 1839 Germany, d 1933 IA). Sophia braided beautiful rugs; Frederick section foreman for Chicago & Milwaukee Railroad; mbrs St.John. No children.

John D. SAHA s/o John Saha & Mary nee Engel; b 1879, d 1943; m 15 Feb 1914 Blanche Ellen Beatty (b 1888, d 1979). Moved to Saha family farm on

Benton-Linn Co IA road. The house was built on the site of an inn that had burned and served as stable for changing horses that pulled the stagecoach from Iowa City to LaPorte and Waterloo, IA. 1930 deep wheel ruts of the coach were still visible in the area. Blanche graduated Coe Academy in Cedar Rapids, IA taught school at Dry Creek before marriage. John raised certified seed grain. The family attended Lincoln Ev. and Atkins Presbyterian Ch. Children:

Glenn – b 1917; South Bend, IN residence

Eleanor – b 1920; Saha homestead residence

Mildred – b 1924; New Berlin, WI residence

Arlo Lee SASS s/o John Sass & Emma A. nee Kreutner; b 31 Jul 1939 bpt & St.Steph; m 18 Jan 1969 Jane Foley (12 Sept 1945) DVD. Arlo continued family tradition of musical talent with his own orchestra. Children:

Amy – b 17 Sept 1975

Lori – b 27 Jul 1979

Beverly SASS d/o Willard John Sass & Betty nee Peters; b 09 Feb 1954; m 07 Apr 1978 Tom Hurn (b 17 Feb 1952). Child:

NN Hurn – NFR

Delaine SASS d/o Elmer William Sass & Rose nee Vesely; b 24 Jun 1953 bpt & con St.Steph Luth Ch; m 14 Mar 1974 Richard Karl Kreutner, her Kreutner and Krug cousin, (b 09 May 1951). Their common Great-Grandfather: William Kreutner; and common Great-Great Grandmother: Wilhelmina Krug. Children:

Matthew Richard Kreutner – b 05 Jan 1978 Cedar Rapids, IA

Michelle Ann Kreutner – b 01 May 1980 Cedar Rapids, IA

Donald Arthur SASS s/o John A. Sass & Emma Anna nee Kreutner; b 03 Mar 1931 bpt St.Steph, con 02 Apr 1944 St.Steph; 1948 Class Atkins High School; farmer; m 14 Aug 1970 LaVonne Lucille nee Willard Jacobsen (b 06 Nov 1935). LaVonne's two sons from 1st m to Gorden J. Jacobsen:

STEPSONS:

James Alan Jacobsen – b 11 Sept 1959 Cedar Rapids, IA;
  m 1980 Connie Roudabush

Gordon Lewis Jacobsen – b 20 Feb 1956;
  m 21 Jul 1979 Kathy Ann Waterman

Elmer William SASS s/o John A. Sass & Emma Anna nee Kreutner; b 17

Dec 1915 bpt and con St.Steph, d 28 Sept 1987 ae71y 9m 11d, bur Oakwood Cem Shellsburg, IA; m 08 Dec 1946 Rose Vesely (b 25 Mar 1924). Farmers. Children:

Sandra – b 18 May 1949; m 21 Aug 1971 Larry Beatty
    (b 16 May 1948)
Delaine – b 24 Jun 1953; m 15 Mar 1974 Richard Kreutner
    (b 09 May 1954)
Edward Elmer – b 28 Oct 1960; Shellsburg, IA residence;
    m 20 Nov 1999 Nancy M. Barger, Cedar Rapids, IA

Frieda SASS d/o Fredrick Johan Heinrich Sass & Anna Gertrude nee Fels; b 06 Jan 1898, d 18 Mar 1991 ae93y 2m 12d; m 1921 Arthur Henry Hueber. Children:

Milton Henry Hueber – m Margaret Tremaine
James Arthur Hueber – m Nancy Holt
Mary Lee Hueber – m Ernie Meyer

*Fredrick Johan Heinrich SASS s/o Fredrick Sass & Karoline nee Burgenhagen; b 18 Jun 1859 Neuendorf, Germany(near Kemmitz Pomerenie) 1877-1887 emigrated to USA, d 05 Aug 1928 ae69y 1m 18d Denver, IA, Bremer Co IA bur 08 Aug 1928 Denver IA Luth Cem, Bremer Co IA; m 27 Sept 1890 St.Steph Benton Co IA to Anna Gertrude Fels; (b 30 May 1860 Löhlbach, Germany bpt 1860 Löhlbach Ch, d 10 Mar 1936 ae75y 5m 11d Bremer Co IA; emigrated to USA; Anna's 2nd m; 1st m Henry Happel) d/o Konrad Fels & Marie Katharina nee Ernst. Children:

Frieda – b 06 Jan 1898, d 18 Mar 1991;
    m 1921 Arthur Henry Huebner
John A.– b 20 May 1892, d31 Jul 1976;
    m 09 Dec 1914 Emma Anna Kreutner
Bertha – b 1901, d 1906 ae5y

John A. SASS s/o Frederick Johan Heinrich Sass & Anna Gertrude nee Fels; b 20 May 1892 bpt and con St.Steph, d 31 Jul 1976 ae84y 2m 11d bur St.Steph Cem; m 09 Dec 1914 Emma Anna Kreutner (b 16 Dec 1895, d 10 May 1965 ae69y 4m 25d bur St.Steph Cem) d/o William Kreutner & Marie nee Moeller. Farmers near Atkins, IA. Children:

Elmer William – b 17 Dec 1915, d 28 Sept 1987;
    m 08 Dec 1946 Rose Vesely
Willard John – b 05 Mar 1928, d 30 Sept 1969;
    m 23 Jul 1950 Betty Peters

Donald Arthur – b 03 Mar 1931;
    m 14 Aug 1970 LaVonne Lucille nee Willard Jacobsen
Arlo Lee – b 31 Jul 1939; m 18 Jan 1969 Jane Foley DVD

Sheryl SASS d/o Willard John Sass & Betty nee Peters; b 16 May 1952 bpt St.Steph; m 21 May 1974 David Waterman (b 22 Dec 1951 bpt St.Steph) s/o Donald Waterman & Eunice nee Fett. Child:
    Kari Michelle Waterman – b 23 Jan 1978

Willard John SASS s/o John A. Sass & Emma Anna nee Kreutner; b 05 Mar 1928 bpt St.Steph, con 1941 St.Steph; 1945 Class Atkins High School, d 30 Sept 1969 ae41y 6m 25d; Professional Musician; m 23 Jul 1950 Betty Peters (b 09 Jan 1931). Children:
    Sheryl – b 16 May 1952; m 21 May 1974 David Waterman
    Beverly – b 09 Feb 1954; m 07 Apr 1978 Thomas Hurn
    Colleen – 06 Oct 1959
    Dean – 08 Jun 1963

Bethann Alice SCHAEFER d/o Lois Ann nee Rinderknecht & Hilbert Christian Schaefer; b 11 Apr 1947; Registered Nurse; m 17 Aug 1968 Stanley Teggatz (b 22 Aug 1946 Dr. of Veterinary Medicine). Children:
    Christopher Teggatz – b 22 Feb 1969; m 21 Sept 1996 Tanya Bruster
    Curt Teggatz – b 08 Oct 1972; m 06 Oct 2001 Susan Miller
    Chad Teggatz – b 09 Jul 1975

Mary Margaret SCHAEFER d/o Lois Ann nee Rinderknecht & Hilbert Christian Schaefer; b 20 Dec 1951; Luth Pastor; m 24 Feb 1974 Douglas Fast (b 28 Dec 1951). Children:
    Cara Fast – b 29 Jan 1979
    Blaine Fast – b 12 Apr 1982

William "Billy" Arthur SCHAEFER s/o Lois Ann nee Rinderknecht & Hilbert Christian Schaefer; b 28 Jul 1953; Iowa Farm Bureau Insurance Salesman; m 21 Jul 1979 Robyn Maas (b 21 Jul 1957). Child:
    Ryan – b 23 Dec 1986

Allan Edward SCHANBACHER s/o Bernard Jacob Schanbacher & Elma Ann Christina nee Krug; b 12 Feb 1939 Parent's farm north of Atkins, Fremont Twp Benton Co IA, bpt 12 Mar 1939 & con St.Steph; Atkins High School; m 30 May 1959 Immanuel Luth Ch, Waterloo, IA to Joyce Elaine

Piehl (b 11 Jul 1939) d/o Edward Piehl & Martha nee Tiedt. Children:
Jeffrey Allan – b 04 Jun 1960, bpt 19 Jun 1960;
    m 01 Sept 1979 Janette Dee Spain
Lori Sue – b 18 Jun 1964, bpt 12 Jul 1964;
    m 18 Nov 1989 Justin Leigh Kithcart
J. Edward – b 26 Jul 1972, bpt 13 Aug 1972, con 23 Mar 1986;
    m 13 Nov 1999 Barbara Ann Kilberg (b 18 Oct 1972)

Amanda Katherina Marie SCHANBACHER d/o Julius Daniel Schanbacher & Gertrude Marie nee Keiper; b 19 Jun 1908 farm Linn Co IA, d 15 Feb 1987 ae78y 8m 1d Cedar Rapids, IA bur St.Steph Cem; m 21 Sept 1933 St.Steph to Edwin Frederick George Schminke (b 07 Feb 1908 Fremont Twp Benton Co IA, d 02 Sept 1990 ae82y 6m 26d bur St.Steph Cem) s/o August Heinrich (Henry) George Schminke & Elizabeth "Lizzie" Katharina Anna nee Rinderknecht; Farmers 01 Mar 1934 until retirement in Atkins, IA 01 Mar 1948. Children:
Richard Edwin Schminke – b 08 Jan 1936 Mercy Hosp
    Cedar Rapids, IA; m 29 Dec 1957 Mary Lou Rauh, TX residence
DuWayne Wilbert Schminke – b 08 Oct 1939 St.Lukes Hosp
    Cedar Rapids, IA; m 04 Feb 1962 Linda Sue Sloan,
    residence Marion, IA

Dorothy Gertrude SCHANBACHER d/o Julius Daniel Schanbacher & Gertrude Marie nee Keiper; b 21 Apr 1923; m Virgil LaClare Gallo (b 30 Apr 1923) s/o Sam Gallo & Helen nee Strickell (older sister of Arlyne Strickell m Adam John Michel). Moved to Modesto, CA. Virgil: Pharmacist. Children:
Cynthia Marie Gallo – b 11 Jul 1950;
    m 31 Jul 1971 Mark David Virtue
Janee' Ann Gallo – b 20 Feb 1954; m 22 Sept 1990 Dennis Linn
Sue Ellen Gallo – b 22 Aug 1955;
    m 14 Oct 1976 Michael Edward Davis

Edward SCHANBACHER s/o Edward Friedrich Schanbacher & Wilma nee Lensch; b 10 May 1952 Cedar Rapids, IA bpt 01 Jun 1952 St.Steph Sponsors: Bernard Schanbacher & Albert Schirm; con 03 Apr 1966 St.Steph; m 03 Jan 1976 Christine C. Harrison (b 29 Sept 1952) d/o Marion Harrison & Joan nee Michael. Farmers east of Atkins, IA. Children:
Timothy Ray – b 04 Jan 1977, bpt 31 Jul 1977 St.Steph
Edward Michael – b 15 Aug 1979, bpt 09 Sept 1979 St.Steph

Edward Friedrich SCHANBACHER s/o Julius Daniel Schanbacher & Gertrude Marie nee Keiper; TWIN b 06 Feb 1916 [TWIN: Wilbert Martin Schanbacker] bpt 27 Feb 1916 St.Steph Sponsors: Henry Haerther and William Happel, con 24 Mar 1929 St.Steph; d 11 Jun 1970 ae56y 4m 5d bur St.Steph Cem; m 30 Nov 1940 St.Steph to Wilma Augusta Lensch (b 02 Mar 1917, bpt 09 Dec 1917 Sponsor: Louis William Lensch & Matilda "Tilly" Fritz, con 06 Jan 1938) d/o Louis Lensch & Matilda nee Fritz. Farmed Schanbacker homestead with twin brother, Wilbert. Children:
 Jane Ann – b 07 Mar 1943 Cedar Rapids, IA;
  m 24 Jun 1967 Hubert Chandler Upton JR., DVD Oct 1997
 Nancy Jean – b 14 Mar 1945 St.Lukes Hosp Cedar Rapids, IA;
  m 01 Apr 1967 Thomas Henry Lange, Atkins
 Glenn Edward – b 10 May 1952 Cedar Rapids, IA;
  m 03 Jan 1976 Christine Lois Harrison

Gilmore Julius SCHANBACHER s/o Julius Daniel Schanbacher & Gertrude Marie nee Keiper; b 10 Oct 1924 Atkins, IA bpt 1924 and con St.Steph; Atkins High School; m 07 Sept 1947 St.Steph to Lolita Marie Gerhold (b 12 Oct 1927 Atkins, IA) d/o Carl Henry Gerhold & Emma Elizabeth nee Happel. Atkins, IA residence. Celebrated 60th Wedding Anniversary. Children:
 Janet Kay – b 30 Jan 1951 Cedar Rapids, IA; bpt 25 Feb 1951
  St.Steph; Sponsors: Mrs Carl Gerhold & Mrs.Dorothy Gallo;
  con 11 Apr 1965 St.Steph
 JoAnn Marie – b 19 Jul 1952 Cedar Rapids, IA;
  m 25 Nov 1978 Thomas Dale Schumacher
 Jean Lynn – b 19 Aug 1957 Cedar Rapids, IA;
  m 21 Dec 1980 Richard Lynn Von Dielingen

Glenn Edward SCHANBACHER s/o Edward Frederick Schanbacher & Wilma Augusta nee Lensch; b 10 May 1952; 03 Jan 1976 Christine Lois Harrison (b 28 Sept 1952). Children:
 Timothy Ray – b 04 Jul 1977
 Edward Michael – b 15 Aug 1979; m 04 Nov 2006 Erica Kae Huber

*Jacob SCHANBACHER b 03 Mar 1852 near Boeblingen, Wittenberg County, Germany, d 08 Feb 1916 IA ae63y 11m 5d bur St.Steph Cem; m in Germany to Maria M. Keller (b 09 May 1845 Germany, d 19 Feb 1928 ae82y 9m 10d, bur St.Steph Cem). 1880 emigrated to USA with their only living child, Mary, ae4y. Chicago, IL residence; Jacob: Stonecutter. When his health failed he decided to farm and wrote to Johann Georg Haerther, friend from Germany living in Iowa Co IA, to ask about farms. After visiting Iowa he decided to purchase the Wieneke farm located west of Cedar Rapids in Linn Co IA. Maria sewed their life savings into the lining of his coat and this made the down payment on the farm. 1892 they moved to Iowa. Jacob's health improved and the Schanbacher family worked very hard. When son Julius married, his parents built a home in Atkins, IA and retired in 1906. Two children:

    *Marie (Mary) Dorothea – b 01 Mar 1876 Boeblingen, Germany;
      d 13 Nov 1965 IA bur St.Steph Cem;
      m 15 Oct 1896 Heinrich (Henry) August Gottlieb Haerther
    Julius Daniel – b 15 Jul 1881 Chicago, IL; d 05 May 1955 IA
      bur St.Steph Cem; m 11 Jan 1906 Gertrude Marie Keiper [TWIN]

Jane Ann SCHANBACHER d/o Edward Frederick Schanbacher & Wilma Augusta nee Lensch; b 07 Mar 1943, bpt 04 Apr 1943 and con Mar 1956 St.Steph; m 24 Jun 1967 St.Steph to Hubert Chandler Upton, DVD Oct 1997. Haymarket, VA residence. Children:

    Scott Chandler Upton – b 12 Nov 1970;
      m 02 Dec 1995 Kathleen Magan O'Reilly
    Kevin Edward Upton – b 28 Oct 1972
    Suzanne Jane Upton – b 14 Sept 1977

Jean Lynn SCHANBACHER d/o Gilmore Julius Schanbacher & Lolita Marie nee Gerhold; b 19 Aug 1957 Cedar Rapids, IA bpt 08 Sept 1957 Grace Luth Ch Blairstown, IA Sponsors: Mrs. Carl Gerhold JR. & Mrs Bernard Schanbacher; con 04 Apr 1971 St.Steph; m 21 Dec 1980 St.Steph to Richard Lynn Von Dielinger JR., Blairstown, IN(b 05 Sept 1951) s/o Richard Lynn Von Dielinger SR. & Marion A. nee Perry. Children:

    Michelle Lynn Von Dielinger – b 31 May 1983, con 21 Mar 1997
    Rachel Lynn Von Dielinger – b 24 May 1985, con 28 Mar 1999

Jeffrey Allan SCHANBACHER s/o Allan Edward Schanbacher & Joyce Elaine nee Piehl; b 04 Jun 1960 St.Lukes Hosp Cedar Rapids, IA bpt 19 Jun 1960 St.Steph Sponsors: Grandfathers Bernard Schanbacher & Edward Piehl; con 17 Apr 1974 St.Steph; Farmer; Jun 2000 Luth Seminary, St.Louis, MO; m 01 Sept 1979 St.Steph to Janette Dee Spain (b 18 Mar 1960; May 2000 Graphic Arts Degree, Mt.Mercy College) d/o Dale E. Spain & Freida nee Brown. Jeanette employed Rockwell-Collins, Cedar

Rapids, IA. Children:

    Jason Bernard – b 21 Oct 1981

    Joel Michael – b 14 Jun 1985

    Elizabeth Anne – b 17 Nov 1987

    James Christopher – b 07 May 1998

JoAnn SCHANBACKER d/o Gilmore Julius Schanbacker & Lolita Marie nee Gerhold; b 19 Jul 1952 Cedar Rapids, IA bpt 17 Aug 1952 St.Steph Sponsors: Mrs. Edwin Schminke & Martha Gerhold; con 03 Apr 1966 St.Steph; m 25 Nov 1978 St.Steph to Thomas Dale Schumacher (b 17 Jan 1944 Jefferson, IA) s/o Walter G. Schumacher & Jessie nee Snouse. Children:

    Eric Thomas Schumacher – b 24 Aug 1981, bpt 04 Oct 1981;

        con 07 May 1995

    Amy Jo Schumacher – b 13 Jul 1985, bpt 04 Aug 1985

John Wilbert SCHANBACHER s/o Eda Barbara Elizabeth nee Rinderknecht & Wilbert Martin Schanbacher; b 17 Sept 1951; m 17 Mar 2000 Eileen Ann nee Hartkemeyer Heyer.

    STEPDAUGHTERS:

    Brenda Ann Heyer – b 12 Jul 1972;

        m 30 Apr 1999 David James Huber. Child: Harrison James Huber

        (b 08 May 2000)

    Julie Ann Heyer – b 30 Mar 1974; m Duane Ogden Farner

        (b 25 Oct 1965). Child – b 24 Nov 2005 Ana Rose Farner

Julius Daniel SCHANBACHER s/o Jacob Schanbacher & Maria M. nee Keller; b 15 Jul 1881 Chicago, IL, d 05 May 1955 ae73y 9m 20d; m 11 Jan 1906 Gertrude Marie Keiper (TWIN b 17 Dec 1886 in SD, d 07 Apr 1950 ae63y 3m 21d) [TWIN: Katherine Keiper]d/o Valentine Keiper & Maria (Mary) Elizabeth Gertrude nee Rinderknecht. Farmers east of Atkins, IA; later retired in Atkins, IA. Children:

    Bernard Jacob – b 16 Mar 1907, d 20 Jun 1976 bur St.Steph Cem;

        m 11 Jan 1933 Elma Anna Christina Krug

    Amanda Katharina Marie – b 19 Jun 1908; d 15 Feb 1987

        bur St.Steph Cem;

        m 21 Sept 1933 Edwin Frederick George Schminke

    TWINS: Edward Friedrich – b 06 Feb 1916, d 11 Jun 1970;

        bur St.Steph Cem; m 30 Nov 1940 Wilma Augusta Lensch

            Wilbert Martin – b 06 Feb 1916; d 03 Nov 2002

bur St.Steph Cem;
  m 14 Sept 1940 Eda Barbara Elizabeth Rinderknecht
Dorothy Gertrude – b 21 Apr 1923; m Virgil LaClare Gallo,
  residence Modesto, CA
Gilmore Julius – b 10 Oct 1924; m 07 Sept 1947 Lolita Marie Gerhold

Lori Sue SCHANBACHER d/o Allan Edward Schanbacher & Joyce Elaine nee Piehl; b 18 Jun 1964 bpt 12 Jul 1964 St.Steph Sponsors: Janet Schanbacher (Mrs. Ronald) & Wayne Piehl (mother's brother) con 19 Mar 1978; Nurse/U.of IA Hosp; m 18 Nov 1989 Justin Leigh Kithcart (b 07 Sept 1965) s/o Ernest Kithcart & LaDonna nee Brown Kithcart Ricklefs. Children:
  Kelsie Leigh Kithcart – b 18 Jun 1992
  Drew Allan Kithcart – b 01 May 1997
  Jackson Ernest Kithcart – b 22 Apr 2001

Merlyn Melvin SCHANBACHER s/o Bernard Jacob Schanbacher & Elma Ann Christina nee Krug; b 21 Sept 1946 Cedar Rapids, IA bpt 13 Oct 1946 & con St.Steph; m 16 Aug 1969 St.John to JoAnne Elaine Koopman (b 02 Apr 1949) d/o Meril Albert Koopman & Agnes Emma nee Senne. Benton Co Farmers near Newhall, IA. Children:
  Brian Allan – b 19 May 1973
  Christina Marie – b 23 Aug 1975;
    m 22 Nov 1998 St.John to Michael Dennis Karr.
    Child: Shelby Jo Karr (b 30 Oct 1999)

Nancy Jean SCHANBACHER d/o Edward Frederick Schanbacher & Wilma Augusta nee Lensch: cf Thomas Henry Lange.

Patricia Sue SCHANBACHER d/o Wilbert Martin Schanbacher & Eda Barbara Elizabeth nee Rinderknecht; b 24 Apr 1944 St.Lukes Hosp Cedar Rapids, IA; m 29 Jun 1968 St.Steph to Ivan Lee Lauck (b 11 Apr 1943 Palo Alto, Co. IA; Mertz Implement, West Bend, IA) s/o Henry Herman Lauck & Ella Emma Louise nee Meyer. West Bend, IA residence. Children:
  Kimberly Sue Lauck – b 04 Sept 1973 Emmetsburg, IA
    m 17 Aug 1996 Leslie Lynn Traub.
    Child: Parker Sue Traub (b 09 Nov 1999)
  John Lee Lauck – b 17 Apr 1975 Emmetsburg, IA
  Greg Alan Lauck – b 21 Apr 1981 Emmetsburg, IA

Robert Alan SCHANBACHER s/o Ronald August Schanbacher SR. & Janet Sue nee Rosdail; b 30 Jul 1965 St.Lukes Hosp Cedar Rapids, IA; m 29 Aug 1986 his Krug cousin Brenda Jo Karr (b 25 Apr 1967 St.Lukes Hosp Cedar Rapids, IA bpt 1967) d/o Dennis Leroy Karr & Jo Ann nee Webert; Robert and Brenda's Great-Grandparents in common: Johann Peter Krug & Anna Katherina nee Michel. Farmers near Newhall, IA. Children:

    Benjamin Robert – b 26 Sept 1989 St.Lukes Hosp Cedar Rapids, IA

    Andrew Michael – b 03 Aug 1992 St.Lukes Hosp Cedar Rapids, IA

    Dustin Raymond – b 04 Jul 1996 St.Lukes Hosp Cedar Rapids, IA

Ronald August SCHANBACHER JR. s/o Ronald August Schanbacher SR. & Janet Sue nee Rosdail; b 21 Sept 1959; 1st m 20 Apr 1979 Jennifer Jordt (b 08 Oct 1959)of Norway, IA, DVD. Farmers near Shellsburg IA. Children:

    Darcy Ann – b 01 Mar 1980

    Neil August – b 18 Jan 1983

2nd m 03 Jul 1993 Ronald August Schanbacher JR. to H. Marie Rowe (b 23 May 1966).

Ronald August SCHANBACHER SR. s/o Bernard Jacob Schanbacher & Elma Ann Christina nee Krug; b 15 Mar 1935 St.Lukes Hosp Cedar Rapids, IA bpt 07 Apr 1935 St.Steph & con St.Steph; m 04 Jun 1955 TrinCR, Cedar Rapids, IA to Janet Sue Rosdail (b 12 Mar 1936) d/o Calvin Rosdail & Opal nee Tow of Cedar Rapids, IA. Farmers near Newhall, IA beginning 1961. Children:

    Steven Michael – b 19 Mar 1957;

        1st m 27 Jun 1975 Lucinda Kay Glime DVD;

        2nd m 06 Mar 1992 Sharon Kay McKibbin Sankey

    Ronald August JR.- b 21 Sept 1959; 1st m 20 Apr 1979 Jennifer Jordt

        DVD; 2nd m 03 Jul 1993 H. Marie Rowe

    Robert Alan – b 30 Jul 1965; m 29 Aug 1986 Brenda Jo Karr

Steven Michael SCHANBACHER s/o Ronald August Schanbacher SR. & Janet Sue nee Rosdail; b 19 Mar 1957; 1st m 27 Jun 1975 Lucinda Kay Glime (b 09 Apr 1957)DVD; d/o Robert Glime of Keystone, IA. Children:

    Gail Lynn – b 08 Apr 1976

    Amy Marie – b 28 Feb 1977

    Michael Lee – b 27 Jan 1979

    Leigh Christine – b 20 Jul 1981

2nd m 06 Mar 1992 Steven M. Schanbacher to Sharon McKibbin Sankey.

Wilbert Martin SCHANBACHER s/o Julius Daniel Schanbacher & Gertrude Marie nee Keiper: cf Eda Elizabeth Rinderknecht.

George William SCHAULL s/o Martin Schaull & Susan nee Edwards: b 1835, d 1913; m Sarah Catherine Baughman. Child:
John Martin – b 1875, d 1950 Benton Co IA

John Martin SCHAULL s/o George William Schaull & Sarah Catherine nee Baughman; b 1875, d 1950 Benton Co IA; moved from Seneca Co, OH to Ladora, IA; m 1899 Ida Slaymaker. Purchased land in Benton Co IA and farmed it until his death. Children:
Clellan – m Anna Brown, Blairstown, IA residents.
    Children: Laurence, Bette, Bonnie, Marlene, Carolyn
Alice – m Lester Stewart.
    Children: Loren, Evelyn, Gerald, Donald, Donald Merle
Edna – m Haddy Hixon; Children: Keith, Dale, Marvin
Lloyd – m Marguerite Thode, Blairstown residents.
    Children: Sandra, Susan

Martin SCHALL s/o Michael Schaull & Rosannah nee Sidenour; b 1800, d 1844; m Susan Edwards. Child:
George William – b 1835, d 1913

Michael SCHAULL s/o Nicolas Schaull JR. & Anna nee Beck; b 1765, d 1840; m Rosannah Sidenour. Child:
Martin – b 1800, d 1844; m Susan Edwards

*Nicholas SCHAULL JR. s/o Nicholas SR. (b 1709 Germany) & Catherine Schaull, Baden, Germany; b 1734 Germany, d 1808; 1752 emigrated to Northampton Co PA; m Anna Beck. Moved to Shenandoah Valley, VA (now WV). Child:
Michael – b 1765, d 1840; m Rosannah Sidenour;

Jane Marie SCHEMPP d/o Dorothy nee Juhnke & Leland Schempp; b 27 Dec 1956; m 27 Dec 1976 Menno, SD to Jay Franklin Reniker. Children:
Jana Mary Reniker – b 01 Mar 1980
Jonathan Jay Reniker – b 18 Oct 1981

Julie Ann SCHEMPP d/o Dorothy nee Juhnke & Leland Schempp; b 16

Apr 1960; 1st m 04 Feb 1984 James Frankman of Sioux Falls, SD s/o Wayne & Dolores Frankman, Sioux Falls, SD. Julie graduate Augustana College. James attended Black Hills State College/South Dakota State U. Rapid City, SD residence. DVD Child:

> Jordan Lee Frankman – b 08 Aug 1986

2nd m 30 Apr 1994 Julie Ann nee Schempp Frankman to Gregory Hoff, s/o Mr. & Mrs. Richard Hoff.

*Heinrich Peter SCHENGEL s/o Balthasar Schengel & Charlotte Luise nee Hohl, Löhlbach, Germany; b 30 Sept 1912 Löhlbach, Germany; bpt & con Löhlbach Ch; d 04 Sept 1996 ae83y 11m 5d Löhlbach; m 16 Mar 1946 Löhlbach Ch to Maria Katharina Gerke (b 19 Mar 1923 Ellershausen, Germany, d 04 Jun 2000 Löhlbach, Germany). Löhlbach, Germany residence in later years with son where Author (Krug fourth cousin) met him in 1995.

> **Horst – b 15 Mar 1948 Löhlbach, Germany;
>   m 19 Sept 1970 Irmgard Ibelshauser
> **Inge – b 05 Nov 19501 m Heinz Scholl

**Horst SCHENGEL s/o Heinrich Peter Schengel & Maria Katharina nee Gerke; b 15 Mar 1948 bpt & con Löhlbach Ch; Maurer (bricklayer); m 19 Sept 1970 Löhlbach Ch to Irmgard Ibelshaser (b 17 Dec 1951 Battenhausen, Germany). Residence: Gruner Weg #16, Löhlbach, Germany. Author visited in their home 1995 and 1999 with the Krug cousins. Children:

> **(Son) Marjo – b 27 May 1978 Bad Wildungen, Germany
> **(Daughter) Ielka – b 18 Jul 1980 Bad Wildungen, Germany

**Inge SCHENGEL d/o Heinrich Peter Schengel & Maria Katharina nee Gerke; b 05 Nov 1951 Löhlbach, Germany; bpt & con Löhlbach Ch; m Heinz Scholl (b 21 Feb 1948, Pfleger [male nurse]). Battenhausen, Kirchplatz residence. Children:

> **Udo Scholl – b 11 Mar 1970 Bad Wildungen, Germany;
> **Anja Scholl – b 21 Apr 1971 Merxhausen, Germany;
>   m NN Boucsein
> **Markus Scholl – b 07 Sept 1973 Battenhausen, Germany
> **Bianca Scholl – b 25 Dec 1973 Battenhausen, Germany
> **Bernd Scholl – b 17 Dec 1975 Bad Wildungen, Germany

David SCHIRM s/o Leona Frieda nee Poock & Eldo August Schirm; m 01 Dec 1951 Janice Hupfeld. Celebrated 50th Wedding Anniversary Pharr, TX

residence. Children (Eleven grandchildren):
- Susan – m George Karam
- Randy D. – m Elaine M. Morrow
- Dan – m Denise
- David – m Chris

Donald C. SCHIRM s/o Fred Schirm of Cedar Rapids, IA; m 07 Feb 1981 TrinCR to Carol A. Carpenter d/o Mr. & Mrs. Alfred Schnieder of Guttenberg, IA. Cedar Rapids, IA residence. Donald employed by Chicago Northwestern Transportation Co.

Edgar SCHIRM s/o Martin Schirm & Carolina "Lena" nee Keiper; b 05 Feb 1917; m Elsie Hessenius residence on Schirm farm eight years before moving to Cedar Rapids, IA. Child:
- Carolyn – NFR

Eldo August SCHIRM s/o Martin William Schirm & Carolina "Lena" B. Keiper: cf Leona Frieda Poock.

*George Martin SCHIRM s/o Johann George Schirm & Anna Maria nee Diehr; b 27 Mar 1821 Germany, d 15 Apr 1896 ae68y 10m 19d; m Anna Maria Gerber (b 01 May 1827, d 15 May 1908 ae81y 14d). Child:
- *Henry Schirm – b 27 Jun 1863 Baden, Germany; d 23 Jun 1939 Cedar Rapids, Linn Co. IA; m 16 Mar 1890 Anna Katherine Rinderknecht

Irvin SCHIRM b 24 Dec 1916 Newhall, IA; m 02 Apr 1938 rural Atkins, IA to Zenolia Meier (b 23 Jan 1922). Celebrated 60th Wedding Anniversary. Children:
- Delores Olanda – b 18 Nov 1938 Newhall, IA; m 31 Aug 1956 Lynn Franklyn Pickering
- Charles – Sioux City, IA residence
- Harold – m Rosemary; Kennett Square, PA residence

*Johann George SCHIRM b 25 Apr 1792 Bahlingen, Germany; m Anna Maria Diehr (b 04 Mar 1798). Child:
- *George Martin – b 27 Mar 1821 Bahlingen, Germany; d Mar 1893; m Anna Maria Gerber

Martin William SCHIRM s/o William Schirm & Anna Gertrude Katherina nee Rinderknecht; b 24 Apr 1889 Hutchinson Co (near Yankton) SD where his parents were homesteaders, d 08 Dec 1979 ae90y 7m 14d Vinton, IA Luth Home for the Aged, bur St.Steph Cem; m 20 Dec 1911 St.Steph to Carolina "Lena" B. Keiper (b 28 Jul 1888 Hutchinson Co, SD d 10 Jun 1980 Vinton IA Luth Home ae91y 10m 13d bur St.Steph Cem) d/o Valentine Keiper & Maria (Mary) Elizabeth Gertrude nee Rinderknecht. Moved to Iowa with his parents and settled just inside Linn Co. Their six sons made a baseball team, later including Schirm cousins. 1942 Martin & "Lena" retired in Cedar Rapids where Martin worked for Co-op Dairy; also city assessor. Son Edgar resided on Schirm farm eight years; oldest son Albert bought the family farm and engaged in dairying until 1978 retirement. Children:

Albert – b 03 Oct 1913; m 12 Jun 1940 Catherine Lensch

Merle – b 25 Oct 1915 Tempe, AZ residence

Edgar – b 05 Feb 1917 Linn Co IA; m 30 Mar 1940 Elsie Hessenius, Cedar Rapids, IA residence

Eldo – b 23 Dec 1918 Atkins, IA d 04 Jun 2007Anamosa, IA; m 23 Aug 1940 Leona Frieda Poock

Lester – b 05 Mar 1921 Colorado Springs, CO residence

Carl – b 04 Nov 1923;m NN Bonesteel, Cedar Rapids, IA residence

Otto William SCHIRM s/o Henrich (Henry) Schirm & Anna Gertrude Katherina nee Rinderknecht; b 13 Jul 1895 Newhall, IA d 11 Oct 1953 ae 58y 2m 28d Cedar Rapids, IA; m 08 Apr 1917 Maria Dorthea Ernst (b 05 Dec 1895 Adair, IA d 23 Apr 1987 ae91y 4m 18d Keystone, IA). Child:

Norine Elizabeth – b 28 Dec 1928 Newhall, IA; m 19 Jun 1949 Robert Lee Canney
Child: Michael Lee Canney b 25 Nov 1951
m 23 Aug 1975 Anita Kay White

Randy D. SCHIRM s/o David Schirm & Janice nee Hupfeld; Garrison, IA; m 22 Aug 1981 Elaine M. Morrow d/o Robb Morrow of Vinton, IA. Randy graduated Iowa State U.; Elaine employed Union Story Bank, Ames.

*William SCHIRM b 1858 Germany; came to USA and settled in the Atkins, IA community, d 1949 IA; m 11 Mar 1887 St.Steph to Anna Gertrude Katherina Rinderknecht (b 01 Jun 1869, bpt 27 Jun 1869 St.Steph (Tauf Reg.p.63) d 19 Feb 1951 ae81y 8m 14d bur St.Steph Cem) d/o Friedrich (William) Wilhelm Rinderknecht & (Mary) Maria Katherina Happel. Homesteaded in Hutchinson Co SD; returned to IA and settled just

a mile inside Linn Co, one mile from Valentine Keiper family. Children:

Martin William – b 24 Apr 1889, d 08 Dec 1979 bur St.Steph Cem;
m 20 Dec 1911 Carolina (Lena) Keiper
Oscar – Appleton, WI residence
Mathilda – b 1908, d 1986; Cedar Rapids, IA residence

*Reimer Nicholas SCHOELERMAN aka Nick Schelerman s/o Peter Schoelerman & Margaretha nee Ahrens; b 27 Sept 1841 Holstein, Germany, bur Keystone, IA Cem; 1863 emigrated to Scott Co Davenport, IA; day laborer; m 04 Dec 1867 Sophia Henrietta Voss (b 04 Jun 1848 Holstein, Germany, emigrated to Davenport, IA with her family in 1853, bur Keystone, IA Cem). Following marriage moved to prairie land northeast of Keystone, Homer Twp Benton Co IA; 1905 retired to Keystone; mbrs Keystone Luth Ch. Children:

Peter – b 1868, d 1919; 1st m 1890 Celia Soehren, 4 children
2nd m 1897 Katie Jansen, 5 children
William – b 1870, d 1943; m 1898 Sophia Jansen, 4 children
John – b 1872, d 1952; 1st m 1895 Mary Mess, 5 children
2nd m 1926 Katie Jansen Schoelerman
Ferdinand – b 1873, d 1943; m 1899 Bertha Norden, 4 children
August – b 1874, d 1919; m 1904 Ella Struck, one daughter
Caroline – b 1977, d 1962; m 1901 Henry Mussman, 2 daughters
Henry – b 1879, d 1919; m Mollie Sindt, 5 children
Cecelia – b 1881, d 1884
Reimer JR. – b 1883, d 1904
George – b 1885, d 1961; m 1909 Rosa Kuhl, 5 children
Herman – b 1890, d 1925; m 1912 Margaret Sindt, 2 sons

*Ernst Heinrich SCHLOEMAN & Anna Marie nee Voss 1847 emigrated from Spenge, Westphalia, Germany with 21 week old son, William, to New Orleans, LA; traveled by riverboat to St.Louis, MO; 1851 by boat to Muscatine, IA, then oxcart to Iowa City, IA to homestead four miles south of Norway, IA. Children:

*William – b Spenge, Westphalia, Germany
John – b St.Louis, MO
August – b near Norway, IA

Annis SCHLOTTERBACK d/o John Schlotterback & Frances nee Gardemann; b 1916; m Lester Werning (b 26 Oct 1911) s/o John C. A. Werning & Mathilda nee Schu;tz. Residence on late John Werning farm

west of Newhall, IA. Children:
- Colleen Werning – m Bill Burrell
- Carol Werning – m Charles Kunstorf

Ardis Rose SCHLOTTERBACK d/o John Schlotterback & Frances nee Gardemann; b 1922; m Leo Kramer. Urbana, IA residence. Children:
- Roger Kramer – NFR
- Marilyn Kramer – NFR
- Marlys Kramer – NFR
- Mardeen Kramer – NFR
- Russel Kramer – NFR
- Monica Kramer – NFR
- Robin Kramer – NFR

Carl SCHLOTTERBACK s/o William Schlotterback & Josephine nee Weichman; b 19 Nov 1897; his mother died giving birth to him and his father let his brother and wife, Jacob and Mary Schlotterback adopt Carl, d 1964; m 19 Mar 1921 Ardis Cummins. Children:
- Kregar – dec'd
- Paul – NFR
- Ardislyn – NFR

Charles C. SCHLOTTERBACK s/o Johann Gottlieb & Christina Schlotterbeck; b 1860 Fremont Twp Benton Co IA, d 1933 ae72y; m 23 May 1888 to Anna Wilhelm (changed to Williams). Anna lived to ae100y (b 1871, d Nov 1971). Farmers southwest of Atkins, 1916 retired in Atkins, IA. Children:
- George – b 1889, d 1946; m Amelia NN
- Frederick J. – b 1896, d 1937; m 10 Apr 1918 Hattie A. Keiper

Frederick J. SCHLOTTERBACK s/o Charles Schlotterback & Anna nee Wilhelm/Williams; b 1896, d 1937 Atkins, IA bur St.Steph Cem; m 10 Apr 1918 Hattie A. Keiper (b 1998 Keiper Homestead, Fremont Twp Benton Co IA bpt and con St.Steph, d 1988 bur St.Steph Cem) d/o Frederick Keiper & Magdalena nee Schminke. Farmers five miles southwest of Atkins, IA until 1929 when moved to Atkins to open a meat market. 1936 Fritz & Hattie were custodians of the new Atkins Public School. Fritz died shortly after he took the custodial job and Hattie remained on as school custodian for several years until she became Atkins Telephone Company operator until 1954 when the conversion was made to dial system. Children:

Frederick C.- b 1919, d 1921

Gordon G. – b 1923, d 1974 m Doris Schirm (b 1923)

Magdalyn – d 1997; m Robert Wayman

2nd m Hattie A. Keiper Schlotterback to James Henry Dye (b 1896, d 1973) cashier of Atkins Peoples Savings Bank. When Henry became an invalid Hattie started the Dye Nursing home and operated it twenty-five years.

Gary SCHLOTTERBACK s/o Gordon Schlotterback & Doris nee Schirm; m Becky Shaffer d/o Robert & Doris Shaffer. Gary employed in heating and air conditioning. Children:

Tonya – NFR

Kelly – NFR

Jeremie – NFR

Gordon G. SCHLOTTERBACK s/o Frederick Schlotterback & Hattie nee Keiper; b 1923, d 1974, bur St.Steph Cem; m Doris Schirm (b 1923) d/o William & Lena Schirm. 15 years employed Fruehauf Trailer Company, Cedar Rapids, IA as a foreman. When the plant closed, Gordon employed at Atkins Elevator, and opened a fertilizer plant. Children:

Sharon – m Ronald Beatty

Nancy – with son Frank's residence Miami, FL

Gary – m Becky Shaffer

Rodney – m Chris Howe

Kevin – m Juliette Burnside

Connie – dec'd

Harold SCHLOTTERBACK s/o John Schlotterback & Frances nee Gardemann; b 1913; m Irene Kramer. Urbana, IA residence. Children:

Karen – NFR

Connie – NFR

Kelly – NFR

Henry SCHLOTTERBACK s/o William Schlotterback & Josephine nee Weichman; b 1883, d 1942; m 1907 Nellie Wallem. Children:

Esther – b 1908, d 1947; m Lawrence Alloway

Lois – b 1914; m 24 Apr 1940 Ivan Anderson

James SCHLOTTERBACK s/o William Carl Schlotterback & Carol nee Hedstrom; b 28 Sept 1962; m 31 Aug 1985 Lisa Heidke. Children:

Ryan – b Jan 1991

Laura – b Jan 1994

John SCHLOTTERBACK s/o William F. Schlotterback & Josephine nee Weichman; b 1889 southwest of Atkins, IA d 1954; m 1910 Frances Gardemann (b 1889, d 1946) d/o Louis & Mary Gardemann. Moved to farm northwest of Newhall, IA; 1933 moved to farm near Urbana, IA. Children:
    Marvin – b 1911; m Lois Langham; Newhall, IA residence
    Harold – b 1913; m Irene Kramer; Urbana, IA residence
    Annis – b 1916; m Lester Werning; farm west of Newhall, IA
    Ardis Rose – b 1922; m Leo Kramer; Urbana, IA residence

Linda Jean SCHLOTTERBACK d/o Robert Dean Schlotterback & Doris Jean nee Kerkman; b 1949; m 1971 Donald John Brecht (b 1947) s/o Rinehart & Dorothy Brecht. Children:
    Molly Lyn Brecht – b 1975
    Megan Jean Brecht – b 1979

Magdalyn SCHLOTTERBACK d/o Frederick Schlotterback & Hattie nee Keiper; d 1997 m Robert Wayman s/o Everett & Evelyn Wayman. Robert administrator 19 years in Benton and Waco Schools, later salesman for Erb's Office Service. Children:
    Thomas Wayman – NFR
    Richard Wayman – NFR

Marvin SCHLOTTERBACK s/o John Schlotterback & Frances nee Gardemann; b 1911; m Lois Langham. Newhall, IA residence. Child:
    John – NFR

Matilda SCHLOTTERBACK d/o William Schlotterback & Josephine nee Weichman; b 1885, d 1973; m 01 Jan 1907 Fred Gardeman. Children:
    Wilma Gardeman – NFR
    Lyle Gardeman – NFR
    Evelyn Gardeman – NFR

Robert Dean SCHLOTTERBACK s/o William F. Schlotterback & Anna E. nee Wallem: cf Doris Jean Kerkman.

Richard Robert SCHLOTTERBACK s/o Robert Dean Schlotterback & Doris Jean nee Kerkman; b 1948; m 1971 Mary Louise Montague (b 1949) d/o Evard & Marcella Montague. Children:

Bryon Arthur – b 1978
Hannah Louise – b 1980

Rodney SCHLOTTERBACK s/o Gordon G. Schlotterback & Doris nee Schirm; m Chris Howe d/o Delwin & Shirley Howe. Rodney employed at Amana Refrigeration. Child:
Jill – NFR

Sharon SCHLOTTERBACK d/o Gordon G. Schlotterback & Doris nee Schirm; m Ronald Beatty s/o Evelyn Beatty Hanson. Ronald farmer and Consolidated Freight dispatcher. Children:
Cindy Hanson – NFR
Cheryl Hanson – NFR
Cari Hanson – NFR

Rev. Thomas P. SCHLOTTERBACK s/o William Carl Schlotterback & Carol nee Hedstrom; b 20 Nov 1959; m 15 May 1982 Jane Hansen. Children:
TWINS: Brooke – b Jan 1990
　　　　Mark – b Jan 1990

William SCHLOTTERBACK s/o Johann Goettlieb & Christina Schlotterback; b 06 May 1859; d 28 Feb 1929 ae69y 8m 22d; bur St.Stephen Cem; 1st m 29 Mar 1882 Josephine Weichman (b 1861, d 19 Nov 1897 [Giving birth] to Carl). Farmers southwest of Atkins, IA on Johann Goettlieb Schlotterback farm. Children:
Henry – b 1883, d 1942; m 1907 Nellie Wallem
Matilda – b 1885, d 1973; m 01 Jan 1907 Fred Gardeman
Clara – b 1887, d 1979; m John Gardeman
John – b 1889, d 1954; m 1910 Frances Gardeman
William Frank – b 06 Oct 1891, d 13 Aug 1980;
　　　m 23 Feb 1916 Anna E.Wallem
Hattie A. – b 1894, d 1986; m 1915 Charles A. Gardeman
Carl – b 19 Nov 1897, d 1964; m 19 Mar 1921 Ardis Cummins
2nd m 1902 William Schlotterback to Martha King (d Jul 1941); retired to Atkins IA.

William Carl SCHLOTTERBACK s/o William Frank Schlotterback & Anna E. nee Wallem; b 15 Sept 1931, bpt & con St.Steph; 1948 Class Atkins High School; 1952 US Navy Korean Conflict; U. of Iowa degree

Electrical Engineering; m 30 Jun 1956 Carol Hedstrom (b 20 May 1932) d/o Rudy & Ethel Hedstrom of North St.Paul, MN. 1959 moved to White Bear Lake, MN, employed by Northern States & Power; members First Evangelical Luth Ch. Children:

    Rev. Thomas P. – b 20 Nov 1959; m 15 May 1982 Jane Hansen

    James – b 28 Sept 1962; m 31 Aug 1985 Lisa Heidtke

William Frank SCHLOTTERBACK s/o William Schlotterback & Josephine nee Weichman; b 06 Oct 1891, d 13 Aug 1980 ae90y 10m 7d; m 23 Feb 1916 Anna E. Wallem (d 13 Apr 1967) d/o Richard & Taletta Wallem. Started farming on Schlotterback homestead; 1930 purchased farm from family estate, added another forty acres; raised hogs along with grain and hay crops. William and Henry Wendel ran threshing ring in partnership north and west of Atkins. 1946 William & Anna retired to home purchased in Atkins, IA. Members Atkins Pleasant Hill Presbyterian Ch; William active in Farm Bureau, Cedar Valley Farm Business Association, Atkins Telephone Company, Atkins Town Council. Children:

    Richard – dec'd

    Doris Mae – b 31 Jul 1920; m 22 Jan 1941 Charles Edward Lensch

    Robert Dean – b 1925, d 03 Jun 2005;

        m 30 Jun 1946 Doris Jean Kerkman

    William Carl – b 15 Sept 1931; m 30 Jun 1956 Carol Hedstrom

Anita Mae SCHLOTTERBECK d/o Delmar Charles Schlotterbeck & Lois Helena Junge; b 1953; 1st m Mark Adyniec. Children:

    Jesse Fielding Adyniec – b 1982

    Sarah Elizabeth Adyniec – b 1984

2nd m Anita Mae Schlotterbeck to Tom Miller. Children:

    Crystal Miller – b 1985

    Brandon Miller – b 1989

    Kendall Miller – b 1996

Beverly Kay SCHLOTTERBECK d/o Delmar Charles Schlotterbeck & Lois Helena Junge; b 1952; m David Michael Stafford (b 1950). Children:

    Eric Michael Stafford – b 1980

    Daniel Stafford – b 1983

    Sheila Kay Stafford – b 1989

Cheryl Ann SCHLOTTERBECK d/o Delmar Charles Schlotterbeck & Lois Helena nee Junge; b 1947; m Steven Raub (b 1946). Children:

Stephanie Ann Raub – b 1966
William Adam Raub – b 1972

Delmar Charles SCHLOTTERBECK s/o George Johann Carl Schlotterbeck & Amelia Christian nee Kerkman: cf Lois Helena Junge.

Denise Dawn SCHLOTTERBECK d/o Delmar Charles Schlotterbeck & Lois Helena nee Junge; b 1961; m Randy Nolan (b 1955). Children:
Lindsay Leigh Nolan – b 1986
Wyatt Charles Nolan – b 1989

Erma Jean SCHLOTTERBECK d/o George Johann Carl Schlotterbeck & Amelia Christian nee Kerkman; b 1926; m George Caspers (b 1924, d 1962). Children:
Jean Marie Caspers – b 1946
Connie Kay Caspers – b 1949; m Leslie Hubert Echols
(b 1946, d 1993). Children: Angela Erma Echols (b 1967);
m Joseph Medwick. Leslie Greg Echols (b 1969)
Brenda Joy Caspers – b 1951; m Michael Joseph Echols (b 1947)
Child: Brandon Gene Echols (b 1986)
Riva Jane Caspers – b 1952; m Doris Ray Echols (b 1949)
Children: Amy Lynn Echols (b 1975),
Ryan Joseph Echols (b 1978), Alicia Jane Echols (b 1981)
Ricky George Caspers – b 1952; m Viginia Whiting (b 1953)
Children: Kimberly Rose Caspers (b 1972), Tracy Ann Caspers
(b 1975), Nicholas Rick Caspers (b 1977)
Randy Ray Caspers – b 1954; Rose Ann Albang.
Child: Patrick Caspers (b 1976)
Debra Sue Caspers – b 1957; m Steven Ray Schmaljohn (b 1955)
Children: Rachel Marie Schmaljohn (b 1980),
Jill Rose Schmaljohn (b 1982),
Timothy Larry Schmaljohn (b 1983)
Rusty Alan Caspers – b 1958; 1st m Julie Ann Aldrich
Children: Jessica Ann Caspers (b 1976), Peter Russell Caspers
(b 1983), Michael Jon Caspers (b May ND)
2nd m Connie Smith

George Johann Carl SCHLOTTERBECK s/o Charles Schlotterbeck & Anna nee Wilhelm/ Williams; b 11 Apr 1889 southwest of Atkins, IA d 1946 bur St.Steph Cem; m 18 Sept 1912 Amelia Christian Kerkman (b 22

Dec 1892, d 14 Mar 1976 ae83y 2m 20d bur St.Steph Cem) d/o Edward John Kerkman & Barbara nee Rinderknecht. Farmed southwest of Atkins, IA until 1931; moved to Atkins where he was a laborer. Children:

Delmar Charles – b 1914; m 1943 Lois Helena Junge;
    Keystone, IA residence
Leona Barbara Anna – b 1916; 1st m Wallace Richard Ness;
    2nd m Virgil Annett of Atkins, IA
Eileen Isabel – b 1920; 1st m Harry Lyons; 2nd m 1990 Art Johnson
Juanita Mae – b 1922; m Reno Walter of Oxford, IA
Edward George – b 1924; m Marguerte McArthur;
    Hiawatha, IA residence
Erma Jean – b 1926; m George Caspers of Anamosa, IA DVD
LaVonne Marie – b 1930; m Karl Lester Whiting, Central City, IA

*Johann Gottlieb SCHLOTTERBECK b 26 Nov 1832 Reichenick, Urack Koeningreich Wurtenberg, Germany, d 1893 on his farm, Benton Co IA, bur Raetz Cem, Atkins, IA; 1854 ae22y emigrated to USA and settled at Utica, NY; m 23 Aug 1854 in NY to Christina (b 1832 Wittenburg, Germany, d 1911 Benton Co IA, bur Raetz Cem, Atkins, IA). Moved to Iowa and farmed southwest of Atkins acquiring land in Section 15, Fremont Twp Benton Co IA dated 08 Dec 1860. Twelve children:

Jane – b 1855, d 1881; m Charles Kunstorf
Jacob – b 1857, d 1931; m Mary Weichman
George – b 1852, d 1931; Never Married
William – b 1859, d 1929; m Josephine Weichman
Charles C. – b 1860, d 1933; m 23 May 1888 Anna Wilhelmi
Albert – b 1862, d 1928; m Hettie Armstrong
Mary – b 1864, d 1928; m Charles Weichman
Pauline – b 1866, d 1920; m Frank Weichman
Caroline – b 1867, d 1927; m Fred Mathias
Johann G. – b 1869, d 1904; Never Married
Elizabeth – b 1872, d 1930; m Henry Schuchmann
Frank – b 1873, d 1925; m Mary Schultz

Juanita Mae SCHLOTTERBECK d/o George Johann Carl Schlotterbeck & Amelia Christian nee Kerkman; b 1922; m Reno Walter (b 1919). Children:

Kevin Walter – b 1950; m Carol Ann Westemier.
    Children: Kristine Lynn (b 1973) Daniel Ray (b 1975)
Duane Walter – b 1952; m Jane Ann Valesky (b 1954).
    Children: Jason Duane (b 1972), Michelle Lee (b/d 1974),

Ryan Edward (b 1976), Lisa Renee (b 1981)
Todd Walter – b 1959; m Lori Jo Gabriel (b 1957).
    Children: Jenny Jo (b 1982), Kate Marie (b 1985)

LaVonne Marie SCHLOTTERBECK d/o George Johan Carl Schlotterbeck
& Amelia Christian nee Kerkman; b 1930; m Karl Lester Whiting.
Children:
    Janet Colleen Whiting – b 1952; m Dave Mannetter
    Lorraine Ann Whiting – b 1954; m Stephen James Burkey
    Peggy Kay Whiting – b 1958; m Jon Dean Barnes

Leona B. SCHLOTTERBECK d/o George Schlotterbeck & Amelia nee
Kerkman; b 12 Oct 1916 rural Atkins, IA d 29 May 2000 ae83y 7m 17d
St.Lukes Hosp Cedar Rapids, IA bur CdrMem; 1975 retired after 22 years
assembly department Rockwell Collins; 1st m 27 Oct 1934 Wallace Richard
Ness (d 1971). Member St.Steph. Children:
    Donna Mae Ness – b 1937; m NN Geater; Children: Judy; Greg
    Betty Ness – b 1939; m Richard Novotny
    Ronald W. Ness – b 09 Dec 1939 Atkins, d 10 Sept 2002 [Cancer]
        1st m Joyce Lange DVD; 2nd m 10 Jun 1989 Carol Brown
    Diane Ness – b 1943; m NN Beatty; Child: Shelley Beatty
2nd m 04 May 1973 Atkins, IA Leona B. nee Schlotterbeck Ness to Virgil
W. Annett.

*Balthasar SCHMIDT s/o Johann Heinrich Schmidt of Romershausen,
Germany; b 23 Oct 1775 Grussen, Germany, d 20 Mar 1832 ae57y 4m 25d
Löhlbach, Germany Hse #56; 1st m 29 Jul 1798 Löhlbach Ch to Anna Guida
Scholl (b 24 Nov 1777 Löhlbach Hse #56, bpt 04 Dec 1777 Löhlbach Ch
Godmother: Anna Guida, father's sister; d 10 May 1823 ae45y 5m 16d
Löhlbach Hse #56;d/o Johann Justus Scholl & Anna Marie nee Möller of
Löhlbach, Germany. Children:
    Johann Nicolaus – b 17 May 1799, d 19 Jun 1800
    Johann Conrad – b 18 Jun 1801, d 19 Jun 1801
    Johann Conrad – 02 May 1802; m 28 Dec 1830 Anna Elis. Schaake
    Johannes – b 14 May 1805, d 19 Apr 1869
    Johann Nicolaus – b 06 Mar 1808, d 12 Mar 1808
    Anna Dorothea – b 16 Mar 1809, d 11 Mar 1828
    Johann Daniel – b 13 Aug 1812
    Johann Jacob – b 27 May 1816, d 28 Aug 1817
    Johann Stephen – b 18 Dec 1818, d 21 Dec 1818

*Anna Elisabeth – b 10 Jun 1820; m 21 Aug 1842 Tobias Ernst
2nd m 23 Mar 1824 Balthasar Schmidt to Anna Catharine Balzer

Catharine SCHMIDT d/o Herman H. Schmidt & Elizabeth nee Spellman; b 1865, d 1925, bur Mound Cem Watkins, IA; m James Wesley Andrew (b 1858 Monroe Co, PA, d 1911 Benton Co, IA bur Mound Cem, Watkins, IA) s/o Samuel & Suzanna Andrew. James operated a livery barn in Newhall, IA. Catharine: charter mbr Newhall Presbyterian Ch. Children:
> Lillian Elizabeth Andrew – b 1884, d 1978;
>> m Arthur Green, Cedar Rapids, IA
> Irving Edward Andrew – b 1887, d 1966; m Emma Meyer
> Edna Lenora Andrew – b 1895, d 1974; m Earl E. Chenoweth
> Franklin James Andrew – b 1898;
>> m Audrey Thompson, Cedar Rapids, IA

Debra SCHMIDT d/o Norman Schmidt & Linda nee Shoemaker; b 27 Jan 1967; m 04 Nov 1989 Michael D. Hoppman (b 01 Dec 1962). Child:
> Daniel J. Hoppman – b 28 May 1992

Doris SCHMIDT d/o Frieda Gertrude nee Happel & Richard Schmidt; b 14 Dec 1930; m 29 Aug 1953 Vince Albrecht (b 03 Jul 1930). Children:
> David Albrecht – b 31 Aug 1956; m 13 Aug 1977 Carol Broman
>> (b 26 Dec 1956)
> Denise Albrecht – b 27 Sept 1959
> Jean Albrecht – b 01 Feb 1961; m 14 Oct 1988 Brian Galligan
>> (b 18 May 1959)

Ellen SCHMIDT d/o Norman Schmidt & Linda nee Shoemaker; b 08 Dec 1962; m 03 May 1986 Steven R. Kay (b 15 Sept 1951). Child:
> James R. Kay – b 26 Nov 1991

Helen Doris SCHMIDT d/o Otto B. Schmidt & Julia M. nee Rammelsberg; b 1907; m Herbert Schroeder. Farmers near Dysart, IA. Child:
> Grace Schroeder – b 1949

*Herman H. SCHMIDT b 1816 os Prussia ns Germany, d 1907 Benton Co IA; 1844 landed in New Orleans, LA; early settler of Clayton Co IA helping to organize town of Guttenberg, IA; m 1852 Elizabeth Spellman (b 1823, d 1890). 1865 moved to Eldorado Twp Benton Co IA; farmer and stockman. Children:

Margaret – b 1855, d 1923; m 1876 Joseph Young
Sophia – b 1857; m NN Warnke
Edward – b 1859; m Ella Hannen
Paul – m to NN Winters
Catharine – b 1865; m James Wesley Andrew
George – m Hanna Waddell

*John SCHMIDT s/o John Schmidt & Florentina nee Kreck of Germany; b 1838 Rosenbeck, Germany, d 1920 Benton Co IA; emigrated 1880's to St.Clair Twp Benton Co IA; m Feb 1866 Josephine Schulte (b 1849 Rosenbeck, Germany. 1861 emigrated with parents; d 1935 Benton Co IA) d/o Charles Schulte & Mary Ann nee Nolte. Farmers near Watkins, IA. Children:

Elizabeth – b 1867, d 1949; m 08 Feb 1893 Charles Nolte
    (b 1867, d 1956). Children: Theodore, Jennie, Leo, Louis, Charles
Mary – b 1868, d 1959; m 1892 Henry Smith (b 1858, d 1909);
Children: George, Florence, Elizabeth, Esmeralda, Cleo, Mineard
Charles – b 1874, d 1960; m May 1900 Katie Spellerberg
    (b 1881, d 1955). Children: Arthur, Elfie, Clayton, Gilbert,
    Delbert, Richard
Gertrude – b 1877, d 1936; m 28 May 1902 David Maag
    (b 1878, d 1953) Son: Forrest
John A. – b 1879, d 1955; m 23 May 1905 Mary Maag
    (b 1885, d 1979). Children: Clifford, Viola,
    Pearl – m Joseph Downes, Hazel
Joseph – b 1881, d 1966; m 07 Feb 1907 Gertrude Schmuecker
    (b 1887, d 1972). Children: Leova, Pauline, Paul, Zeno, Hilda
Margrete – b 1883, d 1894
Rose – b 1885, d 1969;
    m 30 Jan 1907 Henry Schmuecker(b 1879, d 1956);
    Children: Ervin, Celesta, Raphael
Louise – b 1888, d 1962; m 12 Oct 1910 George Stark
    (b 1887, d 1973). Child: Leota; raised Robert Gibney Stark
    (mother died)
William – b 1890, d 1963; m 27 Apr 1915 Mary Delaney
    (b 1895, d 1967). Children: Margaret, Dolores, William JR.,
    Clarence, Robert, Lois, Anna Mae, Alice, Allen
Theodore – b 1893, d 1973; m 17 Jul 1916 Rosetta Arp
    (b 1889, d 1984). Children: Vernon, Laverna, Elaine, Doris,
    Geraldine, Jeanette, Patricia.

Family residence Schmidt homeplace.

Jeff SCHMIDT s/o Audrey nee Happel & Norbert Schmidt; b 28 Oct 1961; m 02 Nov 1985 Penny Hagenow (b 12 Jan 1963). Children:
    Holly – b 07 Dec 1986
    Heide – b 06 Sept 1988
    Zach – b 28 Jun 1991

Julie Kay SCHMIDT d/o Mabel Marie nee Haerther & Rev. Lawrence Arthur Schmidt; b 03 Nov 1969; m 12 Oct 1996 Davenport, IA to Craig Alan Dueker. Child:
    Ryan Paul Dueker – b 24 Jul 1997 Davenport, IA

Kristi SCHMIDT d/o Neils Schmidt & Delores nee Koopman; b 1950; m 1973 Dysart, IA to Mike Hesse. Waterloo, IA residence. Child:
    Matthew Hesse – b 1980

Leona SCHMIDT d/o Frieda Gertrude nee Happel & Richard Schmidt; b 08 Jan 1927; m 29 Aug 1958 Henry Standridge (b 03 Jan 1917m d 20 Dec 1992). Child:
    Karla Standridge – b 01 Jun 1959; m 03 Oct 1987 Matthew Cole

Margaret SCHMIDT d/o Herman H. Schmidt & Elizabeth nee Spellman; b 1855, d 1923; m 1876 Joseph Young (b 1855 Easton, PA, d 1936) s/o Enos Young & Louise nee Bauer. 1866 Joseph came to Benton Co IA with parents and farmed in Section 28 Eldorado Twp. He had a steam engine threshing outfit. Retired in Newhall, IA prob 1907, started hardware and implement store with sons. After Margaret's death Joseph and his daughter built "Youngsville", a restaurant and gas station at the junction of U.S. highway 30 and Iowa 218 where Joseph lived until his death. Children:
    Charles Young – m Verna Blue
    Franklin Young – b 1879, d 1966; m 1902 Mathilda Kerkman
    Elizabeth Pearl Young – b 1882, d 1976; m Andrew Park Wheeler

Norman SCHMIDT s/o Richard Schmidt & Frieda Gertrude nee Happel; b 29 Dec 1932; m 30 Dec 1958 Linda Schoemacher (b 26 Sept 1936). Children:
    Becky – b 11 Oct 1959; m 29 Dec 1984 Kenneth M. Oeltjenbruns
    Ellen – b 08 Dec 1962; m 03 May 1986 Steven R. Kay
    Debra – b 27 Jan 1967; m 04 Nov 1989 Michael D. Hoppman

Otto B. SCHMIDT s/o Gustav Otto Schmidt & Sophie nee Pagel; b 1875 Jackson Co IA, d 1931; educated Valpariso Indiana U.; taught school in Jackson Co IA; m 1897 Julia M. Rammelsberg (b 1875, d 1949) d/o Hugo Herman Friedrich Rammelsberg & Bertha nee Hauschild. Moved to Eldorado Twp Benton Co IA and farmed; 1914 moved to Van Horne, IA where Otto became livestock buyer and president of Van Horne Savings Bank until his death. Children:
    Waldo – b 1900, d 1908
    Helen Doris – b 1907; m Herbert Schroeder
    Ruth Esther – b 1911; m Virgil Hartz

Rebecca SCHMIDT d/o Norman Schmidt & Linda nee Shoemaker; b 11 Oct 1959; m 29 Dec 1984 Kenneth M. Oeltjenbruns JR. (b 16 Oct 1957). Children:
    Elizabeth E. Oeltjenbruns – b 19 Sept 1989
    Sarah L. Oeltjenbruns – b 12 May 1993

Ruth Esther SCHMIDT d/o Otto B. Schmidt & Julia M. nee Rammelsberg; b 1911; m 1935 Virgil Hartz (b 1908 Blairstown, IA) s/o Preston Hartz & Ella nee Ebert. Farmers northwest of Newhall, IA beginning in 1940. Children:
    Marye Hartz – b 1936; m Dr. Wm. R. Cotton MD, Chevy Chase,MD
    Herbert Hartz – b 1943; m Sally Curtis, Cedar Rapids, IA residence

Alan Douglas SCHMINKE s/o Wilfred Walter Schminke "Butch" & Betty Jeanne nee Glick; b 25 Aug 1963 Virginia Gay Hosp Vinton, IA; m 02 Sept 1983 United Ch of Christ, Clarence, IA to Kandace Rae Thomson (b 20 Nov 1962 Clarence,IA) d/o Gary Alan Thomson & JoAnn Lucille nee Seitz. Children:
    Cody Alan – b 06 May St.Lukes Hosp Cedar Rapids, IA
    Chelsea Rae – b 26 Oct 1991

August Heinrich (Henry) George SCHMINKE s/o Jacob Schminke SR. & Anna Katerina nee Ibel: cf Elizabeth "Lizzie" Katharina Anna Rinderknecht.

Carl Henry August SCHMINKE s/o August Heinrich (Henry) George Schminke & Elizabeth "Lizzie" Katharina Anna nee Rinderknecht; b 20 Mar 1920 Fremont Twp Benton Co IA, d 27 Apr 2002; m 14 Sept 1947

TrinCR to Lillian Koss (b 24 Jul 1926 Marion, IA) d/o Edward Adolph Koss & Mary nee Navratil. Third generation farming Schminke homestead. Children:

    Dennis Carl – b 16 Mar 1950 St.Lukes Hosp Cedar Rapids, IA;
        m 28 Nov 1970 Carol Ann Brunssen

    Darwin Lee – b 12 Jul 1952 St.Lukes Hosp Cedar Rapids, IA;
        m 22 Aug 1981 Carla Rae Dallege

Clarence W. SCHMINKE s/o Fred Schminke & Lillian nee Wieneke; b 1898, d 1965; 1st m Margaret Gibney. Children:

    Donald – Council Bluffs, IA residence

    David – Milwaukee, WI residence

    Dr. Clarence – Eugene, OR U. of Oregon Professor

2nd m 1933 of Clarence Schminke to Mabel Voss (b 1908) d/o Joe Voss & Carrie nee Voehl. Farmers and members St.Paul's Catholic Ch, Newhall, IA. Children:

    Carolyn – m Thomas Thomason; Children: Timothy, Tami

    Mary – m Donald Kaliban; Children: Keri, Michael, Mark

    James – Logansport, IN; Children: Sue Ellen, Cathy

Conrad Werner SCHMINKE s/o Jacob Schminke SR. & Anna Katherina nee Ibel: cf Katherina Jeannette Werning.

Daniel Walter SCHMINKE s/o Marlin Richard Henry Schminke & Donna Mae nee Connor; b 11 Mar 1957 Van Horne, IA; m 12 Jul 1980 St.Anthony Park Luth Ch St.Paul, MN to Amy J. Rathman (b 28 Mar 1957 MS) d/o Dr.Paul G. & Sigrid Rathman. Children:

    Brittany Allison – b 15 Apr 1985 Saginaw, MI

    Brooke Lanea – b 02 Nov 1987 Rossau, MN

Darwin Lee SCHMINKE s/o Carl Henry August Schminke & Lillian nee Koss; b 12 Jul 1952 St.Lukes Hosp Cedar Rapids, IA; m 22 Aug 1981 Concordia Luth Ch Cedar Rapids, IA to Carla Rae Dallege (b 17 Apr 1951 Davenport, IA) d/o Harley LaVern Dallege & Rosemary Louise nee Evers, Tipton, IA. Children:

    Danielle Rae – b 22 Oct 1984 Cedar Rapids, IA; bpt Dec 1984
        Concordia Luth Ch; Sponsors: Dennis Schminke & Craig Dallege

    Shawn Michael – b 27 Dec 1986 Cedar Rapids, IA; bpt Feb 1987
        Concordia Luth Ch; Sponsors: Dennis Schminke & Craig Dallege

David Henry SCHMINKE s/o Henry Conrad Schminke & Audrey Laura nee Hartz; b 15 Mar 1944 Vinton, IA; Truck Driver; 1st m 05 Oct 1962 Vinton, IA to Pamela Darlene Primmer (b 31 Oct 1945 Vinton, IA) d/o Carl Eugene Primmer & Betty Jean nee Butler. Children:

Scott David – b 12 Feb 1964 Vinton, IA;
1st m 23 Oct 1982 Tammy Johnson; 2nd m Leanne Maynard
Timothy Carl – b 21 May 1965 Vinton, IA; m 13 Jun 1986 Susan Smith
Christina Lorraine – b & d 9 Sept 1968 Vinton, IA;
bur Evergreen Cem. Vinton, IA
Laura Jean (Addopted) – b 17 Jul 1969 St.Lukes Hosp Cedar Rapids, IA

2nd m 12 Dec 1987 TrinVT David Henry Schminke to Mardean Hilda nee Stein Olson (b 10 Aug 1928 Benton Co IA; 1st m Arthur Hoeppner; 2nd m Robert E.Olson)

Dean Edward SCHMINKE s/o Henry Conrad Schminke & Audrey Laura nee Hartz; b 08 Sept 1947 Vinton, IA; Military Service Nov 1966-Oct 1968 VA & TX; m 08 Jul 1972 St. And to Jane Helen Thompson (b 23 Aug 1950 Virginia Gay Hosp Vinton, IA) d/o Sheldon Ronald Thompson & Bernice June nee Kuhl. Farmers; Children:

Nicholas Dean – b 13 Dec 1979 St.Lukes Hosp Cedar Rapids, IA
TWINS: Alison Joy – b 17 Sept 1982 St.Lukes Hosp Cedar Rapids, IA
Amy Beth – b 17 Sept 1982 St.Lukes Hosp Cedar Rapids, IA

Dennis Carl SCHMINKE s/o Carl Henry August Schminke & Lillian nee Koss; b 16 Mar 1950 St.Lukes Hosp Cedar Rapids, IA; US Army Reserves; m 28 Nov 1970 St.Steph to Carol Ann Brunssen (b 29 Aug 1951 Belle Plaine, IA). Farmers on Wilbert Rinderknecht farm. Children:

Mindy Lynn – b 11 Jul 1972 St.Lukes Hosp Cedar Rapids, IA;
m 20 May 1995 Jay Michael Kimm
Tanya Renee – b 08 Jul 1974 St.Lukes Hosp Cedar Rapids, IA;
m 12 Jun 1999 Daniel DuWayne Reade
Dion Scott – b 18 Sept 1977 St.Lukes Hosp Cedar Rapids, IA;
bpt 16 Oct 1977 and con 12 Apr 1992 St.Steph;
Sponsors: Darwin Schminke & Cindy Lange

Diana Marie SCHMINKE d/o Richard Edwin Schminke & Mary Lou nee Rauh; b 13 Mar 1961 Dallas, TX; m 30 Dec 1988 Zion Luth Ch, Dallas TX to Dr. Charles Kevin Peirce (New Bedford, MA; Urologist) s/o Charles Condil Pierce & Betsy May nee Lord. Child:

Charles Andrew Peirce – b 06 Feb 1991 Houston, TX
Emily Marie Peirce – b 24 Nov 1992
Rebecca Marie Peirce – b 28 Jul 1995

DuWayne Wilbert SCHMINKE s/o Edwin Frederick George Schminke & Amanda Katherina Marie nee Schanbacher; b 08 Oct 1939 St.Lukes Hosp Cedar Rapids, IA; m 04 Feb 1962 Sharon E.U.B. Ch Cedar Rapids, IA to Linda Sue Sloan (b 23 Aug 1942 Cedar Rapids, IA) d/o William Lee Sloan & Leah Irene nee Flitsch of Alburnett, IA. Children:
    Brenda Sue – b 20 Jun 1971 St.Lukes Hosp Cedar Rapids, IA
    Douglas Wayne – b 02 Aug 1973 St.Lukes Hosp Cedar Rapids, IA;
        m 23 May 1998 Kimberly Christine Kelley
    Patricia Lynn – b 11 Oct 1976 St.Lukes Hosp Cedar Rapids, IA;
        m 02 Feb 1975 Bradley Allen Henderson

Edna Katharina Magdalena Schminke: cf George Jacob Haerther.

Edwin Frederick George Schminke: cf Amanda Katherina Marie Schanbacher.

Elaine Leone SCHMINKE d/o Walter Karl Jacob Schminke & Ilma Mildred nee Werning; b 18 Jun 1938 near Van Horne, IA; graduated St.John Luth School; Van Horne High School; m 03 Aug 1957 St.John to Duane Ferdinand Kromminga (b 21 Mar 1933 Keystone, IA; Korean Conflict Veteran, d 01 Jul 2004 ae71y 3m 10d bur Keystone IA Cem) s/o Ferdinand Kromminga & Elsie nee Harder. Farmed near Keystone until 1994 retirement. Children:
    Lori Lynn Kromminga – b 27 Nov 1958 Vinton, IA;
        m 18 Jul 1981 Brian McCulloh
    Kurt Duane Kromminga – b 25 Sept 1963 Cedar Rapids, IA;
        m 08 May 1993 Jane Renae Tucker

Fredrick W. SCHMINKE s/o Jacob Schminke & Anna Katerina nee Ibel; b 31 Dec 1868 on farm in Benton Co southwest of Atkins, IA d 1951; m 24 Apr 1895 Lillian May Wieneke (b 1876, d 1965). Farmers in Atkins community until moving to Atkins in 1941. Fred active school director and Atkins Telephone Company Board; played in Atkins band in 1885. Children:
    William H.(Bill) – b 27 Jan 1987, 13 Mar 1981 bur St.Steph Cem;
        m 18 Mar 1919 Hilda Fox, Atkins, IA residence

Clarence W. – b 1898, d 1965; 1st m Margaret Gibney;
  2nd m 1933 Mabel Voss
Fred JR. – dec'd 1918 ae18y
Harold – dec'd ae4 months
Erma Magdalene – b 03 Mar 1909 in ND; d 21 Nov 1992
  bur St.Steph Cem; m 30 Jan 1929 Paul Julius Haerther;
Mabel – dec'd 1925 ae14y
Lillian – m Glen Weir; 2 daughters

Henry Conrad SCHMINKE s/o August Heinrich (Henry) George Schminke & Elisabeth "Lizzie" Katharina Anna nee Rinderknecht; b 14 Oct 1914 Fremont Twp Benton Co IA, d 29 Nov 2005 ae91y 1m 15d; 1st m 25 Sept 1940 St.Steph to Audrey Laura Hartz (b 27 Jan 1919 Newhall IA, d 14 Feb 1975 ae56y 18d Vinton, IA bur Evergreen Cem Vinton, IA) d/o Harvey William Hartz & Elsie L. nee Siek. Farmers. Children:
  David Henry – b 15 Mar 1944 Vinton, IA;
    1st m 05 Oct 1962 Pamela Darlene Primmer;
    2nd m 12 Dec 1987 Mardean Hilda (Stein) Olson
  Dean Edward – b 08 Sept 1947 Vinton, IA;
    m 08 Jul 1972 Jane Helen Thompson
2nd m 15 Nov 1975 Henry Conrad Schminke to Pauline Anna Catherine Mohr (b 30 Mar 1920 Mt.Auburn,IA) d/o Herman Mohr.

Hilda Gertrude Anna SCHMINKE d/o August Heinrich (Henry) George Schminke & Elisabeth "Lizzie" Katharina Anna nee Rinderknecht; b 12 Feb 1910 Fremont Twp Benton Co IA; m 20 Sept 1934 TrinCR to Walter William Maurer (b 15 Aug 1911 Cedar Rapids, IA; Collins Radio Employment).Child:
  Nadine Ann – b 24 Jun 1938 Cedar Rapids, IA;
    m 20 Sept 1957 Larry Dean Schultz

*Jacob SCHMINKE SR. b 12 Feb 1837, Germany, d 09 Apr 1921 ae84y 1m 28d Benton Co IA bur St.Steph Cem; 1855 emigrated to Cedarville, NY until outbreak of the Civil War. m 1861 Cedarville, NY shortly before enlistment at outbreak of Civil War to Anna Katerina Ibel (b 20 Oct 1833, d 02 Dec 1902 ae69y 1m 12d). Served in infantry two years. 1866 moved to Benton County, IA and homesteaded in 1867. Children:
  Jacob JR. – m Julie Klippe
  Fredrick W. – b 31 Dec 1868, d 1951; m 24 Apr 1895 Lillian Wieneke
  Conrad Werner – b 12 Jun 1871, d 31 Jul 1963;

m 15 Feb 1899 Katherina Jeannette Werning
August Heinrich (Henry) George – b 02 Apr 1876, d 26 Nov 1964;
   m Elizabeth "Lizzie" Katharina Anna Rinderknecht
Magdalena – b 1855, d 1961 bur St.Steph Cem;
   m 25 Nov 1884 Frederich Keiper JR.
Anna C. – b 1867, d 1926; m August Gardemann
Mary – b New York, dec'd ae3y

Janet Lee SCHMINKE d/o Marlin Richard Henry Schminke & Donn Mae nee Connor; b 29 Mar 1961 Van Horne, IA; m 24 Oct 1981 Emanuel Luth Strawberry Point, IA to Michael Andrew Guyler (b 21 Nov 1958 LaGrange, IL) s/o Clarence Guyler & Claire nee Herzog, Seminol, FL. Children:
   Jennifer Leigh Guyler – b 28 Feb 1988 Dunedin, FL

Joan Annette SCHMINKE d/o Wilmer Frederick August Schminke & Helen Cecelia nee Blaha; b 24 Jun 1955 St.Lukes Hosp Cedar Rapids, IA; m 17 Jan 1981 Ascension Luth Ch Marion, IA to Garald Gene Pease (b 31 Dec 1949 Sioux Falls, SD [1st m Jolene Hascke) s/o Garald Jay Pease & Audrey Elizabeth nee Iverson, Sioux Falls, SD. Child:
   STEPCHILD: Aaron Michael Pease– b 10 Feb 1975
      Lukes Air Force Base, AZ
   Emily Lynn Pease- b 27 Nov 1981 St.Lukes Hosp Cedar Rapids, IA

Julie Ann SCHMINKE d/o Marlin Richard Henry Schminke & Donna Mae nee Connor; b 10 May 1954 Van Horne, IA; m 30 Sept 1973 American Luth Ch Strawberry Point, IA, to Terry Lee Minard, DVD. Children:
   Michelle Ann Minard – b 18 Mar 1974 Strawberry Point, IA
   Jessica Lee Minard – b 29 Jun 1979 Elkader, IA, d 17 Aug 1985;
      bur Elkader East Cem.
   Michael Lee Minard – b 16 Dec 1980 Elkader, IA

Kevin Lee SCHMINKE s/o Wilmer Frederick August Schminke & Helen Cecelia nee Blaha; b 10 Jan 1949 St.Lukes Hosp Cedar Rapids, IA; m 04 Aug 1979 St.John Luth Ch Des Moines, IA to Sarah Louise nee Cox Hines (b 12 Apr 1952 Waterloo, IA) [Her 1st m Terrance Hines]d/o Lloyd Montell Cox & Jean Louise nee Netcott. Children:
STEPCHILDREN:
   Heather Louise Hines – b 25 Apr 1971 Des Moines, IA
   Meredith Katherine Hines – b 08 Jan 1976 Cedar Rapids, IA
   John Kevin – b 27 Nov 1980 Ft. Dodge, IA

Michael Lowell – b 12 Aug 1982 Ft. Dodge, IA
Alexandria Lynn – b 28 Jul 1986

Lenore Kathryn Elizabeth SCHMINKE d/o Walter Karl Jacob Schminke & Ilma Mildred nee Werning; b 11 Jul 1920 near Van Horne, IA; m 07 Aug 1949 St.John to Clifford Virgil Thompson (b 09 Dec 1924 Van Horne, IA World War II Veteran) s/o Ralph Virgil Thompson & Joy Evelyn nee Rieke. Farmers near Van Horne, IA. Children:
  Gregory Lee Thompson – b 30 Jun 1950 Vinton, IA;
    m 03 Jun 1972 Susan Kay Olson
  Diane Marie Thompson – b 30 Nov 1951 Vinton, IA;
    m 19 Aug 1972 David Paul Kosbau
  Debra Kay Thompson – b 02 Mar 1954 Vinton, IA;
    m 18 Jun 1977 Michael Arthur Marinelli JR.
  Gary Clifford Thompson – b 09 Apr 1958 Vinton, IA;
    m 21 Jun Julie Ann Magdefrau
  Cora Ann Thompson – b 26 May 1967 Cedar Rapids, IA;
    m 27 Aug 1988 Ron Spading

Leona Barbara Lillian SCHMINKE d/o August Heinrich (Henry) George Schminke & Elisabeth "Lizzie" Katharina Anna nee Rinderknecht; b 24 Mar 1912 Fremont Twp Benton Co IA; m 31 Aug 1938 St.Steph to Clarence Arnold Melhus (b 24 Oct 1911 Norway, IA, d 03 Oct 1948 ae36y 11m 9d bur Norway IA) s/o Edward Melhus & Olisa nee Dyrland. Farmers. Children:
  Kathleen Ann Melhus – b 22 Jun 1939 Mercy Hosp Cedar Rapids, IA;
    m 09 Mar 1958 William Charles Stickney
  Kenneth Clarence Melhus – b 04 Nov 1942 St.Lukes Cedar Rapids,IA
    m 06 Sept 1975 Sheila Gay Rodies
  Carol Leona Melhus – b 18 Dec 1946 St.Lukes Hosp Cedar Rapids;IA
    m 02 Jul 1966 Charles Irvin Schirm

Lois Jeanette SCHMINKE d/o Walter Karl Jacob Schminke & Ilma Mildred nee Werning of Van Horne, IA; b 26 Sept 1932 near Van Horne, IA Benton Co; m 30 Aug 1952 Newhall, IA Luth Parsonage to Grant Anthony Wessling (b 23 Apr 1930 farm north of Marengo, Iowa Co; National Guard Service) s/o William Christian Wessling & Ethel Irene nee Walter. Grant Assistant Purchasing Agent Iowa Manufacturing Company, Cedar Rapids & farmer; Lois secretary Atkins Center of Benton Community School; residence near Atkins, IA. Children:

TWINS: David William Wessling – b 12 Feb 1953;
    m 13 Aug 1977 Kathy Stumpff
        Douglas Walter Wessling – b 12 Feb 1953;
    m 09 Jul 1977 Debra Weichman
Thomas Grant Wessling – b 08 Apr 1955;
    m 12 Jul 1975 Sara Feuerbach
William Bradford Wessling – b 20 Dec 1956;
    m 11 Aug 1984 Mary Fritcher

Marlin Richard Henry SCHMINKE s/o Walter Karl Jacob Schminke & Ilma Mildred nee Werning; b 30 Nov 1928 Eden Twp Benton Co IA; US Army Korean Conflict d 04 Apr 2006 ae77y 4m 5d; m 21 Oct 1951 TrinCR to Donna Mae Connor (b 06 May 1929 Delhi, IA) d/o Harry Connor & Julia Hannah nee Davis. Strawberry Point, IA residence. Children:
    Julie Ann – b 10 May 1954; m 30 Sept 1973 Terry Lee Minard
    Daniel Walter – b 11 Mar 1957; m 12 Jul 1980 Amy J. Rathman
    Janet Lee – b 29 Mar 1961; m 24 Oct 1981 Michael Andrew Guyler

Mindy Lynn SCHMINKE d/o Dennis Carl Schminke & Carol Ann nee Brunssen; b 11 Jul 1972 Cedar Rapids, IA; bpt 20 Aug 1972 St.Steph Sponsors: Darwin Schminke & Corene Messer; con 30 May 1986 St.Steph; m 20 May 1995 St.Steph to Jay Michael Kimm (b 02 Dec 1972) s/o Danny & Marcia Kimm. Children:
    Colton Jay Kimm – b 07 Mar 1997
    Tyler Blake Kimm – b 23 Jan 1999

Richard Edwin SCHMINKE s/o Edwin Frederick George Schminke & Amanda Katherine Marie nee Schanbacher; b 08 Jan 1936 Mercy Hosp Cedar Rapids, IA; 1956 Class Valpariso Tech; 1959 Rockwell, Dallas, TX; m 29 Dec 1957 Luth Ch Alva, OK to Mary Lou Rauh (b 15 Nov 1935 Alva, OK; 1955 St.John College Winfield, KS) d/o Albert J. Rauh & Viola nee Pierboam. Children:
    Daniel Thomas – Stillborn 24 Oct 1988 Cedar Rapids, IA;
        bur CdrMem Cem
    Diana Marie – b 13 Mar 1961 Dallas, TX;
        m 30 Dec 1988 Charles Kevin Peirce
    Sara Marie – b 20 May 1963 Dallas, TX;
        m 20 Jun 1987 David Wayne Krumrei
    Cynthia Marie – b 06 Dec 1965 Dallas, TX

Roy SCHMINKE s/o Conrad Werner Schminke & Katherine Jeannette nee Werning; b 26 May 1904 Eldorado Twp Benton Co IA, d 1973; 1ˢᵗ m 29 Jan 1930 Martha M. E. Bierschenk (b 03 Jan 1910 Eden Twp Benton Co IA, d 27 Jun 1970 ae60y 5m 24d bur St.John Cem) d/o Carl Heinrich (Henry Carl) Bierschenk & Elizabeth nee Kranz. Farmers retiring 1970 in Newhall, IA. Children:

> Glenn Conrad George – b 06 Jan 1931; m 21 Jan 1931 Leta Albers,
>> Belle Plaine, IA. Children: Craig Allan, Douglas Glenn
> Gerald Edmond – b 02 Jun 1932; m 11 Jun 1951 Adah Lois Doyel,
>> Belle Plaine. Children: Connie Velma, Rosemarie Annie,
>> Geraldine Sue, Judith Kay
> Velma Elizabeth Katherine – b 22 Nov 1933;
>> m 20 Jun 1954 Robert Dean Van Scoy, Winterset, IA.
>> Children: Rox Ann, Christine Lynn, Richard David
> Gladys Adala Christina – b 19 Aug 1935;
>> m 06 May 1956 Merl August "Sonny" Hagan JR.. Children:
>> Curtis Lee, Paul August, Dawn Christine, Mary Elizabeth
> Virgil Victor – b 29 Aug 1942; m 02 Sept 1962 Sharon Jeanne Rohlena.
>> Children: Tammy Kay, Teresa Marie, Todd Alan

2ⁿᵈ m 30 Sept 1973 Vinton, IA Roy Schminke to Hazel Bernice (Kraft) Lauterwasser (b 24 Mar 1902 Benton Co IA) d/o Neal & Laura Kraft. Newhall, IA residence; St.John members.

Ruth Ilma SCHMINKE d/o Walter Karl Jacob Schminke & Ilma Mildred nee Werning; b 11 Jul 1940 Virginia Gay Hosp Vinton, IA; m 15 Aug 1959 St.John to Darwin Ray Oehlerich (b 02 Mar 1940 near Dysart, IA) s/o Ray Adolph Oehlerich & Blanche Rose nee Schoelerman. Residence near Keystone, IA. Children:

> Kim Denise Oehlerich – b 22 Jul 1960 Vinton, IA;
>> m 26 Nov 1983 Michael Ray Mollenhauer
> Kathy Dawn Oehlerich – b 15 Feb 1965 Independence, IA;
>> m 30 Jun 1990 Daniel Stockdale
> Kristi Diane Oehlerich – b 07 Jun 1967 Independence IA

Sara Marie SCHMINKE d/o Richard Edwin Schminke & Mary Lou nee Rauh; b 20 May 1963 Dallas, TX; m 20 Jun 1987 Zion Luth Ch Dallas, TX to David Wayne Krumrei (b 12 Feb 1960 Cleveland, OH) s/o Richard Robert Krumrei & Mary Margaret nee Tilgner. Child:

> Nathaniel David Krumrei – b 26 Jun 1991 Dallas, TX
> Benjamin Richard Krumrei – b 06 Jun 1995

Scott David SCHMINKE s/o David Henry Schminke & Pamela Darlene nee Primmer; b 12 Feb 1964 Vinton, IA) 1ˢᵗ m 23 Oct 1982 Tammy Johnson DVD 1984; 2ⁿᵈ m Leanne Maynard, DVD. Child:
   Tiffany Nicole – b 04 Aug 1985 Cedar Rapids, IA

Tanya Renee SCHMINKE d/o Dennis Carl Schminke & Carol Ann nee Brunssen; b 08 Jul 1974 Cedar Rapids, IA; bpt 25 Aug 1974 Sponsors: Diane Sand & Jan Messer; con 27 Mar 1988 St.Steph; m 12 Jun 1999 St.Steph to Daniel DuWayne Reade (b 25 Dec 1973) s/o DuWayne Reade & Brenda nee Brenneman.

Victor J. SCHMINKE s/o Conrad Werner Schminke & Katherine Jeannette nee Werning; b 21 Jul 1911 Eden Twp Benton Co IA bpt St.John; Lincoln High School, Vinton, IA; 1ˢᵗ m 15 Feb 1935 Hazel Price (d 1972) d/o Benjamin Price & Esther nee Helm. Benton Co IA farmers. 1963 retired in Vinton, IA. Children:
   Loreen – NFR
   Lawrence – NFR
   Gary – NFR
2ⁿᵈ m 1973 TrinVT Victor J. Schminke to Dorothy Sattizahn Price d/o Samuel Price & Cecelia Jane nee Elder of Independence, IA.

Walter Karl Jacob SCHMINKE s/o August Heinrich (Henry) George Schminke & Elizabeth "Lizzie" Katharina Anna nee Rinderknecht; b 15 Jun 1903 (Tauf Reg 130-8) Fremont Twp Benton Co near Atkins, IA where he spent youth, d 21 Oct 2003 ae100y 9m 6d m 08 Sept 1927 St.John to Ilma Mildred Werning (b 26 Jan 1906; Newhall High School, d 04 May 2003 ae97y 3m 8d) d/o Martin Werning & Katharina nee Rinderknecht. Farmed northwest of Newhall, IA and raised Chester White hogs beginning in 1940; many championships at hog shows and state fairs. 1963 moved to Newhall and son Wilfred and family occupied farm and carried on Chester White hog business. Celebrated 50ᵗʰ & 75ᵗʰ Wedding Anniversary. Children:
   Marlin Richard Henry – b 30 Nov 1928 Eden Twp Benton Co IA;
      m 21 Oct 1951 Donna Mae Connor
   Lenore Kathryn Elizabeth – b 11 Jul 1930 near Van Horne, IA;
      m 07 Aug 1949 Clifford Virgil Thompson
   Lois Jeanette – b 26 Sept 1932 near Van Horne, IA;
      m 30 Aug 1952 Grant Anthony Wessling
   Vernon – b 18 Mar 1935, near Van Horne, IA; d 05 Feb 1936

bur St.John Cem

Darol George – b 13 Jul 1937, near Van Horne, IA; d 24 Nov 1939
    bur St.John Cem

Elaine Leone – b 18 Jun 1938 near Van Horne, IA;
    m 03 Aug 1957 Duane Ferdinand Kromminga

Ruth Ilma – b 11 Jul 1940 Virginia Gay Hosp. Vinton, IA;
    m 15 Aug 1959 Darwin Ray Oehlerich

Wilfred Walter "Butch" – b 16 Oct 1942 Vinton, IA, d 21 Oct 1984
    m 01 Dec 1962 Betty Jeanne Glick

Wilfred Walter "Butch" SCHMINKE s/o Walter Karl Jacob Schminke &
Ilma Mildred nee Werning; b 16 Oct 1942 Vinton, IA, graduate St.John
Luth School, Van Horne High School, d 21 Oct 1984 Newhall
[Suicide/hanging home place] ae42y 5d bur St.John Cem; m 01 Dec 1962
TrinCR to Betty Jeanne Glick (b 01 May 1942 Orange, CA; Jefferson High
School, Cedar Rapids; School of Beauty Culture) d/o Maynard Glick &
Rosalie nee Flukinger. Farmer:Chester White Hogs. Children:

Alan Douglas – b 25 Aug 1963 Vinton, IA;
    m 02 Sept 1983 Kandace Rae Thomson

Patricia Ann – b 12 May 1965 Vinton, IA;
    m 14 May 1988 David Wayne Sims

Jeffrey Michael – b 01 Aug 1969 Vinton, IA;
    m 22 Jun 1991 Alicia Christine Denny

Matthew Wilfred – b 05 Sept 1978 St.Lukes Hosp Cedar Rapids, IA

William H. (Bill) SCHMINKE s/o Fred W. Schminke & Lillian nee
Wieneke; b 27 Jan 1897, bpt and con St.Steph, d 13 Mar 1981 ae84y 1m
14d; US Army until 1918; m 18 Mar 1919 Hilda M. Fox (b 1899, d 1982).
Lifelong members St.Steph; farmers in Atkins, IA community until 1941
move to Atkins; Bill drove Atkins Public School bus fifteen years; worked
in carpenter trade of C.W. Haerther. No children.

Wilmer Frederick August SCHMINKE s/o August Heinrich (Henry)
George Schminke & Elisabeth "Lizzie" Katharina Anna nee Rinderknecht;
b 01 Dec 1917 Fremont Twp Benton Co IA; Military Service:World War II
1941 European Theatre of Operations until 1945 d 11 Oct 2001 ae83y 10m
10d; 1st m 1946 Helen Cecelia Blaha (b 09 Nov 1923 Vining, IA, d 03 Feb
1981 ae57y 2m 25d St.Lukes Hosp Cedar Rapids, IA [Cancer] bur St.John
Cem) d/o Charles W.Blaha & Vlasta K. nee Kucera. Farmers Benton Co
Fremont Twp 1948-1960, and Eden Twp 1960-1980; 1979 moved to

Newhall, IA. Wilmer became a realtor. Children:

> Dr. Kevin Lee – b 10 Jan 1949 St.Lukes Hosp Cedar Rapids, IA;
>> m 04 Aug 1979 Sarah Louise Hines
>
> Karin Lynne- b 27 Feb 1951, St.Lukes Hosp Cedar Rapids, IA;
>> U. of Wisconsin faculty
>
> Joan Annette- b 24 Jun 1955 St.Lukes Hosp Cedar Rapids, IA;
>> m 17 Jan 1981 Gerald Gene Pease

2nd m 28 Aug 1982 Wilmer Frederick August Schminke to Joan Marie nee Kiernan Shipley (b 07 Nov 1936) d/o Joseph Francis & Laura Etta Kiernan. Children:

> Michael Richard Shipley – b 26 May 1959 Fairfield, IA
>
> Susan Laura Shipley – b 28 Dec 1960 Fairfield, IA;
>> m 09 Sept 1979 Timothy Edward Mostek
>
> Mark Patrick Shipley – b 20 Jun 1962 Fairfield, IA

Dale SCHNADT s/o Marie nee Happel & Elmer Schnadt; b 26 Jul 1947; m 27 Jun 1987 Sue Hoeger (b 12 Dec ND). Children:

> Elizabeth – b 25 Sept 1988
>
> Daniel – b 12 Mar 1992

Phyllis SCHNADT d/o Marie nee Happel & Elmer Schnadt; b 27 Feb 1939; m 02 Sept 1962 Ralph Bolte (b 14 Feb 1939). Children:

> Lynn Bolte – b 19 Jul 1964; m 02 May 1987 Thomas Anderson
>
> Wanda Bolte – b 07 Jun 1966; m 23 may 1992 Robert Walsh III
>> (b 18 Dec 1963)
>
> Dean Bolte – b 13 May 1969

Chris Ann SCHOEPKE d/o Carol Rae nee Poock & Dale William Schoepke; b 09 Dec 1959; m 21 Jun 1986 Burnsville, MN to Brian Lapham. Children:

> Chelsea Lynn Lapham – b 05 Dec 1986
>
> Sarah Renae Lapham – b 07 Oct 1989

**Anja SCHOLL d/o Inge Schengel & Heinz Scholl, Germany; b 21 Apr 1971 Merxhausen, Germany; m NN Boucsein. Children:

> **Svenja Boucsein – b 24 Dec 1990 Frankenberg, Germany
>
> **Lena Boucsein – b 13 Feb 1992 Frankenberg, Germany

**Bianca SCHOLL d/o Inge Schengel & Heinz Scholl, Germany; b 25 Dec 1973 Battenhausen, Germany; m Battenheusen, Germany. Children:

Anna – b 12 Sept 1993 Frankenberg, Germany

*Johann Justus SCHOLL b 25 Jan 1753 Löhlbach, Germany, Hse #56, d 19 Jul 1812 50y 5m 24d Löhlbach Hse #56; m 18 Apr 1775 Anna Marie Möller (b 04 Sept 1756 Löhlbach Hse #4, d 14 Nov 1816 ae66y 2m 10d Löhlbach, Germany, Hse #56). Children:
   *Anna Guida – b 24 Nov 1777 Löhlbach, Germany, Hse #56;
      m 1798 Balthasar Schmidt

**Udo SCHOLL s/o Inge nee Schengel & Heinz Scholl, Germany; b 11 Mar 1970, Master Electrician; m 06 May 1993 Karin Ochse (b 22 Mar 1971, retail trade business). Child:
   **Patrik – b 18 Oct 1997

Allen Donald SCHORNACK s/o Olga Senne & George Schornack; b 1931; m Marilyn Miller (b 1931). Children:
   Marcia Ann – b 1955; 1st m Jerry Osborn. Children: Jess Osborn
      (b 1980), Brian Osborn (b 1982); 2nd m Gary Lourens
   Jan Elizabeth – b 1957; m Rick Koeneman. Child: Jenna Koeneman
      (b 1980)
   Kent Allen – b 1962; m Nancy Whitehead (b 1961). Children:
      Benjamin Allen (b 1990), Zachary Richard (b 1992)

Doris SCHORNACK d/o Olga Senne & George Schornack; b 1919; m Donald Craig (b 1919, d 1987). Children:
   Berdette Elaine Craig – b 1942; m Bruce Zastrow (b 1940). Children:
      1. Roderick Zastrow (b 1962); m Carol Jo Schumaker (b 1962).
      Children: Colton (b 1992), Chandler (b 1996)
      2. Andrea Lee Zastrow (b 1967); m Mark Halbkat. Child:
      Drake Halbkat (b1992)
   Carol Lee Craig – b 1948; m Kenton Eisenbeisz (b 1944)
   Barbara Ann Craig – b 1950; 1st m Terryl Huyck (b 1949). Children:
      Anthony A. Huyck-Morreissey (b1968); m Heidi Haglund
         (b 1967).
      Children: Taylor Huyck-Morreissey (b1993),
      Morgan Huyck-Morreissey (b1996); 2nd m Charles Morreissey
      (b 1949). Child: Sarah Huyck-Morreissey(b1974)

Harold SCHORNACK s/o Olga nee Senne & George Schornack; b 1914; m Agnes Svarstad (b 1911). Children:

Larry – b 1944
Dennis Lynn – b 1951; m Linda Gobler

Howard SCHORNACK s/o Olga nee Senne & George Schornack; b 1915; m Harriet Paulsen (b 1922). Children:
Diana Elaine – b 1950; 1st m Michael Neigar (b 1950). Children: Jennifer Dawn Neigar (b 1969), Jason Michael Neigar (b 1974); 2nd m Randy Gene Swenson (b 1951).
Children: Laura Beth Swenson (b 1980), Cody Nicholas Swenson (b1984)
Peggy Jean – b 1952; m Galen Lahammer (b 1949). Children: Scott Carey Lahammer (b 1973), Jodie Lynn Lahammer (b 1974), Brianna Kay Lahammer (b 1990)
Patti Lynn – b 1956; m Mitch Joslin (b 1957). Children: Brittany Rose Joslin (b 1980), Zachary Kyler Joslin (b 1985), Alexandra Devereau Joslin (b 1989), Dakota Gabrielle Joslin (b 1993)

*Frederick SCHRADER b 1827 Holstein, Germany, bur St.John Cem; emigrated to Davenport, IA; 1870 moved to Big Grove Twp Benton Co IA; 1895 family name changed from SCHROEDER to SCHRADER; m in Germany to Annie Seevis (b Holstein, Germany, bur St.John Cem). Schrader homestead farmed by family for 103 years. Children:
Henry – m Henretta (Hettie)
John – NFR
Peter – NFR
Margaret – NFR
Mary – NFR

George Charles SCHRADER s/o Henry & Henretta (Hettie) Schrader; b 1885, bpt and con 15 Mar 1913 St.And, d 1973 Benton Co IA. bur St.John Cem; m 23 Aug 1904 Gertrude M. Kerkman (b 1886, d 1926 bur St.John Cem) d/o Conrad H. "Coony" Kerkman & Amelia "Emilie" nee Grovert. Farmed Schrader homestead. Children:
Viola – b 1906; m Feb 1925 Laurel Bodzein,
Vernon – b 1908, d 1995; m Helen NN
Helma – b 1910, d 1970; m Gordon NN

Henry SCHRADER s/o Frederick Schroeder aka Frederick Schrader & Annie nee Seevis; m Henretta (Hettie) d/o Jacob & Johanna Knaack.

Farmers north of Van Horne. Youngest child:
George Charles – b 1885, d 1973; m Gertrude M. Kerkman

Viola SCHRADER d/o George Charles Schrader & Gertrude M. nee Kerkman; b 1906 bpt and con Luth Ch; m Feb 1925 Laurel Bodzein. Farmers 30 years. 1980 moved to Vinton, IA. Child:
Nadine V. Bodzein – b 1927; m Clifford Wax

os Schüler in Germany: ns Schueler in Iowa with insertion of letter 'e' English translation.

*Adam SCHUELER s/o Anton Schüler & Anna Catharina nee Bornscheuer; b 16 Jul 1843 Löhlbach, Hessen, Germany; 1870 emigrated to Iowa; brick and stone mason specializing in laying up brick and stone for cisterns; d 23 May 1916 ae72y 10m 7d Atkins, IA bur St.Steph Cem; m 28 Dec 1875 Anna Maria Schirm (b 17 Feb 1849, d 10 Jul 1927 ae88y 4m 23d Atkins, IA bur St.Steph Cem). Farmers east of Atkins before moving to Atkins, IA. Children:
Caroline Katharine – b 1875, d 1968; m Jake Luther; Children: Ella and
  Myrtle
Louise – b 27 Jan 1876, d 17 Jan 1935;
  m 22 Oct 1896 Nicolaus Schueler
Marie – b 1878, d 1889 ae10y
Henry – b 1880; Children: son and daughter
Elizabeth "Lizzie" Marie – b 1882, d 1958; m NN Matter
William – b 1883, d 1961; Never Married
John Adam b 1885, d 1946; Never Married
Adolph – b 1887, d 1918 [killed in France World War I]
Rudolph – b 1889, d 1964; Never Married
Walter – b 1892, d 1894 ae2y
Albert J.- b 1894, d 1966; m Marie Mitchell; Child: Richard

*Andreas SCHULER s/o Luise Katharina nee Alumus Schüler; b 25 May 1798 Löhlbach, Germany, d 20 Jan 1875 Löhlbach, Germany; m 16 Apr 1824 Anna Elisabeth Krug (b 27 Jan 1799 Schwabendorf, Germany, d 10 Apr 1879 ae80y 2m 13d Löhlbach, Germany, Hse #70) d/o Johann Justus Krug III & Anna Elisabeth nee Paar of Löhlbach, Germany. Children:
*Wilhelmina – b 10 Oct 1824 Löhlbach, d 18 Nov 1882 Löhlbach;
  m 16 Jan 1848 Andreas Hohl
Conrad – b 26 Mar 1830, d 1830 Löhlbach, Germany
493

Johann Justus – b 08 Jul 1837 Löhlbach, Germany; d 02 Jan 1868;
m 17 Feb 1867; No children

Anna Marie SCHUELER d/o Nicolaus Schueler & Louise nee Schueler; b
16 Dec 1901; m 09 Sept 1946 Edwin Roe Towne (b 19 Apr 1907 Wiota,
IA) s/o Wallace Towne & Grace nee Roe. Lived in Forsythe, MO. Ann
returned to Atkins, IA in later years. Child:
    Sandra Jean Towne – b 1942; m to NN Smith,
        Cedar Rapids, IA residence

*Anton SCHULER s/o Johann Heinrich Schüler & Anna Gertrud nee
Henkel; b 04 Aug 1814 Löhlbach, Germany; m 14 Apr 1838 Löhlbach Ch
to Anna Cath. Bornscheuer (b 23 Feb 1806 os Alt Heim ns Altenhaina,
Germany). Löhlbach Ch records show family immigrated 1870 to USA.
Children:
    *Karoline – b 07 Jan 1839 Godmother: Karoline Bornscheuer of
        Altenhaina, Germany (b 19 Oct 1822)sister of Anna Cath.;
        m 20 Sept 1896 Johann Daniel Möller
    Johann Karl Anton – b 15 Nov 1841, d 13 May 1842
    Christoph Wilhelm – b 24 Jan 1846

*Conrad SCHULER s/o Johann Christopher Schüler & Luise Katharina nee
Almus; b 24 Apr 1785, d 14 Feb 1851 ae65y 9m 21d; 1st m 13 May 1806 A.
Cath. Menzel (b Rosentahl, Germany, d 09 Jul 1823 Löhlbach, Germany;
2nd m 10 Mar 1824 Elisabeth Scholl. Parents of:
    *Johannes – b 24 Oct 1831; m 1857 Anna Landau

George SCHUELER s/o Tobias Schueler & Milda nee Schaefer; b 1899; m
Elsie Hanneman. Van Horne, IA residence. Child:
    Marian Frances – m to NN Seigfried, Austin, MN

Irene Caroline SCHUELER d/o Nicolaus Schueler & Louise nee Schueler;
b 1907; m Orville Ness (d 1977; Conductor, Milwaukee Railroad at Atkins,
IA). Moved to Marion, IA. Children:
    Duane Ness – NFR
    Cleo Ness – NFR

*Johann Christoph SCHULER b Kleinern, Germany, d 20 Apr 1790
Löhlbach, Germany 35y 6m 3d; master carpenter in Haina, Germany; m
Luise Katharina Almus (b 04 Feb 1756, d 13 Sept 1830 ae74y ym 9d

Löhlbach, Germany, Hse #70) d/o Johann Christop Almus. Blacksmith in Haina, Germany. Children:

Anton – b 10 Feb 1780, d 02 Jan 1844; Löhlbach, Germany Bricklayer;
    m 15 Jan 1805 Catharine Leiss (b 01 Apr 1829,d ae52y)
Johann Heinrich – b 26 Jul 1782, d 26 Feb 1837;
    m 16 Jun 1807 Anna Gertrud Henkel
Conrad – b 24 Apr 1785, d 14 Feb 1851;
    1st m 13 May 1806 Anna Catharina Menzel;
    2nd m 10 Mar 1824 Elisabeth Scholl
Johann Heinrich – b 16 Jul 1788, d 16 Feb 1790

After death of Johann Christoph Schüler, two children were born to *Luise Katharina nee Alumus Schüler:

Anna Catharina Schüler – b 02 Feb 1794, d 22 Aug 1794
*Andreas Schüler – b 25 May 1798 Löhlbach, Germany; d 20 Jan 1875
    Löhlbach, Germany; m 16 Apr 1824 Anna Elisabeth Krug

*Johann Heinrich SCHULER s/o Johann Christoph Schüler & Luise Katharina nee Almus; b 26 Jul 1782, d 26 Feb 1837; m 16 Jun 1807 Anna Gertrude Henkel (b 27 May 1780 Haubern, Germany, d 27 Apr 1832 Löhlbach, Germany). Children:

*Anton – b 04 Aug 1814 Löhlbach, Germany;
    m 14 Apr 1838 Anna Cath. Bornscheuer

*Johannes SCHULER s/o Conrad Schüler & 2nd m to Elisabeth nee Scholl; b 24 Oct 1831 Löhlbach, Germany, d 21 Mar 1874 ae42y 4m 25d Löhlbach, Germany; m 20 Dec 1857 Löhlbach Ch to Anna Landau (b 06 Jul 1829 Löhlbach, Germany). Children:

*Tobias – b 19 Mar 1858 Löhlbach, Germany;
    1st m 23 Apr 1882 Caroline Ritter; emigrated 1896 to USA;
    2nd m in Iowa to Milda Schaefer
Anna Elisabeth – b 10 Sept 1860 Löhlbach, Germany
Conrad – b 07 Jan 1862 Löhlbach, Germany
*Nicolaus – b 12 Jan 1865 Löhlbach, Germany; emigrated to USA IA;
    m Louise Schueler
*Johann Adam – b 18 Jun 1867; emigrated USA to Benton Co IA
Christina – b 03 Sept 1869 Löhlbach, Germany
*Caroline E. – b 13 Apr 1873 Löhlbach, Germany, d 1964 USA IA;
    m 26 Feb 1901 John H. Moeller

*Nicolaus SCHUELER s/o Johannes Schüler & Anna nee Laundau,

Löhlbach, Hessen, Germany; b 12 Jan 1865, Löhlbach, Germany; emigrated USA; d 27 Jul 1911 ae46y [Killed in Threshing Accident] m 22 Oct 1896 Louise Schueler (b 27 Jun 1876, d 17 Jan 1935 bur 20 Jan 1935 ae 58y 6m 21d St.Steph Cem) d/o Adam Schueler & Anna Maria nee Schirm. Children:

Otto – b 1899, d 1907 ae8y
Theodore Johan – b 1900; m Hilda Murken
Anna Marie – b 16 Dec 1901; m 09 Sept 1946 Edwin Roe Towne
Rose Milda – b 12 Jul 1904, d 15 Apr 1990;
    m 31 Mar 1929 Orville Risdal
Irene Caroline – b 1907; m Orville Ness
Elmer – b 1909, d 1975; 1st m Fern Ludeman;
    2nd m Allegra Bush Grady

Rose Milda SCHUELER d/o Nicolaus Schueler & Louise nee Schueler; b 12 Jul 1904 Eden Twp, Benton Co IA, bpt 21 Aug 1904 St.Steph Sponsors Milda Schueler & Caroline Luther con 24 Mar 1918 St.Steph; Fremont #8 School and Luth Parochial School Teacher about six years prior to marriage; cook Atkins Public School twenty-two years; Legion Auxilary; Atkins Women's Club, St.Steph Ch Ladies Society; d Easter Sunday 15 Apr 1990 ae85y 9m 3d Mercy Medical Center, Cedar Rapids, IA; Newhall High School; m 31 Mar 1929 Parsonage of Rev. G. Rickels to Orville Risdal (b & bpt 1906 Norway,IA d 03 Sept 1972; Occupation: Carpenter, Chris Haerther; Risdal & Gibney; school bus driver) s/o Dan & Lena Risdal. Children:

Elaine Risdal – b 13 Apr 1930 Atkins, IA;
    m 16 Apr 1955 Francis Daniel Voss
Donald Eugene Risdal – b 05 Mar 1932 Atkins, IA; m Joan Lee Shaw,
    Atkins, IA residence

Theodore (Ted) Johan SCHUELER s/o Nicolaus Schueler & Louise nee Schueler; b 1900; m Hilda Murken of Boone, IA. Atkins, IA residence, later farmed Boone, IA; moved to Cedar Rapids, IA. Children:

Eleanor – NFR
Norma – NFR

*Tobias SCHUELER s/o Johannes Schüler & A. nee Landau; b 19 Mar 1858 Löhlbach, Germany, d 1937 Atkins, IA; 1st m 23 Apr 1882 Löhlbach Ch Germany to Caroline Ritter (b 30 Dec 1857 Löhlbach Germany, d prob 1896 IA). Children:

*Anna Elisabeth – b 09 Dec 1882 Löhlbach, Germany
*Johann Heinrich – b 20 Mar 1884 Löhlbach, Germany
*Nicolaus – b 09 Mar 1886 Löhlbach, Germany
*Caroline – b 09 May 1888 Löhlbach, Germany
Luise Elisabeth – b 12 Jul 1890 Löhlbach
Löhlbach Ch records show this family emigrated pro 1896 to USA; farmers Benton Co IA.
2nd m Tobias Schueler to Milda Schaefer (b 1866, d 1949). 1922 retired in Atkins, IA. Children:

Hattie – b 1898, d 1979; m Sturley May
George – b 1899; m Elsie Hanneman, Van Horne, IA
William – b 1902; m Olive Schultz
Frances Magdalene Elizabeth Anna – b 26 Jan 1905, d 31 Dec 1968;
    m 16 Nov 1926 Elmer Henry John Keiper

*Wilhelmina SCHULER d/o Andreas Schüler & Anna Elisabeth nee Krug; b 10 Oct 1824 Löhlbach, Germany, Hse #70, d 18 Nov 1882 ae58y 1m 8d Löhlbach; m 16 Jan 1848 Löhlbach Ch to Andreas Hohl (b 03 Apr 1821 Löhlbach, Germany, d 28 Nov 1875 ae54y 7m 25d Löhlbach, Germany). Children:

*Paulus Hohl – b 13 Nov 1848, d 17 Jun 1931; 1st m 16 Feb 1873;
    2nd m 20 Apr 1912 Wilma Karoline Dippel
    (b 13 Mar 1872, d 20 Apr 1934)
Anna Elisabeth Hohl – b 11 Feb 1851 Löhlbach, Germany
Johann Justus Hohl – b 20 Sept 1854 Löhlbach, Germany
Heinrich Hohl – b 04 Aug 1852, d 04 Dec 1938;
    m 08 Feb 1889 Cath. Beyer
Wilhelmina Hohl – b 24 Jan 1861, d 05 Feb 1861 Löhlbach, Germany

Randal Lee SCHULTZ s/o Nadine Ann nee Maurer & Larry Dean Schultz; b 10 Nov 1959 Sacramento CA; m 28 Dec 1985 Decorah, IA. to Ruth Ann Hove. Occupation: C.P.A. Law Degree S.U.I. Child:

Lauren Marie – NFR

Robert Dean SCHULTZ s/o Nadine Ann nee Maurer & Larry Dean Schultz; b 27 Jan 1962 St.Lukes Hosp Cedar Rapids, IA; m 27 Oct 1984 Ft. Dodge, IA to Sheryl LaValley. Children:

Andrew Robert – b 27 Apr 1987 Des Moines, IA
Tyler James – b 1988

Arnold G. SCHULZ s/o Elmer Schulz & Clara nee Werning; b 26 Jul 1915, d 11 Jan 1985 ae69y 5m 17d; m 14 May 1944 Susie Schamber (b 02 Aug 1919) d/o George Schamber & Helen nee Staller. Children:
Janelle – b 06 Nov 1946; m 1970 Norman Custer; Line, NE
Lynn Arnold – b 09 Mar 1957; m 1984 Jolene Heezen; Miller, SD

Janelle SCHULZ d/o Arnold G. Schulz & Susie nee Schamber; b 06 Nov 1946; m 06 Jun 1970 Lime, NE to Norman Custer (b 09 Apr 1940) s/o Seaman Custer of Oshkosh, NE.

Lynn Arnold SCHULZ s/o Arnold G. Schulz & Susie nee Schamber; b 09 Mar 1957; m 30 Mar 1984 Jolene Heezen of Miller, SD. Emery, SD residence. Child:
(Son) – b 29 Dec 1986

Walter SCHULZ s/o Elmer Schulz & Clara nee Werning; b 31 Jan 1923 Clayton, SD, d 25 Jan 1984 ae60y 11m 25d Aberdeen, SD military bur Parkston SD Cem; m 09 Jun 1957 Redfield SD to Lois Thomas (b 20 Jul 1923, d 13 Jun 1978 ae54y 10m 23d) d/o Samuel Thomas & Augusta nee Kroning. Taught school 15 years before work with FMHA office in 1966. World War II Army, Pierre, SD; VFW. Member Ft.Pierre Moose Lodge. Children:
Leann Marie – b 17 Oct 1958; Viborg, SD
Karen – b 15 Nov 1959; Rapid City, SD
Myrna Lou – b 28 Feb 1961;
m 1978 Donald Schladweiler; Brookings, SD
Marlene Kaye – b 18 Jun 1962; Brookings, SD

John SEECK s/o Thies Seeck JR. & Cacilie nee Albers; b 1871, d 1919; m Margaret Balhorn (b 1871, d 1953). Children:
Cecilia – b 1891, d 1969; m William Junge
Carl – b 1894, d 1969; m Edna Schliemann. Children: Wilbert, Lavon
(m Selk), Mardean (m NN Kromminga), John
Emma Esther – b 20 Dec 1898; b 20 Dec 1898;
m 12 Mar 1918 Louie Junge
Hilda – b 1902, d 1950; m Peter Junge. Children: Lola (m Bossler),
Marlys (m Papesh), Corley, Betty (m Kapucian),
Helen (m Jurgens), Mariann (m Fay), Janice (m Sievers),
Shirley (m Peters)
Mable – b 1909; m Clement Bevins. Children: Kathleen (m Novak),

Doris (m Osborn), Ilene (m Strellner), Edward
Esther – b 1909; m Robert Bender.
Anna – m Frank Mussman (b 1871, d 1955); raised Louise
(m Shellenberger) and Arthur

*Margaretha SEECK d/o Thies Heinrich Seeck SR. & Margaret nee Lahan; b 1845 Germany, d 1925 IA; m 1867 Scott Co IA to Eggert Offt. Moved to Benton Co IA; farmers until 1903 move to Keystone, IA. Children:
William Offt – b 1868, d 1956
Susana "Lena" Offt – b 1870, d 1965; m Seebrandt
Anna Offt – b 1872, d 1968; m Eichmeyer
Laura Offt – b 1874, d 1962; m Jammer
Emma Offt – b 1876, d 1974; m Stein
Alfred Offt – b 1877, d 1956
Gustav Offt – b 1879, d 1935
Herman Offt – b 1881, d 1917

*Peter SEECK s/o Thies Heinrich Seeck SR. & Margaret nee Lahan; b 1838 Germany; 1858 emigrated to Scott Co. IA; enlisted in Civil War; settled in Cedar Co IA; 1868 moved to Homer Twp Benton Co IA; m Christina Meyer. Children:
Lena – dec'd infancy
Gustaf – b 1875, d 1964; m Gertrude Shireman, Son: Peter Charles
Ferdinanduait – b 1877, d 1957; m Deborah Collins,
Daughter: Christine
Herman – b 1880, d 1950; Daughter: Carma
Peter – b 1881, d 1943; m Martha Harder, Children: Roy;
Mildred (Slaymaker)

*Thies SEECK JR. s/o Thies Heinrich Seeck SR. & Margaret nee Lahan; b 1842 Germany, d 1923 Benton Co IA; m Cacilie Albers (b 1849, d 1932). Eight children (two lived to adulthood):
John – b 1871, d 1919; m Margaret Balhorn
Anna – b 1875, d 1924

*Thies Heinrich SEECK SR. b 1809 Wohrden, Schleswig-Holstein, Germany, d pro 1870; 1864 emigrated with Thies JR. and Margaretha to Scott Co IA; 1868 moved to Homer Twp Benton Co IA; m in Wohrden, Schleswig-Holstein, Germany, to Margaret Lahan (b 1806 Germany, d 1860 in Germany). Children:

*Claus – b 1832 Germany, d 1855 Benton Co IA; emigrated before father

*Peter Matthies – b 1838 Germany, d 1916 IA; emigrated before father

*Anna – b 1834 Germany, d 1917; emigrated 1865; m Johann Peters, six children; 1911 moved to SD

*Wiebke – b 1840 Germany, d 1921; m Jakob Boge; emigrated 1868

*Thies JR. – b 1842 Germany, d 1923 IA; m Cacilie Albers

*Margaretha – b 1845 Germany, d 1925 IA

Carroll W. SEEMAN s/o Emmett Seeman & Mary Ann nee Sindt; b 14 Jun 1921, d 23 Jan 2000 ae78y 7m 9d bur CdrMem; m Marilyn Meyer d/o Glen Meyer & Velma nee Schulze. Started farming 1947. Children:

Lon Carroll – b 1946; m Mary Marquardt

Larry Glen – b 1950, d 1962

Tracy Lee – b 1960; m Janelle NN

Charles E. SEEMAN s/o Emmett Seeman & Mary Ann nee Sindt; b 1930; US Army Korean Conflict; 2nd m 1966 Ardis Frieden (b 1930) d/o William Frieden & Eliza nee Moor of Elgin. Newhall, IA residence; Plumbing, heating and well business. Children:

Jeff – b 1962

Mary – b 1969

Sherry – b 1970

Donna SEEMAN d/o Emmett Seeman & Mary Ann nee Sindt; b 1925; m Arnold Haar (b 1919) s/o Fred & Emma Haar. Farmers beginning 1950. Children:

Janet Marie Haar – b 1951

Steve A. Haar – b 1955; m Katherine Ternus, Son: Jared (b 1979)

Emmett SEEMAN s/o Emma nee Zornig & August Seeman; b 1898, d 1980; m Mary Ann Sindt (b 1897) d/o William Sindt & Katherine nee Wunder. Farmers near Newhall, IA. Children:

Carroll W. – b 14 Jun 1921 Eldorado Twp Benton Co IA, d 23 Jan 2000 bur CdrMem; m 06 May 1944 Marilyn Meyer

Donna M. – b 1925; m Arnold Haar

Charles E. – b 1910; 2nd m 1966 Ardis Frieden

Lon Carroll SEEMAN s/o Carroll W. Seeman & Marilyn nee Meyer; b 1946; m Mary Marquardt. Newhall, IA residence. Children:

Brian Glen – b 1973; m Jennifer
Bree Janel – b 1977

Debra Sue SELKEN d/o Donna Mae nee Krug & Donald Gene Selken; b 28 Mar 1959 Cedar Rapids, IA bpt 19 Apr 1959 Keystone, IA St.John Luth Ch; 1st m 11 Mar 1978 Rick Selk DVD; 2nd m 13 Aug 1984 Douglas Yates (b 15 May 1956). Children:
Daniella Kay Yates – b 06 Sept 1986
Mathew D. Yates – b 30 Mar 1990

Dianne Marie SELKEN d/o Donna Mae nee Krug & Donald Gene Selken; b 20 Jul 1962, bpt 1962 Keystone, IA St.John Luth Ch; m 17 Apr 1982 St.John Luth Ch, Keystone to Thomas Edward Barfels (b 25 Jul 1962) s/o Thomas Barfels. Children:
Lauren Elizabeth Barfels – b 08 May 1988
Erin Barfels – b 19 Feb 1991

Amanda SENNE d/o John Senne & Katherine nee Kerkman; b 1884, d 1949; m Carl Lehrer Detlefsen (b 1888, d 1959). Children:
Ruth Katherine Detlefsen – b 1909, d 1911
Paula Eliza Detlefsen – b 1910; m Edgar Rutz
Paul Detlefsen – b 1912, d 1971; m Leona Schumann
Walter Detlefsen – b 1914, 1974; m Ida Wolter
Ruth Detlefsen – b 1915; m Harold Kammerer
Ada Marie Detlefsen – b 1919; m Robert Henry Traver
Lois Detlefsen – b 1925; m Richard Marks

Arthur SENNE s/o August Senne & Anna nee Berkholtz; b 1908, d 1973; m Lillian Edlund (b 1908, d 1996). Children:
Janet Ann – b 1936; m Virgil Bluhm (b 1937). Children:
1. Steven Lee Bluhm (b 1956); m Raelene Probst (b 1958). Children:
Nathan Andrew Bluhm (b 1985), Matthew Steven Bluhm (b 1991), Alison Lynel Bluhm (b 1992)
2. Kevin Dale Bluhm (b 1959); m Karen Jensen. Children:
Kelie Kay Bluhm (b 1983), Kindra Ann Bluhm (b 1986)
3. Brandon Charles Scott Bluhm (b 1973)
Sandra Kay – b 1940; m Dr. Samuel G. Kinser (b 1931). Children:
1. Lawrence Kinser (b 1963); m Carol Cahill (b 1967),
2. Ralph Kinser (b 1965)

Karen Sue – b 1942; m Richard Nice (b 1941). Children:
  1. Richard David Nice (b 1971), 2. Matthew Walter Nice (b 1974),
  3. Susan Cayle Nice (b 1979)
Patty Jo – b 1945; m Cecil Wetsel (b 1944). Children:
  1. Julie Anne Wetsel (b 1973), 2. Ryan Wetsel (b 1975),
  3. Kindra Jo Wetsel (b 1979)
Terry – b 1949

August SENNE s/o John Senne & Katherine nee Kerkman; b 1878, d 1936; m Anna Berkholtz (b 1882, d 1947). Children:
  Arthur – b 1908, d 1973; d Lillian Edlund
  Herbert – b 1912; m Nathine Montgomery
  Laurine – b 1917; m Orville Mooberry

*Conrad SENNE b/d Germany; m Katherine (b Germany, d Benton Co IA; Children:
  *John – b 1845 Rodenberg, Germany, d 1928 Benton Co IA;
    m Katherine Kerkman
  *Henry Christop – b Germany; d USA; m NFR;
    Son Titus Matthew Senne; m Martha Scheele
  *Son – b Germany, d USA
  *Son – b Germany, d USA

Fred SENNE s/o John Senne & Katherine nee Kerkman; b 1870, d 1946; m 1897 Elsie M. Bierschenk (b 1872, d 1924) d/o Jacob Bierschenk & Anna Martha nee George. Farmed Eden Twp Benton Co IA farm until his parents moved to Newhall, IA and purchased farm from his father; fourth generation of family farm ownership. Children:
  Herman – b 1899, d 1967; m Elfrieda M. Kranz
    d/o Adam Kranz & Emma nee Emmick
  Irene K. – b 1902, d 1952; m Ervin J. Lauterwasser
  Hilda – b 27 Oct 1906, d 1996; m 12 Feb 1929 Paul Werning
    s/o Anton & Alice nee Nell
  Agnes Emma – b 1912, d 1980; m 02 Oct 1935 Meril Albert Koopman
  Elnora – b 1915, d 1916
  Lillian – b 18 Jun 1917, d 15 Aug 2005 Newhall IA. Never Married

Hannah SENNE d/o John Senne & Katherine nee Kerkman; b 1887, d 1967; m John N. Gluesing (b 1887, d 1970). Children:
  Gilbert Gluesing – b 1912, d 2003; m 1934 Madeline Weichman

Paul Gluesing – b 1915; m Normal Voeltz
Helen Gluesing – b 1923, d 1996; m John Schreckengast

Herbert SENNE s/o August Senne & Anna nee Berkholtz; b 1912; m Nathine Montgomery (b 1923). Children:
 Richard – b 1950, d 1978
 Paul – b 1953, d 1963
 Beth Carla – b 1956; m Mark Lindsay Duff (b 1957). Child:
  Allen Walker Duff (b 1991)

Herman SENNE s/o Fred Senne & Elsie M. nee Bierschenk: cf Elfrieda Kranz.

Hilda SENNE d/o Fred Senne & Elsie M. nee Bierschenk: cf Paul Werning.

Irene K. SENNE d/o Fred Senne & Elsie M. nee Bierschenk: cf Ervin J. Lauterwasser.

*John SENNE s/o Conrad & Katherine NN, Germany; b 1845 Rodenberg, Germany, d 1928 Benton Co IA bur St.John Cem; 1857 emigrated ae12y with his mother, four brothers, and settled in KS; 1868 naturalized U.S. citizen; m 1869 Luzerne, Benton Co IA to Katherine Kerkman (b 1850 near Chicago, IL, d 1941 bur St.John Cem) d/o Johan Conrad Kerkman & Anna Martha nee Werning Shumacher. Lived with her parents for several years three miles west and one and one-half miles north of Newhall, IA; moved to farm in Eden Twp Benton Co IA three miles northwest of her parent's farm. When oldest son married, moved to farm purchased in 1893, four and one-half miles northwest of Newhall, IA where they lived until 1905 or 1906 retirement in Newhall, IA. Children:
 Fred – b 1870, d 1946; m Elsie M. Bierschenk
 Daughter – b/d 1872
 Daughter – b/d 1873
 (Mary) Maria – b 1874, d 1959; m William Paulsen
 Anna – b 1876, d 1963; Never Married
 August – b 1878, d 1936; m Anna Berkholtz
 Martha – b 1881, d 1966; 1st m Conrad Hereth; 2nd m Henry Luiten
 Emma Mina Dorothea – b 1882, d 1952; m 1903 Julius Ernst Taschner
 Amanda – b 1884, d 1949; m Carl Detlefsen
 Hannah – b 1887, d 1967; m John Gluesing
 Olga – b 1889, d 1958; m George Schornack

Laurine SENNE d/o August Senne & Anna nee Berkholtz; b 1917; m Orville Mooberry (b 1920). Children:
    David Mooberry – b 1947; m Joan Chou (b 1947)
    Anne Mooberry – b 1950; m Kenneth Cecil Lamb (b 1948)
        Children: Heather Elsia Lamb (b 1976), Monica Lamb (b 1976)
    Mark Mooberry – b 1952, d 1971

Maria (Mary) SENNE d/o John Senne & Katherine nee Kerkman; b 1874, 1959; m William Paulsen (b 1875, d 1955). Children:
    Arnold Paulsen – b/d 1900
    Frieda Paulsen – b 1901, d 1988; m William Warner
    Irma Paulsen – b 1902, d 1999; m Espa Jones
    Eldo Paulsen – b 1903, d 1980; m Sophia Schnarr
    Olga Paulsen – b 1906
    Mildred Paulsen – b 1910, d 1999; m Ray Meyer
    Emily Paulsen – b 1915, d 1977; m Fred Lange

Martha SENNE d/o John Senne & Katherine nee Kerkman; b 1881, d 1966; 1ST m Conrad Hereth (b 1880, d 1987). Children:
    Esther Hereth – b 1907, d 1987; m Harold Simpson
    Martha Hereth – b 1909; m Henry Brandes
    Ruth Hereth – b 1911; m Carl Koss
    Marie Hereth – b 1913; m Arthur Schatz
    TWINS   Lois Hereth – b 1916, d 1988; m Eugene Wisman
                Lydia Hereth – b 1916, d 1922
2nd m Martha Senne to Henry Luiten (b 1874, d 1954)

Olga SENNE d/o John Senne & Katherine nee Kerkman; b 1889, d 1958; m George Schornack (b 1891, d 1959). Children:
    Harold Schornack – b 1914; m Agnes Svarstad
    Howard Schornack – b 1915; m Harriet Paulson
    Doris Schornack – b 1919; m Donald Craig
    Allen Donald Schornack – b 1931; m Marilyn Miller

Anna SIEPMANN d/o William Siepmann & Gertrude nee Flammang; b 1900, d 1968; m Chicago to Delbert Garwood (b 1901, d 1950). Delbert employed 23 years in Norway, IA for Northwestern Railroad. Children:
    George Garwood – NFR
    Marcella Garwood – m NN Olson

Raymond – Garwood dec'd
Virgil Garwood – NFR
Bernadine Garwood – m NN Marks, dec'd
Merle Garwood – NFR
Illa Garwood – m to NN Duncalf
Dennis Garwood – NFR
Jane Garwood – to NN Himmelsbach

Helen SIEPMANN d/o William Siepmann & Gertrude nee Flammang; b 1898, d 1981; m St.Michael's Ch, Norway, IA to Louis Redelmann. Farmers Waltkins, IA and Norway, IA area; moved to Davenport, IA, Louis: caretaker; Helen: caterer. Child:
Gilbert Redelmann – Chicago, IL residence

Henry SIEPMANN s/o William Siepmann & Gertrude nee Flammang; b 1894, d 1972; 1st m Maybelle McIntier of Belle Plaine, IA (d 1955). Cedar Rapids, IA residence, owner/operator CeMar Roller Skating Rink. Children:
Mary Roberta – NFR
Miriam – NFR
Marvel – NFR
Wayne – NFR
2nd m Henry Siepmann to Mabel Swank; Cedar Rapids, IA residence.

Kate SIEPMANN d/o William Siepmann & Gertrude nee Flammang; b 1887, d 1917; m Tony Miller. Norway, IA residence. Children:
Gilbert Miller – dec'd in infancy
William F. Miller – m Rita Lavelle
Frederick "Fritz" Miller – m Zerelda Barth. Children: Roslyn, Donna, Sally, Caroline; Baraboo, WI residence

Mary SIEPMANN d/o William Siepmann & Gertrude nee Flammang; b 1885 Blairstown, IA d 1940; m 1903 St.Michael's Ch, Norway, IA to John Trojovsky (b 1884, d 1948) s/o Charles Trojovsky & Lena nee Walters. Farmers south of Norway, IA; moved into Norway where John worked for Denniston & Partridge Lumber Yard. Children:
Victor Trojovsky – m Ann Nicola; Children: Orrene, Joanne, Kenneth, Donald; Washington, IA residence
Esther Trojovsky – m 1925 Lloyd Primrose; Children: Robert, Susan, Harold, Gayle; Norway, IA residence
Annette Trojovsky – 1st m Ray Jammer, Keystone, IA;

2nd m George Collignon, Davenport, IA
Harold Trojovsky – m Lorraine Glenn; Children: Hal JR., Jim, Lynn,
    Mary Kay; Harold: Cleveland Indians & White Sox
    Big League Baseball player.

*William SIEPMANN s/o Albert Siepmann & Wilhelmena nee Lang; b 1858 Oberhouse-on-der-Rhine, Germany, d 1928 Benton Co IA; 1880 emigrated to NY; m 1883 in Buffalo, NY to Gertrude Flammang (b 1858, d 1925). 1884 moved to Tipton, IA; 1885 moved to Blairstown, IA; 1887 moved to Norway, IA owning and operating Siepmann Meat Market and milk delivery route. Children:
    Mary – b 1885, d 1940; m 1903 John Trojovsky
    Kate – b 1887, d 1917; m Tony Miller
    John – b 1890, d 1933; butcher in Norway, IA & Sioux City, IA
    Henry – b 1894, d 1972; m Maybelle McIntier
    Bernard – b 1898, d 1974; butcher Norway,IA & Isabel, SD
    Helen – b 1898, d 1981; m Louis Redelman
    Anna – b 1900, d 1968; m Delbert Garwood

Katherine Ambrosia SIERRA d/o Rita Ann nee Campbell & Timothy Lawrence Sierra; b 31 Mar 1977; m 10 Dec 1993 Joseph Clarence Walters V (b 22 Apr 1974). Children:
    Joseph Clarence Walters VI – b 21 Mar 1994
    Michael Timothy Walters – b 01 Jul 1995

Harold SIMPSON b 1904, d 1984; m Esther Hereth (b 1907, d 1987) d/o Martha nee Senne & Conrad Hereth. Children:
    Patricia – b 1926; m Morris Beckmeyer (b 1925). Children:
        1. James (b 1950); 1st m Debra Jeanne Anderson (b 1951);
        2nd m Deborah Delappe. Children: Jennifer Beckmeyer (b1984),
        Megan Elizbeth Beckmeyer (b1986), Kelsey Marie Beckmeyer
        (b 1988)
        2. John Beckmeyer (b 1952)
        3. Robert Beckmeyer (b 1955)
        4. Roger Allen Beckmeyer (b 1961)
    Gladine – b 1928; m Joe Borek (b 1924). Children: 1. Karen Borek
        (b 1949); m David Burke (b 1946). Children: Jason David Burke
        (b 1972), Shana Nicole Burke (b1975)
        2. Keith Borek (b 1951); m Dawn Skindzeil (b 1957). Child:
        Spencer Lane Borek (b 1990)

3. David Borek (b 1956)

Suzanne – b 1929; m James Smith (b 1927, d 1999). Children:
1. Sallie Jane Smith (b 1955); m Christianson
2. Nancy Jo Smith (b 1958); m Michael Helm. Children: Katherine Ann Helm (b1983), Rebecca Helm (b 1986), James Helm (b 1988)
3. Molly Jean Smith (b 1962); 1st m David Maynard. Child: Zachary Maynard (b 1985); 2nd m Jeffery Blaylock

Margaret – b/d 1932

Dale SINDT s/o Lester Sindt & Dorothy nee Sullivan; b 27 Mar 1946; m Carmen Espinoza. Grayslake, IL residence. Children:
Dale Berendt – NFR
Kelly – NFR

Darwin SINDT s/o Lester Sindt & Dorothy nee Sullivan; b 31 Jul 1942; US Navy career before retiring in San Diego, CA; m Jean Nishaharo. Children:
Sheila – m John Loftus
Gregory – NFR
Darin – NFR

Judith SINDT d/o Lester Sindt & Dorothy nee Sullivan; b 04 Mar 1944; m Terry Hertle. Eden Twp Benton Co IA farmers. Children:
Kevin Hertle – NFR
Denise Hertle – NFR

Lester SINDT s/o Henry J. Sindt & Margaret nee Albers; b 04 Oct 1914 near Keystone, IA; Keystone High School; m 28 Dec 1938 Keystone, IA to Dorothy Sullivan (b 06 Feb 1920; Belle Plaine High School) d/o Ray Sullivan & Rosie nee Sklennar. Children:
Duane – b 12 Sept 1939; m Linda Cornutt
Darwin – b 31 Jul 1942; m Jean Nishaharo
Judith – b 04 Mar 1944; m Terry Hertle
Dale – b 27 Mar 1946; m Carmen Espinoza

*Anton "Tony" H. SIMNACHER s/o Joseph Simnacher & Josephine nee Nauer; b 1905 Donauworth, Germany; d 1978 Benton Co IA; 1925 emigrated to Benton Co IA; 1937 naturalized USA citizen; m 1934 Myrtle Ness d/o Hans Ness. Benton Co IA farmers. Children:
Robert – b 27 Dec 1936; m 1956 Phyllis Martin DVD

Bonnie – b 19 May 1939; 1st m 1963 Myron Richart
Gary – b 02 Sept 1945; m 1967 Loretta Lorenz

Bonnie SIMNACHER d/o Anton "Tony" H. Simnacher & Myrtle nee Ness; b 19 May 1939; 1st m 1963 Myron Richart. Children:
Kristi Richart – b 1964; m 1986 Steve Albright
Gena Richart – b 1967; m 1986 Jeff Downs
Tony Richart – b 1974

Gary SIMNACHER s/o Anton "Tony" H. Simnacher & Myrtle nee Ness; b 02 Sept 1945; m 1967 Loretta Lorenz. Children:
Lisa – b 1970
Lori – b 1972

Robert SIMNACHER s/o Anton "Tony" H. Simnacher & Myrtle nee Ness; b 27 Dec 1936; m 1956 Phyllis Martin, DVD. Children:
Becky – b 1957; m 1978 Brian Clark, son: Joshua – b 1981
Kevin – b 1960

David Peter SKERSICK s/o Marie Elizabeth nee Moeller & Kenneth Gerald Skersick; b 02 Oct 1938; Orthodonist, San Juan Capistrano, CA; 1st m 17 Aug 1963 Susan Ruth Bunker (b 28 Mar 1943)DVD 1975. Children:
Tracy Lynn – b 14 Dec 1968; m 22 Apr 1994 Seth Kenney, CA residence
Dayna lee – b 01 Sept 1970; m 05 Jan 1995 Rudy Camarena
(b 07 May 1970)
Michael David – b 15 Mar 1972
2nd m 08 Oct 1976 David Peter Skerick to Sara Post Maxwell (b 17 Nov 1938 Interior Design Studio). San Clemente, CA residence.

Richard Kenneth SKERSICK s/o Marie Elizabeth nee Moeller & Kenneth Gerald Skersick; b 25 Jul 1943; Lt.Col. US Air Force, Ret; 1st m 25 Dec 1970 Christie Cameron Smith (b 08 Mar 1947)DVD 1978. Children:
Karen Marie – b 16 Feb 1974
2nd m 10 Aug 1981 Richard Kenneth Skersick to Pamela Wurzbacher (b 26 Oct 1946) Ft.Worth, TX residence.

William SLOVAK s/o Earl Slovak & Helen nee Harnisch; b 06 Jul 1955; m 22 Apr 1982 Pennie Lou Hamm (26 Dec 1956) d/o Leo & Audrey Hamm. Children:

Belinda Lou – b 29 Sept 1983
Brock Charles – b 05 Nov 1985
Bo William – b 01 Aug 1987

Allen Jane SMITH s/o Mildred nee Juhnke & Curt Smith; b 09 Aug 1962; m 07 Jun 1986 Carla Williams. Child:
Jessica Jo – b 09 Nov 1988

Chris Jay SMITH s/o Mildred nee Juhnke & Curt Smith; b 24 Mar 1961; m 03 Sept 1983 Lisa Christine Shanks of Nora Springs, IA. Children:
Chas Jorden – b 05 Nov 1986
Megan Ashley – b 09 Apr 1989

Jeanette Ann SMITH d/o Mildred nee Juhnke & Curt Smith; b 07 Jan 1964; m 08 Aug 1982 Kevin Wheeler of Clear Lake, IA. Child:
Lonnie Wheeler – b 15 Nov 1983

C.W.E. SNYDER s/o F.E. Snyder & Angeline nee Monismith; U. of Iowa law degree; m Jennie Furnas d/o John Furnas. Benton Co IA doctor. Children:
Lois – Beverly Hills, CA residence
Merle – U. of Iowa medical degree
Donald – U. of Iowa medical degree
Edward – m Mary Ella Blue. Children: Mary Louise, Edward, Ralph
Wallace F. – b 1907; m 1933 Mildred Johnson

*F.E. SNYDER b 1835 Germany; 1851 emigrated to USA ae16y; m 1858 Angeline Monismith. Moved to Belle Plaine, IA soon after town was founded in 1864; Belle Plaine, IA mortician and furniture store business; 1882 F.E. Snyder elected Mayor of Belle Plaine, IA. Children:
Emma – dec'd in infancy
Susan Adeline – dec'd ae11y
Ella – FL resident
C.W.E. – m Jennie Furnas

Wallace F. SNYDER s/o C.W.E. Snyder & Jennie nee Furnas; b 1907 Belle Plaine, IA; d 1944 US Army Captain World War II [Killed in Action in English Channel]; U.of Iowa law degree; m 1933 Mildred Johnson. Children:
Suzanne – Cedar Rapids IA Community Schools educator

Wallace Stephen – Washington D.C. lawyer

Gary Melvin SOUTO s/o Carol Marie nee Rammelsberg & William Souto;
b 04 Sept 1961; m 04 Jul 1986 Robin Lane. Child:
David Lane –b 06 Mar 1992

Jeffrey Nelson SOUTO s/o Carol Marie nee Rammelsberg & William
Souto; b 28 Feb 1960; m 22 Nov 1986 Suzanne Ryan. Children:
Carol Marie – 03 Jun 1988
Jackson Lee – b 18 Jan 1993

Karla STANDRIDGE d/o Leona nee Schmidt & Henry Standridge; b 01
Jun 1959; m 03 Oct 1987 Matthew Cole (b 01 Sept 1957). Children:
Henry Standridge Cole – b 21 Jan 1992
Geneva Valarie Cole – b 18 Oct 1993

Lori Sue STANEK d/o Doris Elaine nee Bayer & Marvin Stanek; b 15 May
1963 Cedar Rapids, IA; m 27 Nov 1993 Robert Newton. Child:
Katherine Jo Newton – b 11 Mar 1995

Wesley David STANEK s/o Doris Elaine nee Bayer & Marvin Stanek; b 30
Mar 1965 Cedar Rapids, IA; m 19 Sept 1992 Cyndi Holleman. Children:
Andrew Devin – b 16 Jul 1992
Alan Jerome – b 03 Aug 1993
Aaron Wesley – b Mar 1995

Craig Wayne STEEGE s/o DeWayne Steege & Delores Marie nee Happel;
b 13 Jan 1949; m 04 Oct 1980 Ann Hageman. Children:
Jenner Elizabeth – b 01 Sept 1985
Eden Ann – b 05 Jun 1989

Darlene STEEGE d/o Reinhardt Steege & Elsie nee Happel; b 08 Dec 1938;
1st m 18 Sept 1960 Leonard Leisinger (b 27 Dec 1935, d 21 May 1983).
Children:
Martha Leisinger – b 15 May 1964;
m 25 May 1985 James Lageschulte (b 07 Oct 1958)
Leah Leisinger – b 28 Mar 1966, d 17 Apr 1967
Barbara Leisinger – b 26 Apr 1968
Cheryl Leisinger – b 04 Apr 1972; m 06 Jun 1992 Brent Hagen
(b 25 Jan 1972)

Keith Leisinger – b 04 Apr 1974
2nd m 11 May 1985 Darlene nee Steege Leisinger to Ray Smith (b 25 Sept 1929).

David Lee STEEGE s/o DeWayne Steege & Delores Marie nee Happel; b 15 Aug 1950; m 18 Oct 1975 Debbie Knipfel (b 29 Jul 1954). Children:
STEPCHILD: Tamara Kay Knipfel – b 04 Jan 1972
Erika Marie – b 08 Jan 1979

Debra Ann STEEGE d/o Leroy Steege & Wilma Malinda nee Happel; b 23 Sept 1950; m 19 Oct 1968 Duane Paul St.John (b 11 Dec 1946). Children:
Stacie Lyn St.John – b 18 Dec 1969
Patrick Ryan St.John – b 20 Jul 1974
Cara Nicole St.John – b 01 Sept 1979

Donna Mae STEEGE d/o Reinhardt Fred Steege & Elsie Minnie nee Happel; b 14 Feb 1946; m 20 May 1947 Larry French (b 29 Jun 1946, d 08 Jan 1997). Children:
Lori French – b 10 May 1968; m Thomas Jeffrey Prince III
Michelle French – b 20 Nov 1970; m 18 Sept 1993 Anthony Hanks
    (b 04 Dec 1968)

Gregory Lynn STEEGE s/o Leroy Steege & Wilma Malinda nee Happel; b 08 Aug 1947; m 27 Aug 1969 Susan Mae Wente (b 25 Oct 1949). Children:
Brent Gregory – b 21 Aug 1971
Ben – b 28 May 1985

Jolyne Kay STEEGE d/o Leroy Steege & Wilma Malinda nee Happel; b 31 Jan 1954; m 06 Apr 1973 Daniel Matthias DVD 22 Oct 1975. Children:
Wendy Lynne Matthias – b 28 Sept 1973
Christopher Matthias – b 30 Jan 1976

Mark Leroy STEEGE s/o Leroy Steege & Wilma Malinda nee Happel; b 30 Apr 1960; m 21 Aug 1982 Teresa Kosted (b 19 Feb 1961). Children:
Scott Andrew – b 23 May 1989
Michelle Renee – b 17 Jul 1990

Eldo William STEIN s/o Henry Stein & Doris nee Burmeister; b 20 Sept 1896 Homer Twp Benton Co IA, d 14 Mar 1932 ae35y 5m 22d; m 21 Sept 1921 Vinton, IA to Hilda Mary Jacobs of Keystone, IA (b 01 Jun 1899

Keystone, IA d 26 Aug 1952) d/o John Jacobs & Augusta nee Mess. Benton Co IA farmers. Children:

Elmer Eldon – b 07 Oct 1926

Mardean Hilda – b 10 Aug 1928

Elmer Eldon STEIN s/o Eldo William Stein & Hilda Mary nee Jacobs; b 07 Oct 1926, Class 1944 Dysart High School; m 22 Sept 1952 Zion Luth Ch, Dysart, IA to Beverly Mae Higgins of Belle Plaine, IA (b 30 Sept 1934 Homer, NE). Benton Co IA farmers. Children:

Brenda – b 1954; m 22 May 1976 Gary Krause.

Children: Michael, Eric, Heather

Gregory – b 1956; m 02 Sept 1978 Catherine Lough.

Sons: Chad, Darren

Darby – b 1958; m 11 Oct 1980 Renee Haefner. Children: Lisa, Brett, Cindy

Randy – b 1961; m 10 Aug 1985 June Covington

Pamela – b 1966; m 13 Sept 1986 Rodney Hare

*Henry STEIN b 25 Aug 1851 Besitz, Mecklenberg, Germany; emigrated with parents ae2y to Davenport, IA; ae17y moved to Keystone, Benton Co IA to farm; m 10 Nov 1874 Vinton, IA to Doris Burmeister (b 02 Jan 1856 Besitz, Mecklenberg, Germany; emigrated ae13y with parents to Davenport, IA then Keystone, IA). Benton Co farmers. Children:

Louis – b 1875, d 1944

Emma – b 1877, d 1935

Alvena – b 1880, d 1941

Anna – b 1882, d 1884

John – b 1884, d 1953

Henry JR. – b 1888, d 1941

Amanda – b 1892, d 1961

Eldo William – b 20 Sept 1896, d 1932

Kay STEIN d/o Wayne A. Stein & Maxine nee Marigold; b 1953; m Mark McMann. Williamsburg, IA residence. Children:

Jodi McMann – NFR

Mike McMann – NFR

Larry STEIN s/o Wayne A. Stein & Maxine nee Marigold; b 1951; m Nancy Clayton. Prior Lake, MN residence. Children:

Wade – NFR

Nathan – NFR
Jessica – NFR

Wayne A. STEIN s/o Albert Stien & Rose nee Hickey; b 1926; US Navy World War II; member of Newhall Fire Department; postal clerk and Newhall Postmaster appointed 1956, retired 1981; m 1949 Maxine Marigold, Newhall teacher, 1961 part-time Postal clerk and 1981 Newhall, IA Postmaster. Children:
>   Greg – b 1950; Mesa, AZ residence
>   Larry – b 1951; m Nancy Clayton; Prior Lake, MN residence
>   Kay – b 1953; m Mark McMann; Williamsburg, IA residence
>   Cindy-b 1956; 1st m Steve Bell; 2nd m Dale Dugenske,
>   Daughter: Amanda
>   Joseph – b 1961; South Bend, IN residence
>   Janice – b 1966; Cedar Rapids, IA residence

Albert "Beanie" STIEN s/o Heldt Stien & Anna Bowers-Baumgartner; b 1899, d 1966; ae4y when mother died; early childhood with half-sister, Anna (Mrs. Fred Weichman); teenage years ventured into livestock buying business with A.A. Boddicker, later with Bill Freeman shipped cattle by rail from Newhall, IA to Chicago, proving unsuccessful in post-World War I economy. Employed Benton Co IA road maintenance over thirty years until retirement. Served on Newhall, IA Fire Department and Newhall Town Council; m 1920 Rose Hickey (b 1899, d 1979) d/o William Hickey & Ellen nee McCormick of Van Horne, IA. Children:
>   Warren – Music Teacher Ionia, MI
>   Wayne A. – b 1926; Newhall, IA Postmaster; m Maxine Mangold

Darlene Mary STIEN d/o Richard Stien & Mary nee Dvorak: cf Charles Richard Rinderknecht.

David STIEN s/o Howard William Stein & Edna nee Risdal; b 1943; m Shirley Reimers. Members St.John. Celebrated 50th Wedding Anniversary. Children:
>   Elizabeth – b 1967; m NN Hickman; Apple Valley MN
>   Stephanie – b 1969; Tony Schreck; Needville, TX
>   Ellen – b 1971; m Larry Kling; Ceylon, MN

Delbert Fredrich STIEN s/o Henry John Stien & Anenia nee Bobzien; b 1919; m 1943 Hazel Schmidt of Watkins, IA (b 1922) d/o John Schmidt &

Mary nee Maag. Farm residence east of Newhall, IA. Children:
  John – b 1944; m Joanne McCoy
  Jean – b 1953; Scottsdale, AZ residence

Douglas Alan STIEN s/o Howard William Stien & Edna nee Risdal: cf Debra Lynn Karr.

Emma STIEN d/o Heinrich Stien & Mary nee Kerkman; b 1883 first girl born in town of Newhall, IA d 1981; 1st m 1903 Otto Richter (d 1916). Children:
  Walter Richter – b 1906, dec'd in infancy
  Lucille Richter – b 1910
2nd m 1924 Emma nee Stien Richter to Henry Broendel s/o Hans Broendel & Anna nee Hassee. Emma made her home the last years of her life at the Luth Home, Perry, IA. Children:

*Franz Heinrich STIEN b 1824 Drage, Schleswig-Holstein, Germany, d 1898 Benton Co IA; 1870 emigrated from birthplace in farming village of Germany with three sons to Benton Co IA; settled with friends from Drage, Germany; purchased farm in Eden Twp Benton Co IA from Joseph Fix in 1870, farmed until his death. Children:
  Franz – 1877 returned to Drage, Germany, where he died
  Peter – b 1852 Germany, d 1930; m Katherine Rath (1865-1950)
  Heldt – b 1851 Germany, d 1922 Benton Co IA

*Heinrich STIEN s/o Peter Stien & Katherina Margareta nee Lass; b 30 Nov 1851 Drage, Schleswig-Holstein, Germany, d 05 Oct 1898 [Typhoid Pneumonia] ae47y 10m 5d at brother Peter Stein's home, bur St.John Cem; 1869 emigrated to Benton Co IA with two brothers and became a blacksmith; m 11 May 1879 St.John to Maria Mary Kerkman (b 06 Jun 1859 Will County, IL, d 24 Oct 1942 ae83y 4m 18d bur St.John Cem) d/o Johan Conrad Kerkman & Anna Martha nee Werning Schumacher; 1880 purchased farm west of Newhall, IA; 1882 purchased two lots east side of Newhall business district and three residential lots, building home one-half block north of the park; 1882 established Newhall blacksmith shop; 1883 purchased thirty acres of land north of the railroad tracks from the Main Street of Newhall, IA; 1898 retired. Children:
  Willie – dec'd infancy
  Anna – b 1880, d 1970; m William Schneckloth
  Emma – b 1883, d 1981; 1st m 1903 Otto Richter;

2nd m 1924 Henry Broendel
Mary – b 1886, d 1965 Never Married; made her home with mother
Henry John – b 1888, d 1968; m 07 Jan 1912 Anenia Bobzien
Tilla – b 1890, d 1982; m Charles Heinrich

*Heldt STIEN s/o Franz Heinrich Stien, Germany; b 1851 Drage, Schleswig-Holstein, Germany; 1870 emigrated to Iowa with father and two brothers; farmed with father many years; prob ae40y, wrote to friend, widow in NJ, to come to Newhall, IA and be his wife. m Anna nee Bowers Baumgartner (d 1902 Benton Co). Her five children: George, Charles, William, Louis, Anna made home on farm north of Newhall, IA. Children of Heldt and Anna:
Mary – b 1896, d 1915
Albert "Beanie" – b 1899, d 1966; m 1920 Rose Hickey

Henry John STIEN s/o Henrich Stien & Mary nee Kerkman; b 01 May 1888, d 02 May 1968 ae80y 1d bur St.John; 1898; m 07 Jan 1912 Van Horne, IA to Anenia Bobzien (b 21 Feb 1891 on farm near Newhall, IA d 23 Oct 1978 ae87y 8m 1d bur St.John Cem) d/o Frederich Bobzien & Alvina nee Zornig. Purchased 480 acres of farmland, retired in Newhall, IA. Children:
Richard Henry – b 1912; m 1937 Mary Dvorak
Howard William – b 1914; m 1943 Edna Risdal
Delbert Fredrich – b 1919; m Hazel Schmidt

Howard William STIEN s/o Henry John Stein & Anenia nee Bobzien; b 20 Jan 1914 Newhall, IA; Newhall High School, d 16 Jan 2003 ae88y 11m 27d University Hosp Iowa City IA bur St.John Cem; m 10 Apr 1943 Luth Parsonage Norway, IA to Edna Risdal (b 1924; Newhall High School) d/o Dan Risdal & Lena nee Dyrland. Farmed two miles east and one-half mile south of Newhall, IA on farm originally owned by her father. Children:
David – b 1945; m Shirley Reimers, Atkins, IA residence
Diane – b 1947; Vadnais Heights, MN residence
Douglas Alan – b 21 Apr 1950; m 06 Aug 1983 Debra Karr

John STIEN s/o Delbert Fredrich Stien & Hazel nee Schmidt; b 1944; m 1971 Joanne McCoy (b 1950). Children:
Darrell – b 1972
Janelle – b 1975

Richard Henry STIEN s/o Henry John Stien & Anenia nee Bobzien; b 1912; m 1937 St.John Parsonage to Mary Dvorak (b 12 Feb 1912 Valtino, Moravia, Czechoslovakia. 19 May 1920 emigrated with mother and siblings to Luzerne, IA) d/o Frank Dvorak & Mary Frances nee Straka of Luzerne, IA; residence a Century Farm west of Newhall, IA. Children:

Donald Richard – b 1939; Atkins, IA residence

Darlene Mary – b 17 Mar 1943;

1st m 10 Sept 1966 Charles Rinderknecht, DVD 1982;

2nd m to Ron Ribble

Roger Henry – b 1948; m 1978 Linda Marie Chambers

Roger Henry STIEN s/o Richard Henry Stien & Mary nee Dvorak; b 1948; Class 1966 Benton Community School; 1968 Kirkwood Community College; m 1978 St.John to Linda Marie Chambers (b 1954; Class of 1973 Danville Community High School; 1975 Kirkwood Community College) d/o Lonnie Chambers & Anna Mae nee Meadower. Atkins, IA residence. Children:

Zachary Roger – b 1979

Jerid Richard – b 1981

**Ralf STOCKER s/o Emilie nee Ernst & Karl Stocker; b 08 Aug 1963 Löhlbach, Germany; m 30 May 1987 Martina Möller. Children:

**Marcel – b 13 Sept 1990

**Mareike – b 18 May 1996

**Wolfgang STOCKER s/o Emilie nee Ernst & Karl Stocker; b 19 Feb 1958 Löhlbach, Germany; m 29 May 1980 Karin Schneider. Children:

**Lars – b 02 Sept 1980

**Christian – b 03 Nov 1986

Elsie Anna STRELLNER d/o Julius Strellner & Julia nee Waterstradt: cf Adam Reinhard Louis aka Louis A. Brehm.

Emma Louise STRELLNER d/o Julius Strellner & Julia nee Waterstradt; b 14 Jul 1908, d 30 Oct 1956 ae48y 3m 17d; m 29 Sept 1926 Iver Johnson (b 11 Jun 1894 Togorp, Sweden, d 07 Jan 1961 ae66y 6m 27d [broke neck in fall down basement stairs]. No children

Esther Florence STRELLNER d/o Julius Strellner & Julia nee Waterstradt: cf Ivan Brandt Reiss.

Francis Marie STRELLNER d/o Julius Strellner & Julia nee Waterstradt: cf
Gerhardt Henry Conrad Krug.

Wilhelmina "Minnie" Gertrude STRELLNER d/o Julius Strellner & Julia
nee Waterstradt: cf Harry Joseph Koopman.

*Jochim STRELLNER b 1841 Schleswig-Holstein, Germany, d 1923
Pasadena, CA, bur Keystone, IA Cem; 1858 emigrated ae17y to
Philadelphia, PA where he mined coal before moving to Davenport, IA;
naturalized U.S. citizen 1875; m 1870 Gertrude Port (b 1851 Fenon,
Germany, emigrated to USA, d 1926 Vinton, IA, bur Keystone, IA Cem).
1907 moved to Pasadena, CA; large landowners Big Grove Twp Benton Co
IA. Gertrude returned to Iowa and lived with daughter, Mrs. George
St.Clair. Children:
    Laura – b 1871, d 1932; m Adam Scheib. Children: John, Lucy
    Henry – b 1872, d 1925; m Carrie Demmel. Children: Helen, Herman,
        Henry, George, William
    Eda – b 1874, d 1907; m Albert Longacre, Child: Nellie
    Julius – b 1875, d 1959; m Julia Waterstradt (b 1877, d 1950). Children:
        Wilhelmina (Minnie), Elsie, Emma, Esther, Frances
    Nellie H. – b 07 Feb 1882, d 20 Apr 1953;
        m 24 Feb 1910 Pasadena, CA George H.St.Clair;
        (b 27 Aug 1872, d 28 Oct 1949) No children.

*Johann Heinrich STREMME prob Totinhausen, Germany; m Anna
Gertrud Maurer. Child:
    *Johannes Stremme – b 1764 Battenhausen, Germany;
        m 10 Apr 1787 Battenhausen, Germany, to Anna Katharina Möller
    d/o Johann Daniel Möller & Anna Elisabeth nee Weber of Battenhausen,
Germany.

Annette Marie SUHR d/o Pearl Evelyn nee Bayer & Arlo Hans F. Suhr; b
30 Sept 1963 Correctionville, IA; m 19 Dec 1982 Luth Ch Anthon, IA to
Greg Allen Nelson (b 14 Oct 1962 Sioux City, IA) s/o Victor Emmanuel
Nelson & Dorothy June nee Hansen. Farmers. Children:
    Michael Allen Nelson – b 09 Jul 1983 Onawa, IA
    Amber Joelle Nelson – b 09 Mar 1985 Sioux City, IA
    Laurie Ann Nelson – b 02 Mar 1989 Sioux City, IA
    Andrea Nelson – b 22 May 1991

Donna Rae SUHR d/o Pearl Evelyn nee Bayer & Arlo Hans F. Suhr; b 05 Sept 1965 Correctionville, IA; m 27 May 1988 Schleswig, IA to Clark Trent Davis (b 11 Jul 1958) s/o Turner Davis & Shirley nee Biebrecht. Farmers. Children:
> Andrea Jean Davis – b 22 May 1991
> (Son) Davis – b 20 Jun 1992
> Amanda Davis – b 28 Dec 1993
> Anna Davis – b 26 Jan 1996

Mark Allen SUHR s/o Pearl Evelyn nee Bayer & Arlo Hans F. Suhr; b 19 Apr 1961 Correctionville, IA; m 01 Oct 1994 Kim Robinson. STEPCHILDREN:
> John Robinson – b 08 Aug 1986
> Melanie Robinson – b 19 Mar 1989
> Jennifer Robinson – b 05 Oct 1990

Jean Susan SUTCLIFFE d/o Corrine Elsie nee Keiper & Joseph Walter Sutcliffe; b 25 Aug 1964 Wichita, KS; m 12 May 1990 Gregory Stephen Weiss (b 30 Nov 1965 Alton, IL) s/o Stanley & Margaret Weiss. Decatur, IL residence. Children:
> Kellen Joseph Weiss – b 28 Jan 1993
> Kavan Gregory Weiss – b 05 Nov 1995

Thomas Joel SUTCLIFFE s/o Corrine Elsie nee Keiper & Joseph Walter Sutcliffe; b 05 Aug 1958; m 05 Oct 1984 Catherine Mary McCubbins (b 11 Mar 1959 Quincy, IL) d/o William McCubbins & Virginia nee Kamphaus. Springfield, IL residence. Child:
> Caitlin Marie – b 22 Oct 1991

Kami Joy SYME d/o Debra Ann nee Bender & Larry Syme; b 03 Aug 1985; m 19 May 2007 Jeff Tam Sing (Hawaiian) s/o Mr. & Mrs. Theodore Tam Sing.

Katie Marie SYME d/o Debra Ann nee Bender & Larry Syme; b 01 Nov 1983; m 26 Jun 2004 Dustin Moon (b 23 Jan 1981) s/o Bill & Linda Moon. Child:
> Hayden Joe Moon – b 05 Mar 2006

Karrah Ann SYME d/o Debra Ann nee Bender & Larry Syme; b 12 Feb

1978 OR; m 21 Feb 1998 Lebanon Mennonite Ch, Lebanon, OR to James
Savage (b 01 Jan 1974) s/o Tim & Sue Savage. Children:
Allye K. Savage – b 18 Apr 1999
Kaleb James Savage – b 21 Oct 2000

Nathanial Jay SYME s/o Debra Ann nee Bender & Larry Syme; b 06 Apr
1976 OR; m 27 May 1995 First Baptist Ch, Lebanon, OR to Alicia Lynn
Kearns (b 16 May 1974) d/o Dick & Dixie Kearns. Children:
Tyler Jay – b 07 Oct 1997
Nikayla Shae –b 08 Feb 2000
Brayden Tri – b 15 May 2002
Lexa May – b 29 Mar 2006

Albert Adolph TASCHNER s/o Johan Gottlieb Taschner & 2nd m Laura
Anna nee Bachman; b 1881, d 1961; m Emma Elizabeth Wohlers (b
1878, d 1945). Children:
Raymond Elmer – b 1902, d 1987; m Mavis Martha Warner
(b 1906).
Harvey – b 1903, d 1948; m Alene Cherrington
Esther Margaret – b 1907, d 1972; m Albert Edward Nordlund
Kenneth Albert – b 1913, d 1977; 1st m NFR;
2nd m Phyllis Margaret Johnson

Amelia Caroline TASCHNER d/o Johan Gottlieb Taschner & 1st m
Wilhelmina nee Schmidt; b 1865, d 1963; m Louis Wagner (b 1858, d
1931). Children:
Ernest Wagner – b 1883, d 1972; m Ina Elizabeth Burns
Rosa Pauline Marie Wagner – m Earl Edward Phillips
Julius Wagner – NFR

Arthur Howard TASCHNER s/o Julius Ernst Taschner & Emma Mina
Dorothea nee Senne; b 1925; m Geraldine Ann Coble (b 1932). Children:
Rhonda Kay – b 1958; m Jeffrey Tenny (b 1958)
Dennis Arthur – b 1961

Betty Jo TASCHNER d/o Herbert August Taschner & Arlene Anna
Marie nee Voeltz; b 1948; m Richard Hardy Nelson (b 1950). Children:
Todd James Nelson – b 1969; m Stephanie Lynn Cheeseman
(b 1967). Children: Trevor Richard Nelson (b 1998),
Rachael Anne Nelson (b 2000)

Tami Lynn Nelson – b 1971; m Darrell Robert Rairdin (b 1971)
Children: Zachary Todd Rairdin (b 2001),
Nina JoAnn Rairdin (b 2002)
Laura Renee Nelson – b 1976; m John Lincoln Mudd (b 1961).
Children: Kassidy Jean Mudd (b 2003),
TWINS: Carson Benny Mudd (b 2005),
Riley Lincoln Mudd (b 2005)

Clara Johanna Maria TASCHNER d/o Johan Gottlieb Taschner & 2nd m
Laura Anna nee Bachman; b 1883, d 1903; m John Peter Paulsen (b
1873, d 1903). Clara died when twins were born; they were raised by
grandparents Johan Gottlieb and Laura Anna nee Bachman. Children:
Ada Pauline Paulsen – b 1901; m G. Melvin Dyrland. Child:
(Adopted) Dorothy Lou (b 1928); m Marlyn Ernest Johnson
Harold Paul Paulsen – 1902, d 1972; 1st m Alma E. Kenter (d 1958)
Children: Dau:m Clair E. Baldwin, Paul E. Paulsen;
2nd m Bessie Irene King (b 1907, d 1971)
TWINS: Clarence Julian Paulsen – b 1903, d 1956;
m Bessie Irene King (1907-1971)
Clement Lucian Paulsen – b 1903

David Leroy TASCHNER s/o Forrest Knuth Taschner & Eva Myrtle nee
Cheney; 1st m Bonnie Uhlmann. Children:
Kathleen Kay – b 1971; m Douglas Chaloupek. Children:
Marcus Robert Chaloupek (b 1994), Brandon Aaron Chaloupek
(b 1996), Owen Douglas Chaloupek (b 2001)
David William – b 1970; 1st m Kari NN; 2nd m Lori NN
Suzanne Renea – b 1972
Robert Edward – m Mari Zimmerman
2nd m David Leroy Taschner to Cynthia "Cindi" Smith (b 1950)

Donald Walden TASCHNER s/o Myron Edwin Taschner & Hazel
Bernice Marie nee Bramow; b 1932; m Barbara Joan Brooks (b 1936).
Children:
Michael Julius – b 1959; m Deborah Denise Brown;
Murray Andrew – b 1961; m Cathleen Mary Bury
Matthew Kirk – b 1952; Rochelle Marie Fraedrich

Eleanor Emilia TASCHNER d/o John August Taschner & Mathilda nee
Grovert; b 1894, d 1988; m Otto Jaroch (b 1891, d 1980). Children:

Gordon Otto Jaroch – b 1919; 1st m Lila Renner;
    2nd m Eleanor Larero; 3rd m Cathleen Marie Janssen
Roger Lawrence Jaroch – b 1922, d 1935

Esther Margaret TASCHNER d/o Albert Adolph Taschner & Emma
Elizabeth nee Wohlers; b 1907, d 1972; m Albert Edward Nordlund (b
1932, d 1999). Children:
    Gordon Albert Nordlund – b 1932, d 1999; m Verlyne Lembke.
        Child: Brian Nordlund (b 1959)
    Marion Nordlund – b 1936; m Ronald Rankin (b 1937). Children:
        1. Laura Joy Rankin (b 1962); m Steven Francis Masters
        (b 1956). Children: Brandon Scott Masters (b 1989),
        Jordan Elizabeth Masters(b 1994)
        2. Gregory Nordlund Rankin – b 1963;
        m Abby Lynne Rosenbaum (b 1962). Child:
        Madison Blon Rankin (b 1994)
        3. Julia Lynn Rankin – b 1970; m Thomas A. Dages (b 1961)

Forrest Knuth TASCHNER s/o Henry Herman Taschner & Anna A. nee
Knuth; b 1908, d 1963; m Eva Myrtle Cheney. Children:
    Phyllis Marie – b 1930; m Lumar Kriz
    Marian Frances – b 1934; m Robert Herman Glandorf
    Patricia Ann – m Willard M. Glandorf
    Forrest William – 1st m Janet Fetter; 2nd m Sharon NN
    David Leroy – 1st m Bonnie Uhlmann; 2nd m Cynthia "Cindi" Smith

*Gottlieb TASCHNER s/o Johan Taschner (b 1768 os Prussia, d 1832 os
Prussia) & Ana Dorthea nee Kruger (b 1779 os Prussia, d 1843 os
Prussia); b 1805 os Prussia; m Anna Catherina Hoeft (b 1800 Hamburg,
os Prussia). 1850 emigrated to USA with children: Heinrich, Johan
Gottlieb, Wilhelmina. Children:
    Christopher Ernst – b 1834 os Prussia, d 1835 os Prussia
    *Heinrich – b 1835 os Prussia
    *Johann Gottlieb – b 1836 Proisen, Prussia, d 1922 Benton Co IA;
        1st m 1859 Wilhelmina Schmidt;
        2nd m 1880 Laura Anna Bachman
    *Wilhelmina – b 1838 os Prussia

Harvey TASCHNER s/o Albert Adolph Taschner & Emma Elizabeth nee
Wohlers; b 1903, d 1948; m Alene Cherrington (b 1903). Children:

Nordeen – b 1928; m Ardella Lynn
Marlys – b 1932; m Horace Clair

Henry Herman TASCHNER s/o Johan Gottlieb Taschner & 1st m
Wilhelmina nee Schmidt; b 1872, d 1952; m Anna Knuth (b 1877, d
1966). Children:
    Leslie J. W. – b 1898, d 1955; m Elsie Elizabeth Kray
    Forrest Knuth – b 1908, d 1963; m Eva Myrtle Cheney

Herbert August TASCHNER s/o Julius Ernst Taschner & Emma Mina
nee Senne; b 1916, d 2005; m Arlene Anna Marie Voeltz (b 1918).
Children:
    Jean Marie – b 1940; m Gordon Earl Stelling
    Marilyn Ann – b 1943; m Paul Edward Mittan
    Betty Jo – b 1948; m Richard Hardy Nelson
    James Herbert – b 1951; 1st m Teresa Ann Boies;
        2nd m Pamela Sue Lester

Ila Jean TASCHNER d/o Myron Edwin Taschner & Hazel Bernice
Marie nee Bramow: cf Donald George August Krug.

James Herbert TASCHNER s/o Herbert August Taschner & Arlene Anna
Marie nee Voeltz; b 1951; 1st m Teresa Ann Boies (b 1953). Children:
    Jill Elisa – b 1975; m Robert W. Hall (b 1975). Children:
        Serina Marie Hall (b 1993), Christopher Thomas Heimsoth
        (b 1995)
    Patrick August – b 1978
    John James – b 1980
2nd m James Herbert Taschner to Pamela Sue Lester (b 1955)

Jan Terese TASCHNER d/o Forrest William Taschner & Janet nee
Fetter; b 1960; m Allan Johnson. Children:
    Nichole Diane Johnson – b 1983
    Michelle Danielle Johnson – b 1984
    Rebecca Jane Johnson – b 1993

Jean Marie TASCHNER do Herbert August Taschner & Arlene Anna
Marie nee Voeltz; b 1940; m Gordon Earl Stelling (b 1940). Children:
    Tina Marie Stelling – b 1963; m Joseph Lawrence Livingston
        (b 1964)

Todd Gordon Stelling – b 1964; m Sue Ellen Kaness(b 1967).
Children: Payton Marie Stelling (b 2000), Ryker Todd Stelling
(b 2004)
Tamara Stelling – b 1966; m Bruce Allen Olson (b 1962). Children:
Steven Christian Olson (b 1993), Justus Alexander Olson
(b 1996)

*Johan Gottlieb TASCHNER s/o Gottlieb Taschner (b 1805) & Anna
Catherina nee Hoeft (b 1800 Hamburg, Germany); b 1836 Proisen,
Hamburg os Prussia ns Germany; bpt & con Germany, d 1922 Benton
Co IA; emigrated ae14y with parents, brother Henry, sister Wilhelmina;
1st m 1859 Highland, WI to Wilhelmina Schmidt (b 1838 os Prussia, d
1880 Benton Co IA) d/o Gottlieb Schmidt. Moved to Iowa Nov 1867,
purchased 160 acres farmland Eden Twp Benton Co IA. Children:
Frederick Wilhelm – b 1861, d 1863 in WI
Marie – b 1863, dec'd infancy in WI
Amelia Caroline – b 1865, d 1963; m Louis Wagner;
John August – b 1868, d 1963; m Mathilda Grovert; Helmet, CA;
Pauline Wilhelmina – b 1870; d 1955; 1st m Thomas Conley;
2nd m Alexander Miller; Child: Arthur
Henry Herman – b 1872, d 1952; m Anna A. Knuth;
Julius Ernst – b 1876, d 1976; m 1903 Emma Mina Dorothea Senne;
2nd m 1880 Vinton, IA Johan Gottlieb Taschner to Laura Anna Bachman
(b 1860, d 1944). Prob 1902 built home in Newhall, IA. Children:
Albert Adolph – b 1881, d 1961; m Emma Elizabeth Wohlers,
De Smet, SD residence;
Rose Lina – b 1882, d 1898; Never Married
Clara Johanna Maria – b 1883, d 1903[At birth of twins];
m John Peter Paulsen;
George Carl Ernest – b 1885, d 1886
Frederick – b 1887, dec'd small child
Matilda Anna – b 1888, d 1918;
m George John Baumgartner, Los Angeles, CA
William Louis – b 1892, d 1936; 1st m Marie Ada Brown;
2nd m Marie Ehrman
Fredrich Elmer – b 1887; m Edna Mort; Son: Vernal M. Taschner,
Laguna Beach, CA

John August TASCHNER s/o Johan Gottlieb Taschner & 1st n
Wilhelmina nee Schmidt; b 1868, d 1963; m Mathilda Grovert (b 1870, d

1950). Children:
- Elsa Wilhelmina – b 1870, d 1892
- Eleanor Emilia – b 1894 1988; m Otto Jaroch
- Elfrieda – b 1898, d 1924
- Sherman Henry – b 1902, d 1993; m Frances Idella Willard

John Carroll TASCHNER s/oJohn August Taschner & Mathilda nee Grovert; b 1930; 1st m Gull Elizabeth Persson (b 1935, d 1990). Children:
- Robert Sherman – b 1959; m Michele Marie Probst
- Karen Elizabeth – b 1964; m John Andrew Chimarusti

Julius Ernst TASCHNER s/o Johan Gottlieb Taschner & 1st m Wilhelmina nee Schmidt; b 1876, d 1976; m 1903 Emma Mina Senne (b 1882, d 1952) d/o John Senne & Katherine nee Kerkman. Implement business in Newhall, IA. Farmed in SD. Children:
- Waldo Julius – b 1904, d 1948; m Wanda Hermina Ella Hageman, Waseca, MN;
- Myron Edwin – b 1907, d 1999; Cedar Rapids, IA residence; m Hazel Bernice Marie Bramow; Howard, SD;
- Clarence Emmett – b 1910, d 1999; m Bertha Emily Hahn; Howard, SD residence
- Herbert August – b 1916, d 2005; Keystone, IA residence; m Arlene Anna Marie Voeltz,
- Arthur Howard – b 1925; m Geraldine Ann Coble;

Karen Elizabeth TASCHNER d/o John Carroll Taschner & 1st m Gull Elizabeth nee Persson; b 1964; m John Andrew Chimarusti (b 1962). Children:
- Rebecca Ann Chimarusti – b 1999
- Maria Elizabeth Chimarusti – b 2002

Kenneth Albert TASCHNER s/o Albert Adolph Taschner & Emma Elizabeth nee Wohlers; b 1913 , d 1977; 1st m NN; 2nd m Phyllis Margaret nee Johnson (b 1922). Children:
- Carol Joyce – b 1945; m Ralph E. Hurlbert (b 1945)
- Joanne Kay – b 1947; m John L. Groves (b 1941, d 2001). Children: Dorothy Ann Groves (b 1974); m Jonathon Michael McAreavey (b 1975), John Vernon Groves (b 1977); m Jennifer Deleft (b 1976)

Ardys Louise – b 1949

Larry Leo TASCHNER s/o Raymond Elmer Taschner & Mavis Martha nee Warner; b 1935; m Mary Jane Evenson (b 1936). Children:
Sandra Jane – b 1956; 1st m Scott Neal Peterson;
2nd m Edward Smith
Randall Larry – b 1958; m Kay Dianne Everson
Sarah Jean – b 1965; m Mark Duane Tatzlaff

Leslie J. W. TASCHNER s/o Henry Herman Taschner & Anna a. nee Knuth; b 1898, d 1955; m Elsie Elizabeth Kray. Children:
Helen Marcella – b 1921, d 1982; 1st m Norman Bryce Newton (b 1919); 2nd m John C. Palmer (b 1910, d 2000). Children: John C Palmer JR., Marge Palmer
Robert L. – b 1924, d 1955; m Jean K. Thompson

Margaret Lorene TASCHNER d/o John August Taschner & Mathilda nee Grovert; b 1928; m Arnold Henry Dickenson (b 1921, d 2006). Children:
Larry Alan Dickenson – b 1949; m Patricia Ann Ostrowski. Children:
Jeffrey Neil Dickenson (b 1977), Brian Joseph Dickenson (b 1979)
Glen Edward Dickenson – b 1951; m Susan Joyce Gardner. Children:
1. Michelle Lyn Dickenson (b 1973); 1st m Steven Robert Veiga (b 1968); 2nd m Mark Lawrence Arvidson (b 1964). Children: Lindsay Arvidson (b 1993), Austin Arvidson (b 1995), Hannah Arvidson (b 2004)
2. Donald Alan Dickenson (b 1974)
3. Ryan Matthew Dickenson (b 1981)

Marian Frances TASCHNER d/o Forrest Knuth Taschner & Eva Myrtle nee Cheney; b 1934; m Robert Herman Glandorf (b 1932). Children:
Debra Lynn Glandorf – b 1961;
m James Edward Walton (b 1963)
Children: Robert Raymond Walton (b 1986)
Rachel Lynn Walton (b 1988)
Rodney Robert Glandorf – b 1962; 1st m NN
2nd m Clover Denise Quigley (b 1959)

Children: Ashley Ellen Shifflett (b 1988)
Ryley Robert Glandorf (b 2003)
Timothy Arnold Glandorf – b 1965; m Theresa Thurkettle (b 1971).
  Children: Regan Elizabeth Glandorf (b 1995),
  Zachary Frank Glandorf (b 2004)
Rebecca Renee Glandorf – b 1971; m Patrick Alan Nehls (b 1972).
  Children: Mackenzie Mariah Nehls (b 1997),
  Ethan Patrick Nehls (b 2001)

Marilyn Ann TASCHNER d/o Herbert August Taschner & Arlene Anna
Marie nee Voeltz; b 1943; m Paul Edward Mittan (b 1943). Children:
  Michael Paul Mittan – b 1968; m Angela Kristine Tonniges.
    Children: Braxton Michael Mittan (b 1994),
    Miranda Kristine Mittan (b 1997), Kyla Breanne Mittan (b 2000)
  Pamela Ann Mittan – b 1970; m Christopher Michael Pippert.
    Children: Nicholas Christopher Pippert (b 1995),
    Weston Michael Pippert (b 1998)

Marlys TASCHNER d/o Harvey Taschner & Alene nee Cherrington; b
1932; m Horace Clair (b 1933). Children:
  David Clair – b 1956
  Daniel Clair – b 1957; m Kim Bushman (b 1961)
  Linda Marlys Clair – b/d 1962

Mary Louise TASCHNER d/o Sherman Henry Taschner & Frances Idell
nee Willard; b 1928; m Clarence Jay Trumpy (b 1924). Children:
  Donna Irene Trumpy – b 1949; m Richard James Scott
  Clifford Robert Trumpy – b 1951; m Riva Sue Klatt
  Virginia Kay Trumpy – b 1958; 1st m Brett Edward Wadleigh
    (b 1958, d 1994); 2nd m Chris Alan Coleman (b 1967)

Matilda Anna TASCHNER d/o Johan Gottlieb Taschner & 2nd m Laura
Anna nee Bachman; b 1888, d 1918; m George John Baumgartner (b
1885, d 1971) partner in Cedar Rapids, IA "Souvenir Lead Pencil"
factory with Archibald C. Stewart. Child:
  Hazel A. Baumgartner – b 1908, d 1991;
    m Clarence Henry Brunsmann (b 1906, d 1976). Children:
    1. Betty Ann Brunsmann (b 1940), 2. Carole S. Brunsmann
    (b 1944); m Edward B. Gill (b 1936). Child: Sheila S. Gill
    (b 1969); 3. David George Brunsmann (b 1950, d 1970);

4. Jack Edward Brunsmann (b 1950)

Matthew Kirk TASCHNER s/o Donald Walden Taschner & Barbara Joan nee Brooks; b 1964; m Rochelle Marie Fraedrich (b 1971). Children:
    Grant Gottlieb – b 2001
    Devin Dakota – b 2003

Michael Julius TASCHNER s/o Donald Walden Taschner & Barbara Joan nee Brooks; b 1959; m Deborah Denise Brown (b 1966). Children:
    Nicohlas Gregory – b 1989
    Alexander Jonathan – b 1991

Murray Andrew Taschner s/o Donald Walden Taschner & Barbara Joan nee Brooks; b 1961; m Cathleen Mary Bury (b 1962). Children:
    Carly Nicole – b 1996
    Anna Catherine – b 1998

Myron Edwin TASCHNER s/o Julius Ernst Taschner & Emma Mina Dorothea nee Senne; b 1907, d 1999; m Hazel Bernice Marie Bramow (b 1912, d 2002). Children:
    Donald Walden – b 1932; m Barbara Joan Brooks
    Ila Jean – b 1934; m Donald George August Krug

Nordeen TASCHNER s/o Harvey Taschner & Alene nee Cherrington; b 1928; m Ardella Lynn (b 1929). Children:
    Kenneth – b 1950; m Linda M. Carner (b 1950). Children:
        Shawn Christopher (b 1974), April Christine (b 1976)
    Victoria – b 1952; m Larry D. Lambrect (b 1950). Children:
        Jacob Harvey Lambrect (b 1981),
        Amoret Margaret Lambrect (b 1982)

Orville Kermit TASCHNER s/o Waldo Julius Taschner & Wanda Hermina Ella nee Hagemann; b 1930; m June Olhoeft (b 1932). Children:
    Beth Ann – b 1958; m Norman Brown (b 1957)
    Andrea – b 1962

Patricia Ann TASCHNER d/o Forrest Knuth Taschner & Eva Myrtle nee Cheney; m Willard M. Glandorf. Children:

Jeffrey Willard Glandorf – b 1963; m Kimberly Feiden. Child:
  Myles Jeffrey Glandorf (b 1997)
Tina Cristine Glandorf – m Steven P. Prusha. Children:
  Garett Paul Prusha (b 1991), Laura Christine Prusha (b 1993),
  Ashley Elizabeth Prusha (b 1998)
Matthew Martin Glandorf – b 1969; m NN. Children:
  Amanda Marie Glandorf (b 1994), Katie Ann Glandorf (b 1996)
Michele Marie Glandorf – b 1969; m Larry McGuire. Children:
  Drew Martin McGuire (b 1992), Emily Elizabeth McGuire
  (b 1994), Melissa Marie McGuire (b 1995)

Randall Larry TASCHNER s/o Larry Leo Taschner & Mary Jane nee
Evenson; b 1958; m Kay Dianne Everson (b 1959). Children:
  Craig Randall – b 1980
  Stacey Ann – b 1982
  Linsey Kay – b 1986
  Tyler John – b 1994

Raymond Elmer TASCHNER s/o Albert Adolph Taschner & Emma
Elizabeth nee Wohlers; b 1902, d 1978; m Mavis Martha Warner (b
1906). Children:
  Larry Leo – b 1935; m Mary Jane Evenson
  Ronald Ray – b 1941; m Donna DeEtta Dugdale
  Marlys – b 1932; m Horace Clair

Renee Ann TASCHNER d/o Robert L. Taschner & Jean K. nee
Thompson; b 1952; m Rick Weeter (b 1950). Children:
  Shane Weeter – b 1983
  Stacy Renee Weeter – b 1986

Robert Sherman TASCHNER s/o John Carroll Taschner & 1st m gull
Elizabeth nee Persson; b 1959; m Michele Marie Probst (b 1962).
Children:
  Nicole Marie – b 1990
  Ashley Victoria – b 1995

Ronald Ray TASCHNER s/o Raymond Elmer Taschner & Mavis Martha
nee Warner; b 1941; m Donna DeEtta Dugdale (b 1941). Children:
  Tamra Rea – b 1962; m Randy Scott Djerf (b 1957). Children:
    Katie Marie Djerf (b 1985), Travis Scott Djerf (b 1988),

Kelly Rae Djerf (b 1990)
Anthony Lee – b 1965; m Jennifer Lea Simondet (b 1965). Children:
    Andrew Mitchell (b 1989), Nicholas John (b 1992)
Teri Ann – b 1975

Sandra Jane TASCHNER d/o Larry Leo Taschner & Mary Jane nee
Evenson; b 1956; m Scott Neal Peterson (b 1954). Children:
    Marty Neal Peterson – b 1975, d 1980
    Michelle Mary Peterson – b 1978
    Melanie Joy Peterson – b 1980
    Marsha Jane Peterson – b 1982; 1st m Edward Smith (b 1988);
        2nd m NFR

Sarah Jean TASCHNER d/o Larry Leo Taschner & Mary Jane nee
Evenson; b 1965; m Mark Duane Tatzlaff (b 1963). Children:
    Jessica Jean Tatzlaff – b 1988
    Dustin Duane Tatzlaff – b 1990
    Casey Ray Tatzlaff – b 1994
    Maridy May Tatzlaff – b 1995

Sherman Henry TASCHNER s/o John August Taschner & Mathilda nee
Grovert; b 1902, d 1993; m Frances Idella Willard (b 1904, d 1993).
Children:
    TWINS: Mary Louise – b 1928; m Clarence Jay Trumpy
             Margaret Lorene – b 1928; m Arnold Henry Dickenson
    John Carroll – b 1930; 1st m Gull Elizabeth Persson;
        2nd m Diana Patricia Percival

Vernal M. TASCHNER s/oFredrich Elmer Taschner; b 1908; m NN.
Children:
    Bruce – b 1932; 1st m Loree Kiklas; 2nd m Clara Hettinger; 3rd m NN;
        4th m Mimi NN; 5th m Mary Kellerman. Children:
        1. Dana Taschner; 1st m Jan. Children: Catherine, Dylan;
            2nd m NN
        2. Scott Taschner

Waldo Julius TASCHNER s/o Julius Ernst Taschner & Emma Mina
Dorothea nee Senne; b 1904, d 1948; m Wanda Herina Ella Hagemann
(b 1908, d 1982). Children:
    Orville Kermit – b 1930; m June Olhoeft

Yvonne Mae – b 1933; m Robert John Burgi

Yvonne Mae TASCHNER d/o Waldo Julius Taschner & Wanda Hermina Ella nee Hagemann; b 1933; m Robert John Burgi (b 1930). Children:
- Tamara Kay Burgi – b 1955; m Timothy Robert Williams (b 1955).
    - Child: Rachel Lynn Williams (b 1982)
- Deborah Mae Burgi – b 1956; 1st m Richard Behnke;
    2nd m Kenneth Gjerde (b 1952).
    - Child: Mark Robert Gjerde (1988)
- Theresa Rae Burgi – b 1963; m Michael Gaffer (b 1958). Children: Jennifer Elizbeth Gaffer (1987), Rebecca Lynn Gaffer (b 1990)

Charles TATGE s/o Christopher Tatge & Sophia nee Collman; m Annis May; Iowa Twp Benton Co IA farmers. Children:
- Nell – music teacher, farmed Iowa Twp Benton Co, IA
- John – m Elsa Gieseke, St.Louis, MO. Children: Jack, Annis
- Lucille E. – m Glenn L. Lyman

*Christopher TATGE b 1830 Germany; 1849 emigrated to USA; m Kendall Co IL to Sophia Collman (b Hanover, Germany). 1855 moved to Iowa Twp Benton Co IA; nurseryman. Children:
- Charles – NFR
- John – NFR
- Martha – NFR
- Edward – NFR
- Lizzie – NFR
- Willie – NFR
- Anna – NFR
- George – NFR

Lucille E. TATGE d/o Charles Tatge & Annis nee May; m Glenn L. Lyman from Belle Plaine, IA s/o Louis & Dora Lyman. Music teachers. Children:
- June C.Lyman – m William Agnew, Holstein, IA. Children: John C. and Patricia
- John B.Lyman – m Florence L. Fuller, Princeton, MO. Children:
    - Alan G. – m Karen Jadley, Geneseo, IL
- Karen J.Lyman – St. Louis, MO

Joel Gene TAYLOR s/o Janet nee Matthias & Mark Steven Taylor; b 03 Jan 1959; m Amy Rodema (b 15 Sept 1957). Child:
Jerold – b 26 Jul 1979

Robert Steven TAYLOR s/o Janet nee Matthias & Mark Steven Taylor; b 18 Sept 1956; m 14 Aug 1976 Darlene May Dietz (b 26 Mar 1957). Children:
Sharon May – b 25 Feb 1978
Nathan Robert – b 02 Sept 1979
Lisa Marie – b 15 Oct 1982
Amanda Marie – b 26 Jun 1984
David Ryan – b 02 Feb 1986

William TAYLOR s/o Janet nee Matthias & Mark Steven Taylor; b 14 Nov 1954; m Beth McGarvey (b 21 Jun 1956). Children:
Amy Taylor – b 24 Jan 1976
Todd Taylor (Adopted) – b 18 May 1986

*Adolph TECKLENBURG b 1866 Buttle, Germany, d 1937; 1881 emigrated to farm northwest of Keystone, Benton Co IA; m 26 Nov 1889 Katherine Bockholt (b 1867, d 1920). Retired to Keystone, IA. Children:
Rose – m Henry Ochlerich
Hannah – m Edward Emmel
Ella – m Herman Paulsen
Herman – Keystone, IA residence
Henry – Cedar Rapids, IA residence
William – clergyman in FL
Hilda – m William McCord
Rudolph – Cedar Rapids, IA residence

Christopher TEGGATZ s/o Bethann Alice nee Schaefer & Stanley Teggatz; b 22 Feb 1969; Dr. of Anesthesiology, Cedar Rapids, IA; m 21 Sept 1996 Tanya Bruster (b 29 Aug 1971 Dr. in Family Practice, Cedar Rapids, IA). Child:
Emma Grace – b 02 Oct 2000

Curt TEGGATZ s/o Bethann Alice nee Schaefer & Stanley Teggatz; b 08 Oct 1972; Dr. Veterinary Medicine, Audubon, IA; m 06 Oct 2001 Susan Miller (b 16 Oct 1970 Dr. in Pediatrics, Cedar Rapids, IA). Child:
Infant – b Nov 2002

Carolyn Ann THEIS d/o Wilmer Theis & Clara nee Sessler; m Darold J. Jacobi. Rapid City, SD residence. Children:
    Timothy Jacobi – NFR
    Tamara Jacobi – NFR

James Wilmer THEIS d/o Wilmer Theis & Clara nee Sessler; m Ruth Ann Huffman. Rochester, IL residence. Children:
    Christopher – NFR
    Jeffrey – NFR
    Melissa – NFR

Judith Elizabeth THEIS d/o Wilmer Theis & Clara nee Sessler; m Tony R. Smith. Atkins IA residence. Children:
    Eric Smith – NFR
    Alexander Smith – NFR
    Nicholas Smith – NFR
    Patrick Smith – NFR

Lydia THEIS d/o Adolph Theis & Anna Marie nee Happel; m Apr 1950 Lamont Larrabee. Westminister, CO residence. Children:
    Linda Larrabee – Denver, CO residence
    LuAnn Larrabee – Redbud, IL residence
    Loren Larrabee – St.Charles, IL residence

Wilmer H. H. THEIS s/o Adolph Theis & Anna Marie nee Happel; b 21 Jan 1914 farm south Atkins, IA; bpt & con St.Steph, d 29 Mar 1996 ae82y 2m 8d bur St.Steph Cem; m 20 Dec 1936 Clara Sessler(b 05 Jul 1915 Wilton, IA d 12 Jun 2006 ae90y 11m 7d Cedar Rapids, IA bur St.Steph Cem) d/o John Sessler & Carolyn nee Grunder. Moved on Adolph Theis farm. Children:
    Carolyn Ann – b 25 Oct 1937; m Darold J. Jacobi, Rapid City, SD
    Judith Elizabeth – m Tony R. Smith, Atkins, IA
    James Wilmer – m Ruth Ann Huffman, Rochester, Ill.
    Jonathan Robert – m 02 May 1981 Leslie Amerling, Castroville, TX

*Heinrich THIELEMANN s/o Justus Thielemann & Katharina nee Vaupel; b 02 Jan 1867 Germany, d 27 Oct 1951 Germany ae84y 9m 25d; m 24 Mar 1894 Anna Katharina Elisabeth Daume (b 04 Aug 1867 Germany, d 06 Mar 1946 ae78y 7m 2d Germany).Parents of:

*Elisabeth – b 18 Sept 1901 Germany, d 14 May 1986 Germany;
m 09 Jan 1925 Löhlbach Ch to Heinrich Paar

*Johannes THIELEMANN s/o Konrad Thielemann & Lucine nee
Schween, Löhlbach, Germany; b 07 Aug 1894, d 1976; m 07 Mar 1920
Löhlbach Ch to Minna Ritter (b 09 Nov 1893, d 1973). Child:
*Karoline – b 27 Sept 1928 Löhlbach, Germany; d 03 Mar 2003
Germany; m 04 Jul 1952 Löhlbach Ch to Wilhelm Hackel,
Löhlbach, Germany (Karoline and Author's Paar common
ancestor: Johannes Paar b 20 Oct 1789, d 04 Jan 1856)

*Justus THIELEMANN s/o Konrad Thielemann & Anna Elisabeth nee
Möller; b 10 Sept 1833, d 20 Feb 1885 ae51y 5m 10d; m 28 May 1860
Katharina Vaupel (b 18 Oct 1837, d 27 Apr 1907 ae69y 6m 9d Löhlbach,
Germany) s/o Justus Vaupel(b 04 Sept 1809, d 05 Apr 1889 Germany
ae76y 11m 12d) & Anna Gertrude Paar (b 07 Apr 1805, d 16 Aug 1886
Löhlbach, Germany ae81y 4m 9d). Child:
*Heinrich – b 02 Jan 1867 Löhlbach, Germany, d 27 Oct 1951
Löhlbach; m 24 Mar 1894 Anna Katharina Elisabeth Daume

*Karoline THIELEMANN d/o Johannes Theilemann & Minna nee
Ritter; b 27 Sept 1928 Löhlbach, Germany, d 03 Mar 2003 ae74y 5m 4d
Germany; m 04 Jul 1952 Löhlbach Ch to Wilhelm Hackel (b 06 May
1925 Hennersdorf, Czechoslovakia; Löhlbach Ch Genealogist d 24 Jan
2005 ae79y 8m 18d Germany) s/o Gustav Hackel & Aloisia nee Fisher.
Celebrated 50th Golden Wedding Anniversary. Children:
**Walter Hackel – b 12 Nov 1953 Löhlbach, Germany;
m 07 Jun 1980 Doris Berg
**Heinrich Hackel – b 15 Mar 1955 Löhlbach, Germany;
Auto Mechanic
**Gerhardt Hackel – b 16 Nov 1958 Löhlbach, Germany;
m 15 May 1985 Karin Kraushaar
Author met this (Paar cousin) family in 1984, 1990, 1995, 1999, 2003.
Wilhelm Hackel researched German ancestors in the records of the
Löhlbach Church.

*Konrad THIELEMANN b 15 Mar 1795 Löhlbach, Germany, d 25 Nov
1865 ae70y 8m 10d Löhlbach, Germany; m 29 Apr 1825 Löhlbach Ch to
Wid/Anna Elisabeth Möller (b 05 Aug 1801 Löhlbach, Germany, d 30
Nov 1855 ae54y 3m 15d Löhlbach, Germany). Child:

*Justus – b 10 Sept 1833 Löhlbach, Germany, d 20 Feb 1885;
  m 1860 Katharina Vaupel

*Konrad THIELEMANN s/o Justus Thielemann & Katharina nee
Vaupel; b 17 Aug 1862 Germany, d 09 Nov 1933 ae71y 2m 23d
Germany; m 28 Feb 1892 Lucine Schween (b 15 Dec 1859 Germany, d
07 Mar 1946 ae86y 2m 20d Germany)Parents of:
  *Johannes – b 07 Aug 1894, d 1976; m 07 Mar 1920 Minna Ritter

*Martha Sophie THIELEMANN d/o Johann Heinrich Thielemann &
Anna Katharina Elisabeth nee Daume, Löhlbach, Germany; b 18 Sept
1901 Löhlbach Hse #38 1/2, bpt and con Löhlbach Ch; m 9/11 Jan 1925
Löhlbach Ch to Heinrich Paar(b 08 Oct 1901 Löhlbach, Germany).
Children:
  **Heinrich Paar – b 10 Mar 1925;
    m 22/24 May 1953 Helene Wilhelmi
  **Adolf Georg Paar – b 24 Dec 1928;
    m 18/19 May 1956 Margit Sieber
  **Anna Martha Paar – b 08 Feb 1932

*Vincent Andrew "Andy" THOMAN s/o Thomas Thoman, 1850's
immigrant from Germany, b 29 May 1863 Iowa Co IA, d 27 Oct 1951 IA
ae88y 7m 2d bur St. Michael's Cem, Norway, IA; m 21 Jun 1892
St.Michael's Catholic Ch, Norway, IA to Anna Meier (b 26 Mar 1871
Norway, IA, d 28 Sept 1970 ae99y, 6m at Marion, IA, bur St.Michael's
Cem, Norway, IA) d/o Meier, 1857 immigrants from Leitmar,
Westphalia, Germany. Farmers until 1928 retirement in Norway, IA.
Children:
  Joseph – b 03 Sept 1893, d 03 Dec 1975; m Elizabeth Gessner.
    Children: Harold, Clarence, Delmar, Vernon
  Magdalena – b 08 Mar 1896, d 03 Nov 1963; m Fred Hasley.
    Children: Sylvan, Lavina, Dale, Robert
  Anna – b 16 May 1899, d 09 Nov 1983; m William Schulte.
    Children: Clarence, Melvin, Audrey, William
  Andrew Philip – b 16 Oct 1901, d 26 Oct 1901
  Donald – b 26 Feb 1906; m Alma Oftedahl.
    Children: Delores, Gerald

Debra Kay THOMPSON d/o Lenore Kathryn Elizabeth nee Schminke &
Clifford Virgil Thompson; b 02 Mar 1954 Virginia Gay Hosp Vinton,

IA; m 18 Jun 1977 Marblehead, MA to Michael Arthur Marinelli JR. (b 17 Jul 1950 Syracuse, NY; Artist/Sculptor) s/o Michael Marinelli SR. Children:
   Krista Noel Marinelli – b 23 Dec 1983 Swampscott, MA
   Lee Michael Marinelli – b 13 Oct 1988 Bever, PA

Diane Marie THOMPSON d/o Lenore Kathryn Elizabeth nee Schminke & Clifford Virgil Thompson; b 30 Nov 1951 Virginia Gay Hosp Vinton, IA; m 19 Aug 1972 St.And to David Paul Kosbau (b 03 Jan 1951 Waverly, IA; Architectural Engineer/Contractor) Children:
   Jennifer Joy Kosbau – b 07 May 1976 Brookings, SD
   Jill Marie Kosbau – b 29 Aug 1978 Brookings, SD

Gary Clifford THOMPSON s/o Lenore Kathryn Elizabeth nee Schminke & Clifford Virgil Thompson; b 09 Apr 1958 Virginia Gay Hosp Vinton, IA; m 21 Jun 1980 Belle Plaine IA to Julie Ann Magdefrau (b 19 Jul 1960 Marengo, IA) d/o Don Magdefrau & Frances nee Backes. Children:
   Wesley Clifford – b 18 Jan 1984 St.Lukes Hosp Cedar Rapids, IA
   Emily Joy – b 18 Mar 1986 Mercy Hosp Cedar Rapids, IA

Gregory Lee THOMPSON s/o Lenore Kathryn Elizabeth nee Schminke & Clifford Virgil Thompson; b 30 Jun 1950 Van Horne, IA; m 03 Jun 1972 Virginia Gay Hosp Vinton, IA to Susan Kay Olson (b 02 Nov 1950) d/o Robert Olson & Betty nee Broad. TX residence. Children:
   Christopher David – b 09 Jun 1976 Dallas, TX
   Tammy Sue – b 08 Jun 1979 Dallas, TX
   Tiffany Ann – b 29 Aug 1981 Dallas, TX

David THURSTON d/o Harlan Thurston & Bernice Ella Louise nee Popenhagen; b 03 Sept 1953; m 14 May 1988 Shirley Biloszly (b 01 Jul 1954). Children:
   Roth A. – b 01 Mar 1989
   Jonathan D. – b 25 Jun 1990
   Mark S. – b 09 Jul 1993
   Susanne J. – b 31 Oct 1996

Marcella THURSTON d/o Harlan Thurston & Bernice Ella Louise nee Popenhagen; b 19 Jun 1949 Cedar Rapids, IA bpt 1949; 1st m 28 Feb 1969 Ronald Warren (b 04 Jan 1947) DVD 1979. Child:
   Ronald Warren JR. – b 12 Aug 1972

2nd m 31 Aug 1993 Marcella nee Thurston Warren to Jerry Emerson.

Steven THURSTON d/o Harlan Thurston & Bernice Ella Louise nee Popenhagen; b 13 Jul 1956; m 19 Dec 1976 Sherri Wonick (b 21 Jun 1958). Children:
    Rebekah A. – b 21 Sept 1980
    Hannah L. – b 26 Feb 1983
    Leah M. – b 06 Nov 1984
    Sarah E. – b 15 Dec 1986

Anne Marna Marie TIBBEN d/o Delores Ann nee Krug & John Tibben; b 11 Dec 1977; m 19 Aug 2000 rural Victor IA to Bradley Dwaye Nelson (b 25 Jan 1976 Greenfield, IA) s/o Ronald & Judy Nelson, Greenfield,IA. Both earned degrees from Iowa State University, Ames, IA. Child:
    Annika Rose Nelson – b 18 Nov 2005 Des Moines, IA
    Matthew DeWayne Nelson – b 17 Aug 2007 Des Moines, IA

Clifford Robert TRUMPY s/o Mary Louise nee Taschner & Clarence Jay Trumpy; b 1951; m Riva Sue Klatt (b 1951). Children:
    Stephanie Marie – b 1974; 1st m Joshua Herrington (b 1975);
        2nd m Robert Lee Taylor (b 1968)
    Robert Jay – b 1976; m Amanda Jayne Valenzuela (b 1975)

Donna Irene TRUMPY d/o Mary Louise nee Taschner & Clarence Jay Trumpy; b 1949; m Richard James Scott (b 1948). Children:
    Steven James Scott – b 1978
    Christine Louise Scott – b 1982

Tamara Kay VAN VLECK d/o Richard Van Vleck & Marjorie nee Campbell; b 30 May 1960; m 20 Mar 1983 David Manson. Children:
    Holly Marie Manson – b 21 Dec 1983
    Kelly Nicole Manson – b 01 May 1986

Timothy Lee VAN VLECK s/o Richard Van Vleck & Marjorie nee Campbell; b 03 Jan 1969; m 17 Jun 1981 Alta Gayle Stanley. Child:
    Curtis Lee – b 19 Dec 1983

Helen Rose VAUPEL d/o Justus Vaupel & Gertrud nee Umbach; b 1919; 1938 Class Vinton High School; rural school teacher; m 1942 Charles

Joseph Birker. Harrison Twp Benton Co IA farmers. Children:
Bonnie Elaine Birker – b 1945; m Jacques Wilson, Washington D.C.
Kenneth Charles Birker – b 1948; m Susan Jones. Sons: Scott, Matt,
   Jeff
Robert Don Birker – b 1951; m Kristie Flickinger,
   Harrison Twp farmers. Children: Justin, Garret, Kahree

*Justus VAUPEL b 04 Sept 1809 Germany, d 05 Apr 1889 ae79y 7m 1d
Löhlbach, Germany; m 26 Dec 1836 Löhlbach Ch to Anna Gertrude Paar
(b 07 Apr 1815 Löhlbach, Germany, d 16 Aug 1886 ae71y 4m 9d
Löhlbach, Germany). Child:
   *Katherina – b 18 Oct 1837 Löhlbach, Germany, d 27 Apr 1907
      Löhlbach; m 28 May 1860 Löhlbach Ch Justus Thielemann

*Justus VAUPEL b 1886 Kuchen, Germany, d 1968 Benton Co IA; m
1912 Gertrud Umbach (b 1890 Kuchen, Germany, d 1979 Benton Co IA)
1914/1915 emigrated with daughter Frieda to Newhall, IA. Benton Co
farmers. Children:
   *Frieda Elisabeth – b 21 Mar 1913 Germany; m 1931 John Epperson
   Carl – b 1916, d 1920 ae4y
   Helen Rose – b 1919; m 1942 Charles Joseph Birker
   Albert Henry – b 1920; m 1942 Viola Walter
   Elsie Martha – b 1925; m 1947 Ralph Wilson

*Katharina VAUPEL d/o Justus Vaupel & Anna Gertrude Paar of
Löhlbach, Germany; b 18 Oct 1837, d 27 Apr 1907 ae69y 6m 9d; m 28
May 1860 Löhlbach Ch to Justus Thielemann (b 10 Sept 1833, d 20 Feb
1885 ae51y 5m 10d). Child:
   *Konrad Thielemann – b 17 Aug 1862, d 09 Nov 1933;
      m 28 Feb 1892 Lucine Schween

Donald Adam VOGT s/o Phyllis Catherine nee Krug & Delbert Dale
Vogt; b 18 Nov 1952 Vinton, IA; 1st m 12 Feb 1977 Newhall, IA to
Maureen Katherine Murray (b 14 Oct 1956, New Hampton, IA d 29 Jan
1989 ae32y 3m 15d [Suicide] Cedar Rapids, IA home, bur 01 Feb 1989
St.Joseph Catholic Cem, Linn Co) d/o Cletus Murray of New Hampton,
IA. Cedar Rapids, IA residence; Donald: Vogt salvage business.
Children:
   Christine Marie – b 06 Aug 1977
   Melissa Lynn – b 11 Nov 1979

2nd m Feb 1995 Donald Adam Vogt to Andie Albert

*Hermann Karl VOGT s/o Ludwig Vogt & Augusta Wilhelmina nee Doll; b 1879 Germany, d 09 Mar 1950 Atkins, IA; m 22 Jan 1902 Helena Mae Wagner of Homestead, IA(d 13 Aug 1973 at home of her daughter Alice). After farming near Vinton, IA for several years, moved to Atkins with young daughter, Ruth Marie. 1912 purchased house on corner east of Presbyterian Ch. Another daughter born in this home. Children:
    Ruth Marie – m Harland Bus; Angola, NY residence
    Alice – m LeRoy Wright; Belle Plaine, IA residence

John Duane VOGT s/o Phyllis Catherine nee Krug & Delbert Dale Vogt; b 25 May 1959. Child:
    Jared – b Jul 1989
    Jennifer – b 29 1994 (mother: Julie Vansickel)

*Ludwig VOGT & wife Augusta Wilhelmina nee Doll 1884 emigrated USA with three children from Rolsdorf, Germany:
    *Hermann Karl- b 1879 Germany;
        m Helena Mae Wagner of Homestead, IA
    *Otto – b 1881 Germany
    *Anna – b 1883 Germany
Settled near Palo, IA where Augusta had relatives and farmed in that vicinity all their lives. Six more children born in USA:
    Minnie – NFR
    Mary – NFR
    Louis – NFR
    Harry – NFR
    William – NFR
    John – NFR

Ronald Dale VOGT s/o Phyllis Catherine nee Krug & Delbert Dale Vogt; b 18 Sept 1952 Vinton, IA; 1st m 07 Jul 1972 Barbra Uridil DVD 1975. Child:
    Sean Dale – b 16 Jul 1973; m 14 Aug 1999 Tina Lynne Ballard
2nd m Jul 1980 Ronald Dale Vogt to Ellen Marie Day DVD
3rd m 14 Apr 1984 Ronald Dale Vogt to Bonnie Zhanek (b 16 Oct 1947) DVD.

Daniel Joseph VOSS s/o Elaine nee Risdal & Francis Daniel Voss; m 23

Jul 1988 Susan L. Waterman. Children:
    Daniel C. – b 08 Jul 1990
    Brian D. – b 11 Sept 1993
    Matthew J. – b 29 Jul 1997

Ellen K. VOSS d/o Elaine nee Risdal & Francis Daniel Voss; m 08 Nov
1986 James M. McDonald. Children:
    Danny McDonald – b 24 Jul 1987
    Megan McDonald – b 10 Mar 1989
    John McDonald – b 24 Jun 1994

James C. VOSS s/o Elaine nee Risdal & Francis Daniel Voss; m 25 Jul
1998 Tamara Fuller. STEPCHILDREN:
    Ashley – b 14 Oct 1986
    Andrew – b 08 Oct 1988
    Josh Busenbark – b 15 Feb 1989
    Caitlin Busenbark – b 05 Sept 1991

Thomas John VOSS s/o Elaine nee Risdal & Francis Daniel Voss; m 06
Feb 1993 Jill Marie nee Grow Runde. Children:
    STEPCHILD: Elise Runde – b 24 Aug 1986
    Madison – b 10 Dec 1996

Ernest WAGNER s/o Amelia Caroline nee Taschner & Louis Wagner; b
1883, d 1972; m Ina Elizabeth Burns (b 1894, d 1962). Children:
    Leland B – NFR
    Vivian L. – b 1914; m NN Manning
    Vernal L. – NFR
    Frances N. – b 1917; m Thomas M. Davis
    Donald Roy – b 1926

Doreen WALTER d/o Betty Lou nee Happel & Jerry Walter; b 03 May
1962; m 02 Jun 1984 Mark Boss (b 26 Feb 1964). Children:
    Megan R. Boss – b 05 Apr 1989
    Sean Boss – b 03 Sept 1991

Louise WARNER d/ Frieda nee Paulsen & William Warner; b 1921, d
1999; m Erwin Wiebold (b 1914). Children:
    Margaret Wiebold – b 1941; m Avery Merriman
    Raymond Wiebold – b 1943; m Donna Brott

Joanne Ruth Wiebold – b 18 Feb 1945;
 m 09 Jun 1963 Lawrence "Larry" Martin Moeller
William Wiebold – b 1949; m Wendy Lee Luken
Kathryn Ann Wiebold – b 1953; m Harold Scheesley

William WARNER JR.s/o William Warner SR. & Frieda nee Paulsen; b
1929; m Elizabeth (Bunny) Morning (b 1927). Children:
 Lynnette – b 1950; 1st m John E. Heisel JR.; 2nd m John Darrow
  (b 1946). Children: Erin Darrow (b 1981), Michael Darrow
  (b 1986)
 Luanne – b 1953; m Gary Lee Frett. Children: Cameron Lee Frett
  (b 1975), Peter Graham Frett (b 1977), Aubrey Frett (b 1980),
  Sebastian Frett (b 1984)
 Richard William – b 1960; m Marlene NN

James Warren WATERMAN s/o Kathryn Marie nee Haerther & Warren
Walter Waterman; b 02 Jun 1956 St.Lukes Hosp Cedar Rapids, IA;
Chemical Engineer Degree Iowa State U.;Phillips Petroleum; m 03 Aug
1985 Redeemer Luth Ch, Bartlesville, OK to Loretta Jo Benson (b 14
Sept 1955 St.Anthony's Hosp Oklahoma City, OK; Graduate
Southwestern Oklahoma State U.; C.P.A.) d/o Lloyd Alvin Benson &
Doris Evelyn nee Miller. Bartlesville. OK residence. Children:
 Bethany Megan – b 17 Dec 1987 Golden Plains Com Hosp,
  Borger, TX
 Matthew James – b 25 Jul 1990 Bartlesville, OK
 Tyler John – b 09 Oct 1993 Bartlesville, OK

Karen Sue WATERMAN d/o Kathryn Marie nee Haerther & Warren
Walter Waterman; b 31 Dec 1959 St.Lukes Hosp Cedar Rapids, IA;
Graduate Central Luth Benton Co & U. of Northern IA; Teacher; m 18
Nov 1989 St.Joseph's Catholic Ch Bellevue, IA to Thomas Joseph
Timmerman (b 26 Jan 1960; Partner in Rotman Motor Co, Maquoketa,
IA) s/o Roman & Cecilia Timmerman. Maquoketa, IA. Children:
 Rachel Marie Timmerman – b 08 May 1993 Dubuque, IA
 Alex Thomas Timmerman – b 01 Jun 1995 Dubuque, IA
 Erica Leigh Timmerman – b 09 May 1998 Dubuque, IA

Kathy Ann WATERMAN d/o Kathryn Marie nee Haerther & Warren
Walter Waterman; b 05 Dec 1957 St.Lukes Hosp Cedar Rapids, IA; bpt
22 Dec 1957 and con 26 Mar 1972 St.Steph; Kirkwood Community

College; m 21 Jul 1979 St.Steph to Gorden Lewis Jacobsen (b 20 Feb 1956 St.Lukes Hosp Cedar Rapids, IA bpt 01 Apr 1956 Hopkinton Methodist Ch Hopkinton, IA, con 27 Mar 1972 St.Steph; Kirkwood Community College; Andrew's Auto Restoration) s/o Gorden F. Jacobsen & LaVonne Lucille nee Willard Sass. Atkins, IA residence. Children:
>   Alexis Katharina Jacobsen – b 04 Oct 1983 Mercy Hosp CR;
>   bpt 30 Dec 1983; con Apr 1997

Sharyln WAX d/o Nadine nee Schrader & Clifford Wax; b 1947; Registered Nurse; m Dr. James Munn. Peoria, IL residence. Children:
>   Stephanie Munn – b 1978
>   Justin Munn – b 1982

Janet Lynn WEBERT d/o Melvin Gottfried Webert & Eleanor Louise Barbara nee Rinderknecht; b 18 Nov 1942 St.Lukes Hosp Cedar Rapids, IA; m 20 Oct 1962 St.Paul Catholic Ch Newhall, IA to James Leroy Boddicker (b 28 Sept 1940 Mercy Hosp Cedar Rapids, IA) s/o Leroy Joseph Boddicker & Geraldine nee Hegewald. Farmers. Children:
>   Janel Lyn Boddicker – b 26 Jul 1963 Mercy Hosp Cedar Rapids, IA;
>   m 24 Jul 1982 Douglas Jay Rathbun
>   Jill Ann Boddicker – b 05 Jun 1965 Mercy Hosp Cedar Rapids, IA
>   Jeffrey James Boddicker – b 17 Apr 1067 Mercy Hosp
>   Cedar Rapids, IA

Jo Ann WEBERT d/o Melvin Gottfried Webert & Eleanor Louise Barbara nee Rinderknecht; b 12 Jul 1945 Virginia Gay Hosp Vinton, IA; m 07 Mar 1964 St.John to Dennis Leroy Karr (b 31 Jan 1945 Virginia Gay Hosp Vinton, IA; Owner Karr Trucking, Newhall, IA) s/o Albert Raymond Karr & Betty June nee Dowler. Children:
>   Deborah Lynn Karr – b 30 Sept 1964 St.Lukes Hosp
>   Cedar Rapids, IA; m 06 Aug 1983 Douglas Alan Stien
>   Brenda Jo Karr – b 25 Apr 1967 St.Lukes Hosp Cedar Rapids, IA;
>   m 29 Aug 1986 Robert Alan Schanbacher
>   Michael Dennis Karr – b 21 Jun 1972 St.Lukes Hosp
>   Cedar Rapids, IA

Judy Louise WEBERT d/o Melvin Gottfried Webert & Eleanor Louise Barbara nee Rinderknecht; b 22 Oct 1948 St.Lukes Hosp Cedar Rapids, IA; m 02 Dec 1967 St.John to Richard Clarence Hertle (b 29 Oct 1938

Eden Twp Benton Co IA) s/o Clarence Johann Conrad Hertle & Elfrieda Christina nee Fiebelkorn. Children:

>Brad Douglas Hertle – b 15 Dec 1968 St.Lukes Hosp Cedar Rapids, IA
>
>Shonda Jo Hertle – b 07 Jan 1972 St.Lukes Hosp Cedar Rapids, IA

Beth WEHRKAMP d/o Yvonne Marie nee Happel & Glenn Wehrkamp; b 18 Dec 1962; m Aug 1990 Robert McWilliams. Child:

>Ryanna McWilliams – b 27 Feb 1992

Pamela WEHRKAMP d/o Yvonne Marie nee Happel & Glenn Wehrkamp; b 12 Jul 1959; m 10 Aug 1985 Steve Egli. Child:

>Megan Egli – b 23 Jun 1986

Amelia WEICHMAN d/o John Weichman & Mary nee Davis; b 1887; m 1914 William Brecht. Children:

>Ruth Brecht – NFR
>
>Arlene Brecht – NFR
>
>Rolland Brecht – b 1920; m 1948 Marian Dill

Byrdine Ann WEICHMAN d/o Victor Dewey Weichman & Bertha M. nee Schirm; b 07 Oct 1932, 1950 Class Newhall High School; m 26 Aug 1951 St.John to Charles Robert Siek (b 09 Jan 1929, 1947 Class Blairstown High School, US Army Korean Conflict; Realtor) s/o Charles Henry Siek & Hilda nee Boddicker of Blairstown, IA. 1953 purchased Blairstown Hardware store; 1969 Plumbing & Heating business; changed to excavating and trenching business. Mbrs Grace Luth Ch, Blairstown, IA. Children:

>Bobbi Jean Siek – b 27 Jul 1954
>
>William Weichman Siek (Adopted) – b 11 Sept 1959

Caroline WEICHMAN d/o John C. Weichman & Mary nee Davis; b 1884, d 1918; m 1904 Albert J. Boddicker (b 1881 St.Clair Twp Benton Co IA, d 1963) s/o Joseph Boddicker & Sophia nee Pieper; first lived in Cedar Rapids, IA moved to farm two and 1/2 miles south of Newhall in Eldorado Twp Benton Co IA. After Caroline's death, Albert sold farm, built home in Newhall, IA moved there in 1922 with daughters. They had housekeeper until 1924. Children:

>Bernice Boddicker – b 1911; Cedar Rapids, IA residence
>
>Marie Boddicker – b 1914; m 1937 Donald Campbell

Lois Boddicker – b 1917; Cedar Rapids, IA residence
2nd m 1924 Albert J. Boddicker to Wilhelmina nee Planken Schrader (b 1889, d 1955). She had son, John Schrader, from a former marriage and came from Germany a few years earlier to keep house for her uncle, Henry Planken, a saloonkeeper in Newhall's early years. John Schrader and his family reside in CA; Child of Albert and Wilhelmina:
    Mildred Boddicker – b 1925; MI residence

Charles WEICHMAN s/o Henry Weichman & Mary nee Schultz; b 1863, d 1939; m Mary Schlotterbeck (b 1864, d 1928) d/o Johann Gottlieb & Christiana Schlotterbeck. Farmers in Fremont Twp Benton Co IA. Children:
    Fred – b 1886, d 1927; m 1911 Anna Baumgartner
    Wilhelmina – b 1887, d 1922
    Elmer – b 1890, d 1922
    Louis – b 1891, d 1976; m Lena Boisen
    Lester – b 1892
    Earl – b 1898; Cedar Rapids, IA residence

David Edward WEICHMAN s/o Harry Weichman & Elizabeth nee Meyer; b 1921 Newhall; 1946 graduate U. of Iowa; 1948 College of Law degree; practiced law in Newhall, IA; Army Air Corps 1942-1945; US Air Corps Reserves 1972 retirement; Iowa State Representative; Newhall JP; Law Clerk, Iowa General Assembly; and other public offices; mbr St.John; Boy Scouts of America.

Debra Joy WEICHMAN d/o Donald Weichman & Shirley L. nee Cahoe; b 1954; m 1977 Douglas Wessling. Child:
    Brooke Wessling – b 1980

Donald WEICHMAN s/o Victor Weichman & Bertha nee Schirm; b 1927; m 1950 Shirley L. Cahoe. Children:
    Debra Joy – b 1954; m 1977 Douglas Wessling
    Cynthia Joy – b 1957

Elma Ellen WEICHMAN d/o John Weichman & Mary nee Davis; b 1889, d 1971; m 1915 Edgar Brecht (b 1892, d 1956). Farmers near Vinton, IA later moving to Quasqueton, IA on a farm. Illness of Edgar forced them to quit farming and move to Newhall, IA where he built a billiard parlor with living quarters upstairs. Edgar in partnership with his brother-in-law, Henry Weichman, in a grocery store across the street from the billiard parlor. Retired to Vinton, IA. Children:

Iver Brecht – b 1916; m 1945 Mary Bissel; Muscatine, IA residence
Virginia Brecht – b 1918; Vinton, IA residence

Emery WEICHMAN s/o John Weichman & Mary nee Davis; b 1897, d 1972; m 1918 Ethel Farrell (b 1897). Children:

Gail – MFR
Phyllis – NFR
Rozella – NFR
Joyce – NFR

Firman WEICHMAN s/o John Weichman & Mary nee Davis; b 1893, d 1938; m 1914 Emma Boddicker (b 1896, d 1926). Children:

Lolita – NFR
Viola – NFR
Edna – NFR
Donald – b 1925, d 1926

Frank WEICHMAN s/o Henry Weichman & Mary nee Schultz; b 1866 Linn Co IA, d 1918 Raetz Cem, Atkins, IA; m 1890 Pauline Schlotterbeck (b 1866, d 1920, bur Raetz Cem, Atkins, IA) d/o Johann Gottlieb & Christiana Schlotterbeck. Farmers and stock raisers, cattle and hogs; acquired several Benton Co IA farms and a tract of land in Hartley Co TX; Frank diretor of Newhall, IA Savings Bank twenty-two years; director school district in Fremont Twp Benton Co IA. Children:

Clarence – b 1890, d 1918
Harry Edward – b 1892 farm near Newhall, IA d 1978;
    m 1914 Elizabeth Maria Meyer
Victor Dewey – b 1898, d 1981; m 1919 Bertha M. Schirm
Irene – b 1903; m Raymond Kelly
Madeline – b 1912; m 1934 Gilbert Gluesing

Fred WEICHMAN s/o Charles Weichman & Mary nee Schlotterbeck; b 1886, d 1967; Farmers in Fremont Twp Benton Co IA; m 1911 Anna Baumgartner (b 1890, d 1963) d/o Louis Baumgartner & Anne nee Bauer. Child:

Gladys – b 1912; m 1968 Harold Carlson

Harry Edward WEICHMAN s/o Frank Weichman & Pauline nee

Schlotterbeck; b 1892 farm near Newhall, IA d 1978; Cedar Rapids Business College; baseball enthusiast playing, managing, umpire on teams; 1st m 1914 Elizabeth Maria Meyer (b 1891, d 1964) d/o Ernst H.F. Meyer & Eliza nee Strankman of Van Horne. Settled on farm at south edge of Newhall, IA; 1941 moved to new home built in Newhall and 1955-1970 established real estate agency. Children:

    Herbert Franklin – b 1917

    David Edward – b 1921

2nd m 1970 Harry Edward Weichman to Marvel nee Hodge Pepmeyer.

*Henry WEICHMAN b 1830 Germany, d 1894; emigrated USA ae24y and settled in PA where he worked in the coal mines; m 1855 Mary Schultz (b 1831 New Caliss, Mecklenburg, Germany, d 1898). 1857 moved to Iowa and settled near Marion, Linn Co IA where they remained until Jan 1866 move to Benton Co IA to purchase wild prairie land in Section 6 and 7 Fremont Twp Benton Co; engaged in farming and improving land. Henry acquired land from Milwaukee Land Company in Newhall, IA build a residence on Main Street. Children:

    Mary W. – b 1885, d 1938; m Jacob Schlotterbeck

    John C. – b 1858 Linn Co IA, d 1938; m Mary Davis

    Charles – b 1863, d 1939; m Mary Schlotterbeck

    Frank – b 1866 Linn Co IA, d 1918 bur Raetz Cem, Atkins;

        m 1890 Pauline Schlotterbeck

    Henry – b 1867, d 1872

    Christian A. – b 1872, d 1952

    Josephine – b 1861, d 19 Nov 1897;

        m 29 Mar 1882 William Schlotterback

    Wilhelmina – b 1870, d 1872

Henry WEICHMAN s/o John C. Weichman & Mary nee Davis; b 1891, d 1975; m 1920 Norma Rogers (b 1889, d 1972). Children:

    Rhoda Ann – NFR

    John – NFR

    James – NFR

John WEICHMAN s/o Henry Weichman & Mary nee Schultz; b 1858 Linn Co IA, d 1938; m 1883 Mary Davis (b 1864 Benton Co IA, d 1950) d/o Henry Davis & Louisa nee Baker. 1919 residence on farm one mile north and 1 ¾ miles east of Newhall for thirty-six years where they built a new home in 1898. Retired in Newhall, IA. Children:

Caroline – b 1884, d 1918; m 1904 Albert J. Boddicker
Louise – b 1885, d 1978; m 1910 August Abraham JR.
Amelia – b 1887; m 1914 William Brecht
Elma – b 1889, d 1971; m Edgar Brecht
Henry – b 1891, d 1975; m 1920 Norma Rogers
Firman – b 1893, d 1938; m 1914 Emma Boddicker
Irvin – b 1895, d 1980; farmed near Newhall, IA
Emery – b 1897, d 1972; m 1918 Ethel Farrell
Leo – b 1899, d 1972

Louis WEICHMAN s/o Charles Weichman & Mary nee Schlotterbeck; b 1891, d 1976; m Lena Boisen. Child:
Marjorie – b 1915, d 1965; m Harold Carlson

Louise WEICHMAN d/o John C. Weichman & Mary nee Davis; b 1885, d 1978; m 1910 August Abraham JR. s/o August Heinrich Abraham SR. & Rosena Louise nee Kramer. Child:
Glenn Abraham – NFR

Madeline WEICHMAN d/o Frank Weichman & Pauline nee Schlotterbeck; b 1912; m 1934 Gilbert Gluesing (b 1912, d 2003) s/o John N. Gluesing & Hannah nee Senne. Farmed twenty-four years two miles south of Newhall, IA; 1958 moved to Newhall; maintenance worker for town and worked for Newhall Grain Elevator twelve years. Children:
Shirley Gluesing – b 1935; m Eldo Meyer
Jo Ann Gluesing – b 1937; m Jack Phelps
Ronald Gluesing – b 1943, d 1957 farm [Tractor Accident]

Marjorie WEICHMAN d/o Louis Weichman & Lena nee Boisen; b 1915, d 1965; m Harold Carlson. Child:
Cheryl Carlson – CA residence

Victor Dewey WEICHMAN s/o Frank Weichman & Elizabeth nee Schlotterbeck; b 17 May 1898, d 1981; m 15 Oct 1919 Bertha M. Schirm (b 20 Feb 1898 Newhall, IA). Children:
Donald Edward – b 09 Sept 1927; m 1950 Shirley L. Cahoe
Byrdine Ann – b 07 Oct 1932 Newhall, IA;
        m 26 Aug 1951 Charles Robert Siek

Scott Alan WELTY s/o Alberta Elizabeth nee Rinderknecht & Gerald Nathan Welty; b 26 May 1959 Guttenberg, IA (Adopted Luth Home) m 10 Jun 1988 St.Joseph Catholic Ch Marion, IA to Amy Kathleen Mitchell (b 14 Jul 1966 Cedar Rapids, IA) d/o Richard Stanley Mitchell & Rosalynn Marie nee Marks. Child:
    Kathleen – b 14 Jul 1966

Sherri Lynn WELTY d/o Alberta Elizabeth nee Rinderknecht & Gerald Nathan Welty; b 28 Jul 1962 Davenport, IA (Adopted Luth Home) m 28 Aug 1982 Concordia Luth Ch Cedar Rapids, IA to Timothy David Patten (b 29 Mar 1960 Cedar Rapids, IA) s/o Morris Gabriel Patten & Ivy Dean nee Aamodt. Children:
    Sarah Elizabeth Patten – b 23 Nov 1989 Emporia, KS
    Zachary Aaron Patten – b 10 Sept 1991 Emporia, KS

Alice WENDEL d/o Conrad Wendel & Nancy nee Lucy; b on Wendel Fremont Twp Benton Co IA farm; m John Raetz. Farmed until retiring to home in Cedar Rapids, IA. Children:
    Robert Raetz – Never Married; residence with parents
    Mary Raetz – m Lynn Doyle; Cedar Rapids, IA residence

Augustus WENDEL s/o Conrad Wendel & Nancy nee Lucy; b 1870 Wendel farm Fremont Twp Benton Co IA, d Sept 1933 farm southwest Newhall, IA; m 1902 Louise Krahling (b 1879, d 1966) d/o Conrad "Con" Krahling & Christiana nee Engles. Farmed near Lake Preston, SD until 1904; returned to Iowa to farm one-half mile west and two miles north of Atkins, Benton Co; March 1911 moved to farm southwest of Newhall, IA where "Gustus" died. Children:
    Alice – dec'd at six weeks in SD
    Harry – b 13 Jun 1904 near Lake Preston, SD;
       m 17 Feb 1938 Letha Doris Risdal
    Anna Martha – b 08 Jan 1906 Canton Twp Benton Co IA,
       d 17 Oct 1988; bur St.Steph Cem;
       m 03 Sept 1930 Carl George Haerther
    Loren – b IA; m 1936 Glenda Melhus, Benton Co IA residence
    Ida – b IA; m Lloyd Peck
    Elwood – b 1914 IA, d 1977; m rural Watkins, IA to E.Faye Higgens

Charles WENDEL s/o Harry A. Wendel & Letha Doris nee Risdal; b 13 Feb 1939; m 26 Jun 1959 Kay Gerke of State Center, IA. Charles employed at Acme Electric Company, Cedar Rapids, IA; Author of two books on antique tractors. Farmed original Wendel homestead southwest of Atkins, Benton Co IA until moving to Amana, IA. Children:

    Steven – b 30 Oct 1961; Atkins, IA farmer

    Lisa – b 30 Dec 1963; m Bruce Seaba, Muscatine, IA

    Rosalyn – b 25 Jan 1966; m Donald Boddicker, Vinton, IA

*Conrad WENDEL b 20 Dec 1838 Sand, Hesse, Germany, d 03 Feb 1896 ae58y Fremont Twp Benton Co IA; 1855 emigrated to USA ae17y and worked ten years in Herkimer Co, NY near city of Ilion, NY; m 1865 Nancy Lucy (b Herkimer Co, New York, d 19 Apr 1924 Atkins, IA). A New York native whose ancestors had established in Herkimer Co prob 1840. Conrad came to Fremont Twp Benton Co IA Aug 1866 and bought eighty acres in Section 28, returning to Herkimer Co, NY to prepare his wife and infant son, William, for the trip to Iowa. Arriving in autumn, logs were hawled from a site two miles north of Shellsburg, IA to build a 12 x 16 foot log cabin on the property while the family lived with the Silas Kimm family. A modern home was built, prob 1880, and it remained until 1956. Children:

    William – b Herkimer Co NY, d 1926; Never Married; well driller

    Cora – b IA; m J.J. Schlotterback, moved to Manly, IA

    Augustus – b 1870 IA, d Sept 1933; m 1902 Louisa Krahling; farmers

    Henry – b IA, d 1942; m 1898 Annie E. Krahling

    Martha – b IA, d 1980 ae100+y; Never Married; seamstress

    Jacob – b IA, d May 1919 [Influenza] Atkins, blacksmith

    Alice – b IA; m John Raetz; farmers

Cora WENDEL d/o Conrad Wendel & Nancy nee Lucy; b Fremont Twp Benton Co IA Wendel farm; m J.J. Schlotterback. Farmers on land later occupied by Karl Wilhelmi, son Edward, and Edward JR. Prob 1910 Cora & husband moved to Manly, IA. Children:

    Homer Schlotterback – NFR

    Raymond Schlotterback – NFR

    Louis Schlotterback – NFR

    Mae Schlotterback – NFR

    Fred Schlotterback – NFR

Douglas Ray WENDEL s/o Loren Wendel & Glenda nee Melhus; b 1943; 1961 Class Newhall High School; m Sally Rae Franck (b 1946)

d/o George Franck & Marion nee Braksiek. Carpenter/owner of business. Children:
> Kelly Rae – b 22 Mar 1966; m 07 Mar 1988 Steven James Heistoffer
> Amy Rae – b 1969

Edwin WENDEL s/o Loren Wendel & Glenda nee Melhus; m Bonnie Boyles. Farmed Wendel family homestead of Loren & Glenda. Children:
> Heidi – NFR
> Jason – NFR
> Casey – NFR

Elwood WENDEL s/oAugustus Wendel & Louisa nee Krahling. b 1914, d 1977; m E.Faye Higgins in rural Watkins, IA. Child:
> Shirley M. – 15 Aug 1935, d 11 Sept 2002
> Janice – m George Alber Hepker, Urbana, IA
> William – m Nancy, Oelwein, IA
> Richard – m Sandra, Urbana, IA

Harry A. WENDEL s/o Augustus Wendel & Louisa nee Krahling; b 13 Jun 1904 near Lake Preston, SD, d 1981; m 17 Feb 1938 Blairstown, IA to Letha Doris Risdal (b 10 May 1909 rural Newhall, IA d 30 Jul 1993 Mercy Medical Center, Cedar Rapids, IA bur Raetz Cem, Atkins, IA). Farmed original Wendel homestead. Children:
> Charles – b 13 Feb 1939; m 26 Jun 1959 Kay Gerke,
>   Amana, IA residence
> Louise – b 06 Mar 1944; m Sherman Kline, Amana, IA residence

Henry WENDEL s/o Conrad Wendel & Nancy nee Lucy; b Benton Co IA, d 1942 Atkins, IA; m 1898 Annie E. Krahling (d 1906). Farmed Wendel homestead until 1922 when moved to Atkins and opened a blacksmith shop operating it until his death. The Atkins Fire Station stands directly on this site. Children:
> Conrad – NFR
> William – NFR

Kelly Rae WENDEL d/o Douglas Wendel & Salley Rae nee Franck; b 22 Mar 1966; m 07 Mar 1988 Steven James Heistoffer. Child:
> Allison Ann Heistoffer – b 03 Feb 1989

Loren WENDEL s/o Augustus Wendel & Louise nee Krahling; m 1936

Glenda Melhus. Farmed one mile south and 1/2 mile east of Jct. 218 and US 30. Children:
    Glenys – NFR
    James – NFR
    Thomas – NFR
    Betty – NFR
    Douglas Ray – b 1943; m Sally Rae Franck
    Edwin – m Bonnie Boyles

*Fredaricka WENDT b 1878 Schwerim, Germany, d 1940 Benton Co IA; m Charles Warner (b 1896 Blairstown, Benton Co IA, d 1953) s/o Hans Warner & Margaret nee Thasiaman. Farmers northwest Eldorado Twp Benton Co IA twenty-five years before moving to Van Horne, IA. Children:
    Clara Marie Warner – b 1896 farm northwest of Newhall, IA
        d 1974; m 1917 John Fred Paulsen
    John Warner – b 01 Jun 1897; m 23 Feb 1919 Hulda Werning
    William Warner – b 1899; m Frieda Paulsen
    Wilma Warner – b 1910; m Frank Gintert

*Christian Wilhelm WENTE s/o Johann Friedrich Wente & Engle Marie nee Bredermeier; b 24 Sept 1813 Germany, d 11 Sept 1882 IA, ae68y 11m 18d bur Maxfield Ch Cem, Bremer Co IA; m Sophie Wilhelma Charlotte Schroeder (b 15 Dec 1823 Reinsdorf, Germany, d 29 Jul 1905 ae81y 7m 13d bur Maxfield Ch Cem, Bremer Co IA). Children:
    *Ernest Christian – b 1855, d Dec 1919; m Engle Mary Wehmhoffer

Ernest WENTE s/o Ernest Christian Wente & Engle Mary nee Wehmhoffer; b 01 Jun 1884, d 12 Mar 1974 ae89y 9m 11d ; m 07 May 1907 Emma Wenthe (b 30 Sept 1887, d 26 May 1960 ae72y 7m 26d). Children:
    Mabel – b 13 Nov 1908, d 17 Sept 1974; m Otis Dappert
        (b 16 Nov 1907, d 15 May 1961)
    Esther – b 03 Jun 1920; m 21 Dec 1941 Elvin Pete Torbeck

*Ernest Christian WENTE s/o Christian Wilhelm Wente & Sophie Wilhelma Charlotte nee Schroeder; b 1855 Germany, d Dec 1919; 1871 came to USA; 1876 returned to Germany after becoming USA citizen; m 12 Sept 1876 Engle Mary Wehmhoffer (b 20 Aug 1850 Hanover, Germany, d Oct 1940 ae90y). Children:

550

Heinrich – b 13 Nov 1877; d ae11y 2m 27 d [Killed by a bull]
Mary Sophia – b 08 Sept 1879 Bremer Co IA, d 31 Jul 1975
    Springfield, OH; m 01 Feb 1900 Conrad Braun
William – b 11 Oct 1881, d 01 Nov 1971;
    m 23 Feb 1905 Matilda Wenthe
Ernest – b 01 Jun 1884, d 12 Mar 1974;
    m 07 May 1907 Emma Wenthe
Louise Sophia – b 22 Sept 1886, d 10 Mar 1971;
    m 19 Dec 1907 Andrew John Happel
Louis – b 25 Dec 1888 Waverly, IA; d 13 Oct 1963 Ft. Collins, CO;
    m and No Children
Minnie Carolyn – b 31 Mar 1891, d 20 Nov 1963

*Johann Friedrich WENTE b 08 Mar 1795 Hse #11 Antendorf Co
Schaumburg, Germany, d 20 Jan 1857 ae61y 10m 12d; m Engle Marie
Bredermeier (b 1791, d 1844). Children:
    *Christian Wilhelm – b 24 Sept 1813, d 11 Sept 1882;
        m Sophie Wilhelma Charlotte Schroeder
    *Wilhelm Christian – b 15 Feb 1816, d 12 Mar 1892

Louise Sophia WENTE d/o Ernest Christian Wente & Engle Mary nee
Wehmhoffer: cf Andrew John Happel.

Mary Sophia WENTE d/o Ernest Christian Wente & Engle Mary nee
Wehmhoffer; b 08 Sept 1879 Bremer Co IA, d 31 Jul 1975 ae95y 10m
23d Springfield, OH; m 01 Feb 1900 Conrad Braun (b 26 Oct 1874
Blasbach, Germany, d 16 Aug 1960 ae85y 9m 22d; 1892 came to
Philadelphia, PA). Children:
    Ernest Braun – b 28 Jan 1901, d 28 Jan 1992;
        m 18 Nov 1933 Ruth Estep (b 1909, d 1990)
    Otillie Louise Braun – b 22 Nov 1902 Diggins, MO;
        d 02 Sept 1989 Denver, CO; m 18 Sept 1923 George Hautum
    William Ernest Braun – b 02 Feb 1904, d 13 Feb 1904
    Katherine Pauline Braun – b 15 Dec 1906 Diggins, MO;
        d 23 Apr 1996 Greely, CO;
        m 07 May 1928 George Coakley Cowherd
    Esther Louise Braun – b 29 Mar 1910, d 28 Jul 1987 in CA;
        m William Rubke (b 13 Oct 1900)
    Walter Arthur Braun – b 08 Oct 1912, d 26 Apr 1995;
        m 27 Nov 1938 Edna Smith

William WENTE s/o Ernest Christian Wente & Engle Mary nee Wehmhoffer; b 11 Oct 1881, d 01 Nov 1971 ae90y 20d; m 23 Feb 1905 Matilda Wenthe (b 10 Jul 1882, d 03 Mar 1973 ae99y 7m 21d). Children:
> Lydia – b 06 Mar 1906, d 29 Jul 1955
> Minnie – b 20 Sept 1907
> Gertrude – b 30 Jan 1910, d 27 Jul 1982;
>> m 31 May 1940 Military Army Chaplain Markus Lohrmann
> Ella – b 13 Nov 1915, d 31 May 1966; m Robert Harris

*Adam WERNING SR.: cf Johann Adam WERNING (GS St.John) s/o Johann Valentin Werning & Anna Martha nee Orth.

Albert WERNING s/o Lawrence Albert Werning & Maxine nee Boddicker; m Linda Womichil. Newhall, IA residence. Children:
> Kristie – NFR
> Aaron – NFR

Albert G. WERNING JR.s/o Albert G.Werning SR. & Hildegard nee Guericke; b 21 Feb 1941; 1st m 08 Jul 1962 Betty Moege (b 27 Mar 1945) d/o Emil Moege & Ida nee Walz/ DVD Dec 1978. Children:
> Tamara Lynn – b 21 Dec 1962; m 1983 Kalvin Kurtenbach
> Albert Douglas III – b 13 Nov 1963; m 15 Aug 1897 Jean Polbreisg
> Michelle Jean – b 26 Jul 1966; m 1987 Kelly Krueger
> Wendy Noel – b 11 Jul 1973
2nd m 25 Apr 1980 Albert G. Werning JR. to Linda Plagman of Mitchell, SD d/o Luella Plagman.

Albert G. WERNING SR. s/o J.A.Wilhelm Werning & Frieda nee Ahrendt; b 24 Feb 1900 Hudson Co SD, d 10 Jul 1970 ae70y 4m 16d Parkston, SD Hospital; m 07 Jun 1925 Clayton, SD to Hildegard Guericke (b 26 Nov 1906, d 27 Mar 1998 ae91y 4m 1d but 30 Mar 1998 Faith Luth Ch, Parkston, SD) d/o Conrad Guericke & Magdelena nee Kretzman. Farmers in Emery, SD area; semi-retired at time of Albert's death. Children:
> Arthur – b 10 May 1926; m 29 Aug 1948 Hilda Huber
> Elma – b 05 Jan 1928, d 24 Jun 1978; m 10 Nov 1946 Harold Huber
> Elmer – b 22 Sept 1929; m 03 Mar 1957 Marcella Winter
> Marvin – b 14 Feb 1932; m 05 Jun 1955 Alvina Konstanz
> Albert G. JR.- b 21 Feb 1941; 1st m 08 Jul 1962 Betty Moege DVD;

2nd m 25 Apr 1980 Linda Plagman

2nd m 28 Sept 1974 Parkston, SD Hildegard nee Guericke Werning to John Buenning(b 15 Oct 1905, d 04 May 1984 ae78y 6m 19d [Heart Disease]s/o Johannes Heinrich Buenning of Melente, Germany.

Albert W. WERNING s/o Justus Werning & Marie nee Krahling; b 04 Aug 1893, d 02 Jul 1938 44y 10m 23d; m 23 Feb 1916 Martha A. Rathje (b 26 Feb 1892, d 30 Jan 1944 ae51y 11m 4d) d/o Johann Heinrich (Henry) Rathje & Anna Rebecca Katherina nee Seeborger. Farmers northeast of Newhall, IA. Children:
    Elwood Henry – b 06 Sept 1917, d 1976;
        m Mary El Ryan; Des Moines, IA
    Lawrence Albert – b 11 Dec 1919; m 1944 Maxine Boddicker
    Edwin – b 24 Nov 1923; d 22 Mar 2002;
        m 12 May 1946 Melba W. Banse (d 16 Dec 1995)
        Vinton, IA residence; No children
    Merrill – b 1928, d 1928

Alice WERNING d/o J.A. Wilhelm Werning & Frieda nee Ahrendt; b 22 Mar 1904, d 14 Mar 1954 ae49y 11m 22d; m 16 Apr 1925 to Arthur Guericke SR. (b 11 Dec 1907, d 02 Sept 1986 ae78y 8m 22d) s/o Conrad Guericke & Magdalena nee Kietzman. Children:
    William Guericke – b 20 Feb 1928, d 12 Dec 1947 [Car Accident]
    Arthur Guericke JR. – b 04 Aug 1930;
        m 17 Feb 1957 Arlene Stoebner
    Alma Guericke – b 17 Nov 1932; m 16 Dec 1956 Roland Presgler
    Alice Guericke – b 11 Feb 1936; m 29 Jun 1955 John Holzworth
    Lena Guericke – b 07 Aug 1938; m 07 Dec 1958 Maynard Winter
    Gilbert Guericke – b 04 Sept 1941; m 18 Jun 1961 Carol Wenzel
    Eldon Guericke – b 16 Mar 1945
2nd m 16 Aug 1959 Arthur Guericke SR. to Justina Kleinsasser nee Hoffman (b 28 Feb 1907). Freeman, SD residence.

Anna WERNING d/o Conrad Werning & Wilhelmina nee Keiper; b 12 Nov 1884; m 26 Apr 1906 Alfred Seefeld (b 07 Dec 1884). Children:
    Apolonia Seefeld – b 16 Mar 1907
    Gladys Seefeld – b 04 Jul 1908
    Evelyn Seefeld – b 08 Oct 1913

*Anna Christina WERNING d/o Johann Adam Werning & Johana

553

Jeanette nee Brehm; b 04 Aug 1840 Dankerode-on-der-Fulda Germany bpt Dankerode Ch, d 1922 Benton Co IA; m 13 Jan 1861 in Dankerode Ch Germany to George Kranz (b 1834 Dankerode-on-der-Fulda Germany bpt Dankerode Ch, d 05 Feb 1912 Benton Co IA) s/o Johann Kranz & Elizabeth nee Wagner. 1869 emigrated to USA, lived near Gibsonburg, OH, prob three years. 1871 traveled west by train when Great Chicago Fire was in progress. Settled on farm one and 1/2 miles northwest of Newhall, IA. Later built home further west and north on same farm. Children:

    *Adam Kranz – b 27 Dec 1862 Germany, d 08 Mar 1941 IA;
        m 24 Feb 1891 Emma Emmick
    Elizabeth Kranz – b 21 Nov 1873, d 13 Nov 1960;
        m 23 Mar 1893 Carl Heinrich Bierschenk

*Anna Martha WERNING d/o Johann Valentin Werning & Anna Martha nee Orth; b 1819, d 1876; 1840 emigrated to USA. While at sea she became acquainted with William Schumacher and her 1st m 1840 in New York. Chicago, IL residence where he died 1847 after seven years of marriage. Children:

    John Schumacher – NFR
    Marlin Schumacher – NFR

2nd m 1847 Anna Martha nee Werning Schumacher to Johan Conrad Kerkman; Six Children: cf Johan Conrad Kerkman.

*Anton WERNING s/o Johann Adam Werning & Johana Jeanette nee Brehm; b 11 Apr 1860 Dankerode-on-der-Fulda, Hessen Nassau, Germany, bpt Dankerode Ch, d 1943 Benton Co IA; 1870 came to USA with his parents; m 12 Mar 1887 Alice Nell (b 07 Nov 1864 Herkimer Co NY, d 1948 IA) d/o Jacob Nell & Ann Elizabeth nee Kimm. Farmed two and 1/2 miles northwest of Newhall, IA where grandson, Loren Werning, resided in later years. Children:

    Marie – b 02 Mar 1888, d 10 Oct 1964;
        m 18 Feb 1911 Berhard Geiken (b 05 Apr 1889, d 13 Jun 1953)
    Matilda – b 29 Nov 1889, d 1931; m 14 Feb 1915 August Bramow
    Leonard – b 25 Jan 1892, d 07 May 1962;
        m 12 Dec 1915 Emma Paulsen
    Wilhelmina "Minnie" Ellen – b 01 May 1894;
        m 1921 Arthur Martin Kerkman
    Arthur Jacob – b 29 Mar 1897, d 21 Jun 1968;
        m 27 Nov 1923 Emma Louise Wiese

Paul – b 29 Jan 1900, d 04 Dec 1970; m 12 Feb 1929 Hilda Senne
Arnold – b 18 Feb 1903; m 03 Dec 1924 Helen Strellner
Melvin – b 22 Dec 1905, d 27 May 1965; m Maurine Kading

Ardith WERNING d/o Delbert Anton Werning & Lusann nee Zobel; m
Rev. Terry Ahlemeyer. Conroy, IA residence where he pastored Luth Ch.
Children:
    Eric Ahlemeyer – NFR
    Michael Ahlemeyer – NFR

Arnold WERNING s/o Anton Werning & Alice nee Nell; b 18 Feb 1903;
m 03 Dec 1924 Helen Strellner. Children:
    El – NFR
    Rose Marie – NFR
    Robert – NFR

Arthur Jacob WERNING s/o Anton Werning & Alice nee Nell; b 29 Mar
1897, d 21 Jun 1968 ae71y 2m 23d; m 27 Nov 1923 Emma Louise Wiese
(b 15 Feb 1900, d 27 Apr 1975 ae75y 2m 12d) d/o William Wiese &
Rosina nee Hertle. Farmers northwest of Newhall, IA. 1965 retired in
Newhall. Children:
    Delbert Anton – b 1924;
        m 28 Apr 1946 Lusann Florence Garnet nee Zobel
    Lorene – m Alfred Karsten; Marengo, IA residence
    Ruth – m Don Huedepohl; Brooklyn, IA residence
    Merlin – m Patricia Tate; Luzerne, IA residence
    Charles – m Beverly Edgeton
    Leroy – m Judy Soden; Cedar Rapids, IA residence
    Duane Melvin – b 1936; m Ruth Floyd
    Wilfred – m Doris Fredrickson; Van Horne, IA residence
    Vernon George – b 1941; m Tammy Pickett

Arthur WERNING s/o Albert Werning SR. & Hildegard nee Guericke; b
10 May 1926; m 29 Aug 1948 Hilda Huber (b 09 Nov 1926) d/o Fred H.
Huber and Anna nee Dubs. Emery area, SD residence. Children:
    Wayne – b 12 Jan 1950
    Dale – b 08 Aug 1951; m 1982 Joan Beitz, Tripp, SD
    Mark – b 12 Nov 1954; m 1983 Kathleen Broge, Tripp, SD

Audrey Anne WERNING d/o Elmer Henry Werning & Rose Marie nee

Moeller; b 30 Jan 1924 Benton Co IA; m 18 Oct 1947 George John
Poelzer (b 12 Mar 1920). Wauwautosa, WI residence. Children:
Susan Jane Poelzer – b 20 Sept 1952 Milwaukee, WI
m 14 Feb 1981 Eric Bruce Weeder
Thomas George Poelzer – b 19 Sept 1953;
m 28 Aug 1976 Sally Ann Kludt
Nancy Ann Poelzer – b 25 Nov 1959;
m 13 Jun 1987 Douglas John Olsen

August J. WERNING s/o Martin Werning & Maria nee Rinderknecht; b
08 May 1879; m 02 Oct 1909 Julie Perie
(b 17 Nov 1882) d/o James Perie. Children:
Robert – b 16 Sept 1910
Lowell – b 27 May 1912
Nadene – b 26 Jul 1914

Chris WERNING s/o Martin Werning & Katharina nee Rinderknecht; b
10 Aug 1887 on farm two miles north of Newhall, IA d 1937; m 16 Mar
1919 Concordia Luth Ch Newhall to Rose A. Grovert (b 10 Dec 1890
farm Eldorado Twp Benton Co IA, bpt 05 Jan 1891 and con 27 Mar 1904
St.John, d 16 Jan 1994 ae104y 1m 6d Virginia Gay Hosp Vinton, IA bur
19 Jan 1994 St.John Cem) d/o Charles Grovert & Elte nee Broendel.
Chris and his brother-in-law, William H. Grovert, partners in Grovert
and Werning Auto Co. Chris director in Newhall, IA bank; members of
St.John; Rose taught Sunday School and was church organist, also
charter member of Newhall's Iowa Federated Woman's Club. No
children.

Christine WERNING s/o Martin Werning & Maria nee Rinderknecht; b
22 Jan 1877, d 28 Aug 1961 ae84y 7m 6d; m 09 Mar 1899 William
Fiebelkorn (b 21 Aug 1875, d Jul 1965) s/o Christian Fiebelkorn &
Ernstine nee Hagemann. Children:
Herbert Fiebelkorn – b 21 Jun 1900, d 01 Sept 1915
Arnold Fiebelkorn – b 01 Jul 1902, d 05 Dec 1918
Walter Fiebelkorn – b 23 Jul 1907, d 17 Sept 1957
Harold Fiebelkorn – b 30 Apr 1916
Wilma Fiebelkorn – b 14 Jun 1918; m 1945 Clare Johnson
NN Fiebelkorn – dec'd
NN Fiebelkorn – dec'd
Lorna Feibelkorn – m Robert Swanson

Clara WERNING d/o J.A.Wilhelm Werning & Frieda nee Ahrendt; b 16 Apr 1891, d 02 Dec 1957 ae66y 7m 14d; m 06 Mar 1913 Elmer Schulz (b 25 Mar 1890, d 23 Sept 1971 ae81y 5m 29d) s/o Herman Schulz & Anna nee Oetter. Children:

Arnold G. Schulz – b 26 Jul 1915, d 11 Jan 1915;
    m 14 May 1944 Susie Schamber
Martin Schulz – b 28 Feb 1918, Never Married
Walter Schulz – b 31 Jan 1923 Clayton, SD; d 25 Mar 1984
    Aberdeen, SD; m 09 Jun 1957 Lois Thomas
Marlin E. Schulz – b 25 Mar 1926, Never Married

Clarence WERNING s/o Martin F. Werning & Clara nee Schultz; b 1906, d 08 Feb 1998; 1st m 26 Feb 1931 Norma Kading (b 1907, d 01 Aug 1937) d/o William Kading & Alvena nee Sindt of Van Horne, IA. Child:

Donald – b 04 Nov 1933, d 10 Apr 1999;
    m 1955 Martha Joanna Baldwin
2nd m 19 Jul 1953 Clarence Werning to Ida nee Bartochek Schlieman (d 1983) of Belle Plaine, IA; farmers until 1964 retirement in Newhall.

*Conrad WERNING s/o Johann Adam Werning & Johana Jeanette nee Brehm; b 07 Aug 1851 Dankerode-on-der-Fulda, Hessen Nassau, Germany, bpt Dankerode Ch, d 1926 Benton Co IA; 1870 emigrated to Benton Co settling in Eldorado Twp near Newhall, IA; m 05 Apr 1875 Wilhelmina Keiper (b 11 Oct 1850 Germany. 1867 emigrated to Atkins IA; d 1920) d/o Frederick Keiper SR. & Katharina nee Mauer. Farmers two and one-half miles northwest of Newhall, IA until retiring 1912 in Newhall. Lifelong mbrs St.John. Children:

Katherina Jeannette – b 09 Jan 1876, d 15 Jan 1953;
    m 15 Feb 1899 Conrad Werner Schminke
Martin F. – b 03 Sept 1877, d 13 Mar 1970; m 1904 Clara Schultz
Maria – b 07 Jun 1880, d 03 Aug 1950;
    m 14 Feb 1901 Herman Feibelkorn
John C.A. – b 12 Jun 1882, d 03 Mar 1957;
    m 26 Feb 1908 Mathilda Schultz
Anna – b 12 Nov 1884; m 26 Apr 1906 Alfred Seefeld
Conrad H. J. – b 04 Mar 1887, d 05 Oct 1956;
    m 06 Mar 1912 Mathilda Paulsen
Elfrieda – b 16 Dec 1891, d 1979; m 03 May 1916 William Grovert

Conrad H.J. WERNING s/o Conrad Werning & Wilhelmina nee Keiper; b 04 Mar 1887 farm two and 1/2 miles northwest of Newhall, IA d 05 Oct 1956 ae69y 7m 1d, bur St.John Cem; m 06 Mar 1912 to Mathilda Paulsen (b 10 Mar 1889, d 1965, bur St.John Cem) d/o Heinrich Paulsen & Alvena nee Grovert. Continued living on farm where he was born until retiring to Newhall, IA. Lifelong members of St.John. Children:
Gertrude – b 01 Apr 1914;
    m Harry Christianson; Dysart, IA residence
Evelyn – b 09 Aug 1915; m Burland Swanson
Lucille – b 16 Aug 1918; m Roscoe Albertson; La Porte City, IA
Willis – NFR

Dale WERNING s/o Albert Werning SR. & Hildegard nee Guericke; b 08 Aug 1951; m 31 Jul 1982 Joan Beitz of Tripp, SD; d/o Elmer Beitz. Children:
Dale Scott – b 15 Nov 1983
Jill Faye – b 30 May 1986

Debra Ann WERNING d/o Marvin Werning & Alvina nee Konstanz; b 02 Mar 1963; m 31 May 1986 Delton Borman. Child:
Alex Randell Borman – b 28 Jun 1989

Delbert Anton WERNING s/o Arthur Jacob Werning & Emma Louise nee Wiese; b 1924; m 28 Apr 1946 Lusann Florence Garnet nee Zobel (b 14 Feb 1926 Ida Grove, IA, d 28 Mar 1983 ae57y 1m 14d [Auto Accident] bur St.John Cem) d/o Louis & Anna Zobel. Farmers west of Newhall, IA until 1963 when moved to rural Van Horne, IA farm. Children:
Ardith – m Rev. Terry Ahlemeyer; Conroy, IA residence
Keith – m Susan Clark; Newhall, IA farmers
Joyce Shirley – b 13 May 1952 Cedar Rapids, IA; d 28 Mar 1983 [Auto Accident]; m 14 Aug 1971 Thomas Elmer Moeller
Barbara – m 1980 Kyle Dee; Cedar Falls, IA residence

Diane WERNING d/o Duane Melvin Werning & Ruth nee Floyd; m David Mudderman. Fairbank, Bremer Co IA residence. Children:
Dustin Mudderman – NFR
Teresa Mudderman – NFR

Donald WERNING s/o Clarence Werning & Norma nee Kading; b 04 Nov 1933, d 10 Apr 1999 ae65y 5m 6d; m 1955 Martha Joanna Baldwin when he was in military service. Children:
Sheryl Sue – b 23 Nov 1960; Pharmacist;
    m 17 Nov 1984 Joel Edward Brehm DVD
Steven – m Jennifer Bickhaus, Indianapolis, IN. Son: Joshua Werning

Dorothy WERNING d/o Leonard Werning & Emma Paulsen; b 26 May 1919; m 23 Jan 1966 Ventura, IA to Elmer Jass. Children:
Lola May Jass – NFR
Doris Jass – NFR

Dorothy WERNING d/o William Werning & Mary nee Guericke; b 16 Sept 1934, d 30 Oct 1981 ae47y 1m 15d; m 02 Oct 1958 Walter Schaeffer (b 04 Aug 1929) s/o Henry Schaeffer & wife nee Bender. Children:
Lynn Walter Schaeffer – b 26 Jul 1959; m/DVD
Timothy Todd Schaeffer – b 09 Jul 1961
Julie Kay Schaeffer – b 30 Aug 1962
Jill Denise Schaeffer – b 07 Aug 1966

Duane Melvin WERNING s/o Arthur Jacob Werning & Emma Louise nee Wiese; b 1936; m Ruth Floyd (b 1938) d/o William & Mary Floyd. Farmers north of Newhall, IA. Children:
Diane – m David Mudderman; Fairbank, IA residence
Douglas – NFR
Mark – NFR
Michael – NFR

Elaine WERNING d/o William Werning & Mary nee Guericke; b 12 Dec 1931, d 07 Jul 1987 ae55y 6m 25d; m 16 Oct 1949 Elmer Wollman (b 03 May 1926) s/o Herman Wollman & Emma nee Melhoff. Parkston, SD residence. Children:
Raymond Wollman – b 18 Feb 1950
Renee Elaine Wollman – b 28 Feb 1953; m 1987 Earl Sheehy, TX
Linda Wollman – b 31 Aug 1955
Carol Pam Wollman – b 03 Oct 1966
Lois Marie Wollman – b 25 Jul 1963; m James Alexander Fanning

Elda WERNING d/o William Werning & Mary nee Guericke; b 09 Mar 1940; m 26 Mar 1961 Marvin Baumiller (b 23 Aug 1936) s/o Reinhold Baumiller & Gerda nee Gerlach. Children:

    Kim Lee Ann Baumiller – b 01 Mar 1962;
        m 10 Oct 1987 Paul Hoffman
    Vicky Lynn Baumiller – b 10 May 1963;
        m 18 Feb 1989 Earl Maier JR.
    Troy Marvin Baumiller – b 14 Aug 1964
    Dawn Marie Baumiller – b 29 Sept 1966

Elfrieda WERNING d/o J.A.Wilhelm Werning & Frieda nee Ahrendt; b 25 Sept 1906, d 31 Aug 1987 ae80y 11m 25d; m 02 Mar 1930 Ruben Buchmann (b 06 Apr 1906, d 20 Feb 1975 ae68y 10m 14d) s/o Fred Buchmann & Elisabeth nee Smitchgall. Children:

    Lydia Mary Buchmann – b 20 May 1931; m 1946 Peter Anderson
    Albert Frederick Buchmann – b 23 May 1935, d 06 Jan 1978
    Esther Martha Buchmann – b 20 Mar 1937;
        m 1968 Marvin Mullennex
    Ruth Mathilda Buchmann – b 01 Sept 1943; m 1963 Robert Wood
    Harold Robert Buchmann – b 20 Aug 1944; m Carol Moehlman

Elfrieda C. WERNING s/o Conrad Werning & Wilhelmina nee Keiper; b 16 Dec 1891, d 1979; Bethany Luth College, Mankato, MN; m 03 May 1916 William Henry Grovert (b 09 Dec 1888, d 02 Jul 1970 ae81y 6m 24d; Tilford Academy, Vinton, IA) s/o Charles Grovert & Elta nee Broendel. Children:

    Lola Grovert – b 25 Jun 1917; m Milton Krumm
    Donald Grovert – b 1923; m Joan Morr
    Dale Grovert – b 1925; m Dortha Stuart

*Elisabeth WERNING d/o Johann Adam Werning & Johana Jeanette nee Brehm; b 29 Nov 1842 Dankerode-on-der-Fulda, Hessen Nassau, Germany, bpt Dankerode Ch, d 09 Apr 1908 IA ae65y 4m 11d; m Easter 1870 to Justus Immeck (b 01 Nov 1839 Germany, d 29 Mar 1914 IA ae74y 4m 19d) s/o Herman Immeck & Martha nee Peter. Residence near Carroll, IA. Seven children:

    Emma Immeck – b 12 Mar 1873, d 25 Sept 1955;
        m 24 Feb 1891 Adam Kranz
        s/o George Kranz & Anna nee Werning
    Jeanette Immeck – b 21 Sept 1874; m 1892 Bernard Maus

Martin Immeck – b 16 Oct 1876; m 1900 Luise Albers
Christine Immeck – b 02 Sept 1878; m 1899 Edward Albers
William Immeck – b 22 Sept 1881; m 1906 Ada Halloway
Maria Immeck – b 25 Mar 1884, d 1918; m 1909 George Meindl
Wilhelmine Immeck – b 10 Mar 1886; m 1907 Fred Wohlenberh

Elisabeth WERNING d/o Justus Werning & Maria nee Krahling; b 01 Mar 1884, d 17 May 1974 ae90y 2m 16d bur St.John Cem); m 24 Sept 1913 John C. Rathje (b 03 Jul 1887, d 1976 bur St.Steph Cem) s/o Johann Heinrich & Anna Rebecca Katherina nee Seeborger. Children:
Arnold Rathje – dec'd at birth
Paul Justus Rathje – b 03 Sept 1916; m Lillian Carter of Vinton, IA
Margarethe Rathje – b 13 Sept 1918; TX residence

Elma WERNING d/o Albert Werning SR. & Hildegard nee Guericke; b 05 Jan 1928, d 24 Jun 1978 ae50y 5m 19d; m 10 Nov 1946 Harold Huber (b 14 Nov 1923) s/o Reinhold Huber & Josephine nee Langle. Emery, SD residence. Children:
James Huber – b 05 May 1947; m 18 Nov 1972 Mary Johnson
Royce Huber – b 02 Jul 1950; m 01 Jul 1979 Lana Schuring
Diane Huber – b 21 Dec 1951; m 16 Aug 1975 Steven Hurd
Curtis Huber – b 01 Sept 1953, d 12 Mar 1954
Galynn Gary Huber – b 18 Jul 1955;
    m 27 Jun 1981 Monica Schneider
Todd Harold Huber – b 07 Jun 1959; 1st m 1984 Lisa Wermers
Grant Douglas Huber – b 31 Aug 1962

Elmer WERNING s/o Albert Werning SR. & Hildegard nee Guericke; b 22 Sept 1929; m 03 Mar 1957 Marcella Winter (b 12 Feb 1933) d/o Edward Winter & Anna nee Maas. Children:
David Kevin – b 05 Aug 1960
Lois Anita – b 07 Mar 1963
Denise Diane – b 02 May 1968

Elmer Henry WERNING s/o Justus Werning & Maria nee Krahling; b 08 May 1898, d 18 Oct 1974 ae76y 5m 10d ; m 15 Dec 1921 Newhall, IA to Rose Marie Moeller (b 03 May 1898 Newhall, IA, d 31 May 1999 ae101y 28d Minneapolis, MN) d/o Peter George Moeller & Anna Marie nee Rinderknecht. Celebrated 50th wedding anniversary. Vinton, IA residence. Children:

Audrey Anne – b 30 Jan 1924; m 18 Oct 1947 George John Poelzer,
    in Milwaukee WI
Phyllis Marie – b 23 Mar 1928; m 22 Jan 1955 LeRoy Henry Jessen

Elwood WERNING s/o Albert Werning & Martha A. nee Rathje; b
1917, d 1976; m Mary El Ryan. Des Moines, IA residence. Children:
    Donna – NFR
    TWINS: Dennis – NFR
           David – NFR

Emma WERNING d/o J.A. Wilhelm Werning & Frieda nee Ahrendt; b
12 Jun 1895; m 14 Jun 1916 William Harnisch (b 28 Sept 1891, d 30 Oct
1957) s/o John Harnisch & Emma nee Dannenbring. Children:
    Mathilda Harnisch – b 19 Mar 1918, d Jun 1997;
        m 12 Sept 1939 LeRoy Campbell
    Melvin Harnisch – b 26 Mar 1921; Never Married
    Wilma Harnisch – b 27 Mar 1923; Never Married
    Margaret Harnisch – b 20 Aug 1925;
        m 26 Sept 1953 John Buckler JR.
    Helen Harnisch – b 06 Aug 1927; m 26 Sept 1953 Earl Slovak
    Esther Harnisch – b 04 Jun 1930; m 24 Jun 1950 Elry Hoefs
    Leonard Harnisch – b 06 Jan 1933; m 28 Oct 1967 Yvonne Erickson
    Alice Harnisch – b 12 Jul 1935;
        m 09 Jun 1956 Maurice Richard Schumacher
    Mildred Harnisch – b 07 Jul 1940

Fred Adam WERNING s/o Martin Werning & Katharina nee
Rinderknecht; b 31 Aug 1885 farm two miles northwest of Newhall, IA d
01 Jun 1938 ae52y 9m1d; m 20 Sept 1917 Anna Steuber d/o Fred
Steuber & Anna nee Hegewald of Cedar Rapids, IA. Fred started in
livery business, 1919 took over the Standard Oil Bulk plant in Newhall,
IA and remained in it until his death. He served on the Newhall town
council and Mayor. Sunday School Superintendent for many years.
Children:
    William F.- b 15 Jan 1920; m Lucille Pieper,Van Horne, IA;
        Keota, IA residence
    Mildred A.- b 1922; m John Hinrichs of Cedar Rapids, IA
    Kenneth R.- b 1924, d 1945 Battle of Bulge WW II,
        Wesel, Germany
    Gerald C.- b 1930; m Marian Ludwick; Liberty, MO residence

Gary Lee WERNING s/o Marvin Werning & Alvina nee Konstanz; b 21 Feb 1958; m 15 Sept 1978 Mitchell, SD to Patricia Kay Moe of Alexandria SD d/o Roy A. Moe & Bertha nee Carlson of Alexandria, SD. Farmers near Emery, SD. Child:
Natala Ann – b 23 Jun 1984

George WERNING s/o Martin Werning & Katharina nee Rinderknecht; b 16 May 1891, d 03 Jul 1949 ae58y 1m 17d; m 11 Jan 1917 Paula Dornseif (b 1895, d 27 Nov 1960) d/o Rev. Philip H.Dornseif & Marie nee Guenther of Wilton, IA. Farmers north of Newhall, IA. Children:
Philip – b 07 Mar 1918, dec'd
Wilmer – b 28 Jul 1919
Waldo – m Ruth Kienow, five children
Dolores – m Fred Lund; Loveland, CO residence
Ronald – NFR

Glenn WERNING s/o Lloyd Werning & Viola nee Knuth; b 1942; m 1964 Marjorie Gahring (b 1941) d/o Merlyn Gahring & Alice nee Dixon. Farmers Eden Twp Benton Co IA where great-grandfather Abraham began farming in 1869. Children:
TWINS: Greg – NFR
Gene – NFR
Barry – NFR

Harvey WERNING s/o Martin F. Werning & Clara nee Schultz; b 14 Jun 1912 home farm where he resided; m 1937 Ruth Augusta Zobel (b 29 Dec 1915 Ida Grove, IA, d 12 Jun 2007 ae91y 5m 14d bur St.John Cem) d/o Louis Zobel & Anna nee Schwenke. Harvey served on Newhall, IA Consolidated School Board. Children:
Marlys – m Robert Frimml
Virgil – m Holly Henricks; Children: Wendy, Kami
Marion – Farmed with parents great-great-grandfather's land.

Hulda WERNING d/o Martin Werning & Katharina nee Rinderknecht; b 12 Mar 1897; m 23 Feb 1919 John Warner (b 01 Jun 1897) s/o Charles Warner & Fredericka nee Wendt. Farmers near Newhall, IA; worked in implement company in Shellsburg, IA; later moved to CA. Hulda retired in CA. Child:
Eleanor Warner – b 09 Jan 1920

Ilma WERNING d/o Martin Werning & Katharina nee Rinderknecht: cf Walter Karl Jacob Schminke s/o August Heinrich George Schminke & Elizabeth Katharina Anna Rinderknecht.

Rev. J.A.Henry WERNING s/o Justus Werning & Maria nee Krahling; b 23 Mar 1882, d Nov 1952 ae70y; m 06 Aug 1907 in NE to Hermine Greinke (b 18 Apr 1887). 1916 Luth pastor at Immanuel Zion, Imperial, Chase Co, NE. Children:
    Norma (Adopted) – b NFR
    Alma (Adopted) – b 1934

*J.A. Wilhelm WERNING s/o Johann Adam Werning & Jeanette nee Brehm; b 17 Dec 1862 Dankerode-on-der-Fulda, Hessen Nassau, Germany, bpt Dankerode Ch, d 11 Nov 1940 ae77y 10m 25d Parkston, SD. After he started school in Germany his oldest brother and a sister emigrated to USA. Two aunts continually wrote emphasizing prospects for young people in the New World when the Civil War and reconstruction days were over. An uncle by marriage showed his sincerity by offering to advance fare for Wilhelm and another sibling. 1870 emigrated with parents to USA. Wilhem continued education in USA attending St.Stephens Christian Day School, Atkins, IA where he was confirmed in Luth faith. He was hired farm laborer until promising prospects of land in western states by statesmen encouraging settling coaxed him in 1887 to the homestead plan of 160 acres for those intending to make their home near Clayton, Hutchinson Co, SD; m 09 Mar 1890 Frieda Ahrendt (b 22 Oct 1867 Eldenav, Mecklemburg-Schwerin Germany; 1873 emigrated to USA; d 25 Sept 1952 ae84y 11m 3d Parkston, SD) d/o Joachin Ahrend & Luise nee Pohlmann of Guttenburg, IA. Farmers until retirement move into Parkston, SD. Nine children:
    Clara – b 16 Apr 1891, d 02 Dec 1957; m 06 Mar 1913 Elmer Schulz
    Martha – b 08 Jun 1893, d 24 Mar 1979;
        m 14 Mar 1912 Otto Dannenbring, Menno, SD
    Emma – b 12 Jun 1895; d ND;
        m 14 Jun 1916 William Harnischl, Wall SD
    William – b 18 Apr 1897, d 04 May 1979;
        m 15 Feb 1931 Mary Guericke
    Albert G. – b 24 Feb 1900 Hudson Co, SD, d 10 Jul 1970
        Parkston, SD; m 07 Jun 1925 Hildegard Guericke
564

Mary – b 09 Mar 1902, d 22 Sept 1988;
    m 16 Apr 1925 Ernest Guericke, Parkston, SD
Alice – b 22 Mar 1904, d 14 Mar 1954;
    m 16 Apr 1925 Arthur Guericke SR.
Elfrieda – b 25 Sept 1906, d 31 Aug 1987;
    m 02 Mar 1930 Ruben Buchmann, Akron, IA
Mathilda – b 24 Feb 1910, d 12 Jan 1986;
    m 22 Jun 1932 Albert Juhnke, Emery SD

James WERNING s/o Lawrence Albert Werning & Maxine nee
Boddicker; m Linda Whittaker; residence Billings, MT. Children:
    Collin – NFR
    Jamie – NFR
    Jimmy – NFR
    Jerad – NFR

*Johann Adam WERNING (GS St.John) s/o Johann Valentin Werning &
Anna Martha nee Orth of Dankerode, Germany; b 16 Aug 1812
Dankerode on-der-Fulda, Kreis Rothenburg, Germany, bpt and con
Dankerode-on-der-Fulda Luth Ch, d 14 Dec 1879 ae67y 3m 29d (GS)
Benton Co IA, bur St.John Cem; m 1839 Dankerode Ch to Johana
Jeanette Brehm (b 28 Sept 1817 Dankerode-on-der-Fulda, Germany, bpt
and con Dankerode Luth Ch, d 21 Sept 1882 ae64y 11m 23d Benton Co
IA, bur St.John Cem) d/o Anton Brehm & Anna Katharina nee
Pfaffenbach. 20 Jun 1868 Martin and Margarethe left Germany via
Bremen, arrived N.Y. 04 Jul 1868, went to Aunt and Uncle Mr. & Mrs.
Conrad Kerkman in IL until Spring 1869 when moved to Benton Co IA.
Johann Adam and Johana Jeanette Werning emigrated to USA on sailing
ship "Dampfer Hansa," arriving Blairstown, IA March 1870; settled on
Benton Co IA farm; helped orangize St.John Luth Ch near Newhall, IA.
Children:
    *Anna Christina – b 04 Aug 1840 Dankerode-on-der-Fulda,
        Germany, d 1922 Benton Co IA;
        m 13 Jan 1861 George Kranz in Germany.
    *Elisabeth – b 29 Nov 1842 Dankerode-on-der-Fulda, Germany;
        d 09 Apr 1908 IA; m Easter 1870 Justus Immeck in Germany
    *Margarethe – b 19 May 1845 Dankerode-on-der-Fulda, Germany;
        d 31 Oct 1906; m 1869 in Germany Henry Luecke
    *Anna Martha – b 25 Dec 1847 Dankerode-on-der- Fulda, Germany
        d 15 Jan 1848 Dankerode-on-der-Fulda, Germany

*Martin – b 01 Dec 1848 Dankerode-on-der-Fulda, Germany,
 d 1919 IA; 1st m 1874 to Maria Rinderknecht (d 1881);
 2nd m 22 Mar 1882 Katherine Rinderknecht (Maria's sister)
*Conrad – b 07 Aug 1851 Dankerode-on-der-Fulda, Germany;
 d 1926 Benton Co IA; m 05 Apr 1875 Wilhelmina Keiper
*Katherina Elisabeth – b 24 Jan 1854 Dankerode-on-der-Fulda,
 Germany; d 13 Jul 1937 Van Horne home, IA, bur St.Steph
Cem;
 m 03 Jul 1874 St.Steph Johann Peter Happel
*Justus – b 04 Oct 1857 Dankerode-on-der-Fulda, Germany;
 d 15 Jul 1936 Bremer Co IA; 1st m 20 Apr 1881 Maria Krahling;
 2nd m 12 Dec 1904 Anna nee Moeller Schneider.
*Anton – b 11 Apr 1860 Dankerode-on-der-Fulda, Germany;
 d 1943 Benton Co IA; m 12 Mar 1887 Alice Nell
*J.A. Wilhelm – b 17 Dec 1862 Dankerode-on-der-Fulda, Germany;
 d 11 Nov 1940 Parkston, SD; m 09 Mar 1890 Frieda Ahrendt

*Johann Valentin WERNING of Dankerode-on-de-Fulda, Hessen
Nassau, os Prussia ns Germany; b 22 May 1785 d 1833 Germany; m 07
Mar 1807 Anna Martha Ort (b & d Germany). Ancestors of Wernings in
IA and SD. Children:
Heinrich – Never Married
*Johann Adam b 16 Aug 1812 Dankerode-on-der-Fulda, Germany
 d 14 Dec 1879 Benton Co. IA;
 m 1839 Johana Jeanette Brehm Dankerode Ch Germany
*Anna Martha – b 1819, d 1876; 1840 USA immigrant;
 1st m 1840 NY William Schumacher;
 2nd m 1847 Johan Conrad Kerkman
Martin – d young
*Anna Elisabeth- 1848 USA immigrant; lived with John Senne &
 Katherine Kerkman, her neice; d 13 May 1903

John C.A. WERNING s/o Conrad Werning & Wilhelmina nee Keiper; b
12 Jun 1882 on farm two and 1/2 miles northwest of Newhall, IA d 03
Mar 1957 ae74y 8m 19d; lifelong resident of Eldorado Twp Benton Co
IA; m 26 Feb 1908 Matilda Schultz (b 08 Jul 1886, d 14 May 1956
ae69y 10m 6d) d/o Henry Schultz & Wilhelmina nee Kunstorf. Settled
on farm two miles east of Van Horne, IA and retired to Newhall, IA;
lifelong mbrs of St.John. Children:
 Viola – b 09 Jul 1909; m 1931 Alfred Otto Koopman

Lester – b 26 Oct 1911; m Annis Schlotterbeck

Julanne WERNING d/o Lawrence Albert Werning & Maxine nee Boddicker; m Warren Clark of Lisbon, IA. Children:
    Lisa Clark – NFR
    Gina Clark – NFR
    Jeff Clark – NFR

*Justus WERNING s/o Johann Adam Werning & Johana Jeanette nee Brehm; b 04 Oct 1857 Dankerode-on-der-Fulda, bpt Dankerode Ch, d 15 Jul 1936 78y 9m 11d Bremer Co IA; emigrated USA a12y with parents and eight brothers and sisters settling in Eldorado Twp Benton Co IA. Justus bought a farm two miles north of Newhall, IA in 1880's; 1st m 20 Apr 1881 Maria Krahling (b 21 Mar 1861 Germany, d 05 Dec 1900 ae39y 8m 14d) d/o John Krahling & Elizabeth. 1903 Justus moved his family to Cedar Rapids, IA. Sons Albert and Elmer later returned to their father's farm. Children:
    Rev.J.A.Henry – b 23 Mar 1882, d Nov 1952;
        m 06 Aug 1907 in NE Hermine Greinke
    Elizabeth – b 01 Mar 1884, d 17 May 1974 bur St.John Cem;
        m 24 Sept 1913 John C. Rathje
    Emilie – b 16 Feb 1886, d 11 Sept 1899
    George – b 10 Aug 1888, d 26 Aug 1890
    Louise – b 20 Oct 1890, d 04 Aug 1973;
        1st m 18 Jun 1913 William Engelmann; 2nd m Frank Krieder
    Albert W. – b 04 Aug 1893, d 02 Jul 1938;
        m 23 Feb 1916 Martha A. Rathje
    Walter – b 27 Nov 1895, d 06 Apr 1897
    Elmer Henry – b 08 May 1898, d 18 Oct 1974;
        m 15 Dec 1921 Rosa Marie Moeller
2nd m 12 Dec 1904 Justus Werning to Anna nee Moeller Schneider (b 02 Jul 1862, d Mar 1946) d/o Johannes Georg Mo(e)ller& Wilhelmina nee Krug.

Katherina Jeannette WERNING d/o Conrad Werning & Wilhelmina nee Keiper; b 09 Jan 1876, d 15 Jan 1953 ae77y 11d; m 15 Feb 1899 Conrad Werner Schminke (b 12 Jun 1871, d 31 Jul 1963 ae92y 1m 19d) s/o Jacob Schminke & Katerina nee Ibel. Children:
    Adelia Schminke – b 1900
    Edmund Schminke – b 1901

Roy Schminke – b 26 May 1904, d 1973;
    1st m 29 Jan 1930 Martha Bierschenk;
    2nd m 30 Sept 1973 Hazel Bernice nee Kraft Lauterwasser
Victor J. Schminke – b 21 Jul 1911 Eden Twp Benton Co IA;
    1st m 15 Feb 1935 Hazel Price;
    2nd m 1973 Dorothy Sattizahn Price
Luella Schminke – b 1917, d Feb 1970

Keith WERNING s/o Delbert Anton Werning & Lusann Florence Garnet nee Zobel; m Susan Clark. Farmed northwest of Newhall, IA. Children:
    Carrie – NFR
    Stacie – NFR

Lawrence Albert WERNING s/o Albert W. & Martha A. nee Rathje; b 11 Dec 1919; m 1944 Maxine Boddicker d/o Albert A."Fish" Boddicker & Julia nee Sevening. Farmed his parents farm fourteen years until it was sold. Purchased and farmed the Al Rammeslberg estate. Children:
    Julanne – m Warren Clark of Lisbon, IA
    Albert – m Linda Womichil; Newhall, IA residence
    James – m Linda Whittaker; Billings, MT residence
    Thomas – b 21 Jan 1954; m Julie Denise Braksiek (Werning cousins)
    Martha – m Robert Finley; Cedar Rapids, IA residence

Leonard WERNING s/o Anton Werning & Alice nee Nell; b 25 Jan 1892, d 07 May 1962; m 12 Dec 1915 Emma Paulsen (b 13 Feb 1893, d 06 Apr 1960 ae67y 1m 24d). Child:
    Dorothy – b 26 May 1919; m 23 Jan 1966 Ventura,IA Elmer Jass

Lloyd WERNING s/o Martin F. Werning & Clara nee Schultz; b 01 Oct 1908 farm in Eldorado Twp Benton Co IA, d Aug 1987 bur St.John Cem; m 1935 Viola Knuth (b 1912; Chairman Benton Co Farm Bureau Women; Benton Co 4-H Committee) d/o Charles Knuth & Mary nee Abraham. Farmers in Eden Twp Benton Co on Knuth farm until moving to Newhall, IA in 1964; members of St.John. Children:
    Russell – b 1936; m 1960 Alice Palmer
    Glenn – b 1942; m 1964 Marjorie Gahring

Louise WERNING d/o Justus Werning & Maria nee Krahling; b 20 Oct 1890, d 04 Aug 1973 ae82y 9m 15d; 1st m 18 Jun 1913 William Engelmann (b 08 Feb 1890).Child:

Jean Elisabeth Englemann – b 27 Jul 1919
2nd m Louise nee Werning Englemann to Frank Krider.

Loren WERNING s/o Paul Werning & Hilda nee Senne; b 1931; m
Delores Weisart (b 1934). Children:
>   Kendall Jo – b 1960; m Sandra Marie Svoboda. Child:
>   Bronson Werning (b 1991)
>   Janelle Kay – b 1961; m Michael George Nissen. Children:
>   Nathan Paul Nissen (b 1988), Sarah Michele Nissen (b 1990)
>   Vaughn Jay – b 1965; m Lisa J. Pingel

Lucille WERNING d/o William Werning & Mary nee Guericke; b 25 Jul
1938, d 08 Aug 1987 ae49y 14d; m 1959 LeRoy Geohring (b 10 May
1933) s/o Andrew Geohring and wife NN nee Krueger. Children:
>   Lisa Marie Geohring – b 14 Oct 1961
>   Leland Jay Geohring – b 21 Sept 1963
>   Curtiss LeRoy Geohring – b 26 Aug 1962
>   Cory Lee Geohring – b 27 Jun 1965
>   Craig Alan Geohring – b 06 Dec 1966
>   Laurie Geohring – b 20 Jun 1973

*Margarethe WERNING d/o Johann Adam Werning & Johana Jeanette
nee Brehm; b 19 May 1845 Dankerode-on-der-Fulda, Hessen Nassau,
Germany, bpt Dankerode Ch, d 31 Oct 1906 ae61y 5m 12d; m 1869 in
Germany to Heinrich F. Luecke (b 12 Sept 1814 Germany) s/o Ludwig
Luecke & Charlotte nee Buda. Lancaster Co NE, north of Cortland NE,
residence. Ten children:
>   William Luecke – b 06 May 1870, d 1946;
>   m 22 Feb 1899 Margaretha Oltmann
>   Henry L. Luecke – b 17 Sept 1871; m 12 Feb 1896 Sophie Fuess
>   Johann Luecke – b 26 Feb 1873, d 09 Aug 1962;
>   m 05 Nov 1902 Mattie Buehler
>   Fred M.Luecke – b 20 Jan 1875, d 1963;
>   m 03 Aug 1902 Nellie Bohlmann
>   Anna M.Luecke – b 21 Aug 1878, d May 1952;
>   m 24 Jun 1899 Gottleib Eberspecher
>   George C. Luecke – b 10 Jul 1880, d 30 Oct 1961;
>   m 24 Jun 1903 Aurelia Brust
>   Jeanette Luecke – b 09 Jul 1882; m 08 Feb 1905 George Raym
>   Mary C.Luecke – b 15 Sept 1884, d 04 Jun 1965;

m 29 Jan 1908 Paul Hahn
Lydia Luecke – b 11 May 1887, d 1891
Emma S.Luecke – b 24 Oct 1889; m 06 Jul 1911 Henry Packard

Maria (Mary) WERNING d/o Conrad Werning & Wilhelmina nee
Keiper: cf Herman Fiebelkorn.

Mark WERNING s/o Albert Werning SR. & Hildegard nee Guericke; b
12 Nov 1954; m 20 Aug 1983 Kathleen Ray Brage of Tripp, SD.
Children:
Blake Matthew – b 23 Mar 1986
Brett Jonathan – b 15 Aug 1987

Marlys WERNING d/o Harvey Werning & Ruth nee Zobel; m Robert
Frimml. Marlys teacher at Atkins, IA Center of Benton Community
Schools. Children:
Linda Frimml – NFR
Jennifer Frimml – NFR
Christopher Frimml – NFR
Matthew Frimml – NFR

Martha WERNING s/o J.A.Wilhelm Werning & Frieda nee Ahrendt; b
08 Jun 1893, d 24 Mar 1979 ae85y 9m 16d bur St.Peter's Luth Cem
Clayton, SD; m 14 Mar 1912 Otto Dannenbring (b 03 Apr 1890, d 10
Sept 1977 ae87y 5m 7d) s/o Henry Dannenbring & Elisabeth nee
Rademacher. Children:
Leonhard Dannenbring – b 13 Dec 1913, d 1989;
m 15 Dec 1940 Leona Huber
Alice Dannenbring – b 02 Apr 1916;
m 19 May 1940 Leonard Buehner
Edmund E. Dannenbring – b 28 Jul 1917; d 25 Jan 1919 [Flu]
Edward William Dannenbring – b 11 Apr 1920;
06 Feb 1922 [Burns]
Arthur Dannenbring – b 31 Mar 1923; m 22 Oct ND Leola Huber
Olga Dannenbring – b 15 Apr 1928; m 19 Jan 1947 Ivan Ibis

*Martin WERNING s/o Johann Adam Werning & Johana Jeanette nee
Brehm; b 01 Dec 1848 Dankerode-on-der-Fulda, Hessen Nassau,
Germany, bpt Dankerode Ch, d 1919 IA; 1868 emigrated USA, first to
uncle and aunt, Mr. & Mrs. Conrad Kerkman in IL; 1870 joined by

parents and other siblings who came to USA to make their home near
Newhall, IA; 1st m 1874 Maria Rinderknecht (b 05 Nov 1856 Germany,
d 03 Apr 1881 ae25y 4m 29d Benton Co IA) d/o Johann Rinderknecht &
Barbara nee Mead. Two children:

Christine – b 22 Jan 1877, d 28 Aug 1961;
  m 09 Mar 1899 William Fiebelkorn
August J.- b 08 May 1879; m 02 Oct 1909 Julia Perie; Norway, IA

2nd m 22 Mar 1882 Martin Werning to Katharina Rinderknecht (b 25 Dec
1864, Atkins IA, d 1933) d/o Johann Rinderknecht & Barbara nee Mead
(sister of his first wife). Continued farming northwest of Newhall, IA
until retiring in Newhall. Twelve children:

Sophia – b 16 Oct 1883, d Apr 1976; m 22 Mar 1907 Henry Stienke
Fred Adam – b 31 Aug 1885, d 01 Jun 1938;
  m 20 Sept 1917 Anna Steuber
Chris – b 10 Aug 1887, d 1937; m 16 Mar 1919 Rose A. Grovert
Martha – b 20 Feb 1888, d 08 Jun 1965; m 31 Oct 1943 Fred Wagley
  (d 12 Jul 1967); retired in Cedar Rapids, IA
George – b 16 May 1891, d 03 Jul 1949;
  m 11 Jan 1917 Paula Dornseif
William J.E. – b 04 Jan 1893; d [Influenza] 1918 Camp Dodge,
  Des Moines World War I
John M. – b 28 Jan 1895, d 1921; farmer; dec'd in young manhood
Hulda – b 12 Mar 1897; m 23 Feb 1919 John Warner
Rev. Walter L.H. – b 28 Sept 1899, d 29 Nov 1984;
  m 01 Sept 1927 Sarah Brammer;
Richard – b 01 Nov 1902, d 1934; m 15 Jul ND Gertrude Persson
Ilma – b 26 Jan 1906; m 08 Sept 1927 Walter Schminke
Myrna – b 19 May 1908, d 16 Apr 1909

Martin F. WERNING s/o Conrad Werning & Wilhelmina nee Keiper; b
03 Sept 1877 Eldorado Twp Benton Co IA farm two and one-half miles
northwest of Newhall, IA d 13 Mar 1970 ae92y 6m 10d bur St.John
Cem; m 1904 Clara Schultz (b 29 Nov 1883, d 31 Jul 1953 ae69y 8m 2d
bur St.John Cem) d/o Henry J. Schultz & Wilhelmina nee Kunstorf.
Farmers until 1938 when retired to Newhall, IA. Martin director of
Newhall State Bank, Mayor of Newhall, 1948 chairman Building
Committee of St.John; Director of Newhall Consolidated School.
Children:

Clarence – b 10 Feb 1906;
  m 26 Feb 1931 Norma Kading of Van Horne, IA

Lloyd – b 01 Oct 1908, d Aug 1987 bur St.John Cem;
    m 1935 Viola Knuth of Newhall, IA
Harvey – b 14 Jun 1912; m 1937 Ruth Zobel

Marvin WERNING s/o Albert Werning SR. & Hildegard nee Guericke;
b 14 Feb 1932; m 05 Jun 1955 Alvina Konstanz (b 10 Aug 1933) d/o
Emil Konstanz & Esther nee Pietz. Emery, SD residence. Children:
    Gary Lee – b 21 Feb 1958; m 15 Sept 1978 Patricia Kay Moe
    Russell Scott – b 05 Feb 1962; m 29 Jun 1984 Carmen Stevenson
    Debra Ann – b 02 Mar 1963; m 31 May 1986 Delton Borman

Mary WERNING d/o J.A.Wilhelm Werning & Frieda nee Ahrendt; b 09
Mar 1902, d 22 Sept 1988 ae86y 6m 18d; m 16 Apr 1925 Ernest
Guericke (b 07 May 1901) s/o Conrad Guericke & Magdalena nee
Kietzman. Children:
    Emma Guericke – b 01 Feb 1926; m 25 Jun 1947 Edmund Rose
    Martin Guericke – b 07 Sept 1928; m 26 Feb 1950 Ladeen Jansen
    Ernest Guericke JR. – b 21 Aug 1930, d 12 Dec 1947 [Car Accident]
    Harold Guericke – b 16 Mar 1940; m 03 Nov 1963 Sharon Gerlach
    Donald Guericke – b 16 Mar 1940;
        m 11 Mar 1962 Charlotte Wuetzer
    Evelyn Guericke – b 05 Jan 1942; m 26 Dec 1960 Gary Walter
    Luverne Guericke – b 01 Nov 1943; m 01 Aug 1986 Gloria Pontzer
    Margaret Guericke – b 06 Oct 1945; m 18 Mar 1977 John Bartell

Mathilda WERNING d/o Anton Werning & Alice nee Nell; b 29 Nov
1889, d 1931; m 14 Feb 1915 August Bramow (b 25 Dec 1893) s/o
Ludwig Bramow.& Minnie nee Warner. Children:
    Ralph Bramow – b 12 Dec 1915
    Elmo Bramow – b 03 May 1918

Mathilda WERNING d/o J.A.Wilhelm Werning & Frieda nee Ahrendt; b
24 Feb 1910, d 12 Jan 1986 ae75y 10m 19d; m 22 Jun 1932 Albert
Juhnke (b 04 Feb 1907, d 03 Aug 2001 ae94y 5m 29d) s/o Julius Junke
& Ida nee Tornow. Parkston, SD residence. Children:
    Elnora Juhnke – b 02 Jun 1933 Parkston, SD;
        m 29 Aug 1954 LeRoy Theodore Bender
    Dorothy Juhnke – b 18 Jun 1936 Clayton, SD;
        m 04 Dec 1955 Leland Schempp
    Mildred Juhnke – b 22 Mar 1938 Clayton, SD;

m 06 Apr 1958 Curt Smith
Marion Juhnke – b 10 Apr 1940 Clayton, SD;
    m 20 Aug 1961 Dallis England
Marvin Juhnke – b 15 Mar 1945, d ND Clayton, SD;
    m 1966 Sandra Kay Hodson

Michelle Jean WERNING d/o Albert G. Werning & Betty nee Moege; b 26 Jul 1966; m 06 Jun 1987 Kelly Krueger. Child:
    Spencer Kelly Krueger – b 28 Aug 1989

Paul WERNING s/o Anton Werning & Alice nee Nell; b 29 Jan 1900, d 04 Dec 1970 ae70y 10m 5d; m 12 Feb 1929 Hilda Senne (b 27 Oct 1906, d 1966) d/o Fred Senne & Elsie M. nee Bierschenk. Children:
    Raymond – b 1930, d 1985; m Doris Boss (b 1924);
        Marion, IA residence. Child: Kimberly Kay Werning (b 1942)
    Loren – b 1931; m Delores Weisart

Phyllis Marie WERNING d/o Elmer Henry Werning & Rose Marie nee Moeller; b 23 Mar 1928 Benton Co IA; m 22 Jan 1955 Leroy Henry Jessen (b 08 Mar 1930. Retired President, Curle Printing). Mound, MN residence. Children:
    Jo Ellen Jessen – b 05 Aug 1955 Minneapolis, MN;
        m 31 Jul 1982 William David Ambrose
    David Lee Jessen – b 27 Dec 1957 Minneapolis, MN;
        m 26 May 1989 Holly Jean Hartloff
    Mark Henry Jessen – b 28 Oct 1962 Minneapolis, MN;
        m 20 Nov 1993 Margaret (Peggy) Ann Lynch
    Lee Ann Jessen – b 04 Oct 1965 Minneapolis, MN;
        m 27 Jun 1992 John Melin, Minneapolis, MN

Richard WERNING s/o Martin Werning & Katharina nee Rinderknecht; b 01 Nov 1902, d 1934; m 15 Jul ND Gertrude Persson (b 18 Jun ND). Richard attended Teachers College, River Forest, IL, taught at Homestead, IA; Edwardville, IL; Maryville, WI. Gertrude taught school after Richard's death and retired near Edwardsville, IL. Child:
    Marian – NFR

Russell WERNING s/o Lloyd Werning & Viola nee Knuth; b 1936; m 1960 Alice Brandt Palmer (b 1937) d/o Paul Palmer & Frances nee Brandt. Russell teacher beginning in 1961, and active in Boy Scouts of

America; Alice teacher at Norway, IA and active in Girl Scouts of America. Children:
David Paul – 1st m Rebecca LaRue DVD;
2nd m 30 Jul 1993 Lynette Jean Meister, Toledo, OH
Mary – m Bradford Miller
Rebecca – NFR

Sheryl Sue WERNING d/o Donald werning & Martha Joanna nee Baldwin: cf Joel Edward Brehm

Sophia WERNING d/o Martin Werning & Katharina nee Rinderknecht; b 16 Oct 1883, d Apr 1976; m 22 Mar 1907 Henry Stienke(b 07 Jun 1884) s/o J.Steinke & Emma nee Schroeder. Farmers northwest of Newhall, later in garage business in Keystone, IA; retired near Houston, TX. Children:
Merill Stienke – NFR
Esther Stienke – NFR
Ruth Stienke – NFR

Tamara Lynn WERNING d/o Albert G. Werning & Betty nee Moege; b 21 Dec 1962; m 08 Jul 1983 Kalvin Kurtenbach. Children:
Magen Adair Kurtenbach – b 21 Dec 1983
Chase Kurtenbach – b 06 Feb 1985

Thomas John WERNING s/o Lawrence Werning & Maxine nee Boddicker: cf his Werning cousin Julie Denise Braksiek.

Vernon George WERNING s/o Arthur Jacob Werning & Emma Louise nee Wiese; b 1941; m Tammy Pickett (b 1944). Residence on Arthur Werning farm northwest of Newhall, IA. Children:
Scott – NFR
Troy – NFR

Rev. Walter L.H. WERNING s/o Martin Werning & Katharina nee Rinderknecht; b 28 Sept 1899, d 29 Nov 1984 ae85y 2m 1d; m 01 Sept 1927 Sarah Brammer (b 08 May ND). 1924 graduate Luth Seminary, St.Louis, MO; received call as traveling missionary in British Columbia where he served twenty-one mission stations; pastorates in Calgary, Alberta, Canada; Decatur, IN; Youngstown, OH. Retired near Sonora, CA. Children:

Margaret – NFR
John – NFR
Ted – NFR

Wilhelmina "Minnie" Ellen WERNING d/o Anton Werning & Alice nee Nell: cf Arthur Martin Kerkman/o Edward Kerkman & Barbara nee Rinderknecht.

William WERNING s/o J.A.Wilhelm Werning & Frieda nee Ahrendt; b 18 Apr 1897, d 04 May 1979 ae82y 16d; m 15 Feb 1931 Mary Guericke (b 05 Mar 1904, d 06 Feb 1949 ae44y 11m 1d) d/o Math Guericke & Wilhelmina nee Harnisch. Children:
    Elaine – b 12 Dec 1931, d 07 Jul 1987;
        m 16 Oct 1949 Elmer Wollman
    Dorothy – b 16 Sept 1934, d 30 Oct 1981;
        m 02 Oct 1958 Walter Schaeffer
    Melvin – b 29 Jan 1936, d 30 Aug 1976
    Lucille – b 25 Jul 1938, d 08 Aug 1987; m 1959 LeRoy Geohring
    Elda – b 09 Mar 1940; m 26 Mar 1961 Marvin Baumiller
    Willie – b 20 May 1943; residence on old Werning farm

David Walter WESSLING s/o Grant Anthony Wessling & Lois Jeanette nee Schminke; TWIN b 12 Feb 1953 Mercy Hosp Cedar Rapids, IA [TWIN: Douglas William Wessling] manager Newhall Branch of Linn Co-op; m 13 Aug 1977 St.Michael's Catholic Ch Norway, IA to Kathy Ann Stumpff(b 30 Jul 1954 Cedar Rapids, IA; Pharmacist degree Creighton U. Omaha, NE) d/o Richard Ora Stumpff & Margaret Ann nee Frimml. Newhall, IA residence. Children:
    Rachelle Ann – b 22 Oct 1979 Mercy Hosp Cedar Rapids, IA
    Erin Renee – b 12 Jan 1982 Mercy Hosp Cedar Rapids, IA

Douglas William WESSLING s/o Grant Anthony Wessling & Lois Jeanette nee Schminke; TWIN b 12 Feb 1953 Mercy Hosp Cedar Rapids, IA [TWIN: David Walter Wessling] m 09 Jul 1977 St.John to Debra Joy Weichman (b 12 Mar 1954 St.Lukes Hosp Cedar Rapids, IA; 1976 Degree Iowa State U.) d/o Donald Edward Weichman & Shirley Lorraine nee Cahoe. Residence Spicer, MN where Doug has sales territory for Princeton Industries. Children:
    Brooke Lorraine – b 09 Mar 1980 Willmar, MN
    Carrie Joy – b 18 Mar 1983 Willmar, MN

Wade Anthony Edward – b 27 Aug 1987 Rice Memorial Hosp
Willmar, MN

Thomas Grant WESSLING s/o Grant Anthony Wessling & Lois Jeanette
nee Schminke; b 06 Apr 1955 St.Lukes Hosp Cedar Rapids, IA; Cedar
Rapids Post Office; m 12 Jul 1975 St.John to Sara Ann Feuerbach (b 11
Nov 1954 Belle Plaine, IA; Teacher) d/o Luverne C.Feuerbach & Leona
Mae nee Katz. Children:
Heidi Mae – b 17 Jan 1976 University Hosp, Iowa City, IA;
    m 27 Nov 1999 St.John to Scott Allan Keiper
Heath Thomas – b 06 Oct 1978 St.Lukes Hosp Cedar Rapids, IA

William Bradford WESSLING s/o Grant Anthony Wessling & Lois
Jeanette nee Schminke; b 20 Dec 1956 St.Lukes Hosp Cedar Rapids, IA;
m 11 Aug 1984 Lakeside Presbyterian Ch Storm Lake, IA to Mary
Katherine Fritcher "Kay"(b 03 Jun 1957 Storm Lake, IA) d/o Theodore
Clifford Fritcher & Doris nee Horslund. Children:
Abigail Ann – b 08 Jan 1987 LaCrosse, WI
Bradford William – b 03 Feb 1990 LaCrosse, WI

Chad Joseph WHEELER s/o Karen nee Heitshusen & Joseph Wheeler; b
01 Feb 1972; m 13 Aug 1994 Kendy Peterson, DVD 1996. Child:
Kathryn Danielle – b 15 Feb 1993
Colton Jospeh – b 04 Apr 1995

Lester G. WHEELER s/o Andrew Park Wheeler & Elizabeth nee Young;
b 1904 Newhall, IA d 1975; m 1928 Leone Boddicker (b 1907) d/o
Albert A "Fish" Boddicker & Julia nee Sevening. Farmers three years
south of Newhall, IA ten years east and forty-two years southwest of
Newhall. 1977 Leone retired to Newhall, IA. Children:
Donald – b 1930; m Joyce Deklotz
Therese – b 1932; m 1955 Eldon Greene
Mary – b 1934; m Gerald E. Johnson

Mary WHEELER d/o Lester G. Wheeler & Leone nee Boddicker; b
1934; m 1958 Newhall, IA to Gerald E. Johnson (b 1933 Montezuma,
IA; Newhall, IA Barber 1961-1975) s/o Ray L. Johnson & Gussie nee
Stephen. Children:
Stephen C. Johnson – b 1959
David A. Johnson – b 1961

Barbara A. Johnson – b 1966

Therese WHEELER d/o Lester G. Wheeler & Leone nee Boddicker; b
1932; m 1955 Eldon Greene (b 1929). Ten children:
    Carol Greene – NFR
    Albert Greene – NFR
    Lawrence Greene – NFR
    Mary Greene – NFR
    Therese Greene – NFR
    Victor Greene – NFR
    Michelle Greene – NFR
    Donald Greene – NFR
    Katherine Greene – NFR
    Daniel Greene – NFR

Tammy Kaye WHITE d/o Joan Kay nee Peacock & Patrick Henry
White; b 19 May 1969; m 10 Sept 1988 Rick McSparen (b 02 Jun 1969).
Children:
    Michael Dean McSparen – b 05 Jul 1989
    Zachary Taylor McSparen – b 19 Jun 1991

Janet Colleen WHITING d/o LaVonne Marie nee Schlotterbeck & Karl
Lester Whiting; b 1952; m Dave Mannetter (b 1952). Children:
    Heidi Christina Mannetter – b 1976
    Traci Renae Mannetter – b 1978
    Katie Colleen Mannetter – b 1982

Peggy Kay WHITING d/o LaVonne Marie nee Schlotterbeck & Karl
Lester Whiting; b 1958; m Jon Dean Barnes (b 1956). Children:
    Melenie Marie Barnes – b 1978
    Jill Nicole Barnes – b 1981
    Jennifer Kay Barnes – b 1986

Sarah WHITLATCH d/o Alice Faye nee Rammelsberg & Robert
Whitlatch; b 13 Sept 1965; m 20 Jan 1990 John Gaeta. Children:
    Ryan Charles Gaeta – b 06 Jan 1992
    Isabella Maxine Gaeta – b 25 Mar 1993

*Barthold WICKERT b 02 Sept 1836 Löhlbach, Germany, d 15 Nov
1910 ae74y 2m 13d Löhlbach, Germany; m 21 Sept 1878 Anne Elisabeth

Wickert of Löhlbach, Germany. Child:
   *Philipp Wickert – b 13 Dec 1883, d 09 Aug 1915; m Karoline
Hesse

**Elke WICKERT d/o Philipp Wicker II & Emilie nee Hesse, Löhlbach,
Germany; b 15 Jul 1953 bpt & con Löhlbach Ch; m 11 Aug 1973
Löhlbach Ch to Heinrich Landau(b 06 Jan 1952 Germany). Child:
   **Anke Landau – b 30 Sept 1975 Germany

**Marlene WICKERT d/o Anna Karoline nee Beyer & Jakob Wickert; b
17 Apr 1939 Löhlbach, Germany, Hse #33, bpt & con 1954 Löhlbach
Ch; m 14 Apr 1961 Civil Ceremony/15 Apr 1961 Löhlbach Ch to Heinz
Böhle (b 19 Jul 1926 Hemfurth, Germany, d 22 Nov 2001 ae 75y 4m 3d
Löhlbach, Germany). Author visited this Paar cousin 1990, 1995, 1999,
2003. Children:
   **Torsten Böhle – b 22 Sept 1961 Bad Wildungen, Germany;
      bpt 05 Nov 1961 con 25 Apr 1976 Löhlbach Ch;
      m 30 Sept 1989 Carola Schafer
   Markus Böhle – b 30 Dec 1964 Bad Wildungen, Germany;
      bpt 14 Mar 1965 Löhlbach Ch; d 04 Dec 1970
      Löhlbach,Germany; bur Löhlbach Cem
   **Ingolf Böhle – b 22 Apr 1972 Kassel, Germany;
      bpt 18 Jun 1972 con 06 Apr 1986 Löhlbach Ch;
      m 28 May 2005 Michaela Waid

*Philipp WICKERT I. s/o Barthold Wickert & Anne Elisabeth Wickert;
b 13 Dec 1883, d 09 Aug 1915 ae31y 7m 27d; m Karoline Hesse (b 19
Apr 1887 Löhlbach, Germany d 17 May 1930 ae42y 8m 28d Löhlbach,
Germany) d/o Peter Hesse and Marie nee Dippel of Löhlbach, Germany.
Child:
   *Philipp Wickert II – b 21 Oct 1915 Löhlbach, Germany;
      m 18 Nov 1950 Emilie Hesse

*Philipp WICKERT II Maurer (bricklayer) s/o Philipp Wickert I &
Karoline nee Hesse; b 21 Oct 1915 Löhlbach, Germany; m 18 Nov 1950
Löhlbach Ch to Emilie Hesse (b 08 Nov 1923 d/o Wilhelm Hesse &
Helene nee Grunewald). Children:
   **Roland – b 01 Jun 1951; m 08/09 Oct 1971 Marlene Paar
      (b 22 Oct 1953)
   **Elke – b 15 Jul 1953; m Heinrich Landau (b 06 Jan 1952)
578

**Roland WICKERT s/o Philipp Wickert II & Emilie nee Hesse, Löhlbach, Germany: cf Marlene Martha Paar.

Jeanette Anne WIDMANN d/o Richard Warren Widman & Eileen nee Kane; b 28 Sept 1959; m 28 Aug 1980 Ronald Arden Blauveldt. Children:
    Ronald Blauveldt – b 01 Jun 1982
    Brandon Blauveldt – b 12 Sept 1984
    Emilee Blauveltdt – b 05 Feb 1986

Rachel Ruth WIDMANN d/o Rev.Richard Warren Widman & Eileen nee Kane; b 17 Oct 1961; m 20 Jun 1981 Joel Wohlseil. Children:
    Benjamin Carl Wohlseil – b 15 Nov 1983
    Jacob Richard Wohlseil – b 27 Feb 1985

Rev. Richard Warren WIDMANN s/o Jeanette Anna Elizabeth nee Happel & Rev. Elmer H. Widmann; b 22 Oct 1931 Iona, MN, bpt 22 Oct 1931 Iona Luth Ch; Luth Clergyman in CA; m 22 Jun 1958 Eileen Kane (b 19 Feb 1933). Children:
    Jeanette Anne – b 28 Sept 1959;
        m 28 Aug 1980 Ronald Arden Blauveldt
    Rachel Ruth – b 17 Oct 1961; m 20 Jun 1981 Joel Wohlseil
    Mary Elizabeth – b 26 Nov 1962
    Jonathan – b 19 Oct 1969
    Faith Louise – b 28 Sept 1972

Melissa Lynn WIEBKE d/o Evelyn Matilda nee Brehm & Larry Lee Wiebke; b 30 Sept 1975 (Adopted 24 Nov 1975); m 04 Oct 1997 Jeremy Jay Jurgens (b 01 May 1976) DVD 2006. Children:
    Gracie Rose Jurgens – b 10 Oct 1998
    Gerik Jaydon Jurgens – b 11 Dec 2001

Edward WIEBOLD of Blairstown, IA s/o parents b in Germany; m Anna Furler (b Switzerland, when young emigrated to USA). Children:
    Lillian – d 1918, bur Good Thunder, MN
    Lavonne – b 24 Dec 1932; m 29 Oct 1950 Edward Leroy Wilhelmi
    Velma – d 1936, bur Homestead, IA
    Gordon – Blairstown, IA residence
    Edward JR. – Blairstown, IA residence

Jo – m Mike Weichman of Van Horne, IA
Gloria – m Don Stenzel of Marion, IA

Kathryn Ann WIEBOLD d/o Erwin Wiebold & Louise nee Warner; b
1953; m Harold Scheesley (b 1952). Children:
    Angela Marie Scheesley – b 1971
    David William Scheesley – b 1974
    Bethany Ann Scheesley – b 1978

Margaret WIEBOLD d/o Erwin Wiebold & Louise nee Warner; b 1941;
m Avery Merriman (b 1939). Children:
    Richard Merriman – b 1963
    Robert Merriman – b 1966

Raymond WIEBOLD s/o Erwin Wiebold & Louise nee Warner; b 1943;
m Donna Brott. Children:
    Rebecca Joanne – b 1970; m Jon Rausenbeger
    Michelle – b 1972

William WIEBOLD s/o Erwin Wiebold & Louise nee Warner; b 1949; m
Wendy Lee Luken (b 1950). Children:
    John Raymond – b 1977
    Jeremy – 1979

*Fred WIESE b and m in Germany to Marie NN, d 1912 Benton Co IA;
emigrated to USA settling in Homestead, Iowa Co IA. Moved to
Williamsburg where Marie died. Fred moved, prob 1909, with his son to
a farm north of Newhall, IA and lived there three years until his death.
Children:
    William – b 1864 in Germany, d 1932 Benton Co IA;
        m 1891 Rosina Hertle

*William WIESE s/o Fred & Marie Wiese; b 1864 Germany, d 1932
Benton Co IA; m 1891 Rosina Hertle (b 1870, d 1945). Farmers near
Homestead, IA and Williamsburg, IA, later moving to farm north of
Newhall, IA prob 1909. About 1920 they retired in Newhall. Children:
    Bertha – b 1891, d 1975; m NN Teggatz of Williamsburg, IA
    Anna – b 1893, d 1960; m MM Willie; Williamsburg, IA residence
    Rose – b 1897; m Elmer Broendel
    Emma Louise – b 15 Feb 1900, d 27 Apr 1975;

m 27 Nov 1923 Arthur Jacob Werning
Elsie – b 1904, d 1919; Williamsburg, Newhall residence
Pauline – b 1909; m 1926 Otto Kaestner, 3 children

*Frederich WILHELM WILLIAMS b 03 Jan 1845 Germany, d 23 Apr
1916 ae61y 3m 20d Benton Co IA; 1867 came to USA and changed his
last name to Williams; settled on farm three miles southwest of Atkins,
IA. He sent to Germany for Sophia Koch(b 24 May 1836 Germany, d 10
May 1912 ae75y 11m 28y Benton Co IA) and they married at Atkins, IA.
Children:
Charles – m Emma Wieditz. Farmers
John Wilhelm – b 1875, d 1939; m Emma Kerkman (b 1881, d 1959)
George Fredrick – b 08 Sept 1879; d 03 Apr 1928 bur St.Steph Cem;
 m 10 Jun 1914 Sophie Christine Haerther
Anna – b 1871, d Nov 1971 Celebrated 100th birthday;
 m 23 May 1888 Charles C. Schlotterbeck. Farmers

*Adam WILHELMI s/o Johann Heinrich August Wilhelmi & Cath.
Anna nee Rose of Löhlbach, Germany; b 03 Oct 1881; m Emilie Hesse
(b 11 Aug 1883, d 15 Jan 1960 ae76y 5m 4d Löhlbach, Germany).
Children:
Helene – b 27 Aug 1910, d 05 Jul 1979; m 24 Sept 1933 Justus Ernst
Katharina Marie "Tina" – b 04 Sept 1912; d 31 Mar 1974;
 Never Married

*Adam WILHELMI s/o Karl Simon Wilhelmi & Anna Cath nee
Schween of Löhlbach, Germany; b 01 Jan 1883 Löhlbach, Germany d 27
Mar 1958 ae75y 2m 23d; m NN Children:
Johannes – m Marie; Child: Adam
Peter – m Hildegard; 2 Children: Dieter and Helmut
Adam – m Margaret; Child: Ruth

Arlene Lucille WILHELMI d/o Peter Wilhelmi & Clara nee Kerkman; b
1919; m Virgil Meyer Andrew. Farmed northwest of Atkins, IA until
retirement in Vinton, IA. Children:
Dennis Ray Andrew – b 1942; m Judy Mattson
Diane Kay Andrew – b 1946; m Lynn Holland.
 Son: Tyrone (b 1970)
Duane Alan Andrew – b 1949; m Cynthia Louise Schmuecher
 Sons: Dustin (b 1973), Damian (b 1982)

Danny Virgil Andrew – b 1954

Carol Rose WILHELMI d/o Walter Peter Valentine Wilhelmi & Rose Elizabeth nee Rammelsberg; b 15 Apr 1939 Fremont Twp Benton Co IA, bpt 1939 and con St.Steph, Atkins High School; m 28 Mar 1959 John Leonard Edwards (b 03 Oct 1936) s/o Leonard Edwards of Vinton, IA. Children:
> Michael John Edwards – b 27 Feb 1960 Cedar Rapids, IA;
>> bpt 17 Apr 1960 St.Steph
> Michelle Edwards – b 28 Sept 1963; 1st m 23 Jun 1984 James Knuth DVD 23 Jun 1984; 2nd m 11 Jul 1992 Christopher Mussman
>> (b 12 Jul 1968)

Donald Jay WILHELMI s/o Edward Leroy Wilhelmi & LaVonne nee Wiebold; b 30 Sept 1955 St.Lukes Hosp Cedar Rapids, IA (TWIN: Ronald Ray Wilhelmi) bpt 30 Oct 1955 St.Steph; m 04 Dec 1976 Nancy Eichenseer (b 30 Apr 1954). Child:
> Miranda Lynn – b 25 Jan 1984 Cedar Rapids, IA

Donald William WILHELMI s/o Walter Peter Valentine Wilhelmi & Rose Elizabeth nee Rammelsberg; b 03 Feb 1929 Parent's Farm Fremont Twp Benton Co IA, bpt 03 Mar 1929 and con 1942 St.Steph, 1946 Class Atkins High School; m 22 Jul 1951 TrinVT to Mae Alpers (b May). Children:
> Terry Michael – b 15 Feb 1954, bpt 23 May 1954 St.Steph
> Debra Jeanne – b 29 Jan 1956 Virginia Gay Hosp Vinton, IA
>> bpt 26 Feb 1956 St.Steph, and had son:
>> Conor Jeffrey Thill (b 05 Nov 1994)
> Kristi Sue – b 20 Aug 1959, bpt 13 Sept 1959 St.Steph
> Steven Donald – b 21 Mar 1964, bpt 19 Apr 1964 St.Steph

Edward Karl WILHELMI s/o Edward Leroy Wilhelmi & LaVonne nee Wiebold: cf Nancy Lynne Keiper.

Edward Leroy WILHELMI s/o Karl F. Wilhelmi & Laura Katherine nee Rammelsberg; b 23 Dec 1929 farm north of Atkins, IA Fremont Twp Benton Co, bpt 12 Jan 1930 and con 1943 St.Steph 1947 Class Atkins High School; m 29 Oct 1950 Grace Luth Ch, Blairstown, IA to LaVonne Wiebold (b 24 Dec 1932) d/o Edward Wiebold & Anna nee Furler of Blairstown, IA. Children:

Edward Karl – b 06 Sept 1951 St.Lukes Hosp Cedar Rapids, IA;
   m 25 Mar 1972 Nancy Lynne Keiper
Vicki LaVonne- b 16 Jan 1954 St.Lukes Hosp Cedar Rapids, IA;
   m 14 Oct 1977 Garth Gardemann
TWINS: Donald Jay – b 30 Sept 1955 St.Lukes Hosp
   Cedar Rapids, IA; m 04 Dec 1976 Nancy Eichenseer
   Ronald Ray – b 30 Sept 1955 St.Lukes Hosp
   Cedar Rapids, IA; m 06 Jun 1981 Mary L. Blankman

Georg Heinrich WILHELMI s/o Johann Heinrich August Wilhelmi &
Cath. Anna nee Rose; b 27 Jul 1867, d 30 Nov 1978 ae81y 4m 3d; m
Marie Elisabeth Wilhelmi (b 19 Aug 1869). Children:
   Anna – b 02 Feb 1895
   Trinchen – b 18 Oct 1899; m G. Gross
   Heinrich – b 14 Dec 1901; m Sophie NN
   Karoline – b 21 May 1905; m H. Goos
   Simon – b 13 Jan 1908; m Marie NN

Glenn WILHELMI s/o Peter Wilhelmi & Clara nee Kerkman; b 1927, d
1962 [Airplane Crash near Garrison, IA]; m Arlene Lois Uthoff. Glenn:
school bus driver, farmer, private airplane license for crop dusting and an
instructor. Children:
   Garry Eugene – m Kathryn Diane Carman
   David Glenn – NFR
   Patti Marie – NFR
   Barbara – NFR
   Kathy Jo – b 1952; m Samuel Dronebarger

*Helene WILHELMI d/o Adam Wilhelmi & Emilie nee Hesse; b 27 Aug
1910 Löhlbach, Germany, d 05 Jul 1979 ae66y 10m 8d Löhlbach,
Germany; m 24 Sept 1933 Löhlbach Ch to Justus Ernst (b 24 Sept 1910
Löhlbach, Germany, d 19 Sept 1994 ae83y 11m 26d Löhlbach,
Germany). Children:
   **Emilie Ernst – b 21 Dec 1933; m 06 Dec 1952 Karl Stocker
   **Erna Ernst – b 03 Aug 1939; m 03 Nov 1961 Ludwig Noll

*Hermann Heinrich WILHELMI s/o Johann Heinrich August Wilhelmi
& Cath. Anna nee Rose; b 04 Dec 1872, d 19 Jul 1945 ae72y 7m 15d; m
Kath. Karol. Luise Barth (b 02 Oct 1875). Children:
   Friederich Wilhelm – b 25 Apr 1901

Heinrich – b 15 May 1904
Johann Adam – b 04 Feb 1907
Simon – b 23 Sept 1909

James Richard WILHELMI s/o Richard Walter Wilhelmi & Betty Sue
McShane; b 04 Mar 1964 Cedar Rapids, IA bpt 29 Mar 1964 St.Steph; m
15 Apr 1989 Diana Lee Lanen (b 07 Sept 1969). Children:
    Richard James – b 31 May 1992
    Sara Nicole – b 23 Apr 1995

Jean Ann WILHELMI s/o Richard Walter Wilhelmi & Betty Sue
McShane; b 14 Aug 1962, bpt 09 Sept 1962 St.Steph; m 13 Sept 1986
Eric William Olsen (b 31 Oct 1966). Children:
    Tobias Charles Olsen – b 27 Dec 1990
    Johanna Nylene Olsen – b 26 Feb 1993

*Johann Adam WILHELMI s/o Johann Heinrich August Wilhelmi &
Cath. Anna nee Rose; b 11 May 1870, d 13 Oct 1959 ae89y 5m 2d; m
Helene Wickert (b 01 Aug 1873, d 12 Oct 1925 ae52y 2m 11d).
Children:
    Heinrich August – b 24 Nov 1900
    Elisabeth – b 12 Mar 1903
    Luise Marie Katharina – b 21 Apr 1905
    Emilie – b 21 Sept 1907
    Heinrich August – b 25 Sept 1909
    Karoline – b 23 May 1912
    Helene Katharina – b 17 Dec 1915

*Johann Adam WILHELMI b 18 Apr 1811 Löhlbach, Germany, d 16
Oct 1873 ae 62y 5m 28d Haubern, Germany; m 27 Dec 1833 Löhlbach
Ch to Anna Elisabeth Kahl (b 16 Dec 1809, d 30 Nov 1877 ae67y 11m
14d Löhlbach, Germany Hse #91). Children:
    Henriette – b 25 Sept 1835; d 13 May 1879 Löhlbach Hse #33;
        m 15 Feb 1862 Justus Beyer
        (b 21 Sept 1838,d 07 Mar 1910 Löhlbach Hse #65)
    Anna Christine – b 21 May 1838 Löhlbach, Germany
    Elisabeth – b 28 Oct 1839; d 08 Dec 1839 Löhlbach, Germany
    *Karl Simon – b 05 Nov 1840; m 25 May 1863 Anna Cath. Schween
    *Johann Heinrich August – b 23 Jul 1843 Löhlbach, d 15 Feb 1903;
        m 25 Mar 1866 Cath. Anna Rose

Johannes – b 26 Oct 1846, d 23 Jun 1898 Elberfeld;
m 29 Jun 1873 Marie Elisabeth Möller
(b 18 Jan 1849, d 30 Oct 1905 Elberfeld, Germany).
Heinrich Adolf – b 29 Apr 1849

*Johann Adam August WILHELMI s/o Johann Simon Wilhelmi &
Christina Elisabeth nee Möller; b 19 Sept 1845 Löhlbach, Germany, bpt
and con Löhlbach Ch; m 12 Jan 1873 Löhlbach Ch to Anna Cath. Goos.
Children:
Christina – b 05 Jul 1874; m 22 Mar 1896 Karl Möller
(b 03 Sept 1868, d 26 Aug 1942)
Conrad – b 06 Oct 1875, d 06 Mar 1876
Friedericke – b 30 May 1877
Karl – b 11 Jan 1879, d 21 Aug 1958
Conrad – b 14 Feb 1881, d 09 Jul 1901
Christina – b 10 Feb 1884
Ferdinand – b 07 Jan 1891
Anna Elisabeth – b 27 Apr 1895

*Johann Daniel WILHELMI s/o Martin Wilhelmi & Anna Gertrud nee
Möller; b 14 Jun 1702 Löhlbach, Germany, d 13 Mar 1773 ae70y 8m
27d Löhlbach, Germany; miller in Löhlbach, Germany and tennant in
Merxhausen, Germany; m 02 May 1729 Anna Guida Landau (b 14 Apr
1709, d 13 Apr 1773 ae64y Löhlbach, Germany) d/o Löhlbach, Germany
miller Simon Laundau. Eleven children.
Johann Heinrich – b 14 Aug 1731, d 17 Apr 1795;
Forester employee of the Count;
m 03 Feb 1769 Cath. Elisabeth Eisentrager. Seven children.
*Johann Heinrich – m 11 Jan 1759 Anne Maria Scherer
Anna Elisabeth – b 22 Feb 1740; m 07 Dec 1759 Joh. Simon Scherer
Anna Gertrud – b 08 Apr 1743; m 08 Oct 1766 Barthold Ritter
Benedict – b 02 Jun 1743, d 20 Dec 1771;
m 16 Feb 1769 Anna Maria Zeiss
Anna Gertrud – b 27 Apr 1747; d 18 Aug 1771 following birth of
child out of wedlock (Leonhardi father of child):
Wilhelmina Lucina b 16 Aug 1771;
m 22 Jan 1796 Johann Casper Sohn

*Johann Heinrich WILHELMI b 06 Dec 1735 Löhlbach, Germany, d 07
May 1807 ae71y 5m 1d Löhlbach, Germany; Occupation: miller; m 11

Jan 1757 Löhlbach Ch to Anna Marie Scherer (b 12 Sept 1739 Löhlbach, Germany d 21 May 1815 ae75y 8m 9d Löhlbach, Germany). Seven children (five died in childhood):

*Johann Simon – b 15 Dec 1756 in Löhlbach mill; d 28 Mar 1842
Löhlbach Hse #3; m 27 Dec 1776 Löhlbach Ch Elisabeth Roder
(b 28 Dec 1760 Löhlbach Hse # 31,
d 10 Mar 1805 Löhlbach House #3)
Anna Gertrude – b 10 Jan 1768, d 21 Nov 1806;
1st m Johannes Kuche, Rauschenberg, Germany; miller.
6 children;
2nd m 1803 wid/o Anna Gertrude to Andreas Eigenbrod.
Child: b 02 Aug 1804, d 29 Feb 1808

*Johann Heinrich WILHELMI b 27 Jul 1782 in Löhlbach, Germany Hse #3, d 20 Feb 1842 ae59y 5m 24d Löhlbach Hse #80; m 12 Nov 1807 Löhlbach Ch to Marie Christina Hesse (b 12 Jul 1784 Löhlbach, Germany Hse #13, d 15 Oct 1839 ae55y 3m 3d Löhlbach, Germany Hse #80). Children:

Henriette Marie – b 06 Apr 1808; d 1811 Löhlbach, Germany
Johann Adam – b 18 Apr 1811, d 16 Oct 1873;
m 27 Dec 1833 Anna Elisabeth Kahl
(b 16 Dec 1809, d 30 Nov 1877 Löhlbach Hse #91)
Anna Christina – b 27 Feb 1874; d 22 Apr 1847 Löhlbach Hse #73;
m 13 Jan 1833 Johann Heinrich Hesse;
(b 09 Jun 1807 Löhlbach Hse #13, d 05 Jan 1895 Löhlbach)
Johann Heinrich – b 16 Oct 1816; d 1817 Löhlbach, Germany
*Johann Simon – b 04 Sept 1878;
d 10 Jan 1865 Lölhbach Hse #119;
m 01 Jan 1845 Christina Elisabeth Möller;
(b 28 Jul 1821, d 11 Jan 1899)
d/o Linen weaver John Adam Möller
*Johann Heinrich – b 03 Aug 1821;
d 04 Feb 1868 Löhlbach Hse #51;
m 08 Feb 1846 Friedericke Kar. Philippine Wien
(b 04 Jun 1829 Löhlbach Hse #51,
d 05 Sept 1896 Löhlbach House #51);
Two sons and two daughters (a daughter emigrated to America)
Katharina Elisabeth – b 07 Aug 1825

*Johann Heinrich WILHELMI s/o Johann Heinrich Wilhelmi & Marie

Christina nee Hesse; b 03 Aug 1821, d 04 Feb 1868 ae46y 6m 1d
Löhlbach Hse#51, Germany; m 08 Feb 1846 Friedericke Kar. Philippine
Wien (b 04 Jun 1829 Löhlbach Hse#51, d 05 Sept 1896 ae67y 3m 1d
Löhlbach Hse#51). Children:
    Hermann Eberhard – b 07 Jun 1848, d 12 Nov 1926;
        m Anna Martha Siegfried (b 10 Oct 1851, d 06 Apr 1900)
    *Anna Elisabeth – b 14 Feb 1851, 1865 emigrated to America
    Caroline Cath. Marie – b 02 Jan 1856, d 31 Oct 1900;
        m 23 Jan 1881 Valentine Rennemann
        (b 16 Oct 1853, d 05 Nov 1926)
    Conrad Friedrich – b 14 Dec 1859;
        m and moved Lehnhausen, Germany

*Johann Heinrich August WILHELMI b 23 Jul 1843 Löhlbach,
Germany, d 15 Feb 1903 ae40y 5m 8d Löhlbach, Germany; m 25 Mar
1866 to Cath. Anna Rose (b 13 Jul 1843, d 26 Aug 1906 ae63y 1m 13d
Löhlbach, Germany) d/o Johann Georg Rose (m 15 Nov 1839 to
Gertrude Elisabeth nee Schufer; made oil from plants in Frankenau,
Germany). Children:
    *Georg Heinrich – b 27 Jul 1867, d 30 Nov 1978;
        m 12 Apr 1899 Marie Elisabeth Wilhelmi (b 19 Aug 1869)
    *Johann Adam – b 11 May 1870, d 13 Oct 1959; m Helene Wickert
        (b 01 Aug 1873, d 02 Oct 1925)
    Herman Heinrich – b 04 Dec 1872, d 19 Jul 1945;
        m Kath. Karol. Luise Barth (b 02 Oct 1875)
    Simon Karl – b 10 Nov 1876
    Adam – b 03 Oct 1881; m Emilie Hesse (b 11 Aug 1883)

*Johann Niclaus WILHELMI JR. s/o Johann Niclaus Wilhelmi SR. (b
1723 Löhlbach, Germany, d 20 Nov 1788 Löhlbach, Germany) & Anna
Gertrud nee Möller (b 1725, d 24 Mar 1793) b 19 Nov 1753 Löhlbach,
Germany Hse #6, d 01 Dec 1807 ae54y 12d; 1st m 04 Oct 1776 Anna
Elisabeth Möller (b 1748 Löhlbach, Germany, d 18 May 1780 Löhlbach,
Germany) two children died young.
2nd m 24 Nov 1780 Johann Niclaus Wilhelmi to Anna Elisabeth
Regenbogen (b 1739, d 04 May 1822 ae83y). No descendants.

*Johann Simon WILHELMI b 15 Dec 1756 in Löhlbach, Germany Mill,
d 28 Mar 1842 ae85y 3m 13d Löhlbach, Germany, Hse #3; m 27 Dec
Löhlbach Ch to Elisabeth Roder (b 28 Dec 1760 Löhlbach, Germany Hse

#31, d 10 Mar 1805 ae44y 2m 10d Löhlbach, Germany Hse #3).
Children:
    Cath.Marie – b 16 Apr 1779; d 06 Jul 1781 Löhlbach, Germany
    *Johann Heinrich – b 27 Jul 1782, d 20 Feb 1862;
        m 12 Nov 1807 Christina Hesse (b 12 Jul 1784, d 15 Oct 1839)
    Anna Gertrud – b 03 Aug 1785; d 06 Jun 1788 Löhlbach, Germany
    Johann Anton – b 18 Oct 1788 Löhlbach, Germany
    Marie Henriette – b 02 Jul 1791, d 21 Oct 1847;
        m 20 Dec 1812 Johann Heinrich Losekamm
        (b 07 Sept 1784, d 01 Jan 1852)
    Wilhelmina Katharina – b 29 Aug 1794;
        d 21 Dec 1868 Löhlbach, Germany
    Anna Gertrud – b 26 Jul 1797 Löhlbach, Germany
    Cath. Elisabeth – b 03 Sept 1800, d 02 Apr 1878;
        m 09 Jan 1831 Johann Eberhard Wien (b 1804)
    Cath. Elisabeth – b 28 Oct 1803; d 01 Mar 1807 Löhlbach, Germany

*Johann Simon WILHELMI b 04 Aug 1818 Löhlbach, Germany, d 10
Jan 1865 ae46y 5m 6d Löhlbach Hse # 119; m 01 Jan 1845 Christina
Elisabeth Möller (b 28 Jul 1821 Löhlbach Hse #41, d 05 Jan 1895 ae73y
5m 11d Löhlbach Hse #119) d/o Adam Möller, a linen weaver. Children:
    *Johann Adam August – b 19 Sept 1845;
        d 13 Dec 1898 Löhlbach, Germany;
        m 12 Jan 1873 Löhlbach Anna Cath.Goos,
        (b 18 Apr 1869, d 22 Jul 1922)
    Adolph – b 02 Nov 1847, d 22 Dec 1854 Löhlbach, Germany
    Konrad – b 30 May 1850 Löhlbach, Germany
    Anna Martha – b 23 Dec 1852, d 06 Aug 1926 Löhlbach;
        m 15 Sept 1875 Johann Heinrich Leininger,
        (b 21 Oct 1850, d 11 Nov 1914)
    Adolph Wilhelm – b 26 Aug 1855, d 30 Oct 1862
    Christine – b 10 Oct 1860, d 15 Oct 1929;
        m 17 Sept 1887 Johann Adam Schmidt.
        (b 02 Jul 1859, d 09 Jun 1928)

*Johann Wilhelm WILHELMI s/o Wilhelmina Cath. Wilhelmi; b 07 Mar
1835 Löhlbach, Germany Hse #3; bpt 11 Mar 1835 Löhlbach Ch
Register #188 (Godfather: Johann Wilhelm Losekamm, his mother's
nephew/son of Johann Heinrich Losekamm) d 16 Dec 1903 ae65y 9m
9dAtkins, Benton Co.IA bur St.Steph Cem; m 12 Sept 1869 Löhlbach Ch

to Marie Elisabeth Shelleberger (b 25 Dec 1840 Germany, d 07 Jun 1913 ae72y 5m 13d Atkins, Benton Co.IA bur St.Steph Cem) d/o Wilhelm Schellberger (cobblestone layer) & Sana nee Ruhwedel. Wilhelm's occupation in Germany: masonry work; two children were born in Germany. 21 Jun 1881 the family emigrated to Baltimore, MD and traveled across country to live with friends near Atkins, IA where their third child was born. Children:

> *Tobias Wilhelm – b 09 May 1870 Löhlbach, Germany;
>> d 04 Feb 1933 Atkins, IA; m Barbara Rinderknecht
> *Carolyn Dorothea – b 30 May 1873 Löhlbach, Germany
> Peter – b Fremont Twp Benton Co IA; m Clara Kerkman

*Johannes WILHELMI s/o Karl Simon Wilhelmi & Anna Cath. Nee Schween; b 25 Oct 1878 Löhlbach, Germany; m NN Rohledu. Children:

> Anna – m Wilhelm; Children: Johannes & Martha.
>> Johannes m Helene; Children: Wilhelm & Heinrich,
>> Martha m Johann; Child: Annemarie
> Liesel – m Adam; Children: Ernst & Maritz; Ernst m Elisabeth.
>> Children: Martin, Peter, Jorg. Maritz m Kathy;
>> Children: Stephen & Judith
> Maritz – m Elisabeth; Children: Wilhelm & Konrad.
>> Wilhelm m Elisabeth; Children: Gerald & Gunter.
>> Konrad m Hilde; Children: Elbe, Rainer, Brigit

John Walter WILHELMI s/o Richard Walter Wilhelmi & Betty Sue nee McShane; b 03 Apr 1973; m 08 Sept 2007 Patricia Dee Harrell (b 18 Nov 1978).

> STEPCHILDREN:
>> Jacelyne Kimber Dee Smith – b 16 Oct 1995
>> Joel Trevo Vaughn – b 14 Aug 2002

*Karl Simon WILHELMI s/o Johann Adam Wilhelmi & Anna Elisabeth nee Kahl; b 05 Nov 1840 Löhlbach, Germany, d 06 Dec 1915 ae75y 1m 1d; m 25 May 1863 Löhlbach Ch to Anna Cath.Schween (b 29 Mar 1839, d 26 Jan 1916 ae56y 9m 28d). Children:

> Anna – b 19 Apr 1864; m NN Euler
> Cath. – b 21 Sept 1866, d 13 Jan 1921
> Marie Elisabeth – b 19 Aug 1869;
>> m 12 Apr 1899 Georg Heinrich Wilhelmi
>> (b 29 Jul 1867, d 30 Nov 1918)

Sophie – b 01 Nov 1872, d 21 Aug 1930;
    m 21 Apr 1895 Maritz Barth (b 13 Jan 1868, d 30 Nov 1918)
Cath. Luise – b 17 Sept 1875, d 01 May 1944; m NN Landau
*Johannes – b 25 Oct 1878; m NN Rohbdu; 3 children
Adam – b 01 Jan 1883, d 27 Mar 1958; m NN; 3 children

Karl Fredrich WILHELMI s/o Tobias Wilhelmi & Barbara Maria nee
Rinderknecht: cf Laura Katherine Rammelsberg.

Kathy Dawn WILHELMI d/o Edward Karl Wilhelmi & Nancy nee
Keiper; b 11 May 1977; m 24 Jul 1999 Daniel G. Schneiderman s/o Jerry
& Pat Schneiderman, Freeport, IL. Child:
    Seth Daniel Schneiderman – b 16 May 2000
    Seward Memorial Hosp, NE

Lenore Katherine WILHELMI d/o Karl Fredrich Wilhelmi & Laura
Katherine nee Rammelsberg; b 28 Oct 1926 north of Atkins, Fremont
Twp Benton Co IA, bpt and con St.Steph; m 27 Feb 1949 St.Steph to
Delmar Herman Pohlman (b 25 Nov 1923). Children:
    Larry Edward Pohlman – b 23 Mar 1950;
        m 12 Sept 1970 Marilyn Hagan
    Steven Delmar Pohlman – b 08 Jun 1953;
        m 15 Jul 1972 Marie Weisert
    Dennis Pohlman – b 16 Apr 1959; m 29 Nov 1986 Pat Biggert
    Gloria Pohlman – b 20 Nov 1960; m 21 Jun 1986 Mark Imhoff

*Martin Wilhelm WILHELMI s/o Johannes Wilhelm Wilhemi (Shepherd
in Halzehausen, Germany) & wife Orthey Bracht; b prob 1662, d 06 May
1731 Lolhbach, Germany; m 13 Nov 1690 in Romershausen, Germany,
to Anna Gertrud Möller (b 1661 Löhlbach, Germany, d 04 Aug 1751
Löhlbach, Germany). Children:
    Johannes – b 01 Apr 1696 Halzehausen, Germany;
        d Löhlbach, Germany Hse #6 (Shepherd in Löhlbach, Germany);
        m 26 Oct 1719 Anna Dehn, seven children
    Johann Niclaus – b 01 Apr 1696 Löhlbach, Germany
    Anna Cath. – b 15 Jul 1705 Löhlbach, Germany
    *Johann Daniel – b 14 Jun 1702 Löhlbach, Germany;
        d 14 Mar 1773 Löhlbach, Germany; m 1729 Anna Guida Landau

Mary Ann Barbara WILHELMI d/o Karl Fredrich Wilhelmi & Laura

Katherine nee Rammelsberg; b 13 Oct 1924 farm north of Atkins, Fremont Twp Benton Co IA, bpt 09 Nov 1924 and con St.Steph; Atkins High School; m 16 Mar 1944 St.Steph to her Krug cousin Marvin Peter Kreutner (b 09 Mar 1917 Shellsburg, IA bpt 1917 and con St.Steph; d 27 Feb 1987 ae69y 11m 18d) s/o Henry Kreutner SR. & Sophia Marie Elisabeth nee Happel. Mary Ann Barbara Wilhelmi and Marvin Peter Kreutner's common Great-Grandparents: Johann Peter Krug & Anna Katharina nee Michel. Farmers. Children:

Lee Marvin Kreutner – b 23 Apr 1945; m 17 Jun 1972 Valerie Head

John Edward Kreutner – b 11 Mar 1946;
1st m 21 Oct 1967 Sheryll Dauenbaugh DVD;
2nd m 12 Feb 1993 Stephanie Bush

Richard Karl Kreutner – b 09 May 1951;
m 15 Mar 1974 Delaine Sass

Randy Lee Kreutner – b 21 Nov 1956; m 27 Jun 1959 Jeanette Hofer

Norma WILHELMI d/o Peter Wilhelmi & Clara nee Kerkman; b 1912; m Cecil Flickenger (b 1906, d 1974). Farmed at Newhall, IA and Vinton, IA before retiring in Vinton. Children:

Wayne Francis Flickenger – b 1934; 1st m Ruth Aann Alcorn.
Children: Bruce (b 1965), Leigh Ann (b 1970);
2nd m Wanda Kay Van Weichel

JoAnn Flickenger – b 1935; m Carl Dennis Michaelson (b 1936)
Children: Craig Michaelson (b 1961),
Jayne Michaelson (b 1963), Lisa Michaelson (b 1973)

Ronald Keith Flickenger – b 1936; m Patricia Ann Deneve (b 1938).
Children: Rhonda Kae (b 1958), Rochelle Marie (b 1962),
Rusty Kevin (b 1963), Ricky Francis (1965)

Karen Kay Flickenger – b 1938; m Dale Leroy Hagen (b 1936).
Children: Denise Hagen (b 1958), Douglas Hagen (b 1961),
Shari Hagen (b 1964)

Larry Robert Flickenger – b 1941; m Sandra Kay Vesley (b 1944).
Children: Larry (b 1962), Lonny (b 1964), Shannon (b 1969)

Rosemary Jean Flickenger – b 1944; m Steven Boisen (b 1939).
Children: David Boisen (b 1970); m Millisa (b 1971),
Jason Boisen (b 1975)

Kristie Lynnette Flickenger – b 1954; m Robert Don Birker
(b 1951). Children: Justin Birker (b 1974),
Kehree Birker (b 1977), Garret Birker (b 1982)

Peter WILHELMI s/o Wilhelm Wilhlemi & Barbara nee Shelleberger; b 1884, d 1967; m Clara Kerkman (b 1886, d 1975) d/o Edward John Kerkman & Barbara nee Rinderknecht. Farmers two and 1/2 miles west of Atkins, IA. Children:

Myron Wilhelm – b 1908; m Fredia Catherine Murken; worked on Rock Island Railroad; son: Roger Wilhelmi

Norma – b 1912; m Cecil Flickinger; moved to Vinton, IA

Arlene Lucille – b 1919; m Virgil Meyer Andrew; farmed northwest of Atkins, IA

Glenn Eugene – b 1927, d 1962 [Airplane Crash]; m Arlene Lois Uthoff

Richard Walter WILHELMI s/o Walter Peter Valentine Wilhelmi & Rose Elizabeth nee Rammelsberg; b 08 Sept 1934 Cedar Rapids, IA bpt 30 Sept 1934 and con St.Steph; Atkins High School, d 06 Jul 1995 ae60y 9m 28d; m 14 Feb 1959 Betty Sue McShane (b 19 Jul 1938). Children:

Jean Ann – b 14 Aug 1962, bpt 09 Sept 1962 St.Steph; m 1986 Eric William Olsen

James Richard – b 04 Mar 1964 Cedar Rapids, IA m 15 Apr 1989 Diana Lee Lamen

John Walter – b 03 Apr 1973 Cedar Rapids, IA; m 08 Sept 2007 Patricia Dee Harrell

2nd m 23 Apr 2005 Betty Sue McShane to Fred Daake.

Ronald Ray WILHELMI s/o Edward Leroy Wilhelmi & LaVonne nee Wiebold; b 30 Sept 1955 St.Lukes Hosp Cedar Rapids, IA (TWIN: Donald Jay Wilhelmi) bpt 30 Oct 1955 St.Steph; m 06 Jun 1981 St.Patrick's Catholic Ch, Watkins, IA to Mary L. Blankman (b 04 Sept 1957) d/o Orville Blankman of Watkins, IA. Children:

Paul Michael – b 16 Dec 1984

Gregory David – b 28 May 1987

Chrystal – b 27 Nov 1988

*Tobias WILHLEMI s/o Johann Wilhelm Wilhelmi & Elisabeth nee Shelleberger; b 09 May 1870, Löhlbach, Germany, d 04 Feb 1933 ae62y 8m 25d Atkins, IA, bur St.Steph Cem; m 25 Apr 1895 Barbara Maria Rinderknecht (b 11 Jan 1875, d 11 Jun 1960 ae93y 5m Atkins, IA, bur St.Steph Cem) d/o Friedrich Rinderknecht & Anna Gertrud nee Happel. Farmers west of Atkins, IA. Children:

Karl Fredrich – b 13 Dec 1896 Fremont Twp Benton Co IA;

d 26 Jul 1985 bur St.Steph Cem;
     m 16 Mar 1921 Laura Katherine Rammelsberg
Ina – b 26 Dec 1898 Benton Co IA;
     m 25 Apt 1931 Walter Dickinson; Cedar Rapids, IA residence
Carolyn – b 02 Apr 1900, d 11 Apr 1900
Walter Peter Valentine – b 06 Dec 1903 Fremont Twp
     Benton Co IA; d 22 Feb 1995 bur St.Steph Cem;
     m 15 Dec 1927 Rose Elizabeth Rammelsberg

Vicki LaVonne WILHELMI d/o Edward Leroy Wilhelmi & LaVonne
nee Wiebold: cf Garth Gardemann.

Walter Peter Valentine WILHELMI s/o Tobias Wilhelmi & Barbara
Maria nee Rinderknecht: cf Rose Elizabeth Rammelsberg.

Charles Dean WILLIAMS s/o Doris Ann nee Rammelsberg & Wendell
Creston Williams; b 25 Nov 1962 Cedar Rapids, IA bpt 23 Dec 1962
St.Steph; m 24 Aug 1985 Valeria Renee Serbousek (b 18 Apr 1963).
Atkins, IA residence. Children:
     Jonathan Charles – b 07 Apr 1987
     Heather Janeice – b 27 Sept 1990
     Jason Jeffrey – b 19 Jun 2001

Dennis Scott WILLIAMS s/o Doris Ann nee Rammelsberg & Wendell
Creston Williams; b 10 Oct 1964, bpt 08 Nov 1964; m 28 Aug 1993
Teresa Ann Brown (b 01 Oct 1964)DVD. Atkins, IA residence. Children:
     Scott Gene – b 09 Dec 1994
     Ashley Ann – b 18 Oct 1996

Eleanor Sophia Wilhelmine WILLIAMS d/o Sophia Christine nee
Haerther & George Fredrick Williams; b 13 Jun 1915; m 21 Sept 1941
Iowa City, IA St.Paul's Luth Ch to J. Neill Delaat (b 17 Jan 1914, d 26
May 1970 ae56y 4m 9d). Children:
     Jacqueline Delaat – b 19 Mar 1943
     Christine Delaat – b 18 Jun 1949; m 07 Sept 1974 Jon Broniarczykt

Elmer G. WILLIAMS s/o John Wilhelm Williams & Emma nee
Kerkman; b 1907; m Sylvia B. Voeltz. Children:
     Maureen – b 1932, d ND; m LeRoy Gardemann
     Donald – b 1935; 1st m Rose Mary; 2nd m Patricia

LeRoy – b 1936; m Phylis
Terry – b 1948

Elsie Barbra WILLIAMS d/o John Wilhelm Williams & Emma nee
Kerkman; b 1917; m Myron Walter Knaack (b 1914). Children:
 Janis Mae Knaack – b 1936; m Ronald Ferguson. Children:
  Rhonda Ferguson (b 1956); m Tom Elias
  Brian Ferguson (b 1967); m Ann Aug
  Boyd Ferguson (b 1960); m Karen Ryan
  Brad Ferguson (b 1965); m Kris Huch
  Eli Ferguson (b 1997)
 Ronald Myron Knaack – b 1942; 1st m Sharon Conkln; 2nd m Nancy
  Children: Suzanne Knaack; m Ryan Heins,
  Sheryl Knaack; m Michael Frey

James Creston WILLIAMS s/o Doris Ann nee Rammelsberg & Wendell
Creston Williams; b 04 Apr 1955, bpt 08 May 1955 St.Steph; 1st m 25
Sept 1976 Stacy Kay Zanka (b 17 Feb 1957) DVD.
2nd m 01 Jun 1983 James Creston Williams to Sandra L. Kirby (b 29 Jan
1957). Child:
 Creston James – b 01 Aug 1987

Linda Ann WILLIAMS d/o Doris Ann nee Rammelsberg & Wendell
Creston Williams; b 08 Feb 1949 Cedar Rapids, IA bpt 20 Mar 1949
St.Steph; m 15 Jul 1972 Ralph Leroy Root (b 03 Sept 1951). Colorado
Springs, CO residence. Children:
 Robert Wendell Root – b 10 Oct 1974;
  1st m 15 Jul 1994 Catherene Sunderland DVD. Child:
  Aeia Kristine (b 13 Dec 1996); 2nd m 16 Sept 2000 Veronica
  (b 21 Mar ND). Children: Regan Renee (b 26 Aug 2001),
  Robert Tristin (b 18 Nov 2002)
 Darby Ann Root – b 24 Jul 1981
 Keeley Maria Root – b 01 Apr 1983

Raymond WILLIAMS s/oJohn Wilhelm Williams & Emma nee
Kerkman; b 1915; m Jean Marie Kell (b 1920). Children:
 Mary Claire – b 1944; m Joe Fair (b 1944). Child: Roberta Lynn Fair
  (b 1967); m Daniel Mitchell
 Ruth Ann – b 1946; m Larry D. Shannon (b 1942). Children:
  John Michael Shannon (b 1969); m Vicky Minsk

Jackie Ann Shannon (b 1974); m Jamie Michael Wagner
Kay Ellen – b 1954

Sherri Lynn WILLIAMS d/o Doris Ann nee Rammelsberg & Wendell Creston Williams; b 08 May 1956 Vinton, IA bpt 10 Jun 1956; m 23 Sept 1978 St.Steph to Scott Michael Peters (b 04 Jul 1958)DVD 1994. Children:
Sarah Lynn Peters – b 03 Apr 1982
Amanda Rae Peters – b 06 Aug 1984

Vernon Frederick WILLIAMS s/o George Fredrick Williams & Sophia Christine nee Haerther; b 19 Feb 1919; m 25 Jul 1941 Viola Fry (b 30 Jan 1913, d 08 Apr 1947 ae34y 2m 9d bur St.Steph). Children:
David Frederick – b 04 Sept 1942; m 22 Jun 1968 Jane Clark
Infant Daughter – b/d 08 Apr 1947 bur St.Steph Cem

William Craig WILLIAMS s/o Doris Ann nee Rammelsberg & Wendell Creston Williams; b 15 Sept 1951 Cedar Rapids, IA bpt 14 Oct 1951 St.Steph; m 07 Jul 1979 Victoria Elaine Reed (b 22 May 1957). Children:
Wendy Marie – b 12 May 1980; m 10 Nov 2007 Chris Smith
Stephanie Lynn – b 08 Jul 1983
Weston Craig – b 09 May 1986

Brian John WILSON s/o Mary Janette nee Krug & Ralph Emerson Wilson; b 04 Apr 1960 St.Lukes Hosp Cedar Rapids, IA bpt 19 Jun 1960 St.Steph Sponsors: Uncle Kenneth Palen & Uncle Allen Postel; Kirkwood Community College; m 18 Apr 1981 United Methodist Ch West Chester, IA to Nancy Ann Duvall (b 29 May 1960) d/o John & Corrine Duvall. Hog farmers, West Chester, IA. Children:
Jessica Leigh – b 10 Mar 1982 Cedar Rapids, IA;
Drake University Degree, Des Moines, IA
Ashley Nicole – b 29 May 1984 Washington, IA;
University of Iowa Degree; m 21 Jul 2007 Jesse Boland
Caleb Jordan – b 13 May 1987 Washington, IA;
Kirkwood Community College, Cedar Rapids, IA
Colton Josiah – b 22 Nov 1990 Washington, IA
Claire Shannon – b 15 Mar 1996 Washington, IA

Julie Rae WILSON d/o Bonita Mae nee Brehm & William Keith Wilson;

b 11 Jan 1954; m 04 Aug 1979 Jay Dee Villont (b 28 June 1952). Children:

    Jordan Tyler Villont (Adopted) – b 16 Feb 1985

    Jarrod Keith Villont – b 14 Jul 1987

    Justin Robert Villont (Adopted) – b 15 Apr 1988

Wendy Ann WILSON s/o Helen Louise nee Bachmann & James Rae Wilson JR.; b 26 Sept 1956; m 31 Jul 1976 Timothy Joe Martin (b 15 Nov 1954) DVD. Child:

    Casey McCutcheon Martin – b 10 Aug 1980

William John WILSON s/o Bonita Mae nee Brehm & William Keith Wilson; b 19 Dec 1956; m 18 Jun 1994 Ronda Houck (b 28 Nov 1959). Children:

    STEPCHILDREN:

        Nicole Elizabeth Houck – b 30 Nov 1986

        Olivia Lauren Houck – b 07 Dec 1988

    Tanner William – b 08 Jun 1995

Deborah Lynn WINDERS d/o Elizabeth Louise nee Rinderknecht & Douglas Lee Winders; b 17 May 1967 Knoxville, IA, bpt 18 Jun 1967 St.Steph; m 13 Aug 1988 William Lee Settlage (b 17 Apr 1966). Children:

    Allison Settlage – b 31 Dec 1991

    Stephen D. Settlage – b NFR

Connie Sue WINTER d/o Lena nee Guericke & Maynard Winter; b 22 Feb 1961; m 29 Jun 1985 Michael Miller. Child:

    (Son) NN Miller – b Nov 1987 in Germany

Nancy Jo WINTER d/o Lena nee Guericke & Maynard Winter; b 03 Mar 1960; m 15 Sept 1984 Joseph Frances Long. Child:

    Amanda Long – b 23 ND 1986

Penny Sue WIRTH d/o Carmen C. nee Rammelsberg & Paul Wirth; b 15 May 1957; m 11 Oct 1985 John Wombacher DVD. Child:

    Hayley Jo Wombacher – b 29 Oct 1990

Michael WIRTH S/O Carmen C. nee Rammelsberg & Paul Wirth; b 18 Nov 1964; m 15 Nov 1997 Heidi Ann Harrison. Children:

Scott Donald – b 01 Jul 1998
Andrew – b 24 Oct 2002

Lois Marie WOLLMAN d/o Elaine nee Werning & Elmer Wollman; b 25 Jul 1963; Registered Nurse; m 08 Oct 1988 James Alexander Fanning of Martin, SD; (Manager of Parkston Coop) s/o James C. Fanning of Tuthill, SD & Jody Fanning of Martin, SD.

Renee Elaine WOLLMAN d/o Elaine nee Werning & Elmer Wollman; b 28 Feb 1953; m 1987 Parkston, SD to Earl Sheehy. TX residence. Children:
    Erin Ann Sheehy – b 17 Mar 1983
    Kevin Earl Sheehy – b 28 May 1985

David Scott WUNSCHEL s/o Lois Ann nee Fix & Russell Stanley Wunschel; b 14 Jul 1969 Carroll, IA; Energy Researcher, Richkand WA. m 09 Jun 2001 Sand Point, ID to Sharon; Children:
    Jacob – b 2003
    Maya – b Dec 2004

DeeAnn Kay WUNSCHEL d/o Lois Ann nee Fix & Russell Stanley Wunschel; b 08 Dec 1959 Carroll, IA bpt and con Carroll, IA; Law Degree U. of Oregon, law practice with her father; 1st m 10 Aug 1985 Brian Taylor DVD Dec 1987. Child:
    Sarah Marie Taylor – b 05 Sept 1986
2nd m 31 Dec 1992 DeeAnn Kay nee Wunschel Taylor to Jeffery Crouse. Child:
    Austin Russell Crouse – b 07 Aug 1993

Lori Lynn WUNSCHEL d/o Lois Ann nee Fix & Russell Stanley Wunschel; b 18 Nov 1964 Carroll, IA bpt and con Carroll, IA; Kansas City University Medical Center nurse; m 05 Nov 1989 Steven Blair Elliott (b 24 Dec 1958). Children:
    Alyssa Elliott – 30 Dec 1995 Kansas City, KS
    Brendon Elliott – b 26 May 1998 Kansas City, KS
    Andrea Elliott – b 17 Nov 2000 Kansas City, KS

Rudolph August WUNSCHEL b 19 Feb 1886 Early, IA, d 15 Oct 1956 Early, IA; m Ruth Elizabeth Adams (b 05 Mar 1897 Elgin, NE, d 31 Aug 1981 Early, IA). Children:

Merle – b 03 Sept 1916, d 19 Aug 1982
Gail – b 15 Oct 1918, d 16 Aug 1989
Marjorie – b 26 Oct 1919
Russell Stanley – b 26 Mar 1927; m 14 Aug 1955 Lois Ann Fix

Steven Rudy WUNSCHEL s/o Lois Ann nee Fix & Russell Stanley
Wunschel; b 03 Feb 1962 Carroll, IA; Modesto, CA Urologist; m 04 Nov
2000 Monterey Bay, CA to Beka Cox; Children:
    STEPCHILDEN:
        Morgan – m and child: Carson – b Oct 2006
        Taylor – Flight School, Tulsa, OK
    Madeline – b Jun 2002
    Liza Murin – b 04 Dec 2004

Christine Marie YOCUM d/o Deanna Marie nee Geiken & Tom Yocum;
b 23 Nov 1981; m Casey Wightman. Child:
    Ava Marie Wightman – b 19 Jun 2006

Colleen YOUNG d/o Marilyn Ruth nee Dietrich & Alan F. Young; b 13
Sept 1963(Adopted Nov 1963) m 04 Aug 1984 Russ Alan Williams
DVD. Children:
    Rhiannon Kae Williams – b 14 Sept 1989
    Jordan Alan Williams – b 08 Jan 1991

Donna Marie YOUNG d/o Philip George Young & Edith Mae nee
Brackett; b 21 Jun 1931 Vinton, IA; m 08 May 1951 Harold Dean
Andrews JR. (b 04 Sept 1930 Urbana, Benton Co IA). Children:
    Lynette Cay Andrews – b 18 Sept 1955 Cedar Rapids, IA
    Wendy Lee Andrews – b 08 Apr 1959 LaMesa, CA
    Cristi Sue Andrews – b 03 Sept 1963 LaMesa, CA

Elizabeth Pearl YOUNG d/o Joseph Young & Margaret nee Schmidt; b
1882, d 1976; m 1902 Andrew Park Wheeler (b 1872, d 1921
[Complications from fall from scaffold] Wheeler Construction Company,
Newhall, IA) s/o Charles H. Wheeler & Janet nee Park. Elizabeth and her
father built "Youngsville" in 1931, a restaurant and gas station at US
highway 30 Junction and Iowa 218 where she spent rest of her life.
Children:
    Lester George Wheeler – b 1904, d 1975; m Leone Boddicker
    Hazel LaVerne Wheeler – b 1906; m Charles I. Crawford, Joliet, IL

Ernest William YOUNG s/o John Philip Young & Marie (Mary) nee Rinderknecht; b 08 Nov 1898 Atkins, IA; m 20 Oct 1928 Jeannette Mandle (b 07 Sept 1905 St.Louis, MO). Children:
    Donald Robert – b 12 Mar 1930 St.Louis, MO
    Norman Edmund – b 18 Sept 1934 St.Louis, MO
    Doris Jean – b 04 Nov 1941 St.Louis, MO

James Philip YOUNG s/o Philip George Young & Edith Mae nee Brakett; b 21 Mar 1928 Cedar Rapids, IA; m 26 Dec 1954 Lea Carol Dankle (b 27 Feb 1933 Red Oak, IA)DVD Fall 1964. Children:
    Tina Carol – b 27 Nov 1958 Iowa City, IA
    Lori Lynne – b 04 Jul 1960 Albuquerque, NM, d 09 Jul 1960
    Susan Marie – b 09 Nov 1961 Albuquerque, NM

John Philip YOUNG s/o Jakob Young & Sophia nee Rinderknecht; b 02 Nov 1865 New York City, NY; d 1928 disappeared in 1907 shortly after the death of his eldest child and was declared legally dead by a Chicago, IL court in 1928 to settle the estate of his brother Jake; m 1890 Marie (Mary) Rinderknecht (b 09 Dec 1870 Benton Co IA, d 15 Aug 1902 ae31y 8m 11d) d/o William Rinderknecht & Maria nee Happel. Children:
    Sophia Marie – b 08 Apr 1891 Atkins, IA d 18 Aug 1907
    Charlotte Martha – b 24 Mar 1893 Atkins, IA; d 15 Mar 1934;
        Never Married
    Philip George – b 05 Aug 1895 Atkins, IA;
        m 16 Jun 1926 Edith Mae Brackett
    Ernest William – b 08 Nov 1898 Atkins, IA;
        m 20 Oct 1928 Jeannette Mandle

Norman Edmund YOUNG s/o Ernest William young & Jeannette nee Mandle; b 18 Sept 1934 St.Louis, MO; m 10 Aug 1957 Carol Jean Meyer (b 19 Oct 1935 Chicago, IL). Children:
    Jeanne Marie – b 13 Oct 1960 Winfield, KS
    Kathleen Ann – b 30 Apr 1963 Winfield, KS
    Janet Lynn – b 29 Mar 1965 Winfield, KS
    Michael Norman – b 19 Mar 1972 Maywood, IL

Philip George YOUNG s/o John Philip Young & Marie (Mary) nee Rinderknecht; b 05 Aug 1895 Atkins, IA d 11 Jul 1952 ae56y 11m 6d; m 16 Jun 1926 Edith Mae Brackett (b 30 Apr 1905 St.Louis, MO, d 14 Feb

1947 ae41y 9m 15d). Children:
    James Philip – b 21 mar 1928 Cedar Rapids, IA;
        m 26 Dec 1954 Lea Carol Dankle DVD
    Donna Marie – b 21 Jun 1931 Vinton, Benton Co IA;
        m 08 May 1951 Harold Dean Andrews JR.
    Robert William – b 29 Sept 1933 Vinton, Benton Co IA;
        m 16 Oct 1960 Dixie Harrington (b 07 Jul 1941 Iowa City)
    Linda Lee – b 10 Aug 1938 Blairstown, IA

Alvina ZORNIG d/o Marx Zornig JR. & Annine nee Haupt; m Frederich
Bobzien Farmers near Newhall, IA. Children:
    Anenia Bobzien – b 21 Feb 1891, d 23 Oct 1978;
        m 07 Jan 1912 Henry John Stien
    Edna Bobzien – NFR
    Nelda Bobzien – NFR
    Dora Bobzien – m Frank Kerkman (b 1896, d 1948)
    Martha Bobzien – NFR
    Royal Bobzien – NFR
    Gilbert Bobzien – NFR
    Laural Bobzien – NFR

*Fred Z0RNIG b Holstein, Germany; emigrated to Iowa and lived in
Benton Co sixty years; m Margaretha Meinert. Farmers southwest of
Keystone, IA. Child:
    Lena – m Herman Franzenburg

*Marx ZORNIG JR. s/o Marx Zornig SR. & Mary nee Wiesel; b 1843
Germany, d 1931 IA; emigrated to Benton Co IA; m Annine Haupt (b
1884, d 1935) d/o Fred & Catherina Haupt. Children:
    Alvina – m Fred Bobzien
    Emma – b 1873, d 1942; m August Seeman
    Fred – dec'd infancy
    Adelia – m NN Petersen
    Herman – US Army Lt.Colonel

Emma ZORNIG d/o Marx Zornig JR. & Annine nee Haupt; b 1873, d
1942; m August Seeman (b 1873, d 1948) s/o John Seeman &
Wilhelmina nee Peters. Farmers and cattle feeders, hunters, trappers,
fishermen. Child:
    Emmett Seeman – b 1898, d 1980; m Mary Ann Sindt

BIBLIOGRAPHY

Atkins Centennial Committee. **Atkins, Iowa Centennial Book,** 1982.

Benton County Historical Society. ***History Of Benton County, Iowa,*** Taylor Publishing Co. Dallas, Texas. 1989.

Buhlow, Ursula. ***Deutches Namen Lexikon,*** Hamburg Records, Germany. 1988.

Jacob, Otto. ***Lohlbach ein Bergdorf im Kellerwald 1200 Year History,*** Gemeinde Haina (Kloster) Kassel, Germany: Druckhaur Thiele & Schwarz GmH.1988.

Krug, Enid Bryner. ***Krug-Michel-Happel-Moeller Reunion Records*** Atkins, Iowa.

Palen, Margaret Krug. ***Genealogical Guide To Tracing Ancestors In Germany,*** Heritage Books, Inc. Bowie, Maryland. 1995

Palen, Margaret Krug. ***Genealogical Research Guide To Germany,*** Heritage Books, Inc. Bowie, Maryland. 1988.

Palen, Margaret Krug. ***German Settlers of Iowa,*** Heritage Books, Inc. Bowie, Maryland. 1994.

Palen, Margaret Krug. ***German Settlers of Iowa, Their Descendants & Their European Ancestors,*** Heritage *Books, Inc. Bowie, Maryland. 2000*

Peitz, Michael &Linda. ***Newhall, Iowa 1882-1982, The First Hundred Years,*** 1982.

---- Adam, 589 Annemarie, 589 Carl, 406
Elisabeth, 589 Ernst, 589 Gordon, 492
Johann, 589 Johannes, 589 Jorg, 589
Judith, 589 Kari, 520 Kathy, 589 Lori,
520 Marilyn, 99 Maritz, 589 Martha,
589 Martin, 589 Peter, 589 Sharon, 521
Stephen, 589 Wilhelm, 589
AAMODT Ivy Dean, 547
AARON Chelsea, 386 Rhonda Jean, 386
389
ABBOTT Brian, 447 Carolyn, 447 Laura,
447 Laura Lyn, 318 Logan, 447 Tony
H, 318 447
ABERNATHY Joan, 72 Keith, 72
ABODEELY Carol Leona, 320 Leslie, 320
Less, 320
ABRAHAM Anna, 1 Anna Katherina, 1
August Heinrich Jr, 1 August Heinrich
Sr, 1 239 546 August Jr, 546 Christine,
359 Dora, 1 Emma, 1 George Jr, 1
George Sr, 1 Louise, 1 546 Margaret, 1
Mary, 1 239 240 568 Peter, 1 Rosena
Louisa, 1 239 Rosena Louise, 546
Wayne, 1 Willard, 1
ABRAM Andrew Timothy, 142 Eric Ryan,
142 Ronald Jack, 142 145 Sharon Ann,
142 145
ACHENBUCH A Elizabeth, 450 Joh
Adam, 450
ACHEY Carol Ann, 236 Robert E, 236
ACKER Elizabeth, 113
ACKLAM Chris, 49 50
ACKLAM Dorothy, 49 50
ADAMS Adrian Craig, 61 Althea Marie,
122 Andrew Kent Avery, 1 Barbara
Juliann, 1 122 137 Christopher Martin
John, 1 Craig Marvin, 61 186 Denise
Michele, 61 186 Herbert, 122 Herbert
Carter, 122 Herbert Howard, 1 137
Howard, 122 Janice, 61 Kent Myron, 1
122 Laurie Ann, 1 122 Marchelle Lynn,
1 122 Marvin, 61 Pauline Elinore, 33
36 Ruth Elizabeth, 77 597
ADDENGAST Gertie, 248 249 Gertrude,
248 249 412
ADRIAN Arthur, 184 Marie, 184

ADYNIEC Anita Mae, 214 472 Jesse
Fielding, 472 Mark, 214 Mark, 472
Sarah Elizabeth, 472
AESCHLIMAN Jennifer Delane, 237
AGAN Brooke Lee, 386 Fred, 386
AGNEW John C, 530 June C, 530 Patricia,
530 William, 530
AGNITSCH Diana, 49 50 Eileen, 49
Frances, 49 Lindsay Dianne, 49 Marni
Jo, 49 Nicole Lee, 49 Thomas, 49 50
AHLEMEYER Ardith, 555 558
AHLEMEYER Eric, 555 Michael, 555
Terry, 555 558
AHREND Joachin, 564 Luise, 564
AHRENDSEN Bryon, 377 Debbie, 377
AHRENDT Frieda, 552 553 557 560 562
564 566 570 572 575
AHRENS Albert Herman Martin, 329
Andrew, 327 Andrew Ludwig
Benjamin, 329 Arthur Henry Conrad,
329 Charles Carl Michael, 327 Charles
Carl Micheal, 329 Edwin, 329 Elfrieda
Viola, 27 Emma, 166 Emma Katherine
Johanna, 329 Goldie Caroline, 26 176
Hans, 27 Katherine, 327 Katherine
Elizabeth, 329 Katie, 327 Margaretha,
71 467 Mary Rose, 329 Mildred Vesta
Otilla, 329
ALBANG Rose Ann, 473
ALBERS Alvin, 2 Amy, 3 Anna, 2 Annie
C, 244 247 Arthur, 2 Betty, 2 Betty, 3
Betty, 294 Brad, 3 Cacilie, 498 499 500
Christine, 561 Cynthia, 2 3 245
Donald, 2 3 294 Edward, 561
Elizabeth, 408 409 Elsie, 2 Emma, 2
Hartwig, 2 Hartwig A, 2 Heimke, 81
Herman, 2 Hiemke, 80 82 Jacob Henry,
2 John, 2 Juston, 3 Katharina, 2
Katherine, 215 Kathleen, 216 Kathryn,
2 Kathy, 434 Kevin, 2 Leta, 487 Luise,
561 Margaret, 2 507 Mark, 2 3 245
Selma, 203 Sheila Ann, 2 270 294
Shiela Ann, 3 Velma, 2 Weibke, 302
ALBERT Andie, 293 538
ALBERTS Cleota, 316 Virgil, 301 316
ALBERTSEN John, 191 Maria, 191 Adam
Roy, 3

ALBERTSON Antonette (Tony), 7 Coreen, 3 Craig A, 372 David L, 3 372 Donald, 3 Donald G, 25 372 Ewald, 372 Joanne, 372 Kay Frances, 3 25 372 Lucille, 558 Nichole, 3 Patricia, 3 372 Peggy Ann, 372 Roscoe, 558 Valerie, 3

ALBRECHT Carol, 476 David, 476 Denise, 476 Doris, 157 476 Frieda Gertrude, 3 Jean, 476 Vince, 3 476 Vincent, 157

ALBRIGHT Kristi, 508 Steve, 508

ALCORN Nancy Sue, 41 Robert Craig, 41 Ruth Aann, 591

ALCOTT Billie, 385 389

ALDEN Anna Emelie, 229 Anna Emilie, 414 Dorothy, 347 Howard Budette, 230 Myrtle Irene, 229 346 348 351 352 Willard Henry, 229 414

ALDRICH Julie Ann, 473

ALLEN Arthur, 382 383 Doris Pauline, 382 383 Eloise Virigina, 118 Nancy, 301 Robert Louis, 382 Sheila Kay, 382 Steven, 331

ALLERS Amanda, 13 200 Carol, 13 Donald, 13 Henry, 13 200

ALLOWAY Esther, 469 Lawrence, 469

ALMUS Johann Christop, 495 Luise Katharina, 264 494 495

ALMUS SCHÜLER Luise Katharina, 493

ALPERS Dorothy, 74 Elte, 368 Elvira, 74 Gerold, 74 John, 368 Mae, 395 582 Pearl, 74 Robert, 74 William, 74

ALT Terese Joy, 102

ALUMUS SCHÜLER Luise Katharina, 495

AMBROSE Daniel Jessen, 210 Jo Ellen, 210 Jo Ellen, 573 Laura Marie, 210 William David, 210 573

AMELSE Michelle Sue, 245

AMENT Glenn, 382 Patricia, 382

AMERLING Leslie, 532

AMJACH Roberta Patricia, 10

AMONSON Bernidane Ann, 10

ANDERSEN Christine Julianna, 18 Ernest, 18 Julie Denise, 26 Marge, 26 Marie Martha, 18 Mark Wayne, 26 Marlyn, 26

ANDERSON Axel, 329 Betty Jean, 3 242 244 C Marie, 393 Caleb Joseph, 3 Christina Julianna, 16 Christine, 16 Colleen Elaine, 78 Collene Elaine, 73 Cora Vlasta, 73 Corinna, 3 42 Craig Daniel, 3 242 Dain, 24 Dale Kermit, 329 330 Debra Jeanne, 506 Diane, 88 Dianne, 90 Donna Jean, 56 Elizabeth Ruth, 31 34 35 36 Ernest, 86 Ethan John, 3 Evelyn Ruth, 31 239 Gertrude, 301 Helen, 437 Henry, 301 Isabella Nicole, 262 Ivan, 469 James Peter, 3 42 Janet, 318 Jason, 3 Joan, 79 Joan Elaine, 42 Jody Sue, 262 292 Joellen Kay, 20 John Hasbrouck, 3 242 244 John Robert, 42 Josephine, 73 June Leona, 20 Kathy Ann, 42 Kathy Marie, 125 241 Kay Karleen, 329 330 Kent Douglas, 242 Kurt, 262 292 Laura, 252-254 Laura Ann, 329 Lois, 469 Lorrene Mae, 71 78 Lydia Mary, 3 42 560 Lynn, 24 490 Mabel, 217 301 Mae, 329 Marlys, 16 Mary, 86 Mattie, 42 Paul Gene, 318 Peter, 3 42 560 Ray, 42 Roger Dean, 20 Stacy Lynn, 3 Teresa Kay, 3 242 Thomas, 24 490 Tyler David, 329 Walter, 329 Warren Carl, 71 73 78

ANDRESEN Julie Denise, 27 Mark Wayne, 27

ANDREW Arlene Lucille, 3 Arlene Lucille, 581 592 Audrey, 476 Catharine, 476 Catharine, 477 Damian, 581 Danny Virgil, 582 Dennis Ray, 3 581 Diane Kay, 581 Duane Alan, 581 Dustin, 581 Edna Lenora, 476 Emma, 476 Emma L, 321 Franklin James, 476 Irvin A, 321 Irving Edward, 476 James, 476 James Wesley, 476 477 Jason, 3 Judy, 581 Julie, 4 Karmen, 3 Kimberley, 3 Kristina Rae, 3 Lillian Elizabeth, 476 Samuel, 476 Suzanne, 476 Virgil Meyer, 3 581 592

ANDREWS Cora, 87 Cristi Sue, 598 Donna Marie, 598 600 Flora, 135 Harold Dean Jr, 598 600 James A, 371 Joan, 323 330 John, 87 Lorene, 135

Lynette Cay, 598 Stella, 87 Susan L, 371 Wendy Lee, 598
ANDRLIK Joseph, 378 Leone, 287 378
ANNETT Leona Barbara Anna, 474 Shelley, 475 Virgil, 474 Virgil W, 475
ANTHES Kaspar John, 405 Louisa Emma, 405 Wilhelmina, 405 407
ANTOR Lelia, 308
APOSTOLIDES Joann Lorraine, 78
APPLETON Janet, 291 Jerry, 291
ARMSTRONG Alice Marie, 4 53 56 Christy, 452 Dorothy Olive, 53 398 Elizabeth, 394 Elton, 53 Fred Bert, 394 Gayle, 7 Hettie, 474 Hettie May, 394 John, 390 Kay Lynn, 4 53 Kimberly, 4 Kimberly Sue, 53 Kristy Ann, 53 Lenard James, 4 53 56 398 Mary, 390 Mary Jane, 273 288 292 383 Mildred, 53 Newton, 452 Ottillie, 390 Sarah, 383 Thomas, 383 Thomas Graham, 383
ARNDT Anna, 224
ARNOLD Ann Elizabeth, 440 Anne Elizabeth, 412 David Dale, 412 441 Ione, 412 Walter S, 412
ARP Rosetta, 477 Theresa, 209
ARVIDSON Austin, 525 Hannah, 525 Lindsay, 525 Mark Lawrence, 525 Michelle Lyn, 525
ASARE Cynthia Marie, 246
ASHING Mabel, 315 316
ASPENGREN Albin H, 337 Lois M, 334 337 Violet M, 337
ATHA Carol Ann, 126 Russell III, 126
AUG Ann, 594
AUGSPURGER Rose Marie, 31 37
AUSTIN Anna, 207 Lois N, 105 Lois Neil, 107 109 111
AVERHOF Anna, 1
AVERY Patty, 52 438
AXELSEN Etta, 75 Heinrich, 77 Mary, 77 Meta, 55 75 77 339 427
BAACK Sophia, 389
BACH Anna, 226
BACHLEY Bertha, 261
BACHMAN Christina, 444 445 Gertrude W, 424 Julius H, 33 Laura Anna, 519-521 523 526 Louise Dorothea, 33

BACHMANN Ashley Brooke, 6 Barbara Jean, 4 Carol All, 4 Carol Ann, 4 Catherine Rose, 5 Catherine Ross, 6 Christina Lee, 5 Donald Charles, 6 Donald William, 4 5 35 Dorothy Agnes, 5 6 35 Dorothy Katherine, 4 6 35 Frances Lorraine, 4 5 6 35 Helen Louise, 5 35 596 Isaac Theodore, 5 James Robert, 5 Julis Jacob Theodore, 6 Julius H, 5 35 Julius Jacob Theodore, 5 35 Kathleen Marie, 4 Lance Alan, 4 5 Louise Dorothea Katherine, 4 5 35 Marilyn Kay, 6 Perla Tina Praxedes, 4 5 Robert Louis, 4 5 6 35 Robert Reed, 5 6 Ruth Elaine, 4 5 35 Ruth Mathilda, 560 Sally Marie, 5 Saundra Ann, 6 Vickie Jo, 5 6
BACHRODT Helen Martha, 432
BACKES Frances, 535
BACKHAUS Henry, 321 Ida, 321
BACKMANN Kathleen Marie, 5
BADE Dorothy Katherine, 5 6 35 Herbert H, 5 6 35 Kathleen Ann, 5 6 Lawrence Mark, 5 Natasha Renee, 5 Nicole Elizabeth, 6 Paul Andrew, 5 Priscilla Faith, 5 Ralph Edward, 5 6 Tara Ann, 6
BADENIN Marie Madeleine, 238
BADER Arlene, 145 162 171 181
BADING Lynn, 96
BADONIN Marie Madeleine, 280
BAGLIEN John L, 290 Nancy Ann, 290
BAIR Duane, 451 Karen Kay, 451 Lonnie, 451 Shannon, 451 Shaun, 451 Sheila, 451
BAKENHUS Evelyn Hattie, 395 Evelyn Hettie, 6 388 Joyce May, 6 388 Lorna Louise, 388 Martha, 388 Ora, 395 Ora Oscar, 6 388 Orville Allen, 388 Oscar Adolph, 388
BAKER Bonnie, 104 366 Cecelia Margaret, 65 Daisy, 190 Francis, 65 Louisa, 51 545 Margaret, 228
BALDWIN Carolyn, 442 Clair E, 520 Danette Lee, 438 442 Martha Joanna, 34 557 559 574 Roger Allen, 442
BALFOUR Virginia, 206
BALHORN Amelia, 6 8 241 Anna, 6-9 142 143 Annie, 7 Antonette (Tony), 7

August, 8 August J W, 6-9 Barbara, 8
Bernice, 8 9 Betty, 7 8 Camille, 8 Carl,
7-9 Charles, 7 8 143 Charles W, 7 8
Clara, 7 8 Dean, 9 Dean William, 7
Diane, 9 Dora, 6-8 Dorliss, 8 Elaine
Eleanor, 7 Elnora Margaret, 7 8 143
Gary, 8 Gayle, 7 Glenda, 8 Helen, 7
Jackoelyn, 8 Jean Ann, 8 Joachin Jr, 6
7 8 Joachin Sr, 8 Joackin, 7 John, 7-9
Linda, 7 8 Margaret, 214 498 499
Merrill, 7 Milo, 8 Minnie, 8 Nancy, 9
Pat, 9 Pearl, 7-9 Randall, 7 Richard
Charles, 7 8 Sharon, 306 Sophia, 7-9 21
Vincent, 8 9 William, 7
BALLAM Corrine Dorothy, 47 233
BALLARD Faith A, 295 Karen Lee, 240
241 Lauren Alyse, 240 Mark S, 241
Mark Sullivan, 240 Shannon Lee, 240
Tina Lynne, 538
BALLHEIM Anna, 360 Michael, 360
Norma Jane, 174 Rosa, 359 360
BALZER Anna Catharine, 476
BANSE Melba W, 553
BARBER Claudia, 246
BARD Janet, 255 256
BARE Becky, 26 79
BARFELS Dianne Marie, 270 501 Erin,
501 Lauren Elizabeth, 501 Thomas,
501 Thomas Edward, 270 501
BARGER Nancy M, 455
BARK Bertha, 261 Floyd, 261 Linda Mae,
261 262
BARKLEY Christy, 259
BARLOW Maxine, 399 401
BARNES Jennifer Kay, 577 Jill Nicole,
577 Jon Dean, 475 577 Melenie Marie,
577 Peggy Kay, 475 577 Renae, 100
149
BARNEY Marie, 16
BARNOSKE Edna, 83 84
BARQUIST Rachelle, 29
BARR Becky Lee, 414 Craig, 414 420
Craig Louis, 439 Rebecca Lee, 420 439
BARRIE Morna Ed, 45
BARTA Cora Vlasta, 73 Joe, 285 Mary,
285

BARTELL John, 120 572 L C, 120
Margaret, 120 121 572 Mary Elizabeth,
121 Sarah Jane, 121
BARTH Kath Karol Luise, 583 587 Maritz,
590 Sophie, 590 Zerelda, 505
BARTHOLMEW Edward, 53 Kay Lynn,
53
BARTHOLOMEW Ann, 4 Brady Jo, 9 24
Brock James, 9 24 Bryce, 4 Ed, 4
James, 24 Jim, 154 Kay Lynn, 4 Lisa
Ann, 24 154 Megan, 4 Paul, 4
BARTHOLONEW James, 9 Lisa Ann, 9
BARTOCHEK SCHLIEMAN Ida, 557
BARTOSH Elizabeth, 229
BARTUSCH Nancy Irene, 48 233
BASCOM Albert Sr, 186 Helen L, 186 187
Joann Catherine, 400 402 403
BASS Christian James, 341 Elisa Jennifer,
341 Jo Ellen, 291
BASSETT Nell Jean, 138
BASTEN Collin, 75 Emily, 75 Mark
Aaron, 75 293 Sharon Arlene, 75 293
BATES Dorothy, 81
BATTEFELD Katharina Elisabeth, 248
326
BATTLES Bertha, 75
BAUER Anne, 544 Evelyn, 72 73 Louise,
478 Michelle, 127 313
BAUGH Toni, 234 237
BAUGHMAN Sarah Catherine, 463
BAUMAN Carol Marie, 9 292 385 Craig,
388 Evalina, 388 Faythe, 388 Fern, 385
388 Fredericka, 39 James, 385 388
Jeffrey, 388 Kerry, 388 Marie, 388
Michelle Lea, 9 385 Rachel, 388 Ralph,
9 292 385 Sanra, 388 Sarah, 388 Scott,
388
BAUMGARTNER Anna, 515 543 544
Anne, 544 Charles, 515 George, 515
George John, 523 526 Hazel A, 526
Louis, 515 544 Matilda Anna, 523 526
William, 515
BAUMILLER Dawn Marie, 560 Elda, 9
560 575 Gerda, 560 Kim Lee Ann, 560
Marvin, 9 560 575 Reinhold, 560 Troy
Marvin, 560 Vicky Lynn, 9 560
BAYER Amy, 12 270 Betty Jean, 11 421
David Lee, 11 Deborah Jean, 11

Delmar Elwood, 9 421 Denise
Michelle, 9 Doris Elaine, 10 421 510
Dorothy Marie, 10 11 222 270 274
Elda Gertrude Louise, 9-12 413 420
Frederkc Henry, 222 Frieda, 221 222
270 Friedrich Henry, 10 11 270 274
George, 221 222 270 Jeffrey Martin, 11
Joel Roger, 11 Julia Marie, 270 Julie
Marie, 10 Kenneth Martin, 270 Lilia,
222 Linda Ann, 10 421 Lucille Jean, 10
421 Lukas Nathan, 9 Marine Mae, 10
421 Martin, 222 Martin Eldred, 11 421
Martin Frederick, 9-12 413 420
Matthew Joseph, 9 Paul Thomas, 12
Paula Marie, 10 Pearl Evelyn, 11 420
517 518 Phyllis Lucille, 11 421
Rebecca Lynn, 12 Robert Fredrich, 11
270 Rose Marie, 421 Timothy Paul, 12
Violette Janette, 12 142 421
BEADLE Andrew Loras, 90 Ann, 8 Debra
Lynn, 90 Elaine Eleanor, 7 Elizabeth
Ann, 90 Leta, 90 Loras John Jr, 90
Loras John Sr, 90 Matthew, 8 Natalee,
7 Robert E B, 7 Shannon, 8 Tyler, 8
BEAKS Leslie, 302 Stephan, 302
BEARD Georgina, 387
BEATTY Blanche Ellen, 64 453 454
Diane, 475 Evelyn, 471 Gertrude
Kathryn, 445 446 Ida, 451 Joe, 90
Joseph Charles, 242 Kristine, 442
Kristine Kay, 186 Larry, 455 Maggie,
90 Mary Ann, 242 Minnie Ella, 242 N
N, 475 Ronald, 469 471 Sandra, 455
Sharon, 469 471 Shelley, 305 306 475
Zoe Kathleen, 223
BECK Addie, 12 Anna, 463 Austin, 12
Burdette, 12 Catharine, 12 Emma, 12
Ethel, 12 Florence, 12 Hazel, 12 Jacob
Jr, 12 Jacob Sr, 12 Jennie, 12 Lillian,
12 Lucille, 12 Mabelle, 12 Mary, 83
Milton, 12
BECKER A Gertraut, 313 Alberta, 207
Amy Elizabeth, 12 268 Andrew Joseph,
12 13 268 292 Angela Kay, 36 37 Anna
Gertraut, 312 Bertram, 211 Bonnie, 208
Deanne Kay, 12 13 268 292 Donald,
207 Dorothy, 268 Elizabeth, 373
Evelyn, 211 Herman, 38 207

BECKER Kelly Anne, 268 Lillian, 38 207
Mary, 373 Matilda, 190 Myron, 207
Nathan Andrew, 268 Sarah Marie, 13
268 Wayne, 207 Wilferd, 268
BECKLER Melissa Lynn, 274 Steven, 274
BECKMAN Dorothy Mae, 361
BECKMEYER Deborah, 506 Debra
Jeanne, 506 James, 506 Jennifer, 506
John, 506 Kelsey Marie, 506 Megan
Elizbeth, 506 Morris, 506 Patricia, 506
Robert, 506 Roger Allen, 506
BECKWITH Ethel Josephine, 378
BEDFORD Della, 185
BEHNKE Deborah Mae, 530 Richard, 530
BEHOUNECK Lori Sue, 95 96
BEHRENS Anna, 135 197 319 Arlene, 23
Carl, 197 Claus, 135 197 319 Curtis
David, 317 Ella Charlotte, 221 226 227
431 Elmer, 197 Harry, 197 Henry
Walter, 135 John, 197 Karl, 23 Louis,
197 Louise, 197 Louise Martha, 13 130
135 197 Mae, 197 Margaret Judith, 13
135 Mark David, 13 Mary Katharine,
221 Mary Lou, 13 135 Mathew
Anthony, 13 Michael William, 13
Michelle Kay, 317 Pauline, 197 255
256 258 260 Walter, 13 130 135 197
William Deitrick, 221 William Henry,
13 135
BEIBERDORF Adina Juliann, 136 Deena,
136 Johanna Sylvia, 123 133
BEIRSCHENK Brandee Lynn, 17 Brian
Conrad, 17 Bridget Marie, 17 Carl
Heinrich, 17 Elizabeth, 17 George A,
17 Henry Carl, 17
BEISEL Anna, 42
BEITZ Clara Amelia, 278 285 288 292
Elmer, 558 Joan, 555 558 Julius, 285
Nettie, 285
BEK Christine Catherine, 131 132
BELL Baylee Theresa, 103 Brent Bell, 103
Cindy, 513 Ethel, 191 Jacqueline
Marie, 103 124 James, 265 Madison
Margaret, 103 Margaret, 103 Marie,
265 Robert, 103 Steve, 513 Thomas
Charles, 103 124
BELLENDIER Mary, 138 139

607

BLANKMAN Mary L, 583 592 Orville, 592
BLASBERG Lois Elaine, 336 349 350
BLATTLER Charles Richard, 274
   Christopher Ryan, 447 Kelsey Rose, 447 Krista, 275 Krista Lynn, 274 Richard, 446 Sue Ellen, 446 447 Tichart, 447
BLAUVELDT Brandon, 579 Emilee, 579 Jeanette Anne, 579 Ronald, 579 Ronald Arden, 579
BLAYLOCK Jeffery, 507 Molly Jean, 507
BLOCK Amy Beth, 103 Helen A, 159 376 377 Teresa, 103
BLOECHER Sandra A, 376
BLOESER Berdina Ann, 21 151 162 Brenda Jean, 21 47 151 Floyd, 21 151 162 Sheryl Rae, 151
BLOMEN Margaret, 106 108
BLOOMQUIST David, 125 134 Jessica, 125 Jessica Jean, 134 Jonathan, 125 Jonathan David, 134 Linda Jean, 125 134 Travis, 125 Travis Neal, 134
BLOUGH Sandra, 74 195
BLUE Mary Ella, 509 Verna, 478
BLUHM Alison Lynel, 501 Brandon Charles Scott, 501 Delwyn Donald, 439 Gloria Lee, 439 Janet Ann, 501 Jennifer Kaye, 438 439 Karen, 501 Kelie Kay, 501 Kevin Dale, 501 Kindra Ann, 501 Matthew Steven, 501 Nathan Andrew, 501 Raelene, 501 Steven Lee, 501 Virgil, 501
BLUMBERG Gary, 257 Sherry, 257
BLUNCK Virginia, 338
BOATWRIGHT John D, 429 John Gatlin, 429 439 Judy Kay, 429 439 Sarah, 429 Therese Ann, 430 Tonya Sue, 429
BOBZEIN Katrina, 380
   BOBZIEN Alvina, 515 600 Anenia, 513 515 516 600 Dora, 231 600 Edna, 600 Fred, 600 Frederich, 515 600 Gilbert, 600 Laural, 600 Martha, 600 Nelda, 600 Royal, 600
BOCK Lenora, 152 181 183
BOCKHOLT Alfred, 7 9 21 Becky, 21 Brady James, 173 Brian James, 160 173 Bucky, 23 James Lee, 21

Katherine, 531 Laura Jean, 159 173 Laverne (Bucky), 9 Laverne Becky, 21 Laverne Bucky, 23 Mako, 21 Marlus, 9 21 Olive, 9 21 23 Sophia, 7 9 21
BODDICKER A A, 513 Albert, 543 Albert A, 247 Albert A Fish, 21 568 576 Albert A Sr, 21 22 Albert J, 22 542 543 546 Angela Gertrude, 436 437 Anna, 21 Antonette, 21 247 Antonette Nettie, 22 Bernice, 542 Bertha, 21 Caroline, 22 542 546 Cyril, 89 Donald, 548 Elizabeth, 21 83 242 244-246 Elwood, 22 78 Emma, 21 544 546 Fish, 21 Geraldine, 541 Helen, 437 Henry John, 22 Hilda, 542 Ida Pauline, 22 Jack, 21 James Leroy, 22 James Leroy, 421 James Leroy, 541 Janel Lyn, 541 Janel Lynn, 22 Janet Lynn, 22 421 541 Jeffrey James, 541 Jill Ann, 541 Joe Ge, 79 John, 21 John Henry Jack, 21 Jolene, 22 Joseph, 541 542 Joseph A, 21 Julia, 21 568 576 Katherina Elisabeth, 25 Lena, 22 Leone, 576 577 598 Lillian, 333 Lois, 543 Luella, 89 Marie, 22 44 46 315 542 Marjorie, 22 78 Mary, 21 Maxine, 25 552 553 565-568 574 Mildred, 543 Nettie, 21 Oralie, 21 Randell, 22 Rhonda, 22 26 78 Rosalyn, 548 Sophia, 542 Wallace, 437 Wilhelmina, 543 William, 21
BODDIKER Elizabeth, 243
BODERMAN Hulda Sophia, 335 336 341 349 353 354
BODKIN Sarah, 40
BODZEIN Laurel, 23 492 493 Nadine V, 23 493 Viola, 23 492 493
BOEHERT Rosine, 315
BOEHMKE Ann, 23 Anna, 21 23 Arlene, 23 Bob, 23 Carolyn, 23 Detlef, 23 Dorothy, 23 Lynold, 23 Mary, 191 192 Olive, 9 21 23 Quinnever, 23 Ruby, 23 Sophia, 23 Thelma, 23 Walter, 23 William, 21 23 Wilma, 23
BOETTCHER Clara, 63 Ella, 179 Ella, 429 Emma, 26 178 Emma Henrietta, 165 179 Gertrude, 63 Leo Henry, 63 148 Lora Lena Lea, 429 Lora Lena Lee, 94

Lucille, 38 Mary, 39 63 Phyllis, 38
Rose, 38 39 580 Tina, 39
BROGE Kathleen, 555
BROMAN Carol, 476
BRONIARCZYKT Christine, 593 Jon, 593
BROOKS Barbara Joan, 520 527
BROOKS Helen, 61 Jerry C, 292 John, 61
Judith Kay, 61 174 Julie Ann, 292
BROSS Alma, 28 Alvena, 39 Alvina, 28
Anna, 39 Caroline, 39 Charles, 39
Clara, 28 Elsie, 28 Emma, 28
Fredericka, 39 Hazel Bernice Marie, 28
Henry, 39 Ida, 39 Johann, 27 39
Kathryn, 39 Letta, 39 Lillian, 28
Martha, 28 Mary, 27 28 39 Sophia, 27
28 39 Wilma, 28
BROTT Donna, 539 580
BROUSE Ruth, 391 394
BROWN Anna, 463 Arthur, 191 Beth Ann,
527 Carol, 357 475 Daniel, 49 Deborah
Denise, 520 527 Denise Vania, 103
Dennis Lee, 103 Elaine, 392 Freida,
459 Harold H, 62 James Mirari, 392
Janet Josephine, 49 Jennie, 191 Kathrin
Terra, 392 Kathy, 59 Kay Elaine, 394
Kevin, 392 394 Kevin Neal, 103 Lael
Anne, 392 Marie Ada, 523 Norman,
527 Patricia Mae, 62 Paulette Sue, 103
Roselyn Edith, 29 37 Teresa Ann, 387
593
BRUCE Eric Louise, 144 Erica Louise, 40
Jason Robert, 40 144 Sally Ann, 40 144
394 Sammie, 40 Stacy Ann, 144 Steve
Dale, 40 144 394
BRUCH Marie, 255-258
BRUGER Fred, 28 Martha, 31 Sophia, 28
BRUNCE Bernadine Elsie, 417
BRUND Ruby Ann, 126
BRUNNER Douglas Bryan, 47 Sheri
Lynne, 47
BRUNS David, 226 Donald, 225 Edwin,
225 228 John Edwin, 226 Maria, 228
Marie, 225
BRUNSMANN Betty Ann, 526 Carole S,
526 Clarence Henry, 526 David
George, 526 Hazel A, 526 Jack
Edward, 527

BRUNSSEN Angela Karen, 316 Carol
Ann, 480 481 486 488 Gaylan Roy,
316 Karen Eileen, 316 Kirk Alan, 316
Ryan, 316
BRUNTJEN Carol Rae, 411 415 Ginnis,
415 Scott, 411 415 Stanley, 415
BRUST Aurelia, 314 569 Margaret, 314
William, 314
BRUSTER Tanya, 456 531
BRYANT Fern Katherine, 223
BRYNER Clifford Leroy, 40 David
Leonidas, 40 Ellen Sophie, 40 41 Enid
Muriel, 40 114 271 276 290 291 297
365 Estella Grace, 41 Ferman Gordon,
41 Frank Arthur Jr, 40 Frank Arthur Sr,
40 41 Hope Lovaire, 40 Ida Mae, 41
Inez Vivian, 40 41 James Monroe, 40
Jay Muirhead, 40 Lucy Evers, 41
Margaret Emma, 40 Mary Caroline, 40
41 Mary Helene, 40 Nellie Ethyl, 41
Sarah, 40 Sarah Caroline, 40 Zee, 41
BUCH Daron Neil, 268 Kelly Anne, 268
BUCHANAN Frances Elizabeth, 65
Millard, 65 Teresa Kay, 3 242
BUCHER Gary, 376 Gary Robert, 376 Jane
Ellen, 376
BUCHHOLTZ Ella, 179
BUCHMANN Albert Frederick, 560 Brian
Will, 41 Carol, 41 560 Cary Lynn, 41
Elfrieda, 41 42 560 565 Elisabeth, 560
Esther Martha, 41 560 Fred, 560
Harold Robert, 41 42 560 Lydia Mary,
3 42 560 Melisse Lee, 41 Ruben, 42
560 565 Rueben, 41 Ruth Matilda, 42
BUCHOLZ Ella, 429
BUCK Barbara, 9 21 Holst, 9 21 Marcia, 9
21 Marlus, 9 21 Robert, 9 21 Ronald, 9
21
BUCKER Carol Melissa, 376 Robert M,
376
BUCKLER Alan Dean, 185 Dale Warren,
185 Dale Webster, 42 John, 42 John Jr,
185 562 John Sr, 185 Jonathan Carl, 42
Lora Marie, 185 Margaret, 42 185 562
Mary Margaret, 42 185 Nellie, 185
Sue, 42
BUDA Charlotte, 569

542 Donald Albert, 22 44 Donald D, 22 44 46 Donald Lynn, 44 Donna Marie, 22 44 Erick George, 46 Eydie Faye, 178 Florence, 444 Gary, 378 Gregory, 46 Jan, 22 46 Janet Lynne, 44 441 John Albert Jr, 45 John Albert Sr, 45 441 Joseph Augustine, 44 Jude Patrick, 45 Julie, 45 Katrina Lynne, 44 Keith Allen, 45 Kevin Paul, 45 442 Kyle Curtis, 45 Lawrence Charles, 45 441 Leroy, 43-45 185 562 Linda, 22 44 Lisa, 44 Lisa Ann, 46 442 Lori Jo, 45 442 M Christine, 45 441 Marie, 22 44 46 315 542 Marjorie, 45 186 536 Mark Patrick, 45 441 Marrisa Ann, 45 Mary Ann, 44 441 Mary Margaret, 46 441 Mathilda, 43-45 185 562 Megan Elizabeth, 45 Michael David, 441 Monica Jean, 45 Morna Ed, 45 Nathaniel Patrick, 45 Pat, 22 44 Patricia Lois, 45 441 Richard Dean, 46 442 Rita Ann, 46 441 506 Robert Lee, 22 46 Rufus, 185 Ruth Marie, 45-47 410 441 Ryan Michael, 45 Sally Classen, 34 300 Sara Jane, 45 442 Sean Stephen, 46 Sharon Kay, 22 46 Shelly, 44 Sierra Kristina, 46 Stephanie Marie, 46 Stephen Francis, 46 442 Therese Marie, 47 441 Tina, 46 Todd, 44 Todd William, 44 Victoria Cecile, 46 William Mckinley, 22 315

CAMPELL Christopher James, 44 Ruth Marie, 44

CANNEY Anita Kay, 466 Michael Lee, 466 Norine Elizabeth, 466 Robert Lee, 466

CARLETON Curtis Hins, 122 Curtis Hins II, 1 2 Curtis Hins III, 1 Florence Katherine, 2 Gregory Scott, 2 Marchelle Lynn, 122 Marchelle Lynne, 1

CARLOCK Marcia Diane, 136 William J, 136

CARLSON Bertha, 563 Cheryl, 546 Gladys, 544 Harold, 544 546 Kay, 324 Marjorie, 546

CARMAN Kathryn Diane, 583

CARMODY Allison Elizabeth, 396 Erin, 396 Joseph, 396 Joseph M, 392 Tammy Jo, 392 396 Thomas Joseph, 396

CARNER Linda M, 527

CARNEY Lonnie, 214 Lonnie, 215 Teresa, 214 215 Terry, 215 Tracey, 215

CARPENTER Carol A, 465

CARROL Andy Michael, 21 Brenda Jean, 21 151 Laura Elizabeth, 21 Michael, 21 151

CARROLL Andy, 47 Brenda Jean, 47 Laura Elizabeth, 47 Michael, 47

CARSTEN Christena, 203

CARSTENS Christena, 203 Heinrich, 71 Sophia, 72 Sophia Marie, 71 72 73

CARSTENSON Ernestine Mary, 230 Tina, 230

CARTE Adrianna Katherine, 134 Clifford Eugene, 133 David James, 127 133 Douglas Donald, 134 Kristina Lynn, 127 133 Lela Jean, 133 Marcial James, 133 Sara Lynn, 133 Tara Jean, 134

CARTER Kathryn, 2 Lillian, 402 561 Lillian C, 402 Martin, 402 Myrtle, 402 Penny, 217

CASEY Mary, 133

CASLAVKA Charlotte, 111 112 Craig, 112 Curtis, 112 Graydon, 112 Sharon, 112

CASPERS Brenda Joy, 473 Connie, 473 Connie Kay, 473 Debra Sue, 473 Erma Jean, 473 474 George, 473 474 Jean Marie, 473 Jessica Ann, 473 Julie Ann, 473 Kimberly Rose, 473 Michael Jon, 473 Nicholas Rick, 473 Patrick, 473 Peter Russell, 473 Randy Ray, 473 Ricky George, 473 Riva Jane, 473 Rose Ann, 473 Rusty Alan, 473 Tracy Ann, 473 Virginia, 473

CASSIDY Mathilda, 230 Tillie, 230

CAVANAUGH Doris, 129 Gloria Susan, 129 137 Lori Jeanne, 129 Richard Jule, 129 137

CAVINESS Brent James, 357 Connie Lou, 273 357 John Ray, 273 357 Jordan Neal, 357

CERVENY Ann, 268 Libbie, 378 Libbie
Ann, 268 269 277 284 289 293 295
Wesley, 268
CESARE Cynthia Marie, 245 Marna
Marie, 245
CETIN Papatya, 76 78 Pat, 76 78
CHALOUPEK Brandon Aaron, 520
Douglas, 520 Kathleen Kay, 520
Marcus Robert, 520 NN, 60 Owen
Douglas, 520
CHAMBERLAIN Margaret Emma, 40
CHAMBERS Anna Mae, 516 Ashlie Reed,
403 Carla Sue, 225 403 Carolyn Jean,
403 Gary Lee, 403 Linda Marie, 516
Lonnie, 516 Todd Michael, 225 403
CHAMPION Nancy Sue, 41 William Dean,
41
CHANCE Douglas, 351 Lorri Sue, 351
CHAPIN Penney, 418 419
CHAUSSE Janet Lucille, 324
CHEESEMAN Stephanie Lynn, 519
CHENEY Eva Myrtle, 520 522 525 527
Eve Myrtle, 521
CHENOWETH Earl E, 476 Edna Lenora,
476 Ida Mae, 41
CHERRINGTON Alene, 519 521 526 527
CHILDS Diane, 120 Michael, 120 Michelle
Rne, 120
CHIMARUSTI John Andrew, 524 Karen
Elizabeth, 524 Marie Elizabeth, 524
Rebecca Ann, 524
CHIZUM Clarinda Isabelle, 288 E Clifford,
288 Marjorie Ann, 288
CHORGHADE Sushila, 133
CHOU Joan, 504
CHRASTIL Margaret, 103
CHRIST Augusta Katharina, 160 Auguste
Katharina, 157 Auguste Katharina, 164
CHRISTENSEN Carl, 72 Charles, 73 Fred,
399 401 Gwen, 304 Kelly Lee, 401
Kristie Kay, 399 401 Leone Marie, 72
Marguerite Ann, 141 Marquerite Ann,
127 138 Phyllis Margaret, 417
CHRISTIANSON Gertrude, 558 Harry,
558 Lela W, 329 Sallie Jane, 507
CHRISTOFFER Joyce, 256
CHRISTOPHER Cheryl, 101 149 Joyce,
259

CHRISTY Diane Kay, 408 Leta Mae, 47
406 408 Patricia Lee, 47 408 Richard
Raymond, 47 406 408 Susan Lynette,
47 408
CHURCH Paula, 154 202
CLABBY Marie Cecelia, 334 351
CLAIR Daniel, 526 David, 526 Horace,
522 526 528 Kim, 526 Linda Marlys,
526 Marlys, 522 526 528
CLANG Patricia Lee, 370 Stan, 370
CLARAHAN Grant Dean, 339 Jim, 339
Sharon Kay, 338
CLARK Becky, 508 Beulah Marie, 382
383 Brian, 508 Bryon, 382 Cathy Rae,
386 397 George, 382 383 Gina, 567
Hobart, 395 Jane, 595 Jeff, 567 Joshua,
508 Julanne, 567 568 Kenneth, 76 77
78 Lisa, 567 Louise May, 395 Norma,
382 Patricia, 382 Peggy Mae, 76 78
Randy Wayne, 78 Shirley, 382 Susan,
558 568 Warren, 567 568 Wendy Jo,
78
CLASSEN Erna Martha Matilda, 233 Hans
John, 233
CLAUSEN Clara, 165 Donna, 232 Erna
Martha Matilda, 232 George L, 232
Hans John, 232 Jeannette, 232 Larry,
232
CLAUSSEN Hilda Christina, 109 330
CLAYTON George, 351 Laurice Diane,
351 Nancy, 512 513
CLEMENS Kathy Lee, 370 Robert Jr, 370
CLINE Elsie Sarah Hannah, 378 379
COAN Mary, 82 367
COBERLY Janet, 369
COBLE Geraldine Ann, 519 524 Lorraine,
234
COBURN Kathleen, 155 160
COGHLIN Beverly, 330 David, 330 Jill, 26
158 John, 330 Kim, 330 Larry, 330
COLE Geneva Valarie, 510 Henry
Standridge, 510 Karla, 478 510
Matthew, 478 510
COLEMAN Chris Alan, 526 Maria G, 416
Virginia Kay, 526
COLLIGNON Annette, 506 George, 506
COLLINS Deborah, 499 Grace Danielle
Kripa, 171 Julie Ann, 162 171 Lauren

617

Elizabeth, 171 Mildred, 174 182 Mrs,
171 Nicole Dawn, 36 37 Theodore
Joseph, 162 171 Thomas Sr, 171
COLLMAN Sophia, 530
COLOSIMO Carolynne, 134
CONDON Mary, 149 155
CONKLN Sharon, 594
CONLEY Pauline Wilhelmina, 523
Thomas, 523
CONNOR Donn Mae, 484 Donna Mae,
480 484 486 488 Harry, 486 Julia
Hannah, 486
CONRAD Charity Eve, 49 Dorothy, 49 50
Earl, 49 Irene, 49 Martha Berth Marie,
413 Martha Bertha Marie, 230 232-237
252 Tamara Kay, 49 Wayne, 49 50
CONRIED Judy Joyce, 43 148 Ronald, 43
148 Whitney Lynn, 43
CONVERSE Henry, 300 Lulu, 300
COOK Irene, 408 Richard, 408
COOMBS Meta, 190
COOP Debra Ann, 235 Dennis Oris, 235
COPE Judith Ann, 244 Stephen, 246
Stephen Paul, 244
COPLEY Ann Grace, 159 Beth Marie, 159
Grace Gertrude, 159 177 Thomas
David, 159 Thomas William, 159 177
CORBIN Loretta, 378
CORNUTT Linda, 507
CORPORON Amanda Ann, 48 Corrine
Dorothy, 47 233 Edith Frieda, 47 233
375 Frank Theodore, 47 48 233 Frieda
Emma Barbara, 47 48 233 Jerome
Noel, 48 Joan, 48 Jon Michael, 47 Kim,
48 Laura Lynn, 48 Leo Frank, 47 233
Lori, 48 Magdelene, 48 233 Max Allen,
48 Max Arvin, 48 233 Meredith Ann,
47 233 Nancy Irene, 48 233 Richard
Allen, 48 Rick, 48 Ruth Ann, 48 233
Sarah Towle, 47 Scott James, 48 Sheri
Lynne, 47 Steven Russell, 47 Thomas
John, 48 Timothy Thomas, 48 233
CORRIGAN Angela Kay, 303 Benjamin
Joseph, 303 Suzanne Marie, 303
COTTON Caroline Ruth, 188 Mary, 188
Marye, 479 William R, 188 Wm R, 479
COTTRELL Bernice, 252 Charles L, 252
COVINGTON June, 512

COWAN Beverly, 320
COWHERD George Coakley, 551
Katherine Pauline, 551
COWLISHAW Ardis Kay, 405 406 407
408
COX Beka, 77 598 Jean Louise, 484 Lloyd
Montell, 484
COX HINES Sarah Louise, 484
CRABTREE Connie, 237
CRAFT Vickie Lee, 123
CRAIG Barbara Ann, 491 Berdette Elaine,
491 Carol Lee, 491 Donald, 491 504
Doris, 491 504
CRANE Darlene C, 55
CRANEY Cecil, 260 Marie Ann, 260 262
Rita, 260
CRANSTON Irene, 87 Robert, 87
CRAVENS Susan Rae, 243 247
CRAWFORD Charles I, 598 Diane, 234
Hazel Laverne, 598
CREECH Michael, 116 Patricia, 116
CRISWELL Thelma, 23
CROGHAM Court Christopher, 138 Mark
Allen, 127 138 Patricia Jane, 127 138
CROLL Anna Martha, 312 Joh, 312
CROMBAUGH Lois, 7 142 143
CROSS Allison Frances, 48 Bruce, 243
247 Daniel, 247 Jessi, 247 Luke, 247
Marie Ann, 15 Norman, 48 Norman
Eugene, 15 207 Raymond Eugene, 15
48 Ruth Ann, 243 247 Susan Jean, 15
48 207 Tonya Kay, 15 48
CROUSE Austin Russell, 597 Deeann Kay,
77 597 Jeffery, 77 597
CROWE David, 219 Gregory, 219 Janine
Cora, 219 Joshua, 219 Luke, 219
CROY Barbara Jane, 227 Barbra Jane, 220
Betty, 220 Wayne, 220
CRULL Lisa Charlene, 410
CRUZ Alberto, 137 205 Ariana Lea, 205
Gabriel Dylan, 205 Martin Richardo,
205 Susan Elisabeth, 137 205
CULPEPPER Kay Elaine, 48 392 394 Lisa
Kay, 48 392 Terry, 48 392 394
CULVER Catherine, 180 184 William
Clarke, 184
CUMBERLIN Penney M, 360 Penny M,
360

618

CUMMING Brandon, 73 Lynne, 73 Shaina, 73
CUMMINS Ardis, 468 471
CURTIS Sally, 188 479
CUSTER Janelle, 498 Norman, 498 Seaman, 498
CUTTRIGHT Frances D, 266
DAAKE Betty Sue, 592 Fred, 592
DAGES Julia Lynn, 521 Thomas A, 521
DAHLHAUSER Bernard John, 48 421 Bernard John Jr, 11 Bernard John Sr, 11 Carrie, 11 48 Joelle Ruth, 11 Kelli Jo, 48 Phyllis Lucille, 11 48 421 Ruthy, 11 Sean David, 11 48
DAHLKE Helen, 120
DAHNKE Henry, 381 John, 381 Minnie, 381 Sophia, 381
DAILY Joan, 292 390 391
DAKER Daryl, 74 Francine, 74
DAKOTA Clara, 319
DALESKE Emma Bertha, 269 283 284 287 Herman F, 284 Johanna, 284
DALLAGE Craig, 480 Carla Rae, 480 Harley Lavern, 480 Rosemary Louise, 480
DALY Catharine, 151 Marcia, 82 409 Michael, 82 409 Noelle, 409
DAMM Elisabeth, 48 George, 48 Johannes, 48 Karoline, 48 364 Karoline Gertrud, 361 362 Katharina, 48
DAMMON Margaretha, 200
DANKLE Lea Carol, 599 600
DANNEN Margaret, 72 Margaret Muller, 72
DANNENBRING Alice, 42 43 48 570 Arthur, 49 50 570 Claudia, 50 Daniel Otto, 50 Debra Ann, 49 50 Diana, 49 50 Dorothy, 49 50 Edmund E, 570 Edward William, 570 Elisabeth, 570 Emma, 562 Harvey, 49 50 Henry, 570 James, 49 Janet Josephine, 49 Jason James, 49 Joanna, 49 50 Joyce, 49 June Leona, 50 Kathy, 49 Leola, 49 50 570 Leona, 49 50 570 Leonhard, 49 50 570 Lucas Len, 50 Martha, 48-50 564 570 Marvin, 50 Matthew Marvin, 50 Olga, 50 208 570 Otto, 48-50 564 570 Patricia Ann, 50 Twyla Lee, 50

DAPPERT Mabel, 550 Otis, 550
DARBY Doris M, 366
DARIN Gregory, 507
DARINGER Alison, 451 Neal, 451 Renea, 395 451 William, 395 451
DARROW Erin, 540 John, 540 Lynette, 540 Michael, 540
DART Jason, 202 Jeff, 202 Linda, 154 202 Robert, 154 202
DATNAUSKUS Marcia Diane, 136 Ronald Allen, 136
DAUENBAUGH Sheryll, 258 591
DAUGHHETEE Ada, 76 Guy, 76 Mildred, 77 Mildred Donley, 76 339
DAUME Anna Katharina, 51 Anna Katharina Elisabeth, 51 532 533 534 Anna Katharine, 51 Anna Martha, 15 51 Johann Adam, 51 Konrad, 15 51
DAVIS Amanda, 518 Andrea Jean, 518 Anna, 518 Bertha, 51 Bethany Ann, 87 Catherine, 333 Clark Trent, 11 518 Cristy Lynn, 87 Donna Rae, 11 518 Elizabeth, 52 Frances N, 539 Henry, 54 545 Henry J Jr, 51 Henry J Sr, 51 Jeremy Michael, 87 Julia Hannah, 486 Lena, 51 54 Lena L, 51 53 55 Louisa, 51 52 54 545 Lucy Evers, 41 Mary, 51 542-546 Michael Edward, 87 457 Shirley, 518 Sue Ellen, 87 457 Ted, 333 Thomas M, 539 Turner, 518
DAVISON Bobby, 369 Donald, 369 James, 369 Jean, 369 Melba, 369
DAWES Ricky Eugene, 17 Shirley Ann, 17
DAY Anita, 52 438 Bernadette, 438 Bertha, 185 Ellen Marie, 293 538 James Edward, 52 438 James Edward II, 52 Janet Ellen, 52 438 Joan, 151 Joan Patricia, 173 174 177 Lisa Lynette, 52 Lloyd Wilmer, 52 412 438 Nina, 438 Nina Mae, 52 412 437 Patty, 52 438 Robert Bruce, 438 Sandra, 52 438 Sarah Autumn, 52 Spencer Thomas, 438 Thomas Allen, 52 438 Tina Marie, 52
DEAL Ann, 36 Ann Marie, 29 37 Anna Marie, 36 Craig Kenneth, 200 Crystal Kay, 200 Debra, 200 Marlene, 200 Robert, 200 Steven Robert, 200

DIELSCHNEIDER Gloria Jean, 341 Nile, 341

DIERCKS Luann R, 183 Luann Ruth, 159 173 174

DIERKS Anna, 189 N N, 416 Roberta Frances, 416

DIERS Christine, 34 Herman, 34

DIESEL Johana, 69

DIETRICH Amy Jo, 59 Andrew, 147 Anna Christina, 58 59 147 Anna Christina Elizabeth, 171 Cole Christopher, 59 Craig Alex, 59 Dake Matthew, 59 Donovan Martin, 58 59 147 Emma, 373 Glenn Howard, 58 59 147 208 Jacqueline, 58 59 Judith, 58 59 Kathy, 59 Kaye, 58 59 Larry Robert, 58 59 Lenora Mae, 58 59 147 Leona Mae, 147 Lois Catharine, 147 Lois Catherine, 58 59 208 Lucille, 65 Marilyn Ruth, 59 147 598 Max Allen, 58 59 Minnie, 147 Pamela Jean, 58 59 205 Randy Lee, 58 Shirlee, 58 59 Timothy Allen, 59 Verlee Ann, 58 59 Walter William, 58 59 147 171

DIETZ Darlene May, 318 531

DILL Arthur, 29 Bertha, 29 Marian, 29 542

DILLING Elizabeth, 112 113 Emma, 113 John, 113

DILLON Alice Ann, 411 418 Hannah Marie, 411 Jeffrey Albert, 411 418 Katherine Lois, 411

DINGEL Catharina Marie, 201 Conrad, 201

DIPPEL Karolina, 201 202 348 Marie, 578 N N, 348 Wilma Karoline, 497

DITTLEMUTH Mary, 204

DIXON Alice, 563

DJERF Katie Marie, 528 Kelly Rae, 529 Randy Scott, 528 Tamra Rea, 528 Travis Scott, 528

DOBOS Deanna, 209

DOCHSCHERR Colleen Mauree, 317 Michael, 317

DOCHTERMAN David, 402 Mark, 402

DOCKEN Lillian, 28 William, 28

DOEBEL Annie, 60 Bertha, 60 Charles, 60 Christian, 60 89 Frank, 60 Fred, 60

George, 60 Lizzie, 60 Maria, 60 89 Mary, 60 88 89 Minnie, 60 Sadie, 60

DOEDER Pauline, 111

DOLAN Andrew James, 99 Christopher Gerald, 95 99 Susan Kay, 95 99

DOLGE Donna Mae, 235 Hilda Marie Emma, 233 235 Lester Henry, 233 235

DOLL Augusta Wilhelmina, 538

DOLLING Gesche, 213

DONLEY Ada, 76 Mildred, 77

DOOSE Amelia, 60 August, 60 Augusta, 60 Dora, 60 Dora Amelia, 60 Emma, 60 Gustave, 60 Ida Dorthea, 60 Johann Jochim Christian, 60

DOOSE John, 60 Marie, 60 See Dohse, 60

DORAN Eugene Felix, 13 135 Gary Eugene, 13 Gina Marie, 13 Kristin Michelle, 317 Lori Lou, 13 Mary Lou, 13 135 Sean Patrick, 317

DORMER Amy, 12 270

DORNSEIF Marie, 154 170 174 184 563 Paula, 563 571 Philip, 184 Philip H, 563

DORTT Beverly, 43 61 186 Burle, 43 Daniel, 43 61 186 Darly Allan, 61 Daryl Allan, 43 Denise Renae, 43 Rawley John, 61 Susan, 43 61 Velma, 43

DOWLER Betty June, 541

DOWNES Joseph, 477 Pearl, 477

DOWNS Gena, 508 Jeff, 508

DOYEL Adah Lois, 487

DOYLE Lynn, 547 Mary, 547

DRAHN Chad Harris, 186 Denis Michele, 61 Denise Michele, 186 Don Lloyd, 61 186 442 Glender Arthur, 186 Irene Ann, 186 Jeffery David, 186 Sharon Louise, 61 186 442

DRAHOS Amy Marie, 305 Brian Michael, 305 Debra Ann, 305 Dorothy, 368 Heather Lynne, 305 Lisa NN, 305 Wilfred, 368 William Michael, 305

DREWITZ Bertha, 119

DRIPPS Mildred M, 243 244 247

DRISCOLL Carrie Loreen, 61 John, 174 John Allen, 61 174 Judith Kay, 61 Julia, 174 Krista Marie, 61 Loreen

Marie, 61 144 174 Norma Jane, 174
Oakley H, 61 144 174
DRONEBARGER Kathy Jo, 583 Samuel, 583
DROSTER Dianne Marie, 350 Forest
William, 354 350 Jill, 350 Marilyn
Jean, 350 354 Mark Allen, 350 Sandy, 350
DRUGG David, 305 Jeffrey David, 305
Matthew Scott, 305 Susan Kay, 305
DUBES Susan Jane, 25 27
DUBS Anna, 555
DUBY Tonya Kay, 15 48
DUCKER Craig Alan, 478 Julie Kay, 478
Ryan Paul, 478
DUEKER Craig Alan, 136 Julie Kay, 136
DUERMYER Kathy Joan, 160 William H, 160
DUEVER Maria Sophia, 330 Sophia, 325
DUFF Allen Walker, 503 Beth Carla, 503
Mark Lindsay, 503
DUFRESNE Chester, 444 Mae F, 233
Pearl, 444
DUGDALE Donna Deetta, 528
DUGENSKE Amanda, 513 Cindy, 513
Dale, 513
DUMBLAUKAS Kari Ann, 266
DUMBLAUSKAS Gail, 101 Kari Ann, 101
Paul, 101
DUMOND Barbara June, 122 127 Charled
Edward, 122 Charles Edward, 127
Edward Leighton, 122 Emily Gabriel,
122 Genelle Mae, 122 Jennifer
Johanna, 122
DUNCALF Agnes Marie, 86 Delbert
George, 86 Illa, 505 N N, 505 Ruth
Ann, 86 423
DUNEK Roberta Clark, 33
DUNKER Shirley, 72 73
DUNSTON Dennis Lynn, 275 Sheryl Kay, 275
DURANT Blanche, 234 W D Ted, 234
DURHAM Catherine Lea, 61 62 David
Leon, 61 Deanna, 267 Debbie, 61
Douglas Leslie, 61 Leon Leslie, 61 62
DURLAM Adam Clark, 347 David O, 347
Jonathan David, 347 Joyce Jean, 347
DURR Dawn, 153 172

DUVALL Corrine, 595 John, 595 Nancy
Ann, 291 595
DVORAK Frank, 516 James, 382 Mary,
415 513 515 516 Mary Frances, 516
Sheila Kay, 382
DYE Hattie A, 222 469 Henry, 469 James
Henry, 222 469
DYRLAND Ada Pauline, 520 Dorothy
Lou, 520 G Melvin, 520 Lena, 515
Olisa, 485
EARLE Emma, 378 Harry, 378
EASON Jennifer Lee, 55 Joseph Michael, 55
EASTMAN Dona, 78
EBERSPECHER Anna M, 313 569 Christ,
313 Elmer Edwin, 313 Florence May,
313 Floyd R, 313 Gottleib, 313 569
Harold G, 313 Homer Hy, 313 John G
K, 313 Kath, 313 Luella A, 313 Myrtle
S, 313 Phoebe K, 313 Verna L, 313
EBERT Don, 38 Ella, 479 Phyllis, 38
ECHOLS Alicia Jane, 473 Amy Lynn, 473
Angela Erma, 473 Brandon Gene, 473
Brenda Joy, 473 Connie Kay, 473
Doris Ray, 473 Leslie Greg, 473 Leslie
Hubert, 473 Michael Joseph, 473 Riva
Jane, 473 Ryan Joseph, 473
ECKARD Johann Jost, 168 Magdalena, 168
ECKHARD Anna Catharina, 175 Johann
Jost, 175 Johann Peter, 167 175
Magdalena, 167 175
ECKMULLER Franziska, 114 447
EDABURN Geraldine, 162
EDGETON Beverly, 555
EDLUND Lillian, 501 502
EDMONDS Brian, 62 Catherine Lea, 61 62
Cheryl Lynn, 63 Corky, 62 Craig, 62
Daniel, 62 Darrell Dean, 62 Darrell
James, 63 Frances Norma, 62 Franes
Norma, 63 Helen Margaret, 62 63 172
Jacqueline Marie, 61 62 371 372 John,
172 Katharina Wilhelmina, 172
Katharina Wilhemina, 62 Leslie, 271
Leslie Alan, 62 Leslie August, 61 62
172 Leslie Everett, 62 Patricia Mae, 62
Prescott Samuel, 62 172 Prescott
Williard, 62 63 172 Roger Wayne, 62

63 Wilma, 271 Wilma Henrietta, 61 62 172

EDSBURN Geraldine, 96

EDWARDS Bryan, 240 Carol, 395 Carol Rose, 582 Carrie Mae, 145 David Alvert, 145 Heather Jean, 240 Jacob Murray, 240 John Leonard, 395 582 Kyle B W, 240 Leonard, 582 Margaret Louise, 145 Margaret Louise Edwards, 144 Martha E, 286 Michael John, 582 Michelle, 582 Raymond L, 286 Susan, 463

EGGERS Anna, 39 Anna M, 63 Clara, 63 Dora, 63 Dorothea, 63 Emma, 63 Henry, 63 John, 63 Mary, 39 63 Rolf, 39 63 William, 63

EGLI Megan, 542 Pamela, 185 542 Steve, 185 542

EHLERS Anna, 222 Anna Elisabeth, 63 146 147 Bertha, 148 Bertha Anna Margaret, 63 147 Bertha Augusta, 275 289 424 Brenda, 388 Esther Wilma Henrietta, 148 Fred, 63 146 147 Frederick Julius, 63 148 George Christian, 148 Henry, 63 147 Herbert, 99 Johannes Heinrich Andreas Nicholas, 63 147 John Peter Hartman, 148 Karl George William, 148 Katie, 388 Laura, 388 Loretta, 99 Marie Gertrude, 63 148 Mary, 98 99 147 Mary Matilda, 63 148 Nell Augusta, 148 Russell, 388 William, 98 William John August, 99 147 Wilma, 99

EHLING Carole, 350 356 Erlisrv, 350 356 Judy, 356 Stephanie, 356

EHMAN Curtis, 351 Julius, 351 Mathilda, 351 Richard, 351

EHMANN Curtis, 345 Julius C, 345 Mathilda, 345 Richard, 345

EHRMAN Marie, 523

EICHENSEER Nancy, 582 583

EICHMEYER Anna, 499

EIDE Jesse, 260 Joshua, 259 Rena, 259 Robert, 259

EIGENBROD Andreas, 586 Anna Gertrude, 586

EILERS Betty, 182 183

EISENBEISZ Carol Lee, 491 Kenton, 491

EISENBRAUN Susan, 43 61

EISENTRAGER Cath Elisabeth, 585

EITENMILLER Debra Ann, 49 50

ELDER Cecelia Jane, 488

ELDRED Carolyn Sue, 269 272

ELIAS Rhonda, 594 Tom, 594

ELLERS Pastor, 342

ELLIOT Sheryl Dianne, 273 357

ELLIOTT Alyssa, 597 Amy Michelle, 356 Andrea, 597 Brendon, 597 Joe, 77 Kent Anthony, 355 Kristine Elizabeth, 77 Lori Lynn, 77 597 Paul Michael, 355 356 Sherry Lyn, 355 356 Steven Blair, 77 597 Timothy Mark, 356

ELLSWORTH Daniel, 402 403 Renee Jo, 402 403 Ross James, 403

ELSNER Patricia Jean, 417 440

ELSON Etta, 263 387

EMANUEL Bonnie, 142 Eric Lee, 142 Kelly Jo, 12 142 Larry, 142 Russell Lee, 12 142

EMCKE Dora, 300 301

EMERSON Ellea Mae, 17 Isabel Irene, 17 Jerry, 377 536 Marcella, 377 536 William James, 17

EMMEL Edward, 531 Hannah, 531

EMMICK Elisabeth, 250 Emma, 230 250-252 502 554 Justus, 250

ENGEL Anna M, 248 Anna Marie, 64 Charles, 64 Christina, 248 249 Eva Rosina, 63 64 George, 64 248 George John, 63 64 Ida, 64 Joe, 64 Johanna, 63 64 John George, 63 64 Mary, 63 64 453 Rosa Marie Elizabeth, 64

ENGELKING Darrell Dean, 234 236 Kyle Dean, 236 Patricia Martha, 234 236 Scott Evean, 236 Vincent Everly, 236

ENGELMANN Louise, 567 568 William, 567 568

ENGLAND Beatrice Ella, 416 Christine Katherina Barbara, 416 425 Dallis, 573 Duane, 190 255 Frederick Louis, 416 Jacqueline, 190 John, 416 425 John Franklyn, 416 Kathleen Marie, 323 Michael, 190 Pamela Ann, 255 Phyllis, 189 190 Roberta Frances, 416 Robin, 190 Rodney, 190 Ronald, 189 190 William Thomas, 416

Robert, 73 Roger, 74 Shirley, 74
Stanley, 74 Stephanie, 74 Steven, 74
Waldemar Conrad, 74 251 Waldmar
Conrad, 73 Walter, 556 William, 73
556 571 Wilma, 75 207 556
FIELDS Brian Scott, 368 Dorothy May,
368 John, 368 Timothy Estill, 368
FILES Hazel, 12
FILLENWORTH Lucille, 440 Ralph Earl,
440 Sandra Gay, 411 440
FINCH Clydene, 385
FINCHEN Joanne, 372
FINK Barbara, 436
FINLEY Martha, 568 Robert, 568
FINTELL Kim, 216
FISCHER Anna Elisabeth, 450 Eleanor
Elizabeth, 410 Johannes, 450 Lillian,
49 119
FISH Linda Luanne, 92 Michael David, 92
Patricia Lou, 75 268 293 Rad, 75 268
293 Sharon Arlene, 75 293 Theresa,
293
FISHER Aloisia, 533 Mildred F, 234
FISTER Ida Dorothea, 230 Jack, 230
FITZGERALD Dan, 24 432 Florence, 452
453 Jacqueline Marie, 24 Jacquline
Marie, 432 Madeline, 24
FIX Amelia, 443 Amelia Louis, 56 Amelia
Louise, 53-55 77 Andrew William, 75
Berhta, 117 Bertha, 75 299 Bertha
Katherine, 75 298 299 Catharina, 76
Christina, 76 Christina Magdelene, 75
76 298 Connor Philip, 78 Daniel
Wayne, 76 David Eugene, 76 Edward
Lee, 75 77 Elizabeth Veronica, 75 298
299 Ella Mae, 77 427 Ella Mae Anna,
434 Ella May, 444 Emily Ruth, 75
Emma, 75 Emma Anna Maria, 77
Emma Anna Marie, 76 352 Emma
Marie, 339 Etta, 75 Flo, 75 Forrest
Edward, 76 78 Fredrick Louis, 76
Georg Jacob, 298 Georg Jakob, 75 76
298 George Jakob, 76 Henry Joseph, 75
Jacob, 75 James Dean, 76 77 Janice, 77
Janice Marie, 75 Joann, 76 Joann
Lorraine, 78 Johann, 75 76 John
Edward, 76 77 339 John Neil, 76 John
P, 75 John Philip, 427 John Phillip, 55

75 76 339 Joseph, 514 Linda, 76 Linda
Kay, 76 Lois Ann, 77 339 597 598
Lorraine, 77 339 Louis Frederich, 77
Louis Frederick, 76 339 352 Louise
Margaretha, 75 Margaretha, 75 76
Maria Christina, 75 Mark Allen, 76
Mary M, 77 Meta, 55 75 77 339 427
Mildred, 77 Mildred Donley, 76 339
Mrs John, 53 Oliver Bruno, 75 Papatya,
76 78 Pat, 76 78 Paul James, 76 Paul
William, 75-78 339 Peggy Mae, 76 77
Philip Guy, 76 78 Philip Karl, 75 Rita
Carol, 76 77 Ruth Ann, 75-78 339
Sarah Anne, 76 Sierra Rhiannon, 78
Susan Marie, 77 78
FLAMMANG Gertrude, 504-506
FLAMMAUG Gertrude, 65
FLANDREAU Kevin, 194 Kristin Leanne,
194
FLECK Dianne Caye, 78 355 356 Paula
Rae, 78 355 Trent Jon, 355 William
Jon, 78 355 356
FLEISHER Alice K, 210 Henry, 210
FLEMMING Hazel Marie, 238 Ralph W,
238
FLETCHER Yvonne, 242 243
FLICKENGER Bruce, 591 Cecil, 591
Joann, 591 Karen Kay, 591 Kristie
Lynnette, 591 Larry, 591 Larry Robert,
591 Leigh Ann, 591 Lonny, 591
Norma, 591 Patricia Ann, 591 Rhonda
Kae, 591 Ricky Francis, 591 Rochelle
Marie, 591 Ronald Keith, 591
Rosemary Jean, 591 Rusty Kevin, 591
Ruth Aann, 591 Sandra Kay, 591
Shannon, 591 Wanda Kay, 591 Wayne
Francis, 591
FLICKINGER Cecil, 592 Kristie, 537
Norma, 592 Rhonda, 160 176
FLITSCH Leah Irene, 482
FLOERCHINGER Viola Minnie, 417
FLOYD Leanna Rose, 396 Leland, 396
Ruth, 555 558 559
FLUKINGER Rosalie, 489
FLYNN Heather Renee, 401 Jonie Lee,
400 401 Matthew, 400 401
FODOR Larry, 121 Nancy Ann, 121

FOLEY Clarence, 77 Eunice, 77 Jane, 454 456 Ruth Ann, 75-78 339
FOLKMANN Christian H, 389 Dean A, 78 389 Diana Kay, 389 Gladys Marie, 78 273 389 Julian Lynn, 78 Julie Lynn, 389 Katelyn Elizabeth, 78 Richard, 78 273 389 Sophia, 389
FOOTE Anna, 315 Anna, 316
FORD Alma, 252 Arthur, 399 401 Charles, 252 Craig, 26 27 Joyce, 251 252 Katharine, 399 401 Lurline Ann, 26 27 Michael Dean, 26
FORRISTALL Colleen Elaine, 78 David Wayne, 78 Dona, 78 George Harlan, 78 Marian Frances, 78 Steven Warren, 78 Tina Marie, 78 Tonaleen Joy, 78 Wayne David, 78
FORTUNE Barbara, 369 Michael, 369
FOSTER Sandra, 337
FOX Anna, 85 Anna, 86 Barbara, 140 Hilda, 482 Hilda M, 489 John, 85 140 Marie Matilda Barbara, 124 127 134 140 Rose, 315 316
FRAEDRICH Rochelle Marie, 520 527
FRAHM Velma, 2
FRANCK Anne-Marie, 79 Barbara, 79 Barry, 22 Barry Kim, 26 78 Becky, 26 79 Charla Francine, 79 Clayton, 79 Darci Sue, 80 Dorthy, 79 Douglas Kenn, 26 79 Elaine Barbera, 79 George, 26 549 George Harlan, 23 26 79 80 176 George W, 79 Gilbert, 79 Gordon, 79 James, 80 Joan, 79 Jodi Jean, 78 Jodie, 23 Jodie Jeanne, 358 Julia, 26 Julia Maie, 79 Julia Marie, 26 Kari Kim, 79 Karrie, 23 Kathleen, 79 Larry John, 80 Marian, 23 Marian Frances, 79 80 176 Marian Francis, 26 Marion, 549 Nancy, 26 80 Rachel Marie, 79 Randall Gilbert, 79 Rhonda, 22 26 78 Rhonda Kay, 79 Richard Arthur, 79 Robbie, 23 Robbie Jan, 78 Ronald Edward, 79 Rosina, 195 Roxanne, 26 79 Ryan Randall, 79 Salley Rae, 549 Sally Rae, 26 79 548 550 Scott Dean, 26 80 Seth Adam, 79 Shane Aaron, 79 Shonda, 79

FRANK Carolyn Sue, 80 385 397 Cecil, 80 Clarence, 80 Clarine, 80 Debra, 80 Diane, 80 Ella, 80 Florence Agusta, 453 Henreitta, 80 Henrietta, 453 Jessika, 385 Judith, 80 Kimberly, 112 Kimberly Nichole, 80 385 Kyle Allen, 385 Lydia, 385 Philip, 80 453 Rosina, 194 196-198 319 Russell, 80 Stacey Allen, 385 397 Stacey S, 80 Vickie Jo, 5 6
FRANKE Anna Katharina, 65 66 Edward F, 65 66 Frederick, 65
FRANK-LITTLE Orion, 80
FRANKMAN Dolores, 464 James, 212 464 Jordan Lee, 464 Julie Ann, 212 463 Wayne, 464
FRANKS Donna Jean, 194 Elisabeth, 42 Lester, 194 Martha Jane, 194
FRANZ Adelle, 167
FRANZENBURG Anita, 250 Arthur, 23 Carol, 81 Carrie, 81 Claus, 80 82 Clause, 81 Darold, 81 Darren, 81 Dean, 82 Donald, 82 Dorothy, 23 81 Faye, 81 357 Gary, 81 Gene, 81 Gina, 81 Heimke, 81 Herman, 81 82 436 600 Hiemke, 80 82 Howard, 81 82 James, 81 Janet, 82 Jason, 81 Jeffrey, 81 Jennifer, 81 Jessica, 81 Joan, 82 John, 80 81 82 Lena, 81 82 600 Lena Margaret, 436 Lois Mae, 271 434 436 437 440 Louise, 80-82 Margretha, 191 Nola, 81 82 Norma, 81 Robert, 81 82 Ruby, 82 409 Ruth, 82 367
FRAY Elizabeth, 261 Fred, 261
FREDERICK Sharon, 53 56
FREDRICK Caryl, 385
FREDRICKSON Doris, 555
FREEBORN Beverly, 260 Teresa, 260 Tracy, 260
FREEEMAN Mary, 332
FREEMAN Amelia, 82 83 206 Ann, 84 August, 82-85 206 Bill, 513 Carolyn, 85 Carolyn (Tina), 332 333 Charles, 83 84 Corleen, 83 84 Dorothy, 83 84 Douglas, 84 Edna, 83 Edna, 84 Elsie L, 83 84 George, 83 247 Gerry, 83 247 Gordon, 84 Gussie J, 83 84 Henry, 83 84 Herman, 84 Howard S, 83 84 Ione,

84 James, 84 Julias, 84 Lila B, 83 84
Marion V, 83 84 Mary, 82 84 85 206
Mary Jane, 83 85 Matilda, 83 Matilda
Ann, 83 247 Pharo, 84 Richard, 84
Roger, 85 Ronald, 84 Sophia, 83 84
Tillie, 83 247 Virgil, 84 William, 83 85
332

FREESE Abigail Lee, 47 Kelly, 408 Kelly
Alan, 47 Patricia Lee, 47 408 Rebeckah
Anne, 47

FREI Mitch, 349 Pattilee Renae, 349

FREIDERICH Johann Peter, 428

FREITAG Anna Elisabeth, 166 Anna
Elisabeth, 282 323 327-329 344
George, 344 Heinrich, 85 Jacob, 85
John, 344 Katharina Elisabeth, 85
Katherina Elisabeth, 328

FRENCH Donna Mae, 85 156 511 Larry,
85 511 Larry R, 156 Lori, 85 511
Michelle, 511

FRETT Aubrey, 540 Cameron Lee, 540
Gary Lee, 540 Luanne, 540 Peter
Graham, 540 Sebastian, 540

FREY Dean, 180 Leo, 397 Michael, 594
Mildred Matilda, 35 Pauline, 118 Rita
J, 180 Sheryl, 594 Susan Kay, 397

FRIEDEN Ardis, 500 Eliza, 500 William,
500

FRIEDERIKE Christel, 52 189

FRIEDRICH Heinrich, 428

FRIEND Edwin, 99 Wilma, 99

FRIESE Harreit Marie, 210

FRIMML Christopher, 570 Jennifer, 570
Linda, 570 Margaret Ann, 575 Marlys,
563 570 Matthew, 570 Robert, 563 570

FRITCHER Anna Lavina, 410 Doris, 576
Mary, 486 Mary Katherine (Kay), 576
Theodore Clifford, 576

FRITZ Anna, 85 86 93 310 August, 85 310
Augusta, 85 Emma, 85 93 Gus, 85
John, 85 Magdalena, 85 Mary, 85
Matilda, 85 Matilda, 310 Matilda, 311
Matilda, 458 Matilda (Tilly), 458 Peter,
64 85 93 Rosa, 164 Tilly, 85 310 311

FRITZPATRICK Andrew, 218 Brouice,
218 Jennifer, 218 Jill, 218 Megan, 218

FROEHLICH Anna, 86 Dale Carl, 86
Ernest, 86 Ester Katherine, 423 Esther

Katherine, 86 Hedwig, 86 Helen Marie,
86 Hugo Herman, 86 423 John, 86 John
D, 423 John Hugh, 86 Kari Lynn, 86
Laura Marie, 86 Loren Hugo, 86 Lori
Ann, 86 Marie Martha, 18 Mary, 86
Ruth Ann, 86 Sharon, 86 Sophia, 86
423 Susan Marie, 86

FROELICH Dale Carl, 423 Helen Marie,
423 Loren Hugo, 423 Ruth Ann, 423
Sharon Laverna, 423

FROST Connie, 14 Myrtle, 241

FRY Cecil R, 407 408 Edward, 115 Jack
Reiss, 408 Leola Wilhelmina, 407 408
Mildred Mathilda, 34 Mildred Matilda,
30 32 Mildred Matilda, 33 Paulina, 115
Rebecca, 115 Rose, 366 Viola, 595
Viola Mae, 140

FRYER Johannes Edna, 120

FRYREAR Edna, 266 Homer, 266

FUEHRER Paula, 156

FUESS Anna, 314 Phil, 314 Sophie, 314
569

FULLER Florence L, 530 Kami Leigh, 160
173 Tamara, 447 539

FULS David, 408 Davie Lee, 47 John
Richard, 47 Matthews James, 47
Rachel Ann, 47 Susan Lynette, 47 408

FUREY Bertha, 311 George, 311

FURLER Anna, 579 582 Chris Alan, 152
Cindy Sue, 26 152 Douglas, 26
Douglas Raye, 152 Kathy, 83 Veda,
217 218

FURNAS Jennie, 509 John, 509

FUSAN John Henry Jr, 188 382 Susan
Jane, 188 382

GABRIEL Lori Jo, 475

GACKER Barbara, 425

GADDIS Julian Lynn, 78 Julie Lynn, 389

GAETA Isabella Maxine, 577 John, 383
577 Ryan Charles, 577 Sarah, 383 577

GAFELLER Arnold George, 124 140
Sophia Christine, 124 140

GAFFER Jennifer Elizabeth, 530 Michael,
530 Rebecca Lynn, 530 Theresa Rae,
530

GAHRING Alice, 563 Marjorie, 563 568
Merlyn, 563

GEFALLER Norma, 382
GEGEL Baria Katharina, 425
GEIGER Alan Eugene, 91 Brian William,
  91 Christina Renee, 91 Eleanor
  Kathleen, 32 91 92 Elizabeth Ann, 92
  Eugene Earl, 91 92 Gina, 91 92 Lea
  Marie, 91 Linda Luanne, 92 Norman
  George, 32 91 92 Ricky Norman, 92
  Suzanne Kay, 91 92 Wendy Jo, 91 92
GEIKEN Anna Margaret, 32 91
GEIKEN Berhard, 554 Cassandra Leigh,
  93 Deanna Marie, 92 93 598 Debbie
  Kay, 92 93 Denise Ellen, 92 93 Dixie
  Lee, 92 93 Eleanor Kathleen, 32 91 92
  Freida Katherine Elizabeth, 33 Frieda
  Katherine Elizabeth, 32 91 92 Greta
  Lou, 32 92 93 Harold Lloyd, 32
  Kimberly Alice, 93 Lucas Aaron, 93
  Marie, 554 Myron Bernard Louis, 32
  92 Steven Allen, 93 Theodore, 32 33
  91-93
GEISSLER Agnes, 233
GEITZ Anna Elisabeth, 93 109 122 322
  325-329 344 Anna Elisbeth, 323 Georg
  Philipp, 325 327 George Philip, 93
  Johann Georg Philip, 327 Johann
  Philip, 93 Katharina Elisabeth, 93 327
GEOHRING Andrew, 569 Cory Lee, 569
  Craig Alan, 569 Curtiss Leroy, 569
  Laurie, 569 Leland Jay, 569 Leroy, 569
  575 Lisa Marie, 569 Lucille, 569 575
GEORG Johannes, 334 Karoline, 334
GEORGE King III, 165
GEORGE Anna Martha, 15 250 502
  Martha Juliann, 33 Martha Julianna, 34
GERBER Anna Maria, 411 465 Charles, 93
  Christina, 93 426 435 Clara Ida, 93 309
  311 Emma, 93 Jacob III, 93 Jacob Jr,
  93 Jacob Sr, 93 Maria, 25 354 Maria
  (Marie), 334-337 340 345 346 349 351
  Marie, 335 Martin, 334 337 351
  Salome, 334 Selma, 334
GERBER MÖLLER Maria (Marie), 335
GERHOLD Adam, 56 Adam F, 93 97 98
  100 424 Alice Hughes, 94 100 Anna
  Katherine, 97 Anna Maria, 412 429
  Anna Sophia Maria, 94 430 Anna
  Sophia Maria Elizabeth, 426 Anna

Sophia Marie, 411 427 Anna Sophia
  Marie Elizabeth, 98 376 420 438 Arlen,
  95 96 98 99 Arlen Gerhold, 96 Ashley
  Nicole, 96 Barbara, 97 Barbara Joan,
  95 96 98 99 Barbara Joann, 96 Carl H
  Sr, 98 150 Carl Henry, 458 Carl Henry
  Jr, 95 100 Carl Henry Sr, 95 99 Carl
  III, 95 98 Carrie, 98 Cheryl Linn, 97
  Conrad George, 97 Curtis Allen, 95 96
  Dianna Lynn, 95 96 Eldred, 97
  Elizabeth, 56 Elizabeth Ann, 100
  Elizabeth Anna, 93 97 98 424 Elsie, 96
  97 253 254 Elva M, 94 Emma
  Elisabeth, 95 98 150 Emma Elizabeth,
  99 458 Emma K, 96 98 151 155 162
  172 Erma, 97 Esther, 97 George, 97
  George Martin, 94 Heinrich, 337 429
  Helen A, 94 98 Henry, 424 Henry IIII,
  97 Henry John, 97 Henry Jr, 96 97 98
  Henry Sr, 25 93 94 96 97 99 345 350
  Jony, 95 Judy, 95 Kathleen, 79
  Kathleen Ann, 97 Kathryn Ann, 95 98
  Kelsey Jo, 96 Linda, 99 Lindsey Marie,
  96 Lolita Marie, 96 458-461 Lora Lee,
  97 Loretta, 94 98 Lori Sue, 95 96 Louis
  C, 94 Louise, 345 349 398 Louise
  Christina, 98 99 399 401 Louise
  Kristine, 25 93-97 99 Lukas Charles,
  100 Lynette, 95 Marie, 94 Marie
  Elizabeth, 53 55 56 Martha, 99 460
  Mary, 95 96 98-100 147 Mary Ellen,
  99 Matthew Curtis, 96 Mrs Carl, 458
  Mrs Carl Jr, 459 Nicholas Henry, 100
  Patricia Elaine, 95 100 Randall, 95
  Richard Warren, 100 Sally Jo, 95 99
  Samuel David, 100 Sophia, 424 Sophie,
  96 97 98 Susan Kay, 95 99 Thomas
  Donovan, 95 100 Wilbert, 56 94 100
  Wilma C, 94 Wilma C, 97
GERKE Kay, 547 549 Maria Katharina,
  201 464
GERLACH Emil, 120 Gerda, 560 Helen,
  120 Sharon, 120 572
GERLOFF Blake, 153 Denise, 153 155
  Perry, 153 155
GERMAN Rajean A, 107

GERNAAT Laurice Diane, 351 Mary Jon, 338 351 Michele Ann, 351 William Clifton, 338 351
GEROLD George, 53
GERTH Douglas, 394 Karen Ruth, 394
GESSNER Elizabeth, 534
GEWECKE Brooke Nicole, 100 Cindy Kay, 396 Dennis, 100 273 396 Kathryn, 396 Lori Ann, 100 396 Rachel Kay, 100 Shirley Ann, 100 273 396 Sterling, 396 Terry Lee, 100 396
GEYER Alice, 404 Anna Juliane, 407 Anna Julianne, 403 George Franklin, 404 James, 404 John, 404 John C, 403 407
GIBNEY Bill, 446 Jacqueline, 88 Margaret, 480 483
GIBSON Beverly, 143 George, 143 Stacee, 143
GIEKEN Anna Margaret, 358
GIELAU Adam Wesley, 101 Alan William, 100 149 Albert Henry, 100 101 149 183 Amy Renae, 100 Anna Marie, 100 101 149 183 Barbara, 101 149 Bryan Alan, 100 Cheryl, 101 149 Emily Ann, 101 Irma Jean, 100 149 Jacquelyn Kristine, 101 Jeffrey Alan, 100 Rachel Mae, 101 Randy Albert, 149 Renae, 100 149 Robert Alan, 101 149 Sharon, 100 149 Sharon Ann, 149 Tyler Jeffrey, 100 Vicky Marie, 101 149 Wesley Ray, 101 149
GIER Anna Katherine, 16 18 19 33 Anna Katherine, 195
GIESEKE Annis, 530 Elsa, 530 Jack, 530
GIGLER Lisa Lynn, 218 William, 218
GILBERT Claude C, 170 172 Katharina Wilhelmina, 170 172 Katharina Wilhemina, 62 Rhonda Sue, 348 Richard, 348
GILL Carole S, 526 Edward B, 526 John, 351 Lorri Sue, 351 Sheila S, 526
GILLETT Aaron Robert, 24 Douglas James, 24 Kevin, 24 Susan Rae, 24 154
GILLIAM Bill, 338 Gregory James, 338 Matthew Dean, 338 Sharon Kay, 338
GILLILAND Marica Jo, 319 Steven, 319

GILLIS Dorothy Olive, 53 99 398 400 401 402
GILLIS RATHJE Dorothy Olive, 398
GILMAN Mike, 22 Mike, 46 Sharon Kay, 22 Sharon Kay, 46
GINTER Hazel C, 449
GINTERT Frank, 550 Wilma, 550
GINTHER Arlo, 43 Judy Joyce, 43 148 Kenneth Joe, 43 148
GIRSCH Janice Kay, 326
GIRSCH Matthew Joseph, 326 Michael, 331 Michael Joseph, 326 Michael Paul, 326 Theresa Maureen, 326
GISH Elaine Louise, 1 Laurie Ann, 1 Laurie Ann, 122 Roger Eli, 1
GJERDE Deborah Mae, 530 Kenneth, 530 Mark Robert, 530
GLANDORF Amanda Marie, 528 Arthur Fredrick, 139 Clover Denise, 525 Debra Lynn, 525 Jeffrey Willard, 528 Johanna Dorthea, 139 Katie Ann, 528 Kimberly, 528 La Dean Meta, 122 Ladean Meta, 123 124 138 139 Marian Frances, 521 Marian Frances, 525 Matthew Martin, 528 Michele Marie, 528 Myles Jeffrey, 528 Patricia Ann, 521 527 Rebecca Renee, 526 Regan Elizabeth, 526 Robert Herman, 521 525 Rodney Robert, 525 Ryley Robert, 526 Theresa, 526 Timothy Arnold, 526 Tina Cristine, 528 Willard M, 521 Willard M, 527 Zachary Frank, 526
GLASGOW Audrey Ann, 101 266 275 David L, 101 266 275 Ella Mikalena, 101 Henrick Elsworth, 101 Jodi Ann, 266 Joel David, 101 266 Kari Ann, 101 266
GLENN Brenna Marie, 42 Haley Nicole, 42 Lorraine, 506 Marilee, 42 Mary Margaret, 42 Patrick, 42 Steve, 42
GLICK Alice M, 101 269 Betty Jean, 479 Betty Jeanne, 489 Delores Ann, 101 269 275 427 Eldora, 399 400 Fred H, 269 Galen Eugene, 101 269 275 427 Jennifer Marie, 101 Joseph Tyler, 101 Maynard, 489 Michael John, 101 269 Odetta Marie, 94 269 Rosalie, 489 Shari Lynn, 101 269

GLIDDEN Frances Norma, 62 Franes
  Norma, 63
GLIENKE David Henry, 306 Kevin David,
  306 Lynn Marie, 306 Sandra Irene, 306
GLIME Lucinda Kay, 462
GLOEDE Darcy Ann, 206 322
GLOVER Mildred Winifred, 391 395
GLUESING Gilbert, 102 103 502 544 546
  Hannah, 102 103 502 503 546 Helen,
  102 503 Jacquelyn Rae, 102 103 Jo
  Ann, 546 Joann, 102 John, 102 103
  John, 503 John N, 502 546 Karmen
  Noreen, 102 103 Madeline, 102 103
  502 544 546 Norma, 102 103 Normal,
  503 Paul, 102 103 503 Paulette Sue,
  103 Ronald, 546 Shirley, 103 546
GOBLER Linda, 492
GOEDKEN Bradley Jerome, 47 Gail Lois,
  47
GOETHALS Jeff, 351 Kimberly Suzanne,
  351
GOETTSCH Bena, 444 445
GOETZ Caroline Mary, 104 123 128
  Caroline May, 103 Clara Mary, 123
  Deborah Joyce, 103 123 Donald
  Charles, 103 104 123 128 Douglas
  John, 103 123 Dustin Thomas, 103
  Elaine Constance, 103 George Joseph,
  123 Jacqueline Marie, 103 124 Ryan
  Charles, 103 Theresa Carol, 123
  Therese Carol, 104
GOLLADAY Alma Ruth, 229 236 Cheryl
  Ann, 229 Elvira Luna, 229 Richard
  Lee, 229 236 William, 229
GOOD Audrey, 104 366 367 Bonnie, 104
  366 Elmer, 366 George, 38 James, 104
  366 Janet, 409 Jo Anne, 366 Joanne,
  104 John, 104 366 367 Judy, 104 366
  Kimberly, 104 Kimberly Rae, 409 414
  Lucille, 38 Wade, 104 Wilber, 409
  Winnie, 366
GOODALL Catherine Ann, 107 Catherine
  Ann Columbia, 109
GOODELL Ann Marie, 437 Mitch Leon,
  437
GOOS Anna Cath, 585 588 H, 583
  Karoline, 583

GORDON Anne, 40 Sarah Caroline, 40
  William Smith, 40
GORKOW Debra Rae, 226 Martin W, 226
GORSCH Carroll, 295 Donna, 295 Jonah
  V, 295 Justin Franklyn, 295 Sarah
  Marie, 295
GORSH Justin Franklyn, 296 Sarah Marie,
  296
GOSLINGA Eric Keith, 264 Kathleen
  Ellen, 264 287
GOUCH Dorothy Griswold, 104 Elsie
  Louise, 104 Louise Marie, 104 Dorothy
  Griswold, 355 Elsie Louise, 355 Louise
  Marie, 135 355 William Griswold, 104
  135 355
GOURLEY Jeremy Lou, 78 Joseph, 78 355
  Nathan Alan, 78 Paula Rae, 78 355
GOYETTE Larry, 351 Michele Ann, 351
GRABAU Adelheid, 106-108 326-328
  Adelheid Kathryn, 106 107 109 Anna,
  104 107 109 Anneke, 106 108 109
  Annete, 106 Anthony Scott, 111
  Arlene, 105 108 Arthur Charles, 105
  107 109 411 Becke, 106 Bernice
  Louise, 325 329 330 Brian Dean, 107
  Byron Zane, 105 110 Carol Renea, 105
  108 Catherine, 106 110 Catherine Ann,
  107 Catherine Ann Columbia, 109
  Christopher Dietrich, 108-111 344
  Christopher Dietrich Sr, 106
  Christopher Jr, 105 111 Claus, 106-110
  Claus Heinrich, 109 111 Claus
  Heinrich Sr, 104 106 326 Claus
  Henrich Sr, 108 Claus Henry, 322
  Claus Henry Jr, 107 Dale Allan, 105
  107 109 111 Dalene Marie, 105
  Deborah Versluis, 107 Didrich
  Wilhelm, 108 Dierck, 106 Dietrich,
  106-109 Dietrich Earl Zane, 105 Dirk,
  110 Douglas Lee, 107 Elizabeth Lee,
  110 Elizabeth Louise, 108 Frances
  Ellen, 105 110 Frederich Henry, 109
  Gerd, 106 110 Gesche, 106 Gesche,
  109 110 Gordon Douglas Kite, 105
  Gretchen Marie, 106 111 Gretje, 106
  Harold Walter Adam, 108 Harold
  Watler Adam, 105 Heinrich, 108
  Heinrich Claus, 109 Heinrich Claus

632

Martin Jr, 109 Henry, 109 111 326 Henry Claus, 108 349 Henry Jr, 109 Henry Sr, 104 106 108 Herman, 106 108 Herman George, 109 330 Herman Jr, 105 107 109 328 329 Hilda, 107 Hilda Christina, 109 Hilda Christine, 330 Hilda Gertrude, 105 109 411 Hinrich, 106 108 110 Irene Louise, 105 107 Jeffrey Allan, 109 Jeffrey Neal, 107 109 Jill Crisann, 109 110 Joel Scott, 110 Johann, 106 109 110 John, 108 Katherine, 104 107 108 Kathleen Marie, 106 Kimberly Donne, 111 Leonard Henry Adam, 105 110 Leonard Morris, 109 110 111 Linda Jean, 110 111 Lois N, 105 Lois Neil, 107 Lois Nell, 109 111 Louise Caroline Marie, 105 108 110 111 344 Lynetta, 107 111 Magarete, 110 Margaret, 106 108 Margarete, 106 107 Margaretha, 106 108 109 111 322 Maria, 107 Maria Magdalena (Lena), 336 337 344 Marie, 105 107 109 328 Mary E, 105 109 Maureen Kay, 106 111 Meta, 106 107 111 322 324 327 330 331 Mildred Anne Minnie, 111 Mimz Anna, 105 Minna, 109 349 Minnie, 107 Morris Allen Kite, 110 111 Norma Jean, 109-111 Ollie, 106 107 109 326-328 Ora Lee, 105 110 Otrav, 108 Pamela, 107 Rajean A, 107 Ruth Katherine, 109 Scott Allan, 107 111 Tibcke, 108 Tibke, 106 108 Titje, 110 Trine, 106 110 Violet, 110 Walter Boyce, 105 Walter Martin, 109 Wilhelmina Marie Meta, 109
GRACK Anna Christina, 67 68 111 169 Anna Elisabeth, 111 Anna Katharina, 111 Johannes, 111 Johannes Jacob, 111
GRADY Allegra Bush, 496
GRAHAM Bernard, 94 Loretta, 94 Mrs Bernard, 56
GRANZBERG Angela Sophia, 351 Gary Robert, 351 Mary Ann, 351 Milinda Bess, 351
GRAU Alvina, 60 Clara, 61 Dora, 60 Dora Amelia, 60 George, 60 Henry, 60 61

Henry Sr, 60 Ida Dorthea, 60 Walter, 61 William, 61
GRAUBAU Arlene, 349 Christopher Dietrich, 349 Christopher Jr, 349 Elizabeth Louise, 349 Gretchen Marie, 349 Harold Walter Adam, 349 Herman, 334 Leonard Henry Adam, 349 Louise Caroline Marie, 349 Maria Magdalena (Lena), 333 Mildred Anne Minnie, 349 Ora Lee, 349 Wilhelmina, 334
GREASER Agnes, 112 113 Agnesia, 112 113 Alfred, 111-113 Anna, 113 Anna Grace, 111-113 Barbara, 113 Carl, 112 Charlotte, 111 112 Christy, 112 Daniel, 112 Douglas, 112 Edna, 112 Elizabeth, 112 113 Emma, 111 113 Gary, 112 George, 112 113 Gregg, 112 Harold, 112 Helen, 112 Idella, 113 James, 112 Janice, 112 Johann Georg, 112 113 John, 113 June, 112 Katherine, 112 113 Lana, 113 Levi Henry, 111 113 Lewis, 113 Lisa, 113 Margaret, 112 113 Maria, 113 Marilyn, 112 Philip, 112 113 Ray, 112 113 Susan, 113
GREEN Arthur, 476 Elda Anna Dorothea, 159 331 Lillian Elizabeth, 476 Merle, 159 331
GREENE Albert, 577 Carol, 577 Daniel, 577 Donald, 577 Eldon, 576 577 Katherine, 577 Lawrence, 577 Mary, 577 Michelle, 577 Therese, 576 577 Victor, 577
GREENLEAF Arno, 113 154 Ashley Lauren, 113 Brian Kettering, 114 Delmar Lewis, 113 154 Dorothy, 113 154 184 Jolle, 114 Karen A, 113 154 Kenneth Allen, 113 Melanie, 114 Michelle, 113 154 Nichole Clara, 114 Vernon, 113 154 184 Wayne Vernon, 154
GREGORY Linda, 22 44
GREINKE Hermine, 564 567
GREVE Lena, 17 38 39 367
GRIEDER Denise, 270
GRIFFIN David W, 287 288 296 Galen, 288 Grant Galen, 287 Karri Lynn, 287 Kerri Lynn, 288 296 Oliva Marie, 287 Velda, 288

634

119 572 Conrad, 552 553 572 Daniel Mark, 119 David Jon, 119 Donald, 119 572 Douglas Arthur, 119 Dustin Grey, 121 Eldon, 553 Emma, 119 451 572 Ernest, 119-121 565 572 Ernest Jr, 572 Evelyn, 119 572 Gilbert, 120 121 553 Gloria, 120 572 Harold, 120 572 Heidi Joy, 120 Hildegard, 552 555 558 561 564 570 572 Jamie Allen, 120 Jane, 119 Jeffrey Jon, 120 Joalyce Jean, 120 Judson Gilbert, 120 Justina Kleinsasser, 553 Kelli Marie, 119 Ladeen, 121 572 Laurie Marie, 119 Lena, 120 553 596 Lula, 119 Luverne, 120 572 Magdalena, 553 572 Magdelena, 552 Margaret, 120 121 572 Mark Daniel, 119 Martin, 121 572 Martin Dean, 121 Mary, 119-121 559 560 564 565 569 572 575 Math, 575 Michael Austin, 121 Michael Jay, 120 121 Michelle Rne, 120 Nancy Ann, 121 Sharon, 120 572 Steven Don, 119 Susan Dawn, 119 Walter, 119 Walter Wallace, 119 Wilhelmina, 575 William, 553

GUERICKE WERNING Hildegard, 553

GUERKE Irene, 49

GUERRERO Cathryn Ann, 356 Fred, 356

GUESE Janice, 61

GUIDA Nn, 164

GUIDER Andrew, 31 Leota Clara Anna, 30 31 33 36 Martha, 31 Yana Roxanna Yanria Ortiz, 30

GUNZENHOUSER Christina Elizabeth, 424 Fred Christian, 424

GUSTAFSON Clare, 259

GUTTENFELDER Bertha, 350 Louise Marie, 350 Martha, 350 N N, 350

GUYLER Claire, 484 Clarence, 484 Janet Lee, 484 486 Jennifer Leigh, 484 Michael Andrew, 484 486

GWINN Judith Juanita, 317

GYSBERS Bonnie Sue, 104 Derk Newell, 104 355 Elsie Louise, 104 355 Linda Diane, 104 Tor Merrill, 104

HAACK Dorothea, 63 Phyllis, 287 296 Rhonda Kaye, 287 296 Russell, 287 296

HAACKER Dorothea, 39 Henry, 39

HAAR Arnold, 500 Donna, 500 Donna M, 500 Emma, 500 Fred, 500 Janet Marie, 500 Jared, 500 Katherine, 500 Steve A, 500

HABER Anna Jo, 308 309 Fred, 308 Joyce, 308 Matthew Benjamin, 308 309

HACHMAN Lynda Frances, 35 Richard, 35

HACHMANN Lynda Frances, 33 Richard, 33

HACKEL Alexander, 121 Aloisia, 533 Doris, 121 533 Gerhardt, 121 533 Gustav, 533 Heinrich, 533 Karin, 121 533 Karoline, 121 533 Markus, 121 Melanie, 121 Stefan, 121 Walter, 121 533 Wilhelm, 121 533

HAEFNER Joel, 451 Kristy, 395 451 Natalie, 451 Renee, 512 Russell, 395 451

HAERTHER (Minnie) Marie Wilhelmina Katherine, 410 418 423 425 441 Adina Juliann, 122 129 136 141 Albert Eberhardt, 121 124 125 136 323 328 Albert Frederick Harman, 136 Amber Marie, 142 Andrea Faye, 138 Andrew William, 123 Anna Magdalene, 133 Anna Martha, 123 137 139 141 547 Barbara Juliann, 1 122 137 Barbara June, 122 127 Benjamin Kline, 126 Bertram William, 122 137 Bette Mae, 122 125 134 140 Bonnie Lou, 122 123 124 139 Brian Keith, 123 139 Brittanie Jean, 126 C W, 489 Cameron Mitchell, 142 Carl George, 123 137 139 141 547 Caroline Johanna, 121 124 125 136 328 Caroline Mary, 104 123 128 Caroline May, 103 Carolynne, 134 Casey Logan, 140 Cheryl Jane, 138 Chris, 446 496 Christ, 124 140 Christ William, 130 Christian, 124 140 Christian Eberhardt, 121 124 130 132 136 139 428 Christine, 427 Christine Barbara, 133 Christine Catherine, 131 132 Christine Wihelmine, 148 Christine Wilhelmine, 124 132 443 Christopher Henry, 140 Christopher John, 127 Cody Lee, 140 Connie Sue, 122 124 125 139 Dale Fredrick, 140 Dale William, 125 131

636

HAMMITT Bill, 229 237 Rebecca Marie, 237 Rita Marie, 229 237 Wesley William, 237
HANBERN Maria, 326
HANEMANN Maria Margaretha, 428
HANFT Diane Marlene, 361 Dorothy Mae, 361 Elizabeth Marie, 361 Jeffrey, 361 John R, 361 Matthew John, 361
HANKINS Barbara Jean, 4 James Lavern, 4 Karla Kay, 4 Kimony Jo, 4
HANKS Anthony, 511 Michelle, 511
HANNEMAN Anna K, 233 234 Charles, 83 84 Dorothy, 83 84 Elsie, 494 497 Kathy, 83 Mary Jo, 83 Regina, 445 Thomas, 83
HANNEN Ellen, 477
HANNENFENT Irene Louise, 105 107
HANS Aunt, 302 Uncle, 302
HANSEN Charlene, 14 Dorothy June, 517 Gertrude, 265 Hans, 265 Jane, 471 472 Jerry Orvelle, 221 226 Orvelle, 226 Patricia Lou, 221 226 Shirley, 226
HANSON Cari, 471 Cheryl, 471 Cindy, 471 Dea, 143 394 Diane L, 155 Edward R, 143 394 Evelyn Beatty, 471 Janet Ellen, 52 438 Jarret Robert, 143 John Douglas, 52 438 Joyce, 308 Karen Lynn, 52 Mary Elizabeth, 52 Norma L, 143 144 292 394 Oscar R, 143 144 Oscar R Jr, 292 394 Rhonda, 143 394 Richard John, 394 Sally Ann, 40 144 394 Vickie, 268 291
HAPPE Elke, 202 Jolante, 144 202 Lina, 144 201 Patrick, 144 Uwe, 144 202 Vanessa, 144 Wille, 201 Willi, 144
HAPPEL (Mary) Maria Katherina, 423 424 466 A Catharina, 164 A Elisabeth, 161 164 A Konigunda, 167 A Kunigunde, 164 A Martha, 167 Abbi, 180 Adam Martin Andrew, 144 145 156 158 163 170 174 Adelle, 167 Alan James, 173 Albert C, 144 151 162 173 Alfred August Christ, 144 145 Alfred W, 145 152 154 159 177 180 185 Alison, 154 Alison Leigh, 153 Allen James, 160 Alvera Gertrude, 142 145 162 Amber Lynn, 175 Andrea, 178 Andreas, 67 68 131 145 147-150 164 166 168 169 176

177 262 307 343 411 423 424 Andreas (Andrew), 350 430 Andreas (Andrew) Sr, 425 Andreas Sr, 170 Andrew, 68 131 145-148 150 164 166 168 176 177 Andrew Adam Jr, 170 Andrew John, 68 146 155-157 168 182 551 Andrew Sr, 149 170 Anna, 68 145 152 168 176 182 183 261 416 Anna Catharina, 161 163 167 169 175 Anna Christina, 58 59 147 Anna Christina Elizabeth, 171 Anna Elisabeth, 63 67 146 147 160 164-167 169 175 312 334 335 Anna Elizabeth, 43 148 161 168 Anna Gertrud, 67 68 70 145-148 158 162 168 169 423 443 592 Anna Gertrude, 426 455 Anna Gertud, 152 168 169 228 Anna Katharina, 67 157 158 160 169 409 412 421 426 Anna Katherina, 146 149 182 271 289 417 425-427 430 431 Anna Katherine, 426 Anna Kathrina, 169 Anna Magdalena Caroline, 166 Anna Margaretha, 169 Anna Maria, 149 166 100 101 149 183 532 Anna Martha, 165 166 169 Annie, 164 166 325 327 Aretha, 182 Arlen, 149 Arlene, 145 162 171 174 176 181 182 Arlin, 155 Armin, 183 Arnetta, 162 177 181 Arnold, 157 Arnold Christian, 150 158 162 Arthur, 157 Audrey, 150 183 478 Audrey Louise, 150 182 200 August, 177 August A, 95 96 144 146 150 172 257 435 August Anton, 151 170 177 179 297 August Konrad William, 152 168 261 Augusta Katharina, 160 Auguste Katharina, 157 164 Barbara, 165 Becky Jo, 151 174 Becky Sue, 156 171 Berdina Ann, 21 151 162 Bertha, 167 228 Beth, 172 Betty, 182 183 Betty L, 156 182 Betty Lou, 152 155 539 Betty Louise, 158 177 Beverly, 152 Beverly Ann, 177 178 Beverly Kay, 183 Bianca Stefanie, 179 Bonnie, 153 155 Bradley Martin, 174 Brenda, 173 Brenda Joyce, 155 156 180 Brenden Lcuas, 150 Brian Christopher, 158 Brian Dennis, 153 Bruce William, 180 Carl, 165 Carl Fred, 165 Carol Ann, 26 152 Carolyn, 180 Carolyn Louise, 153 160 162

Carolyn Sue, 163 175 181 Catharina, 161 Catherine, 180 184 Chari, 180 Charles Conrad, 145 152 159 181 Cheryl, 145 152 Christina, 165 177 184 Christina Marie, 170 266 267 273 275 276 282 297 Cindy Sue, 26 152 Clara, 165 Clara Sophie Anna, 165 Connie, 155 160 Conrad, 145 152 168 176 182 183 261 Conrad August William, 68 Cynthia Kay, 173 Dale Adam, 172 Dana Rae, 175 Darles, 172 Darwin Eugene, 183 David, 178 David Edward, 145 David Lee, 153 173 Dawn, 153 172 Dean Alan, 153 172 Deb, 152 159 Debra Lynn, 158 Delores Marie, 153 162 510 511 Denise, 153 155 182 Dennis Harold, 153 160 Derch John, 153 Derlad Elmer, 155 Diana, 183 Diane, 173 Diane Carolyn, 153 160 Diane L, 155 Dianne, 153 Donald Alfred, 145 154 Donna, 24 145 154 157 172 173 Donna Mae, 154 183 Dorothea, 68 149 Dorothea, 154 155 157 162 168 173 180 181 183 Dorothy, 113 154 176 182 184 Dorothy Claire, 144 156 162 171 Dorothy Fern, 156 162 163 Dorothy Fern, 172 179 181 Dorothy Gertrude, 151 159 177 Dorothy Gertude, 174 178 Dorothy Marie, 154 184 202 Douglas, 155 Edna, 154 182 Edward, 174 Edwin, 182 Edwin John, 154 176 Eileen Joyce, 183 Elaine, 147 149 152 155 160 163 171 Elda, 155 176 183 Elda Ann, 182 Eldon, 153 155 Eleanor May, 96 155 Eleanora Mathilda, 150 182 Eleanora Matilda, 147 Elisabeth, 161 166 Elizabeth, 165 177 277 325 327 335 338 344 Elizabeth Christina, 156 160 161 170 178 279 Elizabeth Crhistina, 148 Elizabeth Jeanette, 131 170 268 271 272 275 277 282 283 289 291 411 Elmer, 145 155 Elmer Derald, 156 180 Elmer Ernest, 147 149 152 155 160 163 171 Elmer Henry Adam, 155 156 161 182 Elsie, 510 Elsie Minnie, 147 156 511 Elvira Marie Christina, 161 Emma, 26 166 178 300 Emma Elisabeth, 95 98

150 Emma Elizabeth, 99 458 Emma Henrietta, 165 179 Emma K, 96 98 151 155 162 172 Engel Magdalena, 165 168 169 Enrique Edward, 177 Ernest, 165 Ervin Henry, 156 Ervin Henry John, 144 162 171 Erwin Henry, 156 162 163 172 179 181 Esther, 38 144 150 153 157 159 183 318 Esther Catherine, 151 170 Esther R, 207 Eulalia Elisabeth, 164 450 Eulalie Elisabeth, 167 Eva Catharina, 161 Eva Catherine, 167 Eva Katherina, 158 Eydie Faye, 178 Florene, 163 180 183 Frank Benjamin, 170 Fred, 157 165 Fred Jr, 157 Fred Martin, 144 Fredrich, 169 Frieda Gertrude, 3 147 157 476 478 Friedrich, 146 Friedrich Hartmann, 157 160 164 Gary, 173 Gary Allen, 26 157 George, 158 167 182 George Andrew, 144 George August Henry, 161 168 George Carl, 164 George Fritz, 166 300 Gerald Marvin, 158 177 Geraldine, 96 150 158 162 Gerdruth, 164 Gertrud, 179 183 Gertrud Anna Elizabeth, 339 344 Gertrude K, 177 330 376 377 Gertrude Katherina, 158 168 Gertrude Mary Christina, 116 158 Gertrude May Christina, 144 Gertud, 164 171 175 Gertud Anna Elizabeth, 167 Glenda, 145 159 Gordon, 159 183 Grace Gertrude, 159 177 Gregory, 152 159 Harlan James, 159 173 174 183 Harold, 157 Harold Conrad, 153 160 162 Harold John August, 160 161 176 Hartmann, 149 Hartmann Johann Balthaser, 157 160 166 Hartmann Peter William, 149 154 155 157 162 168 173 180 183 Harvey, 155 160 Hattie, 157 165 Heather Kisling, 180 Heidi S, 155 Heinrich, 158 161 Heinrich August, 148 156 161 170 178 279 Henrich, 161 Henry, 68 70 161 166 168 228 455 Henry George, 145 150 151 153 156 160 173 177 184 Henry George August, 68 Herbert Louis, 96 162 Herman Andreas Johann Goerge, 151 Hilda, 162 183 321 Hohann Georg Sr, 338 Hulda Caroline, 68 145 150 151

Martin, 178 Martin George, 177 Martin George Valentine, 151 159 174 178 Marvin, 176 182 Marvin Benjamin, 151 158 172 177 Marvin John, 162 177 181 Mary, 93 149 155 165 166 176 352 Mary (Maria), 426 Mary Ann, 145 177 Matthew, 179 180 Maxine Lorraine, 26 27 152 157 179 Melvin G, 26 27 152 157 178 179 Merle Martin, 177 178 Michael Harvey, 174 Michael John, 171 Michael Lynn, 180 Mildred, 174 182 Mildred Esther, 155 156 161 182 Mildred Louise, 161 178 Milton Eugene, 178 182 Nancy, 145 180 Nancy Lue, 178 179 315 Neil Alan, 153 Neoma Margaret, 151 171 178 179 184 Nina, 151 Nina Laura, 177 Paul, 26 178 Paul Friedrich Heinrich, 165 179 Paula, 156 Peter, 171 179 Peter Heinrich Wilhelm, 167 Peter Johann, 276 283 Philip, 150 Phyllis, 96 172 Rachael, 159 Raydean Lee, 157 179 Raymond John Henry, 151 171 178 179 184 Rebecca Lea, 180 Regina, 67 168 Renee Ann, 177 Renee Jo Lynn, 180 Rhonda, 160 176 Richard, 145 180 Richard Henry, 163 180 183 Rickey, 173 Ricky Allen, 155 180 Rita J, 180 253 Rita Jane, 145 Robert, 145 179 180 Robert Quinton, 184 Rodney, 145 173 Ronda, 177 181 Ronda Jean, 153 160 Rosa, 164 Roxanne, 174 Ruth, 144 151 159 162 173 183 257 261 Sally Rae, 175 180 Sandra Kay, 158 Sara Kisling, 180 Scott, 160 182 Shannon Lee, 163 181 Sharen Kay, 160 Sharon Ann, 145 Sharon Kay, 318 Sherry, 182 Shirley, 161 Shirley A, 160 176 Sophia Katharina Elisabeth, 146 164 426 Sophia Marie Elisabeth, 150 255 257 261 591 Sophie, 150 158 162 Sophie Maria Elisabeth, 255 261 Stacy, 173 Starr Layne, 158 Steven, 160 Steven Kent, 150 Susan, 157 159 179 Suzanne, 58 162 173 181 183 Tamara Sue, 162 181 Tamie Jo, 184 Teresa Jane, 152 181 Theodore George, 165 Thomas, 173 183 Timothy Gordon, 178 Todd, 159 Todd James, 163 Tracie Ann, 160 173 Tyler Alan, 158 Verilyn Fern, 156 Verilyn Ferne, 181 Vernon, 181 183 Vernon Ray, 156 182 Victor, 153 178 182 Walter, 154 174 182 Walter Herman, 147 150 182 Walther Johann Heinrich Phillip, 165 Wilhelm, 158 182 William, 149 150 153-155 157 159 162 168 173 180 181 183 228 458 William C, 167 William Hartman Peter, 68 William John, 152 181 183 William Martin, 154 170 174 184 William Raymond, 180 184 William Raymond Jr, 184 Wilma Malinda, 184 511 Yvonne Marie, 145 185 542

HARBOURNE C T, 316 Jaime Farrah, 316 Jane Anne, 316

HARDER Elsie, 482 Henry, 199 Martha, 499 Meta, 199

HARDING June Maxine, 375

HARE Pamela, 512 Rodney, 512

HARFORD Becky Lynn, 124 Steven Lee, 124

HARGER Flo, 75

HARGETT Kay Ann, 245 246 Marcus Robert, 245 Robert, 246 Robert Glen, 245

HARKEMEYER Laura C, 412 413 Marjorie, 74

HARMAN Pamela Joy, 34 Rand Charles, 34

HARMS Carolyn Louise, 153 160 162

HARNISCH Alice, 185 562 Emil Frederick William, 267 Emma, 185 562 Eric Lenard, 185 Esther, 185 200 562 Gail Alein, 267 268 276 290 291 295 296 Helen, 185 508 562 John, 562 Leonard, 562 Margaret, 42 185 562 Martha, 267 Mathilda, 43-45 185 562 Melvin, 562 Mildred, 562 Wilhelmina, 575 William, 185 562 Wilma, 562 Yvonne, 185 562

HARNISCHL Emma, 564 William, 564

HARPER Margaret Amanda, 219 Virginia, 16 193

HARRELL Patricia Dee, 589 592

HARRINGTON Dixie, 600 Julia, 174

HARRIS Amy Suzanne, 186 Beth Ann, 120 121 Brad Alan, 186 Carolyn Ann,

186 442 Charles D, 442 Donna, 232
Ella, 552 Erica Renee, 186 Grace, 442
Grace Marie, 442 Gregory Alan, 186
442 Ken, 121 Kristine, 442 Kristine
Kay, 186 Lisa Marie, 186 Nadine Jane,
186 Nathan Wilson, 186 Nichole
Louise, 186 Patricia Elaine, 186 442
Robert, 552 Robert Dwain, 186 442
Sharon Louise, 61 186 442 Thurman
Cloyd, 186 289 442 Velma Louise, 186
289 442

HARRISON Christine C, 457 Christine
Lois, 458 Heidi Ann, 596 Joan, 457
Marion, 457 Rita Carol, 76 77

HARROD Dana L, 368 David W, 368
Louis C, 368 Sharon Louise, 368
Shirley Ann, 368

HARTI Fred, 266 Laverna, 266 Leonard J,
266

HARTKEMEYER Aflred L, 187 Alfred,
187 Alfred L, 186 187 Alma, 203
Brandon, 357 David, 187 Dick, 187
Edna, 187 Eileen, 187 Elaine, 187
Eldo, 187 Elmer, 187 Emily, 358
Helen, 187 Helen L, 186 187 Jennie,
186 187 Keith, 81 357 Laura C, 187
425 Laverna, 187 Leona, 187 Michelle,
81 357 Tiffany, 358 William C, 186
187

HARTKEMEYER HEYER Eileen Ann,
420 460

HARTL Dan, 188 Fred, 187 432 Julie, 187
Leonard J, 187 432 Luverna, 432
Melissa, 188

HARTLOFF Holly Jean, 210 573

HARTMAN Anna, 82

HARTMANN Meghan Genevieve, 300
Nathan Earl, 300 Olivia Judith, 300
Pamela Jo, 300 Rand Charles, 300

HARTSON Alice M, 101 Linda, 101
Ronald, 101

HARTWICK Wilhelmina, 105

HARTWIG John, 370 Ruth, 370

HARTZ Audrey Laura, 422 481 483

HARTZ Ella, 479 Elsie L, 483 Harvey
William, 483 Herbert, 188 479 Jennifer
Kay, 188 Judy, 54 55 Julie Anne, 188
Mary, 188 Marye, 479 Preston, 479

Ruth E, 188 Ruth Esther, 479 Sally,
188 479 Stephanie, 54 Virgil, 188 479

HARTZLER Lori, 211

HARVEY Alvera Gertrude, 145 162 Cecil
William, 145 162

HARVIGSEN Earl, 65 Juliette Marie, 65

HASCKE Jolene, 484

HASENJAEGER Florence, 228

HASLEY Dale, 534 Fred, 534 Lavina, 534
Magdalena, 534 Robert, 534 Sylvan,
534

HASS Brian Scott, 231 Diane Lee, 231
Jennifer Lee, 231 Sally, 125 Sidney,
231

HASSEE Anna, 39 115 514

HASSTEDT Adelheid, 106 Adelheid
Kathryn, 106 107 109 Andrea Ramah,
188 341 Ashley Elaine, 188 Denise
Elaine, 188 341 Janet Carol, 128 188
341 Joel Craig, 188 341 Joshua Tyler,
188 Mark Wayne, 341 Myron Wilson,
128 188 341 Nathan Alan, 188 Nicole
Ann, 188 Ollie, 106 107 109 Ryan
Craig, 188 Todd Alan, 188 341

HATT Jeannine, 61 372

HATTER Evelyn, 429

HAUCK Susanne, 342

HAUPT Annine, 600 Catherina, 600 Fred,
600

HAUSCHILD Bertha, 116 384 390 479

HAUSER Josephine, 192 Mae, 359

HAUSKINS Carl Julius, 188 337 352 Edna
Elizabeth, 337 352 Enda Elizabeth, 188
Jane Elaine, 188 337 Jean Carol, 337
Joan Edna, 188 337 381 382

HAUSMAN Minna, 235 Minnie, 235

HAUSMANN Minna, 232 234 236 Minnie,
232 234 236

HAUSRETH Bertha, 148

HAUTUM George, 551 Otillie Louise, 551

HAVLIK Cathleen Mary, 303 Raymond
Gerald, 303 Suzanne Marie, 303 304

HAWKER Chad, 370 Lawanna Jean, 370
N N, 370

HAWKINS Patricia, 55 56 Robert S, 55

HAYNER Anna Catharina, 161 163 Anna
Katharina, 158 Anna Katherina, 182

Catharina, 161 Hans, 161 Katharine, 167

HAYNOR Benjamin Charles, 126 Charles Richard, 126 134 Diane Lynn, 126 134 John William, 126 Nathan David, 127

HEAD Valerie, 258 591

HEADLEY Denise Elaine, 188 341

HEARTHER Louise Martha, 197

HEATH Brian, 323 Dawn Rae, 323

HEATHERWICK Sandra Ann, 443

HECKER Anni Elisabeth, 52 189 447 Helene, 114 189 447 Karl Friedrich, 114 189 447

HECKT Anna, 189 Beryl, 189 Carole, 189 Clement, 189 Emma, 189 190 Ernst, 189 190 Fleta, 189 Herbert, 189 James Ernst, 189 Joachim, 189 Margarita, 189 Phyllis, 189 190 Raymond, 189 190 Robin, 190 Rosemary, 190 Ruth, 189 190 Sherwyn, 189 Shirley, 189 William, 189

HEDDING Andrea, 324

HEDSTROM Carol, 469 471 472 Ethel, 472 Rudy, 472

HEEFNER Jeffery, 56 Kara Marie, 56 Leslie Anne, 56 Timothy Allen, 56

HEEZEN Jolene, 498

HEGEWALD Anna, 562 Augusta, 85 Edward, 85 Emma, 85 Geraldine, 541 Magdalena, 85 Robert, 85

HEGGEN Miriam Kareen, 439 441

HEHN Hulda, 137 Mary, 128

HEIBENTHAL Martha, 263

HEIBER Catherine, 333

HEIDE Gertrud, 179 Gertud, 164 171 175

HEIDEN Betty Jo, 431

HEIDKE Lisa, 469

HEIDTKE Lisa, 472

HEIKEN Ruth Ann, 48 233

HEILMAN Barbara, 452 Elisabeth, 426 N N, 452

HEIN Andrew, 284 Carrie May, 272 274 275 282 284

HEINDRICH Anna Maria, 426 428 Heinrich, 426

HEINEMAN Amy Ann, 163 Ann Lee, 163 Eugene, 163 173 Jeanne K, 163 Jeanne Kay, 173

HEINRICH Alfred, 190 Amanda, 190 Arthur, 190 August, 190 Charles, 515 191 Clara, 190 Daisy, 190 Edith, 191 Elsie, 191 Emma, 190 Ethel, 191 Frank, 191 Frederich, 190 George, 190 Gustav, 190 Hattie, 190 Howard, 191 Jennie, 191 Laura, 191 Laurance, 190 Mabel, 191 Mae, 190 Mary, 190 Matilda, 190 Meta, 190 Myrtle, 191 Raymond, 191 Susan, 190 Tilla, 191 515 Wallace, 191 William, 190

HEISE Jayne Helen, 232 Robert, 233

HEISEL John E Jr, 540 Lynnette, 540

HEISTOFFER Allison Ann, 549 Kelly Rae, 549 Steven James, 549

HEITMAN Vera, 234

HEITMANN Alice, 191 Alvena, 191 Caroline, 191 Cecilia, 191 Edna, 191 Elmer, 191 192 Francis, 192 Gale, 191 Heinrich, 191 Herman, 191 Jean, 191 Johann, 191 John, 192 302 John Sr, 191 Katie, 191 Lena, 191 192 302 Louis, 191 Louise, 192 Luke, 191 Margretha, 191 Maria, 191 Martin, 191 Mary, 191 192 Neill, 191 Sue, 191 Wilhelm, 191 Will, 191

HEITSCHUSEN Anna, 226 Erwin George William, 17 Herman F, 226 Karen Marie, 226 Kaye Ann, 226 Madora Gesina, 17 Milda Katherine, 226 Phyllis Jane, 17 Willard Anton, 226

HEITSHUSAN Phyllis Jane, 19

HEITSHUSEN Karen, 576 Karen Marie, 192 Kaye Ann, 192 Milda Katherine, 192 431 Willard Anton, 192 432

HEITZ John A, 209 Linda Marie, 19 209 Mary Lou, 209

HELDT Julie Kay, 102

HELM Esther, 488 James, 507 Katherine Ann, 507 Michael, 507 Nancy Jo, 507 Rebecca, 507

HEMESATH May Elizabeth, 210

HEMME Anna, 321 Henry, 321

HENDERICKSON Alvin, 289 Elizabeth, 205 Joel H, 289 Liberta Sue, 289

HENDERSON Bradley Allen, 482 Laura, 314 Patricia Lynn, 482

643

HESSE Adam, 298 Anna Christina, 586
Christina, 588 Cynthia Jo, 308 309
Elizabeth, 298 Emilie, 198 365 578 579
581 583 587 Helene, 198 578 Johann
Heinrich, 586 Jutta Erika, 52 Karoline,
578 Kristi, 243 478 Marie, 198 578
Marie Christina, 586 587 Matthew, 478
Mike, 243 478 Nancy, 145 180 Peter,
578 Simon, 198 Wilhelm, 198 578
HESSENIUS Elsie, 465 466 Gesina, 53
198 332 Heinrika, 198 Henry, 198
Herman, 53 198 332 John, 198
Margaret, 198 Marie J, 198 332
Minnie, 53 54 198 N N, 414 Tillie, 414
HETTINGER Clara, 529 Dea, 143 394
HEUP Bertha Wilhelmina, 31 33 35
HEYER Amanda, 200 Augusta, 199 200
Bernard Jr, 187 Bertha, 200 Brenda,
187 Brenda Ann, 460 Carl, 199 Eileen,
187 Elisabeth, 199 Ferdinand, 200
Herman, 200 Julie, 187 Julie Ann, 460
Katherine, 368 370 Katrina, 199 Louis,
200 Louise, 199 Ludwig Jr, 199
Ludwig Sr, 199 200 Margaretha, 199
200 Paul, 200 Phillip, 199 200
Wilhelm, 199 Wilhelmina, 13
Wilhelmina, 14 Wilhelmina, 199 200
HEYWOOD Jessica Jean, 134 Leslie
Arnold, 134
HICE Patricia Lois, 45 441
HICKEY Ellen, 513 Rose, 513 515
William, 513
HICKMAN Elizabeth, 513 N N, 513
HICKS Elizabeth, 365
HIGGENS E Faye, 547
HIGGINS Beverly Mae, 512 E Faye, 549
HILDEBRAND Clarence, 380 Margie J,
378-380
HILDEBRANT Margie J, 380
HILL Audrey Louise, 150 182 200 Eddie,
150 Elizabeth Ann, 150 200 Erin
Michelle, 150 Laura Kristin, 150
Robert E, 150 182 200 Waneita, 150
HILLE Fredricka, 114
HILSABECK Carol Ann, 341 David, 341
HIMMAH Andrea Ellen, 232
HIMMELSBACH Jane, 505 N N, 505

HINES Heather Louise, 484 Meredith
Katherine, 484 Sarah Louise, 484 490
HINRICHS Esther, 374 Howard, 374 John,
562 Mildred A, 562
HINTON Dustin Arlo, 91 Nicole Renee, 91
HINTZE Christine, 255 258 David Alan,
86 423 Liza Ann, 86 Mary Elizabeth,
52 Michelle Lynn, 87 Peter John, 52
Sharon, 86 Sharon Laverna, 423
HIRSCHBERG Carolyn Jean, 403
HITCHINGS Lori, 48
HIXON Dale, 463 Edna, 463 Haddy, 463
Keith, 463 Marvin, 463
HOCKADAY Lettie, 115
HOCKEN Harlan, 370 Mark William, 370
Ruth, 370
HOCKING Doug, 349 Pattilee Renae, 349
HODGE PEPMEYER Marvel, 545
HODSON Genevieve, 212 Robert Clyde,
212 Sandra Kay, 212 213 573
HOEFS Clara, 185 Debra, 185 200
Edward, 185 Elry, 185 200 562 Esther,
185 200 562
HOEFT Anna Catherina, 521 523
HOEGER Sue, 176 490
HOEHN Phyliss, 95
HOEPPNER Arthur, 481 Hardean Hilda,
481
HOFER Jeanette, 259 591 Maria Louisa,
225 265
HOFF Gregory, 464 Julie Ann, 464 Mrs
Richard, 464 Richard, 464
HOFFMAN Anita, 200 Carol Jean, 72
Daniel, 200 Edna Margaret, 72 200
Erwin Carl, 200 Howard, 72 200
Justina Kleinsasser, 553 Kim Lee Ann,
560 Larry, 200 Margaret, 156 Nancy,
200 Paul, 560 Quinnever, 23 Rachel
Cashman, 200
HOFMANN David, 137 141 Kathleen, 137
Lawrence, 137 Nicole Suzanne, 137
141
HOGAN Kathleen, 266 276
HOHENSEE Debbie, 102
HOHL Andreas, 201 202 264 493 497
Anna Elisabeth, 497 Cath, 497
Catharina, 201 Charlotte Luise, 201
464 Heinrich, 201 497 Johann Justus,

497 Johann Justus Paulus, 201 202
Johann Peter, 201 Karolina, 201 202
348 Lina, 144 201 Luise Elisabeth, 201
202 Paulus, 201 202 348 497
Wilhelmina, 201 202 264 493 497
Wilma Karoline, 497
HOING Amy, 434 Peggy Jean, 434 436
Wilford, 434
HOLDIMAN Benjamin Thomas, 202
Dorothy Marie, 154 184 202 James,
154 184 202 Linda, 154 202 Nancy,
154 202 Paula, 154 202 Peggy Lynn,
202 Thomas, 154 202
HOLLAND Diane Kay, 581 Herbert Boyd,
325 Lynn, 581 Marianne, 323-326 330
Mary Jane, 325 Tyrone, 581
HOLLANDSWORTH Agnes, 233
HOLLEMAN Cyndi, 510
HOLLENBECK Rose Mae, 389
HOLLERMAN Cyndi, 10
HOLLEY Faye Irene, 125
HOLLIS Erick G, 240 Gregory, 240
Heather Jean, 240 Jean Ann, 240
Melinda Arlene, 240
HOLM Hedwig, 86 Katie, 191 Willie, 86
HOLMES Brian, 393 C Marie, 393 Connie,
202 394 John Richard, 202 391 393
Kathy, 260 Martha, 202 Martha R, 391
393
HOLMS Aaron, 260 Bob, 260 Christine,
260 Nephani, 260
HOLST Alfred, 202 203 Alma, 203
Andreas Julius, 204 Andrew Julius, 203
Anna, 203 Bryon, 203 Carol, 203
Christena, 203 Christina Margaretha,
204 Claus Julius, 202-204 Dora, 203
Earl, 204 Effie, 203 204 Elsabe
Margaretha, 204 Fred, 203 Frieda, 374
Hans Jurgen, 204 Harvey, 203 Hattie,
203 Hedwig, 202-204 Johann, 204
Johann Andrew, 203 Johann Andrew
Julius, 203 John, 203 204 Katherina,
204 Lester, 203 Lillie, 203 Marie, 203
Mary, 203 204 Olga, 202 Ruth, 202
Selma, 203 Stella, 202 203 Victor, 203
Victoria, 203 204 Waldo, 204 374
HOLSTENBERG Lena, 144 145
HOLT Nancy, 206 455

HOLZ Anna Katherine, 97
HOLZWORTH Alice, 118 204 553 Irene
Alice, 118 John, 118 204 553 Marcia
Ann, 118 204 Paulette Pauline, 118 204
Pauline, 118 Theador, 118 Todd
Theador, 118
HOMAN Celeste Joyce, 137 204 Cynthia
Marie, 137 204 Kathleen Jo, 137 204
Lynn Adele, 137 Mildred Arlene, 130
137 204 205 Richard Fredrick, 130 137
204 205 Susan Elisabeth, 137 Susan
Elizabeth, 205
HOMBERGER Liesel, 114
HONNEN Margaret, 314
HONNOLD Darrel L, 58 59 205 Darren L,
59 205 Kelly, 59 205 Michaela Jene,
205 Pamela Jean, 58 59 205 Rylie Jean,
205 Tamitha J, 59 205
HOOVER Helen Teegan, 276 Helen
Teegen, 266
HOPPE Sophia Marie, 71
HOPPENWORTH Bruce Allen, 341 Carol
Ann, 341 Gloria Jean, 341 Jean Marie,
336 341 Leslie Elston, 336 341
HOPPMAN Daniel J, 476 Debra, 476 478
Michael D, 476 Michael D, 478
HORSLUND Doris, 576
HORTON Dee Ann, 393 Jay Robert, 393
Marlene Ann, 386 393 Robert John,
386 393
HOUCK Nicole Elizabeth, 596 Olivia
Lauren, 596 Ronda, 596
HOUGH Kathryn, 102
HOUNKER Marie, 132
HOUSER Joan, 311
HOUSMAN Alta Maria, 266 Charles
William, 266 Loretta Mae, 266 273 276
294
HOVDE Helen Marie, 86 423
HOVE Ruth Ann, 319 497
HOWARD Gathel Edna, 141 Gaythel
Edna, 131
HOWE Chris, 469 471 Colleen, 305
Delwin, 471 Shirley, 471
HOWELL Debra Lynn, 330 Henry, 322
330 Patsy Lee, 322 330
HOYDT Delores F, 25 27 Deolores F, 176
HOYER Thea, 215

HOYT Bernadine, 391 Jennifer, 384
Terence, 384 William, 384 391
HUBBARD Amy Sue, 264 295 Caleb
Marc, 264 Craig Marc, 264 295
Hannah Sue, 264 Irma Jean, 100 149
Mary Ann, 264 Rich, 100 149 Roger,
264
HUBER Albert, 49 Anna, 555 Ashley
Elisabeth, 205 Brenda, 187 Brenda
Ann, 460 Christine Marie, 205 Curtis,
561 David, 187 Diane, 205 561 Elma,
205 552 561 Erica Kay, 458 Fred H,
555 Galynn Gary, 561 Grant Douglas,
561 Harold, 205 552 561 Harrison
James, 460 Hilda, 552 555 James, 205
561 Jeremy James, 205 Josephine, 50
561 Justin Royce, 205 Lana, 561 Laura
Elma, 205 Leola, 49 50 570 Leona, 49
50 570 Lilly, 49 Lisa, 561 Mary, 205
561 Monica, 561 Reinhold, 50 561
Royce, 561 Royce Reinhold, 205 Todd
Harold, 561 Troy Donovan, 205
HUCH Kris, 594
HUCKFELDT Gesche, 106 109 110
HUDEPHOL Misti Lynn, 232 Phil, 232
HUDSON Adeline, 219 Edna, 154 182
Everett Raymond, 62 Faith A, 295
Frank, 267 Frank Junior, 295 George,
219 Joan, 20 Judy, 219 Kenneth, 20
Kristopher Jon, 20 Marc Joel, 295
Marie, 62 Mary, 219 Minerva Ellen,
295 Nancy, 219 Ruth Marie, 267 295
Trisha Sue, 20 Wilma Henrietta, 61 62
172 Zail Howard, 295
HUEBENER Albert T, 206 276 288 Bruce
A, 206 288 Christianne, 288 Jacob A,
206 Lavonne, 206 276 288 Scott W,
288 Teresa, 206 288 Wayne S, 288
Zachariah S, 206
HUEBER Arthur Henry, 455 Frieda, 455
James Arthur, 455 Margaret, 455 Mary
Lee, 455 Milton Henry, 455 Nancy,
455
HUEBNER Arthur Henry, 68 206 455
Douglas Arthur, 206 Frieda, 68 206
455 Gere Keith, 206 Jade, 206 James
Arthur, 206 Kristin Marie, 277 310
Margaret, 206 Mary Lee, 206 321 322

Milton Henry, 206 Nancy, 206 Sloan
Elizabeth, 310 Tiffan, 206 Timothy S,
277 Timothy Sloan, 310 Virginia, 206
HUEDEPOHL Don, 555 Ruth, 555
HUFFER Duane Maynard, 296 James R,
296 Ray, 296 Robert Lloyd, 268 296
Thelma Karlein, 268 296
HUFFMAN Bonnie, 356 Carol Ann, 126
George Lowell, 125 134 Linda Jean,
125 134 Ruth Ann, 532
HUMFIELD Jacqueline, 58 59
HUMPHREY Gary, 446 Judy Ann, 446
Scott Andrew, 446 Timothy Jon, 446
HUNKER Elfrieda, 73
HUNT Mary Helene, 40
HUNTLEY Nancy Lou, 347
HUPEN Engel Magdalena, 165 168 169
HUPFELD Janice, 464 466 Janice, 377
HURD Brent Steven, 205 Christopher, 205
Collin Reed, 205 Diane, 205 561
Galynn Gary, 205 Harold, 205 Monica,
205 Steven, 205 561
HURLBERT Carol Joyce, 524 Ralph E,
524
HURN Beverly, 454 456 N N, 454
Thomas, 456 Tom, 454
HURST Charles Raymond, 440 Marcella
Jean, 272 412 417 419 440 Mary Esto,
440 Randall, 238
HUSSEY Paul Theodore, 440 Peter
Thomas Jr, 440 Peter Thomas Sr, 436
440 Phillip Timothy, 440 Rita Jane,
436 440
HUSTED Albert, 38 82 206-208 Amelia,
82 83 206 Anna, 33 38 207 208 Anna
Mae, 38 82 206-208 Anna Margaret
Elizabeth, 58 Anna Marie, 206 Anna
Marie Dolly, 38 Audry, 208 Bernice,
207 Bert, 38 82 83 206 Charles, 82 206
Dolly, 38 206 Doris, 208 Edna Frieda,
207 Edna Frieda Marie, 14 208 Edna
Grieda Marie, 15 Elizabeth, 38 207
Esther, 38 82 206 Esther R, 207 Frank,
38 207 Fred, 38 207 Frederick, 38 207
George, 207 Jennie A, 75 Jennie Alice,
38 207 211 John, 38 207 Joyce, 207
Lavern, 207 Lillian, 38 207 Lloyd, 207
Lois Catharine, 147 Lois Catherine, 58

59 208 Lucille, 207 Marjorie, 38 208
Martha, 38 Melvin, 38 208 Merle, 208
Richard, 208 Robert F, 207 Roy, 33 38
58 207 208 Stella, 38 208 Wayne, 208
William, 82 206
HUTCHINS Connie Lynn, 324 Dennis,
324 Sara Lynn, 324
HUTCHISON Marlene, 209
HUTTON Laura E, 449
HUYCK Barbara Ann, 491 Terryl, 491
HUYCK-MORREISSEY Anthony A, 491
Heidi, 491 Morgan, 491 Sarah, 491
Taylor, 491
IBEL Anna Katerina, 422 479 482 483
Anna Katherina, 221 480 Katerina, 567
IBELSHASER Irmgard, 464
IBELSHAUSER Irmgard, 464
IBIS Arthur, 50 Charles, 50 208 Cynthia,
50 Ivan, 50 208 570 Luke, 208 Olga,
50 208 570 Sandria, 50 208 Sara, 50
Sara Ann, 208
ILTEN August, 228 Fred, 228 Helen, 228
Lee, 228 Meta, 228 Olga, 228
IMHOFF Gloria, 375 590
IMHOFF Kathryn Ann, 375 Mark, 375 590
IMMECK Ada, 561 Christine, 561
Elisabeth, 560 565 Emma, 560
Herman, 560 Jeanette, 560 Justus, 560
565 Luise, 561 Maria, 561 Martha, 560
Martin, 561 Wilhelmine, 561 William,
561
INMAN Alex Michael, 209 Brenda Lee, 19
208 David Robert, 19 208 Denise Ann,
19 209 Flossie Muriel, 19 Joshua
David, 208 Karen Margaret, 18 19 209
Karen Margert, 208 Lee Alan, 19 209
Linda Marie, 19 209 Marcus Alan, 209
Myron Clarence, 19 Nancy Ann, 19
209 Roger Earl, 18 19 208 209 Seth
Allen, 209
IRVIN Bryan, 388 David, 388 Faythe, 388
Michael, 388 Timothy, 388
ISBELL Edwin, 56 Jake, 261 Kristi, 56
Phyllis Jean, 56 Sherri Lynn, 261
Steven, 56
ISMALI Heather Danielle, 317 Refik, 317
IVERSON Audrey Elizabeth, 484
IWAASHASHI Mako, 21

JABENS Ann Marie, 232
JACK Jennifer, 303 Kathryn M, 87-90
Mary, 88 Niles Verne, 88
JACKSON Charlotte, 235 236
JACOB Frederika, 379
JACOBI Carolyn Ann, 532 Darold J, 532
Elizabeth, 21 Linda, 81 Tamara, 532
Timothy, 532
JACOBS Augusta, 512 Cynthia Marie, 137
204 Evan Lee, 204 Hilda Mary, 511
512 John, 512 John Benjamin, 137 204
Sara Jo, 204
JACOBSEN Alexis Katharina, 541 Alvina,
28 Connie, 452 454 Dain Glenn, 316
Erick Michael, 316 Glen Michael, 316
Gorden F, 541 Gorden J, 454 Gorden
Lewis, 133 541 Gordon Lewis, 454
James, 452 James Alan, 454 Jane
Anne, 316 Kathy Ann, 133 454 540
Lavonne Lucille, 454 541 Lawrence,
28 Luella, 322 331
JADLEY Karen, 530
JAEGER Elizabeth, 192 193
JAGER Anna Elisabeth, 334 335 348 Anna
Guida, 335 Daniel, 335
JAMES Jeffrey, 217 John, 217 Julie, 217
Karen, 217 Loraine, 337 Velma, 337
JAMMER Annette, 505 Laura, 499 Ray,
505
JANKE Brian, 59 205 Tamitha J, 59 205
Tyler Brian, 205 Wyatt Brian, 205
JANSEN Henry, 121 Katie, 467 Ladeen,
121 572 Lena, 121 Sophia, 467
JANSS Alvena, 302 William, 302
JANSSEN Alma, 209 Amelia, 252
Amerila, 209 August George, 209 250
252 Bernice, 252 Cathleen Marie, 521
Christian F, 209 252 Donella, 252
Hilbert, 252 Karl C, 209 Lawrence, 252
Mary, 252 Ruth, 252 Wilhelmine
Elizabeth, 209 250 252
JARMUTH Louise, 28
JAROCH Adam Michael, 209 Barbara, 209
Cathleen Marie, 521 Eleanor, 209 521
Eleanor Emilia, 520 524 Gordon Otto,
209 521 Judy Olive, 209 Lila, 209 521
Matthew John, 209 Molly Sue, 209
Nancy, 209 Neil Leon, 209 Otto, 209

KAMINSKI Kathleen Marie, 243 247
Susan Rae, 247
KAMMERER Brian Michael, 58 Carol
Ann, 56 Diane, 58 Harold, 56 501
Kelly, 58 Lori, 58 Luanne, 58 Melinda,
58 Phyllis Jean, 56 57 Ronald Harold,
58 Ruth, 56 501
KAMMEYER Tracie Ann, 160 Tracie
Ann, 173
KAMPHAUS Virginia, 518
KANE Eileen, 163 579
KANESS Sue Ellen, 523
KANKE Agatha, 218 Brenda, 217 Brett,
217 Carly, 218 Chad, 217 Danny, 217
Darrel, 217 Dean, 217 Deborah, 217
Dennis, 217 Dick, 217 Donald, 217
Dora, 217 Dorothy, 217 Frederick, 217
Frederick August, 217 Fredrick August,
217 Friederich, 217 Gidget, 217 Glenn,
217 Gordon, 217 Irene, 217 Janet, 217
Janice, 217 Jean, 217 Jennifer, 217 Jeri,
217 Jessica, 217 Jock, 218 Joe, 217
John, 217 Jolene, 217 Karen, 217
Kathy, 218 Kendra, 217 Kenneth, 217
Kevin, 217 Kody, 218 Lavonne, 217
Linda, 218 Mabel, 217 Marcella, 217
Martha, 217 Melissa, 217 Michael, 217
Myron, 217 218 Penny, 217 Scott, 217
Shana, 217 Sheryl, 217 Stacy, 218
Steven, 217 Sue Ann, 218 Thomas, 217
Tiffany, 217 Veda, 217 218 Vernon,
217 Warren, 217 Wayne, 217 218
Wilhelmina, 217 William, 217
KANMIN Mary, 165 Wilhelm Christopher,
165 Will, 165
KAPFER Margaret Judith, 13 135
KAPUCIAN Betty, 498
KARAM George, 465 Susan, 465
KARG Eleonora, 87
KARR Albert Raymond, 541 Betty June,
541 Brenda Jo, 462 541 Christina
Marie, 461 Deborah Lynn, 218 541
Debra, 515 Debra Lynn, 514 Dennis
Leroy, 218 421 462 541 Jo Ann, 218
421 462 541 Michael Dennis, 461 541
Shelby Joe, 461
KARSTEN Alfred, 555 Lorene, 555
KASPER Julie Lynn, 43 Michael Justin, 43

KATH Ann Elisabeth, 69 Anna, 69 71
Paul, 69
KATZ Amanda, 230 Anita, 230 Anna M,
219 230 235 Arthur, 218 219 230
Bernice Marie, 218 Cora Ann, 218 219
230 Dorothy, 34 Emma, 230 Ernestine
Mary, 230 Fred, 230 Heinrich
Chrisoph, 219 Heinrich Christoph, 230
235 Henry, 230 Ida Dorothea, 230
Johann Heine, 230 Lawrence, 230
Leona, 230 Leona Mae, 218 576 Louis
Otto, 230 Marie Sophie, 230 Marilyn
Ann, 218 Martha, 34 Martha Mary, 230
Mathilda E, 230 Mildred, 230 Myles,
230 Ralph, 230 Ruth Lillian, 219
Sophia Dorathea, 219 230 Tillie, 230
Tina, 230 William, 230 Wm, 34
KAUFMAN John L, 179 Nancy Lue, 179
KAUFMANN A Martha, 450
KAY Ellen, 476 478 James R, 476 Janice,
331 Johanna, 356 Steven R, 476 478
KEARNS Alicia Lynn, 14 519 Clara, 373
Connie, 288 Dick, 519 Dixie, 519 Milo,
288 373
KEENAN Anna, 199 Indiana, 199
KEENON Denette Helen, 319 Steven, 319
KEIPER Alma M, 219 222 241 Amanda,
228 Ann, 225 Anna, 222 224 228 Anna
Elizabeth, 225 228 264 279 August,
228 Barbara Jane, 227 Barbra Jane, 220
Becky, 225 Bernard, 228 Bernice, 228
Bertha, 167 228 Betty Jane, 220 223
224 226 227 310 431 Bonnie Lynn, 220
223 226 Caitlin Ann, 227 Callan Mae,
227 Cameron James, 227 Carolena, 228
Caroline, 222 Caroline (Lena), 467
Carolina (Lena) B 377 465 466 465
Cheryl, 225 227 Corrine Elsie, 219 220
518 Crystal, 225 227 Delores Irene,
220 223 224 431 Donald Ray, 220 227
Douglas Elton, 220 223 226 Elizabeth,
222 Ella Charlotte, 221 226 227 431
Elmer Henry John, 219 220 222 227
413 497 Esto Magdalene, 210 221 431
Florence, 228 Frances Magdalene, 222
Frances Magdalene Elizabeth Anna,
219 220 222 227 413 497 Fred J, 225
Frederich Jr, 484 Frederick, 222 468

651

Frederick Carl, 221 226 227 Carolina
(Lena) B 377 465 466 Frederick John,
228 264 279 Frederick Jr, 219-223 225
431 Frederick Sr, 221 222 228 557
Frieda, 221 222 270 Fritz, 221
Germaine, 225 Gertrude, 272 Gertrude
Marie, 228 420 457-460 463 Greg, 225
Harriet Charlene, 220 222 309 412 413
429 Hattie, 469 470 Hattie A, 222 223
468 469 Heidi, 223 Heidi Mae, 576
Henry Conrad, 221 223 226 227 431
Hilda, 224 298 Hulda J, 222 223 240
Irvin George, 220 223 224 431 James
Charles, 223-225 227 Janice Irene, 223
224 Jayme, 225 Jayson, 224 Jeanne,
224 Jim, 303 John, 222 224 298 John
George, 224 Josephine Magdalene, 220
Julie Ann, 223 224 June Ann, 224 227
403 Kaitlin, 226 Kate, 220 Katharina,
221 228 557 Katherina, 222 Katherina
Christina Magdalena, 221 227
Katherina Christina Magdalene, 226
Katherina (Katie) Christina Magdalene,
430 431 Katherine, 166 228 460 Katie,
221 226 227 Kimberly, 224 Kristin
Frances, 228 Lawrence J, 225 227 265
Lila M, 222 Lori Sue, 224 225 Louis,
225 265 Lydia, 226 Magdalena, 219-
223 225 431 468 484 Magdalene
Lillian, 222 225 Maj Matthew Clark,
226 Margaret, 228 Maria, 227 228
Maria (Mary) Elizabeth Gertrude, 460
466 Maria Elizabeth Gertrude, 148 222
228 Maria Louisa, 225 265 Marie, 225
265 Mark Andrew, 220 Mary, 222 228
Mary Elizabeth, 225 Matthew Clark,
220 Melanie Suzanne, 220 Meta, 228
Milda Katherine, 192 226 431 Nancy,
590 Nancy Lynne, 226 227 582 583
OJ, 228 Olga, 228 Oswald John Tobias,
228 Otto, 228 Patricia Lou, 221 226
Paula Jo, 220 226 Raymond Conrad,
220 223 224 226 Raymond Conrad
William, 227 310 431 Richard, 224
Sara Jane, 220 Scott Allan, 223 227
576 Sharon Kay, 221 227 Sherry, 225
Stan, 225 227 Steven, 225 Susan, 227
Susan Trachta, 221 Terry, 225 Timothy

Lynn, 221 227 Valentine, 148 222 225
228 460 466 467 Valentine II, 228
Wendy, 224 303 Wendy Kay, 223-225
227 Wilhelmina, 74 222 553 557 558
560 566 567 570 571 Wilma, 264
KEITH Stacy, 307 319
KELL Jean Marie, 232 594
KELLER Eva Rosina, 63 64 Heather
Jeanne, 256 257 Johann Andreas, 64
Joseph Raymond, 256 257 Kate, 64
Katharina Margaretha, 64 Louis John,
257 Lydia, 212 Maria M, 458 460
Marie M, 130 Mary Elizabeth, 257
KELLERHALE Alma, 252
KELLERMAN Mary, 529
KELLEY Kimberly Christine, 482
KELLY Bernice Christene, 255-257
Clarence, 38 208 Elmer Evelyn, 256
Irene, 544 Lavonne, 208 217 Marjorie,
38 208 Mary Agnes, 214 Raymond,
544 Willa Catherine, 256
KEMERER Hazel, 332
KEMME Anna, 229 Charles, 229
Christine, 229 Chrstine, 229 Edward,
229 Elizabeth, 229 Lizzie, 229
Margaret, 229 Richard, 228 229
Virginia Marie, 229 237 238 William,
229
KENNEDY Gordon, 403 Mary Elizabeth,
403
KENNEY Cali, 52 Seth, 508 Tina Marie,
52 Tracy Lynn, 508 Trent, 52
KENTE Anna Dorothea, 364 Ludwig, 364
KENTER Alma E, 520
KERKMAN Adam, 231 Agnes, 233 Alma
Ruth, 229 236 Amelia, 116 231 233
235 475 Amelia (Emilie), 492 Amelia
Christian, 414 473-475 Amelia Rose,
231 Amy Annette, 231 Anita, 229 232
Ann Marie, 232 Anna Emelie, 229
Anna Emilie, 414 Anna K, 233 234
Anna M, 219 230 235 Anna Martha,
230 231 234 235 503 514 554 566
Arthur Martin, 230 231 414 554 575
Barbara, 229-233 235 256 261 413 474
575 592 Bertha, 232 234 321 Blanche,
234 Bonnie, 230 234 Bryan Keith, 233
Carl Edward, 230 233 236 250 251

KIENOW Ruth, 563
KIERNAN Joseph Francis, 490 Laura Etta, 490
KIERNAN SHIPLEY Joan Marie, 490
KIESEL Augusta, 60 Emma, 60
KIETZMAN Magdalena, 553 572
KIKLAS Loree, 529
KILAWEE Cathy, 117 Kevin, 117
KILBERG Barbara Ann, 457
KILBERGER Linda Jean, 110 111
KILBERGER Marlene, 111 Marvin, 111
KILNER Lizzie, 285
KIMM Ann Elizabeth, 554 Colton Jay, 486 Danny, 486 James Allen, 102 Jay Michael, 481 486 Karmen Noreen, 102 103 Kelsey Lee, 102 Lori, 102 Marcia, 486 Mindy Lynn, 481 486 Richard, 102 103 Silas, 548 Sonja Kay, 102 Tyler Blake, 486
KINE Henry, 83 Mary, 82-85 206
KING Barbara Joanne, 31 239 Bessie Irene, 520 Betty Ann, 148 Dawn, 308 Diana, 308 Jennifer Irene, 239 Katie, 238 Kelly Diane Kersten Hurst, 238 Kent, 238 Kersten, 238 Kevin William, 31 239 Marie R, 129 307 Martha, 471 Mary Esto, 440 Maxine, 230 233 234 236 237 Ted L, 148
KINNEY Frank Lawrence, 375 Joanne, 376 Joanne Louise, 375 June Maxine, 375
KINSER Carol, 501 Lawrence, 501 Ralph, 501 Samuel G, 501 Sandra Kay, 501
KINZENBAW Denise, 217
KINZENBOM Denise, 434
KIRBY Sandra L, 387 594
KIRCHNER Ludwig, 238 Marie Madeleine, 238 Wihelmina, 264 Wilhemina, 238
KIRCKPATRICK Jody, 354
KIRKPATRICK Judy, 317
KIRSCHNER Catherine, 448 Ludwig, 280 Marie Madeleine, 280 Wilhelmina, 280
KISLING Chari, 180
KISLING Heather, 180 Sara, 180
KITCHEN Shirley L, 42 Vicki, 49 Vicki M, 42

KITHCART Drew Allan, 461 Ernest, 461 Jackson Ernest, 461 Justin Leigh, 457 461 Kelsie Leigh, 461 Ladonna, 461 Lori Sue, 457 461
KITTING Anna Martha, 450 Joh Henrich, 450
KITZMANN Andrew, 377 Jack, 376 377 Marcie, 377 Norma Lee, 376 377 Ricky, 377
KLAMER Shannon Lee, 163 Wade, 163
KLAMMER Justin, 181 Kory Dean, 181 Shannon Lee, 181 Wade, 181
KLAR Ella Mae, 238 Elmer Jerry, 238 Eva Amelia, 238 George Wilbur, 238 Hazel Marie, 238 Jacob, 238 John, 238 Paul, 238 Paul Leroy, 238
KLATT Riva Sue, 526 536
KLAUSSEN Anna, 314
KLEIN Eva Catherine, 131-133 Ida Catherine, 448 Magdalene, 448
KLEINMAIER Joan Ruth, 58 Joseph Roger, 58 Sarah Jo, 58 Susan, 58
KLENKE Edward Fred, 405 Martha Magdalena, 405
KLEPP Louise, 412
KLINE Ada Jean, 126 Cleora, 298 Earl, 298 Hubert Husted, 126 Kelli Kathleen, 126 129 Louise, 549 M Christine, 45 441 Sherman, 549
KLING Ellen, 513 Larry, 513
KLINGE Karoline, 164 171
KLIPPE Julie, 483
KLIPPEL Anna Elisabeth, 328 Conrad, 328 Susanna, 323 325 327 328 330
KLOEPFER Kath, 313
KLOSTERMANN Anerea, 358 Anerea Leigh, 91 358 Brylee Ann, 358 Bryon, 358 Jaxon James, 91 358 Kale David, 358
KLOVER Gesina, 53 198 332
KLUDT Sally Ann, 375 556
KLUSS Emma, 359
KNAACK Elsie Barbra, 232 594 Esther, 392 Janis Mae, 594 Karolyn, 385 392 Kathryn, 385 Keith, 385 392 Myron Walter, 232 594 Nancy, 594 Ronald Myron, 594 Ryan Heins, 594 Sharon, 594 Sheryl, 594 Suzanne, 594

KNAAK Henretta (Hettie), 492 Jacob, 492 Johanna, 492
KNAIN Ione, 84
KNAUFF Barbara Joanne, 31 239 Daniel James, 31 David Alan, 31 239 Eunice Maye, 31 33 239 Evelyn Ruth, 31 239 Gregory Charles, 239 Jonathan Mark, 32 Karen Maye, 31 239 Sharon Ruth, 31 239 Theodore Charles, 31 33 239
KNEELAND Mary Lou, 311
KNEESKERN Jenny, 452 William, 452
KNIEF Edward George Friederich, 340 Edwin George Friedrich, 334 Hilda, 334 Hilda Anna Marie Sophia, 334 340
KNIGHT Lela Jean, 133
KNIPFEL Debbie, 153 511 Tamara Kay, 511
KNIPP Betty, 284 Betty Ann, 274 275 293 Janice, 242 Marilyn, 242 Russell, 242
KNOCK Alvena, 39 Harvey, 444 Pauline Wilhelmine Louise, 444
KNOKE Christina Margaretha, 204 Wilhelm, 204
KNOLL Cynthia Marie, 245
KNOX Geraldine, 150 158 Philip, 158 Russell, 150 158
KNUCKEY Bonnie Jo, 136 Richard Brook, 136
KNUDSON Michael, 121 Micheal Jr, 121 Nancy Ann, 121 Suzanne Elaine, 121
KNUTH Anna, 522 Anna A, 521 523 525 Charles, 568 Charles Frank, 1 239 240 Clara, 7 8 Elizabeth, 16 Emma, 1 Irvin, 16 James, 582 Mary, 1 239 240 568 Michelle, 582 Viola, 239 563 568 572 573 Wilhelmina, 239 240 William, 239
KOBER Anna Catharina, 428 Anna Maria, 426 428 Anna Marie, 425 Maria Margaretha, 428 Peter, 428
KOCH Jennie, 12 Jes Rosen, 450 Katie, 285 Magdalena, 450 Martha, 300 Sophia, 232 581 Wigand, 450
KOEHL Anna Marie, 64 J Martin, 64
KOEHN Allene Deanna, 219 240 241 Alma M, 219 222 241 Arlene Claire, 223 240 Bill, 219 240 241 Hulda J, 222 223 240 John H, 222 223 240 Karen Lee, 240 241 Kraig William, 241

Kristen Deann, 240 241 Leota, 219 240 Merlon F, 223 Merrell, 219 William G, 219 222 241 William George Jr, 219 240 241 Zoe Kathleen, 223
KOELLE Caroline, 373 374
KOELLING Florene, 163 180 183
KOENEMAN Jan Elizabeth, 491
KOENEMAN Jenna, 491 Rick, 491
KOENIG Dawn Marie, 10 Marie Agnes, 132 Matt, 10
KOENNING Katherine Marie, 377
KOEP Amelia, 6 8 241 Dorothy, 6 241 Jean, 6 Louis, 6 8 241 Mildred, 6 241 Stanley, 6
KOERING Andrew Lee, 241 Arthur Carl, 125 130 241 Darlene Elizabeth, 125 130 241 James Arthur, 125 241 Jason Andrew, 242 Jeffrey Allen, 125 Jerald Arthur, 242 Kathleen Marie, 125 241 Kathy Marie, 125 241 Kelly Ann, 241 Lester H, 125 241 Sally, 125
KOERNER Helen, 119
KOESTER Amanda Gesina Rebecca, 19 Heidi Marie, 202 Jerry, 154 202 Nancy, 154 202 Shelly Lynn, 202
KOHLER Anna Marie, 206 Anna Marie Dolly, 38 Dolly, 38 206 Eugene, 38 206 Lillian, 206 Lucille, 206 Madeline, 206
KOKEMILLER Anna Katherine, 135 355 356 Elizabeth Salome, 124 125 130 137 140 Fred, 164 Katherina Elisabeth, 164
KOLSTED Teresa, 511
KOLSTROM Augusta Christine, 274
KONRAD James, 177 181 Kyle Leon, 181 Ronda, 177 181
KONSTANZ Alvina, 552 558 563 572 Emil, 572 Esther, 572
KOOPMAN Agnes, 247 Agnes Emma, 244 246 461 502 Alfred Otto, 242 243 247 566 Anne, 245 Annie C, 244 247 Betty Jean, 3 242 244 Brenda Ann, 242 Carolyn, 246 Charles Leroy, 242 Cynthia Marie, 245 246 Dale Wayne, 242 247 Daniel Ray, 242 Dean Edward, 242 Delbert, 242 243 Delores, 243 244 478 Dennis Lee, 242 Donald John, 243

23 Fritz, 23 Irene, 469 470 Julie, 142
143 Kenneth, 23 441 Leo, 468 470
Mardeen, 468 Maria, 90 Marilyn, 468
Marlys, 468 Monica, 468 Olive, 23
Rachel, 91 Robin, 468 Roger, 468 Rose
Ann, 290 441 Rosena Louisa, 1 239
546 Russel, 468
KRANTZ Elfrieda, 503
KRANZ Adam, 230 251 252 502 554 560
Anna, 250 560 Anna Christina, 250 553
554 565 Anne Christina, 251 Arnold,
232 Arnold J William, 250 Christina,
250 Edna A, 250 Eizabeth, 15 Elfrieda
M, 502 Elfrieda Martha, 250 Elisabeth,
250 Elizabeth, 16 17 74 193 251 423
487 554 Emma, 230 250-252 502 554
560 Erna Martha Matilda, 232 233
George, 250 554 560 565 George C M,
250 George Jr, 251 252 George Sr, 251
Heinrich George, 250 Hilda, 250-252
Hulda C, 250 Johann, 554 John, 251
Joyce, 251 252 Kathy Jo, 252 Lydia M,
250 Lydia Martha Marie, 230 233 236
251 Maria A, 250 Mariam Jean, 252
Marie Chris, 74 Mark Wilbert, 252
Martin Lee, 252 Merlon G, 251 252
Steven Marion, 252 Viola Martha, 233
Wilbert E, 251 Wilhelmine Elizabeth,
209 250 252
KRAUSE Brenda, 512 Elizabeth Joy, 208
Eric, 512 Gary, 512 Gorden, 50 208
Heather, 512 Johanna, 284 Michael,
512 Sandria, 50 208
KRAUSHAAR Johannes, 279 Karin, 121
533 Marie Elisabeth, 278 279 286
KRAY Bernie, 253 254 Dallas, 252 254
David Roberts, 254 Delbert, 96 253
Edith, 254 Elizabeth, 253 254 380
Elsie, 96 97 253 254 Elsie Elizabeth,
254 522 525 Esther Mae, 254 Fred,
252-254 380 Frederick, 254 George
Arthur, 255 Harry Carl, 253 254 Helen
Lucille, 255 Jake, 252 James Earl, 254
Janet Elaine, 254 Jeffrey, 180 254
Karen, 253 Karl, 96 97 253 254 Katey
Jane, 253 Kathy, 180 253 254 Laura,
252-254 Laurie, 180 253 Meda, 253
254 Merl Andrew, 254 Meta, 254

Michael, 254 Michael J, 180 253 Pat,
252 254 Patricia Jean, 253 Rita J, 180
253 Rita Jane, 145 Rosa Marie, 253
254 379 380 Rose, 254 Rose Marie,
287 Russell Earl, 254 Ruth, 254 Ruth
Marie, 255 Tammy Sue, 252 254 Vera
Ruth, 253 254 Virgil, 96 145 180 253
254 William, 252-254 William Carl
Frederick, 253 254 William Russell,
254
KREBS Anna Martha, 69 Frederick, 69
KRECK Florentina, 477
KREEGIER Henry, 416 Viola, 416
KREGER Eleanor, 259
KREIGEL Brian Scott, 231 Jennifer Lee,
231 Shannon Mara, 231
KREIKEMEIR Charles Robert, 128
Kathryn Ruth, 128
KRETZMAN Magdelena, 552
KREUTNER Adam John, 259 Albert, 197
255 256 258 260 Anna, 145 152 168
176 182 183 261 Ardith Elizabeth, 36
255 262 Becky Ann, 257 Bernard, 255-
258 Bernice Christene, 255-257 Betty
Jo, 255 258 Bill, 261 Brandon William,
259 Brian Lee, 257 Carol Ann, 255 256
Christine, 255 258 Clara, 229 Clara,
237 256 261 414 Clarence, 256 259
261 Cynthia, 255 Dana Therese, 258
David Lee, 255-257 Dawn Marie, 258
Debra Jo, 258 Delaine, 454 455 591
Derek Sean, 256 Diane, 256 257
Donald, 255 256 Donna Jean, 258
Doris Mae, 257 Eileen Freida, 257
Eileen Frieda, 262 Elizabeth, 253 254
261 380 Emma, 68 Emma A, 454
Emma Anna, 256 261 454-456 Floyd,
257 261 Gary Lee, 258 Gerald William,
257 262 Heather Jeanne, 256 257
Helen, 256 259 261 Henry Adam Sr,
261 Henry Jr, 256-258 260 Henry Sr,
150 255 257 261 Henry St, 591 James,
255 258 James David, 258 Janet, 255
256 Jay Robert, 256 Jean, 261 Jeanette,
259 591 Jeanne, 255 258 Jennifer
Christine, 257 Jeremy Michael, 260
John Edward, 258 591 Joyce, 256 259
Julie Marie, 260 Karl Lee, 258 Kristi,

659

Larry, 288 Laura Suzanne, 346 Lauren
Elizabeth, 285 Lavonne, 206 276 288
Leola Anna Elizabeth, 195 270 277 284
296 Leona A, 286 288 384 Lexa Rae,
294 Libbie, 378 Libbie Ann, 268 269
277 284 289 293 295 Liberta Sue, 269
289 Linda Marie, 270 278 Lindsey
Christine, 285 Lizzie, 285 Lloyd, 288
Logan John, 285 Lola Maye, 29 263
274 287 295 Loretta Mae, 266 273 276
294 Louisa, 264 265 274 Louise, 161
278 281 285 290 Louise Elizabeth, 283
289 410 419 420 427 431 442 Louise
Marie, 433 Louise Marie Katherine,
284 289 424 429 441 443 Lucille, 285
Lucy Isabelle, 263 283 292 293 Lyle,
288 Margaret, 291 Margaret Jean, 273
296 Margaret Lovaire, 290 297
Margrate Rebecca, 264 295 Maria
Elisabeth, 279 Marie Elisabeth, 278
286 Marjorie Ann, 288 Mark A, 288
Martha, 263 404 Martha E, 286 Martha
Elisabeth, 279 286 Martin, 263 290
Marvin, 290 Mary, 265 278 285 404
Mary Ann, 268 284 292 Mary Jane,
264 274 275 277 287 288 294-296
Mary Janette, 291 297 595 Matthew
Martin, 295 Maynard Clarence, 268
291 Melissa Lynn, 274 Melvin August,
268 284 291 Minnie, 404 Nadine, 291
Nadine Marcel, 262 276 292 Nettie L,
285 292 383 384 388 390 394 Noreen
Etta, 263 292 Otto, 285 Owen Russell,
296 Pamela May, 275 293 Patricia Lou,
75 268 293 Phyllis Catherine, 263 293
537 538 Rachel Marie, 278 Randall
Ray, 3 270 293 294 Randell Ray, 2
Raymond Henry, 266 294 Rebecca,
294 Rena, 266 294 Renee, 288 Reva
Marjorie, 294 Rhonda Kaye, 287 296
Richard Allan, 270 293 294 Rita Rae,
294 Roger, 346 Roger Gerhardt, 264
274 275 Rogert Gerhardt, 294 Ronda
Lee, 269 295 Rose, 285 Roy, 285 Ruth
Marie, 267 295 Ryan Randall, 294
Sarah Marie, 295 296 Sheila Ann, 2
270 294 Sheryl Kay, 275 Shiela Ann, 3
Sophia, 404 Stephanie, 296 Stephen

Martin, 264 295 Steve Roger, 346
Steven John, 287 296 Sue, 346 Tamara
Suzanne Leisner, 274 295 Thelma
Karlein, 268 296 Thomas, 288 Tobias,
278 Travis James A, 296 Trevor James,
294 Troy Lee, 273 296 Tyler James,
277 Vera Eloise, 266 Vickie, 268 291
Virgil Irvin, 277 287 288 295 296
Virginia, 267 Virginia Beverlyn, 269
272 274 Walter, 285 Walter W A, 268
114 271 276 290 291 297 365 Weston,
296 Wihelmina, 264 Wilhelmina, 24
259 261 264 280 281 297 342 343 345
352 454 567 Wilhemina, 238 William,
297 William August, 40 William
Henry, 282 Zachary Caleb, 296
KRUG PALEN Margaret Lovaire, 365
KRUGER Ana Dorthea, 521 Clara, 28
Harrison, 28
KRUKOW Cory Jon, 347 Julie Kay, 347
355 Kellie Jane, 347 Mitchell, 347 355
Ryan Mitchell, 347
KRUMHOLTZ Kimberly, 56
KRUMM Amy, 299 Andrew, 299 Anna,
224 298 299 Barbara, 298 299 Berhta,
117 Bertha, 299 Bertha Katherine, 75
298 299 Caroline, 299 Christina, 299
Cleora, 298 Dero J, 298 Elizabeth
Veronica, 76 298 299 Fred, 299
George, 299 Jacob, 117 Jacob Jr, 75 76
298 299 Jacob Sr, 298 299 Katherine,
299 Lena, 299 Lola, 117 298 299 560
Louise, 299 Marcy, 299 Martin, 299
Melinda, 117 299 Michael, 117 299
Milton, 117 298 299 560 Opal, 298
Rosa, 299 William, 299
KRUMREI Benjamin Richard, 487 David
Wayne, 486 487 Mary Margaret, 487
Nathaniel David, 487 Richard Robert,
487 Sara Marie, 486 487
KRUSE Bonnie Jean, 126 Kerrie Sue, 126
129 Richard Wayne, 126
KRUSON Mattie, 42
KUCERA Vlasta K, 489
KUCH Alison, 300 Bradley, 300 Donald
Andrew Ernest, 32 34 299 300 Judith
Mildred, 32 34 299 300 Lisa Maree, 34
300 Lori Jo, 34 299 Mallory, 300 Marc

Donald, 34 300 Pamela Jo, 300 Pamela
Joy, 34 Sally Classen, 34 300 Terry
Lynn, 34
KUCHE Anna Gertrude, 586 Johannes, 586
KUCKER Edith, 254 Flossie Muriel, 19
KUDDING Margaret Elisabeth, 312
KUEHL Henrietta, 14
KUEKER Karla, 349
KUELPER Henry, 27 Mary, 27 Naomi
Grace, 25 27 176
KUENY Edward, 373 Elizabeth, 373
KUESPERF Heidi S, 155
KUHL Albert, 300 Anna, 300 Bernice
June, 481 Frank, 300 Henrietta, 300
Henry, 300 Herman, 300 Jochim, 300
Lulu, 300 Margaret Sindt, 300 Martha,
300 Rosa, 195 300 467
KUHNHOLZ Henry, 390
KULISH Viola Gertrude, 65 Wencil, 65
KULKARNI Joyce Gertrude, 128 133
Kimberly Kumud, 133 Shirkant
Vishnu, 133 Shrikant, 128 Sonya Carol,
133 Sushila, 133 Vishnu, 133
KUMMER Bertha Marie, 269
KUNCH Eldon George, 233 Mary Ann,
231 233 236 237
KUNSTOF Emma, 166
KUNSTORF Anna, 300 301 Carol, 301
468 Charles, 300 301 468 474
Charlotte, 301 Curtis, 301 Dora, 300
301 Elizabeth, 300 301 Emma, 300
Evelyn, 26 301 Everett, 301 Henry, 300
301 Ida, 300 Jane, 300 301 474 Mabel,
301 May, 301 Minnie, 301 Nancy, 301
Timothy, 301 Todd, 301 Wilhelmina,
566 571 William, 300
KURG Delores Ann, 101
KURTENBACH Chase, 574 Kalvin, 552
574 Magen Adair, 574 Tamara Lynn,
552 574
KUSCHNEREIT Ann, 227
LACHENMAIER Denise M, 348
LACHENMIER Denise, 337 348
LACKNEY Gertrude Ilene, 122 137 Patricia
Ann, 122 137 William Edward, 122
LADUE Jolene, 451 Wayne, 451
LAGESCHULTE James, 510 Martha, 510

LAHAMMER Brianna Kay, 492 Galen,
492 Jodie Lynn, 492 Peggy Jean, 492
Scott Carey, 492
LAHAN Margaret, 499
LAHN Alfred Hans, 302 Alvena, 302
Beverly, 302 Christine, 302 David, 302
Diane, 302 Donna, 302 Doris, 302
Evelyn, 302 Fred, 191 Fredrich, 302
Fredrick, 302 Frerick, 302 Irene, 302
Jack, 302 James, 302 Jean, 302 John
David, 302 John F, 302 Lena, 191 302
Leslie, 302 Ordinancy, 302 Pamela,
302 Peter, 302 Roger Johnson, 302
Sam, 302 Sarah, 302 Sharon, 302
Susan, 302 Victor Fredrick, 302
Weibke, 302
LAMB Anne, 504 Heather Elsia, 504
Kenneth Cecil, 504 Lisa K, 391
Monica, 504
LAMBRECT Amoret Margaret, 527 Jacob
Harvey, 527 Larry D, 527 Victoria, 527
LAMEN Diana Lee, 592
LANDAU A, 496 Anke, 578 Ann
Elisabeth, 69 70 Anna, 347 494 495
Anna Guida, 585 590 Cath Luise, 590
Elke, 578 Heinrich, 578 Marie, 66 67 N
N, 590
LANDREY Bernie, 253 254
LANDRUS Amy Lee, 91 Dennis Leroy, 20
90 Diana Elaine, 20 90 Holly Renee, 91
Lindsey Kay, 91 Ronald, 90 Virginia,
91
LANDSDOWN Gregory K, 230 Tara L,
230
LANE Robin, 385 510
LANEN Diana Lee, 584
LANG Edna, 143 Glen, 143 Patricia, 143
Thomas, 143 Wilhelmena, 506
LANGE Aaron Michael, 303 Alice, 367
Andrew James, 367 Angela Christine,
302 304 April Ann, 303 305 Cindy,
304 481 Cynthia Diane, 302 304 419
Darci Nicole, 304 David Henry, 303
304 Dorothy, 289 420 Dorothy
Catherine, 289 Dorothy Katherine, 303
304 419 Drew David, 303 Emily, 366
504 Emily Suzanne, 303 Eric John, 303
Fred, 366 504 Fred Lawrence, 367

LEBESCAT Jean (John), 433 Marie, 433
Paulette Marie, 433 438
LECLERE Mary, 252
LECRAW Adrienne, 175 307 Donald, 175
John E, 175 184 307 Lydia, 174 184
307
LEDDER Charles, 269 289 John Robert,
289 Liberta Sue, 269 289 Matthew, 289
LEE Alex Jordan, 126 Debra Sue, 126 134
Heather Marie, 101 Irma Jean, 100 149
Jack Swaney, 126 Jason Alan, 100 Jean
Lee, 101 Keith Allen, 100 149 Linda R
I, 194 Richard Leslie, 126 134 Ruby
Ann, 126 Suzanne Nicole, 126
LEFEBURE Debbie, 53
LEHUE Betty Louise, 158 177
LEICK Carol June, 449 Melvin Louis, 449
LEIDIGH Ashley Nicole, 307 John
William, 171 Judith Kay, 171 180 Judy
Kay, 307 Kim Ellen, 26 171 Laurie
Ann, 171 Lisa L, 171 Nathan Ray, 307
Russell Clare, 171 180 307 Thomas
Russell, 171 Timothy Ray, 26 87 171
307
LEIGH Allyson, 431
LEIMBERER Reta, 16 193
LEININGER Anna Magdalina, 348 Anna
Martha, 588 Johann Heinrich, 588
LEINWEBER Anna Elisabeth, 85
Emanuel, 85 Katharina Elisabeth, 85
Katherina Elisabeth, 328
LEISINGER Barbara, 510 Cheryl, 510
Darlene, 510 Darlene Gladys, 156
Keith, 511 Leah, 510 Leonard, 156 510
Martha, 510
LEISNER Frank, 274 Sharon, 274
LEISS Catharine, 495
LEITNER Harold Louis, 449 Mary
Frances, 449
LEMBKE Ella Sophie, 377 Ella Sophie,
379 John, 377 Sophia, 377 Verlyne,
521
LEMKE Waldena Helen, 138
LENABURG Alma, 129 Amelia Louise,
308 Carisza Marie, 308 Craig Louis,
129 307 Edward Theodore, 129
Geraldine Edna, 129 131 307 308
Henry Kai, 308 Kay Louis, 129 131

307 308 Keith Louis, 129 308 Lelia,
308 Marie R, 129 307 Marta Christine,
308 Zay Christine, 129 308
LENSCH Alex Jo, 308 Anna Jo, 308 309
August Louis, 311 Ava Charlene, 308
Bertha, 311 Bettie, 308 310 311 Bettie
Philomena, 227 Betty Jane, 220 223
224 226 227 310 431 Brian Charles,
311 Catherine, 309 310 311 466 Chad
Michael, 308 309 Charles Edward, 277
308-311 472 Christine, 309 311 Clara,
309 Clara Ida, 93 309 311 Cynthia Jo,
308 309 David Charles, 275 277 308-
310 Dennis Paul, 308 413 429 Doris
Mae, 277 308-311 472 Dorothy, 309
311 Esther, 309 Harold, 309 Inez Mae,
275-277 308 Inez Marie, 310 Joan, 311
John, 308 310 311 John Harry, 93 227
309 Jolene, 308 Jolene Ann, 308 309
413 Kenneth, 311 Kristin Marie, 277
310 Leslie, 309 Lori Ann, 277 310
Louis, 85 310 311 458 Louis William,
458 Margaret, 311 Mary, 310 Mary
Lou, 311 Matilda, 85 310 311 458
Tilly, 85 310 311 Tonya Leigh, 311
Wayne Allen, 309 311 William, 311
William Matthew, 309 310 311 Wilma,
457 Wilma Augusta, 304 310 458-461
LENZ Catherine Louise, 94 412 438
Louise, 412 William Frederich, 412
LEOFFLER Betty Lou, 390
LEONHARDI ----, 585
LERCH Annthaneeya, 102 Jeremy, 102
Sonja Kay, 102
LESS Josephine, 192 Kaye Ann, 192 226
Rachel Ann, 192 Richard Allen, 192
226 Ryan Allen, 192 Vernon Charles,
192
LESTER Pamela Sue, 522
LEWIS Anthia, 106 Becky Sue, 156 171
Don, 382 Edward G Sr, 449 Frances
Kay, 448 449 Laura E, 449 Leonard,
171 Mae, 438 Shirley, 382 Verna Dean,
142 Wendy Gail, 417 423
LICHT Wilma C, 94 97
LIDDLE Kathy Jane, 339 353

663

LIEB Arlene Claire, 223 240 Cheryl, 240 Jacob, 223 240 Jay Edward, 240 Joshua Edward, 240
LIEN Craig, 178 315
LIEN Justin Wayne, 315 Tamara Rae, 178 315
LIGHTFOOT Harold, 111 Jeffrey Scott, 111 Maureen Kay, 106 111 Shawn Dietrich, 111 Thomas, 106 111
LINDBAR Barbara, 335
LINDEMAN Margaret, 112
LINDER Jean, 318 354
LINDHOLM Penny, 324 Scott, 324
LINES Phyllis Jean, 242 244 245 247
LINGELBACH Anna Elisabeth, 160 166 169 Johann, 166
LINGWOOD Frances Lorraine, 4 5 6 35
LINK Bernice, 228 Kristine Mary, 450
LINN Andrew Moon, 87 Dennis, 87 457 Janee' Ann, 87 457 Leslie, 23 Wilma, 23
LINSCOTT Leslie, 231
LINT David, 232 Dennis, 232 Elzo, 232 Gladys, 232
LIPPERT Martha, 154 165 174 182
LITTLE Alex, 385 Andrea Dee, 35 38 Dennis, 80 385 Kimberly Nichole, 385 Orion Frank, 385
LIVINGSTON Joseph Lawrence, 522 Tina Marie, 522
LLOYD A J, 60 Cheryl Jane, 125 138 James Edward, 138 Lizzie, 60 Nell Jean, 138 Paul William, 125 William Edward, 138
LOBEAN Mary, 190
LOBERG Gathel Edna, 141
LOBERG Gaythel Edna, 131
LOCATELLI Makayla Diane, 71 Oreste, 71 Wendy Kay, 71
LOCHARD Lesa, 317 354
LOCKHART Anna Gertrude, 11
LOCKWOOD Aaron Marcus, 408 Connor Scott, 408 Gerald, 58 Haley Kathryn, 408 Kathryn Kay, 407 408 Phyllis Jean, 58 Scott, 407 408
LOEFFLER Betty Lou, 370
LOFFERTY Nellie, 179
LOFTUS John, 507 Sheila, 507

LOGAN Lula, 119
LOHRER Brian, 55 Carrie, 55 Chad, 55 Dennis, 55 Eric, 55 Margaret, 55 Margie, 55
LOHRMANN Gertrude, 552 Markus, 552
LONG Amanda, 596 Donald Alfred, 336 347 Emerson Clayton, 129 Georgia Pauline, 129 Joseph F, 120 Joseph Frances, 596 Judith Lee, 336 347 Mary Caroline, 126 129 131 Nancy Jo, 120 596
LONGACRE Albert, 517 Eda, 517 Nellie, 517
LORD Betsy May, 481
LORENZ Effie, 203 204 Fredrika, 445 446 Loretta, 508
LORMAND Mary Faye, 236 Mary Faye Pope, 252
LOSEKAMM Johann Heinrich, 588 Johann Wilhelm, 588 Katharina Elisabeth, 66 Marie Henriette, 588
LOSH Christopher, 125 Christopher Leslie, 140 Jeffrey, 125 Jeffrey Alan, 140 Jennifer Love, 140 Lonnie, 125 Loren Leslie, 125 140 Susan Lynn, 125 140
LOUGH Catherine, 512
LOUIS Adam Reinhard, 516
LOURENS Gary, 491 Marcia Ann, 491
LOUVAR Georgia Pauline, 129
LOWER A Catharina, 313 A Elisabeth, 313 A Gertraut, 312 313 A Gertrud, 312 A Magdalena, 312 A Maria, 313 A Martha, 312 Andreas, 311 312 Anna, 311 312 Anna Elisabeth, 165 167 175 312 Anna Elizabeth, 168 Anna Gertraut, 312 Anna Maria, 312 Anna Martha, 312 Barbara, 311 Catharina, 311 Catharina, 313 Christian, 312 Christianus, 313 Elisabeth, 312 Gertraut, 311 312 Heinrich, 311 J Jost, 312 Joh Hartmann, 312 Joh Henrich, 313 Johan Adam, 312 Johan Daniel, 312 Johan Jacob, 312 Johan Jost, 313 Johann Jost, 167 312 Johannes, 167 312 313 Johannes Jost, 311 312 John Jost, 312 Magdalena, 312 Margaret Elisabeth, 312 Margaretha, 167 312 313 Maria Elisabeth, 312

LUBBEN Jean, 56
LUCAS Elizabeth, 52 Ferman, 52
LUCIANO Anthony, 436 Anthony Adolfo, 436 Danielle Elizabeth, 436 Joseph Salvatore, 436 Mary Lee, 436 Michael Gennaro, 436
LUCY Nancy, 547 548 549
LUDEMAN Fern, 496
LUDVICEK Emily, 284 Emily Irene, 272 296 Joseph L, 272 292 Mary, 272 292 Mary Ann, 268 284 292
LUDWICK Marian, 562
LUDWIG Dorothy Mae, 127 138 313 Hannah Michelle, 313 Michelle, 127 313 Rudolf, 127 138 313 Susan Marie, 127 Thomas Richard, 127 313
LUECKE Anita, 314 Anna M, 313 569 Aurelia, 314 569 Bruce, 314 Charlotte, 569 Earl, 314 Emma S, 313 570 Erwin Alvin, 314 Esther, 315 Fred M, 314 569 George, 314 George C, 314 569 Gladys, 315 Glen, 314 Glen Gerald, 314 Hazel, 314 Heinrich F, 313-315 569 Henry, 565 Henry L, 314 569 Jeanette, 314 569 Johann, 314 569 Lucille, 314 Ludwig, 569 Lydia, 570 Margaretha, 315 569 Margarethe, 313-315 565 569 Mary C, 315 569 Mattie, 314 569 Nellie, 314 569 Neva Veda, 314 Royal, 314 Ruby, 314 Sophie, 314 569 Viva Margaret, 314 William, 315 569
LUEHR Antje, 115 116
LUGAR Charlene, 103 Deborah Joyce, 103 123 Mark Hadden, 103 123 Richard Green, 103 Taylor Charles Goetz, 103 Tory Marie, 103 Trent Hadden Haerther, 103 Tye Ashley Green, 103
LUITEN Henry, 503 504 Martha, 503 504
LUKEN Wendy Lee, 540 580
LUND Dolores, 563 Fred, 563 Margaret, 1 Overan, 1 Shirley, 215
LUNDIN Ethel, 405 407
LUNDL Gertrude, 301
LUNDVALL Julie, 4 Rick, 4
LUNDY Sandra, 52 438
LUNGER Winnie, 366
LUTE Tina Marie, 78

LUTHER Caroline, 496 Caroline Katharine, 493 Ella, 493 Jake, 493 Myrtle, 493
LUTJEN Chris, 344 347 Elsie, 347 Irene, 347 Katherine, 344 347 Laverne, 348
LUTZ Glenn Eldon, 178 179 315 Joetta Kay, 178 Louis Carl, 178 Nancy Lee, 178 Nancy Lue, 179 315 Pearl, 178 Shirley Ann, 130 139 140 Tamara Rae, 178 315
LUWE Albert, 315 Anna, 22 315 316 Arnold, 315 316 Barney, 315 Charlotte, 315 316 Dale, 316 Delores, 316 Emma, 315 316 Harry, 315 Henry, 315 316 Kathryn, 316 Leland, 316 Lucille, 316 Mabel, 315 316 Mose, 315 Paul, 315 Rose, 315 316 Vinson, 316 Wilhelm, 315 William, 315 316
LUZE Henrietta, 453
LYMAN Alan G, 530 Dora, 530 Florence L, 530 Glenn L, 530 John B, 530 June C, 530 Karen, 530 Karen J, 530 Louis, 530 Lucille E, 530
LYNCH Carol, 400 Kay, 400 Kay Marie, 400 Margaret (Peggy) Ann, 573 Margaret Ann, 211 Monica Ann, 391 394 Patricia, 338 Paul, 400 Peggy, 211 Velma, 43
LYNN Ardella, 522
LYON Margaret, 314
LYONS A'mae Karissa Nicole, 317 Andrew, 317 Anna, 317 Carol J, 317 Daniel Loren, 317 Eileen Isabel, 316 317 474 Harry, 316 317 474 Jane Anne, 316 Judith Juanita, 317 Karen, 317 Karen Eileen, 316 Kari Ann, 317 Lillie Mae, 58 Linda, 317 Loren Harry, 316 317 Matthew David, 317 Patricia Eileen, 317 Peni, 317 Roger Gene, 317 Sharon Kae, 317 Steve, 317
LYTTEN Susan, 320
MAAG David, 477 Forrest, 477 Gertrude, 477 Mary, 477 514
MAAS Anna, 561 Dietrich, 10 Louisa, 406 407 Renee Marie, 10 Robyn, 433 456 Wilhelmina Just, 405 Wilma, 75
MABIE Lynn Marie, 367
MACHHOLZ Kim, 48

MACKIE Emma, 111 113 Mary, 113
Robert, 113
MACLEAN Jean, 302
MACLEOD Willa Catherine, 256
MADAN Betty Ann, 415 Betty Anne, 411
James Clark, 415 James R, 411 415
Jennifer Ann, 415 John William, 209
Marlene, 209 Nancy Ann, 19 209
MADDOX Gloria Ann, 136 James, 98
James Thomas, 95 98 John Edward,
136 Kathryn Ann, 95 98 Leatha, 98
Mackenzie Nicole, 98
MADISON Brian, 259 Richard, 259 Rita,
259
MAGDEFRAU Don, 535 Frances, 535
Julie Ann, 485 535
MAGEE Breann, 318 Colleen Mauree, 317
Darren Joe, 317 Daryl Dean, 317 354
David Joe, 317 354 Debra, 317 318
Elaine James, 318 James Henry, 317
318 354 Jean, 318 354 Jeanette, 318
354 Jody, 354 Joe, 317 318 337 354
John James, 318 Joseph Karl, 318 Judy,
317 Kathy, 317 318 354 Keith Charles,
318 354 Kevin James, 317 Kisley
Lorrine, 318 Lesa, 317 354 Loraine
James, 317 318 354 Mary Jane, 318
354 Michelle Kay, 317 Randall James,
317 318 Tamara Jo, 317 Velma, 317
318 354
MAGNANI Celeste Joyce, 137 204 Nicole
Lynn, 204 Timothy Paul, 137 204
MAHONEY Julie Christine, 138 139
Leroy, 138 Mary, 138
MAIER Earl Jr, 560 Earl Sr, 9 Earl Willis
Jr, 9 Marcella, 9 N N, 9 Vicky Lynn, 9
560
MAIERS Theresa Mae, 450
MAINE Matilda, 327
MAIR Margaretha, 106 108 109 111 322
326
MALLISON Dawn Michelle Kerkman, 237
Sharon Jean, 234 237 William, 234 237
William Zachary, 237
MALLOY Dennis, 143 Donna Mae, 7 143
Julia, 143 Julie, 143 Rose Alice, 30 35
38 Steve, 143 William, 143 William P,
7

MALONE Brenda, 405 407
MANAUGH Amy Annette, 231 Kenneth,
231
MANDERSCHEID Anne Elizabeth, 412
Glenn Orville, 412 Marie Catherine,
412 Orville John, 412
MANDLE Jeannette, 599
MANGELSON Violet, 41
MANGOLD Maxine, 513
MANNETTER Dave, 475 577 Heidi
Christina, 577 Janet Colleen, 475 577
Katie Colleen, 577 Traci Renae, 577
MANNING N N, 539 Vivian L, 539
MANOS Crystal Lynne, 30 38 Harry III,
38 Mark, 30 Mark Alan, 38 Pamela, 38
MANSON David, 45 536 Holly Marie, 536
Kelly Nicole, 536 Tamara Kay, 45 536
MARCOTTE Joseph Denis Michel, 310
Lori Ann, 310 Renaud Alexander, 310
Sebastien Nicholas, 310 Tristan David,
310
MARCOTTI Lori Ann, 277 Michael, 277
MARIGOLD Maxine, 512 513
MARINELLI Debra Kay, 485 534 Krista
Noel, 535 Lee Michael, 535 Michael
Arthur Jr, 485 535 Michael Sr, 535
MARKLAND Madeline Frances, 160
Samuel F, 160 Shirley, 161 Shirley A,
160 176
MARKS Andrea Danielle, 56 Angela
Marie, 56 Bernadine, 505 Bruce
Thomas, 56 Cindy, 56 Dennis Paul, 56
Jordan Ashley, 56 Karen, 56 Kathleen,
56 Kevin, 56 Kimberly, 56 Leslie
Anne, 56 Lois, 56 501 Matthew Travis,
56 N N, 505 Nathan Andrew, 56
Pamela, 56 Richard, 56 501 Richard
Jason, 56 Rosalynn Marie, 547 Sarah
Marie, 56 Steven, 56 Susan Kay, 56
Terry Niel, 56
MARQUARDT Brooke, 7 Herman, 116
Luke, 7 Mary, 500 N N, 7 Natalee, 7
Pauline, 116 158
MARSH Alva Jean, 336 Ethel, 12 James
Richard, 336 John, 12 Leland, 12
Lorraine Trueblood, 336 340 341 347
352 353 Lucille, 12

MARSHALL Bertha, 446 N N, 446 Pat, 252 254 Sally Marie, 5
MARTA Martha, 267
MARTELL Olga, 212
MARTIN Anna, 356 Anna Grace, 111-113 Bessie, 111 Casey Mccutcheon, 596 Daniel Heinrich, 340 Henry, 356 Peggy Lynn, 202 Phyllis, 507 508 Robert E, 111 Timothy Joe, 5 596 Wendy Ann, 5 596
MARTINUSEN Julia, 143
MARTITZ Christine, 451 Francis J, 451
MARTLEY Sarah, 15 393
MARXSEN Bruce Leland, 4 Cale Shawn, 4 Carol Ann, 4 Jamie Leigh, 4
MARY JANE 385
MASON Andrea Catherine, 256 Carol Ann, 255 256 Gregory, 331 Jack, 255 256 Kevin Andrew, 256 Stephanie, 331 Taylor Michel, 331 Terri Lynn, 331
MASTERS Brandon Scott, 521 Diane, 58 Jordan Elizabeth, 521 Laura Joy, 521 Steven Francis, 521
MATA Debra Sue, 71 Jonathan Manual, 71 Joseph Gabriel, 71
MATCHAN Joan Renee, 10 Paul, 10
MATHIAS Alden, 335 Angela, 335 Berdina, 335 Caroline, 474 Dennis, 335 Fred, 474 Mark, 335 Theresa, 335 Tim, 335
MATHIASON N N, 60
MATSON Edwin, 22 Ida, 21 Ida Pauline, 22
MATTER Anna, 135 197 319 Bill, 319 Charles, 319 Elizabeth (Lizzie) Marie, 493 John, 319 John W, 196 319 Katharina, 319 Katharine, 196 N N, 493
MATTHEWS Karen, 56
MATTHIAS Alden, 337 Berdina, 337 Carol, 318 447 Carol Joyce, 157 Christopher, 511 Daniel, 184 511 Esther, 150 153 157 159 183 318 Janet, 318 531 Janet Jean, 157 Jolyne Kay, 184 511 Kenneth Melvin, 157 Leroy William, 157 Maxine Dorothy, 157 307 318 Melvin, 157 183 318 Wendy Lynne, 511

MATTOX Sarah, 429
MATTSON Art, 44 Brooke Renee, 44 Donna Marie, 22 44 Jan, 22 44 Judy, 581 Lucille, 44 Matthew Jan, 44
MAUER Katharina, 221 228 557 Katherina, 222
MAURER Anna Elisabeth, 65-67 319 Anna Gertrud, 517 Anna Guida, 319 Elizabeth, 333 Hilda Gertrude Anna, 319 422 483 Johannes, 319 Nadine Ann, 319 483 497 Walter William, 319 422 483
MAUS Bernard, 560 Jeanette, 560
MAUSEHUND Christine, 115
MAXWELL Sara Post, 508
MAY Annis, 530 Barbara, 209 Hattie, 497 Sturley, 497
MAYER Rose Marie, 9
MAYHEW Andrew Frank, 319 Audrey Laverne, 319 Audry Laverne, 71 Benjamin Merrill, 319 Denette Helen, 319 Frank Arthur, 71 319 Marica Jo, 319 Merrill Emerson, 319 Sarah Louise, 319
MAYNARD David, 507 Leanne, 481 Molly Jean, 507 Zachary, 507
MCAFEE Brian, 237 Gary, 237 Jeremy, 237 Keely Denise, 237
MCALEXANDER Emily Jo, 448
MCAREAVEY Dorothy Ann, 524 Jonathon Michael, 524
MCARTHUR Marguerte, 474
MCBIRNIE Danelle Frances, 349 Jeffery Allen, 349
MCCANDLESS Allie Christine, 249 Esther, 115 Robert B, 249
MCCANN Mary Elizabeth, 257
MCCARTHNEY Cindy Lou, 47
MCCARTY Luanne, 58
MCCHESNEY Sandra, 14
MCCLINTOCK Ann Delores, 284 287 296 Anne Marie, 336 David Miller, 336 Jeannette, 232 Jo Dee, 232 Lyle T, 287 Misti Lynn, 232 Norman Duane, 232 Regina Renna, 232 Wayne David, 232
MCCLURE Ada Jean, 126
MCCLURG Linda Jean Andrews, 371 390
MCCONNAUGHEY Della, 236 John, 236

MCCORD Hilda, 531 William, 531
MCCORMICK Ellen, 513
MCCOY Joanne, 514 515
MCCUBBINS Catherine Mary, 220 518
 Virginia, 518 William, 518
MCCULLOH Allison Lynn, 263 Brian,
 482 Brian Winton, 263 Cleone Rachel,
 263 Lori Lynn, 263 482 Matthew
 Calvin, 263 Ryan Jay, 263 Winton
 Scott, 263
MCCURDY Ruth Marie, 365
MCCURRY Cynthia, 255
MCDANIELS Leslie Jean Delaney, 305
MCDONALD Clare, 393 Danny, 539 Ellen
 K, 446 539 James M, 446 539 John,
 539 Megan, 539
MCDOUGAL Donna, 145 154
MCELHOSE Kim, 178 182
MCGARVEY Beth, 531
MCGINNIS Karolyn, 242 Thomas, 242
MCGIVERN Magdalene Lillian, 222 225
MCGIVERN Peter J, 222 225
MCGOFF Beryl, 189
MCGOHAN Cynthia Louise, 270 285
 Donald, 285 Helen, 285
MCGRANAHAM Sadie, 60
MCGRANAHAN Mabel, 191
MCGUIRE Drew Martin, 528 Emily
 Elizabeth, 528 Larry, 528 Melissa
 Marie, 528 Michele Marie, 528
MCHAFFIE Elfrieda, 196 Hartley, 196
MCHAFFY Camiel, 440 Hanna, 440 Renee
 Ann, 439 440 Samuel, 439 440
MCHATTIE Elfrieda, 195 Hartley, 195
MCHUGH Andrea Michelle, 365 Edward
 Peter, 290 365 Elizabeth, 365
 Raymond, 365 Susan Laurel, 290 365
 Thomas Edward, 366
MCILLRATH Floyd, 372 Karen K, 25 372
MCINTIER Maybelle, 505 506
MCINTOSH Susan Kay, 56
MCISAAC Lucille, 253
MCKEAN Benjamin Isaac, 34 Charles
 Patrick, 34 Desiree Hope, 34 Katharine
 Elizabeth, 34 37 Kirk Andrew, 34
 Patrick, 34 37
MCKECHNIE Joanne, 443
MCKINLEY Chrystal Elaine, 238

MCKINNEY C F, 347
MCKINSTRY Elfreida, 195 196 Jay, 195
 196 Sharon, 196 Sheila, 196
MCLAUD Bret Louis, 102 Chad, 102
 Tamara Lynn, 102
MCLEAN Cole Maxwell, 240 Emma, 240
 Kristen Deann, 240 241 Robert
 Maxwell, 240 241
MCLEOD Eugene, 12 Hazel, 12
MCLINDEN Phyllis, 96 172
MCMAHAN James, 383 Laura, 382 383
 Mary, 383
MCMANN Arlene, 99 Jodi, 512 Kay, 512
 513 Mark, 512 513 Mike, 512 Paul, 99
MCMILLAN Frank, 52 Frankie Mae, 52
 Jaime Sierra, 52
MCNALLEN Evelyn, 207 211 Robert H,
 211 Thomas, 207 211
MCNULTY Alice, 332 333 Gerald, 333
 Lillian, 333
MCQUISTIN Connie Sue, 125 139 Jeffrey
 Robert, 125 Lavelle, 125 Robert, 139
 William, 125
MCROBERTS Jan, 22 46
MCSHANE Betty Sue, 395 584 589 592
MCSPAREN Michael Dean, 577 Rick, 371
 577 Tammy Kay, 371 577 Zachary
 Taylor, 577
MCSWEENEY Charles, 369 370 Michael,
 370 Richard, 370 Ruth, 369 370 Sandy,
 370 Timothy, 370
MCVEY Michelle, 417 437
MCWILLIAMS Beth, 542 Beth Marie, 185
 Robert, 185 542 Ryanna, 542
MEAD Barbara, 124 413 416 428 571
MEADOWER Anna Mae, 516
MEALHAUSER Sophie, 435 William, 435
MEANS Bertha, 51 William, 51
MEARA James, 61 Terry Kay, 61
MEBES Gertraut, 311 312 Hans, 313
MEBUS Anna Catharina, 167 Hartmann,
 167
MEDBERRY Leona, 380 Walter, 380
MEDWICK Connie Kay, 473 Joseph, 473
MEEK Alta, 451 452 Ida, 451 John, 451
MEER Cheryl Ann, 229 David Christopher
 Vander, 229

MEIER ----, 534 Anna, 534 Keith, 150
   Zenolia, 372 465
MEINDL George, 561 Maria, 561
MEINEKE Lenora Mae, 58 59 147 Lillie
   Mae, 58 Paul George, 58
MEINERT Dora, 199 370 Margaretha, 81
   600 William, 199 370
MEIR Dorothea, 137
MEISSNER Anna, 195 197 Dale, 199 332
   Delores, 199 Gerhardt R, 199 Hillis,
   199 332 Marie J, 199 Verla, 199
   William, 195 197
MEISTER Lynette Jean, 574
MELBERG Delores Irene, 220 223 224
   431
MELDREM Tami Jo, 235
MELHOFF Emma, 559
MELHUS Carol Leona, 319 485 Clarence
   Arnold, 319 320 422 485 Edward, 485
   Glenda, 80 182 547-550 Kathleen Ann,
   320 485 Kendra Denise, 320 Kenneth
   Clarence, 320 485 Leona Barbara
   Lillian, 319 320 422 485 Michael
   Jason, 320 Olisa, 485 Sheila Gay, 320
   485
MELIN Jackson Thomas, 211 John, 211
   573 Lee Ann, 211 573
MENDELL Sharon, 211 260
MENGEL Eva Amelia, 238 Henry, 238
   Margaret, 238
MENKE Anna Guida, 319
MENKEL Anna Katharina, 320 Anna
   Marie, 320 363 448 Anna Martha, 320
   448 Eckardt, 320 Johann Peter, 169
   Johann Winter, 320 448 Regina, 67 168
MENTOR Joanne, 397
MENZEL A Cath, 494 Anna Catharina,
   495˙
MEROSHECK Mary Jane, 295
MEROSHEK Charles, 296 Mary Jane, 277
   287 288 296
MERRIMAN Avery, 539 580 Margaret,
   539 580 Richard, 580 Robert, 580
MERRITT Ardith Mae, 320 399 Dillard,
   320 Jack Dillard, 399 Judith Ann, 320
MESS Augusta, 512 Emma, 62 Ernest, 62
   Helen Margaret, 62 63 172 Mary, 467
MESSER Corene, 486 Jan, 488

MEUXAYANAKHAM Some, 37
MEUXAYANAKHOMA Bend, 36 Kellie,
   36 Some, 36 Wayne, 36
MEVEY Nancy, 233
MEYER Abby Jo, 321 Abegail, 369
   Alvina, 378 Andrea Beth, 434 Andrea
   Danielle, 56 Anna, 321 Annie Jean,
   322 Bernard, 39 Bertha, 232 234 321
   Carol Jean, 599 Charles, 369 Christina,
   499 Clara, 321 Connie Jean, 103
   Criston Kay, 103 Dale, 321 Dale
   Herold, 162 Darcy Ann, 206 322
   Debra, 317 318 Diane Lee, 206 321
   Donna, 369 Donna Jean, 369 Eileen
   Freida, 257 Eileen Frieda, 262 Eldo,
   103 546 Elisa, 321 Eliza, 545
   Elizabeth, 543 Elizabeth Maria, 321
   544 545 Ella Emma Louise, 461
   Emma, 287 476 Emma C, 378 Emma
   L, 321 Ernest, 321 Ernie, 455 Ernie A,
   206 321 322 Ernst H F, 321 545
   Evelyn, 369 Florence Lisetta, 257
   Gregg, 321 Gussie J, 83 Harold, 162
   183 321 Henry, 321 Herman, 321
   Hilda, 162 183 321 Ida, 39 321 Jamie,
   369 Janet, 321 Jean Dorothy, 162
   Jillian Louise, 321 John, 321 Julien,
   162 321 Karie, 229 Luanne Rae, 290
   Lucille, 443 444 Magdelene, 75 Marc,
   290 434 Marjorie, 22 78 Mary Lee, 206
   321 322 455 Mathilda, 321 Matthew
   Marc, 434 Merle William, 162
   Michael, 321 Mildred, 369 504 Otto,
   321 Pamela, 418 437 Pharo, 83 84
   Rachel Marie, 103 Randall Milton, 206
   321 Ray, 369 504 Ruth, 370 Samuel
   James, 322 Sean, 56 Shirley, 103 546
   Steven Lynn, 103 Sue, 350 356 Teresa,
   103 Teresa L, 206 321 Theodore, 378
   Theophil, 257 Timothy Harold, 206
   322 Travis Earl, 321 Tyrone, 229
MICHAEL Henry, 282 Joan, 457
MICHAELSON Carl Dennis, 591 Craig,
   591 Jayne, 591 Joann, 591 Lisa, 591
MICHEL Adam, 329 Adam John, 107 457
   Adam John Jr, 322 330 Adam John Sr,
   111 322 324 327 330 331 Adam
   Michel, 322 Adelheid, 326 328

669

133 Diane, 333 Donna, 505 Dora M, 371 Doris Evelyn, 540 Dorothy, 6 241 Douglas Eugene, 104 123 Elizabeth, 333 Ella M, 177 Elsie L, 83 84 Emma, 193 Florence Lisetta, 257 Frederick (Fritz), 505 Frederick M, 376 Gerald (Jerry), 333 Gilbert, 505 Gladys E, 339 340 354 Harry Frank, 339 354 Hazel, 332 Henry, 332 333 Henry N, 397 Ian Douglas, 104 Jane, 145 152 159 181 Joann, 186 John, 28 333 John A, 332 333 Julie, 215 216 Karmen, 3 Kate, 505 506 Kendall, 472 Kyle Lynette, 237 Lana Joy, 21 Lizzie, 251 Louisa, 332 333 Lynelle Jane, 21 Marilyn, 491 504 Mary, 373 408 574 Melinda, 117 299 Michael, 120 596 N N, 596 Pauline Wilhelmina, 523 Ralph, 133 Rhianna Carolyn, 104 Rita, 505 Roslyn, 505 Sally, 505 Sandra Kay, 19 Sara Jo, 21 Sheila, 133 Sonya Carol, 133 Steve, 3 237 Steven, 333 Susan, 113 456 531 Ted Eldo, 19 21 Terry, 333 Thelma Evangeline, 271 Theresa Carol, 123 Therese Carol, 104 Tom, 6 241 472 Tony, 505 506 W Peter, 373 Wayne, 332 333 William (Bill), 332 William F, 505 Zerelda, 505

MILLS Chad, 260 Darwin, 260 Frank, 259 261 Joyce, 260 Kathy, 260 Laura, 260 Rena, 259 Rita, 259 Rosella, 259 261 Ryan, 260

MILOTA Allen James, 262 292 Jade Rui, 262 Jami Oiu, 262 Shelly Renee, 262 292

MINARD Jessica Lee, 484 Julie Ann, 484 486 Michael Lee, 484 Michelle Ann, 484 Terry Lee, 484 486

MINDEMAN Albert, 325 331 Eileen Rose, 331 Rose, 328 Verda Erma Anna, 325 331

MINISH Jean, 6

MINO Janice, 112 Michelle, 112 Rebecca, 112

MINSK Vicky, 594

MIRKLIN Barbara, 452

MITCHELL Amy Kathleen, 410 547 Daniel, 594 Donna Lee, 266 294 Marie,

493 Mary Claire, 594 Minnie, 409 Richard Stanley, 547 Rosalynn Marie, 547

MITTAN Angela Kristine, 526 Braxton Michael, 526 Kyle Breanne, 526 Marilyn Ann, 522 526 Michael Paul, 526 Miranda Kristine, 526 Pamela Ann, 526 Paul Edward, 522 526

MIXDORF Chad, 178 Denise, 178 Hilbert, 145 178 Mary Ann, 145 178

MIZE Bert, 436 Matilda, 436

MOE Bertha, 563 Patricia Kay, 563 572 Roy A, 563

MOEGE Betty, 552 573 574 Emil, 552 Ida, 552

MOEHLMAN Albert, 41 Carol, 41 560 Violet, 41

MOELLER Aaron Thomas, 354 Adam, 333 336 Adam Dean, 339 Adam Sr, 327 343 346 Albert, 347 Albert Adam, 347 Alice Margaret, 338 348 351-353 Alice Verna, 340 341 347 353-355 Alva Jean, 341 Andrew, 351 Andrew Jason, 341 Andrew Martin, 351 Andy, 340 Ann, 335 Anna, 298 Anna Elisabeth, 281 333 335 336 340 342 347 351 Anna Elisabeth (Lizzie), 338 339 Anna Elizabeth, 350 Anna Elizabeth Caroline, 335 Anna Katharina, 342 Anna Maria Katharina, 424 Anna Maria Katharina (Annie), 352 Anna Marie, 298 336-340 350 353 561 Anna Marie Barbara, 335 Anne Marie, 336 Annetta, 337 340 August, 298 Becki Lyn, 348 Berdina, 335 337 Bernard Fred, 335 341 349 353 354 Betty Jean, 215 434 Bonnie Kaye, 336 354 Brian Lee, 348 Byron David, 341 Carl William, 336 340 347 352 353 Carol Sue, 352 Carolina Clara, 346 Carolina Maria, 342 Caroline, 336 Caroline E, 298 347 495 Chad Wendell, 348 Charles, 251 Christopher Martin, 353 Cindy, 341 Clarence, 334 336 Collin, 353 Connie Kay, 338 354 Danelle Frances, 349 Daniel Heinrich Martin, 354 Daniel Heinrich Martin (Henry), 335 337 Daniel Henry Martin,

671

345 Louise Caroline Marie, 344 Louise Elizabeth Salome, 334 Louise Kristine, 25 94-97 99 350 Magdalena, 341 344 Maria, 25 97 346 354 Maria (Marie), 334-337 340 345 346 349 351 430 Maria (Marie) Elisabeth, 424 425 Maria Elisabeth, 25 67 68 146-150 164 166 168-170 177 262 343 423 Maria Katharina, 146 342 343 345 350 Maria Magdalena (Lena), 344 Marie, 67 68 146-150 164 166-170 176 177 262 335 345 Marie Cecelia, 334 Marie Elisabeth, 176 345 585 Marie Katharina, 24 Martha, 334 Martha Johanna, 334 Martin Adam, 334 Martina, 65 516 Mathilda, 345 Nicholas, 381 Peter Fredrich Heinrich, 334 Peter George, 346 Tena, 344 Walter Wilhelm, 334 Wilhelmina, 24 261 343-347 567

MOLONEY Beulah, 385 James, 385

MOLUS Anna Catherina, 356 Anna Catherine, 333 343 346 Maria Elisabeth, 356 Marie Elisabeth, 346 Peter, 346 356

MONCH Catharina, 311 Johan, 311

MONISMITH Angeline, 509

MONTAGUE Evard, 470 Marcella, 470 Mary L, 231 Mary Louise, 470

MONTGOMERY Nathine, 502 503

MOOBERRY Anne, 504 David, 504 Joan, 504 Laurine, 502 504 Mark, 504 Orville, 502 504

MOON Bill, 518 Dustin, 14 518 Hayden Joe, 518 Katie Marie, 14 518 Linda, 518

MOOR Eliza, 500

MOORE Carol Jean, 379 380 Ella Sophie Hannah, 378 Glenn, 408 Kathryn, 39 Mabel, 408 Myron M, 378 Pearl, 178 Roy, 39 Verla, 199 332

MORCH John Bernard II, 133 John Bernard III, 133 Kimberly Kumud, 133 Mary, 133

MORGAN Andrea Sue, 244 Carl B, 244 246 Diana Lynn, 244 Judith Ann, 244 246

MORIS Margaretha, 106 108 109 111 322 326

MORNING Elizabeth (Bunny), 367 540

MORONEY Rita, 260

MORR Anna, 116 Clarence, 116 Joan, 116-118 Joan, 560

MORREISSEY Charles, 491 Morgan, 491

MORRISON Alden, 83 84 Amy, 83 Charles Allen, 232 Corleen, 83 84 Leonard, 83 Linda Marie, 232 Mary, 114 Olga, 83 Sue, 83

MORROW Elaine M, 465 466 Robb, 466

MORT Edna, 523

MORTELL Charles Henry, 10 James William, 10 421 Linda Ann, 10 421 Patrick Martin, 10 Philip August, 10 Roberta Patricia, 10

MORTLAND Carma Sue, 405 406

MORTVEDT Connie Jean, 103 Randy, 103

MOSIER Naomi, 254

MOSTEK Susan Laura, 490 Timothy Edward, 490

MUCH Alvin, 117 Clyde William, 116 117 Irene, 117 Melissa, 117 Nichole, 117 Susan, 116 117

MUCKY Ruthy, 11

MUDD Carson Benny, 520 John Lincoln, 520 Kassidy Jean, 520 Laura Renee, 520 Riley Lincoln, 520

MUDDERMAN David, 558 559 Diane, 558 559 Dustin, 558 Teresa, 558

MUEHLHAUS LANGLO Eva Elisabeth, 407

MUELHAUS LANGLO Eva Elizabeth, 405

MUELLER Esther Wilma Henrietta, 148 Mary Matilda, 63 148 Melinda, 102 Pauline Louisa Augusta, 332 Sophia, 380 381

MUENCH Cynthia Sue, 250 Emily Elizabeth, 250 Gary Edwin, 250 Katherine Christine, 250 Matthew Douglas, 250

MUENSTER Anna Mae Philomena, 450 Dorothy Susan, 448 450 Frank Joseph, 448 Ida Catherine, 448

MUHL Christopher, 443 Regina Jane, 443 Reginald M, 290 443 Verna Jane, 290 442

MUILENBERG Clara, 156

MUIRHEAD George, 114 Mary, 114 Mary Janette, 40 114

MULANAX Christopher, 324 Jeff, 323 Jessica, 324 Steven, 324 Wendy Marie, 323

MULLENNEX Anna, 41 Esther Martha, 41 560 Julius, 41 Marvin, 41 560

MULLER A Maria, 313 Anna Maria, 312 Carole, 350 356 Debra, 356 Donald, 350 356 Edgar, 337 350 356 Gregg, 356 Kathy, 317 318 354 Lucille, 337 350 356 Sandy, 356 Sue, 350 356

MULLIN Catharine, 151 Esther Catherine, 151 170 Frank, 151

MULLINGER Derk, 255 260 Nicole, 260 Susan, 255 260

MUMM Martha Emma, 232 236 Mathew Michael, 236 Mike Steven, 232 236 Patricia Mary, 236

MUMMA Alice Margaret, 338 348 351-353 Mary Rose, 338 Oscar Delavan, 338

MUMN Cindy Sue, 152 Steve, 152

MUNCH Godfather, 312

MUNN James, 541 Justin, 541 Sharyln, 541 Stephanie, 541

MUNOZ Gustavo A, 389 Marcy Ann, 389

MURBACH Margaret, 436

MURKEN Eleanor, 496 Fredia Catherine, 592 Hilda, 496

MURPHY Arleta, 408 Doris, 129 Eileen, 49 Kelly, 59 205

MURRAY Billy, 240 Cletus, 537 Jean Ann, 240 Louie Ethel, 240 Maureen, 293 Maureen Katherine, 537 Roy W, 240 William Keys, 240

MUSCH Eleanora Mathilda, 150 182 Eleanora Matilda, 147

MUSSMAN Ann, 499 Arthur, 499 Caroline, 191 467 Christopher, 582 Frank, 499 Henry, 467 Louise, 499 Michelle, 582

MUSTAPHA Curtis, 260 Ilene, 260 Jack, 260 Kelly, 260

MYERS Stacy Elizabeth, 320 Steven James, 320 Zolina, 320

MYRICK Jill Renee, 6 Julie Kay, 6 Marilyn Kay, 6 Melanie Kay, 6 Mickey Calvin, 6

N N Beth, 403 Christina, 383 Dawn, 399 Donna Fay, 395 Ellen, 379 Frederika, 379 Jessika, 385 Kay, 377 Kelly J, 394 Mahala, 381 Rachel, 372 Sandy, 398 402 Sue, 377 Tammy, 403

NABHOLZ Mary Ellen, 385

NAEVE Anna, 356 Ella, 357 Johanna, 356 Marx, 356

NAGY Ann, 84

NANCE Erma, 332 John Boyd, 332 Paul, 332 Sandra Lee, 332 Tracy Michel, 332

NANNEN Linda, 112

NATZEL Frank, 321 Mathilda, 321

NAUER Josephine, 507

NAVE Carolyn, 296 Dennis, 296 Stephanie, 296

NAVRATIL Mary, 480

NEAL Amy Marie, 357 Beth Ann, 357 Bill, 273 Brenda Kris, 273 Christ Raymond, 273 Connie Lou, 273 357 Evelyn Leta, 266 357 Inez, 273 Jonathan, 37 Rochelle D, 32 37 Sheryl Dianne, 273 357 Wililam Raymond Sr, 266 William Raymond Jr, 273 William (Bill) Raymond Jr, 357William Raymond Sr, 357 William Raymons Sr, 273

NECHANICKY Amber Marie, 102 Ashley Ann, 102 Kathryn, 102 Robert, 102 Shari Lynn, 101 269 Stuart, 101 Stuart, 269

NEELY Glenn, 191 Jean, 191

NEES Andreas, 76 Anna, 76 Margaretha, 75 76

NEHLS Ethan Patrick, 526 Mackenzie Mariah, 526 Patrick Alan, 526 Rebecca Renee, 526

NEIBHOR Mabel, 409

NEIGAR Diana Elaine, 492 Jason Michael, 492 Jennifer Dawn, 492 Michael, 492

NEILS Maria Katharina, 425

NELL Alice, 230 502 554 555 566 568 572 573 575 Ann, 144 Ann Elizabeth, 554

NORRIS Alan, 102 103 Jacquelyn, 102
Jacquelyn Rae, 103 Kaylie Suzanne,
102 Kristen Jay, 102 Kyle Scott, 102
Melinda, 102 Nicole Norma, 102 Scott
Alan, 102
NORTH Susanne, 194
NORTON Jackson Ray, 386 Josie Ann,
386 Mark, 386
NOSIKOVA Ksenia, 338 354
NOSKER Herbert Dean, 366 Kimberly
Beth, 367 Lola Katherine, 366 Robin
Carol, 367
NOVAK Hank, 293 Kathleen, 498
Margaret, 311 Theresa, 293
NOVOTNEY Becky, 357 Betty, 357 Mark,
357 Michael, 357 Richard, 357 Scott,
357
NOVOTNY Betty, 475 Richard, 475
NUECHTERLEIN Elaine, 396 Elaine
Laura, 391 392 394
NUMRICH Ervin E, 219 John Arthur, 219
Monica Ruth, 219 Ruth Lillian, 219
NUSS Terri, 349 350
NUTT Beverly, 260 Ilene, 260 Jesse, 260
261 Mary Ann, 260 Melvin, 260 Verna,
260 261
NYE Annetta, 337 340
NYREEN C W, 213 Michael W, 213
Sandra Kay, 213
OBEREMBT James, 119 Jane, 119
OBERMEYER Marilyn, 361
OBERMUELLER Alana Rae, 92 358
Anerea, 358 Anerea Leigh, 91 358
Anna Margaret, 32 91 358 Cade
Mitchell, 358 Don, 79 Donald Lee, 91
358 Drake Wesley, 358 Fredrick
Waldo, 32 358 Frerick Waldo, 91 Jodi
Jean, 78 79 Jodie Jeanne, 358 Juanita,
91 358 Nancy Jean, 91 Nita, 79 Wesley
Mitchell, 79 358
O'BRIAN Ella Marie, 429 Frederick, 429
Louise, 429
O'BRIEN Ella Marie, 94
OBRIST Karen, 13
OCHLERICH Henry, 531 Rose, 531
OCHSE Anna Katharina, 363 381 Anna
Maria, 48 Karin, 491 Konrad, 381
OCKENFELS Lena, 51

O'CONNOR Beverlyn Kay, 267 272 358
Christine Ann, 267 358 James M, 267
272 358 Rebecca Lynn, 267 358
Timothy James, 267
OCUS Catharina, 167
OEHLER Kathleen Marie, 125 241
OEHLERICH Anna, 358 Blanche Rose,
487 Claus, 358 Darwin Ray, 359 487
489 Harry W, 358 Jay, 359 Joyce, 359
Judith, 359 Kathy Dawn, 487 Kim
Denise, 359 Kristi Diane, 487 Lucille,
359 Ray Adolph, 487 Ruth Ilma, 359
487 489
OEHLERT Francis, 250 Hulda C, 250
OELMANN Farlen, 372 Peggy Ann, 372
OELTJENBRUNS Becky, 478 Elizabeth E,
479 Kenneth M, 478 Kenneth M Jr,
479 Rebecca, 479 Sarah L, 479
OERLY Jane, 356
OETTER Anna, 557
OFFEDAHL Connie Rae, 420 443
OFFT Alfred, 499 Anna, 499 Eggert, 499
Emma, 499 Gustav, 499 Herman, 499
Laura, 499 Margaretha, 499 Susana
(Lena), 499 William, 499
OFTEDAHL Alma, 534 Ervin, 443 Joanne,
443
OHDE Andrea Ellen, 232 Caroline, 189
Dale, 232 Diane, 232 Dorothy, 14
Emma, 189 190 Evelyn, 232 235 Jade
Lexus, 233 Jayne Helen, 233 Margaret,
25 Nancy, 233 Shannon Kathleen, 233
Wayne, 232 235 William, 189
OHLDE Elaine Louise, 1
OHLEN Ann, 359 August, 359 Christine,
359 Dora, 359 Henry, 359 Henry F,
359 Mae, 359
OHRMAN Susan, 398
OHRT Albert J, 360 Anna, 360 Betty Jo,
360 Cheryl Rae, 360 Donald L, 359
Donita Sue, 360 Harold L, 359 Henry,
360 Herman, 359 360 Jama Marie, 360
Johann, 359 360 John, 359 360 Kathryn
Jean, 359 360 361 Kuno, 360 Leta
Mae, 359 360 Lori J, 360 361 Louis H,
360 Margaret, 359 Margaretha, 359
360 Penney M, 360 Penny M, 360
Rickie Duane, 360 Robert Herman, 359

360 361 Roger Lynn, 360 361 Rosa, 359 360 Ruth M, 359 Tana Joyce, 361 Theodore R, 360 Zelda M, 359
OLESON Allison, 204 Paulette Pauline, 118 204 Roger, 118 204
OLHOEFT June, 527 529
OLIVER Laura Jo, 155 180
OLLENDICK Jon, 252 254 Tammy Sue, 252 254
OLMSTED Edna, 191
OLSEN Douglas John, 556 Eric William, 584 592 Jean Ann, 584 592 Johanna Nylene, 584 Nancy Ann, 556 Tobias Charles, 584
OLSON Betty, 535 Bruce Allen, 523 Cleone Rachel, 263 Douglas John, 374 Hardean Hilda, 481 Joann, 325 329 Justus Alexander, 523 Lela W, 329 Leslie Rose, 374 Lester E, 329 Mardean Hilda (Stein), 483 Maurine, 207 211 Nancy Ann, 374 Natalie Susan, 374 Opal, 298 Robert, 535 Robert E, 481 Steven Christian, 523 Susan Kay, 485 535 Tamara, 523
OLTMANN Anton, 315 Ervin, 377 Kath, 315 Marcia, 377 Margaretha, 315 569
OLTROGGE Henry, 436 Maria Sophia Barbara, 435
ONDROZECK Anna, 42 Evelyn, 42 49 Juli Ann, 43 Larry, 42 49 Waldo, 42
ORCUTT Christine, 309 311
ORDONEZ Elizabeth, 177
O'REILLY Beatrice Ella, 416 Kathleen Magan, 459 N N, 416
ORHMAN Susan, 397
ORT Anna Martha, 566
ORTH Anna Martha, 230 552 554 565
ORWIG Emma, 28 Lloyd, 28
OSBORN Benjamin Earl, 44 Brian, 491 Brooke Renee, 44 Doris, 499 Jerry, 491 Jess, 491 Marcia Ann, 491
OSBORNE Gary Eugene, 306 Sara Sue, 306
O'SHEA Mary Rose, 338
OSTERLUND Janis, 143 William, 143
OSTHEIMER Anna, 76
OSTROWSKI Patricia Ann, 525
OTTE Martha, 388

OTTEN Catherine, 106 110 Claus, 110 Tibke, 110 Trine, 106 110
OTTO Deanna, 209 Roger Macarthur, 209
OVERTON Ann Marlene, 361 Diane Marlene, 361 Jamie Kathryn, 361 Kathryn Ann, 361 Lee Richard, 71 361 Marjorie Ruth, 361 Mark Lee, 361 Marlene Ann, 71 361 Mary Marlene, 361 Milford, 361 Robert Mark, 361
OWENS Pat, 22 44
O'WREATHA Bessie, 111
PAAR ----, 447 578 Adolf Georg, 534 Adolf Heinrich, 361 362 364 Andreas, 364 Anna Dorothea, 362 364 Anna Elisabeth, 114 264 278 280 281 297 345 361-364 380 381 493 Anna Elisabeth Karoline, 362 Anna Gertrud, 362 364 Anna Gertrude, 533 537 Anna Katharina, 363 364 448 Anna Katharina Elisabeth, 342 Anna Kunigrunde, 364 Anna Kunigunde, 361 362 364 Anna Martha, 534 Caroline, 90 Elisabeth, 51 361 362 533 Elisabeth Marie, 362 Georg, 364 Georg Heinrich, 361 362 364 Heinrich, 51 90 533 534 Heinrich I, 361 362 364 Heinrich II, 362 Helene, 362-364 534 Herta Elfriede, 363 Jacob, 362 Johann Adolf, 364 Johann Daniel, 362 363 448 Johann Georg, 363 448 Johann Heinrich, 362 364 Johann Justus, 364 Johann Peter, 363 Johannes, 281 362 363 381 533 Johannes I, 363 364 Johannes II, 361 362 364 Karoline, 361 362 364 Karoline Gertrud, 361 362 Katharina Elisabet, 364 Katharina Elisabeth, 363 364 448 Margit, 534 Marlene, 198 578 Marlene Martha, 363 364 579 Martha Sophie, 534 N N, 364 Sophie Friedericke, 362 Tobias, 364
PAARMANN Bill, 390 Ruth Ellen, 390
PACKARD Doris, 313 Emma S, 313 570 George, 313 Gerald, 313 Grace, 314 Henry, 313 570 Mary Jane, 313
PADGETT Alva Jean, 336 341
PADILLA Linda, 116 118
PAGE Chris, 118 Ericka Beth, 118
PAGEL Louise, 429 Sophie, 479

PALAS Elizabeth, 300 301 Regina Renna, 232
PALEN Helen Polly, 290 365 Kenneth, 291 595 Kenneth Raymond, 290 297 365 Lloyd Ira, 290 Magaret Lovaire, 290 Margaret, 291 Margaret Krug, 447 Margaret Lovaire, 297 365 Mildred Cecil, 290 Nancy Ann, 290 Richard Kenneth, 290 365 366 Susan Laurel, 290 365
PALMER Alice, 568 Alice Brandt, 573 Cody Alan, 202 Connie, 202 394 Frances, 573 Helen Marcella, 525 Jeffrey Alan, 202 394 John C, 525 John C Jr, 525 Linda, 100 Lynn Marie, 306 Marge, 525 Matthew, 306 Patricia Elaine, 95 100 Paul, 573 Sara Lynn, 202 Stephen, 100
PAPESH Marlys, 498
PARK Janet, 598
PARKER Charlene, 209 Denise Ann, 19 209 Gary Lee, 400 401 Glenn Robert, 19 209 Jeanne, 384 389 Jimi Jo, 331 Julie Lynn, 400 401 Lloyd Spencer, 413 433 Lorane, 440 Lorane Kathrine Wilhelmine, 413 433 Otis Robert, 209
PARMATER Clifford Earl, 41 Clifford Leroy, 40 41 Elizabeth Helen, 41 Mary Caroline, 41 Nancy Sue, 41
PARRY Art, 43 Ella, 43 Linda, 43 49 Michelle, 43 Randall R, 43 49 Son, 43
PATRICK Amanda Jo, 320 Gary Lee, 350 Judith Ann, 320 Meghan Mae, 321 Paul Bryan, 320 Sandy, 350
PATTEN Ivy Dean, 547 Morris Gabriel, 547 Sarah Elizabeth, 547 Sherri Lynn, 547 Timothy David, 547 Zachary Aaron, 547
PATTERSON Dianne, 428 Larry (Butch), 427 428 Tammara Jo, 427 431
PATTON Sherri Lynn, 410 Timothy David, 410
PAUL Emily Suzanne, 306 Natalie Elizabeth, 306 Richard Joseph, 306 Shirley Beth, 306
PAULEY Gusta, 71 Joseph, 71 Josephine, 72 73 319 361 Josephine Anna, 71

PAULSEN (Mary) Maria, 503 Ada Pauline, 520 Allen, 369 Alma E, 520 Alvena, 558 Alvina, 367-369 Anna, 199 370 Ardis Rose, 366 Arlo, 366 369 Arnold, 504 Audrey, 104 366 367 Ben, 367 Bessie Irene, 520 Beth, 366 Clair E, 520 Clara, 520 Clara Johanna Maria, 520 523 Clara Marie, 366 368-370 550 Clarence Julian, 520 Clement Lucian, 520 Daniel, 366 Daniel Wayne, 17 Darwin, 366 David, 366 Delbert, 366 367 Delbert Henry, 17 423 Deloris, 366 Dona, 366 369 Donald, 82 367 368 Donna Mae, 154 184 Dora, 199 370 Doris M, 366 Dorothy, 368-370 Elaine, 367 Elaine Elizabeth, 17 423 Eldo, 366 504 Elizabeth, 199 367 370 Ella, 199 368 370 531 Ellen, 17 39 366-368 Elte, 368 Emily, 366 504 Emma, 368 554 559 568 Eugene, 366 Frieda, 367 504 539 540 550 Gail, 369 Gary Lee, 370 George, 39 366-368 George H, 17 Glenda, 82 Gordon, 82 Gregory, 82 367 Gretchen, 82 367 Harold Paul, 520 Harriet, 492 Heinrich, 367-369 558 Herman, 199 368 370 531 Herman Jr, 368 Ian, 369 Irma, 368 504 Isabel Irene, 17 James Darwin, 366 John Fred, 366 368-370 550 John Peter, 520 523 Joyce, 366 Joyce Elaine, 17 Katherine, 368 370 Kathy Lee, 370 Katrina, 199 Kay Dee, 366 Lawrence Neil, 366 Lesley, 369 Lloyd, 369 Louis, 77 Lucas, 367 Majory, 369 Maria (Mary), 366-369 504 Marion, 186 Marjorie, 186 Marjory, 369 Marlys, 369 Marx, 368 Mary, 82 367 368 Mary M, 77 Mathilda, 368 557 558 Melba, 369 Mildred, 369 504 Olga, 504 Paul E, 520 Pete, 199 368 370 Richard James, 366 Robert J, 369 370 Robert L, 154 184 Rose, 366 Ruby, 368 Ruth, 82 367 369 370 Shirley, 366 Shirley Ann, 17 Sophia, 366 504 Sue Jong, 366 Terry Lee, 370 William, 366-369 503 504
PAULSON Glenn, 219 240 Harriet, 504 Leota, 219 240 Omar, 240 Sharyl Lee, 240 Stella, 240 Steve, 240

PEACOCK Betty Lou, 370 390
Christopher Michael, 371 Cindi, 370
Harold John, 370 371 390 394 Iris
May, 370 371 390 394 James Patrick,
370 390 Joan Kay, 370 390 577 Linda
Jean Andrews, 371 390 Michael John,
371 390 Patricia Lee, 370 Rebecca
Lynne, 370 Steven Patrick, 370
PEACOCK WHITE Joan Kay, 371
PEAR Dora, 61
PEARSON Edith Frieda, 47 233 Lewis
Arthur, 47 233
PEASE Aaron Michael, 484 Audrey
Elizabeth, 484 Emily Lynn, 484 Garald
Gene, 484 Garald Jay, 484 Gerald
Gene, 490 Joan Annette, 484 490
Jolene, 484
PECK Ida, 547 Joseph Neil, 127 Lloyd,
547 Shelby Lynn, 127
PECKA Phyllis, 96 172
PEETZEE Nell Augusta, 148
PEIRCE Charles Andrew, 482 Charles
Kevin, 481 486 Diana Marie, 481 486
Emily Marie, 482 Rebecca Marie, 482
PELTON Martha E, 286 Will, 286
PENCE Jody, 431
PERCIVAL Diana Patricia, 529
PERIE James, 556 Julia, 571 Julie, 556
PERLMAN Karen Lynn, 52 Lawrence Jay,
52
PERRY Marion A, 459
PERSONS Mildred Cecil, 290
PERSSON Gertrude, 571 573 Gull
Elizabeth, 524 528 529
PETCU Scott Mitchell, 122 Stacey Ann,
122
PETER Ann, 336 Arthur, 336 Bernard, 336
Beverly, 330 Caroline, 336 Caroline
(Carrie), 344 Clara Caroline, 324 328
329 331 332 Clara Caroline Christine,
325 Cleo, 330 Dale, 330 Frederick
Carl, 325 330 Fritz, 325 330 Henry,
328 330 Joann, 330 Louis, 336 344
Magdalena, 338 344 346 Maria Sophia,
330 Martha, 560 Mary, 328 330
Sophia, 325 Verna, 336 Vesta, 330
PETERS Amanda Rae, 595 Ann, 227
Anna, 500 Betty, 454 455 456 Connie

Kay, 338 Hertha, 72 73 Jennifer
Suzanne, 227 Johann, 500 Ladonna,
354 Sarah Lynn, 595 Scott Michael,
387 595 Sharon Kay, 221 227 Sherri
Lynn, 387 595 Shirley, 498 Victor, 354
Wilhelmina, 600 William Frederick,
227 William John Jr, 221 227 William
John Sr, 227
PETERS MANGO Connie Kay, 354
PETERSEN Adelia, 600 Alfred M, 371
Anna, 371 Augusta W, 371 Chris
George, 371 Delia, 371 Della Rae, 269
Dorothy Ann, 213 Dorothy Anne, 214
Duane, 269 Everett, 371 Harriet, 371
Harriette, 371 John F, 371 John Martin,
371 Karl John, 269 Leone, 371 Lillian,
371 Lloyd, 213 214 Lynda, 371 Lynn,
213 Michael, 213 N N, 600 Neil, 213
Patricia, 371 Thomas, 213 Wayne, 213
PETERSON Brian R, 337 Carolyn, 246
Hazel Arlene, 419 Helen Irene, 224
Jennifer Christine, 257 Kendy, 576
Laurie Mae, 337 Marsha Jane, 529
Marty Neal, 529 Melanie Joy, 529
Michelle Mary, 529 Nancy, 26 80 Ruth
Lois, 213 214 Sandra Jane, 529
Sandrda Jane, 525 Scott Neal, 525 529
PETRASALKA Coreen, 3
PETTER Elizabeth, 54 John, 54
PETTY Charlotte Louise, 267 Deanna, 267
James E, 267 Martha, 267 Stephen V,
267 William V, 267
PETTYCOURT Claude L, 177 Ella M, 177
Kathleen, 151 158 172 177
PEYTON Dorthy, 79 Ica D, 79 Jacob E, 79
PFAFFENB ACH Anna Katherina, 30
Anna Katharina, 565
PFAFFENBACK Anna Katharina, 34
PFIFFNER Cheryl Ann, 387
PFLUEGER Nettie, 285
PHEFFER Wilhelmine (Wilma) I, 386 393
Wilhemine I, 265 Wilma, 265
PHELPS Benjamin Ryan, 372 Charles, 62
Charles Ray, 61 Charles Ray Jr, 61 371
Charles Ray Sr, 371 372 Daniel Jack,
102 Deborah Darlene, 102 Donald
Scott, 102 Dora, 61 Gregory Lynn, 61
372 Hannah Darlene, 102 Harry John,

375 590 Marilyn, 375 590 Mary Frieda, 375 Matthew James, 375 Megan Angie, 375 Pat, 590 Patricia Frieda, 47 375 Renee Ann, 375 Steven Delmar, 375 590 Tanya Rachelle, 375

POHLMANN Luise, 564

POHLMEIER Kenneth, 231 Renay Ellen, 231

POKAY Albia, 399 401

POLANSKY Matthew David, 95 99 Nathan David, 99 Sally Jo, 95 99 William Matthew, 99

POLBREISG Jean, 552

POLDBERG Kimberly Alice, 93

POLEGE Lois, 445 Walter, 445

POLK Alvin Ernest, 95 159 375 376 Elsie Katherine Louise, 94 95 159 375 376 James Herold, 375 Jane Ellen, 375 Jeffrey Michael, 375 Joanne Louise, 375 Jordan James, 375

POLLMAN Connie Lynn, 324 Gene, 324

POLYCHRON Adrienne, 175 307 Alexandra Adrienne, 307 Jason John, 307 John Philip, 175 307

POMMIER Angela Marie, 258 Benjamin John, 258 Jeanne, 255 258 Murray, 255 258

PONTZER Gloria, 120 572 Jean, 120 John, 120

POOCK Alvin Ernest, 159 375 376 Amylin Elizabeth, 376 Angie, 376 Anna Elizabeth Caroline, 334 335 Carol Rae, 376 490 Dorothea, 68 149 154 155 157 162 168 173 180 181 183 Dorothy, 176 Dorothy Gertrude, 151 159 177 Dorothy Gertude, 174 178 Elda Anna Dorothea, 159 322 323 326 330 331 Elsie Katherine Louise, 159 376 Ernest, 158 177 330 376 377 Ernest Carl, 168 Gertrude K, 177 330 376 377 Gertrude Katherina, 158 168 Harold Edward, 376 Harold Ernest, 159 376 377 Helen A, 159 376 377 Henry, 158 James Herold, 376 Jane Ellen, 376 Jerry Wayne, 376 Joanne, 376 John, 334 335 Kyle Edward, 376 Leona Frieda, 159 377 464-466 Martha, 334 335 337 340 350 354 Norma Lee, 376 377 Sandra

A, 376 Scott Ervin, 376 Timothy Steven, 376

POOCK MICHEL Elda Anna Dorothea, 331

POOCK See Polk, 95

POOLE Christina, 306

POPE Judith, 58 59

POPE Mary Faye, 236

POPENHAGEN Amanda, 378 Bernice Ella Louise, 287 377 535 536 Carol Jean, 379 380 Carrie, 378 380 Cynthia Jolene, 378 Dane, 378 Ella, 379 Ella Sophie, 377 379 Ella Sophie Hannah, 378 Ellen, 379 Elsie Sarah Hannah, 378 379 Emma, 287 378 Emma C, 378 Ethel Josephine, 378 Fern Melissa, 378 Fred, 379 Fred Herman, 378 Frederick John Martin, 377 379 Frederika, 378 Fredricka, 287 George Conrad, 287 378 George William, 378 Grace, 378 Henry Elmer, 287 378 Jeffrey Karl, 378 380 Jennifer Marie, 379 380 John, 378 John Peter, 377 Joseph, 254 287 379 Joseph August, 253 Joseph C, 379 Joy Harold, 378 Kade, 379 Katherina Elizabeth, 282 287 377-380 Katherine Marie, 377 Katie, 287 Kenneth William, 379 380 Laverle, 379 Lena, 379 Leona, 380 Leone, 287 378 Lida Johanna, 378 Loretta, 378 Louis Carle, 378 379 Margie J, 378-380 Marie R, 379 Nellie Landas, 378 Norman Karl, 378-380 Otto George, 378 Richard Roy, 379 380 Robert James, 379 Rosa Marie, 253 379 380 Rose Marie, 287 Roy Joseph August, 287 379 380 Wilhelm Fredrich, 282 287 377-380

POPP Anna, 358

PORT Gertrude, 517

PORTER Mary Kaye, 56

POSSEHL Arthur, 381 Carl, 380 Christian, 380 Dorothea, 381 Emma Katherine, 381 Frederick, 380 George John Henry, 381 Gustav, 381 Heinrich, 380 Jacob, 380 Joachim, 381 Johann, 380 381 Karl, 380 381 Katrina, 380 Louis Heinrich, 381 Louise Doerzman, 381 Lydia, 381 Mahala, 381 Maria, 380 381

Pearl Ethel, 381 Sophia, 380 381 Vera, 381 Wilhelm, 380

POST Sara, 350

POSTEL Allan, 291 Allan Eugene, 271 297 Allen, 595 Cynthia Ann, 271 Elaine, 291 Elaine Enid, 271 297 Gayle Osborn, 271 Mark Allan, 271 Thelma Evangeline, 271 Thomas Allan, 271

POTTEBAUM Christine, 302

POTTEE Helen, 256 259 261

POWERS Andrea Jean, 211 Brian Frederick, 204 Eric, 204 Hayden Lee Wayne, 47 441 Jeffrey, 211 Kathleen Jo, 137 204 Nova Lynn, 47 Rebecca Erin, 204 Therese Marie, 47 441 Walter Anton, 204 Walton Anton, 137

POYNTER Bryce Lee, 347 Dorothea Mathilda, 347 Lee, 347

PRACHTER Anna Elisabeth, 281 381 Anna Katharina, 363 381 Johann Peter, 363 Johann Peter Jr, 381 Johann Peter Sr, 381 Katharina Elisabeth, 363 381

PRANSKY Elizabeth, 394

PRATHER Carol Ann, 26 152 David, 26 Greg Alan, 152 Shawn David, 152

PREIS Sophie, 196

PRESGLER Alma, 553 Roland, 553

PRESTON Douglas, 374 Helen, 374

PRESYLER Alma, 118 Charlene Alice, 119 Cynthia Helen, 119 Helen, 119 Hubert, 118 119 Roland, 118

PRICE Anthia, 106 Benjamin, 488 Carol Ann, 56 Cecelia Jane, 488 Dan, 106 Debra Jo, 56 Dona, 366 369 Donna Jean, 56 Dorothy Sattizahn, 488 568 Esther, 488 Gretchen Marie, 106 111 349 Hazel, 488 568 Larry, 85 Lori, 85 Matthew Robert, 56 Megan, 85 Rober Jr, 56 Robert Sr, 56 Samuel, 488 Thomas Jeffrey III, 85

PRIMMER Betty Jean, 481 Carl Eugene, 481 Nellie, 10 Pamela Darlene, 481 483 488

PRIMROSE Betty Jo, 255 258 Dora M, 371 Esther, 505 Gayle, 505 Harold, 505 Harriet, 371 Harriette, 371 James, 371 Lloyd, 505 Robert, 505 Susan, 505

PRIMUS Helen, 7

PRINCE Lori, 511 Thomas Jeffrey III, 511

PRINE Kathleen, 194

PRINGLE Amber, 13 Angeline Kay, 13 212 Christina, 13 Karen, 13 Richard, 13 Ronald, 13 212 Steve, 13

PROBST Michele Marie, 524 528 Raelene, 501

PROHOSKY Brenda, 383 Mark, 383

PRUDENZ Marijean, 30

PRUSHA Ashley Elizabeth, 528 Garett Paul, 528 Laura Christine, 528 Steven P, 528 Tina Cristine, 528

PUCKETT Gary, 400 Gary Lee, 401 Julie Lynn, 400 401

PUDENZ Marijean, 30

PUGH Marilyn Monroe, 214

PYLE Christopher James, 382 David William, 188 George Luppert, 188 337 381 382 James George, 188 381 Janet Maria, 188 382 Joan Edna, 188 337 381 382 Robert Carl, 188 Scott Richard, 382 Susan Jane, 188 382

PYLE FUSAN Susan Jane, 382

QUALLS Daniel V, 253 Susan Marie, 253

QUASS (George) Alfred Jr, 383 Alfred, 383 Alfred Jr, 382 Alfred Sr, 382 383 Beulah Marie, 382 383 Donna, 382 Doris Pauline, 382 383 Dorothy, 382 383 Dorothy May, 383 Edward, 383 Elizabeth, 383 George, 382 George Jr, 383 George Sr, 382 James, 382 Joe Edward, 382 John G, 382 383 Laura, 382 383 Mary, 382 383 Stanley, 382 Teresa, 382 Wilhelmin, 382 Wilhelmina, 383

QUIGLEY Clover Denise, 525

QUIMBY Brad, 385 Carolyn Sue, 385 397 Jay, 385 Jay Morgan, 397 Matt, 385

QUINN Rita, 234

RAABE Christina, 383 Dorothea, 383 Fred, 383 Joachin Frederich, 383 Johann Joachim Frederich, 39 John, 383 Louisa, 39 383 Mary, 27 39 383 Sophia, 383

RADEKE Karen, 54 55

RADEMACHER Elisabeth, 570 Kath, 315

RADLOFF Ina Mae, 14

RAETZ Alice, 547 548 Anna, 194 195 197 Clarence, 194 Emma, 194 292 Emma Louise, 275 276 279 288 Gottlieb, 194 Gottlieb, 197 John, 194 547 548 Mary, 547 Robert, 547 Wilma, 194

RAGER Charles Arthur, 355 356 Dianne Caye, 355 356

RAHR Henrietta, 453

RAILSBACK Edna Alice, 94 416 419 432 433 438 Gary, 438 Mae, 438

RAINBOW Frances, 68

RAINWATER Chad, 432 Kathelyn Elizabeth, 432

RAIRDIN Darrell Robert, 520 Nina Jo Ann, 520 Tami Lynn, 520 Zachary Todd, 520

RAMMELSBERG A F, 273 Albert Edwin, 391 394 Alice Faye, 383 577 Alphonsa, 390 Alphonsa Fredrich Emil, 288 Alphonsa Friedrich Emil, 273 383-385 390 Andrew, 391 Anna, 435 Anna Katharine, 394 Anna Katherine, 265 282 386 387 391 393 395 398 435 Anna Maria, 395 Anna Marie, 392 Anne Marie, 390 Ardis, 265 396-398 Arthur, 383 Arthur J, 370 Austin, 386 Ava, 385 Barbara, 386 Barbara Jean, 385 386 388 389 397 Benjamin Kurt, 393 Bernadine, 384 391 Bernice M, 384 391 393 Bertha, 116 384 390 479 Beulah, 385 Bill, 265 Billie, 385 389 Brenda Sue, 391 Brian, 384 Brian Karl, 389 Brooke Lee, 386 Bruce Thomas, 384 395 Carl, 265 Carl (Charles), 384 386 426 434 Carmen C, 288 596 Carol Ann, 389 392 394 397 Carol Marie, 9 384 510 Carolina Catharine Marie, 435 Carolyn Sue, 80 385 397 Caryl, 385 Cathy Rae, 386 397 Cecil, 384-386 388 389 392 395 Cecil Faye, 385 Celeste, 391 Charles, 265 434 Charles (Carl), 390 Charles Fred, 265 386 393 Charlotte, 390 Christopher Lee, 389 Clydene, 385 Cody, 386 Constance, 116 117 265 388 390 Dale, 385 Daniel John, 384 Darlene, 385 386 David, 386 395 435 David Henry, 386 397 Dianne Rose, 397 Donna, 391 Donna Fay, 395

Dori, 389 Doris Ann, 387 388 593-595 Dorothy, 369 370 Dorothy Jean, 387 391 Earl Edward, 273 384 389 396 397 Elaine, 396 Elaine Laura, 391 392 394 Elfriede, 390 Elizabeth, 370 386 Ellen Pauline, 384 395 Elmer Henry, 265 Elmer Henry David, 387 388 397 Emiline, 383 390 Emma, 435 Emma Katherine, 396 Emma Katherine Elizabeth, 266 273 290 384 389 397 Eric, 397 Eric Gerald, 389 Esther, 384-386 388 389 392 395 Esther Mae, 385 388 Eunice Jean, 388 Evelyn Hattie, 395 Evelyn Hettie, 6 388 Fern, 385 388 Florence Ellen, 392 396 397 Floy J, 238 288 Frederich, 390 Gerald Lee, 389 397 Gladys Marie, 78 273 389 Glen, 385 389 Goldie Etta, 265 387 397 Harold Roy, 384 389 396 Hazel, 389 396 Hugo, 116 389 434 Hugo H, 390 391 Hugo Herman Friedrich, 383 390 479 Iris May, 370 371 390 394 Issac William, 395 Ivan L, 286 288 384 Jacob Steven, 391 James Everett, 392 James William, 387 391 395 Jason, 385 Jeanne, 384 389 Joan, 390 391 Joan Lee, 288 Joanne, 397 John, 390 391 John August, 384 391 393 John B, 391 394 John Charles, 391 Jordan Paul, 391 Josie Ann, 386 Julia, 384 390 Julia M, 476 479 Kandace Taylor Hampton, 397 Karen Ruth, 394 Karla Marie, 391 394 Katherine Ruth, 135 386 389 392-395 397 Kathleen Rose, 384 389 396 Kathryn, 385 392 Kay Elaine, 48 392 394 Kelly J, 394 Kenneth Carl, 392 396 397 Kenneth Ralph, 392 395 Kevin Ray, 395 Kristi Kaye, 397 Kurt Marvin, 392 394 Kyla Kay, 387 Kyle L, 394 Larel Jean, 391 Laura Katherine, 265 393 582 590 591 593 Laverne Rose, 396 397 Leanna Rose, 396 Lena, 395 Leona, 390 391 Leona A, 286 288 384 Leonard, 386 Lisa K, 391 Lois Ruth, 15 393 396 Loren, 384 Louise, 117 390 Louise May, 265 384 388 390-392 394 395 Lurel Jean, 387 395 Lynae, 386 389 Magdalena (Lena),

386 435 Marcy Ann, 389 Maria Katharina Barbara, 265 384 426 434 Marie Louise, 392 Marinda, 384 Marlene Ann, 386 393 Martha, 202 Martha R, 391 393 Marvin Fred, 391 392 394 396 Mary, 390 Mary Ann, 391 Mary Jane, 273 288 383 Mathilda Katherine Karoline, 435 Matilda, 384 Matthew Carl, 384 Melvin A, 286 383-385 388 390 394 Merle, 273 Michael Allen, 384 Mildred, 385 Mildred Winifred, 391 395 Monica Ann, 391 394 Nettie L, 285 286 383 384 388 390 394 Norma L, 143 144 394 Ona Lea, 395 Ottillie, 390 Owen Chris, 386 Paul David, 397 Paul G, 391 394 Rachelle Danielle, 391 Ralph Leonard, 384 Ralph Leonard II, 391 395 Ralph Leonard Sr, 265 388 390-392 394 Randy, 395 Rhonda Jean, 386 389 Robert, 389 Rose Elizabeth, 265 395 582 592 593 Rosina Sophia Katharina Christine, 435 Roxy, 385 395 451 Roy Carl Jacob, 135 386 389 392-395 397 Ruby, 384 Ruth, 391 394 Ruth Ellen, 390 Sarah Louise, 389 Selma Ann, 396 398 Shirley Ann, 100 273 396 Sophie, 435 Stacey L, 389 Stephen Carl, 397 Stephen Chet, 393 Susan, 397 398 Susan Kay, 397 Tammy Jo, 392 396 Todd Kenneth, 392 397 Troy Kenneth, 392 Verla Emma, 273 397 Vernon David, 385-387 389 397 Victor David, 396 397 Wilhelm, 265 282 Wilhelmine (Wilma) I, 386 393 Wilhemine I, 265 William, 435 William (Bill) Henry, 396 397 William (Bill) Henry Jr, 398 William Edward, 397 398 William Henry, 265 William R, 265 282 386 387 391 393-395 398 William R (Wilhelm), 435 Wilma, 265
RAMMELSBERG CULPEPPER Elaine, 392
RAMMELSBERG KETTLESON Dorothy Jean, 387
RAMMELSBERG SOUTO Carol Marie, 385

RAMMELSBURG Barbara Jean, 386 Christopher Lee, 386 Earl Edward, 276 Emma Katherine Elizabeth, 276 Vernon David, 386
RAMMESLBERG Al, 568 Alice Faye, 292 Alphonsa Friedrich Emil, 292 Carol Marie, 292 Eunice Jean, 292 Hugo H, 292 Joan, 292 Louise, 158 Mary Jane, 292 Melvin A, 292 Nettie L, 292 Norma L, 292
RANDALL Charles Ernest II, 142 Gretchen Louise, 158 Pamela Kay, 127 142 Sondra Kay, 142 Thomas, 158 Verna Dean, 142
RANDO Karen A, 113 154
RANDOLPH Bill, 412 433 Christopher J, 440 Danna Ann, 440 Lois Ann, 412 433
RANK Mary Katharine, 221
RANKIN Abby Lynne, 521 Gregory Nordlund, 521 Julia Lynn, 521 Laura Joy, 521 Madison Blon, 521 Marion, 521 Ronald, 521
RASK Caroline, 398 399
RASMUSSEN Elizabeth, 38 207
RATH Katherine, 514
RATHBUN Corinne Elizabeth, 22 Douglas, 22 Douglas Jay, 541 Janel Lyn, 541 Janel Lynn, 22 Nichole Elizabeth, 22
RATHJE Adam Jeffrey, 400 Alan Henry, 53 99 398 400-402 Albert H, 398 Albert Henry, 98 99 399 401 Albia, 399 401 Amanda, 402 Andrea Marie, 400 Angelica Renee, 403 Anna, 399 Anna Rebecca, 401 Anna Rebecca Katherina, 400 402 553 561 Ardith Mae, 320 399 Arlene, 99 Arlys Van Langen, 399 400 Arnold, 561 Arthur, 399 401 Beth, 87 88 403 Candice, 398 Caroline, 398 399 Chad Alan, 398 Chelsea Rose, 403 Craig Allen, 398 399 Daniel Edward, 399 Dawn, 399 Dixie Lee, 398-401 Dorothy Olive, 53 99 398 400-402 Elaine Marie, 398 402 Eldora, 399 400 Elisabeth, 401 561 Elizabeth, 399 402 567 Emma, 399 401 Emma Gertrude, 130 398-402 Glen

685

689

690

RUPPRICH Charles Daniel, 453 Florence
  Agusta, 453 Glade, 453 Henrietta, 453
  Mathilde, 453 Noma Lurreen, 453
  Norma Lureen, 210 Rose, 453
  Wilhelmine, 453 William, 453
RUSCH Augusta M, 449
RUSH Austin James, 305 Kathryn Jean
  Elizabeth, 234 Lisa Nn, 305
RUSSELL Elizabeth Mcgregor, 420
RUTAN Carol Ann, 389 397
RUTZ Edgar, 501 Paula Eliza, 501
RYAN Denise, 178 Donna Loy, 338 Karen,
  594 Marie Catherine, 412 Mark, 178
  Mary El, 553 562 Suzanne, 385 510
RYKER Jody, 59
RYSER Pamela, 107
SADLER Leanne Marie, 423 433 Megan
  Elizabeth, 433
SADLER Terry, 423 433
SAEGEBRECHT Frederick, 453 Sophia
  (Tonka), 453
SAGE Amy, 68 Ann Lucille, 68 115 Craig,
  68 Elizabeth, 113 Ernest E, 68 Frances,
  68 James E, 68 115 Patrick, 68
  Timothy, 68
SAHA Anna, 64 Blanche Ellen, 64 453 454
  Edward, 64 Eleanor, 454 Etta, 64
  George, 64 Glenn, 454 John, 63 64 453
  454 John D, 64 453 Katie, 64 Mary, 63
  64 453 Mildred, 454
SALERNO Mary E, 105 109
SALLER Adeline, 219 Alice, 219 Bud, 219
  Charlene, 219 Dorothy, 219 Fred, 219
  230 Herb, 219 Herbert, 219 Lenore,
  219 Sophia Dorathea, 219 230
SALVIATI Jennifer Jean, 247 Jessica
  Elise, 247 Sandra Jean, 247 Stephen,
  247 Stephen Paul, 247
SAMUELSON Elenora Julie, 65 Vernon,
  65
SAND Diane, 488
SANDERS Eunice, 77 Kenneth, 264
  Martin, 264 Wilma, 264
SANDERSFELD Madora Gesina, 17
SANDLER Barbara Joan, 95 96 98 99
  Barbara Joann, 96 Edward Max Sr, 95
  Phyliss, 95

SANDMAN Connor Gregory, 358 Gregory
  John, 358 Greta Louise, 358 Jack, 358
  Judy, 358 Rebecca Lynn, 358
SANDROCK Anna Margarethe, 30
SANKEY Sharon Kay Mckibbin, 462
SANKOT Mary Jane, 325
SANSGAARD Diane, 348
SARTOR Annie Maria, 448 449
  Magdalene, 448 Nicholas, 448
SASS Amy, 454 Anna Gertrud, 70 Anna
  Gertrude, 68 455 Arlo Lee, 454 456
  Bertha, 69 455 Betty, 454-456 Beverly,
  454 456 Colleen, 456 Dean, 456
  Delaine, 259 454 455 591 Donald
  Arthur, 454 456 Edward Elmer, 455
  Elmer W, 259 Elmer William, 454 455
  Emma, 68 Emma A, 454 Emma Anna,
  256 261 454-456 Frederick Johan
  Heinrich, 68 Frederick Johann
  Heinrich, 70 Fredrick, 455 Fredrick
  Johan Heinrich, 455 Frieda, 68 206 455
  Jane, 454 456 John, 68 454 John A,
  256 261 454-456 John Sr, 68 Karoline,
  455 Lavonne Lucille, 454 456 Lori,
  454 Nancy M, 455 Rose, 259 454 455
  Sandra, 455 Sheryl, 456 Willard John,
  454-456
SAUER Earnest George, 105 Frances
  Ellen, 105 110 Ica D, 79 Jerry, 399 402
  Kristie Kay, 399 402 Vesta Alice, 105
SAVAGE Allye K, 519 James, 14 519
  Kaleb James, 519 Karrah Ann, 14 518
  Sue, 519 Terry, 156 181 Tim, 519
  Verilyn Fern, 156 Verilyn Ferne, 181
SCEWE Johnie Jr, 370 Lawanna Jean, 370
SCHAAKE Anna Elis, 475
SCHADE Mardene Lorraine, 244 246
  Robert, 244 246
SCHADLE Kaye, 58 59 Keevan, 216
  Kelly, 59 Miranda, 59 Valerie, 59
SCHAEFER Bethann Alice, 433 456 531
  Hattie, 497 Hilbert Christian, 412 433
  456 Lois Ann, 412 433 456 Mary, 77
  Mary Margaret, 433 456 Milda, 494
  495 497 Robyn, 433 456 Ryan, 456
  William Arthur, 433 William (Billy)
  Arthur, 456

693

SCHAEFFER Dorothy, 559 575 Ella, 43
Henry, 559 Jill Denise, 559 Julie Kay,
559 Lynn Walter, 559 Opal, 43
Timothy Todd, 559 Walter, 559 575
SCHAER Gerald Richard, 134 Lillian
Elizabeth, 134 Susan Betty, 126 134
SCHAFER Anna Juliane, 403 404 405 406
Anna Juliane (Julie), 406 Carola, 23
578 Christina, 263 George, 406 Julia,
406 Maria Elisabeth, 356 Marie
Elisabeth, 346
SCHALL George William, 463 Martin, 463
Susan, 463
SCHAMBER George, 498 Helen, 498
Susie, 498 557
SCHANBACHER Allan Edward, 272 456
459 461 Amanda Katharina Marie, 460
Amanda Katherina, 457 Amanda
Katherina Marie, 422 Amanda
Katherina Marie, 482 Amanda
Katherine Marie, 486 Amy Marie, 462
Andrew Michael, 462 Barbara Ann,
420 457 Benjamin Robert, 462
Bernard, 457 459 Bernard Jacob, 272
283 456 460-462 Bill, 304 Bill Wilbert
Martin, 420 Brenda Jo, 462 541 Brian
Allan, 461 Christina Marie, 461
Christine C, 457 Christine Lois, 458
Cindy, 304 Dorothy Gertrude, 87 457
461 Dustin Raymond, 462 Eda, 304
Eda Barbara Elizabeth, 94 420 460 461
Eda Elizabeth, 463 Edward, 457
Edward Frederick, 458 459 461
Edward Friedrich, 457 458 460 Edward
Michael, 457 458 Eileen, 187 Eileen
Ann, 420 460 Elizabeth Anne, 460
Elma Ann, 272 Elma Ann Christina,
283 456 461 462 Elma Anna Christina,
460 Erica Kae, 458 Gail Lynn, 462
Gertrude, 272 Gertrude Marie, 228
Gertrude Marie, 420 457-460 463
Gilmore Julius, 96 458 459 461 Glenn,
304 Glenn Edward, 458 H Marie, 462 J
Edward, 457 Jacob, 130 458-460 James
Christopher, 460 Jane, 303 Jane Ann,
458 459 Janet, 461 Janet Kay, 458
Janet Sue, 272 462 Janette Dee, 457
459 Jason Bernard, 460 Jean Lynn, 458

459 Jeanette, 459 Jeffrey Allan, 457
459 Jennifer, 462 Joann Marie, 458
Joanne Elaine, 246 272 461 Joel
Michael, 460 John, 187 John Wilbert,
420 460 Joyce Elaine, 272 456 457 459
461 Julius, 228 272 459 Julius Daniel,
420 457-460 463 Leigh Christine, 462
Lolita Marie, 96 458 459 461 Lori Sue,
457 461 Lucinda Kay, 462 Maria, 459
Maria M, 458 460 Marie (Mary)
Dorothea, 399 459 Marie Dorothea,
128 130 138 Marie M, 130 Mary, 128
130 459 Mary Dorothea, 128 132 135
138 Merlyn Melvin, 244 246 272 461
Michael Lee, 462 Mrs Bernard, 459
Mrs Ronald, 461 Nancy Jean, 303 304
419 458 461 Patricia Sue, 420 461
Robert Alan, 462 541 Ronald August,
272 Ronald August Jr, 462 Ronald
August Sr, 462 Sharon Kay Mckibbin,
462 Steven Michael, 462 Timothy Ray,
457 458 Wilbert, 458 Wilbert Martin,
94 458 460 461 463 Wilma, 457 Wilma
Augusta, 458-461
SCHANBACKER Eda, 187 Edward
Frederick, 311 Edward Fredrick, 304
Gilmore Julius, 460 Joann, 460 John,
187 Lolita Marie, 460 Nancy Jean, 304
Wilbert, 187 Wilma Augusta, 304 311
SCHARRCHMIDT Anna, 343 Anna
Christina, 341 Anna Elisabeth, 341
Johannes, 341
SCHATZ Arthur, 504 Bradley Carl, 278
Cynthia Kay, 278 Janice Kay, 268 277
Kenneth C, 268 277 Marie, 504
SCHAULL Alice, 463 Anna, 463 Bette,
463 Bonnie, 463 Carolyn, 463
Catherine, 463 Clellan, 463 Edna, 463
George William, 463 Ida, 463 John
Martin, 463 Laurence, 463 Lloyd, 463
Marguerite, 463 Marlene, 463 Martin,
463 Michael, 463 Nicholas Jr, 463
Nicholas Sr, 463 Nicolas Jr, 463
Rosannah, 463 Sandra, 463 Sarah
Catherine, 463 Susan, 463
SCHEAR Susan Betty, 131
SCHEEL Katharina, 2
SCHEELE Martha, 502

694

SCHEER Dorance, 322 330 Patsy Lee, 322 330

SCHEESLEY Angela Marie, 580 Bethany Ann, 580 David William, 580 Harold, 540 580 Kathryn Ann, 540 580

SCHEETS David, 28 Susan, 28

SCHEETZ Elmer, 252 Ruth, 252

SCHEIB Adam, 517 John, 517 Laura, 517 Lucy, 517 Mary, 33

SCHELERMAN Nick, 467

SCHELLBERG Anna Elisabeth, 362-364 Anna Katharina, 363 448

SCHELLBERGER Sana, 589 Wilhelm, 589

SCHEMPP Albert, 212 Dorothy, 212 463 572 Jane Marie, 212 463 Jerod Albert Lee, 212 Julie Ann, 212 463 Leland, 212 463 572 Olga, 212

SCHEMPP FRANKMAN Julie Ann, 464

SCHENGEL Balthasar, 201 464 Bathasar, 201 Catharina Marie, 201 Charlotte Luise, 201 464 Heinrich, 201 Heinrich Peter, 201 464 Horst, 464 Ielka, 464 Inge, 464 490 491 Irmgard, 464 Johann Peter, 201 Maria Katharina, 201 464 Marjo, 464 Minna, 201

SCHERER Anna Elisabeth, 585 Anna Marie, 586 Anne Maria, 585 Joh Simon, 585

SCHERF Sophia, 377

SCHIEFELBEIN Cathryn, 418

SCHIEL Brett, 60 Dawn Renee, 60 Dennis, 58 59 Verlee Ann, 58 59

SCHIFFER Paula Louise, 326

SCHILD Ann, 241 Dick, 6 241 Donald, 241 Mildred, 6

SCHILDWACHTER A Catharina, 313

SCHILIG Jeanice, 236

SCHILLER Laura, 259 Tim, 259

SCHILLIG Jeanice, 252

SCHILLING Wilhelmina, 217

SCHIMEK Aretha, 182

SCHIRM Albert, 310 457 466 Anna, 228 435 Anna Gertrude Katherina, 411 424 465 466 Anna Katherine, 465 Anna Maria, 411 465 493 496 Bertha, 543 Bertha M, 542 544 546 Beverly, 320 Brian Charles, 320 Carl, 466 Carol A,

465 Carol Leona, 319 485 Carolena, 228 Caroline (Lena), 465 467 Carolina (Lena) B, 377 465 466 Carolyn, 465 Catherine, 310 466 Charles, 465 Charles Irvin, 319 485 Chris, 465 Dan, 465 Danny, 377 David, 377 464-466 Debbie, 377 Delores, 25 372 Delores Olanda, 465 Denise, 465 Donald C, 465 Doris, 469 471 Edgar, 465 466 Elaine, 466 Elaine M, 465 466 Eldo, 159 466 Eldo August, 377 464 465 Elsie, 465 466 Fred, 465 George Martin, 411 465 Gertrude, 228 Harold, 465 Heinrich (Henry), 411 424 466 Henry, 105 465 Hilda, 107 Hilda Gertrude, 105 109 411 Irvin, 320 372 465 Jacob, 64 Janice, 377 464 466 Jeffery Allen, 320 Johann George, 465 Katherine, 105 Kay, 377 Lena, 466 469 Leona Frieda, 159 377 464 466 Lester, 466 Marcia, 377 Maria Dorthea, 411 466 Marilyn, 234 Mark, 377 Martin, 465 466 Martin W, 228 Martin William, 377 465 467 Mathilda, 467 Matthew, 435 Merle, 466 Norine Elizabeth, 466 Oscar, 467 Otto William, 411 466 Randy, 466 Randy D, 465 466 Rosa Marie Elizabeth, 64 Rosemary, 465 Sue, 377 Susan, 320 465 William, 228 424 466 469 Zenolia, 372 465 Zolina, 320

SCHLADWEILER Donald, 498 Myrna Lou, 498

SCHLARBAUM Lori, 102

SCHLIEMANN Alma, 129 Edna, 498

SCHLOEMAN Anna Marie, 467 August, 467 Ernst Heinrich, 467 John, 467 William, 467

SCHLOTFELD Elizabeth, 34 Ludwig, 34

SCHLOTTERBACK Albert, 394 Amelia, 468 Anna, 468 472 Anna E, 231 308 470-472 Annis, 301 467 470 Ardis, 468 471 Ardis Rose, 468 470 Ardislyn, 468 Arnold, 315 Becky, 469 Brooke, 471 Bryon Arthur, 471 Carl, 468 471 Carol, 469 471 472 Charles, 468 Charles C, 468 Chris, 469 471 Christina, 471 Clara, 89 471 Connie, 469 Cora, 548

SCOTT Bessie, 111 Christine Louise, 536
Donna Irene, 526 536 James, 174
Leona, 390 391 Madeline Frances, 160
Richard James, 526 536 Steven James,
536
SCOY Christine Lynn, 487 Richard David,
487 Robert Dean Van, 487 Rox Ann,
487 Velma Elizabeth Katherine, 487
SEABA Bruce, 548 Lisa, 548
SEABROOK Jeanice, 236 252
SEBOR Anna Maria, 428
SEEBORG Christine, 229 Chrstine, 229
SEEBORGER Anna Rebecca, 401 Anna
Rebecca Katherina, 400 402 553 561
SEEBRANDT Susana (Lena), 499
SEECK Ann, 499 Anna, 499 500 Annie, 7
Cacilie, 498 499 500 Carl, 498 Carma,
499 Cecilia, 498 Christina, 499
Christine, 499 Claus, 500 Deborah, 499
Edna, 498 Emma Esther, 213 214 215
498 Esther, 14 200 499 Ferdinanduait,
499 Gertrude, 499 Gustaf, 499 Herman,
499 Hilda, 498 John, 214 498 499
Lavon, 498 Lena, 499 Mable, 498
Margaret, 214 498 499 Margaretha,
499 500 Martha, 499 Mildred, 499 N
N, 7 Peter, 499 Peter Charles, 499 Peter
Matthies, 500 Roy, 499 Thies Heinrich
Sr, 499 Thies Jr, 498-500 Wiebke, 500
Wilbert, 498
SEEFELD Alfred, 553 557 Anna, 553 557
Apolonia, 553 Evelyn, 553 Gladys, 553
SEEGMILLER Angie, 238 Jacob Mikal,
238 Jason Donald, 238 Mikal, 238
SEEMAN Ardis, 500 August, 500 600
Bree Janel, 501 Brian Glenn, 501
Carroll W, 500 Charles E, 500 Donna,
500 Donna M, 500 Emma, 500 600
Emmett, 500 600 Jeff, 500 Jennifer,
501 John, 54 600 Lon Carroll, 500
Mabel Elizabeth, 54 Mary, 500 Mary
Ann, 500 600 Mildred, 53 Sherry, 500
Tina, 39 Wilhelmina, 600
SEENE Martha, 194
SEEVIS Annie, 492
SEHLE Anna Martha, 169
SEIBEL Anna Gerdraut, 249 Anna
Katharina, 157 160

SEIFERT Geoffrey Michael, 13 268
Michael, 13 268 Patricia, 13 268 Sarah
Marie, 13 268
SEIGFRIED Marian Frances, 494 N N, 494
SEILHAMER Elizabeth, 38 207
SEITZ Joann Lucille, 479
SEK Sue Jong, 366
SELCK Allen, 306 Josie Lynn, 306
SELK ----, 498 Chris, 444 Debra Sue, 270
501 Deeanne, 270 277 Delbert, 278
Flossie, 444 Gina, 270 277 Jeanette,
278 Linda, 277 Linda Marie, 270 278
Louie, 444 Rich, 270 Rick, 501 Vera,
444
SELKEN David Jon, 270 Debra Sue, 270
501 Denise, 270 Dianne Marie, 270
501 Donald Gene, 270 277 501 Donna
Mae, 270 277 501 Rudolph, 270
SELTRECHT Bertha, 21 Margaret, 229
SEMELROTH A J, 321 Adam John, 321
Bradley, 206 321 Diane Lee, 206 321
SENNE (Mary) Maria, 503 Agnes, 247
Agnes Emma, 244 246 461 502
Amanda, 56 58 501 503 Anita, 250
Anna, 501-504 Arthur, 501 502
August, 501-504 Beth Carla, 503
Conrad, 502 503 Cynthia Sue, 250
Donald, 250 Douglas Herman, 250
Elfrieda M, 502 Elfrieda Martha, 250
Elnora, 502 Elsie M, 246 250 502 503
573 Emma Mina, 522 524 Emma Mina
Dorothea, 503 519 523 529 Fred, 246
250 502 503 573 Gladene, 250 Hannah,
102 103 502 503 546 Henry Christop,
502 Herbert, 502 503 Herman, 250 502
503 Hilda, 502 503 555 569 573 Irene,
414 Irene K, 305 306 502 503 Janet
Ann, 501 John, 235 501-504 524 566
Karen Sue, 502 Katherine, 235 501-504
524 Laurine, 502 504 Lenore, 250
Lillian, 501 502 Maria (Mary), 366-369
504 Martha, 194 502-504 506 Myron
Edwin, 527 Nathine, 502 503 Olga, 492
503 504 Patty Jo, 502 Paul, 503
Richard, 503 Sandra Kay, 501 Terry,
502 Titus Matthew, 502
SENNNE Olga, 491
SENTZ Clara Johanna, 427

701

SERBOUSEK Valeria Renee, 593 Valerie
Renee, 387
SERCY Dalmer Porter, 336 347 Judith
Lee, 336 347
SERGEANT Kyla Kay, 387 Todd, 387
SESSLER Carolyn, 532 Clara, 149 532
John, 532
SETHER Clara, 185
SETTLAGE Allison, 596 Deborah Lynn,
422 596 Stephen D, 596 William Lee,
422 596
SEVENING Jacob, 22 Julia, 21 568 576
Lena, 22
SEVERIN Marge, 26
SEWARD Suzanne, 162 173
SEYBOLDT Bernadette, 438
SHAFER ----, 407
SHAFFER Becky, 469 Doris, 469 Robert,
469
SHAH Amber Ali, 317 Heather Danielle,
317
SHANKS Lisa Christine, 509
SHANNON Elfriede, 390 Jackie Ann, 595
John Michael, 594 Kimberly Kay, 153
Larry D, 594 Rex, 390 Rick, 153 Ruth
Ann, 594 Vicky, 594
SHARKS Lisa Christine, 213
SHARON Myrtle, 320
SHAW Dave, 409 Edith B, 446 Harold C,
446 Helen Polly, 290 365 Joan Lee,
446 447 496 Martha, 409 Milton
Roberts, 365 Ruth Marie, 365 Tara
Jean, 134
SHEEHY Earl, 559 597 Erin Ann, 597
Kevin Earl, 597 Renee Elaine, 559 597
Lilliam, 12 Lillian, 12
SHELL Lucy Isabelle, 293
SHELLEBERGER Barbara, 592 Elisabeth,
592 Marie Elisabeth, 589 Louise, 499
SHELTON Edwina M, 330 331 Jonathan
Russell, 37 Melinda Sue, 37 Russell
Dean, 37 Sara Elizabeth, 37 Suela
Marie, 37
SHENENBERGER Meda, 253 254 Meta,
254 Naomi, 254 Sylvanus A, 254
SHERWOOD Michelle, 16 18
SHIELDS Donella, 252
SHIFFLETT Ashley Ellen, 526

SHIMP Juanita, 351
SHIPE Dean Allen Jr, 56 Dean Allen Sr, 56
Debra Jo, 56 Laurie Anne, 56 Sherlyn
Ann, 56
SHIPLEY Joan Marie (Kiernan), 422 Mark
Patrick, 490 Michael Richard, 490
Susan Laura, 490
SHIPPEN Bonnie Jo, 136 Ernest, 136
SHIREMAN Gertrude, 499 Mabel, 143
SHIRLEY Fleta, 189
SHOEMAKER Cynthia Diane, 304 419
Darlene, 304 Linda, 157 476 479
Robert, 304
SHONKA Phyllis, 444
SHRADEL Clara Mary, 123
SHRAME Betty, 220
SHUEY Carol, 330 Joann, 330 Kathy, 330
Robert, 330
SHULDT Elmer L, 354 Gladys E, 354
SHUSTER Christopher Wayne, 331 Cindy
Lou, 331 Gary Wayne, 331
SICK Katharine Louise, 151
SICKLER Bonnie Jo, 136 Jerry, 136
SICRA Ron, 112 Sharon, 112 Steve, 112
SIDENOUR Rosannah, 463
SIEBER Margit, 534
SIEGFRIED Anna Martha, 587 Lina, 69 70
SIEK Bobbi Jean, 542 Byrdine Ann, 542
546 Charles Henry, 542 Charles
Robert, 542 546 Elisabeth, 175 Elsie L,
483 Hilda, 542 William Weichman,
542
SIEPMAN Kathleen Marie, 139 Sandra
Lee, 134 139 Stephan Bruce, 139
Stephen Bruce, 134 Thomas Stephan,
139
SIEPMANN Albert, 506 Anna, 504
Bernard, 506 Gertrude, 504-506 Helen,
505 506 Henry, 505 506 John, 506
Kate, 505 506 Mabel, 505 Marvel, 505
Mary, 505 506 Mary Roberta, 505
Maybelle, 505 506 Miriam, 505
Wayne, 505 Wilhelmena, 506 William,
504-506
SIERRA Daniel Julien, 46 Katherine
Ambrosia, 46 506 Lisa Ann, 46 442
Philip Timothy, 46 Rita Ann, 46 441

506 Timothy Lawrence, 46 441 506 Veronica Ann, 46

SIEVERS Janice, 498

SILVEY Arlene, 105 108 349 Florence, 108 Fred, 108

SIMMER Charles, 400 Jeanne Marilyn, 399 400 401

SIMMONS Craig, 379 Drew, 379 Jennifer Marie, 379 380 Thomas, 379 380

SIMNACHER Anton (Tony) H, 507 508 Becky, 508 Bonnie, 508 Gary, 508 Joseph, 507 Josephine, 507 Kevin, 508 Lisa, 508 Loretta, 508 Lori, 508 Myrtle, 507 508 Phyllis, 507 508 Robert, 507 508

SIMON Edda, 447 Hermann, 447

SIMONDET Jennifer Lea, 529

SIMPSON Esther, 504 506 George, 252 Gladine, 506 Harold, 504 506 Margaret, 507 Mariam Jean, 252 Marie, 252 Patricia, 506 Suzanne, 507

SIMS David Wayne, 489 Patricia Ann, 489

SINDELAR (Carl) Charles Martin, 417 Bernadine Elsie, 417 Connie Sue, 416 417 439 Terry Edward, 417 439

SINDT Alvena, 557 Anna, 199 370 Dale, 507 Dale Berendt, 507 Darwin, 507 Dorothy, 2 197 507 Duane, 507 Elmer, 3 Gregory, 507 Henry J, 2 507 Jean, 507 Judith, 195 197 507 Katharina, 2 Katherine, 500 Kelly, 507 Lester, 2 197 507 Linda, 507 Margaret, 2 467 507 Mary Ann, 500 600 Mollie, 467 Sheila, 507 Wilbert H, 2 Wilhelm, 2 Will, 199 William, 370 500

SING Jeff Tam, 14 518 Kami Joy, 14 518 Mrs Theodore Tam, 518 Theodore Tam, 518

SISLEY Ardis, 265 396 397 398 Edgar, 398

SISSLER Fredericka, 27

SIZER Betty, 214 215 Charles Mills, 214 Mary Agnes, 214 Mary Elizabeth, 214 215

SKERSICK Christe Cameron, 350 Christie Cameron, 508 David Peter, 350 508 Dayna Lee, 508 Karen Marie, 508 Kenneth Gerald, 350 352 508 Marie

Elizabeth, 350 352 508 Michael David, 508 Pamela, 350 508 Richard Kenneth, 350 508 Sara, 350 Sara Post, 508 Susan Ruth, 508 Tracy Lynn, 508

SKINDZEIL Dawn, 506

SKLENNAR Rosie, 507

SKORDOS Michael Harry, 367 Robin Carol, 367

SLABY Helen A, 94 98

SLACK Erica, 159 Glen, 145 159 Glenda, 145 159

SLATER Vickie, 213

SLAUGHTER Daniel Preston, 244 Diana Lynn, 244

SLAYMAKER Ida, 463 Linda, 218 Mildred, 499

SLOAN Leah Irene, 482 Linda Sue, 457 482 William Lee, 482

SLONE Magdelene, 48 233

SLOVAK Belinda Lou, 509 Bo William, 509 Brock Charles, 509 Earl, 508 562 Helen, 508 562 Pennie Lou, 508 William, 508

SMETLZER Charlene, 103

SMITCHGALL Elisabeth, 560

SMITH Alexander, 532 Allen Jane, 213 509 Angie, 376 Anna, 335 344 Ardith, 213 Carla, 213 509 Chas Jorden, 509 Cheryl Rae, 360 Chris, 595 Chris Jay, 213 509 Christe Cameron, 350 508 Cleo, 477 Connie, 473 Craig Allen, 32 35 Curt, 213 509 573 Cynthia (Cindi), 520 521 Darlene, 511 Darlene Gladys, 156 Dewey, 213 Donna, 211 260 Doris, 414 Douglas Curt, 213 Edna, 551 Edward, 525 529 Elaine, 335 Elizabeth, 335 477 Eric, 532 Erik Allen, 35 Esmeralda, 477 Ethel Todd, 233 Florence, 477 Gary, 194 George, 477 Grace, 442 Harold, 335 344 Helen B, 418 Henry, 477 Jacelyne Kimber Dee, 589 James, 104 366 507 Jeanette Ann, 213 509 Jesse, 104 Jessica Jo, 509 Jo Anne, 366 Joanne, 104 John T, 52 Jon B, 370 Judith Elizabeth, 532 Justin, 104 Kimberly Suzanne, 351 Lena, 22 Leona Kathleen, 194 Lisa Christine, 213 509 Lorri Sue, 351 Lynda Frances, 32 35

Marsha Jane, 529 Mary, 83 477 Mary Ann, 351 Megan Ashley, 509 Mildred, 213 509 572 Mineard, 477 Molly Jean, 507 Nancy Jo, 507 Natalie Ann, 351 Nicholas, 532 Nina, 151 Nina Laura, 177 Patricia Lee, 370 Patrick, 532 Randy L, 360 Ray, 156 511 Richard, 351 Robert, 335 Sallie Jane, 507 Sandra Jane, 525 Sandra Jean, 494 Sophia, 83 84 Susan, 481 Suzanne, 507 Tony R, 532 Vesta Alice, 105 Vickie, 213 Wendy Marie, 595

SMOCK Charlotte, 315

SNAVELY Becky Lee, 414 Doris, 414 Herman, 414 Nicholas Robert, 414 439 Rebecca Lee, 420 439 Robert, 439 Robert Herman, 420 Robert Herman (Casey), 414

SNELL Etta, 263 387 Goldie Etta, 265 387 397 Julian Franklin, 263 387 Lucy Isabelle, 263 283 292

SNIDER Charles, 398 Dale, 398 Judy, 99 398 Kim, 398

SNIDER-HOLTZ Christa, 398

SNOUSE Jessie, 460

SNYDER Angeline, 509 C W E, 509 Donald, 509 Edward, 509 Ella, 509 Emma, 509 F E, 509 Jennie, 509 Lila B, 83 84 Lois, 509 Mary Ella, 509 Mary Louise, 509 Merle, 509 Mildred, 509 Ralph Wallace F, 509 Susan Adeline, 509 Suzanne, 509 Wallace F, 509 Wallace Stephen, 510

SODEN Judy, 555

SOEHREN Celia, 467

SOHL Gusta, 71

SOHN Johann Casper, 585 Wilhelmina Lucina, 585

SOJKA Susan, 227 Susan Trachta, 221

SOLBERT Cheryle Marie, 58 Jennifer Marie, 58 Karen Sueanne, 58

SOLUM Kathleen, 56

SOMMERS Marie, 62

SOREANO Juliane, 194

SORENSEN Karen, 388 Larry, 388

SORENSON Lynn, 65 212

SOTELO Evalina, 388

SOUKUP Mary Elizabeth, 403 N N, 403 Sue Ellen, 287 Terry James, 287

SOUTHWICK Edwin, 118 Mary Ann, 118 444 Polly Bethel, 118

SOUTO Carol Marie, 292 384 510 David Lane, 510 Gary Melvin, 385 510 Jackson Lee, 510 Jeffrey Nelson, 385 510 Robin, 385 510 Suzanne, 385 510 William, 292 385 510

SOVERN Grace, 54

SPADING Cora Ann, 485 Ron, 485

SPAIN Dale E, 459 Freida, 459 Janette Dee, 457 459

SPEAKER George, 241 Sharyl Lee, 241

SPELLERBERG Katie, 477

SPELLMAN Elizabeth, 476 478

SPENCER Eileen Rose, 331 Hazel, 76 Ted, 331

SPIESS Alison, 4 Ann, 4 Gary, 4 53 Kimberly, 4 Kimberly Sue, 53 Nicole, 4 Robert, 4

SPIRKEL Anna, 314

SPITZ Marie, 89 Wm P, 89

SPOERER Barbara, 435 Friedrich, 423 Johann Martin, 425 Katherina Elisabeth, 423 Maria Barbara, 148 164 384 423 425 428 430 434 435 Maria Margaretha, 425

SPOONER Esther, 157 183 Harold, 157 183

SPOR Maria, 326

SPRATTE Lena, 373 Marie, 373

ST AUBIN Terry Lynn, 367

ST CLAIR George H, 517 Mrs George, 517 Nellie H, 517

ST JOHN Cara Nicole, 511 Debra Ann, 511 Duane Paul, 511 Patrick Ryan, 511 Stacie Lyn, 511

STAAB Anna, 86 Howard, 86

STADEM Myrtle, 441

STAFFORD Beverly Kay, 214 472

STAFFORD Daniel, 472 Darin Joe, 181 David Michael, 214 472 Eric Michael, 472 Joe, 152 181 Justin, 181 Sheila Kay, 472 Teresa Jane, 152 181

STALLER Helen, 498

STALLMAN Germaine, 225 265 Louis, 265

STEVENSON Carmen, 572 Maude Estelle, 156 Mildred Esther, 155 156 161 182 Wilbert Roy, 156
STEWART Alice, 463 Archibald C, 526 Donald, 463 Donald Merle, 463 Evelyn, 463 Gerald, 463 Kimberley, 3 Lester, 463 Loren, 463 Robert, 3 Todd, 430 Tonya Sue, 430
STICKLING Dorothy Louise, 50
STICKNEY Charles, 320 Jon Charles, 320 Kathleen Ann, 320 485 Myrtle, 320 Stacy Elizabeth, 320 Steven William, 320 William Charles, 320 485
STIEFF Carol A, 205
STIEN Albert, 513 Albert (Beanie), 513 515 Anenia, 513 515 516 600 Anna, 513-515 Darlene Mary, 439 513 516 Darrell, 515 David, 513 515 Deborah Lynn, 218 541 Debra, 515 Delbert Fredrich, 513 515 Diane, 515 Donald, 415 Donald Richard, 516 Douglas Alan, 218 514 515 541 Edna, 218 513-515 Elizabeth, 513 Ellen, 513 Emma, 39 514 Franz, 514 Franz Heinrich, 514 515 Hazel, 513 515 Heinrich, 235 514 515 Heldt, 513-515 Henry John, 513 515 516 600 Howar William, 218 Howard William, 513-515 Jacob Douglas, 218 Janelle, 515 Jean, 514 Jerid Richard, 516 Joanne, 514 515 John, 514 515 Katherina Margareta, 514 Katherine, 514 Linda Marie, 516 Lucas William, 218 Maria Mary, 514 Mary, 415 513-516 Maxine, 513 Peter, 514 Richard, 513 Richard Henry, 415 515 516 Roger Henry, 516 Rose, 513 515 Ryan Dennis, 218 Shirley, 513 515 Stephanie, 513 Tilla, 191 515 Warren, 513 Wayne A, 513 Willie, 514 Zachary Roger, 516
STIEN RICHTER Emma, 514
STIEN RINDERKNECHT Darlene Mary, 416
STIENKE Emma, 574 Esther, 574 Henry, 571 574 J, 574 Merill, 574 Ruth, 574 Sophia, 571 574
STILSON Craig, 3 Kristina Rae, 3

STIMSON Anita, 229 Karie, 229 Kent, 229 Ralph L, 229
STJOHN Debra Ann, 184 Duane Paul, 184
STOCK-BETTIN Lorraine, 77 Lorraine, 339
STOCKDALE Daniel, 487 Kathy Dawn, 487
STOCKER Christian, 516 Emilie, 65 516 583 Karin, 65 516 Karl, 65 516 583 Lars, 516 Marcel, 516 Mareike, 516 Martina, 65 516 Ralf, 65 516 Wolfgang, 65 516
STODDARD Tammy, 399
STOEBNER Alma, 119 Arlene, 119 553 Emanuel, 119
STOLL Christina, 165 Ella, 325
STOLTE Donna Loy, 338 Elsie Minnie, 338 346 Faith, 338 Jason Christopher, 338 Jennifer Lynn, 338 John, 338 346 Lavonne Alma, 339 Maureen, 338 Michael John, 338 Myron Dean, 338 Patricia, 338 Robert Lee, 338 Ronald Leigh, 338 Sharon Kay, 338 Stephanie Ann, 338 Virginia, 338
STOLZ Dakota, 142 Hilary, 142 Paul, 12 142 Sherri Lee, 142 Sherrie Lee, 12
STOMBAUGH Deborah Versluis, 107
STONE Angela Denise, 6 Joyce May, 6 388 Michelle Leigh, 6 Wayne B, 388
STONEFIELD Billy, 61 62 Jacqueline Marie, 61 62
STONER Brent, 259 Christy, 259 Janice, 259 Tracy, 259
STORBECK Anthony Clarence, 5 Breanna Katherine, 5 Kathleen Marie, 4 5 Nathan Anthony, 5 Nicholas Arthur, 5
STORMER Marie, 201
STORTY Kathy, 229
STORTZ Kathy, 238
STOVIE Rebecca Lynne, 370 Timothy, 370
STRAKA Mary Frances, 516
STRAMER Jeff, 255 Karmen Jane, 255
STRAMPE Patricia Eileen, 317
STRANKMAN Elisa, 321 Eliza, 545
STRASBAUGH Cindy Lou, 331 Eileen Rose, 331 Lester, 331
STRAUBE N N, 450

STRAUSS Almore L, 105 Anna, 105 107
Christina M, 105 Edward A, 105
Florence M, 105 Henry, 105 Otto E,
105 107 Richard, 105 Robert, 105
Wilhelmina, 105
STRAWN Al, 75 298 Elizabeth Veronica,
75 Elizabeth Veronica, 298
STREETER Anne-Marie, 79
STRELLNER Carrie, 517 Cindy, 216 434
Eda, 517 Elsie, 32 37 517 Elsie Anna,
29 33 264 516 Emma, 517 Emma
Louise, 516 Esther, 517 Esther
Florence, 405 406 407 408 516
Frances, 517 Frances Marie, 269 275
276 294 517 George, 517 Gertrude, 517
Helen, 517 555 Henry, 517 Herman,
517 Ilene, 499 Jochim, 517 Julia, 29
406 516 517 Julia Fredericka Amelia,
275 Julie Fredericka Amelia, 243
Julius, 243 275 406 516 517 Julius D,
29 275 Laura, 517 Minnie, 242 243 246
Nellie H, 517 Wilhelmina Gertrude,
242 243 246 Wilhelmina (Minnie)
Gertrude, 517 Wilhelmina (Minnie),
517 William, 517
STREMME Anna Gertrud, 517 Anna
Katharina, 342 343 517 Johann
Heinrich, 517 Johannes, 342 343 517
Maria Katharina, 146 297 342 343 345
350
STREMME Marie Katharina, 24
STRIBLING James, 357 Justin, 357 Renee,
357
STRICKELL Arlyne, 322 330 457 Charles,
322 Hattie, 322 Helen, 457
STRIMMOEN Olga, 83
STRODE Julie, 45
STRUCK Ella, 467
STRUTZ Mabel Frances, 348
STRUUBE N N, 164
STRUVE Pearl, 7 8 9
STUART Albert, 115 Anna, 21 115
Dortha, 115 560 James C, 21
STUDT Pastor, 282
STUECK Andrea, 81 357
STUMME Elinor Eileen, 348 354
STUMP Anthony, 56 Sherlyn Ann, 56
Tyler Paul, 56

STUMPFF Kathy, 486 Kathy Ann, 575
Margaret Ann, 575 Richard Ora, 575
STURTZ Bertha, 29 Dixie Lee, 92 93 Jill
Marie, 92 Kent, 92 93 Ryan Steven, 92
STURTZ-MYERS Alvina, 60
SUBERGER Anna, 399
SUHR Annette Marie, 11 517 Arlo Hans F,
517 518 Arlo Hans Fredrich, 421 Arlo
Hans Fredrick, 11 Donna Rae, 11 518
Elsa, 11 Hans, 11 Kim, 11 518 Mark
Allen, 11 518 Pearl Evelyn, 11 420 421
517 518
SULLIVAN Dorothy, 2 507 Ray, 507
Rosie, 507
SUMMERS Gloria Lee, 439
SUMMERVILLE Minnie, 28
SUNDERLAND Catherene, 594
SUNDERMEYER Martha Johann, 355
Martha Johanna, 334 339 350 354
SUNDSTROM Ellen Sophie, 40 41 Hedvig
Gustava, 40 John August, 40
SURFACE George Moffett, 257 Tammy
Sue, 257
SUTCLIFFE Caitlin Marie, 518 Catherine
Mary, 219 518 Corrine Elsie, 219 220
518 Ephraim, 382 Hannah, 382 Jean
Susan, 220 518 Joseph Walter, 219 220
518 Margaret Amanda, 219 Mary, 382
383 Thomas Joel, 219 518 Walter
William, 219
SUTLIFF Natasha Renee, 5
SVANOE Myrtle, 441 William Rennard,
441
SVARSTAD Agnes, 491 Agnes, 504
SVOBODA Allison Nicole, 96 Bradley
Scott, 95 96 Dianna Lynn, 95 96 James
P, 294 James Robert Michael, 294
Reva Marjorie, 294 Sandra Marie, 569
Zachary James, 96
SWALES Ronda Jean, 153 160
SWALLEY Sharon, 102
SWANK Mabel, 505
SWANSON Augusta Christine, 274
Burland, 558 Christine, 260 Evelyn,
558 Gaylord, 260 Janet Elizabeth, 272
John Emmanuel, 274 Juliet Elizabeth,
263 270 274 279 Lee, 65 Lorna, 556

Lucy Katherine, 65 Mary Ann, 260
Robert, 556
SWAYSE Gina, 91
SWAYZE Gina, 92
SWENBY Carol J, 317
SWENSON Cody Nicholas, 492 Diana
Elaine, 492 Laura Beth, 492 Randy
Gene, 492
SYME Alicia Lynn, 14 519 Brayden Tri,
519 Debra Ann, 14 212 518 519 Kami
Joy, 14 518 Karrah Ann, 14 518 Katie
Marie, 14 518 Larry, 14 212 518 519
Leona, 14 Lexa May, 519 Nathanial
Jay, 14 519 Nikayla Shae, 519 Robert,
14 Tyler Jay, 519
SYMESKI Gertrude Ilene, 122
SYMONDS James, 294 Janene Rae, 270
294 Karen, 294
TAGGATZ Bertha, 580 N N, 580
TANNER Inez Vivian, 40 41 Mary Janette,
40 114 William Allen, 40
TASCHNER Albert Adolph, 519 521 523
524 528 Alene, 519 521 526 527
Alexander Jonathan, 527 Amelia
Caroline, 519 523 539 Ana Dorthea,
521 Andrea, 527 Andrew Mitchell, 529
Anna, 522 Anna A, 521 523 525 Anna
Catherina, 521 523 527 Anthony Lee,
529 April Christine, 527 Ardella, 522
Ardella Lyn, 527 Ardys Louise, 525
Arlene Anna Marie, 519 522 524 526
Arthur Howard, 519 524 Ashley
Victoria, 528 Barbara Joan, 520 527
Bertha Emily, 524 Beth Ann, 527 Betty
Jo, 519 522 Bonnie, 520 521 Bruce,
529 Carly Nicole, 527 Carol Joyce, 524
Catherine, 529 Cathleen Mary, 520 527
Christopher Ernst, 521 Clara, 529 Clara
Johanna Maria, 520 Clara Johanna
Maria, 523 Clarence Emmett, 524
Craig Randall, 528 Cynthia (Cindi),
520 521 Dana, 529 David Leroy, 520
521 David William, 520 Deborah
Denise, 520 527 Dennis Arthur, 519
Devin Dakota, 527 Diana Patricia, 529
Donald Walden, 520 527 Donna
Deetta, 528 Dylan, 529 Edna, 523
Eleanor, 209 Eleanor Emilia, 520 524

Elfrieda, 524 Elsa Wilhelmina, 524
Elsie Elizabeth, 522 525 Emma
Elizabeth, 519 521 523 524 528 Emma
Mina, 522 524 Emma Mina Dorothea,
503 519 523 527 529 Esther Margaret,
519 521 Eva Myrtle, 520 522 525 527
Eve Myrtle, 521 Forrest Knuth, 520-
522 525 527 Forrest William, 521 522
Frances Idell, 526 Frances Idella, 524
529 Frederick, 523 Frederick Wilhelm,
523 Fredrich Elmer, 523 529 George
Carl Ernest, 523 Geraldine Ann, 519
524 Gottlieb, 521 523 Grant Gottlieb,
527 Gull Elizabeth, 524 528 529
Harvey, 519 521 526 527 Hazel, 270
Hazel Bernice Marie, 28 520 522 524
527 Heinrich, 521 Helen Marcella, 525
Henry, 523 Henry Herman, 521-523
525 Herbert August, 519 522 524 526
Ila Jean, 270 277 278 284 285 293 294
522 527 James Herbert, 522 Jan Terese,
522 527 Janet, 521 522 Jean K, 525 528
Jean Marie, 522 Jennifer Lea, 529 Jill
Elisa, 522 Joanne Kay, 524 Johan, 521
Johan Gottlieb, 519 520 522-524 526
Johann Gottlieb, 521 John August, 117
520 523-525 529 John Carroll, 524 528
529 John James, 522 Julius Ernst, 503
519 522-524 527 529 June, 527 529
Karen Elizabeth, 524 Kari, 520
Kathleen Kay, 520 Kay Dianne, 525
528 Kenneth, 527 Kenneth Albert, 519
524 Larry Leo, 525 528 529 Laura
Anna, 519-521 523 526 Leslie J W,
522 525 Linda M, 527 Linsey Kay, 528
Loree, 529 Lori, 520 Margaret Lorene,
525 529 Mari, 520 Marian Frances, 521
525 Marie, 523 Marie Ada, 523
Marilyn Ann, 522 526 Marlys, 522 526
528 Mary, 529 Mary Jane, 525 528 529
Mary Louise, 526 529 536 Mathilda,
117 520 523-525 529 Matilda Anna,
523 526 Matthew Kirk, 520 527 Mavis
Martha, 519 525 528 Michael Julius,
520 527 Michele Marie, 524 528 Mimi,
529 Murray Andrew, 520 527 Myron,
270 Myron Edwin, 28 520 522 524 527
Nicholas John, 529 Nicohlas Gregory,

708

710

711

URE Christine Lynn, 235
URHAMMER Edward, 285 Lucille, 285
URIDIL Barbra, 293 538
URMY Bertha, 285 288 290
USHER Alta Maria, 266
UTECHT Claris Dean, 263 292 Gary Dean,
    293 Noreen Etta, 263 292
UTHOFF Arlene Lois, 583 592
UTITUS Jeannie, 56 Jeannine, 56
UTTECHT Theresa, 120
VAIL Mary, 252
VALENTA Gary, 218 Susan Gail, 218
VALENZUELA Amanda Jayne, 536
VALESKY Jane Ann, 474
VAMPEL Anna D C, 70
VAN DEE Iowa Ann, 419
VAN HAMME Danelle Marie, 441
    Danielle Marie, 419 Eugene Peter, 419
    Iowa Ann, 419
VAN HEIDEN Betty Jo, 427 432
VAN VLECK Alta Gayle, 53 Curtis Lee,
    536 Marjorie, 536 Richard, 536 Tamara
    Kay, 536 Timothy Lee, 536
VAN VOY Elizabeth, 370
VAN WEICHEL Wanda Kay, 591
VANCE Darles, 172
VANDAGRIFT Martha, 28 Ora, 28
VANDEE Inez, 273
VANDERHAMM Cellen, 50 Claudia, 50
    Wilma, 50
VANDEUSEN Opal, 89
VANHEIDEN Betty Jo, 271
VANSICKEL Jennifer, 538
VANTHOURNOUT Teresa, 452 453
VANVLECK Alta Gayle, 45 Marjorie, 45
    186 Misty, 45 Richard, 45 186 Tamara
    Kay, 45 Timothy Lee, 45 Troy Dean,
    45
VARNADO Joshua Daniel, 216 Judy
    Marie, 216 Justin Mercedes, 216 Reo,
    216
VAUGHN Joel Trevo, 589
VAUPEL Alfred, 193 Anna, 51 193 Anna
    Elisabeth, 15 Anna Gertrud, 362 364
    Anna Gertrude, 537 Anna Martha, 169
    Arnold, 193 Carl, 16 193 537 Elsie
    Martha, 537 Emma, 193 Frieda, 537
    Frieda Elisabeth, 537 Gertrud, 536 537

Helen Rose, 536 537 Henry, 193
    Johann Peter, 169 Justus, 362 364 533
    536 537 Katharina, 362 532-534 537
    Katherina, 537 Kathrina, 16 193
    Louise, 193 Martha, 193 Tobias, 67
VAVENKA Esther, 265
VEIGA Michelle Lyn, 525 Steven Robert,
    525
VELASQUEZ Amy Katherine, 136
VELKY Jennifer Diane, 396
VESELY Rose, 454 455
VESLEY Rose, 259 Sandra Kay, 591
VILETA Elda, 176 Elda Ann, 182 Leo C,
    182
VILHAUER Dick, 83 Mary Jo, 83
VILLONT Jarrod Keith, 596 Jay Dee, 596
    Jordan Tyler, 596 Julie Rae, 595 Justin
    Robert, 596
VIRTUE Christopher David, 87 Cynthia
    Marie, 87 Cynthia Marie, 457 Heather
    Christine, 87 Mark David, 87 457 Peter
    David, 87
VITEK Patricia, 3 372
VITT Ida, 300 Joseph, 300
VOCHELL Grace, 378
VOEHL Carrie, 480 Sophe, 436
VOELTZ Arlene Anna Marie, 519 522 524
    526 Norma, 102 103 Normal, 503
    Sylvia B, 232 593
VOGELER Irene, 217
VOGELGESANG Alfred, 409 Elinor, 409
VOGLER Abigail, 259 Clare, 259 Donald,
    259 Eleanor, 259 Janice, 259 Kathy,
    259 Kim, 259 Laura, 259 Leonard, 259
    261 Loren, 259 Mildred, 261 Sarah,
    259 Sophia, 259
VOGT Alice, 538 Andie, 293 538 Anna,
    538 Augusta, 538 Augusta Wilhelmina,
    538 Barbra, 293 538 Bonnie, 293 538
    Christine Marie, 537 Dale, 249 Delbert
    Dale, 263 293 537 538 Donald, 537
    Donald Adam, 293 537 538 Ellen
    Marie, 293 538 Harry, 538 Helena
    Mae, 538 Herman, 293 Hermann Karl,
    538 Jared, 538 Jeanne, 293 Jennifer,
    538 John, 538 John Duane, 293 538
    Julie, 293 Katherine Jean, 293 Lonnie
    Edward, 293 Louis, 538 Ludwig, 538

714

WEBELHUTH Anna Elisabeth, 111
Johannes, 111
WEBER Anna Elisabeth, 342 Anna
Elizabeth, 517 Heike, 66 Jo Ann, 421
Johannes, 342 Kathryn Jean Elizabeth,
234 Madgalene, 453 Peter, 66 Sarah,
66 Susanne, 342 Theresa, 66
WEBERT Eleanor, 197 Eleanor Louise
Barbara, 272 421 541 Fred Peter, 421
Janet Lynn, 22 421 541 Jo Ann, 218
462 541 Judy, 74 197 Judy Louise, 421
541 Mathilda Meta, 421 Melvin, 197
Melvin Gottfried, 272 421 541
WECKS Eric, 194 Lillian Grace, 194 Mary
Jaylene, 194
WEED Eleanor, 116 Shirlee, 58 59
WEEDER Calvin Magpie Christian, 374
Eric Bruce, 374 556 Susan Jane, 374
556
WEETER Renee Ann, 528 Rick, 528
Shane, 528 Stacy Renee, 528
WEHLING Paula, 307 415
WEHMHOFFER Engle Mary, 550 551 552
WEHR Beverly, 152 Beverly Kay, 183
Charlotte, 152 Gene, 152 183
WEHRKAMP Beth, 542 Beth Marie, 185
Donald D, 185 Glenn, 145 185 542
Karen, 185 Kristin, 185 Pamela, 185
542 Yvonne Marie, 145 185 542
WEICHMAN Amelia, 29 542 546 Anna,
300 301 513 543 544 Audrey, 316
Bertha, 543 Bertha M, 542 544 546
Byrdine Ann, 542 546 Caroline, 22 542
546 Charles, 474 543 544 545 546
Christian A, 545 Clarence, 315 316 544
Cynthia Joy, 543 David Edward, 543
545 Debra, 486 Debra Joy, 543 575
Donald, 543 544 Donald Edward, 546
575 Earl, 543 Edna, 544 Elizabeth, 543
546 Elizabeth Maria, 321 544 545
Elma, 546 Elma Ellen, 28 543 Elmer,
543 Elsie, 316 Emery, 544 546 Emery
J, 306 Emma, 315 316 544 546 Ethel,
544 546 Ethel F, 306 Firman, 544 546
Frank, 474 544-546 Fred, 543 544 Gail,
544 Gladys, 544 Gladys Myrtle, 303
Glenn Abraham, 546 Harry, 543 Harry
Edward, 321 544 545 Henry, 316 543

544 545 546 Herbert Franklin, 303 545
Irene, 544 Irvin, 546 James, 545 Janeen
Kaye, 303 419 Jo, 580 John, 51 542-
545 John C, 542 545 546 Josephina,
471 Josephine, 88 89 468-470 472 474
545 Joyce, 544 Lena, 543 546 Leo, 546
Leona, 316 Lester, 543 Lolita, 233 234
544 Louis, 543 546 Louise, 1 546
Madeline, 102 103 502 544 546
Marjorie, 546 Marvel, 545 Mary, 51
474 542-546 Mary W, 545 Mike, 580
Mrs Fred, 513 Norma, 545 546 Pauline,
474 544-546 Phyllis, 544 Rhoda Ann,
545 Rozella, 305-307 544 Shirley L,
543 546 Shirley Lorraine, 575 Victor,
543 Victor Dewey, 542 544 546 Viola,
544 Wilhelmina, 543 545
WEIDMAN Mary Jane, 318 354 Melinda
Jo, 318 Sam, 318 354 Stasha Lynn, 318
WEIR Glen, 483 Lillian, 483
WEIS Bettie, 308 310 311 Bettie
Philomena, 227 Edward, 310 Minnie
Ella, 242 Theresa, 310
WEISART Delores, 569 573
WEISE Eva Catharina, 161 Eva Catherine,
167 Pauline, 216 434
WEISERT Marie, 375 590
WEISS Amanda Gesina Rebecca, 19
Clarence Henry, 417 Gregory Stephen,
220 518 Jane, 437 443 Jane Myrl, 417
Jean Susan, 220 518 Kavan Gregory,
518 Kellen Joseph, 518 Laurel Emil Sr,
19 Lorane Ann, 20 Lorene Ann, 17 19
423 Margaret, 518 Stanley, 518 Viola
Minnie, 417
WEITERMANN Gretchen Louise, 158
Robert, 158
WEITZ Anita, 52 438
WEITZKAMP Donna, 157 172
WELCH Barbara, 220 226 Beverly, 302
David, 192 Gene, 191 192 John, 192
Mary, 191 192 Paul, 220 226 Paula Jo,
220 226
WELLER A Magdalena, 312 Anna Guida,
335
WELTON Ernest C, 360 Kathryn Jean, 359
360 361 Stells M, 360

WELTY Alberta Elizabeth, 289 410 547
Amy Kathleen, 410 547 Anna Lavina,
410 Cale, 410 Gerald Nathan, 289 410
547 Kathleen, 547 Scott Alan, 410 547
Sherri Lynn, 410 547
WENDEL Alice, 547 548 Amy Rae, 80
549 Anna Martha, 123 137 139 141
547 Annie E, 548 549 Augustus, 547-
549 Betty, 550 Betty L, 156 182
Bonnie, 549 550 Casey, 549 Charles,
547 549 Conrad, 547-549 Cora, 548
Douglas, 26 79 549 Douglas Ray, 548
550 E Faye, 547 549 Edwin, 549 550
Elwood, 547 549 Glenda, 80 182 547-
550 Glenys, 550 Gus, 123 Gustus, 547
Harry, 547 Harry A, 547 549 Heidi,
549 Henry, 472 548 549 Ida, 547
Jacob, 548 James, 550 Janice, 549
Jason, 549 Kay, 547 549 Kelly Rae, 80
549 Letha Doris, 547 549 Lisa, 548
Loren, 80 182 547-549 Louisa, 548 549
Louise, 123 547 Martha, 548 Nancy,
547-549 Richard, 549 Rosalyn, 548
Salley Rae, 549 Sally Rae, 26 79 548
550 Sandra, 549 Shirley M, 549
Steven, 548 Thelma Olga, 231 235
Thomas, 550 William, 548 549
WENDLANDT Sophia, 86 423
WENDT Fredaricka, 369 550 Fredericka,
563 Joyce Elaine, 17 Ronald Lee, 17
WENTE Christian Wilhelm, 550 551 Ella,
552 Emma, 550 551 Engle Marie, 550
551 Engle Mary, 550-552 Ernest, 550
551 Ernest Christian, 550-552 Esther,
550 Gertrude, 552 Johann Friedrich,
550 551 Louis, 551 Louise Sophia, 68
147 155-157 168 182 551 Lydia, 552
Mabel, 550 Mary Sophia, 551 Matilda,
551 552 Minnie, 552 Minnie Carolyn,
551 Sophie Wilhelma Charlotte, 550
551 Susan Mae, 184 511 Wilhelm
Christian, 551 William, 551 552
WENTHE Emma, 550 551 Matilda, 551
552
WENZEL Carol, 120 121 553 Herbert, 120
Johannes Edna, 120
WERMERS Lisa, 561

WERNER Christine, 115 Emma Dora, 115
Henry, 115 Lisa Marie, 127 Steven,
127
WERNING Aaron, 552 Abraham, 563
Adam Sr, 552 Albert, 263 552 562 567
568 Albert Douglas III, 552 Albert G,
564 573 574 Albert G Jr, 552 Albert G
Sr, 552 Albert Sr, 555 558 561 570 572
Albert W, 399 401 402 553 567 568
Alice, 118-120 230 502 553-555 565
566 568 572-575 Alice Brandt, 573
Alma, 564 Alvina, 552 558 563 572
Anna, 298 346 553 557 560 562 566
567 571 Anna Christiana, 251 Anna
Christina, 250 553 565 Anna Elisabeth,
566 Anna Martha, 230 231 234 235
514 552 554 565 566 Anne Christina,
251 Annis, 301 467 470 567 Anton,
230 502 554 555 566 568 572 573 575
Ardith, 555 558 Arnold, 555 Arthur,
552 555 574 Arthur Jacob, 554 555 558
559 574 581 Audrey Ann, 374 Audrey
Anne, 555 562 August J, 556 571
Barbara, 558 Barry, 563 Betty, 552 573
574 Beverly, 555 Blake Matthew, 570
Brett Jonathan, 570 Bronson, 569
Carmen, 572 Carol, 301 468 Carrie,
568 Charles, 555 Chris, 115 117 556
571 Christine, 73 556 571 Clara, 498
557 563 564 568 571 Clarence, 557
559 571 Colleen, 468 Collin, 565
Conrad, 74 222 553 557 558 560 566
567 570 571 Conrad H J, 368 557 558
Dale, 555 558 Dale Scott, 558 David,
562 David Kevin, 561 David Paul, 574
Debra Ann, 558 572 Delbert Anton,
353 555 558 568 Delores, 569 573
Denise Diane, 561 Dennis, 562 Diane,
558 559 Dolores, 563 Donald, 34 557
559 574 Donna, 562 Doris, 555 573
Dorothy, 559 568 575 Douglas, 559
Duane Melvin, 555 558 559 Edwin,
553 El, 555 Elaine, 559 575 597 Elda,
9 560 575 Elfried C, 117 Elfrieda, 41
42 557 560 565 Elfrieda C, 560
Elfriede C, 115 116 299 Elisabeth, 250
401 560 561 565 Elizabeth, 399 401
402 567 Elma, 205 552 561 Elmer, 552

561 567 Elmer Henry, 352 353 555 561 567 573 Elwood, 562 Elwood Henry, 553 Emilie, 567 Emma, 185 368 554 559 562 564 568 Emma Louise, 554 555 558 559 574 580 Evelyn, 558 Fern Katherine, 223 Fred Adam, 562 571 Frieda, 552 553 557 560 562 564 566 570 572 575 Gary Lee, 563 572 Gene, 563 George, 563 567 571 Gerald C, 562 Gertrude, 558 571 573 Glenn, 563 568 Greg, 563 Gregory John, 26 Harvey, 563 570 572 Heinrich, 566 Helen, 555 Hermine, 564 567 Hilda, 502 552 555 569 573 Hildegard, 552 555 558 561 564 570 572 Holly, 563 Hulda, 550 563 571 Ida, 557 Ilma, 564 571 Ilma Mildred, 422 482 485-489 J A Henry, 564 567 J A Wilhelm, 552 553 557 560 562 564 566 570 572 575 James, 565 568 Jamie, 565 Janelle Kay, 569 Jean, 552 Jeanette, 251 564 Jennifer, 559 Jerad, 565 Jill Faye, 558 Jimmy, 565 Joan, 555 558 Johana Jeanette, 170 250 553 554 557 560 565-567 569 570 Johann Adam, 170 250 251-554 557 560 564-567 569 570 Johann Valentin, 230 552 554 565 566 John, 467 575 John C A, 242 467 557 566 John M, 571 Joshua, 559 Joyce Shirley, 338 353 558 Judy, 555 Julanne, 567 568 Julia, 571 Julie, 556 Julie Denise, 25-27 568 Justus, 25 298 346 399 401 553 561 564 566-568 Kami, 563 Katharina, 428 488 556 562-564 571 573 574 Katharina Elisabeth, 146 147 151 170 175 184 276 Katharine Elizabeth, 144 161 172 283 Katherina Elisabeth, 25 566 Katherina Jeannette, 480 484 557 567 Katherine, 566 Katherine Jeannette, 487 488 Kathleen, 555 Kathleen Ray, 570 Keith, 558 568 Kendall Jo, 569 Kenneth R, 562 Kimberly Kay, 573 Kristie, 552 Lawrence, 25 574 Lawrence Albert, 552 553 565 567 568 Leonard, 368 554 559 568 Leroy, 555 Lester, 301 467 470 567 Linda, 552 553 565 568 Lisa J, 569 Lloyd, 239 563

568 572 573 Lois Anita, 561 Loren, 554 569 573 Lorene, 555 Louise, 567 568 Lowell, 556 Lucille, 558 562 569 575 Lusann, 555 Lusann Florence Garnet, 353 555 558 568 Lynette Jean, 574 Marcella, 552 561 Margaret, 575 Margarethe, 313-315 565 569 Maria, 73 74 399 401 556 557 561 564 566-568 571 Maria (Mary), 570 Marian, 562 Marian, 573 Marie, 553 554 Marion, 563 Marjorie, 563 568 Mark, 555 559 570 Marlys, 563 570 Martha, 48-50 564 568 570 571 Martha A, 399 401 553 562 567 568 Martha Joanna, 34 557 559 574 Martin, 428 488 556 562 564-566 570 571 573 574 Martin F, 557 563 568 571 Marvin, 552 558 563 572 Mary, 73 74 119-121 559 560 564 565 569 572 574 575 Mary El, 553 562 Mathilda, 212 242 368 467 557 558 565 572 Matilda, 27 28 212 213 554 566 Maurine, 555 Maxine, 25 552 553 565 567 568 574 Melba W, 553 Melvin, 555 575 Merlin, 555 Merrill, 553 Michael, 559 Michelle Jean, 552 573 Mildred A, 562 Minnie, 230 231 Myrna, 571 Nadene, 556 Natala Ann, 563 Norma, 557 559 564 571 Patricia, 555 Patricia Kay, 563 572 Paul, 502 503 555 569 573 Paula, 563 571 Philip, 563 Phyllis Marie, 210 562 573 Rachel Marie, 26 Raymond, 573 Rebecca, 574 Richard, 571 573 Robert, 555 556 Ronald, 563 Rosa Marie, 567 Rose, 556 Rose A, 115 556 571 Rose Marie, 352 555 561 573 Russell, 568 573 Russell Scott, 572 Ruth, 555 558 559 563 570 572 Ruth Augusta, 563 Sandra Marie, 569 Sarah, 571 574 Scott, 574 Sheryl Sue, 33 34 559 574 Sophia, 571 574 Stacie, 568 Steven, 559 Susan, 558 568 Tamara Lynn, 552 574 Tammy, 555 574 Ted, 575 Thomas, 568 Thomas John, 25 27 574 Troy, 574 Vaughn Jay, 569 Vernon George, 555 574 Viola, 239 242 243 247 563 566 568 572 573 Virgil, 563 Waldo, 563 Walter, 567 Walter L H, 571 574 Wayne, 555

Wendy, 563 Wendy Kay, 223-225 227
Wendy Noel, 552 Wilfred, 555
Wilhelm, 564 Wilhelmina, 74 222 231
553 557 558 560 566 567 570 571
Wilhelmina Ellen, 230 Wilhelmina
(Minnie) Ellen, 414 554 575 William,
559 560 564 569 575 William F, 562
William J E, 571 Willie, 575 Willis,
558 Wilmer, 563 Wilmer Paul, 223
WERNING ENGLEMANN Louise, 569
WERNING SCHUMACHER Anna
Martha, 554
WERNING SHUMACHER Anna Martha,
503
WERTZ Carolyn Mae, 46 442
WERUM Inge, 171 179
WESELOH Donna, 382
WESSELS Gary Michael, 448 Linda Sue,
448
WESSLING Abigail Ann, 576 Bradford
William, 576 Brooke, 543 Brooke
Lorraine, 575 Carrie Joy, 575 David
Walter, 575 David William, 486 Debra,
486 Debra Joy, 543 575 Doug, 575
Douglas, 543 Douglas Walter, 486
Douglas William, 575 Erin Renee, 575
Ethel Irene, 485 Grant Anthony, 485
488 575 576 Heath Thomas, 576 Heidi,
223 Heidi Mae, 227 576 Kathy, 486
Kathy Ann, 575 Lois Jeanette, 485 488
575 576 Mary, 486 Mary Katherine
(Kay), 576 Rachelle Ann, 575 Sara,
486 Sara Ann, 227 576 Sara Anne, 218
Thomas Grant, 218 227 486 576 Wade
Anthony Edward, 576 William
Bradford, 486 576 William Christian,
485
WEST Payton Alexander, 134
WESTEMIER Carol Ann, 474
WESTENDORF Arnetta, 162 177 181
WESTERGAARD Alice, 367 Brandon
Andrew, 367 Debra, 367 Eric Andrew,
367 Ronald A, 367 Terry Lynn, 367
WESTERMANN Anneke, 106 108 109
WESTON Sarah Towle, 47
WETSEL Cecil, 502 Julie Anne, 502
Kindra Jo, 502 Patty Jo, 502 Ryan, 502
WEYER A S, 452 Kate, 452

WHALEY Ferlan, 329 Kristie Lee, 329
WHEELER Andrew Park, 478 576 598
Anna, 371 Chad Joseph, 192 576
Charles H, 598 Colton Jospeh, 576
Don, 192 Donald, 576 Elizabeth, 576
598 Elizabeth Pearl, 478 598 George,
371 Hazel Laverne, 598 Janet, 598
Jeanette Ann, 213 509 Joseph, 576
Joseph Andrew, 192 226 Joyce, 192
576 Karen, 576 Karen Marie, 192 226
Kathryn Danielle, 576 Kendy, 576
Kevin, 213 509 Leone, 576 577 598
Lester G, 576 577 Lester George, 598
Lonnie, 509 Mary, 576 Scott Alan, 192
Therese, 576 577 Timothy Melvin, 192
WHITE Anita Kay, 466 Carolyn, 23 Clara,
44 Clara May, 186 Cynthia Jolene, 378
Jeffrey Scott, 378 Joan Kay, 370 390
577 Joseph William, 371 Kelly, 44
Kevin Dale, 44 Kyle E, 44 Patrick
Henry, 370 390 577 Pearl, 105 Robert,
44 186 Tammy Kay, 371 Tammy Kaye,
577 Ward, 44
WHITEHEAD John, 322 Margaret Jane,
322 Michelle, 113 154 Nancy, 491
WHITING Janet Colleen, 475 577 Karl
Lester, 474 475 577 Lavonne Marie,
475 577 Lorraine Ann, 475 Peggy Kay,
475 577 Ruby, 23 Virginia, 473
WHITLATCH Alice Faye, 292 383 577
Brenda, 383 Brian, 383 Melanie, 383
Robert, 292 383 577 Sarah, 383 577
WHITSON Emma, 315 316 Morris, 315
316
WHITTAKER Linda, 565 568
WICHMAN Chris, 200 Diane May, 155
Eleanor May, 96 155 Elizabeth Ann,
200 Irvin (Dick), 29 Kenneth Karl, 155
Raymond, 96 155 Richard Ray, 155
Taylor Nicole, 200
WICKER Emilie, 578 Philipp II, 578
WICKERT Anna Karoline, 15 114 578
Anne Elisabeth, 577 578 Barthold, 577
578 Claudia, 365 Dirk, 365 Elisabeth
Marie, 362 Elke, 578 Emilie, 198 365
578 579 Helene, 584 587 Jakob, 15 114
578 Karoline, 578 Karsten, 365 Marius,
365 Marlene, 15 23 198 578 Marlene

718

Wilhelm, 583 Fredia Catherine, 592
Friedericke, 585 Friedericke Kar
Philippine, 586 587 G, 583 Garry
Eugene, 583 Georg Heinrich, 583 587
589 Gerald, 589 Glenn, 583 Glenn
Eugene, 592 Gregory David, 592
Gunter, 589 Heinrich, 583 584 589
Heinrich Adolf, 585 Heinrich August,
584 Helene, 362-364 534 581 583 584
587 589 Helene Katharina, 584
Helmut, 581 Henriette, 584 Henriette
Marie, 586 Herman Heinrich, 587
Hermann Eberhard, 587 Hermann
Heinrich, 583 Hilde, 589 Hildegard,
581 Ina, 593 James Richard, 584 592
Jean Ann, 584 592 Johann Adam, 584
586 587 589 Johann Adam August, 585
588 Johann Anton, 588 Johann Daniel,
585 590 Johann Heinrich, 585 586 588
Johann Heinrich August, 581 583 584
587 Johann Niclaus, 587 590 Johann
Niclaus Jr, 587 Johann Niclaus Sr, 587
Johann Simon, 585-588 Johann
Wilhelm, 588 592 Johannes, 581 585
589 590 Johannes Wilhelm, 590 John
Walter, 589 592 Karl, 548 585 Karl F,
582 Karl Fredrich, 265 393 590 592
Karl Simon, 581 584 589 Karoline, 583
584 Kath Karol Luise, 583 587
Katharina Elisabeth, 586 Katharina
Marie (Tina), 581 Kathryn Diane, 583
Kathy Dawn, 226 590 Kathy Jo, 583
Konrad, 588 589 Kristi Sue, 582 Laura
Katherine, 265 393 Laura Katherine,
582 590 591 593 Lavonne, 89 226 393
579 582 592 593 Lenore Katherine,
375 393 590 Liesel, 589 Luise Marie
Katharina, 584 Mae, 395 582 Margaret,
581 Marie, 581 583 Marie Christina,
586 587 Marie Elisabeth, 583 585 587-
589 Marie Henriette, 588 Maritz, 589
Martha, 589 Martin, 585 Martin
Wilhelm, 590 Mary Ann Barbara, 258
Mary Ann Barbara, 259 393 590 591
Mary L, 583 592 Miranda Lynn, 582
Myron Wilhelm, 592 Nancy, 582 583
590 Nancy Lynn, 226 Nancy Lynne,
227 583 Norma, 591 592 Orthey, 590

Patricia Dee, 589 592 Patti Marie, 583
Paul Michael, 592 Peter, 231 414 581
583 589 591 592 Rainer, 589 Richard
James, 584 Richard Walter, 395 584
589 592 Roger, 592 Ronald Ray, 582
583 592 Rose Elizabeth, 265 395 582
592 593 Ruth, 581 Sara Nicole, 584
Simon, 583 584 Simon Karl, 587
Sophie, 583 590 Steven Donald, 582
Tami Renee, 226 Terry Michael, 582
Tobias, 149 393 395 590 592 593
Tobias Wilhelm, 589 Trinchen, 583
Vicki Lavonne, 583 593 Vickie L, 88
Vickie Lavonne, 89 Walter, 395 Walter
Peter Valentine, 265 582 592 593
Wilhelm, 589 592 Wilhelmina Cath,
588 Wilhelmina Katharina, 588
Wilhelmina Lucina, 585
WILHITE Sharon Grace, 208
WILHLEMI Arlene Lucille, 3
WILKINS Bernice, 8 9 John Clifford, 395
Louise May, 395
WILKINSON David, 143 Julie, 143
WILL Jacqueline Gail, 332 Jeffrey
Douglas, 332 Richard Marvin, 332
Timothy Richard, 332
WILLARD Frances Idell, 526 Frances
Idella, 524 529
WILLARD JACOBSEN Lavonne Lucille,
454 456
WILLARD SASS Lavonne Lucille, 541
WILLENBROOK Augusta, 436
WILLENINA Alice, 219 Barbara, 219
Fred, 219 Frederich, 219
WILLER Cecilia, 191 Hans, 191
WILLET Majory, 369 Marjory, 369
WILLIAMS Anna, 468 473 581 Ariel Kay,
36 Ashley Ann, 593 Brianna
Marguerite, 36 Carla, 213 509 Charles,
581 Charles Dean, 387 593 Cheryl
Ann, 387 Clarence, 232 Clarine, 80
Cody, 447 Colleen, 59 598 Creston
James, 594 Daniel Joe, 36 37 David
Frederick, 595 Dennis Scott, 387 593
Diane, 173 Dianne, 153 Donald, 593
Doris Ann, 387 388 593 594 595
Eleanor Sophia, 140 Eleanor Sophia
Wilhelmine, 593 Elmer G, 232 593

WOHLSEIL Benjamin Carl, 579 Jacob Richard, 579 Joel, 579 Rachel Ruth, 579
WOLD Dr, 191 Laura, 191 Sonja, 336
WOLF Susan, 190
WOLFANGER Christina Renee, 91 Darren Eugene, 91
WOLFE Alma Alberta, 320
WOLLMAN Carol Pam, 559 Elaine, 559 575 597 Elmer, 559 575 597 Emma, 559 Herman, 559 Linda, 559 Lois Marie, 559 597 Raymond, 559 Renee Elaine, 559 597
WOLTER Calvin F, 306 Erik Thomas, 306 Ida, 58 501 Kelly Marie, 306 Stella Marie, 306
WOMBACHER Hayley Jo, 596 John, 596 Penny Sue, 596
WOMICHIL Linda, 552 568
WOMOCHIL M Valeria, 446
WONDERLICH Rae, 53
WONDERLICK Deb, 152 159
WONICK Sherri, 377 536
WOOD Elisabeth, 42 Margaret, 145 180 Robert, 42 560 Ruth Mathilda, 560 Ruth Matilda, 42 Thomas, 42
WOODILL Gerald, 191 Myrtle, 191
WOODSON Debbie Ann, 46 Eleanor, 295 George Leon, 46 295 Mary Jane, 264 274 275 294 Sharon Kay, 46 Wendy Renee, 46
WOODWARD Chandler Timothy, 34 299 Diane, 302 Joyce Elaine, 268 Lori Jo, 34 299 Ryder William, 300 Syrena Emma Lena, 299
WOOTEN Carroll Maynard, 141 Irma, 141 Sharon Colleen, 30 32 37 Susan Margareite, 127 Susan Margarite, 137 141
WORDEN Lucille, 440
WORKENSTIEN Sophia, 383
WORTHINGTON Brian Paul, 56 Darrin John, 56 Ellen Leona, 56 Marjorie Ruth, 361 Robert Jr, 56
WRIGHT Alfred, 373 Alice, 538 Arlene, 373 Barry Evan, 432 Berry Evan, 423 Brian Lewis, 432 Carrie Ann, 432 Emma, 373 Emma R, 359 Hazel, 76

Katherine Josine, 423 432 Kristi, 56 Leroy, 538 Leta Mae, 359 360 Lewis N, 359 Linda, 76 153 156 172 Linda Kay, 76 William, 76
WUBBEN Jim, 83 Sue, 83
WUBBENA Alvin, 80 Ella, 80 Kevin, 80 Kim, 80 Korey, 80 Kristy, 80
WUETZER Charlotte, 119 572 Kathy, 49 Lillian, 49 119 Louis, 49 119
WUNDER Katharina, 2 Katherine, 500
WUNROW Jeffery Romaine, 245
WUNSCHEL Beka, 77 598 Carson, 598 David Scott, 77 597 Deeann Kay, 77 597 Gail, 598 Jacob, 597 Kristine Elizabeth, 77 Liza Murin, 598 Lois Ann, 77 339 597 598 Lori Lynn, 77 597 Madeline, 598 Marjorie, 598 Maya, 597 Merle, 598 Morgan, 598 Rudolph August, 77 597 Russell Stanley, 77 339 597 598 Ruth Elizabeth, 77 597 Sharon, 77 597 Steven Rudy, 77 598 Taylor, 598
WUNSCHEL TAYLOR Deeann Kay, 597
WURST Myrtle S, 313
WURTZ Darles, 172
WURZBACHER Pamela, 350 508
WUTZKE Clara, 61 Elfrieda, 28
WYANT Lucille, 44
WYLAM Barbara, 101 149
WYNEK Ann, 268
XE Kim Tran Thi, 128 337
YATES Daniella Kay, 501 Debra Sue, 501 Douglas, 501 Matthew D, 501
YATTON Gertrude Grace, 449
YEAGLE Polly Bethel, 118
YEDLIK Carrie, 112 388 Marilyn, 112 Sara, 112
YILECK Mildred, 53
YOCHEM Patsy Joyce, 336 353
YOCK Joe, 410 Minnie Lois, 410
YOCUM Christine Marie, 92 598 Deanna Marie, 92 93 598 Jeremy Delbert, 92 Tom, 92 93 598 Tommy Merle, 92 Erin Ashley, 306 John David, 306 Michelle Kathleen, 306 Sally Jane, 306
YOST Aletha Dale, 155
YOUNG Alan F, 59 147 598 Amy Christine, 307 Carol Jean, 599 Charles,

478 Charlotte Martha, 599 Colleen, 59
598 Daniel Joseph, 307 Della, 236
Dennis, 55 56 Dione, 109 Dixie, 600
Don, 109 Donald Robert, 599 Donna
Marie, 598 600 Doris Jean, 599 Edith
Mae, 598 599 Elizabeth, 576 598
Elizabeth Pearl, 478 598 Enos, 478
Ernest William, 599 Florence, 116 117
Frank, 117 234 236 Franklin, 478
Geraldine, 87 236 Gregory, 109 110
Jacob, 426 Jacob George, 435 Jake,
599 Jakob, 150 435 599 James Philip,
599 600 Janet Lynn, 599 Jeanne Marie,
599 Jeannette, 599 Jeffrey Alan, 59
Jennifer, 56 Jill Crisann, 109 110 Jody,
59 John Philip, 424 435 599 Joseph,
477 478 598 Kathleen Ann, 599 Lea
Carol, 599 600 Linda Lee, 600 Lori
Lynne, 599 Louise, 478 Margaret, 477
478 598 Maria (Mary) Katharina, 424
Maria Sophia Barbara, 426 435 Marie
(Mary), 435 599 Marilyn Ruth, 59 147
598 Martha, 95 96 144 146 150 172
177 257 435 Mary Lou, 306 307
Mathilda, 117 234 236 478 Michael
Norman, 599 Norman Edmund, 599
Philip George, 598 599 Richard, 56
Robert William, 600 Sharon, 55 56
Sophia, 150 599 Sophia Marie, 599
Steven, 306 307 Susan Marie, 599 Tina
Carol, 599 Verna, 478 Wesley, 236
YOUNGBERG Amy Marie, 210 Edward,
210 Edward Arthur, 210 Eleanor
Hedwig, 210 Jason Melvin, 210 Larry
Edward, 210 221 Mary Alyce, 210 221
YOUNGREN Teresa, 29
ZACK Genelle Mae, 122
ZANDER Evelyn, 336 348 354
ZANKA Stacy Kay, 387 594
ZASTROW Andrea Lee, 491 Berdette
Elaine, 491 Bruce, 491 Carol Jo, 491
Chandler, 491 Colton, 491 Roderick,
491
ZEADOW Florence Ellen, 392 396 397
ZEISS Anna Maria, 585
ZEITER Debra Jane, 318 Don, 318
ZELLER Sandra, 88
ZEMAN Orpha, 229 232
ZHANEK Bonnie, 293 538
ZID Mary Pauline, 291
ZIMMERMAN Donna, 145 173 Laverne
Rose, 396 397 Mari, 520
ZINSER Andrew George, 37 Melissa
Marie, 37
ZOBEL Anna, 558 563 Louis, 558 563
Lusann, 555 Lusann Florence Garnet,
353 555 558 568 Ruth, 570 572 Ruth
Augusta, 563
ZORNIG Adelia, 600 Alvina, 515 600
Anna, 116 Annine, 600 Delia, 371
Dora, 63 Emma, 500 600 Fred, 600
Herman, 600 John, 63 Lena, 600
Margaretha, 81 600 Marx Jr, 600 Marx
Sr, 600 Mary, 600
ZULK Dorothea, 28 Fred, 28